MANORAMA YEARBOOK 2022

57th Year of Publication

Malayala Manorama

Kottayam Kozhikode Kochi Thiruvananthapuram Palakkad Kannur Kollam Thrissur Malappuram Pathanamthitta Alappuzha Mumbai Chennai Bengaluru Mangaluru Delhi Dubai Bahrain Doha

MANORAMA
YEARBOOK 2022

Chief Editor Mammen Mathew
Editor Philip Mathew
Managing Editor Jacob Mathew
Editor-in-charge Thomas Dominic
Assistant Editors Biju Mathai
C Unnikrishna Pillai
Sr. Sub Editor Kenny Jose
Cover Design M M Sabu
Design P G Rajeev

Contributors Index

Circulation Offices

NEW DELHI
Malayala Manorama Co. Ltd., Tej Building, 1st Floor, 8-B, Bahadurshah Zafar Marg, New Delhi-110002 Phone: 01123354920, 23354921

MUMBAI
Malayala Manorama Co. Ltd., Marathon Nextgen Innova Building, A wing, 4th Floor, Off. Ganpatrao kadam Marg, Lower-Parel (West), Mumbai - 400 013. Phone: 022 24900844, 62965900

KOLKATA
Malayala Manorama Co. Ltd, 14 Parasar Road, Near Lake Market, Kolkata - 700029. Phone: 033 24198233, 033 24198048

CHENNAI
Malayala Manorama Co. Ltd, Janpriya Crest (III Floor), No: 113, Pantheon Road, Egmore, Chennai - 600008 Phone: 044 66918530/31

BENGALURU
Malayala Manorama Co. Ltd, 132, 3rd Floor Kantha Court, Lalbagh Road, Bangalore- 560 027 Phone: 080 22247735 Fax. 080 22247736

HYDERABAD
Malayala Manorama Co. Ltd, 6-2-348/10/1, Flat No.101 & 102 Moghal Mansion, Khairatabad, Hyderabad- 500 004 Phone: 040 23314168, 23324692

COIMBATORE
Malayala Manorama Co. Ltd, 1st floor, Sunshine Buildings1056 Avinashi Road, Coimbatore- 641 018 Phone: 0422 2241911, 2245470

Printed and published from Malayala Manorama Press, Kodimatha, Kottayam-686 039 by Mammen Mathew, on behalf of the Malayala Manorama Company Private Ltd. Kottayam - 686 001
Editor: Philip Mathew

Manorama Yearbook is published as independent editions in Hindi, Tamil, Malayalam and Bengali with special focus on the relevant regions.

RNI Reg. No. 40731/1982. **ISSN** 0975-2250 **ISBN** 978-81-954072-7-9

Price ₹ 310 *For Feedback :* ybfeedback@mm.co.in

P B No. 26 Kottayam 686 001 Kerala India
Phone 0481 2563646 2563656 Fax 91- 481- 562479

Be the Best!

India is celebrating *Azadi ka Amrit Mahotsav* -75 years of Independence. We salute all our freedom fighters and martyrs who sacrificed their lives to make India a free country.

We are happy to present Manorama Yearbook 2022 despite all the disruptions caused by COVID-19. The year 2021 was no different from 2020 with a new wave of the pandemic and measures like social distancing, self-masking, sanitising, quarantines, lockdowns, and vaccination drives.

Amid the rising death toll due to COVID-19 pandemic across the globe, India also faced severe natural calamities that caused loss of lives and damage property. After months of uncertainty and economic gloom, we are slowly heading towards the light at the end of the tunnel. The infection rate has come down, the economy is bouncing back, markets are recovering and educational institutions are reopening. We have also completed 100 crore doses of covid vaccination in about nine months since the drive began.

It was a hard fight for everyone. And we didn't give up.

Overcoming many hurdles, our sportspersons too scaled new heights in the Tokyo Olympics and Paralympics. With the spirit soaring high, javelin thrower Neeraj Chopra brought home the first ever Olympic gold in athletics. Our Paralympians returned with the best medal haul ever.

Manorama Yearbook 2022 is power-packed in more than 25 sections with interesting articles by eminent writers that capture the new trends. Honourable President of India Shri Ram Nath Kovind, Dr Shashi Tharoor, Suresh Prabhu, Dr S. Unnikrishnan Nair, Prof. Pranav N Desai, Jayanti Ghose, and Paranjoy Guha Thakurta are some of the prominent personalities who have contributed this year. As for topics, we have write-ups on Gaganyaan, Careers of the Future, Vaccine Diplomacy, and a motivational article on Purpose-driven life and much more.

May you find Manorama Yearbook 2022 helpful to make most of the opportunities that come your way. We have proven it to the world that we are brave and resolute enough to endure every hardship and emerge victorious. Keep doing the best to be the best. There is new hope rising. Stay safe!

Mammen Mathew

Chief Editor

Log on to manoramayearbook.in for daily updates and lot more...

Manorama Yearbook has often been described as "one of the most trusted sources of knowledge" by many. The book, published in five languages, has played a major part in helping tens of thousands of aspirants in cracking many competitive exams in the past six decades. With its updates on facts and figures, the book is an unmissable item on the bookshelves of serious learners.

In 2018, Manorama Yearbook took a digital leap by launching a website. With the positive response from the digital users, we published an app in 2019.

What's new?

The Yearbook retains its glory and charm of the book and the app/website is not an e-book version. Instead, it provides knowledge on the fingertips of the new age users.

The primary focus of the digital version is to provide daily dose of current affairs and explainers mostly suitable for UPSC exam aspirants.

With a user-friendly design and navigation, users can easily browse through various sections like:

- ✓ **Current Affairs**
- ✓ **Special Stories**
- ✓ **Mock Tests**
- ✓ **Quizzes**
- ✓ **Videos**
- ✓ **International Relations**
- ✓ **Indian Polity**
- ✓ **Constitution**
- ✓ **Government Schemes**

Yearbook app available on 

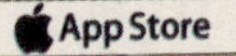

For more details, turn to page no. 20

Contents

01

15-106

India and the World

02

107-128

Government Initiatives

03

129-156

Calander of Events

04

157-256

Current Affairs

05

257-302

Who is Who

06

303-384

Quiztival

07

385-414

Science & Medicine

CONTENTS

10

459-480

Universe, Earth & Space

11

481-490

India Insignia

CONTENTS

12

491- 514

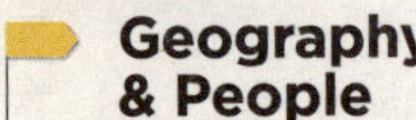

Geography & People

13

515-528

History of India

14

529-544

Space, Security, Energy

15

545-576

Polity & Governance

16

Education & Career

17

Economy

18

Transport & Communication

CONTENTS

19

673-722

India States

20

723-756

World Panorama

21

757-778

Equality, Ethics & Social Justice

22
779-814

Skill Development

23
815-848

International Relations

24
849-944

General Knowledge

CONTENTS

25

945-976

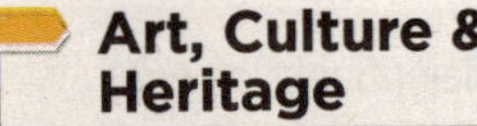

Art, Culture & Heritage

26

977-1008

Sports

01 INDIA AND THE WORLD

- Letter to Young Indians
- Gaganyaan
- India Rising to $5 Tn GDP
- Unsung Freedom Fighters of Indian Independence
- Vaccine Nationalism Vs Vaccine Diplomacy
- The Real Virus Came from Zhoushan
- Making A Mark Abroad
- Reproductive Health in India
- A Purpose-Driven Life
- Beyond Postmodernism
- The Art of Positive Speaking

Arise, The Future Beckons

Letter to Young Indians

Ram Nath Kovind
President of India

In human life, 75 years may look ripe enough, but in a nation's life it would mark a youthful age. Today, India is a nation filled with verve and energy of youth like you whose aspirations will define the course of the future.

Dear young friends,

As you hold the Manorama Yearbook in your hands and mull about the future, you nurse a dream. Like you, I also passed through this phase of life that beheld hopes and anxieties of its time. So how should we describe this beautiful phase of life of our youth whose collective dreams shape the future of the nation?

It is a pleasant coincidence that at a time when you are planning to take a leap forward with a new beginning in life, the country will be celebrating the 75th anniversary of independence. In human life, 75 years may look ripe enough, but in a nation's life it would mark a youthful age. Today, India is a nation filled with verve and energy of youth like you whose aspirations will define the course of the future.

In this context let us recall the values that our forefathers held close to their hearts while fighting for Independence and which formed the bedrock for the building of a new nation born at the midnight of August 15, 1947.

Mahatma Gandhi, Father of the Nation, epitomised all those values. Though with his trademark self-deprecating humour he would call himself as ordinary, his so-called "ordinariness" encompassed the best features of excellence. His exceptional journey to becoming a "Great Soul" was consistently guided by those eternal values – truth and non-violence. And neither of these values was imbibed by him overnight. If it had any beginning it was during his higher studies and early years in what we would today call professional career. In short, what I mean to underline here is that Gandhiji brought about the most radical transformation in his personality when he was in his twenties.

That, usually, is the time of life when all its potential is unexplored and all alternatives are open ahead of you. From the next decade, the range of choices starts narrowing down. Experience is appreciated everywhere – and rightly so, but it comes at the cost of closed options.

As average Indians in your twenties, the question of career is bound to be uppermost in your minds. Under social imperatives or under peer pressure, many of you often equate a 'career' with a 'job', preferably with the assurance of its continuity till superannuation. That is understandable. India's bureaucracy and public sector both require talented, hardworking youngsters. As good governance is always a work in progress, it requires infusion of new thinking, innovation and passionate commitment that can best come from your generation. It is the youth of today who will enhance delivery of public services by deploying new models of administration or futuristic technologies and improve the lives of people.

But a job need not mean a government or public-sector job. Our private sector has contributed immensely to the creation of wealth for all, and it would also need talent to take India's economy to new heights. The more ambitious among you will aim to become not employees but employers. With entrepreneurship they will create new job opportunities.

And a career need not mean a job. In the new century, many of our deeply held notions of 'work' were anyway undergoing changes, and Covid-19 only hastened that process. It forced movement restrictions and lockdowns on us, paralysing economies around the world. As a result, there were job losses and salary cuts, but there was also a rise in the 'gig economy'. In this brave new world, a brave new breed of youngsters is seeking neither jobs nor the financial security of the routine nine-to-five work but a rightful recognition of and remuneration for their unique talents, for their creative vision, for their skills. Instead of safety, their preference is for flexibility. Instead of closing their options, they are exploring more alternatives.

Along with the gig economy, another trend in recent years is work-life balance. A phase when hard work alone was of paramount importance is over in many nations, organisations and sectors. There is increasing focus on accommodating other aspects of life alongside the economically productive work. An employee spending extra hours and weekends on work is replaced by one who cares as much about promotions as about family time. It makes all the more sense in the pandemic time. Work-from-home has its benefits but it also puts working women under a 'triple burden'. They already have the double burden of paid work and 'unpaid work', that is, domestic responsibilities. On top of that,

Student Praying Before Online Pravesanolsavam Fotokannan / Wikimedia Commons / Public Domain (Online class Kerala 2021.jpg

as children attend school from home, their learning has to be supplemented by the parents, and that task usually falls on the mother. The new stress on family time should be welcome for male employees, so that they can share some of the responsibilities of their partners. In any case, studies show that hard work in itself can be even counterproductive and as the number of hours spent on work goes up, productivity comes down in some instances.

Yet another change worth noting is the importance of continued learning. Education, after all, should not be limited to the goal of securing a job. Nowadays, more and more mid-career professionals are returning to campuses to pick up new skills, refresh their perspectives and enhance their careers. With online learning, new horizons have opened up. Securing a livelihood must not put an end to education; indeed, it should free up one's choices to study for the sake of knowledge itself. With massive open online courses (MOOCs), one can pursue education at any and every stage of life. Earlier generations did not have the luxury of accessing multimedia tutorials, on smartphones, about cutting-edge research in healthcare, advances in data sciences or fascinating chapters of Indian history – for that matter about world cultures. It is an exciting quest to embark upon!

Fulfilling work in harmony with other life goals, a meaningful career and livelihood supplemented with intellectual curiosity – this recipe for a meaningful life is incomplete. A crucial element is missing. Every individual is also a citizen. Just as you remain in debt to your family that put you into school and supports you till you stand up on your own feet, you also remain in debt to your larger family – the nation that has put in place the whole framework that facilitates your education and offers you opportunities to earn your livelihood.

To the motherland, I believe, we can never fully repay our debt, but only a part of it. No matter which path you choose, and which career you pursue, you can always pay back to the nation in a variety of ways. What is a nation, after all, but the sum total of fellow citizens? Caring for others, especially the children and the elderly, the poor and the marginalised, is the best way to repay a token of your debt to the nation.

Isn't that what we witnessed everywhere during the most difficult phase of the pandemic? It was a challenge of the most epic proportions, and its impact could have been far worse but for the ordinary citizens who were not so ordinary after all. We all have heard heart-warming accounts of heroic corona warriors who put their own life in danger to save as many lives as they could. Some tragically perished too. Doctors and nurses treated patients, while police personnel and government employees, vegetable vendors and delivery personnel made the day-to-day life less uncomfortable for others.

The pandemic has been an unprecedented crisis, but it may as well be just a warning of a far bigger crisis that is looming over the horizon. Climate change is no longer a matter of scientific research and policy discussions; its impact is already tangible, and we are fast running out of time to keep global warming within feasible limits. The decade of the 2020s could turn out to be the most decisive point. The situation is dire and pessimism won't be out of place, but I remain hopeful. My hope stems from the fact that we have seen what we are capable of when our collective existence was threatened by the coronavirus. Covid-19 has shown what humankind can do if all nations join hands and are guided by nothing other than concern for our common future coupled with respect for science. Nations shared inputs on warnings, treatment protocols, scientific research and finally the vaccines too. India reached out to the needy with medicines, protective equipment and vaccines; and when it needed help the others wasted no time in giving it a hand. Whenever we were told about our ancient saying, "Vasudhaiva Kutumbkam" – the whole world is but just one family, it seemed an abstract ideal, but we have seen how true it is when humankind faced a crisis together, like a family. The pandemic has, thus, taught us exactly those lessons that will come handy for climate action.

At an individual level, meanwhile, it is your duty to spread awareness about

the challenges to the environment and about what each of us can do to save our rivers and our forests. It is neither a tall order nor would it require great sacrifices to nudge ourselves a little every day towards an ecologically conscious lifestyle. To that end, we can find ample guidance from our scriptures and our traditions, which saw nature as the mother of all living beings.

We are blessed in having a heritage that has the Vedas and Upanishads, Mahavira and the Buddha among its early defining points and the lives of Swami Vivekananda and Gandhiji among its exemplars in modern times. They form our moral constellation that helps us find the way whenever darkness engulfs us. Gandhiji's abiding faith in the law of nature taught us to desist from overconsumption, indulgence and to adhere to the discipline of life to nourish all living organisms on this planet. I have no doubt that the world is increasingly realising the necessity of adopting this vision if it is going to save itself from the coming climate apocalypse.

Before I sign off this letter, I thought I should remind you that along with your diligent efforts to look for a brighter future, you are inescapably saddled with another responsibility of preserving and nourishing Mother Nature to protect humanity and biodiversity. The two, in fact, are tied together.

To all of you, I wish a fulfilling life ahead, in the service of the motherland.

Current Affairs videos:
Weekly analysis of important national and international events, presented with special focus on UPSC Prelims and Mains.

Government Schemes:
Comprising comprehensive articles on the major schemes and initiatives of the government of India.

International Relations:
Covering a wide range of topics like India's foreign policies, its relations with other countries, important international conventions, movements, global bodies, etc.

Polity and Constitution:
Featuring in-depth articles on the Indian Constitution, its evolution, historical underpinnings, amendments, etc.

Gaganyaan

Indian Human Space Mission

Dr Unnikrishnan Nair S
Distinguished Scientist, Director, Human Space Flight Centre, ISRO, Bangalore

After the successful unmanned spacecraft Chandrayaan and Mangalyaan in its first missions, Gaganyaan is a national Programme aimed at building expertise in the human-space interface. This article explains what it involves in a manned space missions.

Gaganyaan is the maiden human space flight project of India for carrying Indian astronauts to space and bring them back safely to a predetermined destination on earth. The word "Gaganyaan" literally means "vessel to space". The Gaganyaan has an Orbiting module which has two parts - A Crew module (CM) and a Service module (SM). The Orbiting module will be lofted into space and injected into a 400 km orbit with inclination of 51° by a variant of GSLV MKIII, named as Human rated Launch Vehicle (HRLV). The Crew module is the habitat of astronauts and it has many sub-systems to protect human lives and to provide comfort. The SM will provide all on-orbit support to the Crew module including power, propulsion, stroing of life support system resources, etc.

A new Centre, named as Human Space Flight Centre (HSFC), was created in ISRO at Bangalore in 2019 for sustained and affordable human space flight activities and Gaganyaan is the first project of HSFC.

1.1 Human Rated Launch Vehicle (HRLV):

The Orbital module will be launched by Human Rated Launch Vehicle which is a modified version of GSLV MKIII vehicle, as shown in figure. The HRLV will be made more robust by adding many features like additional redundancy in systems, incorporating an Integrated launch vehicle health management system, improving structural margins, etc.

Typical ascend and descend mission profiles are depicted in figure below.

Challenges for Human Survival in Space:

There are many challenges for human survival in space conditions. The hard vacuum in space of 10-5 to 10-7 Pa, temperature extremes from -100°C to 120°C, dealing with weightlessness of space, threat of galactic radiation as well as high energy impact of micrometeoroid or orbital debris are some of the challenges. These challenges are addressed by various design features. The hard vacuum is managed by providing a leak tight Crew module where standard atmospheric conditions of are maintained. The pressure in Crew module is maintained at one bar and the temperature is within 18 to 25°C; the Relative humidity is within 30 to 70%. These limits are selected to provide comfortable living conditions for the crew.

2.1 Life support system:

The Crew module has a pressurized cabin with a Life support system (LSS) that will provide everything needed for the comfortable stay of humans for a few days including collection and disposition of solid and liquid wastes.

For short duration mission lasting for a few days, the resources like food, water, oxygen etc are carried in special metallic bottles and containers. The astronaut consumes about 0.8 to 1.1 kg of oxygen per day, drinks 2 liters of water and eats about 0.6 kg of solid food. The consumables are stored in suitable metallic bottles in the Orbital module. The oxygen will be stored in a gas bottle at a pressure of 250 bar and it will be regulated and used inside the crew cabin. The food will be packed in air tight bags and stored in stowage area in the Crew module. The water will be carried in sachets with special mouth piece for drinking in space conditions. Each astronaut will give out about 0.96 kg of carbon dioxide per day. The exhaled carbon dioxide, odour emanating from food items, human body, etc will be removed by passing the cabin air through special chemical bed containing activated charcoal and lithium hydroxide beds. The crew will also release per day about 1.2 litres of urine and 0.3 kg of feces. The solid and liquid wastes will be collected in special chemically treated bags, sealed and stored.

Human Rated Launch Vehicle

The thermal environment inside the Crew module will be managed by a Thermal and Humidity Control System. The crew cabin air is passed through special heat exchangers which has special coolant to take the heat from cabin air and

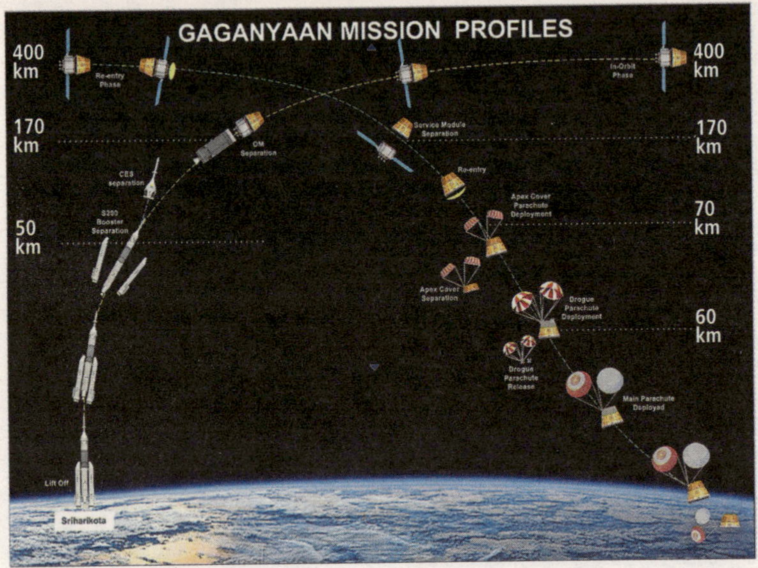

Gaganyaan Mission profiles

the heat will be rejected to space through radiator panels mounted in the SM. The humidity will be managed by allowing the humidity in cabin air to condense at heat exchanger and the condensate will be pumped and stored in special tanks.

It is mandatory for the crew to wear Flight suit during the dynamic phases-that is ascent and descent phases. The Flight suit is a self-supporting lifesaving system, with its own oxygen supply and heat removal systems, and can support the crew life for more than one and a half hours in case of any crew cabin life support system failure. The Flight suit will be pressurized to about 0.4 bar with pure oxygen and the crew will be inhaling pure oxygen.

All the activities related to thermal management, cabin pressure control and air revitalization are automatically performed by the Life support system through a set of sensors and a dedicated redundant Controller.

Space food: There are certain requirements for space food. The food should not create debris that may fly around, the food package should be air tight for avoiding any stray odor in crew cabin, it must be easy to consume in space conditions, food should be tasty and storable for few days without degradation. There are calorific requirements apart from meeting the requirement of balanced diet. Again, the food should be appealing to individual astronaut.

Each crew needs about 3000 kcal of energy per day. The food is usually retort processed to enhance its shelf life. Conventional food items like Katti roll, aloo paratta, vegitable pulav, sooji halva, paneer masala, chappathi, dal fry, biriyani etc can be conveniently packed and used in space. The beverages like tea, mango nectar etc stored in sachets can be used. Also, energy bars, nuts etc can

IMPERIO
FEDERAL BANK
YOUR PERFECT BANKING PARTNER
Live the Imperial Life

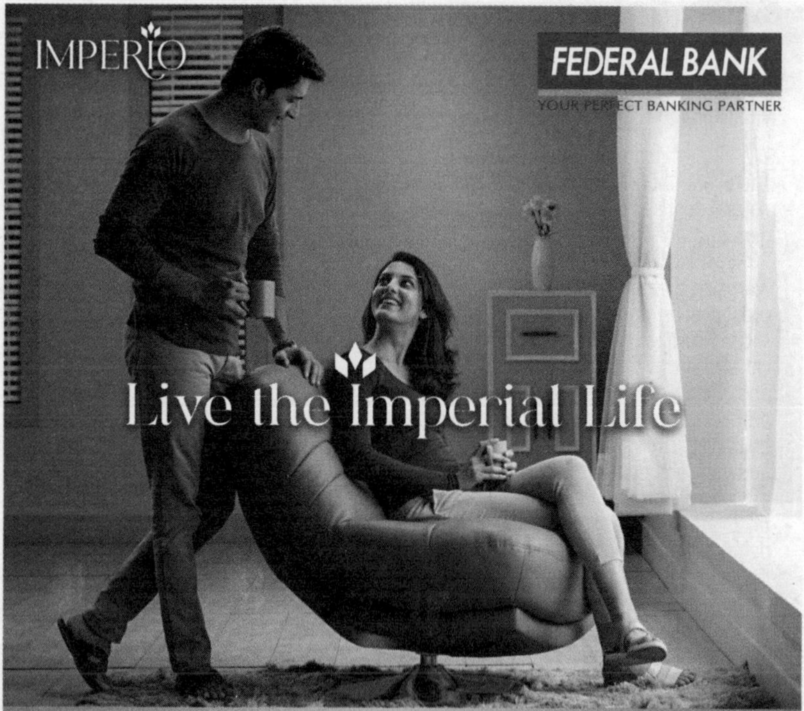

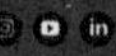

be used depending upon the crew taste and situation.

2.2 Micrometeoroid and Orbital debris:

There are thousands of man-made and natural debris in space causing many dangers to space vehicles and satellites. As of 2020, there are one trillion orbital debris with size greater than 0.1mm moving at great speeds ranging from 7 to 15 km per second. Orbital debris with more than 10 cm size are well tracked and catalogued and there are about 20,000 of them around earth. Whereas details of debris below 10 cm size are difficult to gather and hence special design considerations are implemented in the Orbital module to take care of debris impact. The threat of debris impact is more for large objects like the International space station because of its large area and hence the more likelihood of debris impact. The methodology adopted in debris impact mitigation is to have a double walled construction. Upon impacting the first layer, the debris will be fragmented into many tiny objects thereby splitting the kinetic energy of debris into multiple objects with lesser energy. The second layer will be able to better resist such impact of multiple tiny objects. It is always preferable to avoid any impact of debris by proper selection orbital parameters thereby the threat of debris can be minimized. For debris with size more than 10cm for which tracked information is available, the Orbital module can be maneuvered, using the propulsion thrusters in Orbiting module, and avoid any impact with the approaching debris.

2.3 Radiation in space:

There are many sources of radiation in space. The radiation dose will be different depending up on the orbital parameters like altitude and orbital inclination. Space radiation is made up of three kinds of radiation: particles trapped in the Earth's magnetic field; particles shot into space during solar flares (solar particle events); and galactic cosmic rays, which are high-energy protons and heavy ions from outside our solar system. Earth gets maximum radiation from the Sun. The Sun emits all wavelengths in the electromagnetic spectrum. Giant explosions, called solar flares, occur on the surface of the Sun and release large amounts of energy out into space in the form of x-rays, gamma rays, and streams of protons and electrons. These solar flares can cause serious damage to astronauts and their equipment, even at locations that are far from the Sun.

Galactic Cosmic Radiation (GCR) is a dominant source of radiation that comes from outside the solar system but primarily from within our Milky Way galaxy. GCR is composed of the nuclei of atoms that have had their surrounding electrons stripped away and are traveling at nearly the speed of light.

The radiation is measured in Milli-Sievert (mSv) and astronauts are exposed to ionizing radiation with effective doses in the range from 50 to 2,000 mSv. 1 mSv of ionizing radiation is equivalent to about three chest x-rays.

The walls of Crew module will provide some amount of protection from radiation to the crew inside. The concern of radiation is more when the astronauts step out of the Crew module for space walk or when they stay in space for longer duration, like weeks or months. In Gaganyaan programme, spacewalk is not envisaged and the mission duration is only about a week; hence the radiation threat is minor in nature. The radiation levels will be monitored in the Unmanned missions using special sensors and this data will be used for taking decision on the need for additional radiation shielding to the Orbiting module.

2.4 Weightlessness of space:

Any orbiting body is in a state of perpetual

free fall under Earth's gravitational field. As weight is the reaction of the platform upon which someone is standing, under free fall there will not be any such reaction on the body as the body is freely from falling down. Hence the person experiences weightlessness under free fall. This is sometimes refereed as microgravity or zero gravity condition as the astronaut is not feeling the effect of gravity even though he or she is falling under the gravity of Earth.

Weightlessness causes several key systems of the body to relax, as it is no longer fighting the pull of gravity. Astronauts' sense of up and down gets confused, because the vestibular system no longer can figure out where the ground and the ceiling are. Crewmembers also experience a disruption in their proprioceptive system, which tells where arms, legs and other parts of the body are oriented relative to each other. This disorientation can make astronauts to feel queasy for some time.

The long-term effects of weightlessness can create more trouble for astronauts if they stay in space for weeks to months. Calcium in bones secretes out through urine. As the bones weaken, astronauts are more susceptible to breaking them if they slip and fall, just like people with osteoporosis. Muscles also lose mass. The long-term research carried out in the International Space Station has helped NASA run studies on how astronaut health is affected with time in the weightlessness of space. The effects of weightlessness on body can be countered by doing specially designed exercises in space including cardiovascular exercise.

However, the long-term effect of weightlessness is not applicable to Gaganyaan astronauts, as they are spending a maximum of only seven days in space.

Gaganyaan – The Indian Human Space Mission

The Gaganyaan Orbital module has two parts- the Crew module (CM) and the Service module (SM) as depicted in Figure and weighs about 8000 kg. While in orbit, the OM will be orbiting the Earth with a velocity of about 7800 m/s. After the orbital phase of flight, the OM will be re-oriented for re-entry to Earth and it will be de-orbited by firing the liquid propellant thrusters in the Service module.

The CM is a double walled structure and is the habitat of astronauts. The CM is designed to re-enter the Earth's atmosphere and has an ablative thermal protection system (TPS) to protect it during the intense aerodynamic heating during flight through the atmosphere. An ablat-

Vyomamitra

Even before orbiting astronauts on India's first manned mission to the space, ISRO will let 'Vyomamitra', a 'lady robot', accompany the unmanned Gaganyaan spacecraft in 2022.

Vyomamitra, (Vyoma meaning Space and Mitra meaning Friend, a half-humanoid robot, can talk, monitor module parameters, perform life support operations, do activities like switch panel operations, recognise astronauts, be their companion and converse with them and also respond to their queries.

ing TPS mitigates the incoming heat through phase changes, chemical reactions and material removal. is designed for the CM. during re-entry, the temperature on eternal surface of CM can reach as high as 1600°C. The TPS will ensure that the substrate temperature is not exceeding 120°C under worst case scenario. The temperature inside the crew cabin will be maintained at comfortable levels by the thermal control system.

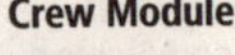

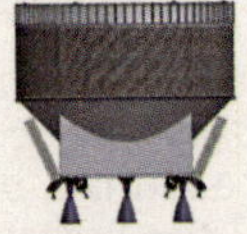

After de-orbiting, the CM will be separated from OM and it will be continuously maintained in the required orientation through the closed loop navigation, guidance and control system. In a controlled manner, the CM will re-enter the Earth's atmosphere. The CM has cluster of small thrusters with 100N thrust level based on green propulsion that will be fired in controlled manner to change the attitude of CM during the re-entry and atmospheric phases of flight.

By virtue of its orbital height and velocity, the OM possess huge amount of energy. More than 99% of CM energy will be dissipated through aerobraking while travelling through the atmosphere. Remaining energy will be killed by deploying a two stage Parachute system. The Parachutes will reduce the CM speed to less than 8 m/s at splashdown in sea.

3.1 Recovery from sea: The CM will be splashing down in sea near the Indian coast. The Arabian sea is comparatively calmer and is the primary choice for landing. As back up, landing option in Bay of Bengal also will be considered. After landing, the coordinates of CM will be passed on to the recovery team waiting in ships. The recovery team will approach the CM and the crew will be recovered. There will be redundant communication and locating systems for easy recovery of crew from sea. The CM has survival packet for each crew that can support the them for nearly two days, however the crew will be recovered in nominal conditions within two hours after the splash down.

3.2 Crew training:

The astronaut training is a crucial part of any human space flight mission. The crew will be familiarized with all conceivable situations that can happen while in flight and they will be trained to face such situation. The training will include class room sessions on different engineering, medical and safety aspects of the mission. The crew will undergo training in weightlessness condition by flying in special aircraft through a parabolic path that will give 25 to 30 seconds of weightlessness duration. In order to familiarize the crew with rescue under abort conditions, they will undergo special survival training in sea, snow, mountain range, desert etc. They will be taught to survive in such situation making use of the survival kit available with them. The crew will also undergo long duration training in special simulators that will mimic the interior of Crew module. The training will address how quickly they can don and doff the Flight suit, how to manually intervene under emergency situation to resolve the issue.

For Gaganyaan, the selected four astronaut candidates have undergone generic space flight training at Russia for about 15 months. The Gaganyaan specific training will be carried out in India at the Astronaut Training Facility being set up at Bangalore.

India Rising to $5 Trillion GDP

Suresh Prabhu
Member of Parliament, Rajya Sabha

In 2019, Prime Minister envisioned to make India a USD 5 trillion economy and global power house by 2024-25. This Article explains the efforts being made to reach the $5-trillion economy in the size of a national economy as measured by the annual GDP.

India, being the world's largest democracy has seen a rapid transformation in recent times. We are one of the world's youngest democracies but still among the fastest-growing nations. India has doubled its GDP to nearly $3 trillion within a decade and is currently the world's sixth-largest economy, and is expected to touch the USD 5 trillion mark in the coming years and progress as a key economic engine in Asia.

India marked its 75 years of Independence recently and we are moving towards creating a New India by 2022 which would be Atmanirbhar (Self-reliant India). Under the able leadership of PM Narendra Modi, India is witnessing the next level of governance and transformation which has never been seen in the entire history of the country. With the "Minimum Government, Maximum Governance" model along with the concept of co-operative federalism, PM Modi is leading India to new heights amidst various challenges including COVID-19.

National Institution for Transforming India (NITI Aayog) is playing a big role in tackling development challenges in the country through policy advocacy. 115

districts have been identified across the nation as aspirational districts and are being ranked based on progress being made (delta ranking) on a real-time basis based on 49 indicators from the 5 identified thematic areas-Health & Nutrition, Education, Agriculture & Water Resources, Financial Inclusion & Skill Development, and Basic Infrastructure. In December 2019, NITI Aayog had released the second edition of the Sustainable Development Goals (SDG) India Index and an online dashboard to track the progress on 17 SDGs of all the States and Union Territories (UTs) on a set of 100 National Indicators. India has made considerable progress especially in SDG 6: Clean water and sanitation by constructing over 11 crore toilets to become open defecation-free (ODF) in five years through Swachh Bharat Abhiyan launched in 2014. PM Modi was conferred the "Global Goalkeeper" award by the Bill and Melinda Gates Foundation in 2019 for this campaign which was also marked Mahatma Gandhi's 150th birth anniversary. Recently, Hon'ble PM was also conferred with the Global Energy and Environment Leadership Award by Cambridge Energy Research Associates (CERA) for his commitment to expanding India's leadership in sustainable development to meet the country's, and the world's, future energy needs.

Industries plays an important role in developing Indian economy. India's Ease of Doing Business (EoDB) rank according to the World Bank's Ease of Doing Business Report 2020 is 63rd among 190 countries. This is a jump of 79 positions from 142nd in 2014 to 63rd in 2019. Among 10 parameters for measuring EoDB, rapid changes have been brought especially in issuing construction permits where India's ranking has improved from 184 in 2014 to 27 in 2019, and ease of getting electricity where the ranking has improved from 137 in 2014 to 22 in 2019.

On the other hand, Foreign Direct Investment (FDI) inflows between April 2014 - September 2019 stood at $319 bn which is nearly 50% of total FDI inflow in the last 20 years. During FY 2020-21, the total FDI inflow of $35.73 billion is the highest ever for the first five months of a financial year. Recently the government has also approved 100 percent FDI through the automatic route in coal mining, 100 percent FDI through the direct route in contract manufacturing, and 74 percent through automatic route in the Defence sector. FDI in India is estimated to reach $100 billion inflow per annum by 2022. This will further boost our domestic manufacturing and will also help in employment generation.

The startup culture in India has seen massive growth with more than 40,000 startups recognized till December 2020 by the Department for Promotion of Industry and Internal Trade (DPIIT) under the Start-Up India scheme launched in 2016. Thousands of young people are aiming to become young entrepreneurs with a wide number of events being organized regularly through Startup India Initiative including boot camps, hackathons, and online competitions. The government's flagship initiatives like Atal Innovation Mission (AIM), have helped advance India's position in the Global Innovation Index from 81 in 2015 to 48 in 2020. Through this initiative, the promotion of a culture of innovation and entrepreneurship across the length and breadth of our country has been started right from school education through setting up of 4870+ operational Atal Tinkering Labs in 660+ districts impacting around 2.5 million students.

The Digital India campaign launched in 2015 has ensured the creation of a digitally empowered society and knowledge economy. Development of broadband highways, universal access to mobile connectivity, public internet access programmes, e-governance among others have seen considerable growth with Aadhaar, Smart Cities Mission, BHIM UPI, RuPay, GSTIn, GeM (Government e-Marketplace), DigiLocker coming under the aegis of the Digital India programme. Through the Bharat Net programme which is also the world's largest rural broadband connectivity program, 2.5 lakh gram panchayats are being connected by a fiber-optic network of which around 1,48,000 connections have been achieved so far. India's Aadhaar has become the world's largest biometric database with almost 125 crore Aadhaar cards being issued so far and is playing a pivotal role in preventing leakages via its integration with the Direct Benefit Transfer (DBT) scheme. Apart from this, through schemes like Jan Dhan Yojana launched in 2014 by the government, 41.38 Crore beneficiaries have banked so far with ₹130,932.33 Crore Balance in beneficiary accounts. Bill Gates recently hailed India's Inclusion policies and called UPI and Aadhaar a phenomenal system that has drastically reduced the cost of money distribution among the poor. According to the 2019 global Multidimensional Poverty Index India has lifted 271 million people out of poverty between 2006 and 2016. Mudra loan scheme launched in 2015 by providing credit up to ₹10 lakh to non-farming and non-corporate micro and small enterprises has helped enable every last mile financer to lend credit to all types of businesses in the country. Pradhan Mantri Kisan Samman Nidhi Yojana launched in 2019 is providing ₹6,000 per year as minimum income support to all farmers. The Agriculture sector reform bills passed by the government last year will further facilitate farmers by providing them new markets, advantages of technology, and helping bring investments and double their income by 2022.

India's Global stature has improved considerably with its election as Chair of the World Health Organization's Executive Board in May 2020 and being elected as a non-permanent member of the United Nations Security Council (UNSC) for a two-year term in June 2020. India is emerging as a global power and is scheduled to host the G20 in 2023.

But today, India faces some major challenges like tackling the COVID-19 pandemic, cross border terrorism and competition from global markets. But it is important to note that India is dealing strategically with all these challenges and has especially dealt with the pandemic better than any country in the world. Even after a number of challenges posed to the economy due to the pandemic, the recent record GDP growth of

20.1% in the previous quarter of this year, is a proof of able management of economy by the finance minister under Prime Ministers guidance. This is India's fastest quarterly growth rate since the mid-1990s. Also, the growth in All India GSDP and Per Capita Income is at a decent rate according to the latest Economic Survey of 2020-21.

We have the highest Covid patient recovery rates of around 95% and a plan in place to vaccinate all of our citizens soon. India manufactures more than 60% of all vaccines sold across the globe and today is the most sought-after destination for manufacturing COVID-19 vaccines. The world's largest distributor of vaccines - Serum Institute of India (SII) is also located in India. Atmanirbhar Bharat economic stimulus relief package of 20 lakh crore amounting to 10% of GDP was released this year to fight the pandemic. 80 crore people were given free food grains till November 2020 under PM Garib Kalyan Yojana and 20 crore women Jan Dhan holders were given ₹500 per month for 3 months. MNREGA wage rate was increased to ₹202 per person per day and is benefiting 13.62 crore families. The new National Education Policy (NEP), 2020 will make India a global knowledge superpower. Today, Artificial Intelligence, Machine learning, and Big Data are setting the path for the future and India is not far away. Through the SWAYAM portal, the government is bridging the digital divide for students who have limited access to the digital revolution and have not been able to join the mainstream of the knowledge economy. Under the 'Make in India' initiative the Micro, Small, and Medium Enterprises (MSME) contribution to the GDP is being targeted to be increased to 50 percent from the existing 30 percent which will create 5 crore jobs in the next few years.

Indian economy has seen a rapid progress in the past 7 years. In my tenure as a Union Minister holding different portfolios with active support from PM Modi, I have taken many initiatives which helped boost economy.

In a short span of time, I have engaged with global leaders and thinkers and have led delegations across the globe for our Nations development. I have joined Rishihood University as its Founding Chancellor and working towards SDG 4: Quality Education and implementing the New Education Policy (NEP). I initiated "The Cooperative Development Forum (CDF)" with seven prominent cooperative leaders who will work towards promoting cooperative movement in the country and boost the rural economy and "The India Bamboo Forum (IBF)" where a voluntary group of 55 committed leaders in the bamboo sector will promote entrepreneurship, research, and trade of high-quality bamboo products in a sustainable manner. "Nisarg Forum" is another actionable programme being carried out to create people's movement nationwide to save environment and conserve water.

Although India is facing unprecedented challenges due to the covid19 pandemic, the rapid vaccination drive has given us a new hope to return to normalcy. Seeing the pace of development works taking place under PM Modi's leadership, I am hopeful that we will overcome all the challenges and create a "New India" by 2022.

Unsung Freedom Fighters of Indian Independence

Dr Vijay Mittal, New Delhi

Our hard-fought freedom was won by many heroes who sacrificed their lives. Many of these freedom fighters are known to us. Here we take a look at 75 freedom fighters who stuck to the cause and never cared to be in the limelight –the unsung heroes.

Any fight for National freedom is hard fought. Similar has been the case in India. Many freedom fighters are known to posterity but quite a significant number remain relatively unknown though their contribution in freedom struggle has been no less. They stuck to the cause and never cared to be in limelight. On the occasion of 75 years of Indian Independence let's take a look at these unsung heroes of our freedom struggle.

1. Ahmadullah Shah (1787-1858) Led in various battles including Battle of Chinhat, seige of Lucknow and Chapati movement.

2. Akkamma Cherian (1909-1982, 'Accamma'): imprisoned twice; once imprisoned with her sister Rosamma Punnose in 1939 during the freedom struggle. She appealed to women to join the struggle, in Kerala.

3. Alluri Sitarama Raju (1897-1924) Led Rampa Rebellion in 1922-24 with support of other local tribals nicknamed Manyam Veerudu (hero of jungles).

Alluri Sitarama Raju

4. Anant Laxman Kanhere (1892-1910) executed for murder of oppressive British officer A M Jackson.

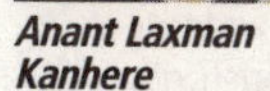

Anant Laxman Kanhere

Annie Besant

5. Annie Besant (1847-1933) freedom fighter from UK, studied Hindu religion, Hindu philosophy from Central Hindu School in Varanasi which was expanded by Madan Mohan Malviya as Kashi Hindu Vishwavidyalaya, laid stress on religion, education, social reforms and politics. Initiated Commonwheel and New India newspapers, was President of Indian National Congress in 1917.

6. Annie Mascarene (1902-1963) activist. arrested several times while compaigning for independence.

7. Aruna Asif Ali (1909-1996). During Quit India Movement she hoisted Indian National Congress flag at Gowalia Tank Maidan in Bombay.

Aruna Asif Ali

8. Ashfaqulla Khan (1900-1927) One of the main mind behind Kakori Conspiracy. He along with Ram Prasad Bismil and Chandrashekhar Azad looted the train carrying British government money in Kakori near Lucknow on August 9 1925. He had escaped but was betrayed by his friend and was later hanged on 19.12.1927.

9. Babu Kunwar Singh (1777-1858) Rajput military commander in Indian rebellion of 1857

10. Badal Gupta (1912-1930) entered Writers Building wearing European outfits and killed IGP of prisons Cl. NS Simpson, notorious for torturing nationalist prisoners.

11. Bagha Jatin (1879-1915) founding member of Anushilan Samiti, convicted in Howrah Shibpur Conspiracy Case, participated in Indo German Conspiracy.

12. Baikuntha Shukla (1907-1934) Revolutionary, executed for murdering a government witness.

13. Batukeshwar Dutt (1910-1965) exploded bombs with Bhagat Singh in Central Legislative Assembly on 8.4.1929 to protest against Trade Dispute Bill and shouted Inquilab Zindabad, arrested and imprisoned for life, initiated hunger strike with Bhagat Singh against maltreatment of Indian prisoners.

14. Begum Hazrat Mahal (1820 – 1879), Took part in 1857 First War of Independence. She took charge of Awadh and Lucknow after her husband had been exiled. Later she had to retreat to Nepal where she died.

Begum Hazrat Mahal

15. Benoy Basu (1908-1930) entered Writers Building wearing European outfits and killed IGP of prisons Cl. NS Simpson, notorious for torturing nationalist prisoners.

16. Bhogeswari Phukanani (1885-1942) Launched revolutionary mass program Bhar Bhuj and was shot down by British.

17. Bipin Chandra Pal (1858- 1932) Nationalist, founding member of Swadeshi movement, compaigned for complete Swaraj and Swadeshi movement.

18. Birsa Munda (1875-1900) He headed Millenarian movement inspiring tribal belt of Bihar and Jharkhand to go against British Regiment in late 19th century. He died at 25 years of age.

Birsa Munda

19. Dadabhai Naoroji (1825-1917) freedom fighter, formed Indian Society and East India Association in London, President of Indian National Congress in 1886, 1993 and 1906. coined the word Swaraj in 1906, member of House of Commons of Britain.

20. Dhan Singh Gurjar (1821-1857) police chief of Meerut, participated in 1857 rebellion, led initial action against British in Meerut.

21. Dinesh Gupta (1911-1931) entered Writers Building wearing European outfits and killed IGP of prisons colonel NS Simpson, notorious for torturing nationalist prisoners.

22. Durgabai Deshmukh (1909-1981) member of Constituent Assembly and Planning Commission of India, took active part in freedom movement.

Durgabai Deshmukh

23. Jatindra Nath Das (1904-1929) died during hunger strike while awaiting trial for Lahore Conspiracy Case.

24. Kamladevi Chattopadhyay (1903-1988) First Indian woman to be arrested by British regime. Social reformer , promoted handicraft and handloom to uplift socio-economic standard of women. She was also the first woman to run for legislative seat in India.

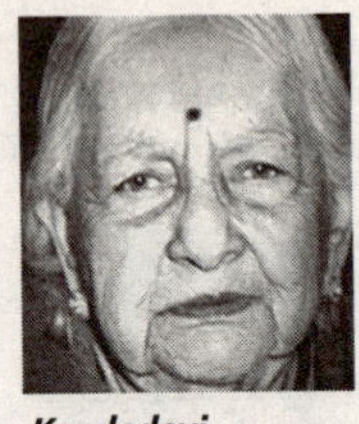
Kamladevi Chattopadhyay

25. Kanaklata Barua (1924-1942). (Birbala) took part in Quit India Movement in 1942. led women volunteers to hoist National Flag at British dominated Gohpur police station. She was shot dead at 18 years of age

26. Kaneganti Hanumanthu (1870-1920) Led Palanadu rebellion against excessive tax, arrested several times and killed by British at 30 years of age.

27. Kanhaiyalal Maniklal Munshi (1887-1971) Took active part in Quit India Movement, founded Bharatiya Vidya Bhavan. He was arrested a number of times during freedom struggle.

Kanhaiyalal Maniklal Munshi

28. K Kelappan (1889-1971) Joined Non-coperation and Quit India movements; held Satyagrahas at Vaikom and Guruvayur.Imprisoned.

29. KE Mammen (1921-2017) A Gandhian from Kerala, participated in Quit India movement. He was president of the Travancore Students Federation and he invoked youth to join the freedom struggle movement. Often referred to as

KE Mammen

the Khadar wearing Kerala Gandhi.

Khudiram Bose

30. Khudiram Bose (1889-1908) Revolutionary, arrested at 15 years of age. Started planting bombs by 16 years of age, made assassination attempt on Douglas Kingsford the chief magistrate of Presidency Court of Alipore.

31. Kittur Chennamma (1778-1829) freedom fighter, Rani of Kittur of former princely state of Karnataka, led Armed force against British East India company in 1824, was defeated in the third war and died in prison.

32. Krishanji Gopal Karye (1887-1910) executed as accomplice in murder of A M T Jackson

Krishanji Gopal Karye

Kushal Konwar

33. Kushal Konwar (1905-1943) president of Sarupathar Congress committee. He was Tai Ahom freedom fighter from Asom, hanged in last phase of Quit India Movement in 1943, mastermind of the troop train derailment and hanged.

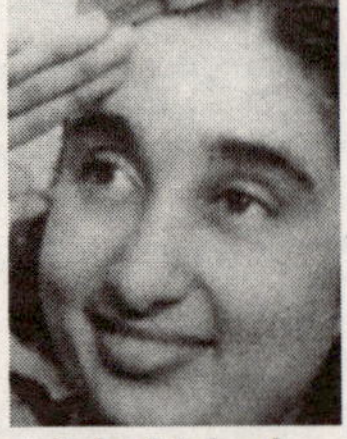
Lakshmi Sahgal

34. Lakshmi Sahgal (1914-2012). An Indian army officer as Captain Lakshmi. World War II veteran, was sent as prisoner to Burma. She founded Rani of Jhansi Regiment under orders of Subhash Chandra Bose.

35. Lala Hardayal (1884-1939) had very sharp and great memory, a book, M A in English and, principal of St Stephen's College Delhi, taught in Saint John College in Oxford, editor of Punjabi newspaper Vande Mataram in Paris, founded the Ghadar party in US.

Madam Bhikaiji Cama

36. Madam Bhikaiji Cama (1861-1936) Parsi. She advocated gender equality and took part in Indian Independence and donated her material possessions to an orphanage for girls. She hoisted first Indian flag at International socialist conference at Stuttgart Germany in 1908. The flag had three horizontal bands. Red, white and green. The red band had lotus flower and seven stars, the white band had Vande Mataram in devanagari and the green band had sun and moon. Started Vande Mataram weekly newspaper from Geneva. She was dead against helping British in First World War.

37. Madan Lal Dhingra (1883-1909) assassinated Curzon Wyllie in England firing 5 shots on his face, cited as First Act of Indian independence in 20th century on August 17 1909.

38. Madhusudan Das (1848-1934) leader of christian community in Odisha, known as Utkal Gaurav, first graduate and advocate of Odisha.

39. Mangal Pandey (1827-1857) From Nagwa India. Indian soldier, played key part before 1857 War of Independence, sepoy in 34th Bengal Native Infantry Regiment of British East India company,

inspired several cinematic productions.

40. Matangini Hazra (1870-1942) (Gandhi Buri). Took part in Quit India and Non Cooperation Movement. She kept shouting Vande Mataram with Indian flag in hand despite being shot thrice and died.

Matangini Hazra

41. Maulvi liaqat Ali (1812-1892) leader of Sepoy Mutiny, captured Khusro Bagh in Allahabad and declared independence of India.

42. Maveeran Alagumuthu Kone Yadav (1710-1759) early chieftain military leader, executed by British in 1759.

43. Parbati Giri - was only 16 but actively in the forefront of all freedom activities, especially the Quit India Movement. She was imprisoned for 2 years for taking part in such activities. Giri served the public socially post independence and was known as the Mother Teresa of Western Orissa.

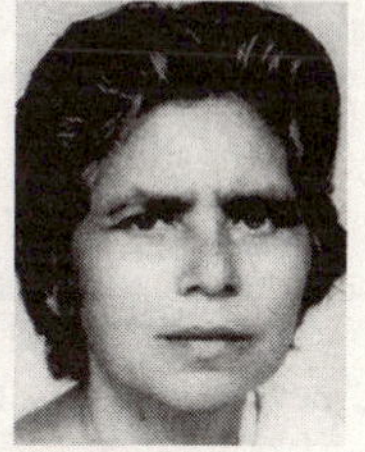

Parbati Giri

44 Pasumpon Muthuramalinga Thevar (1908-1963) leader of socialist All India Forward Bloc, arrested and jailed by British.

45. Peer Ali Khan 1812-1857) In the first war of independence in 1857 he was given death sentence and inspired many to fight for Indian Independence.

Peer Ali Khan

46. Potti Sriramulu (died 1952) Supporter and devotee of Mahatma Gandhi. Gandhi admired his dedication towards humanitarian purposes and remarked". If I could have 11 more followers like Sreeramulu I will win freedom in a year".

Potti Sriramulu

47. Prafulla Chaki (1888- 1908) partner of Khudiram Bose in assassination attempt of Muzaffarpur. Also threw bombs on carriage of chief magistrate Douglas Kingsford but that lead to death of two British ladies. He assumed the name of Dinesh Chandra Roy during the mission but was arrested next day and committed suicide with his own revolver before anybody could harm him.

48. Pritilata Waddedar (1911-1932) Bengali revolutionary, led attack on European Club in Pahartali and committed suicide to avoid capture.

49. Raja Nahar Singh (1821-1858) Jat ruler of Ballabgarh, secured road from Delhi Gate to Bharatpur and drove British away from Pali, Palwal and Fatehpur.

50. Rajkumari Gupta (birth 1902) She took crucial part in Kakori case and worked along with her husband with Mahatma Gandhi and Chandrashekhar Azad. She hid firearms in her undergarments and delivered them holding her 3 year old son. On arrest she was disowned by her marital home.

51. Ram Prasad Bismil (1897-1927) Involved in executing Kakori Kand on

Ram Prasad Bismil

9.8.1925. He wrote various books to spread revolutionary thoughts. wrote patriotic poems in Hindi, Urdu, hIs final letter to his mother is taught to children in many schools. He was executed along with Ashfaqulla Khan on 19.12.1927.

52. Ramadevi Choudhury (1899-1985) Hailed as Maa by people of Odisha, took part in Non Cooperation movement and travelled different villages asking women to participate in Indian Revolution, adopted khadi and worked to uplift harijans.

53. Rani Gaidinliu (1915-1993) Naga spiritual, fought against Naga religious conversion into Christianity. Initiated Heraka movement to drive Britishers away from Manipur at 13 years of age, arrested at 16 years and given life imprisonment. Nehru gave her title Rani, released after 10 years.

Rani Gaidinliu

54. Sangolli Rayanna (1796-1831) Army Chief of Kittur, fought British East India company.

55. Senapati Bapat (1880-1967) He led Mulshi Satyagraha and got the honour of hoisting Indian flag in Pune for first time after Indian Independence. Earlier he had been jailed for vandalism, then turned himself as a satyagrahi and shed path of violence.

Senapati Bapat

56. Seth Harchandrai Vishandas (1862-1928) Sindhi politician, mayor of Karachi, fought for Hindu Muslim Unity, opposed Simon Commission of 1912.

57. Sah Mal (1834-1857) Rebel of Baroda, led 3500 local jat peasants who fought against British soldiers of East India Company

58. Shambhu Dutt Sharma (1918-2016) British Indian army officer, joined Quit India Movement in 1942

59. Shaukat Ali (1873-1938) Revolutionary, campaigned for independence and supplied weapons to revolutionaries.

60. Shivaram Rajguru (1908-1931) Was executed at 22 years of age along with Bhagat Singh and Sukhdev for killing British Police officer J P Saunders.

Shivaram Rajguru

61. Shyamji Krishna Varma (1857 -1947) Nationalist was from a very poor background. Sanskrit literateur, lawyer, greatly influenced by Maharshi Dayanand, founded Indian Home Rule Society, India House and Indian Socialogist in London. Worked with Madam Bhikaiji Cama in Paris, supplied arms to revolutionaries in India, wrote a book "how to make bomb."

62. Sucheta Kriplani (1908-1974) first lady CM of India (Uttar Pradesh). Founder of all India Mahila Congress in 1948 Gandhian, sang Vande Mataram on 15.8.1947 in Constituent Assembly.

Sucheta Kriplani

63. Sukhdev Thapar (1907-1931) executed along with Bhagat Singh and Rajguru, also participated in prison hunger strike of 1929.

64. Tanguturi Prakasam Pantulu. (1872-1957) called Andhra Kesari for

leading protest against Simon Commission in Madras.

65. Tararani Srivastava She led a procession at Siwan police station. When her husband was shot she bandaged His wounds and continued moving forward holding Indian flag high.

Tararani Srivastava

66. TatyaTope (1814-1859) freedom fighter, took part in First War of Independence.

67. Tirot Sing (1802-1835) chief of Khasi people, died fighting British during their attempt to take over Khasi Hills.

Tirot Sing

Tiruppur Kumaran

68. Tiruppur Kumaran (1904-1932) Native of Tirupur near Coimbatore. Nicknamed Kodi Katha Kumaran (Kumar who save the flag.) Founded Desh Bandhu Youth Association. He was killed during protest march for holding flag of Indian Nationalists on 11.1.1932. He was found dead still holding the flag.

69. Titumir (1782-1831) freedom fighter, built a bamboo fort in Narikelberia village which became subject of Bengali folk legend, died of wounds following storming by British forces.

Titumir

70. T V Thomas (1910-1977) one of trade union leaders in Kerala, actively involved in independence movement.

71. Udham Singh (1899-1940) revolutionary of Gadar party assassinated Michael O Dyer in London to revenge Jallianwala Bagh massacre in Amritsar in 1919 assumed name of Ram Mohammad Singh Azad to represent three religions of Punjab also referred to as Shahid A Azam Sardar Udham Singh, hanged in July 1940.

Udham Singh

72. Umaji Naik Khomane (1791-1832) Challenged British rule (1826-32) known as Vishva Krantiveer narveer Raje Umaji Naik.

Umaji Naik Khomane

73. Vanchinathan (1886-1912) revolutionary, killed oppressive tax collector Robert Ashe and committed suicide.

74 Vada Narasimha Reddy (1806-1847) Led an uprising in Andhra Pradesh in 1846 and was executed by British.

75. Veerapandiya Kattabomman. (1762-1799) Tamil chieftain hanged by British on 16th Oct 1799.

Veerapandiya Kattabomman

Timeline

75 Years Since Indian Independence

Azadi Ka Amrit Mahotsav is an initiative of the Government of India to celebrate and commemorate 75 years of progressive India and the glorious history of its people, culture and achievements.

This Mahotsav is dedicated to the people of India who have not only been instrumental in bringing India thus far in its evolutionary journey but also hold within them the power and potential to launch India to the next level, India 2.0, fuelled by the spirit of Atmanirbhar Bharat.

Azadi ka Amrit Mahotsav is an embodiment of all that is progressive about India's socio-cultural, political and economic identity. The *Mahotsav* commenced on 12th March, 2021 – a 75 week countdown to our 75th anniversary of Independence and will end post a year on 15th August, 2023. PM Modi lists 5 pillars for celebrating India's 75 years of independence – "Freedom Struggle, Ideas at 75, Achievements at 75, Actions at 75 and Resolve at 75. "We have to celebrate this festival of 75 years of independence by taking 130 crore countrymen together. Public participation is the core spirit of this event."The country cannot progress by denying anyone's contribution. The country goes forward by accepting and respecting everyone's contributions and we want to follow this mantra, says" the Prime Minister.

On the 75th anniversary of India's independence, let us look at the progress we have made in political, economic, agricultural and environmental programmes besides sports.

Political

1947: The Backdrop After the World War-II (1 Sept. 1939-2 Sept 1945) India witnessed decolonisation, nation-building efforts, rise in developmental and welfare economy, beginning of the Non-Aligned Movement, import-substitution through self-reliance programme and war with neighbours. But at the global stage America emerged in 1945 as the undisputed victor of the war with its large navy, air force, and an army that was rivalled only by that of the Soviets. Hence two great

Role of India during WW-II

powers forming two super-power blocs US and the Soviet Union began an undeclared Cold War between them that stretched from earth to space and from scientific advancement to nuclear race. Their ideology of communism and capitalism emerged as strong point of conflict between each other dividing nations into two halves, politically.

During WW-II, the British had mobilised India's resources for their imperial war effort. And at the same time, in a bid to win Congress support, Britain had promised to give India full independence once the war was over. Britain hoped that a self-governing India would remain part of the imperial defence.

Soon after the end of the WW-II, British officials were exhausted and troops were demoralised. It was clear that Britain lacked the means to defeat a renewed mass campaign by the Congress. In the meantime Mahatma Gandhi and the Indian National Congress organised movements across India to force them to 'quit India' in 1942. By the time the last viceroy, Lord Louis Mountbatten, arrived in India, Jawaharlal Nehru understood the moves of Md. Ali Jinnah who was seeking a Muslim majority state as East and West Pakistan, at the time of transfer of power from British into Indian hands. Anyway that decision was left to Mountbatten to hand-over power.

1947: British India consisted of 17 provinces and 563 princely states. In 1947, India was a country with a large impoverished population, fledgling industries and suffering from food shortages.

Casualities of Soldiers Before and After Independence

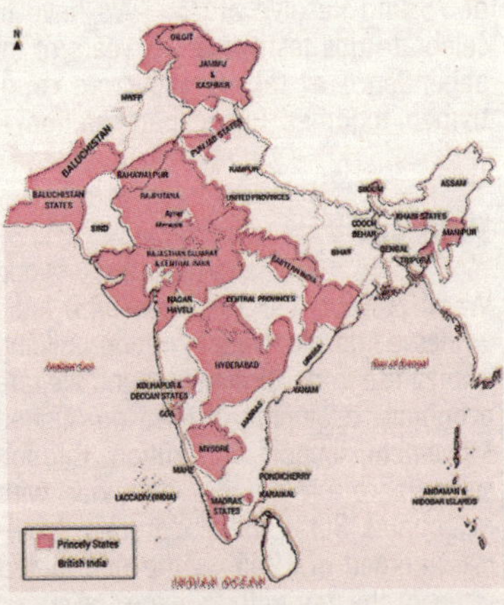

Pre-partition Map of India - before 1947

Our biggest challenges then were that of national integration and nation-building.

•August 14. Britain divides India into two – India and Pakistan; It was midnight on 14 August. At one minute past, as the 15th dawned, India became free. In front of numerous guests in the assembly hall of the Council House, Jawaharlal Nehru, took the Oath of Office as the prime minister of free India.

And then delivered a speech celebrating India's independence.

"Long years ago we made a tryst with destiny, and now the time comes when we shall redeem our pledge, not wholly or in full measure, but very substantially. At the stroke of the midnight hour, when the world sleeps, India will awake to life and freedom. A moment comes, which comes but rarely in history, when we step out from the old to the new, when an age ends, and when the soul of a nation, long suppressed, finds utterance. It is fitting that at this solemn moment, we take the pledge of dedication to the service of India and her people and to the still larger cause of humanity."

Conches were blown, shouts of 'Mahatma Gandhi ki jai!' were heard. While it rained outside thousands danced in the lit and decorated streets of Delhi. And the day after that, the 16th, there was a ceremony at the Red Fort. Probably a million people had gathered there. .Jawaharlal Nehru spoke, beginning with the words 'Jai Hind!', and all roared in response, repeating those words with joy. India national flag, the tricolour, was raised.

•Independence coincided with partition. It was accompanied by violent riots and mass casualties, and the displacement of nearly 15 million people due to religious violence. The partition resulted in migration of about 35 lakh Hindus, Sikhs from West Punjab fearing repression and killing of 10 lakhs in communal violence

and riots

•Oct 22. First War with Pakistan: Pakistan's Operation Gulmarg starts to take

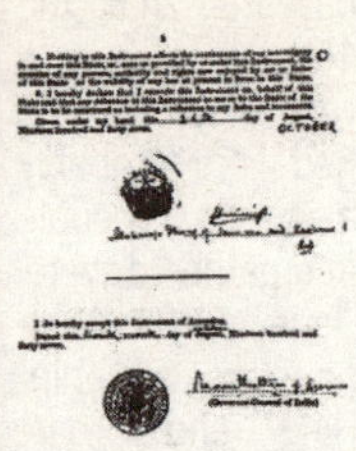

over Kashmir. Armed Lashkar of Pathan tribesmen from Pak NWFP attacked Jammu and Kashmir (J&K). The raiders takes over Muzaffarabad.24. GoI gets the first information of invasion of Kashmir. 26. Raiders enter town of Baramula. Maharaja of J&K Hari Singh signs Instrument of Accession with India in return for defending the kingdom. 27.Governor General of India accepts it. The Indian Army enters the State.

01 Nov. Indian Army recaptures Zoji La Pass. 3 Nov. Raiders reaches close to Srinagar airport but repelled.

•Population: 340 m. Literacy: 41m (12%). 1948: 30. Jan. Assassination of Mahatma Gandhi by Nathuram Vinayak Godse. •Fighting continues as regular Pak army gets involved. 1949: 01 Jan. the war with Pakistan ends when UN negotiated a cease-fire. •Nov. 26 – The Constitution of India was adopted by the Constituent Assembly.• India remained a dominion till 1950.• India records 1m Hindu refugees into West Bengal and other states from East Pakistan. 1950: On 24 Jan. The members of the Constituent Assembly adopted the National Anthem – Jana Gana Mana – written by Rabindranath Tagore in Bengali and later translated into Hindi. •India adopted its new constitution and on 26 Jan., India became a Republic at 10.18 am. A few minutes later, at 10.24 am •Dr. Rajendra Prasad was sworn in as the first President of India. •The first Constitution of India was handwritten in Hindi and in English. It was signed by the members of the Constituent Assembly on 24 January, 1950. 1952: India's 1st general elections. 60% turnout. Jawaharlal Nehru becomes the first elected PM. Potti Sreeramulu dies in his fast-unto-death over demand for statehood for Andhra. It led to formation of state re-organisation commission. 1953 22 Dec. The State Reorganisation Commission (SRC) constituted. 1954: JK's accession to India is ratified by the state's constituent assembly. 1955: The SRC recommends formation of 14 states and 6 UTs. Rajpath was chosen as the permanent venue. This was the first Republic Day parade. 1956 State Re-organisation Act passed. •01 Nov. The State Reorganisation Act implemented- birthing 14 states. Andhra Pradesh, Bombay, Kerala, MP, Madras, Mysore, Punjab and Rajasthan formed linguistically.•Poverty: 65% (215 m). 1957: J&K approves India's constitution, except Communication Defence and Foreign relations.

1962: Chinese Army invades India in Ladakh, and across the McMahon Line in the Arunachal Pradesh. 1965: India's second war with Pakistan over Kashmir. 1968: Madras state renamed as Tamil Nadu. 1971: India fights 3rd war with Pakistan; East Pakistan breaks away from Pakistan and Bangladesh gains independence. 1972: 21 Jan. Meghalaya, Manipur and Tripura formed.•India and Pakistan sign the Simla Pact to sort out disputes

bilaterally. 1973: Anti-royalist riots in Sikkim. 1975: 16 May. Sikkim merged with Indian Unionas the 22nd state.• National Emergency imposed. •PM of Sikkim appeals to India to make Sikkim a state of India. 1977: Emergency ends. First non-Congress government elected at the centre. 1979: The Janata Party government collapses. 1980: The BJP is formed after internal differences in the Janata Party. 1984: Operation Blue Star launched to drive out the Sikh extremists from the Golden Temple in Amritsar. PM Indira Gandhi assassinated by two of her Sikh bodyguards. • The Bhopal Gas Tragedy : leakage of toxic gas from Union Carbide India kills 3,500 people and injures 500,000. 1987: India-Sri Lanka pact signed to establish peace and normalcy in Sri Lanka after tensions between majority Sinhala and minority Tamils. India deploys troops in Sri Lanka to ensure peace. 1988: PM Rajiv Gandhi visits China and meets Deng Xiaoping—the first visit to China by an Indian PM in 34 years. 1989: Outbreak of militancy in J&K. 1990: Cauvery tribunal formed to resolve 150-year-old river water dispute between Karnataka and Tamil Nadu.• VP. Singh government tables Mandal Commission recommendations for 27% reservation for OBC candidates in all levels of government services. 1992: The Babri Masjid demolished. 1993: Serial bomb blasts in Bombay. 1999: PM Atal Bihari Vajpayee visits Lahore, inaugurates the Delhi-Lahore bus.•Indian Airlines flight IC-814 bound to Delhi from Kathmandu–Kandahar in Afghanistan hijacked. Militants Maulana Masood Azhar, Syed Umar Sheikh and Mushtaq Latram Jerger released in exchange for the hostages •Kargil War – Indian army evicts Pak army and militants from the Kargil heights inside the Line of Control in Kashmir. 2000: The states of Uttarakhand, Chhattisgarh and Jharkhand are formed. 2001: Parliament attack– five terrorists of Lashkar-e-Taiba and Jaish-e-Mohammed storm Indian Parliament. 2002: Gujarat communal violence breaks out after a coach of Sabarmati Express was set on fire at Godhra railway station. 2005: Right to Information Act implemented. 2008: Lashkar-e-Taiba carry out a series of attacks at different locations– Taj hotel, Bombay VT, etc. 2010: Aadhaar card issued by Unique Identification Authority of India for the first time. 2011: World's longest running democratic Left rule comes to an end as Mamata Banerjee defeats communists in West Bengal. 2014: The BJP wins a parliamentary majority for the first time; NDA forms government. •India's 29th state, Telangana, is created. Telangana Rashtra Samithi (TRS) forms the first government in the state. 2015: India invites US president Barack Obama to be the chief guest at Republic Day parade, the first time a US president is invited for the event. 2016: PM Ujjwala Yojana launched to provide LPG connections to BPL women. 2017: General and railway budgets merged for the first time. 2018: The Supreme Court recognises the rights of LGBTQI community and scraps the Section 377, decriminalising any sex other than between man and woman.• The Supreme Court permits women of menstrual age entry into Sabarimala temple. 2019: BJP reelected to the Lok Sabha •Parliament passes. Triple Talaq Bill or Muslim Women (Protection of Rights on Marriage) Bill declaring instant triple talaq illegal – attracting a jail term of 3-years for husband. •Modi-led government revokes Article 370 – it gave special status to J&K and bifurcates it into two UTs of J&K and Ladakh. 2020: India fights Covid-19 pandemic–marked by facial mask, lockdown, personal protective equipment kit; job loss of migrant labourers forced them to move to their homes walking hundreds of kms with their family esp. kids and old parents; online learning and work from home•Double and triple lockdown enforced where ever clusters had formed. 2021: Economy reopening.

Economy

1947: India's GDP was a mere 2.7 lakh crore accounting for a paltry 3 per cent of the world's total GDP.. Forex reserve: $2b. Savings rate: 8%.Poverty incidence: 80% (250m). 1950: India's share of the world economy 4.2% 1951: First Five-Year Plan, based on the Harrod-Domar Model of economic growth and focusing on the primary sector, is presented. 1955: The Imperial Bank of India is nationalized to create the State Bank of India. 1956: Second Five-Year Plan, based on the Feldman-Mahalanobis model and focusing on heavy industry, is presented •Industrial Policy Resolution passed by Parliament – marking the beginning of the Licence Raj•Life insurance is nationalised, and the LIC established. 1958: The first Hindustan Ambassador car is produced. 1959: The Rourkela Steel Plant is commissioned. 1961: GDP growth rate: 3.72%. Annual Change -0.79%. 1968: The Foreign Investment Board is established. 1969: 14 leading banks are nationalised that controlled 85% of the country's deposits on 19th July 1969; The Monopolies and Restrictive Trade Practices Act becomes law.

1970: GDP growth rate: 5.16% 1972: GDP growth rate: -0.55%; General insurance is nationalised. 1973: Coal mines and oil companies are nationalised.• The Foreign Exchange Regulation Act is passed. 1974: Oil struck in the first well at Sagar Samrat, off Bombay High. 1978: Housing Development Finance Corporation Ltd, or HDFC, the first specialised mortgage company in India, disburses its first home loan. 1980: Sixth five-year plan marks the beginning of economic reforms• GDP. growth rate: 6.74% •India's first credit card, Central Card, is introduced by the Central Bank of India. 1981: Infosys Ltd

First Maruti Car Roll-out

is incorporated by N.R. Narayana Murthy and six other co-founders. 1982: Indian Oil Corporation commissions India's first public sector petroleum refinery in Guwahati. 1983: GDP growth rate: 7.29%; First batch of Maruti cars rolls out, priced at about $35,000 apiece. 1985: Significant tax reforms are kicked off by PM Rajiv Gandhi with VP Singh as finance minister. 1986: S&P BSE Sensex, India's first equity index, is launched 1987: India's first debit card is introduced by Citi Bank, first ATM installed in Mumbai by HSBC. 1988: Securities and Exchange Board of India (Sebi) is established. (delegated powers in 1992 after the Parliament passed the SEBI Act.) • India has only $5 billion in reserves; 1991: Jan. India pledged 67 tonnes of gold to IMF after forex reserves plunged to a mere $1.2b –just enough for 3 weeks imports. • 24 July- Finance Minister, Manmohan Singh, presented the most significant budget paving the way for the economic reforms, opening India for global markets which liberalised the nation's economy. 1994: Rupee is made convertible on the current account. 1995: GDP growth rate: 7.57%. 1999: GDP growth rate: 8.85% 2000: Privatisation of insurance business with a 26% limit on FDI in the sector. 2002: Competition Act comes into force. 2005: India's reserves by 2005 grows to $300 billion. 2006: India's largest-ever rural jobs scheme, MGNREGS, is launched. 2008: Tata Motors launches Tata Nano, the world's cheapest car. 2009: Aadhaar Card issued with demographic and biometric information, useful for KYC norms and validationa.2010: GDP growth rate: 8.50% 2011: Population below poverty line 60.4% on less than \$3.20/day (2011); 2G scam is exposed. 2016: 8 Nov. the Indian government announced Demonetisation– bans \$500/- and \$1000/- currencies in order to combat tax evasion and black money. 2017: 01 July: Passage of the Goods and Service Tax (GST) Bill ushers in a uniform tax structure throughout the country. GDP by sector: Agriculture: 15.4%; Industry: 23%; Services: 61.5% (2017 est.) 2019: The top 3% of the population still earn 50% of GDP. Public debt 146.886 trillion (US\$2.1 trillion) 69.037% of GDP (2019). Gross external debt \$543.0 B (2019). 2020: GDP growth rate dipped due to the pandemic. India GDP Growth Rate: -7.96% Annual change: -12.01% 2021: GDP at constant (2011-12) Prices in Q1 of 2021-22 is estimated at Rs 32.38 Cr.

Science and Technology

1947: The first step was developing infrastructure for irrigation - for food grain production, electricity and industries.• British education in India exposed Indians to civil and administrative services and the scientists to foreign institutions of excellence. 1951: The first Indian Institute of Technology is set up in Kharagpur. 1956: India's first atomic reactor, Apsara, goes critical at the Bhabha Atomic Research Centre. 1969: Indian Space Research Organisation (ISRO) founded. •Tarapur Atomic Power 320 MW plant, India's first nuclear power plant went operational.

1974: 18 May- India's first successful nuclear bomb tested at Pokhran Test Range (PTR), in Rajasthan, coded 'Smiling Budha'.

1975: April 19 India launches Aryabhata, its first satellite into space • 01 Aug. India's first Satellite Instructional Television Experiment (SITE) begins – 2,400 b/w TV sets came alive in as many villages in six states. 1978: 3 Oct. -The first test tube baby, Durga, in India-is born in Calcutta to Ms Bela Agrawal via in-vitro fertilisation under the care of Dr Subhash Mukhopadhyay . 1983: India's first scientific base station in Antarctica, Dakshin Gangotri, established, near South Pole. •The Integrated Guided Missile Development Program launched to develop a wide range of ballistic missiles. 1984: Rakesh Sharma becomes the first Indian to fly into space. 1988: Maitri, India's first permanent station at the South Pole constructed. •India conducts, Operation Shakti-98 – five nuclear tests in Pokhran, Rajasthan. 2008: India's first unmanned space mission, Chandrayaan-1, reaches the moon. 2009: India launched its first indigenous submarine ballistic missile (SSBN), the INS Arihant. 2013: 5 Nov. - India launched the Mars Orbiter Mission (MOM) 2014: 27 March- India declared a polio free country.•24. Sept. MOM starts orbiting Mars. 2017: 05 June- The first developmental flight of India's heavy lift launch vehicle GSLV Mk-III successfully conducted. 2019: India launches Chandrayaan-2 from Sriharikota, comprising an orbiter, a lander and a rover. •7 Sep. Vikram-lander crashed while descending on moon's surface. 2021: Vaccinated 100 crore persons on 21 October. 2022: ISRO's maned mission to space.

Agriculture and Environment

1947: Food grain Production: 50m tonnes. Agriculture: 54% of India's GDP. 1960: In the mid 1960s, India faced a severe food shortage and nearly escaped from a major famine. India was the largest importer of food, mainly under the PL480 programme of the U.S. 1965: Green Revolution launched to make India self-sufficient in production of food grains, with the first introduction of High Yielding Variety (HYV) seeds in Indian agriculture. *Grey Revolu-

OUR SHARED VISION :
5000 MW by 2023, 12000 MW by 2030 & 25000 MW by 2040
SJVN
POWERING
GREEN GROWTH
HYDRO POWER
WIND POWER
THERMAL POWER
SOLAR POWER
POWER TRANSMISSION
एसजेवीएन
SJVN
PROJECTS IN OPERATION
• 1500 MW Nathpa Jhakri Hydro Power Station
• 412 MW Rampur Hydro Power Station
• 47.6 MW Khirvire Wind Power Station
• 5.6 MW Charanka Solar PV Power Station
• 50 MW Sadla Wind Power Station
PROJECTS UNDER DEVELOPMENT
• 11 Hydro Electric Projects in Himachal Pradesh
• 3 Hydro Electric Projects in Uttrakhand
• 1 Hydro Electric Project in Bhutan
• 2 Hydro Electric Projects in Nepal
• 1 Thermal Power Project in Bihar
• Solar Power Project in Gujarat & UP
• 310 km Double-Circuit Transmission Line
एसजेवीएन लिमिटेड
SJVN Limited
(A Joint Venture of Govt. of India & Govt. of H.P.)
A 'Mini Ratna' & Schedule 'A' PSU | An ISO 9001 : 2015 Certified Company
Regd. Office : SJVN Limited, Shakti Sadan, Corporate Head Quarters, Shanan, Shimla - 171006, Himachal Pradesh (INDIA)
Liaison Office : Office Block, Tower-I, 6th Floor, NBCC Complex, East Kidwai Nagar, New Delhi - 110023 (INDIA)
Website : www.sjvn.nic.in

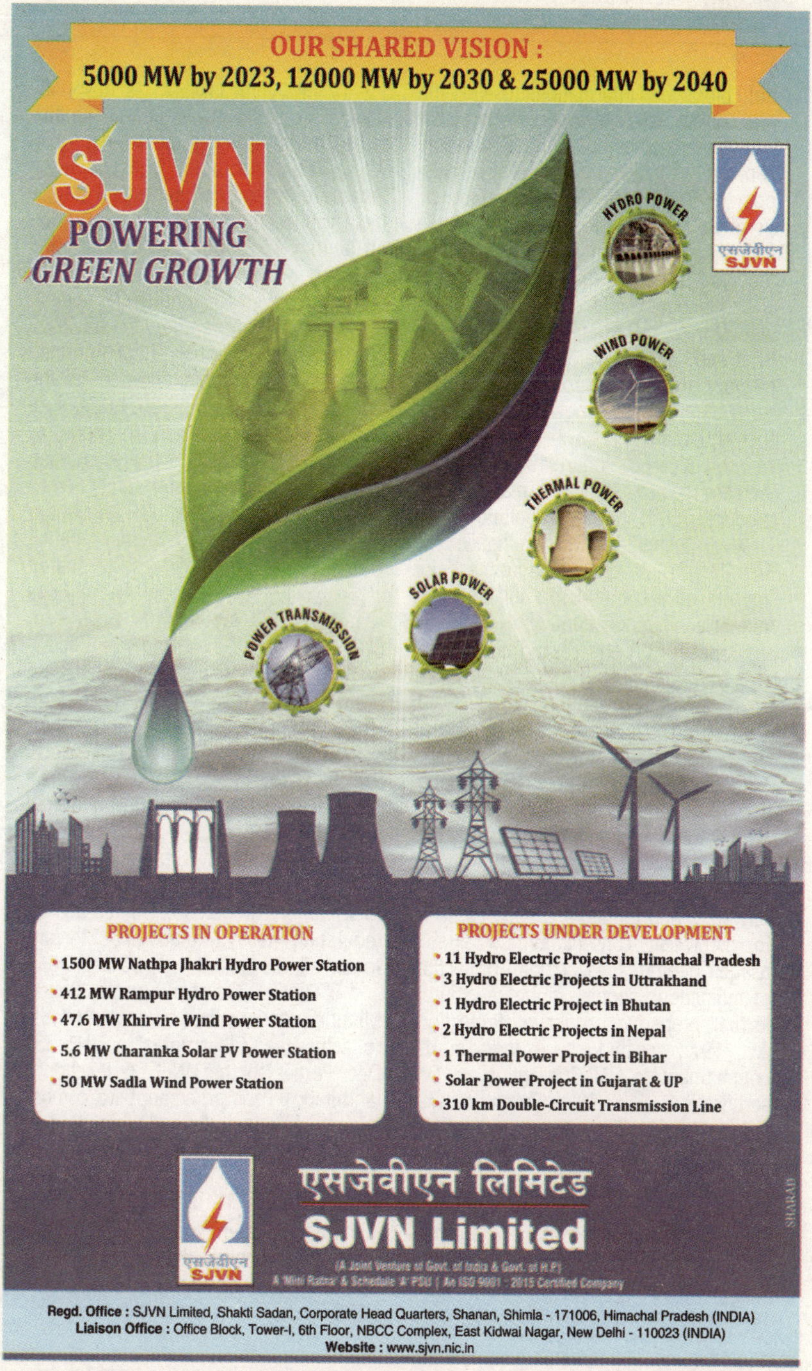

tion: introduced efficient irrigation system and correct use of fertilisers to boost the crop production. 1970: White Revolution: A project of India's National Dairy Development Board (NDDB), initiated by Dr. Verghese Kurien, which transformed India from a milk-deficient nation into one of the world's largest milk producer. 1974: The Chipko movement, (Chipko Andolan), was started by women--Chandi Prasad Bhat and Goura Devi. Sunderlal Bahuguna popularised it as a forest conservation movement at Reni village of Chamoli district, Uttarakhand.

1985: Blue Revolution (1985-1990): To increase the production of fish and marine product. 1986: `Yellow Revolution'. The Oilseeds Technology Mission headed by Sam Pitroda converted India from a major importer to become almost self-sufficient in edible oil production. 1989-90: India signs Basel Convention on Trans-boundary Movement of Hazardous Wastes. 1991: Golden revolution (1991-2003): was started to increase the production of Fruits, Honey and Horticultural produce. *Golden Fibre Revolution: Jute Production. 1992: India became a signatory to Montreal Protocol on Substances that Deplete the Ozone Layer; India signed Convention on Biological Diversity treaty on 5 Jun 1992 and ratified it on 18 Feb 1994 for biodiversity-conservation, sustainable usage, habitat preservation, protection of indigenous people's rights, and intellectual property. * Wildlife (Protection) Act, 1972 enacted. 1994: India makes commitment to UN Convention on Desertification. 1996: *Pink Revolution was led by Durgesh Patel for growing onion and tropical and temperate fruits. *Red Revolution: Tomato Production. Indira Gandhi. *Silver Fibre Revolution: Cotton. *Round Revolution: Potato. 1997: Kyoto Protocol to the UNFCCC Ammendment - Annex-B (at Nairobi, 17.11.2006) India ratifies the second commitment period 2001: Cartagena Protocol on Biosafety under CBD (29, Jan.) India is a signatory to the Protocol and ratified it on Jan. 23, 2003; *Stockholm Convention on Persistent Organic Pollutants, (22 May) -- India ratified the Stockholm Convention on January 13, 2006. 2002: India's first GM crop of three hybrid varieties of Bt cotton approved for commercial release. Brown Revolution: Leather / Cocoa. 2005 *Rotterdam Convention (Prior Informed Consent - PIC), India acceded to the Convention on 24.05. 2006. to promote international cooperation in trade of hazardous chemicals, to protect human health and environmental safety. 2007: India's Rajendra Pachauri, on behalf of IPCC, shared Nobel Peace Prize with Al Gore – for giving scientific evidence that climate change due to both natural and anthropogenic reasons. 2007-2012 Evergreen Revolution: for improving overall production of agriculture. 2010: Nagoya Protocol on Access to Genetic Resources. (Japan 29 October)- India is a signatory to it . 2013: Minamata Conference on regulating heavy metals like Mercury, Japan. - India signed it on 30 Sep. 2014 2014: On 2nd October, Swachh Bharat Mission was launched throughout India to achieve a 'Clean India' . 2015: 12 Dec. Parties to the UNFCCC reached a landmark 'Paris agreement' to combat climate change. India has committed to increase non-fossil fuel power capacity to 40% and boost forest cover to reduce carbon dioxide. 2016: India ratified Paris climate agreement. 2019: Government created Jal Shakti Mantralay to focus on water conservation• PM attended UN Climate Action Summit in New York.

Rajendra Pachauri

2020: Climate Ambition Summit, the 5th anniversary of Paris Agreement. India reiterates its commitment. 2021: Oct31-Nov12 Indian PM to attend COP26 Glasgow UN Climate Summit.

Sports

1951: Independent India hosts its first major sporting event—the Asian Games in Delhi. Goan Lavy Pinto gets gold medals in 100m and 200m sprints. 1952: K.D. Jadhav wins India's first-ever individual Olympic medal at the Helsinki Games.•India win their fifth hockey gold medal at the Olympics. 1956: Neville D'Souza scores a hat-trick against Australia at the Melbourne Olympics. 1980: India wins Olympic gold medal in hockey.1983: India win the 50-over cricket World Cup, beating West Indies in the final. 1987: Sunil Gavaskar becomes the first to score 10,000 runs in Test cricket. 1988: Viswanathan Anand is India's first chess Grandmaster. 1996: Leander Paes gets India's second individual Olympic medal—a tennis bronze in Atlanta—after 44 years. 1997: Mahesh Bhupathi becomes the first Indian to win a Grand Slam title—the French Open mixed doubles with Rika Hiraki of Japan. 1999: •Leander Paes and Mahesh Bhupathi win the French Open doubles. 2000: The first Indian woman to win an Olympic medal, Karnam Malleswari gets a bronze in the 69kg category of weightlifting in Sydney. 2002: Koneru Humpy becomes the first female chess Grandmaster from India; at 15, she is the world's youngest female GM. 2004: Rajyavardhan Rathore is India's first individual silver medallist at the Olympics—in the men's double trap shooting event in Athens.2005: Narain Karthikeyan becomes the first Indian to drive in the Formula One, with team Jordan. • Pankaj Advani wins IBSF World Billiards Championship in Malta. 2007: India win the inaugural cricket World Twenty20 Championship. 2008: Abhinav Bindra becomes the first Indian to win an individual Olympic gold medal in Beijing. •Vijender Singh is the first Indian boxer to win a medal at the Olympics—a bronze in Beijing. 2011: India hosts its first-ever Formula One Grand Prix at the Buddh International Circuit in Greater Noida. 2012: Mary Kom wins a bronze medal in women's boxing at the London Olympics. •Sushil Kumar becomes the only Indian to win two individual Olympic medals, with a silver in wrestling in London after his bronze in Beijing. •Saina Nehwal wins a bronze medal in London Olympics. 2016: P.V. Sindhu wins a silver medal in badminton at the Rio de Janeiro Olympics. •Sakshi Malik becomes the first Indian female wrestler to win an Olympic medal with a bronze at Rio. • Nagpur's visually impaired swimmer, Kanchanmala Pande, becoming the first ever Indian to win a gold medal at the World Para Swimming Championship held in Mexico. 2018: PV Sindhu defeated Nozomi Okuhara in the final to become the first Indian to clinch a World Tour Finals gold.•Vinesh Phogat became the first Indian wrestler to clinch an Asian Games gold in a year in which she also bagged the yellow metal at the Gold Coast CWG; 18-year-old Indian runner Hima Das sprinted to a historic gold at the IAAF World U20 Championship. 2019: India sprint star Hima Das won 5 international gold medals, including one in her favourite 400 mt in just three weeks.

2020: Pandemic restricted sports events.

2021: India wins seven medals. Neeraj Chopra wins gold in Javelin throw.

Indian States and Union Territories by GDP

GSDP is the sum of all value added by industries within each State or UT and serves as a counterpart to the national gross domestic product (GDP). In India, the Government accounts for around 21% of the GDP, agriculture accounts for 21%, the corporate sector accounts for 12% and the balance 48% of the GDP is sourced from small proprietorship and partnership companies, unorganised sector and households.

Rank	State/UT	Nominal GDP ₹ lakh crore (₹ trillions)	USD billion (bn)	Data year
1	Maharashtra	26.61 lakh crore	(US$370 bn)	2020—21
2	Tamil Nadu	20.92 lakh crore	(US$297 bn)	2020–21[3]
3	Uttar Pradesh	17.05 lakh crore	(US$240 bn)	2020–21[3]
4	West Bengal	16.69 lakh crore	(US$232 bn)	2020-21 [6]
5	Gujarat	16.48 lakh crore	(US$230 bn)	2020–21
6	Karnataka	16.38 lakh crore	(US$228 bn)	2020-21
7	Rajasthan	10.21 lakh crore	(US$140 bn)	2020–21
8	Andhra Pradesh	9.73 lakh crore	(US$138 bn)	2020-21
9	Telangana	9.69 lakh crore	(US$137 bn)	2020–21
10	Madhya Pradesh	9.09 lakh crore	(US$130 bn)	2020–21
11	Kerala	8.54 lakh crore	(US$110 bn)	2019–20
12	Delhi	7.98 lakh crore	(US$110 bn)	2020–21
13	Haryana	7.65 lakh crore	(US$100 bn)	2020–21
14	Bihar	7.57 lakh crore	(US$100 bn)	2020–21[7]
15	Punjab	5.41 lakh crore	(US$72 bn)	2020–21
16	Odisha	5.09 lakh crore	(US$68 bn)	2020–21
17	Assam	3.74 lakh crore	(US$50 bn)	2020–21 [8]
18	Chhattisgarh	3.50 lakh crore	(US$46 bn)	2020–21
19	Jharkhand	3.29 lakh crore	(US$44 bn)	2019–20
20	Uttarakhand	2.53 lakh crore	(US$34 bn)	2019–20
21	J&K	1.76 lakh crore	(US$23 bn)	2020–21
22	Himachal Pradesh	1.56 lakh crore	(US$21 bn)	2020–21
23	Goa	0.815 lakh crore	(US$11 bn)	2020–21
24	Tripura	0.597 lakh crore	(US$7.9 bn)	2020–21
25	Chandigarh	0.421 lakh crore	(US$5.6 bn)	2018–19
26	Puducherry	0.380 lakh crore	(US$5.0 bn)	2019–20
27	Meghalaya	0.348 lakh crore	(US$4.6 bn)	2020–21
28	Sikkim	0.325 lakh crore	(US$4.3 bn)	2019–20
29	Nagaland	0.319 lakh crore	(US$4.2 bn)	2019–20
30	Manipur	0.318 lakh crore	(US$4.2 bn)	2019–20
31	Arunachal Pradesh	0.273 lakh crore	(US$3.6 bn)	2019–20
32	Mizoram	0.265 lakh crore	(US$3.5 bn)	2019–20
33	A& N Islands	0.088 lakh crore	(US$1.2 bn)	2018–19
•	**India**	**203.85 lakh crore**	**$3.05 trillion**	**2021**

The following list gives the latest available gross state domestic product (GSDP) figures for all Indian States and UTs at current prices in crores (units of 10 million) or lakh crores (units of 1 trillion) of the Indian rupees. No data is available for the UTs of DNH & DD, Ladakh and Lakshadweep.

Politics of Procurement and Deployment of Covid-19 Vaccines:

Shades of Vaccine Nationalism Versus Vaccine Diplomacy

Prof. (Dr.) Yatish Agarwal
Dean, University School of Medicine,
Guru Gobind Singh Indraprastha University; and Professor, Vardhman Mahavir Medical College & Safdarjung Hospital, New Delhi.
E-mail: dryatishagarwal@gmail.com

This article takes a look at how the race for vaccination has exacerbated tendencies of hoarding – vaccine nationalism – harmful to the global effort in the fight against the pandemic. The politicisation of vaccine distribution is proving counterproductive for democratic practices globally.

Even as the COVID-19 pandemic continues to take a toll on the human race, the battleground has largely shifted to preventive strategy. One, of employing personal protective gear; and two: of development, procurement, and delivery of potent vaccine jabs to checkmate the virus. Given the present small global scales of vaccine production, however, meeting the requirements of a colossal human population of 7.8 million is no mean task. The challenge deepens, given that most vaccines require at least two jabs to instil a primary protection, and very possibly, one or more subsequent booster shots to keep up the immunity.

Vaccine Nationalism

In this trying landscape, the rich nations have further confounded the equation. Muscled by their economic strength and vastly superior scientific and pharmaceutical capabilities, they have forced an unequal run on

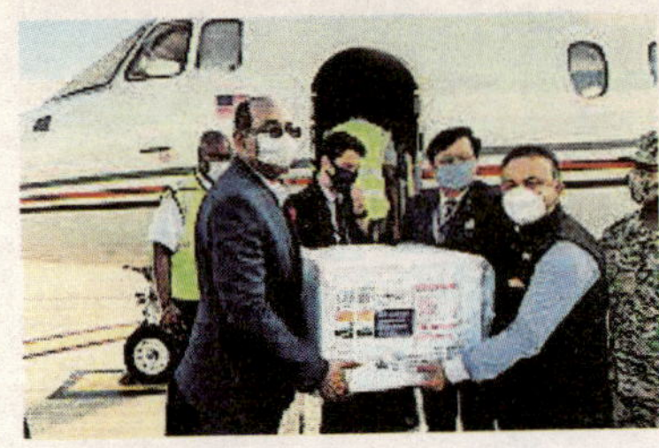

the corona vaccines. In the first phase of vaccine deployment, led by this self-centric approach, the developed countries displayed exacerbated tendencies of hoarding the vaccine as a measure of their state power. This has led to the birth of a new expressive axiom — 'vaccine nationalism', wherein these countries captured a disproportionately large part of the global COVID-19 vaccine supply, and left little or no provisions for the citizens of the third world.

Through investments in vaccine manufacturing and advance purchase agreements, nearly half of the planned 2021 supplies of the leading vaccine candidates were secured by a small contingent of wealthy nations – Australia, Canada, Japan, the United Kingdom, the United States and the European Union. Together, these countries account for just 14 per cent of the global population. Still, by making advance market commitments, they collectively reserved nearly 5 billion vaccine doses. The US has entered into at least six bilateral deals, totalling more than 1 billion doses – more than enough to inoculate the entire American population. The European Union, Britain and Canada have each entered into seven bilateral deals, with the potential of securing enough doses to cover their populations two, four, and six times over, respectively.

Constituting a crass moral failure against such fundamental World Health Organisation declarations as 'Health for All', this phenomenon of vaccine nationalism is set deeply against the very tenet of universal good. This primeval instinct spurred market approach, in fact, may snowball into a situation which could go horribly wrong. The narrow, self-centric, behaviour may not only turn out to be epidemiologically self-defeating and clinically counterproductive, but is also bound to prolong the pandemic by perpetuating the spread of the contagion in and across unprotected populations. If a majority of the world's population will go unvaccinated, the toll of COVID-19 illness and deaths will continue to strike and devastate large parts of the world. In such a setting, the virus is bound to grow and multiply and spawn new virus mutations. These new avatar corona viruses may lead to vaccine resistance, and precipitate a fresh threat to the human race.

Clearly, notwithstanding the compulsions of the democratic governments in developed economies — which must act to suit the electoral politics, and must win the approval of their own people by overtly prioritising the health of their people over those of all others, a fine, delicate balance needs to be struck. Be it from ethical motivations, self-interest, transactional considerations or some mix of all three, these worthy nation states must act to share stockpiles of vaccines, waive patent protections, relax export controls on ingredients used for vaccine production, and reduce vaccine costs for other weaker economies and poor countries.

In practical terms, tailoring such a vaccine continuum is an imperative. Frankly, while ethical frameworks and cosmopolitan humanitarianism may be dismissed without much ado, and building a diplomacy-borne international political clout may easily be given a miss in the present global climate, securing the health and

well-being of human race, including that of one's own population, may be more than a just reward of such vaccine sharing.

Shaping a Vaccine Continuum

If nothing else, the global will to stymie the pandemic must shape a vaccine continuum. This process could be split into three reinforcing but distinct phases: the first that of 'predatory vaccine nationalism', characterised by commandeering and hoarding of vaccine doses exclusively for one's own population, a phenomenon that the rich nations remained committed to till late. This phase was also marked by conservatism, of disallowing protection waivers on vaccine technology patents, and limiting global supply chains to safeguard their selfish interests.

The second phase of the continuum, call it 'benign vaccine nationalism', is a little better. It allows policymakers and governments of worthy nations to continue the prioritization of their populations in regard to vaccine access, but simultaneously inspires them to adopt a restrained approach of providing vaccine doses to populations beyond their borders, largely to their neighbours — for example, the U.S. donating vaccine doses to Canada and Mexico.

The third phase synthesizes the positive features of the first and second phases to yield 'vaccine diplomacy', centring the vaccine needs of populations beyond borders, waiving intellectual property to diversify vaccine production sources, and empowering less-privileged poorer nations to build capacity to produce vaccines on their own and protect their people.

The Global Vaccine Deployment Policy:

A Continuum Approach from "Taking Care of One's Own" to "Striving for Universal Good!"

Vaccine Diplomacy

Eradicating Covid-19 requires nothing less than a universal vision and global leadership. The benefits of vaccination must percolate across large parts of the world if human populations have to develop herd immunity and call a stop to the deadly play of the virus.

Until now, even if only to gain geo-political leverage among the donee countries, three countries have largely experimented with the theorem of vaccine diplomacy — India, China and Russia. But all three have been faulted; that the vaccines they have developed and deployed did not go through sufficiently transparent and rigorous testing, robust clinical trials, and authorisation processes, and the hurry with which they were cleared for emergency human usage was essentially nothing but the other face of vaccine nationalism, whereby these countries tried to assert and build up their international clout.

Be what it may, as the results of the clinical trials establish the safety and efficacy of Indian-born Covaxin and Indian-mass produced Covishield (produced in India under license from Oxford-AstraZeneca), the political leaders of the United States, India, Japan, and Australia have announced during their first virtual Quad Summit that they would supply one billion doses of vaccine to Indo-Pacific countries by 2022 — by scaling up production in India in an effort financed by the other three members of the bloc. This initiative will certainly be welcomed by the recipient countries, but it is apparent that this plan has been formulated in the context of great-power rivalry and is aimed at countering China's large vaccine diplomacy thrust. The Chinese Sinovac and Sinopharm vaccines, however, have still to win people's acceptance and continue to suffer from persistent skepticism both about their safety and efficacy.

Even as the big question of universal access to vaccines continues to be marred by politics, both at the domestic and international platforms, global policymakers have drawn a more profound vaccine diplomacy initiative at the multilateral level.

Formation of COVAX

Under the guidance of United Nations, a COVID-19 Vaccine Global Access facility (abbreviated as COVAX) has been founded. Directed by 'Gavi', the Vaccine Alliance (formerly the Global Alliance for Vaccines and Immunization, or GAVI), the Coalition for Epidemic Preparedness Innovations (CEPI), and the World Health Organisation (WHO), it was set up in December 2020 and is a worldwide initiative. COVAX coordinates international resources to enable low-to-middle-income countries fair and reasonable access to vaccine-sharing

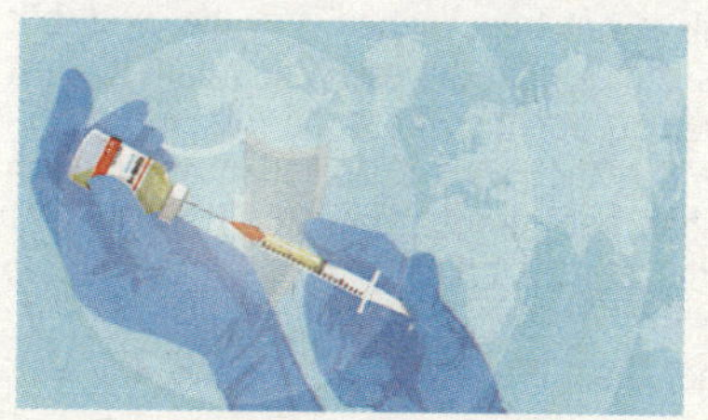

scheme that encourages rich countries to donate vaccines to the poor and to promote effective vaccine diplomacy.

The United Nations Security Council has also passed a resolution that promotes joint international efforts to combat COVID-19 by assisting with health technology and vaccination in regions of armed conflict and humanitarian emergencies. These modest steps to fight the pandemic cooperatively augur well for the global community and hold the promise of bringing the pandemic to a true end.

Much at the same time, scientists across the world continue to toil in their labs and run clinical trails to search out the safety and efficacy of at least a hundred more potentially effective vaccine candidates.

The Winning Secret

The race to defeat the corona virus is finding new and stronger allies with each passing day. Just as in the past, against all pandemics that raged since the advent of life on mother earth, the Homo sapiens must prevail! But as the global pundits have wisely stated, the success will come only if we were to stand united and fight the virus collectively. We could be rich, or we could be poor, but our fates are inextricably linked, and if we wish to win, we must take the winning steps together.

The Real Virus Came from Zhoushan

Pooja Biraia Jaiswal

Courtesy: The Week, issue dated June 13, 2021

With over 244 million cases and about five million dead worldwide, China's responsibility for the fallout of the Coronavirus is significant if the virus was indeed made in Wuhan lab.

This interview of Virologist Dr Li-Meng Yan is republished because she gives clue to world's question about its origin.

Q After our exclusive interview last year, in which you said the Covid-19 virus was man-made, scientists and governments are considering it to be a possibility. New theories have emerged as well. Do you think the samples found from the Yunnan copper mine come closest to SarsCoV-2?

A They say the Bat Woman Shi Zhengli got RaTG13 from a copper mine in Yunnan and, after a bit of modifications, inserted the furin cleavage site to make it the SarsCoV-2 virus. I have actually proved in my reports that this is not true. Yunnan is in the west, but the real virus comes from the east, Zhoushan. It's just a way of diverting attention from the role of the Chinese military. It is the People's Liberation Army which found Zhoushan bat coronaviruses ZC45 and ZXC21 in 2017 in the east of China and it is these viruses that come closest to Sars-CoV-2. These were live viruses. They got them live and kept them live. This was

Military personnel brief Chinese President Xi Jinping at a Covid-19 facility in Wuhan in early 2020

published in their paper at the end of 2017 and it mentioned that these viruses could infect rat brain. I got to know this in January 2020 when I checked the virus sequence. If Sars-CoV-2 was natural, the E protein (Envelop protein) would definitely have had some changes in the genome as it moved from bats to humans. However, SarsCoV-2 has the same identical E protein as ZC45/ZXC21 viruses. So, this is definitely a 'Smoking Gun.' After the Sars1 outbreak in 2003, China realised that coronaviruses could be used to develop a novel bio-weapon. The head of China's Centers for Disease Control, George Gao, and a member of the US National Academy of Sciences organised a collaboration project from 2010 to 2017 to search for a novel animal virus. The WIV lab and Chinese military labs were part of it. They looked at coronaviruses, dengue virus, zika virus, mice virus and bat virus to cause brain haemorrhage and fever, and hoped to find at least two to three types of new viruses every year. Interestingly, we have seen millions of people suffering from neurological illnesses after contracting Covid-19. We virologists never make only one virus in the lab. Experiments always generate mutants. And with the number of scientists in China working on creating bio-weapons, it is difficult to believe that we have only this one type of bio-weapon. There is always a possibility that they will use a new one to attack other countries. Hence, it is important to investigate this aspect so as to prevent an imminent biological warfare.

Q Many scientists have dismissed your theory of creation of Covid-19 as a bio-weapon.

A Interestingly, this is despite my giving them academic, genomic, intelligence evidence. They simply deny it, deliberately choosing to ignore the evidence, because it is in the interest of select scientists and government officials to dismiss the lab origins. This is a novel bio-weapon, not a traditional one. In my second report I define it as an 'unrestricted bio-weapon.' In an official military textbook written by a Chinese bio-weapon expert, along with a PLA general, and published by the military medical press in 2015, they clearly mention that based on the experience from Sars1 the coronaviruses can be used to develop some novel genetic bio-weapons. Its magnitude far exceeds that of anthrax. I sent it to the US intelligence department several months ago. They also say in the book that this novel coronavirus bio-weapon needn't have a high death rate of over 10 per cent—because, if it does, people would immediately realise it is a bio-weapon. But if it is less than 2 per cent, then this kind of weapon will bring in a secondary form of disaster, that is, break down the

First Woman to Join the Indian Foreign Service

extra

The first woman to join the Indian Foreign Service (IFS) was C.B Muthammain in 1949. Prior to her, Vijaya Lakshmi Pandit was appointed as the first woman ambassador of India to the Soviet Union in 1947.

entire health machinery and later disturb the economy and social order. All of this has happened in the world, exactly as mentioned. So the reason it is a novel bio-weapon is that it looks like nature, but it isn't. The US has verified the authenticity of the textbook.

Q So it served as a guide to the scientists working at WIV?

A It doesn't matter whether they read it or not. The concept in itself is enough for virologists to understand. The Wuhan lab is just one of those labs which worked on producing such non-traditional and unrestricted bio-weapons. Behind them is the Chinese Academy of Military and Medical Sciences, which in turn has numerous labs and scientists working in the army but as civil scientists. In China, military-civil fusion projects are very common. This virus has not been made inside just one lab by a single team. It has had a number of teams working on it from labs across China, after which it finally landed in WIV from where it was leaked and went out of control.

Q You published your third report in March this year.

A Yes, it was my attempt at correcting all the misinformation about the origins of the novel coronavirus that has been going on around the world.

Q So, the Yunnan copper mine theory is wrong.

A The copper mine exists. People have gotten infected and suffered from severity of infection and died. But the story that it has a connection with Sars-CoV-2 is not true. It's baseless. That theory only suggests that scientists collected the samples from there simply for some good

Wuhan Institute of Virology

research. There is nothing more to that. RaTG13 or bat coronavirus 4991 doesn't exist there. Only a tiny part of it does, and there is no proof that it is similar to

Covid-19. They have just created a fake virus family and attributed to it the characteristics of the novel coronavirus. They, along with Shi Zhengli, did it because they were desperately looking for a new virus that the country had asked all its scientists to develop. But there was no Sars-like coronavirus from that place. The doctor who examined all those miners, who got infected from the mine and died, presented his observations and clinical data in a thesis which I had access to. Having read that, I can tell you there is no evidence that those patients had died from the novel coronavirus. Their information was right, but the analysis and conclusions were wrong. Just because these Chinese master's and doctoral theses suggesting these things have been translated into English, the media and the world press have taken it. It's just a diversion tactic.

Q They say you've been funded by some groups to toe the line.

A That is completely false. I am in New

Founding of Stanford University  extra

The Leland Stanford Junior University was founded in 1885 by Jane and Leland Stanford in memory of their only child, Leland Jr., who died of typhoid fever at 15.

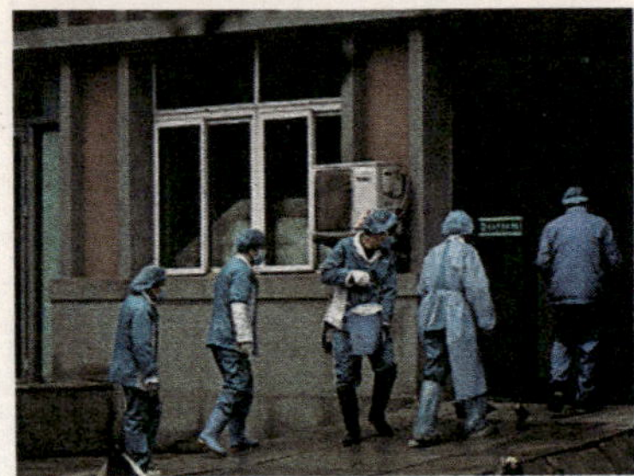

York because I'm safe here. Other than me, the Rule of Law Foundation supports thousands of other scientists. I'm only revealing the truth, which is against the Communist Party of China. I'm a medical doctor, PhD holder and scientist, and so I can fund and support myself very well. My research is totally independent and nobody can buy or manipulate me.

Q Did you expect the US to call for an investigation?

A Yes, that is needed. It came a bit late in the day, though. Because we still do not know which are the other functions they've hidden inside the genome of this virus that could target humans. What made it so much more lethal than the other coronaviruses, impacting several organs of the body so much so that we simply could not come up with the right diagnosis before letting millions

This virus has not been made inside one lab. Several teams worked on it across China, after which it landed in WIV. die. The odds that this virus comes from nature are 1 in 13 billion. We know that in biology, when you do something, you're sure to have some random results show up, alongside the focus research results you expect. That's exactly what must have happened here.

Q Could you explain this virus relation in a bit more detail, please.

A Usually what we do is take the father as the reference point to make the son. Here the son is the Covid-19 virus. The father and the son have similarities, like a same nose, which other people do not have. But in WIV, the Bat Woman created a fake father and then made him look like the son—that is, the Covid-19 virus which was already present. And to make it all look very authentic, they created this huge family of fakes, all of who were curiously born after the son. And then they got themselves published in Nature magazine. Given the reputation of Shi Zhengli in the scientific community, there was no question of refuting her claims. China also made an International Scientific Group that could promote the nature origin theory.

Q Did you face a backlash from the Chinese after you first went public?

A I'm a target even now. They're trying to make my person and voice disappear. Even now, as I continue to live in the US, cyber military people and real people from my country's government try to intimidate me. I cut off my connections with my family last July. The scientific world and mainstream media have been promoting the nature origin, and social media, including Facebook, Instagram and YouTube, has suppressed and discredited (labelled as lies) my reports and interviews. CNN, The New York Times and National Geographic write papers on behalf of the Chinese government by interviewing scientists who have colluded with the government.

extra

India's Diplomatic Network

According to Australian think tank Lowy Institute's Global Diplomacy Index, India's diplomatic network ranks 12th in the world – behind smaller countries such as Turkey, Spain, and Italy.

Making A Mark Abroad: 75 Years of NRIs

Dr. Shashi Tharoor
Member of Parliament for Thiruvananthapuram,
Chairman of Parliamentary Standing Committee on Information Technology

This article looks at Non-Resident Indians and their contributions to the country. It can be measured in terms of their remittances, technological inputs, investments, sharing of knowledge and values.

India is probably the only country in the world that has not only given official recognition to its expatriates, but has even devised a formal acronym for them. NRI, or Non-Resident Indian, is a term that, over the last three decades, has found a firm place in the national vocabulary, though it is yet to be reflected in any dictionary. In my book India: From Midnight to the Millennium, I jokingly suggested that the real debate was whether NRI stood for "Not Really Indian" or "Never Relinquished India". The nearly 25 million people of Indian descent who live abroad fall, of course, into both categories. And in recent years, as the Government has set about cultivating them through generous new policies, the establishment of a Ministry for Overseas Indians Affairs, and annual Pravasi Bharatiya Divas (PBD, or Overseas Indians' Day) events in India, it's clear one can apply a third variant to the acronym – the "Now Required Indians."

I recall a PBD in Mumbai attended by the Vice-Presidents of Suriname and Mauritius, both the former Prime Ministers of Fiji and Trinidad and Tobago, Malaysian politicians and Gulf-based entrepreneurs, tycoons from

Hong Kong and titans from the United States, all united by the simple fact of shared heritage — the undeniable reality that even exiles cannot escape when they look into the mirror. They were united, too, in the words of the typically thoughtful and inspiring inaugural address by then-Prime Minister Manmohan Singh on that occasion, by an "idea of Indianness". It is an idea that enshrines the diversity and pluralism both of our country and of its disapora. In a land that is home to Indians of every conceivable caste and creed, the Pravasi Bharatiya Divas celebrations continue each year to afford to Indians — including former Indians — of every conceivable caste and creed the welcome assurance that they were indeed at home.

Non-Resident Indians have certainly come a long way since the days when Indian Prime Ministers sanctimoniously urged them to be loyal to the foreign countries in which they had settled. As late as 1974, an Indian Foreign Minister told Parliament that "overseas Indians" had chosen to live abroad and so were responsible for their own condition: the Government of India had no obligation towards them. But since then New Delhi has developed expectations of its NRIs, and a reciprocal sense of obligation, too, has followed. Today NRIs are seen as people on whom the motherland – and its elected representatives – have a legitimate claim. It is a claim willingly conceded by many NRIs; for every extremist or secessionist abroad (a category whose numbers are mercifully dwindling), there are a hundred who continue to demonstrate a remarkable degree of interest in, and commitment to, the land of their birth (or of their forebears).

The law that first defined NRIs did so in broad terms - not just Indian citizens resident abroad, but persons of Indian "origin" irrespective of their current nationality. Initially "NRIs" applied to expatriate Indians irrespective of their current citizenship; today the term is restricted to Indian citizens living abroad, whereas people whose emigration has acquired the permanence of foreign nationality are referred to as PIOs, or Persons of Indian Origin. "A Person of Indian Origin (PIO) means a foreign citizen (except a national of Pakistan, Afghanistan, Bangladesh, China, Iran, Bhutan, Sri Lanka and Nepal)", says the government, "who at any time held an Indian passport; Or who or either of their parents/grandparents/ great grandparents was born and permanently resident in India as defined in Government of India Act, 1935 and other territories that became part of India thereafter provided neither was at any time a citizen of any of the aforesaid countries (as referred above); Or Who is a spouse of a citizen of India or a PIO."

% of total remittances

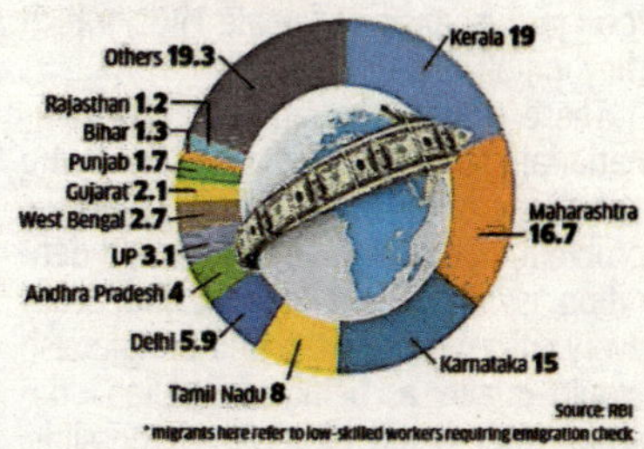

Source: RBI

*migrants here refer to low-skilled workers requiring emigration check

New Delhi's anxiety to define the category as broadly as possible has led to some interesting terminological calisthenics. Not only can anyone with one Indian grandparent declare himself an NRI and claim the benefits of that designation, but the "spouse of a citizen of India, or of a person of Indian origin, shall also be deemed to be of Indian origin though they may be of non-Indian origin". (The semantic sexism of the earlier version, which used the term "wife" instead of "spouse", has been dropped:

the rules now do apply in reverse, to the foreign husbands of female NRIs, which they initially did not.)

These criteria, though liberal by international standards, still omit some who are visibly of Indian origin. One obvious problem, of course, is that if the NRI definition is interpreted literally, practically every citizen of Pakistan and Bangladesh would qualify as being of "Indian" descent. That being politically impossible, exclusions have been made. The NRI definition also disqualifies descendants of some of the earlier waves of Indian migration, mainly in the last century, to such far-flung outposts of Empire as Malaya and Mauritius, Ghana and Guyana, Singapore and Suriname. In most cases, nationals of those countries, though manifestly of Indian origin, are descended from migrants of earlier generations, higher up the family tree than their grandparents. In this era of shrinking planetary distances, many of those expatriate communities have, in recent years, renewed their links to their ancestral lands, and their connection is now recognized in the term "PIO" (for Persons of Indian Origin). So NRIs and PIOs together constitute the Great Indian Diaspora.

There have been four broad waves of diasporic movement from India. The first, in pre-colonial times, featured Indians leaving our shores as travellers, teachers and traders; the second involved the enforced migration of Indian labour as indentured servants of the British Empire; the third, the tragic displacement of millions by the horrors of Partition; and the fourth, the contemporary phenomenon of skilled and educated Indians seeking opportunity and challenge in our globalised world. I would probably divide the fourth wave further into two distinct categories: one of highly educated Indians, often staying on after studies abroad in places like the U.S., and the other of more modestly-qualified but even harder-working migrants, from taxi drivers to shop assistants, who for the most part see their migration as temporary and who remit a larger proportion of their funds home to India than their higher-earning counterparts. But in today's world both sets of "fourth wave" migrants remain closely connected to the matrbhumi: the ease of communications and travel makes it possible for expatriates to be engaged with the country they left behind in a way that was simply not available to the plantation-worker in Mauritius or Guyana a century ago. To tap into this sense of allegiance and loyalty through an organised public gathering was an inspired idea; hence the annual PBDs, supported by a "one-stop shop" in the form of a dedicated Ministry for Overseas Indians. ((MOIA). Though the Ministry was merged by the Narendra Modi government into the Ministry of External Affairs (MEA), a Secretary of the Ministry is still dedicated to the work of the MOIA, and a Minister of State in MEA is usually tasked with giving Overseas Indians the level of political attention their importance deserves.

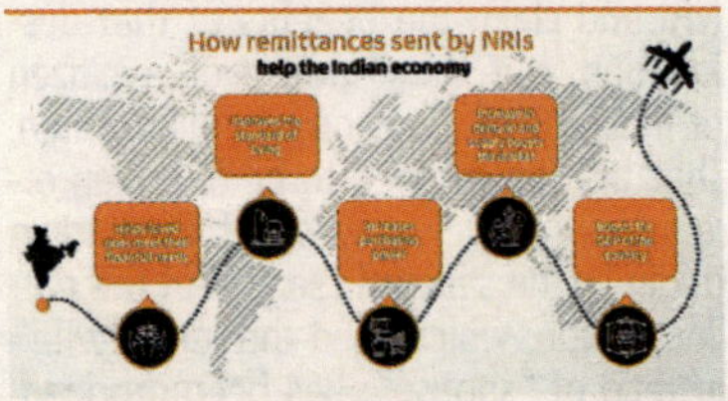

The stories of this "fourth wave" vary. Many of the first Indian emigrants to Britain, for instance, went in search of an education and stayed on to work. Then, from the 1950s on, came less-educated members of the working class, attracted by the liberalization of British entry laws during the labour shortages of the post-war boom years. A third stream of Indi-

How remittances sent by NRIs help the Indian economy

ans came in the 1970s via East Africa, from where many were expelled in the xenophobic fervour that swept some African states after independence. All three groups, and their offspring, have acquired a reputation for hard work, business sense and ethnic clannishness. Their success and, paradoxically, their failure to assimilate fully into British society, have made them ideal NRIs - still owing residual loyalty to their Indian past, and usually well-off enough to do something about it. This has appealed to all those in India who wish to court their support.

In North America, the "waves" took place in a different order. The first Indian immigrants to the US and Canada came as early as the 1890s, when shiploads of Sikhs settled on the Pacific coast and established thriving farming communities in British Columbia and California. Racist entry-legislation - prompted by such events as anti-Indian riots in the state of Washington in 1907 - prevented them from adding to their numbers, however, and it was only a thin trickle of students who came to the US from India after the 1920s. (As late as 1935, signs on the doors of certain California establishments declared, "No jobs for Japs or Hindus".) The number of Indian students began to increase after Independence, and an increasing proportion of them stayed on, bringing high levels of academic attainment and valuable scientific and engineering skills to their new country. By the early 1970s the small but influential Indian minority was estimated as having the highest per capita income of any ethnic group in the United States – the median family income of the Indian American, according to US census figures, exceeds the median income of white Americans by a wide margin. That is still the case in 2020.

It was the more liberal Immigration Act of 1965 that opened the sluice-gates to the United States for Indians. But while the trickle of Indian professionals became a stream, in more recent years it is illegal immigration that has swelled the flow into a torrent. Working-class Indians found their way into the United States for the first time in the late 1970s and early 1980s, toiling on construction sites, taking over newspaper kiosks on street corners, operating run-down motels, cooking and serving in Indian restaurants and driving taxicabs. Their success has been based on the strength of qualities regarded as "typically Indian" - hard work, discipline, self-sacrifice and thrift. The way in which Indians have taken over unprofitable motels across the United States, and run newsstands in New York City or late-night groceries in London, is widely seen as reflective of these qualities. A pair of "amnesties" gave the illegals amongst them the legal status they needed to bring their families over, and today this "underclass" of Indian immigrants accounts for nearly half of the estimated 3,400,000 persons of Indian origin in the United States.

That figure may even be an undercount, omitting as it does many who are still illegal and those who trace their direct descent from another centre of the Indian diaspora, such as the Caribbean. But allowing for the approximations that are inevitable in such an exercise, the Indian-American is now a familiar figure in US politics.

But Indian-Americans are probably behind other Indian immigrants in making major financial contributions to their motherland. In the 1980s and 1990s, remittances home from NRIs - primarily the diligent Indian workers in the countries of the Arab/ Persian Gulf – averaged the equivalent of some 40% of India's annual merchandise exports, or some 3% to 4% of GNP, though both percentages have been dropping in recent years as

India's economy has boomed. (In the state of Kerala, these remittances were responsible for generating a remarkable boom in the real estate and construction businesses, as money was poured in to new housing for NRIs and land values tripled in some areas.) In addition, NRI depositors in Indian banks have frequently bailed out the Government in periods when it was strapped for hard currency. And yes, there are now the millions poured into cutting-edge high-tech businesses in Bangalore or Gurgaon by investors from Silicon Valley. But we shouldn't get carried away — overseas Indians, especially Indian-Americans, still invest a lower proportion of their resources in India than overseas Chinese do in China. Encouraging them to do more — and giving them reasons to do more — is certainly a worthwhile task for Ministry for Overseas Indian Affairs in New Delhi.

Meanwhile, no longer is there much cavil about a "brain drain". The argument that Indians who work abroad are doing a disservice to their country seems to me misplaced, especially in recent years as Indians abroad have given so much more back to their homeland than they could ever have contributed while staying there. The old fears of a "brain drain" seemed to me to have been supplanted by hopes of a "brain gain", as desi software designers and high-tech gurus from Silicon Valley have opened thriving firms in India, employing their countrymen and women, increasing the country's export revenues and pumping up the national GDP. Indians going abroad after their studies have done a great deal to benefit the Indians who stayed at home. And with some second-generation PIOs coming to India to discover the land of their ancestors and even work there, the less euphonious but more accurate term seems to be of "brain circulation".

So it seems otiose to ask: Why do NRIs matter to India?

The answer is simple: as a source of pride, as a source of support, and as a source of investments. It is entirely natural for Indians to take pride in the successes of their erstwhile compatriots abroad. I once remarked rather cruelly to an interviewer that the only country where Indians as a whole did not succeed was India. That is fortunately no longer the case, as signs of Indians' increasing prosperity are increasingly evident everywhere one travels in India, but Indians abroad have certainly given us all a great deal to be proud of. One recent statistic from the U.S. shows that the Indian-American family's median income is over $100,000 a year, the same as Japanese-Americans, but nearly $20,000 higher than the figure for all American families. That kind of success is not merely at the elite end of the scale: in England today, Indian curry houses employ more people than the iron and steel, coal and shipbuilding industries combined. (Many are the ways, indeed, in which the Empire can strike back.)

So we can be proud of the impact Indians have made on foreign societies. But pride is not merely an intangible asset. When I was living in the U.S., I was struck by the extent to which the success of our NRIs has transformed the public perception of India in the U.S. A generation ago, when I first travelled to the U.S. as a graduate student in 1975, India was widely seen as a land of snake-charmers and begging-bowls — poverty marginally leavened by exotica. Today, if there is a stereotypical view of India, it is that of a country of fast-talking high-achievers who are wizards at maths and who are capable of doing most Americans' jobs better, faster and more cheaply in Bangalore. Today "IIT" is a brand-name as respected in certain American circles as

"MIT" or "Caltech". If Indians are treated with more respect as a result, so is India, as the land which produces them. Let us not underestimate the importance of such global respect in our globalising world.

The presence of successful and influential NRIs in so many countries also becomes a source of direct support for India, as they influence not just popular attitudes, but governmental policies, to the benefit of the mother country. A list of successful NRIs would range from the likes of Dr Hargobind Khorana, Nobel Prize winning geneticist, and Dr Subrahmanyan Chandrashekhar, Nobel Prize winning astro-physicist, to the Oscar winning actor Ben Kingsley, the millionaire British industrialist Lord Swraj Paul, and the conductor Zubin Mehta, as well as embrace self-help guru Deepak Chopra and Didar Singh Bains, the United States' biggest peach farmer. The novelist Salman Rushdie has a claim to the designation (and sued successfully for the restitution of property his father had owned in India). Most of India's nationalist leaders, from Jawaharlal Nehru to the anti-Emergency opposition leader Jayaprakash Narayan, were NRIs at one time, though the term had not been invented while they lived abroad.

With increasing affluence and visibility, the Indian-American is also beginning to develop political clout, and that is where the story takes a contemporary turn. In Mauritius, Fiji, Guyana and Trinidad and Tobago, Indians have long occupied the highest offices; but for Portugal and Ireland to have Prime Ministers of Indian descent is remarkable. In Britain, both the current Chancellor of the Exchequer and the Home Secretary are of Indian origin, and for some years Parliament has sported a few, both in the House of Commons and among the nominated nobility in the unelected House of Lords. In the United States, there are now four Indian members of Congress, calling themselves a "Samosa Caucus" in the House of Representatives,and that number was five until Senator Kamala Harris won elevation. It is worth recalling, though, that two Americans of Indian descent, Dalip Singh Saund and Bobby Jindal, did serve three and two terms in the United States House of Representatives respectively in the past. But neither flaunted their Indian-American credentials: Saund kept his first names out of public view (he ran on the slogan "Elect Judge Saund") –and Jindal, who went on to be Governor of Louisiana and an unsuccessful Presidential candidate, conspicuously stayed away from Indian causes, refused to join the India Caucus, and resolutely resisted being identified as Indian.

It was a welcome change, then, when a woman of half-Indian, half-Jamaican descent, proud of her Tamil mother and her "chittis" (aunts) in Chennai, and willing to make and taste dosas with a popular YouTuber (Mindy Kaling, also of Tamil origin), was elected the first woman Vice-President of the USA in 2020. She spoke at length about her Indian ancestry, her visits to her grandfather and their conversations during seaside walks in Chennai. Well-known liberal Indian-American celebrities campaigned for the Biden-Harris ticket. Kamala Harris is Indian-American and yet not wholly so; and for a potential US President, that is a good place to be.

The members of the Great Indian Diaspora are increasingly seizing every opportunity to exercise influence on India's behalf, contribute to India's development and profit from India's growth. Kamala Harris' victory has made it impossible for the world's largest democracy to be ignored by the leaders of the oldest.

75 Years at a Glance

Reproductive Health in India

Dr. Nandini Sahay
Faculty Social Work, Amity University, NOIDA

Reproductive health is a state of complete physical, mental and social well-being. It is not merely the absence of disease or infirmity. This article analyses where India stands in terms of its reproductive health programme, services and approaches.

Reproductive health is a state of complete physical, mental and social well-being and not merely the absence of disease or infirmity, in all matters relating to the reproductive system and to its functions and processes. Reproductive health infers that people are able to have a satisfying and safe sex life and that they have the capability to reproduce and the freedom to decide, when and how often to do so. Reproductive Health implies that every individual has an access to correct information and also have an access to contraceptive methods which are of their choice and are safe to use. This also means that people are able to avail clinical services for healthy pregnancies and safe deliveries. Fertility Regulation, Sexually Transmitted Diseases, Contraceptives' knowledge, Safe Pregnancy and childbirth, antenatal Care, and Menstrual Health issues are included in reproductive health.

Accessibility to reproductive health services helps in abortion safety, upgradation of sexual and reproductive health of adolescents, containing & controlling reproductive tract malaise, and sexually transmitted diseases like HIV/AIDS. Reproductive health wellness envisages a perception that no child is unwanted, no birth is unsafe, none of the youngsters are exposed to HIV/AIDS, and that due respect is meted out to each female. This means that every individual is in a position to achieve a fulfilling & risk-free sex life, regulate their fertility and are able to reproduce without any kind of coercion.

Women from lowest economic strata have to face barriers in availing reproductive health services which leads to early unintended and repeated pregnancies, high maternal mortality, sexually transmitted infections, and other problems. The topic of reproductive and sexual health is shrouded in secrecy because of cultural and traditional issues. This is the reason why in spite of constitutional programmes and policies, the objective looked for remains elusive for a good number of them. A substantial number of pregnancies in India is still unplanned and millions of women still have unmet need of contraceptives. A subgroup, which include adolescents and men are under-served and availability of basket of choice of contraceptives remains a distant dream for these groups.

India's population is growing at a rapid rate and very soon it would surpass China and would become a highest populated country. Indian Government has been encouraging family planning programmes since independence only. In fact our country has been pioneer in instituting government run family planning programme with the objective of downscaling the fertility and retarding population upsurge. In the aftermath of introduction of the programme there has been perceptible decrease in the fertility rate in India

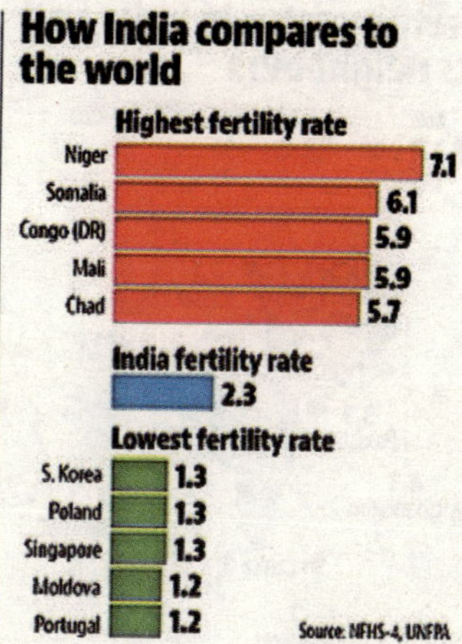

which has come down from 6.4-6.6 lifetime birth per woman in the early 1970s to 3.4 births in the mid 1990s. National Family Health Survey (NFHS-5) revealed that the population of India is said to be stabilising now. The Total Fertility Rate (TFR) in India is decreasing in almost all states except Bihar1.

Since introduction of the family planning programme in 1952, there has been a significant progress in the field of Family Welfare Programmes. Apart from making contraceptive available at doorstep, new programmes were introduced to deal with the issues of sexual health, pregnancy, postpartum care, child care and immunisation. Reproductive and Child Health Programme was also introduced to bring down social and geographical inequalities in accessing and deriving benefits of reproductive and child health services. Since then this programme has gone through different stages, and has included different knacks. In its formative years, the family planning programme aspired for ameliorating the health of mothers and the child. Dispensing clinic-cen-

Fertility rates in India and its neighbours

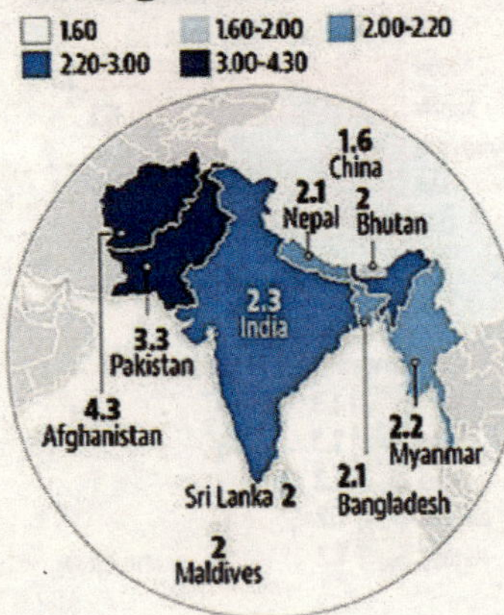

tred family planning service and pursuit of health education were strengthened in the first decade. In subsequent years, the underlying purpose of the initiative was to achieve demographic goals. Because of the growing concern about the human population upswing and its adverse effect on the speed of socio-economic advancement, the focus of the plan veered. The well-being of women and children took a back-stage as the aim tilted on steadying population. Also clinic-centred approach was removed and extension- education was introduced. This programme was amalgamated with health services which was later merged with the maternal and child health programme. Target conforming to specific method and time-frame was introduced which became very coercive during the Emergency period (1975–77). It targeted male members and took recourse to financial inducement, directed at deprived class to undergo sterilization2. Under this program millions of men received vasectomies, which was largely coerced in nature. Research reports revealed that government officials had dragged men to health centres for sterilizations3. The Government was expected to stipulate family planning mandatory and compel its population to limit childbearing to three numbers, if the "state so desires"4. This coercive approach was highly criticised and it forced government to launch family planning programme which was free from any coercion and was voluntary in nature. In 1977, The "Population Policy" was set in motion with an aim to adopt instructive, informative and inspirational attitude to shape family planning as an institution for willing participation.

In 1990, the family welfare policy and programme witnessed a major change in the India. The International Conference on Population and Development in 1994 and the Beijing Women's Conference in 1995 played a major role in policy change. In 1996, method-specific contraceptive was obliterated and a new Target-free Approach was introduced. This was later renamed as the Community Needs Assessment Approach. This new approach believed in decentralised participatory planning.

The year 1997 saw the commencement of Reproductive and Child Health Programme. Aspiring to deliver all-inclusive health services of valued quality, it was to ensure that the recipients feel contended. For rendering the novel scheme affable for the people, it engaged stakeholders which included civil society organisations, Panchayati Raj institutions and private sector to reframe new agenda5. This new approach gave attention to gender issues and focussed on improving availability of infrastructure for mainly female health care.

The National Population Policy further shifted focus to client-based services in February 2000. In March 2001, Government of India introduced an Empowered Action Group with an aim to stimulate

the Programme focussing Reproductive and Child Health care especially in those states which were showing poor socio economic indicators.

The National Population Policy6 was introduced with duo objective of population stabilisation and promotion of reproductive health rights. Further, National Rural Health Mission (NRHM). 2005 was introduced to reduce the maternal and child mortality rates and improve the health systems7. 3 "India's dark history of sterilisation". BBC News. 14 November 2014.

In the 21st century India introduced programs and policies encompassing the field of sexual and reproductive health. This include National Health Policy which was introduced in 2017 with an aim to attain distinctive well-being services for the masses and ensure that such facilities are within reach of everybody. National Youth Policy, 2014 and Rashtriya Kishor Swasthya Karykram , 2014 was instituted for enabling young persons in the age-group of 15 and 29 to excel and distinguish themselves. Further, Ayushman Bharat8 (Healthy India) was launched in 2018 by Government of India. The objective was to transform and upgrade existing health centres and strengthen the outreach services.

Apart from the above mentioned policies various convention and treaties played an important function to safeguard sexual and reproductive health. The International Conference on Human Rights Declaration in 1968, the Alma Ata Declaration in 1978 and the International Conference on Population and Development (ICPD) in 1994 raised a global consensus that reproductive rights are human rights. ICPD introduced Programme of Action which recognised accessibility and availability to comprehensive reproductive health care as a basic human right.

The International Covenant on Economic, Social and Cultural Rights, 1996 (ICESCR) and the Convention on the Elimination of All Forms of Discrimination against Women, 1979 (CEDAW) recognised the role of state in ensuring that women are not discriminated and their rights are protected by the state. Sexual and reproductive health right issues are part of The Sustainable Development Goals (SDGs). The preceding Millennium Development Goals (MDGs) also included several targets which gave importance to reproductive rights. Since India has endorsed the aforesaid accords, pledges and protocols, there is commitment to aver accomplishment of the prescribed goals in true spirit.

In spite of all these programmes, policies and constitutional provisions, reproductive health situation has not achieved the desired level. Lack of accessibility, affordability and availability of reproductive health services have hindered the pace of improvement in reproductive health situation in our country. India is still facing some reproductive health apprehensions which are to be grappled with on the premise that they are compelling. An effort has been made in the succeeding passage to present a few of them.

A very large percentage of pregnancies are either unwanted or mistimed. In 2019, around half (52%) of India's 353 million women who were in the reproductive age group wanted to avoid pregnancy. Out of these, around 27% of them are not using any modern contraceptive method which shows that they have an unmet need for modern contraception9. There is a high unmet need for family planning among currently married women especially among women who are illiterate and who come from lowest economic strata. A very small number of

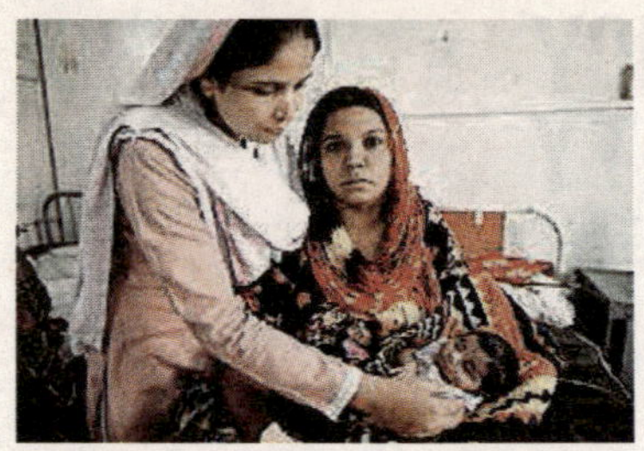

menfolk (only around 1% as per NFHS –III) participate in the process of adoption of contraception. Approximately 134 million women in India use modern contraceptives. Around 77% of them go for irreversible method i.e. sterilization, and a very small percentage of them are using reversible methods. Further, users generally do not have generally information about the possible side effects of any modern methods10. There still exist a gap in coverage of maternal and new born health indicators. Expecting mothers are required to receive proper care during her visits to the health centres at least four times during the pregnancy. As regards post-natal check-up, it is expected to be provided within 24 hours of delivery. But the availability of high-quality maternity care is lacking. These are some of the issues faced by women in India. Moreover high risk cases related to pregnancy do not receive due treatment on time. There is a silence around the topic of Sexually Transmitted Diseases and a general apathy among women to avail of medical attention. In consequence thereof a large number of them remain deprived of the medical care designed to fix infection of sexual and reproductive organs.

A plethora of programmes cutting across the areas of family planning, maternal and child health, adolescent health, etc is introduced by government. An analysis of these programmes, however, showed that there is a lack of proper implementation of these programmes in a human right frame work. Reproductive morbidities including sexually-transmitted diseases, fertility regulation and infertility, lack of access to quality health services, early marriage leading to early and repeated pregnancy are still a neglected area. Our country has manifested its allegiance to betterment of sexual and reproductive health of its citizens in manifold decrees, enactments, and programs. Still a lot remains to be done.

For this an additional budget would be required to for provide a comprehensive set of services which can improve health outcomes. Every individuals should be provided information about basket of choice of contraceptive methods, safe abortion care and how to protect oneself from sexually-transmitted diseases. This would bear desirable fruits.

Further research has revealed that the contraceptive needs of sexually active young people remain largely unmet. They need correct, user-friendly information and services. Their access to information and services can be enhanced by providing information at the educational institutions, community meeting, workplace, clinics, health centres etc. Apart from this budget should be allocated for health workers' training which include ASHA workers (Accredited Social Health Activists), auxiliary nurse midwives, male outreach workers and other fieldworkers who are the primary contact person for women.

Reproductive health programme must be expanded to address health needs of menfolk and counselling sessions should be organised to change their attitude and sensitise them on their role as partner, husbands and fathers.

Multi-sectoral activities should be introduced to enhance status of women as they do not have decision making capacity in sexual and reproductive health

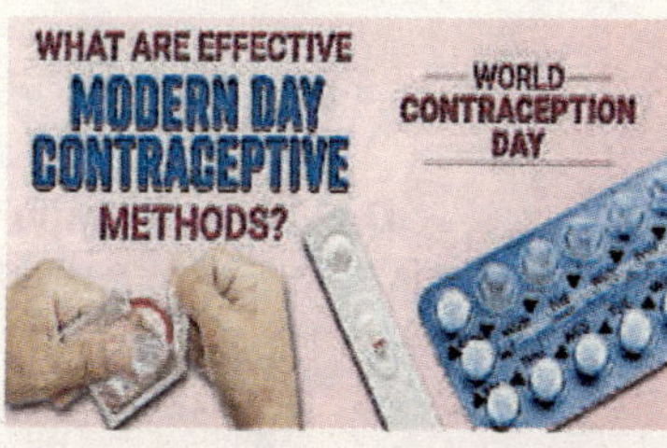

affairs. Stress should be laid on promoting research which could facilitate greater level of comprehension of the way, women and men resolve conflict of emotions. The outcome is expected to quip increased knowledge for all stakeholders. Additionally an inter-sectoral synergy amongst health sector, IEC units needs to be promoted for better results. Programs should be initiated to address the problem of knowledge, attitudes, behaviour and social norms which is creating a barrier around family planning and reproductive health. Government should introduce measures to overcome barriers so that a safe and effective family planning and reproductive health services are available for one and all. Further, Age-appropriate Comprehensive Sexuality Education (CSE), that encompasses issues such as gender relations, roles, identities, body and relationship of the self with the body, disease prevention, amongst others, is widely recognised as the way of enabling children and young persons in schools to become aware about their bodies, personal hygiene, gender identities as well as safe sex practices.

Researchers, advocates and leaders have expressed their concern about persisting toll of the COVID-19 affliction, gender parity as well as sexual and reproductive health globally11. Findings of different research has revealed that during the time of Covid19, access to sexual and reproductive health information and services got restricted and there was an increase in the cases of gender-related outrage and premature marriage, unwanted pregnancies, and maternal mortality. To prevent the spread of deadly virus, lockdown was imposed which impacted women's control over their own reproductive health, undermining family planning programs worldwide12. As per UN's reproductive health agency13 around 12 million women experienced problems in availing family planning services.

There is a need to safeguard women's reproductive health and rights, especially women residing in rural areas where infrastructural inadequacies have been existing even before COVID-19. Telemedicine services for consultations on reproductive health issues can be an important step towards reaching the most vulnerable population. Keeping in mind the issues related to pandemic, government must critically analyse previously framed health policies and introduce new measures for the newly identified challenges amidst COVID. The post-pandemic era can serve as a unique opportunity for radical reforms in India's public health system. New policies should be framed which would focus on prevention of unwanted pregnancies especially among adolescents and strengthen the access and quality in public and private sectors. Antenatal, intranatal, and postnatal care should be improved and capacity of service providers should be built to ensure quality of reproductive health care. Policies and programmes must therefore take cognisance of and comprehensively fulfil to the reproductive rights beyond maternal health and contraception; they must encompass a gamut of imperatives such as nutrition, water, education, non-discrimination, freedom from violence, access to affordable, accessible and quality care for abortion, communicable and non-communicable diseases, as well as access to information.

A Purpose-Driven Life

Dr. Valson Thampu
Former Principal, St. Stephen's College, New Delhi

This article takes a deep dive into our life and tries to explain why a purposeful life is important. In fact, purpose guides decisions, influences behaviour, shapes goals, offers a sense of direction and adds meaning to make life worth living for.

The phrase 'purpose-driven' life enfolds the insight that for life to be 'driven', or dynamic, it has to have 'purpose'. In purposelessness, we drift like flotsam on the sea of life. In such a state, we don't live; we merely exist. Or, as Shakespeare's Macbeth says, we creep from day to day. Our life may be 'full of sound and fury', but may signify nothing. Purposiveness is the best vaccination against futility in life.

As to the shaping influence of purpose on the life of individuals, consider this example. Till a few decades ago, we used to get our knives made by local blacksmiths. Suppose, you went to one such blacksmith and asked him to make a knife for you, he would surely ask: 'What sort of knife? A kitchen knife, a pen-knife, a butcher's knife, or one for mischief?' Why? Because the shape and size of the knife depend on its purpose. As a rule, purpose determines the form of everything. This is true of our life as well. The vitality, beauty and greatness of one's life depend on what one lives for.

Purposes, big or small, conscious or unconscious, underlie all human actions. We farm our land to reap a harvest. We make gardens to beautify our premises. We

Uttar Pradesh
UTTAR PRADESH TOURISM
U.P. nahi dekha
toh India nahi dekha
Awaits You...
With the occurrence of 'Holi', the entire Braj region remains immersed in celebration for days and weeks. Flowers, Laddus, Gulaal and wet colors enlighten this fiesta. Women here, hit the men with sticks or batons which is known as Chhadimar or Lathmar Holi respectively.
Rangotsav
/UttarPradeshTourism /uptourismgov /UttarPradeshTourism /UttarPradeshTourism

laze around, to take a negative example, in the mistaken notion that this amounts to, somehow, having a 'good time'. We skip classes in schools or colleges for the same reason, and based on the same misconception. It is impossible to live well or act sensibly without purpose.

Thinkers on contemporary life agree that the two most widespread epidemics of our times are boredom and depression. There are many reasons why it is so. Space-constraint rules out their full enumeration. For our present purpose, it suffices to note one of them. Today, we have everything to live with, nothing to live for. That is to say, life today is burdened by purposelessness. According to Victor Frankl, the Holocaust survivor and author, life is bearable only if it is meaningful. Meaninglessness sickens life.

'Purpose' pertains to what we live for. We can either live for great purposes, or for trivial indulgences. The words of Jawaharlal Nehru, the architect of modern India, are relevant here. We are small men and women, he said; but the cause we serve is great. And because the cause is great, something of its greatness falls on us.

The modern man, said Albert Einstein, is obsessed with processes to the neglect of purpose. In education, for example, the obsession is with how to teach. What does it mean to educate, is rarely addressed. There is no dearth of efforts and activities. Life is getting busier; but the weariness of futility clogs the life of individuals. Late in life they become remorseful for having lacked a steadfast, shaping purpose in life, which made them drift along and waste their talents and potentialities.

In relation to purpose, there are two categories of people. For the first, their purposes are set by external agencies and sustained by compulsions. They move from one contingent purpose to the next. For example, while in school or college, their purpose is only to pass examinations. After that, it is to get well-paid jobs. Then it is to lead an easy-going life. The drift goes on till they enter the evening of life and begin to feel the pang of not having lived to a worthwhile purpose or cause. As is well said, 'Life becomes worth living, when there is a cause worth dying for'.

The second category of people, who are a minority, are driven by self-embraced purposes. They are responsive to external demands and pressures, but are not determined, or intimidated or overwhelmed by them. Self-set purposes endure life-long. They are related to personal destiny. They inspire and sustain individuals through thick and thin.

To understand this a bit more clearly,

consider the different personality orientations. There are those who are guided by what happened in the past. We call them tradition-directed, or past-directed, individuals. Then, there are those who are directed by external influences. We call them other-directed. Then there are those who are impelled by purposes from within. We call them inner-directed. Finally, there are those who are directed by something larger than themselves. In the religious context we call them God-directed. In the secular context, we call them destiny-driven.

Gandhiji was a God-directed person. He described himself as 'an instrument in the hand of God to lead the people of In-

dia to freedom'. In what follows, I make a few observations on the beneficial role of purpose in human life, based on the life and struggles of the Mahatma.

Consider the Mahatma

It is incredible how much Gandhiji packed into the seventy-eight years of his life! He accomplished more than a million others together would in the same span of time. The lives he influenced, the events he shaped, the issues he addressed, the places he reached, the literature he produced; above all, the strength of character he exemplified! Suppose you remove his profound sense of purpose from all of this: what will be left? Gandhi, minus his over-arching, godly sense of purpose would have been an ordinary person. Consider the following-

(i) Purpose and time

If ever you feel that you are under pressure for time, think of Gandhiji. Think, in particular, of the tens and

thousands of letters he wrote to people in all walks of life; from Adolf Hitler to even ordinary individuals here and there. Gandhi had time, because he steadfastly followed a grand purpose in life. Time is a function of purpose. Ironically, those who lead a purpose-less life, and are drifting, are 'too busy', as we say, 'doing nothing'. It is rightly said that 'only busy (that is, 'active) people have time for anything'. Unlike them, those who drift through life are bored, which means they don't know what to do with the time that's hanging heavy on them. Lovers never excuse themselves from finding time for each other. Why? Because, their prime purpose is to make each other happy. The moment love fails, they begin to be too busy, otherwise.

(ii) Purposiveness, individuality, and strength of character

Some people found being with Gandhi too demanding, taxing and even irksome. Unlike the vast majority of the people who lead a shadowy existence, Gandhiji was a unique, well-defined and powerful personality. He described the secret of this as 'character and soul force'. Life is, in itself, only the raw material. It has to be shaped into something significant through individual action. In religious terminology this is called 'stewardship of life'. As the aphorism has it, 'Life is what God gives to us; personality –that is, what we make of the life given to us- is what we give back to God'.

Purposiveness is the engine of character. This has diverse components. Consider strength of will, without which no good intention can be put to work and realized. What is it that enables us to endure and persevere? Is it not an unwavering sense of purpose? The case of wisdom, or discernment, is likewise. How do we distinguish between right and wrong, and choose the former? Is it not in relation to what we live for? For a student who intends to excel in life, and not merely to pass examinations, there will no debate on whether to use time fully and aright. She or he will welcome hard work as a privilege, not deem it a burden. Challenges and hindrances will not dispirit or demoralize them. Think of the privations that Gandhiji endured. Would he, or anyone else, have endured a fraction of it, unless he was sustained by a firm and steadfast sense of purpose touching the destiny of India?

As a rule, purposiveness is tested and manifested over a period of time. We live

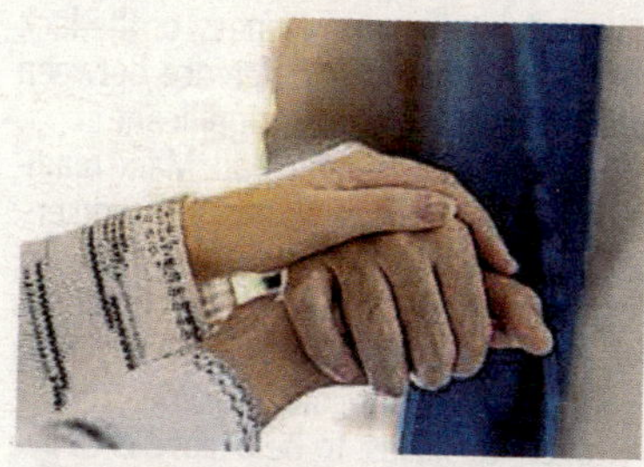

in an age of immediacy. Except in the rare cases of those who are guided by long-terms goals and purposes, most people opt for immediate results and gratifications. This craving for immediate gratification, which makes individuals opt for pleasure rather than personal stature, stems from the absence of a long-term, life-shaping purpose. One may pursue, as seen already, a series of proximate goals, and mistake this for leading a purpose-driven life; whereas the two are mutually contradictory. The difference between the two may be likened, so to speak, to the difference between a life of steadfast fidelity as against one of serial promiscuity. The first steadies the ship of life; the second tosses it on the choppy waters of disenchantment and unrest.

(iii) Purposiveness and discipline

Discipline is not a fashionable word or concept in our times. Yet, it remains the secret of success; and will do so forever. Discipline is the outworking of purposiveness. The need to lead a disciplined life will never be obvious or acceptable to one who drifts from day to day. Remember that scintillating gymnast Nadia Comaneci? She broke on to the global gymnastics stage as none before her had done. She was hailed as a global sensation. But what happened? Her weakness for ice cream undid her. Your brilliance, said Albert Einstein, can take you to the top; but it is your character that keeps you there.

Consider the nearly-superhuman discipline that Gandhi maintained; in particular, his long and excruciating fasts to purify himself. As a token of his earnestness in pursuing the liberation of India, he embraced brahmacharya, which involves the severe discipline, not merely of abstaining from sensual pleasures, but of abiding in the will of God. Brahmacharya means, literally, living, or moving, in Brahma. In the Judeo-Christian terminology this is termed living according to the will of God; or, 'abiding' in God. Such a life respects clearly-defined 'do's' and 'don'ts'. In a state of purposelessness they seem irksomely restrictive of personal freedom. But, from the perspective of purpose-driven life, 'do's' and 'don'ts' are the two terminals of the battery of life between which power flows! A glad and voluntary acceptance of discipline is the hallmark of one who leads a purposeful life.

(iv) Purposiveness and the beauty of life

Young people covet beauty as much as they desire freedom. But, there is no guarantee that they understand both aright. In a culture of instant gratification, freedom is understood mostly as 'freedom from' and beauty is understood in cosmetic terms. As a result, the freedom and beauty of inner life is neglected. There was a beauty to the life Gandhiji that the passage of time will not bedim; whereas beauty of the cosmetic kind proves short-lived. Purpose impacts the substance of freedom. Because Gandhiji

Who Coined the Term "Meritocracy"

"Meritocracy" was coined by Michael Young, a British sociologist, in a book published in 1958. Young feared that a system that rewarded merit—defined as IQ plus effort—could actually be dystopian because the losers would suffer more than ever.

led a purposeful life, he was not only free in himself, but also became the means by which millions were led to freedom. This freedom is not a matter of the absence of restraining external forces, but of the presence of inner resources critically relevant to the given context. It is the freedom to make a beneficial impact on life from which both oneself and others benefit.

Though Gandhiji disliked to be called the Mahatma, that predicate stuck to him; for he was truly one. As Nelson Mandela said, 'India sent a barrister to South Africa; we returned a Mahatma!' What was it that made Gandhi a Mahatma? Was it not the profound, larger-than-the-self, purpose that shaped his life? Arnold Toynbee, easily one of the greatest historians of the last century, said in the evening of his life that he was grateful for 'the singular blessedness of having had a purpose in life'. Small wonder he achieved so much!

(v) Purposiveness: the insurance against the tragedy of waste

The pathos of life consists in the fact, as Hegel pointed out, that wisdom comes too late in life. Human beings, he said, are like owls; they open their eyes only after the sun goes down! There is none who doesn't cherish his or her life. But only a small proportion of human beings attain fulfilment in life, or do justice to their potentials. Most people die without realizing who they could have been.

Nearly in all religious and ethical systems, sloth or laziness is recognized as an enemy to human dignity and fulfilment. Adam Smith, the eminent economist, believed that inertia broods in the DNA of human nature. Most people tend to languish in enervating underutilization of their energies and aptitudes. At the same time, there is no human being, as the American psychologist Thomson pointed out, who does not want to be effective or impactful. It is purposiveness, or the lack of it, that makes the difference between the impactful and the insignificant.

Unlike Adam Smith, Karl Marx maintained that human beings are workers. Everyone works; at least, everyone, except the unemployed. But the conditions of work that prevail –which is his critique of the capitalistic economic order- reduce workers to slaves. To be a slave is to live according to the purposes of others. In that sense, most people are slaves, without knowing it. Very few individuals follow their own dreams; or, as it is put more poetically, 'sing the songs of their own hearts'. When we chase money, position, popularity or power, as against remaining steadfastly true to our personal destiny, we become de facto slaves; successful, suave, sought-after, all right; but slaves, all the same.

(vi) Purposiveness and the human predicament

There are only two possibilities for a human being: either to be in charge of oneself, or to be controlled and manipulated by external forces. We have little control over external circumstances. But, we can control what is internal and personal to us. Key to leading an authentic

life lies here. But most people fail to use this key, for the reason that they are vague about what they live for.

Even with respect to what is personal to us, human beings do not have total control. Or, not everyone has the same extent of control. That is because, apart from other factors, very few have clear self-understanding. It is possible, though, to grow in this respect. But that does not happen in a state of drift. It is purposiveness that strengthens and sustains one's self-mastery, which is basic to success. To lack self-control is to remain vulnerable to manipulations by all and sundry and to succumb to circumstantial pressures. A familiar instance of it is peer-pressure, which affects the weak-willed and the impressionable. It is purposelessness that makes people weak, and keeps them vulnerable. The more purposive we are, the greater the control we have over ourselves; and the greater our self-control the clearer our sense of purpose. Self-mastery and self-understanding reinforce each other and sustain purposiveness in life.

Purposeful Living in a Post-pandemic World

Now to the special relevance of the preceding discussion to our plight in these pandemic days.

Most people feel intimidated and frustrated by what is perceived to be adverse circumstances. They feel even changes in the familiar routine as set-backs. The extent to which we exaggerate the odds and difficulties we face depends on our earnestness of purpose. To the clear-minded and the strong-willed, obstacles could be like the wind under their wings. They feel challenged, stimulated and invigorated. Others react like sensitive plants, fold up, and wait for better days. In this light, let us consider our plight under the pandemic; in particular, in lock-down. Is the present situation only a handicap, an unqualified disadvantage? Or, does it afford scope for preparing ourselves to engage with the life beyond the pandemic more fruitfully?

Consider a somewhat comparable instance. Pearl S. Buck, the novelist, was the daughter of missionary parents, who chose China as their mission field. As a young girl, Pearl was, because of the linguistic barrier, cut off from children of her age group. Her parents being busy with their mission work, she grew up in solitude. She lived in conditions comparable to those of the lock-own. Did this deprivation cripple her?

No! Not in the least. Instead, it enabled her to become an immortal author. While a growing child, Pearl spent all her time in her parent's library, reading all she could. This nourished the creative genius in her. Of course, she did not do so deliberately, but out of compulsion. Unwittingly, she turned a handicap into an opportunity for self-enrichment.

In this context consider a universal tendency in human nature: that of looking for excuses. It is not inappropriate to connect this to the principle of inertia that Adam Smith attributed to human nature. Those who exist from day-to-day purposelessly are apt to waste the possibilities in the given situation. As a rule, no human condition is wholly devoid of positive prospects. What may or may not be present is the willingness to recognize them and the will to engage purposefully

with them so that handicaps are turned, over time, into advantages. Those who fail to do so become adept at inventing excuses. They blame their failures on circumstances. More often than not, adversities are 'blessings in disguise'.

The COVID pandemic can be read in relation to this important fact of life. Life contains ups and down; easy days and hard days. These contraries constitute the full measure of life. The beauty of life is that even in dark days there are glimmers of possibilities. That is why it is said that a crisis is not only danger, but also an opportunity. Purposiveness is the light necessary for seeing the sunshine hidden behind the clouds. Where this is absent, individuals stay fixated on negative aspects and improvise excuses for not doing what they can to make the hard days no harder than they need to be.

Now consider living under the pandemic condition. The fact that we live in locked-down doesn't mean that live has come to a standstill. On the other hand, today life is free of its routine distractions. Surely, it is possible to stay more focussed, utilizing our time and talents to better effect?

Consider the life of a serious researcher, or an author. Don't they live, for all practical purposes, a life similar to what it is in lock-down? A scientist, a creative genius –why, even a spiritual visionary- spends years and decades in focused, solitary research, reflection or meditation, as the case may be. The main difference between their blessed state and ours under the pandemic is that they embrace their way of life voluntarily. Lock-down implies coercion. It is imposed on us.

Read the autobiography of John Stuart Mill. Thanks to his energetic and ambitious father, James Stuart Mill, the historian on India under the British Empire, John led, from his tender years, a life of incredible intellectual rigour. He began to learn Greek at the age of three, Latin at seven, classical literature, philosophy, natural sciences, advanced mathematics and history, thereafter. By the time he was fourteen, he became an author to

reckon with. Admittedly, this is an exceptional case. But I cite this on purpose. John grew up in de facto lock-down conditions. Rather than resent this, he developed a profound respect for his father. In his autobiography he writes that a child, from whom what is more than he can is not demanded, may end up doing less than what can.

Now, here's something that I did not know well-enough when it mattered most. I wish I had; but I was to discover this much later than I should have. If I could go back in time and begin my life all over again, I'd attach utmost importance to living the early years of my life –especially from three to twenty years- as fully and purposively as I can. To the extent that I know that a majority of my

extra

Female Foreign Secretaries of India

In 2001, Chokila Iyer became the first female foreign secretary of India. Since then only two more women have occupied the highest office in the service: Nirupama Menon Rao (2009-2011) and Sujatha Singh (2013-2015).

readers will be young people, I offer them the following thoughts with much affection and profound respect for the potential they hold.

Life's Dichotomy

Life comprises two parts: what is given to us and what we make of it. Jesus Christ taught a parable relevant in this regard: the parable of the talents. Three servants are given talents –the first gets five, the second gets two, and the third, one- by their master. The first two value the talents given to them. The third belittles and buries it. Their destinies diverge accordingly. The sober insight here is that we build ourselves or condemn ourselves based on how purposefully we employ the gifts given to us. Life is the supreme gift. It is God-given. It abounds in possibilities. The given is the ladder to the to-be-attained. What made the all-important difference between the good servants on the one hand, and the unprofitable servant on the other, is their sense of purpose. The good and faithful servants wanted to honour their generous master. The wicked servant was distrustful of, and ungrateful to, the master. Purpose makes the difference between happiness and misery, acceptance and rejection.

One of the most precious resources given to us is time. Lock-down is the condition which affords us plenty of time! We stay at home. No time is lost in traveling or social interactions. This can be

a tremendous advantage to those who know how to use their time gainfully. The best we can do, under this enforced blessing, is to feed and enrich our minds so that when the pandemic ends, as it is sure to, we can resume life with better resources and preparedness.

If only to convince you that I am not merely theorising, but saying this from the truth of my life under the pandemic, let me be, from now onwards, autobiographical. How have I coped with life in lock-down?

Well, my first decision was to take good care of my health; given that it is difficult and hazardous to seek the help of doctors and hospitals in the case of ill-health. At any rate, ill-health is a state of privation in which we cannot use our time or talent optimally. The foremost thing I did in this regard was to incorporate a substantial element of physical labour –hard work that helps to enhance core body strength as well as control health indicators like blood sugar and blood pressure- in my daily life. I was guided in this by the old dictum, 'A sound mind in a sound body'. I wouldn't have done this, if I were not keen to use every hour of my pandemic time for equipping and enhancing myself.

The second thing I did was to invest the remaining time, aside of hours of rest and sleep, into intellectual and creative pursuits. This comprised a blend of reading and writing, both of which involve sustained and deep thinking. My goal was to preserve and enhance inner vitality. I did so, realizing that if I didn't, I could succumb to depression through inactivity and the under-utilization of my mental energies. I can say with sincerity that this has enabled me to turn the pandemic into a blessing in disguise.

All this meant -and that is the third thing I need to mention- maintaining a high degree of self-discipline. Life has taught me that mental concentration is both prophylactic and therapeutic. That is to say, if we increase and enhance our inner coherence we are protected against ill-health to a great extent and healed faster, in case we fall ill. In all of this, I was particularly mindful of the importance of mental state to wellness. As John Milton says in Paradise Lost, "The mind is its own place and, in itself can make a heaven of hell or a hell of heaven".

Now, here's something deeply personal. Why did I do all this? I did so also as a creative protest against the redundancy that is customarily associated with retirement. I am convinced that, whether I am young or old, relevance is what I create for myself. My relevance will not end, so long as I am resourceful enough to relate meaningfully to the needs of the people. How inwardly rich I am, will determine the extent of my relevance. It is I, not others, who decide my relevance or redundancy.

I would not have struck this personal note, but for its direct relevance to the life of young people. We live in a massified society. The more crowded a context, the less significant ordinary individuals in it tend to be. How shall we cope with this? Surely, not by feeling aggrieved and by nursing victimhood. The only sensible way to preserve one's self-worth –irrespective of how old or young one is- is by enhancing and diversifying one's resources. This calls for a sustained investment of time and energy into one's development. The beauty of being human is that one can grow, in some respect or other, till the night descends finally.

If what I have suggested above is to become real and feasible, there is a fundamental issue, or principle, that needs to be regarded. Human beings, as a rule, feel motivated to do their best when they are watched and acknowledged by others. That is why making a public speech, or singing or dancing to an audience, is exhilarating. All these happen in the public sphere. But in lock-down, this public realm vanishes. So, if we derive our motivation only from public acclaim, or human agencies external to us, we are sure to languish and weaken in our resolve. Here's how I cope with this problem: by substituting the public with Providence. Let me explain-

As a human being, I am not only connected to the horizontal world of social relationships which are located in the public domain; but also situated in a vertical relationship with God. In lock-down, I am not seen by my fellow human beings, but I am seen by God. My life I owe to Him. It is my duty to take the best, most inspired, care of it; for sooner or later it has to be returned to God. When I do so, it has to be in its best state.

Admittedly, this option is not relevant to agnostics and atheists. I know no alternatives to offer them, in lieu of what is stated above. They are sure to know better. I commend my thoughts and experiences, in hope and humility, to them too for what they are worth. What matters in the end is if our life is fruitful or not; not the brands we flaunt, or the bravados we bawl. One thing is certain. Life needs to be purposive, if it is to be bearable. Remember Toynbee's memorable words: 'the singular blessedness of having had a purpose in life!'

Beyond Postmodernism

Dr. Merlin Joseph
Assistant Professor, Dept of Sociology, Mithibai College of Arts(Autonomous), Mumbai

This Article traces the evolution of cultural era from the enlightenment period to meta-modernism. Postmodernism has led to an unwrapping of the shifting order in the context of an unholy marriage between human secularism and new age spirituality that is shaping our multicultural world.

Much of liberal thinking finds its roots in enlightenment period in the 18th century. Enlightenment period was the coming of age of reason which marked the beginning of secular humanism. Secular humanism stated that man is the centre of everything and anything outside the purview of the natural order should be accounted as metaphysics and thus should not be considered important. The main tenets of secular humanism is that empirical evidence (data verifiable through sense experience or experimental procedure) should be the only credible methodology whether to study the natural world or the human society. Thus, secular humanism influenced the doctrines of the church by way of biblical higher thinking or higher criticism which led to liberal theology or social gospel.

The influence of Friedrich Wilhelm Nietzsche, the father of Nihilism, further strengthened the cause of secular humanism with the introduction of the doctrine of transvaluation where values do not mean what they mean as objective meaning doesn't exist as humans apparently had killed God. By the middle of the 20th century, countries saw the failure of classical Marxism which defined world history in terms of economic power struggle. Existentialism ruled the roost after the emptiness created by both the world wars. By the end of 1960's postmodernism grew from the ashes of classical Marxism. Post-modernism celebrated deconstruction of institutions, knowledge and objective values. Frankfurt school theorists after re-establishing itself in New York, through the methodology of critical theory tried to redefine marriage and redefine sexual relations. Thus, we see that postmodernists and neo-marxists attacked cultural institutions and not the disparity that merged from economic inequality . Neo-Marxists like Gramsci and Lukas attacked western culture as it depended on religious principles which was a theistic transcendental worldview that emphasised on objective morality. And so religions particularly monotheistic ones were fiercely attacked and was labelled as misogistic, repressive and out-dated. Western universities were a fertile ground for harbouring hostile attacks in the name of liberalism where once upon a time the cosmological, ontological arguments for the existence of God were richly debated. They saw academia the best place to subvert western values but strangely enough western academic institutions were founded by religious people. Truth became relative and moral relativism was used by liberal government and institutions to experiment with various forms of social patterns and phenomenon which eroded the age old institutions of family and marriage.

Western World and Postmodernism

The flourishing of postmodernism in western Europe particularly France took pace in the 1960's. Vocabularies like multiculturalism, pluralism, political correctness, inclusion, prejudice, progressive, safe sex, post-colonial justice, social justice, victimhood, special interest groups are the buzz words of postmodernism. This ideological shift has led to a liberal(liberalism in the west can be anti-religion or indifferent to religion) western worldview which is now marked with cultural wars and identity politics. The fight is pitted between individual against the collective. Collective mob mentality is the norm of the day which is picked by both individual journalists and partisan media houses. Ben Shapiro, American conservative speaker is of the opinion that social media platforms like Twitter and Facebook cater to a crowd without a purpose .He says, "Fundamental human currency is attention, if people do not get good attention they will get bad attention"(Dave Rubin show-podcast, 2017).

The conservatives opine that hierarchy is inverted by the postmodernists, if one is at the top of hierarchy that means the person is oppressive towards other groups and the privilege is undeserved. The below table tells us about the oppressor-oppressed dichotomy. White, heterosexual, males are considered to be the most privileged group while a non-white, transgender would find themselves in the bottom of the order.

This postmodern definition of privilege and under-privilege is very strongly

Table No:1

Elite/Privileged Groups	Targeted Social Groups
White, Adults, Rich, Able-Bodied, Heterosexuals, Protestants	Women, Natives, Latino, Africans, Asians, Queer, Non-Christians

played out in the west. For instance in Canada, an Act to amend the Canadian Human Rights Act and the Criminal Code (Bill C-16, 2016) was passed by its Parliament. The law adds gender expression and gender identity as protected grounds to the Canadian Human Rights Act, and also to the Criminal Code provisions dealing with hate propaganda, incitement to genocide, and aggravating factors in sentencing. This means that under the Act any evidence of discrimination against people on the basis of their gender identify or expression could lead to a criminal offense.

Dr. Jordan Peterson, a professor of psychology at the University of Toronto, criticized the C-16 bill, saying that he was concerned that something he says when he's teaching can be "transformed suddenly into hate speech" under the garb of politically correct culture. According to him, the law would compel speech on people and so he argued that the law could easily be molded as a weapon for hate speech against the LGBTQ members. He said, "These laws are the first laws that I've seen that require people under the threat of legal punishment to employ certain words to speak a certain way, instead of merely limiting what they're allowed to say." In November 2017, Lindsay Shepherd, a teaching assistant at Wilfrid Laurier University, Canada showed a video of Peterson's appeal against the Bill C-16 in her lecture on "Canadian Communication in Context". She was pulled up by the college authorities, stating that she violated Bill C-16 by showing the video in the class and holding a debate among the students.

This amendment is an excellent example of equity of outcome where all the identities should be considered equal and good which is a sign of a politically liberal progressive societies. Gender neutral terms have become a social norm in many western countries. Genderless kindergarten in Sweden are using terms like chest-feeding instead of breast-feeding as an attempt to tone down the historical oppression meted out by the 'privileged group'.

Living in a Post-postmodern World

This fight for identity and recognition has now led to chronic cynicism and treat of tribalism. According to critics, it has led to loss of deeper meaning and depth model. However in midst of this cacophony and chaos, is religion trying to enter through the back door in the materialistic west? Yes and No. In the west, we do not have world religions coming back with vengeance but what we have is a concoction of the ethical values of traditional world religions with a huge dollop of new age spirituality. The vacuum that was created after the death of God movement, is now filled with personalised meaning. Sam Keen, an American author, calls it personal mythology. According to him, "We

Coining of the Term "Postmodernism"  extra

"Postmodernism" was a term coined by Arnold Toynbee early in the 20th century to refer to the last quarter of the 19th century, a time when capitalism and imperialism and Western civilization in general began to decline.

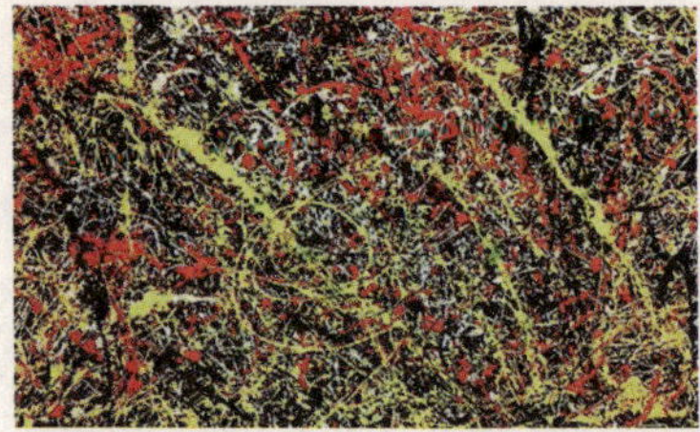

should create our own meaning through our individual stories". In his book, 'In The Absence of God: Dwelling in the Presence of the Sacred', he calls us to have the "courage to wait patiently on the border of agnosticism and faith, forsaking the false certainties promised by the God of traditional religion".

Ihab Hassan states that we have forgotten words like truth, trust, spirit in our academia. However 'spirit' for him is different. For him it certainly is not traditional world religions or occultism. For him, spirit is mystic, a sense of self-emptying, a connection to emptiness or in his own words, "Only through nihilism is nihilism overcome."

However people are still confronted with the million dollar question, 'what is my role in the vast universe'? Several counter-movements to postmodernism has taken place after 2000s to primarily answer this question.

Remodernism is one of them. For Remodernism, spirituality in art is not religion. A Remodernist's job is to bring back God back to art but not as how God was before. Spirituality is in knowing ourselves and focusing on our true relationships with others which ultimately make people happy, so this requires remodernists to depart from postmodern art like deconstruction or conceptual art.

As postmodernism did not give any space to universality of values or spirituality in the production of culture or public sphere, there emerged along with remodernism, a parallel new movement called metamodernism. It explores the many returns of dimensionality. It uses vocabularies like helpful and unhelpful constructs rather than using right/ wrong or above/below.

The new forms of metamodernism realises the importance of meta narratives which is nothing but the awareness that

life is not meaningless and that we aren't merely cogs in the machine. However, the cultural pundits have stopped at the door of religion and are trying their own ways to find meaning and social order through an uncomfortable friendship between secularism and new age spirituality. So are we witnessing the very last days of a Judeo-Christian worldview in the western world and heading to a one world religion through a resurgence of the pre-modern religious ideas and secularism comfortably juxtaposed with science and technology'? Only time will tell.

extra

Gender-neutral 'Mx'

"The gender-neutral 'Mx' is used as a title for those who do not identify as being of a particular gender, or for people who simply don't want to be identified by gender," according to Merriam-Webster. It's pronounced like mix.

Your Words Determine Your Destiny

The Art of Positive Speaking

Dr. John Harrison
Education Influencer, Philosopher, Polymath, Writer, Humanitarian, Counselor

The ability to speak and the words we use are like gateways, fountain and a tree of life. It opens ways, lets cool waters flow and bear sweet fruits. The words that we speak has creative ability and it is reflected in our lives, surroundings and relationships. It can either build and motivate a person or shatter that person. The words we speak has considerable influence on our life-style and even our destiny.

Your words are the architect of your fortune or misfortune, hope you are aware of that. The words we speak have life in them; every spoken word is a seed that brings forth a fruit and a harvest. If the seed (spoken word) is good and you are sowing in fertile soil (lives of people), the fruit or the harvest will be good.

Gateway to Destiny

You can make or mar your life, your future. Your tongue is a pen; use it wisely to write your destiny. You cannot be talking like a slave and expect people to treat you like a king. Your future depends on what you speak today.

Our tongue is the gateway to our destiny. The power of life and death is in your tongue, every word you speak proclaims what you shall have, what you are inviting in your life.

What you proclaim and what you invite with every spoken word shall happen.

Of all the natural gifts given to us by God, the ability to speak or use the words is the greatest. Your words are like the rudder of a ship that controls and steers you in the direction you are going in. Be watchful what you speak and invite in your life.

Wholesome Tongue is a Tree of Life

Good words will bring blessings and prosperity, if you curse yourself or others you are inviting trouble.

Be a "Blessing" to not only yourself, but to your family, and even the world.

Are you choosing your words wisely before you speak? What is it that you are inviting in your life?

Are you speaking prosperity, good health, and abundance upon yourself and others, OR abusing, cursing and thus inviting poverty, sickness, and death upon yourself? Remember a wholesome tongue is a tree of life. Let us refrain our tongues from evil and let our lips speak no guile. Your words have the power to create, thus speak wholesome words upon your life, your family. It makes no difference what condition you are in at present; you can recreate your world by your words. Speak blessings upon yourself daily and see your world, your life being transformed. If there is any area in your life, where you are struggling with darkness, start blessing that area using the right words and the light will manifest and completely obliterate the darkness.

The Fountain of Words

Our mouth is like a fountain from which words flow. A fountain can give you either clean, pure water or dirty water; it cannot give you both. Those who have ears let them hear. The secret lies in speaking (asking) what you want, then expect it believing that you will receive it. Our life mirrors what we speak – producing results after its own kind – be it rotten or sweet. Positive words lead to positive manifestations and vice-versa when it comes to negative words.

The Creative Power of Words

Use the power of words to create or destroy. We can use this power with the words of encouragement, or destructively with the words of despair. Words have energy and power with the ability to help, heal, hinder, hurt, harm, humble, and humiliate. When we speak truth and blessings upon people, words have the ability to change lives. We must be mindful of what we say and how we say it. Words whether written or spoken, have the power to break and destroy environments and relationships; and vice versa. Words are powerful expression tools that can inspire and bring forth a smile, and at the same time make, people shed tears. If we are mindful with our words, we can create a more positive and altruistic world. Words affect our lives, our relationships, our decision-making, our present, and our future. Words can encourage people to achieve greatness. Words can nurture and nourish our minds and our hearts. Words can build your self-esteem. Never speak negatively about yourself or others.

Your linguistic ability helps you in defining the scope of your potential and ability. Do not restrict yourself by using the wrong words.

The Power of Thoughts and Mind

The words we use in our minds very often to describe our lives, our surroundings, our relationships, and ourselves; are some of the most powerful influencing forces in our lives. Keep an eye on your internal dialogue as well and not only your spoken words. If we constantly utter self-deprecating language in our internal dialogue, we are allowing the power of words to work against us. Our whole life is controlled by our words.

Be watchful what you speak !!!

02

GOVERNMENT INITIATIVES

- Select Schemes : 2021-2014
- Intensified Mission Indradhanush 3.0
- PM Umeed Mitra Scheme
- PM Mitra Scheme
- Scheme for Higher Education Youth in
- Apprenticeship and Skills
- AICTE Pragati Scholarship Scheme
- PM Gatishakti Master Plan
- Shram Suvidha
- Saamarth Yoana
- NIPUN Bharan Mission

GoI Schemes and Initiatives

The Government of India initiates specific schemes or yojanas from time to time to address the social and economic problems of the citizens. These schemes are for development or for welfare and are participative or cooperative in nature. Let us take a look at them:

2021

Intensified Mission Indradhanush 3.0 Started on 09 Feb 2021 to * provide immunisation against 12 Vaccine Preventable Diseases - VPD like Whooping cough, Diphteria, Polio, Tetanus, Meningitis, Tuberculosis, Hepatitis B, Pneumonia, Haemophilus influenzae type B infections, Rotavirus vaccine, Japanese Encephalitis -JE, Measles-Rubella-MR, and Pneumococcal Conjugate Vaccine-PVC., to pregnant women and children under 2 years free of cost in India. It will cover hitherto unreached people across 250 districts or urban areas in 29 states/UTs.

PM Umeed Mitra Scheme: An 18- month scheme after completion of a 2-month entrepreneurship development training. The scheme also expects States to identify potential entrepreneurs and ventures that would require financial support and connect them to appropriate markets where their skills will fetch profits and create employment.

PM Mitra Scheme to establish 7 Mega textile parks (holistic integrated textiles processing regions) across Inida to empower textile sector by integrating the currently scattered value chain.

Scheme for Higher Education Youth in Apprenticeship and Skills (SHREYAS) for graduated student to get industrial training and placements.

AICTE Pragati Scholarship Scheme to provide assistance for advancement of girls pursuing technical education.

Senior Able Citizens for Re-employment in Dignity (SACRED) a new online portal of Min. of Social Justice and Empowerment for elderly people to find suitable employment.

PM Gatishakti Master Plan to provide framework for National Infrastructure Pipeline programme and make Indian products more competitive by reducing logistic costs and improving supply chains through a ₹100 crore national plan for multi-modal connectivity.

Shram Suvidha for Labour identification Number (LIN) and people to

Saamarth Yoana To provide 5 lakh certified and trained tyre mechanics by 2022

NIPUN Bharan Mission (5 Jul 2021) by 2026-2027 make sure foundational literacy, like reading, writing and numerical calculations in every child by Class 3. Fund allocation ₹2688 crore annually.

2020

PM SVANidhi Scheme (PM Street Vendor's Atmanirbhar Nidhi)

Launched: 18 July Objective: To facilitate street vendors to access affordable working capital loan provide short term loans (special micro-credit) of upto ₹10,000 for resuming their livelihoods activities,

Website: https://pmsvanidhi.mohua.gov.in/

NISHTHA Teachers Training Program

Launched: 18 July Objective: To improve learning outcomes at the elementary level by motivating and equipping teachers to encourage and foster critical thinking in students.

Official Website: https://itpd.ncert.gov.in/

Aatmanirbhar Skilled Employee Employer Mapping (ASEEM)

Launched: 9 July Objective: To help skilled people find sustainable livelihood opportunities by providing real-time granular information by identifying relevant skilling requirements and employment prospects and enabling opportunities for growth & development. Website: https://smis.nsdcindia.org/

Affordable Rental Housing Complex (ARHC) Scheme

Launched: 9 July Objective: To provide affordable rental accommodation to migrant workers & urban poor in vacant government funded housing complexes converted through a concession agreement for 25 years. Website: https://pmay-urban.gov.in/

SERB Accelerate Vigyan Scheme

Launched: 2 July Objective: Through ABHYAAS program of AV scheme boost Research & Development (R&D) in the country by engaging in High-End Workshops (KARYASHALA) and Research Internships (VRITIKA) potential PG / PhD level students in selected areas / disciplines.

Website: https://acceleratevigyan.gov.in/

Pradhan Mantri Formalisation of Micro Food Enterprises (PM FME) Scheme

Launched: 30 June Objective: To bring in new technology and provide access to information, training, better exposure and formalization of micro food enterprises. Nearly 200,000 micro enterprises will get credit-linked subsidy support.

Website: https://mofpi.nic.in/

Satyabhama – Science and Technology Yojana for Aatmanirbhar Bharat in Mining Advancement

Launched: 15 June

Objective: To promote research and development in science and technology areas in applied geosciences, mineral exploration, mining and allied areas, mineral processing, optimum utilization and conservation of the mineral resources of the country.

Website: http://research.mines.gov.in/

Pradhan Mantri Garib Kalyan Rojgar Abhiyaan

Launched: 18 June 2020 Objective: To empower and provide livelihood opportunities to the returnee migrant workers and citizens in villages in 25 types of works like creation of infrastructure in rural regions of the country.

The resource envelope for PM Garib Kalyan Rojgar Abhiyan is of ₹50,000 crore.

Sahakar Mitra Yojana

Launched: 13 June Objective: Govt. will provide paid internship to youth and ensure availability of assured project loans to young cooperators in the cooperative sector entrepreneurship development ecosystem through capacity development in disciplines including Agriculture and allied areas, IT, Agri-business, Cooperation, Finance, International Trade, Forestry, Rural Development.

Website: https://www.ncdc.in/

Swades Skill Card Scheme

Launched: 4 June Objective: Skill map overseas returning citizens (through Vande Bharat Mission) amid Coronavirus (COVID-19) crisis, and register themselves for Swades Skill Card for future employment opportunities.

Website: http://nsdcindia.org/swades/

Manodarpan Scheme

Launched: 20 July Objective: To provide psychosocial support to school, college, university students for their mental health and well-being during the COVID outbreak and beyond. It has been included in Atmanirbhar Bharat Abhiyan as a part of strengthening human capital and increasing productivity and efficient reform and initiatives for the education sector.

Website: http://manodarpan.mhrd.gov.in/

Aatmnirbhar Bharat Abhiyan

Launched: 12 May Objective: To make India self reliant or self dependent in production and export of goods with special emphasis on economy growth, local production of goods, strengthening supply chain and raising demand of products

(with an economic outlay of ₹20 lakh crore to benefit labourers, farmers, daily wage earners, construction workers, middle class and upper class people.)

(focus on improvement in land, labour, liquidity and laws relating to economy, infrastructure, system, demography, demand and supply chain.)

Pradhan Mantri Swamitva Yojana

Launched: 28 April Objective: To provide bank loans to people on their village property using Drone's technology for survey and the collaborated efforts of the Ministry of Panchayati Raj, State Panchayati Raj Department, State Revenue Department and Survey of India.

Aarogya Setu App

Launched: 17 April Objective: To track and prevent Coronavirus (COVID-19) spread by alerting persons in case they come in proximity with the COVID infected persons. (available to download in 11 languages for android users and iPhone iOS users.

Website: https://play.google.com/store/apps/details?id=nic.goi.aarogyasetu&hl=en_GB

PM CARES Fund (PM's Citizen Assistance and Relief in Emergency Situation Fund)

Launched: March 28, Objective: This national trust is created to meet the distressed and dreadful situation like COVID-19 in times ahead.

PM Garib Kalyan Ann Yojana

Launched: 26 March 2020 Main Objective: To provide food to poor people under the food distribution scheme for stranded migrant workers, daily wage earners who does not have source of income due to COVID-19 lockdown.

Pradhanmantri Garib Kalyan Yojana (PMGKY)

Launched: 25 March Objective: Provide financial assistance and basic facilities to 80 crore people affected by COVID-19.

Pradhanmantri Garib Kalyan Yojana is a new scheme launched by Narendra Modi Government to provide free ration for 3 months and financial assistance to about 80 crore people affected by coronavirus disease or COVID-2019. Under the Garib Kalyan Yojana, the central government will provide free ration to poor, ₹500 per month to women jan dhan account holders, advanced pension for 3 months to all pensioners, increased daily wage for all MGNREGA workers and many other benefits to ease the lives of all affacted people in the country.

2019

Fit India Movement

Launch: 29 August Objective: To increase the awareness among the mass to encourage people to start/increase physical activity and sports in their day-to-day lives.

PM Laghu Vyapari Maan-dhan Yojana or Karam Yogi Mandhan Scheme

Launched: 23 July Objective: ₹3,000 per month as Pension to Retail Traders & Shopkeepers on a voluntary and contributory pension scheme.
Website: https://maandhan.in/

Pradhan Mantri Kisan Mandhan Yojana (PMKMY Farmers Pension)

Launched: 1 June Main Objective: ₹3,000 per month as Pension on a voluntary and contributory pension scheme for all small and marginal farmers (SMF).

Any farmer having land holding upto 2 hectares (5 acres) and belonging to the age group of 18 to 40 years can enroll himself.

Website: https://maandhan.in/ or https://pmkmy.gov.in/

Pradhan Mantri Shram Yogi Maan-dhan Yojana (PM-SYM)

Launch: 1 February Main Objective: ₹3,000 per month to unorganized sector workers who are of 60 years age to ensure old age protection, esp., home based workers, street vendors, mid-day meal workers, head loaders, brick kiln workers, cobblers, rag pickers, domestic workers, washer men, rickshaw pullers, landless labourers, own account workers, agricultural workers, construction workers, beedi workers, handloom workers, leather workers, audio- visual workers and similar other occupations whose monthly income is ₹15,000/ per month or less and belong to the entry age group of 18-40 years are eligible.

Official Website: https://labour.gov.in/pm-sym

PM Kisan Samman Nidhi Yojana

Launch: 1 Feb. Objective: All the farmers with land holding upto 2 hectares of land will get ₹6,000 per year in 3 installments of ₹2,000 each with an outlay of ₹75,000 crore. Website: https://pmkisan.gov.in/

PM Shram Yogi Maan-dhan Yojana (PM-SYM)

Launch: 1 Feb. Objective: To ensure old age protection for unorganised workers whose monthly income is ₹15,000/month or less and belong to the age of 18-40 years. • To provide ₹3,000/month after 60 years of age. Website: https://labour.gov.in/pm-sym

2018

Ayushman Bharat

Launch: 25 Sep. Objective: It is the largest

government-funded healthcare programme in the world with over 50 crore beneficiaries. The Ayushman Bharath programme has two sub-missions PM-JAY & HWCs. •*Pradhan Mantri Jan Arogya Yojana (PM-JAY)*. It provides health insurance coverage for secondary and tertiary level hospitalisa-

National Civil Service Day

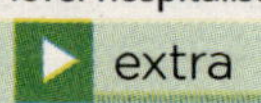

The Government of India chose April 21 as the National Civil Service Day as on this day the country's first home minister, Sardar Vallabhbhai Patel, addressed the newly appointed Administrative Services Officers in 1947 at Metcalf House in New Delhi.

tion worth ₹5 lakh• *Health and Wellness Centres (HWCs)* It aims at improving access to cheap and quality healthcare services at the primary level.

National Youth Empowerment Scheme
Announced: 17 July Objective: N-YES to provide 1 Year compulsory military training with stipend to all the 10th and 12th pass candidates. Govt. will make this training an essential qualification after 10th and 12th class to secure jobs in Defence, Police, and Paramilitary forces. It focuses on providing a disciplined and nationalist Force of Youth.

Ganga Vriksharopan Abhiyan
Launch: 9 July Objective: To plant trees along the river banks of Ganga for reduction in floods, soil erosion and pollution. It will make river Ganga free from dirt and to improve the water level.

Seva Bhoj Yojana (SBY)
Launch: 1 June Objective: It waives off GST on charitable religious institutions' purchase of raw materials such as ghee, edible oil, atta/maida/flour, rice, pulses, sugar, burra for Langar in holy places. Govt. also reimburses the amount spent for providing free food to the public.
Website: https://ngodarpan.gov.in/

PM Jan Vikas Karyakram (PMJVK)
Launch: 2 May Objective: To reduce the gap between the National average and minorities on backwardness parameters. This scheme is Restructured Multi-Sectoral Development Programme (MsDP) and will provide better socio-economic infrastructure facilities in the field of health, education and skill development.
Website:http://www.minorityaffairs.gov.in/

Restructured National Bamboo Mission
Announced: 25 April Objective: To increase the net area for bamboo plantation in non-forest govt. and private lands. Promotion of products development at small, medium and micro levels to give it to larger industries.
Website: https://nbm.nic.in/

PM Universal Social Security Scheme
Announced: 23 April Objective: This social security scheme provides all the social security benefits to the workers across the country. Universal Social Security Cover is going to provide Retirement, Health, Old-age, Disability, Unemployment and Maternity benefits to workers. This scheme is going to provide relief to a million number of under-priviledged workers.
Website: https://labour.gov.in/

Van Dhan Scheme
Launch: 14 April Objective: To harness non-timber forest produce and to utilise true wealth of forest and generate livelihood for tribal people and promote and hold the collective strength of tribals through Self Help Groups (SHGs) to achieve scale.

Nikshay Poshan Yojana
Launched: 1 April Objective: ₹500 per month to all TB patients. Website: https://nikshay.in/

Samagra Shiksha Abhiyan
Announced: 28 March Objective: Govt. has launched Samagra Shiksha Abhiyan to merge – Sarva Shiksha Abhiyan, Rashtriya Madhyamik Shiksha Abhiyan (RMSA) and Teacher Education (TE). This scheme will provide assistance to the states to universalise access to school education from pre-nursery to class 12th. Sabko Shiksha, Acchi Shiksha is the core objective.
Website: http://samagra.mhrd.gov.in/

Agricultural Mechanisation Promotion

Allocation for MGNREGA

extra

The Centre in its Budget allocated ₹73,000 crore to the Mahatma Gandhi National Rural Employment Guarantee Act for the financial year of 2021-'22. This was substantially lower than the actual expenditure of ₹1.11 lakh crore in the fiscal year 2020-21.

Scheme for Crop Residue Management
Launch: 7 March Objective: For in-situ crop residue management – to protect environment from air pollution, prevent loss of nutrients & soil micro-organisms which is destroyed by burning of crop residue. This Scheme will promote retention of nutrients in the soil by using appropriate mechanisation inputs.
Website: https://farmech.dac.gov.in/

PM National Nutrition Mission (Poshan Abhiyan)
Launch: 8 March Objective: To tackle under-nutrition, anaemia, low birth weight and stunting. Under Poshan Abhiyan, all the adolescent girls, pregnant women and children (b/w 6 months to 3 years) will get hot cooked meals. This will realize the dream of "Kuposhan Mukt Bharat".
Website: https://www.icds-wcd.nic.in/nnm/home.htm

Vehicle Scrapping Policy
Launch: 25 March Objective: To scrap 15 years or old vehicles. Govt. is keen to implement Voluntary Vehicle Fleet Modernisation Programme (V-VMP) Policy to reduce pollution in the country. This will also give a boost to vehicle scrap business and thus to make it an automobile industry hub.

Driving Training Centre (DTC) Scheme
Launch: 7 March Objective: To ensure safer roads, enhance driver skills, create employment, provide high level training to commercial vehicle drivers through world class technologies and provide financial support to private participants to setup Driving Training Centers. Website: http://morth.nic.in/

PM Research Fellowship Scheme (PMRF)
Launch: 5 March Objective: To attract the best talent for doctoral studies (Ph.D.) programs of IITs and Indian Institute of Science (IISc) to carry out research in cutting edge science and technology domains with focus on national priorities.
Website: https://pmrf.in/

Solar Charkha Scheme
Announced: 5 February Objective: This Scheme will provide skill training to women and thus will create employment opportunities for them. This scheme will also promote Khadi. The main focus is to promote green energy and reduce pollution by the use of environment friendly khadi fabric.

Kisan Urja Suraksha evam Utthan Mahabhiyan – Kusum Yojana
Announced: 1 February Objective: It was launched to provide solar agricultural pump sets to double the income of farmers by 2022. Now farmers can setup solar agriculture pump sets on their barren land, generate and utilize the energy and sell the excess energy to DISCOMS to earn additional income.

Operation Greens Mission – TOP Scheme

Launch: 1 February Objective: To promote production of Tomato, Onion and Potato and incentivise TOP-processing, compress supply chains, provide an appropriate climate infrastructure for natural preservation of produce, encourage agri-logistics processing facilities and professional management.

Gobar Dhan Scheme (Galvanising Organic Bio-Agro Resources Dhan)
Announced: 1 February Objective: To ensure managing and reusing cattle dung by farmers as compost and fertilisers in agriculture, and as bio-fuel. It will reduce pollution and would result in generating addi-

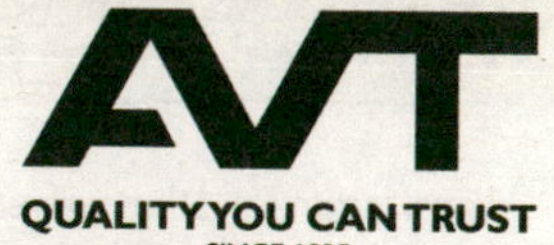
AVT
QUALITY YOU CAN TRUST
SINCE 1925

AVT
pure
Green tea
Infuse Health
loose tea

AVT
Select
CTC DUST TEA

STRENGTH SEALED-IN
STRONGEST TEA
AVT
PREMIUM
Garden Fresh
CTC DUST TEA

AVT
Nature's
Cup
Ayurvedic Tea

AVT
PREMIUM
RICH Coffee Chicory BLEND

tional income and thus will realise doubling farmers income by 2022.

Revitalising of Infrastructure and Systems in Education – RISE Scheme

Announced: 1 February Objective: RISE scheme will promote Infrastructure Development in educational institutions. Govt. will provide low cost funds to all govt. higher educational institutions including Centrally Funded Institutes (CFIs) to promote higher education in schools. Govt. will also open new schools for Scheduled Tribe (ST) candidates and will also promote programmes for teachers to provide quality education to students

PM Rashtriya Swasthya Suraksha Mission (PMRSSM) – **Ayushman Bharat Yojana**

Announced: 1 February Objective: To provide health insurance cover of ₹5 lakh for secondary and tertiary hospitalisation. It would benefit around 10 crore families (50 crore poor citizens) across the country and provide them cashless and paperless treatment in hospitals.

Website: https://www.pmjay.gov.in/

MNRE Rooftop Solar Power Plant Subsidy Scheme

Launch: 29 January Objective: In this scheme, people will get 30% subsidy on the total installation cost under MNRE rooftop solar power plant connections scheme. Citizens can also avail home loans up to ₹10 lakh. People can consume their generated power and also reduce their electricity bills.

Website: https://mnre.gov.in/

Khelo India School Games

Launch: 31 January Objective: To identify sporting talent among school children. In this training, govt. will provide ₹5 lakh to each of the performing candidate and will make them capable of competing at the global level to earn medals for India. Website: http://kheloindia.gov.in/

Stree Swabhiman Initiative

Launch: 27 January Objective: To establish sanitary napkin units for women and girls to promote menstrual hygiene. Govt. will also provide support to village level entrepreneurs and Self Help Groups (SHG). These sanitary pads could be availed from the villages CSC Centers.

Website: http://streeswabhiman.in/

City Liveability Index Programme

Announced: 20 January Objective: To assess the living conditions in 116 cities including 99 Smart Cities and rank them on a National basis. This would be done on the basis of 79 parameters which includes 57 core parameters and 22 supporting indicators to ensure better life for their citizens.

Electoral Bonds Scheme

Launch: 3 January Objective: To ensure that all the political parties are receiving clean money (not black money), Union govt. has launched Electoral Bonds Scheme. Now if anyone wants to donate money to any political party then they can purchase bonds from SBI bank for 10 days in the month of January, April, July and October and pay money in party funds. Most importantly, the name of the owner of the bonds will not be disclosed.

Website: https://www.sbi.co.in/

Aspirational Districts Programme

Announced: January Objective: This scheme is based on 3 pillars – Convergence of Central & State govt. Schemes, Collaboration of Officers & Competition among Districts. 115 Aspirational districts have been identified in India. The primary focus will be on Health & Nutrition, Education, Agriculture & Water Resources, Financial Inclusion & Skill Development, and Basic Infrastructure.

Website: http://niti.gov.in/content/about-aspirational-districts-programme

2017

FAME India Scheme II

Announced: 29 Dec 2017 (FAME India I - 2015) Objective: This scheme envisage all the public transport facilities across the

country like buses, auto rickshaw, taxis to become fully electric under FAME India Scheme II. For this purpose, govt. will provide subsidy on the purchase of new electric vehicles or on the exchange of old petrol / diesel vehicles and on purchasing new electricity (charging) based vehicles.
Website: https://www.fame-india.gov.in/

Market Assurance Scheme
Announced: 27 December Objective: This scheme is meant to ensure price support to rural farmers in case of distress sales. Union govt. will provide 30% compensation to the state govt. for losses in procurement. Farmers will get appropriate price of their crops. This will boost the agricultural production in the state and state govt. have the right to sell the procured goods anywhere.

Atal Bhujal Yojana

Announced: 23 December Objective: This is a mega scheme with ₹6000 crore allocation and is supported by World Bank. It will improve the existing conditions of all river bodies. This will help in raising the ground water level and to meet the agricultural needs of irrigation.

Sustainable Rooftop Implementation for Solar Transfiguration of India
Launch: 22 December Objective: This scheme will provide subsidy to people on installation of solar rooftop. It will increase the use of solar energy in India and residential people can adopt for cleaner electricity generation mechanism.

Scheme for Capacity Building in Textile Sector (SCBTS)
Announced: 21 December Objective: Under this scheme Govt. will provide various training courses compliant to National Skill Qualification Framework (NSQF) under SCBTS. These courses would create jobs in the Textile sector where around 70% of the selected candidates gets salary on wage basis.

GST E-Way Bill (Inter State & Intra State)
Announced: 18 December Objective: National E-Way Bill System is made compulsory for transporters in all the state for movement of goods. To transport the goods Inter State (from one state to another). E-Way Bill is now compulsory for movement of goods within the state, Intra-State and for police verification.
Website: https://ewaybillgst.gov.in/

National Ayush Mission (NAM)
Announced: 18 December Objective: AYUSH stands for Ayurveda, Yoga and Naturopathy, Unani, Siddha and Homeopathy. This scheme will improve health services/ education, up-gradation of hospitals, dispensaries, educational institutions, pharmacies, laboratories and cultivate medicinal plants in the far flung areas. NAM also ensures co-location of various AYUSH services at Primary Health Center (PHCs), Community Health Centers (CHCs) and District Hospitals (DHs).
Website: http://ayush.gov.in/schemes/financial-sanctions/national-ayush-mission

North East Special Infrastructure Development Scheme (NESIDS)
Announced: 16 December Objective: The main aim is to ensure connectivity, power, education, health, water supply, tourism and to promote industrialisation in the NE states. Central govt. will provide 100% funds for this public welfare scheme.
Website: http://mdoner.gov.in/activities/ne-

sids-guidelines

Inter Caste Marriage Scheme for Dalits

Announced: 7 December Objective: Dr. B.R Ambedkar Scheme for Social Integration through Inter-Caste Marriage has been revised to Inter-Caste Marriage Scheme. Under this scheme, govt. will provide ₹2.5 lakh for all marriages in which either a bride or a bridegroom belongs to the Dalit Caste. The primary focus is to put an end to caste system and endogamy.

PM Powerloom Weavers Credit Scheme

Announced: 29 November Objective: Financial Assistance to Powerloom Weavers. All the powerloom weavers will get 90% financial assistance for their work, technology up-gradation by Sustainable and Accelerated Adoption of efficient Textile technologies to Help small Industries (SAATHI) plan. All the beneficiaries will get margin money subsidy of 20% of the total project cost. Long Term Loan at 6% interest would be available.

PM Mahila Shakti Kendras (PMMSK) Scheme

Announced: 22 November Objective: The main objective of this scheme is to empower rural women through community participation by increasing care, protection and development of women across the country. It is designed to improve the child sex ratio, survival of new born girl child, and girls' education.

PM Gramin Digital Saksharta Abhiyan (PMGDISHA)

Announced: 7 October Objective: PMGDISHA scheme aims to empower rural citizens with information, knowledge, skills and make them capable of participating in governance. Basic training would be provided on how to operate computer, digital devices (tablets, smartphones), send and receive e-mails, browse internet, access govt. services, search for information, make digital payment etc.

Website: https://www.pmgdisha.in/

Saubhagya Scheme – Pradhan Mantri Sahaj Bijli Har Ghar Yojana

Announced: September 2017 Objective: This scheme aims to provide electricity to each and every household in the country. Govt. will provide electricity meter connections to all the left out families who have still not received power supply even after 71 years of independence. This scheme will ensure last mile electricity connectivity to all rural and urban houses.

Website: http://saubhagya.gov.in/

Shadi Shagun Scheme

Announced: 9 August Objective: Under this scheme, govt. will provide ₹51,000 as wedding gift to all the girls belonging to minority sections who have completed graduation. This scheme will ensure that girls from backward sections must get necessary higher education before getting married.

PM Matru Vandana Yojana (PMMVY) – Pregnancy Aid Scheme

Announced: August Objective: The pregnant women and lactating mothers will be provided ₹6,000 financial assistance from the central government for the first living child of the family. PMMVY scheme would provide partial compensation for wage loss in terms of cash incentives so that the woman can take adequate rest before and after delivery of the first living child.

Website: http://www.wcd.nic.in/node/712776

extra

PLI Scheme

The Department of Telecom (DoT) notified the PLI scheme for telecom and networking products on February 24, 2021, with a financial outlay of ₹12,195 crore, over the five years.

M Vaya Vandana Yojana

Launch: 4 May Objective: To the senior citizens on attaining the age of 60 years. People can purchase this LIC policy in a lumpsum amount with maximum limit of ₹15 lakh. The plan provides for pension for 10 years, with return of purchase price with interest of 8% at the end of 10 years Pension modes are Monthly / Quarterly / Half-yearly / Yearly.

Website: http://www.licindia.in/

PM Kisan Sampada Yojana

Announced: 18 April Objective: Under this scheme, 7 schemes will get implemented like mega food parks, integrated cold chain and value addition infrastructure, creation/ expansion of food processing/ preservation capacities (Unit Scheme), Infrastructure for Agro-processing Clusters, Creation of Backward and Forward Linkages, Food Safety and Quality Assurance Infrastructure, Human Resources and Institutions

Website: http://mofpi.nic.in/Schemes/pradhan-mantri-kisan-sampada-yojana

Rashtriya Gram Swaraj Abhiyan

Launched 2016-17 Objective: To help Panchayat Raj Institutions deliver Sustainable Development Goals. Rashtriya Gram Swaraj Abhiyan had an allocation of ₹655 crore.

Website: http://rgsa.nic.in

2016

Pravasi Kaushal Vikas Yojana (PKVY)

Announced: 13 December Objective: PKVY will enhance skills of youth in line with the international standards and help them get overseas employment, pre-departure orientation, language training and soft skills.

Website: https://www.msde.gov.in/

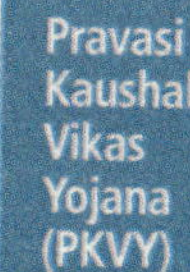

Swachh Surveskshan Program

Launch: 2016 Objective: To encourage a large scale citizen participation in keeping their surroundings and environment clean. This program will create mass awareness among all sections of the society to make towns and cities a better place to live in. This Survey will promote a spirit of healthy competition among towns and cities to improve their service delivery to citizens and to create cleaner cities.

Website:https://www.swachhsurvekshan2018.org/

National Apprenticeship Promotion Scheme (NAPS)

Launch: 19 August Objective: To promote apprenticeship training and to incentivise employers who wish to engage apprentices. This will increase the engagement of apprentices from 2.3 lakh to 50 lakh by 2020. It allows reimbursement of 25% of stipend (max. ₹1500 p.m) to all employers who engage apprentices.

Website: http://apprenticeship.gov.in/

Krishonnati Yojana – Green Revolution

Announced: 11 May 2016 Objective: It covers 11 schemes to enhance agricultural production, impart best holistic practices, introduce latest varities, crop husbandry including micro-irrigation.

Standup India (5 April 2016) The objective of the Stand-Up India scheme is to facilitate bank loans between INR 10 lakh and INR 1 Crore to at least one SC or ST borrower and at least one woman borrower per bank branch for setting up a greenfield enterprise.

Setu Bharatam Project

Launch: 3 March 2016 Objective: To free all national highways from railway level crossings and renovate the old bridges on national highways. Setu Bharatam is an ambitious programme with an investment of ₹50,000 crore to build bridges for safe and seamless travel on National Highways. 208 new "road over bridges / road under bridges" are envisaged for construction, while 1500 bridges will be widened, rehabilitated or replaced.

Website: http://morth.nic.in

2015

UJWAL Discom Assurance Yojana (UDAY)
Launch: 20 November Objective: To obtain operational and financial turnaround of State owned Power Distribution Companies (DISCOMs).The Scheme aims to reduce the interest burden, reduce the cost of power, reduce power losses in distribution sector, and improve operational efficiency of DISCOMs.
Website: http://powermin.nic.in

Gold Monetisation Schemes
Launch: 4 November Objective: To reduce the reliance on gold imports over time. The programme is to lure tonnes of gold from households into the banking system. Under the scheme, people can deposit gold into the banks and earn interest on the value of the gold.

Website: http://finmin.nic.in

Vikalp Scheme
Launch: 1 November Objective: For confirmed accommodation in next alternative train for the waitlisted passengers. Vikalp scheme is available only for the tickets booked through internet for six months and option will be limited to mail and express trains running on Delhi-Lucknow and Delhi-Jammu sectors.
Website: http://powermin.nic.in

Saur Sujala Yojana
Launch: 1 November Objective: Solar Power Irrigation Pumps to Farmers. This scheme provides subsidy on the purchase of solar powered pumps. These subsidised pumps will be of 3HP and 5HP under Saur Sujala Yojana for irrigation and agriculture.

Integrated Power Development Scheme
Launch: 18 September Objective: To ensure 24/7 power for all. The GoI will provide financial support of ₹45,800 crore over the entire implementation period of IPDS under which strengthening of sub-transmission network, metering, IT application, customer care Services, and provisioning of solar panels.
Website: http://www.apdrp.gov.in

PM Khanij Kshetra Kalyan Yojana (PMKKKY)
Launch: 17 September 2015 Objective: To Safeguard Health, Environment and Economic Conditions of the Tribals. PMKKKY is meant to provide for the welfare of areas and people affected by mining related operations, using the funds generated by District Mineral Foundations.

Website: http://mines.nic.in

eBasta Project
Announced: August Objective: This is a common platform where all the teachers, publisher, students come together for e-learning. Basta means school bag. Digital version of school books and study material will be available on the portal. E-Books can easily be downloaded on tablets and computers by students or teachers. Publishers can upload and manage content in the portal.
Website: https://www.ebasta.in/

Sagarmala Project
Launch: 31 July Objective: To transform the existing ports into modern world class ports. The aim is to promote port-led direct and indirect development and to provide infrastructure to transport goods to and

Centre Approves Investment of ₹3345

The Department of Telecom on October 14 approved 31 proposals entailing an investment of ₹3,345 crore over the next four and a half years. The companies selected for the PLI scheme include Nokia India, Dixon Technologies, Flextronics and Foxconn.

Uttar Pradesh
UTTAR PRADESH TOURISM
Deepotsav in Ayodhya
/UttarPradeshTourism
/uptourismgov
/UttarPradeshTourism
/UttarPradeshTourism

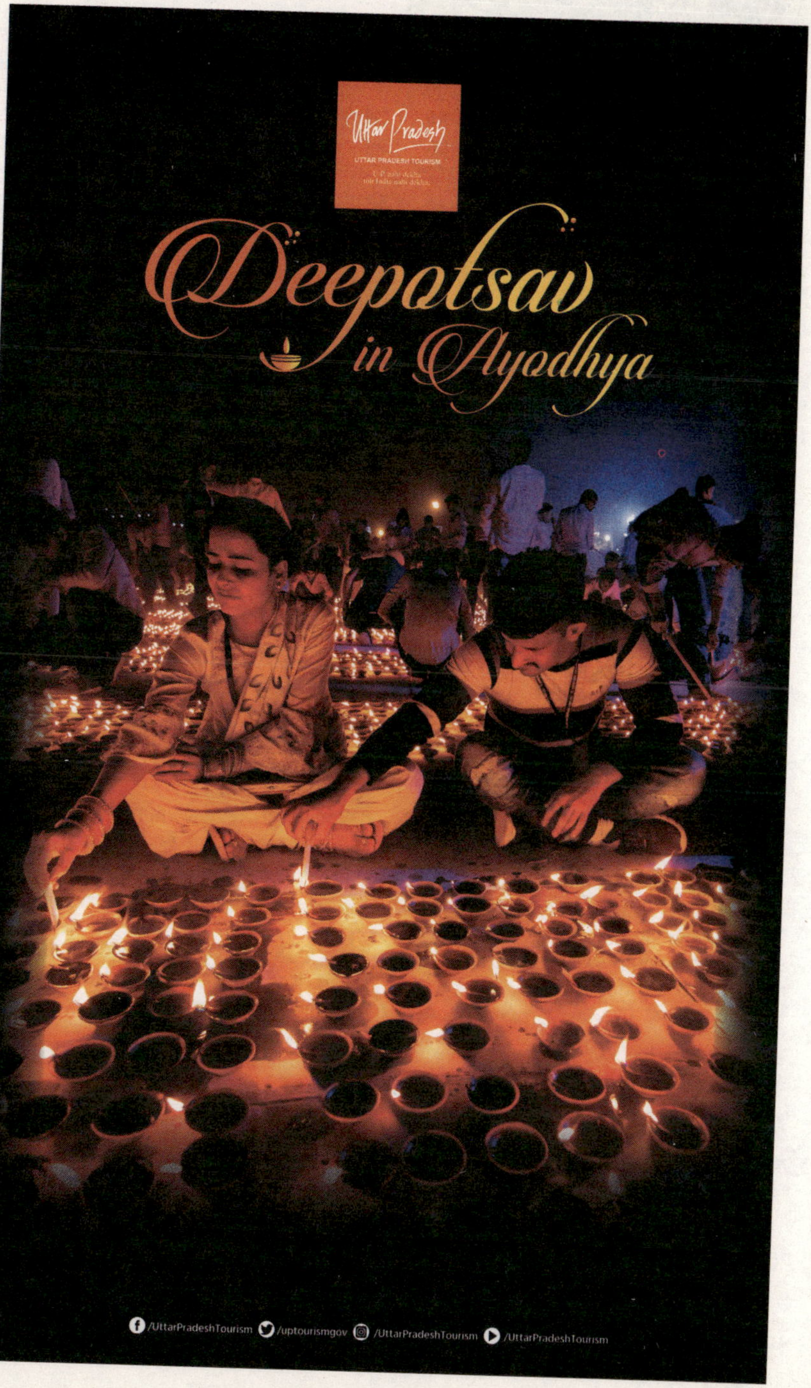

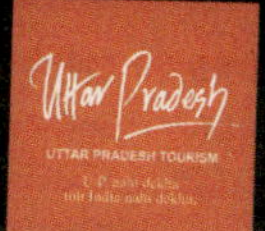

from ports quickly, efficiently and cost-effectively. The Sagarmala Project, is bound to boost the country's economy and the government has lined up about ₹70,000 crore for its 12 major ports only

Website: http://shipping.nic.in

Deen Dayal Upadhyaya Gram Jyoti Yojana (DDUGJY)

Launch: 25 July Objective: DDUGJY will help in providing round the clock power to rural households and adequate power to agricultural consumers The earlier scheme for rural electrification viz. Rajiv Gandhi Grameen Vidyutikaran Yojana (RGGVY) has been subsumed in the new scheme as its rural electrification component.

Website: http://powermin.nic.in

Skill India

Launch: 16 July 2015 Objective: Train over 40 crore people in India in different skills by 2022.The main goal of Skill India Program is to create opportunities, space and scope for the development of talents of the Indian youth. Website: http://skillindia.gov.in

PM Gram Sinchai Yojana (PMGSY)

Launch: 1 July 2015 Objective: Irrigating the field of every farmer and improving water use efficiency to provide `Per Drop More Crop'. All the States and Union Territories including North Eastern States are covered under the programme. The government has approved ₹50,000 crore for the implementation of Pradhan Mantri Krishi Sinchai Yojana for next 5 years, i.e. up to 2020.

Website: http://agricoop.nic.in

Digi Locker

Launch: 1 July Objective: To provide a secure dedicated personal electronic space for storing the documents of resident Indian citizens. Digilocker is a part of Digital India programme, where the Digital Locker reduces the administrative overhead of government departments and agencies created due to paper work besides making it easy for the citizens to receive services and save time and effort as their documents will now be available anytime, anywhere and can be shared electronically.

Website: https://digilocker.gov.in

Digital India

Launch: 1 July Objective: To deliver Government services to citizens electronically by improving online infrastructure and by increasing Internet connectivity. The Digital India programme aims to transform India into a digitally empowered society and knowledge economy.

Website: http://www.digitalindia.gov.in

Smart City Mission

Launch: 25 June Objective: To develop 100 smart cities equipped with basic infrastructure and offer a good quality of life through smart solutions. Assured water and power supply, sanitation and solid waste management, efficient urban mobility and public transport, robust IT connectivity, e-governance and citizen participation along with safety of its citizens are some of the likely attributes of these smart cities.

Website: http://smartcities.gov.in

PM Awas Yojana (PMAY)

Launch: 25 June Objective: The government aims to provide about 5 crore affordable homes to the people belonging to EWS and LIG categories by the year 2022. There is a target of building 2 crore homes in urban area and 3 crore in rural areas across the country. Under the scheme, the government will provide financial assistance to the poor home buyers, interest subsidy on home loan and direct subsidy on homes bought under the scheme.

Website: http://mhupa.gov.in

Atal Mission for Rejuvenation and Urban Transformation (AMRUT)

Launch: 24 June Objective: To improve the quality of life for all (i) ensure that every household has access to a tap with assured supply of water and a sewerage connection; (ii) increase the amenity value of cities by developing greenery and well maintained open spaces (e.g. parks); and (iii) reduce pollution by switching to public transport or constructing facilities for non-motorised transport (e.g. walking and cycling).

Website: http://amrut.gov.in

Pradhan Mantri Rojgar Protsahan Yojana (PMRPY)

Launch: June Objective: In this scheme, govt. pays full employer's contribution towards EPF & EPS both (w.e.f 01.04.2018) for new employment. This scheme will increase the employment base of workers in the establishment and a large number of workers find jobs in such establishments.

Website: https://pmrpy.gov.in/

PM Surakshit Matritva Abhiyan (PMSMA)

Launch: 9 June Objective: PMSMA scheme will provide healthcare facilities for pregnant women across the country. All the pregnant women will receive a minimum package after 4 months of their pregnancy to ensure good health for the new born baby, free health check-up and required treatment every month.

Website: https://pmsma.nhp.gov.in/

Rashtriya Vayoshri Yojana (RVY)

Announced: Budget 2015-16 Objective: Under this scheme, govt. will provide assistive devices to senior citizens who are living below the poverty line and facing age related problems. These includes problem of low vision, hearing, broken teeth, disability etc. All the equipment will be provided to old age persons absolutely free of cost. The devices will include hearing aids, wheelchair, walkers, crutches, tripods, spectacles and dentures.

PM Jeevan Jyoti Bima Yojana (PMJJBY)

Launch: 9 May Objective: This is a government backed life insurance scheme that is aimed at increasing the penetration of life insurance cover in India. The scheme is open and available to all Indian citizens between the age of 18 to 50 years. Under the scheme, the policy holder can get a life insurance cover of ₹2 Lakh with an annual premium of just ₹330 excluding service tax.

Website: http://www.jansuraksha.gov.in

PM Suraksha Bima Yojana

Launch: 9 May Objective: This is a government backed accident insurance scheme aimed at increasing the penetration of accident insurance cover in India. The scheme is open and available to all Indian citizens between the age of 18 to 70 years. Under the scheme, the policy holder can get a life insurance cover of ₹2 Lakh with an annual premium of just ₹12 excluding service tax. All the Indian citizens between 18-70 years of age with a saving bank account are eligible to avail the scheme.

Website: http://www.jansuraksha.gov.in

Revitalising Infrastructure and System in Education

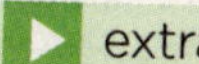

Revitalising Infrastructure and System in Education (RISE) came into being for the sole purpose of improving the infrastructure of government higher education institutions across the country by sanctioning loans.

Atal Pension Yojana

Launch: 9 May Objective: APY is aimed at increasing the number of pension scheme beneficiaries across the country. The scheme is especially targeted to the private unorganised sector and is open to all Indian citizens between the age of 18 to 40 years. Under the scheme, the beneficiary have to make contribution for at least 20 years before he/she can get pension after attaining age of 60 years. The scheme provides a monthly pension of ₹1000 to ₹5000 per month based on the contribution amount.
Website: http://www.jansuraksha.gov.in

PM Ujjwala Yojana

Launch: 1 May Objective: To distribute free LPG connections to the women belonging to 5 Crore BPL families across the country. The scheme provides a financial support of ₹1600 for each LPG connection to the BPL households. This welfare scheme benefited crores of women belonging to the poorest households.
Website: http://www.pmujjwalayojana.com

PM MUDRA Yojana (PMMY)

Launch: 8 April Objective: Financial support for growth of micro enterprises sector. To provide funding to the non-corporate small business sector from all Bank branches across the country. The small businesses/ startups or entrepreneurs can avail loans from the three categories of the scheme – Shishu (< ₹50,000), Kishore (₹50,000–05 L) and Tarun (₹5L to ₹10L).
Website: http://www.mudra.org.in

PM Garib Kalyan Yojana (PMGKY)

Launch: April 2015 Objective: Garib Kalyan Yojana is a Poverty Alleviation Scheme, which is primarily a work shop that you can pay and attend. The effort of the campaign and workshop is to motive and appraise the member of parliaments to help them effectively implement the government run schemes for the welfare of poor in the country.
Website: http://niti.gov.in

Swadesh Darshan Yojana

Launch: 9 March Objective: Develop world class tourism infrastructure. As part of the Swadesh Darshan Scheme, theme based tourism circuits (TBCT) around specific themes such as religion, culture, ethnicity, niche, etc. are identified for infrastructure development across the country.
Website: http://tourism.gov.in

PRASAD (Pilgrimage Rejuvenation and Spiritual Augmentation Drive)

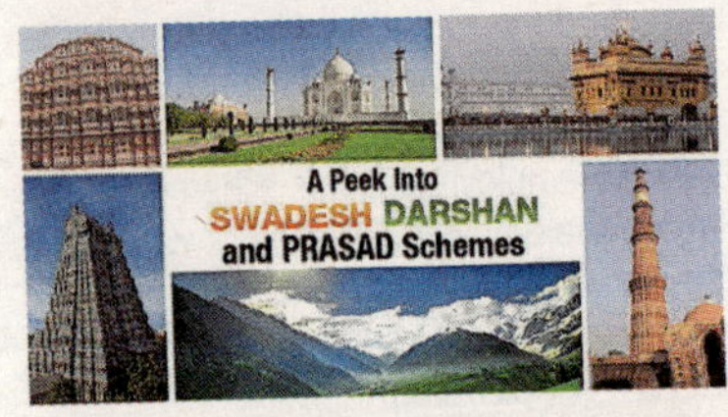

Launch: 9 March Objective: PRASAD scheme aims to create spiritual centres for tourism development within the nation. As part of mission strategy, religious destinations that have potential to be showcased as world-class tourism products are identified and develop world class tourism infrastructure in Amritsar, Ajmer, Amaravati, Dwaraka, Gaya, Kanchipuram, Kedarnath, Kamakhya, Mathura, Puri, Varanasi and Vellankani.
Website: http://tourism.gov.in

National Sports Talent Search Scheme (NSTSS)

Launch: 20 February Objective: To Identify sporting talent among students in the age group of 8–12 years. The scheme is being implemented by the Sports Authority of India (SAI), under the Ministry of Youth Affairs & Sports for spotting talented young children in the age group of 8-14 years from schools and nurturing them by providing scientific training.

Website: http://www.sportsauthorityofindia.nic.in

PM Jan Aushadhi Yojana (PMJAY)

Launch: Objective: Pradhan Mantri Bhartiya Jan Aushadhi Pariyojana, the scheme aims to open 3000 Jan Aushadhi stores to sell drugs at affordable cost. Under the scheme, over 500 medicines will be sold through Jan Aushadhi stores at price less than the market price. Private hospitals, NGO's, and other social groups are eligible to open the Jan Aushadhi stores with a onetime assistance of ₹2.5 Lakh from the central Government.

Website: http://janaushadhi.gov.in

Soil Health Card Scheme

Launch: 17 February Objective: To help farmers to improve productivity from their farms by letting them know about the quality of soil right, its functional characteristics, water and nutrients content and other biological properties besides corrective measures for obtaining better yield.

Website: http://www.soilhealth.dac.gov.in

Beti Bachao, Beti Padhao Yojana

Launch: 22 January Objective: To generate awareness and improving the efficiency of welfare services meant for women. Now Central govt. has extended this BBBP Scheme Pan India Expansion to have as focused intervention and multi-section action in almost 100 districts with low Child Sex Ratio (CSR).

Website: http://wcd.nic.in

PM Sukanya Samriddhi Yojana (PMSSY)

Launch: 22 January Objective: Under the scheme, a savings account can be opened in the name of girl child and deposits can be made for 14 years. After the girl reach 18 years of age, she can withdraw 50% of the amount for marriage or higher study purposes. After the girl completes 21 years of age, the maturity amount can be withdrawn including the interest at rates decided by Government every year. The maximum investment of ₹1.5 Lakh per year can be made while minimum deposit is ₹1000 per year.

Website: http://www.nsiindia.gov.in

National Heritage City Development and Augmentation Yojana (HRIDAY)

Launch: 21 January Objective: Bringing together urban planning, economic growth and heritage conservation in an inclusive manner to preserve the heritage character of each Heritage City. With a duration of 27 months (to be completed by March 2017) and a total outlay of ₹500 crores, the Scheme is being implemented in 12 identified cities namely, Ajmer, Amaravati, Amritsar, Badami, Dwarka, Gaya, Kanchipuram, Mathura, Puri, Varanasi, Velankanni and Warangal. The scheme is implemented in a mission mode.

Website: http://hridayindia.in

'Prakash Path' – 'Way to Light' – The National LED Programme

Launch: 5 January Objective: To distrib-

ute LED bulbs and decrease the power consumption. The programme has been launched to distribute and encourage the use of LED light bulbs to save both cost and consumption.
Website: http://powermin.nic.in

PAHAL – Direct Benefits Transfer for LPG (DBTL) Consumers Scheme
Launch: 1 January Objective: Under it, the LPG consumer can receive subsidy in his bank account through CTC (Cash Transfer Compliant) once he joins the scheme and is ready to receive subsidy in the SB account or a direct benefits transfer for LPG (DBTL) consumers Scheme.
Website: http://dahd.nic.in

National Institution for Transforming India
Launch: 1 January Objective: To foster involvement and participation in the economic policy-making process by the State Governments of India. It replaced 65 year old Planning Commission to act more like a think tank or forum.
Website: http://niti.gov.in

2014

Saksham Aims at all-round development of Adolescent Boys and make them self-reliant, gender-sensitive and aware citizens, when they grow up. It cover all adolescent boys (both school going and out of school) in the age-group of 11 to 18 years subdivided into two categories, viz. 11-14 & 14–18 years. In 2014–15, an allocation of ₹25 crore is made for the scheme. (previously Rajiv Gandhi Scheme for Empowerment of Adolescent Boys)

Mission Indradhanush
Launch: 25 December 2014 Objective: To immunise all children as well as pregnant women against seven vaccine-preventable diseases namely diphtheria, whooping cough (Pertussis), tetanus, polio, tuberculosis, measles and hepatitis B. The aim is to achieve full immunisation in 352 districts which includes 279 mid priority districts, 33 districts from the North East states and 40 districts from phase one where huge number of missed out children were detected.
Website: http://www.missionindradhanush.in

Rashtriya Gokul Mission
Launch: 16 December Objective: To conserve and develop indigenous breeds in a focused and scientific manner. It is a focused project under National Programme for Bovine Breeding and Dairy Development, with an outlay of ₹500 crore.
Website: http://dahd.nic.in

Udaan Scheme
Launch: 14 November Objective: It is a mentoring and scholarship scheme to enable meritorious girl students to transit from schools to higher technical education without much difficulty and also aims to enrich and enhance teaching and learning of mathematics and science at senior secondary school level by providing free online resources for all.
Website: http://mhrd.gov.in

National Bal Swachhta Mission
Launch: 14 November Objective: To provide hygienic and clean environment, food, drinking water, toilets, schools and other surroundings to the children. The Bal Swachhta Mission is a part of the nationwide sanitation initiative of 'Swachh Bharat Mission' launched by the Prime Minister on 2nd October, 2014.
Website: http://wcd.nic.in

Pandit Deendayal Upadhyay Shramev Jayate Yojana (PDUSJY)

Launch: 16 October Objective: To consolidate information of Labour Inspection and its enforcement through a unified web portal, for transparency and accountability in inspections. Shram Suvidha portal was launched under the scheme as a platform to facilitate the implementation of a transparent system for information and database management.
Website: https://www.efilelabourreturn.gov.in

Sansad Adarsh Gram Yojana

Launch: 11 October Objective: Development of model villages called "Adarsh Gram".Under the SAGY, MPs will be responsible for developing the socio-economic and physical infrastructure of three villages each by 2019, and a total of eight villages each by 2024.
Website: http://rural.nic.in

PM Fasal Bima Yojana

Launch: 11 October Objective: Provide insurance cover to rabi and kharif crops and financial support to farmers in case of damage of crops. PMFBY replaced the previous NAIS and MNAIS. Under PMFBY, farmers will have to pay a uniform premium of two per cent for all kharif crops and 1.5% for all rabi crops. The scheme will be implemented from the kharif season of FY 2016.
Website: https://pmfby.gov.in/

Swachh Bharat Abhiyan

Launch: 2 October Objective: To fulfill Mahatma Gandhi's dream of a clean and hygienic India. Swachh Bharat Mission is being implemented by the Ministry of Urban Development (M/o UD) and by the Ministry of Drinking Water and Sanitation (M/o DWS) for urban and rural areas respectively.
Website: http://swachhbharat.mygov.in

Make in India

Launch: 25 September Objective: To encourage multi-national, as well as domestic companies to manufacture their products in India and create jobs and skill enhancement in 25 sectors. The major objective behind the initiative is to focus on job creation and skill enhancement in 25 sectors of the economy. The initiative also aims at high quality standards and minimising the impact on the environment. The initiative hopes to attract capital and technological investment in India.
Website: http://www.makeinindia.com

PM Jan Dhan Yojana (PMJDY)

Launch: 28 August Objective: Under the PMJDY, any individual above the age of 10 years and does not have a bank account can open a bank account without depositing any money.

The scheme is designed to ensure access to financial services such as banking / savings & deposit accounts, remittance, credit, debit cards, insurance and pension in affordable manner. The scheme was targeted for people who are under the Below Poverty Line but is beneficial to everyone who does not have a bank account. The total balance is over ₹34.81 crore PMJDY accounts crossed ₹1.31 trillion (₹1.31 lakh crore) on 20 Aug. 2020.

Website: http://www.pmjdy.gov.in

One Rank One Pension (OROP) Scheme

Launch: NA Objective: To provide same pension, for same rank, for same length of service, irrespective of the date of retirement. Website: http://wcd.nic.in

Namami Gange Project

Launch: 10 July Objective: To integrate the efforts to clean and protect the Ganga river in a comprehensive manner. Namami Gange approaches Ganga Rejuvenation by consolidating the existing ongoing efforts and planning for a concrete action plan for future. The interventions at Ghats and River fronts will facilitate better citizen connect and set the tone for river centric urban planning process.
Website: https://nmcg.nic.in

03

CALENDAR OF EVENTS

Calendar of Events - **India**

2021 was eventful. This section captures the major events chronologically. This time the events are divided into 6 categories like Economics, Politics, Socio-cultural, Awards, Science and General, for a quick-read. It also includes a short note on one item.

January

Economics

28. Centre unveils draft Blue Economy policy.

Politics

01. PM Modi unveils Light House Project, India, Pakistan exchange list of nuclear installations
05. SC approves Central Vista project.
07. J&K L-G Sinha announces industrial package.
11. Heritage panel clears Central Vista.
12. SC stays farm laws, appoints panel to study laws.
13. Centre approves procurement of 83 Light Combat Aircraft.
16. COVID-19 vaccination begins.
17. UK invites PM Modi for G7 summit, PM Modi flags off 8 Statue of Unity trains.
20. Cabinet approves MoU with Uzbekistan in solar energy.
21. India clears vaccine exports to Brazil.
23. India makes Chinese apps ban permanent.
24. India, China hold ninth round of talks, Election Commission launches e-EPIC.
26. India celebrates Republic Day, Red Fort vandalised by protestors over farm laws.
31. India delivers 2 cranes for Chabahar port in Iran.

Science

01. Covishield vaccine gets DCGI approval.
03. India detects first COVID-19 UK variant, India approves Covishield and Covaxin.
05. Government launches toys hackathon.
12. Covishield vaccine first batch leaves SII.

Central Vista

15. DRDO develop India's first indigenous machine pistol.

Socio-cultural

25. Padma Vibhushan: SPB, Shinzo Abe, BB Lal; Padma Bhushan: KS Chithra, Sumitra Mahajan, Ram Vilas Paswan; Padma Shri: Sridhar Vembu, Bombay Jayashri, Dulari Devi, Solomon Pappaiah, Pappammal (Total Padma Awards: 119).
19. Netaji Subhas Chandra Bose's birth anniversary – Parakram Diwas.
28. UP wins Republic Day 2021 parade award.; India approves Covishield (AstraZeneca) and Covaxin (Bharat Biotech).

Sports

19. India wins series against Australia.

Parakram Diwas

The Centre declared the legendary freedom fighter Subhas Chandra Bose's birth anniversary on January 23 as *Parakram Diwas* (day of valour). It has triggered a political row.

- The TMC wanted the day to be celebrated as *Desh Nayak Diwas* (the national hero's day)
- The Forward Bloc, and a section of Bose's family wanted January 23 to be observed as *Desh Prem Diwas* (day of patriotism).

February

Economics

01. Union budget 2021: FM announces Atmanirbhar healthcare system, big boost for roads and infrastructure, National Research Foundation, Vehicle scrappage policy, Improvement of fishing harbours and ports, Fuel and liquor cess imposed.

Politics

02. Lt. Gen. CP. Mohanty takes over as Vice Chief of Army Staff.
03. Centre warns Twitter, Praveen Sinha takes over as CBI chief.
06. Farmers conduct chakka jam.
07. Nanda Devi glacier bursts in Uttarakhand.
08. RS passes J&K Reorganisation (Amendment) Bill, Govt asks Twitter to remove 1178 accounts.
10. Rajya Sabha passes ports Bill.
12. Govt denies conceding territory to China, Mallikarjun Kharge assumes charge as Leader of Opposition in Rajya Sabha.
14. Disha Ravi arrested over Toolkit case, PM Modi hands over Arjun Mk-1A tank to Army.
15. FASTag mandatory, Chinese troops clears Finger 4 heights at Pangong Tso.
17. 24 envoys arrive in Srinagar, Kiran Bedi removed as Puducherry L-G, Cabinet approves Juvenile Justice Act Amendment.
18. L&T delivers 100th K9 Vajra howitzer to Army.
19. India, China complete disengagement at Pangong Tso.
21. India, Maldives sign defence and security pacts.
22. India and Mauritius signs defence agreements.
24. National Urban Digital Mission launched.
25. Govt announces rules for OTT platforms.
26. EC announces elections dates for five states, Kerala, Tamil Nadu elections on April 6, counting on May 2, India & China to establish hotline.
27. Vice Admiral R. Hari Kumar takes over as chief of Western Naval Command.

Science

04. SII inks pact with UNICEF.
05. Balasore gets first thunderstorm research testbed.
07. Govt announces geothermal field development project in Leh, India supplies Covishield to Afghanistan.
19. Helina, Dhruvastra ATGMs successfully test fired.
28. ISRO launches PSLV-C51 with Amazonia-1, India donates advanced digital cobalt therapy machine Bhabhatron-II to Madagascar.

Socio-cultural

02. Aatmanirbharta named Oxford Hindi word of 2020.

Sports

21. Novak Djokovic beat Medvedev to win Australian Open 2021.
24. Motera Stadium renamed after Narendra Modi.
26. India bt England in Test in Ahmedabad.

FASTag

The National Electronic Toll Collection FASTag has been made mandatory for all vehicles in India. Over 80% of all toll collected across NHs is through FASTag. The cost of buying FASTag depend on the type of vehicle. FASTag is valid for 5 years. FASTag digital wallet can be recharged using internet banking, credit or debit cards and UPI. It can be bought online on portals (Paytm, Amazon.in) or on the websites of banks (HDFC, SBI, ICICI, Axis, etc.).

March

Economics

04. Bengaluru and Shimla top Ease of Living Index.

Politics

01. PM Modi takes first dose of COVAXIN, Manpreet Vohra appointed India's High Commissioner to Australia.

02. Lok Sabha-Rajya Sabha TV merged into Sansad TV.

03. Rahul Gandhi terms Emergency was a mistake.

08. China approves first downstream dams on Brahmaputra, MT Swarna Krishna all-women crew makes history.

09. Uttarakhand CM Trivendra Singh Rawat resigns, Modi opens Maitri Setu between India and Bangladesh; freebies galore AIADMK manifesto, IMF lauds India's vaccine policy.

10. Mamata files nomination from Nandigram, Lok Sabha passes National Capital Territory Bill, Tirath Singh Rawat becomes Uttarakhand CM.

12. PM Modi launches Amrut Mahotsav and attends Quad summit, Justice Indu Malhotra retires from SC.

16. Rajya Sabha passes the Medical Termination of Pregnancy Bill, Cabinet approves development finance institution bill.

18. Rajya Sabha passes Insurance Amendment Bill.

19. Lok Sabha passes Mines and Mineral (Development and Regulation) bill, US Defence Secretary Lloyd Austin meets PM.

22. PM Modi launches Catch the Rain campaign.

24. Justice NV. Ramana to take over as 48th CJI.

25. Parliament passes Bill to set up National Bank for Financing Infrastructure and Development, Rajya Sabha approves Delhi UT bill.

26. SC refuses to stay sale of electoral bonds, EC to work on e-voting with IIT-Madras.

Maitri Setu between India and Bangladesh

27. India sends 200,000 doses of COVID-19 vaccines to UNPKF.

29. President signs Centre's Delhi Bill law, Mehbooba Mufti denied passport.

30. President Ram Nath Kovind undergoes bypass surgery.

31. SC panel submits report on farm laws,

Science

01. India starts COWIN portal for vaccine. registration.

03. COVAXIN shows 81% efficacy.

05. DRDO tests Solid Fuel Ducted Ramjet technology.

Socio-cultural

04. PM Modi gets CERAWeek Global Energy and Environment Leadership Award.

11. Brahma Kumaris chief Dadi Hriday Mohini (93) passes away.

15. Statue of Unity crosses 50 lakh visitors mark.

Solid Fuel Ducted Ramjet

SFDR is a missile propulsion system based on the concept of Ramjet engine principle. Unlike solid propellent rockets, the Ramjet takes up oxygen from the atmosphere during flight which makes it light weight, carry more fuel and travel longer distance. DRDO successfully tested SFDR technology from Integrated Test Range, Odisha, on 05 March 2021. This technological demonstrator will enable India to develop long range air-to-air missiles. Presently such technology is available only with a handful of countries in the world.

April

Economics

02. India contributes $300,000 to UN Women.

Politics

02. EC suspends Assam poll officials, Priyanka Gandhi cancels election campaign.
04. Chhattisgarh Maoist encounter kills 17 jawans.
07. PM Modi conducts Pariksha Pe Charcha.
08. PM Modi gets 2nd dose of COVID-19 vaccine, Naxals release abducted CRPF jawan in Chhattisgarh.
11. Centre bans export of Remdesivir.
12. Sushil Chandra appointed Chief Election Commissioner.
13. EC bans Mamata from campaigning for 24 hours, CCI probes WhatsApp's new privacy policy.
14. CBSE cancels Class 10 exams, Maharashtra imposes mini lockdown.
15. India restores e-visa for 156 countries, SC orders CBI probe into ISRO spy case.
16. UK approves Nirav Modi's extradition, Centre eases guidelines for OCI cardholders.
17. Bharat Biotech to make 6 crore Covaxin doses by July.
19. UK PM Boris Johnson cancels India trip, Centre imposes curbs on industrial oxygen, Manmohan Singh tests positive for COVID-19.
20. ICSE cancels class 10 exams.
21. Centre increases production of Remdesivir, Centre credits MSP directly to farmers accounts.
22. PM Modi announces India-US climate partnership, Railways run Oxygen Express trains, India searches for Indonesian submarine.
24. Justice NV Ramana becomes 48th CJI, Congress launches INC TV.
25. PM Cares allots funds for 551 Oxygen plants, Centre asks Twitter to remove COVID-19 posts.
26. Director Chloe Zhao wins Oscars 2021.

Railways Run Oxygen Express Trains to 15 states

27. EC bans victory celebrations, Centre uses Nitrogen and Argon tankers for Oxygen.
28. SII slashes Covidshield price for states to ₹300, COVID-19 vaccine registration begins for 18+, PM Cares fund 1 lakh portable oxygen concentrators.
29. Covaxin state prices cut to ₹400

Science

8. Indian double mutant strain named B.1.617.
12. India approves Sputnik V.
21. Covaxin neutralises double mutant strain.
26. DRDO develops crystal blade technology for aero engines.

Sports

08. Lt Col Bharat Pannu earns Guinness World Records for solo cycling.

Oxygen Express

During the second wave of Pandemic, Oxygen Expresses were started by Indian Railways on 19th April, 2021 to provide respite to Indian states requiring medical Oxygen. More than 35000 MT of LMO was transported to 15 states. Around 480 Oxygen Expresses were operationalised. For the first time ever the Oxygen Express was put into operation to neighbouring country – 200 MT of Liquid Medical Oxygen to Benapole, Bangladesh. India sent 150 MT of LMO to Sri Lanka as well.

MAY

Economics

01. Govt slashes GST on imported oxygen concentrators.

Politics

01. India reports 4 lakh COVID cases.

02. Assembly Election Results: Asom (BJP), Kerala (Left), Tamil Nadu (DMK), Bengal (TMC), Puducherry (NDA); Railways ply Oxygen Express.

03. Green panel clears Central Vista project, NEET-PG exams postponed.

05. Mamata Banerjee sworn in as West Bengal CM, SC quashes Maratha quota law, India gets 3 more Rafale jets.

08. SC forms National Task Force for oxygen allocation.

09. Himanta Biswa Sarma elected as new Asom CM.

12. Kerala women killed in Gaza rocket attack in Israel.

13. UPSC prelims postponed to Oct. 10.

15. Cyclone Tauktae intensifies, Air India starts zeolite cargo flight service.

18. ICMR drops plasma therapy, Bangladesh sends medicines to India.

19. Recovered COVID patients can vaccinate after 3 months, Govt enhances DAP fertiliser subsidy.

20. Pinarayi Vijayan sworn in as Kerala CM with new cabinet, INS Rajput decommissioned, Black fungus (Mucormycosis) declared as epidemic.

22. IMA demands action against Ramdev.

23. Cyclone Yaas hits north Odisha coast.

25. Subodh Kumar Jaiswal appointed CBI Director, Railway suspends wrestler Sushil Kumar.

26. New IT rules comes into effect.

27. PM Modi completes 7 years in office, BVR. Subrahmanyam appointed as Commerce Secretary.

28. Govt gives 15 days to social media companies to submit reports, Lakshadweep reforms triggers controversy.

30. Lt. Nikita Kaul, wife of Pulwama martyr joins Army

31. Delhi HC dismisses plea against Central Vista, Justice Arun Mishra appointed as NHRC head.

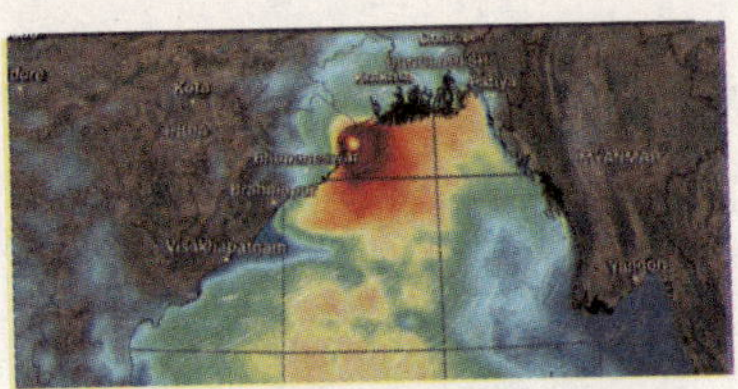

Cyclone Yaas Hits North Odisha Coast

Socio-Culture

13. Govt shuts monuments till May 31.

19. 6 UNESCO heritage sites added in India.

22. Mathematician MS Narasimhan (89) passes away.

Science

01. Sputnik V arrives in India.

08. DCGI approves DRDO's 2-deoxy-D-glucose (2-DG) drug.

14. Sputnik V cost fixed at ₹995 per dose.

17. Govt approves 2-DG for usage.

20. ICMR approves COVID-19 rapid home testing kit.

24. Panacea Biotec begins production of Sputnik-V vaccine.

2-DG

Discovered by the Institute of Nuclear Medicine & Allied Sciences of DRDO and Dr. Reddy's Laboratories has codeveloped an adjunct therapy for Covid-19 – Antiviral and anti-inflammatory drug, 2-deoxy-D-glucose (2-DG). It is administered orally at 45mg/kg twice a day before meals. 2-DG selectively accumulates in virally infected cells because of higher glucose demand and inhibits the energy production required for viral multiplication. 2-DG alters glycosylation of viral glycoprotein, rendering new virions incapable of infecting human cells. It inhibits aerobic glycolysis in the virally infected host cell

June

Economics

04. RBI cuts GDP growth forecast to 9.5%.
09. Cabinet approves 5MHz spectrum for railways.
12. GST slashed on COVID-19 essentials.
16. India grants $100 mn loan to Sri Lanka.
21. Govt ban flash sales on e-commerce sites.

Politics

01. Justice Arun Mishra becomes NHRC chief, CBSE scraps Class XII exams, Mahesh Jethmalani nominated to Rajya Sabha.
02. Cabinet approves Model Tenancy Act, Centre amends pension rules.
04. Defence Ministry clears deal for 6 submarines.
05. India issues final warning to Twitter to comply with IT rules, Raimona becomes Assam's sixth national park.
07. PM Modi addresses nation and announces centralized vaccine policy.
08. India welcomes Maldives UNGA win.
12. Defence ministry approves war history declassification policy.
13. PM Modi calls for one earth, one health at G7 outreach session.
15. Twitter appoints interim Chief Compliance Officer,
16. IT Minister slams Twitter, Cabinet approves OFB corporatisation & Inland Vessels Bill.
17. SC approves CBSE's 30:30:40 formula for Class 12, Amit Shah launches cyber fraud helpline, Cable TV network rules amended, Aashish Chandorkar appointed as India's WTO mission.
23. ED transfers assets of Vijay Mallya, Nirav Modi & Mehul Choksi.
24. PM Modi meets J&K leaders.
25. Twitter blocks Ravi Shankar Prasad's Twitter account.
26. Vigilance Commissioner Suresh Patel becomes CVC.
28. Govt to share CoWIN API with 50 nations, Govt extends AG KK. Venugopal tenure by one year.
30. India toughens stand on EU COVID passport

Lakshmi N. Bora

Socio-Cultural

01. Syed Akbaruddin becomes dean of the Kautilya School of Public Policy.
03. Assamese writer Lakshmi Nandan Bora (91) passes away.
28. P. Sainath awarded 2021 Fukuoka Prize.

Science

07. AIIMS Delhi starts Covaxin trials on Children.
10. ICMR approves Meril's COVID-19 Rapid Antigen test kit.
14. Govt to deploy drones for vaccine delivery.
28. DRDO tests Agni-P nuclear missile.

Sports

18. Milkha Singh (92) passes away.

Twitter Jugglery

Over tweets and accounts linked to the continuing farmers' protests against a series of agriculture reform laws pressure was mounting between the BJP Union government and Twitter. The farmers agitation suddenly turned violent involving a group of protesters on 26 January. The government asked Twitter to remove tweets that used an incendiary hashtag, and accounts allegedly used by Sikh separatist groups. Twitter blocked 500 accounts in response to legal notice by the government but restored it in 6 hours. Twitter soon lost the legal immunity over its failure to comply with the new IT rules.

July

Economics

07. Chinese nationals step down from Paytm board ahead of IPO.
08. Cabinet approves second COVID-19 emergency response package.

Politics

01. Air Marshal VR. Chaudhari takes charge as IAF Vice Chief.
02. SC dismisses Maratha verdict review petitions.
04. Pushkar Singh Dhami becomes Uttarakhand CM.
06. New Governors appointed [Thaawarchand Gehlot (Karanataka), PS. Sreedharan Pillai (Goa), Satyadev Narayan Arya (Haryana), Ramesh Bais (Tripura), Bandaru Dattatraya (Himachal)], CBSE divides 2021-22 academic year into two terms.
07. Union Cabinet expanded with 43 new ministers (Jyotiraditya Scindia, Narayan Rane, Sarbananda Sonowal, Ashwini Vaishnaw, Meenakashi Lekhi, Rajeev Chandrasekhar, Anupriya Patel, L. Murugan among others).
08. Twitter appoints India compliance officer, Ex Himachal CM Virbhadra Singh (87) passes away.
09. WhatsApp places new Privacy Policy on hold.
10. Vietnam appoints NS. Srinivasa Murthy as first Consul General in India.
11. Twitter publishes first compliance report, BJP wins UP block-level polls.
13. NEET exam on September 11, India's first COVID patient tests +ve again, PM Modi reshuffles Cabinet panels.
14. Piyush Goyal appointed Rajya Sabha Leader.
16. Cabinet approves Ayush scheme continuance, Indian photojournalist Danish Siddiqui killed in Afghanistan.
17. Centre revises COVID vaccine procurement rates (Covishield: ₹205, Covaxin: ₹215).
18. Uttar Pradesh cancels Kanwar Yatra.

Pegasus Spyware Fiasco

19. Govt smells global conspiracy behind Pegasus fiasco, Mukhtar Abbas Naqvi appointed Deputy Leader of Rajya Sabha.
21. J&K grants domicile certificates to non-local spouses.
22. Govt announcces COVID-19 portal for orphaned children, Ladakh gets Central varsity.
24. India protest against Pakistan's Drone activities.
26. BS. Yediyurappa resigns as Karnataka CM, UK court declares Vijay Mallya bankrupt.
28. IAF operationalises second Rafale squadron, Rakesh Asthana appointed Delhi Police Commissioner, SC rejects Kerala's petition to scrap Assembly Ruckus case.
29. Centre announces reservation for OBCs (27%), EWS (10%) in national quota Medical seats, Parliament passes Factoring Regulation (Amendment) Bill.

Pegasus
In July, the Indian news website *The Wire*, reported that there were at least 300 Indian phone numbers, including those of human rights defenders, journalists, lawyers, government officials, and opposition politicians, in the leaked global list of 50,000 numbers. These were concentrated in countries known to engage in unlawful and arbitrary surveillance of their citizens and were clients of NSO Group, an Israeli company that develops and sells surveillance spyware called Pegasus.

August

Economics

02. PM Modi launches e-RUPI, Lok Sabha passes insurance Amendment Act.

03. Rajya Sabha passes Insolvency and Bankruptcy Code (Amendment) Bill.

04. RS passes Limited Liability Partnership Amendment Bill.

23. FM launches National Monetisation Pipeline.

24. FM directs Infosys to fix I-T portal glitches by Sept 15.

Politics

02. J&K to deny passport & jobs to persons with adverse police report.

03. CBSE 10 results declared.

09. Defence Ministry denies any deal with NSO, Govt approves vaccination for foreign nationals, Parliament passes DICGC amendment Bill.

10. Modi launches phase-II of Ujjwala scheme.

11. Parliament passes OBC Bill, Rajya Sabha clears general insurance bill.

12. Twitter locks Rahul Gandhi's account,

13. Govt announces plastic items ban in phased manner, Govt announces vehicle scrapping policy.

16. Govt denies Pegasus snoop allegations, Air India evacuates 129 people from Kabul.

17. India announces emergency e-visa for Afghans, India evacuates Kabul embassy staff.

18. SC allows women to take NDA exam, Collegium recommends nine judges for SC, India & Vietnam navy hold exercise in South China Sea.

19. Calcutta HC orders CBI probe into Bengal post-poll violence, India & Australia sign naval cooperation agreement.

22. India buys 70000 assault rifles from Russia.

25. Delta variant AY.12 found in India.

27. Ila Ganesan becomes Manipur Governor, Portal for unorganised workers launched.

e-RUPI Launched

31. India holds first meeting with Taliban.

Science

08. Govt launches COVID-19 vaccine certificate via WhatsApp.

13. Bharat Biotech's intranasal vaccine gets approval.

20. Govt clears Zydus Cadila's 3-dose COVID-19 vaccine, Zycov-D vaccine for kids approved.

26. Centre formulates new Drone policy.

31. Ayush Ministry launches Y-Break app.

Sports

01. Olympics: PV Sindhu defeats Bing Jiao to win Bronze medal.

02. Olympics: Indian women hockey team enters semifinals.

05. India wins Bronze in Mens hockey after 41 years.

08. Neeraj Chopra wins Gold medal in Javelin Throw.

29. India wins two silvers & one bronze at Tokyo Paralympics.

30. Avani Lekhara & Sumit Antil wins Gold at Paralympics.

Delta Variant AY.12

A new sublineage of the SARS-CoV-2 Delta variant known as AY.12 was detected in a number of states in India in Sept. 2020, which caused a big surge of Covid cases. INSACOG, a multi-laboratory, pan-India network that monitor genomic variations in the SARS-CoV-2 by sequencing samples circulating in India described the new sublineage of Delta as AY.4. However, after a revaluation the mutation was reclassified as AY.12.

September

Economics

01. JB Mohapatra appointed CBDT chairman.
09. Ford India stops manufacturing cars.
16. Cabinet clears ₹30600 crore guarantee for bad bank.
20. Facebook appoints Rajiv Aggarwal as Public Policy head.
26. GoM set up to rationalise GST rates.

Politics

01. Schools reopen in Tamil Nadu, Telangana and Delhi.
03. SC Collegium recommends 68 High Court judges.
04. India sends 150 tonnes of oxygen to Sri Lanka.
05. Nipah virus detected in Kerala.
07. ULFA-I favours Assam CM as mediator.
08. Centre approves Women for NDA exams, Cabinet hikes Rabi crops MSP.
09. RN Ravi becomes Tamil Nadu Governor, Banwarilal Purohit in Punjab.
10. India & US to collaborate on new fuels
11. Gujarat CM Vijay Rupani resigns.
12. Bhupendra Patel elected Gujarat CM.
15. PM Modi launches Sansad TV.
17. India sets new record with 2.5 crore COVID-19 vaccination.
18. Punjab CM Amarinder Singh quits:GST council rejects Petrol & Diesel inclusion.
19. Charanjit Singh Channi is Punjab CM.
20. India-Nepal Military Exercise Surya Kiran starts, Raj Kundra granted bail.
21. Air Marshal VR Chaudhari is IAF Chief.
23. Defence Ministry places order for 118 Arjun Mk-1A tanks.
24. PM Modi & Kamala Harris discuss bilateral ties, PM Modi attends Quad Summit in US, UPSC allows unmarried women to apply for NDA.
25. PM Modi addresses UN General Assembly.
26. Cyclone Gulab begins landfall.
27. PM Modi launches Ayushman Bharat Digital Mission, PM Modi visits new Parliament site.

PM Modi-Kamala Harris Discusses Bilateral Ties

28. Defence Ministry orders Ordnance Factory Board dissolution, Kanhaiya Kumar joins Congress, Navjot Singh Sidhu quits Punjab PCC chief.
29. Amarinder Singh meets Amit Shah, Centre extends mid-day meal scheme.
30. Bhabanipur Bypoll election crucial for Mamata.

Science

03. DCGI approves Biological E's COVID-19 vaccine CORBEVAX for kids, India & US signs Unmanned Aerial Vehicle development agreement.
04. DCGI approves Phase-1 trial of Reliance Life Sciences COVID vaccine.
10. Co-WIN UI includes vaccination status

Sports

09. BCCI appoints Dhoni as mentor for T20 World Cup.

Unmanned Aerial Vehicle

India and US signed a project agreement on July 30, 2021 for Air-Launched Unmanned Aerial Vehicle. The main aim of US-DTTI is to bring sustained leadership focus to promote collaborative technology exchange and create opportunities for co-production and co-development of future technologies for Indian and US military forces. Under DTTI, Joint Working Groups on land, naval, air, and aircraft carrier technologies have been established.

October

Economics

08. KV Subramanian steps down as Chief Economic Adviser; Tata Group gets nod to acquire 100% stakes of Air India from Government of India through it's subsidiary Talace Private Ltd, as part of Disinvestment of Public Sector Units in India.

10. Almost eight states in India expects power outage due to reduced stocks of Coal as fuel to power the thermal power stations.

11. India slips down seven places from previous year to reach 101th rank out of 116 in the Global Hunger Index; India extends Line of Credit to Kyrgyzstan.

Politics

01. India imposes action on UK citizens over COVID vaccine, Road projects started in Ladakh.

02. UIDAI opens 166 standalone Aaadhar enrolment centers.

03. Mamata Banerjee wins Bhabanipur bypoll.

02. Eight people including Shah Rukh Khan's son arrested by Narcotics Control Bureau following a drug bust and raid conducted on a cruise vessel named Cordelia chartered between Mumbai and Goa.

03. In the Lakhimpur Kheri, UP, massacre, eight people including four farmers are rammed and killed as Union Minister of State for Home Affairs Ajay Kumar Mishra's son's car runs over protesters who were part of 2020–2021 Indian farmers' protest.

Three members of the party and the driver of the vehicle were then killed by protesters.

04. Farmers vow to intensify their protest against laws aimed at liberalising agriculture, after four farmers were rammed and killed in Uttar Pradesh. A journalist was also found dead near the scene of the violence.

Lakhimpur Kheri Violence

05. Shah Rukh Khan's son Aryan Khan arrested by NCB.

06. Govt revises Ayushman Bharat packages.

07. Indian & UK to carry out joint exercise, PM Modi opens 35 PSA oxygen plants.

09. Centre restricts syringe exports, India & Japan hold bilateral maritime exercise.

11. PM Modi, Boris Johnson hold talks.

12. PM Modi launches multi-modal connectivity masterplan, Amit Khare appointed advisor to PM Modi.

13. Centre enhances BSF powers.

14. India resumes COVID-19 vaccine export.

Science

03. Zydus Cadila fixes ₹1900 for its COVID-19 vaccine.

04. ICMR launches drone-based vaccine delivery.

05. AstraZeneca asks FDA to authorise COVID antibody treatment.

10. Govt allows export of Sputnik Light vaccine.

12. Panel recommends Covaxin for Kids upto 18 years.

17. Twenty-six people are killed and dozens are missing as heavy rains affect the Indian state of Kerala.

Sports

15. Chennai Super Kings wins IPL 2021.

एनटीपीसी
NTPC
Azadi Ka Amrit Mahotsav
Transforming into a
"Sustainable Integrated Energy Company"
India's largest Power Company, NTPC is venturing into new business areas - e-mobility, Waste to Energy, Power Distribution and Green Hydrogen Solutions.
Green H_2
TRASH
Follow us on: /ntpc1 /ntpclimited /ntpcltd1 /ntpclimited /company/ntpc ntpc_limited

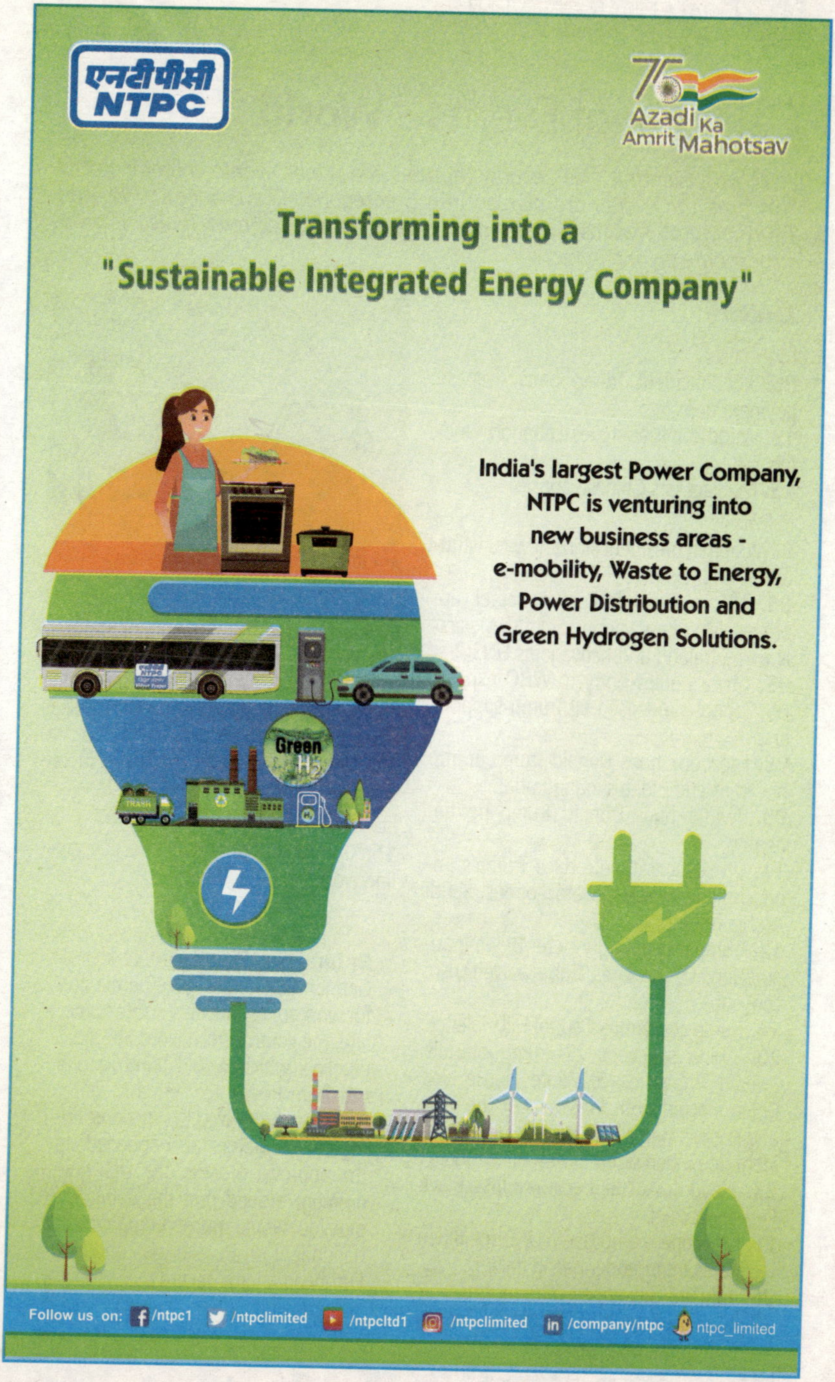

Calendar of Events - **World**

2021 was eventful. This section captures the major events chronologically. This time the events are divided into 6 categories like Economics, Politics, Socio-cultural, Awards, Science and General, for a quick-read. It also includes a short note on one item.

January

Economics

06. US President Trump bans Chinese payment apps.
13. World Bank approves Lebanon funding.
15. US blacklists Chinese apps.

Politics

01. Algerian president signs new constitution, Trump extends H-1B freeze.
05. UK imposes lockdown, Israel approves Moderna vaccine, India, Mexico, Norway, Ireland and Kenya joins UNSC.
06. China denies entry to WHO experts, US Capitol vandalised by Trump supporters.
08. Facebook bans Donald Trump, Trump not to attend Biden's inauguration.
09. Twitter bans Donald Trump permanently.
11. US Democrats introduce Trump's impeachment process, Qatar opens Saudi Arabia border.
12. Trump lifts emergency for Biden inauguration, US declares Cuba as terrorism sponsor.
14. Trump condemns Capitol Hill violence.
20. China sanctions 28 Trump officials, Donald Trump leaves White House; Joe Biden elected 46th President of the USA and Kamala Harris becomes 49th Vice President. Joe Biden signs 17 executive orders.
23. Lloyd J. Austin becomes first Black Pentagon chief.
25. Israel opens embassy in UAE, Joe Biden reinstates transgender ban in military.
26. Italy PM Giuseppe Conte resigns.
27. Russia extends START treaty, Antony Blinken becomes US Secretary of State.
29. WHO team visits Wuhan, UN chief calls for social media regulation, China derecognises British National Overseas passport.
31. Nguyen Phu Trong re-elected in Taiwan.

Joe Biden and Kamala Harris Wins US Election

Science

15. Germany approves Russia gas pipeline work.

Natural Gas Pipeline
German authorities gave permission for work to resume on a subsea pipeline, the controversial Nord Stream 2 pipeline, which would bring natural gas from Russia to Germany. It has been the target of U.S. sanctions. European regulators also speeded up the approval process. The U.S. government argued that the Baltic Sea pipeline would make Europe more dependent on Russian gas and hurt European energy security.

February

Economics

06. IMF supports US stimulus plan.
25. Sri Lanka seeks $2.2 billion from China.
26. Senegal, Morocco, Caymans added to FATF watchlist.
27. US House passes $1.9 trillion COVID-19 relief plan.

Politics

01. Military coup in Myanmar, Suu Kyi detained.
02. UK reports new coronavirus mutation, Sputnik V vaccine shows 91.6% efficacy.
03. US extends START nuclear arms treaty with Russia, WHO team visits Wuhan virus lab, Alejandro Mayorkas is Joe Biden's homeland security secretary.
04. NATO urges Taliban to end violence, Myanmar blocks Facebook.
05. Trump refuses to testify in impeachment trial, Joe Biden ends Yemen war support.
06. Myanmar shuts down Internet.
07. Iran urges US to lift curbs.
08. China arrests Australian Journalist Cheng Lei, US to rejoin UN rights council.
09. China blocks Clubhouse app, New Zealand suspends ties with Myanmar.
11. BBC World News banned in China, Joe Biden orders sanctions against Myanmar.
12. COVID-19 UK strain found in Sri Lanka.
14. US Senate acquits Donald Trump.
16. France passes anti-radicalism bill.
18. US to pay $200 million to WHO, Facebook blocks Australians from accessing news.
19. US reinstates Iran nuclear deal, Biden introduces immigration bill.
21. Joe Biden approves Texas disaster declaration.
22. SC rejects Trump election challenge cases, China urges US to lift trade restrictions.
24. Imran Khan announces defence credit line for Sri Lanka, US confirms Linda Thomas-Greenfield as UN ambassador.
25. Facebook bans Myanmar military accounts.

Suu Kyi Detained by Military

Science

02. Bhavya Lal appointed NASA's Acting Chief of Staff.
13. Pakistan approves CansinoBio COVID-19 vaccine.
14. UAE publishes first photo from Mars probe, Japan approves COVID-19 vaccine.
19. NASA's Perseverance rover makes historic Mars landing.
23. NASA releases first audio from Mars, Sri Lanka orders AstraZeneca doses.

New START Extended

The New START nuclear disarmament treaty's original duration was 10 years (until February 5, 2021), with the option for the Parties to agree to extend it for up to an additional five years. The United States and Russian Federation agreed on a five-year extension of New START to keep it in force through February 4, 2026. It is the last remaining nuclear Russia-USA arms control treaty.

March

Economics

02. US retains hardline approach to China trade.

11. US Congress passes $1.19 trillion COVID-19 relief bill.

13. US court removes Xiaomi from blacklist.

23. Sri Lanka secures $1.5 bn Chinese loan.

Politics

01. EU condemns Myanmar coup, France former President Nicolas Sarkozy convicted.

02. Twitter combats COVID-19 vaccine misinformation with labels & strike policy.

05. YouTube removes Myanmar army channels.

06. Pakistan PM Imran Khan wins trust vote.

07. China asks Biden not to support Taiwan.

08. Australia ends defence cooperation with Myanmar.

09. Nepal ruling party splits, Biden imposes curbs on drone strikes.

10. China launches virus passport.

13. UN urges Somalia to conduct elections.

15. Iran unveils underground missile facility.

17. Joe Biden asks migrants to avoid US, US sanctions 24 Chinese and Hong Kong officials.

22. Riyadh submits ceasefire plan to Yemen's Houthis.

23. Myanmar junta defends crackdown.

24. UAE finance minister Sheikh Hamdan passes away, US Senate appoints Dr. Vivek Murthy as Surgeon General.

25. Suez Canal temporarily halts navigation, Manila sends more ships to South China sea.

26. Georgia passes restrictive voting law.

27. China & Iran sign 25-year strategic pact.

Ever Given Ran Aground in Suez Canal

28. Ever Given container ship registered in Panama ran aground in Suez Canal causing a global shipping traffic jam.

29. Ship stranded in Suez Canal re-floated, Agnes Callamard named Amnesty chief.

30. Palau President Surangel Whipps visits Taiwan.

Science

11. EU approves J&J one-shot COVID-19 vaccine; Denmark, Norway, Iceland suspend AstraZeneca vaccine.

31. Japan wants probe into COVID-19 origin.

Socio-cultural

12. South Africa's Zulu King Goodwill Zwelithini (72) passes away.

The Suez Canal Trade Route

The Suez Canal was blocked for six days after the grounding of Ever Given, a 20,000 TEU container ship. The 400-metre-long vessel was buffeted by strong winds on the morning of 23 March, and ended up wedged across the waterway with its bow and stern stuck in the canal banks, blocking all traffic until it could be freed. As one of the world's busiest trade routes, the canal obstruction had a significant negative impact on trade between Europe, Asia and the Middle East.

April

Economics

01. Saudi Arabia to unveil $3.2 tn investment drive.

Politics

01. Pak court lifts ban on TikTok.
02. EU condemns harassment of foreign media in China.
05. Vietnam National Assembly selects PM and President, Kosovo elects Vjosa Osmani Sadriu as president.
07. Turkey summons China's ambassador, Russia to supply military gear to Pakistan.
08. NZ suspends Indian tourists, Biden restores aid to Palestine.
09. Joe Biden tightens gun control.
10. Iran unveils advanced nuclear centrifuges.
13. Hong Kong amends election laws, US announces troops withdrawal from Afghanistan by September 11.
16. Turkey bans cryptocurrencies, Shaukat Tareen becomes Pakistan's Finance Minister.
17. Shooting at FedEx facility in Indianapolis.
18. Israel and Greece sign record defence deal, Israel lifts mask usage.
20. Former US Vice President Walter Mondale (93) passes away, EU expands sanctions against Myanmar military.
22. UAE bans travel from India, Australia reduces flights.
23. Canada bans flights from India, Pakistan.
24. Japan hosts joint drills with US & France.
26. EU launches legal action against AstraZeneca.
27. COVID-19 Global task force formed with 40 company CEOs in US.
29. US issues Level 4 health alert against India.
30. World's longest pedestrian suspension bridge opens in Portugal.

Prince Philip (left) with Prince Harry

Science

03. SpaceX rocket debris lands at Washington state farm.
06. Sri Lanka buys 6 million Sputnik V vaccines.
09. Prince Philip passes away.
10. Pakistan approves CoronaVac, France advises vaccine mixing.
13. US pauses J&J vaccine.
23. SpaceX launches third crew to space station.
28. Astronaut Michael Collins (91) passes away.
29. Bangladesh approves Sinopharm vaccine.
30. Europe grants Pfizer vaccine trial for children.

Gun Control
The Biden-Harris Administration announces six initial actions including rules to help stop the proliferation of "ghost guns" firearms without serial numbers to address the gun violence public health epidemic. The mass shootings in Boulder killing 10 individuals, 8 in Atlanta and 6 Asian American women – underscored the relentlessness of this epidemic. Gun violence leaves a lasting trauma in communities in US.

May

Economics

05. Britain and India sign ETP agreement.
06. China suspends economic dialogue with Australia.

Politics

01. Daniel Smith becomes US envoy to India, Brazil privatizes water and sewage utility.
04. Bill Gates and Melinda announce divorce, Egypt buys 30 Rafale aircraft from France.
09. Sadiq Khan wins second term as London Mayor.
10. Nepal PM Oli loses vote of confidence, South Sudan President dissolves Parliament.
13. Oli reappointed as Nepal PM, Martin Griffiths becomes UN humanitarian chief.
14. US CDC removes mask mandate for fully vaccinated people.
15. Neera Tanden becomes White House senior adviser.
16. Israel bombs Hamas Gaza chief home.
17. Joe Biden allocated 20 million vaccine does from other nations.
19. Sudan bans travellers from India, EU reopen borders to fully vaccinated travellers.
20. Sri Lankan passes Bill on China-backed Port City, Martha Koome becomes Kenya's first woman chief justice.
21. Israel and Hamas agree to ceasefire, China offers $3 billion COVID-19 aid and vaccines.
22. Nepal President dissolves Parliament.
23. Lithuania quits divisive China group.
25. Iran approves 7 presidential candidates.
27. Joe Biden orders probe into virus origin.
28. Sri Lanka seeks FDI in Port City, NATO conducts massive war games.
29. Vietnam detects new Hybrid variant, Mali court declares Colonel Goita as President.
30. UK PM Boris Johnson marries Carrie Symonds, Sri Lanka faces marine disaster.

Boris Johnson Marries Carrie Symonds

31. China allows couples to have third child, Pak Journalist Hamid Mir banned.

Science

02. SpaceX returns 4 astronauts to Earth.
06. Russia approves Sputnik Light single dose vaccine, Sri Lanka approves Sputnik V.
07. UK advises AstraZeneca alternative for under 40s.
08. WHO approves Sinopharm vaccine.
15. China lands rover on the Mars.
22. Yuan Longping (91), father of hybrid rice passes away.
30. China's space station completes cargo docking.

Three-child Policy

China's population is aging faster than almost all other countries in modern history. In May 2021, China introduced the three-child policy in a further attempt to address the issue. In 2015, a two-child policy was introduced in an attempt to deal with the aging problem.

In 1979, the Chinese government established a controversial one-child policy aimed at curbing the high fertility rate.China's one-child policy lasted from 1980 to 2015.

From 1950 to 2020, the fertility rate in China dropped from 6.11 to 1.3 births per woman.

June

Economics

12. Rebecca Grynspan appointed as UNCTAD head by US.
21. China cracks down crypto mining.
23. Warren Buffett resigns from Gates Foundation.

Politics

02. Iran's largest navy ship catches fire, Isaac Herzog elected Israeli president.
03. Joe Biden announces vaccine sharing plan, Donald Trump permanently closes his blog.
04. Hong Kong seals Tiananmen vigil site, South Korea's air force chief resigns.
05. China blasts US, EU consulates in Hong Kong, Nigeria suspends Twitter.
06. Sri Lanka recovers black box from container ship.
07. China hosts ASEAN ministers.
08. India elected to UN Economic and Social Council, Mahatma Gandhi's great-grandaughter convicted, Russia sanctions Canadian officials.
09. US drops plan to ban TikTok & We-Chat, Australia pushes for Chinese sanctions at WTO.
16. Biden & Putin conduct great power summit, France removes masks outdoors, Israel strikes Gaza.
18. Antonio Guterres re-elected as UN Secretary-General, Israel sends one million COVID-19 vaccines, US locks down Afghanistan embassy.
19. India abstains on UN resolution on Myanmar.
21. Armenia PM wins majority, Iran shut-down nuclear power plant.
24. Joe Biden nominates Cindy McCain to UN food post, Former Philippine President Benigno Aquino (61) passes away.
25. Tibet first bullet train links Lhasa broder with India.
28. Ukraine & US launch Black Sea drills.

Science

01. WHO approves Sinovac, New Zealand signs space agreement with NASA.
08. Major Internet outage hits Guardian, NY Times, Reddit and others.
15. UAE backed troops lands at Yemen base.
17. China launches manned spacecraft Shenzhou-12 to new space station.
24. Microsoft releases Windows 11 with Microsoft Teams, Android support, Auto HDR & Widgets.

Tibet's First Bullet Train

Tibet Gets First Bullet Train

China started operating the first bullet train line in Tibet, linking Lhasa to Nyingchi near the border with Arunachal Pradesh. The 435-km line, on which construction began in 2014, has a designed speed of 160 kilometres per hour and would connect the capital city of the Tibet Autonomous Region to the border city of Nyingchi with a travel time of three and a half hours. Over 90% of the track is 3000 metres above sea-level. China completed construction of a strategically significant highway through the Grand Canyon of the Yarlung Zangbo river, as the Brahmaputra is called in Tibet. This is the "second significant passageway" to Medog county that borders Arunachal.

July

Economics

07. China fines Internet giants.

Politics

01. Pakistan Army inducts VT-4 battle tanks, Former US Defense Secretary Donald Rumsfeld (88) passes away.
05. Hackers demand $70 mn after cyber attack.
06. China's President reshuffles PLA border command leadership, Ethiopia starts filling disputed dam on the Nile.
07. Haiti President Jovenel Moïse assassinated, China deletes LGBT accounts on social media.
08. Japan places Tokyo under emergency.
10. US appoints Los Angeles Mayor Garcetti as Ambassador to India.
13. Sher Bahadur Deuba becomes Nepal PM.
17. Russia unveils new fighter jet at Moscow's air show.
18. Nepal PM wins Sher Bahadur Deuba vote of confidence.
19. US blames China over Microsoft hack.
21. Pedro Castillo becomes Peru president, Israel attacks Lebanon.
22. Israel appoints commission to review NSO, China rejects WHO plan to audit Wuhan labs, France launches vaccine pass.
26. Junta cancels results of Myanmar polls, Tunisian PM Kais Saied sacked by President.
28. US makes masks compulsory for vaccinated people.
30. Danish Siddiqui executed by Taliban.
31. Singapore warns residents for COVID-19 safety violations.

Science

04. Chinese astronauts conduct first spacewalk.
20. Amazon's Jeff Bezos reaches space with Wally Funk (82), Oliver Daemen (18) via Blue Origin.
24. Brazil suspends Covaxin clinical trials.
31. NASA picks SpaceX for Jupiter's moon mission.

Tokyo Olympics Begins

Sports

07. Italy reaches Euro 2020 final.
23. Tokyo Olympics begins.
25. Andy Murray withdraws from Olympics, Sania Mirza-Ankita Raina knocked out.

Vaccine Pass

A vaccine passport is proof that one is tested negative for or been protected against certain infections. It can be digital, like a phone app, or physical, such as a small paper card. One can carry it and show it if required, like before entering into the office, board an airplane, or visit a restaurant, movie theater, or gym.

As the COVID-19 pandemic continues, vaccine passport system has found grounds where companies fully open business to anyone who shows proof of vaccination. Countries have resumed international travel without requiring quarantines, using vaccine pass, in order to boost economies while limiting the spread of the disease.

August

Economics

03. IMF approves increase in funds.
25. World Bank stops aid to Afghanistan.

Politics

01. US COVID-19 eviction ban expires; Kim Jong-un's sister Kim Yo-jong warns South Korea against conducting military drills with the United States, saying that such a move could damage the talks to resolve the Korean conflict.
03. Ebrahim Raisi inaugurated as President of Iran.
08. Israel strikes Gaza, Iran rejects G7 and US allegations on Drone attacks.
10. China recalls Lithuania ambassador.
11. US Senate passes massive infrastructure Bill.
12. Israel opens diplomatic mission in Morocco, Pakistan test fires nuclear ballistic missile.
13. Haiti's presidential election postponed.
15. Taliban enters Kabul, Haiti earthquake kills several people, Israel condemns Poland restitution law.
16. Taliban enters Afghan presidential palace.
17. China slams US over Afghan crisis, Iran appoints Shahram Irani as new Navy Chief.
18. India welcomes ASEAN consensus on Myanmar, Taliban destroy statue of Shiite foe.
19. Russia fines Google.
20. NATO urges Taliban to allow evacuations, China passes three-child policy.
21. US SC halts reinstating Remain in Mexico policy.
22. Israel strikes Gaza.
23. Taliban warns of US.
25. China & Taliban hold first talks, Papua New Guinea bans India flights, US SC reinstates Remain in Mexico policy.
26. UN bans British stamps in Chagos island.

Cuba Recognises Cryptocurrencies

30. Hurricane Ida hits Louisiana.
31. UAE & Turkey discuss relations, Vietnam gives amnesty to 3000 prisoners, UNSC adopts resolution on Afghanistan.

Socio-Cultural

09. Actor Jane Withers (95) passes away.
25. Rolling Stones drummer Charlie Watts (80) passes away.

Science

08. Indonesia's Mount Merapi volcano erupts.
11. China approves first mixed-vaccine trial, Boeing 737 MAX tested in China.
20. NASA halts SpaceX work on lunar lander.
27. Cuba recognises cryptocurrencies.

Cuba Recognises Cryptocurrencies

According to Resolution 215 published in the Official Gazette, the Central Bank has set rules for such currencies and how to license providers of related services within Cuba.The American embargo on the communist state has turned Cuba into a pariah in the global economy. Cuba's decision to join El Salvador in embracing decentralised virtual cash could help the country to circumvent the U.S. sanctions regime, which was dialed up under former President Donald Trump and has been extended.

September

Economics

15. UN pledges $1.2B to help Afghans.
22. Sri Lanka seeks World Bank COVID-19 loan.

Politics

01. Beijing rolls out new data law.
02. China bans reality talent shows, Pakistan shuts Afghanistan border, US SC sustains Texas abortion law.
03. Japan PM Yoshihide Suga resigns.
06. Taliban claim complete control of Panjshir province, Greece creates climate change ministry, Saudi Arabia intercepts Houthi drones.
07. Mullah Akhund heads interim Taliban government.
08. China endorses the Taliban government.
09. Taiwan President commissions naval warship, Donald Trump to work as boxing commentator.
18. Taliban excludes Girls from schools, Former Algerian President Abdelaziz Bouteflika (84) passes away.
19. Taliban replace ministry for women.
23. China sends fighter jets towards Taiwan, US rules out adding India, Japan to AUKUS.
25. Venezuela talks suspended in Mexico City, Protests in Libya over no-confidence motion.
26. Israeli troops kill 5 Palestinians in West Bank, Iceland elects its first female-majority parliament.
27. Social Democrats beat Merkel bloc in German elections, Joe Biden gets COVID-19 booster shot.
28. France & Greece sign defence deal, North Korea fires short-range missiles to sea.
29. Taliban warns US, Nepal introduces third gender category in census, North Korea tests new hypersonic missile.
30. Ethiopia expels seven UN staff.

SpaceX Launches 4 Amateurs to Space

Socio-Cultural

01. Ramon Magsaysay Award: Firdausi Qadri, Muhammad Amjad Saqib, Roberto Ballon, Steven Muncy.

Science

15. South Korea conducts major missile test.
16. SpaceX launches 4 amateurs on private Earth-circling trip.
19. SpaceX capsule lands safely.

Sports

12. Emma Raducanu beats Leylah Fernandez in US Open.
13. Novak Djokovic's record win dream broken by Daniil Medvedev.

New Data Law

China enacted a sweeping new data privacy law that dramatically impacts how tech companies can operate in the country. Officially called the Personal Information Protection Law of the People's Republic of China (PIPL), the law is the first national data privacy statute passed in China. The national privacy law closely resembles the world's most robust framework for online privacy protections, Europe's General Data Protection Regulation, and contains provisions that require any organization or individual handling Chinese citizens' personal data to minimize data collection and to obtain prior consent.

October

Economics

01. EU postpones trade talks with Australia.

04. US launches trade discussions with China.

12. France unveils $35 bn revival plan, China launches biodiversity fund.

13. EU's first green bond raises USD 13.8 billion.

Politics

01. China sends 25 fighter planes towards Taiwan, North Korea test fires anti-aircraft missile.

02. Najla Bouden Romdhane becomes Tunisia's first woman PM.

03. Former Marseille president Bernard Tapie (78) passes away.

04. Fumio Kishida becomes Japan PM.

05. Singapore Parliament approves foreign interference law.

06. Romanian Govt loses confidence vote.

07. WHO ships COVID-19 medical supplies to North Korea.

08. Joe Biden to restore three national monuments.

09. Iran's first president Abolhassan Banisadr (88) passes away, UNHRC declares access to clean environment a human right.

10. Austrian Chancellor Sebastian Kurz steps down, Czech PM Andrej Babis loses polls.

11. Bangladesh & UN sign deal to aid Rohingya, Tunisia new cabinet includes record women, Alexander Schallenberg becomes Austria's chancellor.

13. US to lift Canada, Mexico border restrictions in November.

14. Bhutan, China sign MoU to expedite boundary talks, China warns WHO.

15. India, US begins military exercise in Alaska.

Chinese 25 Fighters Fly towards Taiwan

Socio-Cultural

10. Pulitzer scholar Martin J Sherwin (84) passes away.

12. Holocaust author Eddie Jaku (101) passes away.

Science

01. Australia recognizes Covishield.

04. Russia test-fires new hypersonic missile from submarine.

05. Microsoft pushes Windows 11 to all eligible PCs.

07. WHO rollout first malaria vaccine for children.

13. Blue Origin launches 2nd manned space mission.

15. China launches 2nd crewed mission via Shenzhou-13.

Green Bond

The European Commission has adopted an independently evaluated Green Bond framework, thus taking a step forward towards the issuance of up to €250 billion green bonds, or 30% of NextGenerationEU's total issuance. The framework provides investors in these bonds with confidence that the funds mobilised will be allocated to green projects. The Commission will study its environmental impact. The green bond underlines the need to better direct financial and capital flows to green investments.

CURRENT AFFAIRS

- Current Affairs India
- Current Affairs World
- Newsmakers India
- Newsmakers World
- Places in the News
- Deaths India
- Deaths World
- Records of the Year
- Nobel Prizes 2021

Current Affairs - India

Nitish Kumar Returns as Bihar CM

Nitish Kumar was on November 16, 2020 sworn in as the Chief Minister of Bihar for the seventh time in two decades. He took oath as Bihar chief minister for a fourth straight term at a ceremony which

Nitish Kumar Being Sworn in as Bihar CM

was attended by top BJP leaders, including Union Home Minister Amit Shah and party president JP Nadda. Nitish Kumar was administered the oath of office at Raj Bhavan by Governor Phagu Chauhan, a day after he staked claim for the formation of a new government in the state, armed with unanimous support of all legislators of the NDA despite his party's emaciated tally.

The 69-year-old, who has had a continuous run since November, 2005, except for the period in 2014-15 when Jitan Ram Manjhi kept the chair warm for him, is on course to becoming the longest serving Chief Minister of the state, surpassing the record of Shrikrishna Singh who held the top post since before Independence till his death in 1961.

Kumar was first sworn in as CM in 2000, for a term that lasted barely a week as he failed to muster a majority and returned as a minister at the Centre in the Atal Bihari Vajpayee government.

Five years later, he returned with the JD(U)-BJP alliance winning a majority and upon completion of his tenure returned in 2010 when the coalition won a landslide victory in the assembly polls.

He stepped down in May 2014, owning moral responsibility for the JD(U)s debacle in Lok Sabha polls, only to return in February, 2015 when a rebellious Manjhi was elbowed out.

In November, 2015, the assembly polls were fought and won by the Grand Alliance which then comprised JD(U), Lalu Prasad's RJD and Congress with Kumar back as the Chief Minister.

He, however, abruptly exited the alliance in July, 2017, citing irreconciliable differences with the RJD and resigned as Chief Minister only to return in less than 24 hours armed with the support of the BJP.

The NDA won the state election with a thin majority and got 125 of Bihar's 243 assembly seats, three above the halfway mark. The results were declared on November 10 after counting of votes that went past midnight.

The BJP is the single largest party in the alliance with 74 seats while the JDU secured 43 seats. Other NDA constituents Vikassheel Insaan Party (VIP) and Hindustani Awam Morcha (HAM) won four seats each.

The Mahagatbandhan or Grand Alliance, led by the Rashtriya Janata Dal and its young leader Tejashwi Yadav was hoping for a big victory on the back of exit polls. The Mahagatbandhan comprises the RJD, Congress and Left parties, and most exit polls had given the alliance a clear edge over the Bharatiya Janata Par-

ABAN OFFSHORE LIMITED
OWNERS AND OPERATORS OF JACK UP DRILLING RIGS, DRILLSHIPS AND FLOATING PRODUCTION PLATFORM
The ABAN Group is one of the largest offshore drilling companies in the world with 20 years of experience in offshore drilling. Our key success factors are high level of technical expertise, focus on core competence and best operational practices.
ABAN aims at
● REDEFINING EXCELLENCE ● SCALING NEW HEIGHTS
● SETTING NEW STANDARDS ● CAPITALISING ON OPPORTUNITIES
'Janpriya Crest', 113 Pantheon Road,
Egmore, Chennai - 600 008. INDIA
Tel : 91 44 28195555 Website : www.abanindia.com
aban

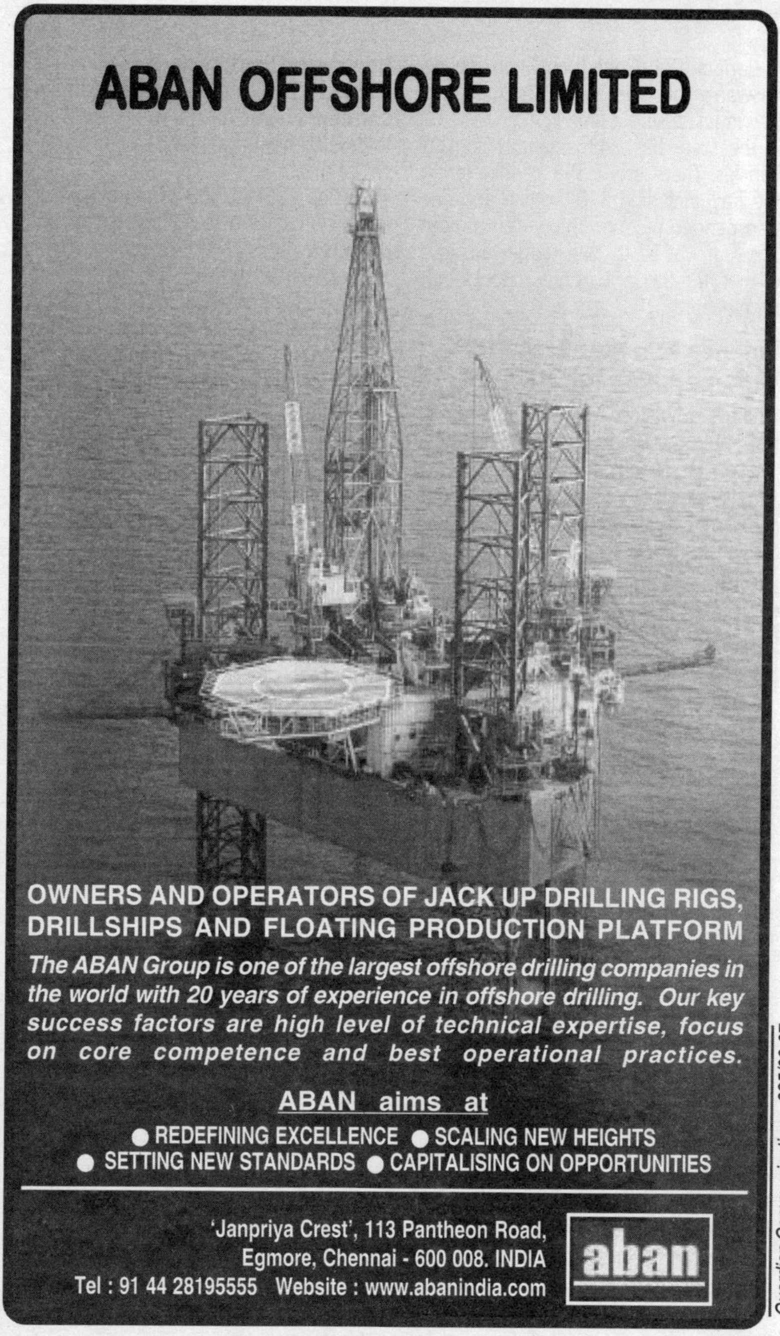

ty–Janatal Dal (United) coalition. Chirag Paswan's Lok Janashakti Party managed to win just a single seat.

The state has 243 assembly constituencies. There are 3,558 candidates in the fray, including 370 women and one transgender person. The voter turnout this year was 57.05% – marginally higher than the 56.66% of the 2015 assembly elections.

Finance Minister Presents Union Budget for 2021-22

Finance Minister Nirmala Sitharaman presented the Union Budget on February 1, 2021.

Nirmala Sitharaman with Anurag Thakur

Presenting the Union Budget for 2021-22, Finance Minister Nirmala Sitharaman said that the Budget proposals for 2021-22 financial year rest on six pillars — health and well-being, physical and financial capital and infrastructure, inclusive development for aspirational India, reinvigorating human capital, innovation and R&D, and 'Minimum Government, Maximum Governance'.

Significant announcements included a slew of hikes in customs duty to benefit Make in India, proposal to disinvest two more PSBs and a general insurance company, and numerous infrastructure pledges to poll-bound States. Fiscal deficit stands at 9.5% of the GDP, and is estimated to be 6.8% in 2021-22. Personal income tax slabs remain as is.

Here are the highlights of the budget for financial year 2021-22:

Health and Sanitation

- A new scheme, titled PM Atma Nirbhar Swasthya Bharat Yojana, to be launched to develop primary, secondary and tertiary healthcare
- Mission POSHAN 2.0 to improve nutritional outcomes across 112 aspirational districts
- Operationalisation of 17 new public health units at points of entry
- Modernising of existing health units at 32 airports, 15 seaports and land ports
- Jal Jeevan Mission Urban aimed at better water supply nationwide
- Strengthening of Urban Swachh Bharat Mission

Education

- 100 new Sainik Schools to be set up
- 750 Eklavya schools to be set up in tribal areas
- A Central University to come up in Ladakh

Infrastructure

- Vehicle scrapping policy to phase out old and unfit vehicles – all vehicles to undergo fitness test in automated fitness centres every 20 years (personal vehicles), every 15 years (commercial vehicles)
- Highway and road works announced in Kerala, Tamil Nadu, West Bengal and Asom
- National Asset Monetising Pipeline launched to monitor asset monetisation process
- National Rail Plan created to bring a future-ready Railway system by 2030
- 100% electrification of Railways to be completed by 2023
- Metro services announced in 27 cities, plus additional allocations for Kochi Metro, Chennai Metro Phase 2, Bengaluru Metro Phase 2A and B, Nashik and Nagpur Metros
- National Hydrogen Mission to be launched to generate hydrogen from

green power sources

- Recycling capacity of ports to be doubled by 2024
- Gas pipeline project to be set up in Jammu and Kashmir
- Pradhan Mantri Ujjwala Yojana (LPG scheme) to be extended to cover 1 crore more beneficiaries

Tax

- No IT filing for people above 75 years who get pension and earn interest from deposits
- Reopening window for IT assessment cases reduced from 6 to 3 years. However, in case of serious tax evasion cases (₹50 lakh or more), it can go up to 10 years
- Affordable housing projects to get a tax holiday for one year
- Compliance burden of small trusts whose annual receipts do not exceed ₹5 crore to be eased
- Duty of copper scrap reduced to 2.5%
- Custom duty on gold and silver to be rationalised
- Duty on naphtha reduced to 2.5%.
- Duty on solar inverters raised from 5% to 20%, and on solar lanterns from 5% to 15%
- All nylon products charged with 5% customs duty
- Tunnel boring machines to attract customs duty of 7%
- Customs duty on cotton raised from 0 to 10%
- Agriculture infrastructure and development cess proposed on certain items including urea, apples, crude soyabean and sunflower oil, crude palm oil, kabuli chana and peas.

Economy and Finance

- Fiscal deficit stands at 9.5% of the GDP; estimated to be 6.8% in 2021-22
- Proposal to allow States to raise borrowings up to 4% of GSDP this year
- A Unified Securities Market Code to be created, consolidating provisions of the Sebi Act, Depositories Act, and two other laws
- Proposal to increase FDI limit from 49% to 74%
- An asset reconstruction company will be set up to take over stressed loans
- Deposit insurance increased from ₹1 lakh to ₹5 lakh for bank depositors
- Proposal to decriminalise Limited Liability Partnership Act of 2008
- Two PSU bank and one general insurance firm to be disinvested this year
- An IPO of LIC to debut this fiscal
- Strategic sale of BPCL, IDBI Bank, Air India to be completed

Agriculture

- Agriculture infrastructure fund to be made available for APMCs for augmenting their infrastructure
- 1,000 more Mandis to be integrated into the E-NAM market place
- Five major fishing hubs, including Chennai, Kochi and Paradip, to be developed
- A multipurpose seaweed park to be established in Tamil Nadu

Employment

- A portal to be launched to maintain information on gig workers and construction workers
- Social security to be extended to gig and platform workers
- Margin capital required for loans via Stand-up India scheme reduced from 25% to 15% for SCs, STs and women

Glacier Burst in Uttarakhand Takes a Heavy Toll

A part of the Nanda Devi glacier broke off in Uttarakhand's Chamoli district on February 7, causing a deluge in the Alaknanda river system that washed away hydroelectric stations, leaving over 200 people dead or missing. The flash flood

Rescue Operations in Uttarakhand

in the Dhauli Ganga, Rishi Ganga and Alaknanda rivers triggered widespread panic and large-scale devastation in the high mountain areas.

Two power projects NTPC's Tapovan-Vishnugad hydel project and the Rishi Ganga Hydel Project were extensively damaged, with scores of labourers trapped in tunnels as the waters came rushing in. Later in the day, 16 men were rescued safely by ITBP personnel from a tunnel near the Tapovan dam.

About two years ago, residents of Raini village had told the Uttarakhand high court that the construction of Rishiganga hydel project could cause damage to those living in the area. In the summer of 2019, villagers filed a public interest litigation in the court, which directed the district magistrate Chamoli and member secretary state pollution control board to constitute a joint team to inspect the Rishiganga Hydroelectric Project site with regard to allegations about the impact on the environment and local people.

The direct cause and source of the glacial lake outburst flood is currently unknown by scientists, though the event could have been triggered by construction projects in the area or climate change.

Uttarakhand, in the western Himalayas, is prone to flash floods and landslides. Some 6,000 people are believed to have been killed in floods in June 2013 which were triggered by the heaviest monsoon rains in decades.

Govt Announces New Social Media Rules to Curb its Misuse

India on February 25 came up with new regulations for social media companies and digital streaming websites to make them more accountable for the online content shared on their platforms, giving the government more power to police it. These regulations are called the Information Technology (Guidelines for Intermediaries and Digital Media Ethics Code) Rules, 2021 (Rules). These Rules will require compliance even by foreign tech-giants operating in India such as WhatsApp, Facebook, Twitter, Netflix, Amazon etc.

Some of the key takeaways from the Information Technology (Guidelines for Intermediaries and Digital Media Ethics Code) Rules, 2021.

Pervasive Internet and Social Media

1. Publishers of news and current affairs content, including aggregators, have to publish a monthly compliance report detailing all the grievances received and what they have done to address it.

2. OTT platforms such as Netflix, Amazon Prime and others now have to classify all content suitable for viewing by age – U (Universal), U/A(above 7), U/A (13+), U/A (16+) and A for Adults.

3. Content put out by OTT platforms

and other online publishers should keep in mind India's sovereignty, relationship with other countries, and these platforms should self-regulate. As part of the oversight committee, a government-designated officer can block access to content.

4. Social media platforms with minimum 50 lakh registered users are classified as significant social media intermediaries and are subject to maximum compliances. All significant social media intermediaries are required to appoint a Chief Compliance Officer, a Nodal Contact Person and a Resident Grievance Officer. Each of the above are required to be Indian residents.

The Rules also necessitate significant social media intermediaries to have a physical contact address in India.

5. Significant social media intermediaries are now required to endeavour to deploy technology-based measures, including automated tools to identify information that depicts rape, child sexual abuse or conduct, or information that has previously been removed.

6. The rules also require maintenance of appropriate human oversight, and periodic review of automated tools.

7. Social media firms should not host or store, and must take down content prohibited in the context of India's sovereignty, integrity, defamation and incitement to offence.

8. If some content is deemed offensive by a court or government, social media firms have to pull it out within 36 hours; 24, if it is sexually offensive content.

9. Messaging services (with more than 50 lakh users) will be required to enable identification of the first originator of information if required by a court order or an order of the Government under Section 69 of the IT Act.

10. There will be three levels of regulation for news publishers – self-regulation, a self-regulatory body, headed by a retired judge or an eminent person, and oversight from the Information and Broadcasting Ministry, including codes of practices and a grievance committee.

Bodies Wash Up on the Banks of the Ganges River

In May 2021, a large number of decomposing bodies, estimated to be in the hundreds, were found floating in the Ganges in Uttar Pradesh and the neighbouring state of Bihar. Disturbing images and videos showed half-burnt and decomposing bodies drifting on the river, shocking the nation that was still reeling from a deadly second wave of Covid-19.

Police Personnel Oversee the Burial of Bodies in Buxar's Chausa Village

While some reports said there were around 10 to 12 bodies, others said there were 40-45 bodies. Some reports placed the number even higher, at 150 bodies. Villagers and officials feared these were Covid fatalities who were thrown into the river. While It could not be ascertained whether all the bodies were of Covid victims, it was widely reported that families were dumping bodies in the river because they did not have the money to pay for cremation. Messages were blared through loudspeakers in river-side villages including Gazipur, Unnao and others, for people not to throw bodies into the river. The government carried full-page advertisements in Uttar Pradesh newspapers exhorting people not to dispose off dead bodies in Ganges river and also offering monetary aid to anyone who could not afford to perform the last rites for their loved ones. Uttar Pradesh government announced a grant of 5,000 rupees to poor families to perform funeral services.The government also asked police to patrol rivers and keep a watch on riverbanks to ensure bodies were not being dumped.

Uttar Pradesh was hit particularly hard by the second wave as a result of its fragile healthcare infrastructure. Experts said the situation could be far worse, as cases were going undetected in rural areas. Denying reports that the number of bodies found in the river was as high as 2,000, an Uttar Pradesh state government spokesperson declined to give a total but said bodies were being found sporadically in groups of 10 to 20.

Maoist Attack in Sukma

At least 22 security personnel were killed after the armed forces came twice under attack by Maoists near Jonaguda village

CRPF Personnel Carry the Coffin of a Soldier Who Lost His Life

in Sukma district of Chhattisgarh on April 3, 2021. Maoists used country-made grenades, rocket launchers and machine guns against the security forces. The death toll was the worst for the security forces fighting the Naxalites since 2017. The deceased personnel included seven from the Commando Battalion for Resolute Action unit (CoBRA) of the CRPF, a unit specially trained for operations in Left Wing Extremist (LWE) areas and 15 from the Chattisgarh Police.

The fighting ensued when Indian security forces, acting on military intelligence, raided a rebel hideout in a densely forested area of Bijapur district. Security forces had got tip-offs that Madvi Hidma, a top Naxal leader, was hiding in Sukma. Hidma is linked with the 2013 Jhiram Ghati killings. It is not yet clear whether the tip-offs were traps to draw security forces to the spot or whether the anto-Naxal operation actually stirred one of the layers that protect Hidma. Hidma's security cover starts from almost one kilometre. The top Maoist leader at the time of the encounter might have been in the vicinity, which triggered the heavy firing.

Big Setback for BJP in State Elections

The results of the 2021 Assembly Elections for the states of West Bengal, Assam, Kerala, Tamil Nadu, and Puducherry turned out to hold some unexpected surprises, some landslide victories, and some new records being broken in political history. While Nandirgam kept people on the edge of their seats till the last minute, Kerala saw an incumbent government making history by being the first to be re-elected in 4 decades. Margins dropped as close to 1,700 votes between a sitting CM and her protege and as high as over 1 lakh for Asom's Health Minister Himanta Biswa Sarma. However, what seemed amiss in the elections was the ability of the Congress party to cover a strong political ground across the 5 states and one Union Territory.

Voting for these elections took place in March and April, just as India started reporting thousands of fresh coronavirus infections every day. On March 14, two weeks before the first phase, there were fewer than 25,000 new cases a day. On March 27 there were around 62,000 and, by April 29, there were well over 3.5 lakh per day. On May 1, new cases reached a record daily high of 401,993, the biggest across the world.

Alongside the Covid spike, leaders of all political parties, including Prime Minister Narendra Modi, led political rallies at which large crowds discarded safety rules on masks and social distancing.

The Trinamool Congress (TMC) — led by India's only woman chief minister Mamata Banerjee — swept the West Bengal assembly polls of 2021 for a third time, winning 213 out of the 292 seats that went to the polls in the state, in a sign of the continued assertion of regional parties in Indian politics, and in a major setback to the Bharatiya Janata Party (BJP).

Riding on a mix of welfare delivery, Bengali sub-nationalism, Banerjee's own popularity and connect with the grassroots, and substantial minority consolidation, the TMC won — but Banerjee lost her own fiercely fought assembly battle in Nandigram, to her former colleague and aide-turned-BJP leader Suvendu Adhikari. She returned as CM — contested and won an election within six months, as constitutionally stipulated, to remain CM.

The Bengal elections were marked by intense competition, political violence, charges of partisanship of institutions, and crowded rallies even as the second wave of Covid hit India.

The BJP — despite a well-resourced

Mamata Banerjee at an Election Rally

and high-profile campaign led by Prime Minister Narendra Modi, promise of greater industrialisation and welfare, and strategy of majority Hindu consolidation — fell way short of its projected claim of winning 200 seats. It, however, emerged as the primary opposition in the state, winning 77 seats — a leap from the three seats it won in the 2016 assembly polls, but a dip from its tally in the Lok

West Bengal 2021

Assembly Election Results Total seats: 292*

Party	Seats won	Vote Share (%)
Trinamool Conress	213	47.94
Bharatiya Janata Party(BJP)	77	38.13
Indian Secular Front (ISF)	1	...
Communist Party of India (Marxist)	...	4.73
Congress	...	2.93
Independent	1	...

* Elections to 2 seats postponed due to death of candidates

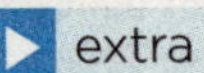

Behind the Name "Chihuahua"

This tiny dog breed is only 15-23 cm high. The ancestor of this small dog was first bred in Mexico. It takes its name from the Mexican state of Chihuahua.

Sabha polls of 2019, which translated into leads in 121 assembly constituencies. In yet another sign of the changing political configuration in the state, the Left parties and the Congress failed to win a single seat.

Among other states that went to the polls, the results were marked by both continuity and change.

In Tamil Nadu, in the first state elections held after former chief ministers M Karunanidhi and J Jayalalithaa passed away, the Dravida Munnetra Kazhagam (DMK)-led alliance, under MK Stalin, won in 159 out of the state's 234 seats.

The DMK returned to power after a decade, riding on a degree of anti-incumbency, Stalin's leadership, alliances, and unease with the BJP. The All India Anna Dravida Munnetra Kazhagam (AIADMK) performed better than expected with the party and its allies winning in 75 seats, with chief minister EK Palaniswami seen as having performed credibly on Covid-19 management — but this was not enough to neutralise the support for the DMK.

MK Stalin

In Kerala, breaking a four-decade-old trend, where power has alternated between two of the state's major political formations, the Left Democratic Front (LDF) led by Pinarayi Vijayan made history by comfortably returning to power for a second consecutive time.

Pinarayi Vijayan

Tamil Nadu 2021

Assembly Election Results — Total seats: 234

Party	Seats won	Vote Share (%)
DMK+		
Dravida Munnetra Kazhagam (DMK)	133	37.70
Congress	18	4.27
Communist Party of India	2	1.09
Communist Party of India (Marxist) CPI(M)	2	0.85
Viduthalai Chiruthaigal Katchi (VCK)	4	...
AIADMK+		
All India Anna Dravida Munnetra Kazhagam (AIADMK)	66	33.29
Bharatiya Janata Party (BJP)	4	2.62
Pattali Makkal Katchi (PMK)	5	3.80

Kerala 2021

Assembly Election Results — Total seats: 140

Party	Seats won	Vote Share (%)
Left Democratic Front (LDF)		
Communist Party of India (Marxist) CPI(M)	62	25.38
Communist Party of India CPI	17	7.58
Kerala Congress (Mani)	5	3.28
Janata Dal (Secular) JD(S)	2	1.28
National Congress Party of India (NCP)	2	0.99
Loktantrik Janata Dal (LJD)	1	...
Congress (S)	1	...
Indian National League (INL)	1	...
Kerala Congress (B)	1	...
Revolutionary Socialist Party (Leninist) (RSP(L))	1	...
Janadhipatya Kerala Congress (JKC)	1	...
Independents	5	
Total	**99**	
United Democratic Front (UDF)		
Congress (I)	21	25.12
Indian Unin Muslim League (IUML)	15	8.27
Kerala Congress (Joseph)	2	...
Kerala Congress (Jacob)	1	...
Revolutionary Marxist Party of India (RMPI)	1	...
National Congress Kerala (NCK)	1	...
Total	**41**	
National Democratic Alliance (NDA)		
Bharatiya Janata Party (BJP)	0	11.30
Total	**0**	

Political observers in the state attributed the win to the government's focused management of Covid-19 and Nipah, as well as floods, during its term.

The Left won 99 of the Kerala assembly's 140 seats, with the Congress-led United Democratic Front (UDF) a distant second with 41 seats. Former Congress president, Rahul Gandhi, is a parliamentarian from the state and had extensively campaigned for the UDF.

The BJP, however, had reason to smile in Asom — where it returned to power despite a united opposition for a second time — under the leadership of chief minister Sarbananda Sonowal and Himanta Biswa Sarma. The BJP largely relied on the government's welfare schemes and

Asom 2021

Assembly Election Results Totat seats: 126

Party	Seats won	Vote Share (%)
Bharatiya Janata Party (BJP)	60	33.0
Asom Gana Parishad (AGP)	9	7.91
United People's Party Liberal(UPPL)	6	...
Congress	29	29.60
All India United Democratic Front (AIUDF)	16	9.29
Bodoland People's Front (BPF)	4	3.39
Communist Party of India (Marxist) CPI(M)	1	0.14

Himanta Biswa Sarma

communal polarisation, where it accused the Congress and the All India United Democratic Front of being sympathetic to illegal Muslim immigrants.

BJP chose Himanta Biswa Sarma as the new leader of the legislative party.

The National Democratic Alliance (NDA) also crossed the majority mark in the Union territory of Puducherry, and the BJP will be a part of the coalition government in the UT for the first time.

Supreme Court Declares Maratha Quota Law Unconstitutional

A five-judge Constitution Bench of the Supreme Court on May 5 unanimously declared a Maharashtra law which provides reservation benefits to the Maratha community, taking the quota limit in the State in excess of 50%, as unconstitutional. The five-judge Supreme Court bench, comprising Justices Ashok Bhushan, L Nageswara Rao, S Abdul Nazeer, Hemant Gupta, and Ravindra Bhat, had earlier on March 26 reserved judgment in the case after a back-to-back hearing for 10 days.

The Bench led by Justice Ashok Bhushan found there was no "exceptional circumstances" or "extraordinary situation" in Maharashtra which required the Maharashtra government to break the 50% ceiling limit to bestow quota benefits on the Maratha community.

The Supreme Court struck down the findings of the Justice N.G. Gaikwad Commission which led to the enactment of Maratha quota law and set aside the Bombay High Court judgment which validated the Maharashtra State Reservation for Socially and Educationally Backward Classes (SEBC) Act of 2018.

The High Court had, in June 2019, re-

Maratha Supporters at a Campaign Rally Demanding Reservation for the Community

duced the quantum of reservation for Marathas from the 16% recommended by the Gaikwad Commission to 12% in education and 13% in employment. The Supreme Court concluded that even the reduced percentages of reservation granted by the High Court were ultra vires.

In fact the Supreme Court held that a separate reservation for the Maratha community violates Articles 14 (right to equality) and 21 (due process of law).

Most importantly, the Supreme Court declined to re-visit its 1992 Indira Sawhney judgment, which fixed the reservation limit at 50%. "We don't find any substance to revisit the Indira Sawhney judgment or referring it to a larger bench. The judgment has been upheld by at least four Constitution Benches," Justice Ashok Bhushan read from his lead opinion on the question of validity of the Maratha quota law.

In 1992, a nine-judge Bench of the court had drawn the "Lakshman rekha" for reservation in jobs and education at 50%, except in "extraordinary circumstances". However, over the years, several States like Maharashtra and Tamil Nadu have crossed the Rubicon and passed laws which allows reservation shooting over 60%. The five-judge Bench had decided not to confine the question of reservation spilling over 50% limit to just Maharashtra. The Bench had expanded the ambit of the case by making other States party and inviting them to make their stand clear on the question of whether reservation should continue to remain within the 50% boundary or not.

Justice Bhushan said that appointments made under the Maratha quota following the Bombay HC judgment endorsing the State law would hold, but they would get no further benefits. Students already admitted under the Maratha quota law would continue. Students admitted to postgraduate courses would not be affected since they were not given reservation.

Cyclone Tauktae Turns Deadly

Cyclone Tauktae, a powerful, deadly and damaging tropical cyclone in the Arabian Sea, became the strongest tropical cyclone to make landfall in the Indian state of Gujarat since the 1998 Gujarat cyclone. Cyclone Tauktae brought extremely heavy rainfall and gale winds over the entire west coast during May 12–May 19. As it travelled between Lakshadweep and Gujarat, the low-pressure system intensified into an 'Extremely Severe Cyclone', moving parallel along the west coast. During its northward journey, Tauktae affected five states — Kerala, Karnataka, Goa, Maharashtra and Gujarat along with two Union Territories — Lakshadweep and Daman & Diu.

Cyclone Tauktae at the Mumbai Coast

Formed in the Arabian Sea, Cyclone Tauktae killed at least 104 people, which is more than the toll from any single cyclone from the Arabian Sea over the last one decade.

States like Andhra Pradesh, Odisha and

What is the Meaning of Tauktae?

The name has been suggested by Myanmar. The name comes from the Burmese language and it means a 'gecko' or a very hitch-pitched lizard.

How Cyclones are Named?

Global bodies like World Meteorological Organisation (WMO), United Nations Economic and Social Commission for Asia, and the Pacific give names to cyclones. Besides, regional specialised meteorological centres (RSMC), as well as tropical cyclone warning centres, also prepare the names of cyclones.

The Indian Meteorological Department (IMD) is among six RSMCs in the world that have been mandated to name tropical cyclones in the north Indian Ocean region.

The WMO and UN ESCAP comprise India, Myanmar, Bangladesh, Sri Lanka, Thailand, Pakistan, and Oman. In 2018, the WMO and ESCAP included five more countries--Iran, Qatar, Saudi Arabia, United Arab Emirates, and Yemen.

In 2020, the IMD released list of 169 new cyclones, which were suggested by 13 countries.

West Bengal along India's east coast have frequently faced the brunt of multiple severe cyclones, such as Fani and Hudhud and the recent Super Cyclone Amphan.

Tauktae was only the second 'Extremely Severe Cyclone' category storm to hit Gujarat in 23 years. Cyclone Tauktae made its landfall east of Diu on May 17 with wind speed ranging between 160–170 km/hr gusting to 185 km/hr. The last cyclone of equal intensity to hit Gujarat was Cyclone Kandla (wind speed 160 to 170 km/hr) that crossed near Porbandar in 1998. The following year, a 'Very Severe Cyclone' formed in the Arabian Sea in May, but it hit the Sindh region of Pakistan.

Climatologically, out of the five cyclones formed annually in the Bay of Bengal and the Arabian Sea, only one develops in the Arabian Sea.

Why Cyclones are Named?

The cyclones are named to make it easier for people to remember and identify the storms. With a name, it is easy to create awareness and to send out alerts, and remove confusion where there are multiple cyclonic systems over a region.

Pushkar Singh Dhami is New Uttarakhand CM

Two term MLA from Khatima in Uttarakhand, Pushkar Singh Dhami was sworn in as the 11th Chief Minister of the State on July 4 in Dehradun.

Dhami, at 45 the youngest Chief Minister yet of Uttarakhand, retained the entire team of his predecessor, Tirath Singh Rawat. Rawat had quit on July 2 ostensibly on being unable to get elected to the Uttarakhand Assembly within the constitutionally stipulated deadline of six months from the date he took over. Tirath Singh Rawat, till then an MP, was sworn in as Chief Minister in March following fierce dissent against Trivendra Singh Rawat. To keep the post, however, Rawat had to win an assembly seat by September 10. Holding a bye-poll amid the Covid pandemic seemed an increasingly distant possibility given that the Assembly polls were due in less than a year's time. Moreover, the Election Commission had recently found itself in the midst of a

Pushkar Singh Dhami Being Congratulated on Becoming Chief Minister

major row over the March-April election in five states held alongside rising infection rates in the second wave.

The state has seen chief ministers change almost ten times in the past 20 years since it was carved out of Uttar Pradesh after a violent agitation in 2000. The only chief minister to complete his tenure of five years was Congress' Narayan Dutt Tiwari who became the chief minister in 2002.

Dhami is not only the youngest chief minister of the state, but also an appointment from Kumaon to the top post. He had worked his way in the BJP hierarchy first in student politics with the Akhil Bharatiya Vidyarthi Parishad (ABVP), the student wing of the Rashtriya Swayamsevak Sangh (RSS), in 1990. He was the officer on special duty (OSD) to his political mentor and former chief minister Bhagat Singh Koshyari when the latter held the post he is holding now. In Dhami's elevation, clearly an attempt is being made to strike the right caste and regional balance in Uttarakhand, as State BJP chief Madan Kaushik is a Brahmin from the Garhwal region, having a Thakur leader from Kumaon as the chief minister is being seen as a good move.

A New Ministry of Cooperation at the Centre

On July 6, the government announced the formation of a separate Union Ministry of Cooperation, a subject that till date was looked after by the Ministry of Agriculture. A media release from the Press Information Bureau said the Ministry of Cooperation will provide a separate administrative, legal and policy framework for strengthening the cooperative movement in the country. "It will help deepen Co-operatives as a true people-based

Dairy Farmers with their Produce at a Cooperative Collections Centre

movement reaching upto the grassroots. In our country, a Co-operative based economic development model is very relevant where each member works with a spirit of responsibility. The Ministry will work to streamline processes for 'Ease of doing business' for co-operatives and enable development of Multi-State Co-operatives (MSCS)," it said.

Agriculture and cooperation are in the

Cooperative Sector at a Glance

A co-operative is an autonomous association of persons united voluntarily to meet their common economic, social, and cultural needs and aspirations through a jointly-owned and democratically-controlled enterprise. Cooperatives range from small-scale to multi-million dollar businesses.

In agriculture, cooperative dairies, sugar mills, spinning mills etc are formed with the pooled resources of farmers who wish to process their produce. The country has 1,94,195 cooperative dairy societies and 330 cooperative sugar mill operations. In 2019-20, dairy cooperatives had procured 4.80 crore litres of milk from 1.7 crore members and had sold 3.7 crore litres of liquid milk per day. (Annual Report, National Dairy Development Board, 2019-20).

In banking and finance, cooperative institutions are spread across rural and urban areas. Village-level primary agricultural credit societies (PACSs) formed by farmer associations are the best example of grassroots-level credit flow. These societies anticipate the credit demand of a village and make the demand to the district central cooperative banks (DCCBs). State cooperative banks sit at the apex of the rural cooperative lending structure. Given that PACSs are a collective of farmers, they have much more bargaining powers than an individual farmer pleading his case at a commercial bank.

NABARD's annual report of 2019-20 counts 95,238 PACSs,363 DCCBs and 33 state cooperative banks in the country. The state cooperative banks reported a total paid-up capital of ₹6,104 crore and deposits of ₹1,35,393 crore, while the DCCBs' paid-up capital stood at ₹21,447 crore and deposits at ₹3,78,248 crore. The DCCBs, whose main role is disbursal of short-term loans to the farming sector (crop loan), distributed ₹3,00,034 crore in loans. The state cooperative banks, which mainly finance agri-processing industries such as sugar mills or spinning mills, disbursed ₹1,48,625 crore in loans. (Annual Report, NABARD, 2019-20)

In urban areas, urban cooperative banks (UCBs) and cooperative credit societies extend banking services to many sectors that would otherwise have found it difficult to get into the institutional credit structure. According to Reserve Bank of India data, the country has 1,539 UCBs whose total capital in 2019-20 stood at ₹14,933.54 crore with a total loan portfolio of ₹3,05,368.27 crore.

state list, which means state governments can govern them. A majority of the cooperative societies are governed by laws in their respective states, with a Cooperation Commissioner and the Registrar of Societies as their governing office. In 2002, the Centre passed a Multi-state Cooperative Societies Act that allowed for registration of societies with operations in more than one state. These are mostly banks, dairies and sugar mills whose area of operation spreads across states. The Central Registrar of Societies is their controlling authority, but on the ground the State Registrar takes actions on his behalf.

The significance of the rural cooperative credit system has been shrinking over the years. The last attempt to provide some fillip was 15 years ago when the Union government appointed and accepted the Vaidyanathan Committee findings and recommendations. After that, except for Kerala state integrating its upper-tier co-operatives into the Kerala Bank, and the recent guidelines issued by the Reserve Bank of India (RBI) for other states to follow a similar model, there has been no policy action.

Basavaraj Bommai is New Karnataka Chief Minister

Basavaraj Somappa Bommai took oath as the new Chief Minister of Karnataka on July 28. In the ceremony at the Glass House of the Karnataka Raj Bhavan in Bengaluru, Governor Thaawarchand Gehlot administered the oath of office and secrecy. Basavaraj Bommai's selection came as BJP's tallest leader in Karnataka, BS Yediyurappa, had resigned as chief minister on 26 July, the day he completed two years in office. Yediurappa was forced to quit amid rumblings of dissatisfaction with his leadership and allegations of misuse of his office for corruption by family members.

Basavaraj Bommai being Sworn in as CM

Bommai was announced as the new Chief Minister of the state following a party meeting the previous day. The 61-year-old Lingayat leader from North Karnataka is a close aide of Yediyurappa and had served as the state home minister under him. Basavaraj Bommai is the son of former Karnataka chief minister SR Bommai, who was removed as the Janata Dal chief minister in 1989 following large-scale defections without being given the opportunity to prove majority on the floor of the House. It was on SR Bommai's petition that a nine-member bench of the Supreme Court, in 1994, imposed restrictions on dismissal of state governments under Article 356 of the Constitution. Basavaraj Bommai began his political career with his father's party and worked with senior party leaders such as HD Deve Gowda and Ramakrishna Hegde before he left and joined the BJP in February 2008.

The selection of Bommai, who is from the Lingayat community, came after several pontiffs from Lingayat mutts in the state had advised the BJP central leadership against removing Yediyurappa, a tall leader of the community. The Lingayat community forms close to 16% of the state's population and has been a loyal vote base for the party. Even though there was speculation of the BJP appointing a leader from a different community, eventually, it zeroed down on the Lingayat leader.

Reservation for OBCs in All-India Quota for Medical Seats

The central government on October 29 announced a 27 per cent quota for the Other Backward Casts (OBCs) and 10 per cent reservation for the Economically Weaker Section (EWS) in the All-India Quota scheme for undergraduate and postgraduate medical and dental courses from the academic year, 2021-22.

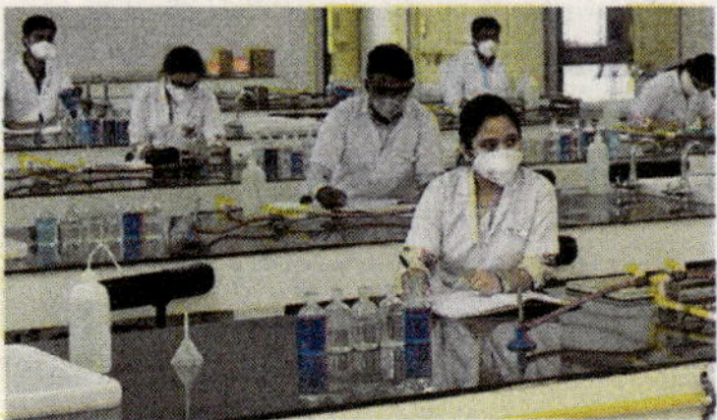

Medical Students in Rapt Attention at a Class

OBC students from across the country shall now be able to take the benefit of this reservation in the AIQ scheme to compete for seats in any state. Being a central scheme, the Central List of OBCs shall be used for the purpose.

The AIQ scheme was introduced in 1986 under the Supreme Court's directions to provide for domicile-free merit-based opportunities to students from any state aspiring to study in a good medical college in another state.

The all-India quota consists of 15 per cent of the total available UG seats and 50 per cent of the total available PG seats in government medical colleges.

Initially, there was no reservation in the AIQ scheme up to 2007. In 2007, the Supreme Court introduced 15 per cent reservation for the Scheduled Castes (SCs) and a 7.5-per cent quota for the Scheduled Tribes (STs) in the scheme.

When the Central Educational Institutions (Reservation in Admission) Act became effective in 2007, providing for a uniform 27 per cent reservation to the Other Backward Classes (OBCs), the same was implemented in all the central educational institutions such as the Safdarjung Hospital, the Lady Hardinge Medical College, the Aligarh Muslim University and the Banaras Hindu University. However, it was not extended to the AIQ seats of the state medical and dental colleges.

In order to provide benefits to students belonging to the EWS category in admission to higher educational institutions, a constitutional amendment was made in 2019, which enabled the provision of 10 per cent reservation for the category. Accordingly, the number of seats in the medical and dental colleges was increased over the next two years (2019-20 and 2020-21) to accommodate this additional 10 per cent EWS reservation so that the total number of seats available for the unreserved category would not see any shortfall. In the AIQ seats, however, this benefit was not extended so far. Therefore, along with the 27 per cent reservation for OBCs, 10 per cent reservation for EWS was also extended in AIQ seats for all the undergraduate/postgraduate medical/ dental courses from the academic year 2021-22.

Over the last six years, the number of MBBS seats in the country increased by 56 per cent from 54,348 in 2014 to 84,649 in 2020 and that of PG seats by 80 per cent from 30,191 in 2014 to 54,275 in 2020. In the same period, 179 new medical colleges were established and the country currently has 558 (289 government and 269 private) medical colleges.

President Kovind Gives Assent to Bill Allowing States to Make OBC Lists

President Ram Nath Kovind granted his assent to the Constitution (105th Amendment) Act 2021, which restores

Lok Sabha in Session to Approve the Bill

the power of state governments to make their own lists of Other Backward Classes. The legislation was passed by the Lok Sabha on August 10 and by the Rajya Sabha on August 11. It was introduced as the Constitution (127th Amendment) Bill but was renumbered later.

The bill was passed in Lok Sabha with 385 members voting in support and no opposition to it. The legislation effectively bypasses a judgement of the Supreme Court that, in May, allowed only the Centre to notify the list of OBCs in India.

Union Social Justice and Empowerment Minister Virendra Kumar, while introducing the Bill in the Lok Sabha, had said there was a need to amend Article 342A of the Constitution to sufficiently clarify that the state and Union Territories' administrations had been empowered to prepare and keep their own list of Socially and Educationally Backward Classes.

The ministry had also noted that amendments had to be made to Articles 338B and 366 to maintain India's federal system. Article 342A deals with the president's power to notify a specific caste as a Socially and Educationally Backward Classes and the power of Parliament to modify the list

Article 366 (26C) provides the definition for a Socially and Educationally Backward Class.

The new Act states that the president would be able to notify the list of Socially and Educationally Backward Classes only for the purposes of the Centre. This list would be prepared and kept by the Centre, and the states and Union Territories would also prepare their own data of the socially and educationally backward classes.

Article 338B deals with the duties, structure and powers of the National Commission for Backward Classes.

The Parliament had in August 2018 passed a constitution amendment bill to give constitutional status to National Commission for Backward Classes.

The 102nd Constitution Amendment Act of 2018 inserted articles 338B, which deals with the structure, duties and powers of the National Commission for Backward Classes, and 342A that deals with the powers of the president to notify a particular caste as an SEBC and the power of Parliament to change the list. Article 366 (26C) defines SEBCs.

The Supreme Court has dismissed the Centre's plea seeking a review of its 5 May majority verdict that held that the 102nd Constitution amendment took away the states' power to notify SEBCs for the grant of quota in jobs and admissions.

Opposition parties had accused the Centre of assaulting the federal structure by taking away the power of the states to identify and list the Other Backward Classes (OBCs).

Government Unveils National Monetisation Pipeline

The government on August 23 unveiled a four-year National Monetisation Pipeline (NMP) which expects to raise ₹6-lakh crore by monetising the operating assets of the Central Government over a four-year period ending FY25.

The NMP is designed to unlock the value of investments in brownfield public sector assets by tapping institutional and long-term capital. So, government-owned roads, railways, power plants, gas pipelines, airports, ports, warehouses et al could be leased out for a specified period to non-government entities. Real estate investment trusts (REITs) and infrastructure investment trusts (InvITs), for instance, are the key structures used to monetise assets in the roads and power sectors. These are also listed on stock exchanges, providing investors liquidity through secondary markets as well. While these are a structured financing vehicle, other monetisation models on PPP (Public Private Partnership) basis include: Operate Maintain Transfer (OMT), Toll Operate Transfer (TOT), and Operations, Maintenance & Development (OMD). OMT and TOT have been used in highways sector while OMD is being deployed in case of airports.

Roads, railways and power sector assets will comprise over 66% of the total estimated value of the assets to be monetised, with the remaining upcoming sectors including telecom, mining, aviation, ports, natural gas and petroleum product pipelines, warehouses and stadiums. In terms of annual phasing by value, 15% of assets with an indicative value of ₹0.88 lakh crore are envisaged for rollout in the current financial year. The NMP will run co-terminus with the National Infrastructure Pipeline of ₹100 lakh crore announced in December 2019. The estimated amount to be raised through monetisation is around 14% of the proposed outlay for the Centre of ₹43 lakh crore under NIP.

What is the list of assets?

The assets on the NMP list include: 26,700 km of roads, railway stations, train operations and tracks, 2,8608 Ckt km worth of power transmission lines, 6 GW of hydroelectric and solar power assets, 2.86 lakh km of fibre assets and 14,917 towers in the telecom sector, 8,154 km of natural gas pipelines and 3,930 km of petroleum product pipelines. In the roads sector, the government has already monetised 1,400 km of national highways worth ₹17,000 crore. Another five assets have been monetised through a PowerGrid InvIT raising ₹7,700 crore.

Also, 15 railway stations, 25 airports and the stake of central government in existing airports and 160 coal mining projects, 31 projects in 9 major ports, 210 lakh MT of warehousing assets, 2 national stadia and 2 regional centres, will be up for monetisation. Redevelopment of various government colonies and hospitality assets including ITDC hotels is expected to generate ₹15,000 crore.

What are the Challenges?

Lack of identifiable revenue streams in various assets, dispute resolution, presence of regulated tariffs in certain sectors and lack of independent sectoral regulators are some hurdles NMP needs to cross. The allocation of assets owned by governments to private investors is often subject to political influence, which can lead to corruption. A regime change should not throw a spanner in the works of NMP projects. Usually, new regimes accuse old ones of corruption and this can lead to legal cases that stretch for years.

Bhupendra Patel Sworn in as Chief Minister of Gujarat

Bharatiya Janata Party leader and Ghat-

Bhupendra Patel being Sworn in as CM

lodia MLA Bhupendra Patel took oath as the 17th Chief Minister of Gujarat on September 13.

The announcement of the 59-year-old BJP leader's name as the Chief Minister-elect at a legislative party meeting of the BJP had come as a surprise for many as the low-profile MLA was not seen to be among the top contenders for the post. Born in Ahmedabad, Patel is a first-time MLA from the Ghatlodia seat, a post previously held by Anandiben Patel, who is currently serving as the Governor of Uttar Pradesh with an additional charge of Madhya Pradesh. He had won his maiden seat by a margin of 1,17,000 votes in 2017, the largest margin in that poll defeating Congress candidate Shashikant Patel. He grabbed more than 72 per cent of the vote share in the Ghatlodia constituency during the 2017 assembly polls.

Patel had served as the Ahmedabad municipal councillor. Patel, who holds a diploma in civil engineering, also served as the chairman of the Standing Committee of Ahmedabad Municipal Corporation and Ahmedabad Urban Development Authority (AUDA).

With Assembly polls in the state scheduled to be held in 2022, BJP went with Patel, a Patidar face for the Chief Minister. He is also a trustee at Patidar organizations Sardar Dham and Vishwa Umiya Foundation. The Patidars are a dominant caste in Gujarat with a sizeable control over the electoral votes. The community also dominates the political economy with a stronghold over education, realty and cooperative sectors.

The party is counting on Patel to navigate the party through tough waters during the upcoming assembly elections in 2022. In the 2017 state election, the BJP won 99 of the state's 182 Assembly seats, Congress got 77 seats.

Farmer Protests Rock the Country

Farmers in the county have posed a unique challenge to Prime Minister Narendra Modi's government, staging huge protests throughout the country against the government's controversial agricultural laws they say could ruin their livelihood.

Women at the Forefront of the Protest

Farmers are the biggest voting bloc in the country, and the agricultural sector sustains about 58% of India's 1.3 billion citizens. Angering farmers could see Modi lose a significant chunk of votes at the next general election in 2024.

In the 1960s, India introduced a system of agricultural subsidies. The government paid for some pesticides and irrigation. That assistance helped farmers boost their crop yields, eventually making India self-sufficient in food. It was called the Green Revolution, and farmers were the heroes at the centre of it.

Since then, while the rest of India has modernized, Indian agriculture has stagnated. Subsidies and rising land prices have allowed a small group of farmers to prosper, but a majority remain poor. There's even been an epidemic of farmer suicides in rural India.

Seeking to help them, Modi's government in September 2020 passed three new agriculture laws: The Farmers Agreement on Price Assurance and Farm Services Act, The Farmers' Produce Trade & Commerce Act, and The Essential Commodities Act. The preamble to the first law says it aims to "protect and empower" farmers to engage with wholesalers, exporters and retailers in a "fair and transparent manner."

These three laws allow farmers and traders to do business outside of government-run wholesale markets that have dominated agriculture since the Green Revolution. The laws also allow them to do business online at prices guaranteed by the government. They say farmers must be paid within three days of selling their crops and cannot have their land confiscated by any buyer or corporation – a protection to allay farmers' fears of losing what is often ancestral property. The laws also establish conciliation boards to mediate trade disputes.

But many farmers don't trust the government. Street protests erupted in November 2020. The demonstrators see the new laws as the first step toward dismantling all the support given to farmers during the Green Revolution.

A big part of that support is the government guarantee of Minimum Support Prices, or MSPs, for 22 staples it considers essential to Indians' nutrition and the agricultural economy. The list includes rice and wheat but not the tomatoes and peppers. A majority of Indian farmers grow crops that are not on that list – and have never enjoyed those price guarantees.

Charanjit Channi is New Punjab Chief Minister

Charanjit Singh Channi was sworn in as Punjab's new Chief Minister on September 20 after Amarinder Singh's dramatic

Charanjit Channi being Congratulated on Becoming CM

resignation just four months before an election in the state. Punjab's first Dalit Sikh Chief Minister took charge with two deputies, both carefully chosen to tie up the Congress's poll math- Sukhjinder Singh Randhawa and Om Prakash Soni.

The Congress is betting on the vote of Dalits, who are 31 per cent of Punjab's population, to counter the opposition Akali Dal, a former BJP ally that has teamed up with Mayawati's Bahujan Samaj Party (BSP) for the polls.

After months of bickering with Sidhu and other rebels, Amarinder Singh resigned on September 18 after the Congress called a sudden meeting of MLAs without informing him. He called Congress president Sonia Gandhi and told her he felt humiliated for the third time this year and "enough is enough". Singh unsurprisingly skipped the MLAs' meet. It is speculated that over 50 MLAs had written to Sonia Gandhi demanding that the "Captain" be replaced as Chief Minister. Singh had fought the party's order to resign.

The Punjab crisis had escalated dramatically over Amarinder Singh's festering feud with Navjot Sidhu. In July, despite Singh's fierce resistance, the party appointed Navjot Sidhu its Punjab chief, but the acrimony stayed barely below the surface.

The truce started unravelling with a row over advisers appointed by Sidhu and their controversial statements, which Amarinder Singh publicly condemned. In

August, four ministers and around two dozen party legislators had raised fresh complaints against Amarinder Singh, telling the leadership that they had no faith in his ability to honour poll promises.

Tatas Win Back Air India

The Tata Group won the bid to acquire debt-laden state-run Air India offering ₹18,000 crore for acquiring 100 per cent shareholding

Tata Sons subsidiary Talace Pvt Ltd emerged as the winning bidder for the debt-laden national carrier after quoting an enterprise value of ₹18,000 crore. The second bidder, a consortium led by Ajay Singh, had quoted an equity value of ₹15,100 crore. The reserve price fixed by the government before opening the bids on September 28 was at ₹12,906 crore. Tatas' bid of ₹18,000 crore comprises taking over of 15,300 crore of debt and paying the rest in cash. Govt will get ₹2,700 cr cash from Tatas for sale of its 100 per cent stake. Tata Sons' winning bid of ₹18,000 crore for Air India was higher than reserve price of ₹12,906 crore set by government.

A group of ministers comprising Home Minister Amit Shah, Finance Minister Nirmala Sitharaman, Commerce Minister Piyush Goyal and Civil Aviation Minister Jyotiraditya Scindia had cleared the winning bid for Air India on October 4. The

ministers approved the highest price bid of M/s Talace Pvt Ltd, a wholly owned subsidiary of M/s Tata Sons Pvt. Ltd for sale of 100% equity shareholding of Government of India in Air India along with equity shareholding of Air India in AIXL and AISATS. The transaction does not include non-core assets including land and building, valued at ₹14,718 crore, which are to be transferred to GoI's Air India Asset Holding Limited (AIAHL).

Jehangir Ratanji Dadabhoy (JRD) Tata founded the airline in 1932. It was called Tata Airlines then. In 1946, the aviation division of Tata Sons was listed as Air India and in 1948, Air India International was launched with flights to Europe.The international service was among the first public-private partnerships in India, with the government holding 49 per cent, the Tatas keeping 25 per cent and the public owning the rest. In 1953, Air India was nationalised.

The stake sale process, which began in January 2020, faced delays due to the COVID-19 pandemic. In April 2021, the government asked potential bidders to put in financial bids. September 15 was the last day for putting in financial bids. Tata Group was among the multiple entities that had put in an initial expression of interest (EoI) in December 2020 for buying the Maharaja.

With previous attempts since 2017 failing to get any significant interest and after receiving feedback from potential investors, the government had in October 2020 sweetened the EoI clause relating to the transfer of Air India's debt to the new investor, giving bidders flexibility to decide on the quantum of humongous debt they want to absorb.

As per the Air India EoI floated by DIPAM in January 2020, of the airline's total debt of ₹ 60,074 crore as of March 31, 2019, the buyer would be required to absorb ₹23,286.5 crore.

The rest would be transferred to Air India Assets Holding Ltd (AIAHL), a special purpose vehicle. Air India has been in losses ever since its merger with domestic operator Indian Airlines in 2007.

The airline will give Tata control of 4,400 domestic and 1,800 international landing and parking slots at domestic airports, as well as 900 slots at airports overseas.

Air India has 141 planes and the best international route network of all the country's airlines. It derives about two-thirds of its revenues from its international business.

Lakhimpur Kheri Becomes a Symbol of Farmer Protests

Eight people, including four farmers, were killed in Tikunia village of Uttar Pradesh's Lakhimpur Kheri district on October 3, after violence over a visit by Union Minister Ajay Kumar Mishra and UP Deputy Chief Minister Keshav Maurya. The farmers were run over by a car that was allegedly part of a convoy of vehicles in which the Union minister of state for home affairs Ajay Mishra's son was travelling. A murder case was registered against Mishra's son and several others

The farmers, who had gathered there to protest against three contentious farm laws, accused the minister's son of driving one of the cars that was involved in the accident, a charge the minister has denied. The protest was being held at that particular spot to block two ministers from visiting.

The situation immediately turned tense with protestors allegedly burning cars and the Uttar Pradesh government deploying heavy police personnel in the village and across the district.

Farmers had gathered in Tikunia to

Ashish Mishra at the Crime Branch Office in Lakhimpur

register their protest by showing black flags to Uttar Pradesh deputy chief minister Keshav Prasad Maurya and Union minister Ajay Mishra, who were visiting the village for a few scheduled government programmes. Tikunia also happens to be the paternal village of Mishra.

According to farmers, they first gheraoed Keshav Prasad Maurya at the helipad and were returning to the road through which the convoy of ministers would move. It was at this point that farmers standing on both sides of the road with black flags were run over by three cars in a convoy in which Mishra's son, Ashish Mishra, and his relatives, were travelling.

The incident was widely condemned by politicians across the spectrum.

Modi Launches Gati Shakti National Master Plan

Prime Minister Narendra Modi on 13 October launched the Gati Shakti National Master Plan for multi-modal connectivity. The ₹100 lakh crore plan, which seeks to speed up and expand infrastructure projects, is intended to enhance the country's self-reliance. The plan aims to lend more power and speed to projects by connecting all concerned departments on one platform.

Prime Minister Narendra Modi Launches Gati Shakti National Master Plan

The Gati Shakti masterplan will use geo-mapping and real-time data in one centralised portal to ensure that key departments and states have visibility over major projects being planned, especially the ones which have multi-sectoral and multi-regional reach. Sixteen central government departments, including Railways, Roads and Highways, Petroleum and Gas, Power, Telecom, Shipping, Aviation and others will be part of this initiative.

The plan will include all existing and planned initiatives of various ministries and departments in one centralised portal. Each and every department will have visibility of each other's activities providing critical data while planning and execution of projects in a comprehensive manner. Through this, different departments will be able to prioritise their projects through cross–sectoral interaction.

The plan includes 11 industrial corridors, achieving a ₹1.7 lakh crore turnover in defence production and having 38 electronics manufacturing clusters and 109 pharma clusters by 2024-25.

The national master plan fixes targets up to 2024-25 for all infrastructure ministries. Like for the Road Transport and Highways Ministry, the target is having national highways of 2 lakh km, completion of four or six-lane national highways of 5,590 km along coastal areas and all state capitals in north-east to be connected with four-lane national highways or two two-lane national highways.

For railways, the target by 2024-25 is to handle cargo of 1,600 million tonnes from 1,210 million tonnes in 2020, decongesting 51 percent of the railway network by completing additional lines and implementation of two Dedicated Freight Corridors (DFCs).

In civil aviation, the target is to double the existing aviation footprint to have a total of 220 airports, heliports and water aerodromes by 2025 which would mean building additional 109 such facilities by then. In shipping, the national masterplan says the target by 2024-25 is to have total cargo capacity to be handled at the ports at 1,759 MMTPA from 1,282 MMTPA in 2020.

The gas pipeline network in the country is aimed to be doubled to 34,500 km by 2024-25 by building an additional 17,000 km long trunk pipeline connecting major demand and supply centres for industries, as per the plan. In power lines, the total transmission network by 2024-25 is targeted to be 4.52 lakh circuit km and the renewable energy capacity will be increased to 225 GW from 87.7 GW presently.

Global Hunger Index Ranks India at 101

The Global Hunger Index published on October 14 ranked India at 101 posi-

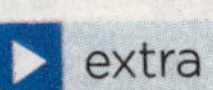

Jai Jawan, Jai Kisan

Lal Bahadur Shastri gave the famous slogan 'Jai Jawan, Jai Kisan' during the 1965 India-Pakistan war to boost the morale of soldiers and the farmers in the backdrop of the crucial war and food paucity.

What is the Global Hunger Index?

The Global Hunger Index (GHI) is published annually as part of a partnership between Concern Worldwide, Ireland's largest aid and humanitarian agency that says it is "dedicated to tackling poverty and suffering in the world's poorest countries", and Welthungerhilfe, which describes itself as "one of the largest private aid organisations in Germany, independent of politics and religion".

The publishers say that the first GHI report was published in 2006 and that it is intended to be "a tool designed to comprehensively measure and track hunger at global, regional, and national levels".

The publishers say that the GHI assesses a country's performance on four component indicators, which reflect the multidimensional nature of hunger — undernourishment, child wasting, child stunting and child mortality — to compile a score that gives an indication as to deficiencies in calories as well as in micronutrients.

A three-step process based on standardisation of scores on each of the indicators and their aggregation yields a country's GHI score on a 100-point 'GHI Severity Scale', where 0 is the best score and 100 is the worst.

tion out of 116 countries. India is also among the 31 countries where hunger has been identified as serious. India ranked 94 among 107 countries in the Global Hunger Index (GHI) released in 2020.

The index calculates the hunger levels and malnutrition across the world. The report for 2021 accessed data from 135 countries but evaluated only 116 of them. The report detailing the index said that there was not sufficient data from the remaining 19 countries.

Only 15 countries fare worse than India. These include Papua New Guinea (102), Afghanistan (103), Nigeria (103), Congo (105), Mozambique (106), Sierra Leone (106), Timor-Leste (108), Haiti (109), Liberia (110), Madagascar (111), Democratic Republic of Congo (112), Chad (113), Central African Republic (114), Yemen (115) and Somalia (116).

Children Having Mid-day Meal at a School

India was also behind most of the neighbouring countries. Pakistan was placed at 92 rank, Nepal at 76 and Bangladesh also at 76.

Current projections based on the Global Hunger Index (GHI) show that the world as a whole — and 47 coun-

Maple Leaf

Maple trees grow across Canada. The country produces 75 per cent of the world's maple syrup, made from the tree sap. A maple leaf can be seen on the Canadian national flag.

tries in particular — will fail to achieve even low hunger by 2030.

The Index tracks key indicators used to measure progress toward Zero Hunger by 2030 at national, regional, and global levels. Based on the values of the four indicators - undernourishment, child wasting, child stunting and child mortality- the GHI determines hunger on a 100-point scale, where 0 is the best possible score (no hunger) and 100 is the worst. Each country's GHI score is classified by severity, from low to extremely alarming.

Somalia has the highest level of hunger according to the 2021 GHI ranking — its GHI score of 50.8 is considered extremely alarming, It is preceded by five countries with levels of hunger that are alarming — Central African Republic, Chad, Democratic Republic of the Congo, Madagascar, and Yemen — and 31 countries that have serious levels of hunger.

"Although GHI scores show that global hunger has been on the decline since 2000, progress is slowing. While the GHI score for the world fell 4.7 points, from 25.1 to 20.4, between 2006 and 2012, it has fallen just 2.5 points since 2012. After decades of decline, the global prevalence of undernourishment — one of the four indicators used to calculate GHI scores — is increasing. This shift may be a harbinger of reversals in other measures of hunger," says the report.

Landslides and Floods in Kerala Cause Huge Loss

Torrential rain battered the coastal state

A Resident Carries a Dog Amid Debris of his Damaged House after Flash Floods

of Kerala in October 2021, causing rivers to swell and flooding roads that left vehicles submerged in muddy waters, with some houses reduced to rubble. The heavy rainfall was caused by a low pressure area over the southeastern Arabian sea and Kerala. As of 19 October 2021, 35 people were killed due to the floods. Kottayam and Idukki were two of the worst affected districts in the state, where days of heavy rainfall had caused deadly landslides.

Home to more than 33 million people, Kerala regularly experiences heavy rainfall during the monsoon months from late May to September. However, flash flooding and landslides have become more frequent and severe in the state in recent years.

In August 2018, at least 324 people were killed and more than 300,000 evacuated after torrential rain battered Kerala, resulting in the worst flooding the state had seen in nearly a century. Some 13 of Kerala's 14 districts were under a red alert, the highest warning level issued during emergencies in India.

Happiest Country in the World

For four consecutive years, Finland has been named the happiest country in the world by the United Nations Sustainable Solutions Network.

Current Affairs - World

Trump Supporters Storm US Capitol

The US Capitol, the seat of American democracy, was stormed by a pro-Donald Trump mob on January 6, 2021, apparently driven by the prospect that they might stop the certification of the 2020 federal election in favour of Joe Biden.

Trump Supporters Storm Capitol

The mob managed to enter the Senate chamber where minutes earlier the election results were being certified. Five people died in the ensuing violence.

Donald Trump praised the mob as "very special" people. The president justified the violence by citing baseless claims of widespread election fraud. In a video that Twitter later deleted from his account, the president urged his supporters to "go home", but also gave legitimacy to the falsehoods that fuelled the attempted insurrection, calling the election "stolen" and telling the angry mob, "we love you".

The breach on US Capitol was the the first since 1814, when the British marched into Washington DC and set it, and other buildings (including the White House) ablaze.

Twitter, Facebook and Instagram locked the president's accounts in order to address misinformation and the incitement of violence. Facebook also announced it would remove all photographs and videos posted from the protest, as well as praise for the protests or calls to bring weapons to the protest or anywhere else in the US.

The Democrats of the House judiciary committee later called for Pence to invoke the 25th amendment and remove Trump from office. The amendment triggers a process during which the vice president becomes president. The fourth section of the amendment, which is the process for removing a president when he is "unable to discharge the powers and duties of his office", has never been used.

Joe Biden Sworn in as the 46th President of the United States

Joseph Robinette Biden Jr. was sworn in as the 46th president of the United States on January 20, 2021, ending one of the most dramatic political transitions in American history. The Chief Justice of

Joe Biden Takes Oath as President

the US Spreme Court John Roberts administered the 35-word oath of office to Biden. Biden is the oldest person ever sworn in as president. Biden turned 78 in November 2020. Before Biden was sworn in as President, Donald J. Trump held the record for the country's oldest chief executive. He was 70 in January 2017, when he became the 45th president of the United States. The inauguration took place at the US Capitol.

Donald Trump, who never formally conceded his defeat, had left the White House on the morning of the inaugural day and was not in attendance, a final display of irreverence for the traditions and norms that have long shaped the presidency. Trump was the first president not to attend his successor's inauguration since 1869. Mike Pence, the outgoing vice-president, was there, joined by the Clintons, the Bushes and the Obamas.

The traditional ceremonies of the transfer of power went off without a hitch, and the widespread, potentially violent right-wing protests that law enforcement had feared around the country did not materialise — a reminder that in spite of the extraordinary circumstances, and rump's explicit efforts to undermine it, American democracy remained intact.

The oaths of office were bookended by Lady Gaga singing the national anthem and Amanda Gorman, a 22-year-old poet, captivating the small crowd with a poem that she finished writing after the riot at the Capitol.

Kamala Harris Sworn in as Vice-President

Kamala Harris, 56, made history on January 20, 2021 when she was sworn in as the first female, first Black and first Indian-origin U.S. Vice-President.The former California senator was sworn in by Justice Sonia Sotomayor, the first Latina on the supreme court.

Kamala Harris Takes Oath as Vice President

Harris's inauguration marks a turning point in American history. Women have run on presidential tickets as would-be vice-presidents but until Joe Biden's win, none were victorious.Harris's elevation fulfills a major goal of Biden's presidential arc: to install people of colour and women in powerful positions in his administration, oftentimes where, historically, only white men have been.

Biden and Harris have described their ideal relationship as similar to that between Biden and Barack Obama when the latter was president. Biden was to be the last voice in the room on any major decision.But that dynamic will not be perfectly replicated. Biden spent decades in the Senate while Harris was in her first term when she first ran unsuccessfully for president and then was selected as Biden's running mate.

Unlike recent vice-presidents, though, Harris is expected to often play a deciding role in the Senate because of the 50-50 split.

Harris will reside at the Naval Observatory, the traditional home of the vice-president. Her husband, Doug Emhoff, will join her there and become the first man married to a vice-president. He will be referred to as the second gentleman.

Kamala Harris, a lawyer, is the former attorney general for California. She attended Howard University in Washington DC for her undergraduate degree and often references her time there.

Harris becomes vice-president with a relatively new team in her office. Her chief of staff, Tina Flournoy, was not a member of her campaign staff. Harris's chief spokeswoman, Symone Sanders, also a woman of colour, served as a top adviser to Biden throughout his successful presidential campaign. Sanders began traveling with Harris near the end of the campaign and stayed on with Harris through the transition.

Supporters of Aung San Suu Kyi Protest Against the Coup

Myanmar's Military Seizes Power in Coup

The military of Myanmar overthrew the country's fragile democratic government in a coup d'état on February 1, arresting civilian leaders, shutting off the internet and cutting off flights.

The coup returns the country to full military rule after a short span of quasi-democracy that began in 2011, when the military, which had been in power since 1962, implemented parliamentary elections and other reforms.

The coup took place in the same week that the Parliament was scheduled to hold its first session since the country's Nov. 8 elections. The election saw a thundering victory for Aung San Suu Kyi and the National League for Democracy (NLD), which won an astonishing 83 percent of the parliamentary seats up for election, while the military's electoral proxy, the Union Solidarity and Development Party (USDP), won a paltry 6.9 percent.

The military refused to accept the results of the election, which was widely seen as a referendum on the popularity of Daw Aung San Suu Kyi. Aung San Suu Kyi, the head of the N.L.D., has been the country's de facto civilian leader since taking office in 2015.

The military detained the leaders of the governing N.L.D. party and Myanmar's civilian leadership, including Aung San Suu Kyi and President U Win Myint, along with cabinet ministers, the chief ministers of several regions, opposition politicians, writers and activists.The coup was effectively announced on the military-owned Myawaddy TV station when a news presenter cited the 2008 constitution, which allows the military to declare a national emergency. The state of emergency, he said, would remain in place for one year.

The coup represents the sudden culmination of civilian-military tensions that have simmered beneath the surface of the country's politics since Myanmar's military-dominated government began to initiate the dramatic political and economic opening of the country in 2011. In some ways, these tensions are baked into the country's 2008 Constitution, drafted and promulgated by the military junta, which guarantees the Tatmadaw the control of three powerful ministries, as well as a quarter of the seats in the Union Parliament.

Even after Aung San Suu Kyi and the NLD won a landslide victory at national elections in 2015, these constitutional provisions ensured that long-standing tensions between the NLD government and the military would continue.

The NLD's massive victory at November's election, and the increasing loss of support for the army-backed USDP, seems to have dramatically sharpened the civilian-military divide, and convinced the army leadership that the Constitution no longer offered sufficient protection against political challenge. Another important factor is the personal ambition of Min Aung Hlaing, who has long harboured ambitions of leading the country, and is slated for mandatory retirement in June.

Donald Trump Acquitted in Second Impeachment Trial

Donald Trump was acquitted by the US Senate in his second impeachment trial

Trump Holds Up a Newspaper with the Headline that Reads "ACQUITTED"

for his role in the 6 January attack on the US Capitol. The Senate voted 57-43 on the question of whether Trump was guilty of inciting an insurrection. Seven Republicans — Richard Burr, Bill Cassidy, Susan Collins, Lisa Murkowski, Mitt Romney, Ben Sasse and Pat Toomey — joined Democrats in voting to convict the president.

Trump was cleared because two-thirds of the Senate would have needed to find the former president guilty for him to have been convicted under the US constitution. After just five days of debate in the chamber that was the scene of the January 6 invasion, a divided Senate fell 10 votes short of the two-thirds majority required to convict high crimes and misdemeanors. Democrats had hoped to convict Trump and then hold a simple majority vote to bar him from holding public office in future. Trump has not ruled out running for president in 2024.

The House impeached Trump in his final days in office, on one charge of "incitement of insurrection" of the siege on the US Capitol. He invited supporters to Washington on the day electoral college votes were being counted, told them to "fight like hell" and encouraged them to go to the US Capitol, Democrats charged. Once the attack on the Capitol turned deadly, placing Vice-President Mike Pence, members of Congress and Capitol Hill employees in danger, Trump violated his oath of office by failing to defend the US government against an attack, the impeachment article alleged.

The attack came after Trump spent weeks trying to overturn the results of the 2020 election. Five people died as a direct result of the assault, including a police officer, and scores more were seriously injured.

Trump is just the third president in US history to be impeached. He is the only president to be impeached twice, and the first former president to face a trial.

Mario Draghi is New Prime Minister of Italy

Mario Draghi, the former European Central Bank chief, was on February 13 sworn in as Italy's prime minister at the head of a unity government called on to confront the coronavirus crisis and economic slump. His government is Italy's 68th government in 75 years. Draghi, a respected figure at home and interna-

Mario Draghi

tionally, managed to convince almost all of Italy's main parties to support his government, with leaders from the far-right League and populist Five Star Movement (M5S) adopting more moderate, pro-European tones in supporting him.

Draghi's appointment ended weeks of political uncertainty triggered after Matteo Renzi withdrew his Italia Viva from a ruling coalition made up of M5S and the centre-left Democratic party because of clashes over how the government was planning to spend the €200bn-plus that Italy was poised to receive from the EU's Covid-19 recovery fund. Renzi's move led to Giuseppe Conte stepping down as prime minister.

Draghi, nicknamed "Super Mario" for his role in saving the euro, also has overwhelming support from the Italian press, which feted him as "a new Italian miracle". Among his first major tasks are accelerating a vaccination programme as Italy strives to emerge from the coronavirus pandemic while at the same time rescuing the economy from the worst recession since the second world war.

China Declares Complete Victory in Eradicating Poverty

President Xi Jinping on February 25 declared that China had scored a "complete victory" in its fight against poverty by lifting over 770 million people out of it in the last four decades. Absolute poverty has been eradicated in the world's most populous country, Xi announced while addressing a gathering held in Beijing to mark the country's accomplishments in poverty alleviation and honour its model poverty fighters.

Xi said that 98.99 million people had been freed from abject poverty after an eight-year campaign and residents of more than 800 counties, with average income under 4,000 yuan (US$619) a year, had been removed from the official poverty list.

Apart from the official narrative, China's success on the poverty-elimination front has also been recognised globally. The World Bank acknowledged back in 2017 the country's "unmatched record", accounting for more than 70 per cent of global success in eradicating extreme poverty since the 1980s.

Farm Workers Harvest Organic Vegetables in a Green House

Poverty alleviation has been a long-term goal for the party since it took power in 1949, and a bedrock foundation for its mandate. Progress has gathered pace along with its opening up and economic reform over the past decades.

About 750m people in China have escaped extreme poverty since 1990. Critics, however, point out that China's extreme poverty line of about Rmb4,000 ($620) in annual income for 2020 — or $2.60 per day in purchasing power parity terms — remains below the level recommended by the World Bank for lower middle-income countries at $3.20 per day.

China Launches 14th Five-Year-Plan

In March of 2021, China's most important annual political meetings took place as thousands of delegates to the National People's Congress (NPC), the national legislature, and the Chinese People's Political Consultative Conference (CPPCC), the top political advisory body, convened for a week at the Great Hall of the People in Beijing. This year's session was particularly significant. The Chinese leadership not only set the national socio-economic and political priorities for 2021, but also approved China's 14th Five-Year Plan (FYP) (2021-2025), the grand strategic blueprint for the next half decade, as well as longer-term goals for 2035.

Formally adopted on March 11, China's 14th Five-Year Plan marks a shift away from the quantitative growth-focus of Beijing's previous plans. Instead, it aims to usher in a more inward-looking "new developmental stage" that targets "quality development."

A Heavy Industries Plant in China

China's five-year plans are a series of social and economic development initiatives issued since the 1950s, which map strategies, put forward targets and set corresponding policy-making directions. They are an important way in which the Communist Party of China (CPC) governs the country.

In 1953, China drew up its first five-year plan when the country needed to build its capacity from scratch. The 1st

Five-Year Plan (1953-1957) set out the basic task of laying the foundations of China's industrialization and completing its socialist transformation. During that period, China successfully produced its first car, its first jet aircraft and the Wuhan Yangtze River Bridge. By the end of 1957, China's total industrial output had increased by 128.6% compared with 1952.

In 1986, China drew up the 7th Five-Year Plan (1986-1990). This plan, devised after the reform and opening-up of China, included for the first time sections on "expanding external economic and technological exchanges" and "investment structure and policy," and also placed the development of science and education in important strategic positions. During the 7th Five-Year Plan period, China's economic system underwent major changes, with the Shanghai Stock Exchange starting operations in December 1990.

In the last five years (2016-2020) of building a moderately prosperous society in all respects, the 13th Five-Year Plan highlighted "innovation" and "reform." It also set out key tasks including targeted poverty alleviation, construction of the Belt and Road Initiative, integration of Hong Kong and Macao into overall national development, and strengthened the crackdown on corruption. By the end of 2020, China's GDP exceeded the threshold of 100 trillion yuan ($15.42 trillion). Meanwhile, the Fuxing bullet trains, Hong Kong-Zhuhai-Macao Bridge, C919 airplane, Chang'e-4 spacecraft, Beidou Navigation System and other achievements have become new icons of China.

China's five-year plans can be said to have charted the path of national economic and social development, and recorded the entire process of the country's growth.

From the 1st to 14th Five-Year Plan, China has been marching toward the same goal, that is, to achieve modernization. The consistency of targets, long-term decisions, stability and continuity of guidelines are distinguishing features of China's governance system.

Now, the new 14th Five-Year Plan and the Long-Range Objectives Through the Year 2035 will lead the Chinese people toward building a great modern socialist country with a brighter future.

First Quad Summit

The leaders of India, Australia, Japan and the United States made history on March 12 when they met virtually in what was the first Quad leaders' summit. Indian PM Narendra Modi, Australian PM Scott Morrison, Japanese PM Yoshihid Suga and US President Joe Biden were the leaders who participated at the meeting.

Virtual Summit of Quad Leaders

The United States, India, Australia and Japan pledged to deliver a billion doses of Covid-19 vaccine throughout the In-

First State Visit by a U.S. President to India

The first state visit by a U.S. president to independent India was by President Dwight D. Eisenhower in 1959. During his trip, Eisenhower addressed both houses of the Indian Parliament and visited the Taj Mahal with Prime Minister Jawaharlal Nehru.

do-Pacific by the end of 2022. This decision at the meeting is widely seen as a bid to counter China's influence in the region. It will allow the group to stake out a role in a region that has been a major beneficiary of Beijing's so-called vaccine diplomacy.

The US will support Indian biopharmaceutical company Biological E Ltd, in scaling up its production capacity to produce at least a billion doses by the end of 2022, including a vaccine developed by the US company Johnson & Johnson.

The US, Japan and Australia also pledged to give at least US$600 million to support the roll-out of vaccines throughout the Indo-Pacific, including "last-mile" vaccine delivery. The countries will also work with the World Health Organization and Covax Facility, its global vaccine drive.

The vaccine initiative was one of several topics discussed at the summit.The US also signalled that the group will play a key role in America's Indo-Pacific policy, at a time of growing tension with China covering a range of issues from trade to human rights. Other Quad countries have also had recent frictions with China. Australian exports have faced a growing number of curbs after it called for an international inquiry into the origins of Covid-19, while India and China were embroiled in a lengthy stand-off along their disputed border in 2020, including the most deadly clash between their armies in decades.

The Quad, officially the 'Quadrilateral Security Dialogue', is a strategic forum between the four nations for exchanging strategic intelligence and conducting joint military exercises. So far, Quad meetings have semi-regularly happened only at the foreign ministers' level. Officially, the grouping was conceived as a space to cooperate for safeguarding joint security and other interests in the Indo-Pacific region. However, observers say that the Quad is geared to counter China's military and economic rise seen in recent decades. Thus, China considers the Quad as an attempt to contain its ambitions and looks at the group as a possible "Asian NATO" of the future.

While the original idea was floated in 2007-08, the initiative only picked up pace in recent years.

The nations hold an annual military drill called 'Exercise Malabar'. However, only the 2007 and 2020 editions saw participation of all four countries together. Between 2014 and 2019, the naval exercise saw participation of only India, US and Japan.

Tanzania Swears in Samia Suluhu Hassan as First Female President

Tanzania's Vice President Samia Suluhu Hassan was sworn in as president on March 18, becoming the first female head of state in the east African country after the death of President John Magufuli. Ms Hassan, 61, was sworn in at State House in the country's commercial capital Dar es Salaam. She assumed the presidency after March 17's announcement of the death of Magufuli, after a more than a two-week absence from public life that drew speculation about his health.

She becomes the only serving female head of state in Africa alongside Ethiopia's President Sahle-Work Zewde, whose role is mainly ceremonial. Among the few other women to hold the post of president in Africa are Ellen Johnson Sirleaf, the Nobel Peace Prize laureate who led Liberia from 2006 to 2018, and Joyce Banda of Malawi, who held office from 2012 to 2014.

Samia Suluhu Hassan

A stalwart in the ruling Chama Cha Mapinduzi (CCM) party, Ms Hassan rose through the ranks from local government to the national assembly over a 20-year political career. She was named Magufuli's running mate in the 2015 presidential campaign, and the pair were re-elected in October 2020 in a disputed poll marred by allegations of irregularities.

Described as a soft-spoken consensus builder, Ms Hassan will also be the country's first president born in Zanzibar, the archipelago that forms part of the union of the Republic of Tanzania. Her leadership style is seen as a potential contrast to that of Magufuli, a brash populist who earned the nickname 'Bulldozer' for muscling through policies and who drew criticism for his intolerance of dissent, which his government denied.

Lasso is Ecuador's New President

Guillermo Lasso, a conservative businessman, was elected as president of Ecuador in the second round of elections held on April 11, 2021. He had contested the 2013 and 2017 elections and had come second. Lasso, the centre-right candidate, got 53 per cent votes as against his opponent, Andres Arauz from the Left, who got 47 per cent votes. In the first round of elections held in February, Arauz was the leader with 32.72 per cent votes while Lasso was second with 19.74 per cent, marginally beating Yaku Perez, the indigenous and environmental activist who had got 19.39 per cent.

CHHATTISGARH MODEL

Economic Development Through Mass Empowerment

80 thousand crore transferred directly to economically weaker sections

Government jobs to more than 4 lakh people

40 lakh families employed through Forest and MNREGA

Rajiv Gandhi Kisan NYAY Yojana -

- Financial aid for various crops, including paddy, in addition to the support price
- Record purchase of 92 lakh metric tonnes of paddy on support price

Rajiv Gandhi Gramin Bhumiheen Krishi Mazdur NYAY Yojana -

- 6 thousand Rupees to more than 10 lakh people every year

Godhan NYAY Yojana -

- The first State Government in the country buying cow dung for 2 Rs. per kilo
- Payment of more than Rupees 100 crore for purchasing cow dung

Purchase of Minor Forest Produce

- Number of Minor Forest Produce purchased at MSP raised from 7 to 52
- Record of highest procurement and purchase in the country, increased collection and support price

Unemployment Rate -

- State unemployment rate now reduced to 3.8% as compared to the National level of 7.6%
- Unemployment rate started reducing from 22%

Industrial Development -

- 1564 new industries established in 33 months, employment to 30 thousand people
- 140 Industrial Units have invested more than Rs. 100 crore

Shri Bhupesh Baghel
Chief Minister, Chhattisgarh

Pro **Active**
Pro **People**

छत्तीसगढ़ शासन

Guillermo Lasso

Lasso's coalition won 31 seats (of which his own party, CREO, got just 12) in the unicameral Congress of 137 members. The leftist coalition (Union for Hope) of Arauz got 48 seats. The Pachakutik party of Yaku Perez got 27 seats, the second-largest group in the Congress. Lasso needs the cooperation of the leftist opposition parties, which have the majority in the Congress, for passing his legislative bills.

President Lasso will face the immediate challenge of dealing with the acute public health and economic crisis caused by COVID-19. He will also have to deal with the huge burden of debt owed to China and the IMF. Income from oil exports, the main foreign exchange earner for the country, has come down due to weak prices and demand.

Both Arauz and his patron, Correa, gracefully accepted the verdict despite the small margin (400,000 votes) of the victor. They did not ask for recount or alleged fraud despite the fact that Lasso himself had refused to accept the 2017 election results with accusations of fraud. He had called on his supporters to protest. But Arauz and Correa showed magnanimity by congratulating the winner and promising to play the role of a constructive opposition.

The peaceful holding of the elections, the non-controversial transfer of power, the absence of gun-totting thugs and extremist rhetoric during the campaign and the prompt acceptance of the verdict by losers are a reflection of the strength and maturity of democracy in Ecuador and Latin America, in general.

Castro Era Ends in Cuba

The Castro era in Cuba came to an end on April 19. Ever since the 1959 revolution, there has been one name at the helm of power in Cuba. That name is Castro - first Fidel and then his brother Raul. On April 16, Raul Castro, at 89, had confirmed his formal resignation as the head of the Communist Party, saying he had "fulfilled his mission, and he was confident in the future of the fatherland." On April 19, President Miguel Diaz-Canel assumed the highest position in government as first party secretary.

According to the Cuban constitution, the Communist Party is the "leading political force of society and of the state." This means that it can set national policy. The first secretary of the Communist Party of Cuba—a post held successively by two Castro brothers (Fidel, then Raúl) for the past six decades—is officially the

Fidel Castro and Raul Castro

extra

Man of Literature

An avid reader and lover of literature, Castro had relationships with many Nobel Prize-winning writers. He cited American Ernest Hemingway's novel *For Whom the Bells Tolls*, about the Spanish Civil War, as an inspiration for his guerrilla tactics.

most powerful political position on the island.

Diaz-Canel, who was party chief in two provinces before joining the national government in 2009, had already succeeded Castro, as president in 2018, and been widely tipped to also take the role of first party secretary - the most powerful position in the country. His election came as part of a broader reshuffle of the party's political bureau at a four-day congress held largely behind closed doors under the banner of "Unity and Continuity".

Fidel Castro, still revered as the country's father and saviour, led the country from 1959 to 2006, when he fell ill and his brother took over. Diaz-Canel was born after the revolution led by the Castro siblings in the 1950s, leading in 1959 to the overthrow of dictator Fulgencio Batista. The PCC congress was held 60 years after Fidel Castro declared Cuba a socialist state, setting up decades of conflict with the United States, which has had sanctions against the country since 1962.

One of the new leadership's first orders of business will be to conduct a nationwide discussion of Raúl Castro's last central committee report, in which he doubled down on existing foreign policy, the need for a single-party system and cautious market reforms to avoid "a restoration of capitalism and dependence on the United States".

President Biden Recognises Armenian Genocide

President Biden on April 24 recognized the mass killings of Armenians more than a century ago as genocide. The United States till recently was careful in not using the term 'genocide' lest it should strain its relationship with Turkey, long a key regional ally and an important partner within NATO. The declaration by Biden reflected his administration's commitment to human rights, a pillar

Activists in Support of Biden's Decision

The Armenian Genocide

When he first coined the term genocide in 1944, Polish lawyer Ralph Lemkin explicitly cited the 1915 extermination of the Armenians as a seminal example. Often called the first genocide of the 20th century, the Armenian Genocide refers to the physical annihilation of the Armenian Christians living in the Ottoman Empire between 1915 and 1916. Prior to those events, the empire had a long history of violence and discrimination against its Armenian population, notably during the Hamidian massacres of the late 19th century. In 1915, there were approximately 1.5 million Armenians living in the Ottoman Empire. By the end of 1916, between 660,000 and 1.2 million of them were killed, either through massacres or from systemic ill-treatment, exposure and starvation.

What is Genocide?

Article Two of the UN Convention on Genocide of December 1948 describes genocide as carrying out acts intended "to destroy, in whole or in part, a national, ethnic, racial or religious group".

of its foreign policy. It is also a break from Biden's predecessors, who were reluctant to anger a country of strategic importance and were wary of driving its leadership toward American adversaries like Russia or Iran.

During World War One, the Germany-aligned Ottoman government accused the Armenians of treachery after suffering a heavy defeat at the hands of Russian forces. Worried that the Christian Armenian population would align with Russia, a primary enemy of the Ottoman Turks, officials ordered mass deportations in what many historians consider the first genocide of the 20th century. On April 24, 1915, Ottoman authorities arrested several hundred Armenian leaders and intellectuals, an event seen by many as the beginning of the massacre. One and a half million Armenians were killed by soldiers and police, or died of starvation and exhaustion in long, cruel marches to concentration camps in what is now northern Syria and Iraq. About 500,000 Armenians survived, and many eventually emigrated to Russia, the U.S. and elsewhere. Turkey claims that 300,000 Armenians died of disease and hunger as they were being deported.

Turkey has acknowledged that widespread atrocities occurred during that period, but its leaders have adamantly denied that the killings were genocide.

So far, about 30 countries have officially recognized the deaths as genocide — among them France, Russia, Canada and Lebanon — according to the Armenian National Institute, a Washington D.C.-based non-profit.

Stampede at Israel Religious Celebration Kills at Least 45

A stampede at a religious festival in northern Israel on April 30, 2021, killed at least 45 people. The stampede occurred during the celebrations of Lag BaOmer at Mount Meron, the first mass religious gathering to be held legally since Israel lifted nearly all restrictions related to the coronavirus pandemic. Worshipers had gathered at the mountain to mark the Lag B'Omer holiday, an annual event where participants sing, dance and light fires in homage to second-century sage Rabbi Shimon Bar Yochai at his burial site.

Jewish Worshippers Walk on Mount Meron, where Fatalities were Reported

Initial reports indicated that a grandstand had collapsed. But as details emerged, it appeared that the crush had occurred after celebrants slipped on stone steps leading into a narrow passageway with a metal-floored slope, setting off what the news site Ynet described as a "human avalanche."

The annual gathering on Mount Meron, which is in the Galilee, takes place near the mystical city of Safed. The Lag b'Omer holiday is linked in Jewish tradition to the Bar Kokhba revolt against the Romans in the second century A.D.

extra

Letters to God Department

The Israel Postal service has a special Letters to God department, for all the letters arriving in Jerusalem from around the world addressed to God. They are opened and placed into the cracks of the Western Wall.

Each year, large numbers of ultra-Orthodox and traditional Jews make the pilgrimage to the mountain for days of festivities. They light bonfires around the grave site of a second-century sage, Rabbi Shimon Bar Yochai, in the hope that they will receive his blessings on the anniversary of his death.

The pilgrimage was held this year (2021) despite warnings from Israeli health officials that it could become a Covid-19 superspreader event. That is what appears to have happened in India when a vast Hindu celebration Kumbh Mela was permitted to take place.

Israel and Hamas Agree to a Ceasefire

Israel and Palestinian militant group Hamas fought for 11 days starting on May 10 in the worst conflict between the two sides since 2014. When both sides agreed to a ceasefire on May 21 following pressure from the U.S. and its allies, the conflict had taken a toll on 248 Palestinians, including 66 children, and 12 Israelis.

Smoke Rises Following an Israeli Air Raid on a Building in Gaza

The genesis of the conflict was the implementation of a court order by Israeli authorities.

In October 2020, an Israeli court had ruled that several Palestinian families living in Sheikh Jarrah—a neighborhood in East Jerusalem—were to be evicted by May 2021 with their land handed over to Jewish families. In February 2021, several Palestinian families from Sheikh Jarrah filed an appeal to the court ruling.

In late April 2021, Palestinians began demonstrating in the streets of Jerusalem to protest the pending evictions and residents of Sheikh Jarrah—along with other activists—began to host nightly sit-ins. In early May, after a court ruled in favour of the evictions, the protests expanded with Israeli police deploying force against demonstrators. On May 7, following weeks of daily demonstrations and rising tensions between protesters, Israeli settlers, and police during the month of Ramadan, violence broke out at the al-Aqsa Mosque compound in Jerusalem, with Israeli police using stun grenades, rubber bullets, and water cannons in a clash with protestors that left hundreds of Palestinians wounded.

After the clashes in Jerusalem's Old City, tensions increased throughout East Jerusalem, compounded by the celebration of Jerusalem Day. On May 10, after several consecutive days of violence throughout Jerusalem and the use of lethal and nonlethal force by Israeli police, Hamas, the militant group which governs Gaza, and other Palestinian militant groups launched hundreds of rockets into Israeli territory. Israel responded with air strikes and later artillery bombardments against targets in Gaza, including launching several air strikes that killed more than twenty Palestinians. While claiming to target Hamas, other militants, and their infrastructure—including tunnels and rocket launchers—Israel expanded its aerial campaign and struck targets including residential buildings, media headquarters, and refugee and healthcare facilities.

On May 21, Israel and Hamas agreed to a cease-fire, brokered by Egypt, with both sides claiming victory and no reported violations. More than two hundred and fifty Palestinians were killed and nearly two thousand others wounded, and at least thirteen Israelis were killed over the eleven days of fighting. Authorities in Gaza estimate that tens of millions of dollars of damage was done, and the United Nations estimates that more than 72,000 Palestinians were displaced by the fighting.

Chile to Draft New Constitution

Independent and opposition candidates have won a key two-thirds of seats in the body that will write a new constitution in Chile.

In May 2021, voters in Chile elected a left-leaning special assembly to draft a new constitution, which is expected to pave the way for a significant increase in social spending and the state's role in the economy while weakening the country's free-market model.

The result of the vote delivered a major blow to traditional, centrist political parties that have ruled Chile since its return to democracy 30 years ago, including President Sebastian Piñera's conservative coalition.

Mr. Piñera's Let's Go Chile group won 37 seats in the 155-member assembly, surprising political analysts as it fell short of securing at least one-third of the delegates needed to have veto power over new articles in the constitution. In total, about 70% of the assembly's seats went to left-leaning groups and independent delegates, most of whom are anti-party leftists.

Chile embarked on replacing its dictatorship-era constitution after protests rocked the nation in 2019. The demonstrations were sparked by high-school students in Santiago upset about an increase in subway fares, but quickly expanded across the nation and to include a range of social grievances such

Supporters of Left-wing Parties Celebrate in Santiago

as inequality, education, healthcare and pensions. The protests often turned violent, as young men burned churches and looted grocery stores while human-rights groups documented many police abuses.

To quell the demonstrations, Piñera agreed to write a new constitution, replacing the one drafted in 1980 during the military dictatorship of Gen. Augusto Pinochet. The election for the special assembly was delayed due to the Covid-19pandemic, which led to a surge in infectionsin 2021 despite one of the world's most successful vaccination campaigns.

The new assembly, which includes gender parity and 17 seats reserved for indigenous delegates, will write a new charter. The new constitution must be approved in a referendum, expected in the second half of 2022.

Opponents of the current constitution say it is illegitimate as it was written during a dictatorship and blame it for stifling social reforms. But many Chileans credit the charter for laying the foundation for years of stability and robust growth that cut poverty amid strong protections for private property and enshrining central-bank autonomy.

Naftali Bennett is Sworn in as Israel PM

Naftali Bennett was sworn in as Israel's new prime minister on June 13, after

Naftali Bennett Greets his Supporters

winning a confidence vote with the narrowest of margins, just 60 votes to 59. His victory ended a 12-year grip on power by former prime minister Benjamin Netanyahu, the country's longest-serving leader.

Bennett became the premier as the leader of Yamina, a right-wing party with only seven seats in Israel's parliament, the Knesset, making him the only prime minister in the country's history with such a small faction. By contrast, Netanyahu's Likud party won 30 seats in March's election. Once again, however, Netanyahu could not cobble together a governing coalition with a majority of the 120 members of Knesset.

Bennett's path to victory seemed all but lost during 11 days of fighting between Israel and Palestinian militants in May, when Netanyahu appeared to scuttle any chances of the opposition parties forming a government to replace him. But Yair Lapid, head of the centrist Yesh Atid party which holds 17 seats, forged the agreements between the different parties that led to the end of Netanyahu's grip on power. The arrangement placed Bennett at the head of a coalition that includes right-wing, left-wing, and Arab parties, united largely by their desire to dethrone Netanyahu.

These disparate interests will challenge the coalition to find common ground on key issues, such as what policy to pursue with the Palestinian Authority in the West Bank or how to manage the relationship with Gaza. The international community, including the United States, are pushing for the renewal of a peace process between the Israelis and Palestinians, but this government is ill-equipped to handle such negotiations, since two of the parties are vocally opposed to the establishment of a Palestinian state.

Instead, Bennett will focus on domestic issues during his two years as prime minister, before he hands the reins to Lapid according to their coalition agreement. These will include the relationship between religion and state, the cost of living, and quality of life issues. Israel also has not passed a budget since March 2018; the newly anointed government has three months to enact one or the Knesset will dissolve and the country will once again head to elections by law.

Takeaways from the Biden-Putin Summit

U.S. President Joe Biden and his Russian counterpart, Vladimir Putin, met in Geneva, Switzerland, on June 16 for their first in-person summit as the relationship between their two countries worsened to its lowest level in decades. The meeting was seen as an effort by both countries to establish ground rules to ease tensions

U.S. President Joe Biden and Russian President Vladimir Putin

in the wake of a series of cyberattacks attributed to Russian hackers, sanctions over Moscow's alleged interference in the 2020 U.S. presidential elections, and a rally of diplomatic expulsions.

After nearly four hours of meetings, Biden and Putin held separate press conferences, where they characterized the summit as productive and outlined a limited range of areas for further discussion on cybersecurity and prisoner exchanges. In a joint communiqué issued after the meeting, the two presidents reaffirmed their commitment to averting nuclear war and announced plans to resume strategic stability talks to lay the groundwork for future arms control negotiations.

Here are some of the key takeaways from the Geneva meeting.

1. Restoration of Diplomatic Ties: The leaders discussed and agreed to the return of US and Russian ambassadors to the embassies in Moscow and Washington respectively.

2. Cyber Security: Another highlight of the meeting was Biden's willingness to engage with Russia in the domain of cyber security. This is an important development given that the U.S. has often linked several cyber-attacks to Russia. This includes alleged interference in the US presidential election in 2016 and 2020. In the weeks leading up to the summit as well, ransom-ware hacks on the Colonial pipeline along the U.S. East Coast and a major U.S. beef producer-JBS, had also been linked to Russia. Both countries have now agreed to delegate experts to start consultations on cyber security. Biden gave Putin a list of about sixteen critical elements of infrastructure that should be 'off limits' for cyber attacks, coupled with a vow to retaliate forcefully if Russia launches such attacks.

3. Arms Control: A joint statement on strategic stability was signed and both sides announced their decision to launch a 'deliberate' and 'robust' integrated bilateral Strategic Stability Dialogue "to lay the groundwork for future arms control and risk reduction measures."

4. Ukraine and NATO: President Biden reaffirmed his support for the Minsk accords. Meanwhile, the NATO statement calls for the full implementation of the Minsk Agreements by all sides, and supports the efforts of the Normandy format and the Trilateral Contact Group.

5. Human Rights and Political Freedom: The issue of Alexey Navalny's alleged poisoning and subsequent imprisonment upon return to Russia was also taken up in the summit. A related issue was that of a ban on Navalny's political network and restrictions on the U.S. funded Radio Free Europe and Radio Liberty which have been designated as "foreign agents" by the Russian government. While Putin in his statements has likened Navalny to any other convict, Biden was more forthcoming in his remarks on the matter. He noted in his media briefing of "disastrous consequences" if Navalny were to die in prison.

Abiy Ahmed Wins Landslide Victory in Ethiopian Election

Prime Minister Abiy Ahmed's Prosperity Party won the most seats in Ethiopia's parliamentary election. Abiy had hailed the June 21 vote as the country's first free and fair election after decades of

Churchill's Iron Curtain Speech

extra

During a speech at Fulton in Missouri in the United States on March 5, 1946, visiting British Prime Minister Winston Churchill proclaimed that Europe was divided by an "Iron Curtain" as the nations of Eastern Europe fell increasingly under Soviet control.

Prime Minister Abiy Ahmed

repressive rule. Abiy's party won 410 of 436 parliamentary seats. The leader of the main opposition Ethiopian Citizens for Social Justice party, Birhanu Nega, lost, while opposition parties won just 11 seats.

The vote was a test for Abiy, who came to power in April 2018 after the former prime minister resigned amid widespread protests. Abiy oversaw dramatic political reforms, but critics say he is backtracking from some promises on political and media freedoms. He also has drawn intense international criticism for his handling of the conflict in the Tigray region has that left thousands of people dead.

The election, which had been postponed twice because of the Covid-19 pandemic and logistical problems, was largely peaceful, but opposition parties decried harassment and intimidation.

The Prosperity party was formed after the dismantling of Ethiopia's former ruling coalition. Disagreements over that decision signalled the first tensions between Abiy and Tigray leaders that finally led to the conflict erupting in November.

No date has been set for voting in Tigray, where the military has been battling forces loyal to the Tigray People's Liberation Front (TPLF), the region's former ruling party, since November 2020. The fighting has displaced 2 million people, and the United Nations has warned of famine conditions in parts of the region.

At the end of June 2021, the TPLF seized control of most of Tigray and the regional capital Mekelle, eight months after the conflict erupted.

The government announced a unilateral ceasefire after days of TPLF advances. The TPLF presented a list of seven demands that it says are a precondition for a ceasefire, including the withdrawal of the military and its allies from parts of Tigray currently administered by the neighbouring region of Amhara, which also claims the land.

The Chinese Communist Party Turns 100

On July 1, 2021, China celebrated the 100th anniversary of the founding of the Chinese Communist Party (CCP). The capstone of the celebrations was the lengthy speech given by Xi Jinping from the top of Tiananmen Gate – the same gate where Mao Zedong had declared the founding of the People's Republic of China on October 1, 1949. According to Xi, China's two centenary goals are to "build a moderately prosperous society in all respects" by 2021 and "build a modern socialist country that is prosperous, strong, democratic, culturally advanced and harmonious" by 2049, the 100th anniversary of the People's Republic of China.

Origin of the Communist Party

Inspired by Russia's October Revolution which broke out in 1917, about a dozen people secretly founded the Chinese Communist Party (CCP) in July 1921 at its first congress in Shanghai, then a French concession.

CCP's Structure

The CCP's structure is as follows. Once every five years or so, a National Party Congress of some 2,000 delegates (the number varies) meets in plenary session to elect a Central Committee of about 200 full members, which in turn meets at least once annually. The Central Committee elects a Political Bureau (Politburo) of about 20–25 full members; that body is the ruling leadership of the CCP. The Political Bureau's Standing Committee of about six to nine of its most-authoritative members is the highest echelon of leadership in the CCP and in the country as a whole. In practice, power flows from the top down in the CCP.

Members of the Party

On June 5, 2021, the Chinese Communist Party (CCP) had about 95.15 million members, making it the second largest political party in the world. The CCP is the sole governing political party in China and it pervades all parts of the Chinese society. Over the years, the number of its members has been increasing constantly. Looking at the professions of CCP members reveals that the party still upholds its tradition as the mouthpiece of the proletariat. Around 27 percent of party members were farmers, herders, and fishermen in 2021. The share of women in the party has been growing in past years and reached around 29 percent in 2021, up from 22.5 percent in 2010. Ethnic minority groups play an important role in the self-representation of the party as a unifying force in the country. Minority groups are comparatively well represented among party members, with a share slightly larger than the minorities' proportion in the total population. However, this share is still well below 10 percent.

How Does One Join the Party

Joining the party is usually an arduous process that can take two to three years. Potential members must apply to their local party organisations, initiating a multi-year process with more than 20 steps to determine their qualification, including submitting a formal application, meeting with the local party organisers and attending party study sessions. Candidates also need a party member to act as a guide and mentor, who they often find through party organisations at their work and schools. After about a year of study, applicants need to pass written tests. They must also pass background checks – those with criminal records or whose family members have such records may fail these. If they pass all of these steps, applicants still have to go through a probation period of at least a year before the party branch decides whether to admit them.

Membership cards

Members must pay dues set at 0.5 per cent to 2 per cent of their income. Under Xi, the party has encouraged party members to wear the party badge to show their affiliation.

South Africa Reels from the Worst Violence Since Apartheid

In July 2021, South Africa was rocked by the worst violence since the nation achieved democracy in 1994. More than

China's GDP

extra

China's economic growth slowed in the July-to-September quarter of 2021, to 4.9% compared with the same period last year. It was down from 7.9% in April-June and rose just 0.2% quarter-on-quarter

350 people died during the riots and property worth $3.3 billion was damaged or destroyed. Hundreds of businesses, including entire malls and key parts of government infrastructure, were burnt down.

The unrest began on July 8 when former President Jacob Zuma started serving a 15-month prison sentence for contempt of court. Supporters in his home province of KwaZulu-Natal set up roadblocks on major highways and burned about 20 trucks. The protests closed the N3 and N2 highways, which link the Indian Ocean ports of Durban and Richard's Bay to the industrial hub of Johannesburg and to Cape Town.

A Scene of Arson in South Africa

The unrest spread within KwaZulu-Natal, where shopping malls and centres were ransacked by mobs that took food, electronics, clothes and liquor. Attacks on retail centres also spread inland to Gauteng province, to Johannesburg, the country's largest city, and to Pretoria, the capital. In Durban and Pietermaritzburg, crowds attacked warehouses for major retailers and factories, which were set alight. Several burned until their roofs collapsed. The unrest lasted for a week until 25,000 army troops were deployed.

Durban has a history of race riots. In 1949, during the apartheid era, 149 people died in clashes between the black majority and people of Indian descent. The apartheid government was happy at the prospect of disunity between blacks and the Indian community.

Extensive damage was done to 161 malls and shopping centres, 11 warehouses, eight factories and 161 liquor stores and distributors, according to the government.

Zambia's Opposition Leader Wins Presidential Election

Hakainde Hichilema was on August 16 declared the winner of Zambia's presidential election. He had failed in five previous attempts at winning the presidency. The incumbent president Edgar Lungu had used every trick up his sleeve to stay in power.

Hakainde Hichilema's election victory is the third time an opposition leader has unseated an incumbent president in Zambia since 1991. The victory bequeaths on the new president and his party, the United Party for National Development (UPND), the immense task of restoring the rule of law, fixing the ailing economy and uniting a divided nation.

Hichilema won the poll with 59.38% of the vote. He secured a 1 million-vote lead over his closest rival and incumbent, Edgar Lungu of the Patriotic Front. Lungu polled 38.33%.

The election was effectively a referendum on Lungu and the conduct of his party during his tenure from 2015 to 2021. Zambians opted to believe in the campaign promises of his opponent.

Hakainde Hichilema

Hichilema promised to grow the economy to alleviate people's suffering, restore the rule of law and end corruption .

Contested Candidacy

Lungu's candidature was controversial and highly contested. He completed his predecessor, the late Michael Sata's unfinished term in 2016. He then served a full five-year term after beating Hichilema in elections held that same year by a narrow margin.

In 2021 Lungu was contesting for office in what some argued would effectively be a third term. The Constitutional Court was thrice petitioned to declare him ineligible. The court ruled in Lungu's favour on all the occasions. It found that he had served only a year, not a full presidential term, between 2015 and 2016 after Sata's death. This made him eligible to contest the polls in 2021.

In the end it was the ballot box that ended his tenure. The arrogance of power displayed by the Patriotic Front in defying the concerns of the country's citizens in the way it ran the affairs of state drove voters to voice their displeasure.

There were a number of reasons the electorate decided to back his opponent.

Zambians were irked by the decline of democracy under Lungu, as shown by intimidation, harassment and arrests of members of the oposition, and critics of the government. Human rights violations were on the rise.

Unemployed young people and households struggling to meet basic needs against escalating prices of essential commodities blamed the government for the worsening conditions

U.S. Withdraws from Afghanistan

The US on August 30 brought an end to its 20-year war in Afghanistan, withdrawing its last remaining troops and concluding a huge and chaotic airlift that evacuated more than 120,000 civilians but left thousands of others stranded.

The withdrawal signalled the end of the longest war in U. S. history, a conflict that began shortly after the Sept. 11 attacks in 2001. The Taliban — which controlled most of Afghanistan at the time — refused to hand over Osama bin

Taliban Special Forces Stand Guard at Kabul Airport

Laden, prompting the United States, allied countries and local fighters to push the hardline fundamentalist group from power. But the Taliban regrouped and kept carrying out insurgent attacks, and the U.S. military began a two-decade process of countering the Taliban and assisting the new Afghan government, leading to more than 2,000 U.S. troop deaths and over $2 trillion in estimated costs. Amid bipartisan weariness over the war, former President Donald Trump struck a deal with the Taliban in 2020 to pull all U.S. personnel from the country by May 2021. Biden extended this deadline by several months but still pushed to leave Afghanistan. As the United States began pulling troops by August 31, the Taliban rapidly took over territory. The U.S.-backed government crumbled more quickly than expected, and the Taliban entered Kabul by mid-August, cementing the group's return to power in Afghanistan after a 20-year-long effort by the United States to defeat it. The U.S. military spent its final weeks in Afghanistan occupying Kabul's airport and flying out evacuees, a mission interrupted by an Islamic State-linked suicide bombing that killed more than 100 civilians and 13 U.S. personnel, likely the war's final American troop deaths.

The Biden administration says it will maintain an ability to conduct airstrikes against terrorist groups in Afghanistan, likely flying from a U.S. military base in the Persian Gulf. The United States has carried out at least two attacks from the air in recent days. A drone strike killed two operatives of Islamic State-Khorasan (a local Islamic State affiliate also known as IS-K or ISIS-K) in eastern Afghanistan on Friday, the Pentagon said, and a Sunday airstrike in Kabul targeted IS-K and reportedly led to several civilian casualties.

Taliban Returns to Power in Afghanistan

The Taliban have returned to power in Afghanistan twenty years after their ouster by U.S. troops, sparking concerns that they will impose harsh rule, neglect to provide basic services, and abuse human rights.

The Taliban on Septembe 7 announced an interim government in Afghanistan, declaring the country an "Islamic Emirate". The Taliban appointed Mohammad Hasan Akhund, a close aide to the group's late founder Mullah Omar, as head of Afghanistan's new caretaker government. The list of cabinet members announced by chief spokesman Zabihullah Mujahid was dominated by members of the group's old guard, with no women included. Abdul Ghani Baradar, the head of the Taliban's political office, was named as the deputy leader while Sirajuddin Haqqani, son of the founder of the Haqqani Network, was appointed as interior minister.

Taliban Leaders in Kabul

Mullah Mohammad Yaqoob, son of Mullah Omar, was named as defence minister. Hedayatullah Badri was named as the acting minister of finance, while Amir Khan Muttaqi, a Taliban negotiator in Doha, was named foreign minister.

The Taliban are a predominantly Pashtun, Islamic fundamentalist group that returned to power in Afghanistan in 2021 after waging a twenty-year insurgency.

Following the U.S.-led invasion that toppled the original regime in 2001, the Taliban regrouped across the border in Pakistan and began taking back territory less than ten years after their ouster. By August 2021, the Taliban had seized most major cities, including the capital of Kabul. The group's swift offensive came as the United States withdrew its remaining troops from Afghanistan as outlined in a 2020 peace agreement with the Taliban.

The Taliban are likely to impose harsh rule despite their pledges to respect the rights of women and minority communities and provide amnesty for people who supported U.S. efforts.

The AUKUS Nuclear Submarine Deal

On September 15, the Biden administration unveiled a historic security partnership in the Indo-Pacific region between the U.S., Australia and the U.K., known as AUKUS. As part of the deal's terms and conditions, the United States and the United Kingdom will help Australia build and deploy nuclear-powered submarines,

Why Nuclear-powered Submarines?

These submarines are much faster and harder to detect than conventionally powered fleets. They can stay submerged for months, shoot missiles longer distances and also carry more.

Having them stationed in Australia is critical to US influence in the region, analysts say.

The US is sharing its submarine technology for the first time in 50 years. It had previously only shared technology with the UK.

Australia will become just the seventh nation in the world to operate nuclear-powered submarines, after the US, UK, France, China, India and Russia.

Australia has reaffirmed it has no intention of obtaining nuclear weapons.

Meanwhile New Zealand said it would ban Australia's submarines from its waters, in line with an existing policy on the presence of nuclear-powered submarines.

as well as share and cooperate on other technologies, such as cyber, artificial intelligence and quantum computing.

One consequence of this deal was Australia cancelling a contract, worth tens of billions of dollars, signed in 2016 with France for diesel-electric submarines.

The cancelling of the contract created a row with France which lost a deal with Australia to build 12 submarines. The new partnership was announced in a joint virtual press conference between US President Joe Biden, UK Prime Minister Boris Johnson and his Australian counterpart Scott Morrison. And while China was not mentioned directly, the three leaders referred repeatedly to regional security concerns which they said had "grown significantly".

The AUKUS partnership also signals a shift in strategy for Australia, whose diplomatic rows with Beijing have resulted in Chinese reprisals in the form of coercive trade restrictions in the past year. The newly formed security pact effectively means Canberra has formally taken sides with the U.S. against China.

Leaders Behind the AUKUS Nuclear Deal

World Bank Suspends its Doing Business Report

On September 16, 2021 the World Bank suspended publication of the Doing Business Report (DBR). The World Bank discontinued the publication of its global business climate index after identifying "irregularities" in its data that may have affected the ranking of four countries. The cancellation follows publication of internal audits and reviews into the irregularities that revealed serious ethical concerns of data manipulation, shattering trust in the DBR.

The annual Doing Business report, launched in 2002, has become an influential global metric to assess the business environment and relative competitiveness of countries. A country moving up in the rankings tends to boost foreign direct investment.

Cancellation of the DBR comes after data irregularities were found in the 2018 and 2020 reports. The four countries most affected by the irregularities in

the 2020 and 2018 reports, were China, Saudi Arabia, the United Arab Emirates and Azerbaijan. Audits revealed serious ethical concerns of data manipulation – shattering trust in the rankings. An explosive external review delivered to the Bank's Board of Executive Directors exposed how senior Bank officials applied pressure to manipulate data in order to improve rankings for select countries.

Notably, the independent report exposed how then-Bank CEO (and current IMF Managing Director) Kristalina Georgieva applied "pressure" to "make specific changes to China's data points in an effort to increase its ranking for the 2018 DBR," at a time the country was expected to increase its financial contribution to the Bank's capital. Then-World Bank President Dr. Jim Yong Kim was also indirectly implicated in the effort to increase China's ranking.

Simeon Jankov, one of the founders of the DBR and a senior Bank official was also incriminated in altering Saudi Arabia's data to boost the country's ranking, in an effort to reward the country for the "important role it played in the Bank community."

Saudi Arabia had previously implemented a series of Reimbursable Advisory Services (RAS) projects – paid advisory services provided by the Bank, some of which focus on improving economic indicators scored on the DBR. Elevating Saudi Arabia to first place in the Top Improvers list was done to "demonstrate the effectiveness of the Bank's efforts and validate the amount of money Saudi Arabia had spent on RAS projects relating to the Doing Business Report."

While shocking, these revelations are not the first charges of data manipulation brought against the Bank's flagship publication. In 2018, the World Bank's then-Chief Economist, Paul Romer exposed how DBR scores for Chile were skewed and politically manipulated to disfavour Michelle Bachelet's progressive government.

Pro-Putin Party Sweeps to Election Victory in Russia

Russia's ruling United Russia party, which supports President Vladimir Putin, retained its majority in parliament in the parliament election held from September 17 to 19. With all the votes tallied, the electoral commission said that United Russia had won 49.83% of the vote. While the pro-Kremlin force got a comfortable majority, it lost the ground it made in the 2016 elections, when it secured 54% of the vote. The Communist Party, which usually supports the Kremlin, garnered nearly 19% of the vote. The pro-Kremlin nationalist LDPR party and the Fair Russia party also each brought in around 7.5% of the vote. A new pro-Putin party called New People also managed to win seats in parliament for the first time, having garnered just over 5% of the vote.

Voter turnout stood at 45.15%, the election commission noted, down from 47.8% in the last election in 2016. United Russia has been the dominant party in the country for decades and it enthusiastically supports Putin, although he has run as an independent candidate since 2018.

Critics of the Kremlin say there were multiple examples of electoral irregularities and fraud in the election, including

Election Officials Engaged in Sorting of Ballots

cases of ballot stuffing and the obstruction of impartial observation of the voting. Navalny's press secretary was among those querying the slow publication of electronic votes in Moscow, where United Russia tends to perform less well than in other regions.

Retaining the party's dominance in the State Duma was widely seen as crucial for the Kremlin ahead of Russia's presidential election in 2024. President Vladimir Putin's current term expires that year, and he is expected either to seek re-election or to choose another strategy to stay in power.

A parliament the Kremlin can control could be key to both scenarios, analysts and Kremlin critics say.

Justin Trudeau is Again Prime Minister

Prime Minister Justin Trudeau won a third term in Canada's snap election held on September 20. But his hope of gaining a majority in the House of Commons was dashed, forcing him to rely on smaller parties, especially the left-leaning New Democrats (NDP) to form a government.

Trudeau's Liberal Party won in 160 of the 338 seats in the House of Commons. That's three more seat than he won in the last election in 2019.The Liberals set a record for the lowest vote share of a party that would go on to form government, winning 32.6% of the popular vote, while losing the popular vote to the Conservatives as they did in 2019. The main opposition Conservatives, under Erin O'Toole, won 119 seats, two fewer than last time.

Overall, the result leaves parliament little changed from what it was before Trudeau called the vote — a stable minority that gives the prime minister license to continue pursuing a pre-election big-spending agenda that had already received parliamentary backing earlier in 2021. In addition, Trudeau should easily find support in the legislature to press ahead with new campaign pledges such as raising taxes on financial institutions and imposing stricter emission rules for the oil and gas sector.

Justin Trudeau

Other initiatives expected to be brought forward quickly include new regulations that will compel media stream services and social platforms like Netflix Inc. and TikTok Inc. to finance and promote Canadian content. Trudeau had

extra

Russia's Largest Political Party

United Russia, founded in 2001, is the country's largest political party. It supports the policies of the Russian president and government.

introduced a bill to regulate the sector in the previous parliament that never won passage through the Senate before the election was called.

The Liberal victory is a historic milestone for Trudeau, marking only the eighth time a Canadian leader has won three successive elections. Trudeau's father, Pierre, also did it. It also represents a comeback of sorts for Trudeau, whose party was trailing in the polls midway through the five-week campaign.

But the outcome is also a rebuke of Trudeau's decision to call a snap election that many Canadians saw as a power grab while the Covid-19 pandemic still rages. It's the second time voters have denied Trudeau full control of the legislature, limiting his freedom to take big risks or govern unilaterally.

China Scores a Victory Over Meng Wanzhou's Release

On September 25, Huawei's chief financial executive Meng Wanzhou was released from house arrest in Vancouver after reaching a breakthrough deal with the U.S. Justice Department. Over the years, Wanzhou's case had become an irritant in straining U.S.-China relations. Around the time Meng took off for Shenzhen, home to Huawei's headquarters, China released two Canadians who had been detained on spying charges. Beijing has repeatedly denied connections between the detention of the two Canadians and Meng's arrest.

Meng Wanzhou, 49-year-old Chief Financial Officer of Huawei Technologies, was arrested on December 1, 2018, at the Vancouver International Airport by the Canadian authorities on instruction from the United States. Wanzhou, daughter of the founder of Huawei Technologies, a Chinese tech company, had joined Huawei in 1993. She had been fighting extradition to the US, since her arrest in 2018.

Wanzhou was accused of bank and wire fraud charges for allegedly misleading HSBC bank in 2013 about Huawei's business dealings in Iran. Huawei allegedly defrauded financial institutions to clear transactions and provide financial assistance to Huawei's Iran-based sister company Skycom — which was against US sanctions imposed on Iran.

Meng, the daughter of Huawei's founder Ren Zhengfei, entered an agreement with the U.S. Justice Department in which she admitted to some wrongdoing while prosecutors deferred wire and bank fraud charges against her and could dismiss the indictment in 2022.

Grand Welcome for Meng Wanzhou at Shenzhen Airport in China

Through a remote court appearance via video on September 24, Meng pleaded not guilty to charges of conspiracy to commit bank fraud, conspiracy to commit wire fraud, bank fraud and wire fraud. However, she admitted to the basic facts underpinning the DOJ's charges, which include "multiple material misrepresentations to a senior executive of a financial institution regarding Huawei's business operations in Iran in an effort to preserve Huawei's banking relationship with the financial institution."

German Election 2021

Germany's parliamentary elections on Sept. 26 signaled the end of Chancellor Angela Merkel's 16 years in power. With Merkel deciding not to seek reelection, it is the first postwar vote where the incumbent chancellor has not fought for a new term. In fact, her absence deeply hurt her Christian Democratic Union party.

With 25.7% of total votes, the Social Democratic Party of Germany (SPD) recorded their best result since 2005, and emerged as the largest party for the first time since 2002. The ruling CDU/CSU, which had led a grand coalition with the SPD since 2013, recorded their worst ever result with 24.1%, a significant decline from 32.9% in 2017. Alliance 90/ The Greens achieved their best result in history at 14.8%, while the Free Democratic Party (FDP) made small gains and finished on 11.5%. The Alternative for Germany (AfD) fell from third to fifth place with 10.3%, a decline of 2.3 percentage points. The Left suffered their worst showing since their official formation in 2007, failing to cross the 5% electoral threshold by just over one-tenth of a percentage point. The party was nonetheless entitled to full proportional representation, as it won three direct constituencies.

With complex governing coalition talks required for the formation of a majority government, the FDP and the Greens are considered kingmakers, and a three-party coalition with either the CDU/CSU or the SPD is a likely outcome. A fifth grand coalition has been dismissed by both the CDU/CSU and the SPD.

Leaders of German Political Parties

Both Olaf Scholz, the SPD's chancellor-candidate, and Armin Laschet of the CDU/CSU have claimed a mandate to try to form a government. Both have their eyes on three-way deals with the Greens and the liberal Free Democrats: either a "traffic-light" coalition led by the SPD or a "Jamaica" combination headed by the CDU/CSU. But after Laschet's wretched campaign, resulting in the CDU/CSU's worst result ever, Scholz has the edge.

Traffic Light Coalition and Jamaica Coalition

The traffic light coalition is so-called because it is made up of the red colour of the SPD, the yellow of the Free Democrats (FPD), and the green of the Greens.

The Jamaican coalition is so-named because it is the colours of the Jamaican flag: the black of the CDU/CSU, green (Greens), and yellow (FDP).

Fumio Kishida Elected as New Japanese PM

Fumio Kishida was elected Japan's 100th prime minister on October 4–just days after the ruling Liberal Democratic Party (LDP) picked him as leader.

The 64-year-old succeeded Yoshihide Suga, who bowed out in September amid anger over his government's COVID-19 response and his insistence to push through with the 2020 Tokyo Olympics.

On Sept. 29, Kishida beat the head of Japan's COVID-19 vaccination programme, Taro Kono, in a poll of LDP lawmakers and rank-and-file party members. His election as prime minister was all-but assured, because the LDP and its allies control the country's legislature, the National Diet.

Kishida, a longtime party stalwart, won the LDP leadership after a deal among party power-brokers—despite

Fumio Kishida

what many political observers say is his lack of personal appeal and much broader public support for Kono. Kishida was supported by one of the LDP's largest factions, but only led Kono by one vote in the first round of party voting.

Kishida's predecessor Yoshihide Suga enjoyed support ratings of about 70% soon after taking office in 2020 but came under heavy fire over his handling of the pandemic. Following Suga's decision to make way for a new face, Kishida beat three contenders for the LDP leadership, paving the way for parliament to formally elect him premier on October 4.

Observers say Japan's new leader will have to address long-standing issues such as the aging population and threats brought on by China's increasing assertiveness in the region, on top of helping the country recover from the COVID-19 pandemic.

Czech PM's Party Loses

Prime Minister Andrej Babis' centrist party narrowly lost the Czech Republic's parliamentary election held on October 8 and 9.

The two-day election to fill 200 seats in the lower house of the Czech Republic's parliament took place shortly after the International Consortium of Investigative Journalists reported details of Babis' overseas financial dealings in a project dubbed the "Pandora Papers." Babis, 67, has denied wrongdoing.

Babiš's ANO party came away with 27.34% of the vote and 72 seats in parliament. This was largely thanks to his support base of older voters and the more deprived regions of northern and western Bohemia and northern Moravia. The Spolu (Together) coalition, which brings together three traditional, right-of-centre political parties, squeaked past ANO with 27.56% of the vote to secure 71 seats in the parliament. The other coalition, that of the Pirate Party and an association of local mayors, gained 15.43% of the vote and 37 parliamentary seats.

The recently created liberal Pirate Party, primarily made up of middle-class professionals, flopped. It had 22 MPs in the parliament before this election and now has just four.

The election result proved a big setback for the country's oldest political party, the Social Democrats. Founded in 1893, they have failed to meet the 5% vote-share threshold to win any seats in parliament, because most of the original social democratic voters voted for Babiš. The Communists, successors to the pre-1989 totalitarian party, are history too.

Leader of Spolu Petr Fiala, Centre, at the Party's Headquarters

Prior to the election, the populist billionaire Babis led a minority coalition government of ANO and the Social Democrats in the Eastern European country of 10.7 million people, which is a member of both the European Union and NATO. He has also governed with the support of the maverick Communists.

Any new government has to win a parliamentary confidence vote to rule, however, and Babis and his potential partner, the Freedom party, don't have enough support for that.

Pandora Papers Expose Hidden Riches of World Leaders and Billionaires

The Pandora Papers is a leak of almost 12 million documents that reveals hidden wealth, tax avoidance and, in some cases, money laundering by some of the world's rich and powerful.

More than 600 journalists in 117 countries were involved in trawling through the files from 14 sources for months, finding stories. The data was obtained by the International Consortium of Investigative Journalists (ICIJ) in Washington DC, which has been working with more than 140 media organisations on its biggest ever global investigation.

The Pandora Papers have uncovered financial secrets of 35 current and former world leaders, more than 330 politicians and public officials in 91 countries and territories, and a global lineup of fugitives, con artists and murderers.

The secret documents expose offshore dealings of the King of Jordan, the presidents of Ukraine, Kenya and Ecuador, the prime minister of the Czech Republic and former British Prime Minister Tony Blair. The files also detail financial activities of Russian President Vladimir Putin's "unofficial minister of propaganda" and more than 130 billionaires from Russia, the United States, Turkey and other nations.

More than 300 Indians also find their names mentioned in the Pandora papers. Anil Ambani, Vinod Adani, Jackie Shroff, Kiran Mazumdar-Shaw, Niira Radia, Sachin Tendulkar and Satish Sharma, among others, figure in the list of Indians in the 'Pandora Papers' revealed so far.

The Pandora Papers leak includes 6.4 million documents, almost three million images, more than a million emails and almost half-a-million spreadsheets.

Why is it Called "Pandora Papers"?

The project is called Pandora Papers because the investigation builds upon previous ICIJ-led collaborations, the Panama and Paradise Papers; the ancient myth of Pandora's Box evokes an outpouring of trouble and woe.

What are Tax Havens?

Offshore tax havens, or offshore financial centres, are generally countries or places with low or no corporate taxes that allow outsiders to easily set up businesses there. Tax havens also typically limit public disclosure about companies and their owners. Because information can be hard to extract, tax havens are sometimes also called secrecy jurisdictions. Financial secrecy is commonly associated with small island territories like the British Virgin Islands or the Cayman Islands, which help shelter wealth from all around the world — hence the "offshore" moniker.

Deaths - India

Soumitra Chatterjee

Soumitra Chatterjee, Bengali superstar and one of India's tallest actors, widely admired for his roles as Apu and Feluda, died at the age of 85 on November 15 in Kolkata. Chatterjee was perhaps best-known for his work with Ray, one of the world's most influential directors and maker of the much-feted Apu Trilogy. The series followed the life of a man who grew up in a Bengali village. The films garnered critical acclaim, winning many awards worldwide, and put Indian cinema on the global map. The third movie of the trilogy, *Apur Sansar*, which released in 1959, was also Chatterjee's debut film. He would go on to star as the lead actor in 14 of Ray's film. Chatterjee was awarded the Dada Saheb Phalke Award, the highest honour in Indian cinema, in 2012 and in 2018, he was given France's highest award, the Legion of Honour.

Tarun Gogoi

Tarun Gogoi, the longest-serving chief minister of Asom who was the mainstay of the state's political scene for nearly two decades, died on November 23 aged 86.As leader of the Congress party in Asom for over 50 years, Gogoi was first elected joint secretary of the All India Congress Committee (AICC) in 1976 under Prime Minister Indira Gandhi. He later served as general secretary of the AICC (1985–90) under Prime Minister Rajiv Gandhi.

Gogoi served six terms as a Lok Sabha MP from Asom. He first represented Jorhat for three terms between 1971 and 1985. He was later elected from Kaliabor in 1991-96 and then 1998-2002. The Kaliabor seat is currently held by his son Gaurav Gogoi.

Ahmed Patel

Ahmed Patel, senior Congress leader and closest political advisor to Gandhi family, died on November 25 aged 71. Patel's loyalty to the party along with his skillset saw him rise to become Rajiv Gandhi's first Parliament Secretary in 1984 following the latter's win in the general elections

During his tenure as head of Congress' Gujarat unit, Patel was responsible for setting up the Gujarat Rahat Samiti to help mobilise its cadres. In 1988, Ahmed Patel was appointed as the secretary of the Jawahar Bhavan Trust – a trust tasked with completing the construction of the Congress' new headquarters on New Delhi's Raisina Road. Patel enjoyed a unique relationship with Congress president Sonia Gandhi and was one of the party's key backroom strategists during the 10-year Congress-led United Progressive Alliance (UPA) rule.

Faqir Chand Kohli

Faqir Chand Kohli– the father of the Indian software revolution, a visionary who saw the future of technology, a mentor to many current top executives, founder and first CEO of Tata Consultancy Services, a master strategist that earned him the sobriquet of 'Bhishma Pitamaha' and a Padma Bhushan awardee --died on November 26 at the age of 96. Kohli was a legend who not only laid the very foundations on which India's prowess as a global software powerhouse has been built, Kohli also led innovations in far-ranging areas including adult literacy, water purification, software engineering, software automation, complex-systems and cybernetics.

Dharampal Gulati

Dharampal Gulati, owner of the household spices company Mahashian Di Hatti—also known as MDH—died on December 3 aged 97. Gulati successfully delivered its spices to every household in the country. The Padma Bhushan awardee expanded its spices kingdom overseas as well.

Ravi Patwardhan

Ravi Patwardhan, actor best known for his work in Hindi and Marathi cinema as well as theatre, died on December 5 aged 84. In his career, which began in the late 1970s, Ravi Patwardhan played a variety of roles in films, TV shows and plays. One of his notable Hindi film roles came in Tezaab. He also starred in movies like *Ankush, Jhanjaar, Bond and Yeshwant.* He was last seen in TV show *Aggabai Sasubai.*

Divya Bhatnagar

Divya Bhatnagar, Hindi television actress, died on December 7, 2020 aged 34. She was best known for her appearance in the daily soap *Yeh Rishta Kya Kehlata.* She was also seen in other television shows like *Jeet Gayi Toh Piyaa Morre* and *Udaan.*

Mangalesh Dabral

Mangalesh Dabral, popular Hindi poet and literary journalist, died on December 9 aged 72. Apart from his five collections of poetry — *Pahar Par Lalten, Ghar Ka Rasta, Ham Jo Dekhte Hain, Awaz Bhi Ek Jagah Hai* and *Naye Yug Men Shatru* — Dabral wrote two collections of prose,

2021 Sakharov Prize for Freedom of Thought

The European Parliament awarded its annual Sakharov prize to Alexei Navalny, Russia's leading opposition figure. The prize is the European Union's highest tribute to human rights defenders.

Lekhak Ki Roti and *Kavi Ka Akelapan*, and a travel diary, *Ek Bar Iowa.* He received the Sahitya Akademi Award in 2000 for *Ham Jo Dekhte Hain.*

Roddam Narasimha

Roddam Narasimha, the legendary aerospace scientist and fluid dynamicist, died on December 14 aged 87. He made significant contribution to the development of computing, aerospace technology as the initiator of the LCA programme, the space programme as the longest-serving member of the Space Commission, and in drafting the country's nuclear doctrine. He is most well-known for his work on fluid dynamics — a study of the flow of fluids (liquid or gas) — that includes modelling cloud flows, structure of shock waves, and fluid dynamics at atmospheric boundaries.He was conferred with the Padma Bhushan, India's third-highest civilian award, in 1987 and Padma Vibhushan, the second-highest, in 2013.

Motilal Vora

Motilal Vora, veteran Congress leader, died on December 21 aged 93. Starting out as a journalist, Vora occupied several key positions including being the Chief Minister of undivided Madhya Pradesh (MP) twice (1985-88 and 1989), health minister in Rajiv Gandhi's cabinet and Governor of Uttar Pradesh (UP) in mid-90s.

Known to be a loyalist of the Gandhi family, Vora served as Congress party's treasurer for 16 years and represented Chhattisgarh in the Rajya Sabha for four terms, until April 2020. Among the rare breed of senior leaders of the All India Congress Committee (AICC) who would be found in party headquarters with unfailing regularity, Vora was well-known for following a simple dictum: never leave behind any paper work when you leave your office for the day.

Sugathakumari

Sugathakumari, renowned Malayalam poet, conservationist and women's rights activist, died on December 25, 2020 aged 86. In 2006, she was bestowed the Padma Shri. In 2013, she was awarded the Saraswati Samman for her poem collection *Manalezhuthu (The Writing on the Sand)*. She also bagged almost all prestigious literary awards in the state, including Kerala Sahitya Akademi Award, Ezhuthachan Puraskaram and Vayalar Award and Odakkuzhal Award.

Dr Mahinder Watsa

Dr Mahinder Watsa, the sexologist whose candid newspaper column made him an urban legend of sorts, died on December 28 aged 96. Dr Watsa, a trained obstetrician-gynaecologist, was 80 when he began writing the now-famous daily sex advice column in the *Mumbai Mirror* newspaper. It quickly drew both interest and censure given that sex is still a taboo subject in most Indian households.

Buta Singh

Buta Singh, senior Congress leader and former Home Minister, died on January 2, 2021 aged 86. Singh, started out as a Communist before switching to the Shiromani Akali Dal, for a short stint and then joined the Congress in the early 1960s. A prominent Dalit leader in the Congress, he was convenor of the All India Congress Committee's (AICC) Harijan cell in 1973-74, after which he became the AICC general secretary in 1978. An eight time Lok Sabha MP, he entered Parliament in 1962 from the Moga Lok Sabha constituency in Punjab. In 1974, Prime Minister Indira Gandhi elevated him to the post of Deputy Minister for Railways. He was considered her close confidante and was involved in Operation Blue Star, which led to much outrage among the Sikh community. Later, as a Union Minister, he was also involved in reconstruction of the Golden Temple.

Madhav Singh Solanki

Madhav Singh Solanki, a veteran Congress leader who served as Chief Minister of Gujarat four times, died on January 9, 2021 aged 93. He was also External Affairs Minister of India during the 1991-92 period. He was a two term MP of Rajya Sabha from Gujarat. He had floated an idea of an alliance of Kshitriya, Harijan, Adivasi (tribal) and Muslim (KHAM) castes and communities in Gujarat for Congress to win elections. He had been the longest serving chief minister of the state before Narendra Modi became CM.

Myadam Kishan Rao

Myadam Kishan Rao, founder of Bambino Agro Food Industries Limited, known for the popular Bambino vermicelli, Ampro and Ganta brands, died on January 12 aged 85. He spearheaded and pioneered the vermicelli industry in India.

Ghulam Mustafa

Ut Ghulam Mustafa, one of the finest Hindustani classical vocalists and torchbearer of the Rampur Sahaswan gharana, died on January 17 aged 89. He was awarded the Padma Shri in 1991, followed by Padma Bhushan in 2006 and Padma Vibhushan in 2018. In 2003 he was awarded the Sangeet Natak Akademi award, the highest Indian recognition given to practising artistes.

Dr V Shanta

Dr V Shanta, renowned Indian oncologist and doyen of cancer care, died on January 19 aged 93. Dr V Shanta was also the chairperson of Adyar Cancer Institute.

The institute is known for providing state-of-the-art health care to all patients, irrespective of their economic condition. Born in 1927, Dr Shanta completed her MBBS from the Madras Medical College in 1949. She went on to specialise in gynaecology and obstetrics. Later in the 1960s, she took training in advanced cancer care in Toronto and the UK. Shantha won several awards including the Padma Shri in 1986, the Magsaysay Award in 2005, the Padma Bhushan in 2006 and the Padma Vibhushan in 2016.

Dwijendra Narayan Jha

Dwijendra Narayan Jha, one of the most erudite and prolific scholars on ancient and medieval Indian history, died on February 4 aged 81.

Akhtar Ali

Akhtar Ali, a former Davis Cup coach and a legendary figure in Indian tennis, died on February 7 aged 83. Akhtar, whose coaching style emphasised on playing aggressive serve and volley game, shaped many careers, including that of the legendary Leander Paes apart from his own son Zeeshan Ali who is India's current Davis Cup coach.

Rajiv Kapoor

Rajiv Kapoor, veteran Bollywood star and son of Raj Kapoor, died on February 9 aged 58. Rajiv Kapoor made his Bollywood debut in *Ek Jaan Hain Hum* back in 1983. He entered movies as a leading actor in Raj Kapoor's last directorial venture *Ram Teri Ganga Maili* in 1985. He starred in several movies including *Aasmaan* (1984), *Lover Boy* (1985), *Zabardast* (1985) and *Hum To Chale Pardes* (1988). He was last seen in the 1990 release *Zimmedaar* after which he turned to producing and directing.

Sandeep Nahar

Sandeep Nahar, actor who starred in Akshay Kumar's *Kesari* and the MS Dhoni biopic, died on February 15 aged 33 .

Captain Satish Sharma

Captain Satish Sharma, former Union minister and Gandhi family loyalist, died on February 17 aged 73. Sharma served as the Union Petroleum and Natural Gas Minister between 1993 and 1996 in the PV Narasimha Rao government. Born on October 11, 1947, in Andhra Pradesh's Secunderabad, Sharma was a professional commercial pilot before joining politics in 1983 at Rajiv Gandhi's behest. He was elected to the Lok Sabha in 1991 from Amethi after Rajiv Gandhi's assassination.From 1998 to 2004, Sharma was the Rae Bareli MP before vacating the seat for Sonia Gandhi. He was later a member of Rajya Sabha from July 2004 to 2016 and represented Madhya Pradesh, Uttarakhand and Uttar Pradesh.

Bhaskar Menon

Bhaskar Menon, the founding chairman and CEO at EMI Music Worldwide who is widely credited for breaking Pink Floyd in the U.S. and presiding over one of Capitol Records' most successful eras, died on Mar. 4, 2021 aged 86. Recruited to EMI in 1956 directly after graduating from Oxford University, Menon went on to join the label's Indian division, Gramophone Company of India, in 1957, before eventually being named chairman in 1969. That same year, he was hired as the head of EMI International, before taking over at Capitol in 1971.

Dadi Hridaya Mohini

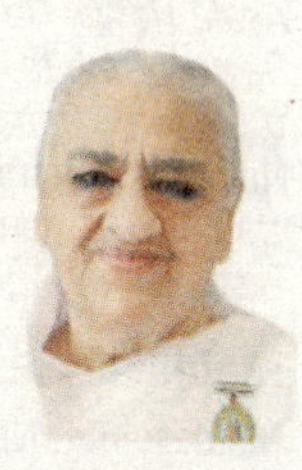

Dadi Hridaya Mohini, chief of the Brahma Kumaris, the world's largest spiritual organisation run by women, died on March 11 at the age of 93 after a prolonged illness.

Laxmipriya Mohapatra

Laxmipriya Mohapatra, noted Odissi dancerr and wife of Kelucharan Mohapatra, died on March 20 aged 86.

GV Ramakrishna

GV Ramakrishna, former SEBI chairman who also held some of the most high-profile jobs in the Indian government over an illustrious career spanning five decades, died on March 20 aged 91.

Anil Dharker

Anil Dharker, noted journalist and writer and founder of Mumbai International Literary Festival, died on March 26 aged 74. In a career spanning over five decades, Dharker had been a columnist and writer, an architect, and a member of the advisory committee of the film censor board. He was also the editor of several publications including *Mid-Day* and *The Independent*. His columns appeared in leading publications both in India and abroad. He was the author of *The Romance of Salt*, a book on Mahatma Gandhi's Dandi March.

Sanjay Chakravarty

Sanjay Chakravarty, the noted shooting coach who has given India some of its finest shooters, including guiding

Non-Fungible Tokens  extra

Non-Fungible Tokens or NFTs are blockchain-certified copies of real world art, music or intellectually-created property that cannot be duplicated. For content creators, NFTs provide a platform to directly reach their patrons, and, in turn, earn from them, much like rare art.

the likes of Olympic medallist Gagan Narang and Anjali Bhagwat, died on April 3 aged 79.

Shashikala

Shashikala, actress best known for her supporting roles in 1960s-70s films like *Aarti, Gumrah* and *Chhote Sarkar*, died on April 4 aged 88.

Satish Kaul

Satish Kaul, the noted Punjabi actor who featured in several Hindi films and shows including *Mahabharat*, died on April 10 aged 74 due to COVID-19 related complications. The actor worked in over 300 Punjabi and Hindi films including *Pyaar Toh Hona Hi Tha, Aunty No 1* and the TV show *Vikram Aur Betaal.*

Vivek

Vivek, popular Tamil actor and comedian, died on April 17 aged 59. He was popularly called 'Chinna Kalaivanar' for his social reformative dialogues in Tamil cinema. Apart from being an actor and a comedian, Vivek was also an activist and a playback singer. He was widely regarded for his performances in movies like *Perazhagan, Run, Saamy, Unnaruge Naan Irundhal, Anniyan* and *Sivaji*, among several others. He acted in over 200 films.He was bestowed with the Padma Shri Award, India's fourth-highest civilian award in the year 2009 by the union government.

Sumitra Bhave

Sumitra Bhave, veteran film director and writer known for her work in the Marathi cinema and theatre, died on April 19 aged 78. In 1985, Bhave made her first short film *Bai*, which was about a woman living in a slum and her survival against all odds. The film won several national awards. In 1995, Bhave and Sukthankar made their directorial debut with *Doghi*, which received the National Film Award. Her other notable works include *Devrai* (2004), *Gho Mala Asala Hawa, Ha Bharat Maza, Astu - So Be It, Samhita, Welcome Home, Vaastupurush, Dahavi Fa and Kaasav*, a National Award-winning film. *Kaasav* was also screened at the Mumbai Film Festival in 2016.

Maidavolu Narasimham

Maidavolu Narasimham, the architect of modern Indian banking and former Reserve Bank of India governor, died on April 20 aged 94. He was known for being the chair of two high-powered committees on banking and financial sector reforms. The first Narasimham Committee Report, presented in 1991, recommended the creation of a four-tier banking structure with three large banks on top.

Shravan Rathod

Shravan Rathod, composer of popular music director duo Nadeem-Shravan, died on April 22 aged 66. Nadeem-Shravan were among the most popular music composers in the 90s, giving chartbuster soundtracks in films like *Aashiqui* (1990), *Saajan* (1991), Shah Rukh Khan starrer *Pardes* and *Raja Hindustani*, headlined by Aamir Khan. After their split in mid 2000s, the duo reunited to compose for David Dhawan's *Do Knot Disturb* in 2009.

Soli Sorabjee

Soli Sorabjee, eminent jurist and former Attorney General of India, died on April 30 due to COVID-19 complications. The 91-year-old had served as the Attorney General for India from 1989-90 and then from 1998-2004. He appeared in several historic cases, including the Kesavananda Bharati case or the Basic Structure Doctrine case. He received the Padma Vibhushan for championing free speech and human rights.

Pandit Devabrata Chaudhari

Pandit Devabrata Chaudhari, sitar maestro died on May 1 of Covid-19 complications at the age of 85. He was a torchbearer of the Senia gharana and performed across the world for over six decades. He has won several honours, including the Padmabhushan, the Padmashree, and the Sangeet Natak Akademi Award for his contribution in the field of music. Besides being a sitarist and composer of eight new ragas, he was also an educationist and author.

Jagmohan

Jagmohan, former Jammu and Kashmir governor, died on May 3 aged 93. Born on September 25, 1927, Jagmohan Malhotra, popularly known as Jagmohan, was a former civil servant who held key positions in his long career. He was the Governor of Jammu and Kashmir and Goa, and the Lieutenant Governor of Delhi. Jagmohan served two terms as Jammu and Kashmir Governor - from 1984 to 89, and then from January to May 1990. He was honoured with the Padma Shri in 1971, Padma Bhushan in 1977 and Padma Vibhushan in 2016.

T.S. Shanbhag

T.S. Shanbhag, owner of the famed Premier Book Shop in Bangalore, died on May 4 aged 84. Started in 1971 on Church Street, Premier Book Shop, had books stacked in every possible corner and was a literature lover's delight. Shanbhag was the first bookseller in the city to offer unsolicited discount.

Ajit Singh

Ajit Singh, the Rashtriya Lok Dal (RLD) president, prominent Jat and farmer leader and former Union minister, died on May 6 aged 82 after battling Covid-19. He was elected to the Lok Sabha six times from Baghpat — twice on a Janata Dal ticket, once from the Congress-supported Bharatiya Kisan Kamgar Party and thrice from the RLD. He had also been a Rajya Sabha member once. Ajit Singh served as Union minister in the governments helmed by V.P. Singh, P.V. Narsimha Rao, Atal Bihari Vajpayee and Manmohan Singh. Ajit Singh's first ministerial assignment was the industries portfolio in 1989 in the National Front government. In 2011, he had been made civil aviation minister in the UPA government.

Prateek Chaudhuri

Prateek Chaudhuri, renowned sitar player, died due to Covid-19 on May 7. His father, veteran sitarist Devbrata Chaudhuri, popularly known as Debu Chaudhuri, had also died due to Covid-19 on May 1.

Indu Jain

Indu Jain, Times Group chairperson, died on May 13 aged 84. Indu Jain was awarded the Padma Bhushan, the third highest civilian honour in the country, in 2016. She was the founder president of FICCI Ladies Organisation (FLO), established in 1983 to promote entrepreneurship and professional excellence among women in India. From 1999, she also served as chairperson of Bharatiya Jnanpith Trust, founded in 1944 by Sahu Shanti Prasad Jain, her father-in-law, to promote literature in Indian languages.The Jnanpith Award, conferred by the Trust annually, is acknowledged to be the most prestigious honour for authors writing in Indian languages.

Sunderlal Bahuguna

Sunderlal Bahuguna, the Gandhian who was the driving force behind the legendary Chipko movement against deforestation that marked a key milestone in Indian environmentalism, died due to Covid on May 21 aged 94.The movement later received the 1987 Right Livelihood Award, often called the "Alternative Nobel Prize". Bahuguna also opposed the construction of the Tehri dam by fasting for 75 days and was able to convince the authorities to reduce the dam height to reduce the submergence area, thereby saving hundreds of trees. In 2009, he was honoured with the Padma Vibhushan.

Buddhadeb Dasgupta

Buddhadeb Dasgupta, the legendary Bengali filmmaker, died on June 10 aged 77. He was known for directing critically-acclaimed films like Uttara, *Bagh Bahadur, Tahader Katha* and *Charachar*. Of all the films he wrote and directed, five movies - *Bagh Bahadur, Charachar, Lal Darja, Mondo Meyer Upakhyan* and *Kaal-*

purush - won the National Awards for Best Film while his 2000's *Uttara* and 2005's *Swapner Din* fetched him the National Film Awards for Best Direction. His poems like *Coffin Kimba Suitcase, Govir Araley, Chhaata Kahini, Himjog, Roboter Gaan* and *Sreshtha Kabita* are still considered as some of the best work in poetry.

Swatilekha Sengupta

Swatilekha Sengupta, who is considered as one of the legendary artists of Bengali theatre, died on June 16. The veteran actress was equally eloquent on stage and in front of the camera. She featured in Satyajit Ray's *Ghare Baire*, Nandita Roy-Shiboprasad Mukherjee directed *Bela Seshe* and *Belashuru*, Raj Chakraborty directed *Dharmajuddha* and others.

Milkha Singh

Milkha Singh, the ace sprinter who was one of independent India's biggest sporting icons, died on June 18 aged 91. The legendary athlete is a four-time Asian Games gold medallist and the 1958 Commonwealth Games champion but his greatest performance remains the fourth-place finish in the 400m final of the 1960 Rome Olympics. His timing of 45.6 sec at the Italian capital remained the national record for 38 years before Paramjeet Singh broke it in 1998. He also represented India in the 1956 and 1964 Olympics and was bestowed the Padma Shri in 1959.

Stan Swamy

Stan Swamy, an 84-year-old priest-activist arrested under an anti-terror law in the Elgar Parishad case, died on July 5 in the middle of his fight for bail on health grounds. Swamy, the oldest person to be accused of terrorism in India, was arrested in October 2020. He was among 15 renowned activists, academics and lawyers, who were charged under a draconian anti-terror law. Swamy had repeatedly denied the charges, saying he was being targeted for his work related to the caste and land struggles of tribespeople in Jharkhand state.The accusations were in connection with violence that broke out in 2018 during an event commemorating a historic battle fought by Dalits (formerly untouchables) against an upper-caste rule.

Danish Siddiqui

Danish Siddiqui, Indian photojouralist, was killed while covering a clash between Afghan security forces and Taliban fighters in Spin Boldak district of Kandahar city on July 6. In 2018, Danish Siddiqui and his colleague Adnan Abidi, as part of the Reuters team, had won the Pulitzer Prize for feature photography for documenting the Rohingya refugee crisis.

Dilip Kumar

Dilip Kumar, one of India's earliest and most famous film actors, died on July 7 aged 98. Kumar acted in more than 65 films over nearly five decades, playing roles that ranged from the iconic to the endearing. He debuted in 1944 in *Jwaar Bhata* but it was the 1949 hit, Andaz, that shot him to fame. Some of his films - *Mela, Naya Daur, Ganga Jumna, Devdas* and *Mughal-e-Azam* - were superhits and won him legions of fans. Kumar essayed a gamut of roles, including a villager, a suave urbanite, a Bengali gentleman and a swashbuckling hero, before moving to paying older, supporting roles in the 1970s. Dilip Kumar was honoured with Padma Bhushan in 1991 and Padma Vibhushan in 2015.

Virbhadra Singh

Virbhadra Singh, former Himachal Pradesh chief minister and senior Congress leader, died on July 8 aged 87. The nine-time MLA and five-time MP, Singh served as Himachal Pradesh's chief minister for six times.

Dr P K Warrier

Dr P K Warrier, doyen of ayurveda medicine and managing trustee of Vaidyaratnam P S Varrier's Arya Vaidya Sala, died on July 10 aged 100. In his nearly seven-decade career, Warrier set a benchmark for the Indian traditional healing system and played a pivotal role for the renaissance of ayurveda.

Yashpal Sharma

Yashpal Sharma, a key member of India's 1983 cricket World Cup-winning side, died on July 13 aged 66. A middle-order batsman, he played 37 Tests and 42 ODIs for India between 1978 and 1985. He was the second-highest run-getter in India's historic 1983 triumph, scoring two half-centuries: an 89 in India's win over West Indies in the group stage, and 61 in the semi-final against England.

Surekha Sikri

Surekha Sikri, the three-time National Award-winning actress, known for her performances in *Balika Vadhu* and *Badhaai Ho*, died on July 16 aged 75. She made her debut in 1978, with the film *Kissa Kursi Ka*. She won the National Film Award for Best Supporting Actress thrice, for her roles in *Tamas* (1988), *Mammo* (1995) and *Badhaai Ho* (2018).

Nandu Natekar

Nandu Natekar, one of the superstars in Indian badminton history, died on July 28 aged 88. The first Indian shuttler to win a tournament overseas — the Selangor International crown in Kuala Lumpur

in 1956, Natekar was among the first batch of the Arjuna Award recipients in 1961 when the awards were introduced. His international achievements included making it to the All England Championship quarterfinals in 1954 and representing India in the Commonwealth Games in Jamaica in 1966.

Gail Omvedt

Gail Omvedt, a scholar renowned for her writings on Dalit history and politics, died on August 25 aged 81. She co-founded Shramik Mukti Dal along with her husband and activist Bharat Patankar. The organisation addresses farmers' problems, deals with displacement caused due to building of dams, drought and caste politics. Omvedt authored over 25 books.

O M Nambiar

O.M. Nambiar, the man who transformed a village girl PT Usha into Asia's golden girl, died on August 19 aged 89. One of India's most famous coaches, Nambiar spotted Usha at a very young age in 1976 and soon began coaching her at the Kannur Sports Division. Under his guidance, Usha began winning medals at the Asian level but his best move was making the sprinter switch to the 400m hurdles before the 1984 Los Angeles Olympics. And Usha almost came very close to winning independent India's first Olympic medal, missing it by one hundredth of a second. Nambiar was conferred the Padma Shri in 2021 and he is also the recipient of the Dronacharya award that he received way back in 1985.

Kalyan Singh

Kalyan Singh, who formed the Bharatiya Janata Party's first government in Uttar Pradesh in 1991, died on August 21 aged 89. Singh, who was accused of criminal conspiracy in the Babri Masjid demolition case for it was during his tenure as chief minister that the 16th century mosque was demolished, also served as the Rajasthan governor between 2014 and 2015.

Nedumudi Venu

Nedumudi Venu, a gifted and versatile actor who essayed a wide range of roles with a remarkable ease across several Malayalam films, died on October 11 aged 73. Born as Kesavan Venugopal, the actor was popularly known by his stage name, Nedumudi Venu. He acted in more than 500 films in his career spanning four decades. Apart from acting, Venu wrote screenplays for many films and directed one film. He won three National Film Awards and six Kerala State Film Awards for his exceptional performances.

Deaths - World

Saeb Erekat

Saeb Erekat, a familiar face in Palestinian politics for 40 years, died from the novel coronavirus on November 10, 2020 aged 65. A longtime adviser to Palestine Liberation Organization Chairman Yasser Arafat, Erekat at the time of his death was secretary-general of the PLO Executive Committee and a close ally of Palestinian Authority President Mahmoud Abbas. Erekat served as chief Palestinian negotiator for decades, struggling to reach agreement with Israel for an end to the occupation of the West Bank and Gaza Strip and the establishment of an independent Palestinian state.

Jan Morris

Jan Morris, the acclaimed British journalist, travel writer and historian who wrote about history's sweep and the details of place with equal eloquence and chronicled her life as a transgender woman, died on November 20 aged 94.

Diego Maradona

Diego Maradona, one of the greatest soccer players of all time, died on November 25 at the age of 60. Regarded as one of the greatest players in the history of the game, Maradona became a household name after inspiring his country to World Cup glory in 1986. He took centre stage at the tournament with a memorable performance against England where he scored an iconic goal that he later described as the "Hand of God. "The diminutive forward out-jumped legendary keeper Peter Shilton and punched the ball into the net. Despite the obvious handball, the goal was allowed to stand because the referee did not see the foul. Later in the game he scored one of the best goals in history after weaving his way past seven English defenders. His glittering career was also marked by numerous controversies and his notorious lifestyle led to alcoholism and addiction.

Mohsen Fakhrizadeh

Mohsen Fakhrizadeh, Iran's top nuclear scientist, died in hospital on 27 November after gunmen fired at his car near Tehran, in an ambush Iran's president has blamed on Israel.

Chuck Yeager

Chuck Yeager, the pilot who took aviation to the doorstep of space by becoming the first person to break the sound barrier more than 70 years ago, died on December 7 at the age of 97. Yeager became

the first person to break the sound barrier on Oct. 14, 1947, while flying the Bell X-1 rocket plane 45,000 feet (13,700 meters) over the Rogers Dry Lake in the Mojave Desert. During the flight, Yeager reached Mach 1.05, or 1.05 times the speed of sound. The aircraft, which he dubbed Glamorous Glennis after his first wife Glennis Yeager, who died in 1990. The Bell X-1 now hangs on display in the Smithsonian Air and Space Museum in Washington. Yeager would go on to fly even faster aircraft, including the Lockheed XF-104, which flew more than twice the speed of sound. His daring test flights were featured in Tom Wolfe's 1979 book *The Right Stuff* as well as the film adaptation and new Disney Plus series by the same name.

John le Carre

John le Carre, the British novelist who captured the cloak-and-dagger intrigue of Cold War espionage in best-selling books such as *The Spy Who Came in From the Cold* and *Tinker Tailor Soldier Spy* died on December 12 aged 89. A former spy with UK intelligence agency MI6, le Carre wrote more than 20 books in a career spanning six decades. His tales of treachery, betrayal and duplicity made George Smiley one of the genre's most well-known secret agents.

Charley Pride

Charley Pride, the pioneering black country singer known for such hits as *Kiss an Angel* Good *Mornin'* and *Is Anybody Goin' to San Antone*, died on December 12 aged 86.

Barry Lopez

Barry Lopez, a seeker and storyteller who plumbed the natural world for its wisdom, exploring the Arctic tundra, the Antarctic waters and spaces in between in voyages that became the stuff of his award-winning books, died on Dember 25 aged 75. An author of nearly 20 books on natural history studies, along with essay and short story collections, Lopez was awarded the National Book Award in 1986 for *Arctic Dreams: Imagination and Desire in a Northern Landscape.* It was the result of almost five years of traveling the Arctic.

Pierre Cardin

Pierre Cardin, the French designer who upended fashion in the 1960s and 70s with his futuristic looks and pioneering approach to merchandise, died on December 29 aged 98. Cardin was well-known for his bold, space-age designs in the late 1950s. Well-regarded by the Parisian haute couture set, he went on to dress 60s luminaries such as Elizabeth Taylor, Brigitte Bardot and the Beatles, whose radical, collarless jackets – inspired by Cardin and worn on *The Ed*

Sullivan Show – became the new standard for a generation still wearing their father's suits.

Brian Urquhart

Brian Urquhart, one of the first employees of the United Nations and who served under a range of Secretaries-General in various roles culminating in his appointment as the Under-Secretary-General for Political Affairs, died on January 2, 2021 aged 101. Urquhart joined the UN at its birth in 1945. Until his retirement in 1986, the long-serving official worked as a principal adviser to five UN secretaries-general, directed 13 peacekeeping operations, recruited 10,000 troops from 23 countries and instituted peacekeeping as one of the core tenets of the Organization.

Tanya Roberts

Tanya Roberts, known for playing Stacey Sutton in the 1985 James Bond film *A View to a Kill* and Midge Pinciotti on *That '70s Show* between 1998 and 2004, died on January 4, 2021 aged 65. Born Victoria Leigh Blum, Roberts had a successful modelling career and appeared in some off-Broadway roles. She made her film debut in 1975 with *The Last Victim.* Thereafter, she appeared in a series of films that attained cult status, including *The Beastmaster* (1982), *Sheena: Queen of the Jungle* (1984), *Body Slam* (1987) and *Night Eyes* (1990).

Michael Apted

Michael Apted, British director of the *"Up"* series of documentaries, as well as *Coal Miner's Daughter, Gorillas in the Mist* (1988), James Bond film T*he World Is Not Enough* (1999) and *The Chronicles of Narnia: The Voyage of the Dawn Treader* (2010), died on January 7 aged 79. Apted directed three actors in performances that drew Academy Award nominations: Sissy Spacek in *Coal Miner's Daughter,* Sigourney Weaver in *Gorillas in the Mist* and Jodie Foster in *Nell,* with Spacek going on to win the Oscar. His *Up* series of documentaries for Granada Television, in which he profiled a varied group of young Britons and revisited them every seven years to what changes time had wrought, topped the list in the 2005 Channel 4 Programme "The 50 Greatest Documentaries."

Ved Mehta

Ved Mehta, celebrated Indian-American novelist who overcame blindness and became widely known as the 20th-century writer most responsible for introducing American readers to India, died on January 9 aged 86. He was a staff writer with the *New Yorker* magazine for more than three decades. Best known for his 12-volume memoir known collectively as *Continents of Exile*, which focused on the troubled modern history of India and his early struggles with blindness, Mehta's 24 books included volumes of reportage on India, among them *Walking the Indian Streets* (1960), *Portrait of India* (1970) and *Mahatma Gandhi and His Apostles* (1977), as well as explorations of philosophy, theology and linguistics. Some of his most fascinating work includes *A Battle Against the Bewitchment of Our Intelligence* (1961), a portrait of British intellectual life and the philosophical debates of the time; *John Is Easy to Please* (1971), a piece about the young linguist Noam Chomsky and the critics of his theory of transformational grammar.

Henry Louis "Hank" Aaron

Henry Louis "Hank" Aaron, the Baseball Hall of Famer who broke Babe Ruth's all-time home run record in the face of racism and became a revered ambassador to the game, died on January 22 aged 86. Aaron famously broke Ruth's longstanding home run record on April 8, 1974, hitting his 715th homer at home in Atlanta-Fulton County Stadium during a game against the Los Angeles Dodgers. He would go on to hit 755 career home runs, a record that stood for 30 years until San Francisco Giants slugger Barry Bonds surpassed the record in 2007 and finished with 762 home runs. Aaron, however, still holds all-time MLB records for RBIs (2,297), total bases (6,856) and extra-base hits (1,477). He ranks third all-time in hits (3,771) and games played (3,298) and fourth in runs scored (2,174).

Larry King

Larry King, giant of US broadcasting who achieved worldwide fame for interviewing political leaders and celebrities, died on January 23, 2021 aged 87. King conducted an estimated 50,000 interviews in his six-decade career, which included 25 years as host of the popular CNN talk show *Larry King Live*. Though King left CNN in 2011, he kept working until his death, hosting *Larry King Now*, a programme that aired on Ora TV, Hulu and RT America. King was recognized with two Peabody Awards and one Emmy Award, among other honours. He was inducted into the National Radio Hall of Fame in 1989 and the Broadcasting Hall of Fame in 1992.

Hal Holbrook

Hal Holbrook, the actor famed for playing the character Deep Throat in *All the President's Men*, died on January 23 aged 95. His other films include award-winning drama *Julia* in 1977, horror classic The Fog in 1980, Oliver Stone's *Wall Street* in 1987 and *The Firm* alongside Tom Cruise in 1993.

Paul J. Crutzen

Paul J. Crutzen, a Dutch scientist who won the Nobel Prize for chemistry for his work understanding the ozone hole and is credited with coining the term Anthropocene to describe the geological era shaped by mankind, died on January 28 aged 87. Crutzen discovered in 1970 that nitrogen pollution was capable of destroying ozone in the atmosphere, a critical layer of that protects living things from the sun's ultraviolet radiation. The implications were potentially dangerous, as this ozone gas thinned into a "hole" above the Southern Hemisphere that threatened to leave millions of people exposed. Crutzen shared the 1995 Nobel Prize in Chemistry for discovering the risk to the ozone layer.

Cicely Tyson

Cicely Tyson, an award-winning icon of the stage and screen who broke barriers for Black actresses with surpassing dignity, died on January 28 aged 96. Her filmography includes some of the most celebrated movies and television shows featuring Black women in major roles: *Sounder* (1972), *The Autobiography of Miss Jane Pittman* (1974), *Roots* (1977), *The Marva Collins Story* (1981), *The Women of Brewster Place* (1989), and *The Help* (2011). President Barack Obama awarded her the Medal of Freedom in 2016. She won three Emmys and many awards from civil rights and women's groups, and at 88 became the oldest person to win a Tony, for her 2013 Broadway role in a revival of Horton Foote's *The Trip to Bountiful.* At 93, she won an honorary Oscar, and was inducted into the American Theater Hall of Fame in 2018 and into the Television Hall of Fame in 2020. She also won a career achievement Peabody Award in 2020. She chronicled her lengthy career in her first memoir, *Just As I Am.*

Tom Moore

Tom Moore, the 100-year-old World War II veteran whose efforts to raise millions for the UK's National Health Service made him a universally adored icon during the first wave of the Covid-19 outbreak, died on February 1 after himself contracting the disease. Known affectionately as Captain Tom, Moore raised almost £33 million ($45 million) by walking laps of his garden in 2020. His exploits united a country frozen in lockdown and made him an unlikely celebrity late in his life, earning him a military promotion, a knighthood from Queen Elizabeth II and a number-one single.

Christopher Plummer

Christopher Plummer, the dazzlingly versatile Canadian actor who starred in *The Sound of Music,* won an Oscar for *Beginners* and was nominated for *All the Money in the World* and *The Last Station*, died on February 5 aged 91. Along with becoming the oldest person to win an Oscar, Plummer also won a pair of Emmys and two Tonys during a nearly 70-year career.

Leon Spinks

Leon Spinks, former world heavyweight champion best known for defeating Muhammad Ali in 1978, died on February 5 at the age 67. Spinks represented the United States during the 1976 Olympics in Montreal, Canada, as a light heavyweight and won a gold medal. He faced Muhammad Ali in Las Vegas, Nevada, on February 15, 1978, winning to become the undisputed heavyweight boxing champion. It was only Spinks' eighth professional bout and one of the greatest upsets in boxing history. Spinks and Ali met again seven months later at the Superdome in New Orleans. Ali won and reclaimed the heavyweight title.

George P Schulz

George P Schulz, President Ronald Reagan's longtime secretary of state, and the oldest surviving former Cabinet member of any US administration, died on February 6 at the age of 100. Schulz, a distinguished fellow at Stanford University, was labour secretary and then the treasury secretary under President Richard Nixon before spending more than six years as Reagan's secretary of state. In the 1980s, he worked diligently to improve relations with the Soviet Union and paved the way for peace treaties in the Middle East.

Jean-Claude Carriere

Jean-Claude Carriere, the prolific French screenwriter and novelist, died on February 8 aged 89. He was best known for his work with Luis Bunuel and Milos Forman. Carriere and Bunuel won an Oscar in 1972 for *The Discreet Charm of the Bourgeoise*, adding to Carriere's best short film Oscar in 1963. His work ranged across cultures, religions and historical periods, from *Cyrano de Bergerac* (1990) to the adaptation of Milan Kundera's *The Unbearable Lightness of Being* (1988). Carriere's 1979 adaption of Gunter Grass's novel *The Tin Drum*, directed by Volker Schloendorff, won another Oscar as well as the Palme d'Or at Cannes.

Chick Corea

Chick Corea, the jazz pianist, improviser and composer, died on February 9 aged 79. Over the decades he won 23 Grammys and 67 nominations for his reinvigoration of jazz.

Carlos Saúl Menem

Carlos Saúl Menem, whose decade-long presidency of Argentina in the 1990s transformed the country, died on February 14 aged 90. One of Latin America's best known and most controversial presidents, who had a flamboyant lifestyle and sported lambchop sideburns, Menem presided over the liberalisation of Argentina's economy. He wholeheartedly embraced the free-market doctrine enshrined in the "Washington consensus" more than any other leader in the region.

Mourid Barghouti

Mourid Barghouti, iconic Palestinian poet and a staunch supporter of the Palestinian cause, died on February 14 aged 76. He was born four years before the state of Israel was created in a village near Ramallah. He spent much of his life in one form or other of exile - which he recounted in the memoir *I Saw Ramallah* that won him an international audience. The memoir was described by his fellow Palestinian writer Edward Said as one of the finest existential accounts of Palestinian displacement.

Rush Limbaugh

Rush Limbaugh, the controversial US radio personality and political commentator who for decades used his perch as the king of talk-radio to alter the landscape of American media and politics, died on February 17 aged 70.

Lawrence Ferlinghetti

Lawrence Ferlinghetti, an acclaimed poet and longtime proprietor of City Lights, the San Francisco bookstore and avant-garde publishing house that catapulted the Beat Generation to fame and helped establish the city as a centre of literary and cultural revolution, died on February 22 aged 101.

Lou Ottens

Lou Ottens, the Dutch engineer credited with inventing the cassette tape and playing a major role in the development of the first CD, died on March 6 aged 94.

John Magufuli

John Magufuli, Tanzania's president who was one of Africa's most prominent covid-deniers, died on March 17 aged 61. Magufuli denied the local spread of Covid-19 in Tanzania, discouraged the mention of the disease by health workers, and claimed without evidence that vaccines were dangerous, suggesting instead that people pray and inhale herb-infused steam.

Nawal el Saadawi

Nawal el Saadawi, an Egyptian author, activist and physician who became an emblem of the struggle for women's rights in the patriarchal Arab world and campaigned against female genital mutilation, which she had endured at age 6, died on March

Homicides in America

There were 21,570 homicides in America in 2020, according to the FBI, up by 29% from 2019. The homicide rate rose from 5.1 to 6.5 per 100,000 people. This was still well below its peak of 9.8 in 1991.

21 aged 89. The feminist author of more than 55 books first spotlighted the issue of female genital mutilation (FGM) with *The Hidden Face of Eve* in 1980. She also campaigned against women wearing the veil, polygamy and inequality in Islamic inheritance rights between men and women.

Bertrand Tavernier

Bertrand Tavernier, the iconic French filmmaker known for such award winning works as *A Sunday in the Country, Round Midnight, Capitaine Conan, It All Starts Today* and *Life and Nothing But,* died on March 25 aged 79. A director, writer and producer, Tavernier made over 30 films, embracing various genres from historical drama to noir, comedy and jazz. Among myriad awards his films have won are the Berlin Golden Bear for 1995's *L'Appat (The Bait)*, a Best Foreign Language Film BAFTA for *Life And Nothing But*, the Cannes Best Director prize with 1984's *A Sunday In The Country* and five Césars as well as a Venice Lifetime Achievement Golden Lion in 2015.

Larry McMurtry

Larry McMurtry, a prolific novelist and screenwriter who demythologized the American West with his unromantic depictions of life on the 19th-century frontier and in contemporary small-town Texas, died on March 25 aged 84. Over more than five decades, McMurtry wrote more than 30 novels and many books of essays, memoir and history. He also wrote more than 30 screenplays, including the one for "*Brokeback Mountain*" (written with Ossana, based on a short story by Annie Proulx), for which he won an Academy Award in 2006. But he found his greatest commercial and critical success with "*Lonesome Dove*," a sweeping 843-page novel about two retired Texas Rangers who drive a herd of stolen cattle from the Rio Grande to Montana in the 1870s. The book won a Pulitzer Prize in 1986 and was made into a popular television mini-series.

Beverly Cleary

Beverly Cleary, the revered children's author who enchanted generations of readers with stories about pesky, curious Ramona and the other young residents of Klickitat Street, died on March 25 aged 104. Trained as a librarian, Cleary didn't start writing books until her early 30s when she wrote *Henry Huggins,* published in 1950. Children worldwide came to love the adventures of Huggins and neighbours Ellen Tebbits, Otis Spofford, Beatrice "Beezus" Quimby and her younger sister, Ramona.

Isamu Akasaki

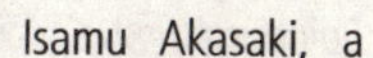

Japanese physicist Isamu Akasaki, a co-winner of the 2014 Nobel Prize in physics for inventing the world's first efficient blue light-emitting diodes, died on April 1aged 92. Akasaki was honoured in

1997 by the Japanese government with the Medal with Purple Ribbon, an honour bestowed on those who have made contributions to academic and artistic developments.

Robert A. Mundell

Robert A. Mundell, a Nobel Prize-winning economist who helped shape economic policy on both sides of the Atlantic as an intellectual architect of the euro and President Ronald Reagan's supply-side tax cuts, died on April 4 aged 88. He was widely regarded as one of the most consequential economists of the late 20th century, his work often compared or even equated with that of John Maynard Keynes and Milton Friedman.

Prince Philip

Prince Philip, Queen Elizabeth II's husband and the Duke of Edinburgh, died on April 9 aged 99. He was the first male royal consort since Queen Victoria's time in the 1800s — and the longest-serving consort in British history. The Duke of Edinburgh, who was born Prince Philip of Greece and Denmark, had four children with his wife of 73 years — Prince Charles, Princess Anne, Prince Andrew and Prince Edward. He will be remembered for his charitable work in particular. In 1956, he established the Duke of Edinburgh's award scheme to encourage young people to become involved in their communities and in outdoor activities.

Bernard Madoff

Bernard Madoff, who was convicted for running the largest known Ponzi scheme in history, died on April 14 aged 82. He had been held at a federal prison in North Carolina in the US, after being sentenced in June 2009 to a 150-year term for engineering a fraud estimated as high as $64.8 billion.

Helen McCrory

Actress Helen McCrory, who is best known for her appearance in the Harry Potter series of films and *Peaky Blinders*, died on April 16 aged 52. She is best known for her roles in the Harry Potter series of films - *Harry Potter and the Half-Blood Prince, Harry Potter and the Deathly Hallows Part 1, Harry Potter and the Deathly Hallows Part 2.* Helen played the role of Aunt Polly in *Peaky Blinders*, a web series streaming on Netflix. She has also starred in the James Bond movie *Skyfall.*

Charles Geschke

Charles Geschke, the co-founder of the software company Adobe who helped develop the Portable Document Format, or PDF, died on April 16 at the age of 81. He and Dr. John

Warnock launched Adobe in 1982 after leaving Xerox. Geschke and Adobe were first known for developing PostScript, a page description language whose power (along with Apple's Macintosh and Aldus' PageMaker) helped establish desktop publishing in the 1980s. He and Warnock are also known for developing the Portable Document Format, or PDF.

Walter Mondale

Walter Mondale, who transformed the role of U.S. vice president while serving under Jimmy Carter and was the Democratic nominee for president in 1984, died on April 19 at 93. He was the first vice president to have an office in the White House and was deeply engaged in both U.S. and foreign policy, working closely with the president. In his 1984 presidential run, Mondale nominated New York congresswoman Geraldine Ferraro as his running mate, making her the first female nominee for vice president of any major American party.

Idris Deby

Idris Deby, Chad's president who ruled the country for more than 30 years and was an important Western ally in the fight against Islamist militants in Africa, was killed on April 20 aged 68 on the frontline in a battle against rebels in the noth.

Alber Elbaz

Alber Elbaz, the Moroccan-born Israeli fashion designer whose playful designs transformed the storied French house Lanvin into an industry darling before his shock ouster in 2015, died on April 24 aged 59 after a battle with Covid-19. A favourite of celebrities like Meryl Streep and Natalie Portman, he rejuvenated Lanvin and had recently started a new venture, AZ Factory.

Michael Collins

Michael Collins, the man who stayed behind aboard the Apollo 11 command module while crewmates Neil Armstrong and Buzz Aldrin descended to the moon and walked into history, died on April 28 aged 90. One of the most articulate astronauts to emerge in the early days of America's space programme, Collins orbited the moon alone on July 20, 1969, when Armstrong and Aldrin touched down on the Sea of Tranquility, the first humans to set foot on another world.

Olympia Dukakis

Olympia Dukakis, a character actress

extra

French Initiative to Cut Carbon Emissions

Emmanuel Macron, the French president, launched a plan called "France 2030", which calls for €30bn ($35bn) to be spent on cutting carbon emissions and boosting industry. It includes a renewed commitment to nuclear power.

best known for her Oscar-winning supporting turn in Norman Jewison's *Moonstruck* and for her role as the wealthy widow in *Steel Magnolias,* died on May 1 aged 89.

Norman Lloyd

Norman Lloyd, the actor, producer and director whose collaborations with Orson Welles, Alfred Hitchcock, Charlie Chaplin, Bertolt Brecht and Jean Renoir made him a legend in Hollywood died on May 11 aged 106.

Yuan Longping

Yuan Longping, the Chinese scientist who developed strains of hybrid high-yield rice that helped alleviate famine and poverty around the world, enabling farmers to feed a growing planet with fewer resources, died on May 22 aged 90. Along with American scientist Norman Borlaug, a Nobel Peace Prize laureate who developed high-yield varieties of wheat, Yuan was frequently cited as a leader of the Green Revolution, in which mid-century agricultural advances helped feed a growing planet.

Josep Almudéver

Josep Almudéver, the last known survivor of the International Brigades who volunteered to fight in Spain's civil war in the hope that they could stop fascism, died on May 23 aged 101. Almudéver was one of many of the brigades' left-wing volunteers who viewed the conflict in Spain as a broader fight against the advance of fascism across Europe, since Franco was also receiving military support from Nazi Germany and Italy.

Eric Carle

Eric Carle, the children's author and illustrator whose classic *The Very Hungry Caterpillar* and other works gave millions of children some of their earliest literary memories, died on May 23 aged 91. His body of work, distinguished by his vividly coloured collage-style illustrations created from hand-painted paper cutouts, spanned more than 70 titles that sold over 152 million copies worldwide in dozens of languages. But his best known by far was *The Very Hungry Caterpillar,* published in 1969, which has been translated into 66 languages and has sold more than 50 million copies. The book has become bedtime reading for generations of parents and their children.

Edward de Bono

Edward de Bono, renowned psychologist and author known for 'lateral thinking'

techniques, died on June 9 aged 88. De Bono's methods and thinking tools have been used by leading corporations (Motorola, IBM and Boeing among some of them), governments, leaders, sportsmen and even school children.

Janet Malcolm

Janet Malcolm, an essayist and journalist known for her work in *The New Yorker*, died on June 16 aged 86. She was revered for her examination of psychoanalysis in essays and critique of her own profession as a journalist. Her debut work was 1981's *Psychoanalysis: The Impossible Profession.* That book was followed by a number of others, including *In the Freud Archives, The Journalist and the Murderer, The Silent Woman, Two Lives* and *Iphigenia in Forest Hills.*

Richard B

Richard B. "Dick" Stolley, the founding editor of *PEOPLE,* whose belief in highlighting stories of ordinary people doing the extraordinary transformed the magazine industry, died on June 16 aged 92. In addition to his lengthy tenure as a magazine editor, Stolley was also known for his reporting work at *Life* magazine, where he helped shed light on the triumphs and tragedies of the civil rights movement in the South — and for famously securing the Zapruder footage of the assassination of President John F. Kennedy in Dallas in 1963.

Kenneth Kaunda

Kenneth Kaunda, Zambia's founding president and a champion of African nationalism who spearheaded the fights to end white minority rule across southern Africa, died on June 17 at the age of 97. Kaunda came to prominence as a leader of the campaign to end colonial rule of his country, then known as Northern Rhodesia, and was elected the first president of Zambia in 1964. During his 27 year rule, he gave critical support to armed African nationalist groups that won independence for neighbouring countries including Angola, Mozambique, Namibia, South Africa and Zimbabwe.

John McAfee

John McAfee, US technology entrepreneur, hanged himself in his prison cell on June 23 after the Spanish high court authorised his extradition to the United States on tax evasion charges. McAfee, 75, was a pioneer of anti-virus software, introducing his eponymous program in the 1980s. He had been indicted in Tennessee on tax evasion charges. He also was charged in a cryptocurrency fraud case in New York.

Benigno Aquino II

Benigno Aquino II, former president of the Philippines, who was the only son of pro-democracy icon Corazon Aquino, died on June 24 aged 61. He was in

power from 2010 to 2016 after a landslide victory. He took charge at a time when the country was struggling with corruption, poverty and ageing infrastructure. Aquino was heir to a political legacy of the parents, the late Senator Benigno Aquino Jr and former president Corazon Aquino, regarded as a bulwark against authoritarianism in the Philippines. His mother, Corazon Aquino, led the 1986 "people power" revolt that ousted Marcos. The army-backed uprising became a harbinger of popular revolts against authoritarian regimes worldwide.

Donald Rumsfeld

Donald Rumsfeld, a proponent behind the U.S. invasions of Afghanistan and Iraq who served twice as Secretary of Defense under President Gerald Ford and President George W. Bush, died on June 29 aged 88. Rumsfeld's long career in government began with three terms in the House of Representatives, in which he voted in favour of the Voting Rights Act of 1965. He was re-elected to a fourth term, but resigned to serve as the Nixon administration's Director of the Office of Economic Opportunity. He later became the U.S. Ambassador to NATO. Rumsfeld continued to serve under President Gerald Ford after Nixon's resignation, first as Ford's White House Chief of Staff and then as Secretary of Defense, the youngest to have ever held the post. Rumsfeld's most well-known and most contentious legacy comes from his second term as defense secretary, this time as the oldest individual to ever hold the post.

Robert Downey Sr.

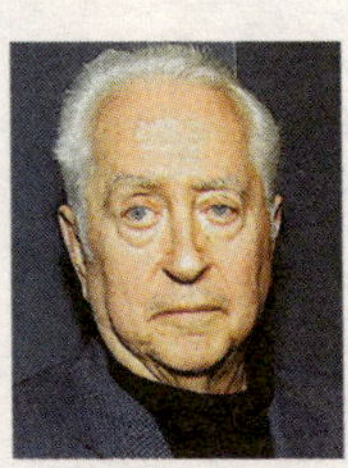

Robert Downey Sr., an actor and filmmaker, and father of Robert Downey Jr., died on July 7 aged 85. Downey began acting in the early 1960s, with *Boogie Nights, To Live and Die in L.A., The Family Man* and *Tower Heist* among his robust credit list. He also appeared in the TV series *1st & Ten* and *Saturday Night Live*, which was his last television credit in 2015. As a director, Downey made films such as comedies *Babo 73, No More Excuses*, *Rented Lips* and *Hugo Pool,* in which Downey Jr. starred in. The filmmaker became well-known for low-budget underground projects such as the 1969 satire *Putney Swope*, in which African American executives take over an all-white agency. He was also active in numerous other departments, from cinematography to producing, writing and editing.

Graham Vick

Graham Vick, a British director who founded Birmingham Opera Company and worked in opera houses around the world, died on July 17 aged 67. He was among the most brilliant, passionate and original opera directors of his generation.

Frenchy Cannoli

Frenchy Cannoli, French hashish evangelist who sought to promote its production as an art form comparable to that of making vintage wine, died on July 18, 2021 aged 64. For nearly half a century he searched for the finest hashish in the world and the very best ways of cultivating, producing and smoking it.

Prof. Steven Weinberg

Prof. Steven Weinberg, the most influential particle physicist in the last five decades, died on July 23 at the age of 88. In 1979 he won a Nobel prize for his work uniting two of nature's fundamental forces, which became a foundation of the standard model of particle physics, the theory that describes all known fundamental particles and forces in the universe.

Jane Withers

Jane Withers, the former child actor who bedevilled Shirley Temple on the screen and went on to star in a series of B movies that made her a box-office champion, died on August 7 aged 95.

Ernst van de Wetering

Ernst van de Wetering, an art historian who was a towering figure in the world of Rembrandt studies and widely regarded as the foremost authority on Rembrandt paintings, died on August 11 aged 83.

Mikis Theodorakis

Mikis Theodorakis, the renowned Greek composer, who scored the 1964 classic film *Zorba the Greek* and was an icon of resistance to the former military junta, died on Septembe 2 aged 96. A prolific talent and political maverick, Theodorakis was revered in his home country for his inspirational music and defiance during the junta that ruled from 1967 to 1974. Theodorakis was perhaps best-known around the world for his film title scores, which also included *Z* in 1969 and *Serpico* in 1973. His work ranged from operas to choral music and popular songs, providing a soundtrack to the life of his country.

Jean-Paul Belmondo

Jean-Paul Belmondo, the French actor who shot to international fame in Jean-

First Country in the World to Adopt the Cryptocurrency

El Salvador is the first country in the world to adopt the cryptocurrency as an official means of exchange; it now uses bitcoin alongside the American dollar.

Luc Godard's revolutionary new wave classic *Breathless*, died on September 6 aged 88. Nicknamed Bébel by French audiences, he became one of the country's biggest box-office stars in the 60s and 70s. Belmondo was a key figure of the outstanding generation of European film-makers of the period, with the series of films he made with Godard – which included *A Woman Is a Woman* and *Pierrot le Fou* – making an indelible mark.

Clive Sinclair

Clive Sinclair, the British inventor who pioneered the pocket calculator and affordable home computers, died on September 16 at the age of 81. His ZX Spectrum computers brought affordable personal computing to the masses and sold in their millions across the world.

Abdelaziz Bouteflika

Abdelaziz Bouteflika, the president of Algeria from 1999 to 2019, died on September 17 aged 84. He led the country out of a ruinous civil war, but was ousted in 2019 amid mass protests against his decision to seek a fifth term.

Abdul Qadeer Khan

Abdul Qadeer Khan, who was considered the father of Pakistan's atomic bomb and who secretly sold nuclear-weapons technology to such states as Iran and North Korea, died on October 10 aged 85. Khan was hailed in Pakistan as a hero for helping the country become a nuclear power on par with rival India. But he was decried by many in the West for his leading role in a proliferation ring that illegally sold nuclear secrets to U.S. adversaries. Khan, who in 2004 admitted to his involvement on national television, was later pardoned by then-President Pervez Musharraf. Yet he remained a revered figure at home.

Gary Paulsen

Gary Paulsen, who inspired generations of young readers with novels about the beauty, wonder and danger of the wilderness — most notably *Hatchet*, about a boy who learns to survive on his own in the Canadian bush — while drawing on his own adventures as a sled-dog racer and restless outdoorsman, died on October 13 aged 82.

Colin Powell

Colin Powell, a US war hero and the first Black secretary of state who saw his trailblazing legacy tarnished when he made the case for war in Iraq in 2003, died on October 18 aged 84.Powell was a dis-

tinguished and trailblazing professional soldier whose career took him from combat duty in Vietnam to becoming the first Black national security adviser during the end of Ronald Reagan's presidency and the youngest and first African American chairman of the Joint Chiefs of Staff under President George H.W. Bush. When he was sworn in as Bush's secretary of state in 2001, he became the highest-ranking Black public official to date in the country, standing fourth in the presidential line of succession.

Edita Gruberova

Edita Gruberova, a soprano who reigned over world opera stages for decades, dazzling audiences with her shimmering pianissimos and vocal pyrotechnics in the works of composers including Donizetti, Verdi and Richard Strauss, died on October 18 aged 74. In a career that lasted more than half a century, from her debut in her native Bratislava, in what is now Slovakia, until her retirement in 2020, Gruberova became recognized as "a spectacularly accomplished coloratura soprano and one of the most beloved stars of her generation," in the description of an obituary published in *Opera News.*

Leslie Bricusse

Leslie Bricusse, an Oscar-winning composer and lyricist who enchanted children with his musical confections for *Doctor Dolittle* and *Willy Wonka & the Chocolate Factory*, seduced their parents with the crooner standards "What Kind of Fool Am I?" and "Who Can I Turn To?" and helped write the title song to the James Bond film *Goldfinger,* died on Oct. 19 aged 90.

Mihály Csíkszentmihályi

Mihály Csíkszentmihályi, world-renowned Hungarian psychologist, died on October 20 at the age of 88. Besides being one of the world's leading researchers on positive psychology, he was best known for introducing flow theory in the 1970s, defining it as a state of mind attained when one becomes fully immersed in an activity.

Halyna Hutchins

Halyna Hutchins, a 42-year-old cinematographer, tragically died on October 22 after being shot in the stomach by a gun fired by actor Alec Baldwin during the filming of the movie *Rust.*

The pistol used by Baldwin during the filming of the movie at Bonanza Creek Ranch in New Mexico was supposed to be a prop, but ended up being loaded.

Hutchins graduated from the American Film Institute in 2015, and had worked on several short films before shooting *Archenemy*, a 2020 feature starring Joe Manganiello. She was named a "rising star" by *American Cinematographer* in 2019.

Newsmakers - India

Disha Ravi

Disha Ravi, a 22-year-old climate activist, emerged as a symbol of the Central government's crackdown on dissent. Ravi's arrest prompted protests throughout the country and renewed concerns of an authoritarian backlash to the farmers' protests that had rocked the country.

She was accused of helping to create and share an online "toolkit" that listed peaceful ways the public could support the protests. The document was later shared online by the Swedish climate activist Greta Thunberg as she joined a litany of global celebrities lending support for the movement. Tens of thousands of farmers were camping out in Delhi since November 2020 to protest new agricultural laws that they say could destroy their livelihoods and leave them open to exploitation by large corporations. Ravi fervently backed the cause, tweeting her support for the farmers. A well-known figure in the country's growing environmental movement, Ravi co-founded the Indian chapter of Thunberg's Fridays for Future (FFF) campaign, an international movement where students skip school on Fridays to protest inaction on climate change. The movement has gained traction in India, with FFF chapters established in most of the states. Ravi was regularly seen at the protests and is known for being increasingly vocal about the issue and her negative view of Modi's environmental policies.

Raj Kundra

Businessman Raj Kundra, husband of actor and businesswoman Shilpa Shetty, was arrested by the Mumbai Police in connection with an adult film racket.

The 46-year-old businessman was booked under relevant sections of the Indian Penal Code, the Information Technology Act and the Indecent Representation of Women (Prohibition) Act and arrested on July 19 by Mumbai's crime branch. He was lodged in the Arthur Road Jail in central Mumbai under judicial custody before being released on bail.

On February 4 2021, the Mumbai police said they had arrested five people for allegedly forcing women into porn movies. They would promise these aspiring actresses, who came to Mumbai from various parts of the country, roles in web series. However, on the day of the shoot, they would change the script and threaten the women to expose themselves. If the women refused, they were asked to foot the bill for the shooting preparations.

Once the movies were shot, the accused made them available on mobile apps, offering subscriptions on the lines of mainstream OTT platforms. They would then put up advertisements on social media platforms. Since pornography is illegal in India, this too was against the law.

Newsmakers - World

Amanda Gorman

Amanda Gorman, 22, became the youngest known inaugural poet when she performed at the 59th the US Presidential inauguration on January 20, 2021. She delivered her original composition, *The Hill We Climb*, at the Capitol in front of President-elect Joe Biden, Vice President-elect Kamala Harris and the entire nation.

Gorman joins a small group of poets who have been recruited to help mark a presidential inauguration, among them Robert Frost, Maya Angelou, Miller Williams, Elizabeth Alexander and Richard Blanco.

At 16, she was named the Youth Poet Laureate of Los Angeles. A few years later, when she was studying sociology at Harvard, she became the National Youth Poet Laureate, the first person to hold the position.

Ngozi Okonjo-Iweala

The World Trade Organization's 164 members on February 15 officially selected Ngozi Okonjo-Iweala, a Nigerian economist and former finance minister, to be its next leader. The first woman and first African to serve as director general, Dr. Okonjo-Iweala assumed the post on March 1 for a renewable term expiring on Aug. 31, 2025. The start of her term at the W.T.O. came at a particularly difficult time for the global trade body, which was created in 1995 to help settle trade disputes, write new trade rules and encourage the flow of goods and services worldwide. WTO has a budget of $220m and staff of 650. As a two-time finance minister in Nigeria she gained a reputation as a tough negotiator during talks to reduce the country's debts. That reputation was consolidated when securing more money for grants and soft loans to poor countries while No 2 at the World Bank.

Hamzah bin Hussein

On April 3, Jordan's King Abdullah II accused his half-brother Hamzah bin Hussein and others of plotting with "foreign parties" to "destabilize Jordan's security." The prince is the oldest son of the late King Hussein bin Talal with his widow, Noor. He had been groomed for the throne by his mother. King Hussein I often publicly expressed his admiration for Hamzah and had planned to name him as his successor. Shortly before King Hussein I died in 1999, he changed his mind, naming his first-born son, Abdullah II, the heir to the throne instead. At the time, Hamzah was still considered too young and inexperienced to take over from his father. In keeping with his father's wish, King Abdullah II made Hamzah crown prince of Jordan. In 2004, however, King Abdullah II surprisingly rescinded this position, instead conferring it to his eldest son: Hussein.

Abdullah had justified this by arguing that he wanted to preserve the liberty of the then-24-year-old Hamzah to pursue careers for which he was more qualified. This move effectively barred him a second time from ascending to the throne.

Liz Cheney

The Republicans House of Representatives in the US voted on May 12 to remove Congresswoman Liz Cheney of Wyoming from her leadership role as chair of the House Republican Conference, due to her constant criticism of former US President Donald Trump and her refusal to endorse his long-debunked claims of election fraud. Her ouster as the third-highest-ranking Republican in the the House points towards Trump's firm grip over the GOP, even six months after he exited the White House. The daughter of former US Vice President Dick Cheney, Liz Cheney is a Congresswoman from Wyoming and a staunch conservative who has served as the chair of the House Republican Conference since 2019, under House Minority Leader Kevin McCarthy.

Cheney has been a long-time critic of former President Trump. In fact, she was among the 10 Republicans in the House who voted in favour of Trump's impeachment over his alleged role in inciting the violence that broke out at the US Capitol building on January 6, 2021.

Alexander Schallenberg

Austria's former foreign minister, Alexander Schallenberg, was sworn in as the country's new chancellor on October 11. Schallenberg took over from Sebastian Kurz, who resigned amid a swirling corruption probe on October 9. Days before, the Green party, which ruled in coalition with Kurz's conservative People's Party (ÖVP), had threatened to break up the government if Kurz wasn't replaced. Schallenberg, 54, is a career diplomat who is a relative newcomer to politics. The son of a former Austrian ambassador, Schallenberg is steeped in diplomacy. Born in the Swiss capital Bern, he spent his childhood in India, Spain and France, where his father took on ambassadorial roles.

Following in his father's footsteps, Schallenberg joined the diplomatic service himself in 1997.

Sandra Mason

Barbados elected Dame Sandra Mason as its very first president, replacing British Queen Elizabeth as head of state. A former jurist who has been governor-general of the island since 2018, Mason was also the first woman to serve on the Barbados Court of Appeals.

Sandra Mason was elected late on October 20 by a two-thirds vote of a joint session of the country's House of Assembly and Senate. In a statement, the government called her appointment a milestone on its "road to republic."A former British colony that gained independence in 1966, the nation of just under 300,000 had long maintained ties with the United Kingdom's monarchy.

But many Barbadians have long agitated to remove the Queen's status –and with it, the lingering symbolic presence of imperialism over its governance.

That finally happenened on November 30, the country's 55th anniversary of independence from Britain, when Mason was sworn in.

Places in the News

Gairsain

Chief Minister Trivendra Singh Rawat on March 4, 2021 declared Gairsain as a new administrative division of the state, a third commissionerate after Kumaon and Garhwal. This was a year after making Gairsain in Chamoli district as the summer capital of Uttarakhand,

Gairsain division will comprise four hill districts, including Almora and Bageshwar (both in Kumaon) and Rudrapyarag and Chamoli (in Garhwal).

Gairsain, a tehsil in Chamoli district, is located nearly 270-km from the existing temporary capital of Dehradun. Even when Uttarakhand was carved out as a separate state from Uttar Pradesh on November 9, 2000, statehood activists had contended that Gairsain was best suited to be the capital of the mountainous state since it was between both Kumaon and Garhwal regions. But it was Dehradun in the plains that was named the temporary capital.

Kakatiya Rudreshwara (Ramappa) Temple, Telangana

On July 25, the United Nations Educational, Scientific and Cultural Organization (UNESCO) inscribed the 13th-century Ramappa in Palampet, Telangana as a World Heritage Site.

Rudreshwara, popularly known as Ramappa Temple, is located in the village of Palampet approximately 200km north-east of Hyderabad, in the State of Telangana. It is the main Shiva temple in a walled complex built during the Kakatiyan period (1123–1323 CE) under rulers Rudradeva and Recharla Rudra. Construction of the sandstone temple began in 1213 CE and is believed to have continued over some

Kakatiya Rudreshwara (Ramappa) Temple in Telangana

40 years. The building features decorated beams and pillars of carved granite and dolerite with a distinctive and pyramidal Vimana (horizontally stepped tower) made of lightweight porous bricks, so-called 'floating bricks', which reduced the weight of the roof structures. The temple's sculptures of high artistic quality illustrate regional dance customs and Kakatiyan culture. Located at the foothills of a forested area and amidst agricultural fields, close to the shores of the Ramappa Cheruvu, a Kakatiya-built water reservoir, the choice of setting for the edifice followed the ideology and practice sanctioned in dharmic texts that temples are to be constructed to form an integral part of a natural setting, including hills, forests, springs, streams, lakes, catchment areas, and agricultural lands.

Harappan Ruins of Dholavira

Dholavira, a Harappan-era city in Gujarat, was conferred the tag of UNESCO World Heritage Site on July 27. The site has been on UNESCO's tentative list since 2014 and the nomination dossier was filed in January 2020. Gujarat now has four world heritage sites — Dholavira, Champaner near Pavagadh, Rani ki Vav in Patan and the historic city of Ahmedabad.

An Aerial View of Dholavira Archaeological Site

Excavated by the Archaeological Survey of India (ASI) in 1967, Dholavira is located in the Rann of Kutch in Gujarat and has been one of the preferred tourist destinations in the State. Dholavira is about 250km by road from the district headquarters of Bhuj (which is also the nearest airport).

The ancient city of Dholavira is one of the most remarkable and well-preserved urban settlements in South Asia dating from the 3rd to mid-2nd millennium BCE (Before Common Era).'

Key characteristics of the site include remains of the water management system, multi-layered defensive mechanisms, extensive use of stone in construction, and special burial structures. Artefacts made of copper, shell, stone; jewellery of semi-precious stones; terracotta, gold, and ivory have been found at the site. Excavations at the site have revealed seven cultural stages detailing the rise and fall of the Indus Valley Civilisation.

India has 40 world heritage properties overall, which includes 32 cultural, 7 natural and one mixed property. Italy, Spain, China, Germany and France are the only other countries that have 40 or more World Heritage sites.

Indian Places in UNESCO's Tentative List of World Heritage Sites

UNESCO included six sites in India on its tentative list of world heritage sites in 2021. The places make it to the tentative list before they are considered for the final nomination. The submissions were made by the Archaeological Survey of India. Satpura Tiger Reserve in Madhya Pradesh, the megalithic site of Hire Benkal in Karnataka, Maratha military architecture in Maharashtra, Bhedaghat-Lametaghat in Madhya Pradesh's Narmada Valley, the riverfront of Varanasi in Uttar Pradesh, and the temples of Kanchipuram in Tamil Nadu are the sites on the list.

1. The Riverfront of the Historic City of Varanasi, Uttar Pradesh

It is one of the most ancient continuously inhabited cities of the world since

Rana Mahal Ghat in Varanasi

at least 1200 BCE. The juxtaposition of the sacred and the mundane, life and death, spiritual and material facets associated with the River Ganga on the Varanasi ghats, embodies a wholly significant interaction between the natural and urban elements of the city.

2. The Temples of Kanchipuram, Tamil Nadu

The temples of Kanchipuram exhibit the creative genius of the Pallava architects in design and scale of construction. The fact that the sculptors did not have any model to follow to create this array of divine imagery makes the temples of Kanchipuram an outstanding example of a first-of-its-kind experimentation in temple architecture.

3. Megalithic Site of Hire Benkal, Karnataka

In Hire Benkal, Karnataka, three clusters of megaliths have stood tall on a castellated granite hillock for over 2,500 years. Studies suggest that over 1,000 megalithic structures lie in the three clusters.

4. Bhedaghat-Lametaghat in Narmada Valley, Madhya Pradesh

Bhedaghat, situated on the Narmada riverside close to Jabalpur, is home to glittering marble rock formations that take on different colours as the light changes through the day. The magnesium limestone rocks on both sides of the Narmada reflect in the clear waters, forming a spectacle of natural light and colour in the area. No such example exists where a river flows freely splitting an enormous mountain of marble.

5. Satpura Tiger Reserve, Madhya Pradesh

Located in Hoshangabad, Madhya Pradesh, Satpura Tiger Reserve is one of the oldest forest reserves in the country. The forest is home to leopards, black bucks, Malabar giant squirrels and sloth bears, among many species. It also houses over 50 rock shelters with paintings that are said to be 10,000 years old.

6. Maratha Military Architecture in Maharashtra

The forts of West India, many of which were built by Chhatrapati Shivaji Maharaj, cover hundreds of acres of land in the area and are known to have been used for guerilla warfare tactics.The nomination lists 14 such forts, including Raigad Fort, Shivneri Fort, Kulaba Fort and Lohagad.The forts of Maharashtra represent Maratha ideology in architectural planning based upon best utilization of hilly terrain and sea. The fortifications and their distinguishing Maratha style of architecture synthesizing Sultanate and Rajput architectural traditions are an exceptional testimony to the cultural traditions governed by the landscape in Maharashtra.

Marble Rocks at Bhedhaghat, Madhya Pradesh

Suez Canal

Suez Canal, a waterway crucial to global trade, was blocked by a massive container ship in March, causing a traffic jam that lasted days. The *Ever Given* is a giant container ship 400m-long (1,312ft) and 200,000 tonnes in weight, with a maximum capacity of 20,000 containers. The ship is owned by container shipping company Evergreen Line. The *Ever Given* was built in 2018. It was carrying 18,300 containers when it, sailing under a Panamanian flag bound for The Netherlands from China, ran aground on March 23. The ship was travelling northward through the Suez Canal to the Mediterranean from the Red Sea when it ran aground in high winds and a dust storm.

The Suez Canal is a crucial global trade passage, providing the shortest warm-water maritime route from Europe to Asia. It's 120 miles long, 79 feet deep and 673 feet wide. Thousands of ships travel through the canal every year. Nearly 19,000 vessels plied the 193km maritime shortcut in 2020, carrying 12% of global trade by volume and around 10% of the world's oil.

Around one million barrels of oil and roughly 8% of liquefied natural gas pass through the canal each day. Prior to the pandemic, trade passing through the Suez Canal contributed to 2% of Egypt's GDP.

Records of the Year

The World's Largest Painting

Sacha Jafri's, The Journey of Humanity, the World's Largest Painting

At 17,000 square feet, Sacha Jafri's *The Journey of Humanity* (2020), an abstraction featuring drips, whorls, and splatters of various hues, is the world's largest painting, as certified by the Guinness Book of World Records. On March 23, The Journey of Humanity sold for $62 million at an auction held in Dubai at Atlantis, The Palm hotel. The sale puts it among the most expensive artworks by a living artist ever sold at auction.

Jafri's plan had initially been to slice up the painting and sell it in 60 segments to raise $30 million to support "global digital equality." Those paintings were intended to have been sold in four auctions.But the work instead ultimately sold as one.

The sale puts Jafri's name among the world's most expensive living artists. The $62 million raised by *The Journey of Humanity* has only been beaten at auction by the works of Jeff Koons, David Hockney and the digital artist Beeple, whose NFT image "Everydays: The First 5000 Days" sold via Christie's for over $69 million in March 2021.

The World's Longest Pedestrian Suspension Bridge

The world's longest pedestrian suspension bridge was officially opened in northern Portugal on May 2, 2021. Hidden between rock-strewn mountains covered with lush greenery and yellow flowers inside the Unesco-recognised Arouca Geopark, the 516 metres (1,700 feet) bridge hangs 175 metres above the fast-flowing River Paiva. Arouca 516 breaks the record for the longest pedestrian suspension bridge, held since 2017 by the Charles Kuonen Bridge at Randa, in the Swiss Alps.

The World's Longest Pedestrian Suspension Bridge in Portugal

Oldest Person to Release an Album of New Material

The Grammy Award-Winning Singer Tony Bennett has created Guinness World Records for being the 'oldest person to release an album of new material' with his album 'Love for Sale'. At the time of the

Covid-19 Pandemic and Drop in Life Expectancy

extra

A study from Oxford University found that the covid-19 pandemic has led to a drop in life expectancy not seen since the second world war in western Europe.

Lady Gaga and Tony Bennett

release of the album of the singer with Lady Gaga, Tony Bennett was 95-years and 60-days-old, according to *Guinness World Records*. The new album of the singer Tony Bennett and Lady Gaga *Love for Sale*, which celebrates the music of Cole Porter, was released on October 1.

The Tallest Living Woman in the World

Rumeysa Gelgi from Turkey has become the tallest living woman in the world, according to *Guinness World Records*. The 24-year-old, who measures 215.16cm, or 7ft 0.7in, had earlier broken the Guinness World Record for the tallest living female teenager in 2014.

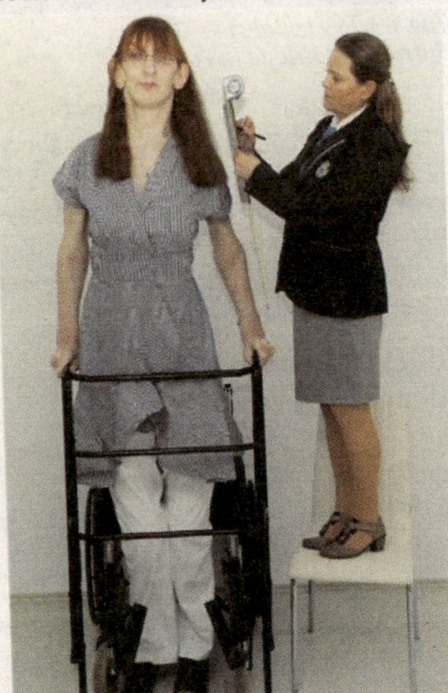
Rumeysa Gelgi, the World's Tallest Living Woman

Gelgi's extraordinary height is caused due to the Weaver Syndrome, a medical condition that accelerates growth and causes abnormalities such as skeletal maturation.The tallest man in the world, Sultan Kosen, is also Turkish.

He was measured at 8ft 2.8in (251cm) in 2018.

The tallest woman to have lived was Zeng Jinlian, from China, who was measured at 8ft 1in (246.3cm) before her death in 1982.

The Oldest Person to Enter Space

Star Trek star William Shatner, at the age of 90 years 205 days, became the oldest person in space (male) on October 13, breaking a record that has stood for almost 23 years.

William Shatner (second form left) with his Fellow Crew

The previous record holder was John Glenn Jr. who was 77 years 103 days old when he was launched into space as part of the crew of Discovery STS-95 on 29 October 1998.

Blue Origin's first space expedition took place in July, with Bezos, his brother Mark Bezos, aviator Wally Funk and Oliver Daeman, the youngest person ever to enter space, aboard the privately funded, reusable spacecraft.

Nobel Prizes 2021

Physiology or Medicine

David Julius and Ardem Patapoutian, two US researchers, won the 2021 Nobel prize in physiology or medicine for work that unlocked the secrets of the sense of

David Julius

Ardem Patapoutian

touch.Through experiments that began in the 1990s, the scientists pieced together how nerve impulses are triggered in the skin so that temperature and pressure can be perceived.

Julius turned to capsaicin, the compound that makes chilli peppers burn, to identify sensors in nerve endings that respond to heat. Meanwhile, Patapoutian studied pressure-sensitive cells and discovered further receptors that respond to being poked and prodded.

Physics

Syukuro Manabe, Klaus Hasselmann and Giorgio Parisi won the prize for physics for their groundbreaking contributions to our understanding of complex phys-

Syukuro Manabe

Klaus Hasselmann

Giorgio Parisi

ical systems – including how humanity influences the Earth's climate. One half of the prize was jointly awarded to Manabe and Hasselmann for their physical modelling of Earth's climate, quantifying variability and reliably predicting global heating. The other half went to Parisi for his discovery of the interplay of disorder and fluctuations in physical systems from atomic to planetary scales.

Chemistry

Benjamin List and David MacMillan were awarded the Nobel Prize in Chemistry 2021 because in 2000 they, independent of each other, they developed a third type of catalysis. It is called asymmetric

Benjamin List

David MacMillan

organocatalysis and builds upon small organic molecules.

Organic catalysts have a stable framework of carbon atoms, to which more active chemical groups can attach. These often contain common elements such as oxygen, nitrogen, sulphur or phosphorus. This means that these catalysts are both environmentally friendly and cheap to produce.

Literature

The Literature prize was awarded to Abdulrazak Gurnah "for his uncompromising and compassionate penetration of the effects of colonialism and the fate of the refugee in the gulf between cultures and continents." Gurnah grew up on one of the islands of Zanzibar before fleeing persecution and arriving in England as a student in the 1960s. He has published 10 novels as well as a number of short stories. Gurnah's novels – from his debut Memory of Departure, about a failed uprising, to his most recent, Afterlives – "recoil from stereotypical descriptions and open our gaze to a culturally diversified East Africa unfamiliar to many in other parts of the world".

Abdulrazak Gurnah

No black African writer has won the prize since Wole Soyinka in 1986. Gurnah is the first black writer to win since Toni Morrison in 1993.

Peace

The Nobel Peace Prize 2021 was awarded jointly to Maria Ressa and Dmitry Andreyevich Muratov "for their efforts to safeguard freedom of expression, which is a precondition for democracy and lasting peace."

"Free, independent and fact-based journalism serves to protect against abuse of power, lies and war propaganda," the Nobel Committee said. "Without freedom of expression and freedom of the press, it will be difficult to successfully promote fraternity between nations, disarmament and a better world order."

The committee considered Ressa and Muratov to be "representatives of all journalists who stand up for this ideal in a world in which democracy and freedom of the press face increasingly adverse conditions".

Ressa, 58, a former CNN bureau chief in the Philippines, and Rappler, the news site she founded in 2012, have faced

Maria Ressa

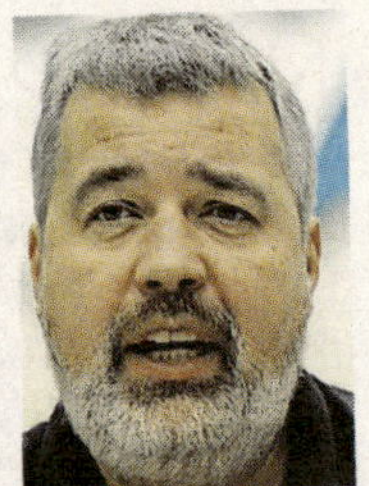
Dmitry Muratov

multiple criminal charges and investigations after publishing stories critical of President Rodrigo Duterte and his bloody drugs war.

Muratov, 59, was one of the founders of the independent newspaper Novaya Gazeta in 1993 and has been its editor-in-chief since 1995.

Economics

The Sveriges Riksbank Prize in Economic Sciences was awarded to three US-based economists: David Card, Joshua D. Angrist

David Card

Joshua D. Angrist

Guido W. Imbens

and Guido W. Imbens. The Nobel Committee awarded half the Prize to David Card for his "empirical contributions to labour economics" and the other half to Guido Imbens and Joshua Angrist "for their methodological contributions to the analysis of causal relationships." This is the first time the economic prize has been divided in this fashion with one half going to one awardee and other half divided across two awardees. In the past, prize money was divided equally between the awardees even if the prize was for different topics as is the case this time around.

05
WHO IS WHO

- A section on Indians and foreigners who have made their mark on different walks of life from business, politics, law, entertainment, science, sports and religion.

WHO IS WHO INDIA

A section on Indians who have made their mark on different walks of life from business, politics, law, entertainment, science, sports and religion.

Abbas, KA (1914–87): Indian film director, novelist, screenwriter, journalist • wrote in Urdu, Hindi and English • one of the pioneers of neo-realistic cinema • *Neecha Nagar, Saat Hindustani, Do Boond Pani*• Palme d'Or, National Award for the Best Feature Film, Ghalib Award.

KA Abbas

Abdullah, Sheikh (1905-82): Indian politician and the founder of National Conference • known as the Lion of Kashmir • former CM of Jammu and Kashmir.

A.C.Bhaktivedanta also called Swami Prabhupada (1896 -1977): Indian religious leader and author who in 1965 founded the International Scociety for Krishna Consciousness, popularly known as the Hare Krishna Movement.

Adiseshiah, Malcolm (1910-94): Development economist and educationist • Dy Director General of UNESCO • Padma Bhushan.

Advani, Lal Krishna (1927): Senior BJP leader and its former president • Deputy PM (2002–04), Leader of Opposition in LS (2004–09), Leader of Opposition in RS (1980) • *My Country My Life* • Padma Vibhushan.

Ahmed, Fakhruddin Ali (1905-77): Freedom fighter and the fifth President of India (1974-77).

Akbar, Jalal-ud-din Muhammad (1542-1605): Mughal emperor of India (1556-1605) known as 'Akbar the Great'• promoted commerce and learning • showed a receptive interest in Hinduism and Christianity • *Akbarnama.*

Akhtar, Begum (1914-74): Singer of Ghazal, Dadra and Thumri genres • known as the 'Queen of Ghazals' • Sangeet Natak Akademi Award, Padma Bhushan (posthumous), Padma Shri.

Akilan (1922-88): (Akilandam, PV): Tamil author noted for realistic writing • journalist and activist • *Chithira Pavai, Vengayin Maindan*• Jnanpith Award (1975).

Ali, Aruna Asaf (1909-96): Originally Aruna Ganguly • independence activist, socialist, publisher • wife of Asaf Ali, India's first Ambassador to US • first Mayor of Delhi (1958) • Bharat Ratna (1997), International Lenin Peace Prize (1964).

Aruna Asaf Ali

Ali, Salim (1896-1987): Indian ornithologist, known as 'The Birdman of India' • The *Fall of a Sparrow* • Padma Vibhushan (1976), Padma Bhushan (1958).

Ambani, Dhirubhai (1932–2002) Originally Dhirajlal Hirachand Ambani • industrialist • Reliance Industries that he set up is India's largest private sector company• Padma Vibhushan (posthumous).

Ambani, Mukesh (1957): Chairman and managing director of Reliance Industries Ltd (RIL) • launched Reliance Jio telecommunication network in 2016.

Ambar, Malik (1548-1626): A former slave from Ethiopia who became a kingmaker in a Deccan Sultanate in Daulatabad.

Ambedkar, Dr Bhimrao Ramji (1891-1956): Indian jurist, social worker, politician, writer, educationist• emancipator of the 'untouchables' and crusader for social justice • headed the drafting body of the Indian Constitution • served as the first law minister of independent India • founded the Republican Party (1956)• Bharat Ratna (1990).

Amrit Kaur, Rajkumari (1889-1964) : Born into the royal family of Kapurthala and educated in England• First woman to join the Union Cabinet, serving as Health Minister for 10 years. In that position, she founded the Indian Council for Child Welfare; helped establish AIIMS, the country's top hospital and medical college and campaigned to prevent malaria, likely saving hundreds of thousands of lives.

Amrohi, Kamal (1918-1993): Urdu-Hindi poet, film director, screen writer• *Mahal, Pakeejah, Razia Sultan.*

Amte, Murlidhar Devidas (Baba Amte) (1914-2008): Indian lawyer and social activist who worked for leprosy patients• Magsaysay award, Templeton Prize, Padma Vibhushan.

Baba Amte

Anand, Dev (1923-2011): Renowned Indian film star, director and producer • *Romancing with Life* (autobiography) • Padma Bhushan (2001), Dada Saheb Phalke Award (2002).

Anand, Mulk Raj (1905-2004): Indian author, novelist, critic • one of the pioneers of Indo-Anglican fiction along with Raja Rao and RK Narayan • *Untouchable, Coolie* • Padma Bhushan.

Anand, Viswanathan (1969): Indian chess grandmaster• won the World Chess Championship in 2007, 2008, 2010 and 2012• won the World Rapid Chess Championship in 2003 and 2017• won the International Grandmaster title in 1988• former No. 1 player• Rajiv Gandhi Khel Ratna, Padma Vibhushan.

Annadurai, CN (1909-69): Former CM of Tamil Nadu, Rajya Sabha MP (1962–67), MLA (1957–62)• eminent writer in Tamil• formed the DMK party.

Arundale, George Sidney (1878-1945): Englishman who adopted India as his home • advocate of national education and the Indian independence movement • married dancer Rukmini Devi.

Aryabhatta (476-550 AD): Indian mathematician and astronomer • India's first satellite was named after him• *Aryabhatiya, Aryasiddhanta.*

Ashapoorna Devi (1909-95): Bengali writer• first woman Jnanpith awardee • *Prothom Pratisruti, Subarnalata, Bakul Katha*• Sahitya Akademi Fellowship.

Ashapoorna Devi

Ashoka the Great: Emperor of the Mauryan dynasty• grandson of Chandragupta Maurya• following the Battle of Kalinga, renounced violence and embraced Buddhism.

Aurangzeb (1618-1707): Mughal emperor of India• helped the empire flourish to the fullest, but estranged Hindus and Sikhs• last of the great Mughal emperors in India.

extra

Sister of Lata Mangeshkar and Asha Bhosle

Usha Mangeshkar, the younger sister of Lata Mangeshkar and Asha Bhosle, came into the spotlight after her devotional songs for the film, *Jai Santoshi Ma.* She was nominated for a Filmfare Best Female Playback Award for the same.

Aurobindo, Sri (1872-1950): (Aurobindo Ghose) Indian philosopher • set up the Aurobindo ashram in Puducherry • developed 'integral yoga' • *The Life Divine*.

Ayyankali (1863-1941): Social reformer who worked for the marginalised in Kerala• founded the *Sadhujana Paripalana Sangham* for the upliftment of dalits.

Azad, Abul Kalam (1888-1958): Freedom fighter • first education minister of free India• *India Wins Freedom*• Bharat Ratna (1992).

Abul Kalam Azad

Azad, Chandrasekhar (1906-31): A revolutionary who was actively involved in the Non-Cooperation Movement and the Kakori Conspiracy.

Azmi, Shabana (1950): Indian film and theatre actress • recipient of five national awards • social activist and former Rajya Sabha MP • Padma Bhushan(2012).

Baba Ramdev (1965): Proponent of yoga, founder of Patanjali Yogpeeth and Bharat Swabhiman Trust• started Patanjali Ayurved, a consumer packaged goods company, based in Haridwar.

Babar, Zahir-ud-din Muhammad (1483-1530): Founder of the Mughal dynasty that ruled northern India for nearly 300 years.

Bachchan, Amitabh (1942): Indian film actor and former MP• the quiz master of *Kaun Banega Crorepati* • *Zanjeer, Sholay, Deewar, Black, Piku, Pink*• Padma Vibhushan.

Bachchan, Harivansh Rai (1907-2003): Hindi poet most known for his work *Madhushala* and autobiography in four volumes *Kya Bhoolun, Kya Yaad Karoon*• Padma Bhushan.

Bahadur Shah II (1775-1862): The last king of Mughal empire• took part in the 1857 Indian War of Independence.

Bahuguna, Sundarlal (1927-2021): Environmentalist most known for leading the Chipko movement and the fight against the construction of Tehri Dam • Padma Vibhushan (2009).

Bajaj, Jamnalal (1886-1942): Industrialist, freedom fighter, social worker• close associate of Mahatma Gandhi• founded the Bajaj group of companies.

Bajaj, Rahul (1938): Indian businessman, politician and philanthropist• chairman of the Indian conglomerate Bajaj Group• MP•Padma Bhushan (2001).

Balasaraswati, T (1918-84): The foremost exponent of bharatnatyam• Padma Vibhushan.

T Balasaraswati

Bandodkar, Dayanand (1911-73): The first CM of Goa after it was returned to India by Portugal• a mine owner• swept the polls in 1963, 1967, 1972.

Bandopadhyay, Padmavathy (1944): The first woman Air Marshal of the Indian Air Force.

Bandopadhyay,Tarashankar(1898-1971): Bengali novelist•Jnanpith award in 1966 for novel *Ganadebata* which was adjudged the best creative literary work published in an Indian language between 1925 and 1959.

Banerjee, Surendranath (1848-1925): One of the first Indians to pass the ICS examination• President of Indian National Congress, twice.

Basavanna: 12th-century Hindu religious reformer and Kannada poet •The Lingayats believe that Basava was the founder of their tradition.

Basu, Jyoti (1914-2010): Veteran CPI(M) leader• CM of West Bengal from 1977 to 2000, becoming the second longest-serving CM in the country.

Bedi, Bishan Singh (1946): Former Indian cricketer, coach• part of the famous 'Indian spin quartet'.

Bishan Singh Bedi

Bedi, Kiran (1949): First woman IPS officer (1972)• social activist• introduced prison reforms in the country• Lieutenant Governor of Puducherry since 2016• Magsaysay Award (1994), United Nations Medal (2004).

Bedi, Rajinder Singh (1915-84): Progressive Urdu fiction writer, playwright• Hindi film director, screenwriter and dialogue writer• Films: *Dastak, Phagun*• Novels: *Ek Chadar Maili Si*• Sahitya Akademi Award (1965).

Beevi Fathima M. (1927): The first woman judge of the Supreme Court (1989).

Behn, Mira (1892-1982): Originally Madeleine Slade• British disciple of Gandhiji• Padma Vibhushan.

Benegal, Shyam (1934): Indian film director• *Ankur, Mandi, Nishant*• Dada Saheb Phalke award (2005), Padma Bhushan (1991). V.Shantaram Lifetime Achievement Award (2018).

Besant, Annie (1847-1933): British woman, staunch supporter of the Indian independence movement• set up the Home Rule League• president of INC (1917)• member of the Theosophical Society of India.

Bezbarua, Lakshminath (1864-1938): Assamese writer• composed Assamese state anthem• *Podum Kunwori*.

Bhabha, Dr Homi J. (1909-66): Indian nuclear physicist• founding director of the Atomic Energy Establishment, Trombay (now, the Bhabha Atomic Research Centre)• the father of Indian nuclear programme• Padma Bhushan (1954), Adams Prize (1942).

Bhagwan Das (1869-1958): Indian theosophist• collaborated in founding the Central Hindu College • founded the Kashi Vidya Peeth • a scholar who wrote 30 books in Sanskrit and Hindi • *The Superphysics of the Great War* • Bharat Ratna (1955).

Bharata Muni (1 BCE-3CE): The father of Indian theatrical art forms• wrote *Natyasastra*, a theoritical treatise on ancient Indian dramaturgy and histrionics, especially Sanskrit theatre.

Bharati, Dr Dharamvir (1926-1997): Hindi poet, author, playwright and thinker• *Gunahon Ka Devta*• Padma Shri, Sangeet Natak Akademi Award.

Bharati, Chinnaswami Subramania (1882-1921): Known as 'Mahakavi'• poet, patriot, writer, journalist, social reformer, philosopher• worked in *Swadesamitran* (Tamil daily)• *Kuyil Pattu* and *Panchali Sapatam*• English works - *Agni and Other Poems* and *Translations and Essays and Other Prose Fragments.*

Bhargava, Manjul (1974): Indian-American mathematician• received the Fields Medal 2014 for outstanding contribution in mathematics• Padma Bhushan (2015), Morgan Prize (1996).

Manjul Bhargava

Bhaskara-I (7 AD): Indian astronomer and mathematician• helped disseminate the mathematical work of Aryabhatta.

Bhaskara-II (1114-1185): Great Indian mathematician and astronomer who was the first to use the decimal system in a written work• *Sidhanta Shiromani.*

Bhatia, Sabeer (1968): Indian-born co-founder of Hotmail• sold Hotmail to

Microsoft in 1998.

Bhatnagar, Shanti Swaroop (1894-1955): Indian scientist considered to be the father of research laboratories• served as the first director-general of CSIR and the first chairman of UGC• Padma Bhushan (1954), Fellow of the Royal Society (1943).

Bhatt, Ela (1933): Activist, lawyer, Gandhian• founded the Self-Employed Women's Association (SEWA)• Magsaysay Award (1977), Padma Bhushan (1986), Right Livelihood Award (1984).

Bhavabhuti (8 AD): A great Sanskrit dramatist• *Malatimadhava*.

Bhave, Vinoba (1895-1982): Advocate of human rights and non-violence• led the Bhoodan movement• Bharat Ratna (1983), Magsaysay award (1958).

Vinoba Bhave

Bhosle, Asha (1933): Playback singer in Hindi cinema• sister of Lata Mangeshkar• first film song: "Chala Chala Nav Bala" • OP Nayyar gave Asha a break in *CID (*1956)• Dada Saheb Phalke Award, Padma Vibhushan.

Bhutia, Bhaichung (1976): One of the best football players from the country• first Indian footballer to sign a contract with a European club• Padma Shri, Arjuna Award.

Bindra, Abhinav (1983): Indian shooter• won gold at the 2008 Beijing Olympics• Padma Bhushan, Rajiv Gandhi Khel Ratna, Arjuna Award.

Birla, Ghanshyam Das (1894-1983): Founder of the Birla empire•A close associate of Gandhi•Founder of the Federation of Indian Chambers of Commerce and Industry(FICCI).

Ghanshyam Das Birla

Birla, Kumar Mangalam (1967): Indian industrialist, chairman of the Aditya Birla Group (since 1995)• chancellor of the Birla Institute of Technology and Science.

Bonnerjee, Womesh Chunder (1844-1906): First president of the Indian National Congress• barrister.

Bordoloi, Gopinath (1890-1950): Independence activist• PM of Assam before independence and later, CM of the Indian state of Assam• one of the makers of modern Assam• educationist• Bharat Ratna (1999).

Bose, Amar Gopal (1929-2013): American-born Indian entrepreneur• founder of the Bose Corporation.

Bose, Jagadish Chandra (1858-1937): Doyen of Indian science• physicist and botanist• founder of the Bose Research Institute, Calcutta• did original work in electricity• identified life in plants, and is also said to have developed wireless telegraphy independent of Marconi• Fellow of Royal Society (1920), Knight Bachelor (1917).

Bose, Khudiram (1889-1908): Indian revolutionary from Midnapore• arrested for attempting to bomb Kingsford's (the magistrate of Muzaffarpur) carriage• hanged at the age of 18.

Bose, Nandalal (1882-1966): Pioneer of modern Indian art• key figure of contextual modernism• Padma Vibhushan.

Bose, Netaji Subhas Chandra (1897-1945): Freedom fighter• formed the In-

Brother of Sarojini Naidu

Harindranath Chattopadhyay was an Indian poet, musician and actor. He featured in films ranging from *Sahib Bibi Aur Ghulam* to *Bawarchi* and Satyajit Ray's *Goopy Gyne Bagha Byne* and *Sonar Kella*. His sister was Sarojini Naidu.

dian National Army in 1943 to fight the British• served twice as Congress president but later ousted• reportedly killed in an air crash, though some disagree.

Bose, Satyendra Nath (1894-1974): Indian physicist after whom the elementary particle Boson is named• best known for his work on quantum physics• Padma Vibhushan.

Brahmagupta (598-665): Indian mathematician and astronomer• the first to give rules to compute with zero• *Brahma Sphuta Siddhanta.*

Buddha, Gautama (6th-4th BC) Born as Siddhartha in Lumbini near Kapilavastu• founder of Buddhism• followers of his teachings are known as Buddhists.

Cama, Bhikaiji (1861-1936): Indian nationalist and advocate of women's rights• best known for unfurling the first version of the Indian national flag at the International Socialist Congress held at Stuttgart, Germany in 1907.

Bhikaiji Cama

Cariappa, Field Marshal KM (1899-93): First Indian Commander-in-Chief of the Indian Army (1949-53).

Chanakya (4th C BC): Also known as Kautilya• statesman and philosopher who helped the Mauryan emperor Chandragupta rise to power• *Arthashastra.*

Chand, Dhyan (1905-79): Indian hockey wizard• won three Olympic gold medals for India (1928, 1932, 1936)• Padma Bhushan.

Chandragupta-II (Vikramaditya) (380-415 CE): Brave emperor from the Gupta period• son of Samudragupta• art, architecture and sculpture flourished during his reign.

Chandra Shekhar (1927-2007): 8th PM of India• formed the Janata Party Socialist• *Dynamics of Social Change.*

Chandrasekhar, Subrahmanyan (1910-95): Indian-American astrophysicist• nephew of CV Raman• Nobel Prize in Physics (1983). Padma Shri (2018).

Chanu, Saikhom Mirabai (1994): Indian female weightlifter from Manipur• won silver medal at the Tokyo Olympics 2020• won gold medal at the World Weightlifting Championship in the US (2017)•Padma Shri (2018).

Mirabai Chanu

Chatterjee, Bankim Chandra (1838-1894): Celebrated Bengali poet, novelist and patriot• composed the national song *Vande Mataram*• *Durgeshnandini, Yugalanguriya, Anandamath, Radharani, Krishnakanter Uil, Debi Chaudhurani, Bisabrksa, Kapalkundala.*

Chattopadhyay, Kamaladevi (1903-88): Social reformer, freedom fighter• resurrected Indian crafts, theatre and literature• set up the National School of Drama• Magsaysay award, Padma Vibhushan, Padma Bhushan.

Chattopadhyay, Sarat Chandra (1876-1938): A popular Bengali novelist and short-story writer• *Debdas, Parineeta, Bordidi, Bindur Chhele, Biraj Bou, Shesh Prasna.*

Chaudhuri, Nirad C. (1897-1999): Indian Bengali-English writer• lived in England• *The Autobiography of an Unknown Indian, A Passage to England*• Sahitya Akademi award.

Chaurasia, Pt Hariprasad (1938): Indian classical player of the *bansuri* or the Indian bamboo flute• Albums: *Call of the Valley, Music of the Rivers, Rasdhara, The Elements: Wind, Flute Duet, Raga Cycle*• Padma Vibhushan.

Chavan, Yashwantrao Balwantrao (1913-

84): The first CM of Maharashtra after the division of Bombay State• instrumental in establishing co-operatives in Maharashtra for the betterment of farmers• writer and advocate of social democracy.

Chawla, Kalpana (1961-2003): American astronaut of Indian origin• first Indian-born woman and the second Indian person to fly in space• flew first on Space Shuttle Columbia (1997)• died in the Space Shuttle Columbia disaster with six others• recipient of the Congressional Space Medal of Honour.

Chembai Vaidyanatha Bhagavathar (1896-1974): One of the greatest (Carnatic) musicians of India• Padma Bhushan, Sangeetha Kalanidhi.

Chidambaram, Rajagopala (1936): Indian physicist most known for his role in the country's nuclear weapons programme as well as coordinating test preparations for the Pokhran I and II• principal scientific adviser to GoI• Padma Vibhushan.

Chopra, Neeraj (1997): Track and field athlete who competes in the javelin. First track and field athlete to win an Olympic gold medal for India. Won gold at the 2020 Tokyo Olympics with a throw of 87.58m in his second attempt.

Neeraj Chopra

Chopra, Yash (1932-2012): Director and producer in Bollywood• Padma Bhushan, Dada Saheb Phalke Award.

Correa, Charles (1930-2015): India's eminent architect and urban planner • Padma Vibhushan, Royal Gold Medal.

Dahia, Ravi Kumar (1997): Indian freestyle wrestler who won a silver medal at the 2020 Tokyo Olympics in the 57kg category. Also a bronze medalist from 2019 World Wrestling Championships and a two-time Asian Champion.

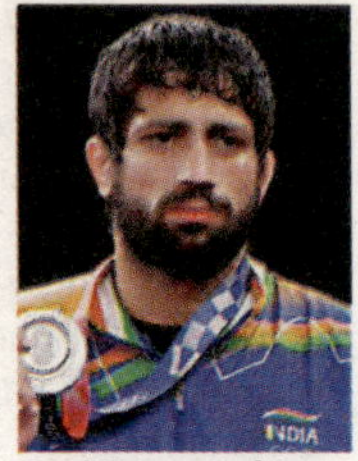
Ravi Kumar Dahia

Dalai Lama (1935): (Tenzin Gyatso) Tibetan spiritual leader• established govt-in-exile at Dharamsala in Himachal Pradesh (1959)• Nobel Peace Prize (1989).

Dara Shikoh (1615–59): The eldest son of the Mughal emperor Shah Jahan. In the war of succession which ensued after Shah Jahan's illness in 1657, Dara was defeated by his younger brother Aurangzeb. Executed in 1659 on Aurangzeb's orders. Translated into Persian the Bhagavad Gita as well as 52 Upanishads.

Das, CR (1870-1925): Nicknamed Deshbandhu• activist, politician, poet, lawyer• founded Swaraj Party in 1923• *Malancha, Mala, Sagar Sangeet.*

Dasgupta, Kamal (1912-74): Eminent Bengali music director, composer and folk artist• *Raga, Thumri* - main elements of his music.

Deendayal, Lala (1844 - 1905): India's first world-class photographer•The ruler of Indore, Maharaja Tukoji II, encouraged him to set up his studio there• was bestowed the title of "Raja Deen Dayal" by the Nizam of Hyderabad•Through his studios across Secunderabad, Indore and Mumbai, Dayal captured an estimated 30,000 photographs of monuments, people, and events.

Deodhar D.B. (1892-1993): The Grand Old Man of Indian Cricket after whom the Deodhar Trophy is named• Padma Bhushan, Padma Shri.

Desai, Morarji Ranchhodji (1896-1995): Indian PM from March 1977-July 1979• Bharat Ratna.

Deshmukh, Nanaji (1916-2010): Social activist who was a leader of the Bharatiya Jana Sangh •worked in the fields of education, health and rural self-reliance• Bharat Ratna (2019).

Nanaji Deshmukh

Deshpande, Purushottam Lakshman (1919-2000): *Maharashtrache Laadke Vyatimatva* - Maharashtra's beloved person• veteran Marathi writer and performer known by his initials Pu. La• Padma Bhushan, Padma Shri, Sahitya Akademi Award.

Deshpande, Vasantrao (1920–1983): Renowned Hindustani classical vocalist• a great performer of Natya Sangeet• Sangeet Natak Akademi Award (1982).

Dev, Acharya Narendra (1889-1956) Nationalist, socialist, scholar• professor at Kashi Vidyapeeth (1925), Vice Chancellor of Lucknow and Banaras Hindu Universities• co-founder of Congress Socialist Party (1934), founder of Praja Socialist Party.

Devi, Shakuntala (1929-2013): Indian math whiz, author• known as human computer• secured a place in the 1982 *Guinness Book of Records* for successfully multiplying two 13-digit numbers in just seconds.

Devi, Sitara (1920-2014): Eminent Indian Kathak dancer• Tagore called her 'Nritya Samragni'• Sangeet Natak Akademi Award, Padma Shri.

Dey, Manna (1919-2013): Eminent Indian playback singer who sang in almost all major regional languages• sang primarily in Hindi and Bengali • Padma Bhushan (2005), Dadasaheb Phalke Award (2007).

Manna Dey

Dhawan, Satish (1920-2002): Scientist, aerospace engineer• served as the director of IISc Bangalore, chairman of ISRO• Padma Vibhushan.

Dhoni, MS (1981): Indian cricketer• captained India in two World Cups• the team won the 2011 World Cup under his captaincy • Rajiv Gandhi Khel Ratna (2017), Padma Bhushan (2018).

Dikshitar, Muthuswami (1775–1835): Poet and music composer• formed the 'Musical Trinity of Carnatic Music' along with Tyagaraja and Shyama Shastri.

Dinkar, Ramdhari Singh (1908-1974): Indian poet known for patriotic poems• Gandhian and advocate of non-violence• *Rashmirathi, Kurukshetra*• Sahitya Akademi Award, Padma Bhushan, Jnanpith Award.

Dorjee, Ang (1970): (also called Chhuldim) Nepali sherpa mountaineer, guide, porter• climed the summit of Mt Everest 19 times• in 1980, he guided Bachendri Pal, the first Indian woman, to reach the summit.

Dutt, Guru (1925-64): Director, writer, producer and actor• *Pyaasa, Sahib Bibi Aur Ghulam, Baazi.*

Dutt, Nargis (1929-81): Hindi actress• married actor Sunil Dutt• nominated to the Rajya Sabha in 1980• *Mother India, Barsaat, Awaara*• National Film award for best actress, Padma Shri.

Dwivedi, Hazari Prasad (1907-79): Hindi novelist, essayist, critic• *Alok Parva, Sahitya Ki Bhumika, Kabir*• Sahitya Akademi Award, Padma Bhushan.

EMS (Namboodiripad, Elamkulam Manakkal Sankaran) (1909-98): First CM of Kerala (1957-59, 1967-69)• CPI(M) general secretary (1978-1992).

Fazal, Abul (1551-1602): One of the *navaratnas* (nine jewels) of the royal court of Akbar• great scholar• *Akbarnama.*

Firaq Gorakhpuri (1896-1982): Originally Raghupati Sahay• one of the most noted contemporary Urdu poets from India• writer, critic• Sahitya Akademi Fellowship, Padma Bhushan, Jnanapith Award.

Fr Chavara (1805-71): Founder of the Carmelites of Mary Immaculate in India•

CMI priests heralded a revolution in the field of education• declared Blessed in 1984• canonised in 2014.

Gadgil, Madhav (1942): Indian ecologist• chairman of the Western Ghats Ecology Expert Panel (2010)• Shanti Swarup Bhatnagar Prize for S&T, Padma Bhushan.

Madhav Gadgil

Gandhi, Ela (1940): Grand daughter of Mahatma Gandhi• peace activist• MP in S. Africa (1994-2004)• ally of ANC party• banned from political activism during apartheid (1975)• worked towards Mandela's release from Pollsmoor Prison in 1990• Padma Bhushan (2007).

Gandhi, Indira (1917-84): PM of India for three consecutive terms (1966-77)• assassinated in 1984 during the fourth term• the only female PM of India till date• Bharat Ratna (1971).

Gandhi, Kasturba (1869-1944): Political activist and wife of Mahatma Gandhi• jailed by the British for political activism• worked for women's rights and welfare• died during imprisonment at Aga Khan Palace in 1944.

Gandhi, Mohandas Karamchand (1869-1948): Father of the Indian nation• 1893-1914: lived in South Africa opposing discrimination against Indians• 1915: returned to India and worked for the Congress party• lived an austere life, devoted to truth, non-violence and worked for Indian independence and unity• assassinated• *The Story of My Experiments with Truth.*

Gandhi, Rahul (1970): President of the Indian National Congress from 2017-19• chairperson of the Indian Youth Congress (2007-17)• Lok Sabha MP from Wayanad.

Gandhi, Rajiv (1944-91): Indian PM from 1984-89 • assassinated• grandson of Jawaharlal Nehru• a commercial pilot-turned-politician• Bharat Ratna (1991).

Gandhi, Sonia (1946): Originally Edvige Antonia Albina Maino• Italian by birth, naturalised in India• wife of former PM, late Rajiv Gandhi• president of the Indian National Congress (1998-2017)• MP from Rae Bareli (2004-).

Ganesan, Sivaji (1928-2001): Legendary actor• acted in around 300 (Tamil, Telugu, Kannada, Malayalam and Hindi) films in five decades• *Veerapandiya Kattabomman, Thevar Magan*• Dada Saheb Phalke Award, Padma Bhushan, Padma Shri.

Ganguly, Kadambini (1861-1923): First female physician of South Asia to be trained in western medicine• one of the first female graduates from the British Empire.

Ganguly, Sourav (1972): Former cricketer and captain of the Indian national team• Current President of the Board of Control for Cricket in India (BCCI)•In 2002, Wisden Cricketers' Almanack ranked him the sixth greatest ODI batsman of all time.

Gargi, Balwant (1916-2003): Punjabi writer who wrote popular plays• Sahitya Akademi Award for *Rang Manch*• *Saunkan, Loha Kutt, Kesro.*

Balwant Gargi

Gavaskar, Sunil (1949): One of the greatest opening batsmen of all time• captained India in 47 Test matches• first person to score centuries in both innings of a Test match thrice• set a world record of 34 Test centuries which was broken by Sachin Tendulkar 19 years later• *Sunny Days* (autobiography), *Idols, Runs 'n Ruins* and *One Day Wonders*• Padma Bhushan, Padma Shri.

Ghalib, Mirza (1797-1869): Originally Mirza Asadullah Khan• one of the greatest Urdu poets ever• was the poet laureate to the last Mughal emperor Bahadur Shah II• poetical works include *Diwan-i-Ghalibin*• notable prose: *Naam-i-Ghalib, Lateif-i-Gaibi* and *Dupshe Kawaiyani.*

Goenka, Ramnath (1904-91): Founder of the Indian Express group in 1932•One of the few journalists to have stood against the Indira Gandhi government during the Emergency period.

Ramnath Goenka

Ghosh, Amitav (1956): Indian-English language novelist•First Indian writer in English to receive the Jnanpith Award •*The Shadow Lines, The Circle of Reason, The Glass Palace, Sea of Poppies, The Hungry Tide*• Sahitya Akademi award, Padma Shri (2007).

Ghosh, Tushar Kanti (1899-1994): Prominent Indian journalist and a distinguished editor• long association with *Amrit Bazar Patrika*• Grand Old Man of Indian Journalism• Padma Bhushan.

Giri, Varahagiri Venkata (1894-1980): 4th president of India• 3rd vice president• advocate of labour and trade union movements• Bharat Ratna (1975).

Godrej, Adi (1942): Indian industrialist and philanthropist• great supporter of the World Wildlife Fund in India• president of the Confederation of Indian Industry (CII) during 2012-13• Padma Bhushan (2012).

Gokhale, Gopal Krishna (1866-1915): Activist and social reformer whom Gandhi regarded as his political guru• founded the Servants of India Society (1905).

Gombu, Nawang (1936-2011): Mountaineer • the first person to scale Mount Everest twice (1963, 1965) • Padma Bhushan, Padma Shri.

Nawang Gombu

Gopalakrishnan, Adoor (1941): Noted Indian script writer and film director• *Swayamvaram, Mathilukal, Kathapurushan, Nizhalkkuthu*• Dadasaheb Phalke Award, Padma Vibhushan, more than 15 national film awards, British Film Institute Award.

Gopi, Kalamandalam (1937): Exponent of Kathakali• performs both virtuous and villainous characters• Kalidas Samman, Sangeet Natak Akademi award.

Gopi Krishna (1935-94): Indian dancer, actor and choreographer• exponent of the Benares *gharana* style of Kathak.

Goswami, Arnab (1973): Journalist• former Editor-in-Chief of *Times Now*• co-founded *Republic TV*• Ramnath Goenka Award (2010).

Goswami, Chuni (1938-2020): Footballer who captained the Indian team which won the gold medal at the 1962 Asian Games. Scored nine goals in 30 international appearances. Also a first class cricketer, playing Ranji for Bengal.

Goswami, Indira (1942-2011): Assamese editor, poet, professor, scholar and writer• pen name: Mamoni Raisom Goswami• *Neel Kanthi Braha, Chinnamastar Manuhto, The Jour-*

Indira Goswami

extra

The Loreto Sisters

The Institute of the Blessed Virgin Mary, more commonly known as the Loreto Sisters, was an organisation, started by Mary Ward in 1609. Mother Teresa belonged to this organisation before founding the Missionaries of Charity in 1950.

ney• Jnanpith Award, Sahitya Akademi Award, Asom Ratna.

Gowda, Deve HD (1933): Indian Prime Minister (1996-1997) in the United Front government• former CM of Karnataka• Janata Dal (S) leader.

Gujral, Inder Kumar (1919-2012): PM of India (April 1997– March 1998) • *IK Gujral: Matters of Discretion: An Autobiography.*

Gulzar (1934): Film director, poet and lyricist• wrote lyrics for films including *Anand, Mere Apne, Omkara, Dil Se, Slumdog Millionaire*• Academy Award for the best original song (2008), Dadasaheb Phalke Award (2013), Padma Bhushan (2004), Sahitya Akademi Award (2002).

Gupt, Maithili Sharan (1886-1964): Hindi poet considered to be one of the pioneers of Khari Boli poetry• *Bharat-Bharati*• Padma Bhushan.

Haasan, Kamal (1954): South Indian film star who gave many blockbusters to Hindi, Tamil, Telugu and Malayalam cinemas• politicial activist who founded the party 'Makkal Needhi Maiam' in 2018• *Apoorva Raagangal, Moondram Pirai, Nayagan, Virumandi, Viswaroopam* • 3 national film awards, Padma Bhushan, Chevalier French Award.

Hangal, AK (1914-2012): Freedom fighter, stage actor and character actor in Hindi films• *Sholay, Aandhi, Shaukeen*• Padma Bhushan.

Hanuman, Guru (1901-99): Legendary Indian wrestling coach who coached many medal-winning wrestlers• Dronacharya Award (1987), Padma Shri (1983).

Hardayal, Lala (1884-1939): Indian revolutionary and scholar• worked for the Gadar Party in San Fancisco (1913) to garner international support for India's freedom.

Harishchandra, Bhartendu (1850-85): Known as the father of modern Hindi literature and Hindi theatre • *Andher Nagari, Bharat Durdasha.*

Hashmi, Safdar (1954-89): Communist playwright, actor, director, lyricist and theorist• associated with street theatre in India• a founding member of Jana Natya Manch in 1973• murdered while performing the street play *Halla Bol.*

Safdar Hashmi

Hazare, Kisan Baburao (1937): Popular as 'Anna'• social activist, Gandhian• organised a mass agitation against widespread corruption and demanded Lok Pal Bill to check it• known for rejuvenating Ralegan Siddhi village in Maharashtra• Padma Bhushan (1992), Padma Shri (1990).

Hazarika, Bhupen (1926-2011): Renowned poet, filmmaker and composer from Asom• famous for his singing of *Borgeet, Bistirno Parore, Snehe Aamar Xoto Shrabonor*• *Rudaali, Darmiyaan, Daman, Indramalati* • Winner of the Bharat Ratna in 2019 *and* Dadasaheb Phalke Award in 1992.

Hedgewar, Keshav Baliram (1889-1940): Founder of Rashtriya Swayamsevak Sangh in 1925.

Hidayatullah, Mohammed (1905-92): Vice President of India (1979-84)• Chief Justice (1968-70).

Huq, AK Fazlul (1873-1962): Founder member of the All India Muslim League • PM of Bengal (1937-43).

Husain, Maqbool Fida (1915-2011): One of the most celebrated and internationally recognised Indian artists, filmmaker and photographer• popularly known as 'MF'• member of Rajya Sabha (1986)• Padma Vibhushan.

Husain, Zakir (1897 -1969): 3rd President of India (1967-69)• second vice president• vice chancellor of Jamia Millia Islamia University • Bharat Ratna.

Hussain, Zakir (1951): Classical tabla virtuoso, musical producer, composer• considered the chief architect of contemporary world music movement• Padma Bhushan, Sangeet Natak Akademi Award.

Idries Shah (1924-96): Born in Shimla• a teacher in the Sufi tradition• author with the pen-name Arkon Daraul• famous for Mulla Nasrudin stories, *The Dermis Probe.*

Idries Shah

Ilaiyaraja (1943): Veteran music composer• music director of over 900 films• composed music for films including *Thalapathi, Nayagan, Thevar Magan, Guru* • Padma Vibhushan, Sangeet Natak Akademi Award.

Irom Sharmila Chanu (1972): Civil rights activist and poet from Manipur• known as the 'Iron Lady' or 'Mengoubi'• led a hunger strike from 2000 to 2016 demanding the repealing of AFSPA from Manipur after the Assam Rifles killed 10 persons in Malom in 2000.

Iyengar, BKS (1918 -2014): Founder of Iyengar Yoga• Padma Vibhushan (2014).

BKS Iyengar

Iyer, Semmangudi Srinivasa (1908-2003): Great musician (Carnatic)• Padma Vibhushan, Padma Bhushan, Sangeeta Kalanidhi.

Jadhav, Khashaba Dadasaheb (1926-84): Wrestler• won bronze at the 1952 Helsinki Olympics in freestyle wrestling.

Jatti, Basappa Danappa (1913-2002): Vice President of India (1974-79)• formerly CM of Mysore and Governor of Odisha.

Jayalalithaa Jayaram (1948-2016) : Indian film actress-turned-politician, AIADMK chief and Tamil Nadu CM (1991-96, 2002-06, 2011-14, 2015-16).

Jayaraman, Lalgudi (1930-2013): Legendary Indian violinist• Padma Bhushan, National Film Award for Best Music Direction.

Joshi, Pandit Bhimsen Gururaj (1922-2011): Hindustani vocalist• led the Renaissance of Indian classical music• Bharat Ratna (2009), Sangeet Natak Akademi Fellowship (1998).

Kabir (1440-1518): Hindi poet who influenced the Bhakti movement• believed in the equality of all religions• *Bijak, Kabir ke Dohe.*

Kakodkar, Anil (1943): Indian nuclear scientist who played a major role in India's nuclear tests• director of the BARC, Trombay (1996-2001)• former chairman of the Atomic Energy Commission• Padma Vibhushan.

Kalam, Dr Avul Pakir Jainulabdeen Abdul (1931-2015): President of India (2002-07)• former scientific adviser to defence minister• called as the Missile Man of India• *Ignited Minds, Wings of Fire, India 2020, Indomitable Spirit, My Journey, Target 3 Billion*• Bharat Ratna, Padma Vibhushan.

Kalelkar, Kaka (1885-1981): Activist, social reformer and journalist•president of Backward Classes Commission constituted in 1953•former VC of Gujarat Vidyapith• authored books in Gujarati, Marathi, Hindi• Padma Vibhushan, Sahitya Akademi Fellowship.

Kalhana (11th C): Kashmiri writer and poet• author of *Rajatarangini*- the book which describes the history of Kashmir up to the tenth century.

Kalidasa (4th-5th CE): Mahakavi• one of the greatest poets and dramatists ever• *Abhigyana Shakuntalam, Kumarasambhava, Meghadoot, Raghuvamsa.*

Kalyanji (1928-2000) -Anandji (1933):

Indian music composer duo from Gujarat• famous for Hindi film soundtracks• Padma Shri.

Kamaraj, Kumaraswami (1903-75): Leader of the Indian national movement• INC President (1964-67)• CM of Tamil Nadu (1954-63)• Bharat Ratna.

Kane, Pandurang Vaman (1880-1972): Indologist, Sanskrit scholar• *History of Dharmasastra*• Bharat Ratna (1963).

Pandurang Kane

Kao, Rameshwar Nath (1918-2002): First chief of the Research and Analysis Wing (RAW), India's external intelligence agency (1969-77).

Kapil Dev Ramlal Nikhanj (1959): Indian cricket all-rounder, former captain of India's World cup winning team and national team coach• record: 100 wickets in the shortest time• first ever player to score 4000 runs and take 400 wickets• Padma Bhushan, Arjuna Award.

Kapoor, Raj (1924-88): Indian film actor, director, producer• *Barsaat, Awara, Shree 420, Sangam*• Padma Bhushan, Dadasaheb Phalke Award.

Kapur, Rippan: The airline purser who in 1979 founded the non-governmental organisation Child Rights and You (CRY).

Rippan Kapur

Kapur, Shekhar (1945): Indian film director• *Bandit Queen, Elizabeth*• Padma Shri, BAFTA Award.

Karanth, Shivaram (1902-97): A literary giant, Yakshagana artist, environmentalist and social activist• wrote novels, plays, travelogues, essays • *Chomana Dudi* •Padma Bhushan, Jnanapith Award, Sahitya Akademi Fellowship.

Karat, Brinda (1947): Communist politician• represents West Bengal in Rajya Sabha• first woman member of the CPI(M) Politburo.

Karat, Prakash (1948): Communist politician• former CPI (M) general secretary (2005-15).

Karmarkar, Narendra (b.1957): Mathematician• He introduced an algorithm in 1984 named after him for solving linear programming problems.

Karnad, Girish Raghunath (1938-2019): Noted Indian playwright, actor and director• chairman of Sangeet Natak Akademi (1988-93)• director of Nehru Centre, London• *Tughlaq, Nagamandala, Hayavadana*• Padma Bhushan, Padma Shri, Jnanpith Award.

Karthikeyan, Narain (1977): First Indian to compete in the Formula One car race• Formula Asia Champion (1996)• Padma Shri.

Karunanidhi, Muthuvel (1924-2018) : Writer and politician • longest tenure as chief minister of Tamil Nadu with 6,863 days in office.

Karve, Dhondo Keshav (1858-1962): 'Maharishi' was an Indian social reformer and educator• worked for women's education and widow remarriage • *Atmawrutta, Looking Back*• Bharat Ratna (1958).

Kattabomman, Veerapandia (1760-99): Chieftain from Tamil Nadu who refused to pay taxes to the British.• fought against the British East India Company, lost and was hanged.

Kelkar, Vijay Lakshman (1942): Economist and academic• served as the chairman of the 13th finance commission and as finance secretary to the GoI (1998-99)• Padma Vibhushan.

Kesavan, Bellary Shamanna (1909-2000): Former head of the National Library of India (Kolkata)• father of Indian National Bibliography• *History of Printing and Publishing in India.*

Khan, Aamir (1965): Bollywood film actor• *Lagaan, PK, Dangal*• Padma Bhushan.

Khan, Alla Rakha (1919-2000): (Qureshi Alla Rakha) A great tabla player, disciple of Mian Qadir Baksh of the Punjab *gharana*• frequent accompanist of sitar virtuoso Ravi Shankar• Padma Shri, Sangeet Natak Akademi Award.

Alla Rakha Khan

Khan, Bismillah (1916-2006): Shehnai maestro from Varanasi• Bharat Ratna (2001).

Khan, Ghulam Mustafa (1931): Hindustani classical musician belonging to the Rampur- Sahaswan *gharana*• *Aagaman*• Padma Vibhushan (2018), Sangeet Natak Akademi Award (2003).

Khan, Khan Abdul Ghaffar (1890-1988): Frontier Gandhi or Badshah Khan• built the Khudai Khidmatgar (Servants of God) movement• opposed the partition of India• Bharat Ratna (1987).

Khan, Shah Rukh (1965): Bollywood film actor, producer• co-owner of KKR IPL cricket team• *Baazigar, Om Shanti Om, Chennai Express, Raees* •Padma Shri, Legion d'honneur.

Khan, Salman (1965): Bollywood film actor• owns Being Human, a charitable organisation• *Bajrangi Bhaijan, Sultan, Ek Tha Tiger.*

Khan, Sir Syed Ahmed (1817-98): Educator and reformer• established the MAO College at Aligarh, the first Muslim university in South Asia• *Essays on the Life of Mohammed* (1870).

Khan, Ustad Allauddin (1862-1972): Composer, sarod player, renowned musician• laid the foundation of the modern Maihar *gharana*• Padma Vibhushan, Sangeet Natak Akademi Fellowship.

Khan, Ustad Bade Ghulam Ali (1903-68): Great classical vocalist• belonged to the Kasur Patiala *gharana* of Punjab• Padma Bhushan, Sangeet Natak Akademi Award.

Khandekar VS (1898-1976): Eminent Marathi novelist• *Yayati, Dondhruva, Ulka, Hirva Chapha*• Jnanpith Award (1974).

VS Khandekar

Khilji, Alauddin (1296-1316): Delhi ruler who ruled north India • his kingdom extended up to the Narmada River.

Khorana, Har Gobind (1922-2011): Indian-American biochemist• shared the Nobel Prize with Robert W. Holley and Marshall Warren Nirenberg in 1968.

Khusro, AM (1925-2003): Economist and intellectual who was the chairman of 11th Finance Commission.

Khusro, Amir (1253-1325): Poet, scholar and Sufi musician• wrote poetry in Persian and Hindavi• known as 'the parrot of India' (*Tuti-e-Hind*), father of Urdu literature and father of qawwali• *Nuh Sipihr, Tughlaq-namah.*

Kitchlew, Saifuddin (1888-1963): Freedom fighter, barrister and associate of Mahatma Gandhi• founder-president of the All-India Peace Council• Stalin Peace Prize..

Kotnis, Dr Dwarkanath (1910-42): One of the five Indian physicians dispatched to China to provide medical assistance during the Second Sino-Japanese war in 1938• regarded as an example for Sino-Indian friendship.

Kovind, Ram Nath (1945): President of India• assumed office on July 25, 2017• Governor of Bihar (2015-17)• RS MP from Uttar Pradesh (1994-2006)• former president of BJP Dalit Morcha (1998-2002)• practised as lawyer at the Delhi High Court.

Kripalani, Acharya JB (1888-1982): Freedom fighter, politician, close associate of Mahatma Gandhi• president of INC (1946)• started Kisan Mazdoor Praja Party and Praja Socialist Party• Wife-Sucheta (1908-74): freedom fighter and the first woman chief minister of India (UP) during 1963-67.

Krishna, Dr Balamurali (1930-2016): Celebrated Carnatic musical genius, singer, composer and instrumentalist• Raga compositions include *Mahati, Sumukham, Trisakthi, Omkari, Rohini, Pratimadhyamavathi*• Padma Vibhushan, Padma Shri.

Krishnamurthi, Jiddu (1895-1986): Indian philosopher of international repute• groomed to be the new 'world teacher' but later rejected the mantle •*The Songs of Life.*

Krishnamurthy, Kalki (1899-1954): Tamil writer, poet, journalist, critic• *Parthiban Kanavu, Ponniyin Selvan.*

Krishnamurthy, Yamini (1940): Bharatnatyam, Kuchipudi dancer• Padma Vibhushan, Padma Bhushan, Padma Shri• *A Passion for Dance.*

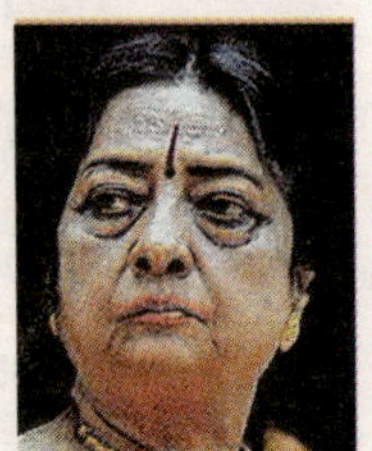
Yamini Krishnamurthy

Kumar, Ashok (Kumudlal Kunjilal Ganguly) (1911-2001): One of the most popular actors of India• *Achhut Kanya, Kismet*• National Film Award for best actor, Padma Bhushan, Dadasaheb Phalke Award.

Kumar, Dilip (1922): One of the greatest actors of all time• producer, screenwriter• known as the tragedy king• famous for bringing realism to film acting• *Andaz, Devdas, Mughal-e-Azam, Deedar*• Dadasaheb Phalke award.

Kumar, Kishore (1929–87): Born Abhas Kumar Ganguly• actor, lyricist, composer, producer, director, screenwriter and scriptwriter• sang in many Indian languages• *Nau do gyarah, Funtoosh.*

Kumari, Meena (Begum Mahjabeen Bano) (1932-72): Indian film actress• known as the tragedy queen• debut film: *Leather Face*• famous movies include *Pakeezah, Dil Ek Mandir, Aarti, Parineeta, Baiju Bawra, Piya Ghar Aaja.*

Meena Kumari

Kurien, Dr Verghese (1921-2012): Engineer and social entrepreneur• Father of White Revolution- India's milk revolution (Operation Flood) and the developer of cooperative milk sector• Magsaysay Award (1963), Padma Vibhushan (1999), World Food Prize (1989).

Lahiri, Jhumpa (1967): English- born American writer of Indian origin• won the Pulitzer Prize (2000) for *The Interpreter of Maladies*• *The Namesake.*

Lal, Durga (1948-90): Renowned Kathak dancer of the Jaipur *gharana* • Padma Shri, Sangeet Natak Akademi Award.

Lalleshwari (1320-1392): Mystic of the Kashmir Shaivism school of philosophy. •Locally known as Lal Ded•creator of the style of mystic poetry called vatsun or Vakhs, literally "speech."

Laxman, RK (1921-2015): Outstanding Indian cartoonist who characterised the 'Common Man'• *The Messenger*• Magsaysay Award (1984).

M.T. (Madathil Thekkepat Vasudevan Nair) (1934): Well-known Malayalam novelist• *Randamoozham, Asuravithu, Kuttiedathi, Kaalam, Naalukettu* and *Iruttinte Athmavu*• Jnanpith Award, Sahithya Akademi award.

Madhok, Balraj (1920-2016): Co- founder of Bharatiya Jana Sangh, national president-1966 • founder-secretary of Akhil Bharatiya Vidyarthi Parishad (ABVP)• *Portrait of a Martyr.*

Madhubala (1933-69): Originally Begum

Mumtaz Jehan Dehlavi• legendary actor• *Mughal-e-Azam, Barsaat Ki Raat, Chalti Ka Naam Gaadi, Jwala.*

Madurai Chinna Pillai: Established a successful banking system in the villages of Tamil Nadu• worked for the upliftment of poor and illiterate women• Stree Shakti Puraskar (1999).

Mahadevi, Akka (1320-1392): One of the early female poets of the Kannada language• A prominent personality in the Lingayat sect of Hinduism.

Mahalanobis, Prasanta Chandra (1893-1972): Economist and statistician• laid the foundation of India's statistical system and economic planning• Padma Vibhushan, Fellow of the Royal Society of London.

PC Mahalanobis

Mahapatra, Kelucharan (1926-2004): Exponent of Odissi dance• trained two generations of world-class dancers• Padma Vibhushan.

Mahasweta Devi (1926-2016): Renowned Bengali writer and activist• *Jhansir Rani, The Breast Stories, Mother of 1084, Old Woman, Imaginary Maps*• Padma Vibhushan, Jnanpith Award, Magsaysay Award, SAARC Literary Award.

Mahavira, Vardhamana (599-527 BCE): The last of the 24 *thirtankaras* who promulgated Jainism.

Mahesh Yogi, Maharishi (1917-2008): Indian yoga expert• led the Transcendental Meditation movement• *Meditations of Maharishi Mahesh Yogi.*

Mahindra, Jagdish Chandra (1892-1951): Industrialist• founded the Mahindra & Mahindra with KC Mahindra and Malik Ghulam Mohammed.

Talat Mahmood

Mahmood, Talat (1924-98): Celebrated ghazal and playback singer• Padma Bhushan (1992).

Malaviya, Madan Mohan(1861-1946): Scholar, leader of the nationalist movement • founder the Banaras Hindu University (1916)• Bharat Ratna (2015).

Malleswari, Karnam (1976): First Indian woman to win an Olympic weightlifting medal (bronze, Sydney)• Padma Shri, Rajiv Gandhi Khel Ratna, Arjuna Award.

Mammootty (Muhammad Kutty Ismail Paniparambil) (1951): Indian film actor, producer• acts primarily in Malayalam cinema• *Thaniyavarthanam, Oru Vadakkan Veeragatha, Mathilukal, Valsalyam, Dr Babasaheb Ambedkar, Ponthanmaada, Pathemari*• Padma Shri (1998), national film award for the best actor (1989, 1993, 1999).

Manekshaw, Field Marshal S.H.F.J. (1914-2008): The first Indian army officer to be promoted to the rank of Field Marshal• popular as Sam Bahadur• Padma Vibhushan (1972), Padma Bhushan (1968).

Mangeshkar, Lata (1929): Melody queen of India, playback singer, songwriter, producer• famous songs include "Sun Sahib Sun", "Chand Apne Safar", "Zindagi Pyaar Ka", "Hum Bhool Gaye Re"• Dadasaheb Phalke Award, Bharat Ratna (2001), Padma Vibhushan (1999).

Mansingh, Dr Sonal (1944): Indian classical dancer specialised in Odissi• credited with the distinction of being the first female dancer to learn Chhau form• Padma Vibhushan.

Bharat Ratna Ceremony in Brabourne Stadium

extra

The Bharat Ratna ceremony is usually held at Rashtrapati Bhavan. But in 1958, a special ceremony for the award was held in the Brabourne Stadium in Mumbai to honour social reformer Dhondo Keshav Karve on his 100th birthday.

Mappillai, KC Mammen (1873-1953): Eminent journalist, social worker and community leader from Kerala • greatly inspired by his uncle Kandathil Varghese Mappillai• In 1938, *Malayala Manorama* (MM) was proscribed and KC Mammen Mappillai imprisoned; MM recommenced in 1947.

Mappillai, Kandathil Varghese (1857-1904): A well-known writer and the founder of *Malayala Manorama* (1888), MM started as a weekly newspaper on March 22,1890, and became a daily on July 2,1928.

Mathew, K. M. (1917-2010): Son of veteran journalist and entrepreneur KC Mammen Mappillai• doyen of Indian media, patriarch of Malayala Manorama group until 2010• Chief Editor, *Malayala Manorama*(1973-2010)• Founder-Chief Editor of *The WEEK*• books: *Annamma, Eighth Ring* (autobiography)• Padma Bhushan, BD Goenka Award.

Maurya, Chandragupta (321-298 BC): Founder of the Mauryan empire in India• spread his empire beyond India• Kautilya (Chanakya) was his minister.

Mavalankar, Ganesh Vasudev (1888-1956): Independence activist • president of the Central Legislative Assembly • first Lok Sabha Speaker.

G V Mavalankar

Mazumdar-Shaw, Kiran (1953): MD of Biocon India, one of the leading biotechnology companies in the world• Padma Bhushan (2005), Othmer Gold Medal, Nikkei Asia Prize.

Meera:(1502–1556): Rajasthani princess, Hindu mystic poet and devotee of Krishna. One of the central poet-saints of the Bhakti movement. A number of compositions by Meera Bai continue to be sung today in India

Mehta, Pherozeshah (1845-1915): Political leader, lawyer and activist• known as the father of municipal government in Bombay• founded the English-language newspaper *Bombay Chronicle* in 1913.

Mehta, Ved (1934-2021): Indian-American writer• blinded at the age of three• *Face to Face*• Fellow of the Royal Society of Literature (2009).

Mehta, Vinod (1941-2015): Indian journalist, founder editor-in-chief of *Outlook*, political commentator, author• *The Sanjay Story*.

Mehta, Zubin (1936): Indian-born musician and music director of the world famous Israel Philharmonic Orchestra and the New York Philharmonic (1978-91)• Praemium Imperiale (2008).

Zubin Mehta

Menon, VKK (1896 -1974): (Vengalil Krishnan Krishna) Defence minister and minister without portfolio in Nehru's cabinet• distinguished himself with incandescent eloquence at the UN on Kashmir issue (1955).

MGR (Ramachandran, Marathur Gopala) (1917-87): Former chief minister of Tamil Nadu• one of the most influential actors in South India• popularly known as 'Makkal Thilagam'• founded the political party AIADMK• *Rickshawkkaran, Adimai Penn, Kudiyirundha Koyil*• Bharat Ratna (1988).

Miranda, Mario (1926-2011) Indian cartoonist and painter• Padma Vibhushan.

Mirza, Sania (1986): India's professional tennis player• formerly World No. 1 in Women's doubles ranking• highest-ranked female player ever from India, peaking at World no. 27 in singles in mid-2007• Arjuna Award, Padma Bhushan, Rajiv Gandhi Khel Ratna.

Mistry, Pranav (1981): Indian computer

scientist known for SixthSense technology.

Mitra, Bimal (1912-91): Bengali writer• wrote more than one hundred novels and short stories• *Saheb Bibi Golam*.

Mitra, Sombhu (1915-97): Stage actor who greatly influenced the Indian theatre scene• a pioneer of Bengali theatre• *Sanmarga-Saparya, Chandbaniker Pala*• Padma Bhushan, Ramon Magsaysay Award, Sangeet Natak Akademi Fellowship.

Mittal, Lakshmi (1950):Indian steel magnate, based in the United Kingdom• chairman and CEO of ArcelorMittal, the world's largest steelmaking company.

Mittal, Sunil Bharti (1957): Telecom entrepreneur• founder-chairman of Bharti Enterprises• Padma Bhushan.

Modi, Narendra Damodardas (1950): PM of India since 2014•third PM after Jawaharlal Nehru and Indira Gandhi to retain power for a second term with full majority in Lok Sabha• elected to Lok Sabha from Varanasi in 2019• former CM of Gujarat (2001-2014).

Modi, Sohrab (1897-1984) Parsi actor, director and producer• directed and produced India's first technicolour film *Jhansi ki Rani* in 1953• Dada Saheb Phalke Award (1980).

Mohanlal (1960): Indian actor, producer• acts mainly in Malayalam films• debut - *Thiranottam* (1978), superstar roles- *Rajavinte Makan; Kalapani; Drisyam; Marakkar, Lion of the Sea*• Padma Shri (2001), Padma Bhushan (2019), five national film awards.

Mookerjee, Syama Prasad (1901-53): Indian political activist, academician, barrister• former minister of commerce and industry (1947-50)• founder-president of Bharatiya Jana Sangh.

Mudgal, Shubha (1959): Hindustani classical singer – *Khayal, Thumri, Dadra* and Indian pop music• Padma Shri (2000).

Shubha Mudgal

Mukesh (1923-76) (Mukesh Chand Mathur): Indian playback singer• popular as being the voice of legendary actor Raj Kapoor• National Film Award for the best male playback singer (1973).

Mukherjee, Pranab (1935-2020): 13th President of India (2012-17)• served as the Union minister of defence (2004-06), Union minister of external affairs (2006-09), deputy chairman of the Planning Commission (1991-96)• Padma Vibhushan (2008).

Mukhopadhyay, Subhas (1919-2003): Bengali poet • edited the Bengali children's periodical *Sandesh* jointly with Satyajit Ray in the 1960s• Sahitya Akademi Award (1964), Jnanpith Award (1991).

Mukhopadhyay, Subhash (1931-81): Physician from Hazaribagh who created the world's second and India's first test tube baby Durga (alias Kanupriya Agarwal) on Oct. 3, 1978 using in-vitro fertilisation.

Munda, Birsa (1875-1900): Indian tribal freedom fighter and a folk hero from the Munda tribe in Jharkhand• spearheaded the Millenarian movement during the British Raj, becoming one of the heroes of the Indian independence movement.

Munda, Jaipal Singh (1903-1970): Politician, prolific writer and sportsman• Member of the Constituent Assembly•

English, August

English, August: An Indian Story is a novel by Upamanyu Chatterjee, loosely based on his experiences as an IAS probationer in a small town in the 1980s. Madna was the name of the fictional town to which he was posted.

Captained the Indian field hockey team to clinch gold in the 1928 summer Olympics in Amsterdam.

Munshi, Kanaiyalal Maneklal (1887–1971): Independence activist, politician, writer, educationist and lawyer from Gujarat• also an environmentalist• initiated the Vanmahotsav in 1950.

Murthy, N.R. Narayana (1946): Indian IT industrialist, co-founder of Infosys (1981), former CEO of Infosys Technologies Ltd• Padma Vibhushan, Padma Shri.

Nadella, Satya (1967) CEO of Microsoft since Feb. 4, 2014• *Hit Refresh: The Quest to Rediscover Microsoft's Soul and Imagine a Better Future for Everyone.*

Nagar, Amritlal (1916-90): A littérateur, journalist, writer in the Indian film industry• *Avshesh, Agni Garbha, Jinke Sath Jiya, Yugavatar.*

Naidu, Sarojini (1879-1949): Freedom fighter, poet, president of the INC (1925)• known as the Nightingale of India• first woman to be appointed a state governor (UP)• *The Golden Threshold, The Bird of Time, The Broken Wing.*

Sarojini Naidu

Naidu, Venkaiah (1949): Vice president of India (2017), minister of parliamentary affairs (2014-16), minister of I&B (2016-17), national president of BJP (2002-04).

Nainsukh (1710-1778): One of the most original and brilliant of Indian painters • An important practitioner of Pahari painting.

Naipaul, Vidiadhar Surajprasad (1932-2018): British writer of Indian descent born in Trinidad• *Miguel Street, A House for Mr. Biswas, A Bend in the River, A Way in the World*• Nobel Prize (2001), Booker Prize (1971).

Nair, Mira (1957): Indian film director, writer and producer• *Salaam Bombay!, Mississippi Masala, Monsoon Wedding, The Namesake, New York, I love you*• Golden Lion, Venice Film Festival (2001), Padma Bhushan.

Mira Nair

Nanak, Guru (1469-1539): Guru, founder of Sikhism and the first guru of Sikhs.

Nanda, Gulzarilal (1898-1998): Gandhian, veteran labour leader• twice acting PM• served as the vice chairman of Planning Commission (1950)• Bharat Ratna (1997).

Nannaya Bhattaraka (Nannayya) (11c.AD): also called Adi Kavi• authored a third of *Andhra Mahabharatam* and the treatise on Telugu grammar *Andhra Shabda Chintamani.*

Naoroji, Dadabhai (1825-1917): Pioneer of Indian nationalism• the first Indian to become a member of the British Parliament• one of the founders of the Indian National Congress• 'Grand Old Man of India'• *Poverty and Un-British Rule in India.*

Narayan, Jayaprakash (1902–1979): (JP or Lok Nayak) Indian independence activist, social reformer, political leader• led the mid-1970s 'total revolution', a movement against PM Indira Gandhi• Bharat Ratna (posthumously, 1999), Magsaysay award (1965).

Narayan, Rasipuram Krishnaswami (1906-2001): Indian writer in English• *The Guide, Swami and Friends, The Man-Eater of Malgudi*• Padma Vibhushan, Padma Bhushan.

Narayan, Shovana (1949): Renowned Kathak danseuse• Padma Shri, Sangeet Natak Akademi Award.

Narayana Guru, Sri (1856-1928): Social reformer from Kerala• worked to improve the life of backward classes• spread the message of equality• *Atmopadesha Satakam, Daiva Dasakam.*

Narayanan, KR (Kocheril Raman) (1920-2005): 10th President of India (1997-2002), Vice President (1992-97)• diplomat (ambassador to China, USA, etc), MP, educationalist (VC, Jawaharlal Nehru University).

Narendra Dev, Acharya (1889-1956): Indian scholar, socialist leader and educationist• leader of the Congress Socialist Party (1934).

Narlikar, Dr Jayant V. (1938): Indian astrophysicist• co-developed the Hoyle–Narlikar theory with Sir Fred Hoyle

Nayudu, Cottari Kanakaiya (1895-1967): First captain of the Indian Test cricket team• Padma Bhushan• the CK Nayudu Award is named after him.

Nehru, Motilal (1861-1931): Lawyer, independence activist, father of Jawaharlal Nehru• twice president of the INC (1919-20, 1928-29)• co-founded the Swaraj Party.

Motilal Nehru

Nehru, Pt Jawaharlal (1889-1964): First PM (1947-64) and the architect of modern India• ardent democrat, internationalist, advocate of scientific temperament and modern technology• *Glimpses of World History, The Discovery of India*• Bharat Ratna.

Nehwal, Saina (1990): Professional badminton singles player• former World No. 1 player• the only female player from India (and overall the second Indian player after Prakash Padukone) to become World No.1• has to her credit over 24 international titles including 11 Superseries titles• Padma Bhushan, Rajiv Gandhi Khel Ratna, Arjuna Award.

Nerella Venu Madhav (1932-2018): Famous mimic from India who imitated celebrities, politicians, local dialects and Nizams• often regarded as father of Indian Mimicry• Padma Shri.

Venu Madhav Nerella

Netravali, Arun (1946): Computer engineer and the former chief of Bell Labs• Padma Bhushan, National Medal of Technology, Marconi Prize.

Nilekani, Nandan Manohar (1955): Indian entrepreneur, co-founder of Infosys and its CEO (2002-07)• former chairman of the Unique Identification Authority of India (UIDAI) • Padma Bhushan.

Nivedita, Sister (1867-1911): Irish-born school-teacher (Margaret Elizabeth Noble) who became a disciple of Swami Vivekananda• joined the Ramakrishna Mission and became a nun• worked for the upliftment of women and the poor, took care of patients during the plague epidemic in Calcutta• *The Master as I saw Him, The Web of Indian Life.*

Nooyi, Indra (1955): Indian-American business woman• CEO of PepsiCo (2006-18)• The first independent female director of the International Cricket Council (ICC) Board• Padma Bhushan.

Oberoi, Mohan Singh (1898-2002): Indian hotelier who owned the international chain of luxury hotels-the Oberoi Hotels and Resorts• Padma Bhushan.

Osho (Bhagwan Rajneesh) (1931-90): Originally Chandra Mohan Jain• Indian godman who set up ashrams in India and in Rajneeshpuram in Oregon, USA• preached the doctrine of Eastern mysticism, individual devotion and sexual freedom.

Paes, Leander Adrian (1973): Indian professional tennis player• won 8 doubles and 10 mixed doubles grand slam titles• won bronze medal in singles in the 1996 Atlanta Olympics• Padma Bhushan, Arjuna Award, Rajiv Gandhi Khel Ratna.

Pal, Bachendri (1954): The first woman in India to scale Mount Everest (1984)• *Everest: My Journey to the Top*• Padma Shri.

Palkhivala, Nani (1920-2002): Eminent Indian jurist and civil rights activist• ambassador to USA (1977-79).

Pandit, Vijayalakshmi (1900-90): Political leader and diplomat• first woman president of UN Gen. Assembly (1953)• first Indian woman to be a minister (UP, 1937)• UK High Commissioner• ambassador to US, USSR, Mexico• Governor, Maharashtra• *The Scope of Happiness: A Personal* Memoir.

Panikkar, KM (1895-1963): Scholar, historian, diplomat• minister in Patiala, Bikaner• ambassador to China, Egypt and France• chairman, States Reorganisation Commission• VC, Kashmir and Mysore Universities.

KM Panikkar

Pant, Govind Ballabh (1887-1961): Freedom fighter• CM of United Provinces (1937-39) and Uttar Pradesh (1950-54)• Bharat Ratna (1957).

Patel, Indraprasad Gordhanbhai (1924–2005): Eminent economist, 14th governor of the RBI (1977-1982)• demonetised ₹ 1000, 5000, 10,000 and gold auctions• Padma Vibhushan (1991).

Patel, Sardar Vallabhbhai (1875-1950): Freedom fighter• the Iron Man of India• played a key role in the integration of India's princely states into the Indian federation• first deputy PM of India• Bharat Ratna (1991, posthumous).

Patel, Vithalbhai (1873–1933): Legislator and political leader• co-founder of the Swaraj Party.

Vithalbhai Patel

Pathak, Surender Mohan (1940): Author, most known for his crime fiction• wrote nearly 300 novels• *Mawali, Dial-100, The 65 Lakh Heist.*

Patil, Pratibha Devisingh (1934): President of India (2007-2012)- the first and only Indian woman to hold the post• Governor of Rajasthan (2004-07).

Patkar, Medha (1954): Noted environmentalist and social worker• works on issues raised by tribals, dalits, women, farmers and the displaced• active participant of Narmada Bachao Andolan• Right Livelihood award.

Paul, Lord Swraj (1931): Britain- based Indian industrialist• owns Caparo - a UK-based steel and engineering group•first person of Indian origin to become the deputy speaker of the House of Lords in UK• Padma Bhushan.

Periyar (E.V.Ramaswami Naicker) (1879-1973): Anti-Brahmin activist, rationalist and orator•In the mid-1920s, he founded the Dravidian Self-Respect Movement.

Phule, Jyotirao (Jyotiba) Govindrao (1827-90): Social reformer and activist• worked for the eradication of caste discrimination and untouchability, and also for the upliftment of the marginalised• founded Satyshodhak Samaj in 1873• Wife Savitribai (1831-97), was a advocate

extra

First Grammy Winner to be Awarded the Bharat Ratna

Pandit Ravi Shankar, who was awarded a Bharat Ratna in 1999, was the first Grammy winner to be awarded the honour.

of women's liberation and education.

Pichai, Sundar (1972): Indian-born American business executive and the CEO of Google Inc. since 2015.

Pillai, Chidambaram (1872-1936): Freedom fighter from Tamil Nadu• established Swadeshi steam navigation company to put an end to British monopoly in shipping.

Chidambaram Pillai

Pillai, Thakazhi, Sivasankara (1912-99): Indian writer (Malayalam)• *Chemmeen, Kayar*• Jnanpith award, Padma Bhushan.

Pookutty, Resul (1971): Sound engineer, sound editor and mixer working for Indian and international films• *Saawariya, Enthiran, Highway, Gandhi: My Father* • Academy Award for sound mixing for *Slumdog Millionaire.*

Pran Krishan Sikand (1920–2013): Film actor popular as 'Pran'• Padma Bhushan (2001), Dadasaheb Phalke Award (2013).

Prasad, Dr Rajendra (1884-1963): Statesman, Gandhian, lawyer and journalist• first president of the Republic of India (1950-62)• Bharat Ratna (1962).

Premchand, Munshi (1880-1936): Hindi writer whose real name was Dhanpat Rai Srivastava• writer of novels and short stories in Hindi and Urdu• referred to as the *Upanyas Samrat* or Emperor of Novelists• *Sevasadan, Rangbhoomi, Ghabon, Nirmala, Godan.*

Premji, Azim Hasham (1945): Businessman, philanthropist• former chairman and now non-executive chairman of the IT giant Wipro• founded the Azim Premji Foundation and University

Pritam, Amrita (1919-2005): Punjabi language writer, poet and novelist• *Kagaz Te Canvas, Pinjar*• Jnanpith Award, Padma Vibhushan, Sahitya Akademi Fellowship.

Puli Thevar: The chieftain who resisted British rule in S. India in the late 1750s and early 1760s• opposed the Nawab of Arcot who was supported by the British• confronted Marudhanayagam.

Puri, Amrish (1932-2005): Indian theatre and film actor most remembered for negative roles• *Mr India, Ghayal, Damini, Karan Arjun, Pardes, Virasat*• Sangeet Natak Akademi Award for theatre.

Qurratulain Hyder (1927-2007): Writer, scholar, editor and translator• made novel a serious genre in Urdu literature• *Aag ka Darya, Aakhir-e-shab ke Hamsafar*• Jnanpith Award.

Qurratulain Hyder

Radhakrishnan, Dr Sarvepalli (1888-1975): India's second president (1962-67), first vice president (1952-62)• scholar, philosopher, writer and statesman• served as a professor at the University of Oxford and as chairman of the UNESCO's executive board (1948-49)• *The Hindu View of Life, Indian Philosophy*• Bharat Ratna, Templeton Prize.

Rafi, Muhammed (1924-80): India's top playback singer who has to his credit more than 20,000 songs• "Chaudavi ka Chand", "Parda Hai Parda" • Padma Shri.

Rahman, AR (1966): Renowned music director• winner of two Oscars (2009), Golden Globe, BAFTA awards• his album *Vande Mataram*, a best-seller• *Roja, Bombay*• Popular Songs - *Maa Tujhe Salam, Jai Ho*• Padma Shri, Padma Bhushan.

Rai, Aishwarya (1973): Indian film actor and beauty queen who won the Miss World title in 1994• *Hum Dil De Chuke Sanam, Raincoat, Jodha Akbar, Provoked, Fanney Khan*• Padma Shri.

Rai, Lala Lajpat (1865-1928): Prominent

freedom fighter and patriot• known as the 'Lion of Punjab' (Punjab Kesari)• *The Story of My Deportation* (1908).

Raj, Dr Kakkadan Nandanath (1924-2010): Indian economist, professor, former VC of Delhi University• played an instrumental role in setting up the Delhi School of Economics• Padma Vibhushan.

Rajagopalachari, Chakravarti (1879-1972): Independence activist, statesman, writer• the only Indian governor-general of independent India• founder and leader of the Swatantra Party (1959)• Bharat Ratna (1954).

Raja Ravi Varma (1848-1906): Painter best known for uniting Hindu mythological subject matter with European realistic historical painting style•One of the first Indian artists to use oil paints and to master the art of lithographic reproduction of his work.

Raja Ravi Varma

Raju, Alluri Sita Rama (1897–1924): Indian revolutionary who was involved in the independence movement• led the ill-fated Rampa Rebellion which witnessed a band of tribal leaders and other sympathisers fighting against the British Raj.

Rajnikanth (1950): Originally Shivaji Rao Gaekwad• Indian actor, Tamil film superstar, politician• known for his mannerism and style• breakthrough film: *Apoorva Ragangal* (1975)• *Muthu, Padayappa, Chandramukhi, Enthiran, Kabali*• Padma Vibhushan, Padma Bhushan.

Ram, Jagjivan (1908–1986): Dy PM (1977–1979)• freedom fighter, social reformer• fought against untouchability and caste discrimination• member of the Constituent Assembly• contributed to the Green Revolution and modernising agriculture• formed Congress (J) in 1980.

Ramakrishna Paramahamsa, Sri (1836-86): Religious leader who taught that God-realisation is the only goal of life• his chief disciple was Swami Vivekananda• Ramakrishna Mission founded after him.

Raman, Dr CV (1888-1970): Indian physicist of international repute• his work in the field of light scattering earned him the Nobel Prize for Physics (1930)• discovered the phenomenon of Raman Effect• knighted in 1929, Fellow of the Royal Society, Bharat Ratna, Lenin Peace Prize.

Ramana Maharshi (1879 – 1950): Indian saint and spiritual teacher who taught a path of self-enquiry and devotion as a means to attain Self-awareness• His original contribution to yogic philosophy is the technique of vichara (self-"pondering" inquiry).

Ramana Maharshi

Ramanna, Dr Raja (1925-2004): Indian nuclear physicist• served as the director of Bhabha Atomic Research Centre and as the chairman of the Atomic Energy Commission• Padma Vibhushan, Shanti Swarup Bhatnagar Prize for Science and Technology.

Ramanujan, Srinivasa (1887-1920): One of the greatest mathematicians from India• made contributions to the theory of numbers• published the first of his papers in the *Journal of the Indian Mathematical Society* in 1911• elected the Fellow of the Royal Society (1918).

Rao, Akkineni Nageswara (1924-2014): Film actor and producer who worked predominantly in Telugu cinema• known for works in biographical films and for donning female roles in the start of his career• *Laila Majnu, Meghasandesham, Premabhishekam*• Dada Saheb Phalke

Award, Padma Vibhushan.

Rao, CNR (1934): Indian scientist• known for solid-state and structural chemistry• Bharat Ratna (2013), Shanti Swarup Bhatnagar Prize for Science and Technology (1969), Legion of Honour (2005).

Rao, Pamulaparti Venkata Narasimha (1921-2004): PM of India between 1991and 1996 whose reign saw the liberalisation of the Indian economy• CM of Andhra Pradesh (1971-73)• *The Insider.*

Rao, Raja (1908-2006): Novelist famous for his contributions to Indian English literature• *Kanthapura, The Serpent and The Rope*• Padma Vibhushan, Sahitya Akademi Award.

Rao, Samarla Venkata Ranga (1918-74): Indian film actor, director and producer in Telugu and Tamil cinemas• popular as Viswa Nata Chakravarthi• *Devadasu, Raju Peda, Karpagam, Prema Nagar.*

Samarla Venkata Ranga Rao

Rashmoni, Rani (1793-1861): Founder of the Dakshineswar Kali Temple, Kolkata• gave considerable charity to the National Library of India and Presidency College.

Rathore, Rajyavardhan Singh (1970): Indian shooter who won the silver medal in men's double trap at Athens Olympics (2004)• also a politician• Padma Shri, Rajiv Gandhi Khel Ratna.

Ravi Shankar, Sri Sri (1956): Spiritual icon and founder of the Art of Living Foundation• Padma Vibhushan.

Ray, Prafulla Chandra (1861-1944): Chemist, teacher, entrepreneur from the Bengal Presidency• founder of India's first pharmaceutical company-the Bengal Chemicals and Pharmaceuticals• awarded knighthood in 1917, Companion of the Order of the Indian empire (1911).

Ray, Satyajit (1921-92): Legendary Indian film director whose films are noted for their realistic portrayal of daily life• *Pather Panchali, Aparajita, Charulata*• Honorary Oscar award, Bharat Ratna, Dadasaheb Phalke Award.

Satyajit Ray

Reddy, Arutla Ramchandra: Indian, known for armed freedom struggle against the rule of Nizam in Hyderabad• joined the poor peasants in Telangana region in the 1940s to throw out the regime in what became a sub-movement in the larger independence struggle of India.

Reddy, Dr Yaga Venugopal (1941): Governor of RBI (2003-08)• Padma Vibhushan (2010).

Reddy, Neelam Sanjiva (1913–96): President of India (1977-1982)• CM (Andhra)• Speaker of Lok Sabha• freedom fighter.

Reddy, Raj (1937): Indian-American computer scientist who did pioneering work in the area of artificial intelligence• Turing Award, Padma Bhushan.

Rita Krocha Famous writer and journalist from Nagaland.

Rituparno Ghosh (1963-2013): Director, actor, lyricist in Bengali cinema• noted for featuring complex themes like gender identity, separation, sexuality• *Unishe April, Choker Bali, Raincoat, Chitrangada*• recepient of over ten national film awards and numerous international awards.

Roy, Arundhati (1961): Author, political activist, environmentalist• the first Indian author to win the Man Booker Prize (*The God of Small Things*)• *The Ministry of Utmost Happiness, The Algebra of Infinite Justice*• Sydney Peace Prize, Norman Mailer Prize.

Roy, Bimal (1909-66): Indian film director noted for his realistic and socialist films such as *Do Bigha Zamin* (1953), *Biraj Bahu* (1954) and *Madhurmati* (1958)•Winner of 11 Filmfare awards.

Roy, Bidhan Chandra Dr (1882 -1962): Freedom fighter, chief minister of West Bengal (1948-62) and prominent physician• considered the architect of West Bengal• Bharat Ratna (1961).

Roy, Jamini (1887-1972): Indian painter from West Bengal• known for developing a decorative, colourful style based on Bengali folk tradition• Padma Bhushan.

Roy, Kamini (1864-1933): Writer, poet and social activist• one of the first women honours graduates in British India• *Mahasweta, Pundorik, Nirmalya, Ashok Sangeet.*

Roy, Prannoy (1949): Journalist and psephologist• co-founder of NDTV.

Roy, Raja Rammohan (1772-1833): Social reformer and scholar• worked for the abolition of *sati*, child marriage and polygamy• founder of Brahmo Samaj.

Rushdie, Salman (1947): Indian-born British writer• His book, *The Satanic Verses*, made Iran's Ayatollah Khomeini declare a fatwa• *Midnight's Children, The Moor's Last Sigh, Shame, Fury, The Golden House*• Knighted in 2007 by Queen Elizabeth II• Man Booker Prize.

Saha, Arati (1940-94): Indian swimmer• the first woman from Asia to cross the English Channel• Padma Shri.

Saha, Meghnad (1893-1956): Indian astrophysicist noted for the development of the thermal ionisation equation• Fellow of Royal Society.

Meghnad Saha

Sahoo, Dr Sarojini (1956): Indian feminist writer, columnist• *Gambhiri Ghara*• Odisha Sahitya Akademi Award.

Sahni, Bhisham (1915-2003): Hindi fiction writer, playwright, translator, teacher• *Basanti, Jharokhe, Bhagya Rekha, Aaj ke Ateet, Tamas*• Padma Bhushan (1998), Sahitya Akademi Fellowship (2002).

Samudragupta (CE 330-380): Son and successor of Chandragupta I• a powerful Hindu king• known as 'India's Napoleon.'

Sane, Pandurang Sadashiv (1899-1950): Freedom fighter, socialist leader and teacher• regarded as the national teacher of India.

Sanjay Leela Bhansali (1963): Indian film director• national film award for the best popular film providing wholesome entertainment (*Devdas*), national film award for the best feature film in Hindi (*Black*), national film award for best direction (*Bajirao Mastani*)• Padma Shri.

Sanjay Leela Bhansali

Sanyal, BC (1902-2003): Eminent Indian painter and sculptor• Padma Bhushan.

Sarabhai, Dr Vikram (1919-71): Indian physicist who helped develop nuclear power in India and initiated space research• regarded as the father of India's space programme• established the Indian National Committee for Space Research (later named ISRO) and the Thumba Equatorial Rocket Launching Station• Padma Vibhushan, Shanti Swarup Bhatnagar Medal.

Saraswati, Dayananda (1824-83): Hindu reformer who fought against social evils• founded Arya Samaj• *Satyartha Prakash.*

Satpathy, Nandini (1931–2006): Indian politician and author• CM of Odisha (1972-1976)• June 9 - Nandini Diwas (National Daughters' Day).

Satyarthi, Kailash (1954): Devout campaigner against child labour• saved over 83,000 children from labour, slavery and trafficking• founder of Bachpan Bachao Andolan• Nobel Peace Prize (2014).

Savarkar, Vinayak Damodar (1883-1966): Indian patriot, philosopher, poet, writer, playwright and politician• leading figure in the Hindu Mahasabha• founded the Abhinav Bharat Society and the Free India Society• *The Indian War of Indian Independence.*

Sawant, Shivaji (1940-2002): Acclaimed Indian writer in Marathi• *Yugandhar, Mrityunjay*• Moortidevi Award.

Sen, Amartya Kumar (1933): Indian economist most known for welfare economics and social choice theory• *Poverty and Famines: An Essay on Entitlement and Deprivation*• Nobel Prize (1998), Bharat Ratna (1999).

Sen, Mihir (1930-97): First Indian to swim across the English Channel• credited with swimming the oceans of five continents in one calender year (1966)• Padma Bhushan, Padma Shri.

Sen, Mrinal (1923-2018): Renowned Indian film director• *Bhuvan Shome, Kharij*• Padma Bhushan, Dada Saheb Phalke Award.

Sen, Suchitra (1931-2014): Indian actress whose pairing opposite Uttam Kumar made history in Bengali cinema• the first Indian actress to be honoured abroad (Moscow international film festival in 1963)• *Saat Paake Bandha*• Padma Shri (1972), Banga Bibhushan (2012).

Sen, Sukumar (1899-1961): The first chief election commissioner (1950-1958) who conducted the general elections in 1951, 52 and 1957 successfully• Padma Bhushan.

Sukumar Sen

Serpa, Kazi Lhendup Dorjee Khang (1904-2007): The first CM of Sikkim who was instrumental in the merger of Sikkim with the Indian Union• Padma Vibhushan, Sikkim Ratna.

Setalvad, Teesta (1962): Indian civil rights activist and journalist• secretary of Citizens for Justice and Peace.

Sethi, Dr PK (1927-2008): Noted Indian orthopaedic surgeon and co-inventor of the 'Jaipur Foot' • Magsaysay Award (1981), Padma Shri.

Sethi, Geet (1961): Professional player of English billiards• amateur snooker player• six-time winner of the professional-level and three-time winner of the amateur-level world championships• Rajiv Khel Ratna, Arjuna Award, Padma Shri.

Shah, Naseeruddin (1950): One of the finest actors in the country • acted as Gandhi in the film *Hey Ram* and as Shivaji in *Bharat Ek Khoj* • *Nishant, Aakrosh, Sparsh, Monsoon Wedding*• Padma Bhushan.

Shahjahan (1592-1666): Son of Jahangir• 5th Mughal emperor of India (1628-58)• brought the Mughal empire to its glory• builder of Taj Mahal, Moti Masjid• owned the Peacock Throne.

Shankar (Shankara Pillai) (1902-89): Indian cartoonist • known for *Shankar's Weekly*, Children's Book Trust and the International Dolls Museum • Padma Vibhushan.

Shankar, Ravi (1920-2012): Internationally known Indian sitar maestro• *My Music, My Life*, 5 Grammy awards, Bharat Ratna.

Shantaram, V. (1901-90): Famous Indian film maker, producer and actor• *Pinjra, Amar Bhoopali, Duniya Na Mane, Navrang*• Dada Saheb Phalke Award, Padma Vibhushan.

Sharada (1945): Indian actress and politician from Andhra Pradesh• also known as 'Urvasi' Sharada• *Thulabharam, Swayam varam, Nimajjanam*• National Film Award - thrice.

Sharma, Dr Shankar Dayal (1918-99): Scholar, freedom fighter, President of India (1992-97)• vice president of India (1987-92)• CM of former Bhopal State.

Sharma, Pt Shivkumar (1938): Santoor maestro• Albums: *Call of the Valley, Rasdhara, The Glory of Strings, Sampradaya, The Inner Path, Varsha: A Homage to the Rain Gods*• Padma Vibhushan, Sangeet Natak Akademi Award.

Sharma, Rakesh (1949): The first Indian cosmonaut to fly into space aboard Soyuz T-11 to the space station Salyut-7 (1984)• Ashoka Chakra.

Shastri, Lal Bahadur (1904-66): Indian politician and Gandhian• succeeded Nehru as PM (June 1964 - Jan 1966)• died in Tashkent• Bharat Ratna.

Shastri, Shyama (1762-1827): Eldest of the trinity of Carnatic music•composed in Sanskrit, Telugu and Tamil•only one among the Trinity to have composed in Tamil.

Shaw, Amit Anilchandra (b.1964): Most powerful politician in the BJP after Narendra Modi. Minister of Home Affairs in the Union Cabinet• Elected to Lok Sabha from Gandhinagar• President of BJP (2014-20).

Sher-Gil, Amrita (1913-41): Indian painter who is known as India's Frida Kahlo• a pioneer in modern Indian art• *South Indian Trilogy, Young Girls.*

Amrita Sher-Gil

Shiva, Vandana (1952): Scholar, environmentalist and author• co-founded Navdanya, a national movement to protect the diversity of living resources, especially native seeds• Right Livelihood Award (1993), Sydney Peace Prize (2010).

Shivaji, Chhatrapati (1627-80): Great Maratha leader and a military genius who fought Mughal emperor Aurangzeb• established a Hindu state in the Deccan• crowned king in 1674• great general and wise ruler.

Shourie, Arun (1941): Journalist, author and economist• served as a consultant to the Planning Commission• Rajya Sabha MP (1998-2010)• served as the editor of *The Times of India* and *The Indian Express*• Magsaysay award, Padma Bhushan.

Shukla, Sri Lal (1925- 2011): Renowned Hindi novelist and an IAS officer from Uttar Pradesh• *Raag Darbari* - translated into 15 Indian languages besides English• detective novel - *Aadmi Ka Zahar*• Jnanpith Award, Sahitya Akademi Award, Padma Bhushan.

Shyamalan, Manoj Night (1970): Acclaimed Indian-born Hollywood filmmaker• *The Sixth Sense, Unbreakable, Split, The Visit.*

Sindhu, Pusarla Venkata (b.1995): Indian professional woman badminton player• first Indian woman to win two Olympic medals (silver in Rio and bronze in Tokyo) • In 2018, she became the first Indian to have clinched the World Tour title.

Singh, Bhagat (1907-31): Indian patriot and revolutionary who was hanged by the British government for participating in the Lahore conspiracy which killed the British official Saunders in 1928, and for bombing the Central Legislative Assembly.

Bhagat Singh

Singh, Charan (1902-87): Fifth PM of India (July 1979- Jan. 1980), Dy. PM (1977-79)• *India's Economic Policy: The Gandhian Blueprint.*

Singh, Dr Manmohan (1932): Indian PM (2004-14), economist, pro-reform and liberalisation leader, former RBI governor and UGC chairman• first Sikh to become PM and get re-elected• Padma Vibhushan, Adam Smith Prize.

Singh, Guru Gobind (1666-1708): The 10th and the last Guru of the Sikhs• founded the Khalsa, the inner council of the Sikhs• believed to be the author of *Dasam Granth.*

Singh, Khushwant (1915-2014): Journalist, writer and parliamentarian• editor of *The Illustrated Weekly of India, The National Herald, Hindustan Times*• *With Malice Towards One and All, History of the Sikhs, Train to Pakistan*• Padma Vibhushan, Sahitya Akademi Fellowship.

Singh, Paramjit (1971): Indian sprinter who broke Milka Singh's 38-year old national 400 m. record in 1998.

Singh, Rajendra (1959):Water conservationist and environmentalist•Known as'waterman of India'•runs an NGO called 'Tarun Bharat Sangh'(TBS) which was founded in 1975•won Maysaysay Award (2001) and Stockholm Water Prize(2015).

Singh, Vishwanath Pratap (1931-2008): PM of India (Dec. 1989 to Nov. 1990)• crusader for social justice• Janata Dal leader.

Sitharaman, Nirmala (b.1959): Minister of Finance and Minister of Corporate Affairs in the Union Cabinet• second female finance minister after Indira Gandhi• She was also India's second female defence minister.

Sobti, Krishna (1925-2019): Hindi fiction writer famous for her 1966 novel *Mitro Marajani*• *Zindaginama, Samay Sargam, Yaaron ke Yaar*• Jnanpith Award (2017), Sahitya Akademi Fellowship (1996).

Krishna Sobti

Sorcar, Protul Chandra (1913-71): Famous magician of India• gained global recognition during 1950s and 60s by performing *Indrajaal*• Padma Shri.

Sreedharan, Elattuvalapil (1932): The Metro Man of India• former managing director of Delhi Metro, former MD of Konkan Railway, principal adviser to Kochi Metro• Knight of Legion of Honour, Padma Vibhushan.

Sreeramulu, Potti (1901-52): Indian revolutionary and Gandhian who is revered as 'Amarajeevi' for striving to create a state for the Telugu-speaking population of Madras Presidency• worked for the welfare of dalits.

Srinivas, Uppalapu (1969-2014): Renowned mandolin player• the youngest to receive the title of Asthana Vidwan (1990).

Srinivasan, Dr MR (1930): Indian nuclear scientist who was instrumental in building APSARA - India's first nuclear research reactor.

Subbarao, Duvvuri (1949): Indian economist, central banker, civil servant• the 22nd Governor of RBI (2008-2013).

Subbier Subramania Iyer (1842-1924): Lawyer, freedom fighter• considered the Grand Old Man of South India.

Subbulakshmi, MS (1916-2004): (Madurai Shan mugavadivu) Famous Carnatic singer• Magsaysay Award (1974), Bharat Ratna (1998).

Subramaniam, C. (1910-2000): Freedom fighter known for his contribution to India's Green Revolution• served as the governor of Maharashtra, as the minister for food and agriculture, finance as well as defence• Bharat Ratna (1998).

C Subramaniam

Subramanyam, Ka. Naa. (1912-88): Renowned Tamil writer and critic• *Oru Nal, Poi Thevu*• Sahitya Akademi Award.

Subramanyam, Padma (1943): Bharatanatyam dancer, scholar, musician, composer, author• Sangeet Natak Akademi

Award, Padma Bhushan, Kalidas Samman.

Sudarshan, Prof. ECG (1931-2018): (Ennackal Chandy George), Indian physicist famous for his particle theory on 'Tachyons'- particles that move faster than light• Padma Vibhushan (2007).

Sultana, Parveen (1950): Indian Hindu-stani classical singer from Asom• Padma Bhushan, Sangeet Natak Akademi Award, Padma Shri.

Sundarayya, Puchalapalli (1913–85): Founding member of CPI (M) and a leader of the peasant revolt or Telengana Rebellion.

Swami Haridas (1480-1575) Classical musician, spiritual poet, esp. of Dhrupad style• founder of the Haridasi school of mysticism.

Swaminathan, MS (1925) (Mankombu Sambasivan): Father of Indian Green revolution• agricultural scientist• chairman, National Commission for Farmers (2004-14)• Padma Vibhushan, Padma Bhushan, Padma Shri, Magsaysay Award, World Food Prize.

Swaraj, Sushma (1952-2019): Politician, lawyer• served as the external affairs minister from 2014-19; 2nd woman after Indira Gandhi to hold the post• leader of Opposition in the 15th Lok Sabha• served as the CM of Delhi.

Tagore, Rabindranath (1861-1941): Indian poet and philosopher• founded Shantiniketan which now is Viswabharati University• wrote national anthems of India - *Jana Gana* and Bangladesh - *Amar Shonar Bangla*• *Sonar Tori, Chaitali, Kalpana, Chitrangada, Gitanjali, Ghare Baire, Chhelebela, Bhanusinha Thakurer Padavali, Manasi*• Nobel Prize (1913)- the first Asian to get it.

Taimur, Syeda Anwara (1936): CM of Assam (1980-81)- the only female CM of the state.

Tandon, Purushottam Das (1882–1962): Indian freedom fighter from UP• remembered for his efforts in achieving the official language status for Hindi• customary title -*Rajarshi*• Bharat Ratna (1961).

Purushottam Das Tandon

Tanvir, Habib (1923-2009): Indian Urdu-Hindi playwright, poet and actor• Plays: *Agra Bazar and Charandas Chor*• Films: *The Rising: Ballad of Mangal Pandey* (2005), *Prahaar* (1991)• Padma Bhushan, Sangeet Natak Akademi Fellowship.

Tata, Jahangir Ratanji Dadabhoy (1904-93): Indian industrialist• the first Indian to get a pilot license• chairman of Air India• Bharat Ratna, Padma Vibhushan.

Tata, Jamsetji (1839-1904): Founder of the Tata Iron and Steel Company• built the Taj Hotel in Mumbai.

Tata, Ratan (1937): Indian industrialist, philanthropist• instrumental in conceiving and producing Nano car• stepped down from the Tata Group in 2012• Padma Vibhushan (2008), Padma Bhushan (2000).

Tegh Bahadur, Guru (1621-75): Ninth Guru of the Sikhs• son of Guru Hargobind• was executed by Aurangzeb after he refused to embrace Islam.

Tendulkar, Sachin (1973): Indian cricketer, former captain• at 16, played his first Test in Karachi• the first batsman to score a double-century in an ODI• the first cricketer to score 100 centuries in international cricket •Became a Rajya Sabha member in 2012• retired from international cricket• Bharat Ratna, Padma Vibhushan, Arjuna Award, Rajiv Gandhi Khel Ratna.

Tendulkar, Vijay (1928-2008): Marathi playwright, writer, political journalist and social commentator• *Kanyadaan, Sakharam Binder, Kadambari*• Padma Bhushan, Sangeet Natak Akademi Award, Kalidas Samman.

Teresa, Mother (1910-97) (Agnes Gonxha Bojaxhui): Christian nun born in Skopje• founded the Missionaries of Charity and devoted life to work for the destitute• Nobel Peace Prize, Magsaysay award, Bharat Ratna.

Thackeray, Bal (1926-2012): Shiv Sena supremo who began his career as a cartoonist.

Tharoor, Shashi (1956): Writer and parliamentarian • Union Minister of State (2009-10, 2012-14)• UN Under-Secretary General (2002-07)• *The Great Indian Novel, An Era of Darkness, Why I Am A Hindu.*

Shashi Tharoor

Thiruvalluvar (1st C): One of the greatest Tamil poets ever• *Thirukkural.*

Tikkana (or Tikkana Somayaji) (1205–1288) The second poet of the 'Trinity of Poets (*Kavitrayam*).

Tilak, Bal Gangadhar (1856-1920): (Lokmanya) Indian patriot and statesman• proclaimed 'Swaraj is my birthright'• *Gita Rahasya.*

Tope, Tantia (1813-59): One of the heroes of the War of Indian Independence in 1857• a brave commander of Nana Sahib's force.

Tripathi, Suryakant (1896-1961): Hindi poet, novelist, essayist and storywriter•Known by his pen name 'Nirala'.

Tulsidas (1532-1623): Hindi poet, composer of devotional songs and kirtans• Masterpiece–*Ramcharit Manas*• Others: *Barvai Ramayana, Parvati Mangal, Gitavali, Vinaypatrika.*

Tyabji, Badruddin (1844-1906): Third president of the INC (1887-88).

Tyagaraja (1767-1847):One of the Trinity of Carnatic music•composed thousands of devotional compositions, mostly in Telugu•of special mention are five of his compositions called *Pancharatna Kritis.*

Uday Shankar (1900-77) Indian fusion dancer, choreographer• Padma Vibhushan, Sangeet Natak Akademi Fellowship.

Upadhyaya, Pandit Deendayal (1916-68): Thinker, politician, social worker• leader of the Bharatiya Jana Sangh.

Deendayal Upadhyaya

Usha, PT (1964): (Pilavullakandi Thekkeparambil), Track-queen of India, the first Indian woman to reach the final of an Olympic event - 400 m hurdles• known as Payyoli Express• runs a sports academy - The Usha School of Athletics• Padma Shri, Arjuna Award.

Vaidyanathan, Nirupama (1977): Retired professional tennis player• first Indian woman to win a round in a grand slam tennis tournament (Australian Open, Jan. 1998).

Vajpayee, Atal Bihari (1924-2018): PM (1998-2004)• parliamentarian, orator, poet, journalist• served as the minister of external affairs (1977-79)• Bharat Ratna, Padma Vibhushan.

Vallathol Narayana Menon (1878-1958): Indian (Malayalam) poet, patriot• founder of Kerala Kala Mandalam • *Badhiravilapam.*

Varma, Raja Ravi (1848-1906): One of the greatest Indian artists• known for uniting Hindu mythological subject matter with European realist historicist painting style• belonged to the royal family of Kilimanoor, Kerala.

Varma, Swati Tirunal Rama (1813-46): Maharaja of Travancore and a great musician• credited with over 500 musical compositions• wrote songs in Sanskrit, Hindi, Telugu, Kannada and Malayalam• composed *Dhrupads, Padams, Khayals* etc.

Vatsyayan, Sachidananda Hirananda (1911-87): (Agyeya) Hindi writer, journalist• *Kitni Navom Me Kitni Bar*• Jnanpith award (1978), Sahitya Akademi Award.

Venkataraman, R. (1910-2009): President of India (1987-92), vice president (1984-87).

Venkatraman Ramakrishnan (1952): Structural biologist• shared the 2009 Nobel Prize in Chemistry for studies on the structure and function of ribosome• Padma Vibhushan.

Venkayya, Pingali (1876-1963): Indian freedom fighter• the designer of the flag from which Indian national flag was adopted.

Verma, Nirmal (1929-2005): Hindi writer, novelist, activist and translator• considered one of the pioneers of *Nayi Kahani* literary movement of Hindi literature• first collection of stories-*Parinde*.

Nirmal Verma

Vidyasagar, Ishwar Chandra (1820-91): Bengali scholar who fought for widow remarriage, women's higher education and against child marriage• father of Bengali prose• *Borno Porichoi, Kathamala, Bodhodoy.*

Vijayan, OV (1930-2005): Political cartoonist and writer in Malayalam• *Khasakinte Ithihasam*• Padma Bhushan.

Visvesarayya, M. (1861-1962): Engineer, educationist, statesman• diwan of Mysore (1912-18)• September 15 is celebrated as National Engineers' Day in his memory• Bharat Ratna (1955).

Vivekananda, Swami (1863-1902): Philosopher, famous for the talk at Chicago Conference of World Religions in 1893• disciple of Ramakrishna Paramahamsa.

Vyarawalla, Homai (1913-2012): India's first woman photo journalist• Padma Vibhushan.

Vyas, Ved: Great Indian Sanskrit scholar who wrote the *Mahabharata,* one of the most revered texts of Hindus.

Williams, Sunita (1965): American astronaut of Indian-Slovenian descent• formerly held the records for the total spacewalks by a woman (seven) and most spacewalk time for a woman (50 hours, 40 minutes)• the second American astronaut of Indian heritage to go into space after Kalpana Chawla• Padma Bhushan, NASA Spaceflight Medal.

Yadav, Santosh (1969): Indo-Tibetan Border Police officer• the first woman in the world to have climbed the Everest twice (1992, 1993)• Padma Shri.

Yashpal: (1903-1976): Hindi author and political commentator• *Jhutha Sach*• Sahitya Akademi Award for *Meri Teri Uski Baat* (1976).

Yechury, Sitaram (1952): Indian Communist leader (CPI-M) who was elected the party general secretary in 2015.

Yesudas, Kattassery Joseph (1940): Indian playback singer, composer and music director• recorded about 50,000 songs in over 17 languages• won the national award for the best male playback singer seven times and the state award over 40 times • Padma Vibhushan, Padma Shri.

Zarina Wahab (1956): Indian actress• *Gopal Krishna, Gharaonda, Chitchor, Adaminte Makan Abu.*

Zarina Wahab

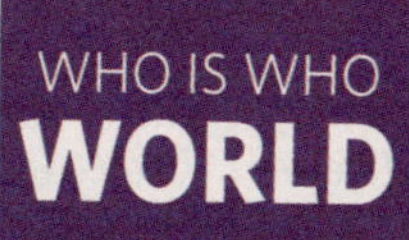

A section on foreigners who have made their mark on different walks of life from business, politics, law, entertainment, science, sports and religion.

Achebe, Chinua (1930-2013): Nigerian novelist. Africa's best-known novelist and the founding father of African fiction• His three novels- Things Fall Apart (1958), No Longer at Ease (1960) and Arrow of God (1964)- span pre-colonial Africa to colonial times to the days before Nigeria's independence from Britain.

Adichie, Chimamanda Ngozi (b.1977): Nigerian author whose work drew extensively on the Biafran war in Nigeria during the late 1960s. Purple Hibiscus, Half of Yellow Sun, Americanah

Aga Khan IV (1936): Spiritual head of 20 million Shia Ismaili Muslims in the world.

Aiken, Howard H. (1900-73): US mathematician who invented the Harvard Mark 1, the forerunner of modern electronic digital computer.

Ali, Muhammad (1942-2016): (Originally Cassius Marcellus Clay) American boxer• the first to win the world heavyweight title thrice.

Muhammad Ali

Allen, Paul Gardner (1953-2018): Billionaire, philanthropist• co-founder of Microsoft Corporation with Bill Gates• founder of the Institute for Artificial Intelligence, Allen Institute for BrainScience• owns sports teams.

Alonso, Fernando Diaz (1981): Spanish Formula One racing driver• twice world champion• one of the greatest F-1 racers ever.

Anastacia (1968): Popular singer and songwriter• known all over the world for her excellence in music and exceptional voice quality• *Not That Kind, Freak of Nature.*

Andersen, Hans Christian (1805-75): Danish fairytale writer, novelist, playwright and poet • *The Ugly Duckling, The Little Mermaid, The Emperor's New Clothes, Thumbelina.*

Arafat, Yasser (1929-2004): Palestinian President until death • leader of PLO (1969-2004) • shared the Nobel Peace Prize in 1994 with Shimon Peres and Yitzhak Rabin.

Armstrong, Neil (1930-2012): American astronaut who became the first man to set foot on the moon (Apollo XI mission) • Presidential Medal of Freedom, NASA Exceptional Service Medal.

Neil Armstrong

Asimov, Isaac (1920-92): US biochemist and writer of non-fiction.

Assange, Julian Paul (1971): Internet activist, journalist, co-founder and editor-in-chief of *WikiLeaks* - a website that publishes comments and sensitive secret information• *Cypherpunks, Underground: Tales of Hacking, Madness and Obsession on the Electronic Frontier.*

Baden-Powell, Robert (1857-1941): Founder of Boy Scouts (1908)• his sister Agnes founded the Girl Guides (1910).

Barnard, Christiaan Neethling (1922-

2001): South African surgeon who performed the first human heart transplant operation.

Beatles, The (Paul McCartney, John Lennon, George Harrison, Ringo Starr) English vocal and instrumental rock'n'roll quartet whose highly original and melodic songs held the attention of youth all over the world in the 1960s.

Beckham, David (1975): Former British football player• married to Victoria Beckham, one of the Spice Girls.

Beethoven, Ludwig van (1770-1827): German musician and composer• his symphonies - nine in number- rank as the greatest ones ever written.

Beyonce Giselle Knowles-Carter (1981): Singer, song writer, actor, dancer, feminist• Albums: *Dangerously in Love, I Am... Sasha Fierce, Lemonade*• acted in: *Dreamgirls, The Pink Panther, Obsessed*• won over 20 Grammy Awards.

Beyonce

Biden Jr., Joseph Robinette (1942): The 46th and current President of the United States. A member of the Democratic Party, he served as the 47th vice president from 2009 to 2017 under Barack Obama.

Bieber, Justin (1994): Canadian, Pop-R&B-teen singer, songwriter, musician, producer, and actor• Album: *My World 2.0, Under the Mistletoe, Purpose, Believe.*

Bolt, Usain (1986) 'Lightning Bolt': Jamaican sprinter• holds the world record for 100 metres, 200 metres and 4x100 metres relay• the first man to win all three events at a single Olympics since Carl Lewis in 1984• retired after the 2017 World Championships• Laureus World Sportsman of the Year (four times), IAAF World Athlete of the Year.

Bradman, Sir Donald (1908–2001): Australian cricket legend• secured 6996 runs in 52 games (average 99.94) including 29 centuries and a record score of 334• inducted into the ICC Cricket Hall of Fame in 2009• *Farewell to Cricket, The Art of Cricket.*

Braille, Louis (1809-52): French educator and inventor of the Braille system (an embossed lettering – touch system of reading and writing for the blind)• turned blind at the age of three and became a teacher for the blind in 1826.

Brown, Dan (1964): American writer known for thriller and mystery fiction• *The Da Vinci Code, Angels and Demons, Deception Point, The Lost Symbol, Inferno.*

Bubka, Sergey (1963): Former pole vaulter from Ukraine who won gold at the 1988 Olympics in Seoul• broke the world record for men's pole vault 35 times.

Cardin, Pierre (1922-2020): French master designer• internationally known for avant-garde style and space-age design• founded his fashion house in 1950• introduced the bubble dress in 1954.

Carey, Mariah (1970): American pop singer• regarded as one of the most prominent singers and songwriters of the 21st century.

Carlsen, Sven Magnus Øen (1990): Norwegian chess grandmaster, World Chess Champion since 2013 and top player in the world• peak rating: 2882, the highest in history• won the Chess Oscars five times, Peer Gynt Prize.

Magnus Carlsen

Carnegie, Dale (1888-1955): American writer famous for self-improvement manuals• *How to Win Friends and Influence People, How to Stop Worrying and Start Living; Lincoln the Unknown.*

Carson, Ben (1951): American neuro surgeon and politician• performed the first successful separation of conjoined twins in 1987.

Caruana, Fabiano (b.1992): Italian American chess grandmaster• became a grandmaster at the age of 14 years, 11 months and 20 days–the youngest grandmaster in the history of both Italy and the U.S. at the time• won the Candidates Tournament 2018, becoming the first American challenger for the undisputed World Chess Championship since Bobby Fischer in 1972.

Carver, George Washington (1861-1943): An African-American scientist, botanist and inventor• developed more than 300 products from peanut, bringing benefits to a lot of farmers and opportunities to industries.

Castro, Fidel (1926-2016): Cuban revolutionary and political leader• overthrew a police-state in 1959• remained in power for the longest period• handed over power to brother Raul on July 31, 2006.

Chan, Jackie (1954): Movie star, stuntman and director from Hong Kong• *Rumble in the Bronx, Rush Hour, The Tuxedo, Shanghai Noon, The Foreigner.*

Chaplin, Charles Spencer (Charlie) (1889-1977): Film actor, comedian, director, screenplay writer, producer• first international screen star with more than 50 years' achievement• Academy Award-three times• *The Kid, City Lights, Modern Times, The Great Dictator, The Circus.*

Chavez, Cesar (1927-1993): The Latino-American civil rights activist• co-founded the National Farm Workers Association• his famous words - '*Si, se puede*' ('Yes, we can' or 'Yes, it is possible')• Presidential Medal of Freedom.

Chekhov, Anton (1860-1904): Russian dramatist and short story writer• *Uncle Vanya, Ivanov.*

Chomsky, Noam (1928): American scholar, commentator on global politics and one of world's most distinguished linguists• *Aspects of the Theory of Syntax, Necessary Illusions: Thought Control in Democratic Societies*• Sydney Peace Prize, Erich Fromm Prize.

Churchill, Sir Winston (1874-1965): British PM (1940-45, 1951-55) and author• *The Second World War, A History of the English-Speaking Peoples, The World Crisis*• Nobel Prize for Literature.

Cole, Nat King (1919-1965): The first African-American performer to host a variety TV show• gifted with one of the most memorable soft baritone voices in music in the jazz genre.

Comaneci, Nadia (b.1961): Romanian gymnast who was the first gymnast to be awarded a perfect score of 10 in an Olympic event•. In 1993 Comaneci became the second person (after Olga Korbut) to be inducted into the International Gymnastics Hall of Fame.

Cook,Tim (1960): CEO, Apple Inc. which produces iPhone, iPad, iPod, MacBook, etc.

Copernicus, Nicolaus (1473-1543): Polish astronomer who put forward the theory that the planets, including the earth, revolve round the sun.

Corbusier, Le (1887-1965): Eminent Swiss-French architect and city-planner• famous for preparing the masterplan for Chandigarh City.

Le Corbusier

Crick, Francis Harry Compton (1916-2004): English molecular biologist, biophysicist, and neuroscientist • co-discoverer of the structure of DNA molecule with James Watson in 1953• Nobel Prize (1962).

Cushing, Harvey (1869-1939): American surgeon whose pioneering techniques for brain surgery improved neuro-surgery tremendously• Cushing's syndrome is named after him• *Life of Sir William Osler* got him the Pulitzer Prize in 1926.

Cyrus, Miley Ray (1992): American teen-idol, actress and recording artist • famous through the TV series *Hannah Montana.*

Miley Ray Cyrus

Dali, Salvador (1904 -1989): Spanish surrealist artist who is known for wide-ranging creative thoughts, from stage design and jewellery to writing poems and essays• *The Persistence of Memory, Metamorphosis of Narcissus, The Temptation of St Antony.*

Darwin, Charles Robert (1809-82): British naturalist who theorised evolution and natural selection through the study of fossils and diverse plant and animal life in and around Galapagos Islands between 1831 and 1836• *The Origin of Species* (1859) and *The Descent of Man* (1871).

Davis, Dwight F. (1879-1945): American tennis player best known as the founder of Davis Cup • played for the US team in the opening contest.

Didrikson, Babe (1911-1956): Named the greatest female athlete of the 20th century by the Associated Press. excelled in a stunning number of sports: track, golf, basketball, baseball, tennis, swimming, bowling and billiards among them. At the Olympics in Los Angeles in 1932, she became the only female Olympian ever to collect individual medals in a running, a throwing and a jumping event (the 80-m hurdles, javelin and high jump)

Diesel, Rudolf (1858-1913): German engineer, inventor of an internal combustion engine which he patented in 1893.

Disney, Walter Elias ('Walt') (1901-66): American cartoonist famous for animated cartoons• opened the Disneyland in 1955• *Pinocchio, Dumbo, Cindrella, Snow White and the Seven Dwarfs*• has a record of winning 22 Oscars.

Djokovic, Novak (1987): Serbian professional tennis player credited with 16 Grand Slam singles titles• one of the greatest tennis players of all time.

Dorsey, Jack (1976): American web developer and businessman • co-founder of Twitter• co-founder and CEO of Square.

Doyle, Sir Arthur Conan (1859-1930): British writer of detective stories • *Stories of Sherlock Holmes, The Lost World.*

Drucker, Peter F. (1909-2005): Austrian-born American management guru and author.

Dylan, Bob (1941): Originally, Robert Allen Zimmerman• US singer and composer• *Blowin in the Wind, Like a Rolling Stone*• Pulitzer Prize (2008), Nobel Prize for Literature (2016).

Bob Dylan

Earhart, Amelia (1897-1937), American aviator, one of the world's most celebrated, who was the first woman to fly solo across the Atlantic Ocean• Her disappearance during a flight around the world in 1937 became an enduring mystery, fueling much speculation.

Edhi, Dr Abdul Sattar (1928-2016): Pakistani philanthropist• called 'the angel of mercy'• founded the Edhi Foundation• operated the world's largest volunteer ambulance network• Gandhi Peace Prize.

Edison, Thomas Alva (1847-1931): American inventor who held 1093 patents for his inventions including the incandescent lamp• created the world's first industrial research lab.

Ehrlich, Paul (1854-1915): German

scientist who worked in the fields of haematology, immunology• known as the father of chemotherapy• founder of the Paul Ehrlich Institute• Nobel Prize (1908).

Einstein, Albert (1879-1955): Physicist whose Theory of Relativity superseded Newton's Theory of Gravitation• his work led to the making of the nuclear bomb• Nobel Prize (1921).

Elizabeth II (1926): Queen of Great Britain and N. Ireland• ascended the throne in 1952• the longest-serving British queen.

Engels, Friedrich (1820-95): German philosopher, socialist• along with Karl Marx, wrote *The Communist Manifesto.*

Ensler, Eve (1953): American playwright, performer, feminist, and activist, best known for her play *The Vagina Monologues.*

Eve Ensler

Evans, Sir Harold Matthew (1928): British-born journalist and writer• editor of *The Sunday Times* (1967-1981)• editor-at-large of the *Reuters* news agency (2011).

Federer, Roger (1981): Swiss professional tennis player• won a record 20 Grand Slam singles titles • set a record with eight Wimbledon titles and five consecutive US Open titles• won the Laureus World Sportsman of the Year award five times, named the ITF World Champion five times.

Fischer, Bobby (1943-2008): American-born chess player• became the youngest to win the Grandmaster title when he received it in 1958• his victory at the World Championship 1972 drew global attention.

Flinders, Matthew (1774-1814): English explorer who discovered a continent and named it Australia.

Frank, Anne (1929-45): Jewish girl who fled Germany with family to escape Nazi persecution• *The Diary of a Young Girl* which she wrote remains a classic of war literature.

Freud, Sigmund (1856-1939): Austrian neurologist and founder of psychoanalysis• *The Interpretation of Dreams, The Ego and the Id.*

Gagarin, Yury (1934-68): Soviet cosmonaut• became the first man to travel into outer space when his Vostok aircraft orbited the earth on April 12, 1961.

Gallup, George Horace (1901-84): Renowned American statistician who studied public opinion through questions put to a representative group - Gallup poll.

Gates, Bill (1955): American computer programmer, billionaire and philanthropist• co-founder of Microsoft Corp.

Gogh, Vincent van (1853-90): Renowned Dutch post-impressionist painter• *The Potato Eaters, Sorrow, The Starry Night, Wheatfield With Crows, Bedroom in Arles.*

Goodall, Jane (b. 1934) : English primatologist and anthropologist • considered to be the world's foremost expert on chimpanzees

Jane Goodall

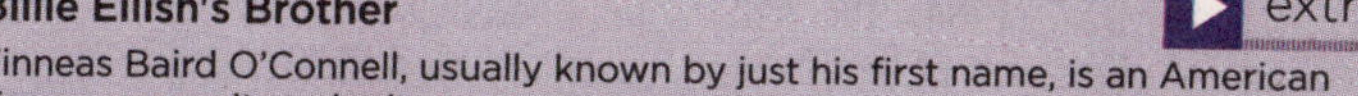
Billie Eilish's Brother extra

Finneas Baird O'Connell, usually known by just his first name, is an American singer-songwriter who has won eight Grammy Awards, but is still lesser known than his sister Billie Eilish.

Gorbachev, Mikhail (1931): Russian and former Soviet politician• president of the Soviet Union (1990-91)• Nobel Peace Prize (1990).

Gorky, Maxim (1868-1936): Russian writer, political activist• founder of social realism• *Mother, The Lower Depths, Children of the Sun, Summerfolk.*

Graf, Steffi (1969): German tennis legend• the first and only tennis player to achieve the Golden Grand Slam (1988)• was ranked World No. 1 by the WTA for a record 377 total weeks• won 22 grand slam singles titles.

Steffi Graf

Graham, Billy (1918- 2018): Celebrated US Christian evangelist famous for Billy Graham Crusades.

Grass, Gunter Wilhelm (1927-2015): German novelist, poet, playwright, graphic artist and sculptor• *The Tin Drum, Dog Years, The Call of the Toad*• Nobel Prize (1999).

Guevara, Ernesto 'Che' (1928-67): Argentine Marxist theoritician, revolutionary, tactician of guerrilla warfare• key figure of the Cuban Revolution• his image remains an icon of leftist radicalism and anti-imperialism.

Hadid, Zaha (1950-2016) Iraqi-born British architect known for her radical deconstructivist designs. In 2004 she became the first woman to be awarded the Pritzker Architecture Prize.

Hamilton, Lewis Carl (1985): British Formula One racing driver• five-time Formula One World Champion (2008, 2014, 2015, 2017, 2018).

Harris, Kamala Devi (1964): The 49th and current Vice President of the United States. She is the first female vice president, the highest-ranking female elected official in U.S. history and the first African American and first Asian American vice president.

Harris, Paul (1868-1947): American who founded the Rotary International in 1905.

Hasina, Sheikh (1947): Bangladesh PM (1996-2001, 2009-)• daughter of Sheikh Mujibur Rahman • Indira Gandhi Prize.

Hassan, Mehdi (1927-2012): Pakistani singer• known as the king of ghazal• Nishan-e-Imtiaz.

Hawking, Stephen (1942- 2018): English theoritical physicist, cosmologist, author• scientific works include the gravitational singularity theorems and the prediction of black hole radiation• suffered from amyotrophic lateral sclerosis (ALS)• *A Brief History of Time, The Universe in a Nutshell, My Brief History*• Presidential Medal of Freedom, Adams Prize, Albert Einstein Award, Copley Medal.

Hillary, Edmund (1919-2008): New Zealand explorer who was the first to climb Mount Everest in 1953.

Hippocrates (460-370 BC): Ancient Greek physician famous for his contribution to the field of medicine• father of medicine.

Hitler, Adolf (1889-1945): Austrian-born German dictator• Chancellor of Germany (1933-45)• known as Fuhrer• killed 6 million Jews.

Ho Chi Minh (1890-1969): Vietnamese revolutionary leader• served as the PM (1945-55) and President (1945-69) of the Democratic Republic of Vietnam• key figure in the foundation of the People's Army of Vietnam.

Hynek, Dr Josef Allen (1910-1986): American astronomer and ufologist famous for his research on UFOs (unidentified flying objects).

Irwin, Stephen Robert "Steve" (1962-2006): Australian wildlife expert, TV personality and conservationist• famous for *The Crocodile Hunter,* a wildlife documentary series.

Isinbayeva, Yelena (1982): The queen of women's pole vault • the first female, from Russia, to cover five metres • Olympic gold (2004, 2008), bronze (2012).

Jackson, Michael (1958-2009): (the "King of Pop" or MJ) - American singer, song-writer, entertainer, dancer, music producer, choreographer, actor and philanthropist • albums: *Thriller, Off the Wall, Bad, Dangerous,* and *History*• 13 Grammy Awards, 26 American Music Awards.

Jesus Christ (4C BC): Born in Bethlehem, Israel• Bible describes him as the Son of God• creator, saviour of the world, Messiah• transformed lives and still inspires songs, ethics, education, medical and social services• His teachings are opposed to injustice, inequality and discrimination.

Jinnah, Mohammed Ali (1876–1948): Pakistani statesman, lawyer• the founder and first governor-general of Pakistan• called the 'great leader'• leader of the All India Muslim League (1913- 47).

Jobs, Steve (1955-2011): Co-founder, chairman and former CEO of Apple Inc.• revolutionised the use of personal computer, iphones, ipods, ipad etc.

Steve Jobs

Jordan, Michael (1963): US basketball legend• played for Chicago Bulls (1984-93, 1995-98)• retired in 1999.

Karpov, Anatoly (1951): Russian chess Grandmaster• world champion from 1975-85.

Kasparov, Garry (1963): Russian chess Grandmaster• the youngest-ever world champion (1985).

Kay, Alan (1940): American computer scientist who pioneered object-oriented programming and graphical user interface design• AM Turing Award (2003).

Keller, Helen (1880-1968): American author and educator of the blind• turned deaf and blind when 19 months old• *The Story of My Life.*

Helen Keller

Kevorkian, Dr Jack (1928-2011): Pathologist who was known as Dr Death for assisting the suicide of terminally ill patients in pain.

Lady Gaga (1986): (Stefani Joanne Angelina Germanotta) US pop-dancer, electronic-rock singer, songwriter, record producer, dancer, activist, actress and philanthropist • *The Fame, Just Dance, Bad Romance, Telephone, Born This Way.*

Lenin (1870-1924): (Vladimir Ilyich Ulyanov) Russian revolutionary leader and statesman• founder of the Russian Communist Party (Bolsheviks)• leader of the Bolshevik Revolution• architect and first head of the Soviet State (1917-24)• founder of the Comintern or Communist International.

Leonardo da Vinci (1452-1519): A great multi-faceted genius from Italy• one of the master artists of the Renaissance•

Lou Gehrig's Disease

extra

Amyotrophic lateral sclerosis ended the career of one of baseball's most beloved players, Lou Gehrig, who stunned the world in 1939 with his admission that he had amyotrophic lateral sclerosis, an incurable neuromuscular disorder.

Mona Lisa, The Last Supper, St Jerome, The Virgin of the Rocks, Leda, Madonna Benois.

Lewis, Carl (1961): American track and field athelete• won nine Olympic gold medals during the 1980s and 90s• won ten World Championship medals including eight gold• set world records in the 100m, 4x100m and 4x200m relays.

Lie, Trygve (1896-1968): Norwegian politician and the first UN Secretary-General (1946-52).

Trygve Lie

Lincoln, Abraham (1809-65): 16th President of USA (1861)• re-elected in 1864• opposed slavery and succeeded in its abolishment• assassinated by John Wilkes Booth.

Luther, Martin (1483-1546): German religious priest and theologian whose teachings led to the Protestant Reformation of the 16th century.

Madonna (1958): (Madonna Louise Ciccone) World's top female pop star, a self-made icon.

Mandela, Nelson Rolihlahla (1918-2013): First black president of South Africa (1994-99)• imprisoned for about 27 years for fighting apartheid• under his leadership, South Africa became a non-racist democracy• *Long Walk to Freedom*• Bharat Ratna (1990), Nobel Prize (1993).

Manto, Saadat Hasan (1912–55) : British Indian-born Pakistani• famous as short story writer, film and radio scriptwriter, journalist• Writing mainly in Urdu, he produced 22 collections of short stories, a novel, five series of radio plays, three collections of essays and two collections of personal sketches.

Maradona, Diego (1960): Argentinian football star• most famous for the 'hand of god' World Cup goal against England in 1986• nicknamed 'the golden boy'.

Marley, Bob (1945-81): (Nesta Robert Marley) Jamaican singer-songwriter famous for crossover reggae albums in US• Rastafarian• infused music with spirituality• *Exodus* (1977).

Marx, Karl (1818-83): German philosopher, sociologist, economist and journalist• propounded the doctrine of Communism-Marxism• with his friend Engels, wrote the *Communist Manifesto* (1848)• *Das Kapital*.

Mayweather, Floyd (1977): Former American professional boxer• as an amateur, he had to his credit a bronze medal in the featherweight division (1996 Olympics), three US Golden Gloves championships and the US national championship at featherweight.

Meir, Golda (1898-1978): First woman to become Israeli Prime Minister (1969-74).

Menuhin, Yehudi (1916-99): One of the greatest violinists of the 20th century.

Messi, Lionel (1987): Argentinian professional footballer, prolific goal scorer• five FIFA Ballon d'Or, six European Golden Shoes, ten La Liga titles, four UEFA Champions League titles.

Michelangelo (1475-1564): Italian painter, sculptor, architect and poet• *The Last Judgement, Bacchus, Pieta.*

Milner, Yuri (1961): Russian billionaire, venture capitalist, physicist.

Mirzakhani, Maryam (1977-2017): Iranian mathematician who became (2014) the first woman and the first Iranian to be awarded a Fields Meda•The citation for her award recognized "her outstanding contributions to the dynamics and geometry of Riemann surfaces and their moduli spaces."

Mohammad, Prophet (570-632): Believed to be the last messenger by Muslims • *The Quran*, the sacred book, was delivered by Jibreel, the angel, to the prophet over 23 years• established Islam.

Marilyn Monroe

Monroe, Marilyn (1926-62): Originally Norma Jeane Mortenson • American film star and charming sex symbol of her times• *The Seven Year Itch, Bus Stop, Some Like It Hot.*

Montessori, Maria (1870-1952): Italian educator and originator of the educational system that bears her name. The Montessori system is based on belief in the creative potential of children, their drive to learn, and the right of each child to be treated as an individual.

Moore, Bobby (1941-93): Soccer legend who captained England to its World Cup triumph in 1966• played 1000 league games• considered the golden boy of English football.

Mozart, Wolfgang Amadeus (1756-91): Austrian composer•hailed as one of best musical geniuses ever• his best works include *The Marriage of Figaro, Don Giovanni* and *The Magic Flute.*

Murasaki Shikibu, *(c. 978 -c. 1014)* Japanese writer and lady-in-waiting who was the author of the Genji monogatari (c. 1010; The Tale of Genji), generally considered the greatest work of Japanese literature and thought to be the world's oldest full novel.

Murdoch, Rupert (1931): US publisher and entrepreneur born in Australia• founder of the News Corporation Ltd.

Murray, Andrew, 'Andy'(1987): British professional tennis player from Scotland• in 2012, he became the first British player since 1977 to win a grand slam singles tournament after winning the US Open• won Olympic singles gold in 2012 and 2016.

Nadal, Rafael 1986): Spanish professional tennis player known as the 'king of clay'• 19 Grand Slam singles titles, Olympic gold in singles (2008), 35 titles in ATP World Tour Masters 1000, Open Era Career Golden Slam• Laureus World Sportsman of the Year (2011).

Navratilova, Martina (1956): US tennis star born in Czechoslovakia• won 18 grand slam singles titles, 31 major women's doubles titles and 10 major mixed doubles titles.

Newkirk, Ingrid (1949): Animal activist who co-founded the People for the Ethical Treatment of Animals (PETA).

Neymar da Silva (1992): Brazillian professional footballer• plays as a forward for Brazil's national team.

Nightingale, Florence (1820-1910): English nurse and the founder of modern nursing• during the Crimean war, she organised a nursing service• known as 'the Lady with the Lamp.'

Nobel, Alfred Bernhard (1833-96): Swedish inventor and philanthropist who discovered dynamite• bequeathed a fund for annual prizes now known as the Nobel Prize.

David Ogilvy

Ogilvy, David (1911 -99): Doyen of the advertising world• founder of the international ad agency Ogilvy & Mather.

Osaka, Naomi (b.1997): Professional tennis player

Murder on the Orient Express

Bruno Hauptmann was executed in 1932 for the kidnapping and death of Charles Lindbergh Jr, the infant son of legendary American pilot Charles Lindbergh. The story inspired the basic plot of Agatha Christie's *Murder on the Orient Express.*

who represents Japan•ranked first in the world by the Women's Tennis Association (WTA)• fist Asian player to hold the top ranking in singles.

Owens, James Cleveland ('Jesse') (1913-80): American athlete and the first man to win four track and field gold medals (100m, 200 m, long jump, 4x100 m relay) in a single Olympics (1936).

Jesse Owens

Pavarotti, Luciano (1935-2007): Italian singer who is popularly known as the King of the High Cs• well-known operatic tenor - a rare voice range.

Peale, Rev. Norman Vincent (1898-1993): American priest who preached positive thinking for more than five decades.

Pele (1940): (Edson Arantes Do Nascimento): Brazilian soccer legend• the first player ever to play for three world championship teams• scored 1281 goals in 1363 games• seven Ballon d'Or awards, FIFA Player of the Century (2000).

Perelman, Grigory b.1966): Russian mathematician• Winner of Fields Medal (2006) and the $1million prize for solving Poincare Conjecture, one of the seven Millennium problems designated by Clay Mathematics Institute.He declined both.

Phelps, Michael (1985): American swimmer• Olympian of all-time highest (28) medals with 23 gold• holds the record for the most gold medals won by an athlete at a single Olympics- 8 golds- in Beijing.

Picasso (1881-1973): Spanish painter, sculptor and ceramicist• one of the originators of Cubism• *Les Demoiselles D'Avignon, Guernica, The Weeping Woman, La Vie, Girl Before a Mirror, Le Reve.*

Pope Francis (1936): (Jorge Mario Bergoglio); The 266th Pope of the Catholic Church (2013)• the first from the Jesuit order and also, from Latin America• Archbishop of Buenos Aires (1998), Cardinal (2001)• popular as Father Jorge• the defender of the poor and disenfranchised• a soccer fan.

Presley, Elvis (1935-77): Popular singer, entertainer and actor best known as the king of Rock 'n' Roll• acted in numerous films• *Love Me Tender, Jailhouse Rock, All Shook Up.*

Quadir, Iqbal Z. (1958): Bangladeshi entrepreneur• taught at the Harvard Kennedy School and the Massachusetts Institute of Technology• championed the role of entrepreneurship and innovations in creating prosperity in low-income countries.

Rahman, Sheikh Mujibur (1920–75): Founding father of the People's Republic of Bangladesh• popularly known as *Bangabandhu* (Friend of Bengal)• first President (1971-72), PM (1972-75).

Reeve, Christopher (1952-2004): Actor best known for the *Superman* movies• an accident in 1995 left him paralysed• *Noises Off, Deathtrap, Street Smart, The Remains of the Day.*

Reuter, Paul Julius (1816-99): German-born pioneer of telegraphic press service• founded the *Reuters* international news agency.

Rihanna (1988): Barbadian singer, actress, and businesswoman. With sales of over 250 million records worldwide, she is one of the best-selling music artists of all time. She has earned 14 number-ones and 31 top-ten singles in the US and 30 top-ten entries in the UK.

Rihanna

Ronaldo, Cristiano (1985): Portuguese professional footballer• plays as a forward for Juventus, the Italian club and the Portugal National Team• five FIFA Ballon d'Or awards, four European Golden Shoe awards.

Rowling, JK (1965): British author of young fantasy, mystery, thriller, magical realism• philanthropist• *Harry Potter* series.

Russell, Bertrand (1872-1970): English philosopher, mathematician and essayist• *The Principles of Mathematics, The Scientific Outlook, The Conquest of Happiness, My Philosophical Development, Power: A New Social Analysis, What I Believe*• Nobel Prize (1950).

Sagan, Carl (1934-96): A multifaceted scientist who left his mark in astronomy, astrophysics, extra-terrestrial science, space and natural sciences• *The Dragons of Eden, Broca's Brain, Cosmos.*

Carl Sagan

Sakharov, Andrey (1921-89): Russian physicist and an advocate of civil liberties • Soviet dissident• designer of thermonuclear weapons• Nobel Prize (1975), Lenin Prize (1956).

Sanger, Larry (1968): American project developer and co-founder of the non-profit encyclopaedia, *Wikipedia*• former editor-in-chief of *Nupedia*.

Savitskaya, Svetlana (1948): Soviet cosmonaut• the first woman to walk in space and to make two space flights.

Schumacher, Michael (1969): German seven-time Formula One world champion• met with a serious skiing accident in Alps in 2013• fully recovered in 2014• holds the record for the most Grand Prix wins (91) and the most races won in a single season (13).

Shakespeare, William (1564-1616): Greatest dramatist and poet of England• wrote 37 plays, 154 sonnets and two poems• *Romeo and Juliet, Julius Caesar, Hamlet, Othello, Macbeth, The Tempest.*

Shakira (1977): A highly successful Columbian pop singer, song-writer, dancer, record producer, choreographer, model• *Laundry Service, Oral Fixation, She Wolf, El Dorado.*

Shakira

Shaw, George Bernard (1856-1950): Irish dramatist and the greatest critic of his age• *Man and Superman, Saint Joan, Pygmalion*• Nobel Prize (1925).

Sobers, Gary (1936) (Sir Garfield St Aubrun Sobers): Legendary West Indian cricketer, all-rounder• highest score- 365- a world record for long time• first to hit 6 sixes in an over in a first class match.

Solzhenitsyn, Aleksandr (1918-2008): Russian novelist, dissident and activist• *Cancer Ward, The Gulag Archipelago, August 1914, One Day in the Life of Ivan Denisovich*• Nobel Prize (1970) .

Spielberg, Steven (1946): One of world's most successful film directors• *Jaws, E.T.–the Extra Terrestrial, Jurassic Park, Saving Private Ryan, Bridge of Spies, The Post*• *Schindler's List* won him the Oscar for the best director (1994) and six other awards.

Steve Jobs' Search for his Biological Father

Mona Simpson is an American novelist who won an award for her novel *Anywhere but Here*. Her second novel, a sequel titled *The Lost Father* was about her search for her biological father, in which she was aided by her brother Steve Jobs.

Stallman, Richard (1953): American who started free software movement• launched GNU Project, Free Software Foundation• pioneered Copyleft -a concept that preserves the right to use, modify and distribute freely.

Suu Kyi, Aung San (1945): Myanmar's champion of democracy, politician, diplomat, author• leader of the National League for Democracy• the first State Counsellor• Nobel Peace Prize, Sakharov Prize, Jawaharlal Nehru Award.

Aung San Suu Kyi

Swift, Taylor Alison (1989): One of the world's leading contemporary recording artists• known for narrative songs about her personal life • sold more than 50 million albums and 150 million single downloads.

Tenzing Norgay (1914-86): The first to climb Mount Everest (1953) along with Edmund Hillary.

Tereshkova, Valentina (1937): Soviet cosmonaut, engineer, politician• in 1963, she became the first woman to make a space flight, aboard Vostok-VI, lasting 3 days.

Thorpe, Ian (1982): Australian swimmer who won five Olympic gold medals and 11 golds in world championships.

Thunberg, Greta (b. 2003): Swedish teenager who skipped school and inspired an international movement to fight climate change. She has become a leading voice, inspiring millions to join protests around the world.

Tim Berners-Lee (1955): Invented WWW-World Wide Web while at CERN in 1989• director of the World Wide Web Consortium (W3C)• knighted in 2004, AM Turing Award (2016).

Toffler, Alvin (1928-2016): American writer, futurist known for the work on revolution in digital and communication technologies and their effects on cultures.

Tolkien, JRR (1892-1973): English writer, scholar, philologist• *The Hobbit, The Silmarillion, The Lord of the Rings.*

JRR Tolkien

Torvalds, Linus (1969): Finnish-American software engineer• principal developer of Linux kernel which became the kernel for operating systems like Android, Chrome OS etc.

Truman, Harry S. (1884-1972): US President (1945-53)• took the decision to drop the first atom bomb.

Trump, Donald John (1946): 45th President of America (2017- 21), businessman, billionaire, TV personality• owns the Trump Organisation.

Turner III, Ted (1938): (Robert Edward) American media entrepreneur, philanthropist• his vision led to the creation of *CNN* (Cable News Network).

Tussaud, Madame (Marie) (1761-1850): French wax modeller• the museum in London with the same name features life-size models of famous people and is now a major tourist attraction.

Ustinov, Sir Peter (1921-2004): British actor, director, columnist, TV presenter, stage designer• *Luther, Around the World in 80 Days*• Academy awards for the best supporting actor (1961, 1965).

Venkatesh, Akshay (1981): Australian mathematician. He is the second Australian and the second person of Indian descent to win the Fields Medal.

Vettel, Sebastian (1987): German racing driver, now driving Formula One for

Scuderia Ferrari• 4-time Formula One World Champion (2010-2013 with Red Bull Racing).

Sebastian Vettel

Vujicic, Nick (1982): Serbian-Australian motivational speaker, born with tetraamelia syndrome a rare disorder characterised by the absence of all four limbs• Christian evangelist.

Wales, Jimmy (1966): American internet entrepreneur• co-founded Wikipedia with Larry Sanger.

Walton, Ernest (1904-95): Irish scientist• along with John Cockcroft, split the atom artificially for the first time in the early 1930s• shared Nobel Prize (1951).

Walton, Sam (1918-92): Business magnate and the owner of Walmart stores, a chain of world's leading departmental stores.

Washington, George (1732-99): First US President (1789-97)• American General who led the revolt against the British and declared American independence.

George Washington

Williams, Serena Jameka (1981): US professional tennis player• The only player to achieve a career Grand Slam in both singles and doubles• Grand Slam: 23 singles, 14 doubles, 2 mixed doubles.

Williams, Venus Ebony Starr (1980): Professional US tennis player• former World No. 1• 7 singles, 14 doubles and 2 mixed doubles grand slam titles• Olympic gold in doubles (2012).

Winfrey, Oprah (1954): American TV talk show host, actress, entrepreneur• first woman to top the *Forbes* magazine list of entertainment millionaires• Presidential Medal of Freedom (2013).

Oprah Winfrey

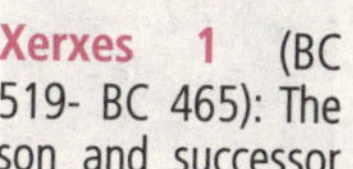

Xerxes 1 (BC 519- BC 465): The son and successor of Darius 1. He is best known for his massive invasion of Greece from across the Hellespont, a campaign marked by the battles of Thermopylae, Salamis, and Plataea. His ultimate defeat spelled the beginning of the decline of the Achaeminian Empire.

Xiaoping, Deng (1904-97): Chinese politician responsible for economic reforms in the country and an opening to the global economy.

Xi Jinping (b.1953): The most powerful Chinese leader since Deng Xiaoping. He worked his way up the party ranks to become a major player in the Chinese Politburo. By 2013, Xi was elected General Secretary of the Communist Party, Chair of the Military Commission and President of the People's Republic of China.

Yeats, William Butler (1865-1939): Irish-poet, dramatist and prose writer. One of the greatest English-language poets of the 20th century.Nobel Prize for Literature in 1923.

Yeltsin, Boris (1931 -2007): President of Russia (1991-99)• the first leader of Russia to be chosen by ballot.

Yew, Lee Kuan (1923-2015): Politician and lawyer who led Singapore to independence. He served as its prime minister from 1959 to1990.During his long rule, Singapore became the most prosperous country in Southeast Asia.

Young, Brigham (1801-77): American religious leader, second president of the Mormon church, and coloniser who significantly influenced the development of the American West.

Young, Neil (b. 1945): Canadian-American singer-songwriter and activist.He is nicknamed the 'Godfather of Grunge' or his undeniable influence on that genre.

Neil Young

Yousafzai, Malala (b.1997): Pakistani education advocate•became an advocate for girls' education when she herself was still a child, which resulted in the Taliban issuing a death threat against her•At the age of 17 in 2014, she became the youngest person to win the Nobel Peace Prize

Yunus, Mohammad (1940): Bangladeshi economist and founder of the Grameen Bank which provides microcredit to clients• Nobel Peace Prize, Magsaysay Award, Gandhi Peace Prize, World Food Prize, Presidential Medal of Freedom.

Zappa, Frank (1940-93): American multi-instrumentalist musician, composer and bandleader. Released more than 60 albums in his 30-year career. Inducted into the Rock and Roll Hall of Fame in 1995.

Zamenhof, Ludwig L. (1859-1917): Polish physician and oculist who created the most important of the international artificial languages--Esperanto.

Zedong, Mao (1893-1976): Chinese communist revolutionary. He was the founding father of the People's Republic of China, which he ruled as the chairman of the Communist Party of China from its establishment in 1949 until his death in 1976.

Mao Zedong

Zellweger, Renee (b.1969): U.S. film actress known for her portrayals of vulnerable characters in films such as Jerry Maguire (1996), Nurse Betty (2000), Bridget Jones's Diary (2001), and Judy (2019). Oscar for best actress for Judy.

Zeta-Jones, Catherine (b.1969): Welch-born actress who showed her acting mettle in a wide range of films, most notably the musical Chicago(2002), for which she won the Academy Award for best supporting actress. Married actor Michael Douglas in 2000.

Zhao, Chloe (b. 1982): Chinese-born filmmaker who made a splash in American cinema with her two independent features, Songs My Brother Taught Me (2015) and The Rider (2018).

Chloe Zhao

Zhou Enlai (1898-1976): Chinese revolutionary statesman• the first Premier of the People's Republic of China (1949- until his death).

Zidane, Zinedine (b.1971): French footballer who won the Golden Ball as the most valuable player in the World Cups of 1998 and 2006.

Zola, Emile (1840-1902): French journalist and novelist known for his series of 20 novels collectively known as Les Rougon-Macquart (1871-93).

Zoroaster (6BC): Iranian religious reformer, prophet and the founder of Zoroastrianism, a part of Parsi religion• author of the holy book *Zend Avesta*.

Zuckerberg, Mark Elliot (1984): American computer programmer• co-founder and CEO of Facebook.

06

QUIZTIVAL

- A quiz featuring 1000 questions and answers on 100 topics related to India ranging from 'First War of Independence' to its latest achievements in Science, Space and Engineering. The quiz also features questions related to Indian history, Politics, Sports, Awards, Books, Literature, National symbols etc.

Quiztival 2022

Snehaj Sreenivas

First War of Independence

1. What connects Sheffield FC, the oldest existing football club in the world, the first elevator by Elisha Otis, University of Bombay & University of Calcutta?
2. This was a major cause of the Sepoy mutiny in 1857. The rule was formulated to impose regulation on the succession of Hindu states in British India. Which rule?
3. He was hanged to death on 8th April 1857. The Indian government issued a commemorative postage stamp with his image in 1984. Identify the person.
4. Among many Hindus, one could lose caste status and religion if they cross the sea. Hence this particular act of 1856 was perceived as an insult to the Hindu community and became a cause for the onset of the 1857 rebellion. Which act?
5. Attack of the mutineers on the Redan Battery on 30th July 1857 was one significant event in the revolt of 1857. In which Indian capital city did it happen?
6. 'Maulana Azad National Scholarship' Scheme was started in the academic year 2003-04 to provide financial assistance to meritorious girl students belonging to national minorities. It was renamed after the lady who revolted against the British in Lucknow. Name her.
7. Born as Ramachandra Pandurang, he was defeated by Colin Campbell and hanged to death in 1859. This Maratha braveheart had won around 150 battles against the British. Who?
8. Queen's Proclamation was a major administrative change that happened in 1858 as a result of the 1857 revolt. This led to the transfer of administration from whom to whom?
9. Though this organization was founded by Atmaram Panduranga, it gained momentum after MG Ranade joined the movement. Founded in Bombay, it worked for social and religious reformation in India. Identify.
10. Identify the person in this picture who has written poems and was called King of Delhi. He spent his last days in Yangon, Myanmar.

Answers

1. All established in the year 1857
2. Doctrine of Lapse
3. Mangal Pandey
4. General Service Enlistment Act 1856
5. Lucknow
6. Begum Hazrat Mahal
7. Tantia Tope
8. From East India company to the British Empire
9. Prarthana Samaj
10. Bahadur Shah Zafar

Prominent Faces

11. The tomb of which famous Indian can be found in Arnos Vale Cemetery, Bristol, United Kingdom?
12. Bethune college in Kolkata was started as Calcutta Female School in 1849. Founded to improve education among women and children, the first secretary to the school was Iswara Chandra Vidyasagar. Who founded this institution?
13. In 1867, this particular place in United Provinces witnessed the formation of a Muslim revivalist organization. Mohammad Qasim Nanautavi and Rashid Ahmed Gangohi were two prominent names among its founders. Identify this city.
14. This person made attempts to revive Hinduism through his preaching and wisdom and therefore, acquired the nickname "Martin Luther of India". Identify the person.
15. People called this person 'Daya Sagar' meaning 'Ocean of Kindness', for his kind-heartedness and generosity. Identify this person who had worked for widow remarriage, abolition of child marriage and polygamy.
16. Har Bilas Sarda was the person behind a path-breaking act named after him, that came into effect in 1930. What was the act all about?
17. The term 'Dalit' in Marathi means broken, crushed. One of the persons behind popularising this term was a social reformer from Maharashtra, founder of Satyashodhak Samaj. Who?
18. India's first university for women was set up in Pune, in 1916. The social reformer who founded this university was awarded Bharat Ratna in 1958. Who?
19. He was the masterbrain behind the set of suggestions to revive and modernise education in India, which was hailed as "the Magna Carta of Indian Education." Identify this person.
20. Identify this person who founded a movement that aimed to establish a modern system of education for the Muslim community during British rule.

Answers

11. Rajaram Mohan Roy
12. John Elliot Drinkwater Bethune
13. Deoband
14. Swami Dayananda Saraswati
15. Iswara Chandra Vidyasagar
16. Minimum age for marriage of girls (14 years) and boys (18 years)
17. Jyotirao Govindrao Phule
18. D K Karve
19. Sir Charles Wood
20. Syed Ahmad Khan

Famous Trials

21. For his provocative articles, he was convicted in the years 1897, 1908 and 1916. In 1908, he was sent in exile to Mandalay with a ₹1000 fine for six years. Who was this famous person?
22. Nandanlal Banerjee was the police officer who arrested the culprits of this famous conspiracy case. The conspiracy was to kill the Chief Presidency Magistrate DH Kingsford of Muzaffarpur. Prafulla Chaki, one of the culprits committed suicide. Who was the other?
23. Basant Kumar Biswas, Amir Chand, and Avadh Behari were some of the names involved in the infamous Delhi - Lahore conspiracy in 1912, headed by Rash Bihari Bose. Who was the target?
24. M N Roy, Muzaffar Ahamed, S A Dange, Shaukat Usmani, Nalini Gupta, Singaravelu Chettiar and Ghulam Hussain were charged for spreading communism and acting against the

British government. With which conspiracy of 1924 would you associate them?

25. Ram Prasad Bismil, Thakur Roshan Singh, Rajendra Nath Lahiri and Ashfaqullah Khan were charged with robbery and murder and hanged to death in the noted Kakori train robbery case. Which revolutionary organisation fuelled the robbery?

26. Name the leader who was sentenced to 50 years in the Cellular Jail in Andaman Nicobar islands for his revolt against the Minto - Morley reforms. He was released in 1924.

27. He was first arrested on 10th January 1908 for declining to leave Transvaal and sentenced to two months' simple imprisonment. Who?

28. Mahatma Gandhi was arrested in 1922 for his three articles in *Young India* against British rule. He was sentenced to six years' imprisonment. Where was he imprisoned?

29. Inspired by the French anarchist Auguste Vaillant who had bombed the French Chamber of Deputies in the year 1893, an Indian freedom fighter bombed the Central assembly in 1929. One of the masterminds behind that bombing was BK Dutt. Who was the other?

30. It was after he was acquitted of the charges in the Alipore Bomb case that this person started a new life. He turned into spirituality and withdrew from active politics to settle in an Ashram in Pondicherry. Who?

Answers

21. Bal Gangadhar Tilak
22. Khudiram Bose
23. Lord Hardinge, then Viceroy of India
24. Kanpur- Bolshevik conspiracy
25. Hindustan Republican Association
26. VD Savarkar
27. Mahatma Gandhi
28. Yervada Jail, Pune
29. Bhagat Singh
30. Aurobindo Ghosh

Indian National Congress

31. A lawyer by profession, he was born on 29 December 1844 at Calcutta. He had presided over the INC session twice; one was in 1892 at Allahabad. Who?

32. This woman addressed the 6th session of INC at Calcutta in 1890. She was the first woman graduate of Calcutta University, also the first female to graduate from a college in Asia, along with Chandramukhi Basu. Who?

33. Lala Lajpat Rai explained his version of the reason behind the formation of INC in his paper *Young India*, in 1916 and said that INC is the brainchild of Lord Dufferin. This particular perspective became famous as a theory. What's the name of this theory?

34. He was the fourth president of the INC and the first non- Indian to hold the position. This Scottish merchant presided over the session at Allahabad. Who is this?

35. He was born in Kutch, in a Khoja Muslim family who were disciples of Agha khan, a title held by the Spiritual leader of the Shia Ismaili Muslims. He was one of the two Muslims who attended the first session of INC held in Bombay. Who?

36. What connect the years 1917, 1925, 1933, 1959 and 1998 in the history of INC?

37. "Congress was tottering to its fall and one of the biggest ambitions in my life is to give it a peaceful demise". This statement by Lord Curzon became partially true when the INC was split into Extremists and Moderates in the session in 1907. Where was it held?
38. It was in 1901 that Mahatma Gandhi attended a Congress session for the first time. He visited the session and expressed his disappointment towards the lack of unity in its functioning. Where was the 1901 session held?
39. The First session of INC was proposed in Pune. But it was held at Gokuldas Tejpal Sanskrit Pathshala, Bombay with 72 delegates. Why?
40. RC Dutt authored the book *Economic History in India* in which he supported the Drain of Wealth theory. This theory was first mentioned in the book *Poverty and un-British rule India*. Identify the author?

Answers

31. Womesh Chunder Bonnerjee
32. Kadambini Ganguly
33. Safety Valve theory
34. George Yule
35. Rahmatullah M Sayani
36. Lady Presidents
37. Surat
38. Calcutta
39. Due to Plague outbreak in Pune
40. Dadabhai Naoroji

Rebellions

41. Political parties such as DMK and AIADMK took their origin from this movement against Brahmanism. Founded by S Ramanathan, the movement was headed by E V Ramasamy. Which movement?
42. A religious order based on Sufism, Hinduism and animism, it was founded by Karim Shah. They revolted against the British during the 1825- 1850s. Identify this socio-religious order founded in Bengal.
43. They were a sect within Sikhism that aimed to purify the Sikh religion. But under Ram Singh, it became politically active and revolted against the British in 1871. Identify this sect.
44. Bankim Chandra Chatterjee's masterpiece *Anandmath* is based on this uprising that lasted for around 50 years. Identify this rebellion which was suppressed in the 1820s.
45. The repercussions of the Khilafat movement in India resulted in an uprising in Kerala that targeted British and Hindu landlords. The Mappila Muslims of Kerala were led by Ali Musliyar and Variyamkunnathu Kunjahammad Haji. What special force was formed by the British to crush the rebellion?
46. *Nil Darpan* is a play written by Dinabandhu Mitra on the suffering of cultivators of this particular plant and a rebellion associated with it. Identify the plant.
47. Ramosi peasant force was founded to get rid of the British from India through armed rebellion. It was founded by a person, who was called the father of

extra

First Couple to be Elected to Parliament

Violet Alva was the first woman to preside over the Rajya Sabha. When she was elected to the Rajya Sabha in 1952, her husband Joachim Alva was in the Lok Sabha, making them the first couple to be elected to Parliament.

the Indian Armed Rebellion. Who?

48. Buddhu Bhagat, Joa Bhagat, Madara Mahato and others were behind this mutiny led by the indigenous people belonging to Chotta Nagpur during 1829-1839.By what name was this revolt/rebellion known?
49. This place in Gujarat is famous for a non-violent movement led by Gandhiji. During this satyagraha, Gandhiji removed his Kathiyawadi turban and became bareheaded afterwards. Which place?
50. Syed Mir Nisar Ali is sometimes called the "Tipu sultan of Bengal" for the Narkelberia uprising against the British. Syed Mir Nisar Ali is well-known by another name. Identify.

Answers

41. Self-respect Movement
42. Pagal Panthis
43. Kuka/ Namdhari
44. Sanyasi rebellion
45. Malabar Special Police
46. Indigo
47. Vasudev Balwant Phadke
48. Kol uprising (Also known as Munda uprising)
49. Kheda
50. Titumir

Newspapers and journals

51. The Grand Old Man of India, Dadabhai Naoroji, started this Gujarati fortnightly to clarify Zoroastrian beliefs and promote Parsi social reforms. Which one?
52. Which 200 plus-year-old newspaper was started as a tabloid with the motto *Quicquid Agunt Homines* which means" Whatever men do'? It was the first newspaper in the then Madras Presidency.
53. Which newspaper was started as a weekly in the name, *The Original Calcutta General Advertiser*? It was started in the year 1780 by an Irish man.
54. *Bombay Darpan* was the first Marathi newspaper started in 1832. *Digdarshan* was the first monthly magazine in Marathi. Who started them?
55. If *Harijanbandu* was in Gujarati, and *Harijan Sevak* was in Hindi, in which language was *Harijan* published?
56. Which weekly published from 1919 to 1931 was edited and published in USA by the India Home Rule League of America under Lala Lajpat Rai?
57. Who started India's first Persian newspaper, the *Mirat-ul-Akhbar* with the help of James Silk Buckingham? *Sambad kaumudi* was another publication by this person in Bengali.
58. Harihar Dutt, a Bengali entrepreneur, started the first Urdu newspaper in 1822. Its name was translated as 'Mirror of the World.' Identify the newspaper.
59. Which mainstream media newspaper started as *the Bombay Times and Journal Commerce* to serve British residents of Western India became a daily in 1851 and was later owned by Bennet, Coleman & Co. Ltd.
60. He started *Bombay Chronicle* in 1913, when his attempt to purchase *Bombay Herald* was thwarted by one of its founders. Who is this person?

Answers

51. *Rast Goftar,* the truth teller
52. *Madras Courier*
53. *Hickey's Bengal Gazette*
54. Balshastri Jambhekar

55. English
56. *Young India*
57. Raja Ram Mohan Roy
58. *Jaim- i-Jahan-Numa*
59. *The Times of India*
60. Sir Pherozeshah Mehta

National Movements and Organizations

61. This organization was formed in 1851 after amalgamating the Landholders Society and the British India Society. It is considered the first political organisation that brought Indians together. Identify.
62. The East India Association was founded in 1866 in London. It had Indians and retired British officials. Who founded this?
63. He is called Rashtraguru and was an open critic of Mahatma Gandhi. He founded Indian National Association in 1876 along with Anand Mohan Bose. Identify this person.
64. Alamelu Mangai Thayarammal was one of the founders of this movement that targeted Brahmin hegemony. It was known as the South Indian Liberation Federation in the beginning. Which movement?
65. Which political party was established by launching a newspaper in the same name which means 'revolt' in Urdu? It was published in Gurumukhi and Urdu scripts.
66. The Bombay Presidency Association was founded in the year 1885. This was started by 3 famous persons who were known as "the three bright boys of Bombay." Who were they?
67. Before 1883, British subjects were exempted from the trial by Indian Judges. This was changed by an act that was introduced in 1883, against which British tea and Indigo planters protested. What was the name of this legislation?
68. During 1946- 47, there was a conflict between Jotedars, the rich peasants and Bhagadars, the sharecroppers in Bengal. The result was the Bargardari bill to regulate money lending and lessen exploitation. Identify the movement?
69. This was established to work as a mediating body between the government and the people of India. Mahadev Govind Ranade, Ganesh Vasudeo Joshi, SH Chiplunkar were the key people behind this.Which organisation?
70. He started the Krishak Mazdoor Praja party in 1951. Spouse of the first woman Chief Minister in India, identify this person who had served as the INC president during the year of independence.

Answers

61. British Indian Association
62. Dadabhai Naoroji
63. Surendranath Banerjee
64. Justice Party movement
65. Ghadar party
66. Badruddin Tyabji, KT Telang, Pherozeshah Mehta
67. Ilbert Bill
68. Tebhaga Movement
69. Poona Sarvajanik Sabha
70. Jiwatram Bhagwandas Kripalani

Kerala

71. With which infamous incident in Kerala history would you associate the orders issued by then Sergeant of the Malabar Police Richard Harvard Hitchcock ?
72. Often considered as the first organised uprising against British rule in the state, this revolt resulted in the death of 133 English soldiers. Name this revolt of 1721.
73. Born as Thampi Velayudhan Chembaraman, this person was the prime

minister of Travancore. How do we better know him.?

74. It is said that Chappathi came to Kerala for the first time because of this protest, when the Akali people who joined this protest brought this dish to Kerala. Which protest?

75.G.Parameswaran Pillai, R.Ranga Rao and N.Raman Pillai were the master brains of this movement. "Travancore for Travancoreans " slogan is related to this movement. Identify.

76.Led by V.T. Bhattathirippadu in 1931 from Trichur to Chandragiri river which lasted for seven days, this event was aimed at the education of poor children. Name the movement.

77.Hailing from Azheekodu in Thrissur district, this freedom fighter is the founder of *Al Ameen* newspaper. His ancestral home has been converted into a museum. Who?

78.C. Kesavan, the freedom fighter and former Chief Minister of Travancore-Cochin, was the chief organiser of this agitation. Representation of Ezhavas, Christians and Muslims in the Legislature was the main aim of this agitation. Identify.

79.The electricity agitation was organised in Trichur town in 1936 as a protest against the Cochin Government to entrust the distribution of electric power in the town to a private company. Who was the Diwan of Cochin during that time?

80.He established the India League in 1928, served as High Commissioner to the United Kingdom and also was India's representative to the United Nations. Identify this former central minister.

Answers

71. Wagon Tragedy
72. The Attingal riot
73. Veluthampi Dalawa
74. Vaikkom Satyagraha
75. Malayali Memorial
76. Yachana Yatra
77. Mohammed Abdul Rahman
78. Nivarthana Prakshoba / Abstention Movement
79. R K Shanmukham Chetty
80. V K Krishna Menon

Mahatma Gandhi

81. What connect the years 1937, 1938, 1939 in the life of Mahatma Gandhi?

82.This was the second of its kind , established by Gandhiji, the first one being the Phoenix settlement in Durban. What?

83.It is said that this book by Henry Salt influenced Gandhiji to be a vegetarian by choice. Name the book.

84. Gandhiji went to South Africa as a legal aide for a particular company. Name the company.

85.This was set up by Gandhiji to assist British soldiers in the second Boer war. What?

86. Calling upon the people in the Kheda district to launch civil disobedience, was later confessed as a huge mistake by Gandhiji in his autobiography. He used a term to express the same, which later gained much fame. Which term?

87. What connect the temples situated in the districts of Nalgonda in Telangana, Mangaluru in Karnataka and Sambalpur in Odisha?

88. Gandhi helped establish three football clubs, in Durban, Pretoria and Johannesburg during his stay in South Africa. All were given the same name. What name?

89.This famous work by Gandhiji exposed

the conditions and human rights violations of Indian workers in South Africa. It was considered as an anti-government publication by the British. Which book?

90. He was Gandhi's personal secretary from 1917 till his death in 1942 and also translated his autobiography into English which was originally written in Gujarati. Identify the person?

Answers

81. Nobel Peace Prize nomination
82. Tolstoy farm
83. *A Plea for Vegetarianism*
84. Dada Abdulla & Company
85. Indian Ambulance Corps
86. Himalayan miscalculation
87. Idols of Gandhiji are worshipped
88. Passive Resisters Soccer Club
89. *The Green Pamphlet*
90. Mahadev Desai

Mixed Bag

91. Known as the Nobel Prize in agriculture, this prestigious award was founded by a businessman named John Ruan.The first awardee was a native of Kumbakonam. Identify the person.
92. Earlier known as Kalka Mail, this train running between Howrah to Kalka was renamed after the popular name of this person whose birthday is celebrated as Parakram Divas (Courage Day) in India. Identify the person.
93. Former Supreme Court Justice Pinaki Chandra Ghose is the first to adorn this post. Which post?
94. The police force of this state is the first to assign a robot in office duties. Identify the state and name the robot.
95. Inaugurated on 28 December 1953 by Maulana Abul Kalam Azad, it is head quartered at Bahadur Shah Zafar Marg in New Delhi. Its motto says 'Knowledge and Science Liberates.' Which Institution?
96. Established by Purno Sangma, and Tariq Anwar and another person, who became its first president, they call themselves as millennial party with a modern and progressive orientation. What and Who?
97. The famous slogan of this institution, *Yogakshemam Vahamyaham*, is derived from *Bhagavad Gita*, which means "Your welfare is our responsibility". Which institution?
98. Popular as temple city of India, this is also counted as one among the first planned cities in India. The modern city was designed by German architect Otto Konigsberger. Name the city which got its name from the word meaning 'Lord of the three worlds'.
99. Built by Maharaja Sawai Jai Singh, this place was once visited by Queen Victoria. To welcome the royal guest the king painted the whole city with a particular colour which represented hospitality. Identify the city mentioned here.
100. Person shown in the picture is known as the 'Snakeman of India.' Name the person.

Answers

91. M S Swaminathan
92. Subash Chandra Bose (Netaji Express)
93. Lokpal

94. Kerala, KPBot
95. UGC
96. NCP and Sharad Pawar.
97. LIC
98. Bhubaneswar
99. Jaipur (Pink city)
100. Romulus Whitaker

Literature

101. This Bengali work of fiction is often considered as the first political novel in India. It first appeared in a monthly called *Banga Darshan* and later was published as a book in 1882. Identify the novel.
102. *Why I am an Atheist* was written by this person in 1930 when he was in Lahore Jail. *Introduction to Dreamland, No Hanging Please Shoot Us* are two among his other works. Who is the author?
103. Founder of Home Rule League Movement in America, Lala Lajpat Rai was a member of Arya Samaj. Name his famous work published in the year 1928.
104. This book, written by the first president of India, was a response to the partition of India. It was first published in 1946. Name the book.
105. *India Wins Freedom* is an autobiographical account by this distinguished scholar of India. Identify the person who was born in Mecca.
106. Originally written in Hindi, this work of Dayananda Saraswathi is considered as a masterpiece. The title of the book can be translated as Light of Truth. Which book?
107. This novel set in the fictional village of Mano Majra, details the repercussions of partition. Name the book.
108. *Gora* is the longest novel written by this person. His artistic works include *Dancing Woman* and *Lady With the Flowers*. Identify this writer.
109. This famous book details the last year of the British Raj, beginning with the appointment of Lord Mountbatten as the last viceroy, and ending with the funeral of Mahatma Gandhi. Identify the book.
110. Born to Ajaib Lal and Anandi Devi as Dhanpat Rai Srivastav, he is referred to as Upanyas Samrat (King Of Essays). His novel detailing the plights of Indian farmers during the freedom struggle is one among the finest novels written in Hindi. Identify the author.

Answers

101. *Anandamath*
102. Bhagat Singh
103. *Unhappy India*
104. *India Divided*
105. Abdul Kalam Azad
106. *Satyarth Prakash*
107. *Train to Pakistan*
108. Rabindranath Tagore
109. *Freedom at Midnight*
110. Premchand

Women

111. The 1917 session held in Calcutta was special in the history of INC. What was special about this session?
112. *Bande Mataram* was written by Bankim Chandra Chatterji in his famous novel, *Anandmath*. Who founded a newspaper of the same name in London in response to the British ban on the poem?
113. Jhalkari Bai was a skilled sword fighter in the women brigade of Jhansi. Mandar, Sundari Bai, Mundari Bai and Moti Bai were other prominent faces

who belonged to this women's brigade. Name this troop.

114. Known as the 'Grand Old lady of Indian Independence', she was born to Upendranath Ganguly and Ambika Devi. She appeared for Batukeshwar Dutt and Bhagat Singh in the Lahore Conspiracy Case. Name this lady who became the first mayor of Delhi after independence.

115. This lady from Hogla, a village in Bengal, was known as Gandhi Buri. She was shot dead by British at the age of 73, while leading a rally of 6000 protesters. The first statue in Kolkata dedicated to a woman revolutionary was that of this braveheart. Identify her.

116. Award for best non-fiction on modern and contemporary India presented by New India foundation is named after this freedom activist. Winner of awards like Magsaysay, Padma Vibhushan etc, her autobiography is '*Inner Recesses, Outer Spaces: Memoirs*. Name this lady.

117. Co-founder of All India Mahila Congress, this lady represented India, in the UN General Assembly as well as ILO. Identify this former professor of Banaras Hindu University.

118. At the age of eight, she took part in her first protest and shouted 'Simon Go Back'. With the help of two friends she set up the Secret Congress Radio, telecasting events happening in India. Who is this lady?

119. She started writing at the age of twelve and her first play was *Mahar Muneer*. She took part in the Second Round Table Conference and also was the president of East African Congress. Name this famous daughter of India.

120. The longest resistance to the British during 1857 was offered by the wife of the deposed Nawab Wajid Ali Shah, who fought as long as she could and finally found asylum in Nepal, where she died in 1879. Identify the woman.

Answers

111. Presided by Annie Besant, the first woman president of INC
112. Madam Bikaji cama
113. Durga Dal
114. Aruna Asaf Ali
115. Matangini Hazra
116. Kamala Devi Chattopadhyay
117. Suchetha Kripalani
118. Usha Mehta
119. Sarojini Naidu
120. Begum Hazrat Mahal

Governor Generals and Viceroys

121. *Frontiers* and *Problems of the Far East* are two famous books by this person who played the key role in Bengal Partition. Who?

122. George Frederick Samuel Robinson is known as the 'Good Viceroy of India'. He repelled the infamous Vernacular Press Act. How do we better know him?

123. He started his career as a clerk in the East India Company and later became the first Governor-General of Bengal. Supreme Court of Kolkata was estab-

Rima Das and *Village Rockstars*

Rima Das directed Village Rockstars, a 2017 Assamese coming-of-age film which won a National Award. It was India's official entry to the Oscars.

lished during his reign. Identify the person.

124.Known as the father of Indian Civil Services, he introduced the Permanent Settlement act. Who?

125.Indian Council Act of 1909 is also known in his name. He had adorned the post of Secretary of State for India. Name the person.

126.Proclaimed as the liberator of Indian Press, this person was born in Calcutta in 1785. He had also served as the governor general of Jamaica as well as Canada. Identify the person.

127.He set up the Charles Wood's Despatch, which is considered as the Magna Carta of English education in India. His annexation policies are said to be one of the major reasons behind the 1857 revolt. Who is this British Lord?

128.Universities at Bombay, Calcutta and Madras were established during the rule of this person who became the first viceroy of India. Identify.

129.Founder of Swatantra Party, he was the last governor general of India. Name this statesman who is one among the first recipients of Bharat Ratna.

130.This World War II hero was killed in a bomb blast by the members of Irish Republican Army. Who?

Answers

121. Lord Curzon
122. Lord Ripon
123. Warren Hastings
124. Lord Cornwallis
125. Lord Minto
126. Lord Metcalfe
127. Lord Dalhousie
128. Lord Canning
129. C.Rajagopalachari
130. Lord Mountbatten

Quotes/Slogans

131.Said to be coined by Hasrat Mohani, this slogan is synonymous with Bhagat Singh.Identify this slogan often heard with revolutionary movements and protests.

132. 'You give me blood I will give you freedom', this famous quote was contributed by a freedom fighter from Cuttack. A degree holder in philosophy, his birthday is celebrated as 'Courage Day 'in India. Who is this person.?

133.This verse from *Mundaka Upanishad* was widely popularised by Madan Mohan Malaviya and later became one of the most famous mottos in India. Which slogan?

134. The famous slogan 'Do or Die' by Gandhiji originated as part of which movement?

135.This person from Mughalsarai met his death while visiting the most populous city in Central Asia. Identify the person and the famous slogan coined by him.

136. This freedom fighter when he was Congress president wrote an article criticising himself under the pseudonym 'Chanakya'. 'Aaram Haraam Hai' is a quote attributed to him. Who?

137.When this person was arrested for participating in non-cooperation movement and brought before the court, he gave his father's name 'as 'Swathantra' and his residence as 'jail'. He once said "If your blood does not rage, it is water that flows in your vein". Who?

138.Known as the father of Indian Unrest, this person proposed the slogan 'Swaraj is my birth right and I shall have it'. Identify the person.

139.These verses from an 1882 novel became more popular than the writer and the novel. Later it was composed into a song by Rabindranath Tagore. Which slogan.?

140.'The desire for revolution is in our

hearts, we shall see how much strength lies in the arms of the enemy'. This is a quote by a firebrand freedom fighter who used to write under the pen name Agyat. Name this founding member of Hindustan Republican Association.

Answers

131. Inquilab Zindabad
132. Subash Chandra Bose
133. Satyameva Jayate
134. Quit India
135. Lal Bahadur Shastri, Jai Jawan Jai Kisan
136. Pandit Nehru
137. Chandrasekhar Azad
138. Bala Gangadhara Tilak
139. Vande Mataram
140. Ram Prasad Bismil

Monuments

141. Said to be built under the concept of Panopticon, in which all the inmates can be watched by a person in the middle, this is now a freedom landmark. Name this monument located in the capital of an island group in India.
142. Mahatma Gandhi, Kasturba Gandhi and Mahadev Desai were imprisoned here right after the announcement of the Quit India Movement. Desai and Kasturba Gandhi both passed away at this place. Identify.
143. This was home to Gandhiji for over a decade and is situated on the banks of a river. Earlier this was called Satyagraha Ashram. Nandini, Vinoba Kutir, Upasana Mandir, Magan Niwas are a few parts of the building. Name the monument.
144. In 1918, lancers from the 15th Cavalry Brigade, from the three princely states, fighting under the leadership of British General Edmund Allenby, defeated the Turkish-German forces. A war memorial known as Teen Murti (statues of 3 soldiers) was constructed to honour them. If two of the soldiers represented Jodhpur and Hyderabad, which princely state is represented by the third.
145. This was built as a secret passage to Shahjahanabad. A plaque here reads "During Mutiny Indian freedom fighters used the gate to attack Britishers by firing cannon balls." What are we talking about?
146. The infamous INA trials took place in this location. It was also known as 'Qila E Mubarak ' which means Blessed Fort. Name the structure.
147. Constructed in Indo–Saracenic style, this is located at Apollo Bunder, near to Chhatrapati Shivaji Marg. This is often referred to as the Tajmahal of the state where it is located. Identify.
148. The landscaping and planting of this famous location was done under Alick Percy-Lancaster, the last Englishman to hold the post of Superintendent of Horticultural Operations, Government of India. Which location?
149. Aruna Asaf Ali is widely remembered for hoisting Indian Flag in Gowalia Tank Maidan as part of Quit India Movement. What is the current name of this place?
150. Originally known as Ochterlony Monument, this was called as 'Cloud Kissing Monument' by Mark Twain. Identify.

Answers

141. Cellular Jail/Kaala Pani Andaman Nicobar
142. Aga Khan Palace
143. Sabarmati Ashram
144. Mysore
145. Kashmere Gate, Delhi
146. Red Fort
147. Gateway of India
148. Raj Ghat
149. August Kranti Maidan
150. Shaheed Minar

National Symbols

151. The second stamp of independent India and the first for domestic use depicted which national symbol?
152. The Great Indian Bustard was considered for this earlier, but later *Pavo Cristatus* was chosen. What is mentioned here?
153. What was launched in April 1973 by the Government of India during Prime Minister Indira Gandhi's tenure and had Kailash Sankhala as the first director.
154. Jyeshtha, Bhaadra, Aswin,Pausha. What are these?
155. The symbol was designed by Udaya Kumar, a student of Indian Institute of Technology Bombay. The Government of India adopted this in 2010.Which symbol?
156. Kesar,Langra,Malda,Pairi,Hapus are the varieties of what ?
157. The official city animal of Guwahati has got another prestigious status, with a national level significance. Which animal? What status?
158. What connects the political party BSP, the Democratic party of USA and the State Road Transport Corporation of Kerala?
159. A Siamese festival called 'Loy Krathong' (Floating Candles) of Thailand is associated with this entity in India.King Bhageeratha of Kosala is said to have brought into Earth. What?
160. This former District Treasury Officer of Vishakhapatnam District is best remembered in India for what contribution?

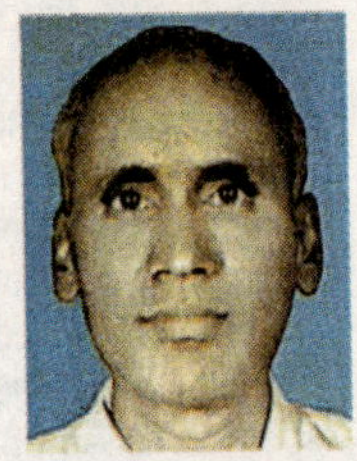

Answers

151. The state seal/National Emblem of India
152. National Bird
153. Project Tiger
154. Months in the National Calendar
155. The Indian Rupee symbol
156. Mangoes
157. Ganges River Dolphin, National aquatic mammal of India
158. Elephant as symbol
159. Ganga
160. Authoring the national pledge of India (Pydimarri Venkata Subba Rao)

Indian National Army

161. Written by Vanshidhar Shukla and composed by Ram Singh Thakuri, it was banned by British in India after World War II as seditious. Name this regimental quick march of INA?
162. INA's brigades/regiments were named after prominent leaders. The women regiment was named after Jhansi Rani. The first three guerrilla regiments were named Subash brigade, Gandhi brigade and Azad brigade respectively. What was the name of the fourth guerrilla brigade?
163. Subhash Chandra Bose was the second commander-in-chief of INA, who was the first commander-in-chief?
164. The most celebrated INA trial was the joint court-martial of Colonel Prem Sahgal, Colonel Gurubaksh Singh Dhillon

and Major General Shah Nawaz Khan, and was publicly held at a particular monument in Delhi. Which monument?

165. An officer of Indian National Army and the Minister of Women Affairs of Azad Hind Government contested in the presidential elections in the year 2002. Name the person.
166. An Officers' Training School for INA officers was set up to provide training to the recruits. A youth wing of the INA, composed of young Indians personally chosen by Bose, were sent to Japan for fighter pilot training. By what nickname were they affectionately known?
167. The INA War Memorial to commemorate the "Unknown Warrior" of the INA was constructed in the year 1945 at the Esplanade Park where the motto of the INA: Ittefaq (Unity), Etmad (Faith) and Kurbani (Sacrifice) is inscribed. In which country can you find it?
168. Col. Hog Toye was the author of one of the first sympathetic western accounts of Indian National Army. Published in 1959, what was the book called?
169. The INA Martyrs' Memorial Complex of Moirang is a war memorial dedicated to the soldiers of Indian Army. In which Indian state is it situated?
170. The Indian National Army was established on 01 September 1942 to secure Indian Independence from British rule. It was formed under the leadership of a person who was born in Purba Bardhaman district of West Bengal. Identify him.

Answers

161. Qadam Qadam Badhaye Ja
162. Nehru brigade
163. Mohan Singh
164. Red Fort
165. Lakshmi Sahgal/ Captain Lakshmi
166. Tokyo boys
167. Singapore
168. *The Springing Tiger*
169. Moirang , Manipur
170. Rash Behari Bose

Acts /Laws

171. Known as the first step taken by the British government to regulate and control the company's affairs in India, this act was introduced by Lord Frederick North on 18 May 1773. Which act?
172. This act was introduced by the British Parliament to correct the defects of the Regulating Act and is also called the East India Company Act of 1784. Which act?
173. This Act separated the revenue administration and the judiciary functions of the company leading to the disappearance of Maal Adalats or revenue courts. Which act of 1793?
174. This emergency criminal law enacted in 1915 was to curtail the nationalist and revolutionary activities of the Indian Independence Movement during and in the aftermath of World War I. Identify.
175. A series of legal acts were passed during 1836 – 1848 in British India under East India Company rule. The acts outlawed the practice of thuggee, which was prevalent in North and Central India. The act also outlawed dacoity, a form of banditry prevalent in the same region. Which is this act?
176. The introduction of this act was a major change in the state of women that prevailed during that period. Ishwar Chandra Vidyasagar played a major role in the establishment of the act. Which is this act?
177. This act was passed during the ten-

ure of Viceroy Ripon and written by Sir Courtenay Pergine Ilbert. The act stipulated that Indian judges could trial Europeans. Which is this act?

178. The Indian Councils Act 1909 was an act of the British Parliament that introduced a few reforms in the legislative councils and increased the involvement of Indians in the governance of British India. It was also called?

179. This law was passed in March 1919 by the Imperial Legislative Council which gave them the power to arrest any person without any trial. It was passed by the British government to increase their grip on power over the people. What is this act called?

180. The Bengal Sati Regulation (Regulation XVII) was passed by the British Government by making the practice of Sati illegal in all of British India, Which Governor-General of India issued this act?

Answers

171. Regulating Act of 1773
172. The Pitt's India Act, 1784
173. The Charter Act of 1793
174. The Defence of India Act
175. Thuggee and Dacoity Suppression Acts, 1836 - 1848
176. Hindu Widow Remarriage Act - 1856
177. The Ilbert Bill - legislative act.
178. Morley-Minto Reforms 1909
179. The Rowlatt Act
180. Lord William Bentinck

Industries

181. This company was established by the Government of India in 1981 and later became a subsidiary of a Japanese Automobile company. The name of the company refers to a Hindu god and it means wind. Identify the Indian company.

182. Situated at Jamnagar, Gujrat this is the largest of its kind in India. Owned by Reliance Industries this was established in1999. What?

183. Ranipet in Tamil Nadu is home to EID Parry Factory. What first of its kind record do they have?

184. Often referred to as 'common man's scooter brand,' this was founded by a honorary magistrate who was also a close aide of Mahatma Gandhi. Which company?

185. Former member of National Information Technology Task Force of India, Prime Minister's Council on Trade and Industries, he was also one among the directors on the board of RBI. He headed NASSCOM from 1992 – 1994 and was also the IT adviser to Thailand. Who?

186. The first one in India was established in 1818 at Fort Gloster near Kolkata but was a commercial failure. The second one was established by KGN Daber in 1854 at Bombay and was named after the city itself. What are these?

187. This PSU company operates and owns five integrated plants at Bhilai, Rourkela, Durgapur, Bokaro and Burnpur and three special plants at Salem, Durgapur and Bhadravathi. Name?

188. The largest and most populous city in Jharkhand and first planned industrial

extra

Jaipal Singh Munda's Many Feats

Jaipal Singh Munda was a member of the Constituent Assembly and a respected political figure. He led India to Olympic glory in field hockey in 1928 in Amsterdam, the first of India's hockey golds.

city in India, it was founded by Jamshedji Tata, and was named Tata Nagar, honouring him. Which city?

189. Born Samuel Evans Stokes Jr., in an American Quaker family, his father was the founder of the Stokes and Parish Machine Company which was a leading manufacturer of elevators in the USA. He reached India, embraced Hinduism and changed his name to Satyananda. He is known as the father of what industry/crop in India?

190. A former minister in Haryana government, she once held the position of Asia's richest woman. Identify this lady who is the chairperson of one of the biggest steel manufactures of India.

Answers

181. Maruti
182. Oil Refinery
183. First Chemical Fertilizer Production Plant in India
184. Bajaj Auto Ltd
185. NR Narayana Murthy
186. Cotton mills
187. SAIL -Steel Authority of India Limited
188. Jamshedpur
189. Apple
190. Savitri Jindal

Mixed Bag

191. Earlier these were known as Rose, Neel and Havlock and now as Netaji Subash Chandra Bose, Shaheed and Swaraj respectively. What are these ?

192. This battle fought between Babur and Mahmud Lodhi in 1529, and named after the river on whose banks it was fought, shares its name with a dress item popular in North India especially in Rajasthan. Name the battle.

193. Rashmi, first of its kind in India created by Ranjeet Srivastava, was inspired by Sophia, a UAE citizen. What are these?

194. This international football tournament is named after the first Indian commander of the Indian Air Force, who is also known as the father of Indian Air Force. Name the tournament.

195. *A Shot at History* is the autobiography of the first Indian who has won the ISSF Blue Cross Medal. Who?

196. CA Bhavani Devi is the first Indian to qualify for this event in Olympics. The foil, the épée and the sabre are three forms of this. Identify the game.

197. Made from Palakkadan Matta rice and a blend of spices, the recipe of this snack is only known to a few families dwelling in the village of Ramassery. Which food item is being mentioned here?

198. General Bipin Rawat is the first to attain this position which was formed in December 2019. Which position?

199. Vostok I was famously associated with Yuri Gagarin and Vostok 6 with Valentina Tereshkova. With which famous Indian can we associate Soyuz –T 11?

200. In 2019 when Narthaki Natraj, a famous Bharatanatyam dancer won this award, she became the first third gender person to win it. Which award?

Answers

191. Islands in Andaman Nicobar
192. Battle of Ghaghra
193. Humaniod Robot (Rashmi is World's first Hindi-speaking Robot)
194. Subroto Mukherjee Cup
195. Abhinav Bindra
196. Fencing
197. Idli
198. Chief of Defense Staff
199. Rakesh Sharma
200. Padma Shri

Bharat Ratnas

201. One of the longest in India, this bridge is named after a Bharat Ratna from Assam.He is also known as Bard of Brahmaputra. Identify the person.
202. This former professor from Vidyanagar College, West Bengal, is also the founder of Rashtriya Samajwadi Party. *The Turbulent Years, The Coalition Years* were books written by him. Name this former defence minister of India.
203. A close associate of Deendayal Upadhyay, this person was born as Chandikadas Amritrao Deshmukh. He was awarded Bharat Ratna in 2019 for his contributions in the field of rural development. How do we better know him?
204. He was the first Chief Minister of Assam post independence. He had also served as the prime minister of the state. Who is this freedom fighter who was conferred with the title 'Lokapriya' by Jayram Das Doulatram?
205. A prominent Indologist, this person wrote the famous book H*istory of Dharmashastra* having around six thousand pages. Name this author.
206. *Looking Back* is the autobiography of this person who founded Samatha Sangh. He also established India's first university for women in 1916. Identify the person.
207. An art director and designer, this person was also called Manik Da. He developed fonts called 'Daphnis, Holiday Script, Ray Ramon and Ray Bizzare'. Who?
208. A member of both Rajyasabha and Loksabha, this person was also a freedom fighter. He also constituted the congress committee which investigated Jallianwala Bagh Massacre case. Identify.
209. He was the premier of United Provinces of Agra and Oudh. He established Prem Sabha, which worked for various social reforms. Identify this Bharat Ratna of 1957.
210. He took part in second Round Table Conference along with Gandhiji and Sarojini Naidu. He was the president of Indian National Congress during the years 1909,1918,1932 and 1933. He was also instrumental in the establishment of Banaras Hindu University. Identify.

Answers

201. Bhupen Hazarika
202. Pranab Mukherjee
203. Nanaji Deshmukh
204. Gopinath Bordoloi
205. Pandu Rang Vaman Kane
206. D V Karve
207. Satyajith Ray
208. P V Tandon
209. G B Pant
210. Madan Mohan Malaviya

National Days

211. Every year approximately two lakh people visit this event. People who visited the same include Malik Ghulam

Muhammad (Governor General of Pakistan), President Sukarno, Queen Elizabeth II, Josip Tito. What is the occasion?

212. Along with January 30, another day is also celebrated as Martyrs' Day in India, honouring the sacrifice of three bravehearts. Which day?
213. This day is commemorated because of an order issued by Brigadier-General Reginald Dyer on 13 April 1919, which marks a tragic event in Indian history. Identify.
214. Samta Diwas emphasizes bringing about equality among all spheres of society. It is observed every year on 5th April, the birth anniversary of a former defense minister of India. Identify the person.
215. Army Day is celebrated in recognition of Field Marshal Kodandera M. Cariappa's taking over as the first Commander-in-Chief of the Indian Army. On which date is it observed?
216. This day is celebrated since 2006 to mark the occasion of Sardar Vallabhbhai Patel's address to this particular group of people, for the first time in1947. He described them as the 'steel frame of India'. Name the day.
217. 4th March marks the day when the NSC was established by the Ministry of Labour, Government of India. Eventhough it was established in 1966, the first observance was held in the year 1972. Which day is this?
218. This day is known as Samvidhan Divas in Hindi and is celebrated on 26 November. Which day?
219. Observed on December 23, this is also the birth anniversary of Chaudhary Charan Singh, the fifth prime minister of India. His tomb is known as Kisan Ghat. Identify the day.
220. This famous sculpture by Carl Fredrik Reutersward, displayed at the UN Visitors' Plaza, depicts a popular ideology proposed by an Indian. His birthday is celebrated as an international day to propagate this ideology. What day?

Answers

211. Republic Day Parade -India
212. March 23
213. Jallianwala Bagh day
214. Jagjivan Ram
215. January 15
216. National Civil Services Day
217. National Security Day
218. National Law Day
219. National Farmers' Day
220. International Day of Non-Violence (2 October)

Movies on Freedom Struggle

221. "Dilli aapki to Ruth bhi aapki," is a famous dialogue from this movie directed by Shyam Benegal in 1979.It was loosely based on Ruskin Bond's *A Flight of Pigeons.* Identify.
222. This was the first Indian movie to premiere in China.The first cut of the film was 7 hours and 30 minutes. The village in which the movie was shot was destroyed in an earthquake on 26th January 2001, six months after the movie was shot. Which film?
223. Three films based on the life of Bhagat Singh were released in the year 2002. Which Indian actor won the National Best Actor Award for playing the role of Bhagat Singh in the film - *Legend of Bhagat Singh*?
224. It is said that Prince Charles became the clapper boy of this film, when he

visited the shooting site. The Amul girl was seen in a sepoy dress and a long mustache, saying 'MAKHAN AAN DE: THE SLICING' as part of publicity campaign for the film. Which film?

225. Rajit Kapoor (1996), Naseerudhin Shah(2000), Darshan Jariwala (2006). What is common to these three actors?

226. Written by Din Dayal Sharma and Buttukeshwar Dutt, this 1965 film is famous for the songs like *Aye Watan*, *Sarfroshi ki Tamanna*. Identify the movie.

227. The director of this film once said that 'this film is his apology to Gandhi.' Shah Rukh Khan, Rani Mukerji, Hema Malini, Girish Karnad, Naseeruddin Shah, Atul Kulkarni, Farida Jalal shared the screen space together in this film. Identify.

228. For enacting the role of this freedom fighter, this actor from Himachal Pradesh won her fourth National award for Best Actress. Identify the movie and actress.

229. This was the first Dolby stereo movie in Malayalam starring Amrish Puri in one among the lead roles. Released in 1996, this was acclaimed nationwide and the protagonist won the State award for best actor in Malayalam. Which movie?

230. *Kranti*, a periodic drama, is said to be the last film of Harikrishna Giri Goswami. He was nicknamed Bharat Kumar for associating with movies of patriotic theme. How do we better know him?

Answers

221. *Junoon*
222. *Lagaan*
223. Ajay Devgn
224. Mangal Pandey
225. Played the role of Gandhiji
226. *Shaheed*
227. *Hey Ram*
228. *Manikarnika*, Kangana Ranaut
229. *Kaalapani*
230. Manoj Kumar

Martyrs

231. A documentary film was released in 2009 based on a revolutionary who died after a 63-day-long hunger strike in Lahore Jail when he was 25 years old. Name this person, one of the youngest martyrs of freedom struggle.

232. In December 1928, Bhagat Singh and an associate, fatally shot a 21-year-old British police officer, John Saunders, in Lahore. Along with Bhagat Singh and Sukhdev this associate was also hanged to death in the year 1931. Identify?

233. Bhagat Singh was a revolutionary socialist who had an extremely high influence in the Indian freedom struggle. What was the name of the organisation he was a member of?

234. This person shot himself after being left with no option of escape after the ammunition was finished. He died at Alfred park in Allahabad. The Colt pistol of this revolutionary is displayed at the Allahabad Museum. Who is he?

235. National Martyrs Memorial is where Sukhdev, along with Bhagat Singh and Rajguru, were cremated. Where is it located?

236. Batukeshwar Dutt was an Indian rev-

 extra

Shree Pundalik's Record

Shree Pundalik was the first full-length Indian film which was released a year before *Raja Harishchandra*. Though *Shree Pundalik* was made earlier, it was shot by a Britisher and was just a photographic recording of a stage play.

olutionary and independence fighter in the early 1900s. He is best known for having exploded two bombs, along with Bhagat Singh, which was the place bombed by them?

237.He composed poems in Urdu and Hindi, under the pen names Varasi and Hazarat. He was involved in the Kakori conspiracy case. Identify this martyr who was hanged at the age of 27.

238.Considered as the first woman martyr of Bengal,this lady had idolized Jhansi Rani. Pahartali European Club was attacked under her leadership where the infamous board which said 'Dogs and Indians not allowed.' was hung.Who was this firebrand?

239. This revolutionary was renowned for his leading role in the 1930 Chittagong armoury raid where he led a gang to raid the police armoury. He was popularly known as 'Master da'. Name the person

240. Authored by Anita Anand, *The Patient Assassin, A True Tale of Massacre, Revenge and the Raj* is a 2019 book based on the life of an Indian revolutionary who was hanged to death on 31 July 1940. Who?

Answers

231. Jatin Das
232. Shivaram Rajguru
233. Hindustan Socialist Republican Association (HSRA)
234. Chandra Shekhar Azad
235. Hussainiwala
236. Central Legislative Assembly in New Delhi
237. Ashfaqullah Khan
238. Pritilata Waddedar
239. Surya Sen
240. Udham Singh

INC Presidents

241. He was the first Indian to be a member of the British House of Lords. His role in materializing the Government of India Act 1919 was significant. Identify this person who presided over the 1915 session held at Bombay.

242. He returned to India from England on 1885, December 28. 15 years later, he became the president of the INC. Soon after, he was appointed as the Chief Justice of Bombay High Court and he retired from politics and joined back in 1914 to associate with the side of moderates. Identify this person, who had advised Gandhi to call off the Civil disobedience movement in 1921.

243. He had contributed around 13 lakh for the establishment of the National Council of Education which later became Jadavpur University. He was the president of the INC session that resulted in the Surat Split. Who?

244. This former INC president had also stood with Pherozeshah Mehta as the maker of the Bombay Municipal Corporation as well as with Gopal Krishna Gokhale as the custodian and watchdog of the country's finance. Identify this person, who embarrassed the government with his criticism of economic policies.

245. Kashmiri Pandit Community declared him an outcast for going to England. He broke the Dharma Sabha to form a new, progressive Bishan Sabha. Identify this person who had served as the INC President of the 26th session held in 1911.

246. This statesman-cum-jurist born on the Malabar coast became the INC president in its Amaraoti session held in 1897. He was instrumental in estab-

lishing the *Madras Review* and *Madras Law journal*. He was knighted in 1912. Identify this President of INC.

247. It was in this particular session held in Amritsar in 1919 that Congress extended support to the Khilafat movement. Who presided over this session?
248. There is a border dispute between Karnataka and Maharashtra over this place. The only INC session which was presided over by Mahatma Gandhi was held at this place in 1924. Which place?
249. The 1914 session was held in Madras. The president of the session was the first president of Mohun Bagan Athletic Club. Who?
250. World Unani day is observed on February 11 to pay tribute to this person for his contributions to Unani medicine in India and the world. He was the acting president of the 36th INC session held at Ahmedabad. Identify this person.

Answers

241. Lord Satyendra Prasanna Sinha
242. NG Chandavarkar
243. Rash Bihari Ghosh
244. Dinshaw Eduljee Wach
245. Bishan Narayan Dar
246. Chettur Sankaran Nair
247. Motilal Nehru
248. Belgaum/ Belagavi
249. Bhupendra Nath Bose
250. Hakim Ajmal Khan

Socio-Religious Movements

251. This organisation was founded by Raja Ram Mohan Roy to campaign against idolatry in 1815. Identify.
252. Tattwabodhini Sabha was established by the founder of the religion called Brahmoism. Who?
253. Founded by Atmaram Panduranga on 31 March, 1867, this establishment encouraged love for god and reverence. Which organisation?
254. Founded by Madame Blavatsky and Col. Olcott in 1875 in New York, this organization started gaining its roots in India in 1879. It is headquartered at Adayar.Identify.
255. In Arabic language this is known as 'Dār al-ʿulūm' which means 'House of Learninig'. It was founded in 1867 by Muhammad ʿĀbid Husayn. Give another name of this movement which aimed at education of Muslims.
256. Hentry Louis Vivian Derozio was a professor of English literature and poet. His famous work is *To India My Native Land*. He was a free thinker and orator and his followers were called 'Derozians. Name the intellectual movement started by him during the 1820s.
257. He started his career as a press employee, then joined East India Company as clerk. He advocated for modern scientific education, especially among Muslims. Muhammadan Anglo-Oriental College (MAOC) which later became the Aligarh Muslim University was set up by him. The educational reform started by him is known as Aligarh Movement.Identify the person.
258. Servants of India Society was found-

extra

Father of Guyana

Cheddi Jagan was a politician who, in 1953, became the first person of Indian descent to be head of government outside of South Asia. He is regarded as the 'father of Guyana'.

ed in 1915 by a person whose 155th birth anniversary was celebrated on 9 May 2021. He also founded the Ranade Institute of Economics. Name this person.

259. Often described as the 'father of Indian Social Revolution', this person and his wife were instrumental in establishing the first girl's school in India. They also founded the organisation called 'Satyashodak Samaj'. Identify this couple.

260. Arya Mahila Samaj, Sharada Sadan are two oraganisations founded by the lady shown in the picture. She was awarded 'Kaiser-i-Hind ' medal by the British government. Identify.

Answers

251. Athmiya Sabha
252. Debendranath Tagore
253. Prarthana Samaj
254. Theosophical Society
255. Deoband Movement
256. Young Bengal
257. Sir Syed Ahmed Khan
258. Gopalakrishna Gokhale
259. Jyothirao Phule and Savitribhai Phule
260. Panditha Ramabhai

Wars and Battles

261. This one-and-a-half-year-long war came to a conclusion with the treaty of Madras. Identify the ruler from Budikote who signed in the treaty along with British.

262. A major site of Carnatic wars, this is a small town in the Thiruvannamlai district of Tamilnadu. When the third Carnatic war took place this place was called Wandiwash. What is the current name of the place?

263. "When you go home, tell them of us and say for your tomorrow we gave our today," is an epitaph written by John Edmonds. Where in India can you locate this.?

264. This was a joint attack by Mir Qasim, Shuja-Ud-Daulah and Shah Alam II against British. In this battle, British won under the leadership of Hector Munro. Treaty of Allahabad was the result of this battle. Identify.

265. One of the earliest examples of India's resistance against the British, this mutiny by Indian sepoys against the British that took place about fifty years before the revolt of 1857 is said to be the inspiration behind the novel *Strangers in the Land* by George Shipway. Which mutiny?

266. This battle known in the name of a traditional warrior community of Odisha was in the news as the former Union Minister Prakash Javdekar suggested 'it should be proclaimed as the first war of Indian Independence instead of the 1857 revolt.' Identify the battle.

267. Which princely state came into existence after the treaty of Amritsar was signed between British East India Company and the Dogra ruler Maharaja Gulab Singh?

268. An important part of the revolt of 1857, this revolt at Kanpur was led by a person who is also known as Dhondu Pant. He was the adopted son of Bajirao II. How do we better know him?

extra

Qutb-ud-din Aibak's Death

The Delhi sultan Qutb-ud-din Aibak lost his life during a match of Polo in Lahore in 1210. However, the rules of Polo were outlined by Akbar only four centuries later.

269.This treaty was signed in 1792 between Lord Cornwallis for British and Tipu Sultan for Mysore, which brought an end to the third Mysore war. Which treaty.

270.This is a memorial dedicated to the battle, which held on 1 January 1818 between Mahar community with the support of British against Peshwa Bajirao II. Name the obelisk.

Answers

261. Hyder Ali
262. Vandavasi
263. Kohima War Cemetery
264. Battle of Buxar
265. Vellore Mutiny 1806
266. Paika Bidroha
267. Jammu and Kashmir
268. Nana Saheb
269. Treaty of Seringapatam (Srirangapatinam)
270. Bhima –Koregoan Pillar

Major Incidents

271.Name the committee appointed by the British government to investigate Jallianwala Bagh Massacre, which let off General Dyer, even though they condemned his act.

272.He was the Labour minister in Winston Churchill government and headed the mission to gather Indian support to British in the Second World War. Identify the person.

273. Lord Birkenhead was the masterbrain behind this commission of which Clement Atlee was a member. Not even a single Indian was member of this and they protested against the same. Boycotting this commission was a major event in Indian history. Which commission is mentioned here.

274. February 1922 marked a special incident in the freedom struggle due to which Gandhiji withdrew the Non Cooperation movement which was launched in 1920. Which incident?

275. Tirur Railway Station was in the news in 2018, owing to a newly-made mural depicting a tragedy which took place on 21 November 1921. Later this painting was removed from the station after protests from certain quarters. What was the event depicted in the painting?

276.After the Third Round Table Conference, a proposal for separate electorates for minorities was suggested by the British Prime minister Ramsay McDonald. What was that called?

277. It was Madan Mohan Malaviya who signed in this pact on behalf of Gandhi with B R Ambedkar. This pact is known by the name of the place where it was signed and which means 'holy' in Sanskrit. Identify

278.*1946: The Unknown Mutiny* is a book by Pramod Kapoor' which is an account of the protest of 1500 low ranking soldiers who were working in HMIS Talwar. They went with the slogans like 'NO FOOD NO WORK' against poor accommodation and disgusting treatment by the British commanders. What is being discussed?

279.In 1947 Lord Mountbatten came up with a plan called Dickie Bird Plan suggesting that provinces can be declared as independent states and they can choose whether to join the constituent assembly. Nehru opposed this using a term. What?

280. What entity named after this lawyer from England has been immortalized in the history of India?

Answers

271. Hunter Committee
272. Sir Richard Stafford Cripps
273. Simon Commission
274. Chauri Chaura Incident
275. Wagon Tragedy 1921
276. Communal Award
277. Poona Pact
278. Royal Indian Navy Mutiny 1946
279. Balkanization (Balkan Plan)
280. Radcliff Line

Independence (Mixed)

281. Vernacular press act 1878 had put restrictions on publications in Native languages. It was intended to prevent criticism against European policies, especially after the second Anglo-Afghan war. Who introduced this act?
282. It was because of his vital role in this satyagraha, Vallabhai Patel earned the title Sardar meaning chief. Which satyagraha?
283. This was first presented at Shimla Conference 1945. This plan suggested that the viceroy's council will have balanced representation of all Indians. It was named after the second last viceroy of India. Name the plan and person.
284. This uprising led by Ram Singh and Bhagat Jawahar Mal in 1845 aimed at the purification of Sikh religion. What was the name of the movement?
285. He is called Rashtraguru and was an open critic of Mahatma Gandhi. He founded Indian National Association in 1876 along with Anand Mohan Bose. Identify this person.
286. This 1907 event which took place on the bank of river Tapti is unforgettable in the history of Indian National Congress. Two camps were formed, one under the leadership of Lal Bal Pal and the other under Gopalakrishna Gokhle. Name this decisive moment.
287. During the First World War, in order to get Indian support, the British, especially Viceroy Linlithgow, put forward a set of proposals, in which for the first time the right of Indians to frame their own constitution was accepted. What was the name of the proposal?
288. This brave freedom fighter from West Bengal is known for shooting the then Bengal governor Stanley Jackson. She is sometimes called 'Agnikanya'. Who?
289. *Kesari* was the Marathi newspaper started by Lokmanya Bal Gangadhar Tilak. Name the English newspaper started by him?
290. This flag represents the party formed by expatriate Indians to overthrow British rule in India. Name the party.

Answers

281. Lord Lytton
282. Bardoli
283. Wavell Plan, Lord Archibald Wavell
284. Kuka Revolt
285. Surendranath Banerjee
286. Surat Split
287. August Offer

288. Beena Das
289. *Mahratta*
290. Ghadar Party

Mixed Bag

291. Acclaimed as the Bible of Modern Hinduism, this set of poems is part of a work which is also called as Jaya. Gandhiji had acknowledged that this set of poems were his spiritual reference book. Name the set of poems.
292. Known as Tsangpo and Dihang, the most popular name of this entity means 'Son of Bhrahma.' Earlier this was known as Lauhitya. What?
293. According to *Bhagavatha Purana*, there are 28 types of this and some of them are Vaitharani, Aveechi, Puyodha, Visasana etc. What are these?
294. Born in Budapest, this lady is famous for her work titled *Young Girls*. She had worked as the assistant editor and a writer at *The Statesman* newspaper. Her trilogy of *Bride's Toilet*, *South Indian Villagers Going to Market* and *Brahmacharis* received wide recognition. Who?
295. This is the most expensive, highest and longest air maintenance field in the world. Identify this place connected by the world's largest all weather pass Khardungla.
296. Kaya, Bala, Graha, Urdhwa, Shalya, Dhanstra, Jara and Vrushya. What are these?
297. Headquartered at New Delhi, this was instituted in 1950. Sukumar Sen was the first Indian to head this institution. What is being discussed here?
298. Smiling Buddha and Operation Shakthi were conducted by India. Who conducted Chagai 1 and Chagai 2?
299. This place is also known as 'Berlin Wall of Asia'. Silly walk was a ceremony, which was conducted here till 2010. Which is this place?
300. "Are ye Serfs or are ye, Freemen, Ye, that grovel in the shade? In your own hands rest the issues! By themselves are nations made! This poem, Old Man's Hope, was penned by a person who founded something significant in India's Independence history. Who?

Answers

291. *Bhagavad Gita* (*Mahabarata* is also known as *Jaya*)
292. Brahmaputra river
293. Types of Hells
294. Amrita Shergil
295. Siachen glacier battlefield
296. Eight parts of Ayurveda(Ashtanga)
297. Election Commission of India
298. Pakistan
299. Wagah Border
300. Allan Octavian Hume

Languages

301. Modi is a script belonging to the Nagari family. When Devanagri rose to prominence, Modi script slowly faded out. Identify the language for which this script was used ?
302. This particular language, which is a mix of Sanskrit and Dravidian, is also known as 'Italian of the East'. Which language?
303. This is the seventh most spoken language in the world. UNESCO declared February 21 as International Mother Language Day to commemorate a movement that took place in 1952 associated with this language. Identify
304. This language is one of the longest palindromes in English and the only Indian language whose name is a pal-

indrome. Which language?

305. This language is taught in more than ten universities in Germany. One may find 100 synonyms for the word 'elephant' in this language. Uttarakhand is the first Indian state to make this an official language. Which language?
306. One of the official languages of Sri Lanka as well as Singapore, this is also one of the oldest languages in the world. The deity in Karaikudi temple is the personification of this language. Name the language.
307. When President Bush was in office he had asked the Congress to allocate 114 million dollars to include this language in curriculum, so that people will get to know about other cultures. This language was earlier known as Apabhramsa. Identify.
308. This is said to be the ancestral language of almost all Indian languages. It was James Princep who deciphered the ancient edicts of Ashoka which was written in this script. Which script?
309. Maithili, Magadhi and Bhojpuri are the three main dialects spoken in this state. Which state?
310. Gopinath Mohanty was the first Jnanpith winner in this language and Pratibha Ray is the first woman to achieve that honour. Which language are we talking about?

Answers

301. Marathi
302. Telugu
303. Bengali
304. Malayalam
305. Sanskrit
306. Tamil
307. Hindi
308. Brahmi
309. Bihar
310. Odia

Statues

311. Constructed by Larsen & Toubro and the Jiangxi Toquine Company this statue is located on a river island called Sadhu Bet between the Vindhya and Satpura Ranges. It was designed by Ram V Suther. Identify the statue.
312. This is the world's second tallest statue of a seated figure, Great Buddha of Thailand being the first. Also called statue of equality, the base of the statue is called Bhadravedi. To whom is this statue dedicated?
313. This sculpture depicts an Indian mythological character. The place where it is located is also named after this character who was the son of Aruna and brother of Sampati. Identify the character.
314. Designed by the famous Indian sculptor V. Ganapati Sthapati, this statue is located in the sea in Kanyakumari. Whose statue is this?
315. This temple and adjacent complex is owned by entrepreneur family of Rama Nagappa Shetty. World's second largest Shiva statue is located here. Identify.
316. Dedicated to the first Teerthankar of Jains, this holds the *Guinness* Record as the world's tallest Jain statue. It's located at Mangi Tungi. How do we better know this statue?
317. The Mahamastakabhisheka Mahot-

sava is an anointing ceremony of this statue which is located at Dharmashala. This ten-day-long festival is a tribute to?

318. This is temple village in Andhra Pradesh where the famous Nandi bull statue and also the snake on the Nagalinga are located. The name of the village can be translated as 'Get up Bird'. Name the village.
319. This famous statue of a brother and sister built by Ramkinkar Baij is situated in front of an apex institution in Delhi. Many people misinterpret it as that of 'Kuber'. Whose statues?
320. This statue of Jesus Christ was in the news a few years back as the statue and the famous church near it were affected by cyclone Gaja and the 2004 tsunami that hit the Coromandel coast. Identify the location of the statue.

Answers

311. Statue of Unity
312. Bhakti Saint Ramanuja
313. Jatayu (Jatayupara, Kollam)
314. Thiruvalluvar
315. Murudeshwar Shiva Statue
316. Statue of Ahimsa
317. Gomateshwara
318. Lepakshi
319. Yaksha and Yakshi
320. Velankanni

Waterfalls

321. Bundla Waterfalls has a magnificent height of 328 feet and is set amidst dense forests, cliffs and tea gardens. In which Indian state is it located?
322. Rajat Prapat waterfall in Hoshangabad district of Madhya Pradesh is a horse tail type waterfall. Rajat Prapat is also known by another name. Identify.
323. Situated between Dharmapuri district of Tamil Nadu and Chamrajnagar district of Karnataka, this is sometimes referred to as the "Niagara Falls of India. Which one?
324. Vantawng Falls with a height of 229 meters is the highest uninterrupted waterfall in Mizoram. It is located in which district of Mizoram?
325. Which three-tiered waterfall in Kerala is also known as Sentinel Rock falls?
326. *Mudalvan*, *Guru*, *Raavan* and *Baahubali* were blockbusters filmed in the pristine surroundings of this waterfall. Which falls once also known by the name "Punnagai Mannan Falls"?
327. Beehad River, a tributary of Tamsa or Tons River, also serves as the course of a famous waterfall. Which waterfall?

Nizamuddin Auliya's Favourite Disciple  extra

Amir Khusrau was the favourite disciple of Nizamuddin Auliya. He was so special to his master that the latter once said, "If the sharia allowed me, I would have liked him to be buried with me in the same grave." Khusrau was also buried in Nizamuddin Dargah.

328. Duduma Waterfall is situated in the border of Koraput and Visakhapatnam districts of India. Which Indian river is associated with Duduma Waterfalls?
329. Ninai Waterfalls is a major tourist attraction in Mohbi, Gujarat. Ninai Falls are located on the watercourse of which river?
330. Which waterfall having Sharavati river as its destination is composed of Raja, Rani, Rocket and Roarer falls?

Answers

321. Himachal Pradesh
322. Silver falls
323. Hogenakkal Falls
324. Serchchip district
325. Soochipara Falls
326. Athirappally Falls
327. Chachai Falls
328. Machkund River
329. Narmada
330. Jog Falls

Dams

331. Built across Mahanadi,this is the longest earthen dam in India. Identify.
332. Known as the 'New Temple of Resurgent India' this is the second largest reservoir in the country. What is being mentioned here?
333. Built on the tributary of Son river, the reservoir of this dam is named after G B Pant. Name this dam located at Pipari, Utter Pradesh.
334. Name the two dams constructed as per the Indus Water Treaty between India and Pakistan which was monitored by UN in 1960.
335. This is the first ever arch dam in India and also one of the largest of its kind in Asia. Identify.
336. Located on Bhageerathi river, this is the eighth tallest dam in the world and the highest in India. Which dam?
337. Banasura Sagar is named after the son of a mythological character immensely popular in Kerala. Identify the character.
338. Built across Kaveri river and located at Thiruchirapalli, this is said to be the oldest dam in India. Name the dam.
339. The lake created by Pong dam in Himachal Pradesh is named after a Mewar king whose horse was also well-known across regions. Who is this king?
340. Identify this person, who was the brain behind this dam which was built around 100 years ago, located in South India. His birthday is celebrated as a public holiday in Tamil Nadu.

Answers

331. Hirakud
332. Bhakra Nangal Dam
333. Rihand Dam
334. Tarbela and Mangala Dam
335. Idukki Dam
336. Tehri Dam
337. Mahabali
338. Kallanai Dam
339. Maharana Pratap
340. John Pennycuick

Mountains

341. Nanga Parbat and Namcha Barwa are considered as the western and

eastern point of this ranges. Its Sanskrit name means 'Abode of Snow'. Which mountain?

342.Kalumar peak is the highest point.An important valley in this mountain range is Pachmarhi, also known as the Rani of this ranges. Identify the ranges.

343.This is the second highest mountain in India and is also famous for Valley of Flowers National Park.Which is this mountain?

344.Home to Mount Abu, the only hill station in Rajasthan, these are the oldest ranges in India. Rivers like Luni, Sabarmati and Banas flow through these ranges.Identify.

345.This is the third highest peak in the world and India's first UNESCO mixed Heritage site. In local language the name means "Five Treasuries of the Great Snow." Name this ranges.

346.This peak is also called Sarvajna Peedom, because the great scholar Sankaracharya meditated here and got enlightenment. Three temples here are dedicated to Uma Devi. Which is this mountain?

347.Barren Island located in Andaman is the only one of its kind in India. What?

348.This is the highest peak in the Western ghats. In the local language the name literally translates into 'Elephant's Hair'. Name this peak.

349.Doddabetta is the highest point in Tamil Nadu. This is also a part of which famous range?

350.This photo went viral in 2020, when the ranges became clearly visible, due to the drop of pollution level. Name the mountain ranges seen in the background which separates Jammu from Kashmir.

Answers

341. Himalayas
342. Satpura ranges
343. Nanda Devi
344. Aravalli
345. Kanchenjunga
346. Kudajadri
347. The only active volcano in India
348. Anamudi
349. Nilgiri Ranges
350. Pir Panjal Mountain Range

Capital Cities

351.This capital city is famous for the largest gathering of women in the world. Greenfield stadium is located here.The city is named after the deity of the most famous temple located in the city. Identify.

352.Even though a capital city,this is located in Guwahati city. It became the capital in 1972 replacing Shillong. Identify the city mentioned here.

353.In Potuguese this city is known as Pongrim. The state was formed in the year 1987. Identify the state and capital.

354.This capital city is known as the silicon valley of India.Famous institutions like ISRO, HAL etc are headquartered here. Which city?

355.Earlier known as Thigoma, the current name of this capital city is said to be derived from Kewhi flowers which is seen abundantly in the mountain ranges of the state. Identify the capital.

356.This city is said to be established by Lakshmana. Bara Imambara is an important monument here. Husainabad clock tower over here is the tallest in the country. Name this city which is known as the Constantinople of the East.

357.The literal meaning of the name of this state is 'thirty six forts' and you can see its symbolic representation in the state's emblem. Identify the capital of this state.

358.A very important pilgrimage in India Harmandir Takht Saheb is located in the heat of this city.In ancient days the city was known as Patliputra. Identify.

359.Home to the Indian cricketer M S Dhoni,this place was the heart of Munda revolt and birth place of Birsa Munda.Name this capital city.

360.This is the logo of Mumbai City FC in Indian Super League. What do the seven stars in the logo represent?

Answers

351. Thiruvananthapuram
352. Dispur
353. Goa and Panjim
354. Bengaluru
355. Kohima
356. Lucknow
357. Nawa Raipur
358. Patna
359. Ranchi
360. The seven islands constituting the capital city of Mumbai.

Scientists

361.He was the first to investigate harmonic nature of sound in Indian instruments.He was also the first Indian to win Nobel for Physics. Identify this person.

362.Born on 19 October 1910 in Lahore, S.Chandrasekhar was awarded the 1983 Nobel Prize for Physics. His work was based on theoretical studies of the physical processes of importance to the structure and evolution of?

363. Tamil Nadu observes 22 December as 'State IT Day' to commemorate the achievements of this person. 'The Man Who Knew Infinity' is a biographical work based on him. Who is this person?

364. Crescograph was invented by this person who wrote *Niruddesher Kahini,* a famous Bengali science fiction work. He also has a crater on moon named after him. Name this person.

365.Considered as the father of India's space programme, he was a native of Ahmedabad. He was awarded the Padma Bhushan in 1966 and the Padma Vubhushan after his death in 1972. Identify the person.

366.*Visva Parichay,* a book by Rabindranath Tagore, is dedicated to this scientist after whom one class of particle is named. Who is person?

367.His birthday is celebrated as 'World Students Day' by UN. A Bacterium discovered in the International Space Station has been named after him. Identify this person.

368.A renowned theoretical physicist and founder of Tata Institute of Fundamental Research (TIFR) which was later named after him, this person is best known as the chief architect of the Indian atomic energy program. Identify him.

369. *Chromosome Atlas of Cultivated Plants* is a reference work for scientists that record the chromosome number of about 100,000 plants, providing knowledge about breeding and evolutionary patterns of botanical groups. Who co–authored this along with Cyril Dean Darlington?

370. Known as 'Father of modern Indian Chemistry', he has established

what is known as the first pharmaceutical company of India. Identify.

Answers

361. C. V. Raman
362. Stars
363. S. Ramanujan
364. Jagdish Chandra Bose
365. Vikram Sarabhai
366. S N Bose
367. A. P. J. Abdul Kalam
368. Homi Jehangir Bhabha
369. E K Janaki Ammal
370. Prafulla Chandra Ray

Dance Forms

371. Around 2000 years old, this was called Dasiattam. Sadir is another form of this. Rukmani Arundale, the first female dancer to be on an Indian stamp, was a prominent practitioner of this dance form. Identify.
372. National dance of Assam shares its name with its national festival. Name it.
373. This classical dance form originated from the village which was earlier known as Kuchelapuri or Kuchelavaram. Which dance form?
374. Odhra Maghadha is said to be the ancient form of this dance style. Evidence of practising of this style was found from caves of Khandagiri and Udayagiri near Bhubaneswar. Identify this dance.
375. Mahapurusha Shankaradeva is believed to be the founder of this dance form. Pat silk and Muga silk are two kinds of sarees used by the dancers of this dance. Name this dance.
376. This dance is based on the 'Lasya' style of Natya Shastra. The songs are in Sopana style. This dance form also celebrates one of the incarnations of Lord Vishnu. Identify this South Indian dance.
377. This is classical dance form of this Indian state which is known as Land of Jewels. Jagoi and Cholom are the two divisions of this dance. Name the dance form.
378. This dance form is associated with the festival Chaitra Parva. It's performed at night with the music played using mohuri and shehnai. This was added in the list of intangible cultural heritage of humanity by UNESCO. Which is this dance form?
379. An inevitable part of Baisakhi festival, this is usually played by men. It is accompanied by songs called Boliyan. Which is this dance form?
380. Birju Maharaj, Sharmila Sharma, Prerana Shrimala, Chitresh Das etc are a few famous faces of this dance form. The literal meaning of the name of this dance form is 'Storyteller'. Identify.

Answers

371. Bharatanatyam
372. Bihu
373. Kuchippudi

Inspiration Behind *Do Aankhen Baraah Haath*  extra

The classic 1957 film *Do Aankhen Baraah Haath*, directed by V Shantaram, won a Silver Bear in the Berlin International Film festival. It was inspired by the story of an open prison in the princely state of Audh in Maharashtra.

374. Odissi
375. Sattriya
376. Mohiniyattom.
377. Manipuri
378. Chhau
379. Bhangra
380. Kathak

Festivals

381. *Cassia Fistula*, commonly known as Golden Shower, is the symbol of this New Year festival. Tamil Nadu celebrates this as 'Puthnadu'. Identify this festival which occurs during the month of April.
382. Eruthazhaval, Manju virattu are two other names of this celebration.Earlier this was a ceremony held to find a capable and strong bridegroom. The current name evolved from the words 'Salli Kaasu'. Which festival?
383. This is celebrated mainly in Barasana village near Vrindavan. The main custom is that men visiting Barsana will be beaten by women folk here using a particular stick or Latt. Name this festival.
384. Gudipawa is one name of the celebration. It is also known as Cheti Chand among Sindhis, Sajibu Nogma Panba among Manipuris, Thapna in Rajastan. How do we better know this?
385. The Goddesses worshipped during this festival are named Shailputri, Brahmcharini, Chandraghanta, Kushmanda, Skandamata, Katyayani, Kalratri, Mahagauri and Siddidatri. Which festival?
386. In the Pori Festival celebrated annually during August, horses are bathed in sweet water, fed rich and healthy food, and decorated beautifully. At the temple of Triloknath, the statue of the Deity is bathed with milk and yogurt. Which Indian state celebrates this?
387. Celebrated to mark the beginning of harvesting season of Rabi crops, this is popular in Punjab and adjacent areas. It is observed a night before Makara Sankranti. Name this fest which is celebrated with a huge bonfire.
388. A monsoon welcoming festival, this is mainly observed by women in the country. As per beliefs it is the union of goddess Parvathi with lord Shiva. Hariyali, Kajari, Hartalika are different forms of this. Which festival?
389. Phauwa, Holla Mohala, Shigmo etc are different names of this festival. The most popular name was derived from the name of a female mythological character associated with Hiranyakashypu. Name the festival.
390. This is a festival of Nagaland. It is held at Naga Heritage village, where all the tribes take part. Identify the fest from the picture.

Answers

381. Vishu
382. Jellikettu
383. Lattimar Holi
384. Ugadi
385. Navaratri
386. Himachal Pradesh
387. Lohri
388. Teej
389. Holi
390. Hornbill Festival

Mixed Bag

391. He was nominated for the Nobel Prize in Literature for five consecutive years between 1933 and 1937.Identify this native of Tiruttani, Tamil Nadu who is credited with some 'First in India'.
392. Rajgruha is the memorial house which has a collection of more than 50000 books collected by a famous Indian social reformer and was one of the largest private libraries in the world till his death. Identify this person who also wrote the book *The Indian Struggle*.
393. This village located in Maharashtra is known for the popular temple of the Hindu God associated with planet Saturn. Due to their undying faith in this Hindu God the houses in this village have no front doors and the locals never feel unsafe. Identify this village.
394. Founded by Harihara and Bukka, the capital of this empire is Hampi which is a UNESCO World Heritage site. Identify the empire.
395. If Mehr Chand Mahajan was the third person and M. Patanjali Sastri was the second person to be in this position, who is the first? What is being mentioned here?
396. River Hiran flows through this forest. The dam built across the river is also called Kamaleswar dam. Identify this forest area.
397. Born to a famous volleyball couple of India, this person is the youngest in India to win an individual Olympic medal. Identify the person who won Arjuna award at the age of 18?
398. Vikram, Vajra, Varad etc are a few vessels owned by this wing. Their motto means Vayam Rakshamah' which means 'We Protect'. Which defense wing?
399. Missile Woman of India is Tessy Thomas and Rocket Man is Dr K Sivan. Who is the Rocket Woman of India?
400. The person in the picture is Talimeren Ao, a doctor by profession from Nagaland. He has a unique distinction in the history of Indian sports. What is it?

Answers

391. Dr. S Radhakrishnan
392. Dr. BR Ambedkar
393. Shani Shingapur
394. Vijayanagara
395. HJ Kania, Chief Justice of Supreme Court
396. Gir Forest
397. P V Sindhu
398. Indian Coast Guard
399. Rithu Karidhal
400. First Indian football team captain.

Prime Ministers

401. National Academy of Administration (Civil Services) is named after this person who was born on 2 October 1904. He is the first person to be posthumously awarded Bharat Ratna. Who is this?
402. A civil engineering diploma holder, this former Prime Minister of India was also called 'Son of Soil'. Both he as well as his son were elected as the Chief Ministers of their state. Who?
403. *Matters of Discretion* is the autobiography of this former Indian ambassador and Information and Broadcasting minister during emergency. One of the popular foreign policy doctrines of India is named after him. Identify.
404. National Good Governance Day is celebrated on the birthday of this first ever non-Congress prime minister who completed the tenure. He was elected to Lok Sabha from four different states. Name this person.

405. Movies called *Art of Impossible*, *One More Day to Live* were based on this person who implemented the report of Mandal commission. Identify.
406. Known as the 'Father of Indian Economic Reforms', he could speak eight local languages and a few foreign languages. He was also the editor of a Telugu weekly magazine namely *Kakathiya Party.* Name this first ever Prime Minister from South India.
407. *The Red Sari* is a famous biography on Edvige Antonia Albina Maino from Lusiana. Who is the famous husband of this person?
408. National Farmers' Day is observed on his birthday Often called as 'Champion of India's peasants', he is the author of books called *Co-operative Farming X-rayed, India's Poverty and its Solution* etc. Who is this?
409. Chanakya was the pen name he used to criticize Prime Minister Jawaharlal Nehru. One of his sisters was the first female president of UN General Assembly. Name this person.
410. Jan Nayak Sthal is the memorial of this prime minister of India who is known as 'Young Turk'. Identify.

Answers

401. Lal Bahadur Shastri
402. H D Deve Gowda
403. I K Gujral
404. A B Vajpayee
405. V P Singh
406. P V Narasimha Rao
407. Rajiv Gandhi
408. Charan Singh
409. Jawaharlal Nehru
410. Chandra Shekhar Singh

Armed Forces

411. Sampriti, Maitree, Mitra, Shakthi and Nomadic Elephant. What are these?
412. This military force is known in the name of a state. It is also known as "Friends of the Hill People," the "Sentinels of the North East." Identify.
413. Vishakhapatnam, Mumbai and Kochi are the three zonal headquarters of which defense force of India?
414. C-448 is a water-jet-propelled interceptor vessel, which is set to be deployed in for patrolling and rescue operations. Which defense wing of India commissioned this project?
415. Coming into existence on 1 December 1965 with KF Rustomji as its first chief and founder, this security wing is called 'India's First Line of Defence.' Which force?
416. This special force is sometimes called 'Orange Army.' Kerala Government published a book called *Orange Book*, detailing the standard operation procedures and emergency function plan of this force, following a few incidents in the state since 2018. Identify the force.
417. This badge was in the news during the 2019 Cricket World Cup, when M S Dhoni wore gloves with the same. It was a badge or logo of the army parachute regiment's special force. What is the name of the badge?
418. This is the highest military honour awarded to the military unit in the country. Name this award presented by

extra

Ravish Malhotra and Rakesh Sharma

Ravish Malhotra was an IAF pilot who later commanded the Hindon Air Force base. He was the other pilot with Rakesh Sharma who was trained to be an astronaut. Sharma was finally chosen to become the first Indian in space.

the Indian President.

419. This was established as Special Service Bureau in 1963. They guard Indo-Nepal and Indo-Bhutan Borders. Give the current name of this force.

420. A biographical movie was released in 2020 based on this officer's life who is popular as Kargil Girl. Who is this?

Answers

411. Joint military exercises of India with different countries.
412. Assam Rifles
413. The Indian Navy
414. Indian Coast Guard
415. Border Security Force (BSF)
416. National Disaster Response Force
417. Balidan Badge
418. Presidents's colour
419. Sashastra Seema Bal
420. Gunjan Saxena

Paintings

421. Pattachitra refers to the folk painting, in the eastern region of India. 'Patta' in Sanskrit means 'Vastra' or 'Clothings' and 'Chitra' means paintings. Pattachitra is one of the ancient art works of which Indian state?

422. This art work is often referred to as Snake Paintings as swirling snakes depict the central character Bihula's tale of love and sacrifice. Which paintings?

423. Mural Painting can be defined as any piece of artwork painted or applied directly onto a wall, ceiling or other permanent surfaces. The word 'mural' was derived from which foreign language?

424. Which disciple of Abanindranath Tagore is also described as an art machine because he produced 20,000 paintings in his lifetime which is about 10 paintings a day?

425. *Days of Glory* and *Mourning en masse* are the famous paintings of which Indian artist, who passed away in 2020 ?

426. Pala School represents the earliest examples of miniature painting in India. The manuscripts of Pala Empire mostly belong to which school of Buddhism?

427. *Rang Rasiya* (2008) and *Makara Manju* (2011) are two films based on this artist who was part of the Chicago World Fair Expo in 1893, famous for the speech of Swami Vivekananda. Name the artist.

428. Head of School of Arts in Shantiniketan, the famous painting of this artist is called 'Gandhi March'. He was asked by Nehru to draw the sketches for awards like Bharat Ratna. Who is this?

429. King Indradyumna who was cursed and ended up in the form of an elephant; a crocodile called Huhu and Lord Vishnu are depicted in this painting. Name the painting?

430. This is a folk painting prevalent in Rajasthan. The style got its name from the local language meaning 'fold'. In this detailed and crowded painting every inch of canvas is used. Identify this style of painting.

Answers

421. Odisha
422. Manjusha
423. Latin
424. Jamini Roy
425. Satish Gujral
426. Vajrayana

427. Raja Ravi Varma
428. Nandalal Bose
429. Gajendra Moksha
430. Phad painting

Books and Authors

431. *Quichottte* is a 2019 novel by Salman Rushdie inspired by a world famous work. Identify.
432. *Art of Fencing and Sword Play* is a book written by this dentist who established Travancore National Pictures. Who ?
433. His mother was blind and when he wrote his autobiography he used his mother's last words as the title. He was the co -founder of a world-famous tech company Mindtree. Identify the book and author.
434. In 1791 German writer Goethe described that ' if heaven and earth combined in one name, that name would be hers'. Title character of which book is being mentioned here ?
435. Which ancient Indian work became the basis for a Syriac translation as *Kalilag and Damnag* and a translation into Arabic in 750 CE as *Kalīlah wa Dimnah*?
436. *Exam Warrior* is a book written to help the students deal with the stress of exams. The braille Version of this book was published on world Braille day by the author of this book. Who is the author?
437. This is a story by Munshi Premchand, which was later made into a film with a unique feature that this is the only Hindi feature film directed by a famous Bengali writer and director. Name the book and director of the movie.
438. The novel was first published as a series in *Kalki* magazine between 1950 and 1954, and book release was done in 1955. Identify this work, widely considered by many to be the greatest novel ever written in Tamil literature.
439. Boria Majumdar is an Indian sports journalist, academician and author. He was in the news in 2014 as the co-author of an autobiography. Identify the book.
440. R Shamasastry was a Sanskrit scholar and librarian at the Oriental Research Institute Mysore. He re-discovered and published this famous book . The title of this book can be translated as 'The Science of Wealth.' Which book?

Answers

431. *Don Quixote*
432. J C Daniel
433. Subrato Bagchi , *Go Kiss the World*
434. *Shakunthala* of Kalidasa
435. Panchathantra stories
436. Narendra Modi
437. *Shatranj ke Khiladi* , Sathyajith Ray
438. *Ponniyan Selvan* by Kalki Krishnamoorthi
439. Sachin Tendulkar : *Playing it My Way*
440. *Arthashastra*

Folk Art/Folklore

441. Bagurumba is a folk dance of Bodo tribes in the state of Assam. This dance

extra

Consecutive National Awards for Best Actress

In 1983-85, Shabana Azmi won three consecutive National Awards for Best Actress, a feat unrivalled in Indian film history. The awards were for *Arth, Khandhar* and *Paar.*

form has a nickname because this dance form is similar to the movement of an organism. Which is the organism?

442. This is a folk art in the Mithila region of Bihar. It is characterised by its eye-catching geometrical patterns. There is also a railway station in Bihar named after this. What is mentioned here ?

443. This is the story of a king who tries to catch a vampire. Every time the vampire asks a riddle and only if the king answers it correctly will he be able to take away the vampire. Which is this famous folklore?

444. Chikka Mela is a group of artists who perform this dance form, on door to door basis other than stage performances. Maddle, Pungi, Harmonium,Chande are the main instruments used while performing this dance. Identify.

445. Kamiacha is an instrument with seventeen strings. Three important strings are made of intestine of goats. Which group traditionally uses this instrument?

446. Ektara is an instrument used in this music.It got its name from a Sanskrit word meaning 'Lunatic'. Lalon Fakir has penned most of the songs in this genre. Identify.

447. This dance form is performed by the women in the Konkan region during Ganesh Chaturthi. It's performed during the month of Bhaadrapada. Which dance ?

448. This is a traditional dance form performed mainly in Rajasthan by Bhil tribe. An adaptation of this dance was shown in a 2018 Hindi movie directed by Sanjay Leela Bansali. Identify the dance form.

449. This folk dance performed by the agrarian community of Haryana has derived its name because of the fact that it is mostly performed in the month of Phalhguna. Which dance?

450. Created by the tribal people from the North Sahyadri Range in Maharashtra, nature and elements in nature often come as the central theme in these paintings. Identify.

Answers

441. Butterfly
442. Madhubani paintings
443. *Vikram and Betal*
444. Yakshagana
445. Manganiyar
446. Baul
447. Fugdi
448. Ghoomer
449. Phag
450. Warli painting

National Parks

451. In 1936, this was called Hailey National Park. During 1950s it was known as Ram Ganga National Park. What is the current name of the park dedicated to a British writer and environmentalist?

452. Popular for one-horned rhinoceros, this park was established when Mary Curzon urged her husband Lord Curzon, to take precautions to protect Rhinos in the region. Identify

453. Which National Park traces its origin to 1931, when a few British mountaineers who lost their way while returning

from a successful expedition to Mt.Kamet, were attracted to the beauty of the area and named it after seeing something over there?

454.This national park is named after a fort adjacent to it. Earlier it was called Sawai Madhopur Game Sanctuary. What is the current name of this Project Tiger reserve?

455.This park got its name from the words meaning 'snake' and 'stream.' Also known as Rajiv Gandhi National park, this was the major hunting destination of Wadiyar dynasty. Identify the park.

456.Swamp deer is the official symbol of this national park which is the first one of its kind in India to have an official symbol. Identify this park which is named after one of the names of Lord Krishna.

457.Hemis is the largest national park in India, famous for snow leopards. Where is this located?

458.Named after a mangrove called 'Sundari,' this is the world's largest coastal mangrove forest. Which national park?

459.Believed to be gifted by Lord Rama to Lakshmana, this fort shares its name with a national park and is situated at Madhya Pradesh. Famous for Royal Bengal Tigers, the name means 'Brother's fort.' Identify.

460. Located in LokTak lake, this national park has got a peculiar ecosystem called 'Phumdis'. Name this UN Conservation area.

Answers

451. Jim Corbett National Park
452. Kaziranga National Park
453. Valley of flowers
454. Randhambore National Park
455. Nagarhole National Park
456. Kanha National Park
457. Ladakh
458. Sunderbans National Park
459. BandhavGarh National Park
460. Keibul Lamjao

Mughal Dynasty

461. He was the first to attain the title 'Ghazi'. His tomb 'Bagh –a- Babun' is situated at Kabul, Afganisthan. Who?

462.Born at Kalpi, his original name was Mahesh Das. He is believed to have got killed in a battle with Afghans. How do we better know him?

463. Dying of falling from the stairs of his own library building, this ruler's name means 'Luck'. His famous associate was Bairam Khan. Identify the ruler.

464.During the reign of Akbar, this was built as a fort and Shah Jahan reconstructed it as a palace. Two of its gates are known as Delhi Gate and Lahore Gate. Which monument?

465.Ram Siya, Sihansah, Rahas, Atma, Chagul, Ilahi, Aftabi.What are these?

466.Which Mughal king was responsible for the executions of his elder brother Dara Shikoh, king Sambhaji and the Sikh Guru Tegh Bahadur?

467.Prominent rival of this ruler was his own son named Khusru. As the rivalry increased he made his son sightless. What is the other name of this ruler who was called 'Salim'?

468. Ralph Fitch is said to be the first Englishman who visited this king. Manzabdari system was established by him. Todar Mal, Abul Fazal, Faizi, Abdur Rahim Khana-i-Khana, Fakir Aziao-Din

and many others belonged to his court. Name this ruler.

469. Located in Aurangabad, this was built in the memory of Dilras Banu. The brain behind this structure is said to be architects Ata Ullah and Hanspat Rai. Which monument?

470. Moti Mahal was one of the important monuments built during his reign. Khuram is another name of this ruler who passed away while he was in prison. Who is this?

Answers

461. Babur
462. Birbal
463. Humayun
464. Agra Fort
465. Coins prevalent during Akbar's reign
466. Aurangazeb
467. Jehangir
468. Akbar
469. Bibi ka Maqbara
470. Shah Jahan

Mythology

471. Bahucharamata Temple in Gujrat is famous for its deity. Seated on a rooster this goddess is also called Bala. Which particular community worships this idol?

472. Mahishasure is the son of Mahishi. It is believed that he had the head of a buffalo. Identify the South Indian city named after this king.

473. According to *Skanda Purana*, King Bhadra Sena built this temple. Situated in Ujjain, it's named after Lord Shiva and is called Kal Bhairav temple. What is peculiar to this temple?

474. Mayamkottu Malancharuvu Malanada Temple in Kollam is one of its kind in India. Even though any rituals do not take place here, people offer toddy and tender coconut to the deity. Which 'villain' is worshiped here?

475. Located on the banks of Godavari, this is believed to be the location where Lakshman cut off Shoorpanaka's nose as asked by Rama. This is also the main stage of Maha Kumbh Mela which occurs in every twelve years. Which place?

476. Kashi Mahakal, the third private train in India, was in the news in the early months of 2020. The Express was in the news when reports came that berth no 64 in coach B5 was reserved for someone forever. Reserved for whom?

477. Buddhi and Siddhi are said to be the consorts of this god who travels on a demigod Kroncha. Vikata is an incarnation of this god. Identify.

478. Founded by Mirza Husayn Ali Nuri, this belief system has no priesthood and does not practise any rituals. Identify the religion.

479. According to beliefs 'Sudhamapuri' is the birth place of Kuchela. A world famous Indian was also born at this place. What is the present name of this place?

480. This award given in the name of a Hindu goddess had Harivamsh Rai Bachan as the first awardee. Which award?

सरस्वती नः सुभगामयस्करत्.

Answers

471. Transgenders
472. Mysuru

473. Liqour is offered to the deity as part of worship
474. Shakuni
475. Nasik
476. Lord Shiva
477. Lord Ganesha
478. Bahai
479. Porbandhar
480. Saraswathi Samman

Sportspersons

481. Itallian club Pallavolo Gebeca had dedicated their home court to this player after his death. Who is this player?
482.In 1987, this player played for a while in the Pakistan team in a practice match.His first test wicket was that of Merv Hughes of Australia. Who is this?
483. Known by the nicknames Prince of Pune, Golden Boy, he is the first player ever to win the title in both short and long formats of snooker. Name this player.
484. He was the second Indian to win the All England Open Badminton Championship and his coach was the first Indian to win the same. Name both.
485. *Unbreakable* is the autobiography of this six times world champion. Nicknamed as 'Magnificent,' this person's first name is Mangte Chungneijang. Who is this?
486. Former member of American club Kansas City Wizards, he became the second-highest active goal scorer in international football behind Christiano Ronaldo in June 2021. Name this player.
487. Pramod Pahan was a name given to this person who was later called Marang Gomke which means 'great leader'. Identify this alumnus of Oxford University who captained the Indian Hockey team that had won the Olympic gold in the year 1928.
488. Hailing from Haryana, she is the first female wrestler from the country to win an Olympic medal. Identify.
489. Born to Vece and Jennifer, this person is one among the Lee-Hesh duo. They have the longest doubles winning record in Davis Cup from 1995 -2010. Name this player who debuted in the Bollywood movie 'Rajdhani Express.'
490. One of the greatest footballers to have played for India, he was the first one from his game to win Arjuna award. Identify

Answers

481. Jimmy George
482. Sachin Tendulkar
483. Pankaj Advani
484. Prakash Padukone and P Gopichand
485. M C.Mary Kom
486. Sunil Chhetri
487. Jaipal Singh Munda
488. Sakshi Malik
489. Leander Paes
490. PK Banerjee

Mixed Bag

491. Twinkle Dwivedi from Lucknow, Calvino Inman from USA, Rashida Khatoon from Patna. These are 3 documented cases of Hemolacria. What condition is that?
492. This person who joined the Congress in 1963, was the only Indian politician to have served as chief minister of two states. Identify him.
493. While serving as the Vice-Chancellor of the University of Calcutta, he acquired air-raid shelters for schools and college students to have their classes functioning. In recognition for his efforts, the Doctorate of Science was conferred upon him in 1944. Who is this?

494. Which famous train that covered the 188-km stretch from Yavatmal to Achalpur in Maharashtra was operated by the Central Province Railway Company (CPRC), founded in 1910 by Killick Nixon?

495. On top of which famous building in India, one can find the statues of Agriculture, Justice, Commerce and Science?

496. Born in Neuchatel, to a Hungarian father and a Russian mother, this person had authored two Sanskrit books and drafted an interpretation of the *Mahabharata*. Identify this author of *Saints of Maharashtra*.

497. The two observation towers on each side of which famous dam are named "Gandhi Minar" and "Nehru Minar"?

498. He wrote an Urdu one-act play called *Karamati* (Wonder worker), the English translation of which had earned him the Saraswati Stage Society prize and medal for the best play of the year in 1912. Identify him.

499. *Bhimayana* is a graphic book written by a group of designers, based on his work 'Waiting for Visa'. A particular sect in Buddhism and the Nagpur International Airport is named after him. Identify him.

500. His Fellow Naxalite P. Krishna Pillai wrote an article hailing him titled "The Bolshevik Hero of Kerala." Identify this person who narrowly escaped from death sentence following the intervention of Gandhiji?

Answers

491. Red coloured tears
492. ND Tiwari
493. Dr.BC Roy
494. Shakuntala Express
495. Writers Building
496. Savitri Khanolkar
497. Hirakud
498. Shanti Swarup Bhatnagar
499. BR Ambedkar
500. KPR Gopalan

Trains

501. Puratchi Thalaivar Dr. M.G. Ramachandran Central Railway Station (Chennai Central) is the longest station name in India. Which are the shortest station names?

502. 'The Dibrugrah (Assam)–Kanyakumari (Tamil Nadu) Express' covers the longest running route in India. It's named after the popular name of Narendra Nath Datta. Name the train.

503. The Red Ribbon Express was launched on 1 December 2007, to create awareness about a particular disease. Which disease?

504. In order to prevent robbery/theft the electronic appliances in the Indian trains work at different rate/volt different from household ones. At what voltage do they work?

505. As on 2021, this is the longest rail-road bridge in India. Constructed by Hindustan Construction Company, the project was announced by Atal Bihari Vajpayee and inaugurated by Narendra Modi in 2018. Name the bridge.

506. To commemorate the 100th birth anniversary of this woman, a special train was launched in 2010. Name the train dedicated to a person born in a capital city called Skopje.

507. This luxury tourist train was launched on 26 January 1982 by the Indian Railways in association with Rajasthan Tourism Development Corporation to promote tourism in Rajasthan. Name it.

508. Designed by Frederick William Stevens from an initial design by Axel

Haig its construction began in 1878, and was completed in 1887, the year marking 50 years of an emperor's rule. Name it.

509. What was started on 22 July 1976 following the Shimla Agreement and ran between Amritsar and Lahore, a distance of about 52 km?

510. Gayatri Devi, the former Maharani of Jaipur, was one of *Vogue*'s 10 most beautiful women in the world. Name the series of trains named after her.

Answers

501. Od (Gujrat) and Ib (Odhisha)
502. Vivek Express
503. AIDS
504. 220 volt
505. Bogibeel
506. Mother Express (named after Mother Theresa)
507. Palace on Wheels
508. Chhatrapati Sivaji Terminus
509. Samjhauta Express
510. Rajyarani Express

Historical Monuments

511. Konark Sun Temple is known as the 'Black Pagoda'. Which monument is known as White Pagoda?
512. Vichitra Mandir, Prakash Mandir and Hawa Mandir belong to which famous monument constructed in the year 1799?
513. Named after one among the Pandavas this UNESCO World Heritage site is situated in Ratapani wildlife sanctuary. Name this considered as India's oldest human art.
514. Home to the oldest Buddhist sanctuary in existence, this site is also famous for monolithic pillars and monasteries. Identify this Mauryan sculpture which is depicted in one of the Indian currencies.
515. Known as the 'City of Victory', this was the first planned city of Mughals. Jama Masjid is an important construction here. Identify.
516. This was commissioned by Hamidah Banu Beegum in memory of her husband. It is said that Edwin Lutyns was inspired by this plot's design while planning the construction of Rashtrapathi Bhavan. Which Mughal architecture is mentioned here?
517. Considered one of the first examples of a republic around the 6th century BCE, Gautama Buddha preached his last sermon from this region. Identify the region in Tirhut division of Bihar, that contains one of the best-preserved of the Pillars of Ashoka, topped by a single Asiatic lion.
518. Situated in the capital city of Uttar Pradesh, this was built by Nawab Asaf–Ud–Daulah and is also known as Asfi mosque. Shahi Baoli, a stepped well here, is as famous as the building. Which construction?
519. Memorial of Akbar's rise over Gujarat, this is also called 'Door of Victory'. Tomb of Salim Chisti can be found adjacent to this. Name this gate.
520. This statue can be seen on the central dome of this building in Kolkata. Made up of Makrana marble, it was King George V, then the Prince of Wales

who laid the foundation of this building. Identify.

Answers

511. Puri Jagannatha Temple
512. Hawa Mahal
513. Bhimbetka Rock Shelters
514. Sanchi Stupa
515. Fatehpur Sikri
516. Humayun's Tomb
517. Vaishali
518. Bara Imambara
519. Buland Darwasa
520. Victoria Memorial

Famous Firsts

521. A former principal of Nehru Institute of Mountaineering,Uttarakhand, Col J.K Bajaj is the first Indian and the first Asian to reach/conquer this region. Robert Scott was the first ever. Which region?
522. Elder brother of Rabindranath Tagore, he was the first Indian to join the Indian Civil Services. Who?
523. Devisingh Ramsingh Shekhawat is the first and only person so far to adorn this position. He is an agriculturist as well as a former lecturer in Chemistry. Identify the particular record he holds.
524. *I Dare* is the autobiography of this former tennis champion. Former United Nation's Police advisor, this native of Punjab has also received UN medal for outstanding service. Who?
525. Located at Bhabha Atomic Research Center (BARC) in Mumbai 'Apsara' is the oldest of its kind in Asia and first in India. What?
526. This was designed by a Hungarian-Russian woman, who was born in Switzerland. Major Somnath Sharma was the first person to win this. What?
527. Known as the 'Iron Lady of Andhra Pradesh', she is the first Indian woman to win a medal at the Olympics. Who?
528. Often referred to as 'Lords of India', this is the first cricket stadium in India. Name this stadium where you can find Ganguly stand.
529. This novel written by Sane Guruji was made into movie by Acharya Atre. It won the Golden Lotus award and became the first film to win the national award. Which film?
530. Identify this Indian physician who became the first Asian to bag a certain title in 1966.

Answers

521. South Pole
522. Satyendranath Tagore
523. First Gentleman of India
524. Kiran Bedi
525. Nuclear Reactor
526. Param Vir Chakra
527. Karnam Malleswari
528. Eden Gardens
529. Shyamchi Aai
530. Reita Faria Powell, the first Indian woman to win the Miss World title.

Awards

531. Odakkuzhal Award instituted by Guruvayurappan Trust in 1968 was named after the first-ever work to win India's highest honour in a particular field. Which prestigious award instituted by a cultural institute founded by Sahu Shanti Prasad Jain is being mentioned here?
532. After which former Indian Prime Minister is India's highest honour for the protection of the environment and national film award for the best debut film of a director named after?
533. The highest award for doctors in India is named after a former chief minister. Who?
534. This prize was established in 1951 by UNESCO with a grant from an Indian

Chief Minister who had participated in the freedom struggle of both India and Indonesia. Identify this prize.

535. This award is named after an Indian scientist who is popularly known as the 'father of research laboratories in India'. Name this award which is dubbed as the' Indian Nobel Prize'.

536. Plaque of this prestigious award in India was designed by a renowned filmmaker who was honoured with an honorary Oscar in 1992. Identify this award.

537. The statuette of this award, which was initially known as the Clare Awards, was designed by N.G.Pansare. Which is this award first introduced in 1954, the same year as the National Film Awards?

538. Kannagi Award, Mata Jijabai Award, Devi Ahilya Bai Holkar Award, Rani Lakshmi Bai Award, Rani Gaidinliu Zeliang Award and Rani Rudramma Devi Award are sub categories of which prestigious award?

539. India's highest sporting honour for coaches is named after Dronacharya. One of the most popular sporting honours in India is named after Arjuna. What name is given to the honorary sports award bestowed by the Government of Karnataka to sports personalities of the nation?

540. In 2020 Anita Kundu was awarded this highest recognition in India for outstanding achievements in the field of adventure on land, sea and air. Name this National Adventure Award named after this 'First achiever'.

Answers

531. Jnanpith Award
532. Indira Gandhi
533. Dr. BC Roy
534. The Kalinga Prize
535. Shanti Swaroop Bhatnagar Award
536. Sahitya Academy Award, Satyajit Ray
537. Filmfare Awards
538. Sthree Shakthi Puraskar
539. Ekalavya Award
540. Tensing Norgay Award

Space Research

541. Pisharoth Rama Pisharoty was a physicist and meteorologist born in Palakkad district in the year 1909. He is considered to be the father of which branch of science in India?

542. The first Indian space satellite was launched in 1975. It was named after an Indian astronomer who developed a phonetic number system with three parts called 'Ganitha, Kala Kriya and Gola'. Who is this?

543. "The St. Mary Magdalene church housed the first office of the Thumba Space Centre. The prayer room was my first laboratory, the bishop's room was my design and drawing office." Whose words?

544. APPLE, the first Indian communication satellite, was launched from French Guiana in 1981. What does APPLE stand for ?

545. If Luna was the project of Soviet Union, Ranger was of US, Kaguya was of Japan and Chang'e was of China, what name was given to India's project?

546. ISRO had launched a geoportal in 2009,which visualizes Satellite Imagery and Maps on earth. What is the name of the app/portal?

547. The 100th birth anniversary of this person was celebrated in 2019 and 2021 marks his 50th death anniversary. He was the first chairman of Indian National Committee for Space Research. Name this person who was one among the founding members of Indian Insti-

tute of Management, Ahmedabad.

548. The record of highest number of satellites launched in a single mission is accredited in the name of ISRO. Satellites of countries like Israel, Kazakhstan, The Netherlands, Switzerland and UAE were launched in this mission. What was the total number of satellites?

549. ANUSAT is the first student satellite launched by ISRO in cooperation with a university from South India. Students and faculty member under the university were involved in the design and development of the satellite. Name the university.

550. This former chairman of ISRO was an active kathakali artist. Identify this native of Irinjalakuda in Kerala.

Answers

541. Remote Sensing
542. Aryabhata
543. APJ Abdul Kalam
544. Ariane Passenger Pay Load Experiment
545. Chandrayaan
546. Bhuvan
547. Vikram Sarabhai
548. 104
549. Anna University
550. Dr. K Radhakrishnan

Political Parties

551. This party was born as a part of protest against a huge corruption case in the country. Established in 2012, the founder of this party is also the youngest chief minister of Delhi. Identify the party and president.

552. Formally established in 1980, this party had only two seats in the next general election of 1984. In 1996 the party had its first prime minister whose birthday is celebrated as Good Governance day in India. Which party?

553. Nicknamed as 'Remote Control', this person started his career as a cartoonist. Salman Rushdie's work *The Moor's Last Sigh* was banned in his state allegedly saying it criticized this person. Who is this?

554. Hemambika temple, situated in Palakad, Kerala is also known as Kaippathi temple in the local language. Which party's symbol is said to have inspired from the unique figure of deity here?

555. Established in 1996, this party got national recognition in 2016 only. Flower and grass is the symbol of the party. Identify this party which is in power since 2011, in one of the eastern states in India.

556. 130 statues of elephants were placed in Noida and Lucknow during the tenure of this former Uttar Pradesh chief minister. It was the symbol of the party founded by Kanshi Ram. Identify the leader and the party.

557. Sachchidanand Vishnu Ghate or SV Ghate was the first General Secretary of this party. M. N. Roy, Evelyn Roy-Trent, Abani Mukherjee were among the few people behind the formation of the party. Identify.

558. Abbreviated MaKaPa in press and media circles, this party was formed in the year 1964 in Calcutta. Which party?

559. This party was formed by Sharad Pawar, Purno Sangma, and Tariq Anwar. A Clock that reads 10:10 is the election

Ram Jethmalani's Legal Career

Ram Jethmalani earned his LLB from Bombay University at the age of 17 and had to get a special exemption to start practising at the age of 18. His books include *Big Egos, Small Men* and *Conscience of A Maverick*.

symbol of the party. Identify.

560. This party was founded as an amalgam of parties opposed to the emergency imposed by Indira Gandhi between 1975 and 1977. Identify.

Answers

551. Aam Aadmi Party and Arvind Kejriwal
552. Bharatiya Janata Party
553. Bal Thackeray
554. Indian National Congress
555. Trinamool Congress
556. Mayavathi, Bahujan Samaj Party
557. Communist Party of India
558. Communist Party of India(Marxist)
559. Nationalist Congress Party
560. Janata Party

State Symbols

561. Maharashtra was the first state to officially declare Blue Mormon (*Papilio polymnestor*) way back in 2015 followed by Uttarakhand (Common peacock), Karnataka (Southern bird wings) and Kerala (Malabar banded peacock). What are all these?
562. *Ailurus fulgens* is the scientific name of an endangered animal which is also the state animal of Sikkim. Identify.
563. The state bird of Rajasthan was once considered to be chosen as the national bird of India instead of peacock. But the decision went in favor of Peacock, one of the reason said being the possibility of mis-pronounciation. Which bird is this?
564. Which state in India declared sparrow as the state animal, marigold as the state flower and peepal as the state tree in the year 2013?
565. It was known as Khira Mohana due to its appearance and has become customary to offer Goddess Lakshmi as prasad on the last day of Rath Yatra. Identify the state and official sweet.
566. This is the national bird of Malaysia and state bird of Arunachal Pradesh and Kerala. Sarawak (Malaysia) is known as the land of these birds. Oriental pied, rhinocerous, black, weathered are some of the varieties. Which bird?
567. This flower/plant is named after a place, where a historic battle took place in 1757. It is also called 'flame of forest'. Name this state flower of Jharkhand.
568. Snow Leopard is the state animal of this state, which was named by Acharya Diwakar Datt Sharma. The only natural ice skating rink in Asia is situated here. Which state?
569. June 22 is the International day dedicated to this animal. This is the state animal of Rajasthan along with 'Chinkara' deer. Identify the animal.
570. Greater Flamingo is the most widespread and largest species of the flamingo family. Official bird of which state?

Answers

561. State Butterflies
562. Red Panda
563. Great Indian Bustard
564. Bihar
565. Odisha, Rasagolla
566. Hornbill
567. Palash

568. Himachal Pradesh
569. Camel
570. Gujarat

Tournaments and Trophies

571. Regarded as the oldest tournament in hockey, this is stationed in Kolkata since 1895. Name?
572. This inter-state cricket championship is named after the first test captain of India. He was the first-ever player to endorse a brand. Who is this?
573. This is the oldest football tournament in Asia. Earlier it was known as Army cup. Which tournament?
574. Ezra cup is named after David Elias Ezra, a former director of RBI.Which sports event is associated with this cup, which is said to be the oldest one of its kind?
575. Whiff–Whaff is an alternate name of this game. Barna-Bellack cup and Ramanujan trophy are associated with this game. Identify.
576. Also known as the Ranji One-Day Trophy, it was started as a limited-overs competition involving teams from the Ranji Trophy plates. It was named after the first Indian player to score triple century in first class cricket. Which tournament is this?
577. It was under Dipak Poddar, India won its first medal ever in the world championship in this game. Holkar Trophy is associated with this game. Identify.
578. Awadhe Warriors, Mumbai Rockets, Pune Pistons, Hyderabad Hunters are teams of which famous league in India?
579. Agha Khan Cup, Rene Frank Cup, Guru Nanak Cup and Ranjith Singh Gold Cup are associated with which game?
580. Runner–up trophy is known as the Kamla Gupta Trophy. The trophy for the second runner up, the Sampangi Cup, was donated by the Mysore Football Association. Which tournament started in 1941 was named after the province of the president of the Football Association Sir Manmatha Nath Ray Chowdhury?

Answers

571. Beighton Cup
572. C K Nayudu
573. Durand Cup
574. Polo
575. Table Tennis
576. Vijay Hazare
577. Bridge
578. Premier Badminton League
579. Hockey
580. SanthoshTrophy

Sobriquets

581. This former capital of Gujarat is known as the Boston of India for its rapid growth and development. Which city?
582. This city situated in the Chota Nagpur plateau has the highest production of steel in the country and therefore is known as the Pittsburg of India. Identify.
583. Damodar river is known as the sorrow of Bengal. Which river is known as the sorrow of Bihar?
584. Kanpur, Ahmedabad and Coimbatore share a common nickname with a European city for their luxurious cotton textile industry. Which city?
585. This city, which is also called 'Deccan Queen,' is home to Lisa Sthalekar, who was the first woman player to score 1000 runs in one day cricket and also to get 100 wickets. Name the city.
586. The automobile capital of India is

also known as the 'Detroit of Asia'. Which city, also known as gateway of South India, are we talking about?

587. Kolkata got this particular nickname after this 1985 novel by Dominique Lappierre. Which nickname?
588. This city is also the Tiger capital of the country. Oranges from here got GI tag and the city is also known as 'Orange city.' Identify.
589. Along with Alappuzha and Srinagar, this city is also known as Venice of the East. Founded by Maharana Uday Singh II, this is also called city of lakes. Name the city.
590. Known as the Scotland of the East, this is where the Booker prize winner Arundathi Roy was born. Which city?

Answers

581. Ahmedabad
582. Jamshedpur
583. Kosi
584. Manchester
585. Pune
586. Chennai
587. City of Joy
588. Nagpur
589. Udaipur
590. Shillong

Mixed Bag -World

591. As part of the proposals/demands for new states based on regional and economic aspirations, if the demand for Kodagu state came from Karnataka, Gondwana came from Madhya Pradesh, demand for Kosal state came from which state?
592. Located in Guntur district, this city is notable for drama, literature and poetry. Identify this city nicknamed as Andhra Paris, which is also the native place of a historical figure from 16th century.
593. As per the tourism department of Jammu and Kashmir, this is the second coldest inhabited place in the world. Identify the place?
594. Besides establishing the first Malayalam printing press, he translated the Bible into Malayalam and published the first English-Malayalam dictionary in 1846 and the first Malayalam-English dictionary in 1849. Identify this person who established one of the oldest colleges in India.
595. Derived from folk music of Punjab and Sindh, it was the folk song of camel-drivers and was developed by Mian Gulam Nabi Shori, a court singer for the Nawab of Awadh, Asaf-Ud-Dowlah. Which musical style?
596. The Nairs of Kerala were classified as a "Martial Race" by the British, but were de-listed after a rebellion that happened in the first decade of 19th century. Who was the leader of this revolt?
597. One of India's oldest fast food restaurant chains, they set up their first restaurant in 1977 and also opened India's first ice cream museum within its ice cream factory in Noida. Which company?
598. Which sparsely populated village, inhabited by Koli fishermen, was then referred to as the village of Koliwadas before the late 19th century?
599. This musical instrument is said to have derived its name from the sound that it makes. Achan, Veekku and Uruttu are three varities. Identify.
600. He was included in the list of the 10

best Captains of the world by English FA in 1953 and also declared as the "Footballer of the Millennium" by AIFF in 2000. Identify this player.

Answers

591. Odisha
592. Tenali
593. Drass
594. Benjamin Bailey
595. Tappa
596. Velu Thampi Dalawa
597. Nirula
598. Dharavi
599. Chenda
600. Sailendra Nath Manna

Union Territories

601. Which region, once under the rule of Chirakkal Raja, was annexed to the British East India Company and was administered from Mangalore after the battle of Seringapattom in 1799 ?
602. The dominant and most spoken language is Bengali with 26% of the population speaking it. The other major languages spoken are Hindi (18.23%), Tamil (17.68%), Telugu (12.81%), Malayalam (8.11%). Other minor spoken languages are Kurukh/Oraon, Munda and Kharia. Which Union territory?
603. Which Union Territory traces its history back to the 17th century following a firman from the Qiladar of Valikondapurarm under the Sultan of Bijapur, with François Martin as the first Governor ?
604. This district traces its ancient history way back to Indo-Greek kings Eukratides, Meanandar and Appollodotes II of the 1st Century B.C. Identify the district annexed by the Portuguese in 1536.
605. Also known as A & N islands or ANI, the Andamans and Nicobars are separated by a channel approximately 150 km wide. Name it.
606. The palace of Kangla was the traditional seat of the Meetei rulers of this region which was made a Union Territory in 1956 and a fully-fledged State in 1972 by the North-Eastern Areas (re-organisation) Act, 1971. Which state?
607. The annual festival known as Yuru Kabgyat is the major attraction of this monastery in Ladakh and mask dance by the lamas are the highlight of the festival. Which monastery, promoted as a "Moonscape" for tourists?
608. Usually performed by men, this is the most popular of the dances of the Minicoy Island of Lakshadweep. Identify this dance form, locally known as 'Bolufeyle?
609. This region was retained by the French following the implementation of Paris Peace Agreement of 1763. An attempt to conquer Cherukallai Military Camp in 1954 is an important event marked in its history. Which Union Territory?
610. This endangered vegetarian mammal is the state animal of Andaman & Nicobar islands. Name it.

Answers

601. Lakshadweep
602. Andaman & Nicobar islands
603. Puducherry
604. Diu

605. Ten Degree Channel
606. Manipur
607. Lamayuru
608. Lava
609. Mahe
610. Dugong

1947

611. In the year 1947, the legislature representatives of the Indian National Congress, the Muslim League, and the Sikh community came to an agreement with Lord Mountbatten on what has come to be known as the Mountbatten Plan. By what date is that plan known?
612. Published on 17 August 1947 its western side still serves as the Indo-Pakistan border and the eastern side serves as the India-Bangladesh border. What is this?
613. Former Commander-in-Chief, Middle East, during the second world war, this person also served as Commander-in-Chief, India, from 1941 to 1943 and then served as Viceroy of India until his retirement in February 1947. Who?
614. In June 1984 Operation Blue Star was carried out by the Indian Army to remove this person and his armed followers from the Golden Temple Complex, resulting ion around 500 deaths. Identify this person born in the year 1947.
615. Known as Bertie among his friends, this person was concurrently the last Emperor of India until August 1947, when the title was changed to 'King of India'. Identify this person.
616. While working as a copywriter for the advertising agency Ogilvy & Mather, he came up with many iconic advertisement taglines. His first novel, *Grimus* (1975), a part-science fiction tale, was generally ignored by the public and literary critics. Identify the person born in the year 1947.
617. With its corporate office at Sansad Marg, New Delhi, and registered office in D N Road, Mumbai, the largest news agency in India was established on 27 August 1947. Identfy.
618. Which famous production company was established by P. S. Ramakrishna Rao and Bhanumathi Ramakrishna in the year 1947 and was named after their son?
619. In August and September of 1947, Gandhi chose to be in Kolkata with some of his followers to put an end to the Hindu – Muslim riots that were going on there.The building where he stayed during those period, has been converted into a museum and has been named Gandhi Bhavan. What was its name?
620. India and Pakistan fought their first war over control of Kashmir, then a kingdom ruled by this person who is known as the last maharaja of Kashmir. Name?

Answers

611. 3rd June plan
612. Radcliffe Line
613. Sir Archibald Percival Wavell
614. Jarnail Singh Bhindranwale
615. King George VI
616. Salman Rushdie
617. The Press Trust of India (PTI)
618. Bharani Pictures
619. Hydari mansion
620. Maharaja Sir Hari Singh

Districts

621. With over 1.11 crore residents, this district ranks number one in population among the districts of India, as per the

2011 Census. Identify this district in Maharashrta.

622. Blessed with many destinations including Ajanta caves, Ellora caves, Daulatabad forts, Bibi ka maqbara etc. this district is named after a ruler whose tomb is placed in the same district. Another district with the same name exists in Bihar. Name the district.

623. Famous for its mangoes, this district shares its name with that of the capital city of Oregon in the USA. Which district?

624. Morena,Guna, Rewa, Niwari etc are a few among the 52 districts in this state which ranks number one in terms of the number of districts. Which state?

625. Which state in India has got only two villages and has been named North & South?

626. Pokhran served as the test site for India's first underground nuclear weapon, ballistic missiles. In which district is it located?

627. Ramnagar, Dharmnagar, Javaharchowk, and Kabirchowk are a few locations in an area situated in the western side of Ahamedabad district. Which area, known across India through a person associated?

628. Sometimes referred to as 'The Land's End', this is the southernmost district in mainland India. Name the district, named after a goddess.

629. With Akbarpur as its headquarters, this district in the Faizabad division of Uttar Pradesh was created in the year 1995 and was named in the memory of a well-known Indian. Name the district.

630. Chauri Chaura incident of 1922 was one of the most unfortunate events during the struggle for independence.

The city is located in a district named after a renowned saint of the Nath Sampradaya. Which is this district.

Answers

621. Thane
622. Aurangabad
623. Salem
624. Madhya Pradesh
625. Goa
626. Jaisalmer
627. Sabarmati
628. Kanyakumari
629. Ambedkar Nagar
630. Gorakhpur named after Gorakhnath

PSUs

631. Exporting to over 70 countries, they have petrochemical products and intermediates under the brand name PROPEL. Identify this Maharatna company with the tagline 'Energy of India'.

632. Dolfin, Trump and Garuda are three brands of an organization having the motto "Transparency makes us different". Identify this company which was formerly known by the name Bombay

extra

Harivansh Rai Bachchan's Trilogy

Madhukalash, *Madhubala* and *Madhushala* were the three works of a specific trilogy by Harivansh Rai Bachchan. All three were inspired by Omar Khayyam's *Rubaiyyat.*

Telecom Limited.

633. Which PSU, administered by the Department of Space, was incorporated as a private limited company owned by the Indian government in the year 1992 with an objective to promote the ISRO's products, services and technologies?

634. This company traces its origin to the discovery of lignite in Rao Bahadur M. Jambulingam Mudaliar's farm artesian well during 1934, who then contacted the authorities to send geologists to the location?

635. Welding Research Institute (WRI) at Tiruchirappalli, Ceramic Technological Institute (CTI) at Bangalore, Centre for Electric Traction (CET) at Bhopal and Pollution Control Research Institute (PCRI) at Haridwar are the four specialized institutes under which PSU established in the year 1964?

636. IPPB received license from RBI in the year 2015 to run a payments bank and in 2016, it was registered as a public limited government company for setting up a payments bank. Which bank with over 4 crore customers ?

637. Incorporated in 1979, this PSU initially operated two plants in Bathinda and Panipat and is India's largest Central Public Sector Enterprise in fertilizer sector. Which company headquartered in Noida?

638. An offshoot of the implementation of National Rail Vikas Yojana, this wholly owned subsidiary of Indian Railways is involved in building rail infrastructure required for the railways. Identify.

639. In 2001, GAIL commissioned a 1415 Km LNG pipe line, then the world's longest and India's first cross state LPG transmission pipeline running from a city in Gujarat to Loni in Uttar Pradesh. Which city?

640. HF-24 Marut, known by the name "Spirit of the Tempest", was the first indigenous fighter aircraft made in India. Who manufactured it in 1960s?

Answers

631. Indian Oil
632. Mahanagar Telephone Nigam Limited
633. Antrix Corporation
634. NLC India Limited (formerly Neyveli Lignite Corporation Limited)
635. Bharat Heavy Electricals Limited
636. India Post Payments Bank
637. National Fertilizers Limited
638. Rail Vikas Nigam Limited
639. Jamnagar
640. Hindustan Aeronautics Limited

Educational Institutions

641. Which institution was established in 1950 in an old Detention Camp in present Paschim Medinipur district?

642. Professor George Robbins of UCLA was invited by the Indian Planning Commission to help in setting up All India Institutes of Management Studies.

Origin of Calcutta Stock Exchange

Though its activities were originally supposed to have started under a Neem tree in the 1830s, the Calcutta Stock Exchange officially started in 1908 and is usually known by the name of the neighbourhood Lyons Range.

Based on his recommendations, two IIMs were established in the year 1961. Name both.

643. The first Chancellor of this university was Amartya Sen and the second one was former Singapore Minister for Foreign Affairs George Yeo. Name this University that has been designated as an "International Institution of National Importance" by the Parliament.

644. 'Taught man what he knew not' is the motto of an educational institution that was established in Aligarh on 29 October 1920 mainly in response to the demand for a new National Muslim University which would be free from pro-British stance.

645. Established in 959 by Jagdish Gandhi and his wife, Bharti, it was recognised by the *Guinness Book of World Records* as the world's largest school, with around 52,000 pre-primary, primary and secondary students distributed across 20 campuses in the city. Which school?

646. Kadambini Ganguly and Chandramukhi Basu were the first two female graduates of the British Empire, who graduated from a women's college located on Bidhan Sarani in Kolkata, known as the oldest women's college in India.Name?

647. Which premier educational institution was established in the year 1956 with the aid of New Zealand government, Rockefeller Foundation, Ford Foundation, as well as from the government of Australia, West Germany and the Dutch government?

648. What was founded by the Church Missionary Society of England, and was patronised by Col. John Munro, the East India Company Resident, and Dewan of Travancore in 1815, with Rev. Benjamin Bailey as the first principal?

649. In the year 1982, Andhra Pradesh Government started the Andhra Pradesh Open University which was later renamed Dr. BR Ambedkar Open University. What first is credited to this University located in Hyderabad?

650. Inspired by the Women's University of Tokyo, this person wanted to establish India's first university for women and thus Shreemati Nathibai Damodar Thackersey Women's University made its humble beginnings in 1916 in Pune. Name this person.

Answers

641. IIT Kharagpur
642. IIM Ahmedabad & IIM Calcutta
643. Nalanda University
644. Jamia Millia Islamia
645. City Montessori school in Lucknow
646. Bethune College
647. AIIMS Delhi
648. CMS College Kottayam
649. First Open University in India
650. Dhondho Keshav Karve

Banks

651. Until its merger with the Indian Bank in 2020, it was the oldest joint stock bank in India. Identify this bank that shows a Triveni Sangam on its logo.

652. Which bank was founded by Maharaja Sayajirao Gaekwad III on 20 July 1908 and has its head office in Vadodara?

653. Which bank was established in the year 1931 in Mangalore and named so since it was established on a Vijayadashami Day?

654. Which Kolkata bank was established by the eminent industrialist, GD Birla during the Quit India movement of 1942 with the idea of organizing a

commercial bank with Indian capital and management?

655. Formerly known as Canara Industrial and Banking Syndicate Limited, this bank was established in Manipal, Udupi in the year 1925. Name the bank.
656. India First Life Insurance Company incorporated in the year 2009 had made more than 2 billion in turnover in just four and half months since it became operational. It was a joint venture between Bank of Baroda and another bank with UK's financial and investment company Legal & General. Which other bank?
657. In 1935, the bank introduced electricity in its head office building by installing oil-powered generator, years before Government's first power project was commissioned at Pallivasal. Which bank that functioned from 1927 to 1960?
658. The first logo adopted in 1955 had a Banyan tree depicting growth, success and stability. However it was abandoned considering the criticism pointing out that a Banyan tree does not let other plants grow within its reach. Which bank?
659. This bank was established in the year 1955 as the initiative of the World Bank, the Government of India and representatives of Indian industry, for providing medium-term and long-term project financing to Indian businesses. Which bank?
660. When it was incorporated as a public company in December 1939, it adopted a short name which was derived from the name of the founder Choonilal Devkaran Nanjee. Which bank ?

Answers

651. Allahabad Bank
652. Bank of Baroda
653. Vijaya Bank
654. Uco bank
655. Syndicate Bank
656. Andhra Bank
657. Palai Central Bank
658. State Bank of India
659. ICICI Bank
660. Dena Bank

Spices

661. Made from peeled, sliced and sun dried green mangoes, this fruity spice powder is used as a citrusy seasoning. Name?
662. This dried latex has got the nick names stinking gum, devil's dung or food of the devils. Identify?
663. Also called Flinders rose,the edible flower buds of this plant is used as a seasoning, and the fruit is usually consumed pickled. Which shrubby plant?
664. In the year 1767, Lord Brown of the British East India Company established an Estate near Anjarakkandy in Kerala, India, which later became Asia's largest estate of its kind. Known for which spice?
665. Chrain is a spicy paste made by grating a root vegetable, used worldwide as a spice and as a condiment. Name it.
666. Known by the names Zyur in Kashmiri and Zero in Sindhi, these seeds have an aromatic odour and bitter taste. Identify this spice that is used as a condiment, and also an ingredient in curry powders, cakes and cheese. Which spice?
667. The seeds of *Apium graveolens,* a marshland plant in the family Apiaceae has been cultivated as a vegetable since antiquity. Leaves and stalks are eaten as a vegetable and also used in cooking. Which plant?

668. Used as a dietary supplement and cosmetic, this compound was named in 1815 when Vogel and Pierre Joseph Pelletier reported the isolation of a "yellow colouring substance" from the rhizomes of turmeric. Which compound?
669. Given its name on account of its foetid bed bug-like smell, this annual herb in the family Apiaceae, is used in cuisines throughout the world. Identify this spice that is also known as Chinese parsley, dhania or cilantro.
670. *Foeniculum vulgare* is a flowering plant species in the carrot family. According to Greek mythology, Prometheus used a giant stalk of this plant to carry fire from Mount Olympus to Earth. Identify the plant.

Answers

661. Amchoor
662. Asafoetida
663. Caper
664. Cinnamon
665. Horseradish
666. Cumin
667. Celery
668. Curcumin
669. Coriander
670. Fennel

Mottos

671. SARVE SANTU NIRAMAYA - may all be free from disease and disability is the motto of which specialist corps in the Indian Army?
672. The motto of which organization has been taken from eleventh chapter of the *Gita*, the discourse given by Lord Krishna to Arjuna on the battlefield of Kurukshetra?
673. Unity & Discipline is the motto of which organization that was inaugurated on 15 July 1948?
674. Originally called "Tiger Force", this special force derived its name from a mythological creature. Their motto can be translated as 'Defense by Offence'. Which force?
675. Termed as the First Line of Defense of Indian Territories, their motto is 'Defense unto Death'. Which organization?
676. Established as the Crown Representative's Police on 27 July 1939, it is the largest Armed Police Force in the country. Identify the organization functioning under the Ministry of Home Affairs, with the motto 'Service and Loyalty'.
677. Second line of defense after the Regular Indian Army, they are nicknamed Terriers and have the motto *Savdhani Va Shoorta,* that can be translated into Vigilance and Valour. Identify.
678. *Sarvatra Sarvottam Suraksha* is the motto of an organization that has been given specific role to handle all facets of terrorism in any part of the country as a Federal contingency force. Which organization?
679. *Vayam Raksāmah* or 'We protect' is the motto of an organization that came into existence on 1 February 1977

extra

National Bravery Awards

An act by 14-year-old Harish Chandra Mehra, on Gandhi Jayanti in 1957 with the PM as witness, resulted in the National Bravery Awards. Mehra, a boy scout, had used his knife to rip open a burning tent, saving hundreds of lives.

following the recommendations from Rustamji Committee. Which organization?

680. Senior-most in the order of precedence of the units of the Indian Army, this regiment is based in the Rashtrapati Bhavan. Their motto is 'Bharat Mata Ki Jai'. Which regiment?

Answers

671. Army Medical Corps
672. Indian Airforce
673. NCC
674. Garud Commando Force
675. Border Security force
676. CRPF
677. Territorial Army
678. NSG
679. Indian coast guard
680. The President's Bodyguard

Postage Stamps

681. What is so special about the Postage stamp with the denomination of Two Rupees, issued on 10th October 1985 to commemorate the 25th anniversary of Border Roads Organization?
682. A postage stamp issued in the year 1960 honoured the first Indian drama to be translated into a Western language. Identify.
683. It was this Padhmabhushan winner who invited Maria Montessori to come up and set up teaching courses thereby marking the beginning of Montessori style of education in India. Identify this woman featured on Indian Postal stamp in the year 1987.
684. Known for setting up the Tuberculosis Association of India, the Central Leprosy and Research Institute and several other health centres across the country, she was the first Health minister to get featured on an Indian stamp. Identify.
685. What was so special about featuring the wife of Bhoj Raj, the crown prince of Mewar on an Indian postage stamp of 1952?
686. If it was coffee in 2018, jasmine in 2008 and rose in 2007, what was it in 2006, the first of its kind? What are these all about?
687. Postage stamps were first used in India in 1852 in this district/province by Sir Bartle Frere, the British East India Company's administrator. Which district/province?
688. The first postage stamp of independent India was issued on 21 November 1947. What was depicted on it?
689. If Sree Narayana Guru was the first Malayali to get featured on an Indian postal stamp, who was the first Malayali woman to get featured?
690. When this stamp was issued on 28th October 1957, to commemorate the 19th International Red Cross Conference in New Delhi, the person depicted was the founder of the Red Cross foundation himself, thereby becoming the first foreigner to get featured on an Indian stamp. Identify

Answers

681. First triangular stamp of India
682. *Shakuntala*
683. Rukmini Devi Arundale
684. Rajkumari Amrit Kaur
685. First woman to be featured on an Indian postage stamp (Mira Bhai)
686. Sandalwood-scented stamps of India
687. Sind
688. Indian National Flag
689. Sister Alphonsa
690. Henry Dunant

Mixed Bag

691. *Burning Bright* is a book by Deepti Priya Mehrotra based on the life of which famous woman from North East India, also known as Mengoubi?
692. The credit for this masterpiece is given to an officer who captured the ruling queen of a kingdom in South India & made her agree the rights for Kingdom's eldest matriarch. Which book?
693. In the year 1960 she became the first woman from the field of sports and games to be awarded Padmashree. Identify her.
694. What first in India has been credited to Cottari Kanakayya Naidu in the year 1932 connected to Indian sports?
695. The address of which organization reads 'Mother House, 54 A, AJC Bose Road, Kolkata, 700016'?
696. Singhi Chaam centres on the Snow Lion, officially recognized as the formal symbol of this state as decreed by spiritual Guru Padamsambhava. Which state?
697. The Mudgal Brahmins of Jodhpur consider themselves to be the descendants of a mythological character, who is the deity of a particular temple in the town of Mandore. The wife of this character is believed to have got her name from this town itself. Which character?
698. The horses of this warrior included Sarangi, Pavan and Badal. She was the only "man among mutineers," as per Sir Hugh Rose, the British general. Which person?
699. What was authored by a district treasury officer in Visakhapatnam in the year 1962 to instill patriotism among the people when the Indo – China war started?
700. Born in Paris, the wife of Ratanji Dadabhoy Tata, is known for being the first woman in India to drive a car, in 1905. Name her.

Answers

691. Irom Chanu Sharmila
692. *Hortus Malabaricus*
693. Arati Saha
694. First Test Captain of India
695. Missionaries of Charity
696. Sikkim
697. Ravana
698. Jhansi Rani
699. National Pledge of India
700. Suzanne RD Tata

Superlatives

701. Earlier Chirapunji used to hold this record, which was later given to a place called Mawsynram. What record?
702. This is the world's largest basaltic crater and bacterial strands found from here show the character of the bacteria found in Mars. In 2020 this was in the headlines as it appeared in pink colour. What is mentioned here?
703. Named after a former prime minister of India, this is the largest of its kind in Asia. Located in Zabarwan range in Srinagar this was earlier known as Model Floriculture centre. Identify.

704. Khadi Prakritik Paint is the first of its kind developed by Khadi and Village Industries Commission. It is eco-friendly, anti-fungal, anti-bacterial and odourless. What is mentioned here?
705. This is the biggest river island in India. The Molai forest reserve here is named after Jadav Molai Payen, who is known as the 'Forest man of India'. Name the place.
706. Built by Maharaja Sawai Jai Singh, this is the largest observatory in the country among all the five. This also has the world's biggest stone sundial. Identify the place.
707. World One, World View, Lodha The Park, Imperial etc situated in Mumbai are part of what superlative in India?
708. With a height of 1493 feet, this waterfall in Nidagodu village in Shimoga district, formed by Varahi river is in the list of tallest waterfalls in India. Name it.
709. Zoological Garden, established on 24th September 1875, is the oldest and biggest zoo in India. Where in Kolkata is it situated?
710. This theatre, credited as the largest cinema hall in Asia during its inception, was one of the landmarks of Madurai. Identify.

Answers

701. Highest rainfall in India
702. Lunar Lake (Largest crater lake in India)
703. Indira Gandhi Tulip garden
704. India's first cow dung paint
705. Majuli Island
706. Jantar Mandir, Jaipur
707. Tallest buildings
708. Kunchikal falls
709. Alipore
710. Thangam Theatre

Daughters of India

711. She is the second woman to adorn this position in India. She is the first female spokesperson of a national political party. Name this former supreme court advocate.
712. This 2020 film starring Deepika Padukone was based on the life of the second winner of International Women of Courage award 2014, from India after Nirbhaya in 2013. Who?
713. Mihir Sen was the first Indian to swim across the English channel. Name the first Asian woman to conquer this feat who was also the first female sportsperson to win Padma Shri .
714. She is the first Indian-born to go to space twice. Her native place is named after a character from *Mahabharata* who was the king of Anga. Who is this lady?
715. SONA is a restaurant group owned by this person who owns the production house called Purple Pebble Pictures. Identify this lady who is also the author of the book called *Unfinished.*
716. Identify the author of these books *The World of Homosexuals; Astrology For You; Super Memory:It can be Yours.*
717. She is the first female ambassador of India to the People's Republic of China. '*Peace is My Dream*' is a commercial album by this former diplomat who published her book of poems called '*Rain Rising.*' Who is this famous Malayali?
718. Sometimes called as 'Eco-Goddess,' she is the founder of Navdanya,' an

organization to protect bio-diversity. *Biopiracy*, *Stolen Harvest* and *Water Wars* etc. are her famous books. Name?

719. During her first term of Chief ministership her salary was Rs 1. The Guinness record for hosting the world's largest luxury marriage reception is in her name. Who?

720. *Jaat Kahan Ho* is the only song from India that has been immortalised alongside the music of Beethoven, Bach and Mozart on the voyager golden record that went to interstellar space. Identify this singer of that song.

Answers

711. Sushma Swaraj
712. Laxmi Agarwal
713. Arati Saha
714. Kalpana Chawla
715. Priyanka Chopra
716. Shakuntala Devi
717. Nirupama Rao
718. Vandana Shiva
719. Jayalalitha
720. Kesarbai Kerkar

GI Tag

721. This city in South India is referred to as Pine Apple city and the Pine Apples grown over here received GI tag in the year 2009. Which city?

722. This rice variety is named after a Hindi word meaning 'Fragrant.' Texmati and Kasmati are a few US varieties of this. Which rice?

723. Known as the perfume capital of India, this place is famous for Damask roses. Perfumes produced from here are also in the GI products. Name this place which was earlier called 'Kanyakabuj.'

724. The Chauri Chaura incident which prompted Gandhi to call off the non-cooperation movement took place in this district of Uttar Pradesh. Identify this place which is also famous for Terracotta painting.

725. Himsagar, Fazli, Malihabadi Dusseheri, Banaganapalle etc are a few varieties of this product, added in the GI products list from various parts of the country. What product?

726. This geographically tagged product since 2007 is also known as Bandha of Odisha. Sambalpur, Bargarh, Sonepur and Boudh are famous for this product. What?

727. These betel leaves from Kerala are of high demand in Indian and foreign markets, especially in Pakistan which is a major export centre. Name?

728. When the application for GI tag for scissors was received from a city in Uttar Pradesh, for the first time, a handmade tool from micro and small and medium enterprises in India has been registered for a geographical indicator GI tag. Which city?

729. The origin of these chappals dates back to 12th century when the King Bijjala and his prime minister Basavanna encouraged its production so as to uplift the cobbler community.Which product?

730. Bavas Miyan is regarded as the father of this entity whereas its origin

traces back to the reign of Tipu Sultan who invited artisans from Persia to train the local artisans in the making of these toys.Identify this GI-tagged product.

Answers

721. Vazhakulam
722. Basmati
723. Kannauj
724. Gorakhpur
725. Mango
726. Odisha Ikat
727. Tirur Betel leaf
728. Meerut
729. Kolhapuri
730. Channapatna Toys

Stadiums

731. This is the biggest stadium in India and is currently known as Vivekananda Yuba Bharati Karirangan. How do we better know this?
732. Which stadium is the home ground of an ISL team called 'Kerala Blasters' and is named after a former Prime Minister?
733. Which stadium in Ludhiana hosted the opening and closing ceremonies of the 2001 National Games and has also been chosen as the home ground of I-League team, RoundGlass Punjab FC?
734. This was earlier known as Auckland Circus Garden, Mar Bagan etc. Also the oldest in the country, it is called Lord's of India.Which stadium?
735. Famous for its cricket ground, this region in Punjab was renamed as SAS Nagar in memory of Sahibzada Ajit Singh. Which place?
736. Constructed in the 1980s, this stadium situated inside the Sardar Patel Sports Enclave in Ahmedabad and owned by the Gujarat Cricket Association has been renamed as Narendra Modi stadium. What was its former name?
737. Which stadium situated in Bhubaneswar near Nayapalli area claims to have the first Olympic standard pink and blue water-based AstroTurf in India?
738. The home ground of Bengaluru FC, this stadium built on top of an old lake, is owned by Karnataka Athletic Association. Name?
739. Lusophone games is a multinational multi-sport event, which involves athletes coming from Portuguese-speaking countries. The 3rd edition was also the first time it was hosted by India. Which stadium was the main venue?
740. The retirement match of Sachin Tendulkar happened in this stadium. It is named after a former BCCI president, politician, and businessman. Who?

Answers

731. Salt Lake stadium
732. Kochi Jawaharlal Nehru stadium
733. Guru Nanak Stadium
734. Eden Gardens
735. Mohali
736. Motera stadium
737. Kalinga Stadium
738. Sree Kanteerava Stadium
739. Fatorda Stadium, Margao
740. Seshrao Krishnarao Wankhede

ISRO

741. This instrument which was part of Chandrayaan and contributed by NASA is also known as M3. It has found small amount of water on the moon's surface. Name the device?
742. The rover in the Chandrayaan II project was named after the Sanskrit word

for wisdom.Identify the word.

743.This was the first-ever mission to go to the south polar region of the moon and it made India,the fourth country in the world to softland on the surface of moon after US, Russia and China. Which project?

744.The Lander, one of the main components of both the Chandrayaan projects, is named after which person ?

745. What was set up by Dr. Vikram Sarabhai in 1962 to formulate the Indian Space Programme, which was then part of the Tata Institute of Fundamental Research?

746. The first attempted launch of an orbital satellite, aboard a Satellite Launch Vehicle, took place on 10 August 1979.What name was given to that mission.

747. On 22 January 2020, ISRO announced a female-looking robot who will accompany the other astronauts in Gaganyaan mission that can detect and give out warnings if environmental changes within the cabin get uncomfortable to astronauts.What name was given?

748. The first dedicated meteorological satellite launched by Indian Space Research Organisation using Polar Satellite Launch Vehicle was on 12 September 2002. What name was given?

749. India's first solar mission has been conceptualized in the year 2008 and has been named after a synonym for sun. Name it.

750. Born in Srinagar, this person is widely regarded as the father of experimental fluid dynamics research in India. Identify this former chairman of ISRO.

Answers

741. Moon Mineralogy Mapper
742. Pragyan
743. Chandrayaan II
744. Vikram Sarabhai
745. INCOSPAR
746. Rohini 1A
747. Vyommitra
748. Kalpana-1
749. Aditya-L1
750. Satish Dhawan

Programmes

751. Aahaar Kranti is a movement launched in April 2021 which is run by Vijnana Bharati and Global Indian Scientists and Techno crafts. What is the aim of this mission?

752.An app was developed by NIMHANS Bengaluru, AFMC Pune, and C-DAC Pune which aims mental well-being of Indian citizens. What name was given to this Mental Health and Normalcy Augmentation System ?

753. Launched in 2016, the beneficiary group of this programme are people belonging to SC, ST and women in India. This scheme facilitates bank loans between Rs10 lakh to ₹1 crore. 'Endeavour and Prosper' is the tagline of this programme. Identify.

754. Shatoot Dam is the second dam to be built by India in Afghanistan as part of New Development Partnership Project. Which is the first one?

755.As part of International Day of Women and Girls in Science, Department of Science and Technology initiated this programme to encourage girls to pursue Science, Technology, Engineering and Mathematics (STEM). Which programme?

756. In 2020, COVID-19 relief package worth 1.70 lakh crore was announced by Government of India under Garib

Kalyan Yojana. In 2021 another relief package worth 27.1 lakh crore was announced. What was the name of that package?

757. Padhe Bharat Badhe Bharat, Shagun Portal are two initiatives under this programme, which was meant for Universalisation of Elementary Education and Education for All. Which programme?
758. Mission Karmayogi is a national capacity building programme launched by Union Cabinet. The programme also has a customized digital learning platform called 'Igot-Karmayogi. Who are the beneficiaries of this programme?
759. Shri Anant Khasbardar of Kolhapur in Maharashra came into limelight following the design of a logo of a programme launched by the Union Ministry in the year 2014. Which programme?
760.Shown below is one of the logos of the largest healthcare insurance schemes in India. It covers around 10 crore poor families. Which scheme?

Answers

751. Awareness on nutritionally balanced diet
752. MANAS
753. Stand Up India
754. Salma Dam
755. Vigyan Jyothi
756. Aatmanirbhar Bharat
757. Sarva Shiksha Abhiyan
758. Civil servants in the country
759. Swachh Bharat Abhiyan
760. Ayushman Bharat

Aviation

761. Headquartered in Gurgaon, it is the largest airline in India by passengers carried and fleet size.Name?
762. Commencing its operations in November 2005, Go Air is a low-cost airline headquartered in Mumbai. Owned by which business group?
763. Operated its first flight in the year 2005, this was earlier launched as an air taxi provider in 1994 and was then called ModiLuft. How do we know it now.
764. Born in the village of Chondi in Maharashtra, Maharani Ahilyabai was the widow of Khanderao Holkar who was killed in the battle of Kumher in 1754. Which airport is named after her?
765. Operating under the UDAAN scheme of central Govt, its parent company Ghodawat Enterprises started its operations in the year 2019 from Kempegowda International Airport in Bangalore. Name it.
766. Tata SIA Airlines Limited, or Vistara, with its hub at Indira Gandhi International Airport is a joint venture between Tata Sons and which other airline?
767. On 21 February 1960, this airlines took delivery of its first Boeing 707 and named it Gauri Shankar, thus becoming the first Asian airline to induct a jet aircraft in its fleet. Which one?
768. Veer Savarkar International Airport operates as a civil enclave, sharing airside facilities with INS Utkrosh of the Indian Navy. In which capital city is it located?
769. Established in 2003, it was owned by the Bengaluru-based United Brew-

eries Group and had started commercial operations on 9 May 2005, on the founder's son Siddharth's 18th birthday, reportedly as a birthday gift. Which air line?

770. Captain GR Gopinath whose business ventures included the Malnad Mobikes Enfield dealership as well as a hotel in Hassan was the winner of the Rolex Laureate Award in the year 1996.He is the co-founder of which airline in India?

Answers

761. Indigo
762. Wadia Group
763. Spice Jet
764. Indore
765. Star Air
766. Singapore Airlines
767. Air India
768. Port Blair
769. Kingfisher Airlines
770. Deccan Aviation (later Air Deccan and then Simplifly Deccan)

Famous Houses

771. Prateeksha, one of the most famous landmarks in Mumbai's Juhu area and Jalsa belongs to which celebrity born in Allahabad in the year 1942?
772. Situated on Lok Kalyan Marg, New Delhi, the official name of this residence complex is Panchavati. Who lives here?
773. Built in 1966 Sahitya Sahavas initially consisted of only three buildings, Abhang, Anandvan and Zapurza. Who was its most famous resident?
774. Known as South Court and Malabar Hill mansion, it was built by a person who left India in 1946. Identify this famous house in Mumbai.
775. Formerly known as Flagstaff House, this was the former residence of Jawaharlal Nehru who stayed here for 16 years until his death in the year 1964. Which house?
776. The owner of this house initially wanted to name it Jannat, but later on named it Mannat.It was previously owned by Keekoo Gandhy, a Parsi from Gujarat. Who is the celebrity owner since 2001?
777. As of 2021, it was deemed to be the world's second most valuable residential property, after Buckingham Palace, and the world's most valuable private residence.Identify this house located on Altamount Road, Mumbai.
778. Jorasanko Thakur Bari was built in the 18th century on the land donated by the Sett family of Burrabazar to Prince Dwarkanath. Which Nobel Laureate was born here?
779. Situated on 8th main, 15th cross in Malleswaram, Panchvati was the name given to this residence by the owner's wife Lokasundari when the couple purchased it in the year 1942. Who was the famous owner?
780. Situated near Hutatma Chowk, Bombay House was built in the year 1924 and was designed by Scottish architect George Wittet. The building houses office of chairman and all top directors of which famous group?

Answers

771. Amitabh Bachchan
772. Prime Minister of India

773. Sachin Tendulkar
774. Jinnah House
775. Teen Murti Bhavan
776. Shah Rukh Khan
777. Antilia
778. Rabindranath Tagore
779. CV Raman
780. Tata Sons

Lakes

781. Which lake, one of the biggest of its kind in Asia, located between Krishna and Godavari deltas spans into two districts, Krishna and West Godavari?
782. Cumbum Lake, also known as Gundlakamma Lake, built on a rivulet upon the Nallamala hills is one of the oldest man-made lakes in Asia. In which state you can find this?
783. Kankaria lake in Gujarat has been wrongly credited as the inspiration behind the logo of a famous entity in India.Which entity?
784. In 2013, which lake near IIM Ahmedabad was renamed 'Bhakt Kavi Narsinh Mehta Sarovar' in memory of Narsinh Mehta?
785. Which lake, mentioned as Mahapadmasaras, traces its etymology to high leaping waves in the afternoons, called Ullola in Sanskrit?
786. This lake , also known as the "Jewel in the crown of Kashmir," was the location for the first floating post office in India and also one of the first floating ATMs in India. Which lake, a tautological name, are we talking about?
787. Largest fresh water lake in Northeast India, it is renowned for its phumdis and also for the Keibul Lamjao National Park, located on this phumdi.Name it.
788. Known as the longest lake in India, it is known as Punnamada Lake in Kuttanad and as Kochi Lake in Kochi. Identify this lake where Nehru Trophy boat race is held.
789. It is the largest salt-producing unit in India whose annual production accounts for more than 9% of India's total production. Identify this lake.
790. This district is referred to as the district of lakes. Three among the four lakes situated in this region are Sattal Lake, Bhimtal Lake, and Naukuchiyatal Lake. Which is the fourth one, that shares its name with the district itself?

Answers

781. Kolleru
782. Andhra Pradesh
783. State Bank of India
784. Vastrapur lake
785. Wular
786. Dal
787. Loktak
788. Vembanad lake
789. Sambar
790. Nainital

Mixed bag

791. Dedicated to Lord Kartik, the Vautha Mela is one of the major religious events in Gujarat. Although it is on par with the famous Camel Fair in Pushkar, the Vautha Mela in Saptasangam, is known for the trading of which animal?
792. Dampier Hodges are imaginary lines passing through West Bengal, which indicates the Northern boundary of the place with the state. This is the only mangrove forest in the world inhabited by tigers. Identify.
793. The Kannada version of Doordar-

shan was launched in 1994. Its name qualifies to be a true cultural ambassador of the state as it could refer to a prominent industry there. Name the channel.

794. Corporate address of which entity in India reads, Exchange Plaza, C-1, Block G, Bandra Kurla Complex, Bandra (E), Mumbai?

795. What has its origins at Bangrabalige valley, Yelaneeru Ghat in Kudremukh in Chikkamagaluru district and was formerly known as the Bantwal and has got a train named after it?

796. This railway station of western railway straddles two states : one half of it is in Maharashtra and the other half in Gujarat.Name the railway station?

797. In 2007, it was voted as the first of Seven Wonders of India in a *Times of India* poll; 49% of the total votes went in favour of it. Identify this structure built around 983 A.D on Vindhyagiri, commissioned by the Ganga dynasty.

798. The region located in the Jaisalmer district literally means "the place of 5 mirages" and is better known for incidents that took place in the second half of 20th century, 24 years apart. Which region?

799. Which former Army General contested the Lok Sabha seat for North-East Bombay as an independent candidate against VK Krishna Menon and J.B. Kripalani?

800. At 23 years she is the first woman recipient of Ashoka Chakra, India's highest peace time gallantry award. She was also honoured by Pakistan with the Tamgha e Insaaniyat award. Identify this braveheart.

Answers

791. Donkeys
792. Sunderbans
793. Chandana
794. National Stock Exchange
795. Netravati river
796. Navapur
797. Statue of Gomateswara (Bahubali)
798. Pokhran
799. Field Marshal KM Kariappa
800. Neerja Bhanot

Military Operations

801. Siachen Glacier, the world's highest battlefield, came under control of Indian Army after this successful operation conducted on 13th April 1984 under the leadership of Lt. Gen. Prem Nath Hoon. This operation was codenamed after which famous literary work from fourth century?

802. Operations Pawan, Viraat, Trishul and Checkmate are associated with a special force of India active during the years 1987 to 1990. Which force?

803.Indian Navy Day is celebrated annually on 4th December to commemorate the Karachi harbour attack of 1971 which is considered as one of the most successful naval victories of India post WW2. In 2019, a Bollywood movie was announced by T-Series based on the same mission. Name the Mission.

804. Operation Cactus was one of the globally appreciated military operations conducted by Indian armed forces in 1988 November against the attempted coup in a neighbouring country. Which country?

805. First-ever emergency of Independent India was declared in September 1948 following the annexation of Hyderabad to Indian Union through Operation Caterpillar. Sardar Vallabhai

Patel had called it as 'Police Action'. The popular name used to refer to this operation is named after which game?

806.R&AW had planned to abduct Jarnail Singh Bhindranwale from Amritsar before Operation Blue Star in 1984 but it was turned down by then Indian Prime Minister Indira Gandhi fearing the casualties. What was the name given for this operation?

807.The air strike by the Indian Air Force (IAF) on a terrorist training camp in Pakistan's Balakot was conducted on 26 February 2019. The date was fixed by then IAF's Western Command head Air Marshal (retd) C Hari Kumar as the date was his birthday. What was the codename of this operation?

808. Operation Madat by Indian Navy, Operation Sahyog by Indian Army and Operation Water Baby by Indian Coast Guard were some of the rescue operations carried out during Kerala flood in 2018. What was the name of the rescue operation carried out by Kerala Police?

809. What was the codename given to both the Liberation of Goa and Daman & Diu from Portugal in 1961 and Kargil victory against Pakistan in 1999 ?

810. Pak-occupied Quaid Post, which was later renamed as Bana Top after one of the only three living Param Veer Chakra recipients Bana Singh, came under India's control through this operation conducted in 1987. It was named after an Indian army officer who was martyred while attempting for the same earlier. What was the codename of this mission?

Answers

801. Operation Meghdoot (Named after the poem *Meghdoot* by Kalidasa)
802. Indian Peace Keeping Force (IPKF)
803. Operation Trident
804. Maldives
805. Operation Polo
806. Operation Sundown
807. Operation Bandar
808. Operation Jalaraksha
809. Operation Vijay
810. Operation Rajiv (Named after 2nd Lt. Rajiv Pande)

Agricultural Institutions

811. In the year 2019 ICAR developed an Integrated Mobile App for Farmers that has interface in 12 Indian Languages. What name was given to that?

812. The sugarcane varieties introduced by this institute, established in the year 1912, occupy more than 90% of total sugarcane cultivated area in India. Name the institute.

813. Formerly known as Imperial Dairy Institute, its headquarters was moved to Karnal in the year 1995. Identify the institute which was conferred deemed to be University status.

814. An autonomous organization engaged in agricultural research on Indian spices, the institute is headquartered in a place called Moozhikkal in Kozhikode district.Identify.

815. National Institute of Natural Fibre Engineering and Technology (NINFET), is an institute for the research of jute and other fibres leading to the diversified use and industrial growth. Where is it headquartered?

816. Which organization, in collaboration with the Government of Maharashtra, implemented a pilot project in the Vidarbha region, based on Brazilian model to enhance the yield in a cost-

effective manner?

817. What was established in the year 1946 at Bidyadharpur, Cuttack, following the Great Bengal famine of 1943 ?

818.As per their website, this is the only research organization in the world dedicated solely to the research on tropical tuber crops. Identify this Institute established in 1963 with its headquarters at Thiruvananthapuram.

819. Pepper Research Station (PRS) under Kerala Agricultural University is one of the oldest institutions of its kind in India. Situated in Kannur district, it is known for developing the world's first artificially pollinated variety of pepper. Name it.

820. Commonly known as the Pusa Institute, it is India's national Institute for agricultural research, education and extension. Identify this institute that was responsible for the research leading to the "Green Revolution in India" of the 1970s.

Answers

811. KISAAN (Krishi Integrated Solution for Agri Apps Navigation)
812. Sugarcane Breeding Institute, Coimbatore
813. National Dairy Research Institute
814. The Indian Institute of Spices Research (IISR)
815. Kolkata
816. Central Institute for Cotton Research (CICR)
817. National Rice Research Institute
818. Central Tuber Crops Research Institute
819. Panniyoor One
820. Indian Agricultural Research Institute

Military Exercises

821. The first edition of Surya Kiran military exercise took place in Mizoram and more than 13 editions have happened ever since.This is a joint military exercise of India with which other country?

822. The first-ever joint military exercise of Indian army with the Japanese army was conducted at Mizoram in the year 2018. What was the name given to it?

823.Which tri - nation exercise of the Indian navy has got the United States and Japan as permanent partners?

824. The annually held naval exercise consists of naval cooperation drills between the French Navy and the Indian Navy. It is held either in the Indian Ocean or Mediterranean Sea. What name has been given to that?

825.This series of Air Force exercises between the Indian Air Force and the United States Air Force used to be conducted in India. Identify this series with Gwalior as the venue for inaugural edition.

826. This multilateral naval exercise hosted by the Indian Navy is a biennial event held in the Andaman and Nicobar Islands. It was first organized in 1995 with the navies of Indonesia, Singapore, Sri Lanka and Thailand participating in the inaugural edition.Name?

827. Biennial military exercise conducted by India and Russia started in 2003. Eventhough the name given to that is that of a mythological character, it is a portmanteau representing the names of both the countries.What name?

828.The joint air force exercise, conducted by the Royal Air Force and the Indian

Air Force starting in the year 2006, is named after a synonym for rainbow. Name?

829. Tiger Triumph is a bilateral tri-service amphibious military exercise involving the armed forces of India and another country. Name the country.

830. Conducted in Lucknow in the year 1960, an exercise called Lal Qila outlined a Chinese attack, and the vulnerabilities of the Indian forces in the eastern sector. It was conceived under a major general known for a 'plan' or 'doctrine' named after him.Identify him.

Answers

821. Nepal
822. Dharma Guardian
823. Malabar
824. Varuna
825. Cope India
826. Milan
827. Indra
828. Indradhanush
829. USA
830. Major General SPP Thorat

Olympics

831. The first-ever participation of India in the Olympics happened way back in 1900 in Paris.The country was represented by an Anglo-Indian who was holidaying in Paris during that time. Identify this legend who had won multiple Olympic medals for India.

832. The first-ever Olympic gold in Hockey came to India in the year 1928.India defeated the hosts in the final to clinch the gold. Who were the hosts?

833. Which Olympic medal winner made his Bollywood debut in the movie *Fugly* in 2014?

834. The first Vice-Chancellor of Delhi Sports University happened to be the first Indian woman to win an Olympic medal.Identify.

835. This world No.1 boxer has been given the top seeding in his category in the Tokyo Olympics. Identify this sportsperson from Rohtak district, Haryana.

836. Joining as a sub-inspector in state police in 1955, he resigned in 1983 as an assistant commissioner of police in Maharashtra.Identify this Olympian who died in a road accident in the year 1984.

837. The youngest Indian participant at the 2000 Summer Olympics in Sydney, his autobiography, *A Shot at History: My Obsessive Journey to Olympic Gold* was published by Harper Sport in the year 2011.Identify.

838. This person, after competing in consecutive Olympics from 1992 to 2016, became the first Indian and only player from his sport to compete at seven Olympic Games. Identify.

839. In the year 2012, who became the only Indian to win two individual Olympic Medals for the country?

840. Which Olympic medal winner was commissioned into the army in 1990 as part of the 9th Grenadiers (Mewar) Regiment and achieved the rank of Colonel in 2009?

Answers

831. Norman Pritchard
832. The Netherlands
833. Vijender Singh
834. Karnam Malleswari
835. Amit Panghal
836. KD Jadhav
837. Abhinav Bindra

838. Leander Paes
839. Sushil Kumar
840. Rajyavardhan Singh Rathore

Arjuna & Dronacharya

841. In the year 1985, the inaugural edition of Dronacharya award was won by three coaches.One was Bhalachandra Bhaskar Bhagwat (wrestling) and another one was Om Prakash Bhardwaj (boxing).Who was the third one representing athletics.?
842.Having represented New Hind sports club, Young Maharashtra XI, Gul Mohar Mills and Mumbai Port in the club level, he played only one first-class cricket match, representing State Bank of India against Hyderabad in the Moin-ud-Dowlah Gold Cup Tournament in 1963. Who is this Dronacharya?
843. The first Indian to be a World champion in any sport, he is a recipient of both Arjuna and Dronacharya award. Identify the person and the sport.
844. In the year 2000, Gopal Purushottam Phadke was the first-ever person from his sport to receive Dronacharya award. Which traditional Indian sport?
845. The first sportsperson to win both the Arjuna Award and Dronacharya Award for football, he captained the Indian team that won a bronze medal at the 1970 Asian Games.Who is this?
846. This nine-time national champion is the first Indian player to be awarded the International Master title in chess, and is one of the key figures in introducing international chess practices to India.Name this Arjuna winner in its inaugural year itself.
847. Published by Penguin books, *A Touch of Tennis: The Story of a Tennis Family* is about three generations of a tennis playing family. Who co-authored the book along with his son and Nirmal Shekar?
848. Appearing in the film *Charitra* with Parveen Babi in 1973, he is the first player to win Arjuna representing his sport. Identify this sportsperson born in Afghanistan?
849.Who competed in seven events at the 1956 Summer Olympics and won the first-ever Arjuna in the year 1961 for gymnastics?
850. This wrestler and coach became the first individual world championship medal winner from independent India in wrestling. Who?

Answers

841. OM Nambiar
842. Ramakant Achrekar
843. Wilson Jones, Billiards
844. Kho Kho
845. Syed Nayeemuddin
846. Manuel Aaron
847. Ramanathan Krishnan
848. Salim Durani
849. Sham Lal
850. Udey Chand

Drinks

851. This drink was launched in 1919 by a company owned by Adduri Ramachandra Raju and Adduri Jagannadha Raju in Ramachandrapuram, East Godavari with a soda machine procured from the British. Identify the drink made popular by the British soldiers during World War-II.
852. Madurai in Tamil Nadu is famous for this cold beverage with its basic ingredients including milk, almond gum, sarsaparilla root syrup, sugar and ice-cream. Name it?
853. It is a sap extracted from the inflo-

rescence of various toddy palms and is obtained by slicing the spathes of the coconut, sago, and Palmyra palm, and scraping the tendermost part, just below the crown. Which drink?

854. A popular drink of Kashmir valley, its name in Kashmiri can be translated into 'sweetened tea.' Identify this drink, also known as Mogul chai, since this tea was introduced in the valley by the Mughal emperors.

855. Literally meaning 'Soul Refresher', this is a concentrated squash formulated in 1906 in Ghaziabad by Naqi Ali Shah. Identify this drink manufactured by Hamdard Laboratories.

856. An appetizer, usually consumed with rice or sometimes drunk after or along with the meals, this is popular in Goa and Maharashtra's coastal region. Identify this drink made from coconut milk, kokum and the dried fleshy skin of *Garcinia indica*, that imparts a deep purple-pink colour to it.

857. Commonly produced in households of Arunachal Pradesh and Assam, this drink is believed to be first developed by the Mising people in Assam. Name this alcoholic drink served during all religious festivals and ceremonies in Assam.

858. A fermented drink of the Angami Nagas, it is commonly consumed by all Naga tribes in the rural regions of Nagaland. Identify this drink, an intrinsic part of traditional Naga cuisine, usually made using ground rice and yeast.

859. Specially relished during summer, Tankaw Toraani is a drink made from one-day-old cooked rice known as anna which is a part of Mahaprasada offered to a particular deity. Which deity?

860. The first product to receive GI recognition in India was for this entity and it was in the year 2004 that GI tags for its unique logo and name were awarded. What are we talking about?

Answers

851. Artos
852. Jigarthanda
853. Neera (Palm nectar)
854. Kahwah
855. Rooh Afza
856. Solkadhi
857. Apo
858. Zutho
859. Lord Jagannath
860. Darjeeling tea

Disasters

861. The novel *Ashani Sanket* by Bibhutibhushan Bandyopadhyay, the novel *So Many Hungers*! by Bhabani Bhattacharya, 1980 film *Akaler Shandhaney* by Mrinal Sen, all these had one disaster as the backdrop. Which one?

862. In the year 1839, an enormous cyclone hit this city, known for its ship

extra

Baroda Dynamite Case and Sushma Swaraj

Sushma Swaraj started her political career with ABVP while reading law and was, along with her husband, a part of George Fendandes's legal defence team in 1975 on the Baroda Dynamite and other cases.

building and repair, and destroyed 25,000 ships and vessels in its bay, and killed around 3,00,000 people. Which city in Andhra Pradesh?

863. The epicentre of this earthquake that destroyed 52 villages and caused around 10,000 deaths was Killari. Which earthquake?

864. Guwahati in Assam, Darjeeling in West Bengal,Malpa in Uttarakhand, Amboori in Kerala, Kedarnath in Uttarakhand and Malin in Maharashtra, all these places were in news connected to which disaster?

865. Aceh (Indonesia), Sri Lanka, Tamil Nadu and Khao Lak (Thailand), all were part of one of the deadliest natural disasters in recorded history. Which one?

866. Watch, Alert, Warning and Outlook are the four stages of warnings issued by IMD for Indian coast. Against which disaster?

867. On 6th June 1981, a train carrying more than 800 passengers derailed and plunged into a river in Bihar, while it was crossing a bridge, making it one of the biggest rail accidents in India. Which river?

868. Which 1999 movie directed by Mahesh Mathai set against the Bhopal gas tragedy examines the irresponsible methods of large corporations and the effects of their actions on common people?

869. Justice TP Garg was the head of the commission set up to investigate the worst-ever fire accident that happened in India, killing around 400 people, gathered at the Rajiv Marriage Palace in Dabwali. In which state did it occur?

870. On 12 November 1996, a Saudi Arabian Airlines Flight 763, and Kazakhstan Airlines Flight 1907, collided over a village around 100 km west of Delhi killing all 349 people on board both planes, making it the deadliest aviation accident to occur in India. Over which village did this happen?

Answers

861. The Bengal famine of 1943
862. Coringa
863. Latur Earthquake
864. Landslide
865. 2004 Boxing Day Tsunami
866. Cyclones
867. Bagmati
868. *Bhopal Express*
869. Haryana
870. Charkhi Dadri

Classical Music

871. Which former jeweler, from Karnataka, who gave away all his material riches to become a servant of Lord Krishna is widely referred to as the Pitamaha of Carnatic music?

872. Saraswati, Pinaki, Bobbili, Chitra, Mohan etc are different types of which musical instrument?

873. According to legend, Lord Muruga, the deity of Tirutani temple, placed a piece of sugar candy in his mouth and

extra

JP Dutta's Refugee

The film *Refugee* by JP Dutta was inspired by a story by Keki N Daruwalla set in the Great Rann of Kutch and titled *Love Across the Salt Desert*. Abhishek Bachchan and Kareena Kapoor made their débuts in the film.

commanded him to sing, thereby starting his musical career. Identify this maestro born in a town called Thiruvarur.

874. Palani Subramaniam Pillai , Ramanathapuram C. S. Murugabhoopathy, and this person are revered as the "Holy Trinity of Mrudangam". Identify the third.

875. Born as Venkata Subrahmanya on 26 April 1762, most of his compositions were devoted to Goddess Kamakshi, a form of Goddess Parvati. How do we better know him?

876. The first Indian who performed in the United Nations General Assembly in 1966, this person's first silver screen appearance was for the movie *Sevasadan* in the year 1938. Identify.

877. Known as Deva vadyam, its name is formulated by the union of the two Sanskrit words meaning 'clay' and 'limb,' as the earliest versions of the instrument were made of hardened clay. Identify.

878. The word comes from a term which means immovable and permanent.This genre in Hindustani music has at least four stanzas, called Sthayi (or Asthayi), Antara, Sanchari and Abhoga. Which genre?

879. The tomb of this musician, who spent most of his life in the court and patronage of the king of Rewa, Raja Ramchandra Singh is situated in Gwalior, near the tomb of his Sufi master Muhammad Ghaus. Identify him.

880. Known as *shata-tantri veena* in ancient Sanskrit texts, this trapezoid-shaped musical instrument has a total of 100 strings. Identify.

Answers

871. Purandara Dasa
872. Veena
873. Muthuswamy Dikshitar
874. Palghat Mani Iyer
875. Shyama Shastri
876. M. S. Subbulakshmi
877. Mridangam
878. Dhrupad
879. Tansen
880. Santoor

Cinema

881. The first Indian film released in India was in Marathi by Dadasaheb Torne on 18 May 1912 at Coronation Cinematograph, Bombay. What was its name?

882. The first silent film in this language, *Keechaka Vadham,* was made by R. Nataraja Mudaliar in the year 1916. Which language?

883. In 1905, he became the Indian representative of Universal Studios and he was a partner of Alexander Cinema in Bombay for over forty years. Identify this gentleman who produced his first silent feature film, *Nala Damayanti,* in the year 1920.

884. Based on a novel by Saadat Hasan Manto and centred around the lives of poor farmers, this movie starring Padma Devi and Zillo was directed by Moti Gidwani. Identify the movie.

885. Known by the sobriquet Chhollywood, the movie industry in this language began in 1965 with the release of the first film *Kahi Debe Sandesh.* Which state?

886. The 1986 movie *Africadalli Sheela* is said to be the first Indian movie to be shot in African forests. Which language?

887. Described by *The Guardian* as "city within a city", it is a popular tourism

and recreation centre, containing natural and artificial attractions including an amusement park. Identify this location visited by around 1.5 million tourists every year.

888. In the year 1971 Prithviraj Kapoor became the third person to win this award, and in 1970, Birendranath Sircar became the second person to win it. Who won it in the inaugural edition in the year 1969? Which award is this?

889. *Jawani Ki Hawa,* a 1959 Hindi crime thriller mostly shot in a train, was the first film produced by this studio established in the year 1934. Name this studio.

890. Director of one of the first indigenously shot 70 mm films in India, this person reached the zenith of his fame through a movie released in the year 1984. Identify the person.

Answers

881. *Shree Pundalik*
882. Tamil
883. Ardeshir Irani
884. *Kisan Kanya*
885. Chhattisgarh
886. Kannada
887. Ramoji Film City
888. Devika Rani, Dadasaheb Phalke Award
889. Bombay Talkies
890. Jijo Punnoose

Mixed Bag

891. This movement was started in Gubbi Gadde, a small village near Sirsi in the (north) Uttara Kannada district, and has forced the forest department to change the forest policy on felling of trees. Name the movement.

892. India's first free dance gurukul, Nrityagram, that taught seven classical dance styles and two martial arts forms, Chhau and Kalaripayattu, was started by her and inaugurated by the then Prime Minister VP Singh in 1990. Who?

893. Which newspaper made its debut on 20 February 1868, started by Sisir Ghosh and Moti Lal Ghosh, from Magura, in Jessore District in present-day Bangladesh?

894. An institute of higher learning in Kolkata, Indian Association for the cultivation of Science, was established in 1876 by Mahendra Lal Sarkar, a private medical practitioner. What was the most famous discovery associated with it?

895. Who, in the year 1992, received an award from his favourite actress Audrey Hepburn from his bed at Belle Vue Hospital in Kolkata?

896. Which famous person became the president of the workers' union at the Tata Steel plant in Jamshedpur for nine years between 1928 and 1937 ?

897. *A Wasted Life – 'The Rise and Fall of the Biscuit King'* was the biographical account of which businessman?

898. With which destination would one associate Magan Niwas, Nandini, Udyog Mandir, Somnath Chhatralaya, Upasana Mandir?

899. Originally from Sanskrit , the name of this dress is a combination of two words meaning 'two', and 'strip of cloth'. Which dress?

900. This physician and microbiologist pioneered AIDS research and prevention in India after diagnosing the first Indian AIDS cases in 1986 along with her student Sellappan Nirmala, Identify.

Answers

891. Appiko
892. Protima Bedi
893. *Amritabazar Patrika*
894. Raman Effect
895. Satyajith Ray
896. Netaji Subash Chandra Bose
897. Rajan Pillai
898. Sabarmati Ashram
899. Duppatta
900. Dr. Suniti Solomon

Memorial Places/Tombs

901. Sometimes called as 'Bhul Bhulaiyan', this tomb was built by Akbar for the person who was executed by his own orders. He was the son of Maham Anga. This is located left to Qutab Minar. Whose tomb is this?
902. Known as Baby Taj, this structure is located on the banks of river Yamuna. This was built for Mirza Giyaz Beg, father of Nur Jahan. Identify.
903. This former teacher had proficiency in languages like Bengali, Croatian, Albanian. Nirmal Hriday is an institution started by this person whose burial place is now a pilgrimage centre. Who?
904. The resting place of M G Ramachandran, J.Jayalalitha and M. Karunanidhi is situated in a location, which is one of the longest of its kind in Asia. Name the location.
905. *Khwab Nama* is a book written by this ruler about his dreams. His original name is Fath Ali. Identify this person whose resting place is called 'Gumbaz'.
906. The fifth prime minister of India is the one to adorn the position for the shortest period in history. He was also called 'Champion of Indian Peasants'. What is his memorial place called?
907. 'Garden of Peace' is the literal translation of memorial place of Jawaharlal Nehru. What do we call this place?
908. This memorial, situated close to Birla Mandir, Necklace Road and Lumbini Park, is maintained by the Buddha Purnima Project Authority under Telangana Government. What is it called?
909. Maha Parinirvan Diwas is observed on the death anniversary of this person who rests in a place called 'Chaitya Bhoomi'. Who?
910. The tomb of which saint born in Iran can be found at the foot of the Taragarh hill?

Answers

901. Adham Khan
902. Itimad-ud-Daulah
903. Mother Theresa
904. Marina Beach, Chennai
905. Tipu Sultan
906. Kisan Ghat
907. Shantivan
908. NTR Gardens
909. B R Ambedkar
910. Moinuddin Chishti

Nicknames/Titles

911. Popularly known as Little Master, he debuted in a Marathi film called *Saavli*

Premachi. Sunny Days, Idols, Runs 'n' Ruins, One Day Wonders are his books. Who?

912. Liberal Party Member of Parliament in the United Kingdom House of Commons between 1892 and 1895, he was referred to as "Unofficial Ambassador of India". Identify.
913. It was A V Smith who is credited with giving this title to Samudragupta. He had won hundreds of battles and said to have lost none. What title?
914. *Tota-e-Hind* translates into 'Parrot of India.' It was the title given to this person whose famous works include *The Nine Heavens, The Book of Tughluq.* Identify the person.
915. One of the fastest goals in the history of International football was scored by this police officer who was also called 'Kala Harin'. Who is this?
916. She is called 'Ding Express' after her native place. She is one of the first Indian sprinters to win a gold medal at an international event. Name the person.
917. P T Usha is called Payyoli Express and Queen of Indian Track and Field. Who is known as Mysore Express?
918. This freedom fighter from Andhra Pradesh, known as Andhra Kesari, was the first chief minister of Andhra state before unification. Who?
919. Dr S Radhakrishnan had praised him as one of the makers of modern India. His original name was Mula Sankara. Identify this person who is called as Martin Luther King of India.
920. Shown below is a person who is popular as 'Mountain Man'. He is from Bihar and is famous for single-handedly carving a path through a mountain. Identify.

Answers

911. Sunil Gavaskar
912. Dadabhai Naoroji
913. Napoleon of India
914. Amir Khusru
915. I M Vijayan
916. Hima Das
917. Javagal Srinath
918. T Prakasham
919. Dayanand Saraswathi
920. Dashrath Manji

Brands

921. Parle G is named after a neighbourhood which is also the name of the railway station in the Western suburb of Mumbai. Which suburb is this?
922. The first-ever outlet of this company was opened in 1996, at Bridge Road, Bengaluru. It later got expanded to places like Pakistan, Vienna, Dubai etc. Identify the company.
923. Once Jawahar Lal Nehru noticed that Indian women were spending too much on foreign cosmetics he asked JRD Tata to come up with a desi brand. This is said to be India's first-ever cosmetic brand. Name.
924. Ravi Modi founded this brand with a capital of ₹10000, which later became a giant men's ethnic wear brand. This company later sponsored a few IPL teams and also 2015 Bangladesh Football League. Which clothing brand?
925. In 1949, K R Sundaram Iyer launched this company to import a very famous product which had the trade mark 'Made Like A Gun'. The first factory was opened in Thiruvottiyur in 1956. Identify the company.
926. 'Gattu' is a famous mascot designed by R K Laxman. For which company did he do this work?
927. Manufactured by Mohan Meakin, Ved Ratan Mohan named it after Bene-

dictine hermits who used to produce the same. What is being mentioned here?

928. By 1945, this brand of butter had hit a record production of 3 million pounds every year and it was synonymous with butter just like Xerox is with photocopy. Identify this brand named after a young Parsi boy Pestonji Edulji Dalal.
929. Which brand was started by seven Gujarati women from Mumbai who lived in Lohana Niwas, a group of five buildings in Girgaum?
930. Identify the company established by Rahul Sharma, Rajesh Agarwal, Vikas Jain, Sumeet Arora in 2008.

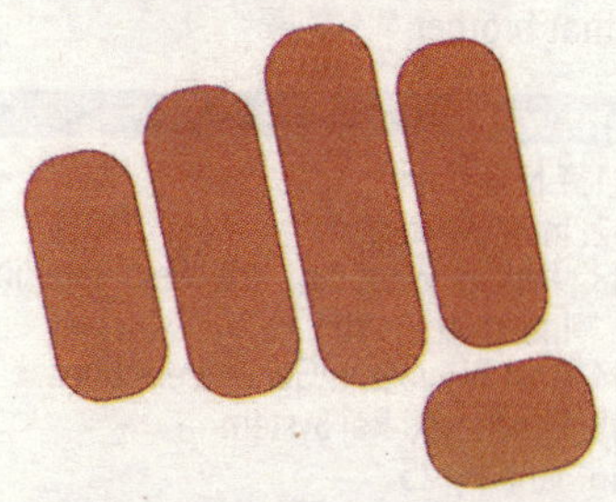

Answers

921. Vile Parle
922. Cafe Coffee Day
923. Lakme
924. Manyavar
925. Madras Motors
926. Asian Paints
927. Old Monk
928. Polson's
929. Lijjat
930. Micromax

Presidents

931. He had served as the president of the constituent assembly of India and also as the first minister of Food and Agriculture in the interim government of 1946. Name this person who is also called Desh Ratna.
932. Which former President, who translated Plato's *Republic* and Edwin Cannan's *Elementary Political Economy* into Urdu, was buried in the Jamia Millia Islamia campus?
933. As the representative of workers, this person had participated in the second Round Table Conference. He was also the governor of Uttar Pradesh and Kerala. Identify this person who was also the acting president of India.
934. This former President had once served as the advocate general of Assam. Who is this?
935. The youngest to occupy Rashtrapati Bhavan, he was the first President elected during a non-Congress regime. Identify.
936. A receiver of Tamra Patra this native of Tanjavore was the eight President of India. Three prime ministers had sworn in during his rule 1987-1992. Who?
937. National Institute of Visual Science and Arts, Kerala is named after this former president, who was a foreign service officer. One of his famous works is '*In the Name of the People: Reflections on Democracy, Freedom and Development*'. Who is this?
938. This former advocate in Delhi High Court contested against Meira Kumar to become the President of India. Name him?
939. This former president had 48 honorary doctorates from universities around the world. Identify this President whose autobiography was translated into 13 languages.
940. B D Jetti was the fifth vice president of India who later became the acting President of the country. Who was the second acting President of India?

Answers

931. Dr.Rajendra Prasad
932. Zakir Hussain
933. V V Giri
934. Fakhruddin Ali Ahmed
935. Neelam Sanjiva Reddy
936. R Venkataraman
937. K R Narayanan
938. Ram Nath Kovind
939. A P J Abdul Kalam
940. Justice Mohammad Hidayatullah

Elections

941. Photographs were added in the voter's identification card when this former cabinet secretary was the Chief Election Commissioner of India. Identify the person.
942. This was first used in India in 1962. Mysore Paints and Varnish Limited is the sole supplier of this. What is mentioned here?
943. Shyam Saran Negi, a school teacher from Himachal Pradesh, holds a very unique record in India. What?
944. K R Narayanan was the first president to break this particular rule in 1998. What did he do?
945. This particular governing system was adopted as per the reports of Balwant Rai Mehta Committee. What?
946. The 11th National Voter's Day was celebrated in 2021. 'Making Our Voters Empowered, Vigilant, Safe and Informed' was the theme of the year. On which date is this observed?
947. A pair of bullocks carrying a yoke was the election symbol of this party in the first-ever general election of India in 1952. Which party?
948. This was introduced in 2013 by Supreme Court of India. One purpose behind this was that more people would show up to cast their vote. It is also said it protects the right to register a negative opinion. What is being mentioned here?
949. This person who contested from Allahabad and defeated a former chief minister in 1984 recorded one of the highest margins ever in the history of Lok Sabha elections in India. Who is this celebrity?
950. Amiya Kumar, an eminent doctor, was the last man to see Rabindranath Tagore alive. His brother's name is also written in golden letters in the election history of India. Identify that brother.

Answers

941. T N Seshan
942. Indelible Ink
943. Person who cast the first vote in Independent India
944. Cast his vote in General elections
945. Panchayati Raj System
946. January 25
947. Indian National Congress
948. NOTA
949. Amitabh Bachchan
950. Sukumar Sen

Jnanpith

951. In the year 1976, when this author won the award for the novel *Prothom Protishruti* (*The First Promise*), the first part of a trilogy, that was one kind of 'First achievement' in the award's history. Who won it?
952. If Umashankar Joshi was the first one to win Jnanpith award for this language, Pannalal Patel the second one and Rajendra Shah the third one, which language are we talking about?
953. *Aag Ka Darya* (*River of Fire*) was a

novel first published in Urdu in the year 1959 in Pakistan, that later on won the Jnanpith award for the author popularly known as "Ainee Apa".Who was this author?

954. *Gyanodaya* was a literary monthly published by the Bharatiya Jnanpith between January, 1949 and February, 1970. When it resumed publication in 2003 its name was given a small change. Identify the changed name.

955. Prof. Shamim Hanfi was the first ever winner of this award given by the Jnanpith trust for senior and celebrated authors above 75 years who have made immense contribution to Indian literature. Name this award.

956. Which award instituted in 1982 is named after the mother of Sahu Santhi Prasad Jain, the founder of Bharatiya Jnanpith?

957. If the first-ever Jnanpith award was presented to Malayalam, the second edition was won by Bengali language. Who was the writer?

958. Winner of the Sahitya Academy award, in the year 1960 for his work Kala Aur Budhdha Chand, he became the first Hindi poet to receive the Jnanpith Award for a collection of his most famous poems titled *Chidambara*. Who is this?

959. In 1956, she became the first woman to win the Sahitya Akademi Award and in 1982 she became the first person to win Bharatiya Jnanpith award for Punjabi language. Identify her.

960. This Jnanpith winner joined San Jose State University in the United States as an Adjunct Professor of Social Sciences and died at San Jose,in the year 1991. Identify him and also identify his language.

Answers

951. Ashapoorna Devi
952. Gujarati
953. Qurratulain Hyder
954. Naya Gyanodaya
955. Jnangarima award
956. Moorti Devi award
957. Tarasankar Bandyopadhyay
958. Sumitranandan Pant
959. Amrita Pritam
960. Gopinath Mohanty, Odia

Automobiles

961. Before launching Nano, dubbed as the world's cheapest car in 2008, Tata launched the first fully indigenous Indian passenger car in the year 1998. What was it called?

962. Literal meaning of this car "she who sits on the lotus" refers to Goddess Lakshmi. Identify the brand known colloquially as the Pad or Fiat.

963. Which company was founded as a steel trading company in the year 1945 in Ludhiana by brothers Kailash Chandra and Jagdish Chandra along with Malik Ghulam Muhammad, the first Finance Minister of Pakistan?

964. The Gurkha is an SUV named after the Gurkha soldiers, manufactured by a company owned by Dr. Abhay Firodia Group, previously known as Bajaj Tempo Motors. Which company?

965. Fondly called the "king of Indian roads", this brand was based on a model first made by Morris Motors Limited at Cowley, Oxford from 1956 to 1959. Which one?

966. If Multix (in collaboration with Polaris) is the lesser-known brand by this company, which is the most popular brand? Also Identify this company whose origin dates back to 1948, when Good Earth Company was established for the distribution and service of im-

ported tractors.

967. Which company was incorporated in 1948 by Raghunandan Saran as a company to assemble and manufacture Austin cars from England and has been named after his son?
968. In 2017 which company partnered with Triumph Motorcycles Ltd, the largest UK-owned motorcycle manufacturer, to build mid-capacity motorcycles in India?
969. Which company established in the year 1982 at Chandigarh was owned by the Sumitomo Corporation and Punjab Tractors Limited, with a technical collaboration with Isuzu and Mazda?
970. Which company was born when the brothers Brij Mohanlal, Dayanand, Satyanand and Om Prakash migrated from their birthplace Kamalia in Pakistan to Amritsar in the year 1944?

Answers

961. Indica
962. Premier Padmini
963. Mahindra & Mahindra
964. Force Motors
965. Ambassador
966. Royal Enfield, Eicher Motors
967. Ashok Motors
968. Bajaj Auto
969. Swaraj Mazda
970. Hero Motors

Beaches

971. Home to many Bollywood celebrities and a significant number of business elite, this beach is known as the "Beverly Hills of Bollywood." Which beach?
972. One of the cleanest beaches in India, this is situated in the Jalalpore taluka, Navsari District, Gujarat. Identify this beach where one can find two monuments of Gandhiji.
973. Situated in Kendrapara district of Odisha, this is the world's most important nesting beach for Olive Ridley sea turtles. Name it.
974. A tag given to environment-friendly clean beaches, equipped with amenities of international standards for tourists, it is a certification by the Foundation for Environmental Education (FEE). Name?
975. Formerly known as Tipu Sultan beach, it has been renamed after the President of a Gulf country. Identify the beach situated in Malappuram district of Kerala.
976. On which coastal city of South India, one can find Ohm beach, named after the Sanskrit letter, the shape of the beach resembling the letter Ohm.
977. This beach was featured among the top 6 best beaches for driving in the world in a BBC article on Autos. Identify this beach considered as the longest Drive-In Beach in Asia.
978. Kailashnath Mahadev statue, the tallest Shiva statue, is in Nepal. On which beach in South India can the second tallest Siva statue be found?
979. Bangaram beach, Kadamat beach and Agatti beach are situated in which Union territory known for its islands?
980. This name is an Anglicised form of 'four channels' or 'four creeks' in

extra

Tagore's Writing

Rabindranath Tagore wrote many of his short stories, in the late 19th and early 20th century, in a bajra or Indian houseboat while traversing the Padma river and its tributaries. He started the English translation of *Gitanjali* on a bajra.

Marathi and is analogous to that of Satpaty, a village in Thane District. Which beach? Also identify this person immortalized in this statue situated over there.

Answers

971. Juhu Beach
972. Dandi beach
973. Gahirmatha Beach
974. Blue Flag
975. Saddam Beach
976. Gokarna
977. Muzhuppilangad beach
978. Murudeswar beach
979. Lakshadweep
980. Chowpatty beach, Tukaram Omble

Forests

981. This state with approximately 80% of its geographical area covered by forests gained Union Territory status in 1972 and had got full statehood in 1987. Which state?
982. If Phoolan Devi is associated with Chambal forest, with which forest would you associate Daku Man Singh and Pan Singh Tomar?
983. Also known as Wayanad Wildlife Sanctuary, this rainforest connects Nagarhole and Bandipur parks in Karnataka and Mudumalai in Tamil Nadu. Name?
984. With which forest would you associate Operation Cocoon launched by the Special Task Force of Tamil Nadu Police to capture the forest brigand Veerappan?
985. Situated in the vicinity of the Aravali hills and Vindhya plateau, this forest is revered for the natural habitat to the significant number of Royal Bengal tigers. Identify this forest in Rajasthan.
986. It is believed that most of the families of this village have been attacked by the man-eater tigers, hence the name Widow Village was given to this village. Identify the forest severely damaged by the cyclone Sidr in 2007, adjacent to which such a village is situated?
987. Which forest situated in the Golaghat and Nagaon regions placed beside the Brahmaputra River on the North and the Karbi Anglong region on the South literally means 'the land of red Goats'.
988. This forest spanning across Chhattisgarh, Orissa and Andhra Pradesh has been the backdrop of many prominent stories mentioned in Ramayana and Mahabharata. Name it.
989. In which state do you find the forests Kanakeswar, Bhandardara, Gautala, Botha and the largest one Tadoba?
990. Molai forest which is located in Majuli Island in Jorhat district of Assam is named after an environmental activist popularly known

extra

Fruit Named After a Famous Victory

The Chausa mango was named after a famous victory that Sher Shah Suri won against the Mughal emperor Humayun in 1539.

as Forest Man of India. Identify him.

Answers

981. Arunachal Pradesh
982. Chambal forest itself
983. Muthanga Wild life sanctuary
984. Satyamangalam forest
985. Ranthambore
986. Sunderbans
987. Kaziranga
988. Dandakaranya
989. Maharashtra
990. Jadav Payeng

Mixed Bag

991. This movie, which has won a total of 102 awards, was added to the *Guinness Book of World Records 2002* edition for winning the most number of awards for a movie. Name it.
992. This art of making jewelry and other handcrafts is known as Scrimshaw. What particular substance is used?
993. The motto of this organization has been taken from the eleventh chapter of the *Gita*, the discourse given by Lord Krishna to Arjuna on the battlefield of Kurukshetra where the great form of the Lord is touching the sky with glory. Which organization?
994. Which Indian automobile brand was incorporated in 1940s in partnership with the first ever Finance Minister of Pakistan Ghulam Mohammed?
995. This commission began its operations in March 2007. Prof. Shantha Sinha was the first chairperson of this commission. Which one?
996. Winner of two national awards for the movies *Lekin* and *Lagaan*, this person is the author of the book *Art of Costume Design* published in the year 2010. Identify the person.
997. One popular story behind the origin of its name is that a violin and some other belongings of Queen Victoria went missing while being unloaded from her ship while on a visit to Mumbai and later were found from this location. Which market is this?
998. Prepared by the First Law Commission, chaired by Thomas Babington Macaulay in 1834, it was adopted by Pakistan, Bangladesh, Colonial Burma, Ceylon, the Straits Settlements (now part of Malaysia), Singapore and Brunei. What is this?
999. This agency set up in 1986 is headquartered in Mahipalpur, Delhi and its motto is 'Empowering Indian Police with Information Technology' Which organization?
1000. The motto of this institution is taken from the *Ishavasya Upanishad* and means 'life eternal through learning'. Identify.

Answers

991. *Kaho Na Pyar Hai*
992. Whale tooth
993. Indian Air Force
994. Mahindra & Mahindra
995. National Commission for the Protection of Child Rights
996. Bhanu Athaiya
997. Chor Bazar
998. Indian Penal Code
999. National Crime Records Bureau
1000. NCERT

SCIENCE AND MEDICINE

Science and Medi-Scan

Hydrogen - Electric Plane

A catchphrase for the transition to a low or zero carbon economy is "electrify everything"–that is, create a world in which most human activities, from manufacturing and construction to transport and tourism, run on electricity generated from low or zero carbon sources such as wind, solar and perhaps nuclear power. In the near and medium term, aviation is, perhaps, foremost among those getting electried.

Before the pandemic, commercial aviation accounted for about 2.5% of global emissions of carbon dioxide (CO_2) accounting for 50% of aviation's contribution to rise in global average temperature. Contrails – watervapour trails from aircraft – are aviation's largest other factor. Importantly in the context of flight, hydrogen packs a lot of energy per unit of mass.

CO_2 emissions per passenger flight have fallen more than 50% since 1990 due to improved engines and operations. But these gains have been overwhelmed by rising volumes of air traffic. It is predicted to reach 10 billion passengers a year by 2050.

Hydrogen, at first glance, looks to be a good solution to the challenge of flying without wrecking the climate. Whether hydrogen is used to power a fuel cell to generate electricity or directly combusted for motive power, the only waste product is clean water.

Importantly in the context of flight, hydrogen packs 3-times more power than conventional jet fuel, and more than a hundred times that of lithium-ion batteries. Hydrogen "is one of the most promising technology vectors to allow mobility to continue fulfilling the basic human need for mobility in better harmony with our environment.

The First Embryo With Human and Non-Human Primate Cells

The journal *Cell*, reported a ground-breaking experiment in which researchers have successfully created the first human-monkey chimera. It describes the first sparks of life (embryogenesis,– how embryos develop) reflected in both human and monkey cells that was cultured for 20 days. Led by Juan Carlos Izpisua Belmonte, a professor in the gene expression laboratory at the Salk Institute for Biological Studies, the study involves understanding the "biggest mystery of human development. While we know a lot about development after we are born, and even a little about what happens during pregnancy, we really don't know anything about human development in the first two or three weeks after fertilization. All we know about early embryogenesis comes from different lab models–from rodents, mice and worms–but we really don't know anything about us."

Learning from the animal world: Belmonte plans to learn the "language" of early human embryo development using this human-monkey model, and then use that to better understand disease–and potentially generate human tissues for organ transplantation.

Question of Ethics: There are serious ethical questions about the implications of combining human cells with those from a different species (even if it is a closely related one like monkeys to create human organs inside monkeys. Creating cross-species mutants to capitalise on specific physical features or characteristics, though not the goal, Belmonte hopes to solve the biological mysteries, and the gaps in knowledge about early development.

The Declassified UFO Report

The US Intelligence Authorization Act - 2021 stipulation mandated the Director of National Intelligence and Secretary of Defense report what the government knows about Unidentified Aerial Phenomena (UAP), to be released to Congress in 180 days. The US UAP Task Force, on June 25, 2021, released a 9-page preliminary assessment stating that they focused on 144 observations of UAP by the US Armed Forces, mostly from US Navy personnel, from 2004–2021. The long-awaited report of mysterious flying objects seen moving through restricted military airspace over the last several decades have been declassified. This is the first time the US government has publicly acknowledged the 140 strange aerial sightings of UAPs and unidentified flying objects (UFOs), by American military forces and others. There were "11 reports of documented instances in which pilots reported near misses with a UAP." The final Report on UFOs, however, was of 17 pages. The Report published by the Office of the Director of National Intelligence, examined 144 reports of UAP, the most direct and substantive US government account ever made public. The UFO report based on the review of 120 incidents infers that •US technology d in most cases and •also does not confirm or rule out alien d. The report points out that "UAP probably lack a single reason and named few categories of potential explanations for the objects observed between 2004 and 2021: Airborne Clutter: "junk — man-made objects cluttering the air, such as balloons or even plastic bags, that are mistaken for craft or affect an operator's ability to identify true targets, such as enemy aircraft. Natural Atmospheric Phenomena: It includes ice crystals, moisture, and thermal variations

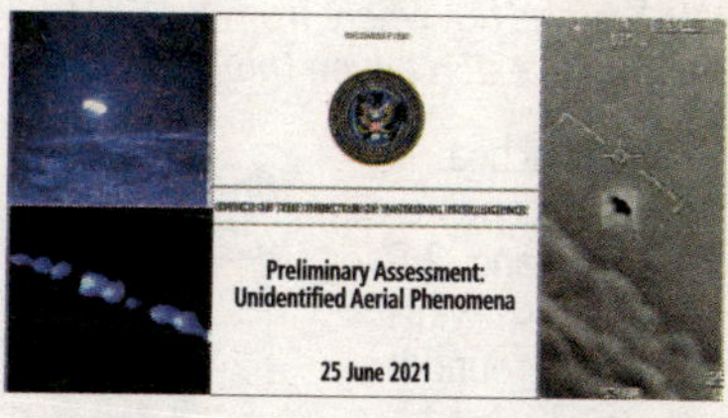

that may register on some infrared and radar systems or cameras and sensors on aircraft or aboard ships at sea. USG or Industry Developmental Programs: Some UAP observations could be attributable to developments and classified programs by US entities or an American corporation. However officials were "unable to confirm" the UAPs are not American technology. Foreign Adversary Systems: Some UAP may be technologies used by China, Russia, or another nation, or a non-governmental entity or aircraft designed by a foreign enemy, making strides in hypersonic technology and directed energy, which "lacked the data" to confirm if the objects reported, were operated by foreign enemy. Other: Most of the UAP described in the dataset probably remain unidentified due to limited data or challenges to collection processing or analysis. It would need extra scientific knowledge to successfully collect on, analyse and characterise some of them.

In short, investigators gave no evidences of sightings that represented either extraterrestrial life or a major technological advancement by a foreign rival. India UFO sightings: 1951 15 Mar: Delhi; 1957 Oct 3: Bihar; 2004 Sep 24: Samudra Tapu; 2007 Oct 29: Kolkata; 2013 Aug 4: Ladakh; 20 Jun:Chennai; 4 Aug- Ladakh & Arunachal Pr.; 2014 Jan 10: Mumbai; 23 July in Lucknow; 2015 Aug 4: Kanpur, UP.

Understanding Our Lungs

We breathe anywhere from 17,000 to 24,000 times a day (or more!), and most of the time we don't even think about it.

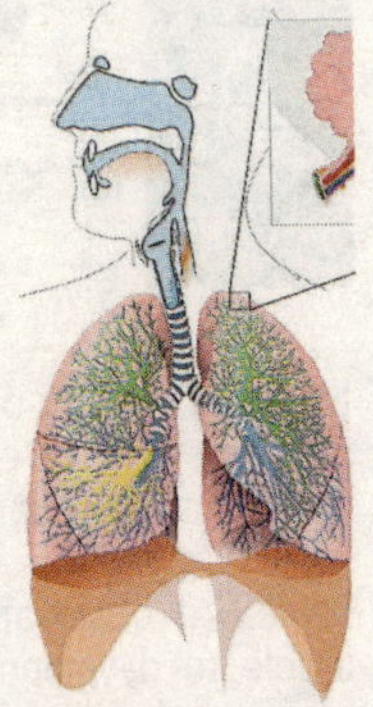

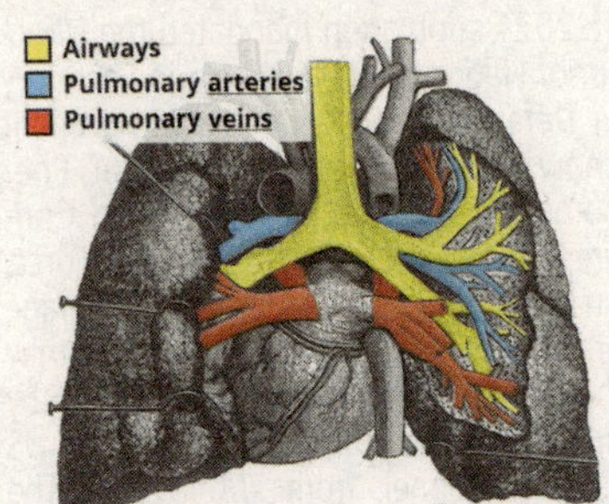

- The Trachea is about 11 centimeters long and 2.5 centimeters wide. Wrapped around it are 16–20 irregular rings composed of hyaline cartilage and elastic fibrous membranes with mucus interior linings, which help provide structure to keep the airway open. At the 5th vertebrae, the trachea divides into two bronchi.
- Division: Our lung have two parts – the left and right lungs, structurally different from each other. The left lung is divided into two lobes: an upper and a lower, and the right lung is divided into three lobes: the superior, the middle, and the inferior.
- Make-up: The lungs are made of a

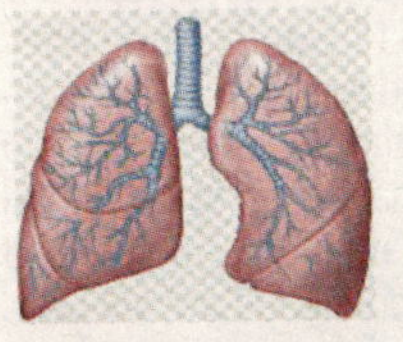

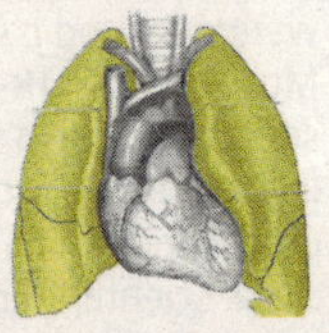

porous spongy texture and are highly elastic. A delicate double layer serous membrane called the pleura covers the surface of the lung and dips into the fissures between the lobes. There is a fluid between the fissures to prevent the lungs from moving and chafing against the thorax wall. The left lung has a indentation (cardiac notch) to accommodate the heart.
- Function: The main function of the lungs is to provide oxygen to capillaries so they can oxygenate the blood.

Fun fact: The total surface area of the lungs varies from 50 to 75 square metres—about the same area as one side of a tennis court!

- Alveoli are tiny, delicate air sacs in which the major and main function of the respiratory system occurs: bringing oxygen into the body and removing carbon dioxide. Tiny pores within the walls of an alveolus allow ventilation with the alveolus next to it. Each lung has about 300 million alveoli. Alveolar sacs are clusters of alveoli, located at the ends of thin airways known as alveolar ducts. The alveoli are surrounded by capillaries.

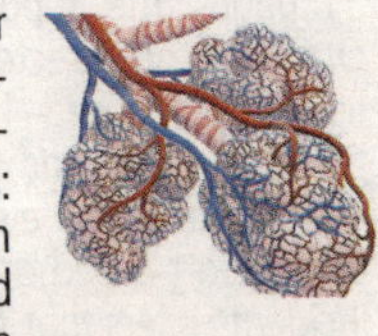

The Largest Living Structure on Earth

The Great Barrier Reef in Australia is known to be the largest living structure on Earth. It spans about 2,000 kilometres and is composed of coral islands and reefs.

Pulmonary Capillaries

The pulmonary arteries branch into arterioles, then into networks of capillaries (tiny blood vessels). Gas exchange occurs across the walls of these capillaries, and the oxygen content of the blood within them rises. The pulmonary veins drain the pulmonary capillaries, carrying oxygen-rich blood to the left atrium of the heart for systemic distribution.

Fun Facts (Respiratory System)

+ You lose a lot of water just by breathing, 17.5 ml per hour!

+ The average time an adult can hold his or her breath is between 30 and 60 seconds.

* According to Guinness World Records, the record for a male voluntarily holding his breath is held by Aleix Segura Vendrell from Spain set in 2016. He held his breath for 24 minutes and 3.45 seconds.

* According to Guinness World Records, the record for a female voluntarily holding her breath is held by Karoline Meyer from Brazil set in 2009. She held her breath for 18 minutes and 32.59 seconds.

• Pulmonary circulation was first described in the 13th century. Arab physician Ibn al-Nafis described the complicated process in 1243.

3D Model for Lungs Developed

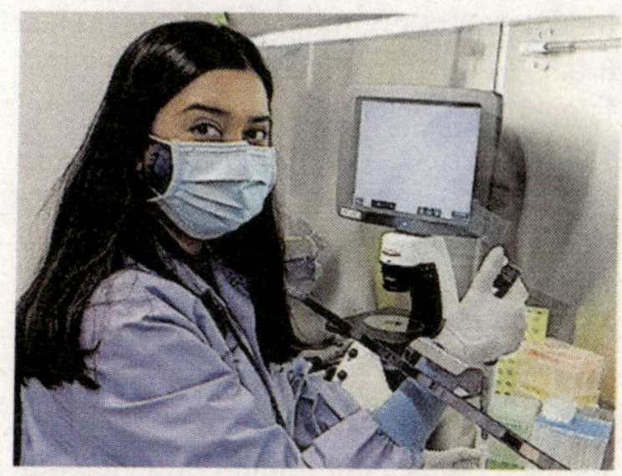

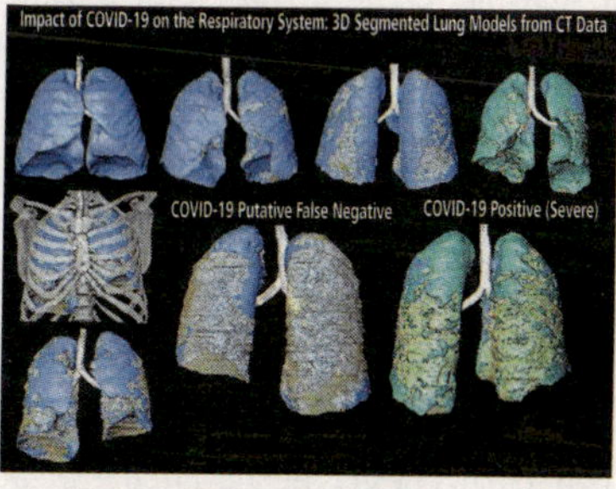

In March 2020, when the Covid-19 hit the world for first wave of, Dr Apoorva Mulay, who hails from Pune, took a challenge to study the impact of the novel coronavirus on the lungs. Using her expertise in model development (simulating an organ in an artificial laboratory environment), Dr Mulay developed 3-dimensional models of the human lungs and studied how SARS-CoV-2 affects it. As a postdoctoral research scientist at the Lung and Regenerative Medicine Institutes at Cedar-Sinai Medical Centre (LA, USA), Dr Mulay's study is the first culture model of the adult human alveoli to be used for studying COVID-19. Dr Mulay found that Covid-19 leads to induction of high levels of inflammation in the stem cells of the alveoli or the bottom part of the lung that is responsible for exchange of oxygen and CO_2 between the lungs and blood, which causes serious symptoms, respiratory failure and death of not just the infected cells, but also the surrounding uninfected cells, leading to lung damage. The Louisiana State University (LSU) team has created 3D digitally segmented models that demonstrate the extent and distribution of the disease. Not only that, but these models could be 3D-printed and used to communicate the impact of the disease to members of the public.

Think Twice: Man has a Second Brain

If you've ever "gone with your gut" to make a decision or felt "butterflies in your stomach" when nervous, you're likely getting signals from an unexpected source: your second brain. Hidden in the walls of the digestive system, this "brain in your gut" is revolutionising medicine's understanding of the links between digestion, mood, health and even the way you think.

Scientists call this little brain the enteric nervous system (ENS). The ENS is known as the "second brain" or the brain in the gut because it is equipped with its own reflexes and senses and can operate independently of the brain and spinal cord, the central nervous system (CNS). The ENS is two thin layers – consists of sheaths of neurons embedded in the walls of the long tube of our gut, or alimentary canal, which measures about 9 metres end to end from the esophagus to the anus. The second brain contains some 100 million neurons, more than in either the spinal cord or the peripheral nervous system.

What Does Your Gut's Brain Control?

Unlike the big brain in our skull, the second brain doesn't help with the great thought processes...religion, philosophy and poetry is left to the brain in the head, but it communicates back and forth with our big brain. According to Jay Pasricha, M.D., director of the Johns Hopkins Center for Neurogastroenterology, whose research on the ENS has garnered international attention – its role in controlling digestion, from swallowing to the release of enzymes that break down food to the control of blood flow that helps with nutrient absorption to elimination." Millions of neurons in the gastrointestinal tract coordinate their activity to generate the muscle contractions that propel waste through the last leg of the digestive system.

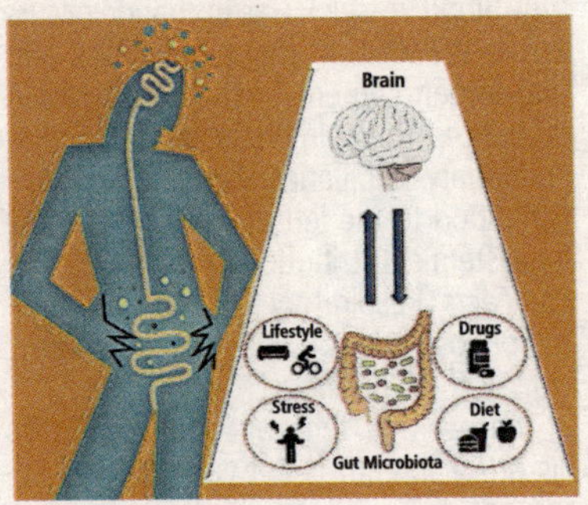

Second Brain Influences Mood, Well-Being

The gastrointestinal tract is sensitive to emotion. Anger, anxiety, sadness, elation — all of these feelings (and others) can trigger symptoms in the gut. The brain has a direct effect on the stomach and intestines. The ENS may trigger big emotional shifts experienced by people coping with irritable bowel syndrome (IBS) and functional bowel problems such as constipation, diarrhea, bloating, pain and stomach upset. In fact, for decades, researchers and doctors thought that anxiety and depression contributed to these problems. But the new studies are finding evidence that irritation in the gastrointestinal system may send signals to the central nervous system (CNS) that trigger mood changes. That explains why a higher-than-normal percentage of people with IBS and functional bowel problems develop depression and anxiety – because up to 30 -40% of the population has functional bowel problems at some point.

New Treatment Opportunities

This new understanding of the ENS-CNS connection helps explain the effectiveness of IBS and bowel-disorder treatments such as antidepressants and mind-body therapies like cognitive behavioral therapy (CBT) and medical hypnotherapy.

Bacteria and Viruses

Antonie Van Leeuwenhoek first observed bacteria in the year 1676, and called them 'animalcules' meaning tiny animal Bacteria are single-celled microorganisms without the nucleus and other cell organelles. So, they are classified as prokaryotic organisms. Some bacteria are good for our bodies – they help keep the digestive system in working order and keep harmful bacteria from moving in. Viruses, are genetic material (DNA or RNA) packaged inside of a protein coating. They need to use another cell's structures to reproduce meaning they can't survive unless they're living inside something else (like a person, animal, or plant).

Difference between Bacteria and Virus

Bacteria	Virus
• Bacteria are generally larger. Size ranges between 900 – 1000nm • Bacteria have a lipopolysaccharide or Peptidoglycan-based cell wall • Bacteria are classified as living organisms Ribosomes are present in bacteria	• Viruses are generally smaller. Size ranges between 30-50nm • Viruses are neither living nor non-living • A virus needs a host to complete its reproductive cycle • Ribosomes are absent in virus • The cell wall is
• Most bacteria can reproduce without a host • Example Diseases: Gastritis, food poisoning, ulcers, meningitis, and pneumonia • Antibiotics are effective for bacterial infections • Antibiotics: Vibrio cholerae, Staphylococcus aureus	absent in viruses. Instead, a capsid (protein coat) is present • Example Disease: AIDS, common cold, influenza, and chickenpox • Antiviral drugs are prescribed for viral infections • Antiviral Drugs: Hepatitis A virus, HIV, Rhinovirus

Endemic, Epidemic, Pandemic

The spread of infectious diseases are by either bacterial or viral agents and are ever-present in society. Infected cases are usually present in numbers below an expected threshold but every once in a while there may be an outbreak, a new strain or a new disease that has a significant impact at either a local or global level. The spread and rate of new cases are classified as: Endemic – is a disease that is present permanently in a region or population.

Epidemic - is an outbreak that affects many people at one time and can spread through one or several communities. •An agent moving between host populations, for example moving from animals to humans (zoonotic diseases) •A genetic change

Endemic Epidemic Pandemic

(mutation) in the infectious agent, eg bacteria, virus, fungi or parasite. • Introduction of new pathogens to a host population. Epidemics can follow predictable patterns, can be monitored, and are predictable.

Pandemic – is an epidemic when the spread is global. •Affects globally •Infects people globally •Often caused by a new virus or a new strain of a virus •Quick spread in humans• high number of deaths • Cause social disruption, unrest and economic loss.

Pandemic Phases and Waves

In nature, influenza viruses circulate continually among animals, especially birds and such viruses might theoretically develop into pandemic viruses

Phase 1 No animal influenza virus circulating among animals have been reported to cause infection in humans.

Phase 2 An animal influenza virus circulating in domesticated or wild animals is known to have caused infection in humans and is therefore considered a specific-potential, pandemic threat

Phase 3 An animal or human animal influenza reassortant virus has caused sporadic cases or small clusters of disease in people, but has not resulted in human-to-human transmission sufficient to sustain community-level outbreaks.

Phase 4 Human to human transmission of an animal or human animal. Influenza reassortant virus able to sustain, community-level outbreaks has been verified

Phase 5 The same identified virus has caused sustained community-level outbreaks in two or more countries in one WHO region

Phase 6 In addition to the criteria, defined in faces five. The same virus has caused sustained Community level outbreaks, at least, one other country in another WHO region

Post Peak Period Level of pandemic influenza in most countries with adequate surveillance have dropped below peak levels

Post Pandemic Period Levels of influenza activity, have returned to the levels seen for seasonal, influenza in most countries with adequate surveillance.

What is a Covid-19 Wave?

Some of the infectious diseases take epidemic or pandemic proportions such as Covid-19 and swine flu. When their progress over time is graphed on paper, they form a crest-trough pattern (showing the incidents of infection peaked at a certain time frame followed by a valley) of an epidemic or pandemic, called a 'wave'. But not all infectious diseases follow this pattern -- like AIDS and TB. There are some other diseases that follow a seasonal wave pattern, like the viruses that cause common cold seasonally. There is no fixed definition of a wave of a pandemic. A pandemic wave is identified on the basis of certain characteristics. For example, Covid-19 pandemic is often compared with the 1918-20 Spanish Flu pandemic in terms of the nature of transmission and expanse of spread. The Spanish Flu had three distinct waves. The recent H1N1 influenza pandemic of 2009-10 had two distinct waves. Covid-19, for example, has seen two nationwide waves in India.

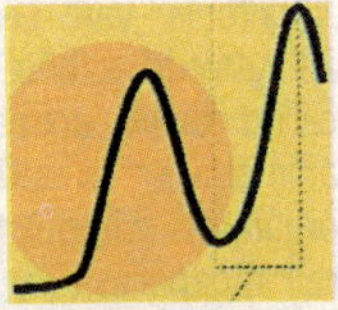

According to the WHO, for one wave of a pandemic to end, "the virus has to be brought under control and cases have to fall substantially Then for a second wave to start, you need a sustained rise in infections". A study, published in February 2021, proposed to offer a working definition of epidemic waves based on R-factor (where R is the reproduction number), the average number of people infected by one infectious person. If R is greater than 1, it indicates a rise in cases of the epidemic or pandemic. "If R is much larger than 1 for a long period, we identify that time period as an upward period, and inversely, If R is much smaller than 1 for a long period, it is a downward period". It means that during the valley time, a pandemic may be laying the seeds for the next wave.

Coronavirus Variants

Viruses constantly change through mutation, and new variants of a virus are expected to occur. Sometimes new variants emerge and disappear. Other times, new variants persist. Multiple variants of the virus that causes COVID-19 have been documented globally during this pandemic.

Viruses change and become more diverse. Scientists monitor these changes, including changes to the spikes on the surface of the virus. By carefully studying viruses, scientists can learn how changes to the virus might affect how it spreads and how sick people will get from it.

B.1.1.7 (Alpha): First detected in the UK and USA in Dec 2020 – was already 50% more contagious than the original coronavirus first identified in China in 2019.

B.1.351 (Beta): Initially detected in South Africa in December 2020.

P.1 (Gamma): P.1 was initially identified in travelers from Brazil in 2020.

B.1.617.2 (Delta): This variant was first detected in India in December 2020.

C.37 (Lamda): It is a SARS-CoV-2 variant, first detected in Peru in Dec 2020. WHO named it Lambda in June 2021

B.1.525 (The Eta) The first cases were detected in December 2020 in the UK and Nigeria. Later found in France, Denmark...

B.1.526 (Iota) was discovered in November 2020, in New York City.

B.1.617 (The Kappa) a mutant variant which was was first detected in India in December 2020.

B.1.621 (Mu) is a new variant first detected in Colobmia in Jan 2021 is now found in 40 countries. Capable of eveding antibodies. WHO rated it a a variant of interest and concern.It has number of mutants.

C.1.2 is a new variant of interest. First identified in May 2021 in S. Africa. Spreads 1.7 times faster. It has 41 mutations per year and found in 7 other countries.

The Delta Variant

The Delta variant has mutations on the spike protein that make it easier for it to infect human cells. It is about 50% more contagious than the Alpha variant. It spread rapidly and is now reported in 104 countries – making up more than 97% of new COVID-19 cases. The average persons Delta spreads to is more than 7 people, as compared with two other people through the original coronavirus strain. The Delta variant may escape protection from vaccines and some COVID-19 treatments.

Rate of Spread of Different Viruses

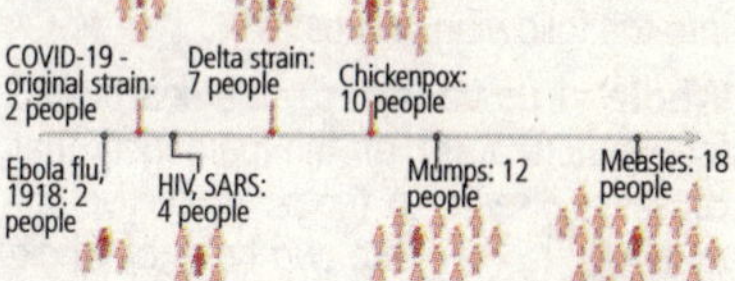

What is the Delta Plus variant? The Delta Plus (B.1.617.2.1 or AY.1), is a "sub-variant" of the Delta version. It has a mutation that allows the virus to better attack lung cells and potentially escape vaccines. First identified in India, Delta Plus has now been found in a dozen countries.

The Symptoms Persistent cough, headache, fever, sore throat, and runny nose seem to be more common. Loss of smell and taste seems to be less common.

Is the Delta variant more deadly? Based on hospitalisations, Yes!

What does the Delta variant mean for the unvaccinated? People who aren't fully vaccinated against COVID-19 are at risk.

What does the Delta variant mean for the vaccinated? Delta variant can cause breakthrough cases, or infections among people who are fully vaccinated.

The Vaccines

The COVID19 vaccines were designed to prevent severe illness, not infection. It intends to prevent hospitalisation and death, the worst outcomes of infection, mainly the damage to the lungs and other organs. The vaccines produce antibodies in the blood that prevent the coronavirus from taking root in those organs. But the infection begins when people inhale or ingest the virus through the nose or the throat. Some antibodies produced by the vaccines do seem to be present in nasal secretions and saliva, and were probably enough to thwart previous variants of the virus. Delta offers a tough challenge. Vaccines, presently, being studied for COVID-19, can be categorised into the following groups:

Whole virus vaccines use a deactivated (attenuated) form of the pathogen that causes a disease to trigger protective immunity to it. There are two types of whole virus vaccines. Live attenuated vaccines use a weakened form of the virus, which can still grow and replicate, but does not cause illness. Inactivated vaccines contain viruses whose genetic material has been destroyed by heat, chemicals or radiation so they cannot infect cells and replicate, but can still trigger an immune response. Both are tried and tested vaccination strategies.

Vector vaccine (Viral vector-based) don't actually contain antigens, but rather use the body's own cells to produce them. In this type of vaccine, genetic material from the COVID-19 virus is placed in a modified version of a different virus (viral vector). When the viral vector gets into your cells, it delivers genetic material from the COVID-19 virus that gives your cells instructions to make copies of the S-protein. Once your cells display the S-proteins on their surfaces, your immune system responds by creating antibodies and defensive white blood cells. In another words, it triggers a strong cellular immune response by T cells as well the production of antibodies by B cells. If you later become infected with the COVID-19 virus, the antibodies will fight the virus. Viral vector vaccines can't cause you to become infected with the COVID-19 virus or the viral vector virus. Also, the genetic material that's delivered doesn't become part of your DNA. The J&J COVID-19 vaccine is a vector vaccine. AstraZeneca of the University of Oxford is a vector COVID-19 vaccine. .

Protein subunit vaccine. Subunit vaccines include only the parts of a virus that best stimulate your immune system. This type of COVID-19 vaccine contains harmless S-proteins. Once your immune system recognises the S-proteins, it creates antibodies and defensive white blood cells.

Messenger RNA (mRNA) vaccine – uses genetically engineered mRNA to give your cells instructions for how to make the S protein found on the surface of the COVID-19 virus. After vaccination, your immune cells begin making the S-protein pieces and displaying them on cell surfaces. This causes your body to create antibodies. If you later become infected with the COVID-19 virus, these antibodies will fight the virus. After delivering instructions, the mRNA is immediately broken down. It never enters the nucleus of your cells, where your DNA is kept. [Pfizer-BioNTech, Moderna use mRNA.]

World First: India's DNA ZyCoV-D

ZyCoV-D is India's first DNA vaccine to be approved anywhere in the world. It uses strands of DNA to prime the immune system against the virus SARS-CoV-2. It is administered into the skin without an injection. It provides 67% protection. If DNA vaccines prove to be successful. It is really the future of vaccinology; an important step forward in the fight to defeat COVID-19 globally.

Q&A

What is Long COVID syndrome?

The vaccination drive for COVID-19 is taking place all around the world including India, even as people of all age groups continue to test positive on a daily basis. While a significant number of patients recover from the coronavirus infection with proper medical treatment after 14 days when the viral vector weakens in the body, unfortunately some discomforting symptoms of COVID-19 linger for several weeks or even months after therapy in some people. Long COVID-19 is not contagious, but it invariably hampers the day-to-day productivity of those affected and they take a long time to regain their optimal health and stamina.

The Symptoms Of Long COVID?
• extreme tiredness or undue fatigue •shortness of breath, heart palpitation, chest pain or tightness • problems with memory and concentration (brain fog) • joint and muscle pain • persistent sinusitis, fever, sore throat, headaches, cold, • anosmia (loss of sense of smell), •ageusia (inability to distinguish tastes) • a decline in nervous system functions due to brain fog, anxiety, depression.

What is Breakthrough Infection?

No vaccine is 100% effective. Dr. Jonas Salk's polio vaccine was 80%-90% effective in preventing paralytic disease. Even for the gold standard measles vaccine, the efficacy was 94% among a highly vaccinated population during large outbreaks. Comparably, clinical trials found the Inactivated cold virus Covishield and Covaxin were 80% and 90% effective at preventing symptomatic COVID-19 and much more protective than initially hoped.

The Efficacy: A vaccine efficacy of 90-95% does not mean that the shot protects 90-95% of people while the other 5% will contract the virus. Vaccine efficacy is a measure of relative risk – you need to compare a group of vaccinated people to a group of unvaccinated people under the same exposure conditions. So if we consider a three-month study period during which 100 out of 10,000 unvaccinated people got COVID-19. We would expect five vaccinated people to get sick during that same time. That's 5% of the 100 unvaccinated people who fell ill, not 5% of the whole group of 10,000.

When people get infected after vaccination, scientists call these cases "breakthrough" infections because the virus broke through the protective barrier the vaccine provides.

How common is COVID-19 infection in the fully vaccinated? Breakthrough infections are a little more frequent than previously expected and are probably increasing because of growing dominance of the Delta variant. But infections in vaccinated people are less and usually said to cause mild or asymptomatic (no symptoms).

What is Flattening the Coronavirus_Curve?

Flattening the curve is a strategy in public health to slow down the spread of the SARS-CoV-2 virus during the COVID-19 pandemic. The curve being flattened is the epidemic curve, a visual representation of the number of infected people needing health care over time. During an epidemic, a health care system can break down when

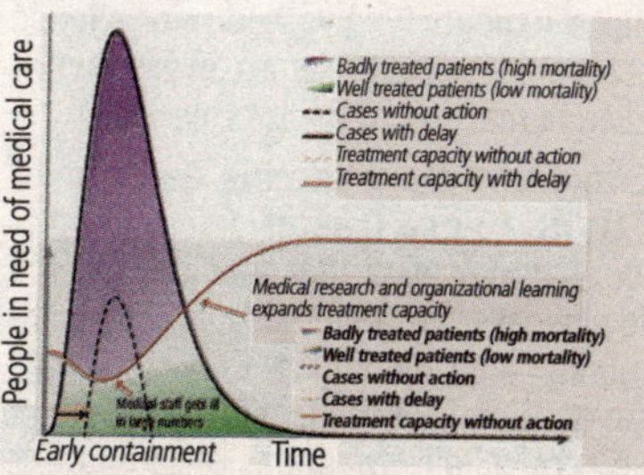

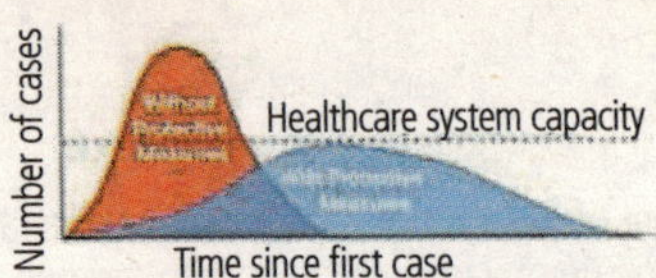

the number of people infected exceeds the capability of the health care system's ability to take care of them. Flattening the curve means slowing the spread of the epidemic so that the peak number of people requiring care at a time is reduced, and the health care system does not exceed its capacity. Flattening the curve relies on mitigation techniques such as hand washing, use of face masks and social distancing.

What are the Benefits of Getting a COVID-19 Vaccine?

A COVID-19 vaccine might: •Prevent you from getting COVID-19 or from becoming seriously ill and dying.• Prevent you from spreading the COVID-19 virus to others • Add to the number of people in the community who are protected from getting COVID-19 — making it harder for the disease to spread and contributing to herd immunity • Prevent the COVID-19 virus from spreading and replicating, which allows it to mutate and possibly become more resistant to vaccines.

What are the Side Effects?

The major one is blood clot in the brain. The other side effects are mild. Some of them are quite common – injection site reactions, fevers, chills, and aches and pains. In a small subset of patients – those patients who've had prior allergic reactions – some patients can experience allergic reaction to the vaccine.

Can a COVID-19 Vaccine Cause COVID-19 in a Person?

No. Keep in mind that vaccines takes a few weeks for your body to build immunity after getting a COVID-19 vaccination. In between, it's possible that you could have symptoms of coronavirus infection after being vaccinated.

Do the COVID-19 Vaccines Protect Against the COVID-19 Variants?

•The COVID-19 vaccines were developed based on the S-protein before it contained the mutations identified in the variants. While research suggests that COVID-19 vaccines have lower efficacy against the variants, the vaccines still appear to provide protection against severe COVID-19. Further research is needed.

•In addition, vaccine manufacturers are also creating booster shots to improve protection against variants.

INDIA: a COVID-19 Vaccine Hub

With global mass COVID-19 vaccination campaigns, there is an emerging gap between rich and poor countries in their capacity to secure sufficient vaccines for their citizens. Wealthy countries have been accused of hoarding vaccines, mostly from Pfzer-BioNTech and Moderna. This has created opportunities for India, China and to an extent Russia to cater to the developing countries.

India has the ability to manufacture >3 billion doses annually. As per the Coalition for Epidemic Preparedness Innovations (CEPI), ~2-4 billion doses of COVID-19 vaccines will be produced by global companies, where India is anticipated to capture a major share on account of its lower vaccine price as compared with its global counterparts. At present, AstraZeneca and Serum Institute of India launched their vaccines; this action was followed by licensed production of foreign vaccines in India like Sputnik V by Zydus Cadila, Dr. Reddy's/Hetero and Bharat Biotech, Biological E, Indian Immunologicals and Mynvax.

Potential Animal Virus for Next Pandemic

The biggest killers of humanity, pathogens, either evolve from old pathogens or jump from other species to humans. The second way, the more common one in history, is born out of our growing contact with animals in the wild and in farms. Scientists have long tracked viruses that can potentially make the leap to people and have published a risk assessment tool for policymakers and researchers to identify such infections, known as zoonotic diseases, or zoonoses. Here 40 viruses are listed that have been evaluated - poses the greatest threat to human health. Potentially, **250 zoonotic viruses** – can spillover from animals to humans and cause disease.

Viruses that are at most risk of spilling over (measured with a risk combining 3 factors –Virus, Environment ,Host)

Lassa virus ^
SARS-COV-2*
Ebola virus ^
Seoul virus •
Nipah virus *
Hepatitis E virus•
Marburg virus ^
Simian immunodeficiency virus *
Rabies virus •
Lymphocyte thortomeningitis virus •
Simian foamy virus •
SARS coronavirus •
Coronavirus229E (Bat strain) ^
Rousettus bat coronavirus HKU9 •
SARS-re!ated betacoronavims Rp3 ^
European bat lyssavirus 1 ^
Andes virus ^
Murine coronavirus •
Puumala virus ^
Cháerephon bat coronavirus/Kenya/KY22/2006 ^
Coronavirus PREDICT CoV-35 *
Borna disease virus *
Longquan Aa mouse coronavirus *
Monkeypox virus *
European bat lyssavirus 2 ^
Laguna Negra virus ^
Eidolon bat coronavirus/Kenya/KY24/2006 ^
Cowpox virus ^
Coronavirus PREDICT CoV-24 *
Macaque Foamy virus•
Rodent coronavirus ^
Sin Nombre virus ^
Human mastadenovirus G*
Coronavirus PREDICT CoV-22*
Reston virus *
Bombali Virus ^
Coronavirus HKU1 ^
Kenya bat coronavirus/BtKY56/BtKY55 ^
Paramyxovirus PREDICT PMV-10 ^
Bat coronavirus 1*

Viruses Detected in India

Two viruses in the SpillOver list have been detected in wildlife in India: Rousettus bat coronavirus HKU9, with a risk score of 8Q:Bat adenovirus isolate 1050597, with a score of 64.

75% of emerging infectious diseases originate from animals

5 L animal viruses have the potential to be zoonotrc, though the viruses in them are not equally risky for us

887 viruses – the ranked database lists, with 38 known to be zoonotic. Influenza would have topped the list, but flu viruses were left out as they are tracked elsewhere

65 experts were consulted to make the list. A weighted average score for each risk factor was assigned based on the experts' opinion on the degree of risk

Note: Host species are only for mammals, birds, reptiles, and amphibians. Risk factors were based on previous spillovers, so new threats. could emerge in the future from different sources. **31** risk factors considered: 9 Host, 16 Virus, 6 Environment.

COVID-19 and Homoeopathy

Dr. Sunil M. Thomas BHMS, DGC, MD (Hom)
Soukhya Speciality Centre for Allergy, Manjadi, Thiruvalla.

Medicine that offers intervention as a preventive or control the quick spread and reducing the severity in any epidemic or pandemic is welcome. This article takes a look at how Homoeopathy addresses COVID-19 as an alternate support to a large population size at the shortest time. Its effectiveness towards Chikungunya, Dengue Fever, Cholera, Spanish flu, acute respiratory syndrome and influenza is proven in the past.

The hottest talk of the century is nothing but COVID-19, since December 2019. This corona virus has infiltrated our homes, and transformed it into quarantine lodges. The virus has made our educational institutions and work places lifeless. The market places and business malls have closed down. The worship places have become deserted. This microscopic virus has created a macroscopic phobia, which weakens our mental status and makes us susceptible to it. It has engrossed our youngsters with anxiety about future, studies and career. Yet another group struggles with depression, due to business failure and financial crisis, leading to suicidal tendency and drug abuse.

What are the common symptoms?

•fever •cough •shortness of breath

Other symptoms: •loss of smell •loss of taste•sore throat •running/ stuffy nose •body pain •headache •chills •fatigue •diarrhea / nausea.

Preventing the spread of COVID-19?

As the age old saying goes, "Prevention is better than cure."

- The SMS: Sanitiser, Mask & Social distancing
- Eat balanced & healthy food; more vegetables & fruits; more fish; more water- hydrate your body; avoid processed & fast foods.

- Have a sound sleep: 6-8 hours of sleep
- Regular exercise: 20-30 mins/day
- Stay connected: through social media - with family members; - friends &relatives
- Healthy mind: have a heart of gratitude; have a timetable for yourself and get yourself engaged; reach out to those in need.
- Homeopathic immunity booster:

In the month of March 2020, the Ministry of Ayush had recommended the use of Arsenicum album 30, a homoeopathic medicine, as an Immunity booster in the fight against COVID-19.

Working of Homeopathic medicine

We've all seen at some point in our lives,a collection of bottled sweet pills. While most have experienced the cure from these Homoeopathic medicines, few others disregard these as placebo. Homoeopathy is based on the principle of 'like cures like.' It is postulated that it works on the principle of 'Hormesis', where a low dose of a drug produces a curative action on the body.

Two studies headed by the IIT Bombay research team (Dr. Jayesh Bellare & Dr. Prashant Chikramane), made ground breaking discovery about the presence of nanoparticles & hormetic activation of Homoeopathic medicines.

A 2014 meta-analysis of placebo-controlled double-blind RCTs (by Dr. Robert Mathie), showed that individualised Homeopathic treatment was 1.5 to 2 times effective than placebo.

Any scientific evidence for Arsenicum album 30?

Artificial intelligence, through computational biology, found that Arsenicum album helps in repairing 16/17 signaling pathways of the human body, that gets affected when a person is infected with novel coronavirus (International Journal of Biomedical Informatics, 2021)

Is there any side effect for Arsenicum album 30?

Since Homoeopathy uses ultra-high dilutions of an active ingredient in low doses, there's 0% chance of any side effects. This is substantiated by the principle of Hormesis.

Was Homoeopathy effective in past epidemics?

Track record of Homeopathy in epidemics

Epidemic	Mortality rate	
	Conventional Medicine	Homeopathic Medicine
Typhus 1813	30%	1.5%
Cholera 1830	40%	7-10%
Cholera 1854	59%	9%
Yellow fever 1850	15%	6%
Yellowfever 1878	50%	5.6%
Diphtheria 1862	83%	16.4%
Cholera 1892	42%	15%
Spanish flu 1918	30%	1.05%

Source: Influenza 1918: Homoeopathy to the Rescue (The New England Journal of Homoeopathy 1998, Vol 7, No. 1)

In 2003,Homeopathic preventive medicine for dengue fever showed a protection rate of 86%, observed in 3 districts of Kerala, India.

Is Homoeopathy effective in treating COVID-19 disease?

Homoeopathy treats the patient in the disease & not just the disease in the person. Therefore, it is effective in symptomatically treating mild to moderate cases of COVID19 & thereby preventing complications. It is been used as a treatment modality in various states of the country.

Homeopathy has also been found effective in treating post-covid complications.

As Homeopathy is a holistic system of Medicine, it effectively treats both the physical and mental states of a person.

Being the second largest system of medicine in the world, Homoeopathy, focuses on developing the body's defense mechanism, rather than targeting the disease agent (bacteria, virus, parasite), thereby promoting perfect wellbeing of the individual, society and the nation.

Human Body Make Up: Curious Facts

The Skeletal System (Bones)

- There are 206 bones in the skeletal system of an adult. Bones of hands and feet alone constitute 50% of the total bones in the human body.
- A new born baby has 300 bones, out of which 94 bones fuse together as he/she grows.
- The largest bone of human body is the femur in the thigh which constitute about 27.5% of a person's stature, average length of this bone is aL 50 cm.
- The shortest bone in the human body is the stapes bone in the middle ear.

Composition of Bones

Organic Matter	33.30%
Phosphate of Lime	51.04%
Carbonate of Lime	11.30%
Flouride of Calcium	2.00%
Phosphate of Magnesia	1.16%
Soda/Chloride of Sodium	1.00%

Muscular System

Muscles are tissues attached to bones and composed of fibres. They are capable of contracting and relaxing to effect body movement.

Total Number of Muscles There are about 630 important muscles in the human body. They account for about 40% of the body weight.

Largest Muscle The bulkiest muscle in the body is gluteus maximus (buttock muscle).

Longest Muscle Sartorius is the longest muscle in the body which originates in the upper part of the hip bone and is attached to the tibia bone of the leg.

Smallest Muscle Stapedius muscle in the middle ear is less than 1/20 of an inch. Muscles • It takes the interaction of 72 different muscles to produce human speech. • One uses 14 muscles to smile and 43 to frown. • The strongest muscle of the body is the masseter muscle, which is located in jaw.

Main Organs

Skin Skin covers the muscles of the body and is said to be the largest organ of the human body. In an adult man skin cover is about 1.9 m^2 and a woman has about 1.6 m^2 of skin. Skin • Each square inch of human skin consists of 600 cm of blood vessels. • Most people shed 20kg of skin in a lifetime. • The thickness of the skin varies from 1/2 to 6 mm, depending on the area of your body. The skin is the largest body organ which stretches across an area of 2 square metres and accounts for approximately 15% of the body weight.

Heart The heart is situated in the centre of the thorax, just behind the breast the breast-bone (sternum) and is enclosed in a tough membrane called the pericardium.

Its average weight is about 340 grams in men and 225 grams in women. Contraction and relaxation mechanism of the ventricles results in a heart beat of about 70-72/ min in males and 78-82/min in females.

Contraction of ventricles is called systole and relaxation is called diastole. Circulation of blood in the body is regulated by the heart. Heart •Our heart beats about 100,000 times/day. • Placed end-to-end all our body's blood vessels would measure about 90,000 kms. • The heart produces enough pressure to squirt blood 900cm. • About 5-6 litres of blood is filtered by 2 million nephrons 37 times a day.

Respiratory System

Lungs A pair of spongy organs consisting of elastic tissues situated in the chest cavity. There are two lungs, the right lung is larger than the left. Together they weigh between 1.18 and 1.19 kg in a healthy adult.

Their main function is to purify blood and supply oxygen to it. The entire blood supply (4.5 to 5 litres) washes through the lungs about once a minute. •If all the airways running through the lungs are connected, they can go up to the length of 2,400 kilometres!

Excretory System

Kidneys The two kidneys are situated in the upper posterior of the abdominal cavity, one on each side of the vertebral column. Each kidney is approximately 10 cm long, 5 cm wide and 2.5 cm thick. They filter nitrogenous waste of the body from the blood and throw it out in the form of urine.

Nervous System

Human Brain •The master organ brain is the control centre of the body, acting just like the CPU of a computer. •Consists of two parts: the brain located in the skull and the spinal cord located in the vertebral column. • The weight of the average human brain triples between birth and adulthood. The final weight of the brain in an adult male is about 1.4 kg (and 1.3 kg in the case of a woman) which averages about 3% of the body weight. • The brain uses about 20% of the oxygen a man breathes, 20% of calories a man takes in, and about 15% of body blood. • Our brain sends messages at the rate of 375 kmph. • The energy used by the brain is enough to light a 10-20 watt bulb. • The average human brain has about 100 billion nerve cells. •Brain remains the least explored human body organ. Though accounting for just 2% of weight, the master organ utilises around 20% of the total oxygen as well as energy required by the body. •With 60% of the dry weight contributed by fats, the brain happens to be the fattiest organ.

Digestive System

Tongue • The five taste zones on our tongue are bitter (back), sour (back sides),

Human Organs

Every organ is derived from one or more of the 4 basic tissue types **Epithelium:** the single layer of cells that line our skin, throat, bowels and internal organs. **Connective**: the turf, fibres and support systems that are found in organs and body systems, **Muscle**: the smooth muscles and skeletal muscles and **Nerve:** tissues that cover them.

80 Organs in the Human Body:

Adenoids
Adrenal glands
Appendix
Arteries
Bladder
Bones
Bone marrow
Brain
Breast
Bulbourethral glands
Clitoris
Cochlear
Colon
Diaphragm
Duodenum
Ears
Epididymis
Esophagus
Eyes
Fallopian tubes
Gall Bladder
Heart
Hypothalamus
Ileum
Interstitium*
Jejunum
Kidneys
Large Intestine
Larynx (voice box)
Liver
Lungs
Lymph Nodes
Mesentery*
Nose
Ovaries
Pancreas
Parathyroid glands
Parotid glands
Pineal gland
Pharynx
Pituitary gland
Prostate
Rectum
Seminal vesicles
Skin
Spinal Cord
Spleen
Stomach
Sublingual glands
Submandibular glands
Teeth
Testes
Thymus gland
Tonsils
Tongue
Trachea
Thyroid
Ureter
Urethra
Uterus
Vagina
Vas deferens
Vulva

salty (front sides), sweet (front) and savory or Umami (middle). Fat is considered as the sixth.

Stomach • We get a new stomach lining every 3-4 days. If we didn't, the strong acids our stomach uses to digest food would also digest our stomach. • The stomach takes 20 minutes to tell the brain that it is full and that one should stop eating. • The small intestine is about 750cm long.• The large intestine is 150 cm long and 3 times wider than the small intestine.

Liver The liver, situated on the right side of the stomach is the largest gland in the human body. It weighs around 1.5 to 2 kgs. The gall bladder is attached to the liver and stores bile produced by it. The liver is responsible for the metabolism of the products of digestion and storage and release of substances (principally glucose) so as to maintain their constant level in blood. •The liver is not only the hottest but also the largest and metabolically most complex internal organ of our body. • The liver is the only major organ in the human body that can regenerate itself if part of it is removed.•The only organs in human body that can float on water are the lungs as they can hold nearly a litre of air at any moment.

Eyes • Each of our eyes has 120 M rods, which help us see in black and white. • Each eye has 6M cones, which help us see in colour. • We blink our eyes about 20,000 times a day • An eyelash lives about 150 days before it falls out. • Women blink twice as much as men. • If one is blind in one eye, he only loses about 1/5 of vision and the sense of depth. • Our eyes are always the same size from birth, but our nose and ears never stop growing.

Growth by Numbers

- Head hair grows 0.35 mm/day
- Wisdom tooth enamel stops growing when you're 12 years old
- Liver cells are replaced every 300 to 500 days
- Fingernails grow 0.1 mm/day
- Skin cells are replaced every 39 days
- The skeleton is replaced every 10 years
- Toenailsgrow Imm/month
- Cerebellum grey matter stops growing between 2.5 and 3 years old
- Heart endothelial cells are replaced ever 6 years
- Heart muscle cells stop growing at 10 years old
- RBC are replaced every 120 days
- Fat storage cells are replaced every 10 years

Nose • The nose can remember 50,000 scents. • When you sneeze, air rushes through your nose at the rate of 156 kmph.

Finger Nail • A finger nail takes about 6 months to grow from base to tip.• The length of the finger shows how fast the fingernail grows. The nail on the middle finger grows fastest. On an average our toenails grow twice as slow as our fingernails. • Hair is made of the same substance as fingernails.

Others

• Babies are born without knee cap. They don't appear till they are 2-6 years of age. • Children grow faster in the spring season. • The thyroid cartilage is more commonly known as the Adam's apple. • It's impossible to sneeze with open eyes. •A pair of feet has 500,000 sweat glands.

Blood Groups

extra

Grouping human blood types can be a difficult process and there are currently around 30 recognised blood types (or blood groups). You might be familiar with the more simplified "ABO" system which categorises blood types under O, A, B and AB.

Disabilities in Learning

What do Albert Einstein, HG Wells, Vincent Van Gogh, Steven Spielberg, Charles Schwab, Steve Jobs, Erin Brockovich, Michael Phelps, Whoopi Goldberg, Hrithik Roshan, Abhishek Bachchan, Boman Irani, have in common? All these celebrities had to grapple with learning disabilities (LD) to be successful in life.

It is sad that children with LD are called 'slow' or 'dumb' even today. Every individual's brain is wired differently. Our education system needs reforms to adapt so that children with LD are able to learn, thrive and become achievers in their own right.

Types of Learning Disabilities

Dyslexia It affects an individual's ability to break words down into phonemes. This affects the development of their skills in reading, writing and spelling. Though such persons are highly intelligent and creative, they still struggle with basic literacy skills, phonics, and pronouncing words. It is quite different from the difficulty in reading caused by non-neurological deficiency with vision or hearing, or due to inadequate reading instruction. It occurs in people of all backgrounds and intellectual levels. About 20% of the population have Dyslexia. They are often very creative and gifted in many areas, such as art, computer science, design, drama, electronics, math, mechanics, music, physics, sales, and sports.

Dysgraphia It refers to (a) the language-based difficulties involved in constructing meaningful and effectively structured expressive writing (b) ongoing weaknesses in spelling and punctuation that affect a student's capacity to express their ideas with clarity – have extreme difficulty getting their thoughts both in order and then down on paper besides face difficulties in basic grammar and spellings. They often have difficulty with the letters p, q, b, and d. They may write inappropriately sized and spaced letters and misspell words in spite of receiving thorough instruction.

Dyscalculia It is a math LD that impairs an individual's ability to learn number-related concepts, perform accurate math calculations, reason and problem solving, and perform other basic math skills. It derails everyday aspects of life involving telling time, counting money, and performing mental calculations.

Dysnomia It is marked by difficulty in recalling words, names, numbers, etc. from memory – needed for oral or written expressive language. They find it difficult to name things like colours, objects, numbers, and letters. They struggle to recall a person's name (even though they recognise the person's face). It interferes with memory and slows processing speed. It can co-occur with other difficulties, esp. accessing, organising, and outputting verbal information. It affects executive functioning and lack of attention. It worsens under stress.

Learning Disabilities in India There are approximately 90 million people with varying degrees of LD and an average class in schools has about 5 students. The incidents in primary school children: Dyslexia: 2-18%, Dysgraphia: 14%, Dyscalculia:14.5%. The prevalence of specific LD was 15.17%, whereas Dysgraphia: 12.5%, Dyslexia: 11.2% and Dyscalculia: 10.5%.

Other Disorders: Auditory Processing Disorder (APD); Visual Perceptual/Visual Motor Deficit; Non Verbal LD. In India, SLD (Special LD) is most likely to exhibit emotional problems mainly due to poor academic performance. Students suffer from these disorders as they are not recognized easily.

Handling Conduct Disorders

Dr Sony Mary Varghese
Assistant Professor in Education, Peet Memorial Training College, Kerala

Conduct disorder has multifactorial causes like biologic, psychosocial and familial, in children. Their behavior goes beyond normal bullying to hurting people. The article aims to point out cognitive emotional interventions that can develop positive attitudes toward oneself and others, besides building connection and commitment to others.

Normal behaviour of a child depends on the child's age, character, and physical and emotional development. If the child's behavior does not match family expectations or is disruptive, it may become a problem or difficulty. Raising a child is difficult, and raising a child with difficulty may disrupt a parents' life. Most parents report having conduct related problems with their children at some time or another. That means conduct problems have become very common among students and adolescents in our society. However the label conduct disorders may only be warranted if those problematic behaviours are persistent and impinge on the basic rights of others, if major age appropriate societal norms are violated or if there is significant impairment in everyday functioning at home or school.

Signs and Symptoms of Conduct Disorders

Children with conduct disorder are often difficult to diagnose because the signs and symptoms of conduct disorders may look similar to those of other conditions, such as ADHD and ODD.One of the hallmarks of conduct disorder is a seemingly callous disregard for societal norms and the rights, feelings, and personal space of other people.

Symptoms of conduct disorder:

- Aggressive behavior, such as cruelty to animals, fighting and bullying
- Destructive behaviour that causes property loss or damage such as firesetting or deliberate destruction of others' property
- Deceitful behaviour, such as shoplifting ,lying,vandalism and theft
- Violation of rules, which may include truancy and running away from home

Drug and alcohol abuse, sexual activity and low self-esteem are also common signs of conduct disorders. Childhood onset conduct disorder may lead to problems like school drop out, alcoholism, drug abuse, juvenile delinquency, adult crime, antisocial personality and marital disruption (Kazdin, 1985, 1987; Wadsworth, 1979; Farrington, 1978; Rutter, 1977; Oltmans, Broderick and O'Leary, 1977; Johnson and Lobitz, 1974; Robbins, 1966). Thus the fact that this disorder continues into adulthood in many cases, conveys conduct disorder to be a serious and life long dysfunction (Webster-Stratton and Dahl, 1995). Kauffmann(1998) noticed that a child with conduct disorders lacks self concept, socio-cognitive skills, assertive skills, problem solving ability, moral values, good interpersonal relationships and good academic performance, which adds to the severity of the disorder. Studies suggest that less than 50% of the most severe cases become antisocial as adults.

Causes of Conduct Disorders

Conduct disorder appears in various forms, and a combination of factors appears to contribute to its development and maintenance. Understanding the various dimensions involved in this disorder, aids in implementing appropriate interventions also. Theoretical researchers points out the factors leading to conduct disorders as genetic predispositions, physiological influences, social, familial influences, environmental influences and individual characteristics. They also pointed out that a negative combination of these factors may predispose young children to exhibit symptoms of conduct disorder.Children who have suffered abuse, parental rejection, or neglect may also be more likely to develop conduct disorder. Research studies noticed that many factors that contribute towards the development of conduct disorders include brain damage, genes, past school failure,low socioeconomic status, background of the family etc. Some children with conduct disorders seem to have a problem in the frontal lobe of the brain which interferes with a child's ability to plan, stay away from harm, and learn from negative experiences.The exact cause behind the problem can be identified through comprehensive assessment followed by diagnosis.

Assessment of Conduct Disorders

Waddell and others (1999) found out that conduct disorders are affecting multiple domains of functioning and shows a high rate of comorbidity with other disorders. This suggests the use of comprehensive assessment in the identification and diagnosis of children with conduct disorders. Comprehensive assessment includes the following aspects:

a) History: Duration of difficulties, their relationship with any specific developmental or situational stressors and any previous attempts to resolve students problems.

b) Specificity: Objective and observable description of students problems.

c) Strengths: Strengths and available resources like family, teachers, peers and other social workers.

d) Intensity: Severity of behavioural problems as they affect academic achievement, social skills and interpersonal relationships.

e) Pervasiveness: Extent to which difficulties occur in different settings.

f) Persistence of the problem: extent to which difficulties have continued despite the use of well planned empirically based and individualized intervention strategies

g) Developmental & Cultural functioning: Current developmental states and extent to which it is different from normal students.

h) Cognitive and Academic functioning: Child's cognitive abilities and academic performance.

i) Environmental factors: People and systems that have an impact on the child, relationship of child with instructional, family and social environment.

Information from all these aspects should be put together to get working hypotheses regarding child's behavioural and emotional functioning, areas of significant impairment like academic achievement, social and communication skills, adaptive behaviour etc., both in and outside the school. Conduct disorders involve a heterogeneous group of behaviours that range in types and severity and ultimately have strong implications for treatment. Furthermore numerous factors can lead to the development of conduct disorders. So assessment should be followed by proper diagnosis.

Diagnosis of Conduct Disorders

Diagnosis comprises collecting a complete social and medical history of the child and the family, interviewing and observing the child and family, interviewing the teachers, examining the socio-economic context of the child's behavior and conducting multiple standardised tests. As conduct disorders is comorbid with ADHD and ODD a differential diagnosis should also be conducted using DSM-IV Diagnostic Criteria. The criteria include

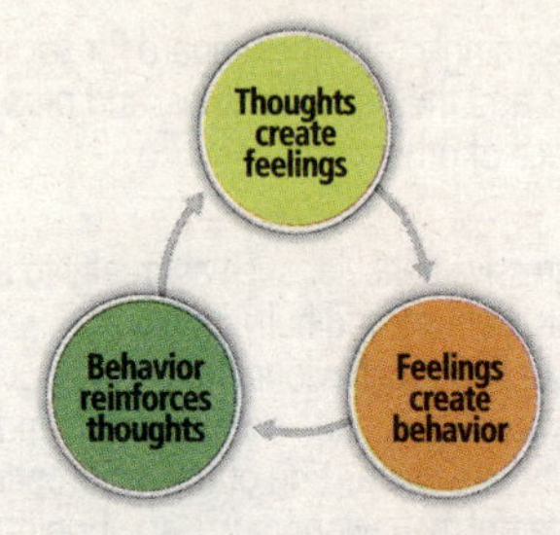

aggression towards people and animals, destruction of property, deceitfulness, theft and other serious violation of social rules. Diagnosis of conduct disorders also requires a persistent behavior pattern in the child in which three or more of the 15 behaviours listed in the criteria should be exhibited by him over a 12-month period. DSM-IV (Diagnostic Statistical Manual-IV) also specifies childhood-onset and adolescent-onset types of conduct disorder depending upon the severity of the disorder. Theoretically adolescent stage is more prone to develop conduct disorders, but researchers noticed that conduct disorders begin under 7 years of age (Scott, 2007). Even though the onset is below 7 years it may not be possible to diagnose at that age due to their inadequate level of social understanding and the allowances that are made for them as a result of it. Apart from this, they lack cognitive abilities to understand the ramifications of their behaviours, which will in turn make it difficult to refer them with a label of conduct disorders. (Frick, 1998). Diagnosis of the genuine cause is an essential step for planning the apt intervention or treatment.

Treatment of Conduct Disorders

Various interventions have been put forward to reduce the prevalence and incidence of conduct disorders. Optimum method appears to be an integrated approach, within a variety of contexts at different developmental stages of the student. The prevalence of conduct disorders is alarmingly wide and appears to be growing around the world and also in India. According to research cited in Phelps and

McClintock (1994), lack of knowledge of appropriate assessment procedures have led to incorrect prevalent rates. The actual rate may well be higher as many students with conduct disorders are not referred so far, due to limited knowledge in this area. Recognising at the right time and acting on symptoms when they appear can minimise the distress experienced by the child and the family. A programme based on Cognitive Emotional interventions can serve as a guideline for both teachers and parents to handle the students with conduct disorders judiciously which may help them to lead a better life.

Cognitive Emotional Interventions

Cognitive emotional intervention is an extended version of Cognitive behavioral intervention which aims at helping individuals to evaluate the basis of their emotional distress and thus reduce the need for associated dysfunctional coping behaviors. Cognitive-emotional exercise is to train an individual to enhance his cognitive control for emotional information processing.

Strategies that are rooted in cognitive change approaches assume that people's problematic emotions and observable behaviour are influenced by their beliefs, attitudes or cognitions. Errors in thinking produce emotional distress and problematic behaviours. So the aim of cognitive emotional interventions is to reduce emotional distress and corresponding maladaptive behaviour patterns through correcting errors in thoughts, perceptions and beliefs. Beeh (1976) observed that changes in behaviour occur once the conduct disordered child's distortions in thinking are unraveled and replaced with alternative more realistic ways of thinking about experiences. Cognitive emotional interventions also stress the importance of self control. Thus children with conduct disorder should become direct agents of their own changes rather than as helpless victims of external events and

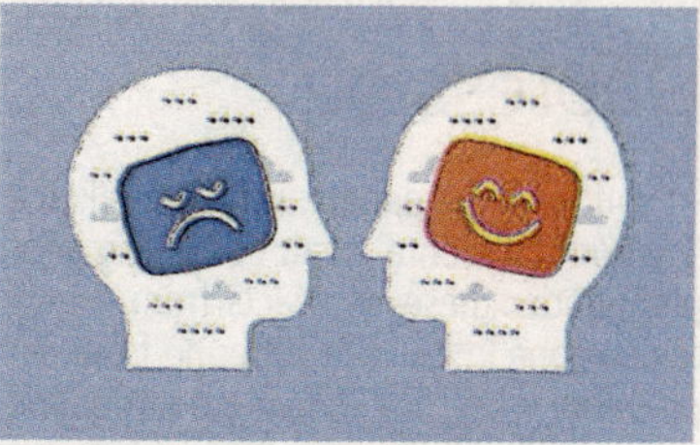

forces.The major strategies that can be adopted under cognitive emotional interventions to correct the thoughts, perceptions and beliefs using cognitive processes are mainly Cognitive restructuring, Cognitive problem solving skills, Thought stopping strategies, Three column technique and Cognitive mapping.All these techniques instructs a child with conduct disorders to replace his self-criticizing thoughts with self-compassionate ones and keep track of their unhelpful thoughts. It will also enable them to recognise their maladaptive emotion coping behaviours and replace them with adaptive coping behaviours.

Students with conduct disorders form a considerable portion of our classrooms. Teachers can identify them and train them to adopt cognitive emotional strategies to ameliorate their conduct problems. Cognitive Emotional Interventions develop positive attitudes toward oneself and others, and also enhances one's own self-efficacy, confidence, persistence, empathy, connection and commitment to others. A number of researches have proved that students with conduct problems could improve their interpersonal relationships with peers and adults after learning cognitive emotional strategies. It also helps to reduce conduct problems, risk-taking behavior, emotional distress thus improving their achievement too. Do remember that early diagnosis and intervention of conduct disorders is vital to prevent further behaviour problems like antisocial personality disorder and juvenile delinquency.

Depression

If you think the pandemic hasn't taken a toll on the mental health of young people, ponder these two facts from a new review: one in four are suffering from depression, while one in five are struggling with anxiety. As the pandemic continues, along with public health safety measures and social distancing, clinically significant anxiety and depression symptoms are likely to continue and to increase especially for youth as well.

According to WHO estimates, the 10 countries with the highest prevalence of depression are: Ukraine (6.3%); United States (5.9%); Estonia (5.9%); Australia (5.9%); Brazil (5.8%); Greece (5.7%); Portugal (5.7%); Belarus (5.6%); Finland (5.6%); Lithuania (5.6%).

10 countries with the lowest rates of depression are: Solomon Islands (2.9%);

Papua New Guinea (3.0%); Timor – Leste (3.0%); Vanuatu (3.1%); Kiribati (3.1%);

Tonga (3.2%); Samoa (3.2%); Laos (3.2%); Nepal (3.2%); Philippines (3.3%)

Depression Rates By Country 2021

Country	Prevalence %	Cases (M)	2021 PopM
Ukraine	6.30	2.87	43.4
Estonia	5.90	0.75	1.32
Australia	5.90	1.31	25.7
USA	5.90	17.49	332.9
Brazil	5.80	11.54	213.9
Portugal	5.70	0.57	10.1
Greece	5.70	0.59	10.3
Lithuania	5.60	0.16	2.6
Finland	5.60	0.29	5.5
Belarus	5.60	0.51	9.4
India	4.50	56.67	1393.4

Depression

Depression is a mental disorder that negatively affects how a person feels, thinks and behaves. Do you know, depression can also lead to death if it gets worse? Depression is the leading cause of disability worldwide, and is a major contributor to the overall global burden of disease. According to WHO more women are affected by depression than men. At its worst, depression can lead to suicide.

Suicide

Depression, is reported to be a major contributor to global suicides. One person commits suicide every 40 seconds globally. In 2015, an estimated 7,88,000 people died due to suicide while many more than this number attempted but did not die. Suicide accounted for close to 1.5% of all deaths worldwide, bringing it into the top 20 leading causes of death. Suicide occurs throughout the lifespan and was the second leading cause of death among 15-29 year olds globally.

The suicide rate varies by WHO Region and by sex, ranging from below 5 per 1L population among females in low- and middle-income countries of the Eastern Mediterranean and American Regions to 20 or more among males in high-income countries and also in the low- and middle-income countries of the African, European and South-East Asian Regions.

Depression: By Age

Childhood Depression

If a child is sad, it doesn't necessarily mean he has depression. It's when the sadness stays with him day after day that depression may be an issue. Or, if the child has disruptive behavior that interferes with normal social activities, interests, schoolwork, or family life, that may also be signs of a problem.

Depression in Teens

A lot of teens feel unhappy or moody. However, when the sadness lasts for more than 2 weeks and a teen has other symptoms of depression, then he may have a problem.

Different Types of Depression

Unipolar major depression

Persistent depressive disorder (dysthymia), when depression lasts for at least 2 years

Disruptive mood dysregulation disorder, when children and teens get extremely irritable, angry, and often have intense outbursts that are more severe than a child's typical reaction

Premenstrual dysphoric disorder, when a woman has severe mood problems before her period, more intense than typical premenstrual syndrome (PMS)

Substance-induced mood disorder (SIMD), when symptoms happen while you're taking a drug or after you stop

Depressive disorder due to another medical condition

Other Specific Features:

Anxious distress. You worry a lot about things that might happen or about losing control.

Mixed features. You have both depression and mania – periods of high energy, talking too much, and high self-esteem.

Atypical features. You can feel good after happy events, but you also feel hungrier, need to sleep a lot, and are sensitive to rejection.

Psychotic features. You believe things that aren't true, or see and hear things that aren't there.

Catatonia. You can't move your body normally. You might be still and unresponsive or have uncontrollable movements.

Peripartum depression. Your symptoms begin during pregnancy or after giving birth.

Seasonal pattern. Your symptoms get worse with changes in the seasons, especially the colder, darker months.

Warning signs include: • Thoughts or talk of death or suicide • Thoughts or talk of self-harm or harm to others •Aggressive behavior or impulsiveness

Symptoms

Doctors diagnose depression when one has someone has the following symptoms for at least 2 weeks: • A depressed mood during most of the day, especially in the morning • feel tired or have a lack of energy almost every day.

• feel worthless or guilty almost every day.•have a hard time focusing, remembering details, and making decisions •can't sleep or you sleep too much almost every day •no interest or pleasure in many activities nearly every day.•often think about death or suicide (not just a fear of death)• feel restless or slowed down.• lose or gain weight. •Feel irritable and restless •Lose pleasure in life

• Overeat or stop feeling hungry • Have aches or pains, headaches, cramps, or digestive problems that don't go away or get better with treatment. •Have sad, anxious, or "empty" feelings.

** While these symptoms are common, not everyone with depression will have the same ones. How severe they are, how often they happen, and how long they last can vary. Such symptoms may also happen in patterns. For example, depression may come with a change in seasons (seasonal affective disorder), fear caused by new environment or future.

Physical Symptoms

Joint pain, back pain, digestive problems, sleep trouble, and appetite changes, slowed speech and movements, too. The reason is that brain chemicals linked to depression, specifically serotonin and norepinephrine, play a role in both mood and pain.

Dementia and Alzheimer's Disease

It is a progressive and sometimes chronic brain condition that causes problems with person's thinking, behaviour, and memory. Dementia itself is not a disease, but a syndrome; its symptoms are common to several brain diseases. It worsens over time. But medications might slow that decline and help with symptoms, such as behaviour changes. The treatments depend on the type of dementia.

Alzheimer's Disease

It is a degenerative brain disease that usually starts in late middle age or in old age, resulting in progressive memory loss, impaired thinking, disorientation, and changes in personality and mood in 60% to 80% people with dementia. It is marked histologically by the degeneration of brain neurons especially in the cerebral cortex and by the presence of neurofibrillary tangles and plaques containing beta-amyloid. Symptoms: memory loss and trouble planning and doing familiar tasks. •mild at first but worsens over a period of years.•confused about where he/she is or what day or year it is • Have problems speaking or writing •Lose things and unable to backtrack to find them • Show poor judgment •Have mood and personality changes

Types of Dementia

Vascular Dementia

In a person with this type of dementia, he or she would have had a major stroke, or one or more "silent" strokes, without them realizing it. The symptoms depend on which part of the brain was affected by the stroke. While Alzheimer's usually begins with memory problems, vascular dementia more often begins with poor judgment or trouble planning, organising, and making decisions. Symptoms: •Memory problems that disrupt your loved one's daily life •Trouble speaking or understanding speech, •Problems recognising sights and sounds that used to be familiar •Being confused or agitated •Changes in personality and mood •Problems walking and having frequent falls

Dementia With Lewy Bodies

Lewy bodies are microscopic deposits of a protein that form in some people's brains. They're named after the scientist who discovered them. In DLB patients these deposits have formed in the part of the brain called the cortex. Symptoms: •Problems thinking clearly, making decisions, or paying attention, •Memory trouble, •Seeing things that aren't there (visual hallucinations), •Unusual sleepiness during the day, •Periods of "blanking out" or staring •Problems with movement, including trembling, slowness, and trouble walking •Dreams where one act out physically, including, talking, walking, and kicking

Parkinson's Disease Dementia

People with the nervous system disorder Parkinson's disease get this type of dementia about 50% to 80% of the time. On average, the symptoms of dementia develop about 10 years after a person first gets Parkinson's. •Like DLB, they have the same symptoms.

Frontotemporal Dementia

In FTD, persons developed cell damage in areas of the brain that control planning, judgment, emotions, speech, and movement. Symptoms: •Personality and behavior changes •Sudden lack of inhibitions in personal and social situations •Problems coming up with the right words for things when speaking •Movement problems, such as shakiness, balance problems, and muscle spasms.

Disorders of Sleep

Millions of people complain about not getting enough sleep. More often than not, stress is the main culprit. However, there are several causes for the sleep deprivation that demand medical attention. Even excess sleeping in itself is a sleeping disorder. Here are five of the most commonly seen sleep disorders and ways you can identify them.

1. Insomnia Insomnia is a condition in which a person is unable to fall asleep and stay asleep for a certain period of time and finds it difficult to wake up early in the morning for a minimum of 3 nights/week for at least 1 month (primary insomnia). Primary insomnia usually has no underlying health condition. It generally occurs due to stress and disruption of sleep schedule. Secondary insomnia occurs as a side effect of an underlying health condition such as arthritis, stroke, overactive thyroid, or as a side effect of certain medications. Regardless of the type, insomniacs have low energy levels. They lack concentration and are hence less productive. Insomnia often leads to anxiety and depression.

2. Narcolepsy Narcolepsy is characterised by excessive daytime sleepiness, hallucinations, drowsiness and sleep paralysis. While the exact cause of narcolepsy remains unknown, it may show up as an autoimmune disorder, because of genetic factors (less common) or as a result of a brain injury (rarely). In the case of narcolepsy, it is claimed that the immune cells attack the hypocretin-containing brain cells. These cells are responsible for maintaining the sleep-wake cycle.

3. Obstructive sleep apnea (OSA) OSA is a condition in which the patient temporarily stops breathing during sleep - at least 5 times every hour for about ten seconds each. These pauses in breathing lead to a drop in the levels of oxygen in the blood. As a result, the person tends to wake up several times during the night. Obesity is one of the major causes of OSA. However, OSA can also occur due to certain endocrine disorders (those that affect hormones), large tonsils and kidney or heart failure.

4. Restless leg syndrome (RLS) or Willis-Ekbom disease (WED) Restless Leg Syndrome is a condition in which the patient gets a strong and irresistible urge to move their legs. The symptoms most commonly show up in the evening and while resting. As a result, the person finds it difficult to fall asleep. RLS is often seen in patients of Parkinson's disease although the cause is not yet known. If one have a family history of RLS, it is highly likely that he or she will get it too.

5. Periodic limb movement disorder (PLMD) PMLD may look quite similar to RLS when it comes to the common signs and symptoms. However, unlike restless leg syndrome, where the symptoms show up when the person is awake, a PMLD patient jerks their leg/s during sleep at a regular interval of 5 to 90 seconds. The patient generally does not know about the condition and often the bed partner describes the symptoms. If you have this condition, you would feel as if you didn't get enough sleep at night and as a result would be sleepy during the day.

Immunity Through Nutrients

On a daily basis, we are constantly exposed to potentially harmful microbes of all sorts.

What is our Immune System? The design of our immune system is complex and influenced by an ideal balance of many factors, not just diet, and especially not by any one specific food or nutrient.

Our immune system, a network of intricate stages and pathways in the body, protects us against these harmful microbes as well as certain diseases. It recognises foreign invaders like bacteria, viruses, and parasites and takes immediate action.

Human Two Types of Immunity:

Innate immunity is a first-line defense from pathogens that try to enter our bodies, achieved through protective barriers, like: •**Skin** that keeps out the majority of pathogens •**Mucus** that traps pathogens •**Stomach acid** that destroys pathogens •**Enzymes** in our sweat and tears that help create anti-bacterial compounds •**Immune system cells** that attack all foreign cells entering the body

Adaptive or acquired immunity is a system that learns to recognise a pathogen. It is regulated by cells and organs in our body like the spleen, thymus, bone marrow, and lymph nodes. When a foreign substance enters the body, these cells and organs create antibodies and lead to multiplication of immune cells (including different types of white blood cells) that are specific to that harmful substance and attack and destroy it. Our immune system then adapts by remembering the foreign substance so that if it enters again, these antibodies and cells are even more efficient and quick to destroy it.

Immune Response Trigger Factors

Antigens are substances that the body labels as foreign and harmful, which triggers immune cell activity. **Allergens** are one type of antigen and include grass pollen, dust, food components, or pet hair. Antigens can cause a hyper-reactive response in which too many white cells are released. People's sensitivity to antigens varies widely. For example, an allergy to mold triggers symptoms of wheezing and coughing in a sensitive individual.

Inflammation is an important, normal step in the body's innate immune response. When pathogens attack healthy cells and tissue, a type of immune cell called mast cells counterattack and release proteins called histamines, which cause inflammation. Inflammation may generate pain, swelling, and a release of fluids to help flush out the pathogens. The histamines also send signals to discharge even more white blood cells to fight pathogens. However, prolonged inflammation can lead to tissue damage and may overwhelm the immune system.

Immunodeficiency disorders can depress or completely disable the immune system, and may be genetic or acquired. Acquired forms are more common and include AIDS and cancers like leukemia and multiple myeloma. In these cases, the body's defenses are so reduced that a person becomes highly susceptible to illness from invading pathogens or antigens.

Autoimmune disorders like lupus, rheumatoid arthritis, or type 1 diabetes are partly hereditary and cause hypersensitivity in which immune cells attack and destroy healthy cells.

Factors that depresses Immune System

Older age: As we age, our internal organs may become less efficient; immune-related organs like the thymus or bone marrow produce less immune cells needed to fight off infections. Aging is sometimes associated with micronutrient deficiencies, which may worsen a declining immune function.

Environmental toxins Smoke and other particles contributing to air pollution, excessive alcohol can impair or suppress the normal activity of immune cells.

Excess weight: Obesity is associated with low-grade chronic inflammation. Fat tissue produces adipocytokines that can promote inflammatory processes. Obesity and impaired T-cells (a type of white blood cell) function, are independent risk factor.

Poor diet: Malnutrition or a diet lacking in one or more nutrients can impair the production and activity of immune cells and antibodies.

Chronic diseases: Autoimmune and immunodeficiency disorders attack and potentially disable immune cells.

Chronic mental stress: Stress releases hormones like cortisol that suppresses inflammation (it is initially needed to activate immune cells) and the action of white blood cells.

Lack of sleep and rest: Sleep is a time of restoration for the body, during which a type of cytokine is released that fights infection; too little sleep lowers the amount of these cytokines and other immune cells.

Immune-Boosting Diet

Probiotic foods: yogurt with live active cultures, fermented vegetables, sp. tea. Prebiotic foods: garlic, onions, asparagus, bananas, and seaweed. A general rule is to eat a variety of fruits, vegetables, beans, and whole grains for dietary prebiotics.

Energy Received from Nutrients: •1 gm. Carbohydrate – 17.1 Kilojoules (4 Kcal)•1 gm. Fat - 38.9 Kilojoules (9 Kcal)•1 gm. Protein – 18.2 kilojoules (4 Kcal) Though carbs, proteins and fats makes up the major part of the diet, vitamins nor minerals can't be missed out.

Healthy Diet

What Are Nutrients?

The very first thing that comes to our mind when we think of nutrition is carbohydrates, proteins, fat, vitamins and minerals. Nutrients are the constituent of food, which helps to perform various functions in the body to lead a healthy life. It can be broadly classified as:

Macronutrients: Nutrients which are needed by the body in large amounts and forms the major portion of the food. It includes Carbohydrates, Proteins, Fat and Water.

Micronutrients: Nutrients that are needed by the body in smaller amounts. Vitamins and minerals belong to this class.

Carbohydrates: the major class of nutrients, and is the body's primary source of energy. It includes sugar, starch and fibers.

Fats/Lipids: group of fatty substances which are not soluble in water and provides a rich source of energy and structure to the body's cells. It includes triglycerides and cholesterol.

Proteins: made of nitrogen containing amino acids, which forms the major structural part of the body's cells. Good quality protein are particularly rich in animal foods.

Water: it is the most essential nutrient needed by the body. It delivers nutrients and removes wastes from the cells. It makes up about 60 – 70 % of the total body weight.

• **Vitamins**: There are a total of 13 vitamins needed for the body. •A, C, D, E, K vitamins and the (8) B complex vitamins forms these 13. •Vitamins are not made in the body, so it must be taken through diet.

The Blood

Blood is a red viscous fluid with numerous suspended cells and proteins, constantly circulating, providing nutrition and oxygen, to the body's cells. It also transports metabolic wastes away from the same cells. There is no substitute for blood. It cannot be manufactured. It is essential to life.

Content On an average, a healthy man has about 5 litres of blood, while a woman has about 500 ml less than a man.

Total Volume About 60-80 ml per kg of body weight.

The Two Constituents:

– blood cells-solid or cellular part : (35%)

– plasma-fluid part: (65%).

Types of Blood Corpuscles (Cells):

1. **RBC** Red Blood Corpuscles are disc-shaped cells without nucleus and contain a pigment called Haemoglobin which gives the red colour to the blood. Haemoglobin is an iron-containing pigment. RBCs are produced in the spleen and the bone marrow. Haemoglobin picks up oxygen in the lungs by forming a chemical compound.

2. **WBC** White Blood Corpuscles are round semi-transparent cells containing a nucleus and are a little larger in size than RBC. The WBC are the 'soliders' of the body's defence system. They combat infection.

Types of Blood Groups

Blood Group	Can donate blood to	Can receive blood from
A	A, AB	A, O
B	B, AB	B, O
AB	Only AB	AB, A, B & O
O	AB, A. B & O	Only O

Grouping In 1900-1902, K. Landsteiner classified human blood into A, B, AB and O. The O group blood can be given to any of the other groups (known as a universal donor). Group AB can receive A, B, AB and O (known as a universal recipient).

Blood Clotting It is a body's defence system to combat bleeding. Plasma contains fibrinogen-a soluble 'protein' which produces the insoluble protein called fibrin essential for blood coagulation which is produced in the liver.

COVID-19 Both Respiratory and a Blood Infection

A recent article in *Elemental at Medium* reports that 40% of deaths from the virus are related to cardiovascular complications. All these COVID-associated complications were a mystery. Bood clotting, kidney damage, inflammation of the heart, stroke, encephalitis (swelling of the brain)– a whole myriad of seemingly unconnected phenomena that you do not normally see with SARS or, frankly, most infectious diseases.

In the April issue of *The Lancet*, a team of scientists found that the SARS-CoV-2 virus can infect and damage the endothelial cells that line the inside of blood vessels and protect the cardiovascular system. The concept that's emerging is that this is a respiratory illness to start with, but it is actually a vascular illness that kills people through its involvement of the vasculature. The article notes that a respiratory virus infecting blood cells before circulating through the body is "virtually unheard of." Other viruses like H1N1 and the original SARS virus, do no spread past the lungs. American and Chinese researchers collaborated to study any association between a severe course of COVID-19 and WBC counts in the body– known to be part of the body's immune system that helps fight infections. COVID-19 pandemic has infected over 40 million people and killed over 1.1 million lives.

INFORMATION TECHNOLOGY

- Potentials of Blockchain Technology
- Reliable Cyberspace
- Data Protection
- India and Cybersecurity
- Data Science and Ethics
- 5G Wireless and Wi-Fi 6
- The Digital Divide
- Digital Economy
- Quantum Communication

Towards Verifiable, Immutable And Secure Operations

Potentials of Blockchain Technology

Dr. Raju Narayana Swamy IAS

Imagine an entanglement! Blockchain promises to solve this problem through a technology that is behind bitcoin, It is an open, distributed ledger that records transactions safely, permanently, and very efficiently. Blockchain would require broad coordination and will take years. This article describes the path that blockchain is likely to follow and explains the great potential it has with greater adoption in years ahead.

What is a blockchain? Blockchain also known as distributed ledger technology has been defined to be a decentralized peer-to-peer network based public encrypted and immutable digital federated ledger system. Working like a shared Google document, the ledger is a public database that records transactions in a permanent fashion and distributes copies to all relevant parties without the need for a third party to authorize the transaction.

The first major use of this technology occurred with the creation of Bitcoin, which is a digital crypto-currency introduced in 2009. The seminal paper that introduced this technology to the world was penned by "Satoshi Nakamoto" (a pseudonym used by the author whose identity is still unknown) and was titled " Bitcoin : A Peer to Peer Electronic Cash System. " Traceability and reliability were the hallmarks set forth by Nakamoto in this innovative method of executing transfers of value between peers.

Transactions are recorded within "blocks" which are stored on each computer in the network. As new blocks are added, they are linked to all preceding transactions. As each computer in the network has its own copy, security of data is improved and vulnerability to cyber attacks is reduced vis-a-vis hitherto used models wherein data is stored in a single central location. It is seen as nearly unhackable because to change any information on it, a cyber attack would have to strike all copies of the ledger simultaneously. Data put into the blockchain cannot be tampered without being noticed.

Blockchains leverage techniques from a field of computer science known as cryptography to sign every transaction with a unique digital signature belonging to the user who initiated the transaction. These signatures are held privately, but are publicly verifiable. This means that if a user with identity A sends money to identity B, anybody can verify that the money was sent by A, but cannot use A's signature for their own transactions. This cryptographic system creates accountability while preventing identity fraud.

Applications of Blockchain

Blockchain is a part of the ever widening canvas of technological developments which range from Artificial Intelligence and Virtualisation to Cloud Computing and Internet of Things. It has begun to make its presence felt in insurance, health care, voting systems, supply chain & logistics , shipping and other sectors too. For instance, NITI Aayog is seriously deliberating on building a new immunisation infrastructure for the country - unified and enhanced by blockchain. Discussions are also in the pipeline on SuperCert- an antifraud identity intelligence blockchain solution for educational certificates. The Gartner Blockchain Spectrum – proposed by Gartner, the research and advisory firm - talks about 3 phases: blockchain inspired solutions (a phase which began in 2012 and will last through the early 2020s), blockchain complete solutions (expected to gain momentum in the market around 2023) and enhanced blockchain solutions.

Smart Contracts

One area where much leeway has been made is smart contracts-self executing contracts wherein the terms can be set out in computer code. The high potential of smart contracts lies in enabling decentralised micropayments such as paying a very small fee in return to accessing small bits and pieces of a digital content (which may be a song or a news article). A classic example is the Ethereum – powered music platform "VOISE" wherein artists upload their music (and set their own prices) and users pay them directly for the music via electronic currency. Mention must also be made of the Open Music Initiative (OMI) announced by the Berklee College of Music in Boston, Massachusetts which aims to build a database in the form of a blockchain seeking to solve the problem of proper identification of right holders.

The Blockchain- IP Interface

IPRs are currently regulated by third party authenticators. These authenticators are governments or administrative bodies of the geographical regions where the IP holder wants to secure and enforce rights. The limiting factor of such a system is its inherent physical limitation. As the market gets more globalised and digitised, it is becoming imperative to look for a more feasible and reliable alternative. The blockchain – IP interface is largely based on the premise that IP management systems could leverage blockchain technology to enforce provable IPRs where verifiable, immutable and secure operations in blockchain could help in the event of disputes. In particular, digital assets such as patents have multiple versions during their life time and blockchains can be used to link all versions of their digital assets and potentially use it for end-to-end life cycle maintenance. No wonder why blockchains are being seriously considered as possible successors to the classic-physical model. In conjunction with AI, particularly domain specific AI, blockchain technology can work wonders. In the realm of certain IP assessments such as likelihood of confusion evaluation in trademark cases or the existence of an inventive step assessment in patent applications, AI-based software can come in handy. As yet another example consider the use of CAD (Computer Aided Design). Taking a photograph of a design from three different angles is sufficient to create a CAD. Such a CAD could be uploaded to a block chain based app that could search the entire database (comprising all designs registered in the history of the IP regime) for similar designs and the right could be granted or denied using an AI based assessment tool.

International Efforts

Internationally, France is the first country to regulate securities transaction on block chain systems. In 2016, Vermont passed legislation declaring that block chain receipts accompanied by written declaration of a person attesting to the details of the transaction are admissible. In 2017 Delaware General Corporation Law was amended to allow organisations to maintain business records using "distributed electronic networks or databases". Arizona amended the Electronic Transactions Act to include blockchain records which "may not be denied legal effect, validity or enforceability". Ohio passed similar Legislation in 2018. In 2018, a Chinese Court (in Hangzhou) recognized blockchain based evidence for the first time. In 2019, the Apex Court of China affirmed the use of evidences stored and verified on blockchain platforms. In India however there is no dedicated law that governs the use and operation of blockchains. However, Section 65B (admissibility of electronic records) of the Evidence Act may be of vital importance.

Challenges

A major obstacle to the widespread use of blockchains is the incredibly high energy consumption. Powering all nodes and simultaneously providing for adequate cooling facilities for a continuous operation becomes an extensively high energy consuming process, making blockchain one of the most expensive databases. Another challenge to be addressed is throughput and band width in the blockchain network. Compared to traditional transaction platforms such as VISA or PayPal, blockchain is significantly slower at this time. For example if we examine the transaction processing capacity of the Bitcoin blockchain, we observe that it can handle 2-5 TPS (transactions per second) as opposed to VISA which can handle 56000 TPS. True, numerous alternatives have been introduced to overcome this challenge through second layer technologies (Segwit update to Bitcoin) but we have miles to go. In particular, the question that arises is: Is the existing network bandwidth enough for block chain transactions to do real-time updates in the systems. Questions of latency/delay in the blockchain network and apprehensions of chocking of bloodline enabled systems in case of huge number of transactions within a fraction of a second also arise. How often should the ledger be updated? What is the least tolerable updating delay that is acceptable? And last but not least, how can we effectively address an attack wherein an adversary disallows a miner's block from reaching all other miners for a long time?

However, the crucial question will revolve around collaborations by industry participants and blockchain developers across the globe towards developing standards and interoperability protocols. True, some work has already started under the aegis of the ISO (International Organisation for Standardisation) which is reported to be working on the ICO/TC307 standards for blockchain and distributed ledger technologies. But that is only a humble beginning. Only when the rules of standardisation are firmly established and are available for use by developers can regulators step in to task of bestowing blockchain with legal status.

On the legal side, the next step will be to commence accepting block chain records as evidence vis-a-vis prior art claims. Thereafter a legislative change that would allow block chain registrations to be deemed registrations should be brought in. Challenges will accrue thereafter too-for instance vis-a-vis laws regulating internet that have been drafted without considering the next layers of future technologies. To address these problems, efforts are needed to map the potential effects of blockchain, determine if they fall under existing laws and if so, how they are so covered. Till these efforts bear fruit, the ambition of block chain technology permeating law and practice will at best remain to be a paper tiger.

Reliable Cyberspace

Kevin Alex Mathews, Heidelberg, Germany

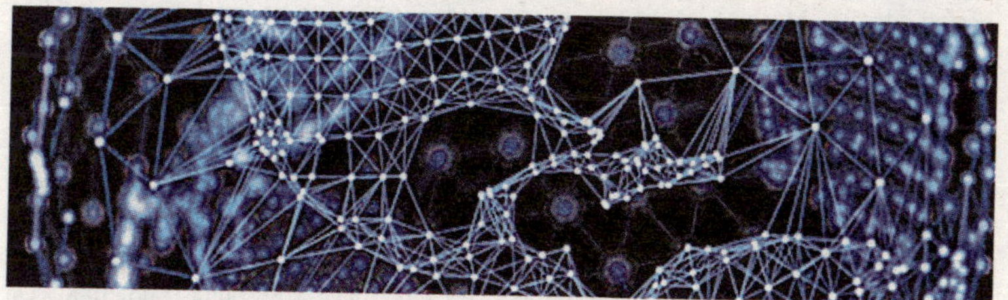

The Internet and social media wield a lot of power in the modern society. It can topple governments, subvert democracies, or corrupt minds if not kept under check. This article takes a look at how people should support and enforce the development of safe, trustworthy as well as fair cyberspace. To answer that, one can examine three aspects — How much privacy can users expect from their online activities? Is it possible for users to trust the content they consume? Does the cyberspace offer fairness without censorship and discrimination?

Digitisation is at the forefront of the technological revolution the world has been witnessing since the turn of the millennium. The digital economy encompasses various technologies such as the World Wide Web, social media, streaming services, smartphones, and personal computers. Businesses are investing heavily in data analytics, cloud computing, and automation. India's digital economy is estimated to constitute 20% of its GDP by the year 2025. In the rush to embrace new technology, we might overlook the risks associated with rapid, uncontrolled deployment of technology. For instance, in January 2021, supporters of Donald Trump attacked the Capitol Building, the seat of the legislative body of the US government. What triggered this act of violence were the tweets posted by Trump on Twitter following his defeat in the presidential election. As an immediate action, the account @realDonaldTrump was permanently suspended from Twitter. This incident shows the influence social media and the Internet in general wield in the modern society. They can topple governments and subvert democracies, if not kept under close scrutiny. We should encourage and enforce the development of safe, trustworthy as well as fair cyberspace. To this end, let us examine the state of the art in online digital media by posing three questions — How much privacy can users expect from their online activities? Is it possible for users to trust the content they consume online? Does the cyberspace exercise fairness by ensuring online content is not censored, and users are not discriminated against on the basis of gender, religion, wealth or political leaning.

User Privacy

Nearly all websites record user activities and meta-data: search terms, pages viewed, chat messages, IP address, time of visit, and duration of session. However, care for user privacy is often not accounted for, especially when the data is collected by parties with vested interests. Machine learning, a set of algorithms that make predictions based on past data, forms the crux of modern digital applications. The principal bottleneck here is the difficulty to obtain high-quality, real-world data. Social media, with its numerous posts, comments, shares and likes, is an excellent source of raw data. A machine learning model that is constructed from this raw data can glean plenty of information with sufficient accuracy. Imagine a young woman from Kerala planning her first-ever adventure trip to the

Himalayas. She is highly likely to have joined online groups that offer assistance to first-time trekkers or shared video clips on mountaineering with her friends. From these activities, a machine learning model can infer the details of the forthcoming trip, even if she never explicitly announces her plan on social media. The recommender system of, say, Amazon can then suggest her a pair of trekking shoes. The recommender system of, say, Airbnb can suggest her an affordable homestay at the foot of the hills. Although such suggestions are useful, the data on social media, which is necessary to make these suggestions, poses great risks to privacy as well as safety. Information about one's behaviour, personality, whereabouts, transactions, and relationships is left out in the open, giving others the freedom to snoop into our lives. Spam emails or unsolicited advertisements form only the tip of an iceberg of threats due to breach of privacy. Cambridge Analytica, a British firm, collected personal data of users through their Facebook application. This data was used, ahead of the 2016 US presidential election, to identify targets for digital campaigning, thereby influence the voters without their consent. In 2013, Edward Snowden, a former employee at the US National Security Agency, brought to light the mass surveillance programmes set up by intelligence agencies across the world. There exist a couple of ways to ensure privacy at the individual level: reducing the use of social media, disabling trackers, deleting cookies after every browsing session, avoiding applications from unreliable sources, and preferring open-source software because of transparency in their inner workings. However, these precautions not only have limitations but also are often not feasible. For instance, few software applications have opensource counterparts. On a larger level, policies to regulate the digital space – collecting, storing, processing, and sharing of data – should be given due emphasis. In 2018, the European Union put into effect the General Data Protection Regulation (GDPR) to keep third-party tracking in check. With a similar objective, the Personal Data Protection Bill (PDPB) 2019 has been introduced, but has yet to pass, in the lower house of the Indian Parliament.

Trust

Until a few years ago,the main sources of information were books, newspapers, radio and television, which are administered by mainstream media and publishing houses. Since then, the role of social media in dissemination of news has increased considerably. According to a 2020 survey conducted by the Pew Research Center, the top ten sources of news for adults in the US included *Facebook, YouTube, Twitter,* and even *TikTok*. With the proliferation of the Internet, anyone having access to a smartphone at least can create content, at times with malicious intent. As a result, it is often difficult to trust the correctness of the videos we watch or the articles we read. The doubt associated with authenticity of online content is of grave concern–it under mines the critical facets of our socio-economic and political life. For instance, the surge in fake news since the past few years hinders access to information, propagates conspiracy theories, and creates confusion among the general public. In 2017, mass distribution of fake news on social media led to a political crisis in Catalonia, a region demanding independence from Spain. To a certain extent, incidents of mob lynching in India could be attributed to rumours circulated on instant-messaging services such as Whatsapp. Trust, or the lack thereof, can decide the fate of a nation as well as a human being. The amount of fake profiles and bots (Internet robots) on social media is staggering. From October to December 2020, Facebook removed 130 crore (1.3 billion) fake profiles worldwide from its platform. A single bot can spawn hundreds if not thousands of fake profiles. These bots have the power to influence public opinion by making a topic trending or downvoting a topic into oblivion. Fake profiles were linked to polarising content in the run up to the European elections in 2019. Through illicit means, it is possible to buy fake views, likes and followers on all major social media platforms. Research and development of automated speech, text, image and video processing systems are progressing at a rapid pace, thanks to artificial intelligence (AI) and sophisticated hardware. As a result, it is becoming increasingly easy to quickly generate fake news on a large scale. In 2019, OpenAI, an AI research company, developed a text generator called GPT2, whose text is indistinguishable from human-written text. Deepfake is a software that can generate fake videos by doctoring people's faces. The consequences will be disastrous if such technologies fall into the wrong hands. Thorough investigation and review, the central aspects of traditional journalism and publishing, are not enforced in cyberspace, especially on social media. Constant attention is necessary while engaging in online activities – to distinguish fact from fiction.

Fairness

Social media platforms are rife with hate speech and offensive language. Numerous forums on websites such as Reddit, where users can discuss anonymously, entertain racism, homophobia and xenophobia. Stack Overflow, the question-answering website for programmers, has been accused of strict gatekeeping, rendering the community unfriendly to newcomers and minorities such as women or people of colour. The Internet is also a breeding ground for offences ranging from trolling, stalking to cyberbullying. In 2015, Free Basics, a service promoted by Facebook's CEO Mark Zuckerberg, promised data access to selected websites free of cost. However, the service was banned in India after numerous protests. Free Basics violated net neutrality by giving preferential treatment, and thus an unfair advantage, to websites that are part of its data plan. At present, a handful of multinational corporations control the entire landscape of services related to the Internet: search, streaming, advertising, and retail. These tech giants have grown large enough to act as gatekeepers of the Internet. Their online influence is often exploited by authorities in power to suppress dissent. In February 2021, *Twitter* blocked accounts that supported the farmers' protest, upon request by the Indian government. Websites take measures to combat abuse, and moderate content. However, the two main challenges in this regard are the large number of users and the enormous amount of data generated daily. For instance, as of May 2019, not only did YouTube have 200 crore (2 billion) active users, but also more than 500 hours of video uploaded every minute. As a result, human moderators don't monitor every user or inspect their submission. Scanning zettabytes of data or flagging inappropriate behaviour is done by AI methods through increased scalability and accuracy. ●

Data Protection

Our data is getting digitised, and we share more information online, data privacy is taking on greater importance. Data privacy relates to how we typically apply the concept of data privacy to critical personal information (personally identifiable information) like Aadhaar numbers, PAN Number, Passport Number, bank account and credit/debit card numbers, PIN/OTP and even basic information, such as full names, addresses and birth dates.

For a business, data privacy could be biometric data of its employees and customers besides information that helps the company operate, it's proprietary research and development data or financial information like it's spending and investments. Cloud backup is becoming more prevalent. Now additional protection has become necessary for even Backup data.

What's Significant! Ever wondered how your financial and personal information is carried, processed or stored while swipng MasterCard / Visa card or use Amazon's services? Well, most of the data tend to be either partly or completely stored outside India. Strangely, about who has access to your data overseas, even Indian government and regulators have limited access to these data. This is what the RBI wants to change through its data localisation rules. When data that should be kept private gets in the wrong hands, bad things can happen. A data breach at a government agency can, for example, put top secret information in the hands of an enemy state.

A breach at a corporation can put proprietary data in the hands of a competitor.

Origin

The genesis of the bill lies in the landmark Puttaswamy v India. judgment, issued on August 24, 2017. In that ruling, India's Supreme Court declared privacy was a fundamental right under the Constitution of India. On September 26, 2018, the Supreme Court asked the government to set robust data protection rules.

Personal Data Protection Bill

The Personal Data Protection Bill was introduced in India's parliament on December 11, 2019, which sets rules for how personal data should be processed and stored, and lists people's rights with respect to their personal information. It also proposes to create an independent new Indian regulatory authority, the Data Protection Authority (DPA), to carry out this law.

• Businesses would have to tell users about their data collection practices and seek customers' consent. Because the bill gives consumers the right to withdraw their consent, businesses would also have to come up with sys-

The World's First Website

Tim Berners-Lee designed his first website while working at Cern (the European Council for Nuclear Research) in 1990 and launched it live to the public in 1991. He published a page that demonstrated how one computer could link to documents on another computer.

tems to allow consumers to do so.

• Consumers has the right to access, correct, and erase their data. The bill also allows consumers to transfer their data, including any inferences made by businesses based on such data, to other businesses. All companies would have to develop ways for consumers to do this.

The bill requires all businesses to make organisational changes to protect data better. These include privacy-by-design principles (an approach in which privacy is a key consideration in how the business is organized), security safeguards, and so on.

• The bill also stipulates that all "sensitive personal data" be stored in India and that "critical personal data" not be transferred out of India. This will distort the market-driven decisions of businesses to access the best data storage services and force such data to be kept locally in India.

• A group of "significant data fiduciaries"—people in charge of checking that data is stored fairly and responsibly—will have extra duties, such as carrying out data audits and appointing data protection officers.

• Lastly, the bill also includes rules about nonpersonal data. Under the bill, the government can require any business to share valuable nonpersonal data (such as aggregate mobility data collected by apps like Google maps or Uber) with the government. The bill is silent on whether businesses will be compensated for their loss. This could have negative long-term consequences on innovation and economic growth.

Global Silicon Chip Shortage

According to Samsung, the world's largest chip manufacturer, the computer chip shortage comes amid rising demand for electronics during the Covid pandemic. Covid-19 has had two major impacts on the availability of computers through the initial closure of factories and then the global surge, including in Australia, for new computers and IT equipment A temporary shutdown in the production of silicon computer chips at the start of the coronavirus pandemic, as well as severe storms in Texas causing more recent delays, has caused worldwide chip shortages, with a knock-on effect for the production of phones, laptops and even automobiles. In the IT sector, there's a serious imbalance in supply and demand of chips, a shortage of one crucial piece of technology, is causing delays in everything from cars and televisions to video game consoles globally.

Apple, the world's biggest buyer of chips, was one of the worst affected companies, delaying the launch of the iPhone 12. Samsung would delay the release of the next Galaxy Note smartphone until 2022.

According to Bloomberg, several companies, including Ford, Toyota, Nissan and General Motors have made changes to their production as a result of the ongoing superconductor shortages. Electric car manufacturer Tesla said in February it was still determining the impact of the shortage. US consulting firm AlixPartners has estimated the shortage could cost carmakers US$61bn (A$82bn) in lost revenue in 2020-21.

India and Cybersecurity

Amidst the tensions at the border, hackers based in China attempted 40,000 cyber attacks on Indian banking and IT sector in the last week of June 2020. India is fast covering ground in the cyber security front. Aided by the rapid influx of global tech companies, indigenous development of digital technologies, and regulatory changes such as demonetisation, pandemic-lockdown, the Indian public and enterprises are pushing for digitisation. It will make enterprises more reliant on their digital data and networks. So, the increasing importance of enterprise data and networks is increasing the need for solutions to protect these valuable assets. To be secure, India will have to be vigilant and resilient, not only by looking at how to prevent and respond to attacks, but by managing cyber risks that would unleash new opportunities.

In the near future, cybersecurity in India will be very different both in terms of emerging problems and the solutions that will be necessary to combat them. Areas like malware and ransomware protection have always been top-of-mind for Indian enterprise cybersecurity teams. Some cybersecurity areas that requires more attention from Indian enterprises, institutions and individuals would be:

(a) Data Loss Prevention There are always threats from hackers and competitors. It is vital to protect data from both insider (data leaks by employees – either willingly or accidentally) and outside threats. As data becomes more valuable, businesses will be required to deploy technologies like next-generation firewalls with data loss prevention capabilities. •personal data protection will become more important due to the increased awareness of data security by the consumers and the enforcement of data privacy laws by the Indian government. •To avoid losing reputation among customers and to escape government-imposed penalties, enterprises will have to implement strong data loss prevention measures in their business networks.

(b) BYOD Management As more people switch to smart mobile computing devices due to even online classes, and work from home, there will be greater threats. Thus, businesses or workplaces will be required to implement clear, strong BYOD policies, as well as next-generation tools to automatically enforce these policies.

(c) Endpoint Protection As the Internet of Things (IoT) expands across different industries, the number of weak spots in their cyber defense will also increase. To prevent the IoT networks from becoming a liability to businesses, they will have to adopt next-generation firewall solutions that can offer comprehensive endpoint protection and give total visibility over their networks.

(d) Proactive Security Majority of Indian enterprises are unprepared with adequate cybersecurity measures. So Indian companies should gear up for implementing a desired level of cybersecurity with cutting edge solutions as outlined below:

Key Technologies for Adoption • AI and machine learning-based cybersecurity solutions to mitigate the risks posed by ever-evolving malware, hacks, and other types of cyber-attacks. • AI-based self-learning applications that will ensure continued protection against evolving risks.

• AI based next-generation firewall solutions that are more contextually-intelligent.

• 7-Layer deeper inspection performing inspection and analyze a broader range of parameters to determine the safety • anticipate potential cyber risks and take measures accordingly.

Data Science and Ethics

The world has entered an era of big data, and the need for its storage also grew. It was the main challenge and concern for the enterprise industries until 2010. The main focus was on building a framework and solutions to store data. Now when Hadoop and other frameworks have successfully solved the problem of storage, the focus has shifted to the processing of this data.

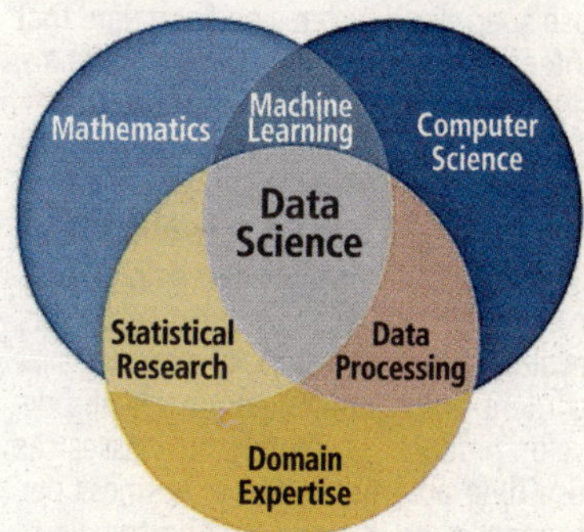

Data Science

It is a blend of various tools, algorithms, and machine learning principles with the goal to discover hidden patterns from the raw data.

Data science is an interdisciplinary field focused on extracting knowledge from data sets, which are typically large (see big data), and applying the knowledge and actionable insights from data to solve problems in a wide range of application domains.

The field encompasses preparing data for analysis, formulating data science problems, analysing data, developing data-driven solutions, and presenting findings to inform high-level decisions in a broad range of application domains.

As such, it incorporates skills from computer science, statistics, information science, mathematics, information visualisation, data integration, graphic design, complex systems, communication and business.

Data Analytics

Data can help businesses better understand their customers, improve their advertising campaigns, personalise their content and improve their bottom lines. The advantages of data are many, but you can't access these benefits without the proper data analytics tools and processes. While raw data has a lot of potential, you need data analytics to unlock the power to grow your business. The term data analytics refers to the process of examining datasets to draw conclusions about the information they contain. Data analytic techniques enable you to take raw data

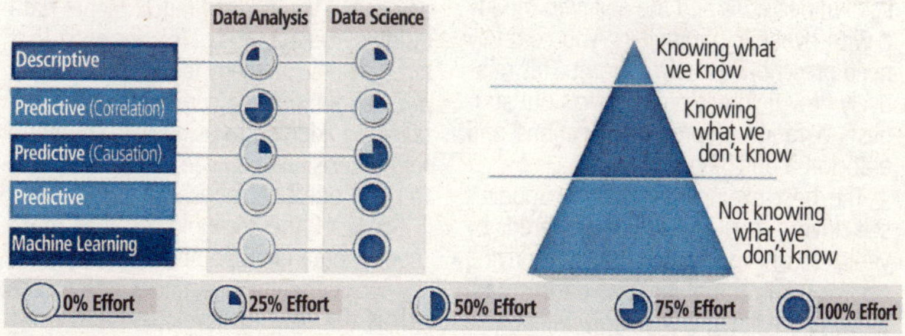

and uncover patterns to extract valuable insights from it.

Today, many data analytics techniques use specialised systems and software that integrate machine learning algorithms, automation and other capabilities.

Data Scientists and Analysts use data analytics techniques in their research, and businesses also use it to inform their decisions. Data analysis can help companies better understand their customers, evaluate their ad campaigns, personalize content, create content strategies and develop products. Ultimately, businesses can use data analytics to boost business performance and improve their bottom line.

So, Data Science is primarily used to make decisions and predictions making use of predictive causal analytics, prescriptive analytics (predictive plus decision science) and machine learning.

Predictive causal analytics – If you want a model that can predict the possibilities of a particular event in the future, you need to apply predictive causal analytics. Say, if you are providing money on credit, then the probability of customers making future credit payments on time is a matter of concern for you. Here, you can build a model that can perform predictive analytics on the payment history of the customer to predict if the future payments will be on time or not.

Prescriptive Analytics: If you want a model that has the intelligence of taking its own decisions and the ability to modify it with dynamic parameters, you certainly need prescriptive analytics for it. This relatively new field not only predicts but suggests a range of prescribed actions and associated outcomes.

The best example for this is Google's self-driving car. The data gathered by vehicles can be used to train self-driving cars. You can run algorithms on this data to bring intelligence to it. This will enable the car to take decisions like when to turn, which path to take, when to slow down or speed up.

Machine learning for making predictions – If you have transactional data of a finance company and need to build a model to determine the future trend, then machine learning algorithms are the best bet. This falls under the paradigm of supervised learning. It is called supervised because you already have the data based on which you can train your machines. For example, a fraud detection model can be trained using a historical record of fraudulent purchases.

Machine learning for pattern discovery – If you don't have the parameters based on which you can make predictions, then you need to find out the hidden patterns within the dataset to be able to make meaningful predictions. This is nothing but the unsupervised model as you don't have any predefined labels for grouping. The most common algorithm used for pattern discovery is Clustering.

Let's say you are working in a telephone company and you need to establish a network by putting towers in a region. Then, you can use the clustering technique to find those tower locations which will ensure that all the users receive optimum signal strength.

Data Analytics Technology

Data analytics is nothing new. Today, though, the growing volume of data and the advanced analytics technologies available mean you can get much deeper data insights more quickly. The insights that big data and modern technologies make possible are more accurate and more detailed. In addition to using data to inform future decisions, you can use current data to make quick decisions.

Some of the technologies that make modern data analytics so powerful are:

Machine learning: Artificial intelligence (AI) is the field of developing and using computer systems that can simulate human intelligence to complete tasks.

Machine learning (ML) is a subset of AI that is significant for data analytics and involves algorithms that can learn on their own. ML enables applications to take in data and analyze it to predict outcomes without someone explicitly programming the system to reach that conclusion. You can train a machine learning algorithm on a small sample of data, and the system will continue to learn as it gathers more data, becoming more accurate as time goes on.

Data management: Before you analyze data, you need to have procedures in place for managing the flow of data in and out of your systems and keeping your data organised. You also need to ensure that your data is high-quality and that you collect it in a central data management platform (DMP) where it's available for use when needed. Establishing a DMP can help ensure that your organisation is on the same page regarding how to organize and handle data.

Data mining: This term refers to the process of sorting through large amounts of data to identify patterns and discover relationships between data points. It enables you to sift through large datasets and figure out what's relevant. You can then use this information to conduct analyses and inform your decisions. Today's data mining technologies allow you to complete these tasks exceptionally quickly.

Big Data Analytics

Big data analytics examines large amounts of data to uncover hidden patterns, correlations and other insights. With modern technology, it's possible to analyze data and get answers from it almost immediately. Big data analytics helps organizations harness their data and use it to identify new opportunities. That, in turn, leads to smarter business moves, more efficient operations, higher profits and happier customers.

3-Way Value Creation: Significant Cost reduction-in storing large amounts of data – plus they can identify more efficient ways of doing business. Faster, better decision making. - analyze information immediately – and make decisions based on what they've learned. New products and services. With the ability to gauge customer needs and satisfaction through analytics comes the power to give customers what they want.

Data Ethics

It is a new branch of ethics that studies and evaluates moral problems related to data (including generation, recording, curation, processing, dissemination, sharing and use), algorithms (including artificial intelligence, artificial agents, machine learning and robots) and corresponding practices (including responsible innovation, programming, hacking and professional codes), in order to formulate and support morally good solutions (e.g. right conducts or right values). Data ethics builds on the foundation provided by computer and information ethics. It highlights the need for ethical analyses to concentrate on the content and nature of computational operations—the interactions among hardware, software and data—rather than on the variety of digital technologies that enable them. And it emphasizes the complexity of the ethical challenges posed by data science. Because of such complexity, data ethics should be developed from the start as a macroethics, that is, as an overall framework that avoids narrow, ad hoc approaches and addresses the ethical impact and implications of data science and its applications within a consistent, holistic and inclusive framework. Only macroethics will provide solutions that can maximize the value of data science for all of us and for our environments.

5G Wireless and Wi-Fi 6

5G is a completely new technology that isn't backwards compatible, which means that new hardware will be needed to broadcast and receive 5G signals. Existing non-5G devices won't be able to connect to 5G networks, even at lower speeds.

According to Forbes, Wi-Fi 6 is reportedly up to four times faster than 5G in certain use cases, so 5G isn't likely to unseat Wi-Fi 6 as the preferred method of connecting to the internet when stationary.

As for use cases, 5G and Wi-Fi 6 each have their niche, but analysts and industry experts have argued that the two complement each other to create a larger, faster, and more accessible internet.

WI-Fi **6** is supposed to make Wi-Fi networks faster, more reliable, and more energy efficient than ever, but what exactly does that mean? Wi-Fi 6 is the Wi-Fi Alliance's name for 802.11ax under its new naming scheme that is designed to make Wi-Fi generations easier to understand for the average computer user. Wi-Fi 6 replaces Wi-Fi 5 (802.11ac), which in turn replaced Wi-Fi 4 (802.11n) as the standard for Wi-Fi speed in 2013.

It's easy to get confused about what Wi-Fi 6 is and how it improves upon older Wi-Fi standards, especially with the coming release of 5G wireless technology at roughly the same time. It would make sense that these two new technologies are somehow related, but that isn't the case. Both promise similar improvements to wireless speed, range, and reliability, but they're distinctly different technologies.

What is Wi-Fi 6?

Wi-Fi 6 is the next evolution of wireless local area network (WLAN) technology. The name Wi-Fi 6 is part of a new naming convention the Wi-Fi Alliance imposed on Wi-Fi standards to make them more easily understood by Wi-Fi users, making it much like the 3G/4G/5G naming convention used by cellular data networks. The new designations have nothing to do with speed, bandwidth capabilities, or other technical benchmarks--they're purely generational.

Behind the Wi-Fi 6 name is the latest version of the 802.11 wireless networking standard: 802.11ax. This new Wi-Fi standard is reportedly up to 30% faster than Wi-Fi 5, but speed hasn't been the main benefit touted by the Wi-Fi Alliance and other industry experts; Wi-Fi 6 also brings lower latency, more simultaneously deliverable data, and improved power efficiency. In order to provide these changes, Wi-Fi 6 is improving on and introducing new technology.

Potential Applications •IoT hardware will benefit from Wi-Fi 6 through improved battery performance, better outdoor operation, and improved range; •Home Wi-Fi, which will be faster and more reliable thanks to increased throughput and superior coverage; • stadiums and other public venues with Wi-Fi will see increased performance • environments with multiple Access Points belonging to different networks (malls, airports, etc.) will have less signal interference to worry about thanks to transmit beamforming.• Wi-Fi 6 may also make wireless last-mile internet connections more plausible due to its superior speeds, ability to handle more users with less latency, and better outdoor performance.

Internet of Things Trending in 2021

The fourth wave of the Industry revolution is about being digitally empowered and driving new technologies and IT services across edge and cloud assets to drive productivity. These technologies include everything from advanced analytics, industrial Internet of Things (IoT) platforms, artificial intelligence, and digital twins and serve the manufacturing sector's core needs. In the last few years, it has been observed that the Internet of Things has boomed. According to industry research, there will be 35 billion IoT devices installed globally by 2021 and 75.44 billion by 2025. Essentially, as a tech-driven network of connected devices, the IoT has the potential to enable data sharing within the system better. Its ability to let machines and equipment to communicate will impact industries..

- The pandemic has significantly enhanced telemedicine resources, and 43.5% of people utilized telehealth facilities in April 2020.

Internet of Things Made Universal in Manufacturing

Due to the pandemic manufacturing industry and other environments with costly machinery have experienced the virtues of remote monitoring first-hand. Remote tracking of machinery has undergone a trial in the post-pandemic era, and many organizations have now embraced these capabilities.

With the help of IoT driven technology, manufacturers and pharmaceutical businesses were able to connect industrial assets this year to remote operations, ensuring business as usual during the pandemic period. The benefits and positive impact promise significant investments flowing in IoT in 2021, according to industry reports.

Connected Devices in Healthcare

The pandemic has significantly enhanced telemedicine resources, and 43.5% of people utilized telehealth facilities in April 2020. One of telemedicine's significant benefits is that it reduces contact between patients, healthcare workers, and other patients. IoT devices help medical workers to have real-time information on patient data while they remain at home.

In coming years there will be a greater need to use connected healthcare solutions to manage illnesses and monitor health. Telemedicine is expected to continue even after the pandemic is over. According to industry experts, there will also be greater interest in digital health devices among consumers due to convivence and more affordable prices, and the technology will grow $185.6 billion by 2026.

Internet of Behaviour

IoB captures the "digital information" of people's lives from various sources, and public or private entities can use that information to influence behaviour. The COVID-19 changed the way many organisations think. Work-from-home and social distancing are the new normal for everyone and staying healthy is one of the topmost concerns. So, we expect to see more IoT technologies in the field that monitors behaviour in various ways to enforce health and safety guidelines. Organisations are taking advantage of technology to monitor consumer and customer behaviours. Some of the useful technological tools here include location tracking, big data, and facial recognition. The Internet of Behaviours (IoB) can be perceived as a people-centric approach to the IoT. This trend highlights the importance of keeping the customers at the center of each organisational strategy to succeed in the long term.

The Digital Divide

The digital divide refers to the gap between demographics and regions that have access to modern information and communications technology (ICT), and those that don't or have restricted access. This technology can include the telephone, television, personal computers and internet connectivity.

The digital divide typically exists between those in urban areas and those in rural areas; between the educated and the uneducated; between socioeconomic groups; and, globally, between the more and less industrially developing countries.

Even among populations with some access to technology, the digital divide can be evident in the form of lower-performance computers, lower-speed wireless connections, lower-priced internet use connections such as dial-up and limited access to subscription-based content.

The digital divide in developing countries includes a lack of access to digital technology and internet service. It can also include a lack of accessibility to modern, high-quality new technologies such as mobile phones and Wi-Fi access.

Bridging the Digital Divide Proponents for bridging the digital divide include those who argue it would improve digital literacy, digital skills democracy, social mobility, economic equality and economic growth.

The UN, for example, has helped to raise awareness regarding the global digital divide through the yearly celebration of World Information Society Day. It has also created the Information and Communication Technologies Task Force in an effort to bridge the global digital divide. However, overcoming the digital divide has not gotten easier, particularly in the aftermath of the COVID-19 pandemic.

India Digital Divide India's digital divide has further deepened because of COVID-19 pandemic. •The nation has the second-largest internet user base in the world with more than 630 million subscribers. It also has the lowest mobile data prices offered anywhere. Despite this, for every Indian citizen with an internet subscription, there is a citizen in a rural area who lacks one. Considering 66% of the population lives in rural areas, there is a sizeable percentage of the country's people living in regions where internet access is minimal.

•Marginalised and vulnerable communities, esp., those living in poverty, could benefit the most from the connectivity and opportunities digital technology provides. By closing the gap in digital access between rural and urban communities in India, the nation will be able to develop and progress more efficiently as a whole.

Digital Access as an Equalizer Digital inclusion is essential in the post-pandemic scenario as the "new normal" becomes more digital than ever. Today, meetings, social events and other large gatherings are moving to online alternatives to practice social distancing and reduce the risk of spreading illness. However, for the many people in India who do not have access to stable internet connections, life is put on standby. As a result, these individuals fall behind as society resumes life online.

Prior to the pandemic, only 23.8% of households across the country had access to the internet. Additionally, there is a wide divide in access between urban and rural households. Of the 66% of India's population that resides in rural communities, only 14.9% have internet access compared to 42% of urban households.

Gender Inequality in India India's digital divide between rural and urban regions contributes to social gender inequality in the society. •36% of Indian males have mobile internet access compared to only 16% of females. This inequality of digital access across genders creates greater dependence on men for women who often rely financially on their spouses in the Indian family context. These women don't afford a device on their own. As the male head of the family is often the only member to possess a digital device, women rely on their spouses to have internet connectivity. This limits what and for how long they may use these devices. Some villages even limit women's use of mobile phones, further hindering their connectivity to social media and educational resources and information. This diminishes women's overall digital empowerment and independence. By limiting women's freedom to use the internet, these villages also restrict the possibility of individual growth and evolution of perspective by blocking access to the digital global network.

Geographical Divide Even geographical differences lead to disparities in internet access. Himachal Pradesh is a remote, mountainous region in the Himalayas and the sparsely populated deserts of Rajasthan are two territories that face higher levels of digital exclusion. Residents of these areas are mostly tribal communities who already experience marginalisation from the rest of Indian society. Therefore a lack of internet access bolsters already existing challenges for these communities. Evidently, the digital divide deepens several other partitions across the societal fabric. In addressing the digital divide, many other related issues would also be resolved.

Divide in Educational Attainment India has the largest student body in the world with 315 million students. This leaves the country with a large amount of responsibility in maintaining education for all students during pandemic-driven school closures. Currently, the COVID-19 outbreak has exposed and expanded the divide between private and government educational institutions.

Private schools in India had less of a challenge transitioning to online learning since the more affluent student population is more likely to have consistent internet access and mobile devices available at home. In comparison, government institutions lack similar access to e-learning solutions. Additionally, the students who attend government-funded schools are more likely to experience inconsistent electricity, poor internet connection or inhospitable housing conditions that prohibit online learning.

The differences in operations between the two institutional groups will result in students receiving different educations during lockdown conditions. This is especially concerning for students enrolled in government schooling as there is increased reliability on parents to continue educating students independently despite potentially lacking the time, resources or intellect. Furthermore, these students will face greater difficulty than their peers at private institutions in finally resuming regular schooling after a long gap.

Closing the Digital Divide The digital divide in India is challenging the nation's current educational methods across its entire student body. The digital divide in India must be addressed and rectified. •Digital connectivity is more necessary than ever before in guaranteeing that students can sustain their studies while schools remain physically closed.

•For starters, an increased financial stimulus for education is necessary to allow greater access to online resources for children who may not have any. This way, schools can rely on and distribute their own digital resources for at-home learning instead of depending on students to have mobile devices at home. Furthermore, this will provide essential funding to education in India, which already receives low government expenditure.

Addressing rising healthcare prices could also help diminish the digital divide in India. Increasing costs push millions of Indians into poverty each year for basic healthcare; this reduces available funds for non-essential spending, including internet subscriptions or mobile devices.

•Other actions are teaching computer science and mathematics in schools to increase digital literacy, expanding broadband connectivity to rural villages and increasing funding for already existing programs, such as the Digital India Project.

Attracting government attention to the indispensability of internet access is crucial. Ensuring uninterrupted internet service for more of the population would launch coronavirus recovery, education and national development forward while ensuring that India's most vulnerable populations are not left behind.

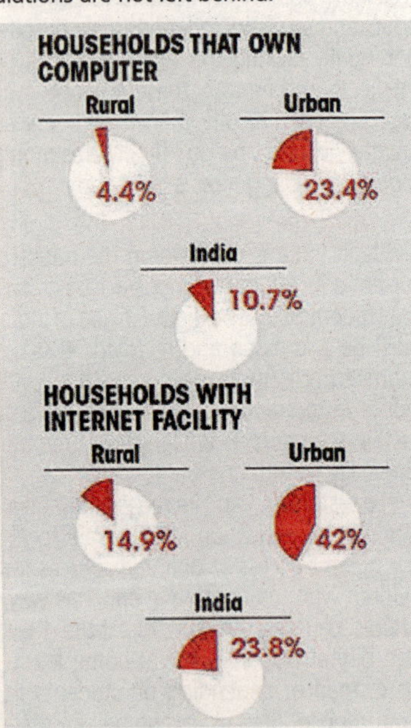

Regional Disparity

* Able to operate computer (%) @ Able to use Internet (%) # State

There is significant difference among states in their ability to access internet and operate computers.

State	● Rural ○	● Urban ○
1. Andhra Pradesh	1.5/10.4	11.6/29.5
2. Asom	3.7/12.1	30.8/46.9
3. Bihar	2.7/12.5	20/38.6
4. Chattisgarh	3.2/10.6	22/34.6
5. Delhi	NA	34.7/55.8
6. Gujarat	4.4/21.1	20.1/49.1
7. Haryana	5.9/37.1	29.5/55.4
8. HP	10.5/48.6	28.3/70.6
9. J&K	3.5/28.7	16/57.7
10. Jharkhand	1.3/11.9	15.6/40.2
11. Karnataka	2/ 8.3	22.9/33.5
12. Kerala	20.1/46.9	27.5/56.4
13. MP	2.3/9.7	17.2/35.4
14. MH	3.3/18.5	27.4/52
15. Odisha	1.8/5.8	17.2/31.2
16. Punjab	9.4/39.4	26.7/57.1
17. Rajasthan	6.4/18.5	26.6/49.9
18. TN	11.6/14.4	24.7/24.8
19. Telangana	1.6/9.9	17.6/41.9
20. Uttarakhand	7/35.2	32.5/64.3
21. UP	4/11.6	22.3/41
22. WB	3.3/7.9	23/36

● Able to operate computer (in %)

○ Able to use internet (in %)

Persons of Age 5 Years and above Who:

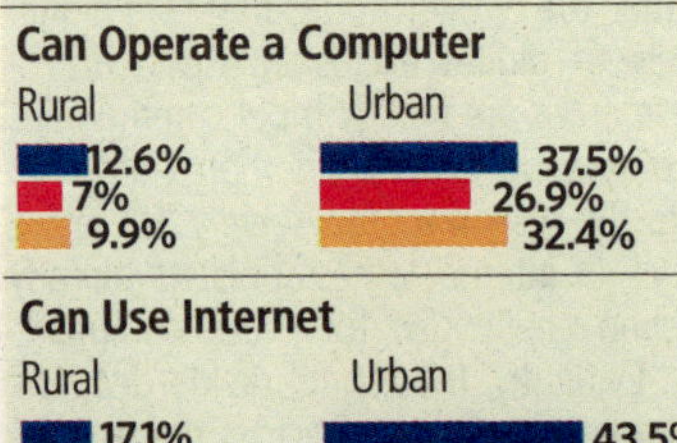

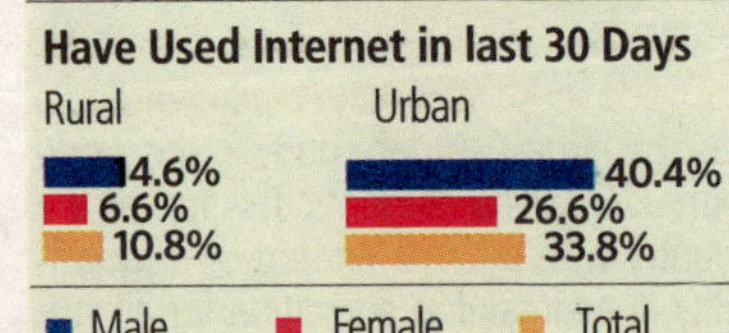

■ Male ■ Female ■ Total

Digital Economy

Digital economy (DE) is a collective term for all economic transactions that occur on the internet. It is also known as the Web Economy or the Internet Economy. With the advent of technology and the process of globalisation, the digital and traditional economies are merging into one.

This concept of DE focuses on digital technologies and computing technologies. It covers all business, economic, social, cultural etc. activities that are supported by the web and other digital communication technologies. The term was first coined in a book *The Digital Economy: Promise and Peril* in the Age of Networked Intelligence by author Don Tapscott in 1995. There are three components of this economy, namely, •e-business •e-business infrastructure •e-commerce. In the last 15 years, we have seen the tremendous growth of digital platforms and their influence on our lives. Now consumers are influenced by things they see on social media (Facebook, Twitter, Instagram) and other such popular websites (YouTube etc). So this economy is a way to exploit this opportunity. Now it is integrated into every aspect of the user's life – healthcare, education, banking, entertainment, etc

Merits of Digital Economy

DE has given rise to many new trends and start-up ideas. Almost all of the biggest companies in the world (Google, Apple, Microsoft, Amazon) are from the digital world. Some merits of the digital economy: 1. Promotes Use of the Internet Today most of our daily work can be done on the internet. The massive growth of technology and the worldwide internet network has contributed to huge investment in hardware, technological research, software, services, digital communication etc. And so DE has ensured that the internet is here to stay and so are web-based businesses.

2. Rise in E-Commerce The businesses that adapted and adopted the internet and embraced online business in the last decade have flourished. The digital economy has pushed the e-commerce sector into overdrive. Not just direct selling but buying, distribution, marketing, creating, selling is easy due to the digital economy.

3. Digital Goods and Services Gone are the days of Movie DVD and Music CD's. Now, these goods are available digitally. There is no need for any tangible products anymore. So is true for services – banking, insurance etc. There is no need to visit your bank if you can do every transaction online. So certain goods and services have been completely digitized in this digital economy.

4. Transparency Most transactions and their payment in the digital economy happen online. Cash transactions are becoming rare. This helps reduce the black money and corruption in the market and make the economy more transparent. In fact, during the demonetisation, the government made a push for online transactions to promote the web economy.

Demerits of Digital Economy

1. Loss in Employment The more we depend on technology, the less we depend on human resources. The advancement of the DE may lead to the loss of many jobs. As the processes get more automated, the requirement for human resources reduces, like online banking. 2. Lack of Experts DE requires complex processes and technologies to build the platforms. Its upkeep require trained professionals. 3. Heavy Investment DE requires a strong infrastructure, high functioning Internet, strong mobile networks and telecommunication. All of this is a time consuming and investment heavy process. In India, development of infrastructure and network is slow, tedious and costly.

Quantum Communication

For the first time in the country, ISRO has successfully demonstrated free-space Quantum Communication over a distance of 300 m. A number of key technologies were developed indigenously to accomplish this major feat, which included the use of indigenously developed NAVIC receiver for time synchronisation between the transmitter and receiver modules, and gimbal mechanism systems instead of bulky large-aperture telescopes for optical alignment.

The Quantum Key Distribution (QKD) technology underpins Quantum Communication technology that ensures unconditional data security through principles of quantum mechanics, which is impossible with the conventional encryption systems. The conventional cryptosystems used for data-encryption rely on the complexity of mathematical algorithms, but the security offered by quantum communication is based on the laws of Physics. Thus, quantum cryptography is considered as 'future-proof', since no future advancements in the computational power can break it.

The free-space QKD was demonstrated at Space Applications Centre (SAC), Ahmedabad, between two line-of-sight buildings within the campus. The experiment was performed at night, in order to ensure that there is no interference of the direct sunlight. The experiment is a major breakthrough towards ISRO's goal of demonstrating Satellite Based Quantum Communication (SBQC), where ISRO is gearing up to demonstrate the technology between two Indian ground stations.

Big Data

Big Data is huge dataset generated at a source (like space rocket launch, nuclear test, super online sales) which can't be managed by traditional RDBMS systems. All social media platforms, Telecom and health care industries deals with huge data usually in petabytes (1024 terabytes or 1 million gigabytes). Data has variety (structure, semi-structured), which flows at high speed. Big Data frame works are designed with concept of distribution of data to handle Big data characters such as 1.Volume (storage space); 2. Velocity (Processing speed–high speed of data accumulation); 3. Verity (structured, semi-structured and unstructured data); 4. Veracity (extracting required data – inconsistencies & uncertainty 5. Value (extract useful data)

Artificial Intelligence

Artificial Intelligence is the science and engineering of making intelligent machines, esp. intelligent computer programs.

What AI Aims •To Create Expert Systems–The systems which exhibit intelligent behavior, learn, demonstrate, explain, and advice its users. • To Implement Human Intelligence in Machines–Creating systems that understand, think, learn, and behave like humans.

AI Domain • Strategy Gaming (chess), where machine can think of options). •Natural Language Processing–to understand natural human language •Expert Systems– (provide explanation and advice to the users). •Vision Systems–used by doctors to diagnose or Police to identify criminals •Speech Recognition •Handwriting Recognition •Intelligent Robots

- Environment Scan
- Global Warming
- SDG: India's Agenda for Development
- The World's First 'Infinite' Plastic
- The Water Cycle is Intensifying
- UN 2021-2030
- IPCC Climate Change 6th Report, 2021
- Disaster Management

Environment Scan

Sundarlal Bahuguna

Noted environmentalist Sunderlal Bahuguna, synonymous with the Chipko movement, passed away on May 8 after testing positive for Covid-19. Shri Sunderlal had been fighting for the preservation of forests in the Himalayas, first as a leader of the Chipko movement and later led the anti-Tehri Dam movement a decade later.

• Born in Maroda near Tehri, Uttarakhand in 1927. • Fought against untouchability •Started organising women from the state in anti-liquor drives from 1965 to 1970. •Adopted Gandhian principles and walked through Himalayan forests for 4,700 km and observed the damage done by mega developmental projects on the fragile ecosystem of the Himalayas and subsequent degradation of social life in villages.

Ghosts Forests

Scientists at the Duke University and the University of Virginia have documented how sea-level rise is triggering forest die-offs in coastal regions. Studying the vegetation in North Carolina, they found that rising seas are inundating the State's coast, and saltwater is seeping further into the land and wetlands. This salty water killed huge swaths of contiguous forest, which is called 'ghost forests'. Using satellite images, scientists have shown that more than 10% of forested wetland within the Alligator River National Wildlife Refuge have been lost in the last 35 years and that the widespread loss of forest has cascading impact on wildlife. Ghosts forests have been witnessed in other parts of the world too.

Famed Darwin's Arch in Galapagos Is.

The iconic arch, named for British naturalist Charles Darwin, that stood at the northernmost tip of the Galapagos Islands, a volcanic archipelago in the Pacific Ocean 965 km west of Ecuador collapsed. Once a part of Darwin's Island, the arch is famed for the variety of underwater life teeming nearby, including schools of hammerhead sharks. The famed natural rock formation in the Galapagos Islands was popular with divers, photographers and cruise-ship tourists, collapsed from erosion.

Fossils of the largest land mammal to ever walk the Earth unearthed

According to a study published in the journal *Communications Biology* by Institute of Vertebrate Paleontology and Paleoanthropology, fossils unearthed in China reveal a new species of giant prehistoric rhinoceros. Paleontologists discovered a complete skull from one rhino and three vertebrae from another, in the Linxia basin in the Gansu Province of northwestern China. The three-foot-long skull of a rhino the size of six elephants came from the largest known land mammal to ever walk the Earth. Taller than a giraffe and roughly the size of six elephants, the rhino towered 23 feet above the ground, and its body was 26 feet long. It weighed roughly 24 tons. The set of bones is 26.5 million years old. The find indicates giant rhinos migrated south, then back north via Tibet, as the climate changed. Genetic analysis revealed that the fossils belonged to a species of giant rhino that scientists had

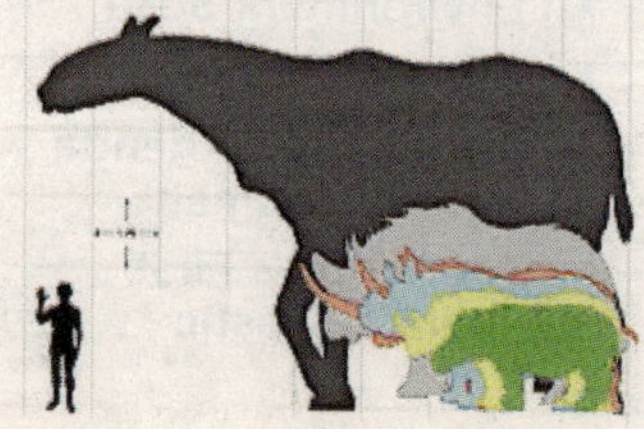

never seen before. The team of researchers from China and the US dubbed the new animal "Paraceratherium linxiaense. Scientists already knew about giant rhinos, or Paraceratherium, which have been found across Asia – in Pakistan, Kazakhstan, Mongolia, and China. But Paraceratherium linxiaense made huge migrations across the continent. In the early Oligocene era, 31 million years ago, when the Mongolian plateau dried up, giant rhinos moved out of the northern Tibetan plateau and they made the trek back north during the late Oligocene.

Gap of 5.5 bn Tonnes of CO_2

Scientist Giacomo Grassi, author of a study on the Gap, published in the journal *Nature Climate Change,* that they have detected a large gap, between the amount of climate-warming emissions that countries report and the amount that independent models say reaches the atmosphere. It is said to be equal to about what the United States emits annually.

The gap of about 5.5 billion tonnes of CO_2 per year arises not because any country is doing anything wrong. Rather, it is due to differences between scientific methods used in national inventories that countries report under the 2015 Paris agreement on climate change and methods used by international models. In the meantime India's percentage CO_2 emissions is reported to have rose faster than the world average.

As countries work to keep their commitments to cut emissions as part of the Paris agreement to limit the global temperature rise to 1.5 degrees Celsius above pre-industrial levels, the discrepancy could become a larger issue. If models and countries speak a different language, assessing country climate progress will be more difficult. The study requires developing country-specific adjustments norms, "but countries that had previously used an incomparable benchmark may eventually need to update their target. It could mean some countries will have to adjust their emissions reductions.

Wildlife Forensic

Pangolins, despite being listed in Schedule I of Wildlife (Protection) Act, 1972 continue to be the world's most trafficked mammal. The primary demand for its scales in the making of traditional East Asian medicines has led to an estimated illegal trade worth $2.5 billion every year.

According to *Forensic Science International,* to enforce the appropriate national and international laws and to track the decline of the species, researchers of Zoological Survey of India (ZSI), Kolkata, have now developed forensic tools to tell apart the scales of Indian pangolin (Manis crassicaudata) and Chinese pangolin (Manis pentadactyla). They characterised the morphological features and investigated genetic variations between the two species by sequencing 624 scales of pangolins and comparing the sequences with all eight pangolin species. Based on the size, shape, weight and ridge counts on the scales, the team was able to categorise the two species. These metric characters can be of immense useful for the law enforcement agencies for taking spot decision during larger seizures.

Green Panel Okay Great Nicobar Plan

The Environment Appraisal Committee (EAC) - Infrastructure of the Ministry of Environment, Forest and Climate Change (MoEFCC) had flagged serious concerns about NITI Aayog's ambitious project for Great Nicobar Island 'Holistic Development of Great Nicobar Island at Andaman and Nicobar Islands' which ignored tribal, ecological concerns. MoEFCC's Parivesh portal show that the 15-member committee headed by marine biologist and former director, Bombay Natural History Society (BNHS), Deepak Apte, made the decision. The proposal includes an international con-

Earth Day Doodle
On the 51st anniversary of Earth Day, Google splashed an animated video doodle highlighting the importance of planting seeds for a brighter and greener future. According to Google, their doodle showed a variety of trees being planted within natural habitats underlined one of the many ways in which people could do their part to keep the Earth healthy for future generations.

tainer transshipment terminal, a greenfield international airport, a power plant and a township complex spread over 166 sq. km. (mainly pristine coastal systems and tropical forests), and would cost ₹75,000 crore.

Greening Investments
Environmental, Social and Governance (ESG) investing are investments that seek positive returns and long-term impact on society, environment and the performance of the business. With picks, you can influence positive corporate behaviour and support companies who are being more discerning. In today's world, investors are not only interested in the financial performance of their investments, but the impact their investments can have in promoting global issues such as climate action, renewable energy, new technology, waste management, recycling and healthcare innovation. ESG or "sustainable" investing is also underpinned by an expectation that companies which score highly on environmental, societal responsibility and corporate governance scales are likely to stay the course and perform well financially - there is compelling commercial rationale behind this too. In 2020, the number of investment funds focused on ESG more than doubled. One demographic particularly drawn to ESG investing is millennials.

Locust Challenge
Of old, locusts have been around, since 32

B.C, at least the time of the pharaohs of ancient Egypt. 2019 witnessed swarms of locust attacking Yemen, Saudi Arabia, SW Iran. and the India-Pakistan border.

What is a Locust? Locusts are part of the grasshopper family. A swarm of just 1 sq. km would contain about 40 million insects. It can eat the same amount of food in one day as 35,000 people, 20 camels or six elephants. They are powerful, long-distance flyers, so they can easily go a hundred plus kilometers in a 24-hour period. They can easily move across countries in a matter of days. It's a major challenge that requires co-ordinated efforts between nations and institutions to control them. In 1988, swarms originating in N Africa crossed the Atlantic Ocean and made it to the Caribbean and S America. Even now, they cross the Red Sea – a distance of 186 miles. India suffered the biggest locust attack in 25 years when it invaded Andhra, Telangana, Karnataka, Haryana, Himachal Pradesh, Punjab and Delhi. Crops were affected in more than 3.5 lakh hectares in various districts of Rajasthan and Gujarat. Crops of mustard, cumin and wheat were devastated in the two states.

Impact on food security Locusts are ravenous eaters. An adult desert locust that weighs about 2 grams can consume roughly its own weight daily. When they do descend, they cause total devastation–they can destroy 50 to 80% of crops depending on the time [of year]. The last large locust outbreak of 2003 lasted until 2005. It destroyed crop worth $2.5 bn.

Fire in the Wild

It is agonizing to learn that six million hectares of forest and more than half a billion animals were lost in the Australia's worst fire season. The primary cause behind the magnitude of the wildfires is attributed to climate change.

It is not without reason that the Anthropocene age is being hailed as the 'Pyrocene' age. Unstoppable fires – took the Amazon, California, Indonesia or Australia by force. Fire deaths and fire refugees, smoked-in and incinerated cities, economic crunches from infrastructural losses and lost tourism are just some of the traits that characterise this age.

In 2020, the tropics lost around 12 million hectares of tree cover, of which 3.64 million hectares was primary forest, the most biodiverse and carbon-dense type of forest. 2019 will be remembered as the year the climate crisis shook everybody, and hopefully also for the mass protests and civic movements against governments and industries failing to respond. Calls to combat the climate emergency were ringing in the ears of delegations from nearly 200 countries at the annual UN climate summit that opened in Madrid on Dec 2. Strangely, the heads of government of the world's biggest emitters were notably absent, including US, China, Russia and Brazil.

Challenges The climate crisis and species extinction are twin challenges with far-reaching consequences. In 2019, a landmark report by IPBES, the Intergovernmental Science-Policy Platform on Biodiversity and Ecosystem Services, warned that more than one million animal and plant species are now threatened with extinction, many within decades. IPS also covered how drought in some areas of Africa would cause famine and migration. The expanding Sahara desert is breaking up families and spreading conflict.

One-fifth of Indian Forests Fire-prone

According to the Forest Survey of India (FSI) 2019 report, about 21.40% of forest cover in India is prone to fires. The forests in the NE-region and central India are most vulnerable. The finding has emerged from a study carried out by the FSI along forest fire points across the country from 2004 to 2017.

Fire-Prone Extremely fire-prone areas account for 3.89% of total forest cover, Very Highly fire prone areas account for 6.01% and Highly fire prone areas for 11.50%.

The reasons for fires are mostlymanmade, particularly in cases where people visit forests and leave burning bidis, cigarette stubs or other inflammable materials. One of the major reasons for forest fires in the NE is slash-and-burn cultivation, or jhoom or jhum cultivation. The fires happen between January and March. The north-east has tropical evergreen forests and, unlike the dry deciduous forests of central India, these are not unlikely to burn easily.• In cases of natural reasons, thunderstorms are the most likely cause. • uncontrolled forest fires can lead to significant loss of cover. • climate change influences forest fire frequency and intensity, resulting in forests becoming highly inflammable.

Green cover While the overall green cover has increased in NE – particularly in Mizoram, Arunachal Pradesh and Nagaland – has decreased.

States recorded a high number of forest fire alerts, (based on MODIS data Nov. 2018 – June 2019): Mizoram 29,547; MP: 2,723 alerts; Maharashtra 2,516; Odisha 2,213, Chattisgarh 1,008.

Global Warming

Global warming, a gradual increase in the average temperature of the Earth's atmosphere and its oceans, is believed to be permanently changing the Earth's climate. There is debate whether global warming is real. But the scientific consensus on climatic changes related to global warming is that the average temperature of the Earth has risen between 0.4 and 0.8 °C over the past 100 years. The increased volumes of carbon dioxide and other greenhouse gases released by the burning of fossil fuels, land clearing, agriculture, and other human activities, are believed to be the primary sources of the global warming that has occurred over the past 50 years. Scientists from the Intergovernmental Panel on Climate have predicted that average global temperatures could increase between 1.4 and 5.8 °C by the year 2100.

Signs of Climate Change

• **Arctic Sea Ice:** Arctic sea ice is declining at a rate of 11.5% per decade. Arctic sea ice reaches its minimum every September. • **Carbon dioxide (CO_2):** It is an important heat-trapping (greenhouse) gas released due to human activities like deforestation, burning fossil fuels, natural processes like respiration and volcanic eruptions. • **Global Temperature:** 2016 is the warmest of the top 10 warmest years since 1880. • **Sea Level:** It is rising 3.16 mm per year. Sea level rise is due to the water coming from the melting of glaciers and the expansion of sea water as it warms up. • **Land Ice:** The land ice sheets in both Antarctica and Greenland are losing mass. The continent of Antarctica has been losing more than 100 cubic kilometres of ice per year, since 2002.

Global Warming Facts

• It is the increase of earth's average surface temperature due to greenhouse gases that collect in the atmosphere.

• Greenhouse gases trap heat and keep it close to the earth's surface making it liveable for humans and animals. However, global warming is due to the over-emission of these gases and fossil fuels.

• With the start of industrial revolution in the 1700's, humans began emitting more fossil fuel gasses (coal, oil, and natural gas) to run our cars, trucks, and factories. .

• There is more carbon dioxide in the atmosphere today than at any point in the last 800,000 years.

• Since 1870, global sea levels have risen by about 8 inches.

• Warming has observable effects on the environment. Glaciers are shrinking, ice on rivers and lakes is drying up, plant and animal have shifted grounds and trees are flowering sooner.

• Heat waves caused by global warming pose a greater risk of heat-related illness and death in human beings.

• It puts coral reefs in danger as the ocean warms resulting in incidents of bleaching.

• Though Americans make up just 4% of the world's population, they produce 25% of the carbon dioxide pollution from fossil-fuel burning – by far the largest share of any country.

SDG: India Agenda for Development

The composite score for each State/UT was computed by aggregating their performance across the goals, by taking the arithmetic mean of individual goal scores. The composite score ranges from 0 to 100 and denotes the overall achievement of the State/UT in achieving the targets under the Goals.

The composite score for India improved, from 60 in 2019-20 to 66 in 2020-21. This indicates that the country overall has progressed forward in its journey towards achieving the SDGs. Nine Goals drive the positive push - 3 (good health and well-being), 6 (clean water and sanitation), 7 (affordable and clean energy), 10 (reduced inequalities), 11 (sustainable cities and communities), 12 (responsible consumption and production), 13 (climate action), 15 (life on land), and 16 (peace, justice, and strong institutions), where India has scored between 65 and 99.

• **Two Goals** - 2 (zero hunger) and 5 (gender equality) demand special attention, as the overall country score is below 50. However, 9 States in Goal 2 and 12 States in Goal 5 moved out of the Aspirant category this year as compared to 2019-20.

The SDG India Index 3.0 score for the States ranges between 52 and 75; for the UTs it belongs to the 62 to 79 band. This presents a notable improvement from 2019-20, when the scores varied between 50 and 70 for the States and 59 and 70 for the UTs.

• **Kerala** retained its rank as the top State with a score of 75. **Chandigarh** too maintained its top spot among the UTs with a score of 79.

• **Tamil Nadu and Himachal Pradesh** took the second spot while **Goa, Ut-**

• Sustainable Development Goals (SDGs) came into being when 193 United Nations member countries adopted a group of 17 goals on 25 September 2015. The aim of the SDG has been cited as to "achieve a better and more sustainable future for all' by the year 2030.
• Came into force on 1st Jan. 2016.
• The SDGs are expected to stimulate developmental actions in areas of critical importance – ending poverty and hunger, providing healthy lives and quality education, achieving gender equality, providing modern energy, promoting sustainable economic growth, reducing inequality etc.
• The 17 SDGs have 169 Targets. Each target consists of 1-3 indicators to measure progress. In total, there are 232 approved indicators envisaged to study compliance.
• The 17 SDGs are evenly distributed and balanced across the 3 dimensions of sustainable development: 6 Social goals (Goals 1 to 6), 5 Economic goals (Goals 7 to 11) and 4 Environmental goals (Goals 12 to 15). A separate goal (Goal 16) on peaceful societies and effective institutions works for the enablers of development. A single goal (Goal 17) on global partnership has also been included to provide financial, technological and systemic support to the developing countries.
• India focusses on the aspect of poverty; infrastructural development, taking development to all sections of society.

tarakhand, Karnataka and Andhra Pradesh shared the fourth spot on the table.

In the other **five Goals** (excluding 14 - life below water, which applies only to **9 coastal States**, and 17 - partnerships for the goals, which is qualitatively analysed), the overall score lies between 50 and 64, including both, indicating the scope for significant improvement in the coming years.

- While in 2019-20, 10 States/UTs belonged to the category of Front Runners (score in the range 65-99, including both), 12 more States/UTs find themselves in this category in 2020-21. **Uttarakhand, Gujarat, Maharashtra, Mizoram, Punjab, Haryana and Tripura** graduated to the category of Front Runners (scores between 65 and 99, including both).
- **Goal 6** has the highest number of Front Runners with 25 States in this category while **Goals 5 and 9** have the highest Aspirants with 14 States each.
- In **SDG 3, SDG 10, SDG 11 and SDG 12**, the country score has moved from the Performer category to the Front Runner category. Among them, **Goal 11** has seen the biggest movement from 53 in 2019-20 to 79 in 2020-21.
- All States have improved their score within a range of 1 to 12 points. **Mizoram, Haryana, and Uttarakhand** are the top gainers in 2020-21, in terms of improvement in score from 2019, with an increase of 12, 10 and 8 points, respectively.

For **Mizoram**, the biggest jumps are in SDG 1 (+13), SDG 3 (+27), SDG 7 (+19), SDG 12 (+37), SDG 13 (+21) and SDG 16 (+18). In the case of **Haryana**, the five goals with biggest improvement are SDG 1 (+22), SDG 7 (+23), SDG 10 (+14), SDG 11 (+32), SDG 12 (+38).

For **Uttarakhand**, the largest rise are in SDG 1 (+10), SDG 3 (+19), SDG 7 (+22), SDG 10 (+18), SDG 11 (+25) and SDG 12 (+32).

Goal-Wise Top State/ UTs

Goal 1: No Poverty: Tamil Nadu, Delhi

Goal 2: Zero Hunger: Kerala, Chandigarh

Goal 3: Good Health and Well-being: Gujarat, Delhi

Goal 4: Quality Education: Kerala, Chandigarh

Goal 5: Gender Equality: Chhattisgarh, Andaman and Nicobar Islands

Goal 6: Clean Water and Sanitation: Goa, Lakshadweep

Goal 7: Affordable and Clean Energy: Andhra Pradesh, Goa, Haryana, Himachal Pradesh, Karnataka, Kerala, Maharashtra, Mizoram, Punjab, Rajasthan, Sikkim, Tamil Nadu, Telangana, Uttarakhand, Uttar Pradesh, Andaman and Nicobar Islands, Chandigarh, Delhi, Jammu and Kashmir, Ladakh

Goal 8: Decent Work and Economic Growth: Himachal Pradesh, Chandigarh

Goal 9: Industry, Innovation and Infrastructure: Gujarat, Delhi

Goal 10: Reduced Inequality: Meghalaya, Chandigarh

Goal 11: Sustainable Cities and Communities: Punjab, Chandigarh

Goal 12: Responsible Consumption and Production: Tripura, Jammu and Kashmir, Ladakh

Goal 13: Climate Action: Odisha, Andaman and Nicobar Islands

Goal 14: Life Below Water: Odisha

State/UT	07	06	12	16	11	03	10	01	15	08	04	02	13	05	09	Composite SDG
KL	100	89	65	80	75	72	69	83	77	62	80	80	69	63	60	75
HP	100	85	77	73	79	78	78	80	68	78	74	52	62	62	61	74
TN	100	87	78	71	79	81	74	86	63	71	69	66	61	59	71	74
AD	100	92	84	77	78	77	74	81	69	67	50	52	63	58	52	72
GA	100	100	47	63	89	72	75	83	59	76	71	78	44	55	68	72
KA	100	85	89	76	78	78	67	68	67	66	64	53	62	57	64	72
UK	100	85	82	86	76	77	77	74	64	63	70	61	60	46	56	72
SK	100	89	76	72	85	62	61	80	73	71	58	69	65	58	52	71
MH	100	90	82	69	87	83	71	66	52	62	64	44	58	51	66	70
GJ	94	93	50	82	87	86	64	66	61	64	52	46	67	49	72	69
TG	100	96	73	71	76	67	67	68	81	73	63	50	43	41	59	69
MZ	100	85	87	81	61	79	64	80	48	51	60	72	66	54	32	68
PB	100	66	71	76	91	77	68	69	48	57	60	73	51	45	69	68
HR	100	80	77	71	81	72	68	69	48	59	64	58	51	43	66	67
TR	83	82	99	80	67	67	85	82	69	57	42	52	41	39	35	65
MN	96	87	89	69	65	68	70	60	60	36	63	64	57	41	35	64
MP	86	88	78	66	81	62	51	44	84	60	45	43	49	55	37	62
WB	98	81	79	81	45	76	71	59	53	57	54	46	39	41	53	62
CT	78	89	64	71	78	60	72	49	65	64	55	37	38	64	36	61
NL	69	87	91	79	48	61	46	73	63	48	39	64	69	48	30	61
OR	80	86	73	59	70	67	66	41	83	48	45	42	70	46	46	61
AR	85	67	77	64	39	64	69	54	93	50	41	66	58	37	31	60
ML	50	75	73	72	51	70	88	77	64	63	48	37	62	51	25	60
RJ	100	54	74	73	81	70	45	63	43	57	60	53	49	39	45	60
UP	100	83	79	79	77	60	41	44	61	53	51	41	39	50	42	60
AS	98	64	66	62	55	59	65	51	78	50	43	41	53	25	39	57
JH	77	83	55	70	71	74	65	36	71	54	45	19	25	51	37	56
BR	78	91	59	73	67	66	48	32	62	50	29	31	16	48	24	52
Union Territories																
CH	100	99	78	73	98	74	100	75	85	70	79	97	61	58	45	79
DL	100	61	50	62	65	90	72	81	81	65	75	63	55	33	66	68
LD	83	100	63	77	56	78	75	61	67	62	62	74	68	58	40	68
PY	98	91	66	86	76	70	62	75	50	68	70	59	23	66	59	68
AN Is.	100	87	73	46	85	68	67	71	72	59	57	45	77	68	23	67
J&K	100	88	95	74	57	70	65	69	52	47	49	71	63	46	42	66
LK	100	84	95	74	57	70	65	79	27	59	49	71	66	46	48	66
DND	71	95	62	75	89	80	66	65	62	57	56	27	18	53	47	62
India	92	83	74	74	79	74	67	60	66	61	57	47	54	48	55	66
Target	100	100	100	100	100	100	100	100	100	100	100	100	100	100	100	100

Aspirant (0-49) **Performer** (50-64) **Front Runner** (65-99) **Achiever** (100)

The heatmap displays the performance of each State/UT on each of the Goals. The States/UTs are arranged in a descending order according to their composite scores. The State/UT with the highest composite score is in the top of their respective list while the one with the lowest score is at the bottom of the list. The columns are arranged according to the average performance of all States/UTs in a certain Goal, with the Goal where all States/UTs have on an average performed well (i.e. Goal 7) being in the left-most column and the Goal where all States/UTs have on an average performed relatively poorly (i.e. Goal 9) being in the right-most column (before the composite score).

The World's First 'Infinite' Plastic

There is one man-made material that we can find in the earth, the air and in the deepest ocean trenches. It is so durable that the majority of what has been created is still present in our ecosystem. Having made its way into the food chain, it permeates our bodies, flowing from our blood into our organs, even finding its way into the human placenta.

It is, of course, plastic, and its durability is what makes the material so useful. Efficiently recycling plastic by conventional means is very difficult, and only 9% of all plastic ever made has been recycled into new plastics. But what if there was a way to turn plastic back into the stuff it was made from? The "next grand challenge" for polymer chemistry – the field responsible for the creation of plastics – is turning plastics back into oil. This process – known as chemical recycling – has been explored as a viable alternative to conventional recycling for decades. So far, the stumbling block has been the large amount of energy it requires. This, combined with the volatile price of crude oil sometimes makes it cheaper to produce new plastic products than to recycle existing plastic.

Every year, more than 380 million tonnes of plastic is produced worldwide. That's about the same as 2,700,000 blue whales – more than 100 times the weight of the entire blue whale population. Just 16% of plastic waste is recycled to make new plastics, while 40% is sent to landfill, 25% to incineration and 19% is dumped. Much of the plastic that could be recycled – such as polyethylene terephthalate (PET), which is used for bottles and other packaging – ends up in landfill. Other plastics – such as salad bags and other food containers – find their way to landfill because they are made up of a combination of different plastics that can't be easily split apart in a recycling plant. Litter dropped in the street and lightweight plastics left in landfill sites or illegally dumped can be carried by the wind or washed into rivers by the rain, ending up in the ocean. Chemical recycling techniques are being trialled across the world. In the UK, Mura Technology has constructed the world's first commercial-scale plant that recycle all kinds of plastic. The most versatile version of chemical recycling is "feedstock recycling". Also known as thermal conversion, feedstock recycling is any process that breaks polymers down into simpler molecules using heat. The UK-based Recycling Technologies has developed a pyrolysis machine that turns hard-to-recycle plastic such as films, bags and laminated plastics into Plaxx. This liquid hydrocarbon feedstock can be used to make new virgin quality plastic. The Plastic Energy plants in Spain transform hard-to-recycle plastic waste, into food-grade plastics. In the US, the chemical company Ineos became the first to use depolymerisation on a commercial scale to produce recycled polyethylene, which goes into carrier bags and shrink film.

Wobble in Moon's Orbit to Cause Floods

Changes in our Moon's orbit along with rising sea levels thanks to climate change could result in record-breaking floods on Earth in the coming years.

NASA revealed this in a recent study in collaboration with researchers from the University of Hawaii. According to the researchers, these floods are expected to begin sometime in the 2030s and last a good 10 years, according to the study.

The National Oceanic and Atmospheric Administration has revealed that in 2019 alone, the US experienced over 600 floods due to high tides. Researchers believe that this number is expected to skyrocket in the 2030s. The flooding is actually expected to occur in clusters that can easily last a month or even more.

How Moon impacts floods on Earth

Even though flooding caused by high tides aren't as harmful as a cloudburst or hurricane, Phil Thompson, assistant professor at the University of Hawaii, who is also the lead author of the study, believes that it's the accumulated effect over time that will have an impact.

If it floods 10 or 15 times a month, a business can't keep operating with its parking lot underwater. People will lose their jobs because they can't get to work. Seeping cesspools will become a public health issue.

Not so surprisingly, the moon wobble phenomenon isn't new. It was first reported in 1728 and is known to occur every 18.6 years. According to NASA, in the first half of the cycle, the Earth's regular tides are suppressed whereas, during the second half, they're amplified.

And right now, Moon is currently in the amplification phase that's resulting in

Sea-level rise is not the same everywhere. In some places sea level is rising by more than the global average while in others it is falling.

flooding in several coastal areas due to higher sea levels caused by climate change. With another decade of the constant rise of sea levels, the consequences would get direr, especially when the Moon's amplification mode is back.

According to researchers, this has the potential to cause flooding on major US coastlines including Hawaii and Guam.

NASA Administrator Bill Nelson, in a statement has warned coastal areas to be prepared for a more flooded future, "The combination of the Moon's gravitational pull, rising sea levels, and climate change will continue to exacerbate coastal flooding on our coastlines and across the world. NASA's Sea Level Change Team is providing crucial information so that we can plan, protect, and prevent damage to the environment and people's livelihoods affected by flooding."

Downtown inundated with water in Guam Is.

The Water Cycle is Intensifying

The world watched in July 2021 as extreme rainfall became floods that washed away centuries-old homes in Europe, triggered landslides in Asia and inundated subways in China. More than 900 people died in the destruction. In North America, the West was battling fires amid an intense drought that is affecting water and power supplies.

Water-related hazards can be exceptionally destructive, and the impact of climate change on extreme water-related events like these is increasingly evident.

In a new international climate assessment published Aug. 9, 2021, the Intergovernmental Panel on Climate Change (IPCC) warns that the water cycle has been intensifying and will continue to intensify as the planet warms. There is an increase in both wet extremes, including more intense rainfall over most regions, and dry extremes, including drying in the Mediterranean, SW Australia, southwestern S. America, S. Africa and western North America. It also shows that both wet and dry extremes will continue to increase with future warming.

Why is the Water Cycle Intensifying?

Water cycles through the environment, moving between the atmosphere, ocean, land and reservoirs of frozen water. It might fall as rain or snow, seep into the ground, run into a waterway, join the ocean, freeze or evaporate back into the atmosphere. Plants also take up water from the ground and release it through transpiration from their leaves. In recent decades, there has been an overall increase in the rates of precipitation and evaporation.

Some Key-points in the Water Cycle • warming temperatures raise the upper limit on the amount of moisture in the air. That increases the potential for more rain.

Understanding this and other changes in

the water cycle is important for more than preparing for disasters. Water is an essential resource for all ecosystems and human societies, and particularly agriculture.

What Does This Mean for the Future?

• both wet and dry extremes and the general variability of the water cycle will increase, although not uniformly around the globe. •Rainfall intensity is expected to increase for most land areas, but the largest increases in dryness are expected in the Mediterranean, southwestern South America and western North America. •Annual average precipitation is projected to increase in many areas as the planet warms, particularly in the higher latitudes.

Annual average precipitation is projected to increase in many areas as the planet

Climate change and regional patterns

Climate change is not uniform and proportional to the level o

Warming will be stronger in the Arctic, on land and in the Nortern Hemisphere

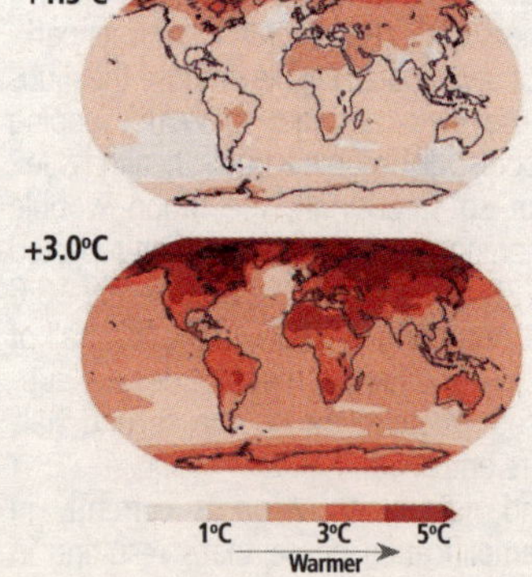

warms, particularly in the higher latitudes. Globally, daily extreme precipitation events will likely intensify by about 7% for every 1°C that global temperatures rise.

Many other important aspects of the water cycle will also change in addition to extremes as global temperatures increase, including reductions in mountain glaciers, decreasing duration of seasonal snow cover, earlier snowmelt and contrasting changes in monsoon rains across different regions, which will impact the water resources of billions of people.

What Can Be Done? Remember that higher greenhouse gas emissions lead to bigger impacts. The IPCC provides the scientific information needed to carefully evaluate policy choices. The results show what the implications of different choices are likely to be marginal. But Limiting global warming to the Paris Agreement target of 1.5°C will require immediate, rapid and large-scale reductions in greenhouse gas emissions. Regardless of any specific target, it is clear that the severity of climate change impacts are closely linked to greenhouse gas emissions. Reducing emissions will reduce impacts. Every fraction of a degree matters.

UN 2021-2030

The marine realm is the largest component of the Earth's system that stabilises climate and support life on Earth and human well-being. However, the First World Ocean Assessment released in 2016 found that much of the ocean is seriously degraded, with changes and losses in the structure, function and benefits from marine systems. The impact of multiple stressors on the ocean is projected to increase as the human population grows towards the expected 9 billion by 2050. In that context the UN has declared 2021-2030 a **Decade of Ocean Science for Sustainable Development** to reverse the cycle of decline in ocean health and gather ocean stakeholders worldwide behind a common framework that will ensure ocean science can fully support countries in creating improved conditions for sustainable development of the Ocean.

2021: Year of Creative Economy for Sustainable Development It aims to promote sustained and inclusive economic growth, foster innovation and provide opportunities, benefits and empowerment for all and respect for all human rights. It was presented by a global grouping of countries, including Australia, China, India, Indonesia, Mongolia, Philippines and Thailand to raise awareness, promote cooperation and networking, encourage sharing best practices and experiences, enhance human resource capacity, promote an enabling environment at all levels as well as tackle the challenges of creative economy.

2020: Year of Plant Health It aims to raise global awareness on how protecting plant health can help end hunger, reduce poverty, protect the environment, and boost economic development.

Carbon Market

When we emit greenhouse gases like carbon dioxide (CO_2), more heat gets trapped in the Earth's atmosphere, raising global temperatures and destabilizing the climate. The political path to stopping that from happening is infinitely more complex – a complexity embodied in one of the main topics of this year's U.N. climate negotiations in Madrid: international carbon markets. The idea is that, under Article 6 of the 2015 Paris Agreement on climate change, if one country pays for carbon emissions to be reduced in a second country, the first country can count those reductions towards its own national targets. If done right, analysts at the Environmental Defence Fund (EDF) say this international emissions trading could almost double global emissions reductions between 2020 and 2035. It could also cut the financial cost of meeting current Paris Agreement emissions pledges, which aim to keep global average temperature rise well below 2 degrees over pre-industrial era, by 59% to 79%.

Therefore, a price is set. A price on carbon helps shift the burden for the damage back to those who are responsible for it, and who can reduce it. Instead of dictating who should reduce emissions where and how, a carbon price gives an economic signal and polluters decide for themselves whether to discontinue their polluting activity, reduce emissions, or continue polluting and pay for it. In this way, the overall environmental goal is achieved in the most flexible and least-cost way to society. The carbon price also stimulates clean technology and market innovation, fuelling new, low-carbon drivers of economic growth.

There are two main types of carbon pricing: emissions trading systems (ETS) and carbon taxes. Under emission trading, a country or a polluter having more emissions is able to purchase the right to emit more. The country or entity having fewer emissions sells the right to emit carbon to other countries or entities. As a result, the most cost-effective carbon reduction methods would be exploited first. A carbon tax directly sets a price on carbon by defining a tax rate on greenhouse gas emissions or – more commonly – on the carbon content of fossil fuels. It is different from an ETS in that the emission reduction outcome of a carbon tax is not pre-defined but the carbon price is.

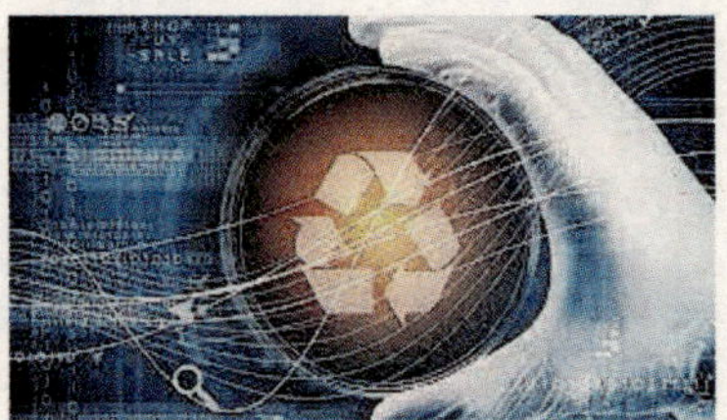

ETS and carbon taxes are a common method for countries to meet their pledges under the Paris Agreement.

Some 40 countries and more than 20 cities, states and provinces already use carbon pricing mechanisms, with more planning to implement them in the future. Together the carbon pricing schemes now in place cover about half their emissions, which translates to about 13 percent of annual global greenhouse gas emissions.

Article 6 controversy: As countries try to hammer out the rules for Article 6, countries are clashing over how strict to make them. Negotiators from the E.U. and many developing nations have accused some countries, including Brazil, Saudi Arabia, Australia and India, of pushing for a system with lax rules for counting emissions reductions and credits, which would make it easier to meet Paris targets, but could undermine global progress on cutting levels of greenhouse gases in the atmosphere.

Drought

Drought affects more people globally than any other natural disaster. Natural disasters usually announce their arrival: Cyclones and floods. These large, sudden events generate destruction on impact–and then they're gone. Drought is different. It doesn't make a big entrance–its impact builds over time. So often described as a "creeping disaster," drought leaves a trail of destruction.

Global Assessment Report on Disaster Risk reduction: Special Report on Drought 2021 says that at least 1.5 billion people have been directly affected by drought during the current century, and its economic cost has been estimated at $124bn (£89bn). The true cost is likely to be many times higher as estimates do not include much of the impact in developing countries. The report will become part of discussions at the next climate talks known as COP26.

People have been living with drought for 5,000 years, but what we are seeing now is very different. Human activities are exacerbating drought and increasing the impact, threatening to derail progress on lifting people from poverty.. Developed countries too have not been immune to drought. The US, Australia and southern Europe have experienced drought in recent years. Drought costs more than $6bn a year in direct impacts in the US, and about €9bn (£7.7bn) in the EU. According to scientists from NASA and NOAA that earth's 'energy imbalance' roughly doubled from 2005 to 2019 in an 'alarming' manner. According to a new research, the earth is trapping nearly twice as much heat as it did in 2005, described as an 'unprecedented' increase amid the climate crisis. 'Energy imbalance' refers to the difference between how much of the Sun's 'radiative energy' is absorbed by Earth's atmosphere and surface, compared to how much 'thermal infrared radiation' bounces back into space.

Environment Events

Internationally, environmental days and events are observed to highlight problems concerning environment and create a general awareness among people so as to prevent further damage to the nature.

Earth Hour: Organised by World Wildlife Fund for Nature, since 23 March 2007, the voluntary one-hour blackout is now held in 3100+ landmarks in 187 nations which is a battle sign against global warming.

Word Environment Day: It was started by the UN General Assembly on 5 June 1972 at the Stockholm Conference on Human Environment. The UN aims to (a) give a human face to environmental issues; (b) empower people as active agents of sustainable and equitable development; (c) encourage communities to change attitudes towards environmental issues; (d) advocate partnership for all nations to enjoy a safer future.

Earth Day: Earth Day began on 22 April 1970 when Sen. Gaylord Nelson began to advocate protecting the environment and increasing awareness on environmental issues. It has inspired big corporations to "go green," encouraging its employees to, use less paper, use alternative heating/cooling systems, use public transportation and urging employees to communicate using green materials. Currently, the sales of hybrid cars and LED lighting systems are quite encouraging.

Earth Charter: It is an international declaration of fundamental values and principles for building a just, sustainable, and peaceful global society in the 21st century.

International Environmental Agreements

The international environmental agreements negotiated in the 20th century reflect commonality of global interests in maintaining the robustness and integrity of our planet and set up procedures through monitoring the health of environment and provide benefits to all parties. Following are some of the major environmental treaties, conventions and protocols that have been negotiated in the 20th century.

International Environmental Treaties

1. International Whaling Convention, 1946 It provides a framework for the regulation of whaling industry and proper conservation of whale stocks.

2. General Agreement on Tariffs and Trade (GATT), 1947 Environment and trade issues move in two directions: environmental protection practices affect trade, and trading practices affect environmental trade. Both are viewed as important elements of sustainable development.

GATT has important implication for environmental protection and it promotes free trade around the glove. Article XX of GATT permits trade restrictions to meet environmental objectives so long as they are not arbitrary or discriminatory.

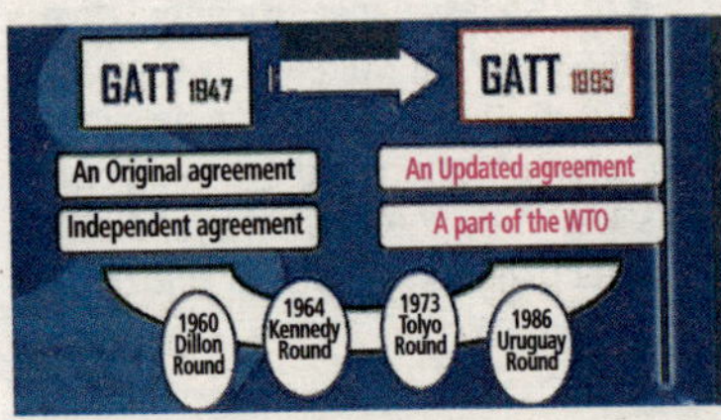

3. Antarctic Treaty, 1959 Under this treaty, any nuclear explosions in Antarctica and the disposal thereof radioactive waste material shall be prohibited. The main aim of this treaty is to keep Antarctica peaceful and free from nuclear and military testing.

4. Ramsar Convention, 1971 It provides framework to prevent the worldwide loss of wetlands through wise use and management of the remaining wetlands. It covers both natural and man-made habitat that can be classified as wetlands. Wetlands include rivers, coral reefs, swamps, marshes, lakes, salt marshes, mudflats, mangroves, coral reefs, fens, peat bogs, or bodies of water – whether natural or artificial, permanent or temporary.

5. The World Heritage Convention, 1972 It is a convention which provides obligation for entire international community to cooperate in concerning the protection of World Cultural and Natural Heritage. Since its approval in 1972, it has become one of the most effective and important mechanisms for the protection of sites and monuments worldwide.

6. London Convention 1972 It is a convention for the prevention of marine pollution by dumping of wastes and other matters.

7. London Convention, 1973 It is a protocol on interference on high seas in case of marine Pollution with Substances other than Oil.

8. Convention on the International Trade in Endangered Species of Wild Fauna and Flora (CITES), 1973 It provides a framework to control international trade on endangered species. It provides protection to more than 30,000 species of animals and plants, whether they are traded as live specimen, fur coats or dried herbs.

9. The International Convention for the Prevention of Pollution from Ships 1973, as modified by the Protocol of 1978 (MARPOL 73/78) It is the major international convention regulating pollution of the marine environment from the ships

due to their operation.

10. The Geneva Convention on Long-Range trans-boundary Air Pollution, 1979 It provides framework to regulate long-range trans-boundary air pollution and haze pollution.

11. UN Convention on the Law of the Sea (UNCLOS), 1982 It provides an international framework regulating use of the world's oceans.

12. Convention for the Protection of the Ozone Layer, 1985 (Vienna Convention) It is a treaty for reducing and eliminating manufacture and use of gases that destroy Ozone in the Earth's atmosphere. The objective: to protect human health and environment against the harmful effect of ozone depletion. As a framework convention it doesn't establish any specific control over the Ozone layer depletion. Instead, it establishes general obligation on parties to protect ozone layer and emphasizes the need for internal cooperation. This convention does not impose any concrete obligations. It only establishes a framework that is needed to be filled in with further actions.

13. Montreal Protocol, 1987 It established a target to reduce and eventually eliminate the production and consumption of substances that cause ozone layer depletion. According to it the countries have to set a target to phase out the ozone depleting substances. However, it provides a special provision for the developing countries.

It recognises the fact that the developing countries have hardly had contributed to the problem, so they have a 10 years delay period in phasing out the production and consumption of ozone depleting chemicals.

14. Basel Convention, 1989 It controls the transboundary movements on hazardous wastes and their disposal.

15. Convention of Biological Diversity, 1992 It imposes obligations to conserve biodiversity in both terrestrial and marine ecosystems. The two main objectives of this convention are the sustainable use of the components of biological diversity and fair and equitable sharing of the benefits arising out of the utilization of genetic resources, including by appropriate access to genetic resources and by appropriate transfer of relevant technologies, taking into account all rights over those resource and to technologies, and by appropriate funding.

16. UN Framework Convention on Climate Change 1992 (UNFCCC) It provides major framework to regulate anthropogenic climate change.

17. Rio Convention, 1992 The main aim of this convention was to alleviate poverty, prevent local environmental degradation and protect the robustness and integrity of the biosphere.

18. Kyoto Protocol, 1997 Under this protocol, which emerged from UNFCCC, an agreement was made between nations to mandate country-by-country reductions in greenhouse-gas emissions

The Goals 1. To secure global net zero by 2050 and keep 1.5°C within reach. Countries will have to put forward ambitious 2030 emissions reductions targets that align with reaching net zero by the middle of the century through accelerated phase-out of coal; curtail deforestation; speed up the switch to electric vehicles; encourage investment in renewables. 2. Adapt to protect communities and natural habitats 3. Mobilise finance. COP26 Must: finalise the Paris Rulebook to accelerate action to tackle the climate crisis through collaboration between governments, businesses and civil society.

UN Framework Convention on Climate Change

The UNFCCC aims to regulate greenhouse gas emissions through international co-operation and agreement to bring emissions to a level that can offset the effects of global warming and climate change. India became a member of the convention in 1992 and went on to ratify it in 1993 – as a developing nation (at that time), India was not bound to commitments for mitigation of greenhouse gas emissions. This changed with the Paris Agreement of 2015 whereby India is committed to attend multilateral negotiations under the UNFCCC. India is moving ahead with policy frameworks that includes the National Environment Policy (NEP) and the National Action Plan on Climate Change (NAPCC).

Agenda 21 is a product of the Earth Summit organised by the UN in Rio de Janerio, Brazil in 1992 to include stakeholders in a non-binding action plan for achieving sustainable development. The stakeholders included local and national governments, business, international organisations, citizen groups and non-governmental organizations. The international community met again ten years later at the World Summit on Sustainable Development and reviewed developments to forge global partnerships for the implementation of Agenda 21. India is signatory to Agenda 21 and has aligned various parts of its development infrastructure: energy, transport, industry, water facilities, climate change policy, forests, biodiversity, ecosystems, marine and coastal management, land policy, agriculture, urban governance, human resource development.

Conference of the Parties (COP): is the supreme decision-making body of the Convention. COP reviews implementation of the Convention, legal instruments that the COP adopts, take decisions for effective implementation of the Convention, including institutional and administrative arrangements.

The UNFCCC deals with the period after the first "commitment period" of the Kyoto Protocol, which expired at the end of 2012. Therefore, negotiations have been mandated by the adoption of the Bali Road Map and Decision 1/CP.13 ("The Bali Action Plan").

The UNCC are yearly conferences where the UNFCCC Conferences of the Parties assess progress in dealing with climate change. • 1995: COP-1, The Berlin Mandate • 1996: COP-2, Geneva, Switzerland • 1997: COP-3, The Kyoto Protocol on Climate Change • 1998: COP-4, Buenos Aires, Argentina • 1999: COP-5, Bonn, Germany • 2000: COP-6, The Hague, Netherlands • 2001: COP-6, Bonn, Germany • 2001: COP-7, Marrakech, Morocco • 2002: COP-8, New Delhi, India • 2003: COP-9, Milan, Italy •2004: COP-10, Buenos Aires, Argentina • 2005: COP-11/CMP-1, Montreal, Canada • 2006:COP-12/CMP-2, Nairobi, Kenya • 2007: COP-13/CMP-3, Bali, Indonesia • 2008: COP-14/CMP-4,Poznan, Poland • 2009: COP-15/CMP-5, Copenhagen, Denmark • 2010: COP-16/CMP-6, Cancún, Mexico • 2011: COP-17/CMP-7, Durban, South Africa • 2012: COP-18/CMP-8, Doha, Qatar • 2013: COP-19/CMP-9, Warsaw, Poland • 2014: COP-20/CMP-10, Lima, Peru • 2015: COP-21/CMP-11, Paris, France • 2016: COP-22/CMP-12/CMA 1-1, Marrakech, Morocco • 2017: COP-23/CMP-13/CMA 1-2, Bonn, Germany • 2018: COP-24/CMP-14/CMA 1-3, Katowice, Poland • 2019: COP-25/CMP-15/CMA-2 Madrid, Spain • 2021: COP-26/CMA-3, Glasgow, UK.

Kyoto-Paris Agreement in Review

The Kyoto Protocol implemented the objective of the UNFCCC to reduce the onset of global warming by reducing greenhouse gas concentrations in the atmosphere to "a level that would prevent dangerous anthropogenic interference with the climate system" (Article 2).

The Kyoto Protocol applies to the six greenhouse gases listed in Annex A: Carbon dioxide (CO2), Methane (CH4), Nitrous oxide (N2O), Hydrofluorocarbons (HFCs), Perfluorocarbons (PFCs), and Sulphur hexafluoride (SF6). The Protocol is based on the principle of common but differentiated responsibilities: putting the obligation to reduce current emissions on developed countries on the basis that they are historically responsible for the current levels of greenhouse gases in the atmosphere.

The Protocol's first commitment period started in 2008 and ended in 2012. All 36 countries that fully participated in the first commitment period complied with the Protocol. A second commitment period was agreed in 2012, known as the Doha Amendment to the Kyoto Protocol, in which 37 countries have binding targets. Some countries withdrew or not put into legal force the Amendment with second round targets and few others have not taken on new targets in the second commitment period. United States did not ratify.

As of May 2020, 138 states have accepted the Doha Amendment, while entry into force required the acceptances of 144 states. Of the 37 parties with binding commitments, 34 ratified.

Negotiations held in the framework of the yearly UNFCCC Climate Change Conferences on measures to be taken after the second commitment period ended in 2020. This resulted in the 2015 adoption of the Paris Agreement – a separate instrument under the UNFCCC.

Adoption of the Paris Agreement in 2015 was the most important diplomatic milestone in the fight against climate change to date. After 20 years of negotiations, 195 countries at COP21 (Dec. 2015, in Paris), agreed to limit global warming.

Takes effect: 4 Nov 2016, 30 days after ratified by 55 Parties representing at least 55% of total GHG emissions.

Global commitments: The 195 countries report their national commitments to combat climate change. From 2020 the progress will be reviewed every 5-years.

Goal: To keep the global temperature increase well below 2 °C compared to pre-industrial levels and continue efforts to limit it to 1.5 °C.

Emissions reduction: Strive for a global peaking of greenhouse gas emissions to achieve carbon neutrality (zero net emissions) quickly.

Transparency: Common frame of transparency to all countries that includes *Information on emissions and *Investment contributions.

Market mechanisms: Countries can use Emissions Trading and Carbon Pricing for emission reduction activities.

Financial commitment: Developed countries must finance developing countries with at least $100,000 million a year starting in 2020 for mitigation and adaptation.

Irrecoverable damages: Support measures for unrecoverable losses (no specific amount of compensations).

Compliance: The Paris Agreement is legally binding and each country establishes the national targets of fight against the climate change.

Climate Change

Climate change refers to significant, long-term changes in the global climate. The global climate is the connected system of sun, earth and oceans, wind, rain and snow, forests, deserts and savannas, and everything people do, too. The climate of a place, say New York, can be described as its rainfall, changing temperatures during the year and so on. But the global climate is more than the "average" of the climates of specific places. A description of the global climate includes how, for example, the rising temperature of the Pacific feeds typhoons which blow harder, drop more rain and cause more damage, but also shifts global ocean currents that melt Antarctica ice which slowly makes sea level rise until New York will be under water. It is this systemic connectedness that makes global climate change so important and so complicated.

Global Warming

Global warming is the slow increase in the average temperature of the earth's atmosphere because an increased amount of the energy (heat) striking the earth from the sun is being trapped in the atmosphere and not radiated out into space.

The earth's atmosphere has always acted like a greenhouse to capture the sun's heat, ensuring that the earth has enjoyed temperatures that permitted the emergence of life forms as we know them, including humans. Without our atmospheric greenhouse the earth would be very cold. Global warming, however, is the equivalent of a greenhouse with high efficiency reflective glass installed the wrong way around. Strangely, the classic proof of this may come from a cooling event that took place some 1,500 years ago. Two massive volcanic eruptions, one year after another placed so much black dust into the upper atmosphere that little sunlight could penetrate. Temperatures plummeted. Crops failed. People died of starvation and the Black Death started its march. As the dust slowly fell to earth, the sun was again able to warn the world and life returned to normal. Today, we have the opposite problem. Today, the problem is not that too little sun warmth is reaching the earth, but that too much is being trapped in our atmosphere. So much heat is being kept inside greenhouse earth that the temperature of the earth is going up faster than at any previous time in history.

Cause and Effect

Heat is energy and when you add energy to any system changes occur. Because all systems in the global climate system are connected, adding heat energy causes the global climate as a whole to change. Much of the world is covered with ocean which heats up. When the ocean heats up, more water evaporates into clouds. Where storms like hurricanes and typhoons are forming, the result is more energy-intensive storms. A warmer atmosphere makes glaciers and mountain snow packs, the Polar ice cap, and the great ice shield jutting off of Antarctica melt raising sea levels.

Signs: Declining Arctic Sea Ice, •Increasing Carbon dioxide (CO2) levels, •Rising Sea level •Land Ice disappearing, Industrialisation, Urbanisation, Deforestation.

Greenhouse gases (GHGs): CO_2, Methane or CH4, Nitrous oxide NO/N2O or simply NOx, Fluorinated gases, Sulphur hexafluoride or SF6, etc.

O3-depleting Substances

The greenhouse warming effects of ozone-depleting substances (ODS) were developed in the 1920s and '30s. These substances acted as a strong supplement to CO_2, the most pervasive greenhouse gas. Its effects have since faded, as they are no longer produced. In the 1980s a hole in Earth's stratospheric ozone layer, which filters much of the harmful ultraviolet radiation from the sun, was discovered over Antarctica. Scientists quickly attributed it to ODS. The world sprang into action, finalising a global agreement to phase out ODS. The Montreal Protocol, as it is called, was signed in 1987 and entered into force in 1989. Atmospheric concentrations of most ODS peaked in the late 20th century and have been declining since. However, for at least 50 years, the climate impacts of ODS were extensive. Now climate mitigation is in action because these substances are decreasing in the atmosphere. In the coming decades, they will contribute very less to global warming.

Ocean De-oxygenation

The ocean is home to majority of the living space on the planet – a blue heart on the planet. If the oceans run out of oxygen, it will mean loss of habitat and biodiversity.

Oxygen levels in the world's oceans declined by roughly 2% between 1960 and 2010. A study by International Union for Conservation of Nature (IUCN) has identified 700 low oxygen zones, up from 45 in the 1960s. By 2100, the oceans are expected to lose 3-4% of their oxygen. It means that the oxygen depletion was not uniform across oceans. In some tropical locations, the loss was upto 40%. The deoxygenation is largely due to climate change along with various human activities like nutrient runoff (a situation where excess nutrients from fertilisers used on farms wash into waterways).

Effects of Oxygen Depletion While jellyfish thrives in low oxygen conditions, oxygen depletion is threatening to larger, fast-swimming marine species like tuna, marlin and sharks. •Low levels of oxygen can affect the cycling of elements like nitrogen and phosphorus that are essential for life on earth. •When oceans absorb CO_2, they become more acidic and less basic. This can dissolve the shells of aquatic life like clams, mussels and shrimps.

•Since mid-1950s, oceans have also absorbed 93% of the heat associated with greenhouse gas emissions leading to mass bleaching of coral reefs. •Besides, warmer water holds less oxygen.

Earth is trapping twice as much heat

NASA warned the Earth is trapping heat at a rate so much higher it's "unprecedented." Researchers from NASA and the National Oceanic and Atmospheric Administration (NOAA) found in a new study that Earth's "energy imbalance approximately doubled during the 14-year period from 2005 to 2019." The energy imbalance is how much heat the Earth absorbs from the sun, compared to how much "thermal infrared radiation" the Earth radiates back into space. According to Norman Loeb, the study's lead author and a NASA investigator, "The magnitude of the increase is unprecedented."

Researchers pointed to human activity as one of the main catalysts.

IPCC Climate Change 6th Report, 2021

The landmark 6th report, Climate Change 2021 released by the UN's Intergovernmental Panel on Climate (IPCC) on 9 August highlights global climate change and the impact it will have on communities across the world.

- The assessment report's stark finding is global temperatures would rise by 1.5-2° celsius from the pre-industrial age in less than 20 years.
- The report predicts almost certain disaster for India and its communities due to extreme weather events like floods, cyclones and heatwaves, spurred by climate change.
- The report states that developed nations have contributed the most to rising global temperatures and must therefore institute swifter curbs on their carbon emissions.
- With reference to absolute carbon emissions, India is now number three in the world after China and USA.

Going by the IPCC's predictions India must take steps in the next few years to minimise climate-related damage to life and livelihood.

- It is almost certain that temperatures will rise across the world, causing heatwaves in many parts.

Predictions for India and Limitations of the Climate Model For India, these heatwaves, also called "extreme heatwaves".

- The heatwaves would damage crops and other forms of agriculture
- It would severely affect human health, even causing scores of deaths across the country.
- There is also an emphasis on the limits of climate models like those predicted by IPCC in the report. Climate models cannot project minutely region-specific phenomenon. For example, it can't say that Odisha will have worse heatwaves than West Bengal. But heatwaves across India will increase, based on the model projected for South Asia.
- The second subject is monsoon patterns across the world, specifically Asia.

However, the existing climate models and their regional models are poor at predicting monsoon rainfall – considered to be one of the world's most meteorologically complicated phenomenon. Indian monsoons even more so.

- Between 1950-2000, there was a decline in Indian monsoons. Various climate models credited this decline to aerosol emissions. However, all climate models now show that monsoon rainfall will increase in the future, not just in India but world over.
- Pluvial floods caused by extreme rainfall as opposed to those caused by other reasons like faulty water management techniques could increase across South Asia and India.
- Flash floods or watersheds after extreme rainfall or urban floods are examples of pluvial floods. The IPCC report predicts that such floods will increase because of excess rainfall.
- IPCC has stated with "medium confidence" that urbanisation leads to intensification of extreme rainfall. The human water mismanagement may lead to increased rainfall. This is an important observation for India as it is a rapidly urbanising country.
- For India, the challenge will be to not just predict excess rainfall due to erratic monsoons, but to also predict areas which will experience extreme drought.
- According to the IPCC report most global analyses are yet to predict increased drought periods across the world, including India. The report also states explicitly that climate models do not have any confidence in projecting drought for the South Asian region.

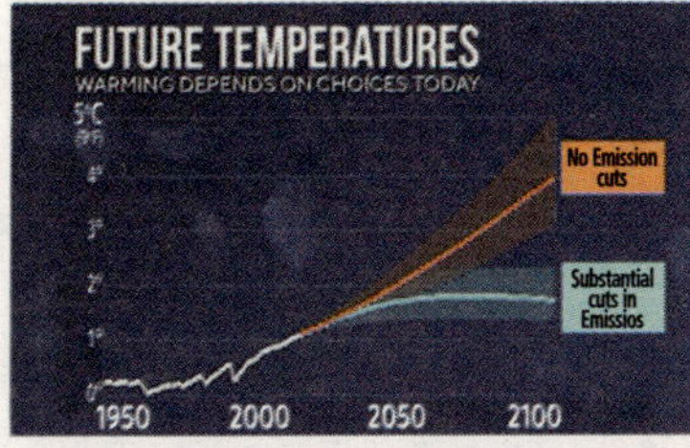

SIXTH ASSESSMENT REPORT ipcc

CO_2 Concentration	Sea level rise	Arctic sea ice area	Glaciers retreat
Highest in at least 2 million years	**Fastest rates** in at least 3000 years	**Lowest level** in at least 1000 years	**Unprecedented** in at least 2 million years

• IPCC Report predicts that India's mountains with snowcaps in Hindukush Himalayas, will show rapid thawing in the next few decades. There is little research to show to what extent the melting glaciers will affect the Indian river system. For example, the glacier melting at a normal pace plus sudden heavy rainfall. Such situational events will have different effects on the rivers.

India's Options

There are three main areas that India needs to work on in terms of its climate policy: •Adaptation to extreme weather events caused by climate change. •A resilience plan, especially for urban areas. •Increase climate services.

A plan for areas facing compound climate extremes, such as how cities like Mumbai and Kolkata were flooded in 2021. The immediate step would be to have a Resilience Plan to face something like this by re-designing the drainage systems and adapt to climate change predictions.

• re-design infrastructure based on these projections.

• Prepare for the event well ahead. For example, what do if a cyclone like Amphan hits a part of the country?

• Urban regions should have a Protocol, a list of immediate steps to be taken to bring the region back on its feet.

• Extend "climate services" to the most vulnerable to the impact of climate change. Climate services are essentially tools that disseminate knowledge of impending or upcoming climate events in a particular region, and also educating the population on preparedness to beat such an event.

A farmer or a fisherman may know about cyclone or drought or heavy rainfall that has been predicted. But they have very little knowledge on how to be prepared for such a calamity which might destroy their entire livelihood.

• Safeguard those who face "compound climate extremes".

A compound extreme event is when one particular region faces multiple extreme weather events, like the Sundarbans in India. There maybe a time period when, say, a cyclone may have hit the region, which will be immediately followed by high tides that will break embankments and cause salt water to enter agricultural fields. This may again be immediately followed by an intense spell of rainfall". The regions expected to experience such compound events should also have a separate resilience plan.

• India is focusing on renewable energy, but a concrete plan for harnessing renewable energy is yet to be chalked out. Again, India is the second highest contributor to global greening, i.e. the world's global green cover. However, most of this green cover is restricted to farmlands and not forests, as is required to contain carbon emissions.

• Forest cover should be planned in specific regions so that they can help in carbon upgrading. This will do a world of good in bringing down carbon levels not just in India's atmosphere, but world over. It may also help if India can commit a deadline to the international community on when it will revise its emission targets and achieve the global promise of zero net carbon.

Disaster Management

There is no country that is immune from disaster, though vulnerability to disaster varies. Disasters involve wide-spread human, material, economic or environmental impacts, which exceed the ability of the affected community or society to cope using its own resources.

Impact on Lives

Any disaster can interrupt essential services, like health care, food supply, water, electricity, sewage/garbage removal, transportation and communications. The interruption can seriously affect the health, social and economic networks of local communities and countries. Disasters have a lasting impact on people long after the immediate effect has been mitigated. If there are no plans for relief work, it can have a negative effect on the disaster victims, on donors and relief agencies. It is important to follow protocols rather than attempt individual efforts.

Disaster Relief

This is a coordinated multi-agency response to reduce the impact of a disaster and its long-term results. Relief activities include rescue, relocation, providing food and water, preventing disease and disability, repairing vital services such as telecommunications and transport, providing temporary shelter and emergency health care.

Disaster Recovery

Once the initial crisis is handled, the communities are still vulnerable. Recovery activities include rebuilding infrastructure, health care and rehabilitation should be blended with development activities, like building human resources for health and developing policies and practices to avoid similar situations in future. It should be in relation to vulnerable people like those with disabilities, elderly people, children and socio-economically marginalised groups.

Four Types of Disasters

Natural disasters: It include floods, hurricanes, earthquakes and volcano eruptions that have immediate impacts on human health and secondary impacts causing further death and suffering from floods, landslides, cyclones, fires, tsunamis, Cold/Heat Wave.

Environmental emergencies: They are man-made disasters like nuclear, chemical, and biological disaster, technological or industrial accidents – involving the production, use or transportation of hazardous material, and forest fires caused by humans.

Pandemic emergencies: It involves a sudden onset of contagious disease that affects health, disrupts services and businesses, brings economic and social costs.

Complex emergencies: It involves a break-down of law and order, looting and attacks on strategic installations, even conflict situations and war.

Disaster Prevention

Not all natural disasters can be prevented, but the risk of loss of life and injury can be mitigated with good evacuation plans, environmental planning and design standards. Hyogo Framework is such a global plan for natural disaster risk reduction. It gives principles, priorities for action, and practical means for achieving disaster resilience for vulnerable communities.

Disaster Preparedness

Preparedness is the only way of reducing the impact of disasters. Community-based preparedness and man management should be a high priority.

10

UNIVERSE, EARTH AND SPACE

- World's Fifth Ocean
- India's Four Astronaut
- Perseverance and Ingenuity
- Ingenuity: The First Helicopter on Mars
- The Rise of SpaceX
- Blue Origin
- The Universe
- The Solar System
- Cyclone, Hurricane, Typhoons, Tornado
- Earthquakes

Space Scan

World's Fifth Ocean

Earth's 71% area is covered in water, and we had learnt only about four oceans — the Atlantic, Pacific, Indian, and Arctic Oceans.

According to Geographer Alex Tait, National Geographic Society, scientists had known for many years that the icy waters around Antarctica form a distinct ecological region defined by ocean currents and temperatures but geographers wondered if it had enough unique characteristics to warrant a name of its own or if it was a colder extension to the Pacific, Atlantic, and Indian Oceans. Besides there was never an agreement internationally, and so it was never officially recognised.

In 1999, the NOAA (National Oceanic and Atmospheric Administration) recognised the Southern Ocean as the fifth body of water. In 2000, International Hydrographic Organisation (IHO) – who ensures that all seas, oceans and navigable waters are properly surveyed, didn't agree. NatGeo considers most of the waters surrounding Antarctica till 60° South (excluding the Drake Passage and the Scotia Sea) make up the Southern Ocean.

Four Oceans or Five?

The fifth ocean is a distinct water body characterised by the powerful Antarctic Circumpolar Current that flows eastward,

perpetually chasing itself around Antarctica. It is also an oceanic ring at the end of the world that connects the Pacific, Atlantic and Indian oceans.

As an important global source for the latest geographic knowledge, even without IHO's official determination, National Geographic updated oceans list based on the science and the conventional acceptance of the Southern Ocean. (@ NatGeo) June 8, 2021

Naming by the Current

While most oceans are defined by their nearby continents, the Southern Ocean is defined by its ocean current called

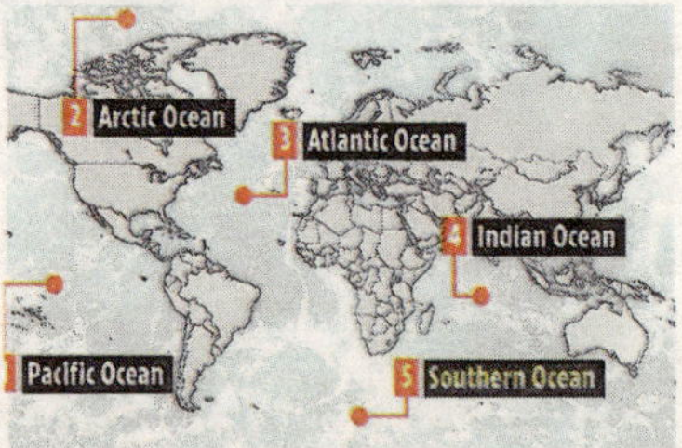

Antarctic Circumpolar Current (ACC), (or the Conveyor Belt). These currents help circulate heat around the Earth and storage of carbon as the cold water sinks to the ocean floor. The ACC would have formed around 34 million years ago when Antarctica broke off from Southern America. It flows west to east around Antarctica and the waters in the south are said to be colder and less salty than those in the north.

India's Four Astronaut

It is like a dream come true! Four Indians flew to space so far – Rakesh Sharma, Kalpana Chawla, Sunita Williams and Sirisha Bandla. Six more persons are in the preparation – four of them are Indians astronauts undergoing training in Russia for the forthcoming manned space mission. Santosh, would be flying in 2022 and Raja, if selected, in 2024 to the moon. India's first human Gaganyaan is scheduled for 2023.

Sirisha Bandla, aeronautical engineer, on 11 July 2021, became the third Indian-origin woman, after Kalpana Chawla and Sunita Williams, to fly into space when she joined Virgin Galactic's first fully crewed suborbital test flight from New Mexico.

Could an Indian be on Moon?

Raja Jon Vurputoor Chari, an Indian -American US Air Force colonel, a graduate of the US Air Force Academy, MIT and US Naval Test Pilot School, is the only Indian-American in the list of Artemis moon-landing programme. The new lunar exploration programme

will land the first woman and next man on the Moon in 2024 and establish a sustainable human lunar presence by the end of the decade. NASA named the 18 astronauts for this mission.

India's First Space Tourist

Sir Richard Branson of Virgin Atlantic and his team's first successful mission to space on July 11, 2021, a dream flight, prove that tourists could fly to space anytime. Santhosh George Kulangara will thus become the first Indian space tourist. They have confirmed his seat as passenger number 38. Santhosh will be allowed to film the entire process of preparations and flight sequences while he spends three hours in zero-gravity environment.

Santhosh, a globetrotter, having visited about 130 countries, thought, why not give space travel a try. The organisers, after numerous rounds of interviews and

tests selected the Malayali in 2007. There were a few setbacks, including the crash of planes during test flights and death of pilots, which delayed the mission. Our best wishes to him!

The Mars Story

Perseverance and Ingenuity

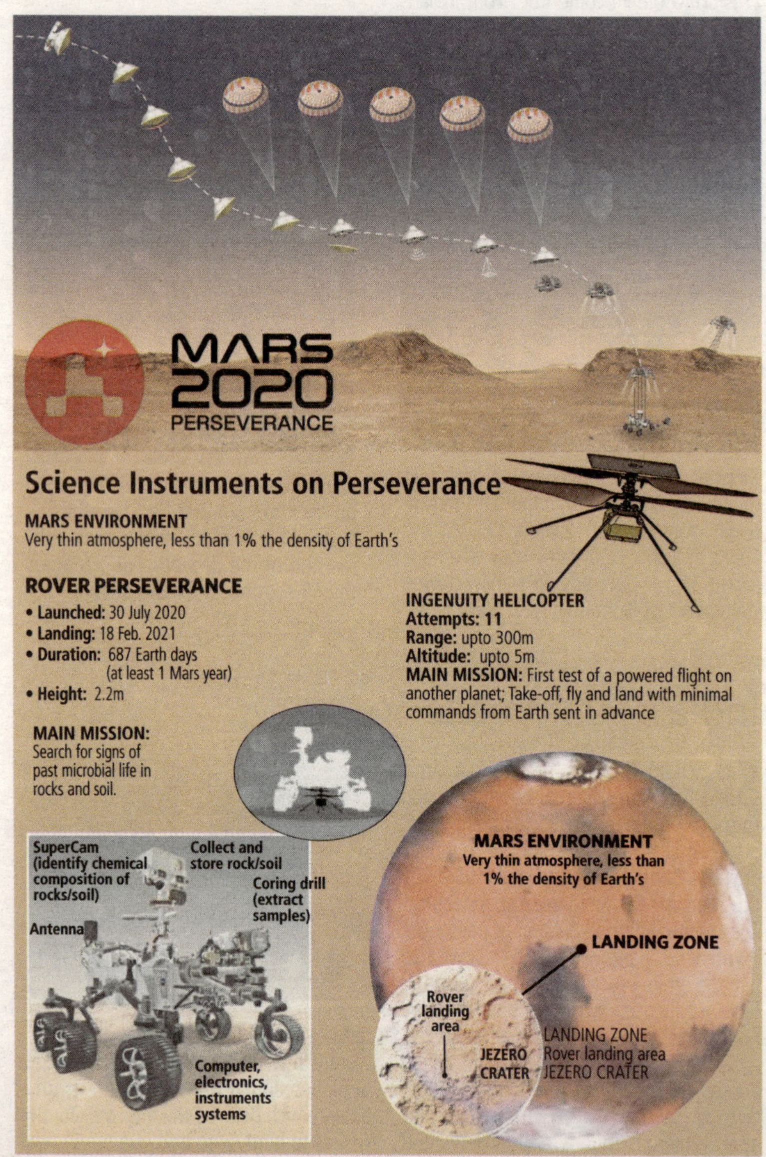

Various Spacecraft Missions on the Mars Surface

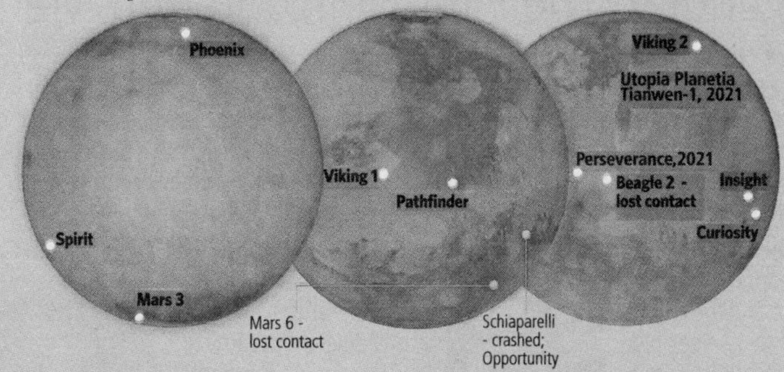

Perseverance Rover

NASA's next-generation Mars rover Perseverance blasted off from Florida's Cape Canaveral on July 30, 2020, atop an Atlas 5 rocket. The new Mars expedition is part of the Mars rover mission, forming part of NASA's Mars Exploration Program that includes the rover Perseverance and the small robotic, coaxial helicopter Ingenuity. The next-generation robotic rover, which is a car-sized six-wheeled vehicle carrying several scientific instruments, landed inside Mars' Jezero Crater on February 18, 2021.

Six weeks later, Ingenuity, the little rotorcraft, deployed from Perseverance's belly began a month-long flight campaign to demonstrate that aerial exploration is feasible on the Red Planet. Ingenuity relied on its own solar-powered battery power to run a vital heater to protect its unprotected electrical components from the freezing and cracking Martian night temperatures. Temperatures on Mars can plunge to -153° Celsius at the poles and 20°C at noon.

Three Rovers

As of May 2021, there were three rovers, operational, on the surface of Mars, the Curiosity and Perseverance rovers, both operated by the NASA, and the Zhurong rover, part of the Tianwen-1 mission by the China National Space Admin. (CNSA).

Eight Orbiters There are 8 orbiters surveying the planet: Mars Odyssey, Mars Express, Mars Reconnaissance Orbiter, Mars Orbiter Mission, MAVEN, the Trace Gas Orbiter, the Tianwen-1 orbiter, and the Hope Mars Mission, have contributed massive amounts of data about Mars.

The Stationary Lander InSight, is searching the deep interior of Mars. Sample return mission for Mars is planned for 2024. In fact, an attempted return mission for Mars' moon by Phobos failed in 2011.

Twelve Probes In all, there are 12 probes currently surveying Mars. The 13th, Ingenuity helicopter, has completed its 5 planned flights. So it is on an extended mission that's focused on showcasing the scouting potential of Mars helicopters. The chopper has completed extended-mission sorties till August 2021.

The Majors •For about 50 years, humanity has sent 49 uncrewed orbiters, probes and landers•Roughly half of all Mars missions failed. • NASA plans the first human landing in Mars by 2030s. •NASA's Curiosity rover found traces of sulfur, nitrogen, hydrogen, oxygen, phosphorus, and carbon (key to life) while drilling a Martian rock. **Earliest Probes**: Viking 1&2: 1976, with an orbiter and a lander. USSR's Mars Prog.1960-73.

Ingenuity: The First Helicopter on Mars

Meet the Indians Behind Perseverance

Mars Perseverance and the Indians
On the Perseverance team alone, there were 12 Indian-origin scientists and eight of whom were women.

Vaneeza Rupani, NASA's first Mars helicopter has a name and the credit goes to 17-year-old Indian-origin girl Vaneeza Rupani. She suggested the name 'INGENUITY' for the helicopter in NASA's "Name the Rover" contest. She is a high school junior from Northport, Alabama.

Dr J. Bob Balaram, an Indian-origin engineer is Chief Engineer. behind Mars helicopter, Ingenuity. Bob Balaram, along with a Stanford professor, in the 1990s, had proposed a "helicopter for Mars. A question, 'could drones fly on Mars?' triggered the idea. Balaram's dream became a reality, when Ingenuity flew. He is an IIT-Madras alumnus, It was a proof-of-concept technology demonstrator. Now they would be able to develop 25-30kg helicopters that can carry science equipment, to go places where no rover can go.

Yogita Shah, was the Avionics Domain Lead for MARS 2020–overseeing the electronic systems for communication, navigation, display on board the spacecraft. An Indian-American scientist is a member of the NASA team that successfully sent the Perseverance rover to the Red Planet.

'Zainab' Nagin Cox, Deputy Team Chief of Engineering Operations for Perseverance Rover, is a Spacecraft Systems Engineer at JPL. She is of Indian origin, born in Bangalore, India, and grew up in Kansas City. Graduated from Cornell University, Masters in Space Operations Systems Engineering from Air Force Institute of Technology. She was a commissioned officer in US Air Force. In 2015, Cox was honored as the namesake for Asteroid 14061 by its discoverers.

Dr Swati Mohan, the Guidance, Navigation and Controls Lead on the NASA Mars 2020 mission. Did research on-orbit operations in the Space Systems Laboratory in MIT and studied Mechanical and Aerospace Engineering at Cornell University.

Dr Vandana Verma, (Vandi Verma), the Indian scientist – the brain behind the Perseverance rover. Did her masters and PhD in robotics from Carnegie Mellon University.

The Rise of SpaceX

Total Launches 127 | Total Landings 89 | Reflown Rockets 68

SpaceX has gained worldwide attention for a series of historic milestones, esp. the unparalleled achievement of rocket reusability (capable of reflight) and vertical landing of rocket on the specified pad. It is the only private company capable of returning a spacecraft from low-Earth orbit.

Makes History

Billionaire Elon Musk created SpaceX in 2002 from the sales of two earlier businesses: software-service internet company Zip2 and online payment provider PayPal. His ultimate goal was to create a Mars settlement company. That said, SpaceX built Dragon cargo ships and Crew Dragon astronaut spaceships for the International Space Station and launched satellites for numerous customers aboard the Falcon 9 and Falcon Heavy rockets.

The story begins in September 2008 when FALCON 1 becomes the first privately developed liquid fuel rocket to reach Earth orbit. • April 2012: Dragon becomes the first private spacecraft in history to visit the space station. In 2012 our Dragon spacecraft became the first commercial spacecraft to deliver cargo to and from the ISS. • December 21 2015: Falcon 9 rocket delivered 11 communications satellites to orbit, and the first-ever orbital class first stage rocket returned and landed at Landing Zone 1. • April 8 2016: the Falcon 9 rocket launched the Dragon spacecraft to the ISS and the first stage returned and landed on the droneship. • March 30 2017: SpaceX achieved the world's first reflight of an orbital class rocket after delivery of the payload, the first stage returned to Earth for the second time. • February 7, 2018: Falcon Heavy made its first launch to orbit, successfully landing 2 of its 3 boosters and launching its payload to space. • March 3, 2019: Dragon docked with the ISS on March 3, becoming the first American spacecraft to autonomously dock with the

SpaceX Starship

Elon Musk built a vehicle that is a game-changer for space travel. Starship, as it's known, will be a fully reusable transport system capable of carrying up to 100 people to the Red Planet. In 2018, Musk rebranded his Mars-colonising spaceflight system as Starship. "Technically, two parts: Starship is the spaceship/upper stage & Super Heavy is the rocket booster needed to escape Earth's deep gravity well

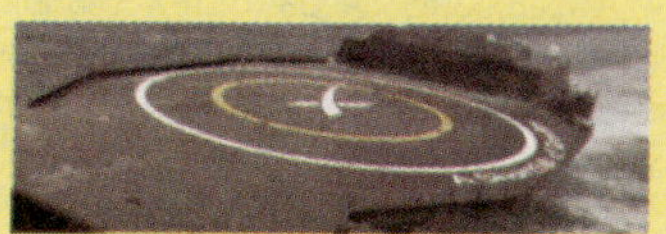

A Shortfall of Gravitas replaced Of Course I Still Love You

Autonomous Drone Ship

SpaceX revealed an autonomous Spaceport drone ship which required no tugboat to take it to the nearby launch site. The platform support Falcon 9 and Falcon Heavy missions launching from Kennedy Space Center and Cape Canaveral Space Force Station, Florida.

orbiting laboratory. May 30,2020: SpaceX became the first private company to take humans to space – atop Falcon 9, with NASA astronauts onboard Crew Dragon's second demonstration mission to and from the ISS. It restored human spaceflight to the US. NASA certified the human spaceflight system for crew missions to and from ISS – making it the first commercial system in history to achieve such a designation.

Inspiration4 It's The first human space-flight for exclusively four private citizens, three-days around Earth, aboard SpaceX Resilience capsule on 15 September 2021. **DearMoon Project** A lunar tourism mission of Japanese billionaire Yusaku Maezawa using SpaceX Starship, a private spaceflight, flying a single circumlunar trajectory around the Moon carrying Maezawa, 8 civilians+two crew members.

Virgin Galactic

The WhiteKnight aircraft, VMS Eve, carried the rocket-powered spaceship VSS Unity (Virgin Galactic Space Unity-22), the vehicle's first fully crewed test flight to space on 11 June 2021 from "Gateway to Space" terminal. British billionaire Sir Richard Branson was accompanied by others including Indian-born Sirisha Bandla, in what Branson has touted as the beginning of space tourism. About 40 minutes after take-off, Unity dropped from the middle of the mothership and ignited its rocket engine to send the crew to the edge of space, about 88 kms high, for about 10 minutes of weightlessness. The plane returned like a commercial airplane to a landing strip at Spaceport America.

Unity 22 Virgin Galactic's Mission

•Branson founded it in 2004. This was the 22nd flight of Unity, but only its 4th launch to space. •The four mission specialists each evaluated different experiences that Virgin Galactic has promised its future customers, many of whom have already reserved trips to space with the company at $250,000 a seat. Branson, took note of enhancing the trip for ticket holders looking for the experience of a lifetime. Beth Moses, ensured everyone is safe in their tests. Sirisha Bandla role was to evaluate the human-tended research experience at various points in the flight profile. Colin Bennett examined Unity's cabin performance,potential enhancements in a weightless environment. •Virgin Galactic mission is the company's second space ship after the first, VSS Enterprise, which broke apart during a 2014 test flight, killing one pilot and seriously injuring another.

Blue Origin

Jeff Bezos owned Blue Origin was founded in 2000 in a remote site in Texas, USA. It planned a crewed sub-orbital spacecraft New Shepard in 2018 and an orbital launch vehicle, New Glen in 2020.

Jul 20, 2021 was a monumental day when Blue Origin successfully completed New Shepard's first human flight with four private citizens onboard. The crew included Jeff Bezos, Mark Bezos, Wally Funk and Oliver Daemen, who all officially became astronauts when they passed the Kármán Line, the internationally recognised boundary of space. Upon landing, the astronauts were greeted by their families and Blue Origin's ground operations team for a celebration in the West Texas desert.

This Historic Mission had many Firsts

The very first seat on New Shepard sells for $28 million. Nearly 7,600 people registered to bid from 159 countries. •Oliver Daemen, 18, the Dutch teenager, after another candidate bidding the $28m ride cancelled at the last minute, got the greatest surprise to find out he was joining the historical flight while on a family holiday in Italy. He became the first ever commercial astronaut to purchase a ticket and fly to space on a privately-funded and licensed space vehicle from a private launch site. He also became the youngest person to fly in space. •Wally Funk, 82, became the oldest person to fly in space. •Jeff and Mark Bezos became the first siblings to ever fly in space together. •New Shepard became the first commercial vehicle under a suborbital reusable launch vehicle license to fly paying customers, both payloads and astronauts, to space and back. By the way New Shepard and New Glen are in memory of Alan Shepard - the second man and first American to travel into space in 1962 and in 1971 to walk on moon abroad Apollo 14. John Glenn - the third American to be in space and first American to orbit the Earth circling three times in 1962.

Wally Funk's Journey to Space

It began in the 1960s when she was the youngest graduate of the Woman in Space Program, which tested female pilots for astronaut fitness. Later known as the "Mercury 13" – thirteen American women successfully underwent the same screening tests as male astronauts selected by NASA for Project Mercury, but never flew to space. Wally, the 82-year-old pilot, now became part of the first crew on New Shepard, and the oldest person ever to fly to space.

Stars, Galaxies, Black Holes...

The Universe: How Little is Known

There are many unknowns regarding the Universe - numerous strange theories and, yes, guesses abound. We would need to understand few concepts to get our head around. Also, it'll be necessary to consider the theorems of some of the most famous physicists in history to be able to understand them.

■ **The Size of Our Universe**: Due to the time limit of the speed of light, some objects may be so far away that light from them hasn't had time to reach us yet. It is therefore postulated that the actual Universe may be far bigger than that portion we can actually observe. This is impossible to verify, however, because, until data does reach us, we just don't know!

■ **What is Our Universe Made Of?**: Believe it or not, the stars, galaxies, nebulae and interstellar dust - visible stuff - collectively make up only 5% of our Universe! Most of the Universe consists of "dark energy", with the next largest portion being "dark matter". These two things are concepts only. In other words, they are invisible and undetectable, so their actual existence can only be theoretical.

They've been "made up", in effect, to explain the gravitational properties of the stars and galaxies, in their relation to the Universe as a whole. The dark matter is said to be pulling the galaxies together, while the dark energy is thought to be driving the Universe's expansion.

It is slightly alarming that most of our Universe is made of something that scientists basically know absolutely nothing about!

■ **Scientific Concepts to be Aware of**: Space-time– When you look round your environment, you see things, obviously, in three dimensions - height, width and depth. Things happen with the passage of time, which is separate from these dimensions.

In outer space, time has to be included as a fourth dimension, linked to the other three. This is because, across the gulfs of the Universe, the flow of time can vary, due to the speed of something relative to its observer and the effect of any local gravitational fields.

Thus, we have the concept of the four-dimensional "space-time", or the "space-time continuum", whereby an object's coordinates are not only "where", but "when", Newtonian Physics and Quantum Mechanics– the everyday world, everything we see around us, is governed by the Newtonian laws of physics, like, when you let go of an object, it falls to the ground. But dealing with inconceivably small particles, the quantum domain, things are very, very different. Everything appears totally random. Particles are popping in and out of existence and some travel faster than the speed of light. The Theory Of Relativity – Albert Einstein took 10 years to formulate this theory. Firstly, the motion of anything is always relative to the position and speed of the observer. That's one concept of "relativity and secondly, the speed of light remains constant under any circumstances (a paradox). But it is not so because at very high velocities, time moves more slowly and length shortens, to keep the light speed constant, relative to the observer ("time dilation), The Planck Length– It's actually 10 million million million million times smaller than an atom. This is a very small measurement of length, considered by some to be the smallest measurable length possible. It's arrived at by combining three fundamental universal constants: the Planck constant, the gravitational constant and the speed of light. As it is derived from universal constants, it is a constant itself, which sort of contradicts Einstein's Theory of Relativity, which proposes that length isn't constant. Either his theory will have to be amended, or the length is too minuscule for it to matter. Heisenberg's Uncertainty Principle–means that some particle interactions, or the particles themselves, are too small or short lived to be measured. Thus it is impossible to predict what they will do or formulate scientific laws about them.

■ **The Shape Of Our Universe:** You may think that, as our Universe originated from a single point as the Big Bang, its subsequent expansion would result in its shape being spherical. Needless to say, it's not as simple as that.

There were three different possibilities proposed for the shape of the Universe - Open, Closed or Flat. To appreciate what each of these mean, we need to understand that the Universe is three-dimensional, expanding in four dimensions. The most our human minds can grasp is a 2-D (two-dimensional) Universe (like the surface of a balloon when it is inflated), expanding in three dimensions. Once you can accept this concept, the three possible Universe shapes might make more sense.

The Closed Universe can be thought of as a sphere, like a ball or a planet, is a three-dimensional sphere, adding depth to the mix. The Universe, however, takes the sphere shape to a fourth dimension which you can't really visualise. The Open Universe is, theoretically, without boundaries. The flat Universe, is also open and without boundaries. The space probe Explorer 80 (or WMAP - Wilkinson Microwave Anisotropy Probe) has measured this fairly accurately and found it to be very close to a value of one. This suggests that we are living in a 4-dimensional flat Universe.

■ **The Colour of Our Universe**: The Universe is black with stars twinkling in it, isn't it? Well, yes, but this colour of our Universe is determined by examining the colour of all the various galaxies and stars in a large portion of the observable Universe and sort of averaging it out.

The result was... beige. Yes, the Universe is beige! Its official name is "cosmic latte", voted upon by the scientists at John Hopkins University, in Baltimore, USA, where the research took place.

■ **Where is the Centre of Our Universe?**: If the Universe was created, in the Big Bang, from a single point, so, if we find where this single point is within the Universe today, then that must be its centre. Seems logical, doesn't it? As you'd expect, that's not the situation at all.

There is no space outside the Universe for it to expand into. There is no existence outside of the Universe. What is actually happening is that space itself is expanding, so, in effect, space is being created with the expansion. Therefore, that original single point has now expanded to be everywhere in the Universe. The centre of the Universe could be – it is everywhere, because "everywhere" originated from the single point

■ **The Fate of Our Universe**: Assuming the Universe is flat, its expansion will continue until one of two things happen.

Firstly, the "Big Freeze", which postulates that, as the expansion continues, the Universe will gradually cool down. It will pass through a "degenerate era", when all star creation ceases, then a "black hole" era. Eventually, these objects will dissolve away, forming the "dark era". Subsequently, the Universe will experience heat death.

Secondly, the "Big Rip". This assumes the existence of a special form of dark energy called "phantom energy". This will simply cause the Universe's expansion to increase at an exponential rate, eventually tearing it apart. All stars and planets would suffer this fate, culminating with all the remaining atoms of matter being destroyed.

SUN Mercury Venus Earth Mars Ceres JUPITER SATURN URANUS

The Solar System

Location: Local Interstellar Cloud, Local Bubble, Orion-Cygnus Arm, Milky Way

FACTS ABOUT THE SUN

- The Sun is one among the 200 billion stars in our Milky Way galaxy
- The mass of Sun : 2 Octillion tons
- The Sun has circled the Milky Way galaxy for about 20 times only since its formation
- The Sun's temperature at its core : 15 million Kelvin
- Each second the Sun loses 5 million tons of material
- It takes up to 50 million years for the energy produced at the core of the Sun to reach its surface.
- The Sun's energy output is 386 billion megawatt
- A total solar eclipse is not noticeable until the Sun is more than 90% covered by the Moon. At 99% coverage, daytime lighting resembles local twilight.
- The longest duration for a total solar eclipse is 7.5 minutes.
- If you weigh 50 kg, your weight on the Sun would be 1353 kg (multiply your actual weight by 27)
- The reaction taking place in Sun is nuclear fusion, same as a Hydrogen bomb.
- Solar flares are violent explosions taking place in the Sun's atmosphere occasionally. Solar flares can reach more than 100,000 miles away from the sun
- Each second 700 million tons of Hydrogen are converted to 695 million tons of Helium and 5 million tons of energy in the form of gamma rays

The Sun is the star at the centre of the Solar System. It is a nearly perfect sphere of hot plasma, heated to incandescence by nuclear fusion reactions in its core, radiating the energy mainly as visible light, ultraviolet light, and infrared radiation.

•Surface temperature: 5,778 K •Mass: 1.989 × 10^30 kg •Radius: 696,340 km •Gravity: 274 m/s² •Age: 4.603 billion years •Distance to Earth: 149.6 million km

- The Sun is getting lighter as it shines? Indeed! By fusion, the sun "burns" about 564 million tons hydrogen per second, resulting in 559.7 million tons of helium. The loss of mass, about 4.3 million tons per second, is transformed into energy. It's only 0.0000000000000000002 % of the sun's entire mass. That weight is turned into energy: equivalent to about 4 trillion Hiroshima bombs every second.

NEPTUNE Pluto Eris Makemake Haumea

CURIOUS FACTS OF SOLAR SYSTEM

1. The hottest planet is not closest to the sun. Mercury has no atmosphere. Venus is!
2. Uranus is tilted on its side
3. Jupiter's moon Io has towering volcanic eruptions 400km into the sky
4. Mars has the biggest volcano ever discovered in the solar system, *Olympus Mons*, 602 km across and 25 km high, or triple the height of Mount Everest, the tallest mountain on Earth.
5. Mars also has the longest valley – *Valles Marineris*, 4,000 km long.
6. Venus is a hellish planet with a high-temperature, high-pressure environment on its surface 50 times faster than the planet's rotation
7. Earth is mostly composed of iron, oxygen, silicon, magnesium, sulphur, nickel, calcium, sodium, and aluminium. In universe, they are merely trace elements, vastly overshadowed by the much greater abundances of hydrogen and helium.
8. Spacecraft have visited every planet – the bulk of the flybys came from NASA's twin Voyager spacecraft, which left Earth in 1977
9. Jupiter has the biggest ocean of any planet, albeit made of metallic hydrogen.
10. The edge of the solar system is 1,000 times farther away than Pluto.

Solar System

Planets 8
Dwarf Planets 5
Moons 200+
Asteroids 1,113,527
Comets 3743

Planets: names by gods

- Mercury: god of commerce, skill, travel, (Roman).
- Venus: goddess of spring, love, beauty (Roman)
- Earth: English-German name for the ground
- Mars: god of war (Roman)
- Jupiter: Ruler of gods and all men (Roman)
- Saturn: god of agriculture (Roman)
- Uranus: god of heavens (Greek)
- Neptune: god of the sea (Roman)

Dwarf Planets

- Pluto: god of the underworld (Roman)
- Ceres: goddess of corn and harvest (Roman)
- Eris: god of discord and strife (Greek)
- Makemake: god of fertility (Polynesia)
- Haumea: goddess of childbirth and fertility (Hawaiian).

The Planets

Planets: There are 8 planets in our solar system: Mercury, Venus, Earth, Mars, Jupiter, Saturn, Uranus and Neptune. All the planets of the solar system move around the sun in fixed elongated paths. Dwarf Planet They are celestial bodies that are (i) rounded in shape and orbits around the sun (ii) has sufficient mass for its self-gravity to overcome rigid body forces so that it assumes a hydrostatic equilibrium (nearly round) shape (iii) has not cleared the neighbourhood around its orbit, and (d) is not a satellite. The 5 recognised dwarf planets are Ceres in the asteroid belt and Pluto, Eris, Makemake and Haumea in the Kuiper belt • Dwarf planets are solid rocky and/or icy bodies. The amount of rock versus. ice depends on their location in the solar system. • They have no rings.

The Earth

All of the planets, except for Earth, were named after Greek and Roman gods and goddesses. However, the name Earth is a Germanic word, which means "the ground"and 1000 years old. •**Earth,** located 1AU from the Sun •The largest and densest of the inner planets •The only planet where life is known to exist •Earth has continuous geological activity where plate tectonics has been observed.•Its liquid hydrosphere is unique among the terrestrial planets. •The atmosphere is radically different from those of the other planets, having 21% free oxygen that supports life. •It has one natural satellite, the Moon, the largest satellite of a terrestrial planet in the Solar System. **Distance from Sun**: 151,645,298 Km **Time the Light Takes from the Sun**: 8.43 mins.

Planet Superlatives

Largest, most massive planet	Jupiter
Smallest, least massive planet	Mercury
Fastest orbiting planet	Mercury
Slowest orbiting planet	Neptune
Longest (synodic) day	**Venus**
Shortest (synodic) day	Jupiter
Most Moons	(67) Jupiter
No Moons	Mercury, Venus
Planet with largest moon	Jupiter
Greatest av. density	Earth
Lowest av. density	Saturn
Strongest magnetic fields	Jupiter
Hottest Planet	Venus
Coldest Planet	Neptune
Most circular orbit	Venus
Planet having moon with most eccentric orbit	Neptune
Deepest oceans	Jupiter
Greatest amount of liquid on the surface	Earth
Retrograde revolution : (East to West) Venus, Uranus, Pluto	

** A Synodic day is the period it takes for a planet to rotate once in relation to the start it is orbiting.*

Planets: names by gods

•**Mercury:** god of commerce, skill, travel, (R). •**Venus:** goddess of spring, love, beauty (R) •Earth: English-German name for the ground •**Mars:** god of war (R) •**Jupiter:** Ruler of gods and all men (R) • **Saturn:** god of agriculture (R) • **Uranus:** god of heavens (G) •**Neptune:** god of the sea (R). DWARF PLANETS : •**Pluto**: god of the underworld (R) •**Ceres**: goddess of corn and harvest (R) •**Eris**: god of discord and strife (G) •**Makemake**: god of fertility (Rapa Nui mythology- Polynesia) •**Haumea**: goddess of childbirth and fertility (Hawaiian). *[Mythology: R: Roman. G: Greek]*

Saturn overtakes Jupiter, becomes the planet with the most moons. Saturn now has 82 moons, 3 more than Jupiter. Saturn now has the most number of moons among planets.

Dwarf Planets

According to the International Astronomical Union, which sets definitions for planetary science, a dwarf planet is a celestial body that -orbits the sun, has enough mass to assume a nearly round shape, has not cleared the neighborhood around its orbit.

CERES: Size: 939.8 kms in diametre
Location: Asteroid Belt
Discovery 1801
Fact: Largest object in the Asteroid Belt

MAKEMAKE: Size: 1432.3 kms in diametre
Location: Kuiper Belt
Discovery: 2005
Moon: MK2
Fact: Second biggest object in Kuiper Belt

ERIS: Size: 2325.5 kms in diametre
Location: outer reaches of Kuiper Belt
Discovery: 2003
Fact: Its discovery started the debate over Pluto's planetary status

PLUTO: Size: 2370 kms in diametre
Location: Near Kuiper Belt
Discovery: 1930
Moons: Charon, Nix, Hydra, Styx
Fact: Pluto day is 6.4 Earth days long

HAUMEA: Size: 1923 x 989.7 kms in diametre
Location: Kuiper Belt
Discovery: 2004
Moons: Hi'iaka, Namaka
Fact: Its moons are name d after the goddess' daughters

The Asteroids

Asteroids: 958,568. Asteroids are classified by their composition – carbon-rich, Silicon-rich, and metal rich – mainly metallic iron and nickel. Most asteroids are irregularly shaped and all have craters. New asteroids are discovered almost on a daily basis. It is estimated that the mineral wealth of the asteroids in the main belt between Mars and Jupiter is about $100,000,000 for every person on Earth. The Asteroid belt is not densely populated – all of the asteroids together only make about 5% the mass of the Moon.

Comets: 3,643. Scientists estimate there are about 1,000,000,000 comets held in the gravitational grip of the sun.

Plutoids' Pluto, Eris, Haumea and Makemake are "plutoids"– a dwarf planet that orbits outside Neptune.

The Kuiper Belt is a region of the Solar System beyond the planets, extending from the orbit of Neptune (at 30 AU) to approximately 50 AU from the Sun. It is shaped like a disk residing in the shell-like structure of the Oort Cloud and full of asteroids ranging in many sizes – home to most dwarf planets.

The Oort Cloud is not really a cloud but a vast shell of billions of comets. It extends three light years from the sun. It is a much more distant region of icy, comet-like bodies that surrounds the solar system, including the Kuiper Belt.

The Moon

The Moon is Earth's only natural satellite, circling the planet at an average distance of roughly 385,000 kms. With a diameter of just under 3,500 km, the cratered surface of the rocky object is one of the most recognisable objects in the sky. A single orbit of our planet takes the Moon 27.3 Earth days - the same amount of time it takes for the satellite to also rotate once on its axis. As a result, half of the Moon's surface perpetually faces Earth. The other half (erroneously called the dark side of the Moon, despite receiving the same amount of sunlight as the more familiar side) was finally seen for the first time in 1959 when the Soviet probe Luna 3 beamed back a grainy set of photographs. This 'tidally locked' orbit is the result of Earth and the Moon pulling on one another, slowing the rotation of each. Earth's own rotation has similarly been affected by the braking effect of the Moon's gravity, adding around 1.4 milliseconds to our day every century.

Moons of Each Planet

Earth-1, Mars-2, Jupiter-79 (53 confirmed, 26 provisional), Saturn- 82 (53 conf., 29 prov.), Uranus - 27, Neptune - 14.

There are currently 174 named moons in our Solar System, orbiting the six outermost planets, with more being discovered and debated every day. Some are more fascinating than others, whether it's their landscapes, features, orbits or environments

Largest Moons in the Solar System

Moon	Planet	Mean diameter
Ganymede	Jupiter	5262 km
Titan,	Saturn	5150 b km
Callisto,	Jupiter	4821 km
Io,	Jupiter	3643 km
Moon,	Earth	3475 km
Europa,	Jupiter	3122 km
Triton,	Neptune	2707 km
Titania,	Uranus	1578 km
Rhea,	Saturn	1529 km
Oberon,	Uranus	1523 km
Iapetus,	Saturn	1471 km
Charon,	Pluto	1210 km
Umbriel,	Uranus	1169 km
Ariel,	Uranus	1158 km
Dione,	Saturn	1123 km
Tethys,	Saturn	1066 km

Lunar Eclipse

During this eclipse the full moon passes partially or wholly through the *umbra* of the earth's shadow. The moon can at times appear reddish esp. during eclipses. For a long-lasting total lunar eclipse of 1 hour and 43 minutes to occur, the moon has to pass through the central part of the Earth's shadow.

Blood Moon

During the total lunar eclipse, Earth fully blocks direct sunlight from reaching the Moon. The only light reflected from the lunar surface has been refracted by Earth's atmosphere. Due to this reddish colour it is called a blood. moon

Blue Moon

Normally, there are 12 full moons per year. A season of 3 months should contain 3 full moons. Whenever there are 4 full moons in a season instead of three, the third of the fullmoons is called a 'blue' moon that happens on average about once in 2.7 years.

Super Moon

It occurs when the full moon is at the closest point of its orbit to the Earth (the perigee) which makes the moon look extra-close, up to 14% bigger and 30% brighter than a full moon at its farthest point from Earth (apogee). Occasionally, two full moons will fall within the same month.

Hubble Space Telescope

In the three decades since shuttle Discovery carried it into orbit on 24 April 1990, the Hubble Space Telescope has changed the way both astronomers and the general public understand the cosmos. More than 550,000 scientific observations were made between 2019-2021.

With the instruments working well and demand for observing time as high as ever, *Hubble* is primed to continue exploring the universe through at least 2025.

Stereographic map charts the diverse astronomical objects that Hubble looked in 30 years.

Among Hubble's most captivating cosmic subjects, first imaged in 1995, are the Pillars of Creation: billowing towers of cold gas and dust in a stellar nursery

Hubble has tracked the slow, steady diminution of the solar system's most famous anticyclone, the great Red Spot in Jupiter.

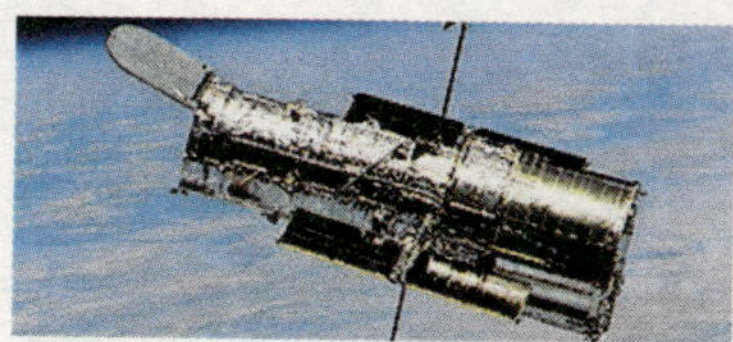

Major Contributions to Science:

- Helped pin down the age for the universe now known to be 13.8 billion years, roughly three times the age of Earth.
- Discovered two moons of Pluto, Nix and Hydra.
- Helped determine the rate at which the universe is expanding.
- Discovered that nearly every major galaxy is anchored by a black hole at the centre.
- Created a 3-D map of dark matter.

Top 3 Hubble facts

- 1. Hubble travels at a speed of 17,500 mph and has covered a distance equivalent to a trip to Neptune, the furthermost planet in our solar system.
- 2. Hubble has peered back into the very distant past, to locations more than 13.4 billion light years from Earth.
- 3. Since its mission began in 1990, Hubble has made more than 1.3 million observations.

- 2003: Capturing more than 2 million galaxies over 2-square-degree field, the Cosmic Evolution Survey is Hubble's largest ever sky survey.
- Measurements of Cepheid variable stars in M81 helped establish one rung of the cosmic distance ladder that has been used to estimate the age of the universe.

Cyclone, Hurricane, Typhoons, Tornado

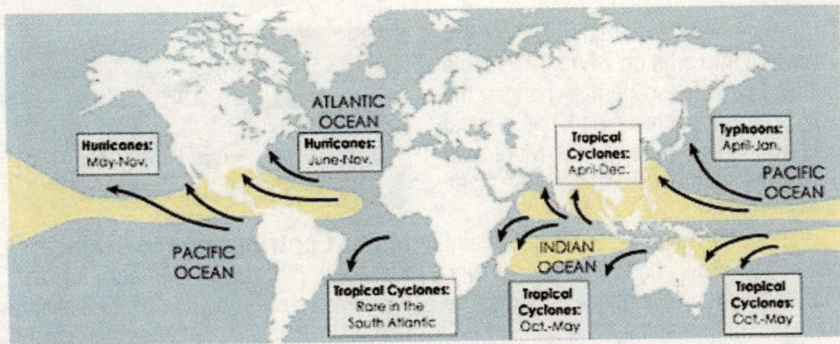

Atmospheric disturbances around a low-pressure area is usually accompanied by violent storms resulting in severe weather conditions.

Tropical cyclone is a deep low pressure area. From around the centre the strong winds spirals and pick up the speeds of 62 Kmph or more. In Northern-hemisphere these winds rotate counter-clockwise and in Southern Hemisphere clockwise.

Classification as per Occurrence: On the basis of the speed of the wind cyclones are classified into five different categories from Category 1 to 5. According to the category of the cyclone the wind speed varies that is from 60 kilometres an hour to about 220 kmph and above.

Tropical Cyclone When the speed of the wind around the low pressure area reach up to 62 kmph.

Super Cyclonic Storm when the speed of the wind exceeds 221 kmph. A fully matured cyclone develops a calm centre.

The Tropical Cyclones that are intense are known as Hurricanes over the Atlantic Ocean and Typhoons over the Pacific Ocean. They are known by different names. For example: dust devils, super cell thunderstorm, tornadoes, tropical cyclones, extra tropical cyclones etc.

Classification as per Speed:

Tropical Depression: A tropical cyclone with maximum sustained winds of 60 kmph or less.

Tropical Storm: A tropical cyclone with maximum sustained winds of 61 to 120 kmph.

Hurricane: A tropical cyclone with maximum sustained winds of 121 kmph or higher. ***Major Hurricane:*** A tropical cyclone with maximum sustained winds of 180 kmph or higher, corresponding to a Category 3, 4 or 5 on the Saffir-Simpson Hurricane Wind Scale.

Typhoons : In the western North Pacific, hurricanes are called so; similar storms in the Indian Ocean and South Pacific Ocean are called Cyclones.

Tornado : A tornado is a violently spiraling funnel cloud that extends from the bottom of a thunderstorm to the ground. It is important not to confuse a tornado with a hurricane or tropical cyclone because tornadoes and hurricanes are very different phenomena. The only similarity between them is that they both contain strong rotating winds that can cause damage.

Origin of Name: '*Cyclone*' is derived from Greek word *cyclos*– coiling of snake.

Earthquakes

An earthquake is the shaking of the surface of the earth resulting from a sudden release of energy in the Earth's interior, usually by sudden movements along fault lines. This movement releases energy that propagates as seismic waves. The size of earthquakes is determined by the amount of energy released in this process. It can range in size between many orders of magnitude and is commonly given as a number on the logarithmic Richter scale. It ranges from so tiny that they are not felt and can be only detected by the most sensitive modern instruments (seismometers) to so strong that entire regions are shaking violently.

•Two Points of Impact:

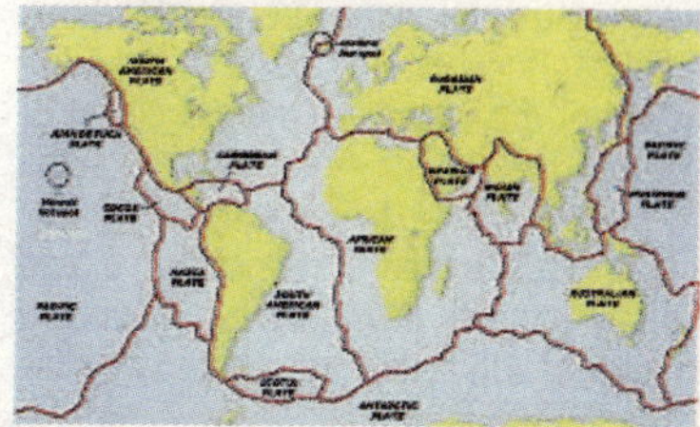

When talking about earthquakes, the hypocenter or focus is the point inside the earth where an earthquake rupture starts. It is often confused with epicenter, which

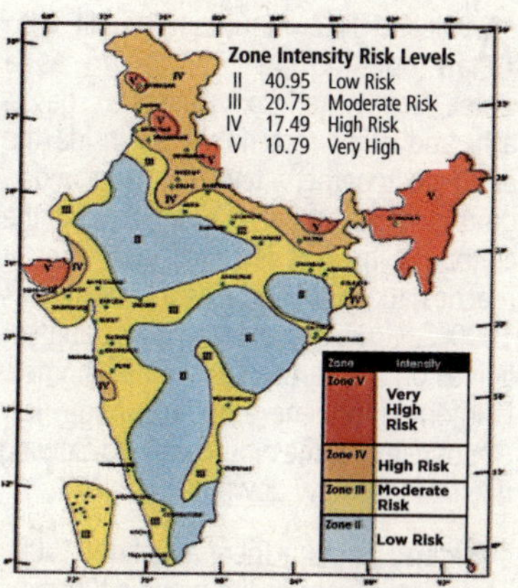

India's Seismic Zone (Four): Zone-II, III, IV and V. Zone V is the most seismically active region, while zone II is the least.

is the is the point directly above it at the surface of the Earth, where the quake is felt strongest.

India lies at the northwestern end of the Indo-Australian Plate, which encompasses India, Australia, a major portion of the Indian Ocean and other smaller countries. This huge plate is colliding against the Eurasian Plate and going under the Eurasian Plate; this process of one tectonic plate getting under another is responsible for making India a earthquake prone country. Some of these occurred in populated and urbanised areas and hence caused great damage. Many go unnoticed, as they occur deep under the Earth's surface or in relatively un-inhabited places.

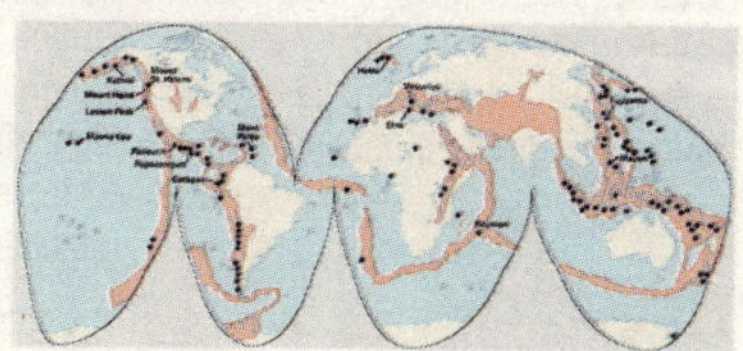

Earthquake Facts:• Each year around 500,000 earthquakes are detected with current instrumentation. About 100,000 of these can be felt. 20,000 are moderate to intense. •Antarctica has the least earthquakes of any continent, but small earthquakes can occur anywhere in the world.•Japan tops the list of the earthquake prone areas and has a long history of disastrous earthquakes since it is situated on the Pacific "Ring of fire".

Volcanoes

A volcano is a mountain or hill with an opening on top known as a crater. Hot melted rock (magma), gases, ash, and other materials from inside the earth mix together a few kilometres underground, and blast out, or erupt, through the crater. The magma is called lava when it reaches the air. Lava may be as hot as 1000°C. Gradually the lava cools and solidifies on the earth's surface making new landforms. In some eruptions, huge fiery clouds rise over the mountain, and glowing rivers of lava flow down its sides.

Volcano Facts: •There are about 1500 active volcanoes in the world.•300 million, or one-in-twenty, people in the world live within the 'danger range' of an active volcano. •About 1,500 different volcanoes have erupted over the past 10,000 years, but only about 60 erupt each year. On any given day, there are about 20 volcanoes erupting somewhere in the world.•Many volcanoes are underwater and erupt onto the sea floor.

Types of Volcanoes – Periodicity

(i) Active- that which is alive now. e.g. Etna, Stromboli, Pinatubo, etc. (ii) Dormant- that which has not erupted for quite some time now. e.g. Vesuvius, Barren Islands. (iii) Extinct- which has not erupted for several centuries/millennia or may not occur in near future.

Mode of Eruption: (i) Explosive or Central- e.g. Hawaiian type, Vesuvius type, Pelean type, etc. (ii) Fissure or quite eruption: lava flows out or floods, mud flow and fumaroles, quietly.

Are earthquakes and volcanoes related? Some, but not all. Most earthquakes are along the edges of tectonic plates. This is where most volcanoes are too. However, most earthquakes are caused by the interaction of the plates not the movement of magma. The magma exerts pressure on the rocks until it cracks the rock. Then the magma squirts into the crack. Once the volcano erupts, magma flow through it causing constant earthquake waves, not always felt.

Comparative Seismic Scale

Intensity	Description	Magnitude	Effects
	(Mercalli Scale)	(Richter Scale)	(RS is calculated in levels of ten to the previous.)
I	Instrumental	1 - 2	Detected only by seismographs
II	Feeble	2 - 3	Noticed only by sensitive people
III	Slight	3 - 4	Resembling vibrations caused by heavy traffic
IV	Moderate	4	Felt by people walking; rocking free standing objects
V	Rather Strong	4 - 5	Sleepers awakened and bells ring
VI	Strong	5 - 6	Trees sway, damage from falling objects
VII	Very Strong	6	General alarm, cracking of walls
VIII	Destructive	6 - 7	Chimneys fall; some damage to buildings
IX	Ruinous	7	Ground cracks; houses begin to collapse; pipes break
X	Disastrous	7 - 8	Ground badly cracked; buildings destroyed; landslides
XI	Very Disastrous	8 - 8.9	Few buildings remain standing; bridges and railways destroyed; water, gas, electricity, telephones disrupted
XII	Catastrophic	9 +	Total destruction; objects are thrown into the air, much heaving, shaking and distortion of the ground topography.

Landforms of the World

Continents - Areawise

Name	Area sq kilometres	% of Earth's area	Population Estimate (million)
Asia	43,998,000	29.5	3879
Africa	29,800,000	20.0	877
N. America	21,510,000	16.3	501
S. America**	17,598,000	11.8	379
Europe	9,699,550	6.5	727
Australia*	7,699,000	5.2	32
Antarctica	13,600,000	9.6	uninhabited

** Australia with New Zealand, Tasmania, New Guinea and the Pacific Islands, (Micronesian, Melanesian and Polynesian Islands) is called Australasia by some geographers, while some others call it Oceania.*
*** includes Caribbean countries*

Continentwise Highest Point

Continent: Peak Height(m)

• Asia:Mt Everest 8 848 •Africa:Kilimanjaro 5963 •N. America: Mt. McKinley 6 194 •S. America: Aconcagua 6 959 •Europe: Mt Elbrus 5 633 •Oceania: Puncak Jaya 4884 •Antarctica: Vinson Massif 4897

Continentwise Lowest Points

Continent: Water body Depth(m)

•Asia: Dead Sea -396.8 •Africa: Lake Assai -156.1 •N. America: Death Valley -85.9 •S. America: Valdes Penin -39.9 •Europe: Caspian Sea -28.0 •Oceania: Lake Eyre-15.8
** Deepest point on land on earth identified under Denman Glacier, east Antarctica at 3.5km (11,500ft) below sea level

Longest Rivers

Name, Nation/ Continent (Basin Area MKm²)	Length (Kms)	Basin Area
Nile, Africa	6695	3.25
Amazon, S. America	6516	6.14
Yangtze Kiang, China	6380	1.72
Mississippi-Missouri, USA	5959	3.20
Ob-Irtysh, Russia	5568	2.97

Indian Rivers: Length (in kms)

• Indus: 3180 •Brahmaputra: 2948•Ganga-Hooghly-Padma: 2620 • Godavari: 1465 •Sutlej: 1372 • Krishna: 1300 •Narmada: 1289 •Chenab: 1086 •Ghaghara:1080.

Shortest Rivers

		(metres)
Ombla river, Croatia:	Europe	30
Roe River, Montana, USA-	N. America:	61
Azuis River, Brazil:	S. America	147

** Basin area of the main river is mentioned*

Principal Peaks

Name	Country	Height (m)
Mt Everest	Nepal-Tibet	8 848
Everest South Summit	-	8750
K2 (Mt Godwin Austen)	India (POK)	8 611
Kanchenjunga	Nepal-India	8 586
Lhotse	Nepal-Tibet	8516

Indian Peaks

•K2 (Mt Godwin Austen):India (POK) 8 611
• Nanga Parbat (Diamir): India 8126 •Gasherbrum: India 8068 •Nanda Devi: India7817
•Mt Kamet: India 7 756.

Oceans of the World

Pacific	166,241,000 sq km
Atlantic	86,557,000 sq km
Indian	73,427,000 sq km
Arctic	9,485,000 sq km

Major Seas

	(sq km)
Arabian Sea	3,862,000
South China	2,974,600
Caribbean	2,515,900
Mediterranean	2,510,000
Bering	2,261,100
Bay of Bengal	2,172,000

Largest Deserts Subtropical

	(sq. km)
Sahara, North Africa	8,600,650
Arabian, Middle East	2,300,000
Great Victoria, Australia	647,475
Kalahari, Southern Africa	582,727
Thar, India/Pakistan	453,232

Deepest Caves

Name	Location	Max.depth
Resseu du Foillis	France	1455
Resseu de la Pierre St.	France	1321
Snezhnaya, Caucasus	Russia	1280

Moon Wobble and Climate Change

Over the past few decades, the Earth's climate has been changing at an unprecedented rate. The cascading impact of rising temperatures can clearly be documented through the dramatic melting of ice sheets and glaciers near the poles. Among the enumerable and widespread repercussions of such melting, one of the scariest is the rising of the sea levels. It has the potential to inundate the coastal regions of the world, effectively impacting the lives of millions of people globally.

Coupled with the climate-change-induced rise in sea levels, the tides in Earth's oceans—which are controlled by the Moon's gravitational pull. The grim projections are detailed in a new first-of-its-kind study conducted by the US space agency NASA, which elucidates how the moon's elliptical orbit around Earth and the moon's wobble effect can lead to considerable changes on our planet.

What is the Moon wobble?
The moon wobble is nothing but a regular swaying in the moon's orbit. It was first documented way back in 1728. This wobble takes over an 18.6-year period to complete, and continues in a cyclic fashion.

Wobble Impact on Earth The moon wobble impacts the gravitational pull of the moon, and therefore, indirectly influences the ebb and flow of tides here on the Earth. In fact, as per the NASA study, each wobble cycle has the power to amplify and suppress the tides on Earth. The lunar cycle is expected to shift again by mid-2030, and in the coming phase, the tides will amplify once again.

The study predicts that the high tide-associated floods–also known as nuisance floods or sunny day floods–may occur in clusters that could last for months or even for longer periods!

El Niño and La Nina

In Spanish, literally, El Niño means 'little boy', It is an oceanic atmospheric phenomenon which causes waters in the equatorial Pacific to warm up abnormally due to weakening of trade winds. • There are periodic warming and cooling of vast stretches of ocean surface. During El Niño years, the Pacific warm pool expands to cover the tropical regions.

Occurance • It is cyclical phenomenon where weather system re-emerges after a gap of about 2 to 5 years in the Pacific ocean and its effects last for about 12 months on an average. • Normally, the sea surface temperatures off S. American west coast range from the 15°C to 25°C. It exceed 26°C in the "warm pool" located in the central and western Pacific.

• El Nino occurs when the threshold value of 0.5°C of Oceanic Nino Index (ONI) is met or crossed for a minimum of five consecutive overlapping seasons of three months each.

La Nina • La Niña occur on an average every 3 to 5 years and can persist for as long as two years. Naturally, it impacts global weather patterns.• La Niña is an oceanic-atmospheric phenomenon that causes the water temperatures in the Equatorial Pacific Ocean become cooler than normal.

Causes •La Niña occurs when the easterly trade winds intensely bring cold water to the surface through a complex series of events along the equator in the tropical Pacific off Peru and Ecuador on the west coast of South America. • The sea surface temperatures along the equator could then fall by -13.88°C below the normal levels. Records suggest that during the 1988-89 La Niña, the sea-surface temperatures (SSTs) fell 4°C below normal.

INDIA INSIGNIA

- National Emblem
- National Anthem
- National Flower
- National Animal
- National Monument
- National Calendar
- National Ration Card
- Our National Flag
- Rank and Precedence
- Indian Currency

The National Insignia

National Emblem: •The Sarnath Lion, at the capital of Asoka's empire, •Adopted as the state emblem of India: 26 January 1950, the day when India became a Republic. •Carved out of a single block of polished sandstone •The Capital is crowned by *Dharma Chakra*, the wheel of the Law.

•In the state emblem adopted by the government only three lions are visible whereas the fourth (in the original) is hidden from view. The wheel appears in relief in the centre of the abacus with a bull on the right and a horse on the left. The bell-shaped lotus has been omitted.

National Emblem

The words, *Satyameva Jayate* (meaning 'Truth alone triumphs') from the *Mundaka Upanishad* is inscribed below the abacus in Devanagari script. It is also the national motto. It is preserved in the Sarnath Museum.

The National Flag

• The Tricolour, comprises three-colour horizontal strip of deep Saffron (Kesari), *(representing courage and sacrifice)* at the top, White *(peace and truth)* in the middle and dark Green *(faith and chivalry)* at the bottom. •The ratio of the width of the flag to its length is 2:3. •In the centre of white band is a wheel, in navy blue. It is a wheel (*Chakra*) with 24 spokes on the abacus of the Sarnath Lion Capital of Ashoka. Its diameter is equal to the width of the white band. •The design of the national flag was adopted by the Constituent Assembly of India: 22 July, 1947. •Flag's use and display are regulated by a code. A new Flag Code of India, 2002, took effect from 26 January 2002. •Provisions for Proper Use: no restrictions for displaying the national flag by members of general public, private organisations, educational institutions. •Prevention of Improper Use Act, 1950, the Prevention of Insults to National Honour Act, 1971 and few other law enacted on the subject are guidelines for using the flag with dignity and pride.

National Anthem: *Jana-gana-mana*
Jana-gana-mana-adhinayaka jaya he
Bharata-bhagya-vidhata.
Punjaba-Sindhu-Gujarata-Maratha-
Dravida-Utkala-Banga
Vindhya Himachala-Yamuna-Ganga
Uchchala-Jaladhi-taranga
Tava Subha name jage,
Tava subha asisa mange,
Gahe tava jaya-gatha,
Jana-gana-mangala-dayaka, jaya he
Bharata-bhagya-vidhata.
Jaya he, jaya he, jaya he,
Jaya jaya jaya, jaya he.

The following is Tagore's English rendering of the stanza:

Thou art the ruler of the minds of all people,
Dispenser of India's destiny.
Thy name rouses the hearts of the Punjab, Sind, Gujarat and Maratha,
Of the Dravid and Orissa and Bengal.
It echoes in the hills of the Vindhyas and Himalayas, mingles in the music of the Jamuna and the Ganges and is chanted by the waves of the Indian Sea.
They pray for the blessings and sing thy praise.
The saving of all people waits in thy hand,
Thou dispenser of India's destiny, victory, victory, victory to thee.

National Song : *Vande Mataram*
•The song is composed by Bankimchandra Chatterjee. • Equal status with *Jana-gana-mana.* •The first sung at a political occasion: 1896 session of the INC.

Vande Mataram,
Sujalam, suphalam, malayaja shitalam,
Shasyashyamalam, Mataram!
Shubhrajyothsna pulakitayaminim,
Phullakusumita drumadala shobhinim,
Suhasinim sumadhura bhashinim,
Sukadam varadam, Mataram!

English translation of the stanza rendered by Sri Aurobindo (in *Sri Aurobindo* birth centenary library popular edition 1972, vol. 8), is

I bow to thee, Mother,
richly-watered, richly-fruited,
cool with the winds of the south,
dark with the crops of the harvests,
The Mother !
Her nights rejoicing in the glory of the moonlight,
Her lands clothed beautifully with her trees in flowering bloom, sweet of laughter, sweet speech,
The Mother, giver of boons, giver of bliss.

National Flower: Lotus
(*Nelumbo Nucifera Gaertn*) •Sacred flower • An auspicious symbol of Indian culture. •Occupies a unique position in the art and mythology of India

Lotus

National River: River Ganga
• The longest in India, flowing over 2,510 kms. •Originates in the Gangotri Glacier in the Himalayas as the Bhagirathi River •Joined downstream by rivers like the Alaknanda, Yamuna, Son, Gumti, Kosi and Ghagra. • Revered in Hinduism as the most sacred river. •The Ganga river

One Nation, One Ration Card
Launch: On pilot basis in 2019. Aim: to provide adequate food grains to the poor sections of the country across the country at very meager rates • It

enables 4 crore migrant workers in India to get cheap food grains with one ration card across the country. •24 States/UTs are connected as on 1st August 2020 covering more than 65 crore beneficiaries

National Currency
The symbol is a combination of both Devanagiri letter 'Ra' and Roman letter 'R' with a stripe cutting at the middle to represent the tricolour.

One Nation, One Tax
The Goods and Services Tax (GST)
Launched : July 1, 2017
Dubbed as : 'One Nation-One Tax'.

One Nation, One Card
National Common Mobility Card (NCMC). Launched: March 4. Aim: the inter-operable transport card will provide seamless urban mobility to commuters across the country – allowing holders to pay for their bus travel, toll taxes, parking charges, retail shopping and withdraw cash.
Dubbed as: 'One Nation-One Card'.

Ganga River

basin is very fertile and is one of the most densely populated areas of the world. • Area: 1,000,000 sq. kms.

National Tree: Indian Banyan Tree *(Ficus Bengalensis)* • It has branches that shoots aerial roots letting it spread like new trees over a large area. • This tree is considered immortal due to the charac-

Banyan Tree

teristic of spreading the whole area with its roots, expanding trunk and its longevity • An integral part of the myths and legends in India. •The banyan tree is the focal point of village life. •The Village Council mostly meets under this tree.

National Animal: Royal Bengal Tiger, • From a specific population of the Panthera tigris tigris subspecies that is native to the Indian subcontinent. •Out of eight existing species, the Royal Bengal Tiger, is the rarest.•The combination of grace, strength, agility and enormous power has earned it the title the national animal of India. •To protect the most dwindling population of tigers in India, 'Project Tiger' was launched in April 1973.

Royal Bengal Tiger

National Fruit: Mango *(Mangifera indica)* •The mango tree is one of the most widely cultivated fruit tree in India. There are over 100 varieties of mangoes, in different sizes, shapes, colours and taste.

National Bird : Indian peacock (*Pavo cristatus)* • It has beautiful velvet feathers and a slender neck. The male is more colourful than the female with a glistening blue breast and neck and a spectacular bronze-green tail of around 200 elongated feathers. [The female is brownish and slightly smaller than the male and lacks tail.]

Indian Peacock

•The dance of the male fanning out the tail and preening its feathers is a gorgeous sight.

National Heritage Animal : Asiatic elephants •In order to increase the population of, the largest mammal species on land, the Min. of Environment has declared it the National Heritage Animal. •Around 60% of them live in India.

National Aquatic Animal : River Dolphin (Platanista gangetica) • It is a critically endangered species in India. •It is put in Schedule 1 of the Wildlife Protection Act, 1972. •Poaching, degradation of its habitat, siltation, pollution and reduced flow of river water are threats to its existence.

River Dolphin

National Monument: India Gate

• The war memorial situated in New Delhi, is the national monument of India, erected in memory of 90,000 soldiers who lost their lives fighting in the World War I and Afghan War for the British Army. Designed by Sir Edwin Lutyens. Earlier, it was called All India War Memorial.

Indian Standard Time (IST)

India has only one standard time. It is 5.5 hours ahead of GMT/UTC, 4.5 hours behind Australian Eastern Standard Time and 10.5 hours ahead of Americal Eastern Standard Time.

National Reptile: King cobra (Ophiophagus hannah) The venomous King cobra is considered a sacred animal in Indian culture. It grows up to 3m.

National Calendar

At the time of independence, the Govt. of India followed the Gregorian calendar based on the Christian era. The National Government adopted the recommendation of the Calendar Reform Committee that the Saka era be adopted as the basis of the national calendar. The Saka year has the normal 365 days and begins with Chaitra as its first month. The days of the Saka calendar have a permanent correspondence with the dates of the Gregorian Calendar, Chaitra 1 falling on March 22 in a normal year and on March 21 in a Leap Year. The National Calendar commenced on Chaitra 1 Saka, 1879 corresponding to March 22, 1957 A.D.

The months of the National Calendar, with their days and the dates of the Gregorian Calendar corresponding to the first day of the Saka month are given below:

Saka	Gregorian
1 Chaitra 30/31 days	March 22/21
1 Vaishaka 31	April 21
1 Jyaistha 31	May 22
1 Asadha 31	June 22
1 Sravana 31	July 23
1 Bhadra 31	Aug. 23
1 Asvina 30	Sept. 23
1 Kartika 30	Oct. 23
1 Margasira 30	Nov. 22
1 Pausa 30	Dec. 22
1 Magha 30	Jan. 21
1 Phalguna 30	Feb. 20

Top Government of India Apps

Our National Flag

The Indian national flag is the symbol of our national pride. It represents the hopes and aspirations of the people of India

Meaning of the Colours and the Chakra:

The Saffron (kesari or *bhagwa)* colour is a symbol of renunciation of material gains, worldly pleasure and dedication to their work. **The White** colour in the centre is light, the path of truth, that guides our conduct. **The Green** colour represents our relation to soil and the plant life here on which all lives depend. **The Wheel** or the *dharma chakra*, in the center of the white colour is the wheel of the law of *satya* or truth, dharma or virtue, is the guiding principle of all those who work under this flag. The Wheel denotes motion and progress, i.e., the dynamism of life and a peaceful change.

The Flag Code

The national flag is governed by the provisions of the Emblems and Name (Prevention of Improper Use) Act, 1950 (No. 12 of 1950) and the Prevention of Insults to National Honour Act, 1971 (No. 69 of 1971). Flag Code of India, 2002 brings together all such laws, conventions, practices and instructions for the guidance and benefit of all concerned.

• The Standard Sizes :

The flag should be made of hand-spun and hand-woven wool/cotton/silk *khadi* bunting. The national flag should be rectangular in shape. The ratio of the length to the height (width) of the flag should be 3:2.

Size Dimensions (mm)

1. 6300	X	4200	6. 900	X	600
2. 3600	X	2400	7. 450	X	300
3. 2700	X	1800	8. 225	X	150
4. 1800	X	1200	9. 150	X	100
5. 1350	X	900			

Correct Display

• Wherever the flag is flown, it should occupy a position of honour and be distinctly placed. • When the flag is to be hoisted on any public building it should be flown on that building on all days including Sundays and holidays and, except as provided in the Code, it should be flown from sunrise to sunset irrespective of weather conditions. The flag may be flown on the public building at night also but it should be only on very special occasions. • The flag should always be hoisted briskly and lowered slowly and ceremoniously. • When the hoisting and the lowering of the flag is accompanied by appropriate bugle calls, the hoisting and lowering should be simultaneous with the bugle calls. • When the flag is displayed from a pole projecting horizontally or at an angle from a window-sill, balcony, or front of a building, the saffron band should be at the farther end of the pole. • When the flag is displayed flat and horizontal on a wall, the saffron band should be upper most and when displayed vertically, the saffron band should be to the right with reference to the flag, i.e., it may be to the left of a person facing it. • When the flag is displayed' on a speaker's platform, it should be flown on a pole on the speaker's right as he faces the audience or flat against the wall above and behind the speaker. • When used on occasions like the unveiling of a statue, the flag should be displayed distinctly and separately. • When the flag is displayed alone on a motor car, it should be flown from a staff, which is fixed firmly either on the middle front of the bonnet or to the front right side of the car.

Incorrect Display

• A damaged or disheveled flag should not be displayed. • The flag should not be dipped in salute to any person or thing.

• No other flag or bunting should be placed

higher than or above or, except as hereinafter provided, side by side with the national flag; nor should any object Including flowers or garlands or emblem be placed on or above the flag mast from which the flag is flown. • The flag should not be used as a festoon, rosette or bunting or in any other manner for decoration. • The flag should not be used to cover a speaker's desk nor should it be draped over a speaker's platform.• The flag should not be displayed with the saffron down. • The flag should not be allowed to touch the ground or the floor or trail in water. • The flag should not be displayed or fastened in any manner that may damage it.

Misuse

The flag should not be used • as a drapery in any form whatsoever except in State/Military/Central Para military Forces funerals hereinafter provided. • draped over the hood, top, sides or back of a vehicle, train or boat.• or stored in such a manner as may damage or soil it.•When the flag is in a damaged or soiled condition, it should not be cast aside or disrespectfully disposed of but should be destroyed as a whole in private, preferably by burning or by any other method consistent with the dignity of the flag. •as a covering for a building. • as a portion of a costume or uniform of any description. It should not be embroidered or printed upon cushions, handkerchiefs, napkins or boxes. •Lettering of any kind should not be put upon the flag. •in any form of advertisement nor should an advertising sign be fastened to the pole from which the flag is flown. •as a receptacle for receiving, delivering, holding or carrying anything except that there should be no objection to keeping flower petals inside the flag before it is unfurled, as part of celebrations on special occasions and on national days like the Republic Day and the Independence Day.

100 Years of our Tricolour

On 02 Aug.1876 Pingali Venkayya was born in Machilipatnam, Andhra Pradesh. He was educated at Cambridge and became a polymath. He met Gandhiji in South Africa. In 1921, Pingali, presented the draft design of the flag to Mahatma Gandhi at the AICC session held at Vijayawada. Gandhiji's approval of his design had made the Swaraj Flag popular and it was in use till 1931. The CWC came up with a new tricolour by replacing the red with saffron, on top, followed by white and then green. A spinning wheel (Gandhi *charkha*) was placed on the white. Post-Independence, a national flag committee under President Rajendra Prasad replaced the *charkha* with the *Ashok Chakra*. India completed 100 years of her Tricolour. Pingali Venkayya, as a freedom fighter designed India's first national flag on March 31, 1921

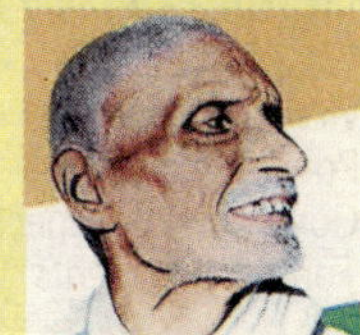

Half-Masting

In the event of the death of the following dignitaries, the national flag should be half-masted at the places indicated against each on the day of the death of the dignitary:

Dignitary	Place or places
President	Throughout India
Vice-President	Throughout India
Prime Minister	Throughout India
Speaker (Lok Sabha)	Delhi
Chief Justice of India	Delhi
Union Cabinet Min.	Delhi, State Capitals
Governor/ Lt Governor	Throughout the State or UT concerned.
Chief Minister	Throughout the State / UT

Display When displayed in a straight line with flags of other countries, the national flag shall be on the extreme right.

Rank and Precedence

List of the rank and precedence of the persons approved by the President (No.33-Pres/79):

- President
- Vice-President
- Prime Minister
- Governors of respective States
- Former Presidents *5A. Dy Prime Minister*
- Chief Justice (CJ) of India; Speaker LS
- Cabinet Ministers of the Union; CMs of States; Former PMs; Leaders of Opposition in RS and LS. *7A. Bharat Ratna winners.*
- Ambassadors Extraordinary and Plenipotentiary and High Commissioners of Commonwealth countries accredited to India; CMs of States & Governors- outside their respective States)
- Judges of Supreme Court. *9A. Chairperson, UPSC; Chief Election Commissioner CAG of India*
- Dy Chairman, RS; Dy CMs of States; Dy Speaker, LS; Union Min. of State {and any other Min. in the MoD}
- Attorney General of India; Cabinet Secretary; Lt Governors of UTs.
- Chiefs of Staff holding the rank of full General or equivalent rank.
- Envoys Extraordinary and Ministers Plenipotentiary accredited to India.
- Chairmen and Speakers of State Legislatures within their respective States. CJs of High Courts within their respective jurisdictions
- State's Cabinet Ministers; CMs of UTs and Chief Executive Councillor, Delhi; Union Dy Min.
- Officiating Chiefs of Staff holding the rank of Lt General or equivalent rank.
- Chairman, Central Administrative Tribunal; Chairman, Minorities Commission; Chairperson, National Commission for SCs; Chairperson, National Commission for STs; CJs of High Courts outside their respective jurisdictions.
- State's Cabinet Ministers; Chairmen and Speakers of State Legislatures outside their respective States; Chairman, Monopolies and Restrictive Trade Practices Commission; Dy Chairmen and Dy Speakers of State Legislatures; Ministers of State in States within their respective States Ministers of UTs and Executive Councilors, Delhi, within their respective UTs. Speakers of Legislative Assemblies in UTs and Chairman of Delhi Metropolitan Council within their respective UTs.
- Chief Commissioners of UTs; Dy Ministers in States; Dy Speakers of Legislative Assemblies in UTs and Dy Chairman of metropolitan Council Delhi.
- Dy Chairmen and Dy Speakers of State Legislatures, outside their respective states. Min. of State in States outside their respective States.
- Members of Parliament.
- Dy Ministers in State outside their respective States
- Army Commanders/ Vice-Chief of the Army Staff or equivalent in other services Secretary to the President. Secretary to the PM. Secretary, Rajya Sabha/Lok Sabha Solicitor General Vice-Chairman,
- Officers of the rank of Lieutenant General or equivalent rank.
- Additional Secretaries to the GoI. CBI; Director General BSF; Director General, CRP; Director, IB; Lt Governors outside their respective UTs.
- Joint Secretaries to the Government of India and officers of equivalent rank. Officers of the rank of Major-General or equivalent rank.

Indian Currency

The new rupee symbol '₹', was officially adopted in 2010. It was derived from the combination of the Devanagari consonant "ra" and the Latin capital letter "R" without its vertical bar. The horizontal parallel lines at the top (with white space between them) are said to make an allusion to the Indian tricolour flag, The first series of coins with the new rupee symbol started circulating on 8 July 2011. It also symbolises nation's economic parity.

Historically speaking, Chanakya, prime minister to the first Maurya emperor Chandragupta Maurya (c 340–290 BCE) in his *Arthashastra*, mentions gold coins as Suvarnarupa, silver coins as rupyarupa, copper coins as Tamrarupa and lead coins as Sisarupa.

New Currency Banknote	**Dimensions** (in mm)	**Base Colour**	**Year of Introduction**	**Motif** (image on the note)
₹10	63X123	Chocolate Brown	Jan 2018	Sun Temple
₹50	66 X135	Fluorescent blue	Aug 2017	Hampi with Chariot
₹100	66 X142	Lavender	Jul 2018	Rani Ki Vav
₹200	66X146	Bright yellow	Aug 2017	Sanchi Stupa
₹500	66X150	Stone grey	Nov 2016	Red Fort
₹2,000	66X166	Magenta	Nov 2016	Mangalyaan

Security Features (**Obverse** : Front)

1. Bleed Lines: Slanting black lines printed on right and left edge of the banknotes.

2. Fluorescent Number Panel: It is printed in fluorescent ink and the optical fibres show up when placed under an ultra-violet lamp.

3. Identification Mark: For visually impaired few shapes are inscribed for various denominations i.e. ₹ 20: Vertical Rectangle, ₹50: Square, ₹100: Triangle ₹ 500: Circle, ₹2000: Diamond.

4. 'INTAGLIO'('to etch'): For the blind people the RBI seal, guarantee and promise clause, RBI Governor's signature are printed

5. Latent Image: A band shows the respective denominational value in numeral ₹2000, ₹500, ₹100, ₹50 and ₹20 notes . It is visible when the note is held horizontally at eye level.

6. Microlattering: It contains 'RBI' in ₹5 and ₹10. On ₹20 and above it contains the denominational value of the notes in micro-letters. It is visible with a magnifying glass.

7. Optical Variable Ink: It is the value in numeral printed with a colour changing ink on ₹500 and ₹2,000 which appears green but turns blue when held at an angle.

8. See-through Register: Will show up number when the note is held against light. A vertical band is placed there which has an accurate back to back registration.

9. Security Thread: A readable, windowed security thread visible on the obverse with the inscriptions 'Bharat' (in Hindi), '2000' and 'RBI'. If held against the light, the security thread on ₹2000, ₹500 and ₹100 can be seen as one continuous line.

10. Watermark: A light and shade effect of Mahatma Gandhi and multi-directional lines in the watermark window.

(**Reverse**: Back)• Year of printing • Swachh Bharat logo and slogan • Panel of 15 languages • Motif of currency.

Currency Notes Down the Ages

1935: RBI formally inaugurated
1938: ₹5, ₹10, ₹100, ₹1,000, ₹10,000
1940: ₹1 reintroduced
1946 : ₹1,000, ₹10,000 withdrawn.
1954 : ₹1,000, ₹10,000 reintroduced & ₹5000 introduced
1978: ₹1000, 5000, 10000 withdrawn
1987: ₹500 introduced in Oct.1998 (birth): ₹1,000 reintroduced.
2016: ₹1,000 withdrawn.
2016: ₹2,000 introduced.
2017: ₹200 introduced
2018: ₹100 introduced

Currency - Banknotes in India are currently being issued in the denomination of ₹10, ₹20, ₹50, ₹100, ₹200, ₹500, ₹2000. These notes are called banknotes as they are issued by the Reserve Bank of India. Currency paper is composed of cotton and cotton rag. The highest denomination note ever printed by the Reserve Bank of India was the ₹10000 note in 1938 and in 1954. These notes were demonetized in 1946 and in 1978.

• **"I promise to pay" Clause**: As per Section 26 of RBI Act, 1934, the Bank is liable to pay the value of banknote.

The Rules • The GoI specifies the denomination of bank notes and its value under sub-section (1) of section 24 of the RBI Act, 1934 and on the recommendation of the central board of directors of the RBI. • GoI vide their Notification no. 2652 dated Nov 8, 2016 have withdrawn the Legal Tender status of ₹500, ₹1,000 • There cannot be banknotes in denominations higher than ten thousand rupees in terms of the current provisions of the RBI Act, 1934. Coins can be issued up to the denomination of ₹1000 in terms of The Coinage Act, 2011. • Printing and Circulation of forged notes are offences under Sections 489A to 489E of the Indian Penal Code and are punishable in the courts of law by fine or imprisonment or both.

Coins

The Government of India has the sole right to mint coins in terms of the Coinage Act, 1906 as amended from time to time. The coins are circulated only through the Reserve Bank in terms of the RBI Act. Coins are minted at the four India Government Mints at Mumbai, Alipore(Kolkata), Saifabad(Hyderabad), Cherlapally (Hyderabad) and NOIDA (UP).

Denominations Presently, coins in India are issued in denominations of ₹1, ₹2, ₹5 and ₹10. Coins of Rupee one and above are called 'Rupee Coins'. Coins can be issued up to the denomination of ₹1000 as per the Coinage Act, 1906. Higher value coin are commemorative coins.

Currency in Circulation 2021

India's currency in circulation stood at 29,390,087.600 INR mn in 03 Sep 2021. It's a decrease from the previous number of 29,438,605.600 INR mn for 27 Aug 2021.

India Reserve Money: Currency in Circulation data is updated daily, averaging 6,920,700.000 INR mn from Oct 1996 to 03 Sep 2021. The data reached an all-time high of 29,909,518.310 INR mn in 11 Jun 2021 and a record low of 1,273,747.200 INR mn in 01 Nov 1996.

GEOGRAPHY & PEOPLE

- Geography of India
- State of Indian Forest
- International Agreements
- Conservation Projects
- Languages in India
- Three Large Religions
- The Minorities in India
- 16th Census of India
- Urbanisation In India
- Rural India

Geography of India

Areawise, India is the seventh largest country in the world in terms of area. It lies on the Indian Plate, which is the northern portion of the Indo-Australian Plate. The country is of a vast size of 3.28 million sq. km. – is often called a sub-continent. The Indian subcontinent is surrounded by three different water bodies and is easily recognisable on the world map.

Extent: 3,214 kilometres (kms) from North to South and about 2,933 kms from West to East.
Kashmir – Kanyakumari: 3214 kms
Rann of Kutch – Arunachal Pradesh: 2933 kms
Southernmost Point: Indira Point (6°45')

Area: 3.28 million sq. kms (2.4 % of world) – 7th largest in area

Length of Coastline: 7,516.6 kms (Mainland + A&N + Lakshadweep)
Mainland Coastline:6100 kms

The Mainland: Situated in S. Asia; N. of Equator.

Latitude (8°4' – 37°6') N
The latitudinal and longitudinal extent of the country is about 30°. The southernmost point of the Indian Territory, (in Great Nicobar Islands) is the Indira Point (6°45'), while Kanyakumari, is the southernmost point of the Indian mainland.

Longitude (68°7'–97°25')E of Greenwich. The country thus lies wholly in the northern and eastern hemispheres.

Central Meridian : Allahabad (82°3')E

Indian Standard Time:- GMT +05:30
Telephone Country Code:- +91.

Common International Borders in South Asia: Afghanistan, Pakistan, China, Bhutan, Nepal, Myanmar, Bangladesh, Sri Lanka.

6 Zones : North, South, East, West, Central, and North East.

Largest Arable land : 2nd after US.
On the basis of its relief features, tectonic history and stratigraphy, India can be divided into several physical units.

Seasons

India is characterised by the tropical monsoon-type climate. Traditionally, India is considered to have six seasons – *Vasanta* (Mar-Apr), *Grishma* (May-Jun), *Varsha* (Jul-Aug), *Sharada* (Sept-Oct), *Hemanta* (Nov-Dec.) and *Shishira* (Jan-Feb).

India experiences three main seasons: (a) *Winter/Cold*: (Dec.-March) (b) *Summer/Hot*: (Apr-May) and (c) Monsoon/Wet: It has two parts – South West (Jun-Sept), and North-East (retreating SW monsoon): (Oct-Nov). Between the two main seasons are Spring (April) and Autumn (Sept).

The coldest winter months are December and January, when the temperature averages around 10-15°C in the NW and 20-25°C towards SE. Summer lasts from April to July, where April/May is the hottest month for the western and southern region, while May is the hottest for the northern regions, averaging 35-45°C.

The Monsoon

India receives 86% of the rain during SW monsoon except SE India (Tamilnadu). It begins in June in Andaman and Nicobar Island, Kerala and Lakshadweep and sweeps across India within the next two months. NE monsoon is a very restricted one mainly experienced in Tamil Nadu. Sometimes it is received in Kerala, Andhra Pradesh and Karnataka.

Physical Regions

Geographically, the mainland, is broadly divided on the basis of a variety of physical terrains. They can be divided into six basic areas:

I. Northern Mountains: These mountains consist of the Himalayas, Hindu Kush and Patkai ranges. They were formed by the collision of the Indian and Eurasian tectonic plates. They act as a natural barrier to the cold katabatic winds (drainage wind that flows downhill) that flow in from Central Asia and are the origins of many of the rivers that flow through the Indo-Gangetic plains.

• In India the most important range is the Himalayan range, since the Hindu Kush lies in the Afghanistan-Pakistan region while the Patkai range lies on the Indo-Myanmar border.

The Himalayas are the world's highest mountain range and the tallest peak in the world, Mount Everest (8849mt), is located here. This range is one of the youngest mountain ranges and extends for almost 2,500 km, from J&K & Ladakh in the north to Arunachal Pradesh in the east. It is made up of three parallel ranges:

• Great or Inner Himalayas: This northernmost range is also known as Himadri. It consists of the most prominent peaks in the Himalayas and the average height of its peaks is a little over 5974 mt. Mount Everest is located here.

• Lesser Himalayas: This range that lies to the south of the Himadri is also known as Himachal or Middle Himalayas. The height of its peaks ranges from 3750 mt to 4480mt.

• Shiwalik Range: This range is also known as the Outer Himalayas since it is the outermost range of the Himalayas. The height of its peaks ranges from 900mt to 1100mt.

2. The Northern Plains: These plains, also known as the Indo-Gangetic Plains or the Great Plains, were created by three river systems—the Indus, the Ganga and the Brahmaputra—and their tributaries such as Yamuna, Chambal, Gomti, Kosi, Beas and Teesta. It is an extremely fertile part of India that is made up of alluvial soil due to the sedimen deposited by the rivers. It covers almost 700,000 sq km of land and is one of the most heavily cultivated areas. The main crop grown here are rice, wheat, sugarcane, cotton and maize. Based on physical features, it can be divided into four sections: a) Bhabar: This belt begins at the foothills of the Shiwalik Range The streams tend to deposit the boulders and pebbles that have carried down with them from the mountain. Due to it high porosity the streams flow underground in this region, b) Terai: This area, which lies south to the Bhabar belt, is a marsh grassland region with thick vegetation where the stream reappear above the ground.

c) Bhangar: This is the largest area of the northern plains and consists of the oldest alluvial soil. They lie above the flood plains of the rivers and have formed in a terrace-like structure

d) Khadar: This area is formed by younger alluvial soil and is replenished every year by the rivers. It is one the most fertil areas of the four categories.

3. The Great Indian Desert

Also known as the Thar Desert, this desert is located in the northwestern area of the Indian subcontinent. It lies mostly in Rajasthan but also extends into parts of Haryana, Punjab and Gujarat. It also extends into Pakistan where it converges with the Cholistan Desert. Most of its rainfall is received during the July-September period and this means, because of the extreme temperatures, the vegetation is scarce and only certain animals can survive under these conditions. The natural vegetation has been classified as Northern Desert Thorn Forest and it occurs in scattered clumps across the desert. Some of the wildlife includes the blackbuck, chinkara, khur, and many species of birds such as eagles, harriers, falcons and buzzards.

Geology of India

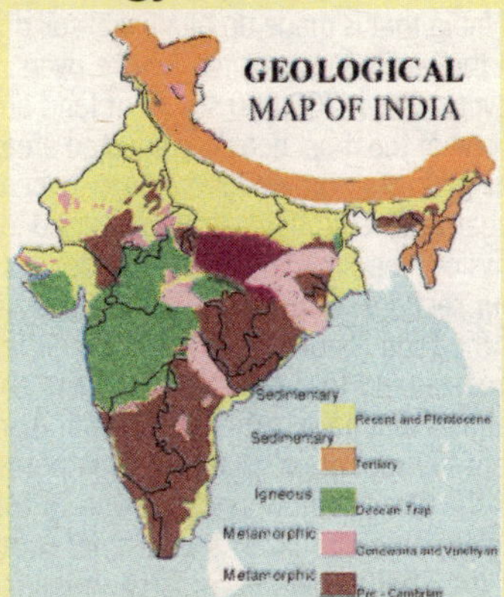

The Standard Geological Eras

•The Pre-Cambrian Supereon - lasted 4 b years+Hadean Eon + Archean Eon+ Proterozoic Eon

Phanerozoic Eon

•The Paleozoic Era (570-225m years old) +Cambrian Period 570m + Ordovician Period 500m + Silurian Period 440m + Devonian Period 395m + Carboniferous Period 345m + Permain Period 280m

•The Mesozoic Era (245-70 m years old) +Triassic Period 225m + Jurassic Period 195m + Cretaceous Period 136m

• The Cenozoic Era (66 m years old to the present) +Palegene Period + Neogene Period + Quaternary Period

• **Pleistocene Epoch**- 1m

• Stone Age

+ Holocene 10,000 years

The Indian Geological Eras:

•The Archean or Early Pre-Cambrian

•The Purana or Late Pre Cambrian

•The Dravidian (400-570 m years old)

•The Aryan (400 m years old to the present)

4. The Central Highlands

This area consists of some of the oldest rock formations. It is divided into three main regions: a) Malwa Plateau; This region lies to the north of the Narmada River and is spread across Rajasthan, Madhya Pradesh and Gujarat. The slope of this region, is indicated by the direction in which the rivers flow, is southwest to northeast. The average elevation of this area is 500mt. Deccan Plateau: The plateau covers most of central and southern India and its average elevation is almost 610mt. It is bordered by two mountain ranges, in the west by the Western Ghats and in the east by the Eastern Ghats. It is separated from the Northern Plains by the Satpura and Vindhya Ranges. Most of the rivers in the Deccan Plateau flow from the west to the east. River Godavari and its tributaries irrigate the northern areas of the plateau, while River Krishna, its tributaries and River Tungabhadra irrigate the middle regions, and the southernmost region is irrigated by River Kaveri. Chota Nagpur Plateau: Located in eastern India, this plateau extends into the states of Jharkhand, Odisha, West Bengal, Bihar and Chhattisgarh. Total area of the plateau : 65,000 sq km. It is made up of three smaller plateaus, the Ranchi, Hazaribagh and Kokdarma plateaus. It is known to have some of the highest levels of mineral resources in India with vast deposits of coal and metal ores.

5. Coastal Plains Along the Indian peninsular there are two coastal plains. a) The Western Coastal Plains: Located between the Western Ghats and the Arabian Sea. Three sections: The Konkan which is the northern part that begins in Mumbai and extends to Goa, the Kannad Plain which is the central stretch that carries on till Karnataka, and the Malabar Coast or southern stretch which runs from Karnataka down the coastal areas of Kerala to the tip of the Indian peninsula. The major rivers of

this area are the Tapi, Narmada, Mandovi and Zuari rivers. b) The Eastern Coastal Plains: Location: between the Eastern Ghats and the Bay of Bengal. Extent: West Bengal to Tamil Nadu. Two parts: the Northern Circars between Mahanadil and Krishna rivers and the Coromandel Coast in the south between the Krishna and Kaveri rivers. Many rivers drain these plains such as the Mahanadi, Godavari, Kaveri and Krishna rivers.

6. The Islands India has two island groups – classified as union territories – a) Lakshadweep: an archipelago in the Arabian Sea 200-300 km off the coast of Kerala. It comprises 36 islands and islets. b) Andaman and Nicobar Islands: They comprise 572 isles that lie in the Bay of Bengal. They are an estimated 1,255 km from Kolkata and 193 km from Cape Negrais in Burma. India's only active volcano, Barren Island, is located here.

7. The Rivers There are 12 rivers that have been classified as major rivers. The total catchment area of which is over 2,528,000 sq km. They originate from either the Himalaya and the Karakoram ranges in the north and in the south, the Vindhya and Satpura ranges, or the Western Ghats. Himalayan rivers are perenial rivers (have constant supply of water due to the snow capped peaks). The rivers that originate from the other two depend on the monsoons. The three main river systems a) The Ganges River System comprises Chambal, Betwa, Ganga, Gomti, Ghaghra, Son, Gandhak, Kosi and Brahmaputra. b) The Indus River System comprise Indus, Chenab, Jhelum, Ravi, Sutlej, and Beas. c) The Peninsular River System comprises many small rivers mainly Narmada and Tapi that flow west into the Arabian Sea. Mahanadi, Godavari, Krishna and Kaveri east flow eastward into the Bay of Bengal.

8. The Gulfs Gulfs are large bays that are a part of an ocean or a sea. India has three

Four Corners of India

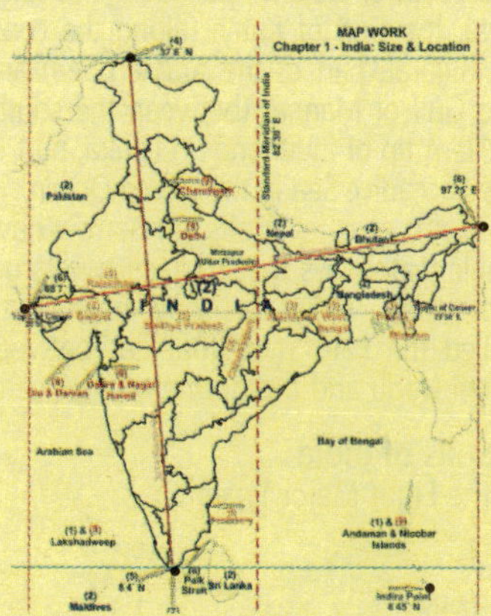

• **The Easternmost Point:** Kibithu is the easternmost point of India and Dong is the easternmost village located in Arunachal Pradesh's Anjaw district, bordering China.

•**The Westernmost Point:** Sir Creek is the western most point of India.

•**The Northernmost Point:** Siachen Glacier in the UT of Ladakh is the northern most point under the Line of Actual control. India claims the entire UT of J&K and Ladakh on the basis of Instrument of Accession signed in 1947. (The northern most point, if we take the whole state accessed, into consideration, is Dafdar in the Taghdumbash Pamir near Beyik Pass in Kanjut in POK.)

•**The Southernmost Point**-Mainland: Kanyakumari is the southernmost Point of Indian mainland, in the state of Tamil Nadu, at the confluence of the Arabian Sea, the Indian Ocean and the Bay of Bengal.

•**The Southernmost Point:** Indira Point at the Great Nicobar island is the southernmost point of land in the territory of India. It was formerly known as Pygmalion Point.

major gulfs, the Gulf of Khambhat (along the coast of Gujarat, part of the Arabian Sea), the Gulf of Kutch (along the coast of Gujarat, part of the Arabian Sea) and the Gulf of Mannar (between the south-eastern tip of India and Sri Lanka, part of the Laccadive Sea in the Indian Ocean).

9. Straits of India Straits are narrow navigable waterways that connect two larger waterways. India has one main strait called the Palk Strait that lies between Tamil Nadu and the northern province of Sri Lanka. It connects the Bay of Bengal with the Palk Bay.

10. The Channels Channels are landforms that are outlined by a shallow and narrow water body. India has one main channel called the Ten Degree Chanel which separates the Andaman Islands from the Nicobar Islands.

11. The Capes Capes are semi-large peninsulas which extend out into a body of water, usually the sea. The two main capes are the Kanyakumari (the southern tip of mainland India) in Tamil Nadu and Indira Point (the southernmost point of India) in the Nicobar Islands.

Soils of India
The Eight Major Types

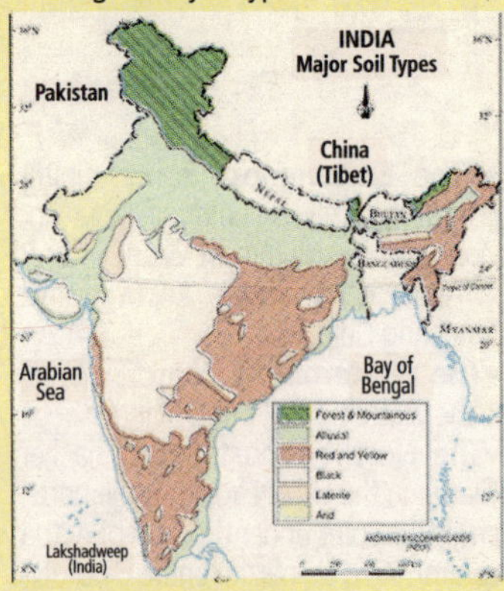

1. Black Soil - 29.7%
2. Red Soil - 28%
3. Alluvial Soil: River plains–Ganges, Brahmaputra, all other rivers - 22%
4. Forest and Mountain Soil - 7.94%
5. Arid and Desert : Dry regions like Rajasthan - 6.1%
6. Laterite Soil - 2.6%
7. Peaty and Marshy Soil - 2.17%
8. Saline & Alkaine Soil - 1.29%

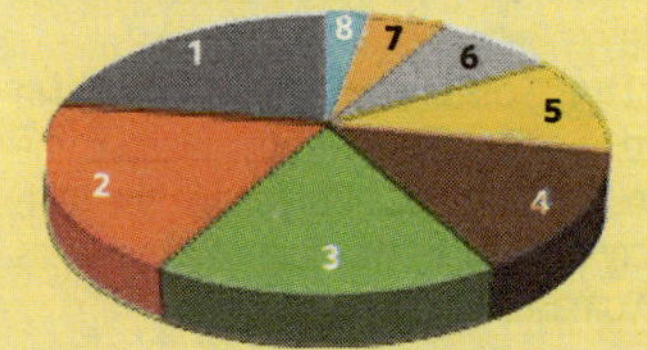

Natural Vegetation

India has six types of forests. • Evergreen (Tropical Forests) – found in areas with 200cm to 300cm rainfall; av. annual temp. 20°C to 27°C; av. annual humidity >80% • Deciduous (Monsoon Forests) – found in places with less rainfall between 150 to 200 cm; mean annual temp between 24°C and 28°C; humidity 75% • Dry Forest– found where rainfall is scanty between 75 to 100 cm; mean annual temp 23°C to 29°C; humidity 50 to 60% • Hill Forests – common in South India and Himalayas • Tidal Forests (Mangrove) – found in the coastal submerged plains of Ganges (Sundarbans), Mahanadi, Godavari and Kerala and • Grasslands (hilly-Himalaya and Deccan hills above 100m)– found in Punjab, Haryana, UP, Bihar, NW Asom and Riverine Grasslands-found along rivers. Available data places India in the tenth position in the world and fourth in Asia in plant diversity. From about 70% geographical area surveyed so far, 47,000 species of plants have been described by the Botanical Survey of India (BSI), Kolkata.

Agriculture India has three crop seasons.
(a) **Kharif**: rice, jowar, bajra, ragi, maize
(b) **Rabi**: wheat, barley, peas, rapeseed
(c) **Zayad** crops: water melon, vegetables

State of Indian Forest

According to the 16th ISFR 2019 (a biennial report published by the Forest Survey of India (FSI)), nearly 25% (one fourth) of India's total land area is now under forest and tree cover. However, there is still a long way to go – more than a decade, before India reaches its target of having 33% of its total area under forest and tree cover. The total forest and tree cover of the country is 807,276 sq. kms. (which is 24.56 % of the geographical area of the country) •The India State of Forest Report 2019 shows an increase of 5,188 sq. km. of forest and tree cover across the country. •However, northeast India continues to lose forests. • The forest area under "recorded forest area" in tribal districts, which are home to about 60 % of India's forests, is decreasing rapid assessment of biodiversity for all states and UTs "maximum tree diversity has been found in tropical wet evergreen semi-evergreen forests of Western Ghats (Tamil Nadu, Kerala and Karnataka) followed by NE states. •Low tree diversity has been noticed in the sub-tropical dry evergreen forests of J&K and forest deficit States like Punjab, Haryana and Rajasthan. Karnataka has the highest tree species richness followed by Tamil Nadu and Andhra Pradesh. •Karnataka has maximum species richness for trees, Arunachal Pradesh has maximum species richness for shrubs and J&K has maximum species richness for herbs. Arunachal Pradesh has the maximum richness of species when all the three types of plants (trees, shrubs and herbs) are taken into account, followed by Tamil Nadu and Karnataka."

Forest Fires: It is quite regular in India. 37,059 fires were detected in 2018. 54.40% of forests in India are exposed to occasional fires and 2.40% to high incidence. 35.71% of India's forests have not yet been exposed to fires.

Biodiversity Hotspots in India

• Himalaya: Indian Himalayan region (and that falling in Pakistan, Tibet, Nepal, Bhutan, China and Myanmar)
• Sundalands: Nicobar group of Islands (and Indonesia, Malaysia, Singapore, Brunei, Philippines) • Western Ghats and Sri Lanka: Western Ghats (and Sri Lanka) • Indo-Burma: North-eastern India, except Asom and Andaman group of Islands (and Myanmar, Thailand, Vietnam, Laos, Cambodia and southern China)

Source: Conservation International www.cepf.net

10 Biogeographic Zones

They are Trans-Himalayan, Himalayan, Indian Desert, Semi-arid, Western Ghats, Deccan Peninsula, Gangetic Plains, Coasts, North-East and Islands. These zones together consist of 26 biogeographic provinces. The aim is to designate one representative site as Biosphere Reserve in each bio-geographic province for long-term conservation.

Biosphere Reserves

India has 18 Biosphere Reserves. •Nilgiri (TN, Kerala, Karnataka) •Nanda Devi (Uttarakhand) •Nokrek (Meghalaya) •Manas (Asom) •Dibru-Saikhowa (Asom); •Sundarban (WB) • Gulf of Mannar (TN) •Great Nicobar (A&N Is.) •Similipal (Odisha) •Dehang-Debang (Arunachal Pradesh); •Khangchendzonga*(Sikkim) •Pachmarhi (MP) • Achanakmar-Amarkantak (Chhattisgarh, MP) •Agasthyamalai (TN, Kerala) •Kachchh (Gujarat) •Cold Desert (HP) •Seshachalam (AP) •Panna (MP).

**The Khangchendzonga Biosphere Reserve is the 11th BR from India, included in the UNESCO's World Network of Biosphere Reserves.*

Forest Cover : 2019

Source: India State of Forest Report 2019 . Area: sq. km.

State / UT	Geographic Area (GA) Sq. km	2019 Total Forest Cover	% of GA	2017 Very Dense Forest Cover	% change from 2017 ISFR
Andhra Pradesh	162,968	29,137	17.88	1,994	3.52
Arunachal Pradesh	83,743	66,688	79.63	21,095	-0.41
Asom	78,438	28,327	36.11	2,795	0.79
Bihar	94,163	7,306	7.76	333	0.10
Chhattisgarh	135,192	55,611	41.13	7,068	0.12
Goa	3,702	2,237	60.43	538	0.36
Gujarat	196,244	14,857	7.57	378	0.68
Haryana	44,212	1,602	3.62	28	0.88
Himachal Pradesh	55,673	15,434	25.81	3,113	2.21
Jharkhand	79,716	23,611	29.62	2,603	0.25
Karnataka	191,791	38,575	20.11	4,501	2.73
Kerala	38,852	21,144	54.42	1,935	4.05
Madhya Pradesh	308,252	77,482	25.14	6,676	0.09
Maharashtra	307,713	50,778	16.50	8,721	0.19
Manipur	22,327	16,847	75.46	905	-2.88
Meghalaya	22,429	17,119	76.33	489	-0.16
Mizoram	21,081	18,006	85.41	157	-0.99
Nagaland	16,579	12,486	75.31	1,273	-0.02
Odisha	155,707	51,619	33.15	6,970	0.53
Punjab	50,362	1,849	3.67	8	0.65
Rajasthan	342,239	16,630	4.86	78	0.35
Sikkim	7,096	3,342	47.10	1,102	-0.06
Tamil Nadu	130,060	26,364	20.27	3,605	0.32
Telangana	112,077	20,582	18.36	1,608	0.80
Tripura	10,486	7,726	73.68	654	0.00
Uttar Pradesh	240,928	14,806	6.15	2,617	0.87
Uttarakhand	53,483	24,303	45.44	5,047	0.03
West Bengal	88,752	16,902	19.04	3,019	0.33
Union Territories					
Andaman & Nicobar Is.	8,249	6,743	81.74	5,678	0.01
Chandigarh	114	22.03	19.32	1.36	2.18
Dadra & Nagar Haveli	491	207	42.16	0	0.00
Daman & Diu	111	20.49	18.46	1.40	0.00
Delhi	1,483	176	13.18	6.72	1.57
J&K, UT of	53, 258	21,122	39.66	4,203	1.68
Ladakh, UT of	169,421	2,490	1.47	78	0.93
Lakshadweep	30	27.10	90.33	0	0.00
Puducherry	490.00	52.41	10.70	0	-2.35
Total	**3,287,469**	**712,249**	**21.67**	**99,278**	**0.56**

Western Ghats

Western Ghats is home to over 5000 species of flowering plants, 139 mammal species, 508 bird species and 179 amphibian species, many undiscovered species.
• It spreads in 6 States: Kerala, Karnataka, Tamil Nadu, Goa, Maharashtra, and Gujarat.

Madhav Gadgil Panel Report, 2011
• Turn entire Western Ghats region into an Ecologically Sensitive Area called Western Ghats ESA of 137000 Km^2.
• Divide ESA into Protected Areas comprising Wildlife Sanctuaries and National Parks + Ecological Sensitive Zones (ESZ) outside the existing protected areas: ESZ-1 and ESZ-2 (highest degree of protection) and ESZ-3.
• Divide the entire Western Ghats ESA into 2200 grids. Assign each grid as ESZ on the basis of ecological significance.
• Establish WGEA as a statutory authority under Environment (Protection) Act 1986 for transparency, openness, stainability and participatory development.
• Demarcate the ESZs based on inputs from Gram Taluk/ Panchayats, Zilla Parishats, and Nagar Palikas, under the overall supervision of a Western Ghats Ecology Authority (WGEA), State level Ecology Authorities and the District Ecology Committees.
• Indefinite moratorium on new environmental clearances for mining in ESZ-1 and ESZ-2.
• Phase out mining from ESZ-1.
• Continue existing mining in ESZ-2 under strict regulation with social audit.
• In ESA-1 and ESA-2, no new Red and Orange category industries (but Green) should be allowed. +Development plans should be tailored to prevalent loc–ality and time bound participation of local communities (adaptive co-management).
• Ecological sensitivity is a human concern and lot of locality specific understanding of what has been happening and what is desirable, is not part of any scientific database. It resides with local communities.

The High-Level Working Group led by K. Kasturirangan prepared a report for protecting the biodiversity of the Western Ghats and addressing the sustainable development agenda for inclusive growth of the "indigenous people".

Kasturirangan Panel Report
•90% of the "natural landscape" be protected under ESA based on the fragmentation of the forests, population density of villages and the richness of the biodiversity in villages. •41% of the W. Ghats is "natural landscape", having low population impact and rich biodiversity and 59% is "cultural landscape" dominated by human settlements and agricultural fields • According to Kasturirangan committee, around 60,000 Km^2 are ecologically sensitive area spread over 6 states. It implies that around 37.5% of the total area of the W. Ghats is ecologically sensitive.
•Businesses and livelihood are important and should continue, but protect the W. Ghats through green and sustainable. economic activities •Initiate an ecosystem service fund to help villages around the forests •Encourage ecotourism for local benefits. • Do Geospatial Analysis for better state (land) policy reforms
• Delimit ecologically sensitive areas using high-resolution maps for people to make decisions about environment.
• Make the so called 'cultural landscape' and 'natural landscape' distinct •Ban mining, quarrying, thermal power plants and polluting industries within 60,000 sq km of the Ghats. •Remove cash crop plantations and settlements from forest area.

India's International Agreements

India is party to many international agreements concerning the management of the environment. Some of them are as follows: •The Antarctic Treaty (Washington, 1959). •Convention on International Trade in Endangered Species of wild fauna and flora (CITES), 1973 • Montreal Protocol on Substances that deplete the Ozone Layer (to the Vienna Convention for the Protection of the Ozone Layer), 1987 • Basel Convention on Transboundary Movement of Hazardous Wastes, 1989 • UN Framework Convention on Climate Change (UNFCCC), 1992 •Convention on Biological Diversity, 1992 •The Nagoya Protocol • Agenda 21 •UN Convention on Desertification, 1994 •Cartagena Protocol on Biosafety •Prior Informed Consent, Rotterdam Convention. **•Other Agreements:** • International Tropical Timber Agreement and the ITT Organisation (ITTO), 1983, 1994 which came into force in 1985 with the formation of the ITTO. India ratified the ITTA in 1996. •Convention on the Protection of the World Cultural and Natural Heritage (Paris, 1972); the Convention on Wetlands of International Importance, especially as Waterfowl Habitat (Ramsar, 1971); the Convention Relative to the Preservation of Fauna and Flora in their Natural State (1933); the International Plant Protection Convention (1951); the International Convention for the Prevention of Pollution of the Sea by Oil (1954); the Convention on the Conservation of Migratory Species of Wild Animals (Bonn, 1979); the Convention on Early Notification of a Nuclear Accident (1986); the UN Convention on the Law of the Sea (Montego Bay, 1982) and the Protocol on Environmental Protection to the Antarctica Treaty (Madrid, 1991) (CEL, Undated). •In India after the UN Stockholm Conference on the Human Environment. in 1976, the 42nd Amendment to the Constitution– Article 48-A, Article 51-A(g). • 2016 International Solar Alliance •2020 13th COP on Migratory species of wild animals, Gujarat.

Conservation Projects

Project Tiger

India is home to 80% of tigers in the world. There are 20 tiger reserves in 17 states. Worldwide there are 3890 tigers (2016 - WWF). Project Tiger was launched in 1973 •to ensure maintenance of the viable population of tigers for scientific, economic, aesthetic, cultural and ecological values, • to preserve for all times, areas of biological importance as a national heritage for the benefit, education and enjoyment of the people. •For estimating tiger population, 93,697 km^2 has been maintained as tiger habitat. The estimated number of tigers in 2018 was 2,967; and in 2006–1411. More Re-

extra

Independence on August 15

Five other countries celebrate their independence on August 15 along with India. They are Bahrain, North Korea, South Korea, Liechtenstein and the Republic of Congo.

serves: Ratapani -MP, Sunabeda-Odisha, Pilibhit -UP, Biligiri Ranganatha Temple-Karnataka, Mukundara Hills-Rajasthan. Sathyamangalam-TN, Nagzira-Navegaon and Bor -Maharashtra, Suhelwa-UP.

Project Elephant

It was launched by GoI in 1991-92 •to protect elephants, their habitat and corridors •to address issues of man-animal conflict • welfare of domesticated elephants, and •technical support to major elephant bearing states. The Project is implemented in AP, Arunachal Pradesh, Asom, Chhattisgarh, Jharkhand, Karnataka, Kerala, Maharashtra, Meghalaya, Nagaland, Odisha, Tamil Nadu, Tripura, Uttarakhand, UP and West Bengal. There were 27,312 (2012 Census) elephants in 2032 Project Elephant reserves exist in 16 States extending to 58,000 sq kms.

Project Rhino

It is a project of the Asom Forest Department and Wildlife Trust of India - International Fund for Animal Welfare (WTI-IFAW)–started in 2006, to repopulate the one horn rhino by relocating them to Manas wild life sanctuary from Kaziranga National Park. Currently, there are 32 rhinos in Manas. 6 will be moved out to Laokhowa-Burachapori WS by 2020.

Project Crocodile

It was launched in 1975 in different States for •protecting the endangered crocodile species like Gharial, Gavialis gangeticus; Mugger crocodile, Crocodylus palustris and Saltwater crocodile. Crocodylus were on the verge of extinction in the 1970s. In 2019, they were 1742.

Project Vultures

Saving Asia's Vultures from Extinction (SAVE) is a group of regional and international organisation that strives to protect South Asian vultures.In 2015 there were 6000 white-backed, 12,000 Long-billed and 1000 Slender-billed.

Project Dolphin

The Gangetic river dolphins is India's national aquatic animal. They are also called the Tiger of the Ganges – an indicator animal which represent healthy river ecosystem in a same position as a tiger in a forest. Their population is 34 in 2019 in India. In 2015 it was 22.

National Forest Policy 2018

Aims : To address the new realities – climate change, human-animal conflict and declining green cover.

The Features: • to bring one-third of India's total geographical area under forest cover through scientific interventions and law enforcement to protect the dense cover. •Meet challenges of climate change. •Public-private participation for afforestation and reforestation activities in degraded forest areas • dedicated quick response teams of well equipped and trained personnel, mobility, strong tie-uo with health and veterinary services, rescue centres, objective and speedy assessment of damage and quick payment of relief to the victims •long-term monitoring and management of wildlife population balance. • Safeguard forest land through restraint on diversion for non-forestry purposes • No oversight of compliance of rules and conditions.

The Largest River Island in the World

Majuli island in Asom holds the *Guinness* World Record for being the largest river Island in the world. The beautiful island is situated on the Brahmaputra River.

Number and Area of National Parks and Wildlife Sanctuaries

State / UT	National Park Number Cover	Area (sq. Km)	Wildlife Sanctuaries Number	Area (sq. Km)
Andhra Pradesh	3	1368.88	13	5942.23
Arunachal Pradesh	2	2290.82	11	7487.75
Asom	5	1977.79	18	1840.14
Bihar	1	335.65	12	2901.67
Chhattisgarh	3	2899.08	11	3760.29
Goa	1	107.00	6	647.91
Gujarat	4	480.12	23	16618.42
Haryana	2	48.25	8	233.21
Himachal Pradesh	5	2271.28	28	6116.10
Jammu & Kashmir	4	3925	15	10243.11
Jharkhand	1	226.33	11	1955.82
Karnataka	5	2795.79	30	6774.81
Kerala	6	558.16	17	1928.24
Madhya Pradesh	10	3656.36	25	7158.42
Maharashtra	6	1273.60	42	7604.44
Manipur	1	40.00	2	184.81
Meghalaya	2	267.48	4	94.10
Mizoram	2	150.00	8	1090.75
Nagaland	1	202.02	3	20.34
Odisha	2	990.70	19	7094.65
Punjab	0	0.00	13	326.60
Rajasthan	5	3947.07	25	5592.38
Sikkim	1	1784.00	7	399.10
Tamil Nadu	5	307.84	29	6157.12
Tripura	2	36.71	4	566.93
Telangana	3	19.62	9	5675.91
Uttar Pradesh	1	490.00	25	5828.12
Uttarakhand	6	4915.44	7	2690.12
West Bengal	6	1981.65	15	1442.12
Union Territories				
Andaman & Nicobar Is.	9	1153.94	96	389.39
Chandigarh	0	0.00	2	26.01
Dadra & Nagar Haveli	0	0.00	1	92.16
Daman & Diu	0	0.00	1	2.18
Delhi	0	0.00	1	27.82
Lakshadweep	0	0.00	1	0.01
Puducherry	0	0.00	1	3.90
Total	**104**	**40501.13 ***	**531**	**117616.71****

*Source: State of Forest Report. • It is about *1.23% & **3..58% of India's total area.*

The People of India

India stands out not just with regard to size and population, but unique in terms of landscape, ethnicity, languages, food, attire, religion and even politics. Here is a snapshot of the country's diversity.

History: The history of India can be traced back to Harappan civilisation. Dravidians, Aryans among many other people group make the population of this country. For centuries the country came to be ruled by native kings, foreign rulers like the Mughals for more than 530 years (1206–1740) and Europeans ruled from1498-1947. Portughese, French, Dutch and British came for trade. British ruled for 200 years. The post-independence story of democracy and development is for all to see.

Politics: India is the largest democracy in the world, a democratic federal republic, with a multi-party system. I

Social Customs: **Naming Conventions** •Many people in India have a 'pet' name or a nickname for family and close friends. • Indians generally address saying *bhai* (brother) and *saheb* (sir), *behenji* (sister) and *memsaheb* (ma'am). It is generally safe to address as 'sir' or 'ma'am.'

Meeting and Greeting It's traditional to greet people using *Namaste* (formal) or *Namashkar* (casual) – place both hands together and bow slightly. Men will shake hands when they meet or as they part. Men may avoid shaking hands with women who are not well acquainted. Indians may hug and often pat each other on the back as a sign of friendship. The educated people would shake hands but for a native person it would not be easy to do it with a foreigner. Indian culture is based on a hierarchical system so elders are greeted first. Religion, caste and social standing all effect greetings.

Personal Space Refrain from standing within an arm's length of others. Do not touch others on their head. Greet the elderly by touching their feet if you would.

Communication style • Pointing, with either one or two fingers, is considered rude. Entire hands (not a pointing finger) are used to point or direct someone's attention •Watch out, head nods can mean yes or no or different, depending on to whom you are interacting. In some places people normally talk loud • Left hand is considered unclean. Be careful not to give anything with left hand •A word in one language can mean different or even a bad word in another.

Visiting a home Always accept water served for drinking or an invitation to dine, unless you have a plausible reason for not attending.

Dining and Food • Food is sacred and is often eaten with the right hand Be careful with non-vegetarian food - depends on where you are and with whom you are •Guests are generally served in a hierarchical order; guest of honour, men and then children (Women may eat later) • Meals often end with a variety of sweets, paan betel nut served with lime and wrapped in a betel leaf or sweets. A host will always serve their guests. Accept whatever you are offered but don't feel obliged to finish everything on your plate. In a restaurant the host generally pays the bill

Taboos •Feet are considered unclean. Avoid wearing slippers inside home. Avoid putting feet on table, books, paper, machines, etc. •Do not let ones feet or shoes touch another person. • Do not kiss with opposite sex. • Winking, ogling and whistling should be avoided. • Ask for permission to sit by the side of a woman on a public transport. Do not smoke at home.

Languages in India

According to the 2011 Census, there are about 122 languages spoken by more than 10,000 people. Of them 22 are the scheduled languages. Other than the 122 languages, the survey has come up with languages that are spoken by less than 10,000 people mainly from tribal areas, nomadic communities and from the interiors of north-eastern part of the country.

History of Languages The earliest language of India was the language of Indus Valley civilisation. The four major language groups of early India are the Dravidian, the Sino-Tibetan, the Austric and Indo-Aryan.

Scheduled Languages: Officially there are 22 recognised languages. The 8th Schedule in the Constitution indicate that all regional languages are statutorily recognised. They are: 1. Assamese 2. Bengali 3. Gujarati 4. Hindi 5. Kannada 6. Kashmiri 7. Malayalam 8. Marathi 9. Odiya 10. Punjabi 11. Sanskrit 12. Tamil 13. Telugu 14. Urdu 15. Sindhi; 16. Konkani 17. Manipuri 18. Nepali 19. Bodo 20. Dogri 21. Maithili 22. Santhali.

Current Classical Languages Tamil (in 2004), Sanskrit(2005), Kannada (2008), Telugu, Malayalam(2013), Odiya (2014).

Classical Languages Criteria

To determine the eligibility of a language to be considered as a classical language the Government of India follows the following criteria • High antiquity of its early texts/ recorded history over a period of 1500-2000 years. • A body of ancient literature/ texts, which is considered a valuable heritage by generations of speakers. • The literary tradition be original and not borrowed from another speech community. • The classical language and literature being distinct from the modern; there may also be a discontinuity between the classical language and its later forms or its offshoots.

Linguistic Classification: (a) Indo-European (b) Indo-Iranian (c) Indo-Aryan

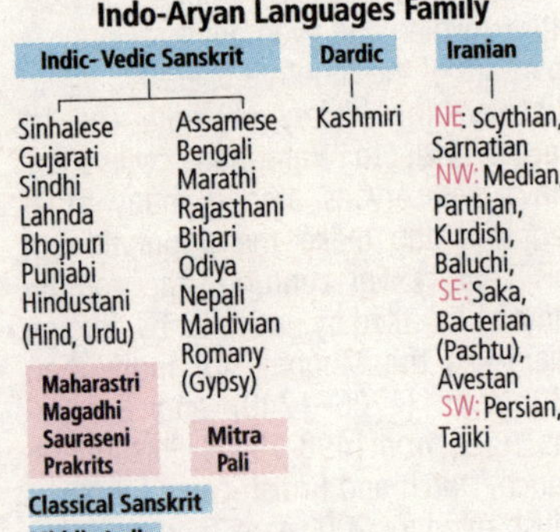

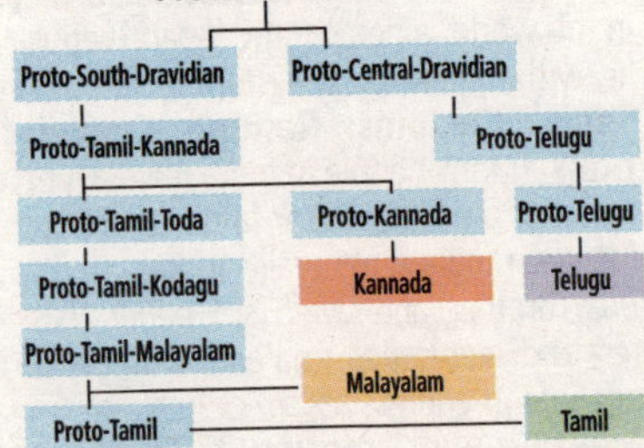

Indo-Aryan languages: The classical language of India, ***Sanskrit*** is a derivative of the Indo-Aryan languages. The Sanskrit literature may be traced back to Rig Vedic period. Its earliest form, Vedic Sanskrit, was spoken by the Aryans. All the classical literature and the Indian epics have been written in Sanskrit. It is the oldest literary language of India and the basis of many modern Indian languages. It is the second official language of Uttarakhand. It is spoken in five villages in India – (a) Mattur or Muttoor–Karnataka (b) Hosahalli–Karnataka (c) Jhiri–MP (d) Mohad–MP (e) Baghuwar – MP.

Proto-Dravidian language: ***Tamil*** was the earliest derivative from the Proto-Dravidian language, followed by ***Telugu, Kannada*** **and** ***Malayalam.*** All these came under the influence of Sanskrit, the least affected one being Tamil.

Extinction: As per *Ethnologue*, India is considered to be home to 453 languages, out of which 14 have been reported to be extinct. According to new study of the People's Linguistic Survey of India, there are • 780 languages and dialects • 96% of 380 languages spoken are endangered • 300 languages have become extinct till now • 220 languages have disappeared in last 50 years • 150 could vanish in the next 50 years. UNESCO classified as many as 191 languages of India are classified as vulnerable.

Scripts: The Writing Systems

All the languages spoken in India do not have associated writing systems. Some of the scripts are Devanagari script–Hindi, Marathi, Angika languages; Gurmukhi–Punjabi; Utkal Lipi–Odiya; Prakrit; Brahmani and Perso-Arabic script–Urdu and sometimes Kashmiri, Saraiki and Sindhi.

Three Large Religions

Of the world religions, according to "The Future of World Religions: Population Growth Projections, 2010-2050," by the Pew Research Center, by 2050, Hinduism will become the third largest religion after Christianity and Islam, making up 14.9% of the world's total population. It is followed by people who do not affiliate with any religion, accounting for 13.2%.

India has given birth to a few religions like Buddhism, Jainism and Sikhism, which exist even today in the world. 97% of all Hindus live in India, Nepal and Mauritius, the three Hindu-majority countries. Zoroastrianism and Judaism have a very long history in India, and each has several thousands of Indian adherents. India has the largest population of people adhering to Zoroastrianism (i.e. Parsis and Iranis) and Bahá'í faith in the world, even though these religions are not native to India. Many other world religions also have a relationship with Indian spirituality, such as the Baha'i faith.

Religious Census 2011

Hinduism	79.8%	96.63 crores.
Islam	14.2%	17.22 crores
Christianity	2.3%	2.78 crores
Sikhism	1.7%	2.08 crores
Buddhism	0.7%	84 lakhs
Jainism	0.4%	45 lakhs
Other religions	0.7%	
No religion	0.2%	

Religion	Population % in 1951	Population % in 1961	Population % in 1971	Population % in 1981	Population % in 1991	Population % in 2001	Population % in 2011
Hinduism	84.1%	83.45%	82.73%	82.30%	81.53%	80.46%	79.80%
Islam	9.8%	10.69%	11.21%	11.75%	12.61%	13.43%	14.23%
Christianity	2.3%	2.44%	2.60%	2.44%	2.32%	2.34%	2.30%
Sikhism	1.79%	1.79%	1.89%	1.92%	1.94%	1.87%	1.72%
Buddhism	0.74%	0.74%	0.70%	0.70%	0.77%	0.77%	0.70%
Jainism	0.46%	0.46%	0.48%	0.47%	0.40%	0.41%	0.37%
Zoroastrianism	0.13%	0.09%	0.09%	0.09%	0.08%	0.06%	n/a
Others	0.43%	0.43%	0.41%	0.42%	0.44%	0.72%	0.9%

Official Language

The Official Language

•The Official Languages Act, 1963, the Official Languages Rules, 1976, and statutory instruments made by the department of official language decides the extent to which, and the areas in which, the union government uses Hindi and English • Judiciary: All proceedings in the Supreme Court and the High Courts, shall be in English • Administration: The union government shall use both Hindi and English in most administrative documents that are intended for the public. • The Union government, acting through the president, can issue certain directives to the state government in relation to the use of minority languages for official purposes. • The Indian Constitution does not specify the official languages to be used by the states for the conduct of their official functions. • The Official Languages Act gives the Governor power, in relation to the language in which the High Court's judgments will be delivered. Implementations: • Communications between different states, or from the union government to a state or a person in a state, shall be regulated by the Official Languages Act and, by the Official Languages Rules. • There should be a translation in Hindi /English in the Official Gazette; of any Central/State Act or of any Ordinance promulgated by the President/ Governor, or bills introduced or amendments to be moved in parliament and for any judgment, decree or order passed or made by the High court for that state.

National Language: Our constitution or our law does not mention a national language. There is a popular misconception among Indians that there is a national language. In the recent past, while rejecting a Public Interest Litigation (PIL) by Suresh Kachhadia, the division bench of Chief

Statewise Official Languages

States/UT	Official Languages	Additional Official Languages
Andhra Pradesh	Telugu	Urdu
Arunachal Pradesh	English	
Asom	Assamese	
Bihar	Hindi	Urdu
Chhattisgarh	Hindi	
Goa	Konkani	Marathi
Gujarat	Gujarati	
Haryana	Hindi	
Himachal Pradesh	Hindi	English
Jammu & Kashmir	Urdu	
Jharkhand	Hindi	Urdu
Karnataka	Kannada	
Kerala	Malayalam	
Madhya Pradesh	Hindi	
Maharashtra	Marathi	
Manipur	Manipuri	English
Meghalaya	English	Khasi
Mizoram	Mizo, English, Hindi	
Nagaland	English	
Odisha	Odia	
Punjab	Punjabi (Gurumukhi Script)	
Rajasthan	Hindi	English
Sikkim	English	
Tamil Nadu	Tamil	English
Telangana	Telugu, Urdu	
Tripura	Bengali	Kokborok, English
Uttar Pradesh	Hindi	Urdu
Uttarakhand	Hindi	
West Bengal	Bengali	Hindi, Urdu, Santhali, Oriya, Punjabi, Nepali
A & N Is.	English, Hindi	
Chandigarh	English, Punjabi, Hindi	
D & NH	Hindi, Gujarati	Marathi
D & Diu	Konkani, Gujarati	
Delhi	Hindi	Punjabi, Urdu
Lakshadweep	English, Hindi, Malayalam	
Puducherry	Tamil, English & Telugu	

Sources: 50th Report of the Commissioner for Linguistic Minorities in India (July 2012 to June 2013) http://nclm.nic.in/shared/linkimages/ NCLM50th Report. pdf

Justice SJ Mukhopadhaya and Justice AS Dave of Gujarat High Court observed that there are no records to suggest that any Provision has been made or Order issued declaring Hindi as a national language of the country. The court pointed out that Part XVII of the Constitution deals with official language and Article 343 states that the official language of the Republic of India is Hindi with English as an additional language for official work and the states can legislate in their own official languages.

Along with Hindi and English, French and Portuguese also enjoy the official language status in some States and UTs.

English Language in India

English is one of the two official languages of India •It serves 3 purposes: (i) Provides a linguistic tool for administrative communication between the union and the state governments. (Hindi is mainly spoken in north India) (ii) Is a linguistic bridge between India and the world. • Used in parliament, courts, media, journalism, education, etc. •It has become the de facto standard for education, research, commerce, social media and online communications.

The Minorities in India

Generally, "minority" means a group comprising less than half of the population and differing from others, esp.the predominant section, in race, religion, traditions and culture, language, etc. Article 30 speaks specifically of two categories of minorities : religious and linguistic.

Religious Minorities: At the national level, all those who profess a religion other than Hindu are considered minorities since over 80% population of the country professes Hindu religion. Muslims form the largest minority. Next to the Muslims are Christians (2.34 %) and Sikhs (1.9 %); while all the other religious groups are still smaller.

Linguistic Minorities: All who speak a language other than Hindi can be treated as linguistic minorities but not so if the state is taken as the unit. Within a state, there may be minorities who speak a language(s) other than the language spoken by the majority in that state. Dialects of a language spoken in a state may proliferate the number of minorities. However, as mentioned earlier, it has been settled in TMA Pai vs. Union of India (2002) that a linguistic minority is determinable with reference to the state as a unit.

Constitutional Provisions Indian Constitution uses the word 'minority' in Articles 29 to 30 and 350A to 350 B– to mean 'any sections of citizens' having a distinct language, script or culture. This may be a whole community living within a majority community. Art. 15 & 16: Prohibits the state from making any discrimination in relation to citizens.. Art. 347: for language spoken by a section of the population of a state

Ministry of Minority Affairs, created on 29 Jan. 2006 to deal with issues relating to the minorities. It is responsible for the administration and implementation of (i) National Commission for Minorities Act, 1992; (ii) Wakf Act, 1995 and (iii) Durgah Khwaja Saheb Act, 1955.

National Commission for Minorities
It is a statutory commission. Commissioner, CLM, 101, 1st Floor, Paryvaran Bhawan, CGO Complex, Lodhi Rd, New Delhi-3.

Indian Demographics

16th Census of India

Population of India, which at the turn of the twentieth century, was only around 238.4 million increased by more than five times in a period of 110 years to reach 1210 million in 2011.•Population of India increased by 3.35 times since independence. India accounts for a meagre 2.4 % of the world surface area yet it supports and sustains a whopping 17.7 % of the world population. Since population of India is increasing at a slower rate than the world, its global share is decreasing. India is the second most populated country in the world. About a fifth of the world's population live here. •It reached the billion mark in 1998. Between 1975–2010, the population doubled.•India is projected to be the world's most populous country by 2024, surpassing China. •India would become the first country to have 1.5b people by 2030. •By 2100, 13.34% of the earth population will be in India, that is 4.42% less than the peak level of 17.76% in 2013.

About Census •The first non-synchronous census was conducted between 1865 and 1872 in different parts of the country.•However, the first synchronous census in India was held in 1881. Since then, censuses have been undertaken uninterruptedly once every ten years. •Since 1949 the census has been conducted by the Registrar General and Census Commissioner of India under the Ministry of Home Affairs, GoI. The Census of India is the largest administrative and statistical exercise in the world.

16th Indian Census, Digitally •According to RGI, for the first time in the 140-year history of the census in India, data would be collected through a mobile app and will be stored electronically by enumerators using their own mobilephone. •The census

The 16th Census Questions :

1. Building Number. **2**. Census House Number. **3**. Predominant material of floor, wall and roof of the census house. **4**. Ascertain use of census house. **5**. Condition of the census house. **6**. Household number **7**. Total number of persons normally residing in the household. **8**. Name of the head of the household. **9**. Sex of the head of the household. **10**. Whether the head of the household belongs to SC/ST/Other. **11**. Ownership status of the census house. **12**. Number of dwelling rooms exclusively in possession of the household. **13**. Number of married couple(s) living in the household. **14**. Main source of drinking water. **15**. Availability of drinking water source. **16**. Main source of lighting. **17**. Access to latrine **18**. Type of latrine **19**. Wastewater outlet. **20**. Availability of bathing facility. **21**. Availability of kitchen and LPG/PNG connection. **22**. Main fuel used for cooking. **23**. Radio/Transistor. **24**. Television. **25**. Access to Internet. **26**. Laptop/ Computer. **27**. Telephone/Mobile phone/smartphone. **28**. Bicycle/ scooter/motorcycle/moped. **29**. car/Jeep/Van. **30**. Main cereal consumed in the household. **31**. Mobile number .

will be conducted in 18 languages out of the 22 scheduled languages (under the 8th schedule) and in English. •There is an option for "Third Gender".

Differences: NPR and Census

NPR collects basic demographic data and biometric particulars. The NPR is a mechanism outlined in a set of rules framed under the Citizenship Act, 1955. **Census** collects data on 29 items : age, sex, marital status, children, occupation, birthplace, mother tongue, religion, disability, and whether they belonged to any Scheduled Caste or Scheduled Tribe. The census is legally backed by the Census Act, 1948.

Census 2011

Population	**1.21 billion** (17.5% of the world)
Male	623.7 million
Female	586.5 million
Literacy	**74.04%**
Male	82.14%
Female	65.46%
Highest	Kerala, Lakshadweep, Mizoram
Lowest	Bihar
Highest – Female	Kerala
Lowest – Female	Rajasthan
Highest – Male	Lakshadweep
Lowest – Male	Bihar
Sex Ratio	**940** – Highest since 1971
Highest (State)	Kerala – 1084
Lowest (State)	Haryana – 877
Highest (UT)	Puducherry – 1038
Lowest (UT)	Dadra& Nagar (775)
Child Sex Ratio	**914**
Highest	Mizoram – 971
Lowest	Haryana – 830
Density of Population	**382** per sq. km
Highest	Delhi > Bihar > WB > UP
Lowest	A & N > Arunachal Pradesh
Most Populous State	**Uttar Pradesh**
Least Populous State	**Sikkim**
Most Populous UT	**Delhi**
Least Populous UT	**Lakshadweep**
Highest Growth of Population	Meghalaya
Least Growth of Population	Nagaland (negative growth)

Quick Facts about the population of India (as of Sept.14, 2021)

Current population: 1,402,844,435

Current male population (51.6%): 724,325,620

Current female population: 678,518,815

Population rank: 2 (17.71% of world population)

Population density: 426.7 per km^2

Sex ratio: 1.07 (724,324,038 men to 678,517,333 women)

Median age: 26.7 years

Births (daily): 45,879

Deaths (daily): 16,657

Child Dependency Ratio: It is a ratio of people below working age (under 15) to workforce of a country.

Child dependency ratio in India is 45.7 %.

Aged dependency ratio: Aged dependency ratio is a ratio of people above working age (65+) to workforce of a country.

Aged dependency ratio in India is 8.4 %.

Total life expectancy (both sexes) at birth for India is 66.8 years.

This is below the average life expectancy at birth of the global population which is about 71 years

Male life expectancy at birth is 65.8 years.

Female life expectancy at birth is 68 years.

India age structure: As of the beginning of 2021 according to our estimates India had the following population age distribution: • percentage of population under 15 : 29.7• percentage of population between 15 and 64 years old : 64.9 • percentage of population 65+ : 5.5

In absolute figures (estimate):

412,614,159 young people under 15 years old (219,190,408 males / 193,423,751 females)

902,111,130 persons between 15 and 64 years old (466,274,997 males / 435,836,133 females)

75,812,098 persons above 64 years old (36,056,634 males / 39,755,464 females)

Source: UN Population Division

Population Forecast

Year	Population	Yearly Change	Median Age	Fertility Rate	Density (/Km²)	Urban Pop %	Country's Share of World Pop	World Popn.	India Global Rank
2020	1,383.1M	1.11 %	28.2	2.30	465	34.0 %	17.74 %	7,795,482,309	2
2025	1,451.8M	0.97 %	29.8	2.19	488	36.2 %	17.74 %	8,185,613,757	1
2030	1,512.9M	0.83 %	31.4	2.10	509	38.5 %	17.69 %	8,551,198,644	1
2035	1,564,.5M	0.67 %	33.0	2.02	526	41.1 %	17.59 %	8,892,701,940	1
2040	1,605.3M	0.52 %	34.5	1.95	540	43.7 %	17.43 %	9,210,337,004	1
2045	1,636.4M	0.38 %	36.1	1.90	550	46.4 %	17.22 %	9,504,209,572	1
2050	1,658.9M	0.27 %	37.5	1.86	558	49.1 %	16.98 %	9,771,822,753	1

Source: Worldometers (www.Worldometers.info). Elaboration of data by United Nations, Department of Economic and Social Affairs, Population Division.

Population Rate of Change

Year	Population (crore)	Change	
		Rate	%
1891	23.60	-	-
1901	23.84	+0.24	-
1911	25.21	+1.37	+5.75
1921	25.13	-0.08	-0.031
1931	27.90	+2.77	+11.00
1941	31.87	+3.97	+14.22
1951	36.11	+4.24	+13.31
1961	43.92	+7.81	+21.51
1971	54.82	+10.90	+24.80
1981	68.33	+13.51	+24.66
1991	84.64	+16.30	+23.87
2001	102.87	+18.23	+21.54
2011	121.07	18.19	17.70
2021	138.00	12.50	

India's Demographic Edge over China

India has 650m people in the working-age group of 25-65, while China has 830m. By 2040, India will have 170m more working-age pople than China.

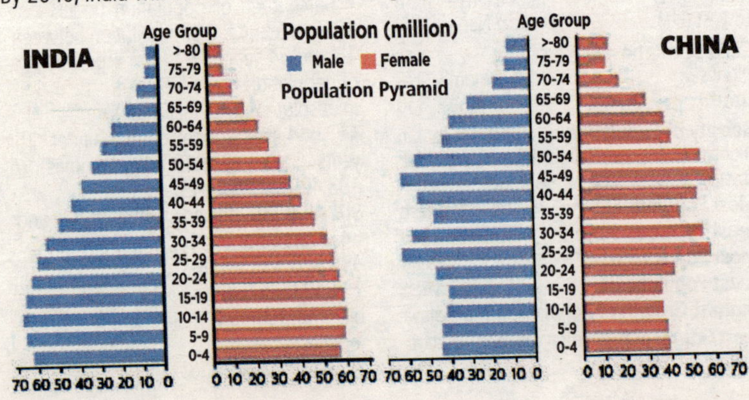

Urbanisation In India

According to the Economic Survey 2020-21 there is an rising trend urbanisation in India. In the process, it has highlighted the several associated challenges with such rapid urbanisation and also gives a glimpse of the various steps that the government is taking to overcome such challenges.

Urbanisation Scenario

In India, urbanisation has become an important and irreversible process, and it is an important determinant of national economic growth and poverty reduction. Its extent can be understood by the following points: • According to Census 2011, India's urban population was 37.7 crores, which is projected to grow to about 60 crores by 2030. • As per Census 2001, only 27.81% of the total population lived in urban areas. This figure rose to 31.16% in the Census 2011. The urban centres are the major engines of economic growth in the country contributing to two-thirds of the country's economic output and are the main recipients of FDI. 70% of future employment is expected to be generated in Indian cities, with emerging cities driving consumption expenditure.

Reasons for Urbanisation Urbanisation in India has been characterised with many negative aspects. Some of the worrying concerns can be seen as follows:

Unplanned Nature of Urbanisation The major lacuna with urbanisation in India has been the lack of planning, leading to very haphazard growth of Indian cities. This has consequently led to urban sprawl and migration (mismanaged expansion of the urban areas) due to the rising population load in the urban areas.

Lopsided Nature of Urbanisation – In India, the major urban centres have been restricted to certain big cities which have grown at the cost of nearby areas. These mega-cities have emerged as the engines of growth, but they have failed to propagate the development to lower-tiered cities. This lopsided growth of urban centres has led to a top-heavy pattern (only major cities growing) devoid of a trickle-down effect (passing growth to lower cities).

No Equity-led Development – The urban centres in India have emerged as areas marked by the stark contrast in the standards of living of the people. Several high rises, modern building is juxtaposed with poor slums and filthy squatter settlements highlighting the huge gap between the lower and upper classes in the urban areas.

Environmental Issues

The concretisation of urban areas has led to the creation of local urban heat islands, with such areas being characterised by a higher temperature as compared to other nearby areas due to increased trapping of heat. High rise buildings also restrict the free movement of air and lead to higher air pollution.

Other Challenges

The rapid pace of urbanisation poses significant challenges to basic infrastructure services such as housing, water supply, transportation, sanitation, solid waste and wastewater management.

Overcome the Challenges

The Ministry of Housing and Urban Affairs (MoHUA) has taken extensive steps to address the problems of urbanisation in India and take advantage of the opportunities provided by the cities. The ministry has devised a three-level strategy for the same.

The Future The UN Department of Economic and Social Affairs (UNDESA) has predicted that the future increase in world's urban population will be concentrated in just a few countries and the absolute growth in urban population is projected to be the highest in India. Thus, in terms of sheer numbers, the largest urban transformation of the 21st century is happening in India.

The Urban Narratives

Definitions: Census of India, 2011

Urban settlement are: •All the places which have municipality, corporation, cantonment board or notified town area committee •All the other places with criteria : (a) A minimum population of 5000 persons (b) At least 75 % of male main working population engaged in non-agricultural pursuits and (c) A density of population of at least 400 persons per square kilometre

•The first category of urban units are known as Statutory Town. These town are notified under law by respective State/UT government and have local bodies.

•The second category of towns are Census Town– identified on the basis of census 2001 data. Cities are urban areas with > 100,000 population. < 100,000 are called towns in India. Census Towns: 3,894

•Urban Agglomeration (UA) are continuous urban spread constituting a town and its adjoining Out Growths (OGs), or two or more physically contiguous towns together with or without outgrowths of such towns. It must consist of at least a statutory town and its total population should not be < 20,000 (2001 Census). There are exceptions when places are treated as UA on the basis of contiguity. Examples: Greater Mumbai UA, Delhi UA, etc. UA in India: 475

Out Growths (OG) are viable unit like a village or an enumeration block made up of such village identifiable with boundaries and location–comprising railway colony, university campus, port area, military camps, etc., come up near a statutory town outside its statutory limits but within the revenue limits of villages contiguous to the town. Out Growths in India: 981.

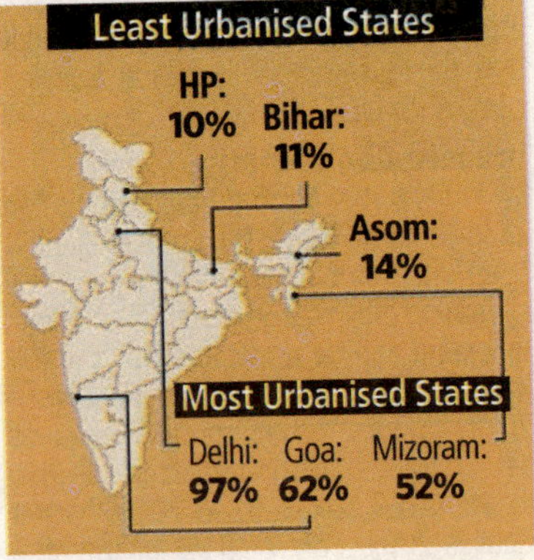

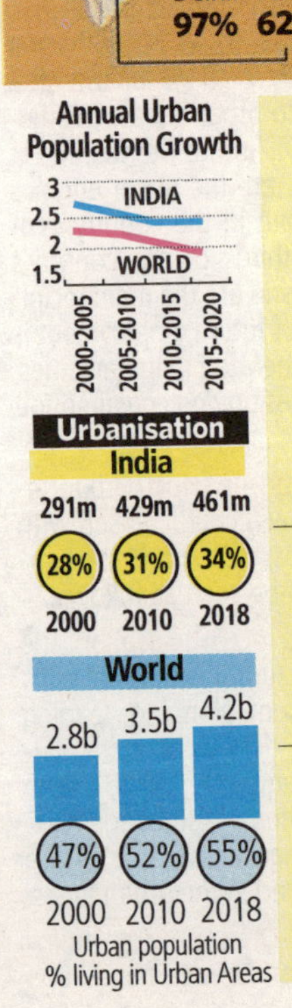

416 m People are expected to live in Indian cities by 2050 (current US population is 332m)

4,041 Statutory towns in India

3,892 Census towns in India

Rural India

Rural population refers to people living in rural areas as defined by national statistical office. It is calculated as the difference between total population and urban population. Aggregation of urban and rural population may not add up to total population because of different country coverages. •India rural population for 2020 was 898,024,053, a 0.29% increase from 2019. •Of the 121 crore Indians (Census 2011), 83.3 crore lived in rural areas while 37.7 crore (approx 32 % of the population) stayed in urban areas. •India rural population for 2017 was 888,881,381, a 0.44% increase from 2016.

For the first time in history, the Census 2011 reported a decline in the population growth rate of rural India. However, at that time India was still predominantly rural, with the urban population being just 30 per cent. Between Census 2001 and Census 2011, the number of Census Towns increased from 1,362 to 3,894. This indicates that people in rural areas are quitting farming or joining non-farm livelihoods. Millions of farmers have quit agriculture and, worryingly, very few from the current generation are entering the sector.

The Shrinking Rural India

Rural and Urban Population (in Crores)

	2001	2011	Difference
India	102.9	121.0	18.1
Rural	74.3	83.3	9.0
Urban	28.6	37.7	9.1

In absolute terms, India is losing farmers. In fact, there are indicators that many rural residents are not taking up farming despite being unemployed and having small lands. This shows that India on the cusp of a major change. In 1970, three-fourths of a rural household's income came from farm sources. After 45 years, in 2015, it is below one-third. Basically, most of the households now earn more out of non-farm sources.

Another concern is that these non-farm jobs are mostly in urban areas. In recent years, these urban employment sources have not been able to meet the surging job demands due to the exodus from agriculture. As the latest economic data points out, manufacturing, construction and other related sectors have not been able to generate employment as they used to earlier. All these sectors are experiencing slowdown.

This leaves us with that big conundrum: We urbanise and celebrate it as a sure shot path to prosperity, but urbanisation doesn't provide basic livelihood to people who have migrated from rural areas. This explains the current slump in demand that is keeping the overall economy down.

Poverty The poverty rate refers to the (percentage) share of the population that lies below the poverty line. Ever since India moved to a high growth trajectory in the 1980s, poverty rates have consistently declined over time. According to a consumption expenditure data reported by the National Statistical Office (NSO) in a report suggests that rural poverty rose nearly 4 percentage points between 2011-12 and 2017-18 to 30% even as urban poverty fell 5 percentage points over the same period to 9%. Given the higher weight of the rural population, the estimated overall poverty rate went up nearly a percentage point to 23% in 2017-18. The rise implies that 30 million people fell below India's official poverty line and joined the ranks of the poor over the past six years. Bihar saw the greatest rise in poverty between 2011-12 and 2017-18, with poverty rate rising by a whopping 17 percentage points to 50.47%. More than 40% of both Jharkhand and Odisha fall below the poverty line.

StateWise Number of Rural Population (As on 01/04/21)

S.No. State Total India	SC 174625057	ST 109546618	GEN 670823993	TOTAL 954995668
1 A&N Islands	0	24539	227665	252204
2 Andhra Pradesh	7190594	2679842	28318051	38188487
3 Arunachal Pradesh	2079	1052069	208556	1262704
4 Asom	2270623	4499939	25015542	31786104
5 Bihar	16687917	1614512	79185073	97487502
6 Chhattisgarh	2859360	8258660	11037411	22155431
7 D&NH- D&D	7735	178065	234618	420418
8 Goa	18110	110175	1008989	1137274
9 Gujarat	2920106	10669916	30369824	43959846
10 Haryana	4075416	3003	14083486	18161905
11 Himachal Pradesh	2005070	448590	5161468	7615128
12 Jammu & Kashmir	886901	1508709	8589003	10984613
13 Jharkhand	4169924	9500392	17450284	31120600
14 Karnataka	8730011	3996091	30970097	43696199
15 Kerala	2747072	487505	25661054	28895631
16 Ladakh	197	245163	9915	255275
17 Madhya Pradesh	9603871	16323329	34322562	60249762
18 Maharashtra	8132818	9653760	49362205	67148783
19 Manipur	47123	1276148	1100952	2424223
20 Meghalaya	15144	3089481	198968	3303593
21 Mizoram	112	671724	3779	675615
22 Nagaland	140	1866505	96099	1962744
23 Odisha	6680253	9404574	21430342	37515169
24 Puducherry	130128	1	428648	558777
25 Punjab	7119824	1980	11298535	18420339
26 Rajasthan	10651855	9405943	37084741	57142539
27 Sikkim	43277	175944	269165	488386
28 Tamil Nadu	11452222	746017	34698552	46896791
29 Telangana	3909523	2962623	13902252	20774398
30 Tripura	641243	1352878	1399939	3394060
31 Uttar Pradesh	38965255	1125836	129705781	169796872
32 Uttarakhand	1523913	278070	5427428	7229411
33 West Bengal	21137241	5934635	52563009	79634885
Total	**174625057**	**109546618**	**670823993**	**954995668**

Note: This data has been uploaded by the respective states after calculating the population based on census 2011 and the decadal growth rate.

13

HISTORY OF INDIA

- Ancient India
- Mauryan Empire
- Gupta Empire
- Foreign Rule of India
- Colonial Rule and the Freedom

Indian History

Ancient India (Pre-historic to AD 700)
Homo erectus activities have been traced in the Indian subcontinent 2 million years ago, and of Homo sapiens since 70,000 BC. But they were gathers or hunters. The first inhabitants of Indian subcontinent might have been tribals like Nagas (North-East), Santhals (East-India), Bhils (Central India), Gonds (Central India), Todas (South India) etc. Most of them are speakers of the Austric, pre-Dravidian languages, such as Munda and Gondvi. Dravidians and Aryans are believed to be immigrants who came later to the sub-continent.

Ancient India It can be classified as Paleolithic, Mesolithic, Neolithic and Chalcolithic period – based on the type of stone/ metal tools people used.

• Paleolithic Period (2 million BC – 10,000 BC):Fire, Tools made up of lime stone, Ostrich Eggs. Major sites: Bhimbetka (M.P), Hunsgi, Kurnool Caves, Narmada Valley (Hathnora, M.P), Kaladgi Basin.

• Mesolithic Period (10,000 BC – 8,000 BC): Major Climatic Change happened, Domestication of animals – Cattle rearing started, Microliths found at Brahmagiri (Mysore), Narmada, Vindya, Gujarat

• Neolithic Period (8000 BC – 4,000 BC): Agriculture Started, Wheel discovered Important site: Inamgaon– an early village. Major Neolithic Sites : Burzahom (Kashmir), Gufkral (Kashmir), Mehrgarh (Pakistan), Chirand (Bihar), Daojali Hading (Tripura/Assam), Koldihwa (UP), Mahagara (UP), Hallur (AP), Paiyampalli (AP), Maski, Kodekal, Sangana Kaller, Utnur, Takkala Kota.

Megalithic Sites: Brahmagiri, Adichanallur.

• Chalcolithic Period (4000– 1,500 BC)
  + Copper Age. Can be considered part of
  + Bronze Age. (Bronze: Copper, Tin)

• Indus Valley Civilisation (2500 – BC 1500): Settlements at Brahmagiri, Navada Toli (Narmada region), Mahishadal (W.Bengal), Chirand (Ganga region)

• Iron Age (BC 1500 – BC 200)

Vedic Period (Aryan migration: 1600 - BC 600) – about 1000 years (Composition of basic books of Hinduism, like Vedas, might have written down later.)

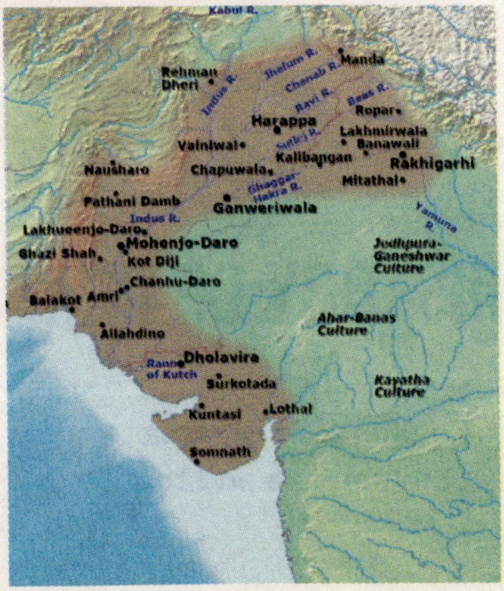

Harappa

One of the earliest urban centres on the Indian subcontinent, Harappa was discovered accidentally in 1921, as was Mohenjo-Daro, a twin city in the lower Indus valley (now located in Pakistan). The sites were

Jainism

550 Birth of Mahavira; Jainism founded.

Buddhism

563-483 Buddha who was Prince Gautama Siddharta of Lumbini, attains nirvana. Magadh Empire – contemporary of both Mahavira and Gautama Buddha. 483 First Buddhist Council held at Sattaparna (Saptaparni) (Rajgriha). 383 Second Buddhist Council at Vaishali.

excavated at the time by D. R. Sahni of Indian Archeological Department headed by Sir John Marshall, and subsequent carbon dating of the remains found there places them in the 3rd millennium BCE.

Harappa was a geometrically-planned brick city built on the banks of the river Ravi. Granaries, grain-pounding platforms, and seemingly workmen's quarters were located near the river, while a walled citadel containing a large tank dominated higher ground. This earliest known civilisation, the Indus Valley Civilisation, derives its name from Harappa.

Dholavira

It is one of the five largest Harappan sites (Mohenjo-daro and Ganeriwala in Pakistan and Dholavira, KalibanganRakigarhi in India) and the most spectacular Indus Valley archeological sites in India. Unlike

Dholavira Site

Harappa and Mohenjo-daro, the city built in Dholavira is built of stones instead of bricks. It had a sustainable resource management scheme. The city was divided into three parts – the citadel, the middle town and the lower town. It is a village located at Khadir bet, Bhachau taluk in Great Rann of Kutch, Gujarat. Bet means island. Locally, Dholavira is called Kotada timba meaning a large ruins of a fortified ancient site. Dholavia is one of the best preserved urban settlements from the period in southeast Asia. It is UNESCO's 40th world heritage site in India.

Magadha Empire

- Bimbisara of Haryanka Kula
- Sisunga dynasty – Kalasoka (Kakavarnin)
- Nanda empire – Mahapadmananda, Dhanananda

King Bimbisara

King Bimbisara, the great monarch of Magadha's rule. Son, Ajatasatru rules (492 BC – 460 BC) the king of the Magadha empire in north India

364 Mahapadmananda, the first ruler of the Nanda Dynasty.

336-323 Alexander the Great conquers Asia, moves to India.

327 Alexander the Great, the Macedonian king invades Punjab (NW India) ruled by king Porus after subduing Syria, Egypt, and Persia.

326 Alexander makes an alliance with Ambhi, king of Taxila and their combined force defeats the Purushottama (Porus) in the Battle of Hydaspes.

324 Dhana Nanda was the last king of Nanda Empire. The conquest of the Nanda Empire under Dhana Nanda by a force under Chandragupta Maurya led to the establishment of the Maurya kingdom – comprised Afghanistan and parts of central Asia.

323 Alexander the Great, dies.

Mauryan Empire

(321-185 BC)

The Mauryas ruled over almost the entire subcontinent of India for the first time as the centralised empire. Writings of Megasthenes and Kautilya, as well as epigraphic, numismatic, and archaeological evidence, illuminate the historical picture.

The founder of the Dynasty, Chandragupta Maurya took peacock as its emblem when supplanted the Nanda rulers in Magadha. He extended his domain far into present-day Afghanistan and consolidated his rule in the entire Indo-Gangetic plain before abdicating in favour of his son Bindusarain 297 B.C.E. Bindusara conquered "the land between the two seas," probably the Deccan , and continued in his father's tradition of tight government for another quarter century. He was succeeded by his son Ashoka , who conquered Kalinga, present-day Orissa , and introduced a novel Buddhist principle of *dharma* or dharma, meaning righteousness based on compassion and non-violence, in his administration. Ashoka was succeeded directly by two grandsons ruling in eastern and western provinces, who were credited with the construction of numerous Jain temples.

321 Rise of the Mauryas (Chandragupta Maurya) in Magadha after defeating Nanda Dynasty and Seleucid empire.
303/5 Chandragupta Maurya defeats Seleukos Nikator and the trans-Indus region transferred to the Mauryas.
298 Bindusara coronated.
272 Ashoka the Great, grandson of Chandragupta Maurya, ascends as emperor of the Mauryan empire.
266 Ashoka conquers and unifies most of South Asia, including Afghanistan.
265 Kalinga War takes place.
232 Ashoka dies.
180 Fall of the Mauryas; Rise of the Sungas under Pushyamitra Sunga.
30 Rise of the Satavahana Dynasty.

Post-Mauryan Kingdoms (Middle Kingdoms): Sunga (181-71 BC), Kanva (71-27BC), Satavahanas (235-100BC), Indo-Greeks, Parthians (19-45AD), Sakas (90BC-150AD), Kushanas(78AD)

The Puranas record the names of other successors, but little is known for certain about them. The rule of the Indo-Greeks in the northwest and the Sunga Kings in Magadha indicate some break up of the Mauryan Empire on or before 180 B.C.E.

Gupta Empire

(c. 320-547 C.E.)

The decline of Kushan and Satavahana power in northern and peninsular India respectively resulted in the emergence of many independent republics and kingdoms in the 3rd century. One such kingdom in the mid-Ganges valley was ruled by Gupta and then his son Ghatotkacha. His son Chandragupta-I assumed the title Maharajadhiraj. symbolic of suzerain power, shortly after marriage to the Lichchavi princess Kumaradevi. Their son, Samudragupta (330-375) engaged in a series of conquests in the north, the west, the Deccan, and the hilly regions of central and eastern India; these are enumerated in Samudragupta's Allahabad pillar inscription. He also established feudatory or diplomatic relations with outlying republics and kingdoms on the subcontinent and in Southeast Asia. Samudragupta issued gold coins

to celebrate his conquests and, more importantly, performed the ashvamedha or horse sacrifice as the overlord of kings.
•The main sources are the standardised coins, stone and iron pillars, inscriptions on stone pedestals and slabs, records of donations to temples, copper plate land grants, and quantities of seals. There are literary sources such as the Puranas, the texts of Kalidasa in Sanskrit, and accounts by foreign travellers, notably the contemporary Fahian, though Huang Tsang and Al Biruni.

Art and Culture of Gupta Period

• Samudragupta was briefly succeeded by his son Ramagupta whose humiliation by the Sakas led to his being ousted by his brother Chandragupta II Vikramaditya who ruled to 412 C.E. Chan dragupta too was a great warrior who extended the frontiers of his Em pire northwest across the Indus into present-day Afghanistan and consolidated his power through all of northern India and part of the Deccan. He issued copious gold coinage. He is the subject of a fine Sanskrit inscription on an iron pillar near Delhi. Chandragupta II, is identified with the legendary Vikramaditya of Kalidasa. His son Govindagupta briefly succeeded before giving place to Kumaragupta I, second son of Chan dragupta II, under whose forty-year rule (415-455) the Gupta Empire reached the greatest height of its glory.
• Evidence of a flourishing culture and

Gupta Kingdom (300–800 AD): Classical Period.
Important ruler of Gupta Period: Samudra Gupta (Indian Napoleon)
Post Guptas: Harshvardana, Vakatakas, Pallavas, Chalukyas. Also, Hunas, Maitrakas, Rajputs, Senas and Chauhans.

economy allowed calling the Gupta period as a "golden age." During that period Sanskrit was the court language; the sciences of Astronomy, mathematics, and medicine developed; treatises on art, dance, music, and sculpture were produced and the artistic achievements of the period to be seen, for example, at Ajanta were high indeed; the great epics Mahabharata and Ranmyana as in the brahmanic tradition were written probably in the form it is used now. •Spirituality allowed orthodox and heterodox faiths like Buddhism and Jainism to coexist. •There are, however, proof of discrimination against women, sudras, and untouchables. Differences of opinion also occur on identifying the origins and caste of the Guptas.

Rajput Dynasties

Rajput (sons of a king) dynasties belong clans: Suryavanshi, Chandravanshi, Agnovanshi, Rishivanshi. They are Chauhans, Chandellas, Gahadavalas, Pratiharas, Tomara, Chaulukyas (Solankis), Paramaras, etc. The Rathores are the major clan descended from Kanauj's Gahadavalas Dynasty. Maharana Sangaof Sisodiya clan, is considered the most powerful among them. They lacked unity and were constantly fought to establish their own supremacy. These conflicts were self-defeating.

Foreign Rule of India

In the late 5th century, the Roman empire collapsed fell into the hands of factions. It was replaced by Byzantine Empire (476CE -1453). One of these different powers was the Ottoman empire (1299-1923). Osman Bay became the chief of the Ottoman tribe in 1284 CE. He founded the Ottoman Empire in 1299 CE. The rule of Suleyman 1 the Magnificent empire reached its zenith in the 16th and 17th century CE. The empire controlled SE Europe, SW Asia and North-Africa. Constantinople was its capital. Throughout the middle ages, Constantinople was Europe's largest and wealthiest city. Now, it is Istanbul, the capital of Turkey.

1. Turkish Invasion

Mahmud of Ghazni (AD 1000-27)

He was the Sultan of the Ghaznavid dynasty of Afghanistan. He was extremely ambitious and was attracted to the wealth of India. He invaded India 17 times from 1001-1025 CE and looted the rich temple towns of Thanesar, Mathura, Dwarka and Nagarkot. His most important expedition was against the extremely rich Somnath temple of Gujarat in 1025 CE. The Somnath Temple was served by 2000 priests. Devotees thronged the temple. It had hundreds of musicians, dancing girls and barbers. Mahmud was amazed by its fabulous wealth.

Mahmud used the wealth to beautify Ghazni building libraries, mosques, gardens, a university and a museum, which also became a centre of fine arts and culture. Mahmud died in 1030 CE leaving behind a large empire. His successors were inefficient and took no interest in India. His invasions had far reaching effects. Punjab became a Muslim territory for nearly 150 years. The economy was devastated as large amounts of wealth were carried away to Ghazni. These invasions paved the way for further invasion- that changed India's history.

The Turkish rule in India was founded by Muhammad of Ghori. His first invasion was directed against Multan in 1175AD.

Muhammad of Ghori (AD 1175-1206)

Muhammad was the governor of the Ghori, a province that laid near Ghazni. He conquered Ghazni in 1160 CE. He was also attracted to the wealth of India. He conquered Punjab, Multan and Sind and attacked Prithviraj Chauhan, the Rajput ruler of Delhi at Tarain in 1191 CE.

In the *First Battle of Tarain*, Prithviraj Chauhan's army had 300 elephants. The Turkish soldiers had never seen an elephant before.

In that fierce battle the Rajput army defeated the Muslim army and Muhammad was badly injured and was captured as prisoner. Prithviraj later on pardoned and released him. However, Muhammad came back the next year to take revenge for his defeat. The two armies met again on the same battlefield and the Second Battle of Tarain was fought in 1192 CE. Muhammad came with a large well-equipped army and attacked the Rajput army in the early hours of morning when they were caught unawares. The Rajputs fought valiantly but were defeated and Prithviraj Chauhan was killed.

The Second Battle of Tarain is believed to be the most significant battle in the history of India as it opened the path for other conquerors into India.

2. Muslim Invasion

Muslim conquests in the Indian subcontinent took place from 12th to 16th century, though earlier Muslim conquests include the invasions into modern Pakistan and the Umayyad campaigns in India, during the time of the Rajput Kingdoms in the 8th century.

Mahmud of Ghazni, the first ruler to hold the title Sultan, who preserved an ideological link to the suzerainty of the Abbasid Caliphate, invaded and plundered vast parts of Punjab and Gujarat, starting from the Indus River, during the 10th century.

After the capture of Lahore and the end of the Ghaznavids, the Ghurid Empire ruled by Muhammad of Ghor and Ghiyath al-Din Muhammad laid the foundation of Muslim rule in India.

Muhammad Ghori appointed Quote-ud-din Aybak as his viceroy in India. Qutb-ud-dinbecame the first Muslim Sultan of Delhi after the death of Muhammad of Ghor and established the Delhi Sultanate. Muhammad Ghori is rightfully called the founder of the Muslim Empire in India. From the latter half of the 16th century, they expanded their kingdom from Agra and Delhi until in the 17th century they controlled nearly all of the subcontinent.

The Five Rulers

Slave Dynasty 1206-1290 – the line of sultans in Delhi who ruled for almost 100 years. It was founded by Qutb al-Din Aibak, a favourite slave of Md. Ghori. The Mamluk dynasty was introduced to India by Qutb Aibak. Ruled 1206-1290.

The Khilji 1290-1320 – a Turk-Afghan dynasty that ruled Delhi for 30 years and controlled a large of Indian sub-continent.

The Tuglaq 1321-1414 – a Muslim dynasty of Turk origin and started by Ghazi Malik over Delhi Sultanate.

The Sayyid 1414-1451 - the 4th dynasty of Delhi Sultanate founded by Khizr Khan governor of Multan

The Lodi dynasty i 1451-1526 – an Afghan dynasty that ruled the Delhi Sultanate. Bahlul Khan Lodi was the first Afghan ruler of India.

The Mughal 1526-1857

[The Suri 1540-1555 replaced the Mughal Empire when Pashtun emperor Sher Shah Suri defeated it in 1540.defeated.]

Medieval India

(AD 700 – AD 1857)

The Mughal Rule of 300 Years

(AD 1526 – AD 1857)

It stretched from the outer edge of Indus basin in the west to Asom and Bangladesh in the east and from northern Afghanistan to Deccan plateau in the south. The first 6 emperors– Babur, Humayun Akbar, Jahangir, Shah Jahan and Aurangzeb changed India. Much of the details are not recorded. 1526: Battle of Panipat, Babur defeats the Sultan of Delhi.

1530: Mughal Emperor Babur dies and is succeeded by his son Humayun. 1540: The Battle of Kannauj. Humayun is defeated by the Afghans (Suri Dynasty), and passes 12 years in exile.

1552: Humayun regains the throne of Delhi

1556: Humayun dies, and is succeeded by his son Akbar. 1556: The Second Battle of Panipat is fought between Hemu (Prime Minister of Adil Shah Suri) and Akbar.

1574: Akbar annexes Bengal 1586: Akbar annexes Kashmir. 1605: Death of the Mughal emperor Akbar. Jahangir to ascend the throne as the fourth Mughal emperor.

1632: Shah Jahan, the fifth Mughal Emperor, begins building the Taj Mahal as a memorial for his wife Mumtaz Mahal.

1646: Shah Jahan builds the Taj Mahal.

1658: Aurangzeb becomes the Mughal emperor. 1674: Forces led by Shivaji defeat Aurangzeb's troops, and establish the Matatha Empire. 1675: Aurangzeb executes the ninth Sikh Guru Tegh Bahadur, starting the Sikh-Muslim feud. 1707: Aurangzeb dies. Bahadur Shah I succeeds. The Decline: *With the death of Aurangzeb* his three sons: Muazzam, Azam and Kam Baksh. were assigned different regions for administrative purposes– as governor of Kabul, governor of Gujarat, and governor of Bijapur respectively. It created differences between them that caused a prolonged war of succession between them causing the great collapse.

Important Battles

1191 **First Battle of Tarain**- Prithviraj Chauhan defeats Muhammad Ghori.
1192 **Second Battle of Tarain**-Muhammad Ghori defeats Prithviraj Chauhan.
1526 **First Battle of Panipat**-Babar defeated Ibrahim Lodi.
1527 **Battle of Khanua**-Babar defeats Rana Sanga.
1539 **Battle of Chausa**-Sher Shah defeats Humayun.
1540 **Battle of Kannauj**-Sher Shah defeats Humayun and captures Delhi.
1556 **Second Battle of Panipat**-Akbar defeats Hemu Vikramaditya.
1576 **Battle of Haldighati**-Akbar defeats Rana Pratap.
1601 **Battle of Asir Garh**-Akbar's last war.
1757 **Battle of Plassey**- Lord Clive defeats Siraj-ud-Daula.
1760 **Battle of Wandiwash**- The British defeats the French in South India.
1761 **Third Battle of Panipat**-Ahmed Shah Abdali defeats the Marathas.
1764 **Battle of Buxar-** The British defeats the combined armies of Mir Qasim, Shuja-ud-daula and Shah Alam.
1767-'69 **First Battle of Mysore**- The British make peace with Hyder Ali and Nizam. The war remains indecisive.
1775-'82 **The First Anglo-Maratha War**- Ends in a long drawn fighting.
1780-'84 **Second Battle of Mysore** – The 4-year-long war between the British and Hyder Ali results in the latter's death (during the war). Tipu Sultan succeeds Hyder Ali.
1790-'92 **Third Battle of Mysore** - The British defeats Tipu Sultan.
1799-**Fourth Battle of Mysore** -Sultan Tipu dies while fighting with the British.
1802-'03 **The Second Anglo-Maratha War** The British defeats Scindia and Bhonsle.
1804-'05 **The Third Anglo-Maratha War** Holkar subjugated by the British.
1817-'18 **The Fourth Anglo-Maratha War** Marathas defeated.

3. European Invasion

Alexander the Great was the first European to invade India. Portuguese Vasco da Gama, 1st Count of Vidigueira, became the next prominent person to undertake the exploration during the reign of King Manuel I in 1495–1499. Vasco da Gama, also became the first European to reach India by sea via the Cape of Good Hope to Calicut in 1498. His voyage to India was the first to link Europe and Asia by an ocean route, connecting the Atlantic and the Indian ocean – the West meeting the Orient. Vasco da Gama sowed the seeds of colonialism in the Indian subcontinent.

Following his steps, other Europeans such as the Dutch, French, Croatians, Austrians, the Danish and English made forays into India in the subsequent years. In fact, the Europeans were initially interested in trading, but a combination of local politics, rivalries among other European nations, and better economic prospects made them switch to full-time imperialism.

It was the English that overcame their European rivals to establish a colonial empire in India. Known as the 'Jewel in the Crown', the Indian subcontinent was one of the prized possessions for the British colonials.

Portuguese Governors

Franusco de Almeida 1505-1509 -First Portuguese Governor, fortified Fort Manual in Cochin; built Anjediva fort.

Afonso de Albuquerque 1509-1515 - Conquered Goa from the Sultan of Bijapur, Adil Shah.

Nuno da Cunha 1529-1538 Made settlements in Madras (San Thome) and Bengal (Hooghly).

The Dutch Settlement

Vereenigde Oost-Indische Compagnie (VOC or the Dutch United East India Company (started in 1602) had settlements on Malabar Coast – Vengurla Port (N. Goa); On Coromandel Coast –

Masulipatnam, Devanampatnam (Fort St David), Pulicat (Fort Geldria) in Bihar-Bengal - Orissa - Patna - Pipli, Chinsurah (Fort Gustavus on the Hooghly)-Balasore.

The Danes 1616 Settlements in Tranquebar in 1620, Serampore in 1676.

The French French East India Company was started by Colbert in 1664. Francois Caron established factory in Surat; Mascara started a factory in Masulipatanam; De la Haye occupied San Thome, Madras. Francois Martin Pondicherry's first Governor- General, 1673; Chandranagar Bengal Settlement, 1690 and Dupleix, 1724.

4. The British Entry

1613-13: British East India Company sets up a trading post at Surat

1757: The British East India Company's private army under Robert Clive annexes Bengal in the Battle of Plassey

1760: The Marathas comprehensively defeat the Nizam of Hyderabad; the Maratha empire reaches its zenith

1761: The Marathas are defeated in the Third Battle of Panipat by the Afghans, bringing an end to their expansion

1766: The Sikhs defeat Ahmad Shah Abdali; establish Sikh rule in Punjab

1766: The First Anglo-Mysore War between Mysore's Hyder Ali and the East India Company

1779: Maratha Mahadji Shinde routs the British at the Battle of Wadgaon

1782: The First Anglo-Maratha War ends with the Treaty of Salbai

1799: The Fourth Anglo-Mysore War ends with the death of Tipu Sultan and the restoration of the Wodeyar dynasty that ruled Mysore earlier

1801: Maharaja Ranjit Singh establishes Khalsa rule of Punjab from Lahore

Struggle for Independence

The national movement was a part of a larger spectrum of national resurgence, which covered almost all aspects of national life, religious, social, educational, cultural and economic. It differed in degree and in kind from region to region, but one common desire animated all regions, namely, gaining independence.

The Beginning of British Dominion

When Lord Dalhousie laid down his office in 1856 and Canning took over as Governor General the British Empire in India had extended to its natural boundaries - from Indus in the west to Irrawady (Burma) in the east and from the Himalayas in the north to Cape Comorin (Kanyakurnari) in the far south.

It was made up of two distinct political segments: •territories directly administered by the East India Co. and •those ruled by Indian princes who owed fealty to the company. For the first time in many years, peace seemed to have settled all over India. The pacifist Lord Canning who succeeded the aggressive Lord Dalhousie as Governor General felt that the calm was ominous.

Modern India (AD 1857 +)

•First War of Indian Independence (1857) •Formation of Indian National Congress (1885) •Formation of Muslim League (1906) •Non-Co-operation Movement (1920)•Civil Disobedience Movement (1930)•Quit India Movement (1942) • Partition of India (1947)

The Revolt of 1857

In the summer of 1857 the massed clouds burst and the entire British dominion in India shook with the Revolt of 1857, which the British historians have dubbed the

Fighting British Forces : Rani Lakshmibai

Viceroys

1.	Lord Canning	1858-62
2.	Lord Elgin-I	1862-63
3.	Sir Robert Napier	1863
4.	Sir William Denison	1863
5.	Sir John Lawrence	1864-1868
6.	Lord Mayo	1869-1872
7.	Sir John Strachey	1872
8.	Lord Northbrook	1872-1876
9.	Lord Lytton I	1876-1860
10.	Marquess of Ripon	1880-1884
11.	Earl of Dufferin	1884-1888
12.	Lord Lansdowne	1888-1894
13.	Lord Elgin II	1894-1898
14.	Lord Curzon	1898-1904
15.	Lord Ernptly	1904
16.	Lord Curzon	1904-1905
17.	Lord Minto II	1905-1910
18.	Lord Hardinge II	1910-1916
19.	Lord Chelmsford	1916-1921
20.	Lord Reading	1921-1925
21.	Lord Lytton II	1925
22.	Lord Irwin	1926-1931
23.	Lord Willingdon	1931-34
24.	Sir John Stanley	1934
25.	Lord Linlithgow	1934-1937
26.	Baron Brebum	1938
27.	Lord Linlithgo	1938-1943
28.	Lord Wavell	1944-1947
29.	Lord Mountbatten	1947-1948
30.	C. Rajagopalachari	1948-1950

Independence Struggle Events

Sepahi Mutiny- *1st war of independence*	1857
Indian National Congress	1885
Swadeshi Movement	1905
Home Rule Movement	1916
Lucknow Pact	1916
Khilafat Movement	1919/1920
Chauri Chaura incident	1922
Non-Cooperation Movement	1920-1922
Swaraj Party	1922
Dandi March	1930
Civil Disobedience Movement	1930
Quit India Movement	1942
Direct Action Campaign	1946

Sepoy Mutiny and the Indian historians, the First War of Independence. True, it began as a mutiny of Indian soldiers against their British commanders but soon it became a fight against British rule. Indian soldiers had broken out in open mutiny against British officers many times previously–in 1806 at Vellore (Madras), in 1842 in Bengal, in 1844 in Sind, then in Bihar and Punjab. None of these had any political overtones but the Mutiny of 1857 differed radically in this respect.

The two elements military and political coalesced in the revolt of 1857. The Indian soldiers having massacred the British personnel in Meerut, marched to Delhi in May 1857. They proclaimed the aged Mughal Emperor Bahadur Shah II as the Emperor of India. Bahadur Shah promptly issued' a proclamation urging upon the people of India–Hindus and Muslims alike.

It is not quite correct to describe the revolt of 1857 as a national revolt. For, at that time, India had not yet become a nation. The revolt itself was the last kick of a dying feudal order, led by a decadent aristocracy. "The idea of a nation and, therefore, of nationality was a bequest of English education."

There is little doubt that the knowledge of English acquired by Indians in every part of the country facilitated communication and expedited the process of national integration. The Indian middle class, steeped in English literature and history, gorged themselves with the ideas of liberty, equality and fraternity which the American War of Independence (1773-1787) and the French Revolution (1789) had glorified.

The Effect of the 1857 Revolt:

•The administration of British India, until then under the control of the Board of Directors of the East India Company, was taken over by the British Government. •Queen Victoria was proclaimed the Empress of India and the Governor General was designated the Viceroy and Governor General.

Independence Struggle Events

Sepahi Mutiny- *1st war of independence*	1857
Indian National Congress	1885
Swadeshi Movement	1905
Home Rule Movement	1916
Lucknow Pact	1916
Khilafat Movement	1919/1920
Chauri Chaura incident	1922
Non-Cooperation Movement	1920-1922
Swaraj Party	1922
Dandi March	1930
Civil Disobedience Movement	1930
Quit India Movement	1942
Direct Action Campaign	1946

•The British Indian army was re-organised. The quota of British personnel in the army was considerably enhanced and the artillery divisions were manned entirely by the British. In addition, many purely British regiments were formed. •The paramountcy of the British Government was proclaimed, ie, all ruling kings and titular princes of India were declared feudatories of the British Crown. This proclamation raised many eyebrows among Indian princes, but there was little they could do in the matter.

With the indigo riots, the agitation for freedom acquired greater momentum. At the same-time, a vernacular Fourth Estate was slowly taking shape to express Indian aspirations.

This resulted in the promulgation of the Vernacular Press Act of 1878 intended to muzzle the periodicals in Indian languages. The reason advanced by Lord Lytton, the Viceroy, was that "the increasingly violent native press was directly provocative of rebellion." The whole of India protested against the Act and appealed to the British government to repeal it. The Act was at last repealed by Lord Ripon in 1882.

Lord Lytton as Viceroy (1874-1880) fathered an offensive brood of laws and regulations. The Arms Act (which exempted Europeans) and the abolition of import duties on British goods were among the more obnoxious performances of Lytton.

Lord Ripon's viceroyalty, otherwise benign, was sullied by the infamous Ilbert Bill. This bill amended the Criminal Procedure Code and specified that only European judges could try European offenders for serious misdemeanours.

In 1883 the agitation over the Ilbert Bill still continued. Surendranath Banerjee was arrested for an article he wrote in the Bengali. Soon arrests of other persons for seditious articles followed. This accumulation of discriminatory laws, arrests and prosecutions, roused the masses.

Some Englishmen in India felt the same way. Henry Cotton and Allen Octavian Hume among them thought that an abiding concord between the government and the people had to be built up.

Hume formed the Indian National Union in 1854. The aim of the Union was "to oppose by all constitutional methods all authorities high and low here or in England, whose acts and omissions are opposed to the principles of the Government of India Act laid down by the British Parliament and endorsed by the British Sovereign."

[* *All unacknowledged quotations in the Section is from The History of the Freedom Movement in India, Vols. I-IV.*]

The Emergence of Nationalism

The new reality led the people to ask a crucial question: what is this country of India and for whom is it meant? The answer that gradually emerged was: India for Indians – all the people irrespective of class, colour, caste, creed, language, or gender. And the country, its resources and systems, were meant for all of them. Then the leaders understood that we surrendered our control over the resources of India and the lives of its people to foreign powers and until this control was ended India could not be for Indians.

This new consciousness emerged in the political associations formed in the 1870s and 1880s. Most of these were led by English-educated professionals such as lawyers like Poona Sarvajanik Sabha, the Indian Association, the Madras Mahajan Sabha, the Bombay Presidency Association, and of course the Indian National Congress. Note the name, "the literal meaning of "sarvajanik" is "of or for all the people" (*sarva* = all + *janik* = of the people). Though many of these associations functioned in specific parts of the country, their goals were stated as the goals of all the people of India, not those of any one region, community or class. They worked with the idea that the people should be sovereign – a modern consciousness and a key feature of nationalism. In other words, Indian people should be empowered to take decisions regarding their affairs.

The Dissatisfaction with imperial rule intensified in the 1870s and 1880s. The Arms Act was passed in 1878, disallowing Indians from possessing arms. In the same year the Vernacular Press Act was also enacted in an effort to silence those who were critical of the government. The Act allowed the government to confiscate the assets of newspapers including their printing presses if the newspapers published anything that was found "objectionable". In 1883, there was a furore over the attempt by the government to introduce the Ilbert Bill. The bill provided for the trial of British or European persons by Indians, and sought equality between British and Indian judges in the country. But when white opposed the government to withdraw the bill, Indians were enraged. The event highlighted the racial attitudes of the British in India.

The need for an all-India organisation of educated Indians had been felt since 1880, but the Ilbert Bill controversy deepened this desire. The Indian National Congress was established when 72 delegates from all over the country met at Bombay in December 1885.

The early leadership – Dadabhai Naoroji, Pherozeshah Mehta, Badruddin Tyabji, W.C. Bonnerji, Surendranath Banerji, Romesh Chandra Dutt, S. Subramania Iyer, among others – was largely from Bombay and Calcutta.

Naoroji, a businessman and publicist settled in London, and for a time member of the British Parliament, guided the younger nationalists. A retired British official, A.O. Hume, also played a part in bringing Indians from the various regions together.

A Nation in the Making

It has often been said that the Congress in the first twenty years was "moderate" in its objectives and methods. During this period it demanded a greater voice for Indians in the government and in administration.

It wanted the Legislative Councils to be made more representative, given more power, and introduced in provinces where none existed. It demanded that Indians be placed in high positions in the government. For this purpose it called for civil service examinations to be held in India as well, other than in London.

The demand for Indianisation of the administration was part of a movement against colonialism, since most important jobs at the time were reserved for some.

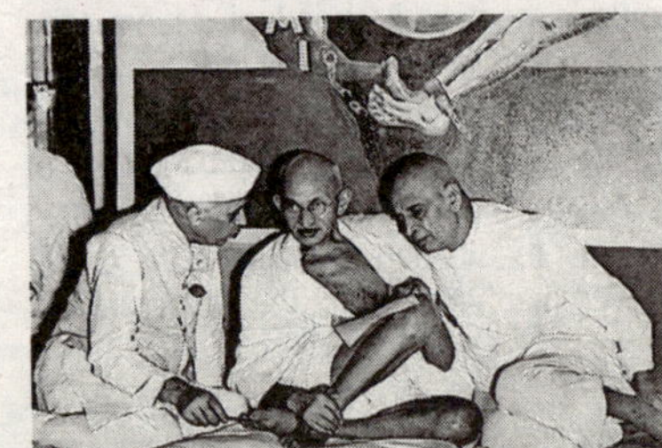

In the Nation Building Process

Colonial Rule and the Freedom

The Arrival of East India Company Traders

British rule in India began in 1757 after the Battle of Plassey, where the British East India Company defeated a large force of the Nawab of Bengal and his French allies on 23 June. East India Company began exercising control over the country and they ruled India for 100 years, until it was replaced by direct British rule (the British raj) as a result of the Indian Mutiny in 1857–58.

The Indian independence movement began during World War I. It was led by Mahatma Gandhi, who wished for a peaceful and nonviolent end to Imperial rule.

Challenges of Independence When India became independent in August 1947, it faced a series of challenges. •As a result of Partition, 8 million refugees had come into the country from what was now Pakistan. •They had to be provided homes and jobs.

Then the princely states, almost 500 of them, each ruled by a *maharaja* or a *nawab*, each of whom had to be persuaded to join the new nation. •The problems of the refugees and of the princely states had to be addressed immediately. •In the longer term, the new nation had to adopt a political system that would best serve the hopes and expectations of its population. •India's population in 1947 was also divided as high castes and low castes, between the majority Hindu community and Indians who practised other faiths. They spoke many different languages, wore many different kinds of dress, ate different kinds of food and practised different professions. *How could they be made to live together in one nation-state?*

To the problem of unity was added the problem of development. In 1947, the vast majority of Indians lived in the villages. Farmers and peasants depended on the monsoon for their survival. So did the non-farm sector of the rural economy, for if the crops failed, barbers, carpenters, weavers and other service groups would not get paid for their services either. In the cities, factory workers lived in crowded slums with little access to education or health care. •Clearly, the new nation had to lift its masses out of poverty by increasing the productivity of agriculture and by promoting new, job-creating industries.

Unification and development •It had to go hand in hand. If the divisions between different sections of India were not healed, they could result in violent and costly conflicts – high castes fighting with low castes, Hindus with Muslims and so on. •At the same time, if the fruits of economic development did not reach the broad masses of the population, it could create fresh divisions – for example, between the rich and the poor, between cities and the countryside, between regions of India that

The Times of India

BIRTH OF INDIA'S FREEDOM

NATION WAKES TO NEW LIFE

Mr. Nehru Calls For Big Effort From People

"INCESSANT STRIVING TASK OF FUTURE"

Assembly Members Take Solemn Pledge

STATE VISIT TO KARACHI

LORD MOUNTBATTEN GREETS PAKISTAN

Mr. Jinnah Re-Affirms Firm Friendship With Britain

FRENZIED ENTHUSIASM IN BOMBAY

Crowds In Festive Mood

The Freedom at Last

were prosperous and regions that lagged behind. •A Constitution was immediately needed. It got drafted between December 1946 and November 1949, through a series of meetings on the country's political future. The meetings of this "Constituent Assembly" were held in New Delhi, but the participants came from all over India, and from different political parties.

The Partition at Last

Though partition of India had been in the making for a long time – were visible in the Hindu-Muslim riots which started as early as 1881. The formation of the All India Muslim League at Dacca (now Dhaka) in December, 1906, provided a focal point for Muslim political aspirations. In 1937, when the Congress and the Muslim League started working provincial ministries, the rivalry between the two organisations came into the open.

The outbreak of the Second World War, which commenced with Hitler's invasion of Poland on September 1, 1939, called for a complete change of policy on both sides- the British Indian Government and the National Congress. India was declared a belligerent nation by Britain on September 3, 1939, and the British Indian administration was placed on a war footing. The war lasted 6 years. The Congress, as a whole supported the democratic allied countries but called for an immediate assurance from Britain, that independence would be given to India, as soon as the war emergency was over. The British Government paid no heed. The Congress ministries resigned in Oct 1939. In March 1940, at its annual session in Ramgarh the Congress demanded complete independence and a Constituent Assembly to draft a constitution for free India. In the same month, the Muslim League at its' Lahore session demanded a separate state for the Muslims of India. In March 1942, the British Government sent Sir Stafford Cripps to India with proposals for a new constitution. The Cripps proposals

Mass Migration Caused by Partition

were found unsatisfactory and were rejected both by the Congress and the League. In May 1942, Gandhiji called on Britain to 'Leave India to God'. In August 1942, the Congress working committee considered Gandhiji's call to Britain and passed the famous 'Quit India' resolution.

The new Labour government set up a parliamentary commission to negotiate the question of Indian independence. Famous as the Cabinet Mission, it announced its constitutional scheme, which implicitly recognised the right of the Muslims to have a state of their own. While the Muslim League accepted the proposals, the Congress rejected it. This was followed by riots. The Great Calcutta Killings of August 16-18, 1946, were the first of the riots. Then followed the killings in West Punjab, where the Muslims were in a majority. In desperation the parties in various consultations demanded the partition of Punjab.

Lord Mountbatten who succeeded Wavell as Viceroy in March 1947, boldly announced the partition of India. The provinces where the Muslims formed the majority were to be constituted into a separate state + Pakistan. Thus, parts of Punjab (West Punjab) and Bengal (East Bengal) and the whole of the provinces of Sind, Baluchistan and the North West Frontier became Pakistan. The rest of India formed another State. The Indian Independence Act, passed by the British Parliament (July 1947), formalised the division of India into two fully independent states + India and Pakistan.

14

SPACE, SECURITY, ENERGY

- Space Initiatives
- Global Space Economy is $447 Billion
- Defence
- Special Security Forces
- Indian Police
- Indian Nuclear Programme
- Energy Sector in India

Space Initiatives

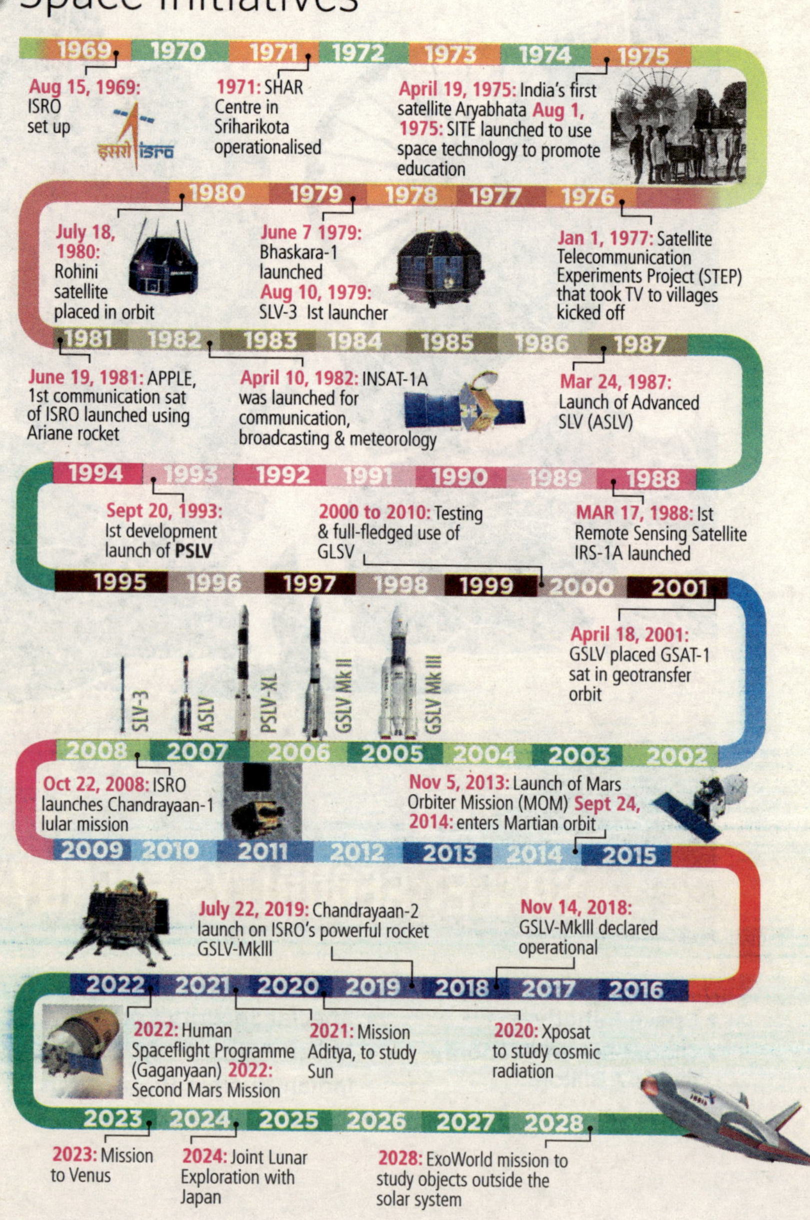

Global Space Economy is $447 Billion

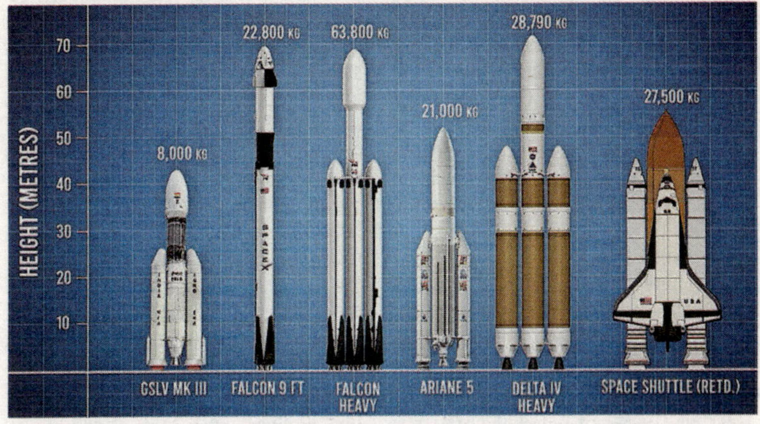

In 2020, India brought in reforms in the space sector, the contribution and participation of the private sector are expected to increase. The government-owned NSIL would take up space missions on a demand model, as opposed to the earlier supply model. The commercial viability of every mission also would be established beforehand. In a major boost for the Indian private sector, he said that India's workhorse rocket, the PSLV, would be made in an end-to-end manner only by companies.

Privatisation of Space Sector

A consortium of L&T and HAL will be the prime contractors. The rest of the ecosystem would play under them. ISRO will no longer procure various parts from 200-plus suppliers and assemble the vehicle. That job will now be entrusted to these two of these companies with help from other current eco partners. All solids and interstages in future would stay with L&T. The liquid along with tankages would be with HAL. Godrej will become a tier-I supplier to HAL, while Walchand will become tier-I supplier to L&T. The first launch of PSLV completely built by industries is planned for 2021. ISRO's other rockets will also follow the same path. According to the Antrix Corporation, despite the pandemic disruption, the global space sector grew by over 4% to reach $447bn in the year 2020. Despite India's wide-ranging capabilities and activities in space, the country captured 2% of this huge market. However, in future when the private sector participates in toto in space activities it would help the country reap the benefits

List of Chairman

1. Vikram Sarabhai	1963 -1972
2. MGK. Menon	Jan 1972 - Sep 1972
3. Satish Dhawan	1972 -1984
4. UR Rao	1984 -1994
5. K. Kasturirangan	1994 -2003
6. G. Madhavan Nair	2003 -2009
7. K. Radhakrishnan	2009 -2014
8. Shailesh Nayak 1Jan	- 12 Jan 2015
9. AS Kiran Kumar	2015 - 2018
10. K. Sivan	2018 -

Heavy Lift Vehicles

To attain total self-reliance in the launch of heavy satellites, weighing above 4 tonnes, and to meet future demands, the ISRO is working on a fleet of five new rockets. The new fleet of rockets are similar to the existing SSLV, PSLV and GSLV and GSLV Mk3 rockets, but they would be powered by more capable, powerful and technologically advanced engines. Presently, India pays and utilises the services of Ariane-5, a foreign rocket, to launch satellites that weigh over 4 tonnes.

This new fleet of heavy-lift rockets would place a payload weighing anywhere between 4.9 tonnes and over 16 tonnes in the Geo synchronous Transfer Orbit (GTO) – an enormous improvement over GSLV Mk3 rocket's 4-ton capability. GTO is an intermediary orbit, 180km at its closest point and 36,000km at its farthest point from the Earth, into which heavy satellites are launched by rockets. After being placed in GTO, the satellites use their onboard propulsion to reach a circular orbit 36,000 km above the earth (equal distance from the earth at any given point of time). Being in the 36,000km circular orbit (Geostationary orbit) allows for communication and monitoring of a large portion of the Earth. Three satellites in GSO orbit are capable of covering nearly the entire globe.

Upgrade

The upgradation of lift capability of GSLV Mk3 to 7.5 tonnes to GTO, is complete. This major upgrade is made possible by the development of two rocket engines: (a) semi-cryogenic engine that burns a special variant of kerosene (dubbed ISROsene) and liquid oxygen; (b) cryogenic engine that burns a mixture of liquid hydrogen and liquid oxygen. The semi-cryogenic engine stage is dubbed as the SC120, and the upgraded cryogenic engine stage is dubbed as the C32. As per ISRO's naming convention for rocket stages, the letter refers to the type of engine fuel-Solid (S), Liquid (L), Semi-cryogenic (SC) and Cryogenic (C) and the accompanying number refers to the mass (in tonnes) of propellant carried. Simply put, a rocket is a combination of multiple engines (stages) that are vertically stacked. The stage will soon be inducted into the rocket, so that India do not have to depend on foreign sources for the launch of heavy communication satellites (weighing over 4 or 5 tonnes).

The configuration of the fleet of five heavy-lift rockets have more powerful rocket stages-SC400 semi-cryogenic stage, the C27 cryogenic stage, and S250 solid rocket booster. Depending on the type of mission, payload to be lifted and rocket required, different variants of engines would be stacked vertically to run a relay race to space. Each stage would detach from the rocket after propelling the rocket to a certain altitude and speed, then the next engine would take over. This process goes on until the satellite (payload) reaches its final orbital destination.

In terms of materials, ISRO is developing carbon-carbon composites, ceramic matrix composite for reusable vehicles, metal-foams for crash landing interplanetary probes, besides crucial components such as solar panels, fibre optics Atomic clocks, deployable antennas, lithium-ion batteries, Application-Specific Integrated Circuits and Micro Electro Mechanical System Devices.

PSLV XL: Height: 44m •Stages: 4 •Lift-off weight: 320 tonnes •Payload mass:1860kg •Orbit:475km Sun Synchronous Polar Orbit; 1300kg in GTO. •Propulsion: Solid & liquid•1st Launch: 20 Sept 1993. Notable: Chandrayaan-1, Mangalyaan, IRS.

GSLV-III •Height: 43.43m •Stages: 3 • Lift-off weight: 640 tonnes •Payload mass: GTO-4000 kg; LEO-10,000 kg •Orbit: GTO. •Propulsion: solid, liquid, Cryogenic 1st Launch: 18 Dec 2014 (suborbital); 5 Jun 2017 (Orbital). Notable: CARE, Chandrayaan-2.

Gaganyaan

Gaganyaan (Sanskrit for SkyCraft), a hugely complex mission to send Indian astronauts to space, is in the making.

ISRO successfully completed a crucial test, Gaganyaan Service Module Propulsion System – System Demonstration Model (SDM), of the Gaganyaan spacecraft's propulsion system, which would help Indian astronauts remain in orbit and also aid their safe return. The expendable rocket's task ends about 16-20 minutes after lift-off and it falls back into the sea (in a phased manner), after ejecting the satellite.

Once placed into orbit, the satellite/spacecraft is an independent entity in space that needs to navigate and propel itself, without the powerful propulsion of the rocket that got it up there. The payload (satellite or the module carrying astronauts) must stay in orbit for a designated mission time, while enduring the harsh conditions of zero-gravity, severe temperature variations, and orbital movement at very high speeds. For example, the International Space Station, which continues to orbit the earth, moves at a whopping 7km/second (27,850km/hour).

While satellites stay in orbit for many years, India's Gaganyaan mission would remain in orbit for up to a week in a designated orbit – requiring use of the spacecraft's own engines. The GSLV Mk3, India's heaviest rocket, is meant to carry the 7.5ton Gaganyaan module into a orbit 170kms from earth and 400kms from earth at its nearest and farthest points in orbit respectively. Thereafter, the Gaganyaan module will be raised to a uniform 400kms low-earth-orbit. Similarly, the same propulsion system would be used to lower the orbit and bring the spacecraft closer to the earth to aid re-entry.

The Gaganyaan integrated module consists of two parts - Crew Module and Service Module. While the crew module will house astronauts, the service module will provide the propulsion to raise the orbit and later lower the orbit. To slow down the spacecraft (traveling at 7.5kms per second) and facilitate re-entry, the five engines are fired on the service module. Once it re-enters earth's gravity, the service module detaches and the crew module alone makes a controlled descent, with its parachutes and crew module propulsion systems.

The Crewed Flight

India's ambitious Human Spaceflight programme requires each propulsion system that goes into the GSLV Mk3 rocket and the spacecraft are undergoing tests. The crew-worthiness tests gives 'Human-rating' of the launch vehicle and its systems, ensuring higher safety and reliability. Four Indian Air Force pilots have been short-listed as prospective astronauts for the Gaganyaan mission– undergoing training in Russia. A separate centre called Human Space Flight Centre has been formed in ISRO for Gaganyaan project. for India's first human spaceflight programme GoI approved $9,023 crore. 1st unmanned mission is scheduled for 2022.

NewSpace India

It is a new Indian space consortium responsible for end-to-end realisation aims 12 numbers per year of solid and liquid fuel-powered stages/engines of the rocket/PSLV, under new contract.

Lunar and Planetary Spacecraft •Chandrayaan-1•Chandrayaan-2 •Mars Orbiter Mission (MOM) •MOM-2 •Chandrayaan-3 & •Shukrayaan-1 (proposed)

Crewed Mission •Gaganyaan

Facilities •Indian Deep Space Network •ISRO Satellite Centre • Telemetry, Tracking and Command Network •Master Control Facility •Satish Dhawan Space Centre •Thumba Equatorial Rocket Launching Station • Satellite Integration and Testing Establishment •VSSC •LPSC • Propulsion Complex

Defence

The Government of India is responsible for protection every part of India and her citizens. The supreme command of the armed forces vests in the President of India. The responsibility of national defence rests with the Union Cabinet.

Indian Army

• It is commanded by the Chief of Army Staff (COAS)–a 4-star general.

• World's 3rd largest military force, has a strength of 1,325,450 personnel. Its force comprises more than 80% of the country's active defence personnel.

•World's largest volunteer army and a reserve of 1,155,000 troops.

• Major military operations: The army has fought 4 wars: 3 with Pakistan and 1 with China. The Indo-Pakistani wars of 1947, 1965 and 1971, the Portuguese-Indian War, the Sino-Indian War, the 1987 Sino-Indian skirmish, the 1999 Kargil War, and the Siachen conflict, 2017 Doklam standoff, 2019 Balkot bombing as a response to Pulwama attack, among others. The other engagements by the army include Operation Vijay, Operation Meghdoot and Operation Cactus.

Structure: The Indian Army follows a regimental system. For operations it is divided into 7 Commands. The basic field formation is called a Division.

Responsibility:•ensure national security and unity •defending the nation from external aggression and threats •maintaining peace and security within its borders, •engage in humanitarian rescue operations (UN peace keeping missions) •during natural calamities •civil wars or coup.

Regiments

A selected list of regiments are – Brigade of the Guards; Parachute Regiment; Mechanised Infantry; Punjab Regiment; the Madras Regiment; the Grenadiers; Maratha Light Infantry; Rajputana Rifles; Rajput Regiment; Jat Regiment; Sikh Regiment; Dogra Regiment; the Garhwal Rifles; Kumaon Regiment; Assam Regiment; Mahar Regiment; Jammu & Kashmir Rifles; Naga Regiment; Gorkha Rifles; the Ladakh Scouts; Rashtriya Rifles; Arunachal Scouts.

Army Aviation Corps: It is part of the Indian Army for tactical air transport, reconnaissance, and medical evacuation, while the Indian Air Force assists the army in troop transport and close air support.

Chief of Army Staff **Manoj M Naravane**

Air Chief Marshal **VR Chaudhari**

Chief of Naval Staff **Karambir Singh**

Director General **K Natarajan**

Chief of Defence Staff **Gen. Bipin Rawat**

Basic Field Formations

Division: Each Division is headed by a General Officer Commanding (GOC) in the rank of Major General. A Division comprises 15,000 combat troops and 8,000 support elements. The Indian Army has 37 Divisions including; 4 RAPIDs (Re-organised Army Plains Infantry Divisions), 18 Infantry Divisions, 10 Mountain Divisions, 3 Armoured Divisions and 2 Artillery Divisions. Each Division composes of several Brigades.

Union Budget for FY 2021-22

The overall defence expenditure planned for FY 2021-2022 is Rs.3,62,345.62 Crore, an increase of Rs.24,792.62 Crore over the Budget Estimates of FY 2020-2021. Clubbing defence pensions, the current allocations become Rs.4.78 Lakh Crore as against Rs.4.71 Lakh Crore in the previous FY, a year-on-year increase of 1.4%. These allocations, including pensions, constitute approximately 2.15% of GDP and excluding pensions, approximately 1.63% of India's projected GDP. The capital outlay for the services Budgeted for (2021-22) • Army : 36481.9 •Navy : 33253.55 • Air Force : 53214.77 • Overall Allocation 135060.72

Top 5 Commissioned Ranks Symbols

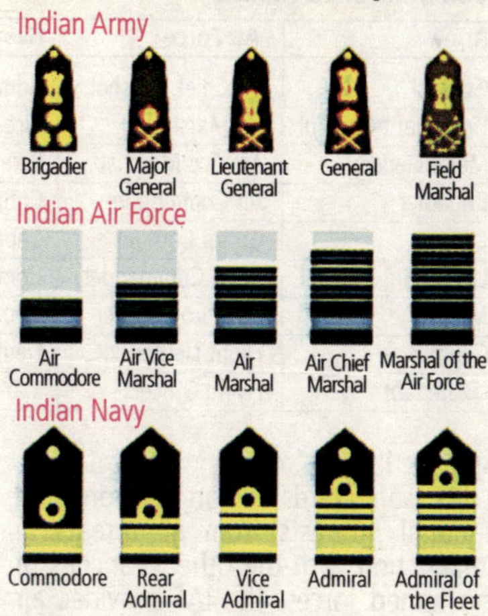

Brigade: A Brigade generally consists of around 3,000 combat troops with supporting elements. An Infantry Brigade usually has 3 Infantry Battalions along with various Support Arms & Services. It is headed by a Brigadier, equivalent to a Brigadier General in some armies. The Indian Army also has 5 Independent Armoured Brigades, which operate directly under the Corps Commander (GOC Corps).

Battalion: A Battalion is commanded by a Colonel and is the Infantry's main fighting unit. It consists of more than 900 combat personnel.

Company: Headed by the Major or Captain, a company comprises 120 soldiers.

Platoon: An intermediate between a Company and Section, a Platoon is headed by a Captain or Lieutenant, or depending on the availability of commissioned officers, even a junior commissioned officer (Subedar). It has a total strength of about 32 troops.

Section: Smallest military outfit with a strength of 10 personnel. Commanded by a non-commissioned officer of the rank of Havaldar or Sergeant.

Commands: The army operates 7 operational commands. Each command is headed by General Officer Commanding-in-Chief with the rank of Lieutenant General. Each command is directly affiliated to the Army HQ in New Delhi. Besides these, army officers may head tri-service commands such as the Strategic Forces Command, Integrated Defence Staff (IDS) and the Andaman and Nicobar Command.

Corps: A corps is an army field formation responsible for a zone within a command theatre. There are 3 types of corps: Strike, Holding and Mixed. A command comprises two or more corps. A corps has Army Divisions under its command. The Corps is the highest field formation in the army.

Indian Air Force

Operational Commands: 5
Functional Commands: 2
Motto: Touch the sky with glory
Size: 127,000 personnel

Commissioned Ranks

Army	Air Force	Navy	Coast Guard
General	Air Chief Marshal	Admiral	Director General
Lieutenant General	Air Marshal	Vice-Admiral	Additional Dir. General
Major General	Air Vice-Marshal	Rear Admiral	Inspector General
Brigadier	Air Commodore	Commodore	Dy. Inspector General
Colonel	Group Captain	Captain	Commandant
Lieutenant Colonel	Wing Commander	Commander	Commandant (Junior)
Major	Squadron Leader	Lieutenant Commander	Dy. Commandant
Captain	Flight Lieutenant	Lieutenant	-no equivalent-
Lieutenant	Flying Officer	Sub-Lieutenant	Assistant Commandant

Approx: 1,588 aircraft

IAF safeguards Indian territory and national interests from all threats in conjunction with the other branches of the armed forces. The IAF provides air support to the Indian Army troops in the battlefield including airlifting. The IAF also operates the Integrated Space Cell along with the civilian Department of Space and the ISRO to utilise the country's space-based resources for military purposes.

Commands: Seven

The President of India is the Commander-in-chief of the Air Force. Chief of the Air Staff with the rank of Air Chief Marshal is the Commander of the IAF.

Operational Commands: Five •Central Air Command, Allahabad; •Eastern Air Command, Shillong; •Western Air Command, New Delhi; •Southern Air Command, Thiruvananthapuram;• S-W Air Command, Gandhinagar.

Functional Commands: • Maintenance Command, Nagpur • Training Command, Bangalore.

Structure

Wings: This formation is intermediate between a Command and a Squadron. It generally consists of two or three IAF Squadrons and Helicopter Units, along with Forward Base Support Units (FBSU). Wings are commanded by a Group Captain.

Squadrons are the field units and formations attached to static locations. A Flying Squadron is a sub-unit of an air force station which carries out the primary task of the IAF. All fighter squadrons are headed by a Commanding Officer with the rank of Wing Commander. Some Transport squadrons and Helicopter Units are headed by a Commanding Officer with the rank of Group Captain.

Flights are sub-divisions of Squadrons, commanded by a Squadron Leader. IAF has service branches for day-to-day operations –Flying Branch, Technical Branch (Engineering), Ground Branch: Logistics, Medical, Meteorological, Admin/Accounts.

Indian Navy

It is the naval branch of the armed forces of India. The Chief of Naval Staff (CNS), usually a four-star officer in the rank of admiral, commands the navy. The primary objective of the navy is to secure the nation's maritime borders besides humanitarian missions, including disaster relief. As of 2018, the Indian Navy had a strength of about 60,000 personnel and a large operational fleet consisting of 2 aircraft carriers, 1 amphibious transport dock, 9 landing ship tanks, 11 destroyers, 15 frigates, one nuclear-powered attack submarine, 14 conventionally-powered attack submarines, 24 corvettes, 7 mine countermeasure vessels, 32 patrol vessels, 4 fleet tankers and various auxiliary vessels.

Commands HQ Location •Western Naval Command – Mumbai •Eastern Naval Command – Visakhapatnam • Southern Naval Command–Kochi.

Indian Coast Guard

ICG started operations on 18 Aug.1978. It is a maritime force that enforces maritime law with jurisdiction over the territorial waters of India, including its exclusive economic zone. The Coast Guard functions closely with Indian Navy, Department of Fisheries, Department of Revenue (Customs) and the Central and State police forces.

Coast Guard Regions • Western Region (W) – Mumbai •Eastern Region (E) – Chennai •North East Region (NE) – Kolkata • North West Region (NW) – Gandhinagar. Each of the regions has districts consisting of Coast Guard Stations, Air Station and Air Enclaves.

Indian Coast Guard Academy: Azhikkal, Kannur district, Kerala. The sailors of ICG are trained with Indian Naval Sailors at INS Chilka. ICG operates a Dornier–maritime surveillance aircraft, HAL Dhruv, HAL Chetak (utility helicopters)

The Integrated Defence Staff (IDS), is an organisation that fosters coordination and enables prioritisation across the different branches of the Indian Armed Forces. It is headed by Chief of IDS – Vice Admiral R. Hari Kumar (2 Dec. 2019). *Role of the IDS*: facilitating functioning of Defence Satellite Control Centre (Integrated Space Cell), the Defence Cyber Agency to look at cyber threats, the Defence Space Agency and the Armed Forces Special Operations Division. HQ IDS: New Delhi.

Integrated Space Cell is operated by the armed forces, the Dept of Space and the ISRO. It aims to utilise the country's satellites for military purposes in coordinaton with all the concerned services.

Highest Order of Security

In India, some high-risk individuals are provided security by the elite squad. Depending on the threat perception to the person, the security is divided into 4 tiers: Z+ (highest level), Z, Y and X.

SPG category – has over 3000 personnel deputed from ITBP, CRPF and CISF. Strength of security detail is Classified. It is provided only to the current and former Prime Minister of India (+parents, spouse and children), Congress interim President Sonia Gandhi, Rahul Gandhi and Priyank Gandhi.

Z+ category has a security cover of 55 personnel [10+ NSG Commando] + [Police Personnel]– armed with Heckler & Koch MP5 submachine guns and modern communication equipment, and each personnel is adept in martial arts and unarmed combat skills.

Z category has a security cover of 22 personnel [4 or 5 NSG Commando] + [Police personnel]

Y category has a security cover of 11 personnel [1 or 2 Commando] + [Police personnel]

X category has a security cover of 2 personnel [No Commando, only Armed Police personnel]

•17 VIPs are provided Z+ protection. •The 'Z' category cover– by Delhi police or ITBP or CRPF personnel and one escort car. •The 'Y' category cover– by 2 personal security officers (PSOs) and •the 'X' category cover – 1 PSO.

Dangers: Indira Gandhi was assassinated by members of her own security detail despite a Z-level security cover. Former Union Minister Pramod Mahajan was shot dead by his brother. Rajiv Gandhi's assassination.

Special Security Forces

Anti-Terrorism Squad Established: 8 July 2004 **Roles**: •gathering information regarding anti-national elements, coordinating with IB, RAW and special State squads, tracking and eliminate activities of mafia, •detect rackets of counterfeit currency notes and smuggling.

Assam Rifles conducts counter insurgency and border security operations in NE.

Border Security Force Established: 1 December 1965. A central para-military force. **Roles**: to guard India's land borders during peacetime• preventing trans-border crimes.

Central Industrial Security Force Established: 15 June 1983. **Roles**: Provide security cover to atomic power plants, space installations, defence units, mints, oil fields and refineries, major ports etc.

Central Reserve Police Force Established: 28 Dec. 1949. **Roles**: •assisting the State/UT in police operations to maintain law and order and contain insurgency. • safety during the general elections.

Commando Battalions for Resolute Action (Cobra) A specialised force within the CRPF. **Roles**: personnels trained and equipped for commando and jungle warfare, • quick operations – mainly in areas affected by Maoist or Naxalites.

Garud Commando Force Established: February 2004. It is an Indian Air Force unit. **Roles**: •protection of IAF installations from terrorist attacks.

Ghatak Force A special unit of the Indian Army. **Roles**: •counter terrorism operations •long range patrols and raids.

Indo-Tibetan Border Police Established: 24 Oct. 1962 **Roles**: •security along the Indo-Tibetan Border. •mountaineering, disaster management, and nuclear, biological and chemical disasters. •UN peacekeeping.

MARCOS A unit of Indian Navy- was seen in action during Operation Pawan and Operation Cactus in 1988 besides deployment in Wular Lake– a terrorists infiltration point.

National Investigation Agency (NIA) **Roles**: •central counter-terrorism law enforcement agency – deals with militancy and insurgency, left-wing extremism, various forms of terrorist attacks and bomb blasts, infiltration from across the borders, complex inter-state and international linkages, smuggling of arms and drugs, pushing in of fake Indian currency, etc.

National Security Guard (NSG) Premier counter-terrorism force, headed by the Director General of the Indian Police Service (IPS). •Also called Black Cats because of the black drill coveralls and balaclavas (assault helmets) they wear. **Roles**: •protecting VIPs, conducting anti-sabotage checks, rescuing hostages, neutralising terrorist threats, engaging terrorists and responding to hijacking and piracy.

Rapid Action Force (RAF) Established: 11 December 1991. Operationalised in October 1992. A specialised wing of the Indian CRPF. It has 10 battalions. **Roles**: •deals with riots during communal violence, and terrorist attacks. •rescue and relief operations during floods, earthquakes, cyclones and outbreak of epidemics.

Research and Analysis Wing (RAW) Established: September 1968. India's external intelligence agency. **Roles**: •counter-terrorism, covert operations •getting information on foreign governments, corporations, and persons.

Special Frontier Force A paramilitary guerrilla force. Governed by RAW.

Special Protection Group (SPG) Established: 1985. **Roles**: •responsible for the security of the PM and other VIPs.

Sashastra Sema Bal A premier paramilitary force in India.

Indian Police

Police are the most visible arm of the State – an index of liberty and rule of law is the strength of a democratic society. Indian Police System is an combination of ancient, Mughal and British policing systems. Various Acts and Enactments promulgated by the colonial rulers powers the system structurally and functionally. The Indian Police Act, 1861 forms the basic foundation of the Indian Police. A Model Police Act, has been formulated and the State governments are in the process of enacting new Police Acts for their respective police organisations.

Functions: •maintenance of public order and peace in society • ensuring protection of citizens •enforces the will of the State.

The State List Police primarily belong to the State list and are identified in relation to their respective States, eg. Kerala Police. Various police matters fall into respective state governments' jurisdiction. As an exception, Delhi Police (of National Capital Region), comes under the Union MoHA.

The Concurrent List : The Indian Police System is horizontally stratified into various cadres and are divided vertically into armed and unarmed branches.

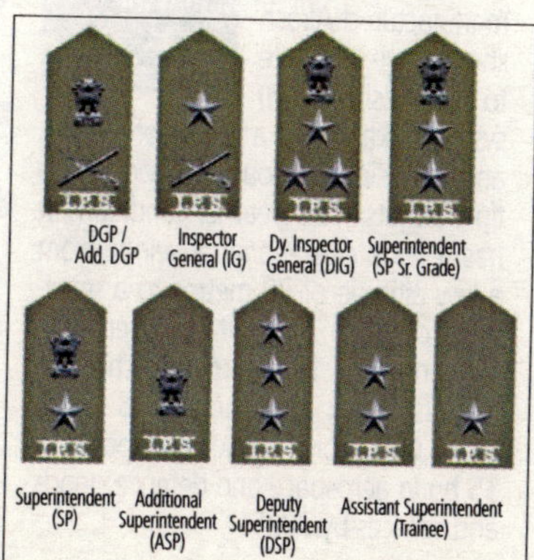

Uniform Colour: Khaki
Service Colour: Dark Blue and Red

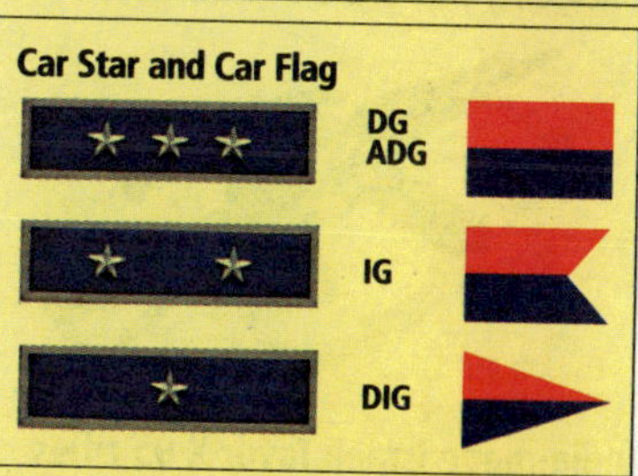

Indian Police Service Officer Rank

CP or DGP Commissioner of Police (State) or Director General of Police[1]

ADL.CP/IGP Additional Commissioner of Police or Inspector General of Police

JCP/DIG Joint Commissioner of Police or Deputy Inspector General of Police

DCP/SSP Deputy Commissioner of Police or Senior Superintendent of Police

DCP/SP Deputy Commissioner of Police or Superintendent of Police

ADL.DCP/ASP Additional Deputy Commissioner of Police or Adl. Supt. of Police

ACP/DSP Assistant Commissioner of Police or Deputy Superintendent of Police

ASST.SP Assistant Superintendent of Police (Probationary Rank: 2 years of service)

ASST.SP Assistant Superintendent of Police (Probationary Rank: 1 year of service)

•[1] Rank insignia of CP/DGP is similar to Spl.CP/ADGP.

Note:
Commissioner of Police designation can only be used by ADL.CP/DIG, JCP/IGP and CP/DGP, where the latter is called Commissioner of Police (State) and the former ones Commissioner of Police (City)• Although DIB is a 4 star post and not a rank, it's given to the senior most IPS officer in Intelligence Bureau.

Defence Acquisitions

AK-103

The Indian Air Force will procure 70,000 AK-103 assault rifles from Russia under an emergency deal of 0 3,000 crore.

India-made Israeli Tavor X 95 rifles

Till recently, India got its Tavor X 95 rifles from the Israel Weapons Industry (IWI). Now, these guns are being made in India and being supplied to the central and state forces

₹48,000 cr. deal to procure 83 LCA

On February 3, MoD awarded a 048,000 crore contract to HAL to supply 83 light combat aircraft (LCA) Mk-1A jets — also called Tejas fighters — to the Indian Air Force. The first Tejas LCA is scheduled to be delivered to the air force in three years. The rest will be supplied 2030.

Israeli SPICE bombs

India has signed a $200 million contract with Israel's Rafael Advanced Defence System. This deal includes the procurement of bomb guidance kits, anti-tank guided missiles, and software-enabled radios. Indian Air Force had employed SPICE kits during the Balakot air strike.

Army seeks high altitude UAVs

The Indian Army ordered an advanced version of SWITCH tactical drones from ideaForge, an Indian company on January 14, which are made to operate in high altitude areas like Ladakh. The deal is worth $20 million (around 0140 crore) and the delivery will take around one year.

'eyes in the sky'

In another boost to 'Make in India', the Defence Acquisition Council gave its go-head for the DRDO to develop six new Airborne Early Warning and Control (AEW&C) planes with a budget of 010,994 crore. They will bridge a critical gap in India's defence preparedness.

HTT- 40 Trainer Aircraft

In addition to the Tejas aircraft, the MoD is looking into procuring HTT-40 trainer aircraft from HAL.

Project 75

The P75I project is a submarine building plan–to build 24 submarines: 18 conventional submarines and six nuclear-powered submarines (SSNs) — as an effective deterrent against China and Pakistan. Currently, India has 14 conventional submarines India and two nuclear-powered submarines — INS Arihant (SSBN, a ballistic missile submarine) and INS Chakra (SSN, a nuclear-powered one) leased from Russia. Six conventional submarines with better sensors and weapons and the Air Independent Propulsion System (AIP) have been approved.

Akash Missile Export

Union Cabinet approved the export of the indigenously developed and manufactured Akash short-range Surface to Air Missile (SAM) system. Akash has a range of 25 km and can simultaneously engage multiple targets in all weather conditions. It has a large operational envelope from a low altitude of 30 metres to a maximum of up to 20 km.It has over 96% indigenisation. India aims to achieve a manufacturing turnover of $25 bn or 01,75,000 crore, including exports of $5 bn in aerospace and defence goods and services by 2025

Indian Nuclear Programme

Nuclear power programme of India is an evolving one. It was formulated by Homi Bhabha in 1950's to secure the country's long term energy independence, through the use of uranium and thorium reserves found in the monazite sands of coastal areas of S. India. •India wants to utilise the rich thorium reserves in meeting the country's energy needs. •India has one of the largest shares of global thorium reserves but has only around 1–2% of the global uranium reserves. •Thorium is not economically viable as global uranium prices are much lower. •Thorium itself is not a fissile material, and thus cannot undergo fission to produce energy. So, it must be transmuted to uranium-233 in a reactor fueled by other fissile materials [plutonium-239 or uranium-235]. •The first two stages, natural uranium-fueled heavy water reactors and plutonium-fueled fast breeder reactors, are intended to generate sufficient fissile material from India's limited uranium resources, so that all its vast thorium reserves can be fully utilized in the third stage of thermal breeder reactors. The 3 stages are: •Pressurized heavy water reactor (PHWR) •Fast breeder reactor (FBR) •Advanced Heavy Water Reactor(AHWR).

Nuclear Supplier Group

NSG is a elite club of 48 nation that seeks to control international non-Proliferation regime through implementation of nuclear and nuclear-related technology and equipment exports. • It was set up in 1974 to counter India's nuclear tests • NSG decision needs full consensus, not simple majority.

China's Checker: China has made India signing the non-proliferation treaty (NPT) a pre-condition to NSG entry. For non-NPT members, the Chinese want some new criteria framed. Countries like China, Turkey, Kazakhstan, Ireland and New Zealand opted for a "process-based"

membership for India.

India and NSG •India sought membership in 2008 – to expand India's civil nuclear sector •In a first, India got a clean waiver from NSG in 2008 to carry out N-commerce despite not having signed the NPT (following India's affirmation of *'No First Use of N-weapons'* policy and its voluntary, unilateral moratorium on N-testing)• India's NSG membership allows access to much-in-demand, nuclear technology.)

NPT

Non Proliferation principle came to be adopted in 1994 whereby a supplier de-

"No First Use" Policy

India first adopted a "No First Use" policy after its second nuclear tests, Pokhran-II, in 1998. •In August 1999, India drafted a doctrine–"nuclear weapons are only for deterrence and that India pursues a policy of "retaliation only". •Recently, during a visit to the Pokharan ranges where India tested its nuclear weapons in 1998, India's defence minister Rajnath Singh indicated that the 'No First Use' doctrine on the use of nuclear weapons will depend on the "future circumstance". It can change in future as no policy is permanently etched that cannot be modified to deal with current realities.•Pokhran witnessed India's two nuclear tests.

NPT Nations

spite rules in the guidelines, allows a transfer only when satisfied that it would not lead to proliferation. •NSG guidelines are internationally legally binding instruments in nuclear non-proliferation like NPT •NPT limits the possession of nukes to the big five countries –US, Russia, UK France and China. India is opposed to this idea and so do not want to sign the NPT.

MTCR

34 nation grouping that controls export of missile technology including drones • Set up in 1987 by Canada, France, Germany, Italy, Japan, the UK and US •India applied for membership in Oct 2015 which was never considered.

Wassenaar Arrangement

The Wassenaar Arrangement (WA) is an elite club of countries which subscribe to arms export controls, similar to the Nuclear Suppliers Group and the Missile Technology Control Regime.

The body came into being in 1996 to succeed the Cold War-era Coordinating Committee for Multilateral Export Controls. The name comes from Wassenaar, a suburb of The Hague, where the agreement to start such a multi-lateral cooperation was reached in 1995.

WA Members : The WA has 42 members – the latest entrant is India. With the exception of China, all the other permanent members of the U.N. Security Council are signatories of the WA.

Working of WA

WA headquarters: Vienna. The goal of the Arrangement is to • promote transparency and greater responsibility in transfers of conventional arms and dual-use goods and technologies • Participants have to ensure that transfers of these items do not contribute to the development or enhancement of military capabilities which undermine the goal • Prevent the acquisition of these items by terrorists.

Wassenaar Control Lists

The Arrangement works according to what it calls WA Control Lists. The con-

trols are subject to ratification by the participants. WA members agree to exchange information on sensitive dual-use goods and technologies and report on such transfers and denials of controlled items to non-participants.

Significance to India

Since it's a non-signatory of the Nuclear Non-Proliferation Treaty, India would look up to the WA membership to boost its credentials to enter NSG. Crucially, China, which stands in the way of India's NSG entry, is not a member of WA.

Are there any Catches?

Critics see WA simply as a Cold War instrument with a different name. According to them Arrangement perpetuates a digital divide by restricting western companies and governments from supplying crucial technologies to emerging markets. The Electronic Frontier Foundation, a digital rights group, has accused the United States of going for even narrower restrictions on technology transfer.

Energy Sector in India

India is the third largest consumer of energy in the world after China and USA but it is not endowed with abundant energy resources. High reliance on imported energy imperils fiscal stability given volatile energy prices, and also impinges adversely on energy security. Achieving 8%-9% economic growth as also meeting the energy requirements of the population at affordable prices, presents a major challenge. It calls for a sustained effort to increase energy efficiency to contain the demand for energy and increase domestic production to keep import dependence at a reasonable level.

The Golden Age of Gas As per International Energy Agency (IEA), if the industry abides by the 'golden rules' proposed by it, the share of gas in the global energy mix could rise from the present levels of 23% to 25% in 2035 overtaking coal (24%), to become the second largest primary energy source after oil (27%). The share of unconventional gas in natural gas could rise from 14% in 2010 to 32% by 2035. Consequently, the emergence of shale gas, holds special relevance for India.

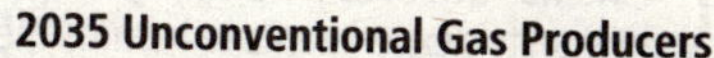

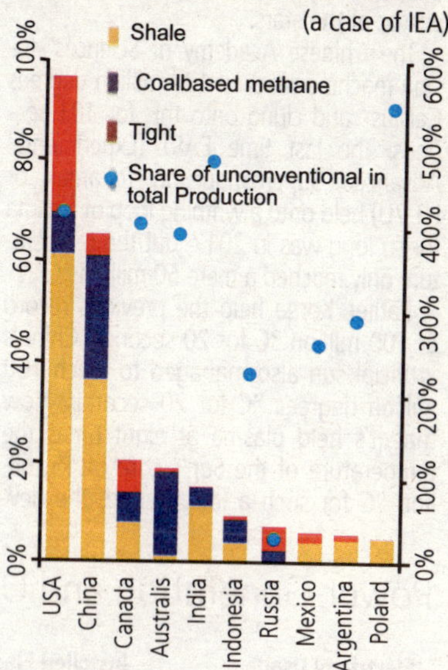

Global Trends in New Gas Sources

Unconventional gas sources are the ones which exist in such reservoirs. They also require specialised technology, depending on the nature of their presence in the specific situation. Traditionally, the following sources of gas have been categorised as un-conventional ones: • Coal bed methane (CBM) • Coal mine methane (CMM) • Shale gas • Tight gas. While the global gas demand is likely to go up by 50% between 2010 and 2035, one third of the above in the year 2035 is likely to come from unconventional sources.

Internationally, unconventional gas, from virtually nil production in 2000 in US, shale gas production has reached a level of 23% in 2010 and is expected to comprise nearly half of total natural gas supply in 2035.

The Source Throughout the world, different types of sedimentary rocks contain natural gas deposits, for example sandstones, limestones and shales. Sandstone rocks often have high permeability, which means that the tiny pores within the rock are well connected and gas can flow easily through the rock. In contrast, shale rocks where gas is trapped as a continuous accumulation throughout a large area usually have very low permeability, making gas production more complex and costly. The shale gas boom in recent years has been due to modern advancement in technology in hydraulic fracturing (fracking) to create extensive artificial fractures around well bores.

'Artificial Sun' Fusion Reactor

China has achieved a new milestone in humanity's experiments to harness the power of the stars.

The Chinese Academy of Sciences' fusion machine reached 120 million degrees Celsius and clung onto this for 101 seconds. The last time EAST (Experimental Advanced Superconducting Tokamak or HT-7U) held onto a writhing loop of plasma for so long was in 2017, but the temperature only reached a mere 50 million °C.

Earlier, Korea held the previous record of 100 million °C for 20 seconds. China's artificial sun also managed to reach 160 million degrees °C for 20 seconds. Now that it's held plasma at eight times the temperature of the Sun's core of 15 million °C for such a long period, the new record has nudged the world ever slightly closer to this elusive, yet highly sought-after clean power source.

According to Southern University of Science and Technology physicist Li Miao, the breakthrough is significant progress, and the ultimate goal should be keeping the temperature at a stable level for a long time.

Nuclear fusion is a great pursuit for a future post-carbon society, but meanwhile, we must do all we can to shift to proven clean power technologies to ensure we can even reach such a future. Every step forward for nuclear fusion certainly is a cause for excitement but there's still a long way to go to get the plasma stable at the required high temperatures.

Power Generation and Use in India

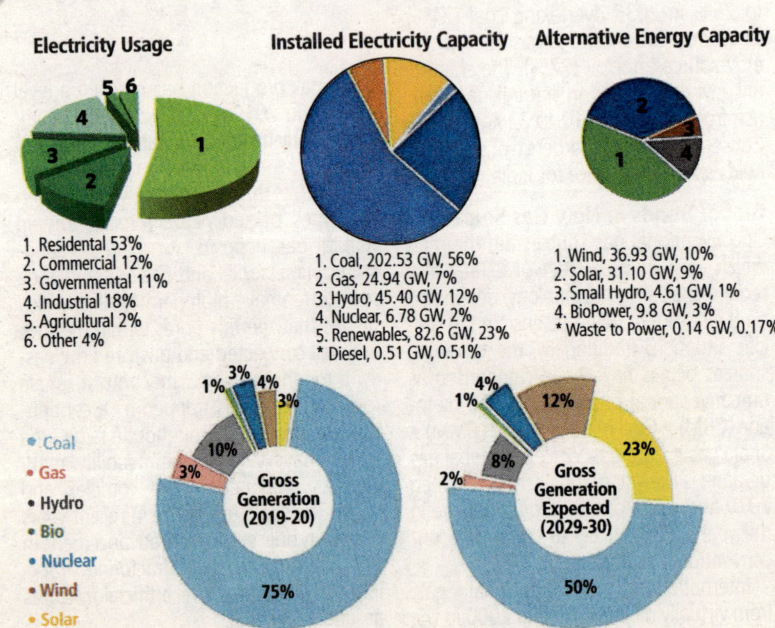

15
POLITY AND GOVERNANCE

- Space Initiatives
- Global Space Economy is $447 Billion
- Defence
- Special Security Forces
- Indian Police
- Indian Nuclear Programme
- Energy Sector in India

The Constitution of India

The Constitution

The word Constitution originates from the Latin word "Constituere" meaning "to establish" and from the Latin adage *salus populi suprema lex* meaning the welfare of people is the supreme law. A Constitution is the framework for the governance of a country which delegates power and authority to the excecutive, the legislative and the judiciary. The purpose of the constitution include conferring powers, rights, functions, principles, restrictions and obligations on individuals as well as the state. It serves maintaining harmonious relations between individuals and the state, and within different organs of the state.It is also an instrument for establishing unity, ensuring citizens rights setting developmental agenda and orderly social change.

The Constituent Assembly (CA)

• Constituted in Nov. 1946 (under the Cabinet Mission Plan 1946.) • Total members - 389 • Members elected indirectly from British India - 296 • Members nominated by princely states. - 93 • It had both Elected and Nominated members. • 1st meeting of CA: Dec.9, 1946. • Muslim League boycotted the CA. • Temporary president of the Assembly - Dr. Sachidanand. • Permanent President of the Assembly - Dr. Rajendra Prasad. Vice President of the Assembly - H.C. Mukherjee. Constitutional Advisor to the Assembly - Sir B.N.Rau

Important Committees

Committee	Chairman
Drafting Committee	: Dr. BR Ambedkar
Flag Committee	: JB. Kriplani
Union Constitution Committee	: Jawaharlal Nehru
Provincial Constitution Committee	: Sardar Vallabhbhai Patel
Union Powers Committee	: Jawaharlal Nehru
Committee on Fundamental Rights and Minorities	: Sardar Vallabhbhai Patel
Special Committee to Examine the Draft Constitution	: (Chairman: Alladi Krishnaswamy Iyer)
Expert Committee on Financial Provisions	
Ad-hoc Committee on Supreme Court	
Ad-hoc Committee on National Flag	
Committee on Chief Commissioners' Provinces	

Drafting Committee

It consisted of 7 members– • Dr. B.R. Ambedkar (Chairman) •N. Gopalaswami Ayyangar •Alladi Krishnaswamy Iyer.•Dr. K.M. Munshi• Syed Muhammad Saadullah •N. Madhava Rao •T.T. Krishnamachari

The Drafting Committee took less than 6 months to prepare its draft. In all it sat only for 141 days. Indian Constitution was formed by a Constituent Assembly in a long time of 2 years, 11 months & 18 days.

Enactment & Enforcement The constitution was adopted on Nov. 26,1949. It contained a Preamble, 395 Articles and 8 Schedules. Now, it has 447 Articles and 12 Schedules. It came into force on January 26,1950 - the first Republic Day.

Features The public document originally had 395 articles divided into 22 parts and 8 schedules. •Lengthiest written Constitution •Supremacy of Constitutions •Republican form of govt. •Secularism • Federal character: Sovereignty of the Country, Parliamentary democracy •Fundamental Rights •Directive Principles.

Flexibility of the Constitution • Supreme in all respects •Can be amended •Separation of powers •Federal nature• Judicial Supremacy •Emergency Provisions.

Salient Features of the Constitution

1. Written Constitution and the Supremacy of the Constitution.
2. Preamble - narrates Justice, Equality, Individual Dignity, Fraternity and National Unity and aspirations of the Indian people.
3. Republic: Sovereign country with a parliamentary democracy where people have the right to elect their own leaders and form their own government.
4. Government: India has a federal system of government in which the different states or provinces of the country have powers to make their own laws and decisions. People vote to choose their rulers through election.
5. Fundamental Rights and Duties: The 6 Rights of citizens which no government can deny. Denial or violation of these rights will invite judicial intervention. There are also 11 duties to be performed by the citizens.
6. Secularism: The principle of secularism– •There shall be no 'State Religion' • The government guarantees freedom of faith and worship to all citizens.
7. Independent and Impartial Judiciary: •All citizens are equal before the law • Justice to be ensured to all sections of the society. •The Supreme Court serves as a guardian of the constitution.
8. Universal Adult Franchise •The system of election of representatives by adults, •Voting right to all above the age of 18.
9. A Welfare State: • Provides equal social, economic and political opportunities to all citizens •Employment and adequate income, food, clothes, shelter and health care so that the citizens can live a peaceful life •The aged, destitute, weaker and marginalised are protected and saved from exploitation.
10. It is federal in form but unitary in spirit.
11. It is neither too flexible (as some provisions require special majority for amendment) nor too rigid (as some provisions can be amended by a simple majority) .

Pillars of the Constitution: Legislature, Executive and Judiciary (known as 'Doctrine of Separation of Power' (Lord Montesquieu). Thus, the Constitution of India is a public document that is considered as the voice of the people. •The Constitution of India is the lengthiest and most detailed compared to any constitution in the world. Today, India is a secular state – a state that does not uphold a particular religion on its own and Articles 25 to 28 give shape to this secularism. It provides for a single citizenship for the whole of India. There is no citizenship for each state. There are 6 Fundamental Rights in the Constitution.

Constitutional Provisions Adopted from Countries British Constitution •Parliamentary form of Govt.; Bicameral legislature •The idea of the Rule of Law •Prime Minister •Council of Ministers •Institution of Speaker •Law-making procedure •CAG •Single citizenship United States Constitution •Written constitution •Charter of fundamental rights •Federal structure of Govt. •Supreme Court; power of judicial review and independence of the judiciary; impeachment of president, judges of both SC and HC •President as the executive head •The post of Vice President- as RS Chairman Soviet Constitution •The idea of the Fundamental Duties (also found in Japanese and Chinese constitutions)• The Planning Commission and Five-Year Plan Canadian Constitution •A Quasi-federal form of Govt. (Federal system with a strong Union Govt.) •The Idea of Residual Powers Australian Constitution •Joint sitting of RS and LS• The idea of the Concurrent List • Centre-State relation •Freedom of trade and commerce inside India S. African Constitution •Constitutional Amendments; election of RS MPs. Germany Constitution •Proclamation of Emergency •Ballot system French Constitution •Republic •Ideals of Liberty, Equality and Fraternity Irish Constitution •Enunciation of Directive Principles of State Policy• Presidential election and nomination of RS MPs. •Federal structure, Governor's office, emergency powers.

The Constitution: Parts

In this section the articles in the constitution are grouped as follows:

Part I – States and union territories
Part II – Citizenship
Part III – Fundamental Rights
Part IV – Directive Principles of State Policy
Part IVA – Fundamental Duties
Part V – The Union
Part VI – The States
Part VII – States in Part B of the first schedule (repealed)
Part VIII – Union Territories
Part IX – Panchayats
Part IXA – Municipalities
Part IXB – Co-operative societies
Part X – Scheduled and tribal areas
Part XI – Relations between the union and the states
Part XII – Finance, property, contracts and suits
Part XIII – Trade and commerce within India
Part XIV – Services under the union and states
Part XIVA – Tribunals
Part XV – Elections
Part XVI – Special provisions relating to certain classes
Part XVII – Languages
Part XVIII – Emergency provisions
Part XIX – Miscellaneous
Part XX – Amending the constitution
Part XXI – Temporary, transitional and special provisions
Part XXII – Short title, date of commencement, authoritative text in Hindi and repeals

The Preamble, with the words "socialist" and "secular", and 'integrity' was added in 1976 by the 42nd amendment.

Schedules

Schedules are basically categories that facilitate governance and policies.

First Schedule (Articles 1, 4): Includes States and UTs, changes in their borders and the laws used to make that change.

Second Schedule (Articles 59(3), 65(3), 75(6), 97, 125, 148(3), 158(3), 164(5), 186 and 221) – Includes the salaries of public officials, judges, and the CAG.

Third Schedule (Articles 75(4), 99, 124(6), 148(2), 164(3), 188 and 219) – Forms of oaths – Includes the oaths of office for elected officials and judges.

Fourth Schedule (Articles 4(1) and 80(2)) – Includes details the allocation of seats in the Rajya Sabha (upper house of Parliament) by state or union territory.

Fifth Schedule (Article 244(1)) – Includes provisions for the administration and control of Scheduled Areas and Scheduled Tribes (requiring special protection).

Sixth Schedule (Articles 244(2) and 275(1)) – Includes provisions made for the administration of tribal areas in Assam, Meghalaya, Tripura, and Mizoram.

Seventh Schedule (Article 246) – Includes Central government, state, and concurrent lists of responsibilities

Eighth Schedule (Articles 344 (1) and 351) – Includes Official languages

Ninth Schedule (Article 31-B) – Includes validation of certain acts and regulations

Tenth Schedule (Articles 102 (2), 191(2)) – Includes Anti-defection provisions for MPs and MLAs.

Eleventh Schedule (Article 243-G): Panchayat Raj (rural local government)

Twelfth Schedule (Article 243-W): Municipalities (urban local government).

Citizenship

The Constitution does not provide a comprehensive provision regarding citizenship in India. Articles 5 to 11 under Part II of the Constitution describes classes of persons who could be considered the citizen of India at the time of commencement of the Constitution that is on 26th January, 1950. The Constitution leaves everything about the citizenship to be regulated by law made by Parliament.

The Constitution Article : Provisions

Article 5: Citizenship at the commencement of the Constitution; **Article 6:** Rights of citizenship of certain persons who have migrated to India from Pakistan; **Article 7**: Rights of citizenship of certain migrants to Pakistan; **Article 8:** Rights of citizenship of certain persons of Indian origin residing outside India; **Article 9:** Persons voluntarily acquiring citizenship of a foreign State not to be citizens; **Article 10**: Continuance of the rights of citizenship; **Article 11**: Parliament to regulate the right of citizenship by law.

Indian Citizenship Act, 1955

It provides for the acquisition and loss of Indian citizenship after the commencement of the Constitution. This Act has been amended four times so far by the Citizenship (Amendment) Acts of 1986, 1992, 2003 and 2005.

Acquisition of Indian Citizenship

The Citizenship Act 1955 provides for the acquisition of Indian Citizenship in five ways; i.e. birth, descent, registration, naturalisation and incorporation of territory.

a. By Birth. Any person born in India, on or after 26th January 1950 but prior to the commencement of the 1986 Act on 1st July 1987, is a citizen of India if either of his parent was a citizen of India at the time of the birth. Further, those born in India on or after 3rd December 2004 are considered citizens of India only if both their parents are citizens of India or if one parent is a citizen of India and the other not an illegal migrant at the time of their birth.

b. By Descent. Person born outside India on or after 26th January 1950 but before 10th December 1992 are citizen of India by descent if their father was a citizen of India at the time of their birth. Persons born outside India on or after 10th December 1992 are considered as citizen of India if either of their parents is a citizen of India at the time of their birth. From 3rd December 2004 onwards, person born outside India shall not be considered citizens of India unless their birth is registered at an Indian consulate within one year with the permission of the Union government.

c. By Registration. Any person, who is not a citizen by virtue of the Constitution or the provisions of the Citizenship Act and belongs to any of the following categories, can apply for registration as a citizen. However, he must have resided in India for at least seven years immediately before making an application for registration as a citizen. They are •a person of India origin who is ordinarily in India for 7 years before making application for registration. (throughout the period of twelve months immediately before making application and for six years in the aggregate in the 8 years preceding the 12 months). • a person of Indian origin who is ordinarily resident in any country or place outside undivided Indian; • a person who is married to a citizen of India and is ordinarily resident in India for seven years before making an application for registration; • minor children of persons who are citizens of India; • a person of full age and capacity whose parents are registered as citizen of India. • a person of full age and capacity who, or either of his parents, was earlier citizen of independent India, and has been residing in India for one years immediately before making an application for registration;

d. By Naturalisation. A foreigner, on application for naturalisation, can acquire Indian citizenship provided he satisfies certain conditions like having normally resided for at least 12 years in India in a period of 14 years before making an application.

Other conditions are: • That he is not a citizen or subject of a country where Indian citizens are prevented from becoming citizens by naturalisation; •2. that he renounces his citizenship of the other country; • that he has either resided in India and/or been in government service for 12 months immediately preceding the date of application; • that during 14 years prior to these 12 months, he has either resided and/or been in government services for not less than 11 years; • that he is of good character; • that he has an adequate knowledge of a language recognised by the Constitution; • that after naturalisation he intends to reside in India.

If the Union government feels that the applicant has rendered distinguished service to the cause of science, philosophy, art, literature, world peace or human progress, it may waive all or any of the above conditions for naturalisation in his case.

e. By Incorporation of territory. If any new territory becomes a part of India, the GoI, the GoI shall notify the persons of that territory to be citizens of India.

Loss of Indian Citizenship

The Citizenship Act, 1955 lays down the three modes by which an Indian citizen may lose his/her citizenship. They are 1. Renunciation is a voluntary act by which a person after acquiring the citizenship of another country gives up Indian citizenship. 2. Termination takes place by operation of law when an India citizen voluntarily acquires the citizenship of another country. Then he automatically ceases to be an Indian citizen. 3. Deprivation is a compulsory termination of the citizenship obtained by Registration or Naturalisation. The citizenship is deprived on the basis of an order of the GoI, if citizenship is acquired by fraud, false representation and concealment of material fact or being disloyal to the Constitution, etc.

Citizenship Amendment Act (CAA)

The bill, now an Act (12 Dec 2019), makes it easier for the minority immigrants of 6 communities i.e. Hindus, Sikhs, Buddhists, Jains, Parsis, and Christians, "forced or compelled to take shelter in India due to persecution on the ground of their religion" from Pakistan, Bangladesh and Afghanistan, to become citizens of India. The Act allows granting the refugees of the six communities Indian citizenship after residing in India for five years.

The Fundamental Rights

• The Right to Equality • Right to Freedom • Right against Exploitation • Right to Freedom of Religion • Cultural and Educational Rights •Right to Constitutional Remedies

The Fundamental Duties (Art.36–51)• It is mentioned in Article 51A under Part IV-A of the Constitution. It was adopted in 1976 by the 42nd Amendment Act. •To abide by the Constitution and respect the ideals and Institutions •To respect the National Flag and the National Anthem •To realize and follow the essential ideals of secularism, democracy and non-violence •To preserve the culture and heritage •To protect the sovereignty, unity and integrity of the nation •To safeguard the public property •To defend the country even at the cost of our life •To protect natural resources •To avoid dowry, gambling, and other social evils •To strive towards excellence in the respective spheres of activities of the individuals.

The Federal Structure of India

The federal structure of the Indian system of governance is a three-tiered system, each tier having executive functions. According to the Constitution of India, the Union or the Central Government is the highest executive body of India. It delineates some of its powers to its constituent political units which are comprised of the State Governments in each state. This is the second tier in the structure. In other words, each state is vested with exclusive executive powers, managed by the ruling governments in each state. The third tier in the federal structure, is the local-level governance of the Panchayats and Municipalities.

The Union Government is divided into three main sections: the executive, the legislature and the Judiciary

Administrative Structure of India

Government of India
State Government(s)
Division(s)
District(s) (*Zill-Parishad*)
Municipal Corporations (Mahanagar-Palika
Municipality(s) (Nagar-Palika)
City Council(s) (Nagar-Panchayat)
Block(s) (Tehsils)
Ward
Villages (Gram Panchayat)

President

Presidential election of 2017 gave India a new President. He is the first citizen of the country and the executive head of the state. He is also the Supreme Commander of the Armed Forces.

Eligibility – Citizen of India; should be aged 35 years; should have qualified for election as a MP of Lok Sabha (LS); should not hold any office of profit under Union/State government or any local authority.

Term: 5 years. Also eligible for re-election.

Election Elected by an electoral college by taking into account the value of vote of MLAs and MPs.

Oath – by chief justice of India or senior most judge of supreme court.

Functions – Executive powers (appointments, ask to prove majority in LS, Supreme Commander of the Armed Forces, can declare war or conclude peace, on the advice of the Union), Legislative powers (Summons and addresses dissolution, nomination, hold joint sessions, give assent to Bills, issue ordinance), Emergency powers (National Emergency (Art. 352); Failure of constitutional machinery in a State (Art. 356); Financial

Emergency (Art. 360), Residual powers (sign international agreements, supreme commander of armed forces) and Judicial powers (seek advice, grant pardon, reprieves or remissions of punishment to any person who has been convicted by a Court of Law).

Term of Office and Emoluments: The President holds office for a period of 5 years. The emoluments are drawn from the Consolidated Fund of India and are, therefore, not votable by the Parliament. He can be re-elected. The presidential retreat houses: The Retreat in Chharabra, Shimla and Rashtrapati Nilayam (President's Place) in Hyderabad.

The Vice President

Eligibility: Citizen of India; should be aged 35 years or above; should have qualified for election as a MP of Rajya Sabha (RS); should not hold any office of profit under Union/ State government or any local authority.

Term: 5 years. Also eligible for re-election.

Election: Elected by an electoral college consisting of the MPs of both Houses of Parliament and according to the system of proportional representation by means of the single transferable vote.

Oath: Administered by the President.

Functions (a) Ex-officio chairman of RS (b) suspend or adjourn the business of the RS (c) issue direction to the Chairman of various committees (d) as Acting-President when vacancy occurs in the office of the President due to his resignation, removal, death or otherwise.

Removal (a) by a resolution of the RS passed by an absolute majority (b) agreed to by the Lok Sabha (LS) and a 14-days advance notice period.

Prime Minister, Council of Ministers

•The Prime Minister is appointed by the President who also appoints other ministers on the advice of Prime Minister – called the Council of Ministers, collectively responsible to the Lok Sabha, to aid and advise the President in the exercise of his functions.

•The Council of Ministers comprises Ministers who are members of Cabinet, Ministers of State (independent charge), Ministers of State and Deputy Ministers.

•The Prime Minister communicates to the President all decisions of Council of Ministers relating to administration of affairs of the Union and proposals for legislation and information relating to them.

Salary of Prime Minister: According to Article 75 of the Constitution of India, the salary of the Prime Minister is decided by the Parliament and revised from time to time. As on 31 July 2012 the monthly pay and allowances of the Prime Minister of India was ₹ 1,60,000 (US $2,600).

Legislature

Union Legislature is called Parliament. It consists of President and two Houses- known as Rajya Sabha (Council of States) and Lok Sabha (House of the People). Each House has to meet within six months of its previous sitting. A joint sitting of two Houses can be held in specific cases.

Rajya Sabha

• It is a permanent body • It is the upper house of the parliament • The term of MPs are 6 years • The Rajya Sabha is not subject to dissolution; 1/3 MPs retire every second year • Rajya Sabha shall consist 250 members (238 representatives of the States and of the UTs, elected indirectly and 12 members nominated directly by the President from among persons having special knowledge or practical experience in respect of such matters as literature, science, art and social service • The presiding officers are the Chairman or the Deputy Chairman. Vice President is the ex-officio chairman of the RS.

Lok Sabha

• It is the lower house of the parliament.

• It is composed of representatives of people chosen by direct election on the basis of adult suffrage • The maximum strength of the House envisaged by the Constitution is now 552 (530 MPs to represent the states, 20 MPs to represent the UTs and not more than two members of the Anglo-Indian community to be nominated by the President, if, in his opinion, that community is not adequately represented in the House).

• The MPs are elected for 5 years. • The presiding officers are the Speaker and Deputy Speaker.

• Following the Constitution's 84th Amendment Act, 2001 the total number of existing seats as allocated to various states in the Lok Sabha on the basis of the 1971 census shall remain unaltered till the first census to be taken after the year 2026.

State Legislature

It could be Bicameral (Legislative Council and Legislative Assembly) or Unicameral (Legislative Assembly) •In a Bicameral system, there will be a Vidhan Parishad (Upper house) or Legislative Council and Vidhan Sabha (Lower House) or Legislative Assembly. •The Vidhan Parishad's maximum strength would be 1/3rd of the total number of MLAs. •The minimum strength would be 40 MLAs. • It elects its members indirectly for a term of 6 years • 1/3 of them retire every second year.

• The Vidhan Sabha, the Lower House, can have a maximum strength of 500 MLAs and a Minumum of 60 MLAs. • MLAs are directly elected and for a term of 5 years.

Panchayati Raj

The term Panchayati Raj in India (PRI) signifies the system of rural local self government. It has been established in all the States of India by the Acts of the state Legislatures to build democracy at the grassroot level. It is entrusted with rural development. It was constitutionalised through the 73rd Constitutional Amend-

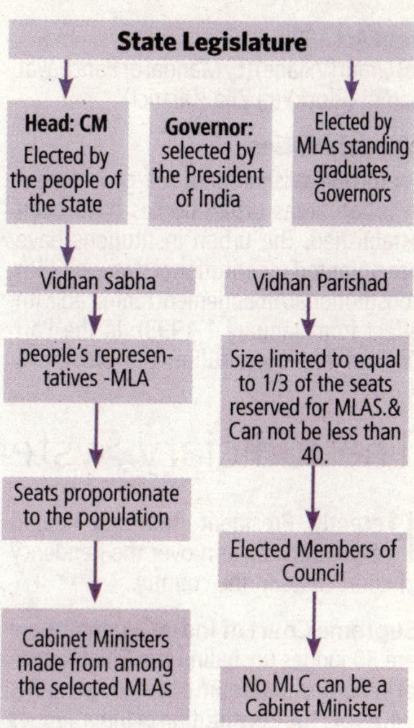

Union Territory

Delhi, Dadra & Nagar Haveli and Daman Diu, Chandigarh, Andaman & Nicobar, Puducherry, Lakshadweep, J&K, Ladakh

Head: CM

Elected by the people of the state

>> Vidhan Sabha

> people's representatives -MLA

> Seats proportionate to the population

Head: Lt. Gov.

Governor: selected by the President of India

> Delhi and Puthuchery has Vidhan Sabha (Legislative Assembly)

ment Act 1992. 3 Types of Panchayati Raj (a) Gram (Village) (b) Mandal or Panchayat Samiti (Block) (c) Zila (District)

Municipalities

For the establishment of self-government in urban areas urban bodies have been established. The urban institutions have been granted constitutional status by 74th constitutional Amendement (enforced with effect from January 1,1993). In the Part IX A of the Constitution the provisions for Municipalities have been made from Article 243 P to 243 ZG. Besides a 12th Schedule also has been incorporated in the Constitution, which contains 18 subjects relating to the jurisdiction of Municipalities. As per this Constitutional Amendment 3 types of urban institutions have been established on the basis of population they are– (d) Nagar Panchayat for a transitional area. (e) Municipal council for a smaller urban area. (f) Municipal corporation for a larger urban area.

The Judiciary System

Recently, President Ramnath Kovind expressed concern over the pendency of court cases in the country.

Supreme Court of India Currently there are 30 judges (including the Chief Justice of India) and maximum possible strength is 34. As per the Constitution of India, judges of the Supreme Court retire at age of 65. Justice Sharad Arvind Bobde is the 47th Chief Justice of India. • As on 1 March 2020, the apex court had 60,469 cases pending. The high member of five or more judge constitutional bench matters that are pending: 551. (5-bench: 402; 7-bench: 13; 9-bench: 136.)

High Court (in each state). Nearly 46 lakh cases are pending before 25 High Courts across the country where 396 posts of judges, out of a sanctioned total of 1079, are vacant. Among the 25 High Courts, the pendency of cases in the highest in Allahabad HC – the biggest High High Court of the country – at 7.32 lakh cases, followed by the High Court of Punjab and Haryana (5.41 lakh), Rajasthan (4.72 lakh). As many as 2.48 lakh cases are pending in the Karnataka High Court. The least number of cases pending are in the Sikkim High Court (237 case), followed by Meghalaya High Court (1,114 cases).

• In the lower courts, the pendency of cases is an astounding 3.19 crore where there are 5,443 fewer judges than the sanctioned strength of 23,597 judges.

• Every state is divided into judicial districts presided over by a District and Sessions Judge. A District Judge is one who presides over a civil case, and a Sessions Judge is one who presides over a criminal case. They are the highest judicial authority below a High Court judge. Below it are courts of civil jurisdiction, in each state.

• District and Sessions Judge's Court: (Over 2067 D and S Judges and 1375 Senior Civil Judges and Chief Judicial Magistrates). • Metropolitan Magistrate's Court • City Civil and Sessions Courts • Subordinate Judge's Court (Civil) • Provincial Small Cause Court • Court of Session (Criminal) • Munsiff's Court (About 4307 Munsiffs Judges) • Nyay Panchayats • Subordinate Magistrate's Court • Panchayat / Adalats • Judicial and Executive Magistrates.

Legislative Process

First Reading

Introduction of a Bill*

Publication of the Bill in Official Gazette

Second Reading

First Stage In the first stage there is discussion on the principles and provisions of the Bill and a motion is passed that: • It is taken into consideration by the House; or •it is referred to Joint Committee of the Houses with the concurrence of Lok Sabha; or •it be circulated for eliciting public opinion

Second Stage •Clause by clause consideration of the Bill as introduced or •as reported by the Select/Joint Committee.

Third Reading

Discussion of motion that the Bill (or the Bill as amended) be or returned (to the Lok Sabha, in case of a Money Bill).

* *Since the inception of Department- related Standing Committee, a new practice has evolved. Now a days, Bills are referred to the concerned Department - related Committees for examination and report thereon by the Presiding Officers once they are introduced in the House.*

Bills

•Government Bills • Private Members' Bills

Original Bills (having new proposals, ideas or policies)

Amending Bills (to modify, amend or revise existing Acts)

Consolidating Bills (to consolidate existing Acts)

Expiring Laws (Continuance) Bills (to continue Acts which will expire after a specific date)

Repealing and Amending Bills (to repeal outdated Acts)

Validating Bills (to give validity to certain actions)

Bills to replace Ordinances; Money and Financial Bills; Constitution Amending Bills

Tribunals in India

Tribunals are institutions established for discharging judicial or quasi-judicial duties. Objectives •To reduce case load of the judiciary •To bring in subject expertise for technical matters •Have the same level of independence from the executive as the judiciary. Several tribunals were established under different Acts since 1980s. The Tribunals Reforms (Rationalisation and Conditions of Service) Bill, 2021 was introduced in Lok Sabha in February. As the Bill was pending at the end of the session, an Ordinance with similar provisions was promulgated in April 2021. They abolish nine tribunals and transfer their functions to existing judicial bodies (mainly High Courts). The Income Tax Appellate Tribunal was established as the first Tribunal in India in 1941. Some others are • Central Administrative Tribunal •Armed Forces Tribunal •National Green Tribunal •Railway Claims Tribunal •Securities Appellate Tribunal

Lok Adalat

न्याय सब के लिए

ACCESS TO JUSTICE FOR ALL

Lok Adalat or the people's court is meant to address public grievance in a participative, accommodative way with fairness, transparency, efficiency and lack of animosity.

Constitutional and Non-constitutional Agencies

Finance Commission This constitutional body is made for distributing financial resources between centre and states. The Finance Commission, according to Article 280, is constituted by the president once in 5 years and it comprises a chairman and four other members appointed by the president.

Comptroller and Auditor-General (CAG) The CAG is the custodian of the entire financial system of the country. The President appoints the person for a period of 6 years or till the age of 65 years and the rank matches that of a Supreme Court judge. It is his duty see that no money is spent outside the Consolidated Fund of India or a state without the authority of proper legislation. The CAG report is presented to the president or the governor, as the case may be, and is finally laid before the parliament or the respective State assembly. He audits all expenditure from the contingency Funds, public accounts of the union and the states, all trading, manufacturing, profit and loss accounts, receipts and expenditure, collection of revenue, allocation of revenue, etc., of the Union or State.

Attorney General (AG) The Attorney General is the highest legal officer of the goverment of India and is appointed by the President. He can hold office during the pleasure of the president. His qualification should be like that of a judge of the Supreme Court. Though AG is not a member of the Cabinet, he has the right to address in the House of Parliment. However, he does not have any right to vote. For performing his official duties the AG is entitled to audience in all courts in India. He gives advice on all legal matters and performs other duties of a legal character, referred to him by the President from time to time. He appears before the Supreme Court and various High Courts in cases involving the Goverment of India.

Advocate General Each state has an Advocate General who is similar to Attorney General of India. He is appointed by the governor of the respective state and can hold office during the pleasure of the governor. A person qualified to be a High Court judge can be appointed Advocate-General. He has the right to address and take part in the proceedings of the state legislative assembly but cannot vote. His functions are similar to those of the Attorney-General.

Election Commission It is an independent body instituted by the Constitution of India to hold free and fair parliamentary elections, assembly elections, president's and vice-president's elections.

Make-up: It comprises Chief Election Commissioner and such other commissioners as the President decides, from time to time. The CEC and other Election Commissioners are appointed by the President for 6 years.

Public Service Commissions Union Public Service Commissions (UPSC) is an independent constitutional body meant to recruit civil servants at the union level. It comprises a Chairman and members for 6 years or until age of 65 years. They are appointed by the President and the President can also remove them. It conducts examinations for appointment to the services of the union and helps the states in operating schemes of joint recruitment.

State Public Service Commission recruit civil servants at the state level. The service conditions of SPSCs members are determined by governor whereas service conditions of Joint PSC are determined by President. The chairman and members of SPSC are appointed by the respective governments and are appointed for 6 years or until age of 62 years.

National Commission for Scheduled Castes and Tribes The President appoints a National Commission for SCs & STs – comprises a chairman, a vice-chairman and 5 other members. The 65th Amendment Act 1990, gives this Commission contitutional status. It has power to investigate every matter relating to the rights and protection provided for SCs and STs under the Constitution and also evaluate the working of the safeguards. It can enquire specific complaints with regard to the denial of rights and safeguards of SCs and STs.

National Commission for Backward Classes The President appoints a commission, under Article 340, to investigate the conditions of the socially and educationally backward classes. After constitution was instituted two 'Backward Class Commissions were appointed - Kaka Saner Kalelkar Committee and BP Mandal Committee. The Commission recommends removal of all problems of Backward Classes so as to raise their social educational and economic standard to a higher level.

NITI Aayog

National Institution for Transforming India (NITI Aayog replaced the Planning Commission) is a think tank that provides policy recommendations. NITI Aayog provides governments at the Union and State levels with appropriate and timely strategies and advice on key elements like national and international, economic front, dissemination of best practices, infusion of new policy ideas and specific issue-based support. Structure: Prime Minister is its chairman.

Lokpal In India, Lokpal is an anti-corruption institution who can investigate on complaints received from individuals against maladministration by public authorities. The position of Lokpal is conceived as the country's watch dog.

Lokayukta At the state level, the anti-corruption institution is called Lokayukta. He/she is appointed by the Governor of the respective state and the term of office is for 5 years or 65 years of age, whichever is earlier.

National Human Rights Commission

In 1993, NHRC as a statutory body, to act as the watch dog of human rights was established in India.It deals with the rights relating to life, liberty, equality and dignity of the individuals guaranteed by the constitution or embodied in the international covenants, enforceable by courts in India. The commission is a multi-member body comprising a chairman and four members. The Chairman and members are appointed by the President. They hold office for a term of 5 years or until they reach the age of 70 years.

List of Important Amendments

As of August 2021, there has been so far 105 amendments to the Indian Constitution (since it was first enacted in 1950). There are three types of amendments to the Constitution of India of which second and third type of amendments are governed by Article 368. The first type of amendments includes that can be passed by "simple majority" in each house of the Parliament of India. The second type of amendments includes that can be effected by the parliament by a prescribed "special majority" in each house. The third type of amendments includes those that require, in addition to such "special majority" in each house of the parliament, ratification by at least one half of the State Legislatures.

Types of Amendments The Indian Constitution is the most amended national constitution in the world.

There are three types of amendments to the Constitution of India of which second and third type of amendments are governed by Article 368.

The first type of amendments includes that can be passed by "simple majority" in each house of the Parliament of India.

The second type of amendments includes that can be effected by the parliament by a prescribed "special majority" in each house; and

The third type of amendments includes those that require, in addition to such "special majority" in each house of the parliament, ratification by at least one half of the State Legislatures.

1st Amendment (1951): Added Ninth Schedule. This amendment provided several new grounds of restrictions to the right to freedom of speech and expression and the right to practise any profession or to carry on any trade or business as contained in Article 19 of the Constitution.

7th Amendment (1956): Re-organisation of States (14 States, 6 UTs).

9th Amendment (1961): Gave effect to the transfer of certain territories to Pakistan in pursuance of the agreement between Governments of India and Pakistan.

31st Amendment (1973): The total strength of Lok Sabha was increased from 525 to 545 (on the basis of Census 1971)

38th Amendment (1975): It sought to make a declaration of Emergency non-judiciable and placed beyond the jurisdiction of courts, the Ordinances and Proclamation of Emergency issued by the President and Governors.

39th Amendment (1975): Placed beyond judicial scrutiny, the election of President, PM and Chairman to either House of Parliament.

42nd Amendment (1976): The working of the Preamble was changed from "Sovereign Democratic Republic" to read as: Sovereign Socialist, Secular Democratic Republic" and changed the description "unity of the nation" to "unity and integrity of the nation". It laid down 10 Fundamental Duties for all citizens.

44th Amendment (1978): The restoration of life of Lok Sabha and State Assemblies to 5 years.

52nd Amendment (1985) Added 10th Schedule which contains provisions as to disqualification on ground of defection.

61st Amendment (1989): Reduced the voting age from 21 to 18 years.

73rd Amendment (1992): Panchayati Raj Bill passed. Constitution of panchayats at village and other levels. Direct elections to all seats in Panchayats and reservation of seats for the SCs and STs and fixing of tenure of 5 years for Panchayats.

74th Amendment (1993): Nagarpalika bill passed. A new Part IX-A relating to the Municipalities was incorporated in the Constitution of 3 types of Municipalities, i.e., Nagar panchayats for areas in transition from a rural area to urban area, Municipal Corporations for larger urban areas. Reservation of seats for SC, ST and women.

85th Amendment (2001): Amended Article 16(4A) to provide for consequential seniority in promotion by virtue of rule of reservation for the government servants belonging to the SCs and STs.

86th Amendment (2002): It provides for (i) insertion of a new article 21A that the State shall provide free and compulsory education to all children of the age of six to fourteen years in such manner as the State may, by law, determine.

88th Amendment (2003): It provides for the insertion of a new Article 268A which states that taxes on services shall be levied by the Government of India and such tax shall be collected and appropriated by the Govt. of India and the States in the manner provided in clause (2).

89th Amendment (2003): It provides for the amendment of Article 338 and insertion of a new article 338A which provides that there shall be a National commission for ST.

91st Amendment (2003): It provides that the total number of Ministers, including the PM, in the Council of Ministers shall not exceed 15% of the total number of members of the Lok Sabha.

93rd Amendment (2005): In this Amendment, a provision has been inserted that the State (i.e., parliament or other legislatures) can make laws for the advancement of the SC, ST or the OBCs of citizens in matters of admission to educational institutions, including private unaided institutions.

95th Amendment (2010): Extended the reservation of SC and ST seats in Lok Sabha and State Assemblies from 60 to 70 years.

99th Amendment (2015): It provides for formation of a National Judicial Appointment Commission.

100th Amendment (2015): It provides for amending First Schedule, that deals with acquisition of certain territories of Bangladesh following agreement between India and Bangladesh.

101st Amendment (2017): The Constitutional 101st Amendment Act, 2016, contains the provisions necessary for the implementation of GST Regime. The amendment Act contains 20 amendments. The important changes made in constitution (new articles / amended articles) via this law are Article 246 (A), Article 269A, and Article 279-A. Changes in the 7th Schedule are in the Union List and State List.

102 Amendment (2018): It gives constitutional status to National Commission for Backward Classes addition of Articles 338B, 342A and a Clause 26C. It removed Article 340 and modified Article 338 and 366.

103 Amendment (2019): The Reservation Act provides for a maximum of 10% reservation for economically weaker sections of citizens of classes other the classes mentioned in Clauses 4 & 5 of Article 15 (other than socially and educationally backward SCs and STs) and in amendment added Clause 6 under Article 15 and Clause 6 under Article 16.

104 Amendment 2020: To extend the reservation of seats for SCs and STs in Lok Sabha and Vidhan Sabha (State Assemblies) from 70 years to 80 years. It removed the reserved seat for the Anglo-Indian community in the LS and State Assemblies. The amendment of Article 334 was passed on 25th January.

105th Amendment (2021): It restores the power of State Governments to identify and specify Socially and Economically Backward Classes (SEBCs). It received the assent of the President of India. The Constitution (127th amendment) Bill 2021 was passed by the Parliament on 11th August, 2021.

Salaries

This is a list of Government positions and the monthly Salaries it draws and emoluments in the Indian order of precedence

Position **Basic Pay/month Other Emoluments & Allowances**

President ₹ 5L + Other allowances
Vice-President ₹ 4L + Other allowances
Prime Minister ₹1.6L (like a LS/RS MP) + allowances as a MP + Other allowances
Governors of States ₹ 3.5L + Other allowances
Chief Justice of India ₹ 2.8L + Other allowances
Judges of Supreme Court ₹ 2.5L + Other allowances
Chief Election Commissioner of India ₹ 2.5L + Other allowances.
Comptroller and Auditor General of India ₹ 2.5L + Other allowances
Chairman, Union Public Service Commission ₹ 2.5L + Other allowances
Cabinet Secretary of India ₹ 2.5L + Other allowances. Senior-most civil servant in GoI
Chiefs of Staff (Army, Air, Naval) ₹ 2.5L + Other allowances. Senior-most Armed Forces personnel in the rank of General and equivalent ranks
Chief Justice of High Courts ₹ 2.5L + Other allowances
Judges of High Courts ₹ 2.25L + Other allowances
MPs ₹ 1.0L + Parliament office allowance ₹ 45,000 + Parliament session allowance ₹2,000 per day + Constituency allowances ₹ 45,000.
Lieutenants Governor (UTs) ₹ 1.1L + Other allowances
Chief Ministers The salary vary from state to state (as of 2019)
Telangana ₹ 4.10L; Delhi ₹ 3.90L; UP ₹3.65L; Maharashtra ₹ 3.40L; Andhra Pradesh ₹3.35L; Gujarat ₹ 3.21L; Himachal Pradesh ₹3.1L; Haryana ₹2.88L; Jharkhand ₹ 2.72L; MP ₹2.55L; Chhattisgarh ₹2.3L; Punjab ₹2.3L; Goa ₹2.2L; Bihar ₹2.15L; West Bengal ₹2.10L; Tamil Nadu ₹2.05L; Karnataka ₹2.0L; Sikkim ₹1.9L; Tripura ₹1.85L; Kerala ₹1.85L; Mizoram ₹1.84L; Rajasthan ₹1.75L; Uttarakhand ₹1.75L; Odisha ₹1.6L; Meghalaya ₹1.5L; Arunachal Pradesh ₹1.33L; Asom ₹1.25L; Manipur ₹1.20L; Puducherry ₹1.2L; Nagaland ₹1.1L.
MLA (Art. 164): Highest ₹2.5L (Telangana); Lowest 20,000 (Tripura, Meghalaya)+ others
Secretaries (GoI), **Sp. Secretaries** (GoI)**, Vice Chief of Army Staff/Commanders** ₹ 2.25L + Other allowances. (in the rank of Lieutenant General and equivalent ranks in Indian Armed Forces)
Chief Secretaries of State Governments, Add. Chief/Sp. Chief Secretaries ₹ 2.25L + Other allowances. Senior-most civil servant (State Government)s)
Additional Secretaries (GoI) ₹1.82L (Min. Pay) to ₹ 2.24L (Max. Pay) + Other allowances.
Principal Secretaries (State Governments) ₹ 1.82L (Min. Pay) to ₹ 2.24L (Max. Pay) + Other allowances
Joint Secretaries(GoI), **Major General** and equivalent ranks in Indian Armed Forces ₹1.44L (Min. Pay) to ₹ 2.18L (Max. Pay) + Other allowances
Secretaries (State Governments) ₹1.44L to ₹2.18L +Other allowances

** *Notes:* The salary includes the Basic Pay, Dearness Allowance and House Rent Allowance.

The Electoral System

Election Commission of India is a constitutional institution created under Article 324 of the Constitution of India. It came into being on January 25, 1950. The Constitution provides for the Election Commission to be a multi-member body, depending upon the requirements from time to time. Since its creation, the Commission was a single member body. From 16.10.1989 – 01.01.1990 it was

Sushil Chandra

Rajiv Kumar

Anup CP

Present Election Commission: Sushil Chandra is the Chief Election Commissioner. EC: Rajiv Kumar and Anup CP.

First Chief Election Commissioner Sukumar Sen served from 21.03.1950 – 19.12.1958.

First Woman Chief Election Commissioner Ramadevi VS was CEC from 26.11.1990–11.12.1990. Her successor was TN Seshan.

Union Electoral Map

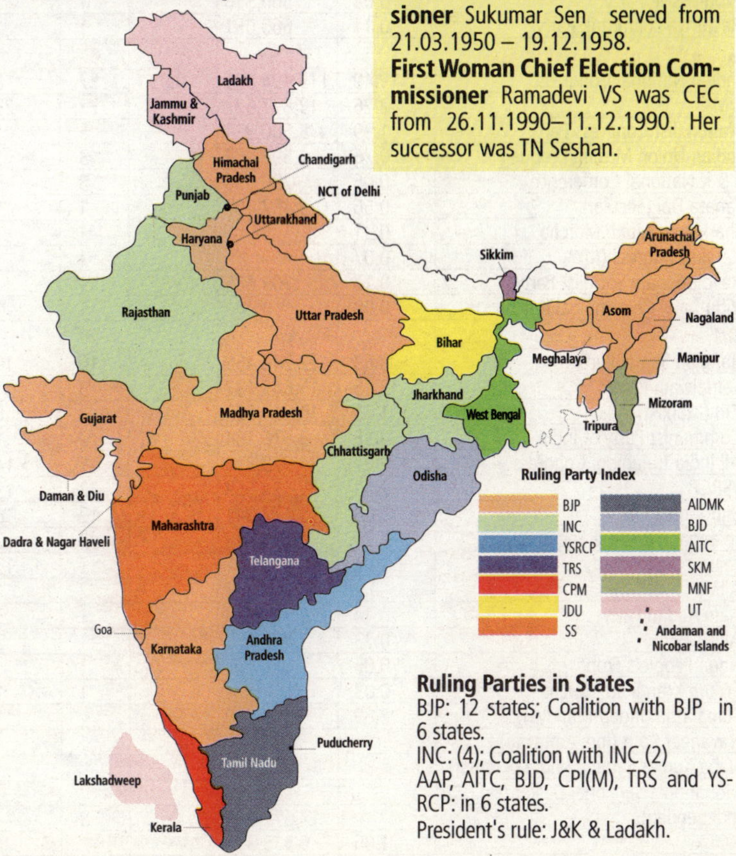

Ruling Parties in States

BJP: 12 states; Coalition with BJP in 6 states.
INC: (4); Coalition with INC (2)
AAP, AITC, BJD, CPI(M), TRS and YSRCP: in 6 states.
President's rule: J&K & Ladakh.

17th Lok Sabha Election Results (2019)

Alliance / Party	Votes			Seats	
	Share %	Total	Swing	Won	Swing
National Democratic Alliance				**353**	
BJP	37.36	229,075,170	6.02	303	21
Shiv Sena	2.1	12,858,904		18	
Janata Dal (United)	1.46	8,926,679		16	14
Lok Jan Shakti Party	0.52	3,206,979		6	
Apna Dal (Sonelal)	0.17	1,039,478		2	
Shiromani Akali Dal	0.62	3,778,574		2	2
AIADMK	1.28	7,830,520		1	36
All Jharkhand Students Union	0.11	648,277		1	1
Mizo National Front	0.04	224,286		1	1
National People's Party	0.07	425,986		1	
Nationalist Democratic Progressive Party	0.08	500,510		1	1
Rashtriya Loktantrik Party	0.11	660,051		1	1
United Progressive Alliance				**92**	
Indian National Congress	19.49	119,494,885	0.03	52	8
DMK	2.26	13,877,622		23	23
Nationalist Congress Party	1.39	8,500,331		5	1
Indian Union Muslim League	0.26	1,592,467		3	1
J & K National Conference	0.05	280,356		3	3
Janata Dal (Secular)	0.56	3,457,107		1	1
Jharkhand Mukti Morcha	0.31			1	1
Kerala Congress (M)	0.07			1	
Revolutionary Socialist Party	0.12	709,685		1	
Viduthalai Chiruthaigal Katchi	0.08			1	1
Others				**97**	
Bahujan Samaj Party	3.63	22,246,455		10	10
Samajwadi Party	2.55	15,647,182		5	
CPI (Marxist)	1.75	10,744,779		3	6
Communist Party of India	0.58	3,576,184		2	1
All India Trinamool Congress	4.07	24,929,325		22	14
YSRCP	2.53	15,534,558		22	13
Biju Janata Dal	1.66	10,172,041		12	8
Telangana Rashtra Samithi	1.26	7,696,848		9	2
Telugu Desam Party	2.04	12,513,061		3	13
AIIMM	0.2	1,201,542		2	1
Aam Aadmi Party	0.44	2,716,629		1	3
All UDF	0.23	1,402,088		1	2
Naga People's Front	0.06			1	
Sikkim Krantikari Morcha	0.03			1	1
Sumalatha (Indep-Mandya)	2.69	703,660		-	1
Navaneet Kaur (Ind, Amravati)		510,947			
Naba Kumar Sarania (Ind, Kokrajhar)		484,560			
Mohanbhai Sanjibhai Delkar (Ind,D&NH)		90,421			
Independents		14,677,631		3	
NOTA	1.06	6,513,315			

Parliament Seat Division

converted into a three member body. From 2 Jan. 1990 to 30 Sep 1993 it was a single member commission and again since 01.10.1993, the Commission has been a three-member body, consisting of the Chief Election Commissioner and two Election Commissioners. Election Commission of India conducts elections to the offices of President & Vice President of India, both houses of Parliament (Lok Sabha & Rajya Sabha), State Legislative Assemblies and State Legislative Councils. The first Chief Election Commissioner was appointed on March 21, 1950.

Election Types

General Election: Lok Sabha
Election to Rajya Sabha
Election of Presidents and Vice Presidents
Assembly Election: State Assembles
Bye-Election: on Vacancy
Elections in Local government bodies

State Assembly Party Position (25.09.2021)

Andhra Pradesh: 2019-2024

Total Seats: 175

YSRCP............ 150
TDP.................. 23
JSP..................... 1

Arunachal Pradesh: 2019-2024
Total Seats: 60

BJP 48
Congress........... 4
JD (U) 7
NPP 4
AITC 1

Asom: 2021-2026
Total Seats: 126

BJP 59
AGP.................. 9
BPF................... 3
INC.................. 27
AIUDF............. 15
Others 1

Bihar: 2020-2025
Total Seats : 243

JD(U) 43
BJP 74
RJD.................. 75
LJP..................... 2
INC.................. 26
CPI(ML)............ 12
AIMIM 5
HAM 4
VIP 4
Others.......... 6 V:2

Chhattisgarh: 2019-2024
Total Seats: 90

BJP 14
INC.................. 70
BSP.................... 2
JCC 4 V:0

Delhi : 2020-2025
Total Seats : 70

AAP 62
BJP 8
INC.................... 0
Ind..................... 0

Goa: 2017-2022
Total Seats : 40

Congress........... 5
BJP 27
MGP 1
GFP 3
NCP 1
Ind..................... 3

Gujarat: 2017-2022
Total Seats: 182

BJP 112
INC.................. 65
NCP 1
BTP.................... 2
Ind.............. 1, V1

Haryana: 2019-2024
Total Seats: 90

BJP 40
Congress.......... 31
INLD 1
JJP 10
HLP..................... 1
Ind............. 7. V:1

Himachal Pradesh: 2017-22
Total Seats: 68

BJP 43
INC.................. 19
CPI-M 1
Ind.............. 2 V. 3

Jharkhand: 2019-2024
Total Seats : 81

BJP 26
JMM 30
INC.................. 18
Ind. 2
Others......... 3. V:0

Karnataka: 2019-2024
Total Seats: 224

BJP 119
INC.................. 68
JD (S).............. 32

Others......... 0. V:2

Kerala: 2021-2026
Total Seats : 140

LDF.................. 91
-CPI-M............. 59
-CPI................. 17
-JD (S)............... 2
NCP.................. 2
-Kerala Congress (B).................... 1
RMPI.................. 1
C (S) 1
UDF.................. 47
-INC.................. 21
-IUML.............. 15
-K. Cong. (M)..... 5
-Kerala Congress (Jacob)............. 1
BJP.................... 0
Ind 6. V:0

Madhya Pradesh: 2019-2024
Total Seats: 230

BJP 125
INC.................. 95
SP..................... 0
Ind............. 0. V:3

Maharashtra: 2019-2024
Total Seats: 288

BJP 106
Shiv Sena......... 57
Congress.......... 44
NCP................ 53
MNS 1
CPM 1
SP...................... 2
PWPI 1
Others............. 17

Manipur: 2017-2022
Total Seats: 60

INC.................. 17
BJP 24
NPF 4
Others....... 7. V:11

Meghalaya: 2018-2023
Total seats: 60

INC................ 17
NPP 21
UDP.................. 8
PDF 4
BJP 2
HSPDP 2
NCP 1
KHNAM 1
Ind. 2

Mizoram: 2018-2023
Total Seats: 40

Congress........... 5
MNF 27
Zoram Peoples Movt................ 6
BJP 1

Nagaland: 2018-2023
Total Seats : 60

NPF 25
NDPP.............. 20
BJP 12
NPP 0
JD (U) 0
Ind.................... 1

Odisha: 2019-2024
Total Seats: 147

BJD............... 113
BJP 22
INC..................... 9
Others 1. v:1

Punjab: 2017-2022
Total Seats: 117

SAD (Badal)..... 14
BJP 2
INC.................. 80
AAP 16
Others 0 V.3

Rajasthan: 2019-2024
Total Seats: 200

INC............... 106
BJP 71
BTP.................. 2
RLP.................. 3
Others............... 0
Ind.................. 12

Sikkim: 2019-2024
Total Seats: 32

SKM 19
SDF.................. 1
BJP 12

Tamil Nadu: 2021-2026
Total Seats : 234

AIADMK........... 66
DMK 133
INC................. 18
VCK.................. 4
PMK 5. V:0

Telangana: 2018-2023
Total Seats: 119

TRS............... 103
AIMIM 7
BJP 2
INC.................... 6
Vacant 1

Tripura: 2018-2023
Total Seats: 60

BJP 36
CPI-M 16
IPFT 7
Vacant 1

Uttarakhand: 2017-2022
Total Seats: 70

BJP 56
INC.................. 10
Ohers...........2 V. 2

Uttar Pradesh: 2017-2022
Total Seats: 403

BJP 305
BSP................. 18
INC.................... 7
SBSP.................. 4
Apna Dal-S 9
Vacant 8

West Bengal: 2021-2026
Total Seats : 294

AITC 211
INC.................... 0
CPM 0
BJP 74
AIFB 2
CPI 1
GJM-T 1............ 3
Others.......... 1 V. 7

Puduchery: 2021-2026
Total Seats: 30

INC................... 2
DMK.................. 6
AINRC............. 10
AIADMK............ 0
Others............... 6

Jammu & Kashmir
(has been bifurcated into UT of J&K and Ladakh. The Assembly has been dissolved. They are now governed by Governors.)# **1**

Centre-State Relations

The basic provisions regarding the distribution of powers between the union and provincial governments are in Part XI and XII of the constitution. Both the Union and the states derive their authority and powers – Legislative, Executive and Financial from the constitution. A total of 56 Articles beginning Article 245 to 300 deal with the state relations.

Centre-State Relation Committees (a) Setalvad Com. (1966) (b) Rajamannar Com. (1969) (c) Sarkaria Com. (1983)

Centre-State Division of Legislative powers Union List (97 subjects); State List (66 subjects); Concurrent List (52 subjects).

Select Subjects from the Lists

Union List (a) atomic energy and mine resources (b) extradition (c) banking (d) insurance. (e) stock exchanges and future markets. (f) patents, inventions and designs,copyright; trademarks, merchandise marks. (g) census (h) corporation tax (i) any other matter not enumerated in lists including any tax not mentioned in either of those lists.

State List (a) public order (b) local government (c) public health and sanitation (d) libraries, museums and other similar institutions (e) agriculture (f) fisheries (g) gas and allied works (h) markets and fairs (i) captivation taxes.

Concurrent List (a) Criminal law (b) Criminal procedure (c) Preventive detention (d) Marriage and divorce (e) Transfer of property other than agricultural land. (f) Contracts (g) Civil procedure (h) Contempt of court, but not including contempt of the Supreme Court (i) Prevention of cruelty to animals (j) Economic and social planning (k) Legal, medical and other professions (l) Electricity (m) Archaeological sites.

Zonal Council In 1956, five Zonal Councils were formed on the basis of recommendation of States Reorganization Commission – North, South, East, West and Central and the sixth zonal council–North-east was set up in 1971.

Aims: (a) to promote collective approach and sorting out common problems of the member states. (b) for cooperation in implementing development plans.

Inter-State Relations

The Inter-State Council is a constitutional body mandated to investigate and advise on disputes between states and to facilitate coordination between states and the centre. It is headed by the Prime Minister. It is set up on the basis of provisions in Article 263 of the Constitution by a Presidential Order, 1990, based on the recommendation of Sarkaria Commission.

The Inter-State Council has as members finance ministers of states.

Inter State Council Members: Prime Minister, Chairman; CMs of all states; CMs of UTs with legislative assemblies; Administrators-UTs; Six union cabinet ministers, including home minister, to be nominated by prime minister and Governors of states under president's rule.

The Major Disputes: • A major problem is over how taxes are to be shared between different states • The southern states complaint about the terms of reference of the 15th Finance Commission, in effect, seems like punishment for their better economic performance • The river water dispute • The dam issue • The border issues • Common State capitals • The linguistic issues • The migrants and labour issue •The cross border crime, narcotics, trafficking and the smuggling issues.

The eGovernance

Time and again it has been noted that e-Governance initiatives adoption and success varied across geography, mainly on account of prevalence of diversity in India. The pandemic has added a new component to the citizens' relationship with the government. What is it? eGovernance! The world bank defines e-Government as "...the use by government agencies of information technologies (such as Wide Area Networks, the Internet, and mobile computing) that have the ability to transform relations with citizens, businesses, and other arms of government. These technologies can serve a variety of different ends: better delivery of government services to citizens, improved interactions with business and industry, citizen empowerment through access to information, or more efficient government management.... Moreover the availability of smartphones made the difference. " On the other hand, e-Governance has been referred to as the use of Information and Communication Technologies (ICTs) by the public sector with an aim to making the government accountable, increase and promote transparency, enhance information and service delivery and encourage participation of citizen in the decision making process.

Due to the ongoing COVID-19 epidemic, which was declared a pandemic by the WHO on March 11, 2020, e-Governance initiatives have gained interest among the governments across the world at unprecedented levels, especially in case of a large country like India which has to cater to a population of almost 1.3 billion people. As a response to the pandemic, like most of other countries in the world, India too had resorted to a nationwide lockdown. The Government of India initially announced a 21 days nationwide lockdown beginning from March 25, 2020, which was further extended Statewise in a graded manner in 2021 with a view to prevent the Stage-III spread of virus in the country. At present, India has started to open up its economy in a phased manner and is currently going through Phase-V (as on October 2020) of the unlocking with travel restrictions being relaxed. Up till now India, has registered 3.36Crore total confirmed cases of COVID-19 with 4.47 lakh fatalities (as on Sept 25, 2021)

In its fight against Covid 19, India has leveraged e-Governance for various kinds of information dissemination, tracing and monitoring activities. One such notable initiative is the ArogyaSetu app which is a contact tracing, syndromic mapping and self-assessment digital service (https://aarogyasetu.gov.in/). The app had seen 16,25,00,000 downloads, as on October 30, 2020, since its launch in May 2020. Another such e-Governance initiative was the e-Pass service delivered through the service plus framework and was used by 17 states of India to provide movement e-Pass services during COVID-19 pandemic (https://serviceonline.gov.in/epass/). In another such use of e-Governance, information on availability of hospital beds, related to Covid-19 treatment, was made available by Delhi Government. The said initiative was coupled with a helpline number to raise grievance, in case the patient in not admitted in a treatment facility . e-Governance services have helped India in responding to the Covid-19 situation in an expeditious manner and has continued to act as a strategic asset in the fight against Covid-19.

India has made numerous efforts related to launch and adoption of e-Governance initiatives, which has been introduced in various fields..Furthermore, post COVID, the importance of e-Governance initiatives in the lives of citizens at large, has witnessed a paradigm shift both in applicability as well as acceptance. The enforcement of social distancing by Central as well as Local governments in the past year has led to enhanced role of e-Governance initiatives in delivering critical to common services/facilities to the citizens at large. Every time the government uses an e-governance technology, it results in more efficiency, lesser costs, lesser manpower requirement and lesser physical presence of humans in the job at hand.

The biggest achievement of Digital India has been its tremendous success in ensuring digital inclusion for all in India. India is able to reach almost all citizens including those living in rural and remote areas, with completely online digital services. Technology has been a great enabler for governance and service delivery to citizens and businesses. India's vision is to transform India into a digitally empowered society and grow our digital economy to reach at least USD 1 trillion. So E-governance possibilities in India for the post-COVID-19 era are great and still emerging.

Probity in Governance

Probity in governance is essential for an efficient and effective system of governance and for socio-economic development. It demands ensuring procedural integrity. It is concerned with procedures, processes and systems rather than outcomes.

The best probity processes do not however guarantee an institution be immune from problems or criticism. It requires that the institution act ethically, impartially, honestly and with fairness. To make probity in governance, government must eliminate corruption. The other requirements are effective engagement of rule of law, and regulations governing every aspect of public life and, a fair implementation of those laws. Surely, a proper, fair and effective enforcement of law is the fruit of discipline. Sadly for India, discipline has not been there in the public life and sphere. According to Gunnyar Myrdal, the Scandinavian economist-sociologist, 'no real progress is possible without discipline.' Discipline implies public and private morality and a sense of honesty. In the Western nations a man who rises to positions of higher authority develops greater respect for laws, but in our country it is found wanting. Here, the mark of a person holding high position is the ease with which he can ignore the laws and regulations. We are being swamped by a culture of indiscipline and untruth; morality, both public and private, is at a premium.

To improve the situation some legislative measures can be designed to ensure probity in governance. Instilling a sense of discipline among the citizens is more the function of the society, its leaders, political parties and public figures and less a matter which can be legislated upon. For that purpose g-governance is contemplated.

e-Governance is about carrying out the functions and achieving the results of governance by using IT network to ensure equitable access to public services and the benefits of economic growth to all. It brings transparency in government dealings, accountablity for its activities and faster responses as part of good governance. **e-Pramaan** is a national e-Authentication framework, facilitating security for users accessing various government services on mobile and fixed platforms.

Indian Penal Code

The IPC was enacted in 1860, while the Indian Evidence Act came into effect in 1872 and the CrPC in 1973.

The current provisions of the CrPC give the state, victim and the accused the right to appeal against lower court judgements before a higher court, in order to avoid any miscarriage of justice. However, this clause has led to inordinate delays in certain cases, like the 2012 Nirbhaya gang-rape and murder where the convicts are using legal remedies to seek relief from capital punishment. The new laws should reflect the modern reality and they should be in accordance with democratic aspirations of the people and provide speedy justice to women, children and the weaker sections of people

The Home ministry, in consultation with the Bureau of Police Research and Development (BPR&D), is considering amendments to the Indian Penal Code (IPC), Code of Criminal Procedure (CrPC) and Evidence Act, and these are among the proposals being looked into. Some of the features of the inquisitorial system could be adopted to strengthen the current adversarial system to make it more effective. This was among the recommendations of the 2003 Malimath committee, set up by the then home minister LK Advani to suggest reforms on the criminal justice system.

Under IPC, classifications like blue collar, white-collar, black-collar, red collar and green-collar crimes have been suggested to equip and empower the police to deal with complex dynamics of internal security. Another suggestion is on setting up of modus operandi bureaus at the national and state levels to study the technique of crime and the mentality of criminal.

Crime in India Report (NCRB), 2017

• Crime against women: 3,59,849 cases of were reported in the country. UP topped the list with 56,011 cases followed by Maharashtra with 31,979 cases and West Bengal 30,002. • Crimes per 1 lakh population Delhi topped the list in terms of, with Kerala the second highest.

Crime against women The number of crimes committed against women have increased in 2017 by 6% compared to 2016 and by 9% compared to 2015. Majority of cases under crimes against women were registered under •Cruelty by Husband or his Relatives: 27.9% •Assault on Women with Intent to Outrage her Modesty: 21.7%. •Kidnapping & Abduction of Women:20.5%. •Rape' (7.0%).

Rioting: Total: 58,880. Bihar: 11,698;UP - 8,990; Maharashtra:7,743.

Metropolitan city Crimes Hyderabad :2.7% of the overall national figure;.National capital: 40.4% of the crimes in metros occurring in the city. Bengaluru (8.9%), Mumbai (7.2%) and Chennai (3.6%).

Crime against the elderly Tamil Nadu topped the country in murder, against senior citizens. Maharashtra reported incidents of robbery and snatching targeting elders. Tamil Nadu:188 senior citizens murdered (62 senior citizens were victims of attempt-to-murder) Maharashtra: 152 (66 senior citizens were victims of attempt-to-murder) UP: 127.

Cyber Crime A 77% rise in the number of cyber crime cases was observed in 2017 compared to 2016. Uttar Pradesh, Maharashtra and Karnataka registered the maximum number of such cases.

Road Accidents Delhi: 1,451 victims in 1,317 accidents caused due to negligence, while Chennai was in second place with 1,404 victims in 1,312 road accidents. Of these, 176 were hit-and-run cases.

Non-bailable Offences under the IPC

Section 121- Waging or attempting to wage war, or abetting the waging of war, against the Government of India •**124A**- Sedition •**131**- Abetting mutiny or attempting to seduce a soldier, sailor or airman •**172** Absconding to avoid service of summons •**232**- Counterfeiting Indian coin •**238**- Import or export of counterfeiting Indian coin •**246**- Fraudulently diminishing weight of coin •**255**- Counterfeiting of government stamp •**274**- Adulteration of drug •**295A**- Deliberate and ,malicious act intended to outrage religious feelings of any class, by insulting religious beliefs •**302**- Punishment for murder •**304**- Punishment for Culpable homicide not amounting to murder •**304B**- Dowry death •**306**- Abetment of suicide •**307**- Attempt to murder •**308**- Attempt to commit culpable homicide •**369**- Abduction of child under the age of 10 years •**370**- Trafficking of person •**376**- Punishment for Rape •**376D**- Gang rape •**377**- Unnatural offence •**379**- Punishment for theft •**384**- Punishment for extortion •**392**- Punishment for robbery •**395**- Punishment for dacoity •**406**- Punishment for criminal breach of trust •**411**- Dishonestly receiving stolen property •**420**- cheating and dishonestly inducing delivery of property •**489A**- Counterfeiting currency notes or bank notes •**498A**- Husband or relatives of husband of a woman subjecting her to cruelty.

Bailable Offences Under the IPC

Section 140- Wearing soldier's garb, sailor, airman •**144**- Punishment for unlawful assembly •**154**- Owner or occupier of land on which unlawful assembly is held •**158**- Owner or occupier land on which unlawful assembly is held •**166**- Public Servant disobeying direction under law •**167**- Public servant framing incorrect document •**177**- Furnishing false information •**181**- False statement on oath to public servants •**186**- Disobedience to order duty promulgated by public servant •**189**- Threat of injury to public servant •**191**- Giving false evidence •**195A**- Threatening any person to give false evidence •**203**- Giving false information with respect to an offence •**210**- Fraudulently making false claim in court •**223**- Escape from confinement or custody negligently suffered by public servant •**213**- Taking gift, to screen an offender from punishment •**228**- Intentionally insult or interruption to public servant sitting in judicial proceedings •**264**- Fraudulent use or false instrument for weighing •**269**- Negligent act likely to spread infectious disease dangerous to life •**279**- Rash driving or driving on a public vehicle •**283**- Danger or obstruction in public way or line of navigation •**292**- Sale of obscene book •**297**- Trespassing on burial places •**304A**- Punishment for causing death by negligence •**309**- Attempt to commit suicide •**318**- Concealment of birth by secret disposal of body •**323**- Causing hurt •**349**- Using force •**354D**- Stalking •**363**- Punishment for Kidnapping •**417**- Punishment for Cheating •**426**- Punishment for Mischief •**447**- Punishment for Criminal trespass •**465**- Forgery •**477A**- Falsification of accounts •**489C**- Possession of forged currency notes or banknotes •**494**- Marrying again during lifetime of husband or wife •**496**- Marriage ceremony fraudulently gone through without lawful marriage •**498**- Enticing or taking away or detaining with criminal intent •**500**- Punishment for Defamation •**506**- Criminal intimidation •**509**- Word, gesture or act intended to insult the modesty of a woman •**510**- Misconduct in public by drunken person.

The Changing Face of Federalism in post-Independent India

Apoorv Agarwal

India's current political order could be described as 'quasi-federal' or 'cooperative federalism' but remarkably different from the past by a new-found pathway of Centre-State equilibrium. This article takes a look at the socio-political transition that the country has experienced in last 75 years.

Should India be described as a federal state, a unitary state or a combination of both? The purists may consider this a debatable terrain; however, the truth is the founding fathers, while framing free India's Constitution, chose to employ the term 'Union of states', rather than 'federalism' or the spirit of its stricter mould.

The choice may have been dictated by historic reasons: One, wherein an absolute or centralised bureaucratic, monarchic or feudal rule gave way to Government of India Act, 1935, which, a little later, became the precursor of independent India's Constitution; and two, the way in which the nation was born, wherein instead of a number of independent sovereign states with well demarcated territories taking a decision to join hands to form a federation, the country was founded by the formation of states by amalgamating a number of small princely states. The parliament had the power to admit new states, create new states, alter their boundaries and their names, and unite or divide the states.

The idea of need for a stronger centre, actuated by a powerful central leadership, may well have also stirred the pot of 'Union of states'. It is not surprising, therefore, that the earlier day political commentators preferred to describe the Indian State as 'unitary' rather than 'federal'.

Nonetheless, if a stock is taken of the socio-political transition that the country has experienced in last 75 years, India's current political order could be best described as 'quasi-federal' or 'cooperative federalism'. A polity that once saw one-party dominance across both houses of parliament and all states has yielded to times when regional parties, propped to serve the interests of different ethnic, cultural and linguistic groups, have become strong and wish to assert themselves, thereby forming the basis for a newfound Centre–states equilibrium.

Colour the landscape a little more, allow the more recent elements of free market trade and the competition of economic liberalisation, and the expression yet again may stand metamorphosed to 'cooperative federalism,' a spirit much more contemporary and exciting!

Understanding Federalism

Derived from the Latin term foedus, "federal" means "covenant". Central to the ideas of contract, obligation, and undertaking, and drawing on the premise of collaboration, reciprocity, and mutuality, federalism postulates a political organisation, which unites separate states or other polities within an overarching political system that allows each entity to function effectively without being subordinate to the other. It is marked by certain fundamental features, namely, the supremacy of the country's Constitution; clearly defined spheres of authority with a clear division of powers between the Union and the state governments; the existence of an independent judiciary to determine the issues between the Union and the states, or between one state and another; and adherence to a strict procedure if the Constitution is to be amended. The Constitution of the country reigns supreme, and the Supreme Court carries authority as its guardian and interpreter.

The federal system ensures a constitutionally binding political theorem to serve regional and local interests. The states exercise a range of autonomous powers and enjoy some measure of representation in central government through the Rajya Sabha (Council of States). The "articles" relating to the relations between the Union and the states are described

Distribution of legislative subjects between the Union and the States under the Seventh Schedule of Part XI of the Indian Constitution

Where the Union Government holds Power

- Defence
- Foreign affairs
- Armed Forces
- Atomic energy
- Citizenship and Extradition
- Currency, coinage; forex
- Banking and insurance
- Reserve Bank of India
- Union Public Service Commission
- Election Commission
- Foreign trade
- Public debt
- Income-tax, Custom and Excise Duty
- Central Bureau of Intelligence
- Railways, Shipping and Airways
- National Highways
- Ports and National Waterways
- Posts and telegraphs, telephones, wireless and broadcasting

Union and State (Concurrent) Powers

- Criminal Law with certain limitations
- Education
- Forests
- Trade unions
- Industrial and Labour Disputes
- Marriage and divorce
- Adoption and Succession
- Bankruptcy and insolvency
- Weights and Measures
- Protection of Wild Animals and Birds
- Food adulteration
- Administration of Justice

Where the State Governments hold Power

- Public Order
- Police Forces
- Prisons and Reformatories
- Public Health and Sanitation
- Hospitals and Dispensaries
- Agriculture
- Water resources
- Land revenue, records and policies
- Variety of State Taxes
- State Trade and Commerce
- Industries subject to certain provisions
- State Public Services
- State pensions
- State Public debt
- Fisheries
- Village Administration
- Crematoriums and Burial grounds

in part XI of the Indian Constitution. While Articles 245 to 255 take care of the distribution of legislative powers, the distribution of administrative powers is dealt with in articles 256 to 261 of the Constitution.

The Constitution provides for a three-fold distribution of legislative subjects between the Union and the states, viz., List-I (the Union List), List-II (the State List) and List-III (the Concurrent List) in the Seventh Schedule (Venn diagram). Nonetheless, the subjects in the Union list have increased, and the number of subjects in the State list has shrunk over time.

A core objective of federalism is the decentralisation of administration. In December 1992, with the passing of 73rd and 74th constitutional amendments, the third tier of government – with Centre being tier one and the State government being tier two – was created at Panchayats and Municipalities. This novel feature of a three-tier government is unique to Indian federalism and is a recipe tailored to meet the specific needs of the country.

Distribution of Powers

(i) Union List. The Union list includes such subjects on which the parliament has exclusive power to legislate. The areas include defence, armed forces, atomic energy, foreign affairs, citizenship, railways, shipping and navigation, airways, posts and telegraphs, telephones, wireless and broadcasting, currency, foreign trade, inter-state trade and commerce, banking, insurance, control of industries, regulation and development of mines, mineral and oil resources, elections, audit of Government accounts, Constitution and organisation of the Supreme Court, High Courts and Union Public Service Commission, income tax, customs and export duties, duties of excise, corporation tax, taxes on the capital value of assets, estate duty and terminal taxes.

(ii) State List encompasses the following subjects: maintaining public order, police forces, public healthcare and sanitation, transport, land policies, electricity in the State, village administration and a host of others. The state legislature has exclusive power to make laws on these subjects; however, vide Articles 249, 250, 252, and 253, certain situations exist under which the Union government can legislate in the areas which fall under this list.

(iii) Concurrent List describes the powers shared among the Union and the States. The following subjects fall under this umbrella: education, forest, trade unions, labour welfare, economic and social planning, contracts, bankruptcy and insolvency, trustees and trusts, marriage and divorce, adoption, succession, civil procedure, transfer of property other than agricultural land, contempt of court, drugs and poisons, adulteration of foodstuffs, newspapers, and books and printing press.

(iv) Residuary subjects. Subject matters which do not fall under any of the three lists are known as residuary subjects. Some provisions in the Constitution permit the parliament or state legislative assembly to legislate in such areas. Still, excluding such provisions per Article 245, the power to legislate on such subjects rests entirely with the parliament per Article 248. The parliament can legislate on such residuary subjects by following the procedure laid down under Article 368 and take it as a constitutional amendment.

Executive Powers

The Union and states have independent executive powers. The Union government cannot override the constitutional rights of a State government. It is, however, the Union's duty to ensure that every state government functions following the provisions of the Constitution as per Article 355 and Article 256. If a State violates the Constitution, the Union government can impose Presidential rule under Article 356, and the President takes over the State's administration with ex post facto consent of the Parliament per Article 357.

Financial Powers

The state governments possess financial autonomy for meeting the expenditure on public spending as per Article 282. At the same time, Article 293 allows the States to borrow without limit without consent from the Union government. However, the Union government can insist upon compliance with its loan terms when a State has outstanding loans charged to the consolidated fund of India or a federally-guaranteed loan.

At the Centre of fiscal federalism is the Finance Commission, a constitutionally mandated body. The President of India constitutes a Finance Commission every five years. Set up under Article 280 of the Constitution, its core responsibility is to evaluate the state of finances of the Union and State Governments, recommend the sharing of taxes between them, and lay down the principles determining the distribution of these taxes among States. Its working is characterised by comprehensive and intensive consultations with all levels of government, thus strengthening the principle of coopera-

1. The Union parliament has the unilateral discretion to reconstruct the boundaries of the states.
2. Both Union and State governments must follow a single Constitution.
3. The powers listed under the Union list far outweigh those in the State list.
4. In case of a deadlock between the Union and states over subjects in the concurrent list, the Union law prevails.
5. The Union parliament can also legislate on any state subject under extraordinary circumstances.
6. The Union government possesses sweeping economic supremacy in terms of resources and can exercise its discretion in allocating resources to the states.
7. The Union Government has unfettered power in appointing the Governors in the states and can dissolve the State governments by proclaiming president rule.
8. Unlike the U.S.A., the Indian Constitution only allows single citizenship of the Union of India.
9. The provisions of a single system of courts, all-India public services, integrated audit machinery, and integrated election machinery, all-powerful Union-run institutions of governance, load the dice favouring a powerful centre.

tive federalism. Its recommendations are also geared towards improving the quality of public spending and promoting fiscal stability.

Influence of Political Factors in Shaping Indian Federalism

Caught in the crossfire of rapidly changing socio-political forces raising their heads through different periods of the republic, the Indian Federal System has been under immense pressure. It faces many difficulties in adapting the constitutional theory and practice to the emerging global situation where divergent forces of globalism and localism are struggling for equilibrium. Since its birth, the federal discourse has sailed through several setbacks, repairs and reinforcements at different periods since its inception.

The Fundamental Bias for Centralised Federalism

Article 1 describes India as a 'Union of States, and not 'Federation of States'. The states in India do not have the right to secede. Being indestructible, the federation, therefore, is called a 'Union'. Essentially then, by its very Constitution at the time of its birth, Indian Union has been a unitary state with subsidiary federal features rather than a federal state with subsidiary unitary features. Table 1 presents the key provisions of the Indian Constitution that reflect a distinct bias in favour of the Union government.

Table 1: Constitutional Provisions which favour the Centre

Growing Phenomenon of Rising Regional Assertiveness

Over the years, while a constitutionally strong centre has ruled the federal structure in Indian polity and has tried to promote cultural homogeneity and improve federal governance in all the Indian states, the unequal development between the states and lack of socio-economic and political opportunities in society has struck contrary notes in the discourse of unitary federalism in India. The federal states, challenged by various restrictions imposed upon their power and autonomy, have sought to assert their interests and influence, and this rising regional assertion has caused a distinct disquiet in the Indian federal discourse.

Passing Through Distinct Phases of Political Landscapes

1952–1967: The Period of Inner-Party Federalism

In this immediate post-independence period, despite Pandit Jawaharlal Nehru's plebiscitary leadership and mass appeal, the influence of the regional leaders within the Congress party and the rise of linguistic autonomy movement marked the regional assertion over the national politics, which consolidated the federal spirit. The Congress was the dominant party both at the Centre and the States. The co-existence of national and State leadership in their respective realms of influence was a consensual model of "inner-party federalism" that marked the era of Congress dominance. This led to the triumph of linguistic diversity observed by the creation of the linguistic states and adoption of bilingualism by the Union government; wherein, it was decided that English, along with Hindi, would continue to be used for all official purposes of State communication in the country, while surrendering the initial proposal of declaring Hindi as the national language. During this period, the issues relating to centre-state relations and the evolving federal dynamics mainly were addressed within the organisational fold of the Congress.

However, the dissolution of the Communist government led by E.M.S. Namboodiripad in Kerala in 1959, by the Centre under Nehru's premiership, was the first sign of more confrontationist federalism. If the states were to come under the rule of the parties that were opposed to the national ruling party at the Centre, consensual federalism could suffer.

1967–1989: The Rise of Centralised Conflictual Federalism

This period was marked by the Congress party losing its steam in many states and the split of the party in 1969, though it continued to reign supreme at the Centre. Many regional parties and anti-Congress coalitions formed governments in the states. A new era of directly conflictual federal dynamics emerged between the Congress-led Centre and the opposition parties-led state governments. The centralisation of power, wherein Congress leader Indira Gandhi became all-powerful, impacted India's federal dynamics in two ways: the erosion of Congress's political base and the encroachment of regional autonomy.

Invoking Article 356, Mrs. Gandhi dissolved state governments led by opposition parties and installed Congress governments. The favour was returned by the Janata government when it came to power at the Centre in 1977. It dissolved the Congress-ruled state governments to install Janata party-led governments in the states. This frequent misuse of Article 356 by the Centre to tame the "recalcitrant" states reduced the autonomy of states to a farce, giving rise to a new brand of conflictual federalism. Rising regional sentiments against the Union government led to the birth of violent political movements in Assam, Kashmir, Mizoram and Punjab in the late 1970s and early 1980s; the Centre-State relations became a casualty.

The wheel turned back in 1984 when the Rajiv Gandhi led-government took office. Adopting a reconciliatory approach, the government tried to accommodate the regional aspirations of decentralisation and greater autonomy. This strengthened the federal spirit, and, as a result, the affected states gradually achieved stability.

1989–2014: The Birth of Multiparty Federalism

With the eclipse of the Congress party in the 1989 national elections, India became home to a new coalition politics era. The first few coalition governments were a failure; however, from 1999 to 2014, the National Democratic Alliance (N.D.A.–I) and United Progressive Alliance (U.P.A.–I & U.P.A.–II) provided stability. The powerful regional and state-level actors congregated to support either of the national coalition groups. This exercise benefited their respective states and increased their political power and recognition in their states and at the national stage. With this, the national and regional political narratives bonded, leading to the evolution of a pluralist, decentralised, multi-party federalism.

This era was a harbinger of major economic reforms. The economy became open, liberal, deregulated and market-driven, which freed it of the shackles of license, permit and quota raj. The state governments discovered economic autonomy and were free to initiate business endeavours and bring in foreign investments to their respective states.

Much at the same time, the Supreme Court in the S.R. Bommai vs Union of India case gave a landmark judgement. In a single stroke of judicial safeguard, it created immunity for the state governments against the arbitrary use of Article 356 by the Union government. The central government was robbed of its wilful power with which it had always breathed heavily on the necks of the state governments.

The era, however, was not without its tussles. National issues like foreign policy, national security decisions, and economic reforms saw a new tug of war between regional and national parties which held warring interests. Still, compelled by the compulsions of coalition dharma, the juggernaut of multi-party federalism rolled on.

2014– The Return of the Dominant Party Federalism

This came about in 2014, with the Bharatiya Janata Party (B.J.P.) emerging as a significant new national political force. Soon after being sworn in, the government took critical steps aimed at strengthening the states. Firstly, born of the thought that states must discover active involvement and that cooperative federalism must shine, the Planning Commission was replaced by the Niti Aayog. Secondly, the long in waiting Goods and Services Tax (G.S.T.) was implemented. By doing so, the Centre and states become equal fiscal partners in sharing a joint indirect tax base. At the same time, a G.S.T. Council was formed to create a consensus amongst the states regarding all decisions. Thirdly, the Union government accepted the 14th Finance Commission recommendations to give the states a 42 per cent share of the funds from the central pool compared to the previous 32 per cent.

However, over time, the new avatar B.J.P. government had begun to employ the tactics that the Congress party, when in power, was slandered for. Be it engineering defections in ranks of other parties to muster majority, capture power and form state governments; the partisan role of Union government appointed Governors in opposition-ruled states; the proclamation of President Rule in the states like Arunachal Pradesh, Uttarakhand and Jammu and Kashmir; the Governor's role in government formation in states like Goa, Manipur and Maharashtra; or the Union government's intervention in the states by directly monitoring and politically appropriating the centrally sponsored schemes — each bespeaks of the centralising intentions of a dominant Union government. Such is its singular dominance that such debatable policies like demonetisation, abrogation of Article 370, changing the political status of Kashmir, and the passing of Citizenship Amendment Act (C.A.A.) 2019 have brooked little resistance.

With many of the regional actors rallying to back the nationalist policy decisions of the central government, this marks the beginning of a new era of 'national federalism' in India. Be it the more recent farm laws (farm reforms 2020); or the central government's approach towards procurement and distribution of COVID-19 vaccines, the assertion of the Union over the state governments has been almost palpable.

Where the Salvation lies

A well-thought-out, detailed book of the Constitution and an independent, active judiciary are two of the staunchest allies of a balanced federal design. While the autonomy of states, national integration, centralisation, nationalism, and decentralisation — each has a case, an even-handed approach towards the federal dynamics, where neither extreme political centralisation works nor chaotic political decentralisation dominates, where states enjoy autonomy but do not play so truant that national unity stands threatened, must be the goal that the founding fathers had enunciated. At the same time, penning Article 1 (1) of the country's Constitution: India, Bharat, shall be a Union of States! The journey of being a sovereign republic that began some seventy-five years ago must head for a true success story!

16

EDUCATION AND CAREER

- Jobs Of The Future
- How to Ace the 'Essay' Test?
- Online Education: Opportunities and Challenges
- Education
- National Education Policy 2020

Jobs Of The Future

Jayanti Ghose, Career Counsellor

Tomorrow's high school and college graduates will be journeying into the professional unknown because they will be taking up jobs which don't even exist today. Here are 20 jobs that are likely to be in demand in the next five to ten years.

For India, the Fourth Industrial Revolution has brought with it the opportunity to leapfrog many stages of development. It is characterized by a fusion of technologies- blurring the lines between the physical, digital, and biological spheres. It's a fusion of advances in artificial intelligence (AI), robotics, the Internet of Things (IoT), 3D printing, genetic engineering, quantum computing, and other technologies. It's given us GPS, facial recognition, voice activated virtual assistants and so on.

In the 21st century, the pace of change has been faster as it has been riding on the shoulders of fast-paced changes in the last quarter century. Many of the new jobs that are appearing are a consequence of experimentation and complementarity, rather than replacing existing jobs. The development of human-like robots, AI, advanced genomics, 3D printing, collaboration of humans and machines, biomedical advancement, faster and ever-expanding internet are among the drivers of changes which are opening up possibilities of newer jobs.

Tomorrow's high school and college graduates will

be journeying into the professional unknown because they will be taking up jobs which don't even exist today, but may come up in the next five to ten years, and not necessarily uniformly across all parts of the country or the world, or in every sector/ industry.

1. Wearable Technology Therapist

Most of us are aware of wearables such as smart watches, fitness trackers, or smart glasses, but mainly for personal use. These are also very useful for health monitoring, especially for

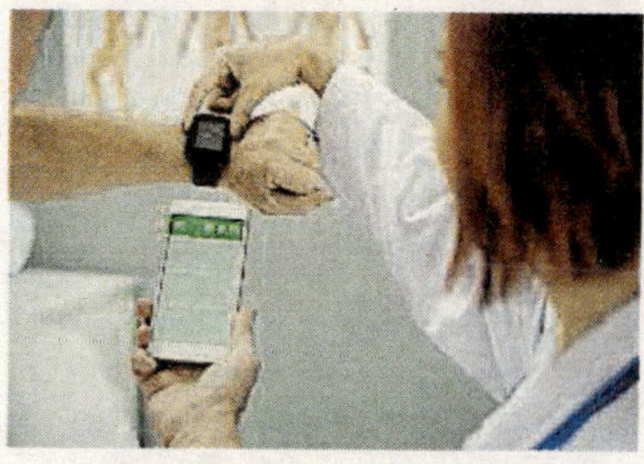

assisting people with disabilities. With wearables becoming more widely used and affordable across the world, an entire career as a Wearable Technology Therapist may soon emerge. Psychotherapists using AI and research to harness wearables would be able to monitor the emotional health of their patients to provide more personalised therapy. The advancement of wearable technology and the possibilities of using AI in healthcare will lead to further specialised wearable technology experts. A digitally-enabled medical / rehabilitation practitioner will have a more trusting, personalised and transparent relationship with the users of wearables.

Skills: Critical thinking, analytical skills, technical aptitude, emotional and social awareness.

Preferred Qualifications: Medical/ rehabilitation training and certification in data science /AI tools to handle the digital health workplace.

IISc Bangalore, Taipei Medical University, Harvard University and online course providers like Future Learn, etc. offer short courses/ certifications.

2. Nostalgist

Spaces for elderly living designed to reflect the surroundings of their times would make them feel comfortable in their twilight years. Nostalgists combining historical research with interior design skills would help the elderly living communities or wealthy elderly get their spaces designed to reflect their favourite decades. It could be recreating a living room of the 1980 or a kitchen of the 1960s, to help recreate happy memories for the elderly clients. Nostalgists would develop virtual reality experiences to help the elderly, especially those suffering with dementia, return to familiar environments from their past.

Skills: Strong communication and problem solving skills, creativity, interest in history, and eye for historical detail and keen interest in historical research

Preferred Qualifications: Interior design, environmental or set design and insights from virtual reality experience creation and carers for the aged.

3. Robot Ethicist

Robot ethics, also called machine ethics, studies the ethical problems that arise with the design, operation, con-

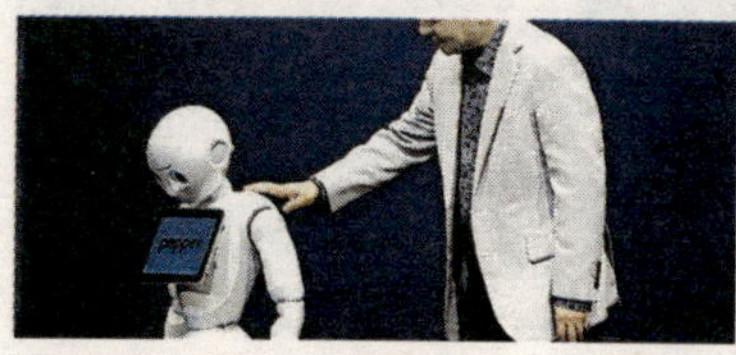

trol and use of robots in real life. It is focused on ensuring that behaviour of machines towards human users, and perhaps, with other machines, as well, is ethically acceptable. Robot ethicists engagements include robot rights (that people have moral obligations towards machines, particularly AI), weaponisation of AI, and robot morality. Robot Ethicists will be responsible for holding robotic engineers and robot designers to a code of ethics to ensure that they assume responsibility regarding the ethical consequences of their creations. They will be examining the legal implications of robots whether as service robots or lethal robots. Robots are and will remain -in the foreseeable future- dependent on human ethical scrutiny as well as on the moral and legal responsibility of humans.

Skills: Strong analytical, risk assessment, communication and critical thinking skills, moral courage, the ability for networking and collaboration.

Preferred Qualifications: MBAs learn business law and ethics, but engineers, designers, developers with industry experience could take up online courses on business ethics for contemporary understanding of ethics as relevant to digital technologies for this emerging role.

4. Ethical Sourcing Officer/ Manager

Ethical sourcing officers will be hired when corporations decide to have their

decisions guided by what is ethical and not just what is profitable. They would ensure that the allocation of corporate incomes aligns with the standards set by customers and employees by investigating, tracking, negotiating, and forging agreements around the automated provisioning of goods and services, to ensure ethical agreement with stakeholders. They will have to undertake research and head a team of analysts to gather, examine and provide the information for the successful implementation of the shareholders values.

Skills: Teamwork skills, tact, diplomacy, thirst for innovation, strong analytical skills, commercial awareness, negotiating and networking skills.

Preferred Qualifications: Background and experience in law, business, governance, or philosophy.

5. Haptic Coder

Haptics engages people's sense of touch to enhance the experience of

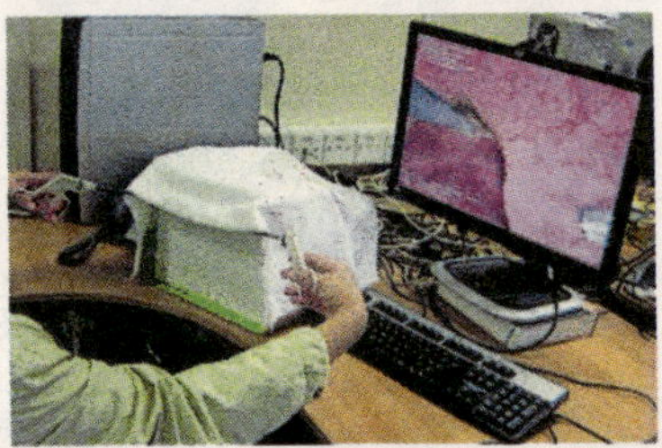

interacting with on-screen interfaces. Our common experience of haptics is vibration in our phones. Haptic devices are graspable, wearable and touchable. Haptic technology based devices are used across diverse applications like mobile, medicine, education, rehabilitation, industrial, sports, gaming, cameras, etc. People are waking up to the importance and potential of haptics, hence, haptics coders will be in demand in the future.

Skills: Inquisitiveness, mathematical ability, problem solving and communication skills

Preferred Qualifications: Electrical and Computer Engineering with insights from Human Factors engineers would be helpful to understand how people interact with current or prototype technologies.

6. HR Data Detective

This new role is expected to open up in the next five years or so as organisations become more data driven to make information led decisions. HR Data Detectives would be required to source, sift, and investigate people from many sources including human capital management and HR information system

data, employee surveys, time-tracking and learning management systems, benefits portals, compensation; and succession planning. This will help find clues on how to solve common HR problems and grow efficiencies. They will also transform unstructured information such as employee sentiment, text, video or voice inputs into usable data sources.

Skills: Excellent communication and analytical skills, curious, relentless, resilient and diplomatic.

Preferred Qualifications: A basic degree in math, physical science, philosophy, economics, law, or accountancy, with mandatory SQL, Python, and cloud capabilities.

7. Smart Home Design Managers

With the incorporation of smart home technology, we will soon need Smart

Home Design Managers who will work with architects, engineers as well as clients to design connected homes that offer their inhabitants a seamlessly connected environment using the latest integrated technology. Keeping abreast of the latest technology, they will find unique ways of integrating the same in an aesthetically pleasing and eco-friendly manner.

Skills: Excellent communication skills, keen interest in smart home technologies, the ability to build rapport with high net worth individuals, and strong sales skills.

Preferred Qualifications: Professional training in and experience in architecture, and ongoing incorporation of the latest developments in technology for smart homes.

8. Man Machine Teaming Manager

The new workforce of the future will be defined by man-machine collaboration which would be the new hybrid work-

force. This holds the potential to transform industries, businesses, workplaces and jobs. The role of Man Machine Training Manager would be to develop an interaction framework for machines and humans to mutually communicate their capabilities, goals and intentions and come up with a task planning system for human-machine collaboration. Passion for advancing human-robot cooperation strategies in a dynamic business environment would be what would drive the Man Machine Teaming managers of the future. They will have to defines roles and responsibilities and set the rules for how machines and humans should coordinate to complete a task.

Skills: Leadership, communication and collaboration skills.

Preferred Qualifications: Degree in Neuroscience or Experimental Psychology followed by a master's degree in HR or Computer Engineering with some years of experience in human robot interaction or machine learning, or robotics.

9. Sustainable Building Regulator

As per current estimates, we will run out of oil in the next fifty years. Hence, scientists are shifting emphasis to move to sustainable and renewable energy sources like solar and wind power which are becoming more accessible and cheaper. Storing solar power effectively is still not within easy reach, but hopefully, by 2050, the hurdles would be crossed. With the growing consciousness and emphasis on more sustainable energy in the coming de-

cades, it is just a matter of time before Sustainable Building Regulators will be in demand. Their job would be to ensure that buildings are fully environmentally sustainable and free from fossil fuels. Government and private sector organizations are increasingly committing to building and operating net zero energy buildings to significantly reduce dependence on fossil fuels.

The code for sustainable homes as a national standard for the sustainable design and construction of new homes has to be laid down with the aim to reduce carbon emissions and promote higher standards of sustainable design above the current minimum standards set out by the building regulations. Sustainable Building Regulators must be well-versed in the regulations and their implications.

Skills: Attention to detail, the ability to build relationships with a range of people, such as project managers and contractors, ability to manage client expectations around sustainability issues, flexibility to work under pressure, responding to changing legislation and project and programme demand. Creative thinking and problem-solving skills numeracy and literacy skills.

extra

Careers in FinTech

FinTech, in layman's terms, refers to the design and delivery of financial products and services using disruptive technologies in order to reduce cost, improve efficiency and provide better personalised service.

Preferred Qualifications: Degree in construction, electrical or environmental engineering along with higher certification or master's in sustainable energy or renewable energy, etc.

Masters in Sustainable Energy Engineering at IIT Kanpur, KTH Sweden, Reykjavik University Iceland, Joint Nordic Masters in Innovative Sustainable Energy, University of Nottingham UK, Lund University Sweden, etc. could be a suitable base.

10. Robot Counsellor

Robot counsellors will become necessary as the wealthy go on to own robots to act as caregivers, or servants in their homes. Robot counsellors will help them decide on the right model to suit the family's needs and priorities. When a particular robot does not work

out for the family, the robot counsellor will have to identify better options.

Skills: Interpersonal and customer service skills, keen understanding of technologies that change household routines, deep-seated knowledge of social work, understanding of diverse cultures and generational relationships, especially in the context of robots providing living assistance.

Preferred Qualifications: Psychology and counselling education combined with knowledge of robots meant for different household / personal needs.

11. Freelance Biohacker

Biohacking is biological experimentation using biology with the mind-set of a hacker. It's a broad concept en-

compassing ways to enhance human body, health, cognitive performance, improving health and well-being customised to personal needs. For exciting bioscience projects in the future, freelance biohackers will be playing a key role in tasks that cover the gamut of hunting for the next model of antibiotics to developing genetically modified wildlife. Major drug companies, bioscience companies as well as university research departments will be using them to piece together complicated DNA-based answers to several of the fundamental questions of diseases emerging in ten years, from remedies for various cancers in different populations to vaccines for brand new epidemics fuelled by our globalised way of life and accelerating climate change. Freelance biohackers will boost major medical breakthroughs because, unlike experts in academic institutes, they could spend time brainstorming and indulging in creative, blue sky thinking without worrying about teaching and publishing papers.

Skills: Sharp scientifically inclined minds with the ability to work naturally, non-competitively, and collaboratively with large virtual teams working on open source software programme platforms connected by the internet. Eye for detail, innovative thinking, talent for intuitive open-minded thinking not limited by preconceptions.

Preferred Qualifications: Biological science education but not confined to traditional science and medicinal disciplines. An understanding of medical and scientific methodology, combined with education in advanced data analytics.

12. Data Waste Recycler

This technology job may not exist now, but organisations are already looking

into hiring data trash engineers owing to the astounding amounts of data that is collected worldwide. The next decade will see the emergence of Data Waste Recyclers or Data Trash Engineers whose brief would be to transform data that may have absolutely no foreseeable use into treasure. As part of routine data management process, data may be recommended for deletion. However, if this is mined, refined and distributed, data trash can be profitable. The era of big data is likely to continue in the next decade, therefore, this job can be a potential long-term employment source.

Skills: Strong interpersonal and cross organisational collaboration skills, written, verbal and visual communication skills and attention to detail.

Preferred Qualifications: Post-graduation in statistics, computer science, applied mathematics and experience with data analysis and data mining tools and statistical packages.

13. Garbage Designer or Waste Reclamation/ Upcycling Specialist

Using trash/ garbage to create new, better quality items is referred to as upcycling. It is what the Garbage Designers in the future would be doing. They would be designing ways to make new items with very little waste so that the upcycling attempt is both efficient and successful. They'd design practical, useful objects from things we've thrown away. This future job would help us to live in a more environmentally friendly way.

Skills: Creative skills, well-developed communication and interpersonal skills to work successfully across diverse industries with cross-disciplinary teams. Keen interest in the environment and in industrial design, problem solving and digital skills with attention to detail.

Preferred qualifications: Materials Science and Engineering and familiarity with the manufacturing process.

Insolvency Professionals

Insolvency Professionals are hired by companies in the dissolution process of the firm, partnership, or LLPs. During the bankruptcy situation, insolvency professionals play a key role in helping to liquidate the assets and other settlement processes for their clients.

14. Space Tourism Operator

Space tourism is an exciting development in travel and tourism that many are keenly looking forward to, beyond using virtual reality software. Virgin Galactic, Blue Origin and Space X are companies developing space tourism.

Of course, when it actually takes off (pun intended), only the super wealthy will be able to afford it at first. Space tourism seeks to give tourists the ability to become astronauts and experience space travel for recreational, leisure, or business purposes. To begin with, it would be a form of adventure tourism. Space Tourism Operators will take shuttle–loads of tourists into orbit, visit space stations, and beyond. They will work with shuttle pilots, space traffic control systems operators and spaceport personnel.

Skills: Strong interpersonal and logistical skills, entrepreneurial and marketing skills, organising ability, healthy and fit.

Preferred Qualifications: Knowledge of locations in our solar system is important, but there are no formal requirements as of now. However, someone with training in astronomy or space science or related fields would be a good fit.

15. Entomicrobiotech Cleaners

While cleaning up the thousands of oil spills of crude or refined petroleum products scientists have discovered that certain insects and bacteria love to consume petrochemicals. Wax worms are known to be able to eat their way through polyethene which is used to make plastic bags and water bottles. Entomicrobiotech Cleaners would be farming these bacteria and insects and deploying them in cleaning up the environment.

Skills: Strong interest and knowledge of the biology of insects and bacteria, and the way to keep them healthy. They would not be put off by bugs and the liquid nutrients which are used for growing bacteria, and be prepared to travel for their work.

Preferred Qualifications: Entomology, Micro biotechnology and allied fields, combined with knowledge / use

of analytical algorithms

16. Data Farmers

Data farming involved growing data from computer models, which can then be analysed using statistical and visualisation techniques. We know that farmers cultivate the land and try to get the best yield by manipulating the environment using crop rotation, pesticides, fertiliser, etc. In the same way, Data Farmers manipulate simulation modes to their advantage. They are bulk data analysts who use algorithms to their advantage so as to extract meaningful extrapolations from stochastic data comparisons. What they are able to learn from it can help businesses, the community and government predict trends for developing new products and services, regulate commerce and environmental strategies.

Skills: Strong problem solving and analytical skills, creativity and cognitive flexibility combined with excellent programming and algorithmic design skills. While freelancing they'd need to be entrepreneurial.

Preferred Qualifications: Computer science, Engineering, Mathematical and allied disciplines.

17. Extinct Species Revivalist

Extinct species revivalists will try to synthesize a complete strand of DNA as the extinct animal's genome. They could play a critical role in recreating species which have already become extinct and reintegrating them into their natural habitat. Extinct species revivalists come up with inventive and innovative methods of resurrecting extinct animals. Usually, the goal is to undo the harm that mankind has caused the earth.

Skills: Strong verbal and written communication skills, critical thinking, problem solving and analytical thinking, proficiency with computers especially scientific databases, team work skills as also the ability to work independently and do research.

Preferred Qualifications: Evolutionary Biology, Wildlife Ecology, Life Sciences, Genetics and allied fields.

18. Fusionist

Fusionists will be the job of the future where they would act as bridge between art, engineering, research, science and other disciplines. They'd be able to bring all of them together through communication and design, create innovative ideas, experiences and provide solutions to complex problems. They will be employed across different industries, where they will act as bridges between people with specialist disciplinary knowledge.

Skills: Strong communicators with excellent listening, written and oral communication skills, with the ability to understand technical concepts from different disciplinary areas and blend the knowledge and skills of different team members to complete a project.

Preferred Qualifications: Design

training with experience of working in multi-disciplinary teams and keeping abreast of the latest technology and research.

19. AI Personality Designer

An AI Personality Designer will create

experimental interactions between humans and machines. They may be working within or alongside companies specialising in technology, to help make an interactive, AI-based product feel user-friendly and engaging. They will work with artificial intelligence and code it to become more useful to humans—and to be more like humans, including building in relevant cultural references or personality details such as sarcasm and humour. It's difficult to tell how this career will transpire and being relatively new, specific requirements of the role will vary.

Skills: Copywriting or journalism skills, fascination with the world around us, interested in human psychology, good in communicating with different personality types, with a keen interest in coding, science and emerging technologies.

Preferred Qualifications: Computer science, cognitive science theory and robotics.

20. AI Educator

The future in which there will be household robots and digital assistants in the workplace, people will have to learn how to work with them. AI Educators will teach people how machines learn and adapt so that they can use the robot or digital assistant effectively. They will teach their clients how to 'feed' the right data and how to interact with them to get the right answers and service from them. AI Educators will teach their clients how to make the best use of AI.

Skills: Excellent interpersonal skills, digitally literate, with teaching skills and strategies for working with different kinds of clients. Good practical knowledge of robot/digital assistant interaction

Preferred Qualifications: Engineering degree with basic knowledge of Machine Learning

I must say that it has been an exciting journey for me exploring, researching and writing about these amazing opportunities awaiting today's high school and college students. It may seem like stepping into the unknown for you since many of these job openings do not have a structured path for training, but for those entering the future job market, being ready to cope with technological and transformational changes ahead is the skill to develop. The most sought-after abilities and skills are typically human, like solving complex problems, critical thinking and emotional intelligence, to name just a few. Workers will be appreciated for their flexibility, creativity and collaborative spirit. Therefore, the development of a portfolio of abilities and skills would be the best form of education for the jobs of the future. Today's students should be focused on the ability to learn, to work independently and an entrepreneurial attitude. Fall in love with learning to learn and you will always be employable. Social, mobile, analytic and cloud (SMAC) skills/ platforms will help you to stand out.

How to Ace the 'Essay' Test?

Dr Sebastian Narively, Pala

The essay can mean the difference between winning or losing a decisive examination or a challenging job. Here are the important points to bear in mind while writing the essay paper for different competitive exams.

The essay is "a loose sally of the mind; an irregular indigested piece, not a regular and orderly composition," defined Samuel Johnson, a towering literary genius of the eighteenth century. It might have been so in the days of the French writer Michel de Montaigne, acclaimed as the Father of the Essay, John Dryden, acknowledged as the Father of English Literary Criticism, and Johnson himself. Of late, the essay has scaled unprecedented heights as a yardstick par excellence in the assessment and grading of students, especially the aspirants of high-level competitive examinations. The main reason is that it can test different attributes of a candidate such as general background knowledge, reasoning ability, observation and power of expression, besides the knowledge acquired through reading and personal experience.

The essay is a discursive composition on any subject conveying the author's points of view. This literary form originated in France and gradually conquered the English literary scene with Francis Bacon in the seventeenth century. It had a steady ascent in popularity in the late seventeenth and early eighteenth centuries, mostly because of the decline of drama, especially the artificial comedy. The essay became more popular with the advent of newspapers in the first decade of the eighteenth century. Daniel Defoe's *Review*, the tri-weekly *The Tatler* and the popular periodical *The Spectator,* through editorials and other articles facilitated its rise. The contributions of luminaries of the eighteenth century like Daniel Defoe, Jonathan Swift, Charles Lamb, William Hazlett, Walter Landor, besides Addison and Steele, elevated the essay as the most popular form of literature capable of dealing with the widest range of subjects. This recognized genre continued its onward march braving challenges from the novel in the hands of Henry Fielding and Jane Austen , and reached a comfortable footing in the twentieth century, mainly headed by versatile stalwarts like Aldous Huxley and T.S. Eliot.

Essays are of three types – descriptive, narrative and analytical, and the components of all these types are subject knowledge, sequential thought, imagination, observation, vocabulary, reasoning and reflection. Of these varieties, the descriptive (e.g., 'On Going a Journey' by William Hazlitt) and the narrative patterns ('Dream Children: A Reverie' by Charles Lamb) seem to be less popular of late, compared to the analytical type. The analytical or expository essay is subdivided into the discursive essay ('Soliloquies in *Hamlet*') and the polemical type ('Prohibition Should be Legalised').

Irrespective of its objective, the essay should be informative as well as interesting. In a quality essay, information has to be balanced by illustration, accuracy by originality, and authority by personality. Variety in presentation, especially that of the opening paragraph, will invite special attention of the reader. Essays should deviate from the tedious conventional mode and be pleasurable and rich in detail. The style should not be too passionate or overenthusiastic while enlisting favourite viewpoints. The tone of writing should be cheerful but not facetious.

The essay can mean the difference between winning or losing a decisive examination or a challenging job. The main objective of the essay paper in the UPSC Civil Services Examination is to assess the thought process

of the candidate, along with the way in which she/he thinks and airs the thoughts within the stipulated time frame. On getting the question paper candidates have to relax sufficiently, plan the answers logically and organise an effective presentation. If you are het up about the paper and symptoms of tension such as a high pulse rate or a blank mind crop up, an easy breathing exercise helps ease the overanxiety and regain mental equilibrium. If any question still arouses tension, spare it for the time being and proceed to the next one.

Preparation

Candidates should acquire adequate general knowledge well in advance through extensive exploration of the internet, newspapers, books, general and subject-special magazines like *Yojana, Economic Survey* etc.. The National Digital Library of India, a perennial storehouse of about 50 million learning resources including e-books, theses, audio and video lectures, web courses etc is a real boon to prospective aspirants. Reading also enhances language skills which should be periodically updated using a standard dictionary and a thesaurus. Keep a notebook in which to put down striking ideas, stimulating expressions, quotes and anecdotes that can be capitalised on as and when required. Suggestive expressions like a

pipe dream, astronomical prices, relax into delicious indolence etc give an edge to the composition.

Since the natural sequence of reading is writing, aspirants should practise writing essays on a variety of topics. Train the fine art of bold omission of inessentials and judicious selection of points of prime relevance since relevance like brevity is the soul of wit. It is good to adopt the precise, analytical style of rated leader writers of reputed dailies. As the adage goes, practice makes perfect. A mentor having reasonably good general knowledge and editing skills, preferably someone who has cracked the UPSC exam, has to be identified to evaluate the practice essays. Time management also has to be primed during this evolutionary span.

Selection of Questions

Questions are to be reread and selected scrupulously with a "desirability grading." If there is choice, prefer questions or topics of which you have personal experience. Misreading a question can tilt the answer with irrelevant details and unsought statistics. One way in which careful reading of the question can be ensured is by underlining the keywords of the question. If the question is worded as a question, a definite answer has to be provided sooner or later. It is better not to give a cut-and-dried answer, an absolute "Yes" or "No." Instead, clearly indicate your preference. After identifying the pick of the bunch, go through the instructions once again ensuring that your selection conforms with them.

Needless to say, a high-risk question involves greater chances of winning or losing the game. If justice is done to it, a risky question yields higher dividends, drawing greater appreciation for the candidate's daring. A high-risk question requires the budget of extra time for planning and choosing the details. If you are not confident, prefer low-risk options. The enthusiasm for being adventurous regarding one question should not spoil the scope of the other answers.

On scrutinizing the questions, the candidate has to think on how to answer each question. Jot down in point form, all relevant ideas on the answer paper itself. This gives the examiner an additional dimension of the candidate's insight. If time runs out, the warm-hearted examiner will appreciate the points mentioned even if they could not be elaborated.

Structure of the Essay

In order to ace the essay paper, the write-up should be of sound matter presented with a felicitous choice of words. Innovative subheadings give a

scholarly look to the essay. The standard format of writing a research paper like underlining scientific terms, putting titles of books and stories in double inverted commas, positioning the full stop within the quotation marks etc. is to be followed. The structure of the essay, comprising a beginning, a middle and an end, has to be adhered to, based on a well-thought-of plan. Ensure that the introduction gives a clue to the major line of argument to follow, the body of the essay displays a logical flow of thoughts and the conclusion tenders the main contents in a nutshell.

The introduction can begin with a real-life anecdote, a story, a question, a striking quotation or a definition of the keywords in the question. Of these, it is the anecdote or the story that has a greater appeal on account of its clearer touch of humanity and warmth. A link sentence or a question will effect a smooth transition from one paragraph to another. The technique of signposting, briefly flagging what is to come, helps the examiner judge the direction of thought. Ideas are to be substantiated through real-life examples, recent statistics, relevant constitutional provisions etc. Even on a controversial topic, the tone of the writing should be impersonal, irrespective of individual views or loyalties.

A well-prepared plan helps add new details, shift the emphasis and shed irrelevancies. If a digression is required, the prethink enables a safe return to the original track. The scheme also facilitates the allotment of adequate time to each point and monitor the progress of the arguments. Your stance on the issue or attitude to the question is to be expressed early enough without holding it in suspense for a telling climax. State your preferred opinions in razor-sharp wit, augmented with examples in support, discussing opposing arguments, if any. Better not to stick slavishly to the view implied in the question or to totally disagree. Facts and figures quoted should be accurate but not too elaborate or excessive. Abstract statements and broad generalisations are to be anchored with specific cases. However humorous or imaginative you are, your comic muse is to be kept under control while dealing with a serious essay topic like "Should Capital Punishment be Abolished or Not?"

Handwriting also is a major feature of offline examinations. A stylish, cursive writing has its own advantage, besides legibility.

Language Skills

A good essay demonstrates the fundamental qualities of good writing: clarity, conciseness and simplicity through crisp and powerful sentences. Technical terms and complex words like acronyms and abbreviations are to be explained. Long winding sentences and grandiloquent phrases are to be avoided. "In literature as in finance", as Washington Irving observes, "much paper and much poverty exist." The essay cannot compromise basic grammar, spelling and diction or choice of words and shades of meaning. The practice of qualifying views repeatedly with phrases like 'It seems to me' and 'As far as I am concerned' creates only an adverse impression.

Points to Steer Clear of

Since a natural, unaffected style is what the examiner prefers, a bombastic and highfalutin language is to be shunned. A flowery or decorated style is outmoded; so also are slang and euphemism (a polite expression used instead of an upsetting one). Avoid stating the obvious and repeating the same phrase, and choose striking metaphors which

are illustrations in miniature. Never ever parade irrelevant scholarship. It is appreciable to have the courage of conviction, but too many superlatives will become self-stultifying. New words entering the language frequently from American English, also linked to technology, are not to be used when it is too early. The essay is to be written in plain British English. Words and spellings in American English, if used, should be consistent. Indianism like 'godown' (warehouse) and without coffee (diet coffee) is regarded sub-standard.

L.A. Hill, noted English essayist, enumerates a few defects to be kept clear of. "Avoid jargon (e.g. re your letter to hand, meaning 'with reference to the letter which I have received from you'), officialese (e.g. it is apprehended that, meaning 'I suppose'), hackneyed expressions (e.g. Adam's ale for 'water'...), rhetorical flourishes (e.g. This is a subject of great importance to many people nowadays, and therefore one which I feel I should discuss seriously and honestly...), empty verbiage (e.g. I feel obliged to add that, doubtless, many people appreciate that it is a matter of the greatest importance that information about possible cases of cruelty to children should be passed on to the appropriate authorities immediately.) and circumlocutions (e.g. I will cause investigations to be made with a view to ascertaining the information, instead of 'I will find out')."

The essay has to be concluded in an optimistic, futuristic note. Arguments are to be consummated in three or four sentences following which the vision for the future may be presented. The conclusion is a wrap-up of the arguments presented in a fresh mode of expression. No new point is to be discussed while toting up the views already elaborated. It is a prudent strategy to include some inspiring thought from the speeches of world leaders like Winston Churchill or John F Kennedy. Prime Minister Narendra Modi's favourite phrase "Reform-perform-transform" also motivates. Oft-quoted last lines of famous poems like "If winter comes, can spring be far behind?" ('Ode to the West Wind' by Shelley) or last words of celebrities like "Service to others is the rent that we pay for our room in the hereafter" (Muhammad Ali) can give the conclusion a stronger impact.

Last impression, they say, is the lasting impression. The last ten to fifteen minutes of the exam should be assigned for meticulously editing the essay, scrutinising the facts and figures, matter and manner. Reinforced with the confidence that the fine-tuned product will elevate you to heights of success, put the pen down.

Online Education: Opportunities and Challenges

Muralee Thummarukudy &
Neeraja Janaki

COVID-19 saw the biggest disruption of education in the history of humankind. A comprehensive look at the dramatic growth in online education, its impact on teaching and learning and its future potential.

COVID-19 saw the biggest disruption of education in the history of humankind. According to the UNESCO estimates, education of more than 1.6 billion students in more than 190 countries were disrupted in 2020 and not even half of them have returned to the classrooms even after a whole year. As countries are still going through second, third or fourth wave of COVID-19, it is not clear when students across the globe will be able to get back to their classes. This article explores the dramatic growth in online education, its impact on teaching and learning and its future potential. In order to understand the opportunities and challenges of online education in Kerala, the authors conducted an online survey of students, teachers and parents in November 2020 about 6 months after the conventional education was disrupted. So along with global literature review, some local sample survey results are also presented here.

Like all crises before, the COVID-19-induced-

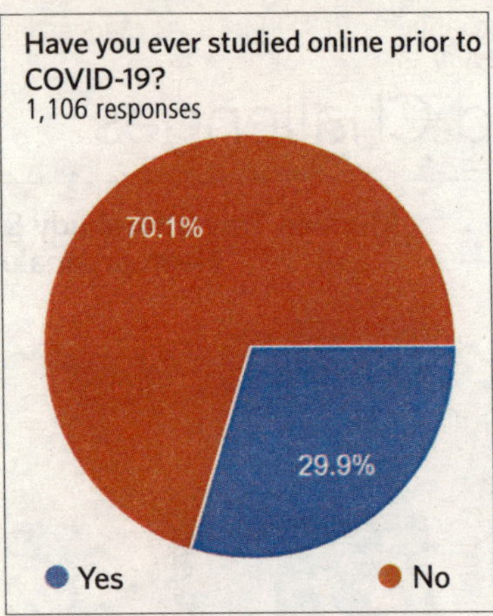

Student Response

breakdown in conventional education also created a breakthrough in the domain of online education. Education in Kerala went completely online using television, tabs, computers or mobile as hardware and zoom, team and many other software platforms. However, in a survey that we conducted in Kerala, six months after the introduction of online teaching, 70% of the students and 80% of the teachers mentioned that they had, respectively, neither studied nor taught online prior to the COVID-19 period. This is both surprising and shocking considering that online education avenues were open since early 2000s and Massive Open Online Courses on many topics were available free from 2010 onwards.

Growth of Massive Open Online Courses

There is still considerable academic debate on which was the first Massive Open Online Course in history. As the name indicates, a massive open online course has four critical features: it must be an academic course, it must be massive, it must be open and it must be online. There is no specific definition on the term "massive,' with many courses these days crossing the million learners mark, while some other MOOCs hardly make it into 1000 learners. The term 'open' is also subject to interpretation. 'Open' does denote one or more of the following: that it is accessible to people in most parts of the world, it has limited entry restrictions and also that it is mostly free.

One of the first and most accepted MOOCs which fit the above bill was the course "Artificial Intelligence" by Sebastian Thrun and Peter Norvig from Stanford University in the fall of 2011. More than 160,000 people from around the world signed up to learn this course jointly, and it was the first time in history that a course was so well-received by that many students. Surprised and elated by the success of this course, Sebastian Thrun teamed up with other partners to start an online learning platform UDACITY in 2011. In 2012, the online platform Coursera was founded and media started referring to 2012 as the Year of MOOC. There were initial speculations that online courses will soon make universities redundant and education globally accessible and even free. However, the financial model of MOOC never took off and most platforms were struggling even when COVID-19 hit the global academic scene.

Online Learning Since COVID-19

There has been explosive growth of online learning since start of COVID-19, especially since March 2021 when most of the world went into lockdown. Parents, academicians and governments around the world scrambled to ensure that children's education continued and also that both children and

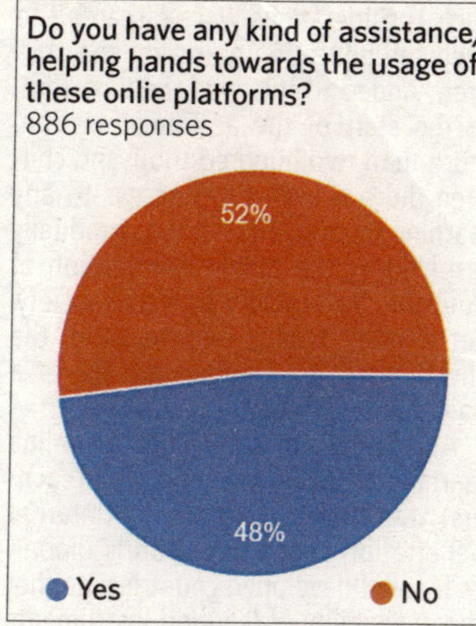

their parents did not suffer psychological trauma due to disruption of education. Around the world, teachers led this revolution armed with whatever tools they had in their hand, and with limited or no support from their parent institutions. A survey in Kerala in September showed that 52% of the teachers received no training to go online. In response to whether they received any kind of financial support or incentives for doing online courses, considering the additional cost of data and platforms, 90% of the teachers answered negative.

It is not only the teachers who were unprepared to deal with online education. There was no preparedness from the side of the academic institutions or the Government. No online platforms were contracted to provide the backbone of online learning. In Kerala, the school system was relatively better prepared, based on the investments made in the IT@School system, which soon evolved to KITES (Kerala Infrastructure and Technology Enabled School) School and its dedicated education channel (VICTERS). By broadcasting the course contents on these platforms at pre-announced slots, millions of children in the schools who followed the Kerala Syllabus were able to learn the topics from some of the best teachers. However, no such systems were available for students of non-Kerala syllabi and higher education. Teachers in every institution had to improvise using whatever technological skills, equipments, or platforms they had. Consequently, teachers used whatever platforms they found or were familiar with. Even in the same institution, each teacher used a different platform, creating completely avoidable difficulties for the learners.

While the teachers around the world heroically adapted themselves to provide some sort of educational continuity to their wards, it was the systems that did not catch up. Online teaching and classroom teaching are essentially two different types of activities and sending a pre-recorded class session over WhatsApp or providing live PPTs on Zoom is no substitute for face-

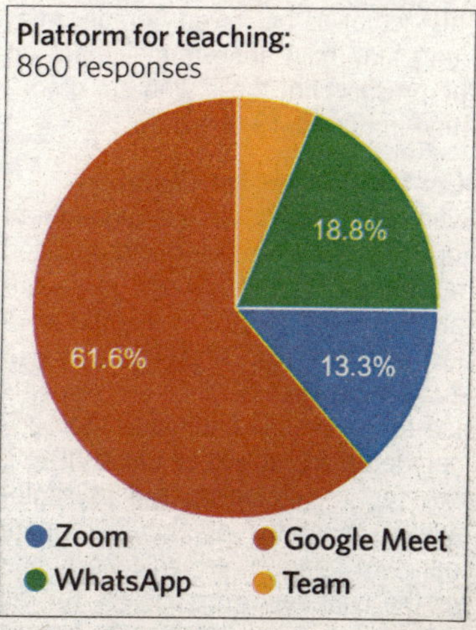

to-face learning. While this certainly helped to continue some degree of transfer of knowledge to the children, the second and perhaps even more important part of educational experience – that of socialization of the learners – was wholly neglected. The teachers received no guidance on how this can be achieved online. The techniques for measuring learning were not up-to-date in order to deal with the online situation and subsequently, the lack of proctoring. Governments around the world were pleased to merely continue providing some kind of education and elicit minimal complaints from parents and children. This led to the "grade inflation phenomenon" across the world. In the United Kingdom as normal examinations were cancelled and grading was based on internal examinations, 10-15% inflation of A grades was projected. In Kerala Technological University, the pass percentage for the 2016-2020 batch was 46.5 percent as against 36.4 the previous year (though this was excluding that of the supplementary results as it was not available when course results were announced.) This actual or perceived "grade inflation" may have long-term impact on the prospects of those who are graduating in COVID-19 times.

Key Challenges for Children

Even as teachers were struggling to cope up with preparing lessons and delivering it to the learners in an unfamiliar medium, the students were having their own challenges. In our study, more than 58% of the students had to use mobile phones as their primary learning tool. Prior to COVID-19, most ophthalmologists and psychologists were of the opinion that more than two hours of screen time is bad for the well-being of children. But all such considerations were discarded to keep the education going for the children. Added to this was the woe that, at the start of the academic session, more than two hundred thousand children did not even have access to any learning instrument. This was gradually resolved by the timely intervention of both the Government and civil society. Yet a good twelve months after, the shortage of learning instrument is a daily fact in Kerala.

Another major challenge for online learning (both for students and teachers) was that of connectivity. Internet penetration varies significantly globally. In most developed countries, neither the availability of learning instruments nor access to bandwidth was an issue. This was not the case in developing countries. While Kerala fares better in connectivity than the rest of India, for most students, the main route of connection was mobile data plans, which are often unreliable and expensive. Only 17% of the students responded that they had access to very good in-

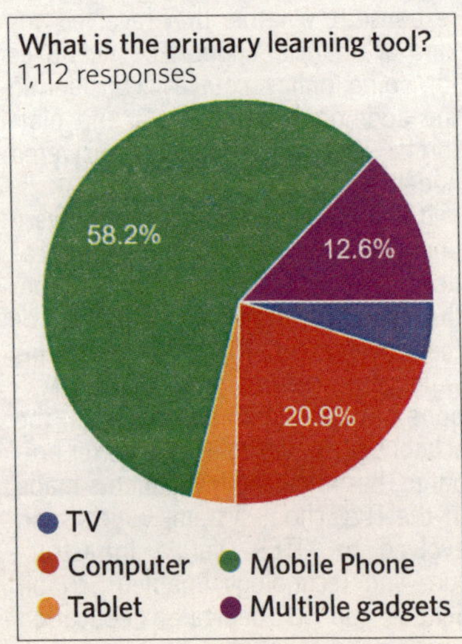

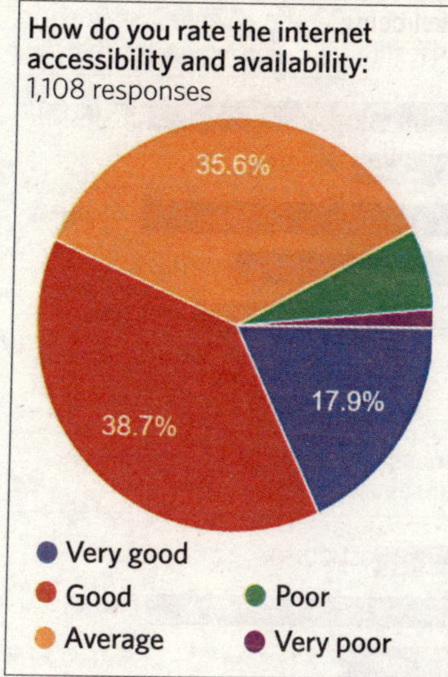

ternet connection. Nearly 44% of the respondents had either average or below average internet connectivity, not an ideal situation for online learning under a lockdown condition.

Positive Features of Online Learning

It must be added there were many positive features to the online learning that were reported by students, parents, and teachers. There was the natural consensus that the lack of travel was the biggest boon. Most respondents felt that their confidence in using digital media increased during this period. The surprising finding was the improvement of learning in the case of children with disability. This may be because such children had opportunity to attend classes right in the safe and comfort zone of their own homes.

Children also reported favorably in terms of factors such as their security and well-being. A large proportion of students (48%) felt that the behavior of teachers improved in the context of online learning: possibly as they were aware that they were on camera and were possibly being watched by the parents of the students. There was relief among students about the absence of bullying from peers. Nearly 40% of the students responded that absence of harassment in public transport was a major relief to them, thanks to the online learning environment.

Interestingly, many students felt that there were areas that showed marked improvement with online learning. Learning things visually, from expert teachers, and the opportunity to listen to recorded lectures, if needed, more than once, improved comprehension. Students also reported improved collaboration between students in the online environment. They also got ex-

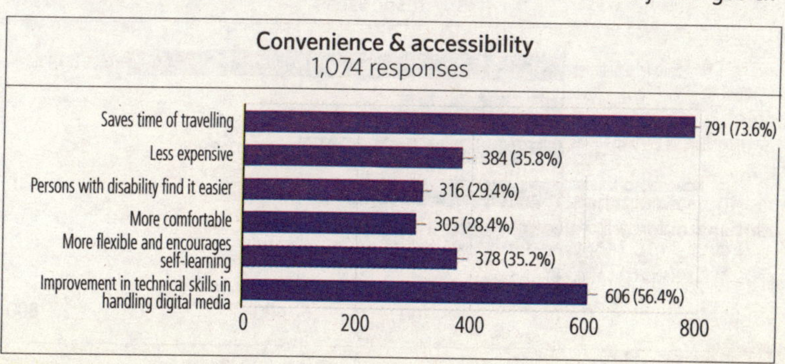

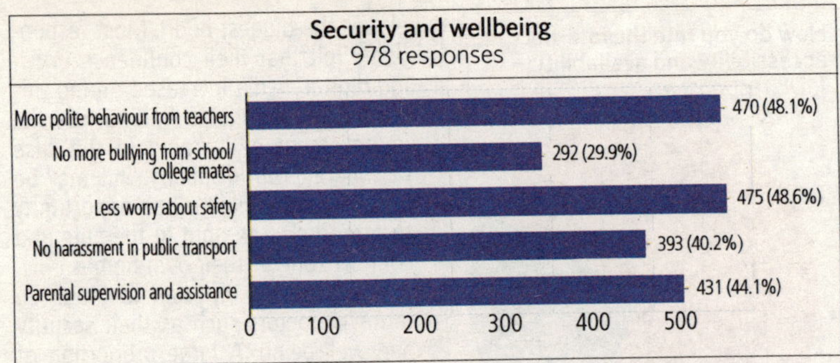

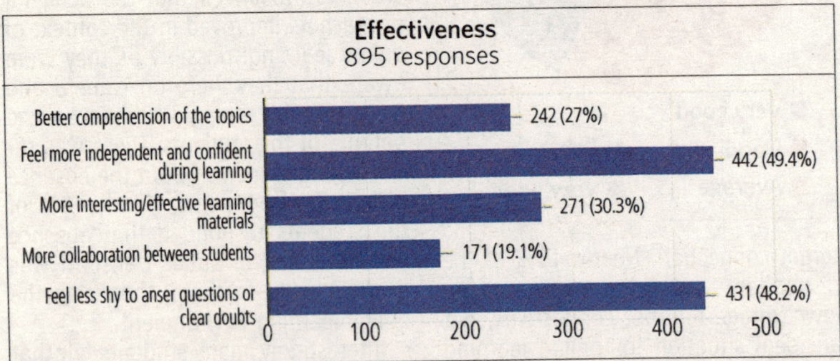

posure to learning materials from other countries and felt more empowered to ask questions and clarify doubts in chat as against seeking attention to ask a question in a real classroom.

The opinions of the students are also shared by the teachers when it comes to some of the conveniences of online learning. Close to 40% teachers reported that they get more time to prepare for the classes and less time is wasted on miscellaneous activities.

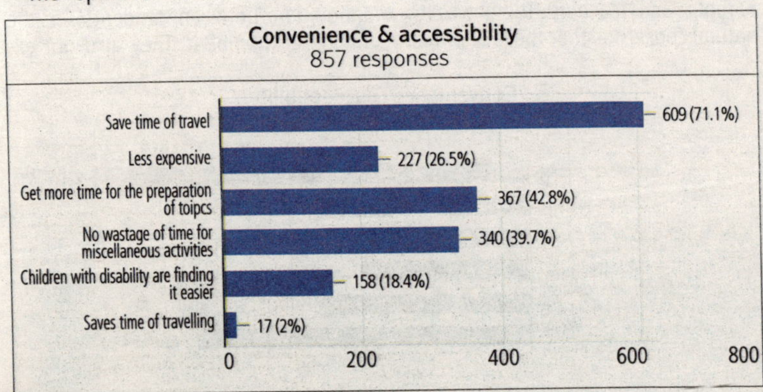

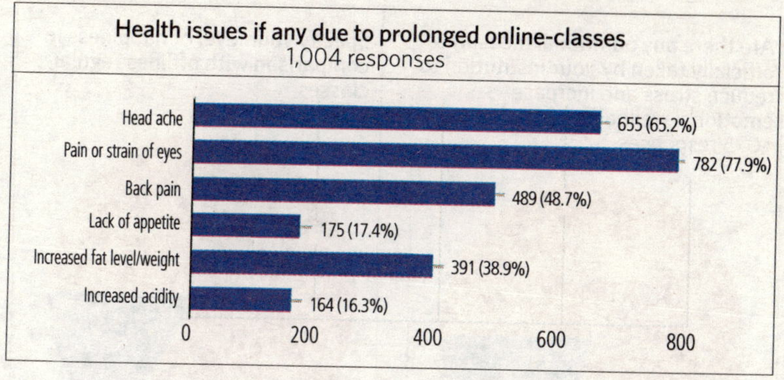

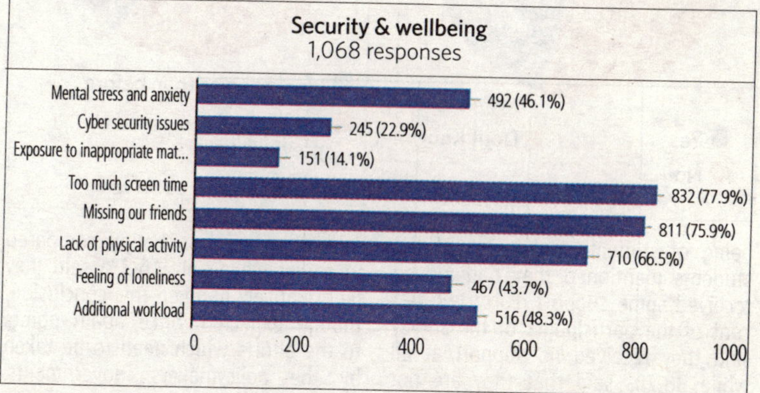

Health Issues Associated with Online Learning

Online learning, combined with lockdowns as experienced in most countries, meant that students were constrained in their homes, with little physical mobility. No specific guidance on how to set up their learning instrument was available. Many families did not, and do not, have the space to create appropriate learning environment for children. Children reported that they suffered a series of physical illnesses during the period from when their online classes began. As expected, strain of the eyes (77.9%) was reported the most, closely followed by headache and back pain. Close to 40% of the students recorded increased weight, a matter of concern that should be addressed immediately by introducing indoor training exercises, even as part of curriculum.

Children also felt mental stress during the COVID-19 period. Seventy seven per cent of the students reported that they missed their friends and more than 46% felt mental stress and anxiety. Many students expressed concern about cyber security issues and exposure to inappropriate materials online.

When asked if there was any action taken by their institutions to reduce stress and increase emotional well-

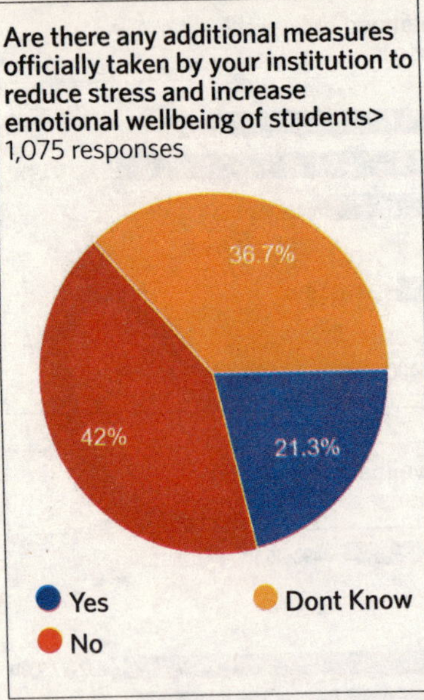

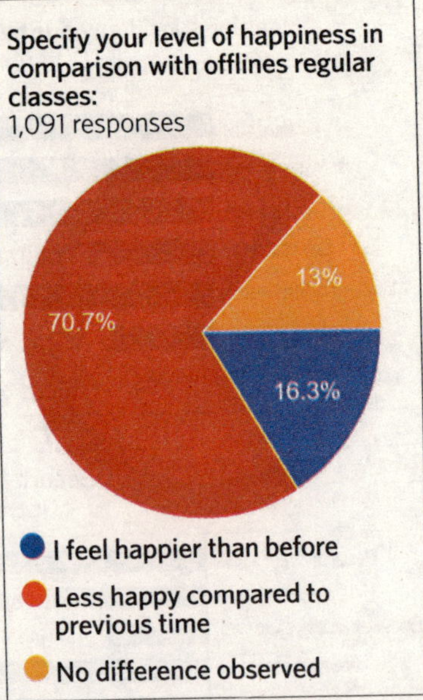

being of students, only 23% of the students mentioned they had indeed received some support. Forty two per cent of the participants of the survey said they received no support at all while 36.7% said that they are not aware of such measures, which in effect meant that they did not receive it even if it existed. It is a matter of concern that majority of the students did not receive any counselling support during the lockdown period while pursuing online learning. These are crucial observations and matters to be kept in mind while thinking about the future of online learning.

When asked how they feel, in comparison to their previous experience of classroom learning, more than 70% said they feel less happy compared to earlier while only 16.3% said they feel relatively happier. This conclusion, though expected, once again points to the efforts which need to be taken by the policymakers, governments, educational institutions, communities, and families to help students thrive through such unprecedented, challenging times.

Teachers' Perspectives

When teachers were asked about effectiveness of online learning, they mostly reacted negatively. A good majority of them complained that it is difficult to ensure attendance as well as attention in the class and 33.5% complained that students are not co-operating well

Enterprise Data Architects

Data architects and stewards provide data management services for the enterprise at a strategic level while ensuring data quality, accessibility, and security. They are the ones who create blueprints for data management, pipelines and its repositories at a strategic level.

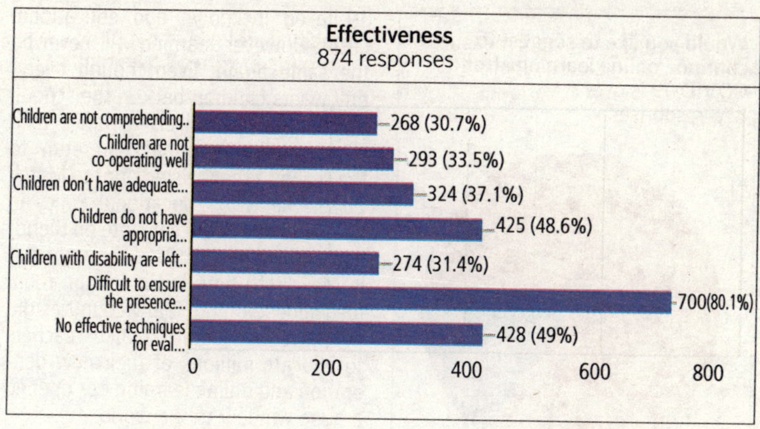

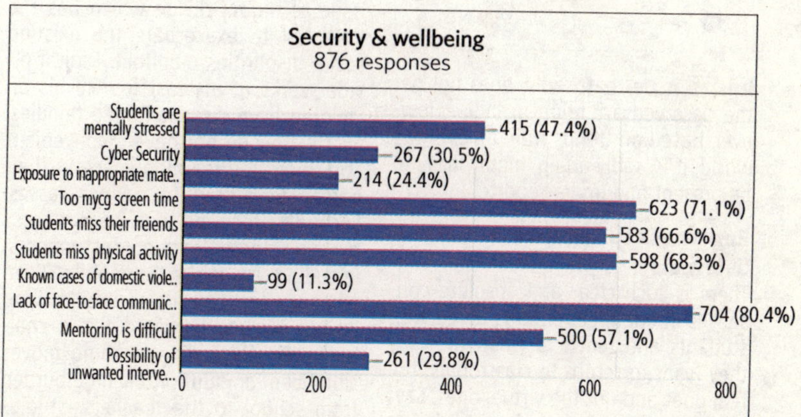

with online classes. A good number of them were rightly concerned that there was no effective way of evaluating the students and 30.7% felt that the students may not be comprehending correctly.

Teachers felt that students were feeling stressed and not getting enough physical activity while being confined to home, having their classes online. They also expressed concern that youngsters could be exposed to cyber security issues and or inappropriate content. Some teachers had apprehensions of domestic violence that some children may be battling with.

Space Tourism

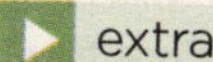

A growing number of businesses are vying to get a pie of the budding space tourism industry. Some big players engaged and hiring in this field are Virgin Galactic, SpaceX, Blue Origin, Orion, Orion Span (Space Hotel) and Boeing.

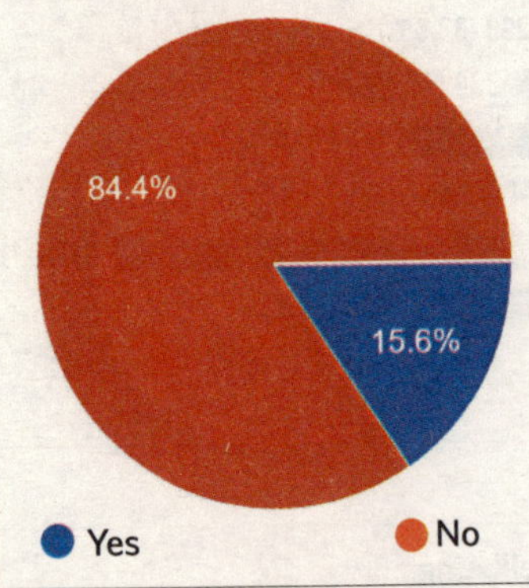

It is an issue that, sadly, does not get the deserved attention in India. However, based on trends from all over the world, it is, sadly again, highly likely to be present and under-reported.

Eagerness to Return to 'Normalcy'

There is such clear and absolute consensus in one area: parents agree with students and teachers when they say they want to return to classrooms; the real ones and not the virtual ones. Seventy-five percent of students and sixty percent of teachers mentioned that they are eager to go back to school. Interestingly, most parents, a whoppingt 84% of them, want their children to return to schools.

Future of Online Learning

With vaccination rates picking up, humanity will get over the COVID-19-linked lockdown and educational crises. However, learning will never be the same again. Even though everyone wants children back in the school, teaching is more likely to move to a blended learning format than return to the scenario that existed prior to March 2020. The New Educational Policy in India and the "Concept Note on Blended Learning" which UGC brought out in May 2020 both leave enough room for online learning. Many countries did not have adequately trained teachers to educate millions of their new generation and online learning has opened a huge window to the world.

The world will need to tackle the issue of digital divide which has the potential to exacerbate the existing social disparities manifold. Digital divide works at at least four levels on children from disadvantaged families. Firstly, they do not have a convenient and dedicated learning space in their homes to attend to online classes. Secondly, they do not have access to appropriate learning instruments, including TV, tablet or mobile. Even when the first two are secured, having an appropriate bandwidth is a challenge. Finally, online learning moves significant amount of teaching burden from school to the teachers. Studies in America shows that the level of involvement of parents in their children's education during COVID-19 period is unparalleled. In such situation, if a parent is not able to help the child with their daily lessons, the chance of the child to adapt to online learning reduces enormously, thus pushing you greater disadvantage.

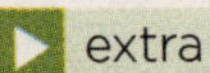

Space Medicine/Psychology

It is the practice of medicine for astronauts in outer space. A large part of it involves mitigating the physiological changes caused by weightlessness as well as psychological issues.

Education

Before 1976, education was the exclusive responsibility of the states. The Constitutional Amendment of 1976, which included education in the Concurrent List, was a far-reaching step. The substantive, financial and administrative implication required a new sharing of responsibility between the Union government and the states. While the role and responsibility of the states in education remained largely unchanged, the Union government accepted a larger responsibility of reinforcing the national and integrated character of education, maintaining quality and standard including those of the teaching profession at all levels, and the study and monitoring of the education requirements of the country.

The Central government plays a leading role in the evolution and monitoring of educational policies and programmes, the most notable of which are the National Policy on Education (NPE), 1986 and the Programme of Action (POA), 1986 as updated in 1992. The modified policy envisages a National System of education to bring about uniformity in education, making adult education programmes a mass movement, providing universal access, retention and quality in elementary education, special emphasis on education of girls, establishment of pace-setting schools like Navodaya Vidyalayas in each district, vocationalisation of secondary education, synthesis of knowledge and inter-disciplinary research in higher education, starting more Open Universities in the states, strengthening of the All India Council of Technical Education, encouraging sports, physical education, yoga and adoption of an effective evaluation method, etc. Besides, a decentralised management structure had

also been suggested to ensure popular participation in education. The POA lays down a detailed strategy for the implementation of the various policy parameters by the implementing agencies.

The National System of Education as envisaged in the NPE is based on a national curricular framework, which envisages a common core along with other flexible and region-specific components. While the policy stresses widening of opportunities for the people, it calls for consolidation of the existing system of higher and technical education. The POA lays down a detailed strategy for the implementation of the various policy parameters by the implementing agencies. It also emphasises the need for a much higher level of investment in education of at least six per cent of the national income.

The government has taken a number of major initiatives during the 11th Five Year Plan. Some of the new initiatives in the school and literacy sector and Higher and Technical Education sector include enactment of Right to education, launching of Saakshar Bharat, evolving a national curriculum framework for teacher education, introducing a system for replacement of marks by grades at the secondary stage in schools affiliated to Central Board of Secondary Education (CBSE) based on recommendations of Yash Pal Committee and National Knowledge Commission, establishment of 14 Innovation Universities aiming at world class standards, setting up 10 new National Institutes of Technology, launching of new Scheme of Interest subsidy on education loans taken for professional courses by the economically weaker students, academic reforms (semester system), choice-based credit system, regular revision of syllabi, impetus to research, etc.

In order to ensure all-round development in the field of education, the ministry of human resource development was created on 26 September 1985. Currently the ministry has two departments namely: (1) Department of School Education or literacy (ii) Department of High Education which deals with university education, technical education, scholarships and promotion of languages, books and copyrights.

Universities and Colleges

Indian higher education is a highly complex and fragmented system. One of the major reasons for its current dismal state is the presence of multiple regulators with varying quality and standards of monitoring and assessment. Under the Ministry of Human Resource Development (MHRD) at the Centre, the University Grants Commission (UGC) and the All India Council of Technical Education (AICTE) have been regulating the majority of the country's universities, affiliated colleges, technical and management institutes. Besides, there are other regulators, including the Bar Council of India (BCI), Medical Council of India (MCI), National Council for Teacher Education (NCTE), and Indian Council of Agricultural Research (ICAR), that set norms and standards for professional courses such as law, medicine, and agriculture. State universities and affiliated colleges, which enroll more than 90 percent of India's student population that avail of higher education, however, must abide by these national regulators as well as align themselves with the state government authorities and their regulations.

India currently has 993 universities, 39931 colleges, 3440 Polytechnics, 291 institutes offering PGDM and 3759 Teacher Training institutions. These universities and their affiliated colleges are often criticised for being substandard as they are overwhelmingly underfunded and mired in politics of both the state and the central governments. This is because the chairpersons/heads of these institutes are invariably political appointees under the respective University Acts. These are also the institutes regulated by the UGC. Among other issues, UGC has been criticised by academics for misutilisation of power and mismanagement of funds (Yash Pal committee, 2009 and Hari Gautam Committee, 2015).

extra

Youngest Congress President

Maulana Abul Kalam Azad was the youngest Congress president. He was elected the Congress president at the age of 35. Azad presided over the special Delhi session of the Congress in 1923.

Number of Recognised Educational Institutions in India

States	2018-19				2018-19						
	Up to Higher Secondary	Up to Secondary	Up to Upperprimary	Only Primary Schools	Universities/ University level Institutes	Colleges	Technical Education (Polytechnics)	PGDM	Nursing	Teacher Training	Institutes under Ministries
Andhra Pradesh	2182	12513	9427	39499	41	2678	154	7	253	406	1
Arunachal Pradesh	161	302	1299	2031	10	37	6	0	0	5	0
Asom	2229	7568	12008	44519	22	544	23	1	25	27	1
Bihar	4931	3666	37894	42733	33	840	54	4	59	31	1
Chhattisgarh	4391	2702	16370	32811	28	760	1	3	40	26	1
Gujarat	7388	4846	30065	12282	72	2232	10	9	142	141	8
Haryana	4973	3176	5500	9885	48	1038	145	11	21	35	8
Himachal Pradesh	2463	1726	2771	11252	26	336	35	0	26	18	0
Jammu & Kashmir	1266	3200	10136	15106	15	293	53	0	25	23	1
Jharkhand	1575	3351	16529	24453	25	313	38	6	26	5	0
Karnataka	5489	15388	31802	25554	65	3670	302	23	524	415	9
Kerala	2962	1927	4680	7132	23	1348	73	5	161	197	1
Madhya Pradesh	9205	8262	49622	86975	65	2191	64	21	121	129	3
Maharashtra	10042	17404	29922	52574	62	4340	669	61	557	959	13
Manipur	246	914	1084	2600	6	92	2	0	6	11	1
Meghalaya	350	1418	3553	9348	10	63	3	0	7	8	1
Mizoram	186	683	1540	1504	3	32	2	0	4	9	0
Nagaland	185	577	800	1190	5	67	5	0	3	8	0
Odisha	2398	9488	21837	34994	28	1062	128	8	168	65	2
Punjab	5159	4484	5122	13872	32	1063	182	2	154	57	2
Rajasthan	20067	10587	36463	38766	83	3156	189	9	55	210	4
Sikkim	108	146	314	722	7	19	2	0	1	4	0
Tamil Nadu	7943	5828	9411	35970	59	2466	496	9	111	292	8
Telangana	2399	11847	7356	20753	24	1988	152	11	153	184	2
Tripura	453	669	1245	2578	4	52	0	0	4	4	1
Uttar Pradesh	19162	12083	80624	161366	79	7078	358	69	264	216	6
Uttarakhand	2450	1341	5430	14338	36	438	111	3	31	13	2
West Bengal	7372	3338	9249	77869	45	1371	146	14	74	210	12

States	2018-19				2018-19						
	Up to Higher Secondary	Up to Secondary	Up to Upperprimary	Only Primary Schools	Universities/ University level Institutes	Colleges	Technical Education (Polytechnics)	PGDM	Nursing	Teacher Training	Institutes under Ministries
A&N Islands	66	50	81	217	0	8	0	0	0	0	0
Chandigarh	96	72	41	20	3	25	3	1	0	3	0
D & N Haveli	24	23	131	168	0	8	0	0	1	0	0
Daman & Diu	24	24	42	50	0	10	0	0	0	2	0
Delhi	1769	367	872	2695	27	180	17	13	22	41	12
Goa	114	404	61	907	3	57	8	1	0	1	0
Lakshadweep	13	2	15	15	0	0	0	0	0	0	0
Puducherry	179	197	83	280	4	76	9	0	1	4	0
All India	130020	150573	443379	827028	993	39931	3440	291	3039	3759	100

Source: Source:Department of School Education & Literacy and AISHE 2018-19

Note: na: not available

School Infrastructure

The progress in school and higher education infrastucture is given in the table below. The physical infrastructure of more than 9.72 lakh government elementary schools has improved significantly. Out of these, 90.72 per cent have girls' toilet, 93.7 per cent have boys' toilet, 95.9 per cent have provision of drinking water facility, 88.1 per cent have hand wash facility, 82.1 per cent have wash (drinking water, toilet and hand wash) facility, 84.2 per cent have medical check-up facility, 20.7 per cent have computer, 67.4 per cent have electricity connection and 83.8 per cent have library .

Increase in Number of Recognised Schools, Colleges and Universities Infrastructure

Year	Primary and Upper Primary schools (in lakhs)	Secondary and senior secondary schools (in lakhs)	Colleges	Universities
2011-12	11.93	2.12	34852	642
2018-19	12.7	2.76	39931	993

Source: Economic Survey 2020-21

National Education Policy 2020

The Union Cabinet chaired by the Prime Minister Narendra Modi on 29 July approved the National Education Policy 2020. The new policy aims to pave way for transformational reforms in school and higher education systems in the country. This policy will replace the 34 your old National Policy on Education (NPE),1986.

The NEP 2020 aims at making " India a global knowledge superpower."

The Cabinet has also approved the renaming of the Ministry of Human Resource Development to the Ministry of Education.

The NEP cleared by the Cabinet is only the third major revamp of the framework of education in India since independence.

The two earlier education policies were brought in 1968 and 1986.

Highlights

School Education

- Universalization of education from preschool to secondary level with 100% Gross Enrolment Ratio (GER) in school education by 2030.
- NEP 2020 will bring 2 crore out of school children back into the main stream through open schooling system.
- The current 10+2 system to be replaced by a new 5+3+3+4 curricular structure corresponding to ages 3-8, 8-11, 11-14, and 14-18 years respectively.
- It will bring the hitherto uncovered age group of 3-6 years under school curriculum, which has been recognized globally as the crucial stage for development of mental faculties of a child. The new system will have 12 years of schooling with three years of Anganwadi/ pre schooling.
- Emphasis on Foundational Literacy and Numeracy, no rigid separation between academic streams, extracurricular, vocational streams in schools; Vocational Education to start from Class 6 with Internships
- Teaching up to at least Grade 5 to be in mother tongue/ regional language. No language will be imposed on any student.
- Assessment reforms with 360 degree Holistic Progress Card, tracking Student Progress for achieving Learning Outcomes
- A new and comprehensive National Curriculum Framework for Teacher Education, NCFTE 2021, will be formulated by the NCTE in consultation with NCERT. By 2030, the minimum degree qualification for teaching will be a 4-year integrated B.Ed. degree .

Higher Education

- Gross Enrolment Ratio in higher education to be raised to 50% by 2035; 3.5 crore seats to be added in higher education.
- The policy envisages broad based, multi-disciplinary, holistic Under Graduate education with flexible curricula, creative combinations of subjects, integration of vocational education and multiple entry and exit points with ap-

propriate certification. UG education can be of 3 or 4 years with multiple exit options and appropriate certification within this period.

- Academic Bank of Credits to be established to facilitate Transfer of Credits
- Multidisciplinary Education and Research Universities (MERUs), at par with IITs, IIMs, to be set up as models of best multidisciplinary education of global standards in the country.
- The National Research Foundation will be created as an apex body for fostering a strong research culture and building research capacity across higher education.
- Higher Education Commission of India(HECI) will be set up as a single overarching umbrella body for the entire higher education, excluding medical and legal education. HECI to have four independent verticals - National Higher Education Regulatory Council (NHERC) for regulation, General Education Council (GEC) for standard setting, Higher Education Grants Council (HEGC) for funding, and National Accreditation Council(NAC) for accreditation. Public and private higher education institutions will be governed by the same set of norms for regulation, accreditation and academic standards.
- Affiliation of colleges is to be phased out in 15 years and a stage-wise mechanism is to be established for granting graded autonomy to colleges. Over a period of time, it is envisaged that every college would develop into either an Autonomous degree-granting College, or a constituent college of a university.

Other Changes

- An autonomous body, the National Educational Technology Forum (NETF), will be created to provide a platform for the free exchange of ideas on the use of technology to enhance learning, assessment, planning, administration.
- NEP 2020 emphasizes setting up of Gender Inclusion Fund, Special Education Zones for disadvantaged regions and groups
- New Policy promotes Multilingualism in both schools and higher education. National Institute for Pali, Persian and Prakrit, Indian Institute of Translation and Interpretation to be set up
- The Centre and the States will work together to increase the public investment in Education sector to reach 6% of GDP at the earliest.

Unprecedented Consultations

NEP 2020 has been formulated after an unprecedented process of consultation that involved nearly over 2 lakh suggestions from 2.5 lakhs Gram Panchayats, 6600 Blocks, 6000 ULBs, 676 Districts. The MHRD initiated an unprecedented collaborative, inclusive, and highly participatory consultation process from January 2015.

In May 2016, 'Committee for Evolution of the New Education Policy' under the Chairmanship of Late Shri T.S.R. Subramanian, Former Cabinet Secretary, submitted its report. Based on this, the Ministry prepared 'Some Inputs for the Draft National Education Policy, 2016'.

In June 2017 a 'Committee for the Draft National Education Policy' was constituted under the Chairmanship of eminent scientist Dr. K. Kasturirangan, which submitted the Draft National Education Policy, 2019 to the Hon'ble Human Resource Development Minister on 31st May, 2019. The Draft National Education Policy 2019 was uploaded on MHRD's website and at 'MyGov Innovate' portal eliciting views/suggestions/comments of stakeholders, including public.

14

ECONOMY

- Economic Survey: 2020-21
- Improving Ease of Doing Business Ranking
- Economy - Timeline
- Privatization: Is it a Boon or a Bane
- Banking, Insurance and Capital Market
- Unicorns in India

Economic Survey 2020-21

State of the Economy

The economy witnessed a sharp contraction in GDP of 23.9% in the first quarter and of 7.5% in the second quarter of

Key Indicators

Data Categories	Unit	2017-18	2018-19	2019-20	2020-21
GDP and Related Indicators					
GDP at current market prices	₹ lakh crore	171.0	189.7	203.4[a]	194.8[b]
GDP at constant market prices	₹ lakh crore	131.8	139.8	145.7[a]	134.4[b]
Growth Rate	%	7.0	6.1	4.2[a]	-7.7[b]
GVA at current basic prices	₹ lakh crore	155.1	171.4	183.4[a]	175.8[b]
GVA at constant basic prices	₹ lakh crore	120.7	128.0	133.0[a]	123.4[b]
Growth Rate	%	6.6	6.0	3.9[a]	-7.2[b]
Gross Savings	% of GDP	32.4	30.1	na	na
Gross Capital Formation	% of GDP	34.2	32.2	na	na
Per Capita Net National Income (at current prices)	₹	1,15,293	1,26,521	1,34,226[a]	1,26,968[b]
Production					
Foodgrains	Million tonnes	285.0	285.2	296.7[c]	144.5[c]
Index of Industrial Production (growth)	%	4.4	3.8	-0.8	-15.5[d]
Electricity Generation (growth)	%	5.4	5.2	1.0	-4.6[d]
Prices					
WPI Inflation (average)	%	3.0	4.3	1.7	-0.1[e]
CPI (Combined) Inflation (average)	%	3.6	3.4	4.8	6.6[e]
External Sector					
Merchandise export Growth (in US$ term)	%	10.0	8.8	-5.1	-15.7[e]
Merchandise Import growth (in US$ terms)	%	21.1	10.4	-7.7	-29.1[e]
Current Account Balance	% of GDP	-1.8	-2.1	-0.9	3.1[f]
Foreign Exchange Reserves (end of year)	US$ Billion	424.4	411.9	475.6	586.1[k]
Average Exchange Rate	$/ US$	64.45	69.92	70.90	74.64[j]
Money and Credit					
Broad Money (M3) growth (annual)	%	7.8	10.2	10.1	12.4[g]
Scheduled Commercial Bank Credit (growth)	%	10	13.3	6.1	6.1[g]
Fiscal Indicators (Centre)					
Gross Fiscal Deficit	% of GDP	3.5	3.4	4.6[h]	3.5[i]
Revenue Deficit	% of GDP	2.6	2.4	3.3[h]	2.7[i]
Primary Deficit	% of GDP	0.4	0.4	1.6[h]	0.4[i]

Notes: na: Not Available a: Provisional estimates b: First advance estimate c: (Fourth AE for 2019-20 and first AE for 2020-21, d: (April-November) 2020, e: (April-December) 2020, f: (April-September) 2020, g: as on December 18, 2020, h: Provisional Actuals, i: Budget estimates, j: End of December 2020, k: As on 8th January 2021.

2020-21.Overall, GDP is expected to decline by 7.7% in 2020-21 as compared to the growth of 4.2% in 2019-20.The survey projects nominal GDP growth of 15.4% and real GDP growth of 11% in 2021-22.

Agriculture and Allied Activities

• India's Agricultural (and Allied Activities) sector has shown its resilience amid the adversities of COVID-19 induced lockdowns with a growth of 3.4% at constant prices during 2020-21 (first advance estimate)

• The share of Agriculture and Allied Sectors in Gross Value Added (GVA) of the country at current prices is 17.8% for the year 2019-20 (CSO-Provisional Estimates of National Income, 29th May, 2020)

• Gross Capital Formation (GCF) relative to GVA showing a fluctuating trend from 17.7 % in 2013-14 to 16.4 % in 2018-19, with a dip to 14.7 % in 2015-16

• Total food grain production in the country in the agriculture year 2019-20 (as per Fourth Advance Estimates), is 11.44 million tonnes more than that during 2018-19

• The actual agricultural credit flow was ₹13,92,469.81 crores against the target of ₹13,50,000 crores in 2019-20. The target for 2020-21 was ₹15,00,000 crores and a sum of ₹ 9,73,517.80 crores was disbursed till 30th November, 2020:

1.5 crore dairy farmers of milk cooperatives and milk producer companies were targeted to provide Kisan Credit Cards (KCC) as part of Prime Minister's Aatma Nirbhar Bharat Package after the budget announcement of February 2020.

As of mid January 2021, a total of 44,673 Kisan Credit Cards (KCCs) have been issued to fishermen and fish farmers and an additional 4.04 lakh applications from fishermen and fish farmers are with the banks at various stages of issuance.

• The Pradhan Mantri Fasal Bima Yojana covers over 5.5 crore farmer applications year on year:

Claims worth ₹90,000 crore paid, as on 12th January, 2021.

Speedy claim settlement directly into the farmer accounts through Aadhar linkage.

70 lakh farmers benefitted and claims worth ₹8741.30 crores were transferred during COVID-19 lockdown period.

• An amount of ₹18000 crore have been deposited directly in the bank accounts of 9 crore farmer families of the country in December, 2020 in the 7th installment of financial benefit under the PM-KISAN scheme.

• Fish production reached an all-time high of 14.16 million metric tons during 2019-20:

GVA by the Fisheries sector to the national economy stood at ₹2,12,915 crores constituting 1.24% of the total national GVA and 7.28 % of the agricultural GVA.

• Food Processing Industries (FPI) sector growing at an Average Annual Growth Rate (AAGR) of around 9.99 % as compared to around 3.12 % in Agriculture and 8.25 % in Manufacturing at 2011-12 prices during the last 5 years ending 2018-19.

• Pradhan Mantri Garib Kalyan Anna Yojana: 80.96 crore beneficiaries were provided foodgrains above NFSA man-

dated requirement free of cost till November, 2020.

Over 200 LMT of foodgrains were provided amounting to a fiscal outgo of over ₹ 75000 crore.

- AatmaNirbhar Bharat Package: 5 kg per person per month for four months (May to August) to approximately 8 crore migrants (excluded under NFSA or state ration card) entailing subsidy of ₹3109 crores approximately.

Industry and Infrastructure

The industrial sector is estimated to decline by 9.6% in 2020-21. Within the sector, highest decline is estimated in construction (12.6%) and mining (12.4%). The contribution of the industrial sector to GVA has declined from 32.5% in 2011-12 to 25.8% in 2020-21.

The Index of Industrial Production (IIP) growth declined by 15.5% between April-November 2020 as compared to growth of 0.3% during same period in 2019. IIP is a measure of industrial performance that assigns a weight of 78% to manufacturing, 14% to mining and 8% to electricity. Out of 407 items in IIP, the number of items which observed growth increased from 28 in April 2020 to 171 in November 2020, thereby, indicating a sharp economy recovery.

The National Infrastructure Pipeline was launched with an investment plan of ₹111 lakh crore over five years (2020-25). The project is aimed at increasing growth, competitiveness and employment. The state governments, central government, and the private sector will invest 40%, 39%, and 21% in the project respectively. The major share of the funds will be given to: (i) energy sector (24%), (ii) roads (18%), (iii) urban infrastructure (17%), and (iv) railways (12%).

Service Sector

The services sector accounts for over 54 % of India's GVA and nearly four-fifths of total FDI inflow into India. The sector's share in GVA exceeds 50% in 15 out of 33 States and UTs, and is particularly more pronounced (greater than 85%) in Delhi and Chandigarh. Services sector accounts for 48% of total exports, outperforming goods exports in the recent years.

Major Services

In the wake of the Covid-19 pandemic, most of the sub-sectors of the services sector witnessed a contraction in growth during 2020-21. Aviation and tourism declined sharply in 2020. Only 2.46 mil-

Performance of Key Sub-sectors in India's Servcice Sector

Sub Sector	Indicator	Unit	Year 2016-17	2017-18	2018-19	2019-20	2020-21
IT-BPM*	IT-BPM service revenues:	US$ billion	139.9	151.4	161.8	174.53(E)	—
	Exports	US$ billion	116.1	125.1	135.5	146.6(E)	—
	Domestic	US$ billion	23.8	26.3	26.3	28(E)	—

Sub Sector	Indicator	Unit	Year				
			2016-17	2017-18	2018-19	2019-20	2020-21
Aviation**	Airline passengers:	million	158.4	183.9	204.2	202(P)	—
	Domestic	million	103.7	123.3	140.3	141.6	22.77#
	International	million	54.7	60.6	63.9	60.4	—
Telecom	Wireless phone subscriptions[a]	million	1,170.2	1,183.4	1,161.8	1,157.8	1,151.81##
	Wireless internet subscriptions[a]	million	400.6	472.7	582.8	720.7	—
Tourism	Foreign tourist arrivals[b]	million	8.8	10.0	10.6	10.9(P)	2.46###
	Foreign exchange earnings from tourism[b]	US$ million	22.9	27.3	28.6	30.1(P)	6.16###
Shipping	Gross tonnage of Shippinga	million	11.6	12.6	12.8	12.68^	12.75@
	Number of ships[a]	number	1,316	1,384	1,405	1,431^	1,453^^
Ports	Port traffic	million tonnes	1,133.7	1,208.6	1,276.8	1307.2	777.04#
	Cargo capacity	million tonnes	2,147.6	2,307.4	2,405.9	2,522.9	2,529.1(P)

Sources: Telecom Regulatory Authority of India (TRAI), Department of Telecom, Ministry of Tourism, Ministry of Shipping, Ministry of Civil Aviation, Ministry of Electronics and Information Technology, NASSCOM.

Notes: *Including Hardware and excluding e-commerce; **Domestic passengers carried by scheduled Indian carriers on scheduled domestic services and international passengers carried by scheduled Indian and foreign carriers to and from the Indian territory; a: As of March of ensuing financial year; b: On calendar year basis; # For Apr-Nov 2020 period; ##: As of Oct 2020; ###: Jan-June 2020; @: As of June 2020: ^ As of March 2020; ^^: As of November 2020; P-Provisional. E- Expected.

lion foreign tourists arrived in India during January-June 2020 as compared to 5.29 million during January-June 2019. Consequently, foreign exchange earnings from tourism declined to US$ 6.16 billion during the first six months of 2020 as compared to US$ 14.19 billion during the corresponding period in 2019. Domestic passenger traffic too dropped to 22.77 million during April-November 2020 from 95.7 million during the corresponding period in 2019. In the ports sector, cargo traffic at ports fell by 10.09 per cent to 777.04 million tonnes (MT) during April-November period of the current fiscal compared to 864.32 MT during April-November 2019.

FDI Inflows into Services Sector

India improved its position from 12th in 2018 to 9th in 2019 in the list of the world's largest FDI recipients according to the latest World Investment Report 2020 by United Nations Conference on Trade and Development (UNCTAD). FDI into India recorded almost 17 per

Gross FDI Equity Inflows* into Services Sector					
Services Sub-sectors	Share in Gross FDI Equity Inflows into Services Sector in 2019-20 (per cent)**	Gross FDI Equity Inflows (US$ million)			
		2018-19	2019-20 2019	April-Sep 2020	April-Sep
Financial, Business Outsourcing, R&D, Courier, Tech Testing & Analysis	9.54	9,158	7,854	4,455	2,252
Computer Software & Hardware	74.34	6,415	7,673	4,025	17,554
Trading	4.02	4,462	4,574	2,143	949
Telecommunications	0.03	2,668	4,445	4,280	7
Information & Broadcasting	0.68	1,252	823	196	161
Hotel & Tourism	1.20	1,076	2,938	859	283
Hospitals & Diagnostic Centres	0.69	1,045	635	376	163
Education	2.56	777	3,245	216	604
Retail Trading	5.21	443	472	243	1,230
Consultancy Services	0.46	411	1,047	473	110
Sea Transport	0.61	279	199	173	144
Air Transport	0.41	191	918	114	97
Agriculture Services	0.25	88	46	23	60
Gross FDI Equity Inflows into Services Sector (US$ million)		28,265	34,868	17,577	23,612
Change from Previous Year (per cent YoY)		-2.4	23.4	33.1	34.3
Gross FDI Equity Inflows into India (US$ million)		44,366	49,977	26,096	30,004
Share of Services sector in Gross FDI Equity Inflows (per cent)		63.7	69.8	67.4	78.7

Source: Department for Promotion of Industry and Internal Trade (DPIIT)
Note: *Excludes re-invested earnings.

cent jump during April-September 2020 over the corresponding period last year, despite the global slowdown, the COVID-19 pandemic, lockdown measures and supply chain disruptions. Services sector, being the largest recipient of FDI in India, witnessed a strong growth during April-September 2020. The gross FDI equity inflows (excluding re-invested earnings) into the services sector jumped 34 per cent YoY during April-September 2020 to reach US$23.61 billion, accounting for almost four-fifth of the total gross FDI equity inflows into India during this period (***see table in page 614***). The jump in FDI equity inflows was driven by strong inflows into the 'Computer Software & Hardware' sub-sector, wherein FDI inflows increased to US$17.55 billion which is over 336 per cent higher over the corresponding period last year. High growth in FDI inflows was also present in sub-sectors such as 'Retail Trading', 'Agriculture Services', and 'Education'.

Health

Health insurance coverage has increased under the Ayushman Bharat Pradhan Mantri Jan Arogya Yojana (AB-PM-JAY). The proportion of health insured households between 2015-16 to 2019-20 increased by 54% in states that implemented AB-PM-JAY and decreased by 10% for states which did not implement the scheme. During this period, infant mortality rate decreased by 20% in states that implemented AB-PM-JAY whereas in states that did not implement AB-PM-JAY, infant mortality rate declined by 12%.

India has one of the highest levels of out-of-pocket expenses as a share of total health expenditure. The survey observes that increasing the spending on public health from 1% of GDP to 2.5-3% of GDP will help in reducing the out-of-pocket expenses from 65% to 30%.

Credit Rating

The survey noted that India's credit rating does not reflect the country's fundamentals in terms of GDP growth, inflation, government debt as a % of GDP, among others. It observed a bias in ratings against emerging economies like India and China. Credit rating maps the probability of default, reflecting the willingness and ability of borrower to meet debt obligations. India has no history of sovereign default (demonstrating willingness to pay), and the foreign exchange reserves are greater than the total external debt of the country (demonstrating ability to pay). Poor sovereign credit ratings have adverse impact on inflow of foreign investments.

Innovation

India ranks 48th among 131 countries for innovation, its highest-ever rank, but more work is needed on research and development (R&D) from the private sector. According to the Global Innovation Index (GII), India's ranking has improved from 81st in 2015 to 48th in 2020. India ranks first in Central and South Asia and third among lower middle-income group economies. The government expects businesses to produce more patents and original research, and says it does "a disproportionate amount of heavy-lifting on R&D by contributing 56 percent of the gross expenditure on R&D, which is three times the average contributed by governments in the top ten economies". In comparison, the business sector contributes 37 percent of the gross expenditure on R&D compared to an average 68 percent in the top 10 economies globally.

Startups need to play a key role in fostering innovation and increasing India's share of patents globally. "The Startup India campaign of the Government of India recognises entrepreneurship as an increasingly important strategy to fuel productivity growth and wealth creation in India. This assumes greater importance in the context of enhancing private participation in innovation in India - in terms of contribution to gross expenditure on R&D, R&D personnel and researchers, and share in patents filed in the country," the survey said.

India ranks 107th in the education sub-segment, mainly on account of ranking 118th on pupil-teacher ratio in secondary education; 115th on new business per thousand population in ages 15-64; 108th on tertiary Innovation.

India performed well regionally and in its income category, ranking first in the GII rankings in Central and South Asia and third amongst lower middle-income group economies. India performed above expectation for its level of development.

India ranks 27th on Knowledge and Technology Outputs and 31st in Market Sophistication, its highest rankings among the various categories. It ranks 55th in Business Sophistication, 60th in Human Capital and Research, 61st in Institutions, 64th in Creative Outputs and 75th in Infrastructure.

The Bare Necessities

Since the 1950s, when Pitambar Pant advocated the idea of "minimum needs", the idea that economic development can be viewed as a process of providing the "bare necessities of life" to citizens has been around in India. A family's ability to access bare necessities–such as housing, water, sanitation, electricity and clean cooking fuel–have therefore been regarded as an important barometer of economic development in academic and policymaking circles.

The "bare necessities" of housing, water, sanitation, electricity and clean cooking fuel are jointly consumed by all the members of a household. They, therefore, touch the life of every member in the household. As these are durable assets, they deliver services to the household over long periods of time. Access to clean drinking water, safe sanitation and clean cooking fuel also have direct linkages with health of the members in the household. Access to these saves time for a household, which they can utilise in productive activities such as education and learning.

In order to improve access to "the bare necessities," successive governments have made constant efforts. The network of schemes designed to deliver these necessities include inter-alia the Swachh Bharat Mission (SBM), National Rural Drinking Water Programme (NRDWP), Pradhan Mantri Awaas Yojana (PMAY), Saubhagya, and Ujjwala Yojana. These schemes were equipped with new features such as use of technology, real time monitoring, geo-tagging of assets, social audit, embedded digital flow of information, and direct benefit transfers wherever possible. These features improved the transparency in governance and enhanced the efficiency and effectiveness of the schemes.

extra

History of Economic Survey

Presenting Economic Survey before the Union Budget is a longstanding tradition. It was first presented in 1950-51 and submitted in the Lok Sabha along with the Budget until 1964. In 1964, the ministry started to release the survey a day before budget day.

Steps Towards Improving Ease of Doing Business Ranking

Dr. Jose Sebastian
Former Faculty, Gulati Institute of Finance and Taxation

A comprehensive look at the 'Ease of Doing Business Index' and its constituents and the various steps taken by the Union Government and different states in improving the ranking.

Countries across the world are trying to attract investment by initiating reforms in areas where the regulatory environment make the process of doing business difficult. Established by the World Bank Group, the Ease of Doing Business (EoDB) index is a ranking system widely used across the world to compare countries in terms of their business friendliness. In the EoDB index, 'higher rankings' (a lower numerical value) indicate better, usually simpler regulations for businesses and stronger protection of property rights. The first part of this article discusses in detail the concept of EoDB and the major strides India has made during the last few years. In the second part, an attempt has been made to compare states in terms of the EoDB ranking keeping the structure of the underlying economies in the background.

The Concept of Ease of Doing Business : A Brief History of its Origin and Development

Due to a variety of reasons, the performance of countries and regions within countries differs in attracting industrial investment. Development financial institutions like World Bank have devoted considerable attention in understanding the factors behind this difference. One of the earliest attempts in this direction was the report prepared jointly by three leading economists at the World Bank Group, Simeon Djankove, Michael Klein and Caralee McLiesh. This report on the ease of doing business titled "Doing Business in 2004: Understanding Regulation" was brought out in 2004. Ranking of countries was first introduced in the report " Doing Business 2006". Since then countries have been ranked every year and the latest report is "Doing Business 2020". Higher rankings (a low numerical value) indicate better, usually simpler, regulations for businesses and stronger protections of property rights. Over the years, the ranking of countries in "Doing Business Index" has emerged as an important benchmark in investment decisions of international investors and development finance institutions.

"Doing Business 2020": Major Highlights

Latest in the series of reports, "Doing Business 2020" presents data for 190 economies and aggregates information from 12 areas of business regulation:

1. Starting a Business of all
2. Dealing with Construction Permits
3. Getting Electricity
4. Registering Property
5. Getting Credit
6. Protecting Minority Investors
7. Paying Taxes
8. Trading across Borders
9. Enforcing Contracts
10. Resolving Insolvency
11. Employing Workers
12. Contracting with the Government

On the basis of each of the above mentioned parameters, rankings and weights are used to develop an overall EoDB ranking. A high EoDB ranking indicates that the regulatory environment is more conducive for starting and operating businesses.

Table 1: **India's Ranking in Various Parameters**

Parameter	**Ranking Among 190 Countries**	**Score out of 100**
Starting a Business	136	81.6
Dealing with Construction Permits	27	78.7
Getting Electricity	22	81.4
Registering Property	154	47.6
Getting Credit	25	80.0
Protecting Minority Interests	13	80.0
Paying Taxes	115	67.6
Trading Across Borders	68	82.5
Enforcing Contracts	163	41.2
Resolving Insolvency	52	62.0
Overall	63	71.0

Source: https://www.doingbusiness.org/en/data/exploreeconomies/india

Ease of Doing Business Ranking: Where Does India Stand?

Among 190 countries, India ranked 63rd in Doing Business 2020. The details are presented in table-1.

India's Efforts at Improving EoDB Ranking

By systematic efforts, India has improved her ranking in EoDB from 142 in 2014 to 63 in 2020. India has earned a place among the world's top 10 improvers for the third year in a row. In 2014, Government of India launched an ambitious programme of regulatory reforms with the objective of making it easier to do business in India. The program has gone

a long way in creating a more business-friendly environment in the country. This was part of a mission to achieve the vision of Prime Minister Narendra Modi of bringing India within the top 50 countries in the Doing Business rankings. As part of this, an analysis of leading comparable countries was undertaken to understand the global best practices. Subsequently, a detailed roadmap was developed and 7 Ministries/ Departments were appointed as nodal Ministries/Departments across 10 indicators.

The aim was to create a conducive business environment by streamlining the existing regulations and processes and eliminating unnecessary requirements and procedures. For improving efficiency, technology has been identified as the key driver. To deliver seamless services to the businesses, multitude of regulatory reforms has been implemented by Central and State Governments after an extensive Government Process Re-engineering exercise.

India's Major Achievements

Some of the major achievements of India's efforts are the following.

Construction Permits: India's ranking on this parameter has improved from 184 in 2014 to 27 in 2019. This improvement has been mainly on account of a decrease in the number of procedures and time taken for obtaining construction permits in India.

Getting Electricity: India's ranking on this parameter has improved from 137 in 2014 to 22 in 2019. It takes just 53 days and 4 procedures for a business to get an electricity connection in India.

Apart from these significant improvements, among the 190 economies, India ranks 13th in Protecting Minority Investors and 25th in Getting Credit.

Central Government Initiatives

Following are the major initiatives taken by the Central government towards improving India's rank in EoDB.

1. Starting a Business

a. For incorporation of companies Permanent Account Number (PAN), Tax Deduction & Collection Account Number (TAN), Director Identification Number (DIN) have now been merged into a single form (SPICe).

b. For companies with an authorised capital of up to ₹15 Lakh, incorporation fee has been eliminated.

c. There was a five-page form and other attachments for reserving the name of the Company with the Ministry of Corporate Affairs. These have been simplified into a simple web service with only three fields to be filled.

d. Shram Suvidha portal as a common online service with no physical touch point makes available registration under Employee State Insurance Corporation (ESIC) and Employee Provident Fund Organisation (EPFO).

e. In Mumbai and Delhi, there is no requirement of inspection before registration under the Shops & Establishment Act.

f. Appropriate amendments have been made in Companies Act to eliminate the requirement of a common company seal.

2. Dealing with Construction Permits

a. Fast track approval system for issuing building permits with features such as Common Application Form (CAF), provision of using digital signature and online scrutiny of building plans goes a long way in eliminating corruption. Municipal Corporations of Delhi and Greater Mumbai have introduced this.

b. Delhi has introduced uniform building by-laws which permits risk-based classification regimes for different building types. There is also a provision of deemed approval of sanctioning building plans within 30 days.

c. Between Doing Business 2018 and 2020 reports, the time for construction permits has been reduced from 128.5 to 98 days in Mumbai and from 157.5 to 113.5 days in Delhi.

d. The total number of procedures has been reduced to 19 in Mumbai and 11 in Delhi.

e. Cost of obtaining construction permits has been reduced from 23.2% to 5.4% of the economy's per capita income.

3. Trading Across Borders

a. In order to facilitate trade, the Central Board of Excise and Customs (CBEC) has implemented the 'Indian Customs Single Window Project'. This has enabled the Importers and exporters to lodge their Customs clearance documents electronically at a single point. The government has launched 'PCS1x' which aims to integrate 27 maritime stakeholders at one platform.

b. For both import and export of goods, the number of mandatory documents required for customs purposes has been reduced to three.

c. An online application system, e-Sanchit, allows traders to file all documents electronically.

d. The electronic self-sealing of the container at the factory has helped to reduce time and cost for exporting firms.

e. The frequency of custom inspections has been significantly reduced by computerized risk management system.

f. Central Board of Indirect Taxes and Customs has provided a facility for Advance Bill of Entry (Advance Import Declaration).

4. Enforcing Contracts

a. In Mumbai and Delhi, Commercial Courts and Appellate Division of High Courts have been established.

b. National Judicial Data Grid(NJDG), provides case data including case registration, cause list, case status and orders/ judgements of courts district-wise across the country. Since 2015, NJDG is open to the public.

c. In Delhi and Mumbai, new cases in district courts are assigned to Judges randomly through an automated system.

d. In district courts of Delhi and Mumbai, e-filing of cases has been introduced.

e. A case management tool has been developed with the functionality of sending a notification to lawyers, viewing court orders/ judgments, tracking the status of cases, semi-automatically generate court orders etc.

5. Getting Credit

a. A geographically unified electronic registry known as Central Registry of Securitization Asset Reconstruction and Security Interest (CERSAI) provides for registration by asset type. Since 2017, CERSAI has started providing search through debtor's name.

b. Securitization and Reconstruction of Financial Assets and Enforcement of Security Interest (SARFAESI) (Central Registry) Rules, 2011 has been amended to include additional types of charges, including a security interest in - immovable property by the mortgage, hypothecation of plant and machinery, stocks, debt including book debt or receivables, intangible assets, patent, copyright, trademark, under-construction building.

c. The definition of property has been widened to include immovable as well as intangible and this allows CERSAI to register these additional charges.

6. Getting Electricity

a. If no Right of Way (RoW) is required, electricity connection is provided within 7 days. Where RoW is required, connection is provided within 15 days.

b. In Delhi, Service line cum Development charges are now capped at USD 339.84.

c. For getting an electricity connection, the number of documents has been reduced to two. No physical documents are accepted.

d. The total number of procedures required for electricity connection has been reduced to 3 in Delhi and 4 in Mumbai.

7. Registering Property

a. Both in Mumbai and Delhi, all sub-registrar offices have been digitized and their records have been integrated with the Land Records Department.

b. All property tax records have been digitized in Mumbai. After registration, property is mutated automatically. The digitization of property records ensures transparency and permits citizens to ascertain the history of transactions in digital mode.

c. Online service charges for search at Registrar of Companies reduces the time taken for this procedure significantly.

d. Both in Delhi and Mumbai, statistics regarding the number of land disputes at Revenue Courts are available online.

8. Resolving Insolvency

a. India's first comprehensive legislation on corporate insolvency, the Insolvency and Bankruptcy Code of 2016, has introduced new dimensions in resolving insolvency in India.

b. Under Fast-track Corporate Insolvency Resolution Process (CIRP) for mid-sized companies, the process for insolvency shall be completed within 90 days with a maximum grace period of another 45 days.

9. Paying Taxes

a. For mid-sized companies, corporate tax has been reduced from 30% to 25%.

b. Option has been given for Domestic companies for concessional tax regime @ 22% (effective tax rate: 25.17% inclusive of surcharge and cess). Such a company cannot claim any income tax incentive or exemption. Such companies are not liable to pay the Minimum Alternate Tax (MAT).

c. For new domestic manufacturing companies, the tax rate is now 15% (17.01% inclusive of surcharge and cess). The concessional tax regime is available for Companies that have been incorporated on or after 1st October 2019, making fresh investment in manufacturing and commencing production on or before 31 March 2023. However, such companies cannot avail of any other income tax exemption/ incentive under the Income-tax Act.

d. A company that does not opt for the above concessional tax regime and avails any tax exemption/ incentive shall continue to pay tax at pre-amended rates. However, the option of availing of the lower tax regime of 22% can be opted for after the expiry of tax during the holiday/ exemption period. Once the same has been opted for, it cannot be subsequently withdrawn by the taxpayer. MAT rate for companies availing exemptions/ incentives has been reduced from 18.5% to 15%.

e. For Indian taxpayers, robust IT infrastructure of online return filing is made available.

f. The Goods and Service Tax came into effect on 1 July 2017. It has subsumed eight taxes at the Central and nine taxes at the State level.

g. A fully online module for electronic return filing with online payment has been developed by the Employee State Insurance Corporation (ESIC). This has considerably reduced the time to prepare and file returns.

h. There remains no physical touch point for document submission to income tax authorities with the introduction of the e-verification system.

i. The GST filers now have only two returns instead of three returns.

Measures in Progress

a. Resolving Insolvency : As more insol-

vent companies opt for reorganization plans instead of liquidation, there is increased usage of Fast-track Corporate Insolvency Resolution Process (CIRP).

b. Enforcing Contracts: Through dedicated commercial courts, there is faster resolution of commercial disputes.

c. Registering Property: Digitization of land records and maps is expected to bring transparency on encumbrances and ease the process of registering property.

d. Generating Electricity: Government of India has initiated a campaign to improve regulatory and process framework in the power sector. It is aimed at reduction in entry barriers in the distribution industry and making it license-free.

e. Starting a business: The new companies registered through the Agile platform of Ministry of Corporate Affairs are also facilitated to register under ESI Act, through the common transaction.

f. Dealing with Construction permits: Central Public work department (CPWD) has introduced 49 new & emerging technologies to enhance the speed of work. Enterprise Resource Planning is under implementation and is expected to be completed by 2021. It will ensure transparency and increase efficiency.

Doing Business 2019: Ranking of States

While several initiatives have been launched at the Central level to improve the ranking in EoDB, States differ widely in introducing reforms. The state-wise

Table-2 **State-wise Ranking in Doing Business 2019**

State	Rank	State	Rank
Andhra Pradesh	1	Punjab	19
Uttar Pradesh	2	Assam	20
Telangana	3	Jammu and Kashmir	21
Madhya Pradesh	4	Andaman and Nicobar	22
Jharkhand	5	Dadra and N. Haveli	23
Chhatthisgarh	6	Goa	24
Himachal Pradesh	7	Mizoram	25
Rajastan	8	Bihar	26
West Bengal	9	Puducherry	27
Gujarat	10	Kerala	28
Uttarakhand	11	Arunachal Pradesh	29
Delhi	12	Chandigarh	29
Maharashtra	13	Manipur	29
Tamil Nadu	14	Meghalaya	29
Lakshadweep	15	Nagaland	29
Haryana	16	Odisha	29
Karnataka	17	Sikkim	29
Daman and Diu	18	Tripura	29

Source: http://eodb.dipp.gov.in

ranking in EoDB are presented in table-2.

Department for Promotion of Industry and Internal Trade(DPIIT) has launched several initiatives to improve the EoDB at the state level. It consists of 301 reform points across 15 areas.

Structural Composition of State Economies

There is wide variation across states

Table-3 **Sectors Falling Under Primary, Secondary and Tertiary Sectors**

Sector	Economic activity
Primary	1. Agriculture, forestry and fishing 2. Mining and quarrying
Secondary	1. Manufacturing 2. Electricity, gas, water supply and other utility services 3. Construction
Tertiary	1. Transport,Storage,Communication and Services related to broadcasting 2. Financial services 3. Real estate, ownership of dwellings And professional services 4. Public administration 5. Other services

in the composition of the underlying economy. The structural composition of Gross State Domestic Product (GSDP) is widely used to analyse the peculiarities of states' economies. In table-3, the economic activities falling under primary, secondary and tertiary sectors are presented.

The Net State Value Added of all the above economic activities is known as Net State Domestic Product (NSDP) or State Income. Sectoral composition of NSDP of major states for 2019-20 is presented in table-4.

Table-4 shows that the contribution of primary sector ranges from 9.93% in the case of Kerala to 46.79% in the case of Madhya Pradesh. Andhra Pradesh, Rajasthan, Odisha, Chhattisgarh and Punjab are the other major states with more than 30% of NSDP being contributed by primary sector. In the case of secondary sector, the contribution ranges from 15.69% in the case of Telangana to 49.54% in the case of Uttarakhand. Gujarat, Tamil Nadu, Chhattisgarh and Jharkhand are the other major states having more than 30% share in secondary sector.

By and large, the tertiary sector domi-

Table-4 **Shares of Primary, Secondary and Tertiary Sectors in the NSDP of Major States in 2019-20 (Current Prices)**

(Base:2011-12)
(Percentage)

State	Primary Sector	Secondary Sector	Tertiary Sector
Andhra Pradesh	42.02	16.05	41.93
Asom*	29.71	23.43	46.86
Bihar	23.86	16.84	59.30
Chhattisgarh	31.06	30.92	38.02
Gujarat	20.26	42.94	36.80
Haryana	19.86	29.38	50.76
Jharkhand	24.74	30.92	44.34
Karnataka	11.92	21.94	66.14
Kerala	9.93	25.17	64.90
Madhya Pradesh	46.79	17.30	35.91
Maharashtra	14.06	27.55	58.39
Odisha	31.45	27.24	41.31
Punjab	30.39	23.67	45.94
Rajasthan	32.96	20.04	47.00
Tamil Nadu	13.72	32.69	53.59
Telangana	19.02	15.69	65.29
Uttarakhand	10.37	49.54	40.09
Uttar Pradesh	26.18	26.11	47.71
West Bengal	25.49	18.83	55.68

Source: Worked out using data from " Handbook of Statistics on the Indian Economy-2019-20", Reserve Bank of India.

nates the economies of most Indian states. Except Chhattisgarh, Gujarat and Madhya Pradesh, in all major states, the share of tertiary sector is more than 40%. The share of Karnataka at 66.14% is the highest among major states.

Impact of Disasters and Pandemic on the Economies of States

Though it is extremely difficult to predict the impact of disasters and pandemics on the economies of states, some general observations can be made. The state economies are highly interdependent. While agricultural production is concentrated in certain states, food processing industries may be located in other states due to a variety of factors. In recent years, the impact of climate change is increasingly felt across the world. Economies with high share of agriculture often bear the brunt of intermittent floods, droughts and pest attacks. Any reduction in the area and production of food crops will impact the whole national economy. Food inflation can impact on the competitiveness of the country's products in the international market. In order to prevent food prices from going out of control, the country may have to import food materials. This will adversely affect the balance of payment position. Some of the agricultural products are raw materials for industries. Any fall in the production of such agricultural raw materials can affect the economies of states where manufacturing industries are concentrated.

Pandemics like Covid-19 and the resultant lockdowns affect the national economy in varying degrees. A lot depends upon the nature of the pandemic and the steps taken by the government to prevent the spread of the disease. Where the disease spread is fast and wide, the intensity of preventive steps like lockdown and isolation will be high. Manufacturing industries and construction sector which uses migrant labour will be immediately affected as migrant workers would want to return to their home states. Supply chain disruptions will affect most manufacturing industries during lockdowns. On the other hand, services based on information and communication technology may not be severely affected as they can switch over to 'work from home' mode. In the 'trade, hotels and restaurants' sector, perishables will be impacted more than non-perishables. However, during prolonged lockdowns, a significant portion of non- perishable merchandise will be lost. Pandemics generally benefit industries manufacturing medicines, vaccines, hospital equipments and preventive materials.

Generally speaking, the service sector-oriented economies, especially based on information and communication technology, are more resistant to disasters and pandemic than economies with primary and secondary sector orientation.

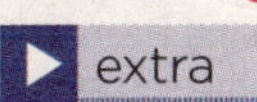

Food Production in India

Food production in India which stood at around 54.92 million tonnes in 1950 has risen to around 305.44 million tonnes in 2020-21.

Economy - Timeline

November 2020

Union Cabinet Gives its Nod to Merge Lakshmi Vilas Bank with DBS Bank India

1. Revenues from the Goods and Services Tax surpasses ₹1.05 lakh crore in October, up 10% from a year ago, and the highest recorded since February 2020 • Unified Payments Interface (UPI), the flagship payments platform of the National Payments Corporation of India (NPCI), records over two billion transactions in October 2020, a milestone that highlights the faster adoption of digital payments in a post-Covid-19 world.

2. Manufacturing PMI for October surges to 58.9, the highest reading since May 2010 • October sees an all-time high in eWay bill generation, at 641 lakh.

3. The government allows income-tax exemption to Abu Dhabi's sovereign wealth fund (SWF), MIC Redwood 1 RSC, for making long-term investments in India in specified priority sectors of infrastructure.

4. State Bank of India reports a 52 per cent jump in second quarter standalone net profit at ₹4,574 crore (₹3012 crore in the year-ago quarter) on the back of lower loan loss provision burden and higher net interest income • At 54.1, Services PMI expands in October after 8 months •The Enforcement Directorate files a prosecution complaint, also known as charge sheet, against ICICI bank's former chief executive officer and managing director Chanda Kochhar, husband Deepak Virendra Kochhar, and nine others in connection with a money laundering case involving the private lender and Videocon Group.

5 The National Payments Corporation of India (NPCI), which manages Unified Payment Interface (UPI), decides to allow Facebook-backed messaging service WhatsApp to go live on UPI in the multi-bank model.

6. The Securities and Exchange Board of India gives nod to the mutual fund industry's request for a new 'flexicap' category, with the freedom to invest across market capitalisations.

8. In October 2020, the Indian pharma market clocks a strong 9.6 per cent growth after growing by 4.5 per cent in September and 2.2 per cent in August.

9. Pfizer announces that an early analysis of its coronavirus vaccine trial suggests the vaccine is robustly effective in preventing Covid-19.

10. With contributions of ₹7,904 crore, Wipro's Azim Premji tops the list of philanthropists in India for 2020, followed by HCL Technologies Founder-Chairman Shiv Nadar.

Azim Premji

11. The Centre decides to bring all content streamed on OTT platforms such as Netflix and Amazon Prime Video, besides news and current affairs content on digital platforms, under the ambit of the Information and Broadcasting Ministry • The government unveils a production-linked incentive scheme to encourage domestic manufacturing investments in 10 more sectors, with an estimated outlay of about ₹1.46 lakh crore over the nest five years.

12. Finance Minister Nirmala Sitharaman announces a fresh set of relief and stimulus measures for the economy worth ₹1.19 lakh crore • Consumer price index (CPI)–based inflation, or retail inflation, rises to 7.61 per cent in October, highest since May 2014.

13. India's exports fall 5.12 per cent to $4.89 billion in October, after recording positive growth in September, on account of drop in shipments of petroleum products, gems and jewellery, leather and engineering goods.

14. The combined market capitalisation of all listed and traded companies on the BSE reaches all-time high of ₹169.3 trillion. At 88 per cent currently, India's market cap- to - gross domestic product (GDP) ratio is now at the highest level in the last 12 quarters.

15. Fifteen Asia-Pacific nations, including China, signs the world's biggest trade agreement, the Regional Comprehensive Economic Partnership (RCEP).

16. The wholesale price index-based (WPI) inflation rises to an eight-month high of 1.48 per cent in October.

17. The Reserve Bank of India places Lakshmi Vilas Bank under moratorium and announces a draft scheme for its amalgamation with DBS Bank India Ltd (DBIL) •Foreign brokerage Goldman Sachs upgrades its India gross domestic product (GDP) forecast to a contraction of 10.3 per cent in FY21, as against its earlier estimate of negative 14.8 per cent growth.

18. SEBI asks NSE to raise corpus of its investor protection fund to ₹1,500 crore.

19. A consortium led by Oaktree Capital Management proposes fund infusion of $2 billion (₹15,000 crore) in Vodafone Idea, as the telecom operator seeks funds for capital expenditure and debt servicing.

20. An Internal Working Group of the RBI proposes allowing large corprates to promote banks but with legislative safeguards. It also suggests increasing the cap on promoter stake after 15 years of operations to 26 per cent from 15 per cent currently.

21. State-owned Punjab & Sind Bank says its board has approved a proposal to raise up to ₹5,500 crore by issuing shares on a preferential basis.

22. Direct Benefit Transfer (DBT) mechanism helped save nearly ₹37,000 crore under various schemes during the financial year 2019-20, says government.

23. AstraZeneca-Oxford vaccine shows up to 90% efficacy.

24. In another blow to Chinese mobile applications functioning in India, the government bans 43 such apps, including the popular online retail portal AliExpress, belonging to Jack Ma-owned e-commerce giant Alibaba Group.

25. The Union Cabinet gives its nod to merge Lakshmi Vilas Bank with DBS Bank India.

26. Bombay High Court denies stay on merger of Lakshmi Vilas Bank with DBS Bank India.

27. The contraction in the Gross Domestic Product slows to 7.5 per cent in the July-September period. The contraction during the April-June quarter was 23.9 per cent. With two successive quarters of decline in the Gross Domestic Product, India officially enters a technical recession.

30. Data giant S&P Global Inc agrees to buy IHS Markit Ltd in a deal worth $44 billion that will be 2020's biggest merger, creating a heavyweight in the increasingly competitive market in financial information.

December

RBI Keeps Policy Rates Unchanged

1. Reinforcing the economic recovery trend, goods and services tax collection surpasses the ₹1-trillion mark for the second consecutive month with a collection of ₹1.049 trillion in November, as against ₹1.05 trillion in October.

2. The UK's drug authority grants an emergency licence to the Covid-19 antidote developed by American pharma major Pfizer along with Germany's BioNTech.

3. The Reserve Bank of India directs HDFC Bank to temporarily halt all its digital launches as well as the sourcing of new credit card customers, following various outages the bank faced due to technical glitches in the past two years.

4. The Reserve Bank of India keeps its policy rates unchanged and promises to continue its accommodative stance this fiscal year and into the next.

5. Consumer confidence remains very low in November 2020 compared to a year ago, as reflected in the Current Situation Index (CSI), according to the Reserve Bank of India Consumer Confidence Survey.

6. E-invoicing under goods and services tax (GST) picks up space right in the second month of its roll-out, with bill generation posting 17 per cent growth in November over the previous month.

7. Coffee Day Enterprises Ltd, the owner of the Cafe Coffee Day chain, appoints Malavika Hegde, the wife of founder and former chairman VG Siddhartha, as its chief executive officer.

Malavika Hegde

8. Agricultural trade in the country is severely hit with most of the 6,946 APMC mandis closed on account of the Bharat bandh called by farmers protesting against controversial farm laws.

9. India could be the fastest-growing Asian economy in calendar year 2021, according to Nomura. The foreign research and brokerage house expects the Indian economy- as measured by gross domestic product(GDP)–to grow 9.9 per cent in 2021, eclipsing China (2021 GDP growth pegged at 9 per cent) and Singapore (7.5 per cent) during the period.

10. In a significant development, the 109-year-old TVS Group decides to restructure its family holdings in the group companies.

11. India's industrial activity touches an eight-month high in October, posting growth for a second straight month, led by significant expansion in consumer goods, electricity and infrastructure goods.

12. American drug–maker Pfizer and its German collaborator BioNTech receive an emergency-use authorisation on their Covid-19 vaccine, making it the first to get off-the-blocks in the US.

13. Securities and Exchange Board of India (Sebi) defers the plan to halve the trade settlement cycle to one day (T+1).

14. Inflation based on the Consumer Price Index (CPI) moderates to 6.93 per cent in November from 7.61 in the previous month, according to the data released by the Ministry of Statistics and Programme Implementation • The wholesale price index (WPI)-based inflation rate rises for the fourth consecutive month and firms up at 1.55 per cent in November –a nine month high, as manufactured products turn costlier • 14. Ola Electric announces a ₹2,400-crore investment plan to set up, what it calls, the "world's largest" electric scooter manufacturing plant in Hosur, Tamil Nadu.

15. S&P Global Ratings raises India's growth projection for the current financial year to (-)7.7 per cent from (-)9 per cent estimated earlier on rising demand and falling Covid-19 infection rates.

16. The Securities and Exchange Board of India (Sebi) paves the way for fintech companies and other start-ups to set up asset management companies by tweaking the eligibility criteria.

17. Advance tax paid by companies in the December quarter rises by 50 per cent compared with the corresponding period lasy year, owing to a low base effect.

18. Reliance Industries and its partner BP announce their first gas finding at the R cluster, an ultra-deep-water gas field in block KG D6, off the east coast of India.

19. The United States gives the green signal to its second Covid-19 vaccine, this one from biotech company Moderna.

20. Stressed low-cost airline SpiceJet seeks a one-time debt restructuring, apart from ₹500-crore in a working capital loan, from YES bank.

21. Global stocks tumble amid panic selling as a new strain of coronavirus emerging from the UK leads to fresh travel restrictions, casting a cloud over the prospects of economic recovery.

22. The Centre, in a first move of its kind, issues ₹5,500 crore in zero-coupon bonds for recapitalising Punjab and Sind Bank and allows it to park the paper in its held-to-maturity (HTM) category at face value rather than the discounted market rate.

23. In a major setback, the Indian government loses an international arbitration case to energy giant Cairn Plc over the retrospective levy of taxes, and is asked to pay damages worth $1.2 billion (₹.8,842 crore) to the UK firm.

24. India challenges in Singapore an international arbitration tribunal's verdict overturning its demand for ₹22,100 crore in back taxes from Vodafone Group Plc.

26. The Finance Ministry clarifies that the mandatory payment of at least one per cent of the tax liability in cash will affect less than half a per cent of total GST assessees. The rule intends to curb the menace of fake invoice.

27. The Comptroller and Auditor General of India (CAG) writes to the Reserve Bank of India, seeking details of the performance of state-run banks after their recapitalisation over the past five years.

28. The Income Tax Appellate Tribunal quashes an earlier order of the Commissioner of Income Tax against three major Tata trusts, thereby restoring tax exemption for the largest shareholder of the $100-billion conglomerate.

29. Tata Sons increases its stake in AirAsia India to 83.67 per cent from 51 per cent till now.

30. The Union Cabinet approves exporting the indigenous Akash air defence missile.

31. The output of the eight-industry core sector drops by 2.6 per cent in November, as against the contraction of 0.1 per cent in September and 0.9 per cent in October.

January 2021

BSE Sensex Hits the 50,000 Milestone

1. Signalling a strong economic recovery, GST collection in December hits an all-time high of ₹1,15,174 crore.

2. The Labour Ministry issues draft standing orders for manufacturing, mining and services sectors. Sleeping on duty, habitual late attendance among 23 types of misconduct defined.

3. India's drug regulator gives its final approval to the Oxford-AstraZeneca and Bharat Biotech coronavirus vaccines for restricted use in an emergency situation.

4. Manufacturing activity expands further in December as the Purchasing Managers Index (PMI) moves a tad higher to 56.4, against 56.3 in November.

5. The Supreme Court, in a majority judgement, gives its go-ahead to the multi-crore Central Vista redevelopment project, which proposes to build a new Parliament three times bigger than the existing 93-year-old heritage building and modify the use of 86.1 acres of land for India's power corridor.

6. The government announces that the next round of telecom spectrum auctions will be held in March • Services PMI falls to 52.3 in December from 53.7 in November.

7. The economy is expected to contract 7.7 per cent in 2020-21, according to the first advance estimate released by the government.

8. The benchmark indices rise, marking their tenth successive week of gains, the longest such streak since June 2009 • The country's foreign exchange reserves surge by $4.483 billion to touch a record high of $583.324 billion in the week ended December 25.

10. Earnings through central excise duty registers over 47 per cent growth during the first eight months of the current fiscal year 2020-21. Collection from central excise duty during the April-November period of FY2020-21 is more than ₹.1.96 lakh against over ₹1.32 lakh during the corresponding period of FY 2019-20.

11. India signs the much-awaited first purchase agreement for the government-sponsored Covid vaccination programme with Pune-based Serum Institute of India • The Reserve Bank of India's Financial Stability Report (FSR) of December 2020 states that banks' gross non-performing assets may rise sharply to 13.5 per cent by September 2021, and escalate to a 23-year high of 14.8 per cent by September, and escalate to a 23-year high of 14.8 per cent, nearly double the 7.5 per cent in the same period of 2019-20, under the severe stress scenario.

12. The Supreme Court stays the implementation of the three agricultural Acts till further orders and constitutes a four-member committee to resolve the impasse over the laws between Centre and protesting farmers • The consumer price index (CPI)-based inflation rate moderates to 4.59 per cent in December, down from 6.93 per cent in November and 7.61 per cent in October • Official data shows that the recovery in industrial output seen in October is an aberration as it contracts again in November by 1.9 per cent.

13. The Union Cabinet clears the purchase of 83 Tejas fighters worth more than ₹45,000 crore.

14. The combined market capitalisation of all listed companies in India crosses the country's GDP for the first time in 10 years. The ratio on the BSE reaches ₹197.7 trillion, against India's nominal GDP at current prices of around ₹190 trillion during the year ended December 2020 •The wholesale inflation rate softens to a four-month low of 1.22 per cent in December as food items enter deflationary zone.

15. India's foreign exchange reserves rise by $758 million to reach a record high of $586.082 billion in the week ended January 8.

16. Jet fuel, or ATF, price is hiked by 3%–the fourth increase in two months–on firming international oil prices.

17. In a major relief for embattled fund house Franklin Templeton, over 90 per cent of investors vote in favour of the closure of six suspended debt funds • China's economy expands in 2020 by 2.3%, the slowest pace of growth since the end of Mao Zedong's Cultural Revolution in 1976.

18. India asks WhatsApp to withdraw its latest terms of service and privacy policy, saying the proposed consolidation of sensitive information exposes its citizens to security risks.

19. Karnataka retains its position as the top-ranking major State in NITI Aayog's India Innovation Index 2020, which ranks States based on how they support innovation and new technologies.

21. The BSE Sensex, a guage of the performance of India's leading 30 stocks, hits the 50,000 milestone for the first time.

22. The Reserve Bank of India proposes to introduce a scale-based regulatory framework for non-banking financial companies to segregate larger entities and expose them to a stricter set of "bank-like" rules.

24. A group of investors of Franklin Templeton Mutual Fund approaches the Supreme Court with a plea to declare the recent e-voting conducted by the fund house 'illegal.'

25. The Centre releases ₹12351.5 crore to 18 States as grants to rural local bodies for 2020-21, taking the total grants released for such bodies this year to ₹45,738 crore • SEBI asks Franklin Templeton to explain the 'unusual withdrawals' from the six debt schemes before it announced the suspension of redemption in them on April 23, 2020.

27. Aditya Birla Fashion and Retail Ltd acquires 51 per cent stake in luxury designer brand Sabyasachi.

28. Hit by high prices and the unprecedented Covid pandemic, India's gold demand in 2020 plunges to the lowest in 25 years at 446 tonnes •The US economy contracts 3.5% in 2020, its worst show since World War II.

29. The Economic Survey says that the Indian economy will rebound to 11 per cent real GDP growth next fiscal on the back of a V-shaped recovery post lifting of the lockdown and the ongoing round of mega Covid vaccination drive.

31. GST collections touch an all-time high of ₹1,19,849 crore in January.

February

FM Presents Budget with Focus on Infrastructure and Healthcare

1. Nirmala Sitharaman presents an expansionary Budget for 2021-22, with a push for infrastructure and healthcare spending.

Nirmala Sitharaman with the Budget Papers

2 January exports rise 5.37% to $27.24 billion.

3. Market regulator SEBI bars Future Group CEO Kishore Biyani from accessing the securities market for one year over alleged breach of insider trading regulations •The Sensex closes above the 50,000 mark for the first time as the Budget-fuelled rally continues for the third straight session.

4. The sum of the market value of BSE-listed companies crosses ₹200 trillion for the first time.

5. The Reserve Bank of India keeps its policy rates unchanged, assures the bond market of ample liquidity and promises an 'accommodative' stance as long as necessary.

6. Madras High Court sets aside order restraining Patanjali from using 'Coronil' trademark.

7. Adani Group completes the purchase of 23.5 per cent stake in Mumbai International Airport from two South African entities in a first step towards acquiring majority control in India's second busiest airport.

8. The Indian markets surge for a sixth day, with the Nifty closing above the 15,000-mark for the first time • Yields on the 10-year benchmark Government Securities (G-Sec) softens about 4 basis points after the Reserve Bank of India announces that it will purchase four G-Secs aggregating ₹20,000 crore, a move aimed at keeping G-Sec yields in check.

9. After cracking down on cement companies, the Competition Commission of India launches a probe against steel companies for forming a cartel to increase prices consistently over the last seven months • The exit from equity mutual funds continues for the seventh month in a row, with a net outflow of ₹9,253 crore in January.

10. In a relief to Ravi Narain and Chitra Ramkrishna, the two former longest-serving bosses of the National Stock Exchange (NSE), market regulator SEBI drops charges of fraud against them in the co-location scam case regarding tick-by-tick data system.

11. The government increases the upper and lower caps on airfare by up to 30 per cent in a move that's expected to push up tariffs and improve the financials of airlines hit hard by the pandemic.

12. Retail inflation, based on the Consumer Price Index, touches a 16-month low of 4.06 per cent in January.

13. The board of ONGC approves creation of a new wholly-owned subsidiary company for gas business that could be used to bid and buy gas from the firm's own oil fields subject to necessary approvals.

15. The National Association of Software and Services Companies pegs the Indian IT industry's revenue during FY21 at $194 billion, up from $190 billion in FY20.

16. Tata Group signs a deal to acquire a 68 per cent stake in Bigbasket, an online supermarket backed by Alibaba Group Holding Ltd, for nearly ₹9,500 crore.

17. The Cabinet approves a ₹12,195-crore Production-Linked Incentive (PLI) scheme for telecom equipment manufacturing, to promote Made-in-India gear and networking products • The Securities and Exchange Board of India eases the listing norms for large companies: large companies can now divest a minimum 5 per cent in the IPO, instead of 10 per cent and they will also get 5 years, instead of three, to raise the public float to 25 per cent.

18. The Reserve Bank of India clears the ₹34,250-crore acquisition of Dewan Housing Finance Corporation (DHFL) by the Piramal group.

19. The Government affirms that it would not just file an appeal against the arbitration award given to Cairn Energy but also contest related legal suits.

20. The Employees Provident Fund Organisation adds around 53.70 lakh subscribers during the first three quarters of FY 2020-21.

22. A new fraudulent transaction of ₹6,182.11 crore is unearthed in Dewan Housing Finance Corporation Ltd, which is set to be acquired by the Piramal Group.

23. Reliance Industries announces that it plans to carve out its oil-to-chemicals (O2C) business into an independent unit with a $25-billion loan from the parent.

24. The Union Cabinet approves the Production Linked Incentive (PLI) schemes for the pharmaceuticals and IT hardware sectors, entailing an outlay of ₹15,000 crore and ₹7,350 crore, respectively • The government lifts an embargo on the grant of government businesses to

private sector banks.
25. The government notifies the much-awaited Information Technology (Intermediary Guidelines and Digital Media Ethics Code) Rules, 2021. The Rules mandate firms to appoint a grievance officer, disclose the originator of the mischievous information and remove content depicting nudity or morphed pictures of women, within 24 hours.
26. India exits 'technical recession' with GDP growth estimated at 0.4 per cent in the third (October-December) quarter of 2020-21.
27. Prime Minister Narendra Modi makes a call for promoting 'Handmade in India', especially for items such as toys, with a thrust on 'Make in India' initiative as a response to the growing global demand for handicrafts.

March

Cabinet Approves Increase in FDI Limit in Insurance from 49 Per Cent to 74

1. The Goods and Services Tax (GST) collections reach over ₹1.13-lakh crore in February, which is 7 per cent higher than in the corresponding month of the last fiscal year.
2. The telecom spectrum auction concludes after bidding for a day and a half, with the Centre garnering ₹77,814.8 crore in revenues. Mukesh Ambani-led Reliance Jio is the biggest bidder, acquiring 488.35 MHz of spectrum for ₹57,122.65 crore, followed by Bharti Airtel which bid for 355.45 MHz of spectrum for ₹18,698.75 crore. Vodafone Idea bid for only 11.8 MHz of airwaves for ₹1,993.4 crore.
3. Covaxin, the country's first indigenous Covid-19 vaccine candidate, shows 81 per cent interim clinical efficacy in Phase-3 trials • Services hit the fast lane in February as the Purchasing Managers' Index (PMI) races to 55.3 against 52.8 for January.
4. Wipro, in one of its biggest acquisitions so far, signs an agreement to acquire London-based Capco, a global management and technology consultancy, for $1.45 billion.
5. The country's forex reserves increase for the second consecutive week, touching $584.554 billion as of February 26, up by $ 689 million.
7. LIC agrees to shed its shareholding in IDBI Bank, a move which will enable the government to completely exit from the bank and ease the process of strategic disinvestment.
8. Government collects ₹54,346 crore under *Vivad se Vishwas* scheme to resolve tax disputes amounting to ₹98,328 crore by taxpayers till March 1.
9. The Organisation for Economic Co-operation and Development (OECD) raises the projection for India's economic growth rate by 4.7 percentage points at 12.6 per cent for 2021-22.
10. The Cabinet approves changes to the Insurance Act for increasing the foreign direct investment (FDI) limit in insurance to 74 per cent from the current 49 per cent.
11. The government kicks off its privatisation drive, with the NITI Aayog, a body headed by the prime minister, submitting its first list of about 12 public sector undertakings to be privatised.
12. India's retail inflation surges to a three-month high of 5.03 per cent in February as against 4.06 per cent in January • The Index of Industrial Production declines by 1.6 per cent in January on a year-on-year basis, as against 1.56 per cent growth in the previous month.
13. The Finance Ministry notifies a new format for the Securities and Exchange Board of India's annual report. Income and expenditure will be required to be part of the annual report as against the

existing provision of presenting the annual account statement separately.

14. Inflation based on Wholesale Price Index (WPI) doubles to 4.17 per cent in February, as against 2.03 per cent in January.

16. The Cabinet clears a bill to set up a government-owned development finance institution (DFI) with initial paid-up capital of ₹20,000 crore so that it can leverage around ₹3 trillion from the markets in a few years to provide long-term funds to infrastructure projects as well as for development needs of the country • Mutual funds are set to be net sellers of Indian equities for the first time in the past seven financial years, having sold stocks worth about ₹1.27 trillion so far in 2020-21, making it the highest net sales on record in a financial year.

17. The Centre's direct tax revenue exceeds the revised Budget target for the first time in four years on the back of robust advance tax mop-up for 2020-21. Net direct tax collection stood at ₹9.18 trillion as of March 16, exceeding the ₹9.05 trillion revised Budget target.

18. The Centre announces the much-awaited vehicle scrapping policy: State governments to be advised to offer road tax rebate of up to 25% for personal vehicles and manufacturers to provide 5% discount on purchase of a new vehicle against the scrapping certificate.

19. Investments via participatory notes (P-Notes) rise to a 33-month high at ₹91,658 crore (over $12 billion) in February, according to data released by SEBI.

20. National Pharmaceutical Pricing Authority (NPPA) fixes the price of 81 medicines, including off-patent anti-diabetic drugs, helping to pass on the benefits of patent expiry to patients.

21. The Centre permits imports of 4 lakh tonnes of tur and 1.5 lakh tonnes of moong for FY21-22, to meet the shortfall in domestic supplies.

22. The market regulator SEBI allows mutual funds to meet its norms on valuation of perpetual bonds in a time-bound manner with the life span of bonds increasing over the years.

23. The Supreme Court directs banks and financial institutions to refund the compound interest collected on EMIs during the loan moratorium period, from March 1 to August 31, 2020.

24. Venu Srinivasan decides to step down as Chairman of TVS Motor Company in January 2023. He will be replaced by Ralph Speth, former chief executive officer of Jaguar Land Rover.

25. SEBI announces a slew of measures including making it easier for start-ups to list, tightening de-listing rules to allow transparent price discovery, and removing the list of restricted activities or sectors from the definition of venture capital undertaking to provide flexibility to Alternative Investment Funds (AIF).

26. The Supreme Court sets aside the NCLAT decision reinstating Cyrus Mistry as Executive Chairman of Tata Sons, ruling in favour of the multi-billion dollar salt-to-software conglomerate.

Cyrus Mistry

27. India delivers on its promise of 2,00,000 doses of COVID-19 vaccines for the United Nations Peace-keeping Force (UNPKF) worldwide, sending a shipment bound for Copenhagen.

29. The *MV Ever Given* is refloated and the Suez Canal reopened to traffic, sparking relief almost a week after the huge container ship got stuck and blocked a major artery for global trade.

30. FTSE Russell puts India's government bonds on the watchlist for potential inclusion in the FTSE Emerging Government Bond Index (EMGBI).

31. The Centre keeps the inflation target of the monetary policy framework unchanged at 2-6 per cent for the next five years, until the fiscal year 2025-26.

April

IMF Raises its Projection for Economic Growth in 2021-22 to 12.5 Per Cent

1. The Union Government reverses the move to lower interest rates on small savings schemes • Goods and services tax revenues touch an all-time high in March, with the government collecting nearly ₹ 1.24 trillion.

2. Gross personal income tax (inclusive of refunds) posts a 2.5 per cent year-on-year growth during FY21.

4. Ethanol blending in India reaches more than 7.2 per cent– the first time it has reached this level–in the first four months of the ethanol supply year 20-21 (December to November), putting the country on course to meet the target of 10 per cent blending by 2022.

5. The government amends the Insolvency and Bankruptcy Code (IBC) through an Ordinance, enabling prepackaged resolution schemes for micro, small, and medium enterprises (MSMEs) and allowing corporate debtors to propose a resolution plan for the stressed company.

6. The International Monetary Fund (IMF) raises its projection for India's economic growth in the 2021-22 financial year by one percentage point to 12.5 per cent • Reliance Jio Infocomm enters into a ₹1037.6-crore spectrum trade with Bharti Airtel.

7.The Reserve Bank of India unveils a ₹1-lakh crore secondary market Government Security Acquisition Programme (G-SAP), committing for the first time its balance-sheet to the conduct of Monetary Policy.

8. Equity-oriented mutual fund schemes in March report net inflows of ₹9,115 crore.

9. The fuel demand contracts by 9.1 per cent in the financial year ended March 31, the first since 1998-99 •Direct tax collections in 2020-21 at ₹9.45 lakh crore, register a nearly 5 per cent growth over the Revised Estimate of FY21.

11. India bans exports of antiviral drug Remdesivir, used to treat moderate to severe Covid-19, amid rising domestic demand and reports of shortages from states.

12. The BSE Sensex tanks 1,708 points or 3.44% driven by the fear of fresh pandemic effects, taking the rupee past the ₹75 mark against the dollar • Amid vaccine shortage forcing many inoculation centres to shut down, Russia's Sputnic V gets the nod of the Subject Expert Committee (SEC) for emergency use • India's retail inflation accelerates to 5.52% in March 2021 from 5.03% in February • Industrial production declines for the second month in a row at a faster rate of 3.6 per cent than the 0.9 per cent in the previous month.

13. The Centre's indirect tax collections rise by more than 12 per cent to ₹10.71 trillion in 2020-21 compared to ₹9.54 trillion in the previous year, even as goods and services tax mop-up declines by 8 per cent.

15. Wholesale price index-based inflation, led by soaring prices of fuels and those of manufactured goods, rises to a 8-year high of 7.4 per cent in March against 4.17 per cent in February and 2.51 per cent in January • India's merchandise exports surge to $34.45 billion, up 60 per cent year-on-year in March, on the back of a low base in the lockdown-hit month in 2020.

16. China's economy surges to a record 18.3 per cent in the first quarter of 2021, riding on strong domestic and foreign demand and aided by recovery from a low base in early 2020 when Covid-19 stalled the world's second-largest economy.

17. India's pharmaceutical exports grow at a record 18 per cent to reach $24.44 billion in the year ended March 31, 2021, as a result of the Covid-19 pandemic.

18: TCS, Infosys and Wipro together hire 72,259 employees in FY 2020-21 compared with 49,888 the previous year.

19. India allows Covid vaccination for all above 18 years of age starting May 1.

20. Domestic rating agency ICRA cuts its 2021-22 growth estimate of Indian economy by 0.5 per cent on the upper end to 10- 10.5 per cent against the 10-11 per cent estimated earlier.

21. Serum Institute of India says it would price its Covid-19 vaccine at ₹400 per dose for States and ₹600 for private hospitals.

22. Rating agency Fitch Ratings affirms India's long-term foreign-currency issuer Dafault Rating at 'BBB-' with a negative outlook.

23. The Central government decides to distribute 5 kg of additional grain free of cost to all the 800 million beneficiaries under the National Food Security Act (NFSA), in May and June.

24. The government waives the customs duty and the health cess for three months on import of medical oxygen and a slew of equipment related to production of the gas.

25. The Centre bars the use of liquid oxygen for any non-medical purpose and asks manufacturing units to maximise its production and make it available to the government for medical use.

26. The Reserve Bank of India caps the tenure of managing directors (MDs) and chief executive officers (CEOs) of private banks at 15 years.

27. Commercial banks and urban commercial banks will have to rope in at least two auditors unaffiliated with each other and have to take prior approval of the Reserve Bank of India for appointment or reappointment of statutory auditors on an annual basis, according to the central bank.

28. Serum Institute of India lowers Covishield vaccine price for States from ₹400

to ₹300 per dose •Food-delivery platform Zomato files for ₹8250 crore initial public offering (IPO).

29. Bharat Biotech reduces the price of Covaxin, an indigenously developed Covid-19 vaccine, by 33 per cent for State governments to ₹400 a dose.

30. The growth of eight key infrastructure segments reaches a 32-month high of 6.8 per cent in March compared to a year earlier, mainly due to a low base.

May

The Centre Releases ₹ 9,000 Crore to Gram Panchayats in 25 States

2. India's merchandise exports nearly treble in April to $30.21 billion, an increase of 197.03 per cent year-on-year, mainly due to the low-base effect as Covid-induced nationwide lockdown a year ago had halted economic activities.

3. India's manufacturing sector activity is largely flat in April, as rates of growth for new orders and output ease to eight-month lows amid the intensification of the COVID-19 crisis. The seasonally adjusted IHS Markit India Manufacturing Purchasing Managers' Index (PMI) was at 55.5 in April, little changed from March's reading of 55.4.

4. Number of open job positions at the end of April drops 31% from March to touch the lowest level in 2021, according to data from official company job pages on LinkedIn and direct postings on top job boards • President Joe Biden throws his support behind waiving intellectual property rights for COVID-19 vaccines, bowing to mounting pressure from Democratic lawmakers and more than 100 other countries, but angering pharmaceutical companies • In an effort to reduce the stress on small businesses and MSME sector amid the unprecedented Covid surge hitting the nation, RBI announces a set of measures targeted at offering relief for such cash-starved enterprises.

6. Sales of daily groceries, essentials, electronics and automobiles decline sharply in April compared with March, indicating faltering demand amid surging Covid infection cases.

7. Tamil Nadu Chief Minister Stalin announces a Covid pandemic time relief of ₹4,000 for the people of the state, a cut in Aavin milk rate, and free travel for women in state-run buses, all promises made by his DMK ahead of the 6 April Assembly elections. • Life insurance companies see a 44.76 per cent rise in new business premium (NBP) in April due to low base in the same period last year.

Stalin

8. Jeff Bezos sells about $2.5 billion of Amazon.com Inc. stock, his first big disposal in 2021 after offloading more than $10 billion worth of shares in 2020.

10. The Centre releases ₹9,000 crore to gram panchayats in 25 States to help fight the Covid-19 pandemic.

11. The 2020 results of China's once-a-decade census shows the population of mainland China increased 5.38% to 1.41 billion, its slowest 10-year growth rate since modern census-taking began in 1953 •Liquid funds of debt funds see a net withdrawal of ₹84,202 crore in the March quarter, the only quarter in 2020-21 that sees outflow in fixed-income or debt category.

12. Passenger vehicle wholesales in India decline by 10 per cent to 2,61,633 units in April 2021 as compared to March 2021 as COVID-19-led restrictions across various states impact demand, according to auto industry body SIAM.

13. Restrictions imposed by states due to the second wave of Covid-19 and the inability of the economy to absorb labour force result in a loss of 7.35 million jobs in April, pushing up the country's unemployment rate to 8% compared with 6.5% in March, according to the Centre for Monitoring Indian Economy.

14. Prime Minister Narendra Modi releases the eighth installment of over ₹20,000 crore to more than 9.5 crore farmer beneficiaries under the Pradhan Mantri Kisan Samman Nidhi (PM-KISAN) scheme.

15. UK's Cairn Energy Plc brings a lawsuit in a US court against Air India to recover $1.72 billion from the Indian government which an international arbitration tribunal had awarded after overturning levy of retrospective taxes.

17. India's wholesale price inflation (WPI) surges to an 11-year high of 10.49 per cent in April compared to 7.39 per cent recorded in March.

18. Indian Information technology and business services record an year-on-year growth of 5.41% in 2020. The sector is expected to grow at 7.18% between 2020 and 2025.

19. China bans the country's institutions

from providing cryptocurrency services.

20. The unemployment rate shoots up to 14.5% in the week ended May 16, 2021, the highest in the last one year, compared to 8% in April, the Centre for Monitoring Indian Economy says.

22. Total dues owed by electricity distribution companies to power producers fall 3.4 per cent to ₹78,379 crore in March 2021 as compared to the year-ago period, showing a reversal of discoms' growing outstandings.

24. Banking tech startup Zeta becomes the latest unicorn in India after raising $250 million from SoftBank's Vision Fund 2, valuing the startup at $1.45 billion • Domestic ratings agency Icra forecasts a 2 per cent GDP growth in the fourth quarter of 2020-21, and a 7.3 per cent contraction for the full fiscal year •World's leading fashion luxury goods company Louis Vuitton Moet Hennessey (LMVH) owner Bernard Arnault dethrones Amazon founder Jeff Bezos as the world's richest man.

25. Barclays pegs India's economic growth for fiscal 2021-22 (FY22) – as measured by gross domestic product (GDP) – at 7.7 per cent in the bear-case scenario, if the country is hit by the third wave of the Covid pandemic going ahead.

26. Amazon buys MGM, the Hollywood studio behind the James Bond and Rocky franchises, for $8.45bn as the battle for global streaming supremacy reaches new heights.

27. The size of the Reserve Bank's balance sheet, which is reflective of activities carried out by it in pursuance of currency issue function as well as monetary policy and reserve management, increases by 6.99 per cent during the nine-month period ended March 31, 2021. The size of the balance sheet increases by ₹3,72,876.43 crore from ₹53,34,792.70 crore as on June 30, 2020 to ₹57,07,669.13 crore as on March 31, 2021.

28. Cementing its foray into the online grocery market, Tata Sons, through its subsidiary Tata Digital Limited acquires a majority stake in BigBasket.

29. The European Medicines Agency approves the Pfizer-BioNTech Covid-19 vaccine for the 12-15-year age group.

30. The government expands the scope of the ₹3-trillion Emergency Credit Line Guarantee Scheme (ECLGS) by including support for onsite oxygen generation plants and declaring civil aviation as an eligible sector.

31. The Centre's fiscal deficit for the financial year 2020-21 settles at 9.2 per cent of the gross domestic product, marginally below the government's revised target of 9.5 per cent.

June

The World Bank Projects India's Economy to Grow 8.3 Per Cent in 2021 and 7.5 Per Cent in 2022

1. Global rating agency Moody's Investors Service scales down its 2021-22 Gross Domestic Product (GDP) growth forecast for India to 9.3% from 13.7% projected earlier.

2. India's merchandise trade deficit shrinks to an eight-month low, as imports over the month amounts to $38.53 billion, 68.54% over May 2020 and 17.47% lower than May 2019.

3. Airlines in India are likely to post a consolidated loss of $4.1 billion in financial year (FY) 2022, forecasts aviation consultancy CAPA.

4. The Reserve Bank of India (RBI) revises its real GDP projection for India from 10.5 percent to 9.5 percent in 2021-22 amid second wave of Covid-19 and localised lockdowns.

5. Quantum, the first non-fungible token (NFT) ever created, the origin of a craze that is sweeping the art market, goes on sale at Sotheby's. "Quantum" is an octagon-shaped animation by New York artist Kevin McCoy. •The goods and services tax collections for May clock ₹1,02,709 crore, making itthe eighth straight month of colletions crossing ₹1 lakh crore mark.

6. More than 9.2 lakh children in India are "severely acute malnourished', with the most in Uttar Pradesh followed by Bihar, according to government data.

7. The Securities and Exchange Board of India (Sebi) directs mutual funds (MFs) to introduce another label called as potential risk class matrix to help investors assess risk better.

8.The World Bank projects India's economy to grow 8.3 per cent in 2021 and 7.5 per cent in 2022.

9. The Centre raises the minimum support price for kharif crops for the 2021-22 crop season (July-June) by an average 3.7 per cent.

10. The Reserve Bank of India accepts the long-standind demand of banks and White Label ATM operators (WLAO) for a hike in interchange fee in view of increasing cost of ATM deployment and maintenance.

11. Industrial production rises by a whopping 134.44 per cent in April on a low YoY base against 24.14 per cent in March, data released by the National Statistical Office show.

13. Direct tax collections, net of refunds, stand at ₹1.62 trillion up to June 11 in the fiscal year 2021-22 against ₹87,000 in the same period in 2020-21.

14: Retail inflation accelerates to a six-month high of 6.3 per cent in May • India's wholesale inflation hits a record high of 12.94 per cent in May, driven by continued rise in fuel and commodity prices and low-base effect • Shares of Adani Group companies come under heavy selling pressure following a report that the accounts of three foreign portfolio investors that own group stocks have been frozen by depository firm NSDL.

15. Merchandise exports grow 69.35 per cent year-on-year in May to $32.27 billion on account of low-base effect as well as rising demand from external markets.

16. The advance tax collection of corporation tax and personal income tax grows 146 per cent in the first quarter of 2021-22 compared to the same period in the last fiscal.

17. Satya Nadella is named chairman of Microsoft Corporation.

Satya Nadella

18. The Reserve Bank of India gives "in-principle" approval to Centrum Financial Services Ltd (CFSL) to set up a small finance bank (SFB), which will take over the beleagured Punjab and Maharashtra Cooperative Bank (PMC Bank).

19 The Finance Ministry notifies the relaxed minimum public offer norms for large companies planning to enter the stock market. The Central government says companies with a market cap exceeding ₹1 trillion will have to dilute ₹5000 crore and at least 5 per cent of their m-cap.

20. The Securities and Exchange Board of India asks PNB Housing Finance not to go ahead with the ₹4,000-crore stake sale to a clutch of investors, led by private equity firm Carlyle Group, until the housing finance company undertakes valuation of its shares.

21. India administers a record 82.7 lakh doses of Covid vaccine, the first day of changed policy regime where the Centre supplies vaccines free of cost to States to all citizens above 18 years of age.

22. The National Company Law Tribunal

clears the Kalrock-Jalan plan to revive Jet Airways, while rejecting the consortium's demand for historicity of airport slots.

23: Moody's slashes India's growth projection to 9.6 per cent for calendar year 2021, from its earlier estimate of 13.9 per cent • The Enforcement Directorate manages to recover for public sector banks assets worth ₹9,041.5 crore, representing about 40 per cent of the total loss to the PSBs caused by three scamsters– Vijay Mallya, Nirav Modi and Mehul Choksi.

24. Reliance Industries Ltd announces a mega entry into green energy • S&P Global Ratings cuts India's growth forecast for the current fiscal year 9.5 per cent, from 11 per cent last year.

25. In a first acquisition of a listed company by any Indian unicorn, digital health care start-up PharmEasy's parent, API Holdings, buys a majority stake of 66.1 per cent in Thyrocare for ₹4,546-crore.

27. SEBI postpones implementation of the skin-in-the-game norms for the employees of mutual funds to October instead of the earlier notified deadline of July 1.

28. Government unveils a ₹6.28-trillion package to revive the economy which includes a new credit guarantee scheme for health, tourism and microborrowers, besides expanding the Emergency Credit Line Guarantee Scheme (ECLGS) by half to ₹4.5 trillion and extending the Atmanirbhar Bharat Rozgar Yojana.

29. The Securities and Exchange Board of India (SEBI) overhauls the norms pertaining to the appointment, removal, and remuneration of independent directors in order to curtail the sway of promoters over them.

30. The finance ministry reimposes expenditure curbs on monistries and government departments for July-September quarter • Brazil suspends a $324- million vaccination deal with Bharat Biotech.

July

IMF Scales Down India's Growth Projection from 12.5 Per Cent to 9.5 Per Cent

1. The covid second wave and the consequent local lockdowns push manufacturing activity into the reverse gear in June, with the Purchasing Managers' Index (PMI) dipping to 48.1 for the month.

2. India records the highest-ever exports of $95 billion during April-June, up 85 per cent YoY and 18 per cent higher than the first quarter of the fiscal year 2019-20.

4. According to RBI data, unsold housing inventory levels come down to 7 lakh units at March 31, 2021 from about 8.5 lakh units in first quarter of FY 2019-20.

5. The Purchasing mangers' Index (PMI) for services crashes to a 11-month low of 41.2 in June, down from 46.4 in May.

6. Goods and services tax (GST) collection falls below the ₹1-trillion mark in June– the first time in nine months– as the second wave of Covid-19 disrupts economic activities in the country.

7. Fitch Ratings cuts India's growth forecast to 10 per cent for the current fiscal, from 12.8 per cent eastimated earlier.

8. The Union Cabinet approves a ₹23,123-crore financial package for improving health infrastructure in the country to fight the pandemic.

9. A break in the South-West monsoon early in June affects Kharif sowing in many parts of the country, with the overall coverage falling 10 per cent until July 8 compared with the same period a year ago.

11. Twitter releases its first compliance report under the new IT Rules • Foreign Portfolio Investors (FPIs) pour in ₹57,675 crore in the first six months of 2021 compared to the ₹96,457 crore in the first six months of 2019.

12. Retail inflation remains over 6 per

cent for the second successive month though it eases a tad in June to 6.26 per cent from 6.30 per cent in May.

13. S&P Global Ratings keeps India's sovereign rating unchanged at the lowest investment grade of 'BBB-' for the 14th year in a row.

14. India's wholesale inflation continues to remain elevated, even as it moderates to 12.07 per cent in June from a record high of 12.94 per cent in May • The Reserve Bank of India bars global card player Mastercard Asia/ Pacific Pte Ltd from onboarding new domestic customers on its network from July 22 over non-compliance with local data storage guidelines.

15. The Centre releases ₹75,000 crore of the ₹1.59-trillion crore estimated as goods and services tax (GST) shortfall in a single investment, to facilitate capital spending by states.

16. Reliance Retail Ventures Ltd (RRVL) acquires a controlling stake in 25-year-old search engine platform Just Dial for ₹5,719 crore.

17. The Pension Fund Regulatory and Development Authority (PFRDA) amends the Pension Fund Regulations to allow foreign companies to hold– directly or indirectly– up to 74 per cent in pension funds.

19. The government informs Parliament that the market regulator and customs authorities are investigating Adani Group for non-compliance with rules.

20. Food delivery major Swiggy closes a $1.25-billion fund-raise, marking the first investment in the category by SoftBank Vision Fund 2.

21. India's edtech giant Byju's acquires US-based digital reading platform Epic for $500 million.

22. The Union Cabinet approves a proposal to allow 100 per cent foreign direct investment in public sector refiners.

23. The Supreme Court dismisses the petitions of Vodafone Idea and Bharti Airtel seeking correction of alleged errors in calculating the dues linked to adjusted gross revenue (AGR).

25. Insolvency regulator IBBI caps the number of assignments of corporate insolvency that an insolvency professional can handle at a time at 10 as part of its efforts to ensure that mandates don't get concentrated in fewer hands.

27. The International Monetary Fund sharply scales down India's economic growth projection by 300 basis points for the current fiscal year to 9.5 per cent from 12.5 per cent estimated earlier.

28. The Union Cabinet clears the Deposit Insurance and Credit Guarantee Corporation Bill, 2021 which will allow depositors to withdraw up to ₹5 lakh in 90 days if a bank is under moratorium.

30. The Finance Ministry reports a fiscal deficit of 18.2 per cent of the Budget Estimate for the April-June quarter, the lowest since 2010-11.

31. Inflows into the equity schemes of mutual funds in the June quarter increase to ₹19,508 crore against an outflow of ₹4,672 crore in the March quarter.

August

Government to Monitise Assets Worth ₹ 6 Trillion

1. The goods and services tax collection recovers to a three-month high in July, exceeding the ₹1.1 trillion-mark.

2. The IHS Markit Manufacturing Purchasing Managers' Index (PMI) rises to 55.3 in July from 48.1 in June, well above the 50-level separating growth from contraction. • Merchandise exports from India rise to $35.17 billion in July - the highest in nine years.

5. Finance Minister moves a bill in the Lok Sabha to repeal retrospective taxation of capital gains from sale of assets located in India by entities registered abroad.

6. The RBI's Monetary Policy Committee maintains status quo on the policy repo rate.

8. India exports 8 lakh tonnes of coal to its neighbouring nations, including Nepal, in the fiscal year ended March 2021.

9. E-commerce giant Amazon and Infosys co-founder N R Narayana Murthy's Catamaran Ventures "mutually decide" to not continue their joint venture beyond the end of its current term.

11. Ten major lenders, including State Bank of India, ICICI Bank, Canara Bank and Standard Chartered Bank for the first time join hands to set up an online platform for trading of corporate loans in the secondary market.

12. Retail inflation falls to a three-month low of 5.59 per cent in July from 6.26 per cent in June.

13. Prime Minister Narendra Modi formally launches the National Automobile Scrappage Policy which will not only phase out old vehicles but also will attract investments of about ₹10,000 crore.

15. Ola Electric launches its much-awaited keyless electric scooter, priced at 99,999 (ex-showroom in Karnataka, inclusing FAME II), considered to be among the cheapest among competition.

16. Wholesale inflation declines for the second consecutive month to 11.6 per cent in July from 12.7 per cent in June.

17. In a partial relief to HDFC Bank, the largest private sector bank of the country, the Reserve Bank of India allows the lender to issue new credit cards.

18. The Union Cabinet approves a new ₹11,040-crore mission to boost domestic palm oil production, which includes a minimum support price-like mechanism for growers.

19. ONGC invites global bids for 43 oil and gas fields.

20. The world's first DNA-plasmid vaccine, the three-dose one for Covid-19 developed by Zydus Cadila, receives emergency-use authorisation from the Drugs Controller General of India (DCGI) for use in adolescents 12 years old and above.

23. Finance Minister announces a pipeline of assets the government is looking to monitise to collect about ₹6 trillion to partly fund its ambitious infrastructure projects over four years ending 2024-25.

26. Aviation regulator Directorate General of Civil Aviation lifts a ban on Boeing 737 MAX aircraft, two and a half years after it was grounded globally.

27. The Securities and Exchange Board of India restrains Kotak Mahindra Asset Management Company from launching any new fixed maturity plans for six months.

28. In a move to bring in one vehicle registration valid across the country, the government introduces a new registration mark called the Bharat Series (BH), effective September 15.

29. The board of Bharti Airtel approves fund-raising to the tune of ₹21,000 crore, mainly to make payments towards adjusted gross revenue (AGR)-related liabilities due in 2021-22.

30. The combined turnover of Tata Sons' 40 biggest unlisted subsidiaries is up 17.8 per cent YoY to ₹80,720 crore in FY21 from ₹68,538 crore a year ago.

31. India's economy grows by a record 20.1 per cent in the April-June quarter of the fiscal year 2021-22 against a contraction of 24.4 per cent in the corresponding previous period.

September

Ford India to Stop Manufacturing Vehicles in India

1. GST collection moderates in August to ₹1.12 trillion as against ₹1.16 trillion in July, but exceeds the ₹1-trillion mark for the second month as economic activity gains pace with a decline in Covid-19 cases. • IHS Markit Purchasing Managers' Index (PMI) for manufacturing falls to 52.3 in August from 55.3 in July.

2. India exports goods worth $33.14 billion in August, up 45.17 per cent on-year, as demand continues to remain robust from other countries.

3. Private sector life insurer HDFC Life announces it is acquiring Exide Life Insurance for ₹6,687 crore, in a bid to enhance its proprietary channel.

4. SBI Mutual Fund emerges the first fund house to have Assets Under Management (AUM) of ₹6 lakh crore.

5. The top five digital-only brokers corner more than half of the industry's active base, signifying a seismic shift in the pecking order among domestic brokerages. Zerodha, Upstox, Angel One, 5 Paisa and Groww have a market share of over 53 per cent until the end of July, with a cumulative tally of 12.6 million active clients.

6. Maruti Suzuki India announces a 1.9% increase in prices of almost its entire range of vehicles.

7. Stock markets in India can soon transfer shares and money into client accounts in under 24 hours with SEBI set to usher in a T+1 (today plus one) settlement cycle for equity transactions from January 1, 2022.

8. The Union Cabinet approves a ₹10,683 crore Production Linked Incentive (PLI) scheme for the textile sector.

9. Ford India will stop manufacturing vehicles in India but will retain the engine-making and technology services business (Global Business Services) as part of restructuring its India operations.

11. The Centre cuts the import duty on edible oils—mainly palm group of oils, soyabean oil and sunflower il—as part of its plans to control surging cooking oil prices and inflation.

12. Zomato shuts down its grocery delivery pilot even as it bets on its investment in Grofers to generate better outcomes than the company's marketplace model of grocery delivery.

13. Retail inflation cools to a four-month low of 5.3 per cent in August from 5.59 per cent in July, led by subdued prices of food articles and a high base effect.

14. Wholesale inflation rises to 11.39 per cent in August, from 11.6 per cent in July, despite a fall in prices of food items as inflation in manufactured items and non-food articles such as oilseeds and minerals remain elevated.

15. Vodafone Idea Ltd gets a big breather with the Cabinet clearing proposal for giving telcos a moratorium on their adjusted gross revenue dues as well as spectrum payments progressively for the next four years.

16. The World Bank Group scraps its flagship publication, the 'Doing Business' report. This report publishes the influential annual ranking of countries on the Ease of Doing Business (EDB) index.

18. India's vaccination count crosses 80-crore mark, a day after the country clocks its highest 24-hour vaccination tally of 2.5 crore jabs.

20. Exports of software services, including services delivered by foreign affiliates of Indian firms, record 2.1% growth during FY21 and stands at $148.1 billion, as per a Reserve Bank survey.

21. The Asian Development Bank cuts its forecast for India's GDP growth in 2021-22 to 10%, from 11% projected earlier.

22. Zee Entertainment Enterprises Ltd announces a merger with Sony Pictures Networks India.After the merger, Sony will invest $1.57 billion and will be the majority shareholder with 52.93% controlling stake and the rest of the 47.07 stake will be controlled by Zee shareholders.

The Merits and Demerits of Privatisation

Dr. Jose Sebastian
Former Faculty, Gulati Institute of Finance and Taxation

Private sector investment is the driver of modern economic growth. There is also a growing trend across the world to privatise public assets to accelerate economic growth. A look at the merits and demerits of privatisation and also the issues involved in privatising public sector assets.

Introduction

It is a widely acknowledged fact that private sector investment is the driver of modern economic growth. Countries across the world vie with each other to attract private sector investment by trying to improve the 'ease of doing business index'. There is also a growing trend across the world to privatise public assets to accelerate economic growth. This article discusses the various aspects of promoting private sector and also the issues involved in privatising public sector assets.

Role of Private Sector in an Economy

History of economic development of countries across the world has convincingly shown that the presence of natural and human resources alone will not lead to faster economic growth. In order to transform the natural and human resources into marketable commercial products and services, individuals with entrepreneurial traits are essential. For historical and sociological reasons, most less developed countries are not endowed with entrepreneurial resources. To overcome this constraint, governments of these countries offer several incentives to foreign and local entrepreneurs to set up enterprises. Tax concessions, land, electricity and water at subsidized rates are some of such incentives. However, promoting private sector is not an unmixed blessing. There are pros and cons in any aggressive promotion of private sector.

Merits in Promoting Private Sector

In the absence of a vibrant private sector, a less developed country does not have any other option other than promoting public sector enterprises. While public sector is essential in certain sectors, it is neither feasible nor practical to establish public sector enterprises in all areas. First, the less developed countries do not have adequate investible capital.

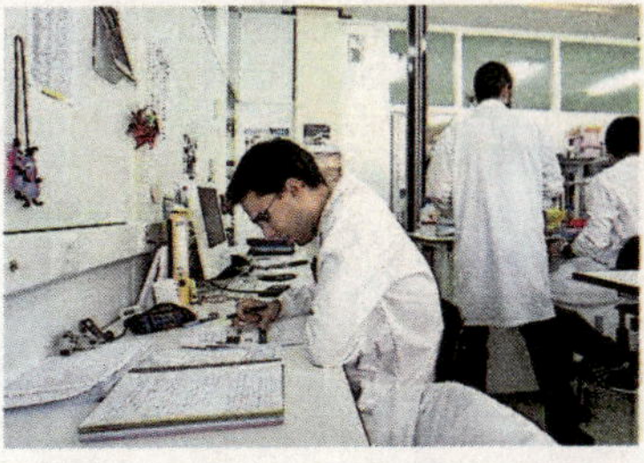

Second, public sector enterprises often function in a protected environment and therefore does not reflect the true costs and benefits to society. Protected from external competition, the public sector enterprises will not innovate and languish as technological laggards. Third, it is almost impossible to prevent political interference in the functioning of the public sector enterprises and the associated corruption and wastage of scarce public resources.

Promoting private sector enterprises has several advantages. First, The private companies, driven by profits as they are, have an incentive to cut costs and be more efficient. Second, in order to be competitive, the private companies have to innovate and come out with new technology, products and services. They invest in research and development and this benefits the whole society in terms of more efficient and cheaper products and services. The progress made in recent history in the fields of health, information and communication technology etc. have transformed human life dramatically. Both in developed and developing countries, private sector is the major provider of employment. A study undertaken by International Finance Corporation in 2013 found that 90% of jobs in developing countries are in the private sector.

Private sector is the single largest contributor to government revenues. Private sector enterprises pay taxes such as corporate tax, goods and services tax and excise duty. The employees of the private sector pay personal income tax, property tax, profession tax etc. Governments experience reduction in tax revenue during periods of prolonged recession as private income and consumption shrink.

Demerits of Promoting Private Sector

As pointed out earlier, aggressive promotion of private sector is not without harmful effects. As private sector companies are driven by profit motive, they sometimes fail to take into account the long term interests of the society. Protecting the environment is part of the long term goal of a society. A private sector company may not be sensitive to environmental concerns and may pollute land, waterways and air. Uncontrolled exploitation of natural resources by the private companies have caused environmental catastrophe in many less developed countries. It is in the interest of the company to ignore environmental concerns as Installing pollution control mechanism will add to the cost of production and in turn will reduce their profits. Providing decent working environment and decent wages to workers is part of the social agenda of a modern society. But private companies driven by short term profit motive are less likely to spend resources on improving working environment or paying decent wages.

Quality of products and services is another area of concern. Cut-throat competition in the market forces private sector companies to churn out products and services of questionable quality. Private sector enterprises generally have a short-term vision. They are less likely to invest in projects with long gestation period and low profit. This is one of the reasons why many such projects are in the public sector. The extent of competition in the market is the main factor that forces private sector firms to produce products and services at competitive prices and quality. In the absence of competition, the private sector companies may fleece customers and make supernormal profits.

The above demerits however do not mean that private sector should not be promoted at all. Governments across the world have put in place regulations so that these demerits are minimized. In order to make the private sector comply with environmental standards, governments across the world have put in place stringent laws for setting up and running enterprises. In India, Green Tribunal at the national level and State level Pollution Control Boards maintain strong vigil on industries. For food and non-food items, different quality standards are prescribed. Consumer protection legislations ensure that the rights of consumers are protected. For workers, governments enact several legislations aimed at ensuring minimum wages, provident fund, health and accident insurance and safety measures at work place. However, in regulating private sector, what is required is a measured approach. Too many regulations, procedures and formalities may strangulate private sector and make the entrepreneurial process difficult. Countries across the world now try to improve their ranking in World Bank's 'Ease of Doing Business' ranking. Private entrepreneurs may choose to move to countries with more business-friendly environment. There may be a tendency on the part of the entrepreneurs to concentrate their activities in sectors where regulation is relatively less or nil. Business activities like trade, real estate or dealings in financial products become attractive for them at least in the short run. But from society's point of view, these activities do not add much value in terms of employment or income. Manufacturing on the other hand, provide more employment and income and ensure utilization of the natural resources. On the other hand, a lax regulatory framework for the private sector will be detrimental to the long term interests of the society. Transparency and accountability of regulatory institutions go a long way in minimizing corruption and red tape.

Public- Private Partnership

Public- Private Partnership(PPP) is an emerging form of infrastructure development model which seeks to minimize the demerits of public sector and private sector while maximizing the merits of both. Public–private partnership projects have been implemented in many

countries with varying success rates for development of infrastructure such as building and equipping of schools, hospitals, transport systems, and water and sewerage systems. There are various models of PPP. Some of the major among them are Operation and Maintenance Contract, Build-Operate- Transfer (BOT), Build-Own-Operate-Transfer (BOOT) and Build-Own-Operate(BOO).

Though PPP as a model has gained acceptance across the world, the effectiveness of PPPs as cost-saving or innovation-producing ventures has been called into question by numerous studies. A common problem with PPP projects is that private investors obtained a rate of return higher than that of government even though most or all of the income risk associated with the project was borne by the public sector. New forms of PPP have evolved over the years to overcome some of the demerits. Asset Monetization, Global Public- Private Partnership, Partnership with Non-Profit Organisations, Product Development Partnership and Public Private Community Partnership are some of the major forms of emerging PPP.

Public Sector Enterprises

Both in developed and developing countries, public sector enterprises (PSEs) play a vital role in the economy. PSEs have strong economic rationale. In the early stage of development of a country, there are certain sectors or activities where the private sector is reluctant to enter.

Lumpy investment, long gestation lag and low profit are some of the reasons. Examples are railway and road infrastructure, strategic goods and services like postal services, banking, arms manufacturing and politically sensitive businesses like broadcasting. Government will have to come forward to start public enterprises in all such areas. Government may supply merit goods like public health and school education either directly or through state-owned enterprises.

Growth of Public Sector Enterprises in India

At the time of independence from the colonial rule, India was primarily an agrarian country with a weak industrial base. Bombay Plan, a set of proposals prepared by eight leading industrialists in 1945, had proposed state intervention in the industrial development of the country. India's Second Five Year Plan (1956–60) and the Industrial Policy Resolution of 1956 emphasized the development of public sector enterprises(PSEs). The major objectives for the setting up of PSEs was to accelerate the growth of core sectors of the economy; to serve the equipment needs of strategically important sectors; and to generate employment and income. In the subsequent Five Year Plans, PSE expansion was carried out vigorously covering various sectors and backward regions of the country. According to Comptroller and Auditor General's(CAG) Report tabled last year, the government had an investment of ₹3,57,064 crores in shares of 420 government companies and corporates by the of March 2018. The market value of shares held by government in 42 listed PSEs was ₹13,63,194 crores.

Public sector units led to the development of large number of ancillary industries across the country and thus paved the way for industrialisation of the country. As part of New Economic Policy of 1990s, Government of India began disinvesting public sector enterprises. The policy of disinvestment has been carried forward by subsequent governments. Though disinvestment has not been a runaway success, government could mobilize substantial resources through this way and this has helped to tide over fiscal stress to some extent.

Privatisation

Depending upon the context in which it is used, the word privatisation may mean different things. In common parlance, privatisation is moving something from the public sphere into the private sphere or government selling state-owned businesses to private interests. It may also mean privatisation of services or government functions, where private entities are tasked with the implementation of government programs or performance of government services.

Though several privatisation initiatives were there in the pre-20th century, privatisation on a massive scale began under Margaret Thatcher in the United Kingdom and Ronald Reagan in the United States. In the subsequent years, countries in Latin America and Europe followed privatisation path. The collapse of Soviet Union paved the way for massive privatization of public assets in Russia and East European countries.

Depending upon the extent of capital market development, there are different models of privatisation. Where there is an established capital market capable of absorbing the shares, privatisation through the stock market is more likely to be the method used. A market with high liquidity makes privatisation easy. On the other hand, if the capital markets are insufficiently developed, it would be difficult to find enough buyers. The shares may have to be underpriced, and the sales may not raise an amount equivalent to the fair value of the company being privatised.

Merits of Privatisation

Studies show that entrepreneurs operating in competitive markets are more efficient than government in delivering

many goods and services. This tends to lead to improved quality, lower prices, less corruption and red tape and quicker delivery. The proponents of privatisation attribute following specific merits.

- State-run industries tend to be bureaucratic as they have little incentive to improve their function. In many countries, even loss-making PSEs are given budgetary support on political grounds.
- The motive to make profit makes private entrepreneurs to produce goods and services more efficiently.
- A private enterprise will be more sensitive to the tastes and preferences of customers than a PSE. The former will be quick to come out with new products and services through innovation.
- PSEs are prone to corruption as de-

cisions are made primarily for political reasons. The decision making body like Director Board are often composed of politicians and bureaucrats.

- PSEs are forced to recruit less efficient staff on political grounds and this affects their financial viability.
- Private enterprises are accountable to the shareholders and to the consumers and therefore are keen to meet their needs. The managers of PSEs are accountable to politicians. This distorts their investment decisions.
- Political interference or populist policies of the ruling party affects the functioning of the PSE in various functions like purchase of raw materials, recruitment of workers and pricing of products.

Demerits of Privatisation

Opponents of privatisation have advanced very strong arguments against privatization. According to them, certain public goods and services should remain primarily in the hands of government in order to ensure that every citizen has access to them. Public health, basic education, law enforcement are some of them. When government provides society at large with public goods and services, there are positive externalities. Providing these services is the basic function of any government. Even though private companies are capable of providing similar goods or services alongside the government, opponents of privatization are skeptical about completely transferring the provision of public goods, services and assets into private hands. Following are their major arguments.

- The profits of PSEs are a major source of revenue to the government. Even when they make losses, they pay indirect taxes like excise and sales tax to state exchequer. Since PSEs have little incentive to evade tax, it serves as a ready source of revenue to governments.
- The profits of the private enterprises go to the owners and shareholders. Often, the private enterprises resort to tax evasion and other malpractices to remain competitive in the market.
- When essential services like public health, water supply and basic education are privatized, the poor and marginalized who cannot afford to pay for the cost will be denied these services.
- Highly subsidized essential services by the government play a major role in reducing inequality in society.
- Private enterprises will try to cut cost by reducing the number of workers or by adopting mechanization.
- Private enterprises may compromise on the quality of goods and services to maximize profits.

Results of Privatisation from Across the World

Several studies have been undertaken on privatization in the developed and developing countries. Depending upon the model of privatisation adopted and the political situation of the country, the outcome has been different. Some empirical studies suggest that privatisation could also have very modest effects on efficiency and quite regressive distributive impact. Some economists hold that although the efficiency gains of privatisation are associated with welfare costs, it can be mitigated to a large extent by appropriate government intervention like redistribution. According to a World Bank study, "privatisation in competitive industries with well-informed consumers consistently improved efficiency".

In Russia and Latin America, privatisation was accompanied by large-scale corruption during the sale of the state-owned companies. Unfair gains were made by those with political connections and this discredited privatisation in these regions.

Privatisation in Strategic Sectors

While privatisation of PSEs in most sectors may not be problematic for a government, privatisation of PSEs in strategic sectors like Defense, Transport and Communication etc. raises serious issues. Since these sectors are closely connected with the security of a country, government has to consider all aspects before privatising PSEs. For this reason, governments across the world keep certain activities exclusively for the public sector. Accordingly, PSEs engaged in the production of certain goods and services are rarely privatised.

It is against this background that the privatisation policy announced by Union Government in 2021-22 budget has to be seen. Government has announced its resolve to push for an aggressive privatization policy of public sector enterprises which would seek to unlock their potential to create wealth in India's economy. According to the policy, there will be a bare minimum presence of PSEs in four strategic sectors, namely atomic energy and defence, transport and telecommunications, power and petroleum, and banking and insurance while PSEs in non-strategic sectors will either be fully privatised or closed down.

Making Privatisation more Successful

One of the challenges facing countries embarking on privatisation is how to make it a success. The success of a privatisation programme has to be evaluated against its objectives. If the objective is revenue or sale proceeds, the focus of the evaluation will be whether public assets received the price it should have received in a fair and transparent sale process. If the objective is industrialisation and employment generation, how much revenue the government receives in the sale process may not be an immediate consideration. A privatisation process that fetches high revenue to the government may not be considered a success if the privatized assets fail to create employment and income in the economy. If buyers of industries in prime locations convert the land for real estate purposes, the impact on the economy could be discouraging. Similarly, if privatised assets are utilized for starting industries which have serious environmental impact, the long term social benefits may far outweigh the revenue impact.

All these suggest that in order to make privatisation a success, the policy makers should be clear about the objectives. While framing the objectives, all dimensions like revenue, employment and income and environmental impact will have to be factored in. There should be clarity about the purpose for which the asset will be utilised and the long term impact on the economy. Clearly, such an approach will affect the revenue potential and also the speed of the privatisation process.

Another way to make privatisation a success is to learn from the experience of countries with comparable circumstances. This helps the policy makers to avoid many costly mistakes. To a large extent, the success of privatisation depends on the extent of transparency and accountability. The civil society, media and the political parties are to be taken into confidence before embarking on privatisation.

Banking, Insurance and Capital Market

Banking in India dates back to thousands of years. Several of India's ancient texts including those in the Vedic period mention bank lending functions. The modern banking system in India has its roots in the colonial era starting in the 1800s. India's public sector banks (PSBs) are essentially legacy banks from the colonial period that were subsequently nationalized. For example, India's largest Public Sector Bank (PSB), State Bank of India (SBI), was founded as Bank of Calcutta in 1806, took the name Imperial Bank of India in 1921 and became state-owned in 1955. The remaining PSBs in India were formed through two waves of nationalizations, one in 1969 and the other in 1980. After the 1980 nationalization, PSBs had a 91 per cent share in the national banking market with the remaining 9 per cent held by "old private banks" (OPBs) that were not nationalized.

Gross Non-performing Advances (GNPA) ratio (i.e. GNPAs as a percentage of Gross Advances) of Scheduled Commercial Banks decreased from 8.2 per cent at the end-March 2020 to 7.5 per cent at end-September 2020. Restructured Standard Advances (RSA) ratio of Scheduled Commercial Banks increased from .36 per cent to 0.41 per cent during the same period. Overall, the Stressed Advances ratio of SCBs decreased from 8.6 per cent at end March 2020 to 7.9 per cent at end-September 2020.

GNPA ratio of Public Sector Banks (PSBs) decreased from 10.25 per cent at

the end-March 2020 to 9.4 per cent at end-September 2020 and the Stressed Advances ratios decreased from 10.75 per cent to 9.96 per cent during the same period. Net NPA ratios also declined and stood at 2.1 per cent for SCBs and 2.85 per cent for PSBs as at end-September 2020.

Capital to risk-weighted asset ratio (CRAR) of SCBs increased from 14.7 per cent to 15.8 per cent between March 2020 and September 2020 on account of improvement of CRAR of both public and private sector banks. SCBs' annualised Return on Assets (RoA) recovered from 0.07 per cent to 0.64 per cent during first half (HI) of 2020-21, while their annualised Return on Equity (RoE) recovered from 0.78 per cent to 7.68 per cent during the same period. The RoA and RoE for PSBs became positive in June 2020 and continued to be positive in the quarter ended September 2020, after recording negative profitability ratios from March 2016 to March 2020 (*see table on page 652*). This is mainly on account of moratorium granted and asset classification stand still order by the Supreme Court.

The World Bank Scraps 'Doing Business Report'

On September 16, the World Bank Group scraped its publication, the 'Doing Business' report owing to Chinese pressure to influence the report through IMF. This report publishes the influential annual ranking of countries on the Ease of Doing Business (EDB) index.

NPAs, CRAR, RoE, RoA of Public Sector Banks and Private Sector Banks (Amount in crore; Rates and Ratios in per cent)								
Public Sector Banks					**Private Sector Banks**			
Reporting Date	Gross NPAs	Capital Ratio (CRAR)	Return on Equity	Return on Total Assets	Gross NPAs	Capital Ratio (CRAR)	Return on Equity	Return on Total Assets
Mar-17	6,84,732	12.14	-1.92	-0.12	91,915	15.53	11.79	1,27
Mar-18	8,95,601	11.66	-14.01	-0.87	1,25,863	16.43	9.98	1.09
Mar-19	7,39,541	12.20	-10.97	-0.66	1,80,872	16.07	5.49	0.60
Mar-20	6,78,317	12.85	-3.92	-0.25	2,05,848	16.55	3.20	0.35
Sep-20	6,09,129	13.51	4.33	0.26	1,88,191	18.21	10.04	1.10

Source: Offsite Returns, Global Operations, RBI

The net profit (profit after tax) for PSBs increased from ₹(–) 25,941 crore at end-March 2020 to ₹14,688 crore at end-September 2020. Similarly, the net profit (profit after tax) for private sector banks increased from 19,113 crore at end-March 2020 to 32,762 crore at end-September 2020. Overall, for SCBs, the net profit (profit after tax) increased from ₹11,322 crore at end-March 2020 to ₹59,426 crore at end-September 2020.

The focus on resolution of stressed assets had to take a backseat during the year on account of the outbreak of the Covid-19 pandemic. Government had suspended the initiation of fresh insolvency proceedings under Section 7, 9 and 10 of Insolvency & Bankruptcy Code 2016 for defaults arising on or after March 25, 2021. Reserve bank announced loan moratorium from March 1, 2020 to August 31, 2020, asset classification dispensation and special resolution framework for Covid-19 related stressed assets. In respect of borrowers to whom moratorium was granted, the period during which such facilities were granted was permitted to be excluded from the calculation of days past due for the purpose of asset classification or out of order status, as the case may be. Further, RBI announced a Resolution Framework for Covid-19 related Stress to enable the lenders to implement a resolution plan in respect of eligible corporate exposures without change in ownership, and personal loans, while classifying such exposures as Standard, subject to certain conditions. Under the resolution plans that could be invoked under the above window, lenders are permitted to grant additional moratorium of up to two years. RBI had appointed a committee under K.V. Kamath for making recommendations on the required financial parameters to be factored in resolution plans. Also, MSME accounts classified as Standard where the aggregate exposure of banks and NBFCs was ₹25 crore or below as on March 1, 2020, were permitted to be restructured without a downgrade in the asset classification, subject to certain conditions. Notably, the Supreme Court issued an interim order dated September 3, 2020 specifying that "the accounts which were not declared NPA till 31.08.2020 shall not be declared NPA till further orders."

The above measures, which provided asset classification reliefs to borrowers, would affect the true recognition of financial stress on the borrower accounts. However, the larger objective of financial stability in the wake of pandemic demanded prudential forbearance which was exercised through clear boundaries and disincentives embedded in the above reliefs. Moreover, the risk recognition has not been completely suspended as the lenders are required to make provisions of at least 10 per cent in respect of accounts which availed of asset classification benefits under the above reliefs.

Insurance Sector

The performance and potential of insurance sector is assessed using two indicators–Insurance penetration and Insurance Density. Insurance penetration is calculated as percentage of insurance premium to GDP and Insurance density is calculated as ratio of insurance premium to population.

In India, Insurance penetration which was 2.71 per cent in 2001 has steadily increased to 3.76 per cent in 2019. In contrast, insurance penetration in Asia, i.e., Malaysia, Thailand and China was 4.72, 4.99 and 4.30 per cent respectively in 2019. As of 2019, the penetration for Life insurance in India is 2.82 per cent, the penetration for Non-Life insurance is much at 0.94 per cent. Globally insurance penetration was 3.35 per cent for the life segment and 3.88 per cent for the non-life segment in 2019. Although the penetration is lower in India for both, it is particularly low for Non-life insurance as compared to other countries.

The insurance density in India which was US$ 11.5 in 2001 reached to approximately US$ 78 in 2019. The comparative figures for Malaysia, Thailand and China in 2019 were much higher at US$ 536, US$ 389 and US$ 430 respectively. Density for Life insurance is US$ 58 and Non-Life insurance is much lower at US$ 19 in 2019 in India. Globally insurance density was US$ 379 for the life segment and US$ 439 for the non-life segment respectively in 2019. United States has particularly high insurance density in the Non-Life category. India has extremely low insurance penetration as compared to global average and other comparable countries.

Penetration and Density in Life Insurance

Particulars	2013	2014	2015	2016	2017	2018	2019
Insurance Penetration(in per cent)	3.10	2.60	2.72	2.72	2.76	2.74	2.82
Insurance Density (in USD)	41.0	44.0	43.2	46.5	55.0	55.0	58.0

Source: SwissRe, Sigma various issues

Penetration and Density in Non-Life Insurance

Particulars	2013	2014	2015	2016	2017	2018	2019
Insurance Penetration(in per cent)	0.80	0.70	0.72	0.77	0.93	0.97	0.94
Insurance Density (in USD)	11.0	11.0	12.0	13.2	18.0	19.0	19.0

Source: SwissRe, Sigma various issues

During 2019-20, the gross direct premium of Non-Life insurers $1.89 lakh crore, as against $1.69 lakh crore in 2018-19, registering a growth of 11.45 per cent. Within non-life category, motor and health segments primarily are the main contributors to industry to report this growth. Life insurance industry recorded a premium income of ₹5.73 lakh crore in 2019-20, as against ₹5.08 lakh crore in the previous financial year, registering a growth of 12.75 per cent. While renewal premium accounted for 54.75 per cent of the total premium received by the life insurers, new business contributed the remaining 45.25 per cent.

Capital Markets

1. Primary Markets (Equity)

A. Public Issue

The year 2020-21 (upto December) witnessed an increase in resource mobilisation through public issue compared to the similar period for previous year. During April-December 2020, although the number of companies raising money through public issue reduced to 33 from 49 in the same period last year, ₹31,086.64 crore were mobilised during this period as compared to ₹10,950 crore in the similar period of previous year indicating an increase of 183.9 per cent in resource mobilisation over the period. Similarly, resource mobilisation through rights issues during 2020-21 (upto December) increased to ₹60,906.90 crore from 16 rights issues as compared to ₹51,865.86 crore from 13 issues in April-December.

Primary Market Resource Mobilization through Public and Rights Issues

	2019-20(Upto December)		2020-21(upto December)	
Issue Type	No. of Issues	Amount (₹crore)	No.of Issues	Amount (₹crore)
Public Issue (Equity)	49	10,949.99	33	31,086.64
Rights Issue (Equity)	13	51,865.86	16	60,906.90
Total Public Issue	62	62,815.85	49	91,993.54

Source: BSE, NSE and SEBI

extra

Foreign Exchange Reserves

India's forex reserves, which stood at ₹1,029 crore in 1950-51, now stands at ₹46.17 lakh crore. In fact, India's forex reserves in 1991 stood just at $1.2 billion, which was barely enough to finance the country's imports even for just 3 weeks.

B. Private Placement

The year 2020-21 (upto December) witnessed a decrease in resource mobilisation through private placement route compared to that during the similar period for previous year. In April-December 2020, there were 183 issues mobilising ₹91,631.33 crore through private placement compared to 229 issues raising ₹1,79,443.86 crore during the same period last year.

Primary Market Resource Mobilization through Private Placements				
Issue Type	**2019-20** (Upto December)		**2020-21** (Upto December)	
	No. of issues	Amount (₹ crore)	No. of issues	Amount (₹ crore)
QIPs Allotment (Equity)	9	34,028.55	21	64,148.50
Preferential Allotment (Equity)	220	1,45,415.31	162	27,482.83
Total Private Placement	229	1,79,443.86	183	91,631.33

Source: BSE, NSE and SEBI

In the year 2019-20 (upto December), resource mobilisation through preferential allotment route was substantially more than that through Qualified Institutional Placement(QIP) route. However, there was a reversal in this trend in April-December 2020. During this period, there were 21 QIPs and 162 preferential allotments raising ₹64,148.50 crore and ₹27,482.83 crore respectively, as compared to 9 QIPs and 220 Preferential allotment raising ₹34,028.55 crore and ₹1,45,415.3 crore respectively during the corresponding period of the previous financial year.

2. Primary Markets (Debt)

The total debt issuance in primary market rose by 29.7 per cent to 5.99 lakh crore during 2020-21 (upto December) as compared to 4.63 lakh core in the corresponding period of the previous year. During April-December 2020, the amount raised through private placement of debt increased by 32.2 per cent to ₹5.95 lakh crore. During the same period, the amount raised through public debt issues declined by 67 per cent to ₹3,871.7 crore.

Primary Market Resource Mobilisation Through Debt Issues				
Issue Type	**2019-20 (Upto December)**		**2020-21(Upto December)**	
	No. of Issues	Amount (₹crore)	No. of Issues	Amount (₹crore)
Public Issue (Debt)	27	11,746.11	10	3,871.70
Private Placement (Debt)	1295	4,49,939.71	1540	5,95,044.66
Total Debt Issue	1322	4,61,685.82	1550	5,98,916.36

Source: BSE, NSE and SEBI

Bilateral Netting of Qualified Financial Contracts Bill was passed and has become operational since October 1, 2020. Prior to this legislation, India did not have a legal framework for bilateral netting. Netting enables two counter parties in a bilateral financial contract to offset claims against each other to determine a single net payment obligation due from one counter party to others. Besides aiding the stability of the financial markets, bilateral netting will help in development of corporate debt market in India and freeing the capital in the system.

Mutual Funds Activities

There was a net inflow of ₹2.76 lakh crore into the mutual funds industry during 2020-21 (upto December), as compared to a net inflow of ₹1.82 lakh crore in the corresponding period of last year. The net assets under management of all mutual funds increased by 16.9 per cent to 31.02 lakh crore at the end of December 31, 2020 from ₹26.54 lakh crore at the end of December 31, 2019.

Mobilisation of Funds by Mutual Funds (Amount in ₹ lakh Crore)

Period	No. of Folios (cr)	Gross Mobilization	Redemption	Net Inflows	Net AUM at the end of the period
2019-20#	8.71	154.67	152.85	1.82	26.54
2020-21#	9.43	65.47	62.71	2.76	31.02

Source: SEBI Note: # Upto December 31 of respective financial years.

Unicorns in India

The number of Indian unicorns – privately held companies worth $1 billion or more – continues to balloon. A record 15 Indian startups became unicorns in the first half of the calendar year 2021; nine more reached unicorn status in July and August.

That is more new unicorns created in India in just two months than the eight that emerged in all of 2020. It brings the country's total to 57, closing the gap with China, which boasts about 160 unicorns, which in turn is second only to the U.S., with roughly 400.

Among the nine Indian companies that became unicorns in July and August, five are engaged in business-to-business (B2B) services, two are in online education, one is a crypto asset exchange and one is an online used car marketplace aimed at consumers. Their composition reflects the recent rapid expansion of India's B2B sector. Eight of the 15 startups that became unicorns in the first half of the year were also B2B companies.

A quick look at the newest unicorns is revealing. Zetwerk, which crossed the $1 billion valuation threshold in a late-August funding round, has brought a variety of manufacturing suppliers and subcontractors online. OfBusiness, which reached a valuation of $1.5 billion at the end of July, is an online B2B trading platform specializing in industrial materials – including steel, plastics and cement – along with grains and other foodstuffs.

BharatPe, which was valued at $2.8 billion at the end of July, is a mobile payments platform that allows vendors to accept various QR code payment applications such as Paytm and PhonePe with a single QR code.

TRANSPORT & COMMUNICATION

- Postal Services
- Telecommunications
- Transport
- Media
- Use and Misuse of Social Media in India

Postal Services

The modern postal system was established in India by Lord Clive in 1766 and it was further developed by Warren Hastings in 1774. The expansion of its network was made during 1786 to 1793. For the first time, the post offices were regulated through an Act of 1837 on a uniform basis to unite all the post office establishments throughout the then existing three Presidencies into one all-India service. Thereafter, the Post Office Act of 1854 reformed the entire fabric of the postal system and the post offices of India were placed on the present administrative footing on 1st October 1854. This was the time when the first postage stamp valid across the country was issued at an affordable and uniform rate of postage, fixed by weight and not by distance. Since then, the Post Office touched the life of every person of the country. Even though the British established the post office for imperial interests, it along with the railways and telegraph, became one of the greatest engines of social development.

The statute presently governing the postal services in the country is the Indian Post Office Act, 1898. In the mid-19th century, the post office served as facilitator of travel with its conveyance systems and by maintaining the dak bungalows and dak serais. Mail order services were started with the value payable system introduced in 1877, while fund remittances at the doorstep became possible from 1880 through money order services. With the introduction of the Post Office Savings Bank in 1882 banking facilities were accessible to all and by 1884 all government employees were covered by the postal life insurance. Besides providing postal communication facilities, the post office network has also provided facilities for remittance of funds, banking and insurance services since the latter half of the 19th century.

The Indian Postal network is the largest postal network in the world with approx. 155,015 post offices. On an average, a post office serves an area of 21.56 sq. km^2 and a population of 7,753. Post offices in the country are categoried as Head, Sub and Branch post office. Branch post offices are mostly located in rural areas and are manned by Gramin Dak sevaks. The sub post offices are Departmental offices located in both rural and urban areas. Head post offices are located in important town and cities mostly at district levels.

The country has been divided into 23 postal circles, each circle headed by a Chief Postmaster General. Each circle is divided into regions, headed by a Postmaster General and comprising field units known as Divisions. These divisions are further divided into subdivisions. In addition to the 23 circles, there is a base circle to provide postal services to the Armed Forces of India headed by a Director General. One of the highest post offices in the world is in Hikkim, Himachal Pradesh operated by India Post at a height of 14,567 ft (4,440 m).

Telecommunications

The wireless telephony constitutes 98.3 per cent of all subscriptions whereas the share of landline telephones now stands at only 1.7 per cent. The overall teledensity in India stands at 86.6 per cent at the end of November 2020, whereas teledensity in rural and urban areas are 59.1 per cent and 139.0 per cent respectively.

Internet and broadband penetrated both in urban and rural area at a rapid pace. The number of internet subscribers (both broadband and narrowband put together) stood at 776.45 million at the end of September 2020 as compared to 636.73 million in March 2019. The wireless data usage grew at exponential rate during the calender year 2019 and was at 76.47 Exa bytes. During January-September 2020, it had already reached 75.21 Exa bytes. Average wireless data consumption per subscriber per month increased from 9.1 GB in March 2019 to 12.2 GB in June 2020. The reduced cost of data could enable affordable internet access at a rapid pace. As on June 2020, the cost of wireless data stood at 10.55 per GB.

The GoI has taken various initiatives including BharatNet for achieving the goal of Digital India programme. Under the project, network infrastructure is being established for Broadband Highways, accessible on a non-discriminatory basis to provide affordable broadband services to citizens and institutions in rural areas, in partnership with States and the private sector. As on 15.01.2021 about 4.87 lakh kms of optical fiber cable has been laid to cover 1.63 lakh Gram Panchayats (GPs) and nearly 1.51 lakh GPs have become service ready.

Transport

Roads

Road transport is the dominant mode of transportation in the country. The share of the transport sector in the GVA for FY19 was about 4.5 per cent of which the share of road transport contributed roughly 67 per cent.

The road network is the backbone of the transport system in India and it is very well integrated with the multi-modal system of transportation, which provides crucial links with airports, railway stations, ports, and other logistical hubs.

With 63.86 lakh kms of rural-urban roads and national-state highways, India is next only to the United States of America that has a road network of 66.45

National Highways Distribution As on 01.03.2019

State/ Union Territory	Existing NH length in Km	State/ Union Territory	Existing NH length in Km
1 Andhra Pradesh	6,913	19 Meghalaya	1,156
2 Arunachal Pradesh	2,537	20 Mizoram	1,423
3 Asom	3,909	21 Nagaland	1,548
4 Bihar	5,358	22 Odisha	5,762
5 Chandigarh	15	23 Puducherry	27
6 Chhattisgarh	3,606	24 Punjab	3,274
7 Delhi	157	25 Rajasthan	10,342
8 Goa	293	26 Sikkim	463
9 Gujarat	6,635	27 Tamil Nadu	6,742
10 Haryana	3,166	28 Telangana	3,795
11 Himachal Pradesh	2,607	29 Tripura	854
12 Jammu & Kashmir	2,423	30 Uttar Pradesh	11,737
13 Jharkhand	3,367	31 Uttarakhand	2,949
14 Karnataka	7,335	32 West Bengal	3,664
15 Kerala	1,782	33 A & N Islands	331
16 Madhya Pradesh	8,772	34 Dadra & Nagar Haveli	31
17 Maharashtra	17,757	35 Daman & Diu	22
18 Manipur	1,750	**Total**	**1,32,499**

lakh km.

During the decade ending in FY19, the national highways recorded a CAGR of 7.25 per cent followed by rural roads (6.25 per cent) and urban roads (4.27 per cent). The pace at which roads have been constructed has grown significantly from 12 kms per day in 2014-15 to 30 kms per day in FY19 before it moderated in FY20. The decline in the construction of road per day in FY21 is mostly on account of the COVID-19 shock. With the unlocking of the economy, construction of roads is expected to return back to the high pace attained before COVID-19.

The total length of National Highways was 1.32 lakh km as on March 1, 2019.

Railways

The first railway on Indian sub-continent ran over a stretch of 21 miles from Bombay to Thane. The formal inauguration

ceremony was performed on 16th April 1853, when 14 railway carriages carrying about 400 guests left Bori Bunder at 3.30 pm. The first passenger train steamed out of Howrah station destined for Hooghly, a distance of 24 miles, on 15th August, 1854, heralding the beginning of railway transport on the Eastern side of the sub-continent. In south the first line was opened on 1 July, 1856 by the Madras Railway Company. It ran between Vyasarpadi Jeeva Nilayam (Veyasarpandy) and

Walajah Road (Arcot), a distance of 63 miles. In the North a length of 119 miles of line was laid from Allahabad to Kanpur on 3rd March 1859. The first section from Hathras Road to Mathura Cantonment was opened to traffic on 19th October, 1875. These were the small beginnings which in due course developed into a network of railway lines all over the country. By 1880 the Indian Railway system had a route mileage of about 9000 miles.

Indian Railways (IR) with over 67,580 route kms, is the third-largest network in the world under single management. During the FY20, Indian Railways carried 1.2 billion tonnes of freight and 8.1 billion passengers — making it the world's largest passenger carrier and fourth-largest freight carrier.

Revenue earning freight loading (excluding loading by Konkan Railway) by Indian Railways in FY20 was 12,084 lakh tonnes, registering a decrease of 1.1 per cent over FY19. The passenger traffic was 80,857 lakhs in FY20 registering a growth of (-) 4.2 per cent over FY19.

The Railways accorded the highest priority to safety and took various measures on a continuous basis to prevent accidents and to enhance safety. As a result, the number of train accidents has come down from 104 in FY17 to 55 in FY20 despite a substantial increase in the traffic volume carried by the Indian Railways during the same period.

The GoI has allowed the private players to operate in the Railways sector through the PPP mode under the "New India New Railway" initiative. The initiative is expected to garner an investment of about ₹30,000 crores from the private sector. Ministry of Railways has identified over 150 pairs of train services for the introduction of 151 modern train sets or rakes through private participation. The private entity shall be responsible for financing, procuring, operating, and maintenance of the trains and shall have the freedom to decide on the fare to be charged from its passengers. The private entities that would undertake the project is being selected through a two-stage competitive bidding process. The bidding process is expected to be completed by May 2021 and the private trains are likely to be introduced in 2023-24

Port and Shipping

The ports and shipping sector is the backbone of international shipment of goods and services. It not only facilitates

international trade but also reduces the cost of international shipping and waiting period at the ports. In India, around 95 per cent (68 per cent) of total volume (value) of international trade is transported by sea.

India is endowed with a rich coastline of approximately 7500 km and has a strategic location on key international maritime trade routes. To harness and unleash the potential benefit of navigable waterways, the GoI has embarked on the ambitious Sagarmala Programme to promote port-led development in the country and reduce logistics costs for trade.

The Sagarmala program had identified 500+projects under four pillars - 211 port modernization projects, 200 port connectivity projects, 32 port-led industrialization projects, and 62 coastal community development projects which can unlock the opportunities for port-led development and are expected to mobilize more than ₹3.59 lakh crores of infrastructure investment. Between July 2019 to October 2020, 37 Sagarmala projects worth ₹8,461 crores have been completed which comprise 17 projects of port modernization worth ₹2,721 crores, 14 port connectivity projects worth ₹5,372 crores and 6 coastal community development projects worth ₹368 crores.

The installed capacity of major ports in India has increased to 1534.91 MTPA in March - 2020 as compared to 871.52 MTPA in March-2014. The major ports handled traffic of 704.82 MT during FT20. GoI has also been striving to improve operational efficiencies of major ports through mechanization, digitization, and process simplification. The average turnaround time in FY20 improved to 61.75 hours as against 126.96 hours in FY11 and 96 hours in FY15 . The average output per ship berth day has increased from 12,458 tonnes in FY15 to 16,433 tonnes in FY20. Unlike the preconceived notion that the port which contributes more in total traffic has a higher turnover time, the evidence suggests that the average turnover time is not significantly associated with the volume of traffic handled by the port. Irrespective of total traffic there are some major ports that are efficient on turnaround time and vice-versa.

Civil Aviation

The aviation market of India is one of the fastest growing in the world. India's domestic traffic has more than doubled from around 61 million in FY 14 to

around 137 million in FY20, a growth of over 14 per cent per annum. From the third largest domestic aviation market, it is expected to become the third largest overall (including domestic and international traffic) by the year FY25.

Despite the severe challenges posed by Covid-19, the Indian aviation industry has persevered through the crisis and demonstrated long-term resilience and full commitment to serve. The Vande Bharat Mission was launched on 7th May 2020 to evacuate stranded Indians across the world. It has thus reported over 30 lakhs passenger arrivals by 13 December 2020, with over 27 lakhs facilitated through chartered flights and Air India Group, making it the largest evacuation mission in human history. The air cargos took the lead in transporting life-critical supplies to the remotest corners of India under the Lifetime Udan initiative and also in seamlessly handling the imports of essential medical supplies.

Air passenger travel and aircraft movements are predicted to reach the pre-Covid level in early 2021 as a result of swift and decisive interventions and effective measures put in place by the Government. Government has also entered into air-links or air transport bubble arrangements with 23 countries to facilitate the movement of passengers between the respective countries and India.

Media

Print Media

The origin of newspapers in India dates back to the eighteenth century. India's first newspaper Hicky's *Bengal Gazette* or the *Calcutta General Advertiser* was published in English in Calcutta by James Augustus Hicky on 29 January 1780. Hicky's *Bengal Gazette* was the first English language newspaper, and indeed the first printed newspaper, to be published in the Indian sub-continent.

In 1789, the first newspaper from Bombay (now Mumbai), the *Bombay Herald* appeared, followed by the *Bombay Courier* in the following year. Later, this newspaper merged with *The Times of India* in 1861. The first newspaper published in an Indian language was the *Samachar Darpan* in Bengali on 23 May 1818. The first Hindi newspaper, the *Samachar Sudha Varshan* started its circulation in 1854. The era of Kannada newspapers started in the year 1843 when Hermann Mögling, a missionary from Basel Mission published the first Kannada newspaper called *Mangalooru Samachara* from Mangalore. The first Malayalam newspaper *Rajyasamacharam* was started by Dr Herman Gundert in 1847. First Marathi daily *Dyanprakash* was started on 12 February 1849, which lasted for 100 years. The first Tamil newspaper, *Swadesamitran,* started as a weekly in 1882 and became a daily in 1889.

As per the Registrar of Newspapers for India (RNI), the number of registered publications in the country as on 31st March 2018 stood at 1,18,239, registering a growth of 3 per cent in 2017-18 over the previous year. However, growth of circulation of publications contracted by 11.9 per cent in 2017-18 over the previous year. The total circulation of publications in the country during 2017-18 was 43 crore of which Hindi, English and Urdu publications were 19.56 crore, 5.34 crore and 2.52 crore respectively.

As per the 2021 FICCI-EY report on media and entertainment, print advertising revenues fell 41% in calenda year 2020 while subscription revenues declined by 24%. In 2019, the print industry was worth ₹29,570 crore; this dropped to ₹18,990 crore in 2020 and is likely to rake in revenues worth ₹23,710 crore in 2021. Further, PwC's Global Entertainment & Media Outlook 2021-2025 suggests that the industry is estimated to have a CAGR of 1.82% until 2025.

The government had spent ₹429 crore on print media advertising in 2018-19, which shrunk to ₹295 crore in 2019-20. It further fell to ₹197.49 crore in 2020-21. Due to the pandemic, the Audit Bureau of Circulation (ABC) has not been able

Fear of Running Out of Reading Material!

extra

There's a word for the fear of running out of reading material! Abibliophobia (noun) is the fear of running out of things to read, according to *Macmillan Dictionary.*

to conduct their circulation audits for the last two years. The DAVP rates are indexed based on these audited numbers. .

Television

Doordarshan is India's Public Service Television Network and the television vertical of Prasar Bharati. It is one of the largest broadcasting organisations in the world in terms of studios and transmitters. Doordarshan serves its mandate through its three tier programme services – National, Regional and Local. National programmes emphasise on events and issues of interest to the entire nation. These programmes include news, current affairs, magazine programmes and documentaries on science, art, culture, environment, social issues, serials, music, dance, drama and feature films.

TV advertising has continued to expand in 2020, despite COVID, reaching ₹35,015 crore. India is the fourth-largest market globally after the US, China and Japan. Further expansion at a 7.6% CAGR will take TV ad revenues to the level of ₹50,586 crore in 2025. Multichannel advertising will account for nearly 92% of the total TV advertising market in 2025. Online TV advertising will make modest inroads in the forecast period, with broadband penetration remaining extremely low at 7.3% of households.

Radio

All India Radio is India's Public Service Radio Broadcaster and the Radio vertical of Prasar Bharati. Serving its mandate to inform, educate and entertain its listeners, All India Radio is living up to its motto of 'Bahujan Hitaya: Bahujan Sukhaya'. It is one of the largest broadcasting organisations in the world in terms of number of languages of broadcast and the spectrum of socio -economic and cultural diversity it serves. AIR's home service comprises 470 broadcasting centres pan India, which covers nearly 92% of country's area and 99.19% of India's total population. AIR produces programmes in 23 languages and 179 dialects.

The opening of private FM radio since 1999 has not only resulted in providing good quality of reception to radio listeners, but also helped encouraging local talent and generating employment to large number of people in various cities. As on May 2019, 380 Private FM channels are operational in 107 cities spread across 27 States and 3 Union Territories. The Government has announced policy guidelines on expansion of private

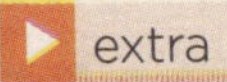

The First Magazine

The first publication which can be called a magazine was the German *Erbauliche Monaths Unteretungene*, launched in 1663. It was a literary and philosophical publication, and after its release, several other periodicals with similar content and topics, were published.

FM Radio broadcasting (Phase-III) wherein the Ministry of Information and Broadcasting will auction 683 channels in 236 cities in subsequent batches. Community Radio Stations are set up with the involvement of various educational institutions and civil society organizations. At present, 250 Community Radio stations have been operationalized. It is proposed to establish at least one CRS in each district with priority to coastal districts and aspirational districts.

Music, Radio & Podcast: India's total music, radio and podcasts market revenues dropped in 2020 to ₹4626 crore, as the pandemic stripped almost ₹522 crore from the country's live music sector. Digital channels account for almost 90% of the recorded music market. And, like elsewhere, streaming is the most-popular category. Ad -supported streaming is the dominant digital product in India, generating ₹1088 crore in 2020, almost twice the sum reported from subscription revenue (₹581 crore). The growth for the overall segment is predicted at 19.1% CAGR 2020-25 to reach ₹11026 crore.

Internet Advertising: India is the fastest-growing Internet Advertising market in the world at a CAGR of 18.8% during 2020-2025. Growth in mobile ad revenue overtook wired revenue in 2019 and is expected to be 74.4% of the total internet advertising revenue of ₹30,471 crore by 2025. In 2020 revenue from mobile internet advertising in India was ₹7331 crore and will rise to ₹22,350 crore in 2025 – increasing at a 25.4% CAGR. This makes India the fastest-growing mobile ad market in the world, reflecting the potential for growth, with over half the population yet to take up a mobile Internet subscription in 2020.

Video Games & Esports: The gaming market in India continues to enjoy exceptional growth and shows enormous potential. Video games and esports revenue reached ₹11,250 crore in 2020 and is set to expand to ₹24,213 crore in 2025, at 16.5% CAGR. India's gaming market is dominated by the social/casual category, which accounted for 77% of all video games and esports revenue in 2020. India's esports market is small but as awareness grows and, crucially, the mobile esports offering becomes stronger, this sector will see rapid expansion, at a 31.6% CAGR over the forecast period.

Films: Box-office revenues plunged by 75% year-on-year in a COVID-hit 2020 to ₹2652 crore. Local producers turned to digital streaming to make up the shortfall. Box-office revenue is expected to recover and grow at a CAGR of 39.3% grossing up ₹13,857 crore by the end of 2025. The overall segment comprising box-office and cinema advertising is predicted to grow back to pre-covid level by mid of 2023.

Use and Misuse of Social Media in India

Paranjoy Guha Thakurta

The widespread use of the social media, especially among the youth, is having a profound impact on community values and social norms in ways that are both beneficial and deleterious. A look at the growth and development of social media in India and the issues relating to privacy, freedom of expression and government regulation over the internet.

With the rapid growth in the use of the internet in India, an increasing number of persons in the country is using social media platforms for personal communications as well as for mass communications. Social media platforms, including WhatsApp, Facebook, Twitter, and Instagram, are being deployed for a wide variety of purposes: from political messaging, social interaction, and education, to spreading misinformation, propaganda, and pornography. The positive and negative aspects of the internet and social media are akin to the proverbial double-edged sword that cuts both ways, or a sharp knife or scalpel that has the potential to both heal and kill. The widespread use of the social media, especially among the youth, is having a profound impact on community values and social norms in ways that are both beneficial and deleterious. Closely related to the phenomenal spread of social media use are issues relating to privacy, freedom of expression and government regulation over the internet. The government of India is at present embroiled in numerous disputes, including legal tussles, with international digital monopolies on these issues; the differences seem unlikely to be resolved in a hurry.

India's "mediascape" has changed considerably in less than a decade. These changes have become even more dramatic after the onset of the Coronavirus pandemic and the accompanying economic downturn. Printed newspapers and periodicals are closing faster than ever before. Advertising flows from private corporate entities to the media have come down drastically. Journalists are being thrown out of their jobs or being asked to accept deep salary cuts while expenditure on reportage, research and investigations have shrunk significantly.

Growth in the Use of the Internet

The environment for dissemination of information has undergone a major transformation with the exponential growth in the use of the internet across the world and also in this country. Almost everywhere in India, there are more SIMs (subscriber identity modules) in mobile cellular phones than human beings—according to the Telecom Regulatory Authority of India, in 2020, the number of "subscribers" had reached 1.18 billion, of which the number of wireless subscribers stood at over 1.17 billion. The current population of India is estimated at around 1.4 billion. There is a rural-urban digital divide in many parts of India but this gap in the use of the internet between those who reside in cities and towns, and those who live in villages, is narrowing. This is on account of various government schemes like BharatNet and Digital India that are encouraging more and more people to use the internet and the social media.

Transformation of the Indian Media Landscape

The rapid transformation of the Indian media landscape in the last few years has been unparalleled. The media has changed, and continues to change, the way we communicate, get entertained and how we are impacted by, and respond to, larger social, economic and political processes that are at play. The success of streaming platforms like Netflix and Amazon Prime, the loud and highly opinionated television news anchors we are bombarded with every evening and, the unrelenting stream of WhatsApp forwards some of which egg on mobs to take the law into their own hands—are all manifestations and symptoms of the unprecedented flow of information and the explosion in the reach of mass media platforms. Since a lot of information is supposed to be "free," the exponential growth of the internet has been accompanied by the dissemination of fake, false, hateful and incendiary speech at scales and speeds never witnessed before.

Lowering of Data Tariffs

Perhaps the biggest game-changer responsible for the proliferation of the digital media in India has been the low-

First Newspaper-Cum-Magazine in India

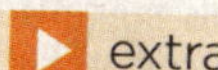

Pundit Jugal Kishore Shukla started the first newspaper-cum-magazine in India in Hindi language and named it *Udant Martanda*. Its first copy was launched on 30 May 1826 in Calcutta. The paper was in Khari Boli and Brij Bhasha dialects of Hindi.

ering of data tariffs which has resulted in not just increasing internet penetration but also much better access and faster speeds for use and for downloading data (although internet speeds in the country are lower than international averages). These facilities have for the first time become available to a large section of the country's population on their mobile phones. It was estimated that there are an estimated 504 million internet users in India who are above the age of five years in May 2020. This figure had exceeded 620 million by January 2021 and is expected to rise further in the years ahead. Most users of the internet also use social media – the two have become virtually indistinguishable.

The Facebook-owned application, WhatsApp, claimed it had at least 400

million users in the country in July 2019. According to more recent government data, in 2021, WhatsApp has at least 530 million users in India. In comparison, the number of users of WhatsApp was 250 million at the end of 2018. When Facebook opened its first office in India in 2011, it had only 15 million users. This number kept growing rapidly and jumped from 100 million in 2014 to over 220 million by the end of 2018 – this figure is expected to rise to over 500 million by 2025. India, the second most-populous country on the planet, is also the second biggest market for social media platforms the world over since the most-populous country, China, has shut out most of the major US-based digital conglomerates from that country, such as Facebook, Twitter and Google.

The number of persons eligible to vote in India stood at around 900 million during the Lok Sabha elections that concluded in May 2019 – this was the rough size of the population over the age of 18 on January 1, 2019. These numbers highlight the importance of mobile internet and social media in India at present. Not surprisingly, the social media has become as important (if not, more important) than the traditional "mainstream" media (daily newspapers, periodicals, radio and television channels) in propagating and disseminating not just facts, information, and opinions, but also half-truths and untruths that seek to influence social behaviour, political preferences and electoral outcomes. There is every reason to believe that the use of the social media has increased on account of the pandemic and the countrywide lockdown from 24 March 2020, simply because people are travelling less and remaining at home for longer periods than before.

Consequences of Fake News

Internet penetration ensures that we are constantly connected to one another and consume online content in a way that we never have before. Misinformation has been the malaise of the modern world but in a country like India which has low literacy in general – according to the 2011 census, close to one out of four Indians could not read or write her or his name – and media literacy in particular, the consequences of consuming huge volumes of fake and false information can be damaging to the working of world's largest democracy. As NDTV India's popular anchor and winner of the Magsaysay Award Ravish Kumar puts it, for a large section of the youth in India who have been deprived of quality education in schools and colleges of some repute and credibility, they are being "educated" in WhatsApp University. The spread of disinformation, which is distinct from misinformation, in the sense that the latter signifies that false, fake, and half-true information is deliberately disseminated to serve political or commercial objectives, is also on the rise.

According to a study in the 10th edition of the Digital News Report 2021 prepared by Reuters Institute, respondents interviewed stated that while WhatsApp, YouTube, and Facebook are widely used for obtaining news, there have also been "serious problems with misinformation and hate speech." The report added that individual members of the ruling Bharatiya Janata Party (BJP) and groups aligned with the party "are alleged to systematically spread false and misleading information via social media and other platforms." In late-2020, Facebook India's policy head Ankhi Das resigned after accusations that the company deliberately took a lenient line on ruling party supporters who allegedly violated hate speech rules with anti-Muslim posts.

A very substantial portion of both the mainstream media and the digital social media platforms has been disseminating information that shows India's Prime Minister Narendra Modi and the BJP in a positive light while simultaneously targeting the Opposition in an unusual "reversal of roles" in a democracy where journalists are expected to ask difficult questions of those in power in order to fulfil their role as "watchdogs" of society. On the contrary, by becoming "lapdogs," those who are part of the godi (literally meaning lap) media in India are acting in a manner that is no different from those who work for advertising agencies or public relations firms.

The Prime Minister has also deliberately chosen to turn a blind eye to many of his so-called "supporters" on social media spreading disinformation and indulging in hateful and incendiary speech. As for the social media, it can be said without fear of contradiction that supporters of the Hindu nationalist, right-wing BJP have been far more adept than supporters of other political parties in using WhatsApp, Facebook and other digital platforms – that wield monopoly power over information flows on social media – to spread disinformation and hate speech that demonises the Muslim minority in particular and also those belonging to other minority communities.

New IT Guidelines

The government's decision to bring in the Information Technology (Intermediary Guidelines and Digital Media Ethics Codes) Rules, 2021, has generated considerable controversy in recent months. The rules led to a sharp confrontation between Twitter and the Union Ministry of Electronics and Information Technology (MEITY). Other digital platforms, such as Google, Facebook, and WhatsApp, have had to comply with requirements of recruiting India-based employees to address legal compliance issues and deal with grievances related to content distributed, even as some of them have disputed the legal validity of the rules. Representatives of these global digital companies have had to appear before

The First Women's Magazine  extra

The first women's magazine was released in London by the name *The Lady's Mercury*. It was published for only four weeks in 1693. The first issue of the periodical was issued on 27 February 1693 by its founder, publisher, editor John Dunton.

committees of lawmakers and answer queries raised by police personnel.

Ravi Shankar Prasad, the then Union Minister for Law, Justice and Communications (including MEITY) stated that Twitter had lost its "safe harbour" status as an "intermediary" and would be held legally liable for content posted on the platform. WhatsApp has filed a petition in the Delhi High Court claiming that the new information technology (IT) rules violated the right to privacy by demanding it break end-to-encryption, while Google has approached the same court, challenging the definition of what constitutes a "media platform." Digital news outlets like The Wire and The Quint have also challenged the rules on various grounds, including that these go beyond the scope of the parent law, the Information Technology Act, 2000. At the time of writing, the Kerala High Court was hearing a petition from the portal Live Law, which has alleged that the IT rules are arbitrary, vague, and place disproportionate restrictions on digital news media organizations.

WhatsApp claims it neither knows what is being distributed by whom, nor does it know who receives the text, video, still pictures and audio messages. WhatsApp spokespersons have claimed on many occasions that it will have to completely change or overhaul its technology and "compromise" the privacy of users if it discloses information on senders and receivers of messages. This, in turn, means that even if law-enforcing agencies seek the Facebook-owned organization's support to track perpetrators of heinous crimes, it will not get its cooperation. This is what has been opposed by the government.

Three special rapporteurs of the United Nations have asked the Indian government to review the rules relating to traceability of first originator, intermediary liability, and executive oversight of digital media content on the ground that they violate the rights to privacy and to freedom of speech. The rapporteurs have claimed that terms like "fake news" and "content that may mislead or cause any injury" are not rigorously defined and could lead to a "chilling effect" constraining the independence of the media. It was further pointed out that the new IT rules were brought into force without a discussion in Parliament.

Right to Free Expression and Privacy

The right to free expression and right to privacy are both guaranteed by the Constitution of India and these rights are also present in the International Covenant on Civil and Political Rights to which the Indian government is a signatory and to which Prime Minister Modi recently reaffirmed his government's commitment. The government's critics argue that the rules are vague: the definition of "reasonable restrictions" on the right to free expression in Article 19(2) of the Constitution is open to myriad interpretations on what is violative of "national sovereignty," the country's "integrity," "friendly" relations with other countries and public order.

Moreover, the UN rapporteurs and others have contended that the new IT rules could lead to the imposition of arbitrary and harsh controls based on which intermediaries can be made to take down content and that the rules also violate privacy by demanding that encryption be removed to identify originators of messages on platforms like WhatsApp. The government, on the other hand, claims that encryption needs to be broken to check terrorists and those who commit heinous crimes.

The measures taken by WhatsApp to check misuse of its platform have been relatively ineffective. It has reduced the number of times one individual can forward the same message to five users and in cases, of messages already distributed widely, only to one user or group of users. In the rest of the world, this number was reduced to 20 but it was brought down to five in India. However, these numbers do not tell you the full story because a single "user" can be a group and a group can have up to 256 participants. This means that a WhatsApp message can theoretically be forwarded to five groups at a time, with each group having, say, 250 participants—in other words, by five clicks on a user's mobile phone she or he can reach out to 1,250 participants. The gamut of activities that entail the use of WhatsApp for commercial and political messaging is very well organised and well-funded—many groups are formed, and these activities are outsourced. WhatsApp new privacy policy for its business customers in India has also aroused controversy.

In July 2018, a committee led by Justice (retired) B N Srikrishna submitted a report that argued in favour of enacting a new law for personal data protection. A draft bill was included as part of the report, which was presented in Parliament in December that year and then referred to a standing committee. The standing committee's report was awaited at the time of writing. There was a crucial change in the version of the bill brought by the government from the one in the Srikrishna committee report. Whereas the committee had stated that government agencies could collect personal data when "necessary" and in a manner that was "proportionate" – this last word has been replaced by the word "expedient" in the government bill, resulting in criticism by, among others, Justice Srikrishna himself.

Internet Shutdowns

India leads the world in terms of internet shutdowns. The shutdowns in Jammu & Kashmir were the longest in the country. Access to regular as well as high-speed internet facilities was denied. After the Modi government abrogated Article 370 of the Constitution of India on August 5, 2020, and the erstwhile state of Jammu & Kashmir was divided into two Union territories, there was a communications blockade with no internet services available to the residents of the region. Following legal interventions in the Supreme Court and international criticism, 4G (or fourth generation) telecommunications services were restored after a gap of 18 months in February 2021. The functioning of the media in this region has become a crucial marker of how democracy is actually practiced in India and how journalists are able to uphold the rights of citizens.

The internet has ensured that we are constantly connected to one another and consume online content in a way that we never have done before. The fact that social media platforms have provided immense benefits to ordinary citizens cannot be denied. The ease of sharing information among peers, family members, friends,

First Really Successful Magazine in the United States

extra

The first really successful magazine in the United States was the *Saturday Evening Post*. This weekly magazine first hit the newsstands in 1821 with very wide circulation. *Saturday Evening Post* featured famous artists and authors.

and professional acquaintances has gone up manifold. This ease of communicating goes beyond remembering birthdays and anniversaries. During the pandemic, many Indians obtained information that was critical and of life-saving importance, information on healthcare and medical facilities. At the same time, as has been already emphasized, the double-edged sword that the social media can be also meant that these digital platforms were misused and abused to spread fake and false information. The Director General of the World Health Organisation Tedros Adhanom Ghebreyesus has remarked that the planet was facing not just a pandemic but an "infodemic" as well.

There have been many reported cases of mob lynching in the last few years, some which have been triggered by rumours circulating on WhatsApp groups. The data available before us is nothing short of alarming. According to a BBC analysis published in April 2019, at least 31 people had been killed by then on account of WhatsApp fuelled mob attacks.

Countering Online Fake News

In response to the proliferation of misinformation and disinformation in India, a number of fact-checking organisations have come up in recent years and some of these have received the support from international companies and foundations. Mainstream or "legacy" media organisations have also set up fact-checking teams. Among the organizations that are focussed on countering online fake news in the country is the Ahmedabad-based AltNews headed by Pratik Sinha which was launched in February 2017.

Government authorities have on many occasions asked digital media platforms to block posts containing both information and opinion, including those put out by activists, journalists, and political opponents of the ruling dispensation. DIGIPUB News India Foundation, an association of digital news organizations that was formed in 2020, has argued that the new IT rules give excessive control to the government to remove news content online. India has consistently slipped in the "press freedom index" of Reporters Without Borders (RSF or Reporters San Frontieres) in the last few years, and currently occupies142nd position out of 180 countries – the most recent report of the RSF for 2021 report observes that journalists in India are facing harassment, trolling and threats of rape and violence on social media. In addition, authorities are resorting to the use of colonial-era laws on sedition laws on journalists and activists for criticising government organizations and political functionaries. The US-based non-governmental organization Freedom House changed India's status from "free" to a "partly free" country in 2021.

Even as the use of social media continues to rise at a rapid pace, it is not clear if the government of India will reconsider the IT rules or be compelled to modify or change these after court directives. What is also difficult to anticipate is whether the management, administration, regulation, and governance of global digital conglomerates that own these profit-maximizing social media platforms, can be left in the hands of a few government officials. The impact of the internet on human society in general and Indian society in particular, continues to evolve extremely fast.

19

INDIA STATES

- The Union of India
- State Symbols
- Ready Reckoner
- State-Wise Capital Outlay
- India: Biggest, Highest, Largest, Smallest

The Union of India

India is the 7th largest country in the world. It is a union of states and union territories. For the purpose of administration, the country is divided into 28 states, and 8 centrally administered union territories including the national capital territory of Delhi. Delhi, J&K and Puducherry are Bicameral. **ISO 3166-2:** IN state code is shown along with state's names. **Districts**: In 2020 there were 739 districts. There were 640 in the Census 2011 and the 593 in the Census 2001.

The District information may vary because of administrative reorganisation and nonavailability of latest data from official sources. **J&K and Ladakh became two UTs on 31st August 2019 (the birth anniversary of Sardar Vallabhbhai Patel who merged more than 560 princely states nto one Union in Independent India. * In Jan 2020 Dadra and Nagar Haveli and Dam and Diu were merged as a single UT.*

Political Map of India with State Population
As released by GoI : Not to Scale

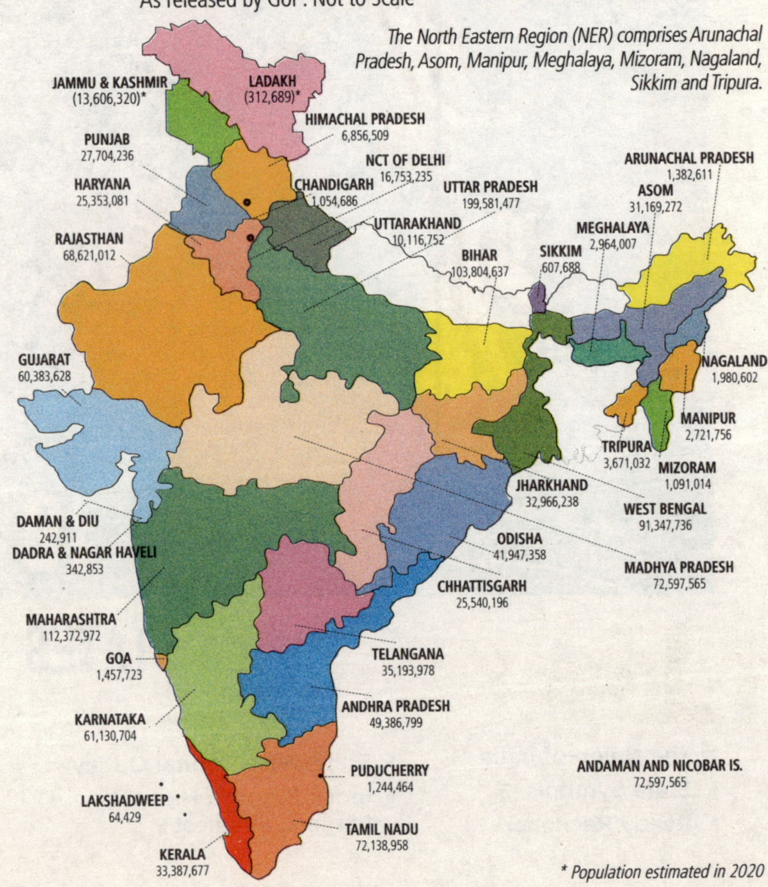

State Symbols

Every state /UT has their own symbols to represent it. They are listed below with their common name, scientific name and images.

1. Andhra Pradesh

Jasmine

Blackbuck

Rose-ringed Parakeet

Animal: Blackbuck (Antilope cervicapra)
Bird: Rose-ringed Parakeet
Trees: Margosa (Azadirachta indica)- Neem
Flowers: Jasmine (Jasminum Officnale)

2. Arunachal Pradesh

Lady's Slipper

Gayal

Great Hornbill

Animal: Gayal (Bos frontalis)
Bird: Great Hornbill (Buceros bicornis)
Trees: Hollong (Dipterocarpus macrocarpus)
Flowers: Lady's Slipper (Cypripedioideae)

3. Asom

Foxtail Orchid

One-horned Rhino

White-winged Wood Duck

Animal: One-horned Rhino (Rhinoceros unicornis)
Bird: White-winged Wood Duck (Cairina scutulata)
Trees: Hollong (Dipterocarpus macrocarpus)
Flowers: Foxtail Orchids (Rhynchostylis gigantea)

4. Bihar

White Orchid

Gaur

House Sparrow

Animal: Gaur (Bos gaurus)
Bird: House Sparrow (Passer Domesticus)
Trees: Sacred Fig (Ficus religiosa)
Flowers: White Orchid-tree (Bauhinia acuminata)

5. Chhattisgarh

Wild Buffalo

Bastar Hill Myna

Animal: Wild Buffalo (B. bubalis arnee)
Bird: Bastar Hill Myna (Gracula religiosa)
Trees: Sal (Shorea robusta)

6. Goa

Gaur

Black-crested Bulbul

Animal: Gaur (Bos gaurus)
Bird: Black-crested Bulbul (Pycnonotus gularis)
Tree: Asna (Terminalia elliptica)

7. Gujarat

Marigold

Asiatic Lion

Greater Flamingo

Animal: Asiatic Lion (Panthera leo persica)
Bird: Greater Flamingo (Phoenicopterus roseus)
Tree: Mango (Mangifera indica)
Flower: Marigold (Tagetes erecta)

8. Haryana

Lotus

Blackbuck

Black Francolin

Animal: Blackbuck (Antilope cervicapra)
Bird: Black Francolin (Francolinus francolinus)
Tree: Peepal (Ficus religiosa)
Flower: Lotus (Nelumbo nucifera)

9. Himachal Pradesh

Animal: Snow Leopard (Uncia uncia or Panthera uncia)
Bird: Jujurana/Western Tragopan (Tragopan melanocephalus)

Rhododendron Snow Leopard Western Tragopan

Tree: Deodar (Cedrus deodara)
Flower: Rhododendron (Rhododendron ponticum)

10. Jammu and Kashmir (UT of)

Lotus Kashmir Stag Black-necked Crane

Animal: Kashmir Stag (Cervus elaphus hanglu)
Bird: Black-necked Crane (Grus nigricollis)
Tree: Chinar Tree (Platanus oreintalis)
Flower: Lotus (Nelumbo nucifera)

11. Jharkhand

Parrot Tree Indian Elephant Asian Koel

Animal: Indian Elephant (Elephas maximus indicus)
Bird: Asian Koel (Eudynamys scolopacea)
Tree: Sal (Shorea robusta)
Flower: Parrot Tree (Butea monosperma)

12. Karnataka

Lotus Indian Elephant Indian Roller

Animal: Indian Elephant (Elephas maximus indicus)
Bird: Indian Roller (Coracias benghalensis)
Tree: Sandalwood (Santalum album)
Flower: Lotus (Nelumbo nucifera)

13. Kerala

Golden Shower Indian Elephant Great Hornbill

Animal: Indian Elephant (Elephas maximus indicus)
Bird: Great Hornbill (Buceros bicornis)
Tree: Coconut (Cocos nucifera)
Fruit: Jackfruit.
Flower: Golden Shower (Cassia fistula)

14. Madhya Pradesh

Parrot Tree Barasingha Asian Paradise Flycatcher

Animal: Barasingha (Rucervus duvaucelii)
Bird: Asian Paradise Flycatcher (Terpsiphone paradisi)
Tree: Banyan (Ficus benghalensis)
Flower: Parrot Tree (Butea monosperma)

15. Maharashtra

Jarul Indian Giant Squirrel Green Pigeon

Animal: Indian Giant Squirrel (Ratufa indica)
Bird: Yellow-footed Green Pigeon (Treron phoenicoptera)
Tree: Mango (Mangifera indica)
Flower: Jarul (Lagerstroemia speciosa)

16. Manipur

Siroi Lily Sangai Mrs. Hume's Pheasant

Animal: Sangai (Cervus eldi eldi)
Bird: Mrs. Hume's Pheasant (Syrmaticus humiae)
Tree: Indian Mahogany (Toona ciliata)
Flower: Siroi Lily (Lilium mackliniae)

17. Meghalaya

Lady's Slipper Clouded Leopard Hill Myna

Animal: Clouded Leopard (Neofelis nebulosa)
Bird: Hill Myna (Gracula religiosa)
Tree: White teak (Gmelina arborea)
Flower: Lady's Slipper (Cypripedioideae)

18. Mizoram

Red Vanda

Himalayan Serow

Mrs. Hume's Pheasant

Animal: Himalayan Serow (Saza)
Bird: Mrs. Hume's Pheasant (Syrmaticus humiae)
Tree: Iron Wood (Mesua ferrea)
Flower: Red Vanda

19. Nagaland

Rhododendron

Gaur

Blyth's Tragopan

Animal: Gaur (Bos gaurus)
Bird: Blyth's Tragopan (Tragopan blythii)
Tree: Alder
Flower: Rhododendron

20. Odisha

Ashoka

Sambar

Indian Roller

Animal: Sambar (Rusa unicolor)
Bird: Indian Roller (Coracias benghalensis)
Tree: Ashwatha (Ficus religiosa)
Flower: Ashoka (Saraca asoca)

21. Punjab

Blackbuck

Northern Goshawk

Animal: Blackbuck (Antilope cervicapra)
Aquatic Animal: Indus Dolphin
Bird: Northern Goshawk (Accipiter gentilis)
Tree: Shisham/Indian Rosewood

22. Rajasthan

Rohira

Chinkara

Camel

Indian Bustard

Animal: Chinkara (Gazella bennettii), Camel
Bird: Great Indian Bustard (Ardeotis nigriceps)
Tree: Khejri (Prosopis cineraria)
Flower: Rohira (Tecomella undulata)

23. Sikkim

Noble Orchid

Red Panda

Blood Pheasant

Animal: Red Panda (Ailurus fulgens)
Bird: Blood Pheasant (Ithaginis cruentus)
Tree: Rhododendron (Rhododendron Niveum)
Flower: Noble Orchid (Cymbidium goeringii)

24. Tamil Nadu

Glory Lily

Nilgiri Tahir

Emerald Dove

Animal: Nilgiri Tahr (Nilgiritragus hylocrius)
Bird: Emerald Dove (Chalcophaps indica)
Tree: Palmyra Palm (Borassus)
Flower: Glory Lily (Gloriosa superba)

25. Telangana

Tangedu Puvvu

Deer

Indian Roller

Animal: Jinka (Spotted Deer)
Bird: Indian Roller (Pala Pitta or Blue Jay)
Tree: Jammi Chettu (Prosopis Cineraria)
Flower: Tangedu Puvvu (Tanner's Cassia)

26. Tripura

Nag Kesar

Phayre's Langur

Green Imperial Pigeon

Animal: Phayre's Langur (Trachypithecus phayrei)
Bird: Green Imperial Pigeon
Tree: Agar (Gelidium amansii)
Flower: Nag Kesar (Mesua ferrea)
Fruit: Queen Pineapple

27. Uttarakhand

Brahma Kamal

Musk Deer

Himalayan Monal

Animal: Musk Deer (Moschidae) • Bird: Himalayan Monal (Lophophorus impejanus) Tree: Burans (Rhododendron arboreum) Flower: Brahma Kamal (Saussurea obvallata)

28. Uttar Pradesh

Palash

Swamp Deer

Sarus Crane

Animal: Swamp Deer (Rucervus duvaucelii) Bird: Sarus Crane (Grus antigone) •Tree: Ashoka Tree (Saraca asoca) •Flower: Palash (Butea monosperma)

29. West Bengal

Night-flowering Jasmine

Fishing Cat

White-breasted Kingfisher

Animal: Fishing Cat (Prionailurus viverrinus) Bird: White-breasted Kingfisher (Halcyon smyrnensis)•Tree: Devil Tree (Alstonia scholaris)•Flower: Night-flowering Jasmine (Nyctanthes arbor-tristis)

30. Andaman & Nicobar Islands (UT)

Dugong or sea cow

Andaman wood pigeon

Animal: Dugong or Sea Cow •Bird: Andaman Wood Pigeon (Columba palumboides) Tree: Andaman Padauk

31. Chandigarh (UT)

Dhak Flower

Indian Grey Mongoose

Indian Grey Hornbill

Animal: Indian Grey Mongoose (Herpestes edwardsii) •Bird: Indian Grey Hornbill (Ocyceros birostris) •Flower: Dhak Flower (Butea monosperma) •Tree: Mango Tree (Mangifera indica)

32. Delhi (NCT)

Nilgai

House Sparrow

•Animal: Nilgai (Boselaphus tragocamelus) •Bird: House Sparrow (Passer Domesticus)

33. Lakshadweep (UT)

Butterfly Fish

Noddy Tern

•Animal: Butterfly Fish (Chaetodon decussatus) •Bird: Noddy Tern (Anous stolidus) •Tree: Bread Fruit (Artocarpus incisa)

34. Puducherry (UT)

Cannonball Flower

Blackbuck

Asian Koel

Animal: Squirrel (Funambulus palmarum) Bird: Asian Koel (Eudynamys scolopaceus) Tree: Bael Fruit Tree (Aegle marmelos) Flower: Cannonball Tree's Flower

Other State Symbols:

•Andhra State Fish: Murrel (Channa Striata); Fruit- Mango (Maamidi Pandu); Song- Maa Telugu Thalliki •Asom State Song: O Mur Apunar Desh •Goa State Fish: Grey Mullet or Shevitto •Gujarat State Song: Jai Jai Garavi Gujarat •Karnataka State Butterfly: Southern Birdwing; Song-Jaya Bharata Jananiya Tanujate •Kerala State Fish: Green Chromide; Fruit- Jackfruit •MP State Fish: Mahasheer •Maharashtra State Butterfly: Blue Mormon; Song- Bande Utkala Janani •Rajasthan State Plant: Cactus •Tamil Nadu State Butterfly: Tamil Yeoman; Fruit- Jackfruit; Song- Tamil Thai Valthu •Telangana State Fish: Korameenu; Fruit- Mango (Maamidi Pandu); Song - Jay Jaya He Telangana •Tripura State Fruit: Queen Pine Apple •Uttarakhand State Butterfly: West Himalayan Common Peacock; Song- Uttarakhand Devabhumi Matribhumi

Ready Reckoner: Categorywise Rank of States

Rank	Population	Area	Density	Literacy	Sex-Ratio	Urban Pop.
1	UP	Rajasthan	Delhi	Kerala	Kerala	MP
2	Maharashtra	MP	Chandigarh	Lakshadweep	Puducherry	Maharashtra
3	Bihar	Maharashtra	Puducherry	Mizoram	TN	Odisha
4	WB	UP	Daman & Diu	Goa	AP	Gujarat
5	MP	J&K*	Lakshadweep	Tripura	Chhattisgarh	Rajasthan
6	TN	Gujarat	Bihar	Daman & Diu	Telangana	Jharkhand
7	Rajasthan	Karnataka	WB	A&N Is.	Manipur	Chhattisgarh
8	Karnataka	AP	Kerala	Delhi	Meghalaya	AP
9	Gujarat	Chhattisgarh	UP	Chandigarh	Odisha	WB
10	AP	Odisha	D&NH	Puducherry	Mizoram	Karnataka
11	Odisha	Tamil Nadu	Haryana	HP	HP	Asom
12	Telangana	Telangana	TN	Maharashtra	Goa	Meghalaya
13	Kerala	Bihar	Punjab	Sikkim	Karnataka	Nagaland
14	Jharkhand	West Bengal	Jharkhand	TN	Uttarakhand	J&K
15	Asom	Arunachal	Asom	Nagaland	Tripura	Tripura
16	Punjab	Jharkhand	Goa	Uttarakhand	Asom	Mizoram
17	Chhattisgarh	Asom	Maharashtra	Gujarat	Jharkhand	Bihar
18	Haryana	HP	Tripura	Manipur	WB	Manipur
19	Delhi	Uttarakhand	Karnataka	WB	Lakshadweep	Arunachal
20	J&K*	Punjab	Telangana	D&NH	Maharashtra	TN
21	Uttarakhand	Haryana	Gujarat	Punjab	Nagaland	Kerala
22	HP	Kerala	AP	Haryana	MP	Uttarakhand
23	Tripura	Meghalaya	Odisha	Karnataka	Rajasthan	HP
24	Meghalaya	Manipur	MP	Meghalaya	Arunachal	D&NH
25	Manipur	Mizoram	Rajasthan	Odisha	Gujarat	Sikkim
26	Nagaland	Nagaland	Uttarakhand	Asom	Bihar	UP
27	Goa	Tripura	Chhattisgarh	Chhattisgarh	UP	Lakshadweep
28	Arunachal	A&N Is.	Meghalaya	MP	Punjab	A&N Is.
29	Puducherry	Sikkim	J&K*	UP	Sikkim	Daman & Diu
30	Chandigarh	Goa	HP	J&K*	J&K*	Goa
31	Mizoram	Delhi	Manipur	Andhra Pradesh	A&N Is.	Punjab
32	Sikkim	Puducherry	Nagaland	Telangana	Haryana	Chandigarh
33	A&N Is.	D&NH	Sikkim	Jharkhand	Delhi	Haryana
34	D&NH and	Chandigarh	Mizoram	Rajasthan	Chandigarh	--
35	Daman&Diu	Daman&Diu	A&N Is	Arunachal Pr.	D&NH	Delhi
36.	Lakshadweep	Lakshadweep	Arunachal Pr.	Bihar	Daman&Diu	Puducherry

Source: Census 2011. * J&K have been bifurcated and made two UTs. ** DNH and DD have been merged

Note: The details on UT of J&K and Ladakh in this section are inconsistent in terms of ranking because of administrative reorganisation and non-availability of latest data from official sources.

Ready Reckoner:

States Compared to World Countries: By Population

Rank	State	Population 2018	Population 2011	2018-2011 Absolute	2018-2011 %	Share %	Country	World Rank
1	Uttar Pradesh	228.959	199.812	29.147	14.59	17.15	Brazil	5
2	Maharashtra	120.837	112.374	8.463	7.53	9.05	Japan	12
3	Bihar	119.461	104.099	15.361	14.76	8.95	Japan	12
4	West Bengal	97.694	91.276	6.418	7.03	7.32	Vietnam	15
5	Madhya Pradesh	82.342	72.626	9.715	13.38	6.17	Germany	17
6	Rajasthan	78.230	68.548	9.682	14.12	5.86	Turkey	20
7	Tamil Nadu	76.481	72.147	4.334	6.01	5.73	Turkey	20
8	Karnataka	66.165	61.095	5.070	8.30	4.96	UK	22
9	Gujarat	63.907	60.439	3.467	5.74	4.79	France	23
10	Andhra Pradesh	52.883	49.576	3.306	6.67	3.96	Myanmar	27
11	Odisha	45.429	41.974	3.455	8.23	3.40	Argentina	31
12	Telangana	38.472	35.004	3.468	9.91	2.88	Poland	37
13	Jharkhand	37.329	32.988	4.340	13.16	2.80	Canada	38
14	Kerala	35.330	33.406	1.924	5.76	2.65	Morocco	41
15	Asom	34.586	31.205	3.380	10.83	2.59	Saudi Arabia	41
16	Punjab	29.611	27.743	1.868	6.74	2.22	Nepal	49
17	Chhattisgarh	28.566	25.545	3.021	11.83	2.14	Yemen	51
18	Haryana	27.388	25.351	2.036	8.03	2.05	Madagascar	51
19	Uttarakhand	11.090	10.086	1.004	9.96	0.83	Haiti	86
20	Himachal Pradesh	7.316	6.864	0.452	6.59	0.55	Hong Kong*	105
21	Tripura	4.057	3.673	0.383	10.45	0.30	Moldova	132
22	Meghalaya	3.276	2.966	0.309	10.43	0.25	Mongolia	137
23	Manipur	3.008	2.855	0.152	5.35	0.23	Albania	138
24	Nagaland	2.189	1.978	0.210	10.65	0.16	Gambia	146
25	Goa	1.542	1.458	0.84	5.77	0.12	Bahrain	153
26	Arunachal Pradesh	1.528	1.383	0.144	10.45	0.11	Bahrain	153
27	Mizoram	1.205	1.097	0.108	9.91	0.09	Cyprus	159
28	Sikkim	0.671	0.610	0.61	10.01	0.05	Macao*	166
UT								
1	Puducherry	1.375	1.247	0.127	10.23	0.10	Trinidad and Tobago	154
2	Chandigarh	1.126	1.055	0.71	6.75	0.08	Cyprus	160
3	A.& N.Islands	0.419	0.380	0.39	10.35	0.03	Malta	177
4	D.& N.Haveli	0.378	0.343	0.35	10.26	0.03	Belize	180
	and Daman & Diu	0.220	0.243	-0.23	-9.52	0.02	Sao Tome and Principe	187
5	Lakshadweep	0.71	0.64	0.006	10.46	0.01	Dominica	205
6	Jammu & Kashmir	13.635	12.541	1.093	8.72	1.02	Guinea	75
7	Laddakh							
8.	NCT of Delhi	18.345	16.787	1.557	9.28	1.37	Kazakhstan	64
	INDIA	**1,335.14**	**1,210.85**	**124.28**	**10.26**	**100**	**India**	**2**

Ready Reckoner:
States Compared to World Countries: By Area

Rank	State	Area (Sq Km)	Share %	Country	World Rank
1	Rajasthan	342,239	10.41	Congo	64
2	Madhya Pradesh	308,252	9.38	Oman	71
3	Maharashtra	307,713	9.36	Oman	71
4	Uttar Pradesh	240,928	7.33	Uganda	81
5	Jammu & Kashmir	222,236	6.76	Guyana	85
6	Gujarat	196,244	5.97	Senegal	88
7	Karnataka	191,791	5.83	Syria	89
8	Andhra Pradesh	162,970	4.96	Tunisia	93
9	Odisha	155,707	4.74	Tunisia	93
10	Chhattisgarh	135,192	4.11	Greece	97
11	Tamil Nadu	130,060	3.96	Nicaragua	98
12	Telangana	112,077	3.41	Honduras	103
13	Bihar	94,163	2.86	Hungary	110
14	West Bengal	88,752	2.70	Jordan	112
15	Arunachal Pradesh	83,743	2.55	Austria	114
16	Jharkhand	79,716	2.42	Czech Rep	116
17	Asom	78,438	2.39	Czech Rep	116
18	Himachal Pradesh	55,673	1.69	Croatia	127
19	Uttarakhand	53,483	1.63	Croatia	127
20	Punjab	50,362	1.53	Costa Rica	129
21	Haryana	44,212	1.34	Estonia	132
22	Kerala	38,852	1.18	Bhutan	136
23	Meghalaya	22,429	0.68	El Salvador	152
24	Manipur	22,327	0.68	El Salvador	152
25	Mizoram	21,081	0.64	El Salvador	152
26	Nagaland	16,579	0.50	Swaziland	158
27	Tripura	10,486	0.32	Lebanon	169
28	Sikkim	7,096	0.22	West Bank	171
29	Goa	3,702	0.11	Cabo Verde	175
UT					
1	A. & N. Islands	8,249	0.25	Cyprus	170
2	D.& N. Haveli	491	0.015	Andorra	491
3	Puducherry	490	0.015	Andorra	491
4	Chandigarh	114	0.00347	Jersey	224
5	Daman & Diu	111	0.00338	Jersey	224
6	Lakshadweep	30	0.00091	Macau	236
7	NCT of Delhi	1,483	0.045	Faroe Is	182
	INDIA	**3,287,469**	-	-	-

Ready Reckoner: State and UT

State/UT	Capital	% National Population	Per Capita (2012-13)	Budget Outlay (BE) ₹ in crore	FY
1. Andhra Pradesh	Amravati	4.08	123664	2,24,789	2020–21
2. Arunachal Pradesh	Itanagar	0.11	119481	19,261	2018–19
3. Asom	Dispur	2.58	67303	99,419	2019–20
4. Bihar	Patna	8.58	34409	2,11,761	2020–21
5. Chhattisgarh	Raipur	2.11	237599	95,650	2020–21
6. Goa	Panaji	0.12	375550	21,056	2020–21
7. Gujarat	Gandhinagar	4.99	156527	2,17,287	2020–21
8. Haryana	Chandigarh	2.09	180174	1,42,343	2020–21
9. Himachal Pradesh	Shimla	0.57	150285	49,131	2020–21
10. Jharkhand	Ranchi	2.72	59799	85,429	2019–20
11. Karnataka	Bengaluru	5.05	161936	2,37,893	2020–21
12. Kerala	Thiruvananthapuram	2.76	163475	1,44,265	2020–21
13. Madhya Pradesh	Bhopal	6.00	74590	1,86,865	2018–19
14. Maharashtra	Mumbai	9.29	165491	4,04,794	2019–20
15. Manipur	Imphal	0.22	58501	13,731	2018–19
16. Meghalaya	Shillong	0.24	73291	TBA	2020–21
17. Mizoram	Aizawl	0.09	128998	9,492	2018–19
18. Nagaland	Kohima	0.16	90168	TBA	2020–21
19. Odisha	Bhubaneshwar	3.47	74234	1,50,000	2020–21
20. Punjab	Chandigarh	2.29	128890	1,54,805	2020–21
21. Rajasthan	Jaipur	5.67	92076	2,25,731	2020–21
22. Sikkim	Gangtok	0.05	270572	7,051	2018–19
23. Tamil Nadu	Chennai	5.96	150036	3,00,390	2020–21
24. Telangana	Hyderabad	2.90	159856	1,82,914	2020–21
25. Tripura	Agartala	0.30	-	TBA	2020–21
26. Uttarakhand	Dehradun-W, Gairsain-S	0.84	157643	53,526	2020–21
27. Uttar Pradesh	Lucknow	16.49	51014	5,12,860	2020–21
28. West Bengal	Kolkata	7.55	83126	2,55,677	2020–21
29. Delhi (NCT)	New Delhi	1.35	300793	60,000	2018–19
30. Andaman&Nicobar	Port Blair		136824	-	
31. Chandigarh	Chandigarh	0.09	237599	-	
32. Dadra & N.Haveli	Daman	0.05	-	-	
and Daman & Diu**			-	-	
33. Lakshadweep	Kavaratti	0.01	-	-	
34. Puducherry	Pondicherry	0.10	185141	TBA	2020–21
35. Jammu & Kashmir*	Srinagar-S, Jammu-W	1.04	78163	95,666	2018–19
36. Laddakh	Leh				

S- Summer/W- Winter; @Per Capita Net State Domestic Product at Factor Cost at Current Prices (2016-17) * J&K made UTs ** Merged *Source:* Directorate of Economics & Statistics of respective State/UT.. NCT: National Capital Territory

Ready Reckoner: Districts and Towns

Sl. No.	State/UT	Districts (new districts)	Sub Districts	No. of Towns: Statutory Towns	No. of Towns: Census Towns	No. of Villages
1	Andhra Pradesh	13	1128	125	228	27800
2	Arunachal Pradesh	25	188	26	1	5589
3	Asom	34	153	88	126	26395
4	Bihar	38	534	139	60	44874
5	Chhattisgarh	32	149	168	14	20126
6	Goa	2	11	14	56	334
7	Gujarat	33	225	195	153	18225
8	Haryana	22	74	80	74	6841
9	Himachal Pradesh	12	117	56	3	20690
10	Jammu & Kashmir*	20	82	86	36	6551
11	Jharkhand	24	260	40	188	32394
12	Karnataka	30	176	220	127	29340
13	Kerala	14	63	59	461	1018
14	Madhya Pradesh	55	342	364	112	54903
15	Maharashtra	36	355	256	279	43663
16	Manipur	16	38	28	23	2588
17	Meghalaya	11	39	10	12	6839
18	Mizoram	11	26	23	0	830
19	Nagaland	12	114	19	7	1428
20	Odisha	30	476	107	116	51313
21	Punjab	24	77	143	74	12581
22	Rajasthan	33	244	185	112	44672
23	Sikkim	4	9	8	1	452
24	Tamil Nadu	38	215	721	376	15979
25	Tripura	8	40	16	26	875
26	Uttar Pradesh	75	312	648	267	106774
27	Uttarakhand	13	78	74	42	16793
28	West Bengal	23	341	129	780	40203
29	A & N Islands	3	9	1	4	555
30	Chandigarh	1	1	1	5	5
31	D & N Haveli and Daman & Diu **	3	3	3	11	84
33	Lakshadweep	1	10	0	6	21
34	NCT of Delhi	11	27	3	110	112
35	Puducherry	4	8	6	4	90
36	Ladakh	2				
	Total		**5924**	**4041**	**3894**	**640937**

Source: Census of India, 2011 *J&K split and made two UTs ** UTs merger in Jan 2020

Ready Reckoner: Statewise Distribution of Area, Population, Literacy, Sex Ratio, Density, Decadal Growth Rate

India/State/UT #	Total Popn. (Million)	Males (Million)	Females (Million)	Literacy % T	Literacy % M	Literacy % F	Sex Ratio	Density (/ sq.km)	Decadal Gro.Rate
INDIA | **Area (sq. kms)**	1,210.85	623.27	587.58	-	-	-	943	382	17.72
Andhra Pradesh | 160,205	84.58	42.44	42.13	67.0	74.9	59.1	993	398	11.10
Arunachal Pradesh | 83,743	1.38	0.71	0.66	65.4	72.6	57.7	938	17	25.92
Asom | 78,438	31.20	15.93	15.26	72.2	77.8	66.3.	958	397	16.93
Bihar | 94,163	104.09	54.27	49.82	62.8	71.2	51.5	918	1,102	25.07
Chhattisgarh | 1,36,034	25.54	12.83	12.71	71.3	80.3	60.2	991	189	22.59
Goa | 3,702	1.45	0.73	0.71	88.7	92.6	84.7	973	394	8.17
Gujarat | 196,024	60.43	31.49	28.94	78.0	85.8	69.7	919	308	19.17
Haryana | 44,212	25.35	13.49	11.85	75.6	84.1	65.9	879	573	19.90
Himachal Pradesh | 55,673	6.86	3.48	3.38	82.8	89.5	75.9	972	123	12.81
Jammu & Kashmir| 2,22,236	12.54	6.64	5.90	67.2	76.8	56.4	889	124	23.71
Jharkhand | 79,714	32.98	16.93	16.05	66.4	76.8	56.2	948	414	22.34
Karnataka | 1,91,791	61.09	30,96	30.12	75.4	82.5	68.1	973	319	15.67
Kerala | 38,863	33.40	16.02	17.37	94.0	96.1	92.1	1,084	859	4.86
Madhya Pradesh | 3,08,000	72.62	37.61	35.01	69.3	78.7	59.2	931	236	20.30
Maharashtra | 307,713	112.37	58.24	54.13	82.3	88.4	75.9	929	365	15.99
Manipur | 22,327	2.85	1.43	1.41	76.9	83.6	70.3	985	128	18.65
Meghalaya | 22,429	2.96	1.49	1.47	74.4	76.0	72.9	989	132	27.82
Mizoram | 21,081	1.09	0.55	0.54	91.3	93.3	89.3	976	52	22.78
Nagaland | 16,579	1.97	1.02	0.95	79.6	82.8	76.1	931	119	-4.47
Odisha | 1,55,707	41.97	21.21	20.76	72.9	81.6	64.0	979	269	13.97
Punjab | 50,362	27.74	14.63	13.10	75.8	80.4	70.7	895	550	13.73
Rajasthan | 3,42,225	68.54	35.55	32.99	66.1	79.2	52.1	928	201	21.44
Sikkim | 7,096	0.61	0.32	0.28	81.4	86.6	75.6	890	86	12.36
Tamil Nadu | 1,30,058	72.14	36.13	36.00	80.1	86.8	73.4	996	555	15.60
Telangana* | 1,14,840				66.4	74.9	57.9			
Tripura | 10,491.69	3.67	1.87	1.79	87.2	91.5	82.7	960	350	14.75
Uttar Pradesh | 2,40,928	199.81	104.48	95.33	67.7	77.3	57.2	912	828	20.09
Uttarakhand | 53,484	10.08	5.13	4.84	78.8	87.4	70.0	963	189	19.17
West Bengal | 88,752	91.27	46.80	44.46	76.3	81.7	70.5	950	1,029	13.93
NCT of Delhi # | 1,483	16.78	8.98	7.80	86.2	90.9	80.8	868	11,297	20.96
A & N Islands | 8,249	0.38	0.20	0.17	86.6	90.3	82.4	876	46	6.68
Chandigarh # | 114	1.05	0.58	0.47	86.0	90.0	81.2	818	9,252	17.10
Dadra & Nagar Haveli# | 491	0.34	0.19	0.14	76.2	85.2	64.3	774	698	55.50
and Daman & Diu # | 112	0.24	0.15	0.09	87.1	91.5	79.5	618	2,169	53.54
Lakshadweep # | 32	0.06	0.03	0.03	91.8	95.6	87.9	946	2,013	6.23
Puducherry # | 479	1.24	0.61	0.63	85.8	92.1	80.7	1,037	2,598	27.72

* Andhra refers to undivided state as existed at the time of Census 2011. Telangana state was formed in 2014. So its figure is separately added with * for making comparison. Literacy: T-total, M-male, F-female

Ready Reckoner: Life Expectancy and Poverty Rate

State/UT	Life Expectancy (2010-14)			Poverty Rate (2011-12)	
	Male	Female	Total	Persons*	Percent
Andhra Pradesh	66.3	70.8	68.5	7.88	9.20
Arunachal Pradesh				0.49	34.67
Asom	62.7	65.5	63.9	10.13	31.98
Bihar	67.8	68.4	68.5	35.82	33.74
Chhattisgarh	63.3	66.3	64.8	10.41	39.93
Goa		-		0.08	5.09
Gujarat	66.6	71.0	68.7	10.22	16.63
Haryana	66.3	71.3	68.6	2.88	11.16
Himachal Pradesh	69.3	74.1	71.6	0.56	8.06
Jammu and Kashmir	70.9	74.9	72.6	1.33	10.35
Jharkhand	66.2	66.9	66.6	12.43	36.96
Karnataka	66.9	70.8	68.8	12.98	20.91
Kerala	72.0	77.8	74.9	2.40	7.05
Madhya Pradesh	62.5	66.0	64.2	23.41	31.65
Maharashtra	69.9	73.6	71.6	19.79	17.35
Manipur			-	1.02	36.89
Meghalaya			-	0.36	11.87
Mizoram			-	0.23	20.40
Nagaland			-	0.38	18.88
Odisha	64.7	67.1	65	13.85	32.59
Punjab	69.7	73.8	71.6	2.32	8.26
Rajasthan	65.5	70.2	67.7	10.29	14.71
Sikkim			-	0.05	8.19
Tamil Nadu	68.6	72.7	70.6	8.26	11.28
Tripura			-	0.52	14.05
Uttarakhand	69.1	74.5	71.7	1.16	11.26
Uttar Pradesh	62.9	65.4	64.1	59.82	29.43
West Bengal	68.9	71.6	70.2	18.50	19.98
A&N Islands			-	0.00	1.00
Chandigarh			-	0.24	21.81
D&N Haveli **			-	0.14	39.31
Delhi	72.0	74.7	73.2	1.70	9.91
Daman & Diu **			-	0.03	9.86
Lakshdweep			-	0.00	2.77
Puducherry			-	0.12	9.69
All India	**66.4**	**69.6**	**67.9**	**269.78**	**21.92**

* Persons: Person in Million ** UTs Merged in Jan 2020

Source : Planning Commission, National Sample Survey Organisation (NSSO), Government of India.

Ready Reckoner: Political and Judicial

Sl. No.	States	High Court Bench (No. of Judges)	Principal Seat / Permanent Strength	Approved/Total
1	Andhra Pradesh	Andhra	Hyderabad (27)	46/61*
2	Arunachal Pradesh	Guwahati	(Bench:Itanagar) •	18/24*
3	Asom	Guwahati	Guwahati (19) •	18/24*
4	Bihar	Patna	Patna (35)	40/53
5	Chhattisgarh	Chhattisgarh	Bilaspur (14)	17/22
6	Goa	Bombay	Mumbai (Bench: Panaji)•	
7	Gujarat	Gujarat	Sola (Ahmedabad) (31)	39/52
8	Haryana	Chandigarh	Chandigarh (54)•	64/85*
9	Himachal Pradesh	Himachal	Shimla (8)	10/13
10	Jharkhand	Jharkhand	Doranda, Ranchi (14)	19/25
11	Karnataka	Karnataka Dharwad,	Bengaluru (Bench: Gulbarga) (29)	47/62
12	Kerala	Kerala	Kochi (36)	27/38
13	Madhya Pradesh	Madhya Pr.	Jabalpur (Bench: Gwalior, Indore) (35)	40/53
14	Maharashtra	Bombay	Mumbai (Bench: Aurangabad and Nagpur) (74)	71/94
15	Manipur	Manipur	Imphal (3)	4/5
16	Meghalaya	Meghalaya	Shillong (3)	3/4
17	Mizoram	Guwahati	Guwahati (Bench: Aizawl)•	
18	Nagaland	Guwahati	Guwahati (Bench: Kohima)•	
19	Odisha	Odisha	Cuttack (18)	20/27
20	Punjab	Punjab	Chandigarh •	64/85*
21	Rajasthan	Rajasthan	Jodhpur (Bench: Jaipur) (37)	38/50
22	Sikkim	Sikkim	Gangtok (3)	3/3
23	Tamil Nadu	Madras	Chennai (Bench: Madurai) (54)	56/75
24	Telangana	Telangana	Hyderabad • (42)	46/61*
25	Tripura	Tripura	Agartala (4)	
26	Uttarakhand	Uttarakhand	Nainital (10)	9/11
27	Uttar Pradesh	Allahabad	Allahabad (Bench:Lucknow) (91)	76/160
28	West Bengal	Calcutta	Kolkata (34)•	54/72
	States >>		(Circuit Bench: Jalpaiguri)	532
	Union Territories >>			
1	Andaman & Nicobar	Calcutta	Kolkata (Bench: Port Blair)•	
2	Chandigarh	Chandigarh•		
3	Dadra & Nagar Haveli and Daman & Diu	Bombay	Mumbai •	
4	Lakshadweep	Kerala	Kochi•	
5	Puducherry	Madras	Chennai•	
6	NCT of Delhi	Delhi	New Delhi (38)	45/60
7	Jammu&Kashmir	J&K	Srinagar/Jammu (12)	13/17
8	Ladakh	--		
*	Nominated			
	Total >>	**24**		

NCT: National Capital Territory • High Courts and Benches Status: as on August. 2017 # Women

Seat LS	RS	Legislative Assembly	Council	1st-Governor	1st-Chief Minister
25	11	175	56	Sir CM Trivedi	Tanguturi Prakasam
2	1	60	--	Bhishma Narain Singh	Prem Khandu Thungon (acting); R.D. Pradhan
14	7	126	--	Sir MS Akbar Hydari	Srijut Gopinath Bardoloi
40	16	243	75	Jairamdas Daulatram	Srikrishna Sinha
11	5	91*	--	Dinesh Nandan Sahay	Ajit Jogi
2	1	40	--	Gopal Singh	Dayanand B. Bandodkar.
26	11	182	-	Mehdi Nawaz Jung	Jivraj N. Mehta
10	5	90		Dharma Vira	Bhagwat Dayal Sharma
4	3	68		S Chhakravarti	Yeshwant Singh Parmar
14	6	81	--	Prabhat Kumar	Babulal Marandi
28	12	225*	75	J Wodeyar	K.Chengalaraya Reddy
20	9	141*	--	B Ramakrishna Rao	EMS Namboodiripad
29	11	231*	--	MM Pakvasa	Ravi Shankar Shukla
48	19	289*	78	Sri Prakasa	Yashwantrao Chavan
2	1	60	--	Braj Kumar Nehru	M Koireng Singh
2	1	60	--	Braj Kumar Nehru	Williamson A. Sangma
1	1	40	--	Hiteshwar Saikia	L. Chal Chhunga
1	1	60	--	Vishnu Sahay	Shilu Ao
21	10	147	--	Kailash Nath Katju	Harekrishna Mahatab
13	7	117	--	Sir C Madhavlal Trivedi	Gopichand Bhargava
25	10	200	--	G Nihal Singh	Gokul Lal Asawa
1	1	32	--	Bipen Bihari Lal	K L Dorjee Khangsarpa
39	18	235*	--	Sir Archibald E Nye	O.P. Ramaswami Reddiar
17	7	120	34	ESL Narasimhan	K. Chandrasekhara Rao
2	1	60	--	Braj Kumar Nehru	Sachindra Lal Singh
5	3	70	--	Surjit Singh Barnala	Nityanand Swamy
80	31	404*	100	Sarojini Naidu	Govind Ballabh Pant
42	16	295*	--	C Rajagopalachari	Prafulla Ghosh
241	4031	454			
13	4			Governor	Chief Minister
1	--	--	--	Manohar Lal Kampani (Lt. Governor)	
1	--	--	--	-- (Administrator*)	--
2	--	--	--	R.V. Mudras (Adm*)	--
1	--	--	--	U.R. Panicker (Adm*)	--
1	1	1	30	S L Silam (Lt. Governor)	Edouard Goubert
7	3	70	--	(Lt. Governor)	
-	4	89	36	--	--
		2	12	--	--
545	**245**				

Ready Reckoner : Chief Produce, and Industries

Sll	States	Major Crops	Production* Rice	Wheat
1.	Andhra Pradesh	Rice, Jowar, Bajra, Ragi, Maize	7234	--
2.	Arunachal Pradesh	Rice, Maize, Wheat, Mustard	285	8
3.	Asom	Rice, Tea, Jute	5223	29
4.	Bihar	Rice, Wheat, Cotton, Jute	6357	3987
5.	Chhattisgarh	Rice, Wheat, Maize, Pulses, Jute	6322	135
6.	Goa	Rice, Ragi	1	20
7.	Gujarat	Rice, Wheat, Bajra,Cotton, Wool	1831	3059
8.	Haryana	Rice, Wheat	4006	10354
9.	Himachal Pradesh	Wheat, Maize	125	646
10.	Jammu & Kashmir	Rice, Wheat, Silk, Wool, Dry Fruits, Saffron	517	314
11.	Jharkhand	Rice, Maize	3362	330
12.	Karnataka	Rice, Wheat, Tobacco, Sunflower, Cotton,Silk	3541	261
13.	Kerala	Rice, Coconut, Pepper, Cardamom	562	17104
14	Madhya Pradesh	Rice, Wheat, Silk, Sugar	3625	1308
15	Maharashtra	Wheat, Rice, Cotton	2946	
16	Manipur	Rice, Maize	334	
17	Meghalaya	Rice, Maize	298	0.8
18	Mizoram	Rice	61	
19.	Nagaland	Rice	454	5.6
20	Odisha	Rice	8298	0.7
21	Punjab	Wheat, Rice	11107	15050
22	Rajasthan	Wheat, Bajra Jowar, Marble	366	9823
23	Sikkim	Wheat, Rice, Millets	20	0.4
24.	Tamil Nadu	Rice, Pulses	5728	--
25	Telangana	--	4441	7.0
26	Tripura	Rice, Sericulture	747	0.3
27	Uttarakhand	--	604	654
28	Uttar Pradesh	Rice, Wheat, Maize	12168	22417
29	West Bengal	Rice, Potato, Jute	14677	939
	A&N	Paddy, Pulses, Oilseeds, Coconut	--	--
	Chandigarh	Wheat, Maize, Paddy	--	--
	D&NH and DD	Paddy, Ragi, Millets, Jowar, Wheat, Pulses		
	Delhi	Wheat, Bajra, Jowar	--	26
	Lakshdweep	Coconut, Sweet Potato		
	Puducherry	Rice, Pulses, Coconut, Cotton	53	--

Source: Ministry of Road Transport and Highways, Government of India; *Source:* Ministry of Railways, GoI.

Chief Industries	Per Capita Net State Domestic Product at Factor Cost* (Constant Prices) (₹)		(Current Prices) (₹)	
	2016-17	2017-18	2016-17	2017-18
Iron, Steel, Jute, Pharmaceuticals, Ship-building, Aircraft	113796	-	136824	-
Plywood, Handicraft	96374	106545	123664	142054
Oil Refinery, Fertiliser, Paper	86818	-	119481	-
Sugar, Paper, Silk, Leather	52416	-	67303	-
Mining, Iron, Cement	25950	28485	34409	38860
Fisheries, Ship-building	207000	-	237599	-
Cement, Paper	68321	71581	84265	92035
Dairy, Automobile Engg., Sugar	249555	264697	300793	329093
Forest products	308823	-	375550	-
	131853	-	156527	-
Iron and Steel, Cement, Paper	143211	-	180174	-
Aircraft, Glass, IT	119387	125607	150285	160719
Ship-building, Paper, IT	62145	-	78163	-
Cement	49174	50562	59799	63754
Leather, Automobile Eng. Aircraft, Pharma.	124093 1	34118	161936	181788
Handicraft	128550	-	163475	-
Handicraft	53047	-	74590	-
Handicraft	133141	140997	165491	180596
Paper, Plywood	46756	-	58501	-
Iron and Steel, Aluminium	58826	63354	73291	79807
Bicycle, Sports goods, Sugar, Paper, Wool	101877	-	128998	-
Textile, Cement, Sugar	63568	-	90168	-
Leather, Food	63674	67522	74234	80991
Leather, Automobiles, Iron-Steel, Cement	127105	134591	185141	198046
Paper, Cement, Fashion items	105386	-	128890	-
Handloom	72072	76146	92076	100551
Tourism	206178	218333	270572	297765
Sugar, Leather, Metal, Glass work	117806	126179	150036	166934
Tea, Sugar, Chemicals and Fertilisers	122684	134402	159856	181034
Handicrafts, Fisheries	-	-	-	-
Food Products, Textiles, Machinery	38934	40815	51014	55339
Manufacturing, Engineering	132464	139435	157643	173820
Tourism, Pharmaceuticals, Metallurgy	61245	65978	83126	95562
IT, Telecommunication, Manufacturing, Tourism	80		--	183
Coir and Tourism				
Engineering, Tourims, Textiles	64		89	22

*Production of Rice/Wheat for 2014-15 in Thousand Tonnes   Base 2011-12

State-Wise Capital Outlay (₹ Billion)

States	2014-15	2015-16	2016-17	2017-18 (RE)	2018-19 (BE)
I. Non-Special Category					
Andhra Pradesh	152.8	114.1	141.7	151.8	228.8
Bihar	181.5	239.7	272.1	359.8	324.2
Chhattisgarh	66.2	79.5	94.7	127.4	144.5
Goa	12.4	16.2	16.4	37.2	41.9
Gujarat	241.6	241.7	223.6	276.5	303.4
Haryana	37.2	69.1	68.6	137.7	157.8
Jharkhand	55.4	81.6	107.8	127.4	123.1
Karnataka	196.2	207.1	281.5	312.3	352.5
Kerala	42.5	75.0	101.3	86.7	103.3
Madhya Pradesh	118.8	168.4	272.9	281.5	293.4
Maharashtra	195.2	227.9	255.5	320.0	363.0
Odisha	110.7	170.9	184.7	215.6	245.7
Punjab	31.2	30.6	43.5	43.9	63.9
Rajasthan	161.0	219.9	169.8	225.4	257.4
Tamil Nadu	178.0	189.9	207.1	243.0	282.8
Telangana	83.7	135.9	333.7	254.5	333.7
Uttar Pradesh	533.0	644.2	697.9	573.4	742.4
West Bengal	98.8	124.2	113.4	215.6	257.6
II. Special Category					
Arunachal Pradesh	14.8	19.9	15.4	50.0	78.8
Asom	39.1	26.9	55.0	148.6	145.7
Himachal Pradesh	24.7	28.6	35.0	41.0	42.4
Manipur	13.3	12.4	14.9	25.6	22.5
Meghalaya	11.2	11.1	12.9	17.3	15.6
Mizoram	9.3	7.1	9.1	20.7	19.8
Nagaland	10.2	10.6	10.7	16.4	13.4
Sikkim	9.8	6.3	7.2	19.5	13.0
Tripura	28.3	31.9	33.0	26.5	26.9
Uttarakhand	49.4	42.2	49.5	55.5	65.8
All-States	**2719.1**	**3333.8**	**3921.9**	**4707.1**	**5377.9**
Memo item:					
NCT Delhi	44.0	47.2	37.5	38.5	54.7
Puducherry	6.1	4.4	4.5	5.7	4.4
Jammu and Kashmir*	51.3	73.3	82.9	219.5	256.7

RE: Revised Estimates. BE: Budget Estimates.

* J&K has been bifurcated into two UTs in 2019. The figures of the corresponding period mentioned above.

Source: Handbook of Statistics on State Government Finances-2010' and 'State Finances: A Study of Budgets', Reserve Bank of India, various issues.

extra

The First Budget

The first Budget of independent India was introduced on November 26, 1947. It was presented by R.K. Shanukham Chetty, India's first Finance Minister.

1. Andhra Pradesh (AP)

Governor: Bishwabhushan Harichandan
CM: YS Jagan Mohan Reddy, YSRCP

CM

Governor

Date of Formation: Andhra Pradesh Reorganisation Act 2014 (Telangana Act). [The Bill, though rejected by AP Legislative Assembly, was passed by Lok Sabha and Rajya Sabha]. On 2 June 2014 Andhra Pradesh was bifurcated to create Telangana state. Earlier Andhra State was carved out of Madras Presidency on 01 Oct. 1953 and Andhra Pradesh State was formed on 1 Nov. 1956;

Chief Languages: Telugu, Urdu, Banjara.
Main Towns: Visakhapatnam, Vijayawada, Guntur, Nellore, Kurnool, Kadapa, Kakinada, Vizianagaram, Nandyal, Machilipatnam, Tenali, Hindupur, Madanapalle, Guntakal.

No. of Districts: 13

District	Area (sq km)	Population (2011)	Headquarters
Rayalaseema Region			
Anantapur	19,130	4083315	Anantapur
Chittoor	15,152	4170468	Chittoor
Kadapa (YSR)	15,359	2884524	Kadapa
Kurnool	17,658	4046601	Kurnool
			Andhra Region
E. Godavari	10,807	5151549	Kakinada
Guntur	11,391	4889230	Guntur
Krishna	8,734	4529009	Machilipatnam
			Sri Potti Sriramulu
Nellore	13,076	2966082	Nellore
Prakasam	17,626	3392764	Ongole
W. Godavari	7,742	3934782	Eluru
Srikakulam	5,837	2699471*	Srikakulam
Visakhapatnam	11,161	4288113+	V. Patnam
Vizianagaram	6,539	2342868	Vizianagaram

(There are variations in figures after bifurcation)

* 83.8% of the population live in rural areas.
+ 67.5% of the people live in urban areas

No. of Tehsils: 670
No. of Gram Panchayat/ Police Stations: 13180
No. of Villages: 17521 No. of Urban Towns: 94

Transport and Communications: (a) **Road Length:** The AP R&B network constitute 69051 km; NH 4472 (4.97% of the national total). It forms a part of Golden Quadrilateral Project. State highway: 10519 km Pandit Nehru Bus Station (PNBS) in Vijayawada is one of the largest bus terminals in Asia. (b) **Railway Length:** 5,107 km. Main Railway Stations: Vijayawada, Visakhapatnam, Guntakal, Renigunta, Vijayawada railway station; *Two Railway Zones*: SC Railway zone, East Coast Railway zone (c) **Airports:** Visakhapatnam Airport is the only airport in the state with international connectivity; 4 domestic airports: Vijayawada, Rajahmundry, Tirupati and Puttaparthi. (e) **Ports:** Visakhapatnam- is the headquarters of Eastern Naval Command base; Other ports:

Legislative Assembly, Andhra Pradesh

Krishnapatnam Port (Nellore), Gangavaram Port and Kakinada Port. Gangavaram Port.

2. Arunachal Pradesh (AR)

CM

Governor

Governor: Brig. (Dr.) BD Mishra
CM: Pema Khandu, BJP

www.arunachalpradesh.gov.in

China
ARUNACHAL PRADESH
Bhutan
Itanagar
Myanmar
Asom
Nagaland

Date of Formation: 20 Feb 1987 a State; on 20 Jan 1972 a UT was created from parts of Asom and renamed as Arunachal Pradesh. Till 1972, it was known as North East Frontier Agency (NEFA). Got elected Legislative Assembly on 15 Aug 1975.

Chief Languages: Arunachal Pradesh houses over 50 distinct dialects, mostly of the Sino-Tibetan language family. Monpa, Miji, Aka, Sherdukpen, Nyishi, Apatani, Tagin, Hill Miri, Adi, Digaru Mismi, Idu-Mishmi, Khamti, Miju-Mishmi, Nocte, Tangsa, Wancho.

No. of Districts: 25

District	Area (sq km)	Population (2011)	Head-quarters
Changlang	4,662	147951	Changlang
UpperDibang Valley	13,029	7948	Anini
Lower Dibang Valley	4,149	53986	Roing
East Kameng	4,134	78413	Seppa
West Kameng	7,422	87013	Bomdila
East Siang	4,005	99019	Pasighat
West Siang	8,325	112272	Along
Upper Siang	6,188	112272	Yingkiong
Lohit	2,402	145538	Tezu
Lower Subansiri	10,135	82839	Ziro
Papum-Pare	2,875	176385	Yupia
Tawang	2,172	49950	Tawang
Tirap	2,362	111997	Khonsa
Upper Subansiri	7,032	83205	Daporijo
Lower Subansiri	3,460	82,839	Ziro
Anjaw	1,249	21089	Hawai
Kurung Kumey	6,040	89717	Koloriang
Longding	-	-	Longding
Namsai	-	-	Namsai
Kra Daadi			Jamin
Rima			
Lower Siang	-	-	Likabali
Itanagar	-	-	Sagalee
Leparada	-	-	-
Hayuliang	-	-	-

No. of Tehsils: 188
No. of Gram Panchayat/ Police Stations: 5191
No. of Village: 5590 No. of Urban Town: 26

Main Towns: Aalo (Along), Itanagar, Naharlagun, Pasighat, Tezu.

Transport and Communications: (a) **Road-NH: 2,537** kms (1.93% of country's total NH) (b) **Main Railway Stations:** Bhalukpong; (c) **Airports:** Itanagar, Daparjio, Ziro, Along, Tezu, Pashigat.

3. Asom (AS)

CM

Governor

Governor: Jagdish Mukhi
CM: Himanta Biswa Sarma (BJP)

www.assam.gov.in

China
Arunachal Pradesh
Bhutan
WB
ASOM
Dispur
Nagaland
Meghalaya
Myanmar
Manipur
Bangladesh
Tripura
Mizoram

Date of Formation: 26 Jan 1950 - Asom became a State.

Chief Languages: Assamese (Asamiya/ Asomiya), Bengali, Bodo, Karbi.

No. of Districts: 34

District	Area (sq km)	Population in lakhs(2011)	Head-quarters
Baksa	2,400	953773	Baksa
Barpeta	3,245	1693190	Barpeta
Bongaigaon	1,724	2060550	Bongaigaon

Cachar	3,786	1736319	Silchar
Charaideo	-	-	Sonari
Chirang	1,469	481818	Chirang
Darrang	3,481	908090	Mangaldoi
Dhemaji	3,217	688077	Dhemaji
Dhubri	2,838	1948632	Dhubri
Dibrugarh	3,381	1327748	Dibrugarh
Dima Hasao	4,888	213529	-
Goalpara	1,824	1008959	Goalpara
Golaghat	3,502	1058674	Golaghat
Hailakandi	1,327	659260	Hailakandi
Jorhat	2,851	1091295	Jorhat
Kamrup	4,345	1517202	Amingaon
Kamrup-Metropolitan	1,272	1260419	Guwahati
E.Karbi Anglong	10,434	965280	Diphu
W.Karbi-Anglong	-	-	Hamren
Karimganj	1,809	1217002	Karimganj
Kokrajhar	3,129	886999	Kokrajhar
Lakhimpur	2,277	1040644	N.Lakhimpur
Majuli	880	167304	Garamur
Morigaon	1,704	957853	Morigaon
Nagaon	3,831	2826006	Nagaon
Nalbari	2,257	769919	Nalbari
Sivsagar	2,668	1150253	Sivsagar
Sonitpur	5,324	1925975	Tezpur
South Salmara-Mankachar	568	555114	Hatsingimari
Tinsukia	3,790	1316948	Tinsukia
Udalguri	1,852	832769	Udalguri
Hojai		931218	Sankardev Nagar
Biswanath	1100	58000	B. Chariali
Bajali	-	253816	Pathsala

No. of Tehsils: 184

No. of Gram Panchayat/ Police Stations :3,502

No. of Village: 26,532 No. of Urban Town: 90

Main Towns: Guwahati-Dispur, Tezpur, Silchar, Jorhat, Dibrugarh, Sibsagar, Karimganj, Tinsukia, Diphu, Dhemaji, Nagaon, Marigaon, Barpeta, Goalpara, Dhuburi, Bongaigaon, Nalbari, Dhubri, North Lakhimpur, Balipara, Matia.

Transport and Communications: (a) **Road Length:** 37,515 km; NH - 3,909 (2.98% of the national total) (b) **Railways:** Length 2,284.28 km.; (c) Main Railway Stations: New Bangaigaon, Maligaon, Guwahati, Rangia, Lumding, Jorhat; (d) **Airports:** Lokopriya Gopinath Bordoloi Airport-Guwahati, Salonibari-Tezpur, Mo-hanbari-Dibrugarh, Kumbhrigram -Silchar, Rawriah-Jorhat, Silonibari-N. Lakhimpur.

4. Bihar (BR)

CM

Governor

Governor: Phagu Chauhan

CM: Nitish Kumar (JD-U)

Date of Formation: 26 Jan. 1950 state. Province-15 Aug 1947; Bifurcated 15 Nov 2000 to create Jharkhand).

Chief Languages: Hindi, Urdu, Angika, Bhojpuri, Magadhi, Maithili.

No. of Districts: 38

District	Area (sq km)	Population (2011)	Head-quarters
Araria	2,830	2806200	Araria
Arwal	637	699563	Arwal
Aurangabad	3,389	2511243	Aurangabad
Banka	3,020	2029339	Banka
Begusarai	1,918	2954367	Begusarai
Bhagalpur	2,569	3032226	Bhagalpur
Bhojpur	2,395	2720155	Arrah(Ar(a)
Buxar	1,703	1707643	Buxar
Darbhanga	2,279	3921971	Darbhanga
Gaya	4,976	4379383	Gaya
Gopalganj	2,033	2558037	Gopalganj
Jehanabad	932	1124176	Jhanabad
Jamui	3,098	1756078	Jamui
Kaimur(Bhabhua)	3,362	1626900	Bhabhua
Katihar	3,057	3068149	Katihar

Khagaria	1,486	1657599	Khagaria
Kishanganj	1,884	1690948	Kishanganj
Lakhisarai	1,228	1000717	Lakhisarai
Munger	1,419	1359054	Munger
Madhepura	1,788	1994618	Madhepura
Madhubani	3,501	4476044	Madhubani
Muzaffarpur	1,419	4778610	Muzaffarpur
Nalanda	2,355	2872523	Biharsharif
Nawada	2,494	2216653	Nawada
Paschimi Champaran	5,228	3922780	Bettiah
Patna	3,202	5772804	Patna
Purbi Champaran	3,968	5082868	Motihari
Purnia	3,229	3273127	Purnia
Rohtas	3,851	2962593	Sasaram
Saharsa	1,687	1897102	Saharsa
Samastipur	2,904	4254782	Samastipur
Saran	2,641	3943098	Chhapra
Sheikhpura	689	634927	Sheikhpura
Sheohar	349	656916	Sheohar
Sitamarhi	2,294	3419622	Sitamarhi
Siwan	2,219	3318176	Siwan
Supaul	2,425	2228397	Supaul
Vaishali	2036	3495249	Hajipur

No. of Tehsils 534

No. of Gram Panchayat/ Police Stations 9989

No. of Village 44935 No. of Urban Town 138

Main Towns: Arrah, Aurangabad, Bagaha, Begusarai, Bettiah, Bhagalpur, Bihar Sharif, Buxar, Chapra, Darbhanga, Dehri, Dinapur Nizamat, Gaya, Hajipur, Jamalpur, Jehanabad, Katihar, Kishanganj, Motihari, Munger, Muzaffarpur, Patna, Purnia, Saharsa, Sasaram,

Transport and Communications: (a) **Road Length:** 5,031 of NH forming 3.83% of the country's total; (b) **Main Railway Stations:** Patna, Gaya, Muzaffarpur, Samastipur, Barauni, Katihar, Chapra; (d) **Airport:** Patna.

Legislative Assembly, Bihar

5. Chhattisgarh (CG)

Governor: Anusuiya Uikey

CM: Bhupesh Baghel (INC)

Date of Formation: 1 Nov. 2000 - became the 26th state when it was carved out of MP.

CM

Governor

Chief Languages: Chhattisgarhi, Hindi

No. of Districts: 32

District	Area (sq km)	Population in lakhs(2011)	Head-quarters
Bastar	10,376	1411644	Jagdalpur
Bijapur	6,555	255180	Bijapur
Bilaspur	8,569	2662077	Bilaspur
Dantewada, D.Bastar	9,055	532791	Dantewada
Dhamatari	4,081	799199	Dhamtari
Durg	8,702	3343079	Durg
Janjgir Champa	4,467	1620632	Janjgir
Jashpur	6,457	852043	Jashpur
Kabeerdham	3,958	822239	Kabeerdham
Kanker, U. Bastar	6,434	748593	Kanker
Korba	5,769	1206563	Korba
Koriya	5,978	659039	Baikunthpur
Mahasamund	4,963	1032275	Mahasamund

Narayanpur	6,640	140206	Narayanpur
Raigarh	6,528	1493627	Raigarh
Raipur	13,445	4062160	Raipur
Rajnandgaon	8,023	1537520	Rajnandgaon
Sarguja	16,034	2361329	Ambikapur
Sukma	-		Sukma
Kondagaon	-		Kondagaon
Gariaband	-		Gariaband
Balouda-bazar	-		Balouda-bazar
Baloud	-	-	Baloud
Bemetara	-		Bemetara
Mungeli	-		Mungeli
Surajpur	-		Surajpur
Balrampur	-		Balrampur
Manendragarh	-		Manendragarh
Mohla Manpur	-		Mohla Manpur
Sakti	-		Sakti
Sarangarh	-		Bilaigarh
Gaurella-Pendra-Marwahi			Gaurella

No. of Tehsils 149
No. of Gram Panchayat/ Police Stations 9856
No. of Village 20133 No. of Urban Town 189
Main Towns: Ambikapur, Bhilai Nagar, Bilaspur, Birgaon, Dhamtari, Durg, Jagdalpur, Korba, Mahasamund, Raigarh, Raipur, Rajnandgaon.
Transport and Communications: (a) Road Length: 3,606 km of NH making 2.75 % of the national total; SH-5,240 km (b) Railway Length: 1,053 km; (c) Main Railway Stations: Raipur, Bilaspur, Durg, Korba, Raigarh, and Rajnandgaon; (d) Airports: Raipur, (Airstrips: Bilaspur, Bhilai, Jagdalpur, Ambikapur, Korba, Jashpurnagar and Rajnandgaon).

6. Goa (GA)

Governor: P.S. Sreedharan Pillai
CM: Pramod Sawant (BJP)

CM

Governor

Date of Formation: On 30 May, 1987 Goa was split into the state of Goa and UT. of Daman and Diu.
Chief Languages: Konkani and Marathi.
No. of Districts: 2

District	Area (sq km)	Population (2011)	Head-quarters
North Goa	1,736	817761	Panaji
South Goa	1,966	639962	Margao

No. of Tehsils 11
No. of Gram Panchayat/ Police Stations 391
No. of Village 391 No. of Urban Town 14
Main Towns: Vasco, Bicholim, Chimbel, Cuncolim, Curchorem-Cacora, Curti, Davorlim, Mapusa, Margao, Mormugao, Panaji, Penha-de-Franca, Ponda, Quepem, Sancoale, Taleigao.
Transport and Communications: (a) Road Length: NH - 264km forming 0.22% of the country's total; state highways-279 km, district roads-815 km.; (b) Railways: Goa is linked with Mumbai, Mangalore and Thiruvananthapuram through the Konkan railway; Vascoda Gama is connected to Bengaluru and Belgaum on SC Railway- exclusively for goods traffic. (c) Main Railway Stations: Margoa, Canacona, Balli, Verna, Karmali, Thivim, Pernem; (d) Airports: Dabolim International (29km from Panaji); (e) Chief Port: Mormugao, Dona Paula, Panaji. Minor Port: Panaji, Tiracol, Chapora Betul, Talpona.

Legislative Assembly, Goa

7. Gujarat (GJ)

Governor: Acharya Devvrat
CM: Bhupendrabhai Rajnikant Patel, (BJP)
Date of Formation: 1 May 1960
Chief Language: Gujarati

CM Governor

No. of Districts: 33

District	Area (sq km)	Population (2011)	Head-quarters
Ahmedabad	8,087	7208200	Ahmedabad
Amreli	7,397	1513614	Amreli
Anand	2,941	2090276	Anand
Banas Kantha	10,757	3116045	Palanpur
Bharuch	6,527	1550822	Bharuch
Bhavnagar	9,981	2877961	Bhavnagar
Dohad	3,646	2126558	Dohad
Dangs	1,764	226769	Ahwa
Gandhinagar	2,163	1387478	Gandhinagar
Jamnagar	14,125	2159130	Jamnagar
Junagadh	8,846	2742291	Junagadh
Kheda	4,219	2298934	Nadiad
Kachchh	45,652	2090313	Bhuj
Mehsana	4,384	2027727	Mehsana
Narmada	2,755	590379	Rajpipla
Navsari	2,209	1330711	Navsari
Panch Mahals	5,220	2388267	Godhara
Patan	5,730	1342746	Patan
Porbandar	2,298	586062	Porbandar
Rajkot	11,203	3799770	Rajkot
Sabar Kantha	7,390	2427346	Himatnagar
Surat	4,327	6079231	Surat
Surendranagar	10,489	1755873	Surendranagar
Vadodara	7,549	4157568	Vadodara
Valsad	3,035	1703068	Valsad
Tapi	3,435	806489	Vyara

* New districts : 7. Aravalli has been carved out of Sabarkantha, Gir Somnath out of Junagadh, Botad out of Bhavnagar and Ahmedabad, Chhota Udepur from Vadodara, Dwarka from Jamnagar, Morbi from Rajkot, Jamnagar and Surendranagar and Mahisagar from Panchmahals and Kheda.

No. of Tehsils 225

No. of Gram Panchayat/ Police Stations 13658

No. of Village 18403 No. of Urban Town 195

Main Towns: Ahmedabad, Amreli, Anand, Anklesvar, Bharuch, Bhavnagar, Bhuj, Botad, Deesa, Dohad, Gandhidham, Gandhinagar, Godhra, Gondal, Jamnagar, Jetpur Navagadh, Junagadh, Kalol, Mahesana, Morvi, Nadiad, Navsari, Palanpur, Patan, Porbandar, Rajkot, Surat, Vadodara, Valsad, Vapi, Veraval.

Krishi Mahotsav is very famous event related to agriculture where farmers are given vital information on modern techniques and scientific methods of farming.

Transport and Communications: (a) Road Length: 77690 km.; NH: 6,635 making 5.05% of the country's total (b) Main Railway Stations: Ahmedabad, Vadodara, Bharuch, Valsad, Navsar, Surat, Dahod, Nadiad, Bhavnagar, Bhuj, Jamnagar, Rajkot, Mehsana, Himatnagar, Palanpur; (c) Airports: There are about 20 airports in the state. Ahmedabad International, Vadodara, Bhavnagar, Bhuj, Surat, Jamnagar, Rajkot; (d) Port: Gujarat has 41 minor and intermediate ports and one major port – Kandla port. Alang port is famous for ship breaking.

8. Haryana (HR)

Governor: Bandaru Dattatreya
CM: Manohar Lal Khattar (BJP)
Date of Formation: 1 Nov 1966 State – carved out of Punjab
Chief Languages: Hindi, Punjabi.

CM

Governor

No. of Districts: 22

District	Area (sq km)	Population (2011)	Head-quarters
Ambala	1,574	1136784	Ambala
Bhiwani	4,778	1629109	Bhiwani
Faridabad	2,151	1798954	Faridabad
Fatehabad	2,538	941522	Fatehabad
Gurugram	2,714	1514085	Gurgaon
Hissar	3,983	1742815	Hissar
Jhajjar	1,834	956907	Jhajjar
Jind	2,702	1332042	Jind
Kaithal	2,317	1072861	Kaithal
Karnal	2,520	1506323	Karnal
Kurukshetra	1,530	964231	Kurukshetra
Mahendragarh	1,899	921680	Narnaul
Panchkula	898	558890	Panchkula
Panipat	1,268	1202811	Panipat
Rewari	1,594	896129	Rewari
Rohtak	1,745	1058683	Rohtak
Sirsa	4,277	1295114	Sirsa
Sonipat	2,122	1480080	Sonipat
Yamunanagar	1,768	1214162	Yamunanagar
Nuh	1874	1089406	Nuh
Palwal	1359	1040493	Palwal
Charkhi Dadri			Charkhi Dadri

No. of Tehsils 83

No. of Gram Panchayat/Police Stations 6651

No. of Village 6835 No. of Urban Town 179

Main Towns: Ambala, Bahadurgarh, Bhiwani, Jind, Kaithal, Palwal, Rewari, Sirsa, Thanesar.

Transport and Communications: (a) Road Length: 35,303 km; NH: 3,098km making 2.36% of the national total (b) Main Railway Stations: Kalka, Ambala, Panipat, Kurukshetra and Rohtak, Jind, Jakhal. Hissar (Jagadhari - railway workshop). (d) Airports: Pinjore, Karnal, Hissar, Bhiwani, Narnaul.

9. Himachal Pradesh (HP)

Governor: Rajendra Vishwanath Arlekar

CM: Jai Ram Thakur, (BJP)

CM

Governor

Date of Formation: 25 Jan. 1971 (after Statehood Act was passed on 18 Dec. 1970); UT - 1 Nov. 1956; Province -15 Apr 1948.

Chief Languages: Pahari, Hindi, Punjabi, Kinnauri.

No. of Districts: 12

District	Area (sq km)	Population (2011)	Head-quarters
Bilaspur	1,167	382056	Bilaspur
Chamba	6,528	518844	Chamba
Hamirpur	1,118	454293	Hamirpur
Kangra	5,739	1507223	Dharamsala
Kinnaur	6,401	84298	Reckong Peo
Kullu	5,503	437474	Kullu
Lahaul & Spiti	13,835	31528	Keylong
Mandi	3,950	999518	Mandi
Shimla	5,131	813384	Shimla
Sirmaur	2,825	530164	Nahan
Solan	1,936	576670	Solan
Una	1,540	521057	Una

No. of Tehsils 117
No. of Gram Panchayat/ Police Stations 3211
No. of Village 20693 No. of Urban Town 56

Main Towns: Baddi, Chamba, Dharamsala, Kullu, Mandi, Nahan, Paonta Sahib, Shimla, Solan, Sundarnagar

Agriculture: 70% of population is engaged in agriculture. Its production make 22.1% of state's GDP. It is also called the Fruit Bowl of India.

Transport and Communications: (a) **Road Length:** 33171 km. (2010) NH-2,607km forming 1.99% of the country's total (b) **Main Railway Stations:** The only broad gauge railway station is Una; two narrow gauge lines are Pathankot to Joginder-nagar and Kalka to Shimla; (c) **Airports:** Bhuntar (Kullu Valley), Jubbarhatti (Shimla) and Gaggal (Kangra).

10. Jharkhand (JH)

Governor: Ramesh Bais
CM: Hemant Soren (JMM/UPA)

CM Governor

Date of Formation: 15 Nov 2000 (State created from part of Bihar)

Chief Languages: Hindi, Urdu, Kurmati, Santhali, Ho, Kurukh, Sadri, Mundari, Khariya, Malto, Nagpuria, Bengali.

No. of Districts: 24

District	Area (sq km)	Population (2011)	Head-quarters
Bokaro	2,861	2061918	Bokaro
Chatra	3,706	1042304	Chatra
Deoghar	2,479	1491879	Deoghar
Dhanbad	2,075	2682662	Dhanbad
Dumka	3,716	1321096	Dhumka
Garhwa	4,044	1322387	Garhwa
Giridih	4,887	2445203	Giridih
Godda	2,110	1311382	Godda
Gumla	5,321	1025656	Gumla
Hazaribagh	4,519	1734005	Hazaribagh
Kodarma	1,311	717169	Kodarma
Lohardaga	1,491	461738	Lohardaga
Pakur	1,806	899200	Pakaur
Palamau	4,015	1936319	Daltonganj
Paschimi Singhbhum	5,290	1501619	Chabasa
Purbi Singhbhum	3,553	2291032	Jamshedpur
Ranchi	4,963	2912022	Ranchi
Sahibganj	1,706	1150038	Sahibganj
Latehar	3,660	725673	Latehar
Jamtara	1,802	5,44,856	Jamtara
Saraikela Kharsawan	2,725	1063458	Seraikela
Simdega	3756	599813	Simdega
Ramgarh	1211	949159	Ramgarh
Khunti	2611	530299	Khunti

Legislative Assembly, Jharkhand

No. of Tehsils 259

No. of Gram Panchayat/ Police Stations 4581
No. of Village 32584 No. of Urban Town 41

Main Towns: Jamshedpur, Dhanbad, Ranchi, Bokaro Steel City, Deoghar, Phusro, Hazaribag, Giridih, Ramgarh Cantonment, Medininagar, Chirkunda

Transport and Communications: (a) **Road Length:** 4,311km, including NH 2711km making 2.56% of the country's total and SH 2,711km; (b) **Main Railway Stations:** Ranchi, Bokaro, Dhanbad,

Jamshedpur, Muri, Deogarh; (c) Airports: Ranchi, Jamshedpur.

11. Karnataka (KA)

Governor: Thawar Chand Gehlot
CM: BS Bommai (BJP).
Date of Formation: 1956, Nov 1- received statehood; 1 Nov. 1973 renamed as Karnataka; 15 Aug.1947 - declared Mysore state.

CM Governor

Chief Languages: Kannada

No. of Districts: 31

District	Area (sq km)	Population (2011)	Head-quarters
Bagalkot	6,575	1890826	Bagalkot
Bengaluru	2,190	9588910	Bengaluru
Bengaluru Rural	5,815	987257	Bengaluru
Belagavi	13,415	4778439	Belagavi
Bellari	8,450	2532383	Bellari
Bidar	5,448	1700018	Bidar
Vijayapura	10,494	2175102	Vijayapura
Chamarajanagar	5,101	1020962	Ch.nagar
Chikkamagaluru	7,201	1137753	Chikkama-galuru
Chitradurga	8,440	1660378	Chitradurga
Dakshina Kannada	4,560	2083625	Mangalore
Davanagere	5,924	1946905	Davanagere
Dharwad	4,260	1846993	Dharwad
Gadag	4,656	1065235	Gadag
Kalaburagi	16,224	2564892	Kalaburagi
Hassan	6,814	1776221	Hassan
Haveri	4,823	1598506	Haveri
Kodagu	4,102	554762	Madikeri
Kolar	8,223	1540231	Kolar
Koppal	7,189	1391292	Koppal
Mandya	4,961	1808680	Mandya
Mysuru	6,854	2994744	Mysuru
Raichur	6,827	1924773	Raichur
Shivamogga	8,477	1755512	Shivamogga
Tumakuru	10,597	2681449	Tumakuru
Udupi	3,880	1177908	Udupi
Uttara Kannada	10,291	1436847	Karwar
Ramanagara	3,556	1082739	Ramanagata
Chikkabellapura		1254377	Chikkabella-pura
Vijayanagara	5,644	1353628	Hospete
Yadgir	5,160	1172985	Yadgir

No. of Tehsils 180
No. of Gram Panchayat/ Police Stations 6050
No. of Village 29490 No. of Urban Town 220

Main Towns: Bengaluru, Mysuru, Hubballi-Dharwar, Mangaluru, Belagavi, Kalaburagi, Davanagere, Bellari, Vijayapura, Shivamogga, Tumakuru, Bidar, Chikkmagaluru, Chitradurga, Gadag, Betigeri, Hassan, Hosapete, Kolar, Raichur, Udupi. Bengaluru has one ofthe largest biotechnology clusters in India. Karnataka produces 31,229 million units of electricity. The state produces 101L tonnes of Horticulture produce and is one of the major milk producers in India.

Transport and Communications: (a) Road Length: 2,15,849 km; NH: 7,335km making 5.59% of the country's total; SH-9590 km (b) Railway Length: 3172 km. Namma Metro rapid transport system was operationalised on 1 Mar. 2014. Now it runs on green line and purple line between MG Road-Baiyappanahalli station and Peenya Industry to Mantri Square Sampige Road station. Konkan Railway is the coastal link between Mumbai and Mangaluru, operational since 1 May, 1998; (c) Main Railway: Stations Bengaluru, Mysuru, Tumakuru, Hosur, Hassan, Mandya, Bellari, Hubballi, Vijayapura, Kalaburagi, Belagavi, Dharwad; (d) **Airports:** Bengaluru-Devanahalli, Belagavi, Mangaluru, Hubballi; (e) **Port:** New Mangaluru port is the main all-weather seaport. 10 minor ports. Maritime Coastline: 300km.

12. Kerala (KL)

Governor: Arif Mohammed Khan.
CM: Pinarayi Vijayan (LDF).
Date of Formation: 1 Nov. 1956- Renamed Kerala; Travancore-Cochin state formed: 1 July 1949; Malabar merger: 1 Nov. 1956.

CM

Governor

Chief Language: Malayalam

No. of Districts: 14

District	Area (sq km)	Population (2011)	Head-quarters
Alappuzha	1,414	2121943	Alappuzha
Ernakulam	3068	3279860	Kochi
Idukki	4,358	1107453	Painavu
Kannur	2,966	2525637	Kannur
Kasargode	1,992	1302600	Kasargode
Kollam	2,491	2629703	Kollam
Kottayam	2,208	1979384	Kottayam
Kozhikode	2,344	3089543	Kozhikode
Malappuram	3,550	4110956	Malappuram
Palakkad	4,480	2810892	Palakkad
Pathanamthitta	2,637	1195537	Pathanamthitta
Thiruvananthapuram	2,192	3307284	Thiruvananthapuram
Thrissur	3,032	3110327	Thrissur
Wayanad	2,131	816558	Kalpetta

Legislative Assembly, Kerala

No. of Tehsils 63
No. of Gram Panchayat/ Police Stations 1058
No. of Village 1459 No. of Urban Town 95

Main Towns: Kochi, Kozhikode, Thrissur, Malappuram, Thiruvananthapuram, Kannur, Kollam, Kottayam, Alappuzha, Perintalmanna, Palakkad.

Transport and Communications: (a) **Road Length:** 3.18 lakh km; Metros services started in Kochi since 2017. NH: 1,782kms forming 1.36% of the country's total; (b) **Railway Length:** 1,257km; (c) **Main Railway Stations:** Thiruvananthapuram, Kollam, Chengannur, Kottayam, Alappuzha, Ernakulam, Trissur, Palakkad, Kozhikode, Kannur, Kasargod.

(d) **International Airports:** Thiruvananthapuram, Nedumbassery, and Karipur (Kozhikode). Kannur International Airport became functional from 9th December 2018 at Mattannur. (e) **Port:** Kochi. (f) **Inland Waterways:** As a part of National Waterways No. 3, there are 3 routes totaling a distance of 205 km.: West Coast -Kottapuram to Kollam, Udyogmandal - Kochi to Pathalam, and Champakara - Kochi to Ambalamugal. There are 33 dams. 18 of them are irrigation dams. Kerala is a power deficit state. 60% of power is purchased from other states. All the villages have been electrified.

Education: The first fully literate municipal town in India–Kottayam (1989); the first district–Ernakulam in 1990. Kerala became the first fully literate state in India in 1991 with 89.9% literacy among adults. Kottayam–the land of 3 'L's: letters, latex and lakes, is famous for being the headquarters of at least 5 newspapers besides many other publications.

13. Madhya Pradesh (MP)

Governor: Mangubhai Chaganbhai Patel

CM: Shivraj Singh Chouhan (BJP)

Date of Formation: 1 Nov. 1956 merged with Madhya Bharat, Bhopal, and Vindhya Pradesh (and separating Marathi-speaking Vidarbha region) to form Madhya Pradesh state. MP was bifurcated in 1 Nov 2000 to form Chhattisgarh. Post independence, Nagpur was the first capital. In 1956 Bhopal was made the new capital.

CM

Governor

Chief Language: Hindi

No. of Districts: 55

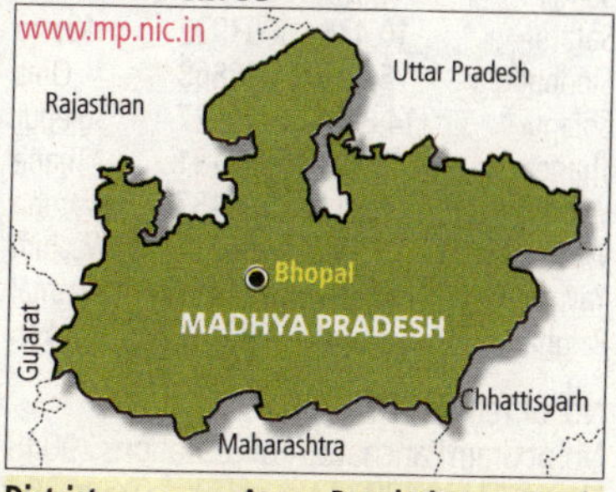

District	Area (sq km)	Population (2011)	Head-quarters
Ashoknagar	4674	844979	Ashoknagar
Alirajpur	-	728677	Alirajpur
Anuppur	3746	749521	Anuppur
Balaghat	9,229	1701156	Balaghat
Barwani	(5,432)	1385659	Barwani
Betul	10,043	1575247	Betul
Bhind	4,459	1703562	Bhind
Bhopal	2,772	2368145	Bhopal
Burhanpur	2,473	756993	Burhanpur
Chhatarpur	8,687	1762857	Chhatarpur
Chhindwara	11,815	2090306	Chhindwara
Damoh	7,306	1263703	Damoh
Datia	2,038	786375	Datia
Dewas	7,020	1563107	Dewas
Dhar	8,153	2184672	Dhar
Dindori	7,427	704218	Dindori
Guna	11,065	1240938	Guna
Gwalior	5,214	2030543	Gwalior
Harda	(3,339)	570302	Harda
Hoshangabad	10,037	1240975	Hoshangabad
Indore	3,898	3272335	Indore
Jabalpur	10,160	2460714	Jabalpur
Jhabua	6,782	1024091	Jhabua
Katni	(4,947)	1291684	Katni
Khandwa(E.Nimar)	10,779	1309443	Khandwa
Khargone (W.Nimar)	13,450	1872413	Khargone
Mandla	13,269	1053522	Mandla
Mandsaur	9,791	1339832	Mandsaur
Morena	11,594	1965137	Morena
Narsinghpur	5,133	1092141	Narsimhapur
Neemuch	4,267	825958	Neemuch
Panna	7,135	1016028	Panna
Raisen	8,446	1331699	Raisen
Rajgarh	6,154	1546541	Rajgarh
Ratlam	4,861	1454483	Ratlam
Rewa	6,134	2363744	Rewa
Sagar	10,252	2378295	Sagar
Satna	7,502	2228619	Satna
Sehore	6,578	1311008	Sehore
Seoni	8,758	1378876	Seoni
Shahdol	14,028	1064989	Shahdol
Shajapur	6,196	1512353	Shajapur
Sheopur	6,606	687952	Sheopur
Shivpuri	10,278	1725818	Shivpuri
Sidhi	10,256	1126515	Sidhi
Singrauli	2200	1178132	Singrauli
Tikamgarh	5,048	1444920	Tikamgarh
Ujjain	6,091	1986597	Ujjain
Umaria	(4,026)	643579	Umaria
Vidisha	2,742	1458212	Vidisha
Agar Malwa	2,785	571275	Agar
Chachaura	1,850	370000	Chachaura
Maihar	-		

No. of Tehsils 342

No. of Gram Panchayat/ Police Stations 24262

No. of Village 55011 No. of Urban Town 405

Main Towns: Indore, Bhopal, Jabalpur, Gwalior, Ujjain, Sagar, Dewas, Satna, Ratlam, Rewa, Bhind, Betul, Chhatarpur, Chhindwara, Guna, Khandwa, Khargone, Morena, Murwara, Singrauli, Vidisha.

Transport and Communications: (a) Road Length: 58,423 km. NH: 4709 kms making 6.68% of the nation's total; SH 10,501 km; (b) Main Railway Stations: Bhopal, Bina, Gwalior, Indore, Itarsi, Jabalpur, Katani, Ratlam and Ujjain; (c) Airports: Bhopal, Gwalior, Indore, Khajuraho.

Famous for Chanderi sarees, Bhimbetka caves and the cave paintings, forts, Khajuraho temples, Bedaghat marble rocks, Ujjain Kumbh mela, legendary singers like Tansen, Baiju Bawra, tribal population forming 21%.

14. Maharashtra (MH)

Governor: Bhagat Singh Koshyari

CM: Uddhav Balasaheb Thackeray (SS)

CM

Governor

Date of Formation: May 1, 1960 -the state of Bombay was bifurcated into Maharashtra and Gujarat. [15 Aug 1947- Bombay Province was restructured into State].

Chief Languages: Marathi.

No. of Districts: 36

District	Area (sq km)	Population (2011)	Head-quarters
Ahmednagar	17,034	4543083	Ahmednagar
Akola	5,431	1818617	Akola
Amravati	12,235	2887826	Amravati
Aurangabad	10,106	3695928	Aurangabad
Beed	10,692	2585962	Beed
Bhandara	3,890	1198810	Bhandara
Buldana	9,680	2588039	Buldana
Chandrapur	11,417	2194262	Chandrapur
Dhule	8,061	2048781	Dhule
Gadchiroli	14,477	1071795	Gadchiroli
Gondiya	5,430	1322331	Gondiya
Hingoli	4,526	1178973	Hingoli
Jalgaon	11,757	4224442	Jalgaon
Jalna	7,715	1958483	Jalna
Kolhapur	7,692	3874015	Kolhapur
Latur	7,166	2455543	Latur
Mumbai City	157	3145966	Mumbai City
Mumbai (Sub.)	446	9332481	Mumbai(Sub.)
Nagpur	9,810	4653171	Nagpur
Nanded	10,545	3356566	Nanded
Nandurbar	5,035	1646177	Nandurbar
Nashik	15,539	6109052	Nashik
Osmanabad	7,550	1660311	Osmanabad
Parbhani	6,511	1835982	Parbhani
Pune	15,637	9426959	Pune
Raigad	7,162	2635394	Alibag
Ratnagiri	8,196	1612672	Ratnagiri
Sangli	8,577	2820575	Sangli
Satara	10,475	3003922	Satara
Sindhudurg	5,222	848868	Oras
Solapur	(14,886)	4315527	Solapur
Thane	9,563	11054131	Thane
Wardha	6,311	1296157	Wardha
Washim	5,150	1196714	Washim
Yavatmal	13,594	2775457	Yavatmal
Palghar	5,344	2990116	Konkan

No. of Tehsils 357

No. of Gram Panchayat/ Police Stations 29048

No. of Village 43937 No. of Urban Town 264

Main Towns: Mumbai, Pune, Nagpur, Nashik, Vasai-Virar, Aurangabad, Solapur, Bhiwandi, Amravati, Ahmadnagar, Akola, Bhusawal, Ichaikaroji, Jalgaon, Jalna, Kolhapur, Latur.Mumbai Metropolitan region include Navi Mumbai, Thane, Kalyan, Bhiwandi, Panvel, Virar, Pen, Ulhasnagar, Ambarnath, Dombivili and Vasai. Mumbai is the financial capital of India. 65% of population are agriculture workers.

Transport and Communications: (a) Road Length: 2.43L km. NH: 4376kms forming 13.52% of the country's total. SH: 34,157 km., 50,256 km. of major district roads, and 106,601 km of village roads; (b) Mono Rail, India's first, started running on 2 Feb 2014 between Wadala Depot and Chembur. (c) Railway Length: 5,983 km. (d) Main Railway Stations: Chhatrapati Shivaji Railway Terminus (Victoria Terminus-VT) station; Bandra, Thane, Vasai, Khurd, Pune, Solapur, Satara, Jalgaon, Bhusaval, Nagpur, Kholapur, Kudal; (e) Airports: 3 International Airports: Chhatrapati Shivaji International Ap. (BOM), Pune Int. Ap. (PNQ); Dr. Babasaheb Ambedkar Int. Ap. Nagpur (NAG), and 5 domestic airports: Nanded, Akola, Aurangabad, Shirdi, Kholapur. (f) Port: Mumbai.

15. Manipur (MN)

Governor: La. Ganesan
CM: N Biren Singh (BJP)

CM

Governor

Date of Formation: 21 Jan 1972 State; (after 1971 NE Areas Reorganisation Act)

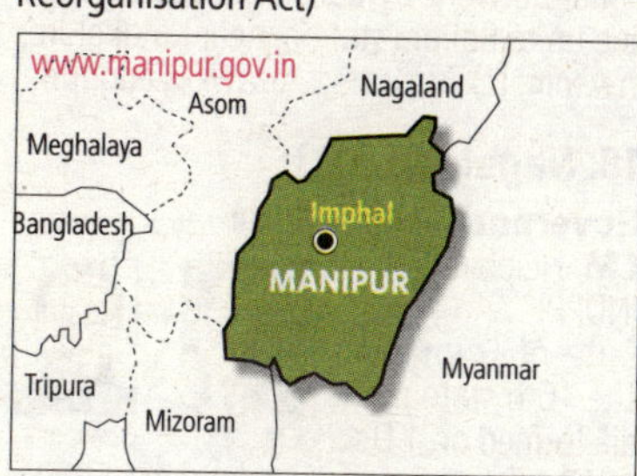

Chief Language: Meiteilon (Manipuri).

No. of Districts: 16

District	Area (sq km)	Population (2011)	Headquarters
Bishnupur	496	240363	Bishnupur
Chandel	3,313	144028	Chandel
Churachandpur	4,570	271274	Churachandpur
Imphal East	709	452661	Porompat
Imphal West	519	514683	Lamphelpat
Senapati	3,271	354972	Senapati
Tamenglong	4,391	140143	Tamenglong
Thoubal	514	420517	Thoubal
Ukhrul	4,544	183115	Ukhrul

No. of Tehsils 38

No. of Gram Panchayat/ Police Stations 2557 No. of Village 2583 No. of Urban Town 32

Main Towns: Imphal, Kakching, Mayang Imphal, Thoubal, Ukhrul.

Transport and Communications: (a) Road Length: 12618 km; NH: 1,750kms making 1.33% of the nation's total NH 39 connects Nagaland and Myanmar, NH53 connects Asom and NH 150 connects Mozoram. (b) Main Railway Stations: Jiribam-225 kms from Imphal; Tupul; Imphal Railway. Station to complete soon.(d) Airports: Imphal- second largest in the NE.

16. Meghalaya (ML)

Governor: Satya Pal Malik
CM: Conrad Kongkal Sangma (NPP).

CM

Governor

Date of Formation: 21 Jan 1972 state (after 1971 NE Areas Reorganisation Act)

Chief Languages: Garo, Khasi, English.

No. of Districts: 11

District	Area (sq km)	Population (2011)	Headquarters
East Khasi Hills	2,820	824059	Shillong
West Khasi Hills	5,247	385601	Nongstoin
Ri-Bhoi	2,376	258380	Nongpoh
South Garo Hills	1,849	142574	Baghmara
West Garo Hills	3,715	642923	Tura
East Garo Hills	2,603	317618	Williamnagar
SW Khasi	1341	110152	Mawkyrwat
West Jaintia Hills	1693	270352	Jowai
East Jaintia Hills	2115	122939	Khliehriat
SW Garo Hills	822	170794	Ampati
North Garo Hills	1113	118325	Resubelpara

Legislative Assembly, Meghalaya

No. of Tehsils 39
No. of Gram Panchayat/ Police Stations 6406
No. of Village 6851 No. of Urban Town 10
Main Towns: Jowai, Nongstoin, Shillong, Tura, Williamnagar.
Transport and Communications: (a) Road Length: 9350 km. NH: 1,156kms forming 0.88% of country's total; six NH passes by (b) Railway: None; (c) Airports: Umroi, 35 km from Shillong

17. Mizoram (MZ)

Governor: Kambhampati Hari Babu
CM: Zoramthanga (MNF)
Date of Formation: 20 Feb 1987; 23rd state

CM

Governor

Chief Languages: Mizo, Kuki and English

No. of Districts: 11

District	Area (sq km)	Population (2011)	Head-quarters
Aizawl	3,576	404054	Aizawl
Champhai	3,186	125370	Champhai
Kolasib	1,283	83054	Kolasib
Lawngtlai	2,557	117444	Lawngtlai
Lunglei	4,538	154094	Lunglei
Mamit	3,025	85757	Mamit
Saiha	1,400	56366	Saiha
Serchhip	1,422	64875	Serchhip
Hnahthial			Hnahthial
Khawzawl			
Saitual			

No. of Tehsils 29
No. of Gram Panchayat/ Police Stations 809
No. of Village 830 No. of Urban Town 23
Main Towns: Aizawl, Lunglei , Champhai, Kolosib, Saiha, Serchhip, Lawngtlai.
Transport and Communications: (a) Roadways serve as the most important means of communication, transportation of goods and passengers within the state, inter-state and with international borders. Road Length: 6349 km; 1,156 kms making 0.88% of the national total (b) Main Railway Stations: For the first time Mizoram has been linked to the national network by building a broadguage line up to Bairabi station, near Katakal Jn., in Asom; (c) Airports: Aizawl - Lengpuri.

18. Nagaland (NL)

Governor: Jagdish Mukhi
CM: Neiphiu Rio (NDPP)
Date of Formation: The 16th state of India formed on 1 Dec. 1963 (after State of Nagaland Act 1962)

CM

Governor

Chief Languages: Angami, Ao, Chang, Konyak, Lotha, Sangtam, Sema and Chakhesang. The state is inhabited by 16 major tribes. Two threads common to all,

are language and religion - English and Christianity.

No. of Districts: 12

District	Area (sq km)	Population (2011)	Head-quarters
Dimapur	927	379769	Dimapur
Kohima	3,144	270063	Kohima
Phek	2,026	163294	Phek
Mokokchung	1,615	193171	Mokokchung
Mon	1,876	250671	Mon
Tuensang	4,228	196801	Tuensang
Wokha	1,628	166239	Wokha
Zunheboto	1,255	141014	Zunheboto
Kiphire	1255	74033	Kiphire
Longleng	885	50593	Longleng
Peren	2300	94954	Peren

No. of Tehsils 114
No. of Gram Panchayat/ Police Stations 1213
No. of Village 1435 No. of Urban Town 19.
Main Towns: Kohima, Phek, Mon, Wokha, Mokokchung, Tuensang, Zunheboto.
Transport and Communications: (a) Road Length: 24709 km; 1,548kms of NH 39 & 61, forming 1.18% of the national total (b) Main Railway Stations: Dimapur- 215 km from Imphal; (c) Airports: Dimapur.

19. Odisha (OD)

Governor: Prof. Ganeshi Lal
CM: Naveen Patnaik - (BJD)

CM Governor

Date of Formation: 1 April - Odisha day. 15 Aug 1947: Orissa Province; 26 Jan 1950: Orissa State; Renamed Orissa as Odisha: gazetted -1 Nov. 2011.
Chief Language: Odiya (Oriya)

No. of Districts: 30

District	Area (sq km)	Population (2011)	Head-quarters
Angul	6,375	1271703	Angul
Bolangir	6,575	1648574	Bolangir
Balasore	3,806	2317419	Balasore
Bargarh	5,837	1478833	Bargarh
Bhadrak	2,505	1506522	Bhadrak
Boudh	3,098	439917	Boudh
Cuttack	3,932	2618708	Cuttack
Deogarh	2,940	312164	Deogarh
Dhenkanal	4,452	1192948	Dhenkanal
Gajapati	4325	575880	Paralakhe-mundi
Ganjam	8,206	3520151	Chhatrapur
Jagatsinghpur	1,668	10,57,629	Jagatsinghpur
Jajpur	2,899	1826275	Jajpur
Jharsuguda	2,081	579499	Jharsuguda
Kalahandi	7920	1573054	Bhavanipatna
Kandhamal	8021	731952	Phulbani
Kendrapara	2,644	1439891	Kendrapara
Keonjhar	8,303	1802777	Keonjhar
Khurda	2,813	2246341	Khurda
Koraput	8,807	1376934	Koraput
Malkangiri	5791	612727	Malkangiri
Mayurbhanj	10,418	2513895	Baripada
Nabarangpur	5,291	12187626	Nabarangpur
Nayagarh	3,890	962215	Nayagarh
Nuapada	3,852	606490	Nuapada
Puri	3,479	1697983	Puri
Rayagada	7,073	961959	Rayagada
Sambalpur	6,657	1044410	Sambalpur
Subarnapur	2,337	652107	Subarnapur
Sundargarh	9,712	2080664	Sundargarh

No. of Tehsils 477
No. of Gram Panchayat/ Police Stations 7066
No. of Village 51442 No. of Urban Town 107
Main Towns: Bhubaneswar, Cuttack, Raurkela, Brahmapur, Sambalpur, Puri, Baleshwar, Bhadrak, Baripada.
Transport & Communications: (a) Road

Length: 3596km NH:5,762kms making 4.39% of the nation's total. state express highways; 3,855 km SH; (b) **Railway Length:** 2,339 km-broad-guage and 91 km narrow-guage lines; (c) **Main Railway Stations:** Bhubaneswar, Puri, Cuttack, Behrampur, Bolangir, Raurkela, Sambalpur; (d) **Airports:** Bhubaneswar. (e) **Ports:** Paradeep (major) and Gopalpur (all-weather)

Culture: (a) **Dances:** Odissi, Chau, Mahari, Gotipua. Dalkhai (tribal dance), Ghoomra, Ranapa and Chhadaya (folk dance); (b) **Music:** Four varieties- Chitrapada, Dhruvapada, Panchal and Chitrakala. Podi singing. (d) **Festivals:** Rath Yatra (Puri), Shraban Purnima, Ashokastami, Chandan Yatra, Snana Yatra and Konark festival; (c) Handloom products of silk and tussar, silver filigree work (tarkashi), Pat chitra paintings, golden glass work. (e) **Craft:** Applique work of Pipli, sand sculpturing in Puri, palm leaf painting, horn (cattle) work are unique to this place.

20. Punjab (PB)

Governor: Banwarilal Purohit
CM: Charanjit Singh Channi (INC)

Date of Formation: 1966 Sept Statehood after Punjab Reorganisation Act and trifurcation of the state. After 1955 PEPSU states were merged.

CM

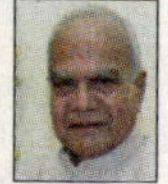
Governor

Chief Language: Punjabi.
No. of Districts: 24

District	Area (sq km)	Population (2011)	Head-quarters
Amritsar	5,075	2490891	Amritsar
Bhatinda	3,377	1388859	Bhatinda
Faridkot	1,472	618008	Faridkot
Fatehgarh Sahib	1,180	599814	Fatehgarh Sahib
Firozepur	5,865	2026831	Firozepur
Gurdaspur	3,570	2299026	Gurdaspur
Hoshiarpur	3,310	1582793	Hoshiarpur
Jalandhar	2,658	2181753	Jalandhar
Kapurthala	1,646	817668	Kapurthala
Ludhiana	3,744	3487882	Ludhiana
Mansa	2,174	768808	Mansa
Moga	2,216	992289	Moga
Muktsar Sahib	2,615	902702	Muktsar
Patiala	3,218	1892282	Patiala
Rupnagar	2,117	683349	Rupnagar
Mohali	1093	986147	Mohali
Nawanshahr	1266	614362	Roop Nagar
Sangrur	5,021	1654408	Sangrur
Tarn Taran	2449	1120070	Tarn Taran
Barnala	1410	596294	Barnala
Fazilka	3113	1180483	Fazilka
Pathankot	929	676598	Pathankot
Malerkotla			
Shahid Bhagat Singh Nagar			Nawanshahar
Shahibzada Ajit Singh Nagar			Mohali

No. of Tehsils 77
No. of Gram Panchayat/ Police Stations 12458
No. of Village 12645 No. of Urban Town 155.

Main Towns: Ludhiana, Amritsar, Jalandhar, Patiala, Batinda, SAS. Nagar, Hoshiarpur, Moga, Pathankot, Batala, Abohar, Barnala, Firozpur, Hoshiarpur, Moga, Muktsar, Phagwara, SAS. Nagar.

Transport and Communications: (a) **Road Length:** 71742 km, NH: 2630 kms; SH-1133 km; Dist. Rd. 1826 km(b **Railway Length:** 3726.06 km; (c) **Main Railway Stations:** Patiala, Jalandhar, Amritsar, Bhatinda; (d) **Airports: Amritsar** (Rajajasansi) Intl. Airport (Amritsar), Chandigarh (Mohali), Patiala, domestic flight started at Sahnewal, Ludhiana.

Culture: (a) **Dances:** Bhangra, Gidda and

Legislative Assembly, Punjab

Thumar, (b) Fairs and Festivals: Besides Gurpurab, Lohri, Dussehra, Diwali, and Holi, there are Maghi Mela at Mukatsar (Jan), Rural Sports at Kila Raipur (Feb), Basant at Patiala in February, Holla Mohalla at Anandpur Sahib in March, Baisakhi at Talwandi Saboo in April, Urs at Rauza Sharif at Sirhind in August, Chappar Mela at Chappar in September, Skeikh Farid Agam Purb at Faridkot in September, Ram Tirath at Village Ram Tirath in November, Shaheedi Jor Mela at Sirhind in December, Harballah Sangeet Sammelan Baba Sodal at Jalandhar in December. There are three heritage festivals at Amritsar, Patiala, Kapurthala celebrated every year and are very popular among the tourists. Harballah Sangeet Sammelan (Jalandhar); (c) Crafts: Pulkari embroidery on bed sheets, durries, shawls, jerseys.

21. Rajasthan (RJ)

Governor: Kalraj Mishra

CM: Ashok Gehlot (INC)

CM

Governor

Date of Formation: 1 Nov 1956 Rajasthan (statehood);

Chief Languages: Rajasthani, Hindi, Gujarati

No. of Districts: 33

District	Area (sq km)	Population (2011)	Headquarters
Ajmer	8,481	2584913	Ajmer
Alwar	8,380	3671999	Alwar
Banswara	5,037	1798194	Banswara
Baran	6,955	1223921	Baran
Barmer	28,387	2604453	Barmer
Bharatpur	5,066	2549121	Bharatpur
Bhilwara	10,455	2410459	Bhilwara
Bikaner	27,244	2367745	Bikaner
Bundi	5,550	1113725	Bundi
Chittorgarh	10,856	1544392	Chittorgarh
Churu	16,830	2041172	Churu
Dausa	2,950	1637226	Dausa
Dholpur	3,034	1207293	Dholpur
Dungarpur	3,770	1388906	Dungarpur
Ganganagar	7,944	1969520	Ganganagar
Hanumangarh	12,690	1779650	Hanumangarh
Jaipur	11,588	6663971	Jaipur
Jaisalmer	38,401	672008	Jaisalmer
Jalore	10,640	1830151	Jalore
Jhalawar	6,219	1411327	Jhalawar
Jhunjhunu	5,928	2139658	Jhunjhunu
Jodhpur	22,850	3685681	Jodhpur
Karauli	5,014	1458459	Karauli
Kota	5,481	1950491	Kota
Nagaur	17,718	3309234	Nagaur
Pali	12,387	2038533	Pali
Partapgarh	4189	868231	Partapgarh
Rajsamand	4,768	1158283	Rajsamand
S. Madhopur	5,043	1338114	S.Madhopur
Sikar	7,732	2677737	Sikar

Legislative Assembly, Rajasthan

Sirohi	5,136	1037185	Sirohi
Tonk	7,194	1421711	Tonk
Udaipur	13,419	3067549	Udaipur

No. of Tehsils 244
No. of Gram Panchayat/ Police Stations 15134
No. of Village 44785 No. of Urban Town 189

Main Towns: Jaipur, Jodhpur, Kota, Bikaner, Ajmer, Udaipur, Bhilwara, Alwar, Bharatpur, Pali, Sikar, Sawai Madhopur, Hanumangarh, Gangapur, Beawar.

Economy: Rajasthan is second only to Jharkhand in terms of mineral wealth in India. It produces 79 varieties of minerals. 57 minerals are commercially extracted. Power installed capacity is 15989 MW.

Transport and Communications: (a) **Road Length:** 207019 km; NH:9,999 kms forming 7.61% of the nation's total (b) **Railway Length:** 5871 km; BG: 4801km, MG: 86.76km, NG: 983.71km(c) Main Railway Stations: Jaipur, Jodhpur, Kota, Bikaner, Sawaai Madhopur, Bharatpur; (d) **Airports:** Jaipur, Jodhpur.

Culture: (a) **Dances:** Khayal (dance-music), Ghumar during Teej and Gangaur festivals, Panihari, Chari, Kachchi Ghori; (b) **Festivals:** Camel Festival - Bikaner is organised every year. Deepawali, Vijayadashami, Holi, Teej, Gangaur (Jaipur), Urs of Ajmer Sherif and Galiakot, Christmas; (c) **Fairs:** tribal Kumbh of Bene-shwar (Dun-garpur), Ramdeora (Jaisalmer), Mahavir fair at Shri Mahavirji in Sawai Madhopur, Janbeshwari Fair (Mukam-Bikaner), Kartik Poornima and Pushkar Cattle Fair-Ajmer and Shyamji Fair (Sikar); (d) **Craft:** Bandhini (tie and dye) work, block printing, hand-knotted woollen carpets, massoria work, gharas kagzi pottery, pichwais (painting on cloth), phads (cloth scroll painting), lacquer-works.

22. Sikkim (SK)

Governor: Ganga Prasad
CM: Prem Singh Tamang (SKM)

CM

Governor

Date of Formation: 16 May 1975. Statehood
Chief Languages: Nepali, Lepcha, Bhutia, and Limbu.

No. of Districts: 4

District	Area (sq km)	Population (2011)	Head-quarters
East	954	281293	Gangtok
North	4,226	43354	Mangan
South	750	146742	Namchi
West	1,166	136299	Gyalshing

No. of Tehsils 9
No. of Gram Panchayat/ Police Stations 452
No. of Village 452 No. of Urban Town 8.

Main Towns: Gangtok, Namchi

Economy: The state produces 22240 tonnes of fruits, Vegetables: 78820, Cut Flowers and planting material numbering 230Lakh.

Transport & Communications: (a) **Road Length:** 3672 km; NH: 463ms making 0.35% of the nation's total(b) **Main Railway Stations:** No stations - the closest ones are Siliguri (114 km) and New Jalpaiguri (125 km); (c) **Airports:** Gangtok, Bagdogra and a new greenfield airport at Pakyong. Helicopter service between Gangtok and Bagdogra.

Culture: (a) **Dances:** Mask dances of Bhutias, Nepalis and Lepchas are famous; (b) **Festivals:** Bumchu (Jan/Feb) at Tashidang Monastry, Maghey Sankranti, Durga Puja, Chaite Dasai (Nepali), Pang Lhabsol (worship snow covered Kanchenjunga) and Losar (Bhutias), Namsoong and Tendong Hlo Rum Faat (Lepchas); (c) **Crafts:** Woollen carpets, with Tibetan designs, rough blankets, saris, cane and bamboo works, wood carving, handmade paper and silver works.

23. Tamil Nadu (TN)

Governor: Banwarilal Purohit
CM: M. K. Stalin (DMK)

CM

Governor

Date of Formation: 14 Jan. 1969 the state was renamed Tamil Nadu; 1956: Madras Province was bifurcated to create separate Andhra; 15 Aug 1947 Madras Province with Andhra came into existence.

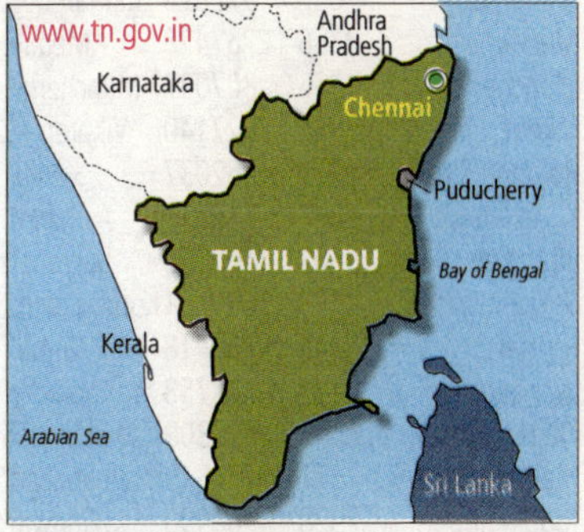

Chief Language: Tamil.

No. of Districts: 38

District	Area (sq km)	Population (2011)	Headquarters
Ariyalur	1,944	752481	Ariyalur
Chennai	174	4681087	Chennai
Coimbatore	7,469	3472578	Coimbatore
Cuddalore	3,706	2600880	Cuddalore
Dharmapuri	9,622	1502900	Dharmapuri
Dindigul	6,058	2161367	Dindigul
Erode	8,209	2259608	Erode
Kancheepuram	4,307	3990897	Kancheepuram
Kanyakumari	1,684	1863174	Nagercoil
Krishnagiri	5,143	1883731	Krishnagiri
Karur	2,901	1076588	Karur
Madurai	3,696	3041038	Madurai
Nagapattinam	2,417	1614069	Nagapattinam
Namakkal	3,404	1721179	Namakkal
Nilgiris	2,549	735071	(Ootty) Udagamandalam
Perambalur	1,750	564511	Perambalur
Pudukkottai	4,651	1618725	Pudukkottai
Ramanathapuram	4,175	1337560	Ramanathapuram
Salem	5,425	3480008	Salem
Sivagangai	4,143	1341250	Sivagangai
Thanjavur	3,476	2402781	Thanjavur
Theni	2,869	1243684	Theni
Thiruvannamalai	6,190	2468965	Thiruvannamalai
Thiruvarur	2,377	1268094	Thiruvarur
Tirunelveli	6,810	3072880	Tirunelveli
Tiruvallur	3,550	3725697	Tiruvallur
Trichirappalli	4,511	2713858	Trichirappalli
Thoothukudi	4,621	1738376	Thoothukudi
Vellore	6,077	3928106	Vellore
Villuppuram*	7,190	3463284	Villuppuram
Virudhunagar	4,283	1943309	Virudhunagar
Tirupur	4720	2471222	Tirupur
Kallakurichi	3520	1682687	
Tenkasi	2916	1407627	
Mayiladuthurai	1172	918356	
Chengalpattu	2945	2556244	
Ranipet	2234	1210277	

No. of Tehsils 216

No. of Gram Panchayat/ Police Stations 12632

No. of Village 16278 No. of Urban Town 822

Main Towns: Chennai, Coimbatore, Madurai, Tiruchirappalli, Tiruppur, Salem, Erode, Tirunelveli, Vellore, Thoothukkudi, Dindigul, Hosur, Kanchipuram, Karur, Nagercoil, Ranippettai (Ranipet), Sivakasi, Thanjavur, Udhagamandalam (Ooty)

Transport and Communications: Metro Rail project is in progress. The Mass Rapid transport is a big relief to the commuters. (a) Road Length: 62,294km; NH: 6,742kms making

5.13% of the nation's total(b) Railway Length: 3846km; (c) Main Railway Stations: MGR Chennai Central, Madurai, Tiruchirapalli, Coimbatore, Erode, Salem, Jolarpetai, Katpadi, Arakkonam, and Tirunelveli; (d) Airports: Meenambakam International, Chennai; Madurai, Tiruchirapalli, Coimbatore, Salem; (e) Ports: Chennai and Thoothukudi (Tuticorin), Cuddalore, Nagapattinam.

Culture: (a) Dances: Bharathanatyam, Kalashetra, Kollattam, Kummi, Kavadi, Karagams; (b) Festivals: Pongal (harvest), Chitirai-Madurai, Adipperukku (on river banks during sowing season), Mahamagam fest, Dance festival-Mamalapuram, Kanthuri festival, Karthigai festival, Navaratri festival, Music Festival. At the Natyanjali Dance Festival, the temple city of Chidambaram pays special tribute to Lord Nataraja the 'Cosmic Dancer'.

24. Telangana (TG)

Governor: Tamilisai Soundararajan
CM: K Chandrasekhar Rao.(TRS)
Date of Formation: 2 June 2014
No. of Districts: 33

CM

Governor

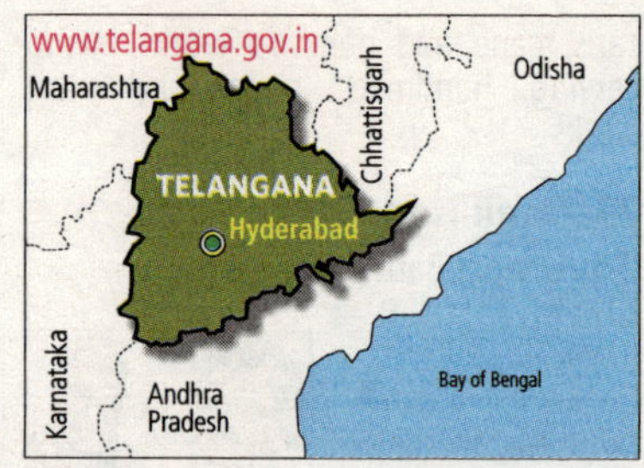

District	Area (sq km)	Population (2011)	Headquarters
Adilabad	16,128	2737738	Adilabad
Hyderabad	217	4010238	Hyderabad
Karimnagar	11,823	3811738	Karimnagar
Khammam	16,029	2798214	Khammam
Mahaboob nagar*	5285	1486777	Mahaboob nagar
Medak	9,699	3031877	Sangareddy
Nalgonda	14,240	3483648	Nalgonda
Nizamabad	7,956	2552073	Nizamabad
Ranga Reddy	7,493	5296396	Hyderabad
Warangal	12,846	3522644	Warangal
Siddipet	3632	1012065	Siddipet
Jangaon	2188	566376	Jangaon
Jayashankar*	6175	711434	Bhupalpalle
Jagtial	2419	985417	Jagtial
Warangal (Rural)	2175	718537	Warangal
Warangal (Urban)	1309	080858	Warangal
Yadadri	3092	73448	Bhongir
Peddapalli	2236	795332	Peddapalli
Kamareddy	3652	972625	Kamareddy
Medak	2786	767428	Medak
Mancherial	4016	807037	Mancherial
Vikarabad	3386	927140	Vikarabad
Rajanna Sircilla	2019	552037	Sircilla
K. Asifabad	4878	515812	Asifabad
Suryapet	3607	109965	Suryapet
B. Kothagudem	7483	1069261	Kothagudem
Nirmal	3845	709418	Nirmal
Wanaparthy	2152	577758	Wanaparthy
Nagarkurnool	6545	893308	Nagarkurnool
Mahbubabad	2877	774549	Mahbubabad
Jogulamba	2928	60990	Gadwal
Medchal-Malkajgiri	1084	2440073	Shamirpet
Mulugu	3881	294671	Mulugu
Narayanpet	4.86	41752	Narayanpet

No. of Tehsils 459
No. of Gram Panchayat/Police Stations 9530
Villages: 10582 No. of Urban Town: 71

Major Cities: Hyderabad, Warangal, Nizamabad, Karimnagar and Ramagundam.

Transportation: Roads: NH: 3,795 kms forming 2.89% of the country's total TSRTC is well connected with all cities and villages. Mahatma Gandhi Bus station, Hyderabad, Jubilee Bus Station, Secunderabad, and Inter City Bus Terminal at Miyapur-Hyderabad provide good service. Railways: It comes under the South Central Railway zone with Secun-

Legislative Assembly, Telangana

derabad as the zonal Headquarters. Airports: Rajiv Gandhi International Airport is an international airport, Hyderabad.

Culture: A blend of Persian traditions, carried over from the Mughals and Nizams and with the south Indian traditions and customs.

25. Tripura (TR)

Governor: Satyadev Narayan Arya
CM: Biplab Kumar Deb (BJP)

CM

Governor

Date of Formation: 21 January 1972.

Chief Languages: Bengali, Kokborak and Manipuri.

No. of Districts: 8

District	Area (sq km)	Population (2011)	Head-quarters
Dhalai	2,552	377,988	Ambassa
North Tripura	1,422	422,370	Dharamnagar
South Tripura	2,152	433,737	Belonia
West Tripura	3,033	1,724,619	Agartala
Sipahijala	-	484,233	Bisramganj
Khowai	1,377	327,391	Khowai
Gomati	-	436,868	Udaipur
Unakoti	687	298,574	Kailashahar

No. of Tehsils 44
No. of Gram Panchayat/ Police Stations 1109
No. of Village 900 No. of Urban Town 16

Main Towns: Agartala, Belonia, Kumarghat, Kailashahar, Udaipur, Khowai and Kamal-pur.

Transport and Communications: (a) Road Length: 1997 km; NH: 854 kms making 0.65.% of the total (b) Railway

Length: 64 km; (c) Main Railway Stations: Railway line has been extended to Agartala. Manughat, Dharamnagar; (d) Airports: Agartala.

Culture: (a) Dances: Bamboo dance, Garia, Lebang Boomain, Hozagiri, Bizu, Hai-Hak, Cheraw, Wangala; (b) Festivals: Makar Sankranti, Poush Sankranti Mela, Garia Puja, Hozagiri, Mansa Mangal, Ker and Karachi Puja, Ganga Puja, Christmas, Buddha Purnima, Ashokasthami at Unakoti, Sarad festival, Rash Leela, Jhulan Jatra, Rath Jatra; (c) Crafts: Bamboo handicrafts esp. sitalpatti (mats), lasing-phee (quilt like weaving), terracotta and cane. Costume: Pachra, Risha.

26. Uttarakhand (UK)

Governor: Gurmit Singh
CM: Pushkar Singh Dhami (BJP)

CM

Governor

Date of Formation: 9 Nov. 2000 as Uttaranchal; renamed Uttarakhand in 2007.

Chief Languages: Hindi, Garhwali, Kumaoni.

No. of Districts: 13

District	Area (sq km)	Population (2011)	Head-quarters
Almora	3,139	621927	Almora
Bageshwar	1,696	259840	Bageshwar
Chamoli	7,520	391114	Gopeshwar
Champawat	2,004	259315	Champawat
Dehradun	3,088	1698560	Dehradun
Pauri Garhwal	5,329	686527	Pauri
Hardwar	2,360	1927029	Hardwar

Nainital	3,422	955128	Nainital
Pithoragarh	7,169	485993	Pithoragarh
Rudra Prayag	2,439	236857	Rudra Prayag
Tehri Garhwal	3,796	616409	New Tehri
Udham Singh Nagar	3,055	1648367	Rudrapur
Uttarkashi	8,016	329686	Uttarkashi

No. of Tehsils 78
No. of Gram Panchayat/ Police Stations 16411
No. of Village 16827 No. of Urban Town 75

Main Towns: Dehradun, Hardwar, Roorkee, Haldwani-cum-Kathgodam, Rudrapur, Kashipur, Rishikesh, Pithoragarh, Ramnagar, Kichha, Manglaur, Jaspur.

Transport and Communications: (a) Road Length: 33,914 km.; NH: 2,949kms making 2.25% of the total (b) Main Railway Stations: Dehra Dun, Hardwar, Roorkee, Kotdwar, Kashipur, Udhamsingh Nagar, Kathgodam, Haldwani; (c) Airport Jolly Grant (Dehra Dun). Airstrips: Pantnagar (Udham Singh Nagar), (Naini-Seni (Pithoragarh), Gauchar (Chamoli) and Chinyalisaur (Uttarkashi) - are being built. Pawan Hans service: Rudraprayag to Kedarnath.

Culture: (a) Dances: Langvir Nritya, Barada nati, Jhora and Choliya; (b) Music: Mandal, Panwara, Khuded, Thadya, Jhoda. (c) Festivals: Kumbh Mela / Ardh Kumbh Mela (Hardwar- every 12th / 6th year interval); Devidhura Mela (Chamawat), Nanda Devi Mela (Almora), Gauchar Mela (Chamoli), Baisakhi & Maga Mela (Uttarkashi), Uttaraini Mela (Bageshwar), Vishu Mela (Jaunsar Va-

Legislative Assembly, Uttarakhand

var), Peerane-Kaliyar (Roorkee), Nanda Devi Raj Jat Yaatra -every 12th year, and Puranagiri Mela. (d) Craft: Kumaoni art, Aipan painting, Peeth wall painting, Alpan Rangoli.

27. Uttar Pradesh (UP)

Governor: Anandi Ben Patel
CM: Yogi Adityanath (BJP)

CM

Governor

Date of Formation: 26 Jan, 1950, Uttar Pradesh became a state. 15 Aug. 1947 United province was formed.

Chief Languages: Hindi and Urdu.

No. Districts: 75

District	Area (sq km)	Population (2011)	Headquarters
Agra	4,027	4380793	Agra
Aligarh	3,650	3673849	Aligarh
Allahabad	5,482	5959798	Allahabad
Ambedkar Nagar	2,350	20,26,876	Akbarpur
Azamgarh	4,054	4616509	Azamgarh
Baghpat	1,321	1302156	Baghpat
Bahraich	4,420	3478257	Bahraich
Ballia	2,981	3223642	Balia
Balrampur	3,349	2149066	Balrampur
Banda	4,460	1799541	Banda
Barabanki	4,402	3257983	Barabanki
Bareilly	4,120	4465344	Bareilly
Basti	2,688	2461056	Basti
Bijnor	4,561	3683896	Bijnore
Budaun	5,168	3712738	Budaun
Bulandshahar	4,352	3498507	Bulandshahar
Chandauli	2,541	1952713	Chandauli

Chitrakoot	3,164	990626	Chitrakoot
Deoria	2,538	3098637	Deoria
Etah	4,446	1761152	Etah
Etawah	2,311	1579160	Etawah
Faizabad	2,341	20,88,928	Faizabad
Farrukhabad	2,181	1887577	Fatehgarh
Fatehpur	4,152	2632684	Fatehpur
Firozabad	2,361	2496761	Firozabad
Gautam Buddha Nagar	1,442	1674714	Gautam BuddhaNagar
Ghaziabad	1,148	4661452	Ghaziabad
Ghazipur	3,377	3622727	Ghazipur
Gonda	4,003	3431386	Gonda
Gorakhpur	3,321	4436275	Gorakhpur
Hamirpur	4,282	1104021	Hamirpur
Hardoi	5,986	4091380	Hardoi
Hathras	1840	1565678	Hathras
Jalaun	4,565	1670718	Orai
Jaunpur	4,038	4476072	Jaunpur
Jhansi	5,024	2000755	Jhansi
Amroha	2,249	1838771	Amroha
Kannauj	2,093	1658005	Kanauj
Kanpur (Dehat)	3,021	1795092	Akbarpur
Kanpur (City)	3,155	4572951	Kanpur
Kanshi Ram Nagar	-	1438156	Kanshi Ram Nagar
Kaushambi	1780	1596909	Kaushambi
Kushinagar	2,906	3560830	Podarauna
Kheri	7,680	4013634	Kheri
Lalitpur	5,039	1218002	Lalitpur
Lucknow	2,528	4588455	Lucknow
Maharajganj	2,952	2665292	Maharajganj
Mahoba	2884	876055	Mahoba
Mainpuri	2,760	1847194	Mainpuri
Mathura	3,340	2541894	Mathura
Mau	1,713	2205170	Mau
Meerut	2,590	3447405	Meerut
Mirzapur	4,521	2494533	Mirzapur
Moradabad	3,718	4773138	Moradabad
Muzaffarnagar	4,0084	138605	Muzaffarnagar
Auraiya	2,015	1372287	Aurraiya
Pilibhit	3,499	2037225	Pilibhit
Pratapgarh	3,717	3173752	Pratapgarh
Rae Bareilli	4,609	3404004	Rae Bareli
Rampur	2,367	2335398	Rampur
Saharanpur	3,689	3464228	Saharanpur
Sant Kabir Nagar	1,646	1714300	Khalilabad
Sant Ravidas Nagar	1,015	1554203	Bhadhohi
Shahjahanpur	4,575	3002376	Shahjahanpur
Shrawasti	2,458	1114615	Shrawasti
Siddharth Nagar	2,895	2553526	Navgarh
Sitapur	5,743	4474446	Sitapur
Sonbhadra	6,788	1862612	Robertsganj
Sultanpur	4,436	3790922	Sultanpur
Unnao	4,558	3110595	Unnao
Varanasi	1,535	3682194	Varanasi
Bheem Nagar	2,422	-	Sambhal
Shamli	1,240	-	shamli
Hapur	1,124	-	Hapur
Kasganj	1993	-	Kasganj

No. of Tehsils 312

No. of Gram Panchayat/ Police Stations 74626

No. of Village 107040 No. of Urban Town 650

Main Towns: Kanpur, Lucknow, Ghaziabad, Agra, Varanasi, Meerut, Allahabad, Bareilly, Aligarh, Moradabad, Bulandshahr, Faizabad, Etawah, Farrukhabad (cum-Fatehgarh), Hapur, Mathura, Mau, Muzaffarnagar, Rampur, Rae Bareli, Sambhal, Shahjahanpur.

Transport and Communications: (a) **Road Length:** 1,46728 km. NH: 3820kms making 8.94 % of the nation's total, SH-8449km, District Rd.-119726km; (b) **Main Railway Stations:** Lucknow (main junction), Agra, Kanpur, Allahabad, Mughalsarai, Jhansi, Moradabad, Varanasi, Tundla, Gorakhpur, Gonda, Faizabad, Bareilly, and Sitapur; (c) **Airports:** Lucknow,

Kanpur, Varanasi, Allahabad, Agra, Jhansi, Bareilly, Hindon (Ghaziabad), Gorakhpur, Sarsawa, Fursatganj (Rae-Bareilly).

Culture: (a) **Dances:** Kathak; (b) **Music:** Thumri, Kajri, Birha, Ghazal, Qawali, Rasiya, Marsiya, Hari and Chaiti. (c) **Festivals:** The biggest congregation, perhaps of the world, Kumbha Mela is held in Allahabad every 12 years and Ardhkumbh mela, every 6 years. Magh Mela is also held at Allahabad Sangam in January. Among other fairs is the fortnight long Jhoola fair of Mathura, Vrindavan and Ayodhya, when dolls are placed in gold and silver jhoolas or cradles. A dip in the Ganga on Kartik Poornamasi is considered holy and there are big congregations at Garhmukteshwar, Soran, Rajghat, Kakora, Bithur, Kanpur, Allahabad, Varanasi and Ayodhya. A famous cattle fair is held at Bateswar in Agra district. Dewa in Barabanki district has became famous because of the Muslim saint Waris Ali Shah.

Crafts: Silk saree and brocade (Banarasi silk), chikankari - hand stiched design, zardosi work, metalware, woodcarving, wood work inlaid with brassware on black sheesham, marbleware, glasswork, glaze pottery, etc.

28. West Bengal (WB)

Governor : Jagdeep Dhankhar
CM: Mamata Banerjee (AI TMC)

Date of Formation: 15 Aug 1947 Province; 26 Jan, 1950 State (until 1956: Part A)

CM Governor

Chief Language: Bengali

No. of Districts: 23

District	Area (sq km)	Population (2011)	Headquarters
Bankura	6,882	3596292	Bankura
Birbhum	4,545	3502387	Suri
Bardhaman	7,024	7723663	Bardhaman
Kolkata	185	4486679	Kolkata
Cooch Behar	3,387	2822780	Cooch-Behar
Darjeeling	3,149	1842034	Darjeeling
Hooghly	3,149	5520389	Chinsurah
Howrah	1,467	4841638	Howrah
Jalpaiguri*	6,227	3869675	Jalpaiguri
Malda	3,733	3997970	Englishbazar
Paschim Medinipur	9295	5943300	Medinipur
Purba Medinipur	4,061	5094238	Purba Medinipur
Purulia	6,259	2535233	Purulia
Murshidabad	5,324	7102430	Berhampore
Nadia	3,927	5168488	Krishnagar
Purulia	6,259	2927965	Purulia
North 24 Parganas	4,094	10082852	Barasat
S. 24 Parganas	9,660	8153176	Alipore
Uttar Dinajpur	3,140	3000849	Raigunj
Dakshin Dinajpur	2,219	1670931	Balurghat
Alipurduar	3,383	1700000	Alipurduar
Kalimpong	1,053	251642	Kalimpong
Sundarbans			
Basirhat			
Purba Burdhman	5,432	4835532	Burdman
PaschimBurdhman	6603	2882031	
Jhargram	3,037	1136548	Jhargram

No. of Tehsils: 360
No. of Gram Panchayat/ Police Stations 3556
No. of Village 40895 No. of Urban Town 147

Main Towns: Kolkata, Kharagpur, Durgapur, Asansol, Murshidabad, Howrah, Bardhaman, Siliguri.

Transport and Communications: (a) 3,664 of NH making 2.79% of the nation's total; (b)Main Railway Stations: Howrah, Asansol, Sealdah, Bandel, Bardhaman, Kharagpur, New Jalpaiguri. Kolkata's Metro Rail commissioned in 1995 is operationalised on 3 lines: BLUE-(East-West, underground) Howrah to Phool-Bagan, RED-(East-West, elevated) Phool Bagan to Salt Lake Sector 5 and GREEN-the single North South corridor between DumDum to Tollygunge; (d) Airports: Dum Dum International (Kolkata), Bagdogra, Kalaikunda, Panagarh, Malda, Barrackpore, Behala, Balurghat and Coochbehar; (e) Ports: Kolkata and Haldia.

Culture: West Bengal is known for its textiles; handlooms; Murshidabad and Baluchari silk sarees; Kantha embroidery; cane and bamboo work, leather craft, clay dolls & toys, masks, sholapith works; (a) Dances: Chhau (Purulia), Rabindra Nritya, Gaudiya nritya; (b) Music: Baul, Rabindra Sangeet, lokgeet. (c) Festivals/ Fairs: Boi Mela (International Book Fair at Milan Maidan, Jan/Feb), Netaji Bose Day- Jan 23, Durga puja-the most important festival along with Kali puja or Diwali. Swadeshi Mela-Feb 25 at Ektapur, Poush Mela-Dec, Ramkeli- June. Vasant Panchami, Lakshmi puja, Saraswati puja, Holi, Sivaratri, Janmashtami, Id-ul-Fitr.

29. Andaman & Nicobar Is. (AN)

Lt. Governor: Devendra Kr Joshi

Date of Formation: 1 Nov, 1956- UT.

Lt. Governor

Until the colonisation of India, Andaman Islands were inhabited by 4 Negrito tribes viz., the Great Andamanese, Onge, Jarawa & Sentinalese and 2 Mongoloid tribes viz., Nicobarese and Shompens.

Chief Languages: Local dialects, Nicobarese, Bengali, Hindi, Nicobarese, Telugu, Tamil and Malayalam.

No. of Districts: 3

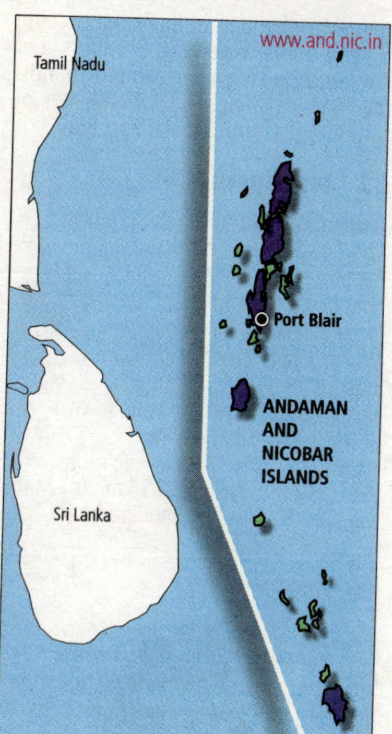

District	Area (sq km)	Population (2011)	Head-quarters
South Andaman	3,181	237586	Port blair
Nicobar	1,841	42,026	Car Nicobar
N & Mid.Andaman	3,227	105539	Mayanunder

No. of Tehsils 9

No. of Gram Panchayat/ Police Stations 79

No. of Village 559 No. of Urban Town 1

Main Towns: Shyamnagar, Nabagram, Mayabunder, Uttara, Checkpoint, Herbertahad, Bamboo Flat, Wrightmyo, Port Meadows, Wandoor.

Transport and Communications: (a) Road NH: 330 kms. The islands are accessible by air and sea. It is well connected to Kolkata, Chennai by air and by sea to Kolkata, Chennai and Visakhapatnam. The UT's transport system serves 9 major islands from Diglipur to Campbell Bay. Andaman Trunk Road services connects Rangat, Mayabunder and Diglipur using 3 ferry boats. There are 5 wharfs and 41 jetties linking all inhabited islands; (b) There is a network of 866 km of tarred roads; (c) Airports: Port Blair.

30. Chandigarh (CH)

Administrator: Banwarilal Purohit

Administrator

Chief Languages: Hindi, Punjabi and English
No. of Districts: 1
No. of Tehsils 1
No. of Gram Panchayat/ Police Stations 10
No. of Village 10 No. of Urban Town 1
Main Towns: Chandigarh
Transport and Communications: (a) Road Length: NH-15.275 km.; (b) Main Railway Stations: Chandigarh; (c) Airports: Chandigarh.

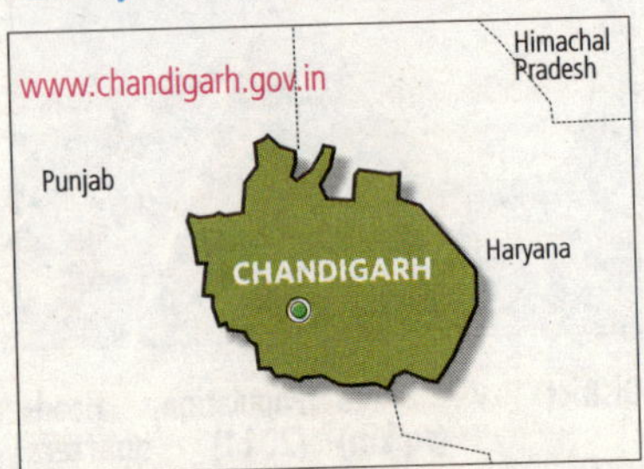

Culture: Festivals: Lodhi, Baisakhi

31. Dadra & Nagar Haveli and Daman & Diu (DD)

Administrator: Praful Patel In 2019

Administrator

Date of Merger: 26 Jan 2020 (according to Merger of UTs Bill, 2019tabled in the Parliament on 26 Nov. 2019).
Capital : Daman town
Area: 603 sq. km
History: DNH Formation: UT on 11 Aug 1961 - liberated from Portuguese on 2 Aug. 1954.
DD Formation: 19 Dec.1961- liberated from Portuguese control / 30 May 1987-

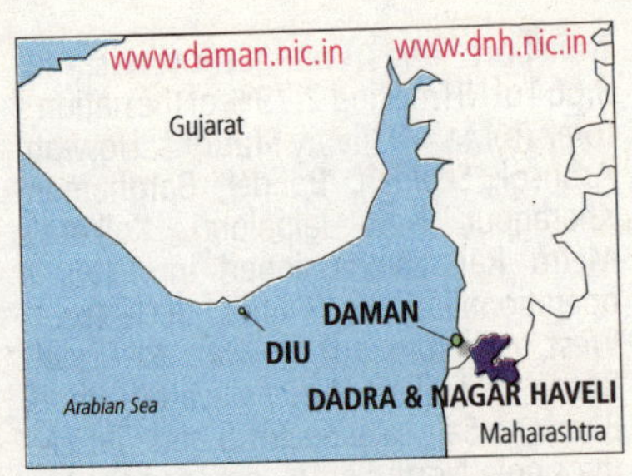

UT when Goa attained statehood
Chief Languages: Bhili, Gujarati, Bhilodi, Marathi and Hindi
No. of Districts: 3

Districts	Area	Pop (2011)	Density
Daman	72	190856	2650
Diu	40	52056	1301
Dadra & Nagar Haveli	491	342853	698
Total	603	585764	971

No. of Tehsils 1
No. of Gram Panchayat/ Police Stations 22
No. of Village 93 No. of Urban Town 3
No. of Tehsils 2
Main Towns: Silvassa, Daman, Diu
Transport and Communications: (a) Road Length: about 700 km; NH: 50 kms (b) Main Railway Stations: Vapi for Silvassa and Daman and Delvada for Diu; ((c) Airports: Mumbai and Daman, Diu.
Economy: (a) Minerals: Salt; (b) Industries: Fishing, tourism, and distillery.
Culture: Festivals: Diwaso, Bhawada, Kali Puja.

32. Lakshadweep (LD)

Administrator: Praful Patel

Administrator

Date of Formation: 1 Nov 1956 Laccadive, Minicoy, and Amindivi Islands union territory (separated from Madras) 1 Nov 1973. Renamed Lakshadweep (LD)
Neighbouring States/UTs:[1+1] Kerala, Mahe (Puducherry). Sea: Arabian Sea.
Chief Languages: Jeseri (a), Mahal and Malayalam.

No. of Districts: 1. The entire group of islands is considered one district and divided into four tahsils.
No. of Tehsils 10
No. of Gram Panchayat/ Police Stations 10
No. of Village 26 No. of Town 1

Major Islands: Kavarati, Agati, Minicoy, Andrott, Kalpeni, Amini, Kadamatt, Kiltan.

Transport & Communications: These islands and Kochi are linked by air and ship. By ship it takes 18-20 hours, and by air 30 minutes; (a) Airports: Agatti; (b) Port: Kavaratti, Minicoy, Agatti, Kadamatt, Kalpeni.

33. Puducherry (PY)

Lt. Governor: Tamilisai Soundararajan
CM: N. Rangasamy

CM

Lt. Governor

Date of Formation: 7 Jan.1963 – became a Union Territory.

Chief Languages: Tamil, Telugu, Malayalam, English and French.

No. of Districts: 4

District	Area (sq km)	Population (2011)	Headquarters
1. Karaikal	161	200314	Karaikal
2. Mahe	9	41934	Mahe
3. Puducherry	290	946600	Puducherry
4. Yanam	20	55616	Yanam

No. of Tehsils 8
No. of Gram Panchayat/ Police Stations 32
No. of Village 95 No. of Urban Town 6

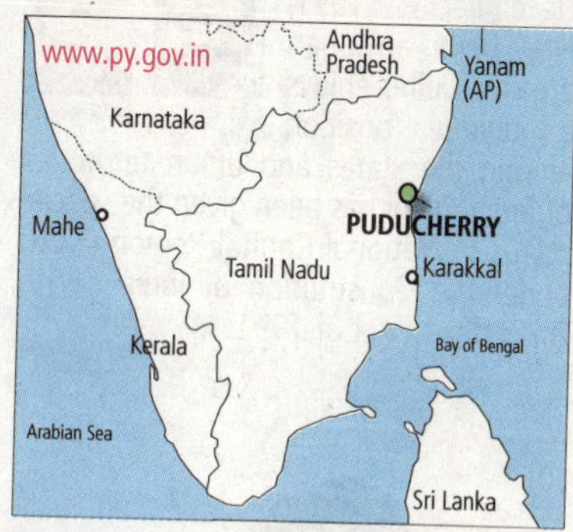

Main Towns: Puducherry, Karaikal, Yanam, Mahe.

Transport and Communications: (a) Road Length: 2,443 km.; NH: 64kms (b) Main Railway Stations: Villupuram Jn. (nearest railway link.); (c) Airports: (nearest-Chennai); (d) Port: Puducherry.

Culture: (a) Dances: Podikazhiattam; (b) Festivals: Mascarade - a mask festival, Mar-Apr); Masimagam (Feb-Mar), eve of

Legislative Assembly, Puducherry

extra

Statue of Mahatma

At Promenade Beach, in Puducherry, the statue of Mahatma Gandhi with a height of 4m is the third-largest in the entire world. The statue was built by sculptor Roy Choudhary. It was placed in the year 1965, opposite to the Old Pier.

French Bastille Day- is marked by flags and parade; (c) Crafts: Hand-printed textiles, Kalakari batik, marbling work, handmade paper, bronze work.

34. Delhi (DL)

Lt. Governor: Anil Baijal
CM: Arvind Kejriwal

CM

Lt. Governor

Date of Formation: December 1991; New Delhi, an urban area in Delhi, enjoys a unique position among the states and union territories of India. Delhi has been given the special status of National Capital Region (NCR) under the Constitution of India's 69th Amendment Act of 1991.

The political administration of the 'union territory,' or NCT of Delhi, resembles more of a state of India, with its own legislature, high court and an executive, led by the Lieutenant Governor of Delhi and Council of Ministers headed by a Chief Minister. The Government of Delhi is the supreme governing authority of the National Capital Territory of Delhi and its 11 districts. The present Legislative Assembly of Delhi is unicameral, consisting of 70 members of the Legislative Assembly who are directly elected from territorial constituencies in the NCT. Lieutenant Governor of Delhi is appointed by the President of India as an agent of President unlike the head of state (like governor), on the advice of the Central government.

Legislative Assembly, Delhi

Some aspects of administration is jointly administered by the union government and the local government of Delhi. The Parliament of India, the Rashtrapati Bhavan, Cabinet Secretariat and the Supreme Court of India are located in the municipal district of New Delhi besides the regional Delhi High Court, along with the Small Causes Court for civil cases; the Magistrate Court and the Sessions Court for criminal cases. The Delhi Police is headed by the Police Commissioner but it does not fall under Delhi state government. It reports directly to union home ministry. The city is administratively divided into eleven police-zones, which are subdivided into 95 local police stations.

The National Capital Territory of Delhi (NCT) includes the Delhi metropolitan area with five local municipal corporations; North Delhi Municipal Corporation, South Delhi Municipal Corporation, East Delhi Municipal Corporation, NDMC and DCB. The former MCD was divided into three smaller Municipal Corporations – North Delhi, South Delhi and East Delhi.The NCR includes towns like Gurgaon, Noida, Ghaziabad, Faridabad, Neharpar (Greater Faridabad), Greater Noida, Sonepat, Panipat, Karnal, Rohtak, Bhiwani, Rewari, Baghpat, Meerut, Alwar, Bharatpur and other nearby towns. Since 1956, direct Union control was implemented until it was re-established in 1993. The first legislative assembly of

Delhi was constituted in Nov 1993 after the Council of Ministers was replaced by the Delhi Legislative Assembly through the Constitution Act 1991 and by the Government of National Capital Territory of Delhi Act, 1991, the Sixty-ninth Amendment to the Indian constitution declaring the Union Territory of Delhi as National Capital Territory of Delhi. Chief Languages: Hindi, Punjabi, Urdu and English.

No. of Districts: 11
North-883418, North East-2700000
North West-3651261, East-1707725
West-2531583, South-2733752
South West-2292363, Central-578671
New Delhi-133713, South East-
Shahdara-

No. of Tehsils 27.
No. of Gram Panchayat/ Police Stations 230.
No. of Village 230 No. of Urban Town 33.
Main Towns: New Delhi, Delhi Cantt, Palam, Mehrauli, Shahdara, Alipur, Badaali, Nazafgarh, Narela.
Transport and Communications: (a) Road NH: 80 kms. Inter-State terminuses: Kashmere Gate, Sarai Kalen Khan and Anand Vihar; (b) Railways: Delhi Metro, started on 24 Dec. 2002, with 137 stations in April 2014. It is operational in 7 coloured lines - RED-Rithala to Dilshad Gardens; BLUE-Vaishali/Noida to Dwaraka Sec. 21; YELLOW-Jahangirpuri to HUDA City; GREEN-Mundaka to Kirti Nagar/Inderlok; ORANGE-Rajiv Chowk to Dwaraka Sec 21 via IGI Airport; VIOLET- Central Secretariat to Badarpur and Airport Express.; (c) Main Railway Stations: Delhi (DLI)., New Delhi (NDLS), Delhi Cantonment (DEC) Hazrat Nizamuddin (NZM); Anand Vihar Terminus (ANVT), Delhi Sarai Rohilla (DEE) (d) Airports: Indira Gandhi International Airport, Domestic flight -Palam and for training Safdarjung.
National Museum: Nehru Memorial Museum, Craft Museum, National Museum of Natural History, National Museum of Modern Art, Central Cottage Industries Emporium (Janpat), States Emporia (Baba Kharak Singh Marg), Dili Haat - handicrafts.
Culture: (a) Festivals: Roshnara festival, Shalimar festival, Qutab festival, Winter Carnival, Garden Tourism & Mango festival. Besides International Industrial Exhibitions, Automobile Exhibitions, Defense Exhibitions, etc.

35. Jammu & Kashmir (JK)

Lt. Governor

Governor: Manoj Sinha
Date of Formation: 26 Oct. 1947 (the day when Maharaja Hari Singh signed Instrument of Accession in favour of Indian Union). Dogra rulers reigned here for long. POK: 78114 Km^2. 5180 sq km given to China by Pakistan.China occupies 37555 km^2.
Chief Languages: Urdu (official), Kashmiri, Dogri, Pahari, Balti, Ladakhi, Pun-

Origin of Jammu & Kashmir

extra

According to the history of Jammu & Kashmir, Maharaja Hari Singh was the last ruling Maharaja of the princely state. Srinagar was founded by Emperor Ashoka and not the Mughal emperor Jahangir.

Legislative Assembly, Jammu & Kashmir

jabi, Gojri, Dadri.

No. of Districts: 20

District	Area (sq km)	Population (2011)	Head-quarters
Anantnag	2,917	1070144	Anantnag
Badgam	1,371	735753	Badgam
Bandipora	398	385099	Bandipora
Baramula	4,190	1015503	Baramula
Doda	4,500	409576	Doda
Ganderbal	1,945	297003	Ganderbal
Jammu	3,097	1526406	Jammu
Kathua	2,440	615711	Kathua
Kishtwar	7,737	231037	Kishtwar
Kulgam	1,097	422786	Kulgam
Kupwara	2,379	875564	Kupwara
Poonch	1,674	476820	Poonch
Pulwama	1,090	570060	Pulwama
Rajouri	2,630	619266	Rajauri
Ramban	1138	283313	Ramban
Reasi	1517	314714	Reasi
Samba	910	318611	Samba
Shopian	612,87	265960	Shopian
Srinagar	294	1269751	Srinagar
Udhampur	2380	555357	Udhampur

Main Towns: Srinagar, Jammu, Anantnag, Udhampur, Baramula, Sopore, Kathua, Bandipura, Leh.
Transport and Communications: (a) **Road Length:** 25,578 km.; NH: 2,423km making 1.85% of the nation's total. NH 1A that connects the state to the rest of India is 400 km long. (b) **Main Railway Stations:** Jammu, Udhampur. The railway line has been extended to Srinagar and Qazigund-Bani in Ramban dist. (c) **Airports:** 3– Sheikh-ul-Alam International-Srinagar, Jammu.

36. Ladakh (LA)

Lt. Governor

Governor: Lt Gov. Radha Krishan Mathur
Date of Formation: August 2019. It was formed by bifurcating J&K.

No. of Districts 2

District	Area (sq km)	Population (2011)	Head-quarters
Kargil	14,036	143388	Kargil
Leh	45,100	147104	Leh

No. of Tehsils: 11
No. of Villages: 243
Main Town: 2
Panchayat: 193; Blocks: 31.

Legislative Assembly, Ladakh

India: Biggest, Highest, Largest, Smallest

Biggest Monolith Statue Gometeshwar Statue
Biggest Mosque Jama Masjid at Delhi
Biggest Stadium Yuva Bharti (Salt Lake) Stadium, Kolkata
Deepest River Valley Bhagirathi, Alaknanda
Densest Populated State West Bengal
Fastest Train Vande Bharat (Train 18) between New Delhi and Varanasi at 180 kmph
Highest Airport Kushok Bakula Rimpochee Airport, Leh (J&K) - 3256m above mean sea level
Highest Civilian Award Bharat Ratna
Highest Battle Field Siachin Glacier
Highest Dam Tehri Dam on river Bhagirathi, Uttarakhand (260.5m high)
Highest Gallantry Award Param Vir Chakra
Highest Gateway Buland Darwaza at Fatehpur Sikri (53.6 metres high)
Highest Lake Tso Lhamo or Cholamoo lake 5330 msl, N. Sikkim; Devtal Lake, Garhwal (Uttarakhand)
Highest Peak Karkoram-2 / K-2 (8611m)
Highest Rainfall Mausinram near Cherrapunji (1082 cms per annum)
Highest Road Road at Khardungla, (in Leh-Manali Sector)
Highest Tower Qutb Minar, Delhi, 88.4m
Highest Waterfall Gersoppa Waterfall (292 meters high) in Mysuru
Largest Animal Fair Sonepur (Bihar)
Largest Auditorium Sri Shanmukhanand Hall (Mumbai)
Largest Botanical Garden Indian Botanical Garden, Shibpur, Kolkata, WB
Largest Cave Amarnath (J&K)
Largest Cave Temple Kailash Temple, Ellora (Maharashtra)
Largest Church Saint Cathedral (Goa)
Largest Delta Sundarbans Delta, W. Bengal
Largest Desert Great Indian Desert (Thar), (Rajasthan)
Largest District Kachchh, Gujarat
Largest Dome Gol Gumbaz, Bijapur-44m
Largest Fresh Water Lake Kolleru Lake (Andhra Pradesh)
Largest Gurudwara Golden Temple, Amritsar
Largest Lake (Saline Water) Chilka Lake, Odisha
Largest Lake (Freshwater) Wular Lake, Kashmir
Largest Man-Made Lake Govind Vallabh Pant Sagar (Rihand Dam)
Largest Museum India Museum, Kolkata
Largest Planetarium Birla Planetarium, Kolkata
Largest Plateau Deccan Plateau
Largest Populated City Mumbai
Largest Port Mumbai
Largest Public Sector Bank State Bank of India
Largest River Island Majuli (Brahmaputra River, Asom)
Largest River without Delta Narmada and Tapti
Largest State (Area) Rajasthan
Largest State (Population) Uttar Pradesh
Largest Zoo Zoological Garden, Kolkata.
Longest Beach Marina Beach, Chennai
Longest Canal Indira Gandhi Canal or Rajasthan Canal (Rajasthan)
Longest Cantilever Span Bridge Howrah Bridge
Longest Dam Hirakud Dam, Odisha
Longest Glacier Siachen 76km, Indo-Pak border.
Longest Electric Railway Line Delhi to Kolkata via Patna
Longest National Highway NH-44 (North-South NH) Srinagar to Kanyakumari - 3745 km
Longest Platform Gorakhpur, UP -1366.33m (Kollam, Kerala-1180.5m; Kharagpur,

WB-1072.5m in Length) - also the longest railway station in world

Longest Railway Route Dibrugarh to Kanyakumari: Vivek Exp. 4,286 km; 82:30 hrs

Longest River Bridge Dhola-Sadiya (on Brahmaputra), 9.15km (Asom); 3.55km longer than Bandra-Worli Sea Link, Mumbai (5.6 km).

Longest River Ganga (2640 km)

Longest Tributary River of India: Yamuna

Longest Road Grand Trunk Road

Longest Road Tunnel Chenani-Nashri Tunnel-9.28km, J&K).

Longest Railway Tunnel Pir Panjal Rly. Tunnel, (Jawahar tunnel), (J&K).

Oldest Church St.Thomas Syro-Malabar Church at Palayur, Trichur (Kerala)

Oldest Museum Indian Museum, Kolkata - 1814

Oldest Observatory Jantar Mantar, Delhi

Oldest Petroleum Refinery Digboi, Asom

Smallest State (Area) Goa

Smallest State (Population) Sikkim

State with Longest Coastline Gujarat

State with Longest Coastline of South India Andhra Pradesh

State-wise Largest Area Under Forest MP

Tallest Building Imperial Tower- I, II Mumbai; 254 m.

Tallest TV Tower Fazilka, Punjab

The Highest Tourist Spot in India Siachen Base Camp; Trek Area Saltoro Ridge of Siachen Base Camp to Kumar Logistics Base

World's Tallest Statue Statue of Unity, 182 m., at Sadhu Bet island, Gujarat.

World's Most Expensive Residential Property Antilia, Mumbai. $1 bn

World's Highest &Coldest Battlefield Siachen

Tourists at Siachen Base Camp

Social Indicators (2018)

State/UT	CBR	CDR	IMR
Andaman & Nicobar Is	11.2	5.3	9
Andhra Pradesh	16.0	6.7	29
Arunachal Pradesh	17.9	6.0	37
Asom	21.1	6.4	41
Bihar	26.2	5.8	32
Chandigarh	13.3	4.3	13
Chhattisgarh	22.5	8.0	41
Dadra & Nagar Haveli	22.9	3.8	13
Daman & Diu	19.6	4.5	16
Delhi	14.7	3.3	13
Goa	12.4	5.9	7
Gujarat	19.7	5.9	28
Haryana	20.3	5.9	30
Himachal Pradesh	15.7	6.9	19
Jammu and Kashmir	15.4	4.9	22
Jharkhand	22.6	5.4	30
Karnataka	17.2	6.3	23
Kerala	13.9	6.9	7
Lakshadweep	15.3	5.6	14
Madhya Pradesh	24.6	6.7	48
Maharashtra	15.6	5.5	19
Manipur	14.3	4.5	11
Meghalaya	22.1	5.8	33
Mizoram	14.8	4.1	5
Nagaland	12.9	3.5	4
Odisha	18.2	7.3	40
Puducherry	13.7	6.9	11
Punjab	14.8	6.6	20
Rajasthan	24.0	5.9	37
Sikkim	16.3	4.5	7
Tamil Nadu	14.7	6.5	15
Telangana	16.9	6.3	27
Tripura	13.0	5.5	27
Uttar Pradesh	25.6	6.6	43
Uttarakhand	16.7	6.2	31
West Bengal	15.0	5.6	22
All India	**20.0**	**6.2**	**32**

Foot Note: •Crude Birth Rate means number of live birth per 1000 women in a year. •Crude Death Rate means number of death per 1000 person in a year. •Infant Mortality Rate means number of death of infant of less than one year per 1000 live birth. •Neo-Natal Mortality Rates means number of infant death less than 7 days of life per 1000 live birth.

Source: Sample Registration System, Bulletin, various issues, Office of the Registrar General and Census Commissioner, Ministry of Home Affairs, Government of India.

20

WORLD PANORAMA

- List of Countries by Continent
- Countrywise Heads of State
- Profile of Select Countries
- The United Nations
- UN Organisations
- The European Union
- International Organisations

List of Countries by Continent

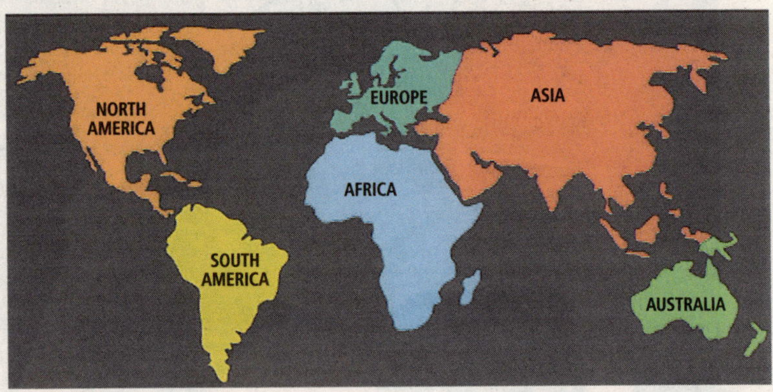

AFRICA (54)

Algeria
Angola
Benin
Botswana
Burkina Faso
Burundi
Cabo Verde
Cameroon
Central African Republic
Chad
Comoros
Congo (Dem. Rep.)
Congo, Republic of
Djibouti
Egypt
Equatorial Guinea
Eritrea
Ethiopia
Gabon
Gambia
Ghana
Guinea
Guinea-Bissau
Ivory Coast
Kenya
Lesotho
Liberia
Libya
Madagascar
Malawi
Mali
Mauritania
Mauritius
Morocco
Mozambique
Namibia
Niger
Nigeria
Rwanda
Sao Tome and Principe
Senegal
Seychelles
Sierra Leone
Somalia
South Africa
South Sudan
Sudan
Swaziland
Tanzania
Togo
Tunisia
Uganda
Zambia
Zimbabwe
Afghanistan
Armenia
Azerbaijan
Bahrain
Bangladesh
Bhutan
Brunei
Cambodia

ASIA (47)

China
Cyprus
East Timor
Georgia
India
Indonesia
Iran
Iraq
Israel
Japan
Jordan
Kazakhstan
Korea (north)
Korea (south)
Kuwait
Kyrgyzstan
Laos
Lebanon
Malaysia
Maldives
Mongolia
Myanmar
Nepal
Oman
Pakistan
Philippines
Qatar
Saudi Arabia
Singapore
Sri Lanka
Syria
Tajikistan
Thailand
Turkey
Turkmenistan
United Arab Emirates
Uzbekistan
Vietnam
Yemen

EUROPE (43)

Albania
Andorra
Austria
Belarus
Belgium
Bosnia and Herzegovina
Bulgaria
Croatia
Czech Republic
Denmark
Estonia
Finland
France
Germany
Greece
Hungary
Iceland
Ireland
Italy
Latvia
Liechtenstein
Lithuania
Luxembourg
Macedonia
Malta
Moldova
Monaco
Montenegro
Netherlands
Norway
Poland
Portugal
Romania
Russian Federation

World Time Zones

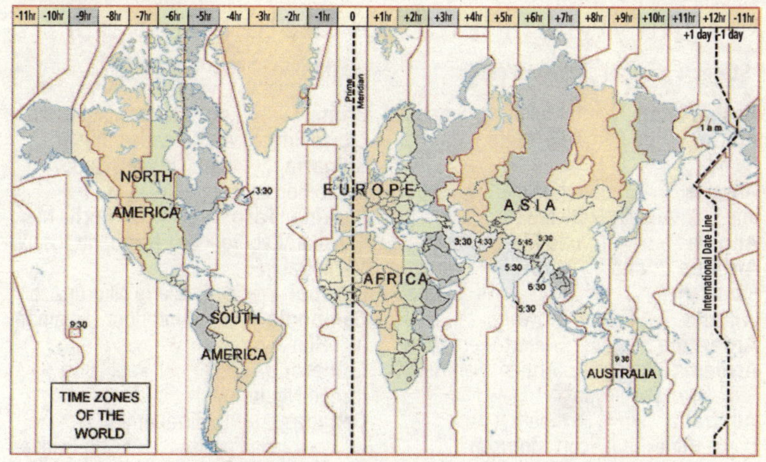

World Population 7,874,965,825

Top 10 Countries	Population (6/8/2021)	Area (km²)	Density	Growth Rate	World %	Rank
China	1,444,598,488	9,706,961 km²	149/km²	0.34%	18.34%	1
India	1,394,469,466	3,287,590 km²	424/km²	0.97%	17.69%	2
United States	333,068,517	9,372,610 km²	36/km²	0.58%	4.23%	3
Indonesia	276,586,642	1,904,569 km²	145/km²	1.04%	3.51%	4
Pakistan	225,538,787	881,912 km²	255/km²	1.95%	2.86%	5
Brazil	214,106,098	8,515,767 km²	25/km²	0.67%	2.72%	6
Nigeria	211,817,683	923,768 km²	229/km²	2.55%	2.68%	7
Bangladesh	166,430,187	147,570 km²	1,127/km²	0.98%	2.11%	8
Russia	145,910,405	17,098,242 km²	9/km²	-0.02%	1.85%	9
Mexico	130,367,414	1,964,375 km²	66/km²	1.03%	1.65%	10

San Marino
Serbia
Slovakia
Slovenia
Spain
Sweden
Switzerland
Ukraine
United Kingdom
Vatican

N. AMERICA (23)
Antigua and Barbuda
Bahamas
Barbados
Belize
Canada
Costa Rica
Cuba
Dominica
Dominican Rep.
El Salvador
Grenada
Guatemala
Haiti
Honduras
Jamaica
Mexico
Nicaragua
Panama
St Kitts and Nevis
St Lucia
St Vincent and the Grenadines
Trinidad and Tobago
USA

S. AMERICA (12
Argentina
Bolivia
Brazil
Chile
Colombia
Ecuador
Guyana
Paraguay
Peru
Suriname
Uruguay
Venezuela

OCEANIA (14)
Australia
Fiji
Kiribati
Marshall Is.
Micronesia
Nauru
New Zealand
Palau
Papua New Guinea
Samoa
Solomon Islands
Tonga
Tuvalu
Vanuatu

Note: Only UN member states are listed. In this list, countries are classified according to political criteria, using the geoscheme created by the United Nations Statistics Division.

Countrywise Heads of State (As on 05.08.2021)

State	President	Prime Minister

Afghanistan Dy PM: Mullah AG Baradar
Albania President: Ilir Meta PM: Edi Rama
Algeria President: Abdelmadjid Tebboune PM: Abdelaziz Djerad
Angola President: João MG Lourenço
Antigua and Barbuda Queen: Elizabeth II Governor-Gen.: Sir Rodney Williams PM: Gaston Browne
Argentina President: Alberto Fernández
Armenia President: Armen Sarkissian PM: Nikol Pashinyan
Australia Queen: Elizabeth II Gov. Gen.: David Hurley PM: Scott Morrison
Austria President: Alexander Van der Bellen Federal Chancellor: Sebastian Kurz
Azerbaijan President: Ilham Aliyev PM: Ali Asadov
Bahamas, The Queen: Elizabeth II Governor-General: Sir Cornelius A. Smith PM: Hubert Minnis
Bahrain King: Sheikh Hamad bin Isa Al Khalifa PM: Prince Khalifa bin Salman Al Khalifa
Bangladesh President: Abdul Hamid PM: Sheikh Hasina
Barbados Queen: Elizabeth II Gov. Gen.: Dame Sandra Mason PM: Mia Mottley
Belarus President: Alexander Lukashenko PM: Roman Golovchenko
Belgium King: Philippe PM: Sophie Wilmes
Belize Queen: Elizabeth II Gov. Gen.: Sir Colville Young PM: Dean Barrow
Benin President: Patrice Talon Prime Minister - Lionel Zinsou
Bhutan King: Jigme Khesar Namgyel Wangchuck PM: Lotay Tshering
Bolivia Interim President: Jeanine Áñez
Bosnia and Herzegovina President: Zeljiko Komsic Chairman of the Council of Ministers: Šefik Džaferovic
Botswana President: Mokgweetsi Masisi
Brazil President: Jair Bolsonaro

State	President	Prime Minister

Brunei Sultan and PM: Hassanal Bolkiah Crown Prince - Al-Muhtadee Billah
Bulgaria President: Rumen Radev PM: Boyko Borisov
Burkina Faso President: Roch Marc Christian Kaboré PM: Christophe Joseph Marie Dabiré
Burundi President: Pierre Nkurunziza
Cambodia King: Norodom Sihamoni PM: Hun Sen
Cameroon President: Paul Biya PM: Joseph Ngute
Canada Queen: Elizabeth II Governor General: Julie Payette PM: Justin Trudeau
Cape Verde President: Jorge Carlos Fonseca PM: Ulisses Correia e Silva
Central African Rep. President: Faustin-Archange Touadéra PM: Firmin Ngrebada
Chad President: Idriss Deby
Chile President: Sebastián Piñera
China General Secretary of the Communist Party: Xi Jinping President: Xi Jinping Premier: Li Keqiang
Colombia President: Iván Duque Marquez
Comoros President: Azali Assoumani
Congo, Democratic Republic of the President: Félix Tshisekedi PM: Sylvestre Ilunga
Congo, Rep. President: Denis Sassou Nguesso PM: Clement Mouamba
Cote D'Ivoire : President: Alassane Dramane Ouattara; PM: Amadou Gon Coulibaly
Croatia President: Zoran Milanovic PM: Andrej Plenkovic
Cuba First Secretary of the Communist Party: Raúl Castro President: Miguel Díaz -Canel PM: Manuel Marrero Cruz
Cyprus President: Nicos Anastasiades
Czech Rep. President: Miloš Zeman PM: Andrej Babiš
Denmark Queen: Margrethe II PM:

Mette Frederiksen
Djibouti President: Ismaïl Omar Guelleh PM: Abdoulkader Kamil Mohamed
Dominica President: Charles Savarin PM: Roosevelt Skerrit
Dominican Republic President: Danilo Medina
East Timor President: Francisco Guterres PM: Taur Matan Ruak
Ecuador President: Lenin Moreno
Egypt President: Abdel Fattah el-Sisi PM: Moustafa Madbouly
El Salvador President: Nayib Bukele
Equatorial Guinea President: Teodoro Obiang Nguema Mbasogo PM: Francisco Pascual Obama Asue
Eritrea President: Isaias Afwerki
Estonia President: Kersti Kaljulaid PM: Juri Ratas
Eswatini King: Mswati III PM: Cleopas Dlamini
Ethiopia President: Sahle-Work Zewde PM: Abiy Ahmed Ali
Fiji President: Jioji Konrote PM: Frank Bainimarama
Finland President: Sauli Niinistö PM: Sanna Marin
France President: Emmanuel Macron PM: Edouard Philippe
Gabon President: Ali Bongo Ondimba PM: Julien Nkoghe Bekale
Gambia President: Adama Barrow
Georgia President: Salome Zourabichvili PM: Giorgi Gakharia
Germany President: Frank-Walter Steinmeier Fed. Chancellor: Angela Merkel
Ghana President: Nana Akufo-Addo
Greece President: Katerina Sakellaropoulou PM: Kyriakos Mitsotakis
Grenada Queen: Elizabeth II Gov. Gen.: Dame Cécile La Grenade PM: Keith Mitchell
Guatemala President: Alejandro Giammattei
Guinea President: Alpha Condé PM: Ibrahima Kassory Fofana
Guinea-Bissau President: Umaro Sissoco Embaló PM: Nuno Gomes Nabiam
Guyana President: David Granger PM: Moses V. Nagamootoo
Haiti President: Jovenel Moise PM: Joseph Joute
Honduras President: Juan Orlando Hernández
Hungary President: János Áder PM: Viktor Orbán
Iceland President: Guðni Th. Jóhannesson PM Katrín Jakobsdóttir
India President: Ram Nath Kovind PM: Narendra Modi
Indonesia President: Joko Widodo
Iran Supreme Leader: Ali Khamenei President: Hassan Rouhani
Iraq President: Barham Salih PM: Mustafa Al-Kadhimi
Ireland President: Michael D. Higgins Prime Minister - Leo Varadkar
Israel President: Reuven Rivlin PM: Naftali Bennett
Italy President: Sergio Mattarella PM: Giuseppe Conte
Ivory Coast President: Alassane Ouattara PM: Patrick Achi
Jamaica Queen: Elizabeth II Gov. Gen.: Sir Patrick Allen PM: Andrew Holness
Japan Emperor: Naruhito PM: Shinzo Abe
Jordan King: Abdullah II PM: Omar Razzaz
Kazakhstan President: Qasym-Zhomart Toqaev PM: Askar Mamin
Kenya President: Uhuru M Kenyatta
Kiribati President: Taneti Maamau
Korea North, NDE: Supreme leader: Kim Jong-un
Korea, South: President - Moon Jae -in; Prime Minister - Chung Sye-kyun
Kuwait Emir: Nawafal -Ahmad al-Jaber Al -Sabah PM: Sheikh Sabah Al-Khalid Al -Sabah

Nawafal-Ahmad al-Jaber Al-Sabah

Kyrgyzstan President: Sooronbay Jeenbekov PM: Kubatbek Boronov
Laos President: Bounnhang Vorachith PM: Thongloun Sisoulith

Latvia President: Egils Levits PM: Krišjanis Karinš
Lebanon President: Michel Aoun PM: Hassan Diab
Lesotho King: Letsie III PM: Moeketsi Majoro
Liberia President: George Weah
Libya PM: Fayez al-Sarraj
Liechtenstein Prince Regnant: Hans-Adam II Head of Government: Adrian Hasler
Lithuania President: Gitanas Nauseda PM: Saulius Skvernelis
Luxembourg Grand Duke: Henri PM: Xavier Bettel
Macedonia, North President: Stevo Pendarovski PM: Oliver Spasovski
Madagascar President: Andry Rajoelina PM: Christian Ntsay
Malawi President: Lazarus Chakwera
Malaysia King: Abdullah of Pahang PM: Muhyiddin Yassin
Maldives President: Ibrahim Md. Solih
Mali Interim President: Ibrahim Boubacar Keita PM: Boubou Cisse
Malta President: George Vella PM: Robert Abela
Marshall Islands President: David Kabua
Mauritania President: Md. Ould Ghazouani PM: Ismail Ould Bedde Ould Cheikh Sidiya
Mauritius President: Prithvirajsing Roopun PM: Pravind Jugnauth
Mexico President: Andrés Manuel López Obrador
Micronesia President: David W. Panuelo
Moldova President: Igor Dodon PM: Ion Chicu
Monaco Sovereign Prince: Albert II Minister of State: Pierre Dartout
Mongolia President: Khaltmaagiin Battulga PM: Ukhnaagiin Khurelsukh
Montenegro President: Milo Dukanovic PM: Dusko Markovic
Morocco King: Mohammed VI Head of Government: Saadeddine Othmani
Mozambique President: Filipe Nyusi PM: Carlos Agostinho do Rosário
Myanmar President: Win Myint State Counsellor: NA
Namibia President: Hage Geingob PM: Saara Kuugongelwa Amadhila
Nauru President: Lionel Aingimea
Nepal President: Bidhya Devi Bhandari PM: Khadga Prasad Sharma Oli
Netherlands King: Willem-Alexander PM: Mark Rutte
New Zealand Queen: Elizabeth II Gov. Gen.: Dame Cindy Kiro PM: Jacinda Ardern
Nicaragua President: Daniel Ortega
Niger President: Mahamadou Issoufou PM: Brigi Rafini
Nigeria President: Muhammadu Buhari
Norway King Harald V PM: Erna Solberg
Oman Sultan: Haitham bin Tariq Al Said Dy PM: Fahd bin Mahmoud al Said
Pakistan President: Arif Alvi PM: Imran Khan
Palau President: Tommy Remengesau.
Palestine President: Mahmoud Abbas PM: Mohammad Shtayyeh
Panama President: Laurentino Cortizo
Papua New Guinea Queen: Elizabeth II Governor General: Bob Dadae PM: James Marape
Paraguay President: Mario Abdo Benítez
Peru President: Martín Vizcarra Prime Minister: Vicente Zeballos
Philippines President: Rodrigo Duterte
Poland President: Andrzej Duda President of the Council of Ministers: Mateusz Morawiecki
Portugal President: Marcelo Rebelo de Sousa PM: António Costa
Qatar Emir: Sheikh Tamim bin Hamad Al Thani PM: Sheikh Khalid bin Khalifa bin Abdul Aziz Al Thani
Romania President: Klaus Iohannis PM: Ludovic Orban
Russia President: Vladimir Putin PM: Mikhail Mishustin
Rwanda President: Paul Kagame PM: Édouard Ngirente
Saint Kitts and Nevis Queen: Elizabeth II Gov. Gen.: Sir Tapley Seaton PM: Timothy Harris

Saint Lucia Queen: Elizabeth II Governor- General: Sir Neville Cenac PM: Allen Chastanet
Saint Vincent and the Grenadines Queen: Elizabeth II Gov. Gen.: Dame Susan Dougan PM:. Ralph Gonsalves
Samoa PM: Tuilaepa Aiono Sailele Malielegaoi
San Marino Captain Regent: Gian Carlo Venturini Captain Regent: Marco Nicolini
São Tomé and Príncipe President: Evaristo Carvalho PM: Jorge Bom Jesus
Saudi Arabia King: Salman bin Abdulaziz Al Saud Deputy PM:
Senegal President: Macky Sall PM: Mohammed Dionne
Serbia President: Aleksandar Vucic PM: Ana Brnabic
Seychelles President: Danny Faure
Sierra Leone President: Julius Maada Bio Chief Minister:
Singapore President: Halimah Yacob PM: Lee Hsien Loong
Slovakia President: Zuzana Caputová PM: Eduard Heger
Slovenia President: Borut Pahor PM: Janez Janša
Solomon Islands Queen: Elizabeth II Gov. Gen.: Sir David Vunagi PM: Manasseh Sogavare
Somalia President: Mohamed Abdullahi Mohamed PM: Hassan Ali Khayre
South Africa President: Cyril Ramaphosa
S. Sudan President: Salva Kiir Mayardit
Spain King: Felipe VI President of the Government: Pedro Sánchez
Sri Lanka President: Gotabaya Rajapaksa PM: Mahinda Rajapaksa
Sudan: Abdel Fattah al-Burhan PM: Abdalla Hamdok
Suriname President: Desi Bouterse
Switzerland President: Guy Parmelin
Sweden King: Carl XVI Gustaf PM: Stefan Löfven
Syria President: Bashar al-Assad PM: Hussein Arnous
Tajikistan President: Emomali Rahmon PM: Kokhir Rasulzoda

Tanzania President: Samia Suluhu Hassan PM: Kassim Majaliwa

Samia Suluhu Hassan

Thailand King: Maha Vajiralongkorn PM: Prayut Chan-o-cha
Togo President: Faure Gnassingbé PM: Komi Selom Klassou
Tonga King: Tupou VI PM: Pohiva Tu'i'onetoa
Trinidad and Tobago President: Paula-Mae Weekes PM: Keith Rowley
Tunisia President: Kaïs Saïed PM: Elyes Fakhfakh
Turkey President: Recep Tayyip Erdogan
Turkmenistan President: Gurbanguly Berdimuhamedow
Tuvalu Queen: Elizabeth II Gov. Gen.: Sir Iakoba Italeli PM: Kausea Natano
Uganda President: Yoweri Museveni PM: Ruhakana Rugunda
Ukraine President: Volodymyr Zelensky PM: Denys Shmyhal
United Arab Emirates President: Sheikh Khalifa bin Zayed Al Nahyan PM: Sheikh Mohammed bin Rashid Al Maktoum
United Kingdom Queen: Elizabeth II PM: Boris Johnson
United States President: Joe Biden
Uruguay President: Luis Lacalle Pou
Uzbekistan President: Shavkat Mirziyoyev PM: Abdulla Aripov
Vanuatu President: Tallis Obed Moses PM: Bob Loughman
Vatican City Sovereign: Pope Francis President of the Governorate: Cardinal Giuseppe Bertello
Venezuela President: Nicolás Maduro
Vietnam President: Nguyen Phu Trong PM: Nguyen Xuan Phuc
Yemen President: Abdrabbuh Mansur Hadi PM: Maeen Abdulmalik Saeed
Zambia President: Edgar Lungu
Zimbabwe President: Emmerson Mnangagwa.

Profile of Select Countries

Rank	Country	2021 Population	Growth Rate	Area	Density (km²)
1	China	1,444,216,107	0.34%	9,706,961	148/km²
2	India	1,393,409,038	0.97%	3,287,590	416/km²
3	USA	332,915,073	0.58%	9,372,610	35/km²
4	Indonesia	276,361,783	1.04%	1,904,569	142/km²
5	Pakistan	225,199,937	1.95%	881,912	246/km²
6	Brazil	213,993,437	0.67%	8,515,767	25/km²
7	Nigeria	211,400,708	2.55%	923,768	218/km²
8	Bangladesh	166,303,498	0.98%	147,570	1,105/km²
9	Russia	145,912,025	-0.02%	17,098,242	9/km²
10	Mexico	130,262,216	1.03%	1,964,375	65/km²

Top Ten Countries by Nominal GDP (at Current US Dollar Exchange Rates)

Country	Nominal GDP (in trillions)	PPP Adjusted (in trillions)	GDP Annual Growth (%)	GDP Per Capita (in thousands)
USA	$21.43	$21.43	2.2%	$65,298
China	$14.34	$23.52	6.1%	$10,262
Japan	$5.08	$5.46	0.7%	$40,247
Germany	$3.86	$4.68	0.6%	$46,445
India	$2.87	$9.56	4.2%	$2,100
UK	$2.83	$3.25	1.5%	$42,330
France	$2.72	$3.32	1.5%	$40,493.9
Italy	$2.00	$2.67	0.3%	$33,228.2
Brazil	$1.84	$3.23	1.1%	$8,717
Canada	$1.74	$1.93	1.7%	$46,195

Country	Capital/ Location, Continent	Area (sq km)	Population (million)	Currency	p.c.i. ($) IMF 2021 E	HDI Rank 2020 •High •Low
Afghanistan	Kabul / Asia	652,230 Landlocked	33.435	Afghani	592	169
Argentina	Buenos Aires / S. America	2,780,400 (coastline) 4,989	44.17	Peso	9,122	46
Australia	Canberra / Australia	7,692,024 (coastline) 25,760	24.698	Australian dollar	62723	8•

World Population History Timeline

Year	Population	Growth Rate
-10000	4,000,000	--
-8000	5,320,000	0.01%
-5000	22,500,000	0.05%
-4000	46,750,000	0.07%
-2000	27,000,000	0.07%
-1000	50,000,000	-0.06%
-800	100,000,000	0.35%
-500	100,000,000	0.00%
-400	157,500,000	0.46%
-200	202,000,000	0.12%
1	235,000,000	0.08%
500	198,500,000	-0.01%
1000	278,600,000	0.19%
1500	458,800,000	0.23%
2000	6,145,000,000	1.43%
2010	6,958,000,000	1.25%
2020	7,715,000,000	1.15%

World Population	Growth
1:	235 million
1000:	278 million
1500:	458 million
1650:	500 million
1750:	700 million
1804:	1 billion
1850:	1.2 billion
1900:	1.6 billion
1927:	2 billion
1950:	2.55 billion
1955:	2.8 billion
1960:	3 billion
1970:	3.7 billion
1985:	4.85 billion
2000:	6.14 billion
2010:	7 billion
2025:	8 billion

Human Development Index

Three dimensions of human development •the health (a long and healthy life), •education (knowledge), and •income (decent living standards), in a given country provides a measure of human development which is comparable between countries and over time. •The 2020 indicators :life expectancy at birth; expected years of schooling for children; mean years of schooling for adults; and gross national income; per capita. The indicators are used to create a health index, an education index and an income index.

- Very high (> 0.800)
- High (0.700-0.700)
- Medium (0.550-0.699)
- Low (< 0.549)
- Data unavailable

Date of Formation	Government Type	Life Expectancy	Literacy (%)	Language (%)	Religion
19.8.1919	Presidential Islamic Republic	60.5	38.15	Pushtu Persian	Muslim-99.7
9.7.1816	Presidential Republic	76.3	98.08	Spanish Italian	Christian-85.2 unaffiliated - 12.2 Muslim - 1
1.01.1901	Parliamentary democracy (Fed. parliament) constitutional monarchy	82.8	99	English	Christian-67.3 unaffiliated - 24.2 Buddhists-2.7 Muslim - 2.4

Country	Capital	Area (sq km)	Population (million)	Currency	p.c.i. ($)	HDI rank •High •Low
Austria	Vienna/ Europe	83,871 Landlocked	8.64	Euro	53859	18
Bahrain	Manama / W. Asia	765 (Island)	1.42	Bahraini dinar	24294	42
Bangladesh	Dhaka / S. Asia	147,570	164.919	Taka	2122	133
Belgium	Brussels / Europe	30,528 (coastline) 66.5	11.471	Euro	50103	14
Bhutan	Thimphu / S. Asia	38,394 Landlocked	.795	Ngultrum	3,296	129
Brazil	Brasilia / S. America	8,515,767 (Coastline) 7, 491	212.161	Real	7011	84
Canada	Ottawa / N. America	9,984,670 (Coastline) 202,080	36.826	Canadian dollar	49222	16
Cen. African Republic	Bangui / Africa	622,984 Landlocked	5.012	CFA Franc	552	188•
Chad	N'Djamena / Africa	1,284,000 Landlocked	14.453	CFA Franc	8741	187•
Chile	Santiago / S. America	756,102 (coastline) 6,435	18.385	Chilean peso	15,617	43
China	Beijing / Asia	9,572,900 (coastline) 14,500	1,397.955	Renminbi	11,819	85
Hong Kong	*Victoria / Asia*	*2,755 (coastline) 733*	*7.474*	*Hong Kong dollar*	*49,036*	*4•*
Congo, D.R. of(Zaire)	Kinshasa / Africa	2,344,858 (Coastline) 37	79.424	Congolese franc	500	175

Date of Formation	Government Type	Life Expec-tancy	Literacy (%)	Language (%)	Religion
1156	Fed. Parlia Republic	81.5	98	German	Christian-80.4 unaffiliated - 13.5 Muslim-5.4
15.8.1971	Constitutional monarchy	76.9	95.7	Arabic, English, Farsi, Urdu	Muslim -70.3 Christian - 14.5
26.3. 1971 16.12.1971 (Victory day)	Parliamentary republic	71.8	61.54	Bangla	Muslim-89.8 Hindu-9.1
4.10.1830	Federal parliamentary democracy; constitutional monarchy	81.1	99	Dutch French German– all official	Christian-64.2 unaffiliated-29 Muslim-5.9
8.8.1949	Constitutional monarchy	69.8	64.88	Dzongkha Tshanglakha Lhotshamkha	Buddhist- 74.7 Hindu -22.6
7.9.1822	Federal presidential republic	75	92.58	Portuguese (official), Spanish, French	Christian-88.9 unaffiliated-7.9 Folk religion - 2.8
1.7.1867	Federal parliamen-tary democracy (constitutional monarchy)	82.2	99	English French	Christian-69 unaffiliated - 23.7 Muslim- 2.1
13.8.1960	Presidential republic	52.5	36.75	French Sangho	Christian-89.5 Muslim-8.5 unaffiliated - 1
11.8.1960	Presidential republic	53.1	40.17	French Arabic, Sara	Muslim-55.3 Christian-40.6
18.9.1810	Presidential republic	80.5	97.29	Spanish	Christian-89.4
1.10.1949 (People's Republic established)	Communist state	76.1	96.37	Mandarin Chinese Wu, Min Cantonese	unaffiliated- 52.2 Folk religion-21.9 Buddhist- 18.2
-	*Presidential limited democracy*	-	*93.5*	*Chinese (Cantonese) English (both official)*	*Chinese folk religion, Buddhism Taoism*
30.6.1960	Semi-Presidential republic	59.8	77.28	French, Kiswahili Lingala Kikongo Tshiluba	Christian-95.8 unaffiliated-1.8

Country	Capital	Area (sq km)	Population (million)	Currency	p.c.i. ($)	HDI rank •High •Low
Congo. Rep.	Brazzaville / Africa	342,000 (Coastline) 169	4.736	CFA Franc	2,505	149
Costa Rica	San Jose C. America	51,100 (Coastline) 1,290	4.925	Costa Rican colon	11806	62
Cote d' Ivoire (Ivory Coast)	Yamoussou-kro(official), Abidjan (de facto)	322,463 (Coastline) 515	23.231	CFA Franc	2567	162
Cuba	Havana / N. Atlantic	109,884 (Coastline) 3,735	11.445	Cuban peso	NA	70
Denmark	Copenhagen / Europe	43,094 (Coastline) 7,314	5.729	Danish krone	67218	10
Egypt	Cairo / N. Africa	1,002,450 (Coastline) 2,450)	93.943	Egyptian pound	3832	116
Estonia	Tallinn / Europe	45,227 (Coastline) 3,794	1.312	Euro	26740	29
Fiji	Suva / Pacific	18,272 (Island)	.899	Fijian dollar	5069	93
Finland	Helsinki / Europe	338,424 (Coastline) 1,250	5.557	Euro	54330	11
France	Paris / Europe	640,679 (Coastline) 4,853	64.986	Euro	44995	26
Germany	Berlin / Europe	357,114 (Coastline) 2,389	81.133	Euro	51860	6•
Ghana	Accra / Africa	238,533 (Coastline) 539	28.112	Cedi	2,374	138

Date of Formation	Government Type	Life Expectancy	Literacy (%)	Language (%)	Religion
15.8.1960	Presidential republic	64.7	79.31	French Lingala Monokutuba Kikongo	Christian-85.9 Unaffiliated- 9 Folk religion - 2.8
15.9.1821	Presidential republic	79.6	97.75	Spanish (official), English	Christian-90.9
7.8.1960	Presidential republic	50.97	43.11	French and tribal	Christian-44.1 Muslim-37.5 Folk religion- 10.2
20.5.1902	Communist state	79.1	99.71	Spanish	Christian - 59.2 unaffiliated - 23
parliamentary monarchy constitutional monarchy	Parliamentary constitutional	80.6	99	Danish	Christian - 83.5 unaffiliated - 11.8 Muslim-4.1
28.2.1922	Presidential republic	70.9	75.23	Arabic	Muslim - 94.9 Christian-5.1
20.8.1991	Parliamentary republic	77.6	99.82	Estonian	Unaffiliated - 59.6 Christian- 39.9
10.10.1970	Parliamentary republic	69.9	93.7	English, Fijian, Hindi	Christian-64.4 Hindu-27.9 Muslim-6.3
6.12.1917	Parliamentary republic	81.1	99	Finnish Swedish	Christian-81.6 unaffiliated- 17.6
486 (Unification by Clovis)	Semi–presidential republic	82.4	99	French	Christian- 63 unaffiliated - 28 Muslim-7.5
3.10.1990 (unification W.Germany & E.Germany)	Federal parliamentary republic	81	99	German	Christian- 68.7 unaffiliated- 24.7 Muslim-5.8
6.3.1957	Presidential republic	62.4	76.57	English African languages + Akan, Ewe	Christian-74.9 Muslim-15.8 Folk religion-4.9

Country	Capital	Area (sq km)	Population (million)	Currency	p.c.i. ($)	HDI rank •High •Low
Greece	Athens / Europe	131,990 (Coastline) 13,676	10.976	Euro	19,673	32
Honduras	Tegucigalpa D.C / C. America	112,492 (Coastline) 832	8.292	Lempira	2,586	132
Hungary	Budapest / Europe	93,033 Landlocked	9.86	Forint	18075	40
India	New Delhi / S Asia	3,287,263 (Coastline) 7,000	1340.809	Rupee	2,191	131
Indonesia	East Kalimantan SE Asia	1,904,569 (Coastline) 54,716	262.763	Rupiah	4,256	107
Iran	Tehran / W Asia	1,648,195 (Coastline) 2,440	81.525	Iranian Rial (Local: Toman)	8034	70
Iraq	Baghdad / W Asia	438,317 (Coastline) 58	37.653	Iraqi dinar	4632	123
Ireland	Dublin / W Europe	70,273 Island	4.753	Euro	94556	2•
Israel	Jerusalem / W Asia	20,770 (Coastline) 273	8.246	Israeli new shekel	47602	19
Italy	Rome / S Europe	301,336 (Coastline) 7,600	60.113	Euro	34997	29
Japan	Tokyo / E Asia	377,930 (Coastline) 29,751	126.732	Yen	42928	19
Jordan	Amman / W Asia	89,342 (Coastline) 26	7.769	Jordanian dinar	4,358	102
Kenya	Nairobi / E Africa	580,367 (Coastline) 536	47.4	Kenyan shilling	2129	143

Date of Formation	Government Type	Life Expectancy	Literacy (%)	Language (%)	Religion
25.3.1821	Parliamentary republic	81	97.68	Greek	Christian - 88.1 unaffiliated - 6.1 Muslim - 5.3
15.9.1821	Presidential republic	74.6	88.48	Spanish Amerindian dialects	Christian - 87.6 unaffiliated -10.5
1000 (Date of unification)	Parliamentary republic	75.9	99.05	Hungarian	Christian - 81 unaffiliated -18.6
15.8.1947	Federal parliamentary republic	68.3	72.13	Hindi (official), English	Hindu-79.5 Muslim-14.4 Christian- 2.5 Others - 2.3
17.8.1945	Presidential republic	69.1	93.88	Indonesian	Muslim-87.2 Christian - 9.9 Hindu - 1.7
1.4.1979	Theocratic republic	75.5	86.84	Persian (Farsi), Azeri, Turkic & Turkic dialects,	Muslim-99.5 Kurdish, Arabic
3.10.1932	Federal parliamentary republic	68.9	79.68	Arabic and Kurdish	Muslim-99
6.12.1921	Parliamentary republic	81.4	99	English and Irish (official)	Christian-92 unaffiliated - 6.2
14.5.1948	Parliamentary democracy	82.5	97.8	Hebrew (official), Arabic	Jewish-75.6 Muslim-18.6 unaffiliated - 3.1 Christian-2
17.3.1861	Parliamentary republic	82.7	99.15	Italian	Christian- 83.3 unaffiliated -12.4 Muslim - 3.7
660 B.C.	Parliamentary constitutional monarchy	83.7	99	Japanese	unaffiliated- 57 Buddhism, Shinto - 36.2
25.5.1946	Parliamentary constitutional monarchy	74.1	96.66	Arabic, English	Muslim-97.2 Christian - 2.2
12.12.1963	Presidential republic	63.4	77.96	English and Kiswahili (official)	Christian - 84.8 Muslim- 9.7 unaffiliated-2.5

Country	Capital	Area (sq km)	Population (million)	Currency	p.c.i. ($)	HDI rank •High •Low
Korea (North)	Pyongyang /E Asia	120,538 (Coastline) 2,495	25.461	North Korean won	NA	
Korea (South)	Seoul / E Asia	100,210 (Coastline) 2,413	51.129	South Korean won	34866	23
Kuwait	Kuwait City /W Asia	17,818 (Coastline) 499	4.101	Kuwaiti dinar	25290	64
Latvia	Riga / Europe	64,559 (Coastline) 498	1.955	Euro	19284	37
Lebanon	Beirut / W Asia	10,452 (Coastline) 225	6.071	Lebanese pound	2802	92
Libya	Tripoli / N Africa	1,759,540 (Coastline) 1,770	6.392	Libyan dinar	3617	105
Liechtenstein	Vaduz / Europe	160 Doubly landlocked	.038	Swiss franc	-	19
Lithuania	Vilnius / / Europe	65,300 (Coastline) 90	2.843	Euro	22245	34
Luxembourg	Luxembourg City / Europe	2,586 Landlocked	.587	Euro	131782	23
Madagascar	Antanana-rivo / SE Africa	587,041 (Coastline) 4,828	24.979	Ariary	521 180	164
Malaysia	Kuala Lumpur / SE Asia	330,803 (Coastline) 4,675	31.243	Ringgit	11,604	62

Date of Formation	Government Type	Life Expectancy	Literacy (%)	Language (%)	Religion
15.8.1945	Communist state	70.6	100	Korean	unaffiliated - 71.3 Other religions-12.9 Folk religion - 12.3 Christian-2
15.8.1945	Presidential republic	82.3	97.9	Korean	Unaffiliated-46.4 Christian-29.4 Buddhist - 22.9
19.6.1961	Constitutional monarchy	74.7	96.15	Arabic (official), English	Muslim - 74.1 Christian-14.3 Hindu - 8.5
21.8.1991	Parliamentary republic	74.6	99.8	Latvian, Russian	Christian-55.8 unaffiliated -43.8
22.11.1943	Parliamentary republic	74.9	93.94	Arabic, French, English	Muslim-61.3 Christian- 38.3
24.12.1951	Transitional government	72.7	91.02	Arabic	Muslim-96.6 Christian - 2.7
23.1.1719	Constitutional monarchy	80.06	100	German	Christian - 91.9 Muslim - 5 unaffiliated - 2.9
11.3.1990	Semi-presidential republic	73.6	99.8	Lithuanian	Christian -89.8 unaffiliated-10
1839	Constitutional monarchy	82	100	French, German, English, Luxembourgish	Christian-70.4 unaffiliated -26.8 Muslim-2.3
26.6.1960	Semi-presidential republicq	65.5`	64.6	Malagasy and) French (official)	Christian-85.3 unaffiliated- 6.9 Folk religion-4.5 Muslim - 3
31.8.1957	Federal constitutional monarchy	75	94.64	Malay English Chinese Tamil	Muslim- 63.7 Buddhist- 17.7 Christian-9.4 Hindu- 6 Folk religion - 2.3

Country	Capital	Area (sq km)	Population (million)	Currency	p.c.i. ($)	HDI rank •High •Low
Maldives	Male / Indian Ocean	300 (Coastline) 644	.376	Rufiyaa	11801	95
Mauritius	Port Louis / SW Indian Ocean	2,040 (Coastline) 177	11,281	Mauritian rupee	9639	66
Mexico	Mexico City / C. America	1,964,375 (Coastline) 9,330	130.126	Mexican peso	9246	74
Micronesia	Palikir / S. Pacific	702 (Coastline) 6,112	.104	US dollar	3,821	136
Mongolia	Ulan Bator / E. Asia	1,564,110 Landlocked	3.033	Togrog	4,172	99
Morocco	Rabat / W. Africa W. Saharan territory)	446,550 (excluding (coastline)	35.12	Dirham	3,415	121
Mozambique	Maputo / SE Africa	801,590 (Coastline) 2,470	28.673	Metical	425	181•
Myanmar	Nay Pyi Taw /SE Asia	676,578 (Coastline) 1,930	54.872	Kyat	1,423	147
Namibia	Windhoek / SW. Africa	825,615 (Coastline) 1,572	2.529	Namibian dollar	4371	130
Nepal	Kathmandu / S. Asia	147,181 Landlocked	29.204	Nepalese rupee	1,236	142
Netherlands	Amsterdam / Europe	41,850 (Coastline) 451	17.081	Euro	58003	8•
New Zealand	Wellington / S. Pacific	270,467 (excluding dependencies) (Coastline)	4.609	New Zealand dollar	47499	14

Date of Formation	Government Type	Life Expectancy	Literacy (%)	Language (%)	Religion
26.7.1965	Presidential republic	78.5	99.3	Dhivehi (official), English	Muslim-98.4
12.3.1968	Parliamentary republic	74.6	90.62	Creole Bhojpuri French	Hindu-56.4 Christian - 25.3 Muslim-16.7
16.9.1810	Federal presidential republic	76.7	94.38	Spanish, Amerindian languages	Christian - 95.1 unaffiliated - 4.7
3.11.1986	Federal republic	69.4	89	English local languages	Christian-95.3 Folk religion - 2.7
11.7.1921	Semi-presidential republic	68.8	98.38	Mongolian	Buddhist - 55.1 unaffiliated - 35.9 Folk religion - 3.5 Muslim - 3.2
2.3.1956	Parliamentary constitutional monarchy	74.3	72.37	Arabic, Berber, French languages	Muslim-99.9
25.6.1975	Presidential republic	57.6	58.77	Emakhuwa Portuguese	Christian - 56.7 Muslim-18 unaffiliated -17.9 Folk religion - 7.4
4.1.1948	Parliamentary republic	66.6	93.09	Burmese	Buddhist-80.1 Christian-7.8 Folk religion - 5.8
21.3.1990	Presidential republic	65.8	81.94	English, Afrikaans, German, Oshivambo, Herero Nama	Christian-97.5 unaffiliated-1.9
1768	Federal parliamentary republic	69.2	64.66	Nepali, Maithili, Bhojpuri	Hindu-80.7 Buddhist-10.3 Muslim-4.6
1579	Parliamentary constitutional monarchy	81.9	99	Dutch	Christian- 50.6 unaffiliated - 42.1 Muslim-6
26.9.1907	Parliamentary democracy; constitutional monarchy	81.6	99	English, Maori	Christian - 57 unaffiliated -36.6 Hindu - 2.1

Country	Capital	Area (sq km)	Population (million)	Currency	p.c.i. ($)	HDI rank •High •Low
Nicaragua	Managua /C. America	130,373 (Coastline) 910	6.212	Cordoba	1,877	128
Niger	Niamey / W Africa	1,267,000 Landlocked	20.505	CFA franc	633	189•
Nigeria	Abuja / W Africa	923,768 (Coastline) 853	186.388	Naira	2,432	161
Norway	Oslo / N. Europe	323,802 (Coastline) 25,148	5.345	Norwegian krone	81995	1
Oman	Muscat / W. Asia	309,500 (Coastline) 2,092	4.717	Omani rial	16212	60
Pakistan	Islamabad / S. Asia	881,912 (Coastline) 1,046	194.11	Pakistani rupee	1,260	154
Panama	Panama City / C. America	75,417 (Coastline) 2,490	4.038	Balboa	13690	57
Papua New Guinea	Port Moresby / SE Asia	462,840 Island	7.813	Kina	2,737	155
Paraguay	Asuncion / S. America	406,752 Landlocked	6.784	Guarani	5,146	103
Peru	Lima / S. America	1,285,216 (Coastline) 2,414	32.068	Nuevo sol	6678	79
Philippines	Manila / SE Asia	300,000 (Coastline) 36,289	102.849	Philippine peso	3,646	107
Poland	Warsaw / Europe	312,679 (Coastline) 440	38.895	Zloty	16930	35
Portugal	Lisbon / Europe	92,090 (Coastline) 1,793	10.349	Euro	25065	38

Date of ormation	Government Type	Life Expectancy	Literacy (%)	Language (%)	Religion
5.9.1821	Presidential republic	74.8	82.81	Spanish, English	Christian- 85.8 unaffiliated– 12.5
.8.1960	Semi-presidential republic	61.8	28.7	French, Hausa, Djerma	Muslim-98.4
.10.1960	Federal presidential republic	54.07	59.56	English, Hausa, Ibo, Yoruba	Christian - 49.3 Muslim-48.8 Folk religion -1.4
.6.1905	Parliamentary constitutional monarchy	81.8	100	Norwegian, krone	Christian-84.7 unaffiliated - 10.1 Muslim-3.7
650	Absolute monarchy	76.6	94.75	Arabic	Muslim-85.9 Christian- 6.5 Hindu-5.5
4.8.1947	Federal parliamentary republic	66.4	56.44	Urdu, Punjabi, Sindhi, Baloch, Pashto	Muslim-96.4 Hindu - 1.9 Christian-1.6
11.1903	Presidential republic	77.8	95.04	Spanish, English	Christian-93 unaffiliated-4.8
.9.1975	Parliamentary democracy constitutional monarchy	62.9	64.23	English, Tok Pisin, Hiri Motu	Christian-99.2
.5.1811	Presidential republic	74	95.56	Spanish, Guarani	Christian-96.9 Folk religion - 1.7 unaffiliated - 1.1
.7.1821	Presidential republic	75.5	94.47	Spanish, Quechua, Aymara	Christian - 95.5 unaffiliated - 3 Folk religion - 1
.6.1898	Presidential republic	68.5	96.28	English, Filipino	Christian-92.6 Muslim- 5.5 Folk religion 1.5
.11.1918	Parliamentary republic	77.5	99.7	Polish	Christian - 94.3 unaffiliated - 5.6
43	Semi-presidential republic	81.1	95.42	Portuguese	Christian-93.8 unaffiliated-4.4

Country	Capital	Area (sq km)	Population (million)	Currency	p.c.i. ($)	HDI rank •High •Low
Qatar	Doha / W. Asia	11,586 (Coastline) 563	2.340	Qatari riyal	59143	45
Russia	Moscow /Europe & Asia	17,098,246 (Coastline) 37,653	144.019	Ruble	11,654	52
Saudi Arabia	Riyadh / W Asia	2,149,690 2,640 (coastline)	32.546	Riyal	22,700	40
Senegal	Dakar / W Africa	196,722 (Coastline)531	15.569	CFA franc	1,622	168
Singapore	Singapore / SE Asia	719 (coastline)	5.837	Singapore dollar	64103	11•
South Africa	Pretoria (administrative) Cape Town (legislative) Bloemfontein (judicial) / Africa	1,221,037 2,798 (coastline)	55.432	Rand	5444	114
Spain	Madrid / W. Europe	505,992 (Coastline) 4,964	46.397	Euro	30996	25
Sri Lanka	Colombo / S. Asia	65,610 (Coastline) 1,340	20.917	Sri Lankan rupee	3,830	72
Sweden	Stockholm / Europe	450,295 (Coastline) 3,218	9.935	Krona	58977	7•
Switzerland	Bern / Europe	41,284 Landlocked	8.499	Swiss franc	94696	2•
Syria	Damascus / W. Asia	185,180 (Coastline) 193	18.747	Syrian pound	2807	151
Tajikistan	Dushanbe / C. Asia	143,100 Landlocked	8.72	Somoni	810	125

Date of ormation	Government Type	Life Expec-tancy	Literacy (%)	Language (%)	Religion
.9.1971	Absolute monarchy	78.2	97.75	Arabic, English	Muslim-67.7 Chrisitian-13.8 Hindu -13.8
4.8.1991	Semi-presidential federation	70.5	99.72	Russian	Christian-73.3 unaffiliated- 16.2 Muslim-10
3.9.2932	Absolute monarchy	74.5	94.65	Arabic	Muslim-93 Christian - 4.4 Hindu - 1.1
.4.1960	Presidential republic	66.7	55.66	French, Wolof	Muslim-96.4 Christian-3.6
8.1965	Parliamentary republic	83.1	96.83	English, Malay, Mandarin, Tamil	Buddhist-33.9 193 Christian 18.2 Unaffiliated 16.4 Muslim -14.3
.5.1910	Parliamentary republic	62.9	94.26	11 official languages including English, Afrikaans, Sesotho, Setswana, Xhosa & Zulu	Christian- 81.2 unaffiliated-14.9 Muslim- 1.7 Hindu-1.1
92	Parliamentary constitutional monarchy	82.8	98.09	Spanish, Catalan, Gallego, Euskera	Christian - 78.6 unaffiliated-19 Muslim - 2.1
.1948	Presidential republic	74.9	92.63	Sinhala, Tamil, English	Buddhist-69.3 Hindu - 13.6 Muslim-9.8 hristian-7.3
.1523	Parliamentary constitutional monarchy	82.4	99	Swedish	Christian67.2 unaffiliated - 27 Muslim -4.6
.1291	Federal republic	83.4	99	French, German, Italian, Romansch	Christian- 81.3 unaffiliated-11.9 Muslim-5.5
4.1976	Presidential republic	64.5	86.43	Arabic Kurdish Armenian	Muslim-92.8 Christian-5.2 unaffiliated-2
1991	Presidential republic	69.7	99.7	Tajik Uzbek Russian	Muslim-96.7 Christian-1.6

Country	Capital	Area (sq km)	Population (million)	Currency	p.c.i. ($)	HDI rank •High •Low
Tanzania	Dodoma / E Africa	945,087 (Coastline) 1,424	55.070	Tanzanian shilling	1,104	163
Thailand	Bangkok / SE Asia	513,120 (Coastline) 3,219	68.771	Baht	7,702	79
Ukraine	Kiev / Europe	603,500 (Coastline) 2,782	44.676	Hryvnia	3,984	74
United Arab Emirates	Abu Dhabi / W Asia	83,600 (Coastline) 1,318	9.426	Dirham	35171	31
United Kingdom	London / Europe	242,495 (Coastline) 12,429	65.62	Pound	46344	13
United States of America	Washington D.C. / N. America	9,526,468 (Coastline) 19,924	327.087	Dollar	68309	17
Uruguay	Montevideo / S. America	176,215 (Coastline) 660	3.461	Spanish	15653	55
Uzbekistan	Tashkent / Asia	447,400 Doubly landlocked	30.623	Uzbek	1,775	106
Venezuela	Caracas / S. America	916,445 (Coastline) 2,800	31.842	Bolivar	1542	113
Vietnam	Hanoi / E. Asia	331,212 (Coastline) 3,444	95.675	Dong	3609	11
Zambia	Lusaka / Africa	752,612 Landlocked	16.682	Kwacha	974	14
Zimbabwe	Harare / Africa	390,757 Landlocked	16.026	S. African Rand; US D	1684 166	15

Date of Formation	Government Type	Life Expectancy	Literacy (%)	Language (%)	Religion
26.4.1964	Presidential republic	61.8	80.32	Kiswahili, English	Christian-61.4 Muslim-35.2 Folk religion1.8
238	Constitutional monarchy	74.9	96.66	Thai	Buddhist-93.2 Muslim- 5.5
4.8.1991	Semi-presidential republic	71.3	99.7	Ukrainian Russian	Christian-83.8 unaffiliated-14.7 Muslim - 1.2
.12.1971	Federation of monarchies	77.1	93.83	Arabic	Muslim-76.9 Christian- 12.6 Hindu -6.6 Buddhists-2
284	Parliamentary constitutional monarchy	81.2	99	English Welsh Scottish Gaelic	Christian-71.1 unaffiliated - 21.3 Muslim -4.4 Hindu -1.3
7.1776	Constitutional federal republic	79.3	99	English, Spanish	Christian-78.3 unaffiliated-16.4 Jewish- 1.8 Buddhists- 1.2
.8.1825	Presidential republic	77	98.42	Spanish	Christian-57.9 unaffiliated-40.7
).1991	Presidential republic	69.4	99.59	Uzbek, Russian	Muslim-96.7 Christian-2.3
'.1811	Federal presidential republic	74.1	95.36	Spanish	Christian-89.3 unaffiliated - 10
.1945	Communist state	76	94.5	Vietnamese, French, English, Chinese	Folk religion-45.3 unaffiliated - 29.6 Buddhists- 16.4 Christian - 8.2
10.1964	Presidential republic	61.8	63.4	English, Bemba, Lozi, Nyanja, Tonga	Christian-97.6
4.1980	Semi-presidential republic	60.7	86.5	English Shona Sindebele	Christian 87 unaffiliated 7.9 Folk religion 3.8

The United Nations

The United Nations (UN) was established in 1945. UN was born after the devastation of the World War II : •to provide a forum for its members to express their views •to host negotiations for governments to find areas of agreement and solve problems together •to take action on the issues confronting humanity, such as peace and security, climate change, sustainable development, human rights, disarmament, terrorism, humanitarian and health emergencies, gender equality, governance, food production, etc. **Members** • 193 member states. South Sudan is the newest member - joined in July 2011. Three that are not members of the UN: Kosovo (not recognised by enough UN members), Taiwan (country's place was taken by China in 1971) and Vatican (religious reasons). Potential members are recommended by the Security Council. They are admitted by a two-thirds majority vote in the General Assembly. ***Structure*** •Six main bodies.: **i.**General Assembly, **ii.** Security Council, **iii.** Economic and Social Council, **iv.** International Court of Justice (World Court), **v.** Trusteeship Council, and **vi.** Secretariat. •HQ of 5 bodies are at UN headquarters in New York, USA. The ICJ HQ is at The Hague, in the Netherlands.

UN Building, New York

1. Security Council • 5 permanent member nations: China, France, Russia, the UK and the US. •10 *Non-permanent members* are elected for 2-year terms by the General Assembly (with end of term date) ***Functions***: •Ensure global peace and security •Impose economic sanctions •Authorise the use of force in conflicts •Oversees peacekeeping operations. •*Non-Council Member States*: More than 50 UN member states have never been members of the Security Council. A State which is a Member of the UN but not of the Security Council may participate, without a vote, in its discussions when the Council considers that country's interests are affected.

Current Members

The Council is composed of 15 Members: Five Permanent Members and 10 Non-permanent Members elected for two-year terms by the General Assembly (with end of term year): Estonia (2021); India (2022); Ireland (2022); Kenya (2022); Mexico (2022); Niger (2021); Norway (2022); Saint Vincent and the Grenadines (2021); Tunisia (2021); Viet Nam (2021).

Both Members and non-members of the UN, if they are parties to a dispute being considered by the Council, may be invited to take part, without a vote, in the Council's discussions; the Council sets the conditions for participation by a non-member State.

2. Economic and Social Council •It spearheads the UN's economic, social, humanitarian and cultural activities •It oversees the work of commissions which deals with human rights, population growth, technology and drugs, among other issues. • Its 54 members are elected by the General Assembly.

3. International Court of Justice (World Court) •The court is the main judicial body of the UN •It is tasked with settling legal disputes submitted to it by states. •The court's 15 judges are elected by the General Assembly and the Security Council. •The court's decisions are binding, although nations have sometimes refused to accept its rulings. **HQ**: Dutch city of The Hague.

4. Secretariat The Secretariat has about 9,000 Secretariat staff are drawn from 170 countries. • undertakes work of the UN – administering the programmes and policies like research, translation and media relations.

5. Trusteeship Council The council, made up of the five permanent Security Council members, agreed in 1994 to meet "as occasion required". • Suspended its activities in 1994 when the last of the UN's trust territories, Palau in the south Pacific, became independent.

UN Peacekeeping Forces

The UN Peacekeeping Forces (Blue Berets or Blue Helmets) include soldiers, police officers, and civilian personnel. • employed to maintain or re-establish peace in an area of armed conflict. • engage in conflicts between states and in struggles within states. • The UN Peacekeeping Forces were awarded the 1988 Nobel Prize for Peace. Annual

United Nations University

The UN University (UNU), established in 1973, is the academic and research arm of the UN. HQ: Tokyo, Japan, with diplomatic status as a UN institution. •Since 2010, UNU grants degrees. •It is a bridge between the UN and the international academic, policy-making and private sector communities.

The UN Flag shows a world map as seen from the North Pole, surrounded by olive branches– an icon of peace. It was officially adopted in 1947.

The Secretary-General: Serves as the chief administrative officer of the UN. Term: 5 years.

Secretaries-General So Far

•1946-'52 Trygve Lie (Norway) •1953-'61 Dag Hammarskjöld (Sweden) •1961-'71 U Thant (Myanmar) •1972-'81 Kurt Waldheim (Austria) •1982-'91 Javier Perez de Cuellar (Peru) •1992-'96 Boutros Boutros-Ghali (Egypt) • 1997-2006 Kofi Annan (Ghana) •2007-'16 Ban Ki-Moon (S. Korea) •2017 Antonio Guterres (Portugal)

UN and India

India was one of the founding members of the United Nations that signed the Declaration by UN at Washington, D.C. on 1 January 1942. India also participated in the UN Conference on International Organization at San Francisco on 25 and 26 June 1945. As a founding member of the UN, India supports the purposes and principles of the UN and has contributed considerably in implementing the goals of the Charter, and the evolution of the UN's specialised programmes and agencies.

India has been a non permanent member of the UN Security Council for 8-terms (totaling 16 years), with the most recent being the 2021–22 term. India is a member of G4, group of nations who back each other in seeking a permanent seat on the Security Council and advocate in favour of the reformation of the UNSC. India is also part of the G-77.

India is a charter member of the UN and participates in all of its specialised agencies and organizations. India has contributed troops to UN peacekeeping efforts in Korea, Egypt and the Congo in its earlier years and in Somalia, Angola, Haiti, Liberia, Lebanon and Rwanda in recent years, and more recently in the South Sudan conflict.

UN Organisations

UNDP (UNs Development Programme) works in nearly 170 countries and territories. **Aim** To eradicate poverty, reduce inequalities and build resilience so countries can sustain progress and achieve the Sustainable Development Goals.

UNICEF (UNs Children's Fund) **Aim** To provide humanitarian and development assistance to children and mothers.

UNHCR (UNs High Commissioner for Refugees) **Aim** UNHCR protects refugees worldwide and facilitates their return home or resettlement.

WFP (World Food Programme) **Aim** To eradicate hunger and malnutrition. It is the world's largest humanitarian agency. Every year, WFP feeds almost 80 million people in around 75 countries.

UNODC (UNs Office on Drugs and Crime) – UNODC helps Member States fight drugs, crime, and terrorism.

UNFPA (UNs Population Fund) **Aim** Delivering a world where every pregnancy is wanted, every birth is safe, and every young person's potential is fulfilled.

UNCTAD (UNs Conference on Trade and Development) is the United Nations body responsible for dealing with development issues, particularly international trade – the main driver of development.

UNEP (UNs Environment Programme) **Aim** To act as a catalyst, advocate, educator and facilitator to promote the wise use and sustainable development of the global environment.

UNRWA (UNs Relief and Works Agency for Palestine Refugees) **Aim** To help in the area of education, health care, relief and social services, camp infrastructure and improvement, microfinance and emergency assistance, during armed conflict. It has contributed to the welfare and human development of Palestine refugees.

UN Women **Aim** To focus on gender equality and women's empowerment.

UN-Habitat **Aim** To promote socially and environmentally sustainable human settlements development and the achievement of adequate shelter for all.

UN Specialized Agencies

They are autonomous organizations working with the UN through negotiated agreements. They were created by the UN to meet emerging needs.

World Bank **Aim** To focus on poverty reduction and the improvement of living standards worldwide by providing low-interest loans, interest-free credit, and grants to developing countries for education, health, infrastructure, and communications, among other things. It works in over 100 countries.

IMF (International Monetary Fund) **Aim** To foster economic growth and employment by providing temporary financial assistance to countries to help ease balance of payments adjustment and technical assistance. Currently it has $28 billion in outstanding loans to 74 nations.

WHO (World Health Organization) It is the directing and coordinating health related matters internationally. **Aim** To the attainment by all peoples of the highest possible level of health.

UNESCO (UNs Educational, Scientific and Cultural Organization) **Aim** To focus on everything from teacher training to helping improve education worldwide to protecting important historical and cultural sites around the world.

ILO (International Labour Organisation) **Aim** To promote international labour rights based on international standards on the freedom to associate, collective bargaining, the abolition of forced labour, equality of opportunity and treatment.

FAO (Food and Agriculture Organisation) leads international efforts to fight hunger. **Aim** To negotiate agreements between developing and developed countries and a source of technical knowledge and information to aid development.

IFAD (International Fund for Agricultural Development) **Aim** To focus on rural poverty reduction, working with poor rural populations in developing countries to eliminate poverty, hunger and malnutrition; raise their productivity and incomes; and improve the quality of their lives.

IMO (International Maritime Organisation) **Aim** To create a shipping regulatory framework, address safety and environmental concerns, legal matters, technical cooperation, security, and efficiency.

WMO (World Meteorological Organization) **Aim** To facilitate the free international exchange of meteorological data and use it in aviation, shipping, security, and agriculture, among other things.

WIPO (World Intellectual Property Organization) **Aim** To protect intellectual property throughout the world through 23 international treaties.

ICAO (International Civil Aviation Organization) **Aim** To develop standards for global air transport and assists its 192 Member States in sharing the world's skies to their socio-economic benefit.

ITU (International Telecommunication Union) **Aim** To connect all the world's people – protect and support everyone's fundamental right to communicate

UNIDO (UNs Industrial Development Organization) **Aim** To promote industrial development for poverty reduction, inclusive globalization and environmental sustainability.

UPU (Universal Postal Union) **Aim** To ensure a truly universal network of up-to-date products and services.

UNWTO (World Tourism Organization) **Aim** To promote responsible, sustainable and universally accessible tourism.

Other Entities

UNAIDS It is co-sponsored by 10 UN system agencies: UNHCR, UNICEF, WFP, UNDP, UNFPA, UNODC, the ILO, UNESCO, WHO and the World Bank. **Aim** To stop and reverse the spread of HIV/AIDS.

UNISDR (UNs Office for Disaster Reduction) **Aim** To serve as the focal point in the UNs system for disaster reduction.

UNOPS (UNs Office for Project Services) **Aim** To successfully implement its partners' peacebuilding, humanitarian and development projects globally.

Related Organizations

IAEA (International Atomic Energy Agency) **Aim** To work with its member states and multiple partners worldwide to promote the safe, secure and peaceful use of nuclear technologies.

IOM (International Organization for Migration) **Aim** To assist in management of migration, to promote international cooperation on migration issues, to assist in the search for practical solutions to migration problems and to provide humanitarian assistance to migrants in need, including refugees and internally displaced people.

WTO (World Trade Organization) **Aim** To negotiate trade agreements, and a place where member governments try to sort out bilateral trade problems.

OPCW (Organisation for the Prohibition of Chemical Weapons) is the implementing body of the Chemical Weapons Convention (CWC). **Aim** To help member states create a world free of chemical weapons.

The European Union

The European Union (EU) is a political and economic union.

Comprises 27 member states primarily in Europe

Total Area : 4,233,255.3 km2

Total Population: 447 million

A monetary union was established in 1999, coming into full force in 2002, and is composed of 19 member states which use the euro currency.

Share of world population, 2020: 5.8%

Density: 106/km2

EU - nominal (GDP) : US$17.1 trillion in 2021 (constituting approx 18% of global nominal GDP)

All EU countries have a very high Human Development Index (UNDP) (2019): Very High - 14th (Increase 0.911)

Citizenship: The union and EU citizenship came through Maastricht Treaty (came into force in 1993).

Official languages: 24

The official seat of the European Parliament - Strasbourg

Time zone: UTC to UTC+2 (WET, CET, EET)

Origin: The European Coal and Steel Community (ECSC) and the European Economic Community (EEC), established, respectively, by the 1951 Treaty of Paris and 1957 Treaty of Rome. The Inner Six were the original member states (came to be known as the European Communities): Belgium, France, Italy, Luxembourg, the Netherlands, and West Germany. • Treaty of Rome: 1 January 1958 • Single European Act: 1 July 1987 • Treaty of Maastricht: 1 November 1993 • Treaty of Lisbon: 1 December 2009 • Last polity admitted : 1 July 2013 (Croatia) • Last polity withdrawn: 31 January 2020 (United Kingdom)

The Members: Austria, Belgium, Bulgaria, Croatia, Cyprus, Czech Republic, Denmark, Estonia, Finland, France, Germany,

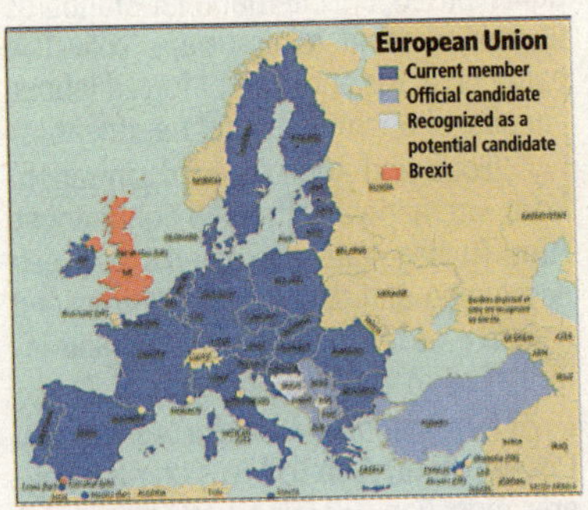

Greece, Hungary, Ireland, Italy, Latvia, Lithuania, Luxembourg, Malta, the Netherlands, Poland, Portugal, Romania, Slovakia, Slovenia, Spain, Sweden.

The Capital of EU : Brussels, Belgium.

The EU Administration: The European Parliament, the Council of the Union, European Commission, the Court of Justice, the Court of Auditors.

The EU motto: "United in diversity"– first came into use in 2000.

The Euro (€) : 19 out of 27 EU member countries use Euro as the sole official currency – collectively known as the Eurozone.

The European flag: A circle of 12 gold stars on a blue background symbolises the identity and the ideals of unity, solidarity and harmony among the peoples of Europe.

The European Anthem: Friedrich von Schiller's lyrical poem "the Ode to Joy," composed by Ludwig Beethoven in 1823, symbolising the EU and Europe as a whole.

Government: Intergovernmental

• President of the Commission: Ursula von der Leyen • President of the Parliament: David Sassoli • President of the European Council: Charles Michel

• Presidency of the Council of the EU: Slovenia

International Organisations

Organisation

African Union (AU) HQ Addis Ababa, Ethiopia Head of Org. Chairman: Felix-Antoine Tshisekedi Tshilombo Established 26.05. 2001 Membership: 55 countries on the African continent. Aim: To strengthen ties between African countries and safeguard their independence

The Arab League HQ Al Tahrir Sq., Cairo, Egypt Head of Org. Sec. General Ahmed Aboul Gheit Established 22.03.1945 Membership: 22- Algeria, Bahrain, Comoros, Djibouti, Egypt, Iraq, Jordan, Kuwait, Lebanon, Libya, Mauritania, Morocco, Oman, Palestine, Qatar, Saudi Arabia, Somalia, Sudan, Syria, Tunisia, UAE, and Yemen. Aim: To safeguard interest, independence and sovereignity of Arab member-states

The Asian Development Bank (ADB) HQ Metro Manila, Philippines Head: President: Takehiko Nakao Estd. 22.08. 1966 Membership: 67 (48 regional and 19 non-regional members) Aim: ADB launched the Asian Development Fund (ADF) with a view to providing concessional credits to needy members.

Asian Infra-structure Investment Bank (AIIB) HQ Beijing, China Head: Sec. -General: Alberto Ninio Estd. 25.12. 2015 Membership: 86 Aim: It is an international multilateral developmental institution to provide finance to infrastructure projects in the Asia region

The Association of South East Asian Nations (ASEAN) HQ Jakarta, Indonesia Head: Sec-General Dato Lim Jock Hoi Estd. 08.08 1967 Membership: (10) Brunei Darussalam, Cambodia, Indonesia, Laos, Malaysia, Myanmar, Philippines, Singapore, Thailand, Vietnam. Aim: To accelerate economic progress and maintain the economic stability of SE Asia

Bank for InternationalSettlements (BIS) HQ Basel, Switzerland Head: General Manager Jens Weidmann Membership 60 central banks (Countries represented in each continent: Europe - 35, Asia - 13, S. America - 5, N. America - 3, Oceania - 2, and Africa - 2) Aim: To provide banking services to central banks and other international organisations; (fosters international monetary and financial cooperation)

BRICS HQ Shanghai Head: Chairman, Narendra Modi Estd. 2009 Membership: (5) Brazil, Russia, India, China and South Africa. Aim: To achieve regional economic growth and work as a bridge between the devoloped and devoloping countries.

Commonwealth of Independent States (CIS) HQ Minsk, Russia Head: Secretary General Aleksey Sergeyev; Executive Secretary: Sergey Lebedev Estd. 1991Membership: 9 member states and 1 associate state Aim: Military and Economic alliance and to reach a supranational union. Also called the Russian Commonwealth; was established through Belavezha Accords (1991) and subsequent the Alma-Ata Protocol (1991) and Free Trade Area agreement (2012).

Gulf Cooperation Council (GCC) HQ Riyadh, Saudi Arabia Head: Secretary General Dr. Nayef Falah Mubarak Al-Hajraf Estd. 25 May 1981 Membership (6) Saudi Arabia, Kuwait, the United Arab

Emirates, Oman, Qatar and Bahrain. Aim: To boost economic cooperation between members and, through collective security, to guard against any threat from neighbouring states and from Islamic terrorism.

Group of Seven (G7, earlier G8) HQ Taormina, Italy Estd. 1973 Membership: 7 (as Russia is suspended) France, Germany, Italy, Japan, UK, USA, Canada, EU ("nonenumerated" participant since 1980s). It is an informal bloc of major industrialized economies and democracies. Aim: To tackle global challenges through discussion and action with no headquarters, budget or permanent staff

Group of 77 Head: Chairmanship Guyana. 21 Jan. 2020 Estd. 15 June 1964 Membership: a coalition of 134 developing nations. (But China does not consider itself to be a member. So all official statements are issued in the name of The Group of 77 and China). Aim: To promote collective economic interest and increase negotiating capacity in UN

Group of 24 (G-24) Estd. 1971 Head: Akbar Komijani Membership: A chapter of the G-77. Aim: to coordinate the positions of developing countries on international monetary and development finance issues and to ensure that their interests were adequately represented in negotiations on international monetary matters. Every member of the G-24, except for Mexico, is also a member of the G77

Group of Twenty (G20) Head: Chairman: Japan Abe Shinzo (2019) Estd. 26 Sept 1999 Membership: An international forum for the governments and central bank governors fromArgentina, Australia, Brazil, Canada, China, the European Union, France, Germany, India, Indonesia, Italy, Japan, Mexico, Russia, Saudi Arabia, South Africa, South Korea, Turkey, the United Kingdom, and the United States Aim: To bring together industrialized and developing economies to discuss key issues in the global economy and promote international financial stability.

The International Air Transport Association (IATA) HQ Montreal, Canada Estd. 1945 Head: Director -General Willie Walsh Members International and domestic airlines. Aim: To promote safe, regular and economical air transport and to provide a forum for collaboration.

INTERPOL HQ Lyon, France Head: Sec -General: Jürgen Stock; President: Kim Jong Yang Estd. 1923 Members 192 countries Aim: To facilitate cross-border police cooperation, and supports and assists all organisations, authorities and services whose mission is to prevent or combat international crime. Motto: Connecting police for a safer world.

New Development Bank (NDB) HQ Shanghai, China Head: President Marcos Prado Troyjo Estd. July 2014 (established by the BRICS states) Membership: Brazil, Russia, India, China, South Africa Aim: To contribute to development plans established nationally through projects that are socially, environmentally and economically sustainable.

North Atlantic Treaty Organisation (NATO) HQ Brussels, Belgium Head: Secretary General Admiral Rob Bauer Estd. 4 April 1949 Membership: 29 states (intergovernmental military alliance for collective defence) Aim: Mutual defence in response to an attack by any external party.

Organisation of Arab Petroleum

Exporting Countries (OAPEC) HQ Kuwait Head: Secretary General Ali Sabt Ben Sabt Estd. 1968 Membership: Kuwait, Libya and Saudi Arabia, Algeria, Bahrain, Egypt, Iraq, Qatar, Syria, Tunisia and the UAE. Aim: Organise cooperation in oil development and regional integration, provide legitimate means to preserve the members' individual and collective interest within the industry and provide access to consumer markets on fair and reasonable terms.

Organization of the Petroleum Exporting Countries (OPEC) HQ Vienna Head: Secretary General Mohammad Sanusi Barkindo Estd. Sep 1960 Membership 15 Aim: To unify the petroleum policies of its Member Countries and ensure the stabilization of oil markets to secure regular supply of petroleum to consumers, a steady income to producers and a fair return on capital for those investing in the petroleum industry.

Organisation for Economic Cooperation and Development (OECD) HQParis, France Head: Secretary General Mr Cormann Estd. Reformed Sep. 1961 *(formerly OEEC, Formed: 16 April 1948)* Membership 36 Aim: to stimulate economic growth and world trade by raising the standard of living in member countries and by coordinating aid to less developed countries.

Organisation of Islamic Cooperation (OIC) HQ Jeddah, Saudi Arabia Head: Secretary-General Hissein Brahim Taha Estd. 1969 Membership 57 Aim: To preserve Islamic social and economic values; promote solidarity amongst member states and increase cooperation in areas of development.

The Shanghai Cooperation Organisation (SCO) HQ Beijing, China Head: Secretary General Vladimir Norov Estd. 15 June 2001Membership 8 member states, 4 observer states, 6 dialogue partners, 4 guest attendances Aim: A Eurasian political, economic, and security alliance for cooperation in political affairs, economics and trade, scientific -technical, cultural, educational spheres and safe- guard regional peace

World Trade Organisation (WTO) HQ Geneva Switzerland Head: Director -General: Ngozi Okonjo-Iweala Estd. 01.01.1995 Membership 164 Aim : Regu- late international trade

Non-governmental Organisations

Amnesty International (AI)
HQ London, UK Head: Secretary General Thomas Hammarberg Estd. July 1961 Membership 7 million members and supporters Aim: Legal advocacy, Media attention, direct-appeal campaigns, research, lobbying

The International Committee of the Red Cross (ICRC) HQ Geneva, Switzerland Head: Dir. General: Robert Mardini Estd. 17.02.1863 Membership Signatory State parties to Geneva Conventions (1949) and Additional Protocols (Protocol I, Protocol II) of 1977 and 2005 and 25-member committee Aim: Protecting victims of conflicts

International Red Cross and Red Crescent Movement HQ Geneva, Switzerland Head: President: Peter Maurer; Secretary General: Eljadj As Sy Membership 17 million volunteers, members and staff worldwide Aim: To protect human life and health, to ensure respect for all human beings, and to prevent and alleviate human suffering.

Greenpeace International Amsterdam Head: Exe. Dir.: Jennifer Morgan. Board Chair: Ayesha Imam Estd. 1971 Aim: Environmentalism and Peace.

World Rating Indexes

World Happiness Index: It is a measure of happiness on the basis of factors that support happiness. caring, freedom, and generosity, health, Income, good governance. 2021 Top Countries 1. Finland, 2. Iceland 3. Denmark 4.Switzerland 5. The Netherlands. India – 139/149.

Ease of Doing Business Index: This index ranks countries on ease of getting electricity, construction permits, registering property, protecting investors, getting credits, employing workers, cross-border trading, paying taxes, enforcing contracts, resolving insolvency. 2021 1. New Zealand, 2. Singapore, 3. HongKong 4. Denmark. India:116

Global International Property Index: It measures analyses the IP climate in 53 global economies.. 2020 1.Switzerland. 2. Sweden. 3. USA. 4. UK. 5. Netherlands .India 2020 – 40/50; 36/40 (2019)

Social Progress Index: It measures the extent to which countries provide for the social and environmental needs of their citizens. 2020:1.Norway, 2. Denmark, 3. Finland.4. New Zealand. India:117 (56.8)

Global Peace Index 2021: The GP) gives us trends of global violence, less peacefulness and relative position of nations'/ region's peacefulness. Produced by the Institute for Economics and Peace (IEP) • Total Countries – 163 • Top – Iceland • India – 135th. •Bottom – Afghanistan 2019: 1. Iceland, 2. New -Zealand, 3. Portugal. India – 141/163.

World Economic Freedom Index:It is an annual index that measure the degree of economic freedom in the nations. 2020: 1. Singapore, 2. Hongkong, 3. New Zealand. India –105/180 countries.

Global Competitiveness Report:The GCR annually "assesses the ability of countries to provide high levels of prosperity to their citizens–indicating how productively a country uses available resources. 2019: 1. Singapore 2. USA, 3.Hongkong. 4. Netherlands. 5. Switzerland. India – 39/138 countries.

Global Innovation Index: 2020 The most Innovative Economies 1. Switzerland 2. Sweden 3. USA 4. UK 5. Netherlands.

Sustainability Index: 2020.(UN& WHO): takes into account carbon emision and ability of children to live healthy lives. 1. Norway 2. S. Korea. 3. Netherlands. India-77.

Other India Rankings

Index Ranking/Total Countries

IMD World Competitiveness Index 2021 ·Released by the Institute for Management Development (IMD) India rank – 43rd/Total Countries – 64 •Top – Switzerland

Global Peace Index 2021 Produced by the Institute for Economics and Peace (IEP) • Total Countries – 163

• Top – Iceland •India – 135th•Bottom – Afghanistan

World Giving Index (WGI) 2021 ·Released by the Charities Aid Foundation's (CAF)• Total Countries – 114 • India – 14th •Top – Indonesia•Bottom – Japan

Chandler Good Government Index (CGGI) 2021 •Total Countries – 104 •India – 49th • Top – Finland

Energy Transition Index 2021 · Released by -World Economic Forum (WEF) • Total Countries – 115 •India – 87th • Top – Sweden

World Press Freedom Index 2021 · Released by – Reports Without Borders (RSF) •Total Countries – 180•India – 142 •Top – Norway •Bottom – Eritrea stands at 180

Inclusive Internet Index 2021 •Released by – Facebook-Economist Intelligence Unit (EIU) •Total Countries – 120 •India – 49th

Global Gender Gap Index 2021 · Released by – World Economic Forum • Total Countries – 156 •The rank of India – 140th • Top – Iceland

21

EQUALITY, ETHICS & SOCIAL JUSTICE

Women in Politics

Women in Parliament: The countries are ranked and colour-coded according to the percentage of women in unicameral parliaments or the lower house of parliament, as on 1 Jan. 2021.

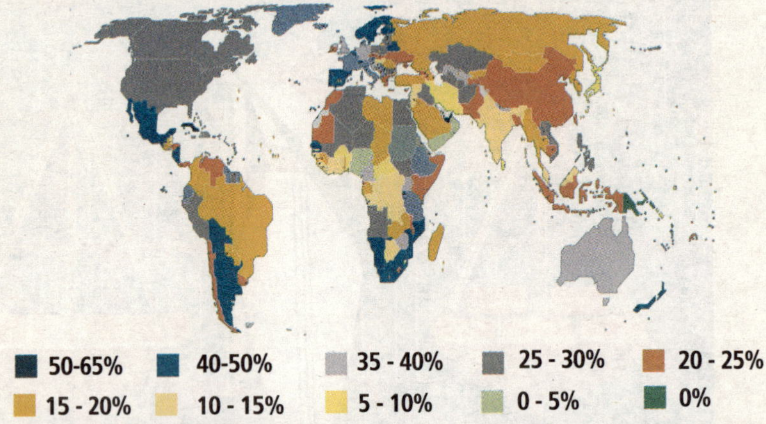

The "Women in politics: 2021" map shows all-time highs for the number of countries with women Heads of State or Heads of Government, as well as for the global share of women ministers.

Despite increases in the number of women at the highest levels of political power, widespread gender inequalities persist: progression in women holding ministerial portfolios has slowed, with just a small increase to from 21.3 % in 2020 to 21.9 % in 2021; the number of countries with no women in government has increased; and only 25.5 % of national parliamentarians are women, compared to 24.9 % the year before.

The map is created by the Inter-Parliamentary Union (IPU) and UN Women which represents global rankings for women in executive, government, and parliamentary positions as of 1 January 2021.

Women Heads of State 1 (9/152 = 5.9%) and women heads of government (13/193 = 6.7%) Bangladesh (HG), Barbados (HG), Denmark (HG), Estonia (HS), Ethiopia (HS), Finland (HG), Gabon (HG), Georgia (HS), Germany (HG), Greece (HS), Iceland (HG), Lithuania (HG), Nepal (HS), New Zealand (HG), Norway (HG), Peru (HG), Rep. of Moldova (HS), Serbia (HG), Singapore (HS), Slovakia (HS), Togo (HG), Trinidad and Tobago (HS)

Women Speakers of Parliament* (58/277 = 20.9%)Women deputy speakers of parliament (165/582 = 28.3%):

Andorra, Antigua and Barbuda, Argentina, Azerbaijan, Bahamas, Bahrain, Bangladesh, Belarus, Belgium (2 chambers), Belize (2 chambers), Bosnia and Herzegovina, Bulgaria, Chile, Equatorial Guinea, Eswatini, Finland, Gabon, Gambia, Indonesia, Italy, Jamaica, Japan, Kiribati, Laos, Latvia, Lesotho, Liberia, Lithuania, Madagascar, Malawi, Mexico, Mozambique, Netherlands, Norway, Peru, Poland, Republic of Moldova, Romania, Russia,

World and Regional Averages of Women in Parliament

	Single house or lower house	Upper house or Senate	Both houses combined
World average	25.6%	24.8%	25.5%
Regional averages			

Regions* are classified by descending order of the percentage of women in unicameral parliaments or the lower house of parliament.

	Single house or lower house	Upper house or Senate	Both houses combined
Nordic countries	44.5%	—	—
Americas	32.2%	33.0%	32.4%
Europe (Nordic countries included)	30.5%	30.2%	30.4%
Europe (Nordic countries not included)	29.1%	30.2%	29.3%
Sub-Saharan Africa	25.0%	23.9%	24.9%
Asia	20.8%	17.6%	20.4%
Middle East and North Africa	19.3%	11.2%	17.8%
Pacific	18.0%	44.9%	20.9%

* The composition of IPU regional groupings – https://data.ipu.org/content/regional-groupings.

Portfolios held by Women Ministers 1432 portfolios in 193 countries

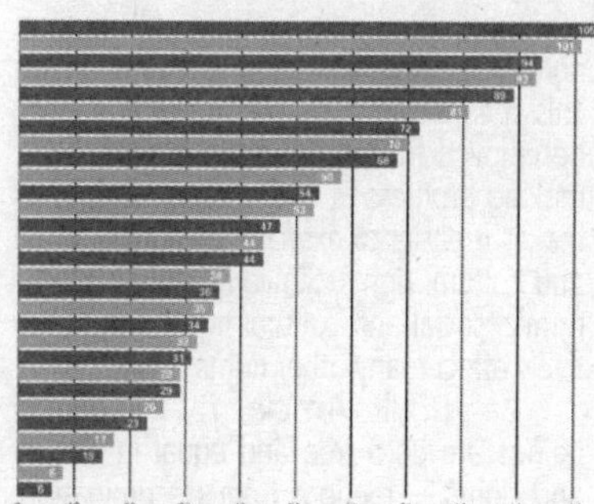

Environment/Natural Resources/ Energy • Social Affairs • Family / Children / Youth/ Elderly/Disables Employment/Labour/ Vocational Training • Education • Culture • Home Affairs, Immigration(including Integration and Refugees) • Women's Affairs / Gender Equality • Trade/Industry • Foreign Affairs (including Development Assistance) • Research and Development / Science and Technology • Agriculture / Food/Forestry/Fishing • Public Works / Territorial Planning • Health • Justice • Tourism • Public Administration /Public Service • Sports • Housing and Urban Affairs • Communications/ Telecommunications/Postal Affairs • Local Government • Defence and Veteran Affairs • Economy / Development • Human Rights • Finance/ Budget • Information/ Media • Transport • Parliamentary Affairs • Population

Rwanda, Saint Lucia, Saint Vincent and the Grenadines, South Africa, Spain (2 chambers), Togo, Trinidad and Tobago (2 chambers), Turkmenistan, Uganda, USA (2 chambers),** Uruguay, Uzbekistan, Viet Nam and Zimbabwe.

Of the 224 chambers in 163 countries for which information is available, 117 have at least one woman deputy speaker. 1 Only elected heads of state have been taken into account.

* Out of a total of 272 parliamentary chambers, two have 2 additional Speakers and three have 1 additional Speaker, for a total of 279 Speakers. At 1 January 2021, there were 2 vacancies.
** The woman Vice President became President of the Senate upon her taking office on 20 January 2021, as a result of the November 2020 elections.
•(HS-Head of State; HG-Head of Government)

Human Rights

The rights we have simply by virtue of our existence as human beings – which are not granted by any state. These universal rights are inherent to all of us, regardless of nationality, sex, ethnic origin, color, language, religion, caste, or any other status. They range from the most fundamental – the right to life – to those that make life worth living, such as the rights to food, education, work, health, and liberty.

The Universal Declaration of Human Rights (UDHR) – the first legal document on fundamental human rights to be universally protected, was adopted by the UN General Assembly in 1948. The UDHR, continues to be the foundation of all international human rights law. Its 30 Articles provide the principles and building blocks of current and future human rights conventions, treaties and other legal instruments. The UDHR, together with the 2 covenants make up the International Bill of Rights – (i) the International Covenant for Civil and Political Rights, and (ii) the International Covenant for Economic, Social and Cultural Rights.

The Universal Declaration – the idea that powers change in the world. The 30 Rights (to ensure all people gain freedom, equality and dignity) are •Free and equal •Freedom from discrimination •Right to life •Freedom from slavery •Freedom from torture •Right to recognition before the law •Right to equality before the law •Access to justice •Freedom from arbitrary detention •Right to a fair trial •Presumption of innocence •Right to privacy •Freedom of movement •Right to asylum •Right to nationality •Right to marriage and to found a family •Right to own property•Freedom of religion or belief •Freedom of Expression •Freedom of assembly •Right to partake in public affairs •Right to social security •Right to work •Right to leisure and rest •Right to adequate standard of living •Right to education •Right to cultural, artistic and scientific life •Right to a free and fair world •Duty to your community •Rights are inalienable

The Salient Features Universal The principle of universality of human rights is the cornerstone of international human rights law i.e., we are all equally entitled to our human rights. This principle is repeated in many international human rights conventions, declarations, and resolutions.

Inalienable Human rights are inalienable. They should not be taken away, except in specific situations and according to due process. For example, the right to liberty may be restricted if a person is found guilty of a crime by a court of law.

Indivisible, Interdependent All human rights are indivisible and interdependent. This means that one set of rights cannot be enjoyed fully without the other – like , making progress in civil and political rights makes it easier to exercise economic, social and cultural rights. Similarly, violating economic, social and cultural rights can negatively affect many other rights.

Equal UDHR ***Article 1***: "All human beings are born free and equal in dignity and rights." Freedom from discrimination, set out in ***Article 2***, is what ensures this equality.

Non-discriminatory Non-discrimination cuts across all international human rights law and is present in all major human rights treaties. Two core instruments: •the International Convention on the Elimination of All Forms of Racial Discrimination, and •the Convention on the Elimination of All Forms of Discrimination against Women.

Rights and Obligations

All countries have ratified at least 1 of the

9 core human rights treaties, and 1 of the 9 optional protocols. 80% of States have ratified 4 or more. This means States have •obligations and duties under international law to respect, protect and fulfill human rights. •must refrain from interfering with or curtailing the enjoyment of human rights. • should protect individuals and groups against human rights abuses. •take positive action to facilitate the enjoyment of basic human rights.

As individuals, we are entitled to our human rights – but, we should also respect and stand up for the human rights of others.

Int. Conventions against Discrimination: Racial-1966, Women-1979, Torture and Punishment- 1984, Children-1989, Migrant workers-1990, Disabilities- 2006.

India: Constitution of India through the Preamble, Fundamental Rights and Directive Principles guarantees human rights.

Childrens Rights

Children's rights were recognised after the 1st World war, with the adoption of the Declaration of Geneva, in 1924. The process of recognition of children's rights continued thanks to the UN, with the adoption of the Declaration of the Rights of the Child in 1959. Children and young people have the same general human rights as adults and also specific rights that recognise their special needs. Children are human beings and are the subject of their own rights. They are neither a property of anybody nor are they helpless objects of charity.

The Convention on the Rights of the Child sets out the rights for children to develop to their full potential as an individual and as a member of a family and community, with rights and responsibilities appropriate to his or her age and stage of development. Thus the focus is on the whole child, recognising, a basic quality of life as right of all children, rather than a privilege enjoyed by a few.

Importance: •The healthy development of children is crucial to the future well-being of any society. Because they are still developing, children are especially vulnerable – more so than adults – to poor living conditions such as poverty, inadequate health care, nutrition, safe water, housing and environmental pollution. The effects of disease, malnutrition and poverty threaten the future of children and therefore the future of the societies in which they live.

•The costs to society of failing its children are huge

Social research findings show that children's earliest experiences significantly influence their future development. The course of their development determines their contribution, or cost, to society over the course of their lives.

Protection of Children from Sexual Offences (POCSO)

Many a times they are exploited and their innocence compromised through abuse. In order to effectively address the heinous crimes of sexual abuse and sexual exploitation of childrenthrough less ambiguous and more stringent legal provisions,

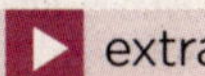

Parental Leave in the Nordic Countries

In the Nordic Region, ensuring that both parents are able to combine work with raising a family has long been a policy priority. On average, parents have the right to 345 days' parental leave per child.

the Ministry of Women and Child Development championed the introduction of the Protection of Children from Sexual Offences (POCSO) Act, 2012.

The Act defines a child as any person below eighteen years of age, and regards the best interests and well-being of the child as being of paramount importance at every stage, to ensure the healthy physical, emotional, intellectual and social development of the child. It defines different forms of sexual abuse, including penetrative and non-penetrative assault, as well as sexual harassment and pornography, and deems a sexual assault to be "aggravated" under certain circumstances, such as when the abused child is mentally ill or when the abuse is committed by a person in a position of trust or authority vis-à-vis the child, like a family member, police officer, teacher, or doctor. People who traffic children for sexual purposes are also punishable under the provisions relating to abetment in the Act. The Act prescribes stringent punishment graded as per the gravity of the offence, with a maximum term of rigorous imprisonment for life, and fine.

Bare Acts related to Children

- Commissions for Protection of Child Rights (Amendment) Act 2006
- Commission For Protection of Child Rights Rules, 2006
- Commissions for Protection of Child Rights Act, 2005
- Right of Children to Free and Compulsory Education Rules , 2010
- Right of Children to Free and Compulsory Education Act 2009
- Protection of Children From Sexual Offences Rules, 2012
- The Juvenile Justice (Care and Protection of Children) Act 2015,Rules, 2016
- THE JUVENILE JUSTICE (CARE AND PROTECTION OF CHILDREN) ACT, 2015
- Protection of Children From Sexual Offences Act, 2012
- Juvenile Justice (Care and Protection of Children) Amendment Act, 2011
- Juvenile Justice (Care and Protection of Chidlren) Rules, 2007
- Juvenule Justice (Care and Protection of Children) Amendment Act, 2006
- Juvenile Justice (Care and Protection of Children) Act, 2000
- Child Labour (Prohibition and Regulation) Rules, 1988
- Child Labour (Prohibition and Regulation) Act, 1986
- Children (Pledging of Labour) Act, 1933
- Bonded Labour System (Abolition) Act, 1976
- Factories Act, 1948
- Guardians and Wards act 1890. Hindu Minority and Guardians Act 1956
- Immoral Traffic (Prevention) Act, 1956
- Medical Termination of Pregnancy Act, 1971
- Mines Act, 1952
- National Food Security Act, 2013
- Prohibition of Child Marriage Act 2006
- Prenatal Diagnostic Techniques (Regulation and Prevention of Misuse) Act, 1994
- Young Persons (Harmful Publication) Act, 1956.

Women: The Equal Half

India's population is 1.38 b. (2020) and women population share is 48.04%. We find that the labour force participation rate for women had a decadal fall from 36.7% in 2005 to 26% in 2018, with 95% (195m) women employed in the unorganised sector. Comparatively, the men's labour force participation rate is four times that of women at 76.08% in 2019. On the Global Gender Gap Index by World Economic Forum, India has fallen four places from 2018, now ranking 112 of 153 countries, largely due to its economic gender gap. Among its South Asian neighbours, India has now the lowest labour force participation, falling behind Pakistan and Afghanistan which had half of India's FLFP in 1990. Raising women's participation in India's labor force by 10 percentage points between now and 2025, requires bringing 68 million more women into the labor force. The question is - will India be able to reach that mark? While it is good to speak about the '$5-trillion economy,' if this has to come to pass a lot more needs to be done to bring more women into the workforce. Looking at the state of the women who are presently in the workforce, the reports are not encouraging. According to Monster Salary Index 2016 Gender pay report, the overall gender pay gap in India was 25% in 2016. Men earn hourly median gross wage of ₹345.8, whereas women only receive ₹259.8. It is important that this gender pay gap is addressed too. The McKinsey Global Institute report says, 'The power of parity: How advancing women's equality can add $12 trillion (has a potential of 26%) to global growth by 2025'.

Equal in Education and Opportunities

After the UN's Beijing Declaration and Platform for Action pledged to take the

necessary steps to "remove all obstacles to gender equality and the advancement and empowerment of women," support for gender equality is strong around the globe. Across 34 countries surveyed by Pew Research Center, a median of 94% think it is important for women in their country to have the same rights as men, with 74% saying this is very important. •While women around the world embrace the idea of gender equality, at least four-in-ten think men generally have more opportunities than women in their country when it comes to getting high-paying jobs (a median of 54% across the 34 countries surveyed) and being leaders in their community (44%). •People see more equity in access to a good education – a median of 81%, believe men and women in their country generally have the same opportunities in this area – and expressing their political views (63% say men and women have the same opportunities). No more than 6% say women have more opportunities than men in any of these realms. •Despite widespread support for gender equality around the world, a notable share (a median of 40% across the countries surveyed) thinks men should have more right to a job than women when jobs are scarce; 56% disagree with this notion. In some countries, men are more likely than women to say men should have preferen-

tial treatment when jobs are scarce, with double-digit gender differences in Kenya, Nigeria, Bulgaria, South Africa, Israel, Slovakia, Italy, Argentina and the Czech Republic.
•Tunisia is the only country surveyed where people say women have a better life than say men do, although similar shares say women enjoy the same quality of life. In most of the 34 countries surveyed, women are more likely than men to say men have a better life in their country.

Gender Neutral Laws, Equal Legal Rights

Historically, the importance of gender neutral laws has led to many changes in the social structure of the society. The relation between laws and religion, in India, are interlinked as the former derives its legislative backing from the latter. Equality for women has been recognised since colonial rule, as early as in 1925. The Commonwealth of India Bill, 1925, in clause 7 demanded for equality before the law and provided that there be "no disqualification or disability on the ground of only sex", along with the provision that all persons were to have equal right to the use of "roads, courts of justice, and all other places of business or resort dedicated to the public".

Constitutional Provision

The earliest case in India pertaining to women's right was Air India v. Nargesh Meerza where the Supreme Court held that the regulation of Air India pertaining to termination of an air hostess if she were to get pregnant within 4 years of service was held to be arbitrary and unconstitutional. This judgment is etched in history of women rights as an beacon for organisations to regulate the working condition of women on par with their male counterparts.

Article 15(3) of the Constitution empowers state to make special laws for protection of women and children rights. The reason for such law is that "women's physical structure and the performance of maternal functions place her at a disadvantage in the struggle for subsistence and her physical well-being becomes an object of public interest and care in order to preserve the strength and vigour of the race."

• In Dattatraya v. State, it was held that educational institutions established by the State exclusively for women, or the reservation of seats for women in a college- does not offend Article 15(1).

• In Rajesh Gupta v. State of U.P, the Court held that reservation of 50% of posts in favour of female candidates is not arbitrary.

The above judgments are a clear example of how judiciary has recognised and has safeguarded the rights of women in India in public life and at work place.

• The case of Vishaka and Ors. v. Sate of Rajasthan and Ors where the court laid down guidelines

Women Hit Harder by Pandemic

A recently released report shows that the pandemic pushed 96 million people into extreme poverty in 2021, 47 million of whom were women and girls. This brings the total number of women and girls living on US $1.90 or less, to 435 million.

The pandemic-induced poverty surge also widens the gender poverty gap – meaning, more women are pushed into extreme poverty than men. This is especially the case among those aged 25 to 34, at the height of their productive and family formation period. In 2021, it is expected there will be 118 women aged 25 to 34 in extreme poverty for every 100 men aged 25 to 34 in extreme poverty globally, and this ratio could rise to 121 poor women for every 100 poor men by 2030.

Poverty •Women earn less •have fewer savings •are disproportionately more in the informal economy •have no access to social protections •have to drop out of the labour force •make single-parent households.

Fallouts of Covid-19 on Children

C S Jaswant Kaur

This write-up discusses the after-effects of the pandemic, on children and adolescents. Many of them suffered in terms of losing their dear ones, unable to have proper meals, having to return to their village with their migrant-parents, and unable to continue with their education. The psycho-socio pressure has pushed some to child labour or even child marriage.

For a second time, we were under lockdown. The year 2021 sparked a new hope. We had a vaccine in place. Except in a few states like Kerala and Maharashtra, the invisible virus seemed to have lost its potency, forcing people to believe that the worst had passed. No one was sure that it would return with more force and vigour. In the end, corona came back throttling the overconfidence of those who thought they had won over it.

At the time of writing this piece, the number of confirmed Covid-19 cases has come down drastically. However, Kerala continues to cause concern. Unlike the beginning of the year, people have started getting vaccinated. Yet, the fear of a third wave looms large.

Amidst all this, a lot of people have lost their lives. A lot of children lost either or both of their parents. A large number of people have lost their spouses. Many families have been going through a devastating phase of their lives with job losses and reduced income. Several decades of development has fizzled out in these two years when the pandemic ruled the roast.

Loss on Education

Just before the corona virus hit the country, we took pride in the fact that India has achieved a record- enrolment in the schools. In fact, the recent UDISE+ report shows that the gross enrolment ratio (GER) for elementary education stood at 97.78 per cent in the year 2019-20. Not only this, the drop-out ratio reduced to 1.45 per cent at the primary level and 92.80 per cent children transitioned from primary to upper primary. The pandemic has reduced the school to a smartphone, leaving many children out of its scope. With less than 30 per cent people having a smartphone, one can imagine how connected children would be to education. Even now, many states have not opened their schools. A field study conducted by Azim Premji Foundation during the last lockdown, showed loss in learning outcomes just in a few months after the pandemic. The study covered 16,067 children in 1,137 public schools in 44 districts across five states.

The table below shows the crux of the findings:

Findings of the Study

Learning Loss in Language

- 92 per cent of the children lost at least one specific language ability from the previous year across all classes
- Illustratively, these specific abilities included describing a picture or their experiences orally; reading familiar words; reading with comprehension; writing simple sentences based on a picture
- 92 per cent in class 2, 89 per cent in class 3, 90 per cent in class 4, 95 per cent in class 5 and 93 per cent in class 6 have lost one specific ability from the previous year

Learning Loss in Mathematics

- 82 per cent of the children have lost at least one specific mathematical ability the previous year across all classes
- Illustratively, these specific abilities include identifying single- and two-digit numbers; performing arithmetic operations; using basic arithmetic operations for solving problems; describing 2D/3D shapes; reading and drawing inferences from data.
- 67 per cent of children in class 2, 76 per cent in class 3, 85per cent in class 4, 89 per cent in class 5, and 89 per cent in class 6 have lost at least one specific ability from the previous year.

Source: Loss of learning during the pandemic: Field studies in Education published by Azim Premji University in February 2021

Nutritional Loss

Children not only lost access to schools but also to the mid-day meals. Many a time, food was the only attraction for parents to enrol children in government schools, making it the main source of nutrition for children. Another survey con-

ducted by the same Foundation revealed that 77 per cent of households were consuming less food during the lockdown and 47 per cent had no money to buy even a week's ration.

Child Labour, Child Abuse, Child Marriage and Adolescent Girls

Another study conducted by a Delhi-based organisation, Protsahan India Foundation in collaboration with other NGOs like Deepalaya, shows that children and adolescent girls were not safe even within the four walls of their house. One of the four children reported that she was being abused by one of her close relatives. This is contrary to the recent data published in the national crime records bureau (NCRB) report 2020, which shows a stark dip in crime against children and adolescents. The difference can easily be attributed to the fact that children had no or limited access to child protection agencies during the lockdown. No reporting, unfortunately, means no crime for NCRB.

Similarly, the study reveals that close to 20 per cent of the children, essentially girls, were forced to do some kind of labour to keep their house running, be it selling vegetables or doing petty jobs to earn money. Not only this, around 17 per cent of the girls, who are traditionally considered a burden, were married off or traded for money. Many of them expressed a similar fear.

While child marriage is illegal, children rarely know about their rights. They end up managing a relationship, which is forced upon them by the choices of their parents.

When it came to saving money, 46 per cent of the girls, who had developed a habit to use sanitary napkins for managing menstruation switched to using cloth, readily available at home. This speaks volumes about the kind of hygiene they would have maintained as the study is silent on the kind of precautions these girls used for using cloth.

Two-thirds of the respondents revealed that they faced gender-based discrimination in view of inadequate resources. Boys were given preference for food, online education, Internet access etc. There is an increased fear of girls being forced to drop out of school as marriage has become a priority for the parents of 26 per cent adolescent girls.

Psycho-social Effects

Soon after the second wave, when people were worried about the increasing number of children, who might have lost one or both parents and social media was full of unsolicited and unverified requests for adoption of children, the national commission on protection of child rights tabled a report. The report showed that the pandemic orphaned 3,621 children. More than 27,000 children lost one of their parents and 274 children were abandoned. The data may seem grossly inadequate but the fact is that these children have been passing through the worst phase of their lives. It also raised a question on the inadequacy of our child protection system.

Government Schemes

Under pressure, various state governments announced several schemes for supporting orphaned children. These schemes promised to provide a monthly support of ₹2,000 to 5,000 to meet their education expenses. Of course, institutionalisation is the last resort as per various international conventions, treaties and even under the domestic legislation – the Juvenile Justice Act. But are these schemes adequate?

No. One, these schemes did not cover children who lost one parent. In many cases, the deceased was the sole earning member of the family. What will happen to such children? The government did not think about it. Two, these schemes are often inaccessible because of various reasons. Many do not even know about the existence of any such scheme. Even if they know, they either do not know the process of availing of these benefits or do not have adequate documents like a death certificate or proof showing that the death happened due to Covid-19.

The Central government, too, announced a package of supporting orphaned children with a fixed deposit of ₹10 lakh for meeting the long-term education needs of the children. Once they turn 18, they will be given monthly support for five years, after which they will be able to withdraw the corpus of ₹10 lakh.

The schemes announced by both the Central and state governments complement each other. They can meet both long-term and short-term needs of the children. But there is no clarity whether the children can avail of benefits under both. The Centre has told the Supreme Court that the family of everyone who died of Covid-19 would be given ₹50,000. However, the money will have to be shelled out by the state governments concerned.

A report published by Save the Children, another non-government organisation, shows that less than 25 per cent of the people have necessary documents to avail of the benefits listed under these schemes. Many do not have income proofs, bank accounts, Aadhar cards etc.

Again, these schemes have missed the need for incorporating into them a component of psycho-social counselling and an emotional connection with the children. They do not have a monitoring mechanism either.

While the above information is based on data collected by several NGOs, the government has not come up with con-

crete data on the after-effects of Covid-19 on children. The government and the state child protection agencies have not devised any solutions for issues faced by them. It is high time that the government chalks out a plan for their rescue and rehabilitation. The local bodies can be entrusted with the responsibilities of conducting remedial education and initiating health care and psycho-socio-counselling. This inaction will cost us dearly in the near future. The voices of children should be heard and acted upon.

The Third Gender

The third gender, are persons whose gender identity or gender expression differs from the assigned sex. In 2014, India recognised transgenders as the third sex. For the first time India's 2011 Census yielded the first official count of transgender population, at more than 490,000. •55,000 came from parents who identified their children as transgender • During the voter registration process, only 28,341 people registered as belonging to the third gender, but the census indicates a inflation in numbers. In India, this number could be 7 times higher •The low literacy rate in the transgender community is 46% in comparison to 74% literacy in the overall population. • The rights of transgenders are "largely compromised" and they live in isolation within households or as communities. • There is rampant societal gender discrimination in public space, work place or institutions. • Transgenders face identity crisis in a "gender-specific India", where everything has a gender identification including public utilities like toilets, security check at airports, ration card, PAN card, driving license, etc.

• Transgenders are harassed by their classmates and even teachers, a reason why they discontinue studies. •Transgenders are at times gang raped •They can't approach a police station fearing harassment. •Some of them present themselves as male to avoid rapes. •There is no legal support to a transgender for entering in to a marriage, having spouse and setting up of own family. •They are denied an accommodation, both on rental or in a hotel. •2% of them stay with parents. •89% qualified ones among them don't get employment opportunities • About 92% of them are deprived of the right to

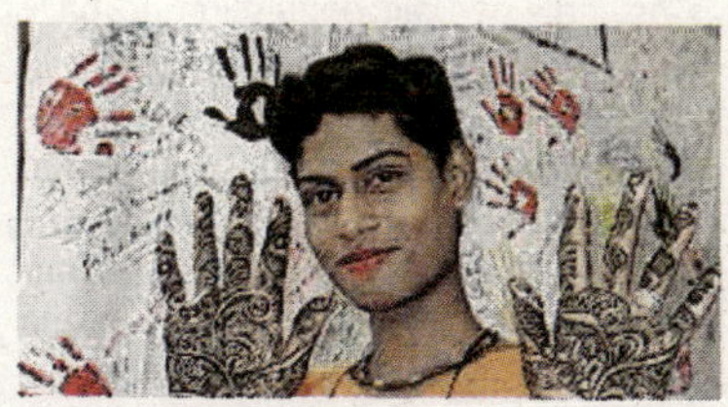

participate in any form of economic activities – even qualified ones are refused jobs compelling them to either beg, extortion or choose sex work. •23% are compelled to engage in sex work which has high health related risks.•With Government support and social acceptance transgenders can lead a dignified life.

Rights and Protection

In 2014, the Supreme Court of India recognised roughly half a million trans individuals as a third gender, giving a separate identity. The Transgender Persons (Protection of Rights) bill prohibits discrimination against transgender persons with regard to things like education, employment and the ability to rent or buy property. It gives transgender persons a "right to self-perceived identity"– but requires them to register with the government if they want to be officially recognised as "transgender" (provided they submit proof of gender to the government). They often face stigma and systematic exclusion in education and employment, difficulty to access health care and face disproportionate public violence and police brutalities. As a result, some feel they have no alternative but to turn to sex work; HIV prevalence among India's transgender community is 26 times higher than the national rate.

The Dalits

The roots of Dalit oppression go back to the origins of the caste system in Hindu religion. The philosophy of caste is contained in the Manusmriti, a sacred Hindu text dating from the second century BCE. 'Untouchable' outcast communities were forbidden to join in the religious and social life of the community and were confined to menial tasks that were viewed as polluting, such as animal slaughter and leatherworking.

The word "Dalit," meaning "oppressed" or "broken". Dalits are members of the lowest social strata in the Indian caste system – the Shudras (tenant farmers and servants).

Deep Discrimination

An 'untouchable' can never ascend to a higher caste order within their lifetime;

An 'untouchable can marry only a fellow 'untouchable' and can not eat in the same table or room and share drink from the same well . • They are not allowed to touch those of higher classes because of their 'uncleanliness' in the eyes of those of the higher order • They are banned from entering certain places of higher communities, touching their belongings or doing several activities like drawing water from village wells because their touch would taint the water for everyone else.

• They face discrimination and violence

Dalits, Statistically

• 4 states account for nearly 50% of the country's dalit population: 2011 census. UP stands first with 20.5% of the total scheduled caste (SC) population, Next is West Bengal with 10.7%

• Bihar with 8.2% and Tamil Nadu with 7.2 % come third and fourth. Dalits form around 16.6% of India's population.

• The 2011 census recorded nearly 20.14 crore people belonging to various scheduled castes in the country. As per the 2001 census, the number was 16.66 crore. The dalit population showed a decadal growth of 20.8%, whereas India's population grew 17.7% during the same period.

• There are around 9.79 crore women among the total SC population, and the sex ratio works out to 946 females per 1000 males. Nagaland, Lakshwadeep and Andaman and Nicobar islands have no scheduled castes among their population. Though UP has the largest chunk of the total SC population, Punjab has the largest share of dalits in its population at 31.9%. Himachal Pradesh and West Bengal follow Punjab with 25.2% and 23.5%. In Tamil Nadu, dalits account for about 18% of the population.

• Many scheduled caste families don't own land or any other property

• Though there is an increase in the population of dalits in the country, many states with a considerable number of dalits don't have any legislation to protect the interests of the community. Dalit empowerment is very poor in many states.

from members of higher castes – even raped and killed • They face discrimination particularly to get jobs, admission for education, and getting marriage partners.

• Many a times an 'untouchable' can not enter a Hindu temple or be taught to read. •They are allowed to live outside village boundaries and can not walk

through the neighborhoods of higher caste members. Earlier, if a Brahmin or Kshatriya approached, an 'untouchable' was expected to throw himself or herself face down on the ground, to prevent even their unclean shadows from touching the higher caste.

Income and Wealth Inequality

In India not only are there a rural-urban and gender bias but also a socio-religious component. Hindu High Castes (HHCs) boasts four times (41%) more wealth than those classified as Scheduled Castes (SCs)–almost double their population size of 22.28%. The next biggest slice of the wealth pie is cornered by Hindu Other Backward Classes (HOBCs) at close to 31%, a little less than their population size (35.66%). And, as expected, SCs and STs own substantially less share of assets (11.3% combined) as compared to their population size (over 27%).

• Under Hindu beliefs, jobs that involved death polluted the workers' souls, making them unfit to mingle with other people. India's 'untouchables' perform religiously polluting work that nobody else want to do, such as preparing dead bodies for funerals, tanning hides, and killing rats or other pests. Indians believe that people born as 'untouchables' is a punishment, the result of misbehavior in previous lives.

The caste system and the oppression of 'untouchables' still hold some sway in Hindu populations. Even some non-Hindu social groups observe caste separation too.

Dalit Rights Movement

Indian reformers took up the cause of untouchability. Jyotirao Phule coined the term "Dalit" as a more descriptive and sympathetic term for the Untouchables. During India's push for independence, activists such as Mohandas Gandhi also took up the Dalits' cause. Gandhiji called them the "Harijan," meaning "children of God," to emphasie their humanity.

Following independence in 1947, India's new constitution identified groups of former untouchables as "scheduled castes," singling them out for consideration and government assistance. Ninety years after the term was coined, the Dalits have become a powerful political force in India and enjoy greater access to education. Some Hindu temples allow Dalits to serve as priests. Although they still face discrimination from some quarters, the Dalits are untouchable no longer.

Understanding Disability

The complex, dynamic and multi-dimensional mien of disability indicates the vulnerability and marginalization of the people with disabilities. According to the International Classification of Functioning, Disability and Health (ICF) disability are the relations between an individual's health condition and various personal and environmental factors. The health conditions include any physical, neurological or mental health issues, whereas personal factors comprise of disability-related prejudices, discrimination, etc and environmental factors cover lack of infrastructure and inaccessibility that contribute to any type of disabilities. Against this backdrop, disability discourses centre around the negative notion on disability and focuses mainly on health and physical differences. Alternatively, the social model of disability is a collective approach of our society regarding the discriminatory social attitude towards disability resulting in issues related to social justice.

The Worldwide Scenario

According to the World Report on Disability, more than 1 billion people in the world live with some form of disability, of whom nearly 200 million experience considerable difficulties in functioning. In the years ahead, disability will be an even greater concern because its prevalence is on the rise. This is due to ageing populations and the higher risk of disability in older people as well as the global increase in chronic health conditions such as diabetes, cardiovascular disease, cancer and mental health disorders. Across the world, people with disabilities have poorer health outcomes, lower education achievements, less economic participation and higher rates of poverty than people without disabilities. This is partly because people with disabilities experience barriers in accessing services that many of us have long taken for granted, including health, education, employment, and transport as well as information. These difficulties are exacerbated in less advantaged communities.

Indian Scenario of Disability

The Disability Census 2011 covered eight types of disability in Indian scenario – 1. In seeing 2. In hearing 3. In speech 4. In movement 5. Mental retardation 6. Mental illness 7. Any other 8. Multiple disabilities.

• According to the 2011 Disability Census report, the percentage of the disabled population has significantly increased in both rural and urban area during the last decade. •44.1% females and 55.9% males have disability. The decadal increase in proportion was reported to be higher among females.

• In India, 1.67% of the 0 to 19-age population has a disability. 35.29% of all people living with disabilities are children. Only 1% of children with disabilities have access to school where 1/3rd of most disabilities are preventable.

• Census of 2011 also noted that the older population consists of about 8.6% of the total population who suffers from some sort of disability due to deterioration of health conditions. Thus these three categories are considered as vulnerable among the vulnerable and are mostly marginalised in terms of access to various facilities and even oppressed and neglected segments of our society.

But the third category of the population is not covered in the disability census data as the older population is not covered under the different categories of disabilities.

Refugees Worldwide

Today, there are more refugees and internally displaced people (IDPs) than at any point since World War II. Driven from their homes by conflict, persecution, environmental calamity, or dire economic straits, these refugees—more than half of whom are children—have been deprived of their statehood, material possessions, and in many cases, their loved ones. They seek solace in purpose-built refugee camps and unplanned settlements, where they wait out their displacement, or attempt to begin life anew.

The world is witnessing the highest levels of displacement on record – an unprecedented 79.5 million people forcibly displaced worldwide in 2019. •Half of them is under 18 years. •1% of the world's population is displaced. •80% of the displaced people are in countries or territories affected by acute food insecurity and malnutrition • 73% are hosted in neighbouring countries like Afghans in Pakistan and Rohingyas in Bangladesh •68% of the refugees originate from 5 countries •40 % of the displaced people are children 85% of them are hosted in developing countries. **•Top source countries:** Syria: 6.6m, Venezuela: 3.7m, Afghanistan: 2.7m, S. Sudan: 2.2m, Myanmar: 1.1m.

•Top hosting countries: Turkey: 3.6m, Columbia: 1.8m, Pakistan: 1.4m, Uganda:1.4m, Germany:1.1m.

•There are 4.2m stateless people, who have been denied a nationality and access to basic rights such as education, healthcare, employment and freedom of movement. •2m are asylum seekers •0.1m resetled in 26 countries •UNHCR, is the UN agency that works among them.

World's 10 Largest Refugee Camps

•Most of the world's refugee camps were temporary facilities. It has grown into city-proportion. •Refugee camps are symbols of human suffering • The huge size of these settlements depict the severity of forced displacement around the world. • these camps are also places of optimism as inhabitants consider these camps a way to safety and prosperity.

2018 Status: Kutupalong in Cox's Bazaar, Bangladesh Population 886,778 Rohingya from Myanmar due to Religious prosecution. Bidi Bidi in N. Uganda Population: 285,000 Sudaneses from S. Sudan following civil war Dadaab, Kenya Population: 235,269 Somalians due to civil war Kakuma, N. Kenya Population: 184,450 Somalians and Suadanese due to civil war Nyarugusu in Kigoma, Tanzania Population: 139,630 Refugees fleeing DR Congo and Burundi Jabalia, N. Gaza City on Gaza Strip Population: 119,486 Zaatari, N. Jordan Population: 80,140 Syrians due to civil war Yida, S. Sudan {Population: 70, 331 Sudanese from S. Sudan Katumba, Tanzania Population: 66,416 Burundians who fled Hutu genocide Pugnido, W. Ethiopia Population: 63,262 Sudanese from S. Sudanese due to violence outbreak Panian, Pakistan Population: Afghans due to internal strife.

Integrity

Integrity is a characteristic that many of us value in ourselves, and it's one we look for consistently in our leaders. But what does it really mean to have integrity?

Integrity is always doing the right thing, even when no one is looking, and even when the choice isn't easy. When we live our lives with integrity, it means that we're always honest, and we let our actions speak for who we are and what we believe in. Integrity is a choice we make, and it's a choice we must keep making, every moment of our lives.

Importance of Integrity

- We never have to spend time or energy questioning ourselves. When we listen to our hearts and do the right thing, life becomes simple. Our life, and our actions, are open for everyone to see, and we don't have to worry about hiding anything.
- We gain the trust of our leaders, our colleagues and our team. We're dependable, and, when we hold ourselves accountable for our actions, we become role models for others to follow.
- Integrity is a hallmark of ethical leadership – people who live and work with integrity are more likely to be considered for promotions.

Developing Integrity

Step 1: Define Your/organisation's core Values –So, these are the values that, no matter what the consequence, you're not going to compromise on.

Step 2: Analyse Every Choice You Make

If you want to be sure ask two questions:

i. "If my choice was printed on the front page of the newspaper for everyone to see, would I feel OK about it?"

ii. "If I make this choice, will I feel OK with myself afterwards?"

Honesty and integrity aren't values that you should live by when it's convenient; they're values that you should live by at all times– be it big choices or little choices; the choices everyone sees, or the choices no one sees.

Step 3: Encourage Integrity

People with integrity are humble, they have a strong sense of self, they have high self-esteem, and they're self-confident. These values will uphold you when you come under intense pressure from others to make the wrong choice.

Build your Self-confidence and Self-esteem

Spend time getting to know yourself, and what you believe in. Develop friendships and work relationships with others who demonstrate integrity, and who will support your decisions.

Learn how to be assertive

When you defend an ethical position from an adult point of view, without whining or being aggressive:

- Avoid white lies.
- Learn to take responsibility for your actions.
- Keep your word, and don't make promises that you know you can't keep. (Keep in mind that in times of fear, disaster and chaos, the temptation is even greater to make a wrong choice. Use these opportunities to demonstrate your true character.)
- Avoid seeming self-satisfied or priggish when you're acting with integrity: stay humble and down-to-earth, don't look for approval, and, where you sensibly can, try to let people save face.

Applied Ethics

Ethics is concerned with •what is good for individuals and society •a set of rules that describes acceptable conduct in society •a guide to moral daily living and helps us judge whether our behaviour can be justified •society's sense of the right way of living our daily lives. It does this by establishing rules, principles, and values on which we can base our conduct. The concepts most directly associated with ethics are truth, honesty, fairness, and equity.

Ethics may be a societal concern but it is of critical importance to the professions that serve society. Because physicians, judges, lawyers, engineers, managers, teachers, health-care workers, small retailers, clerks, drivers, etc. provide services that affect our welfare, they develop codes of ethics that establish standards for behaviour. For example, the types of standards found in professional codes of ethics include: an lawyer or physician maintaining client-patient confidentiality or an accountant not using client information for personal gain

Critical Dilemmas Ethics helps in sorting out certain dilemmas:

- how to live a good life
- our rights and responsibilities
- the language of right and wrong
- moral decisions - what is good and bad?
- how not to hurt others by ones actions.

Understanding Ethics

Ethical theories are categorised into three areas: metaethics, normative ethics and applied ethics.

Meta-ethics deals with the nature of moral judgement. It looks at the origins and meaning of ethical principles.

Normative ethics is concerned with the content of moral judgements and the criteria for what is right or wrong.

Applied ethics looks at controversial topics like war, corruption, human trafficking, animal rights, drug peddling and capital punishment

Benefits of Ethics

•Ethics provides good tools for thinking about moral issues.

•Ethics provides a moral map. For e.g.,think of abortion and euthanasia. Because these are such emotional issues we often let our hearts do the arguing while our mind just go with the flow. So ethics provides us with a framework, to find our way that is in the best interest of all.

• Ethics pinpoints a disagreement. When there are arguments about any moral issue, ethical principles will reveal that what they disagree about is just one particular part of the issue, and that they broadly agree on everything else. That can hint at a way for them to resolve their problem.

What it does not do Ethics, sometimes, may not provide people with the sort of help that they really want. Ethics also doesn't always show the right answer to moral problems. At times, ethics can give several options but many people would like to have single right answer to ethical questions. They find moral ambiguity hard to live with because it forces them to take responsibility for their own choices and actions, rather than falling back on convenient rules and customs.

At the heart of Ethics It is a concern about something or someone other than ourselves and our own desires and self-interest. So when a person 'thinks ethically' they are giving at least some thought to something beyond themselves. Therefore, ethics is concerned with other people's interests, with the interests of society, with God's will for the "ultimate good", and so on.

Ethics Vs. Morality It is not only about the morality of particular courses of action–what is good and bad. It is also about the goodness of individuals and what it means to live a good life.

5 Key Areas in Ethics for Decision Making

Values

Values are defined as the acts, customs, and institutions that a group of people regard in a favorable way. Statements of value typically contain words of approval, disapproval, and obligation. Some of these words might be good, bad, should, and should not. However, value judgments do not have to contain specific value words. "That is a lie" does not contain a particular word of disapproval, but the implication that a lie is wrong is understood.

Values are what really matter to us most–what we care about. For instance, faith and prayer, respect for the environment, and working hard for a wage or pay are three values that evoke a response in many people.

Morals

Morals are a set of rules or mode of conduct on which society is based. Certain moral elements are universal, such as the laws forbidding homicide and the basic duties of doing good and furthering the well-being of others. With morals serving as the underpinning of society, there are four points we should remember. •Moral rules are important: It helps society function in a civilised way. •Morality consists of universal rules: They apply to everyone, everywhere, and are recognised by everyone as being necessary. •Morals are objective: They do not consider personal preferences. Right is right and wrong is wrong. •Morality affects other people: Morality involves considering the well-being of others as reflected by the Golden Rule in the Bible: "Do unto others as you would have them do unto you."

Integrity

It is about honesty and sincerity. Integrity is a moral code in daily decision making. When people and businesses possess integrity, it means they can be trusted. On the other hand, companies that lack this quality mislead customers with false advertising or inferior products/services. They think only about profiteering. They be tested by law and will suffer the consequences.

Character

How we think and act is not just about ethics. It is also about character. Character drives what we do when no one is looking. A person with character has high morals and will act morally in all situations by choice, not force. A person with character will honor his or her commitments. Character pertains to organisations, as well. A company with high character is worthy of trust and respect, acts honestly, and stands by its promises.

Laws

The law is a series of rules and regulations that helps people. •Laws protect people from the most blatant and despicable affront to morality, such as murder, rape, and theft. •Laws provide us a sense of right and wrong and guide our behavior, but not always. While murder is against the law, the law does not always stop someone from killing another out of hatred, anger, or in defense of a personal ideology. •Laws are gives a notion of justice and tend to be specific, yet vary within different societies. •Laws have a connection to morality, ethics, and values. But, not all laws are ethical.

Sadly, laws at the wrong hands have legalised slavery, segregation, sexism, and apartheid. Although these laws might have reflected society's values at the time they were enacted, they can not nor will they ever justify immoral behaviour. Likewise in business, it is not unlawful to lie to a coworker or on a job application, but both are ethically wrong. These concepts thus should form the foundation of trust upon which ethical governance and business practice is built.

Women Achievers

Historic Moment in SC for Women

In a historic moment for gender representation, three women – Justices Hima Kohli, BV Nagarathna and Bela M Trivedi, took oath as judges of the Supreme Court. They are among the nine new appointees to the Supreme Court. With their appointments, the Supreme Court has four women judges - the highest ever - among 33 judges.

Justices BV Nagarathna, Hima Kohli Bela M Trivedi

The Supreme Court has had 11 women judges (including the new appointments) in its history so far. Justice Hima Kohli was elevated from the post of Chief Justice of the Telangana High Court. At the Supreme Court, she will have a term till September 2, 2024. Justice BV Nagarathna is the daughter of former Chief Justice of India ES Venkataramiah, Justice BV Nagarathna from Karnataka High Court is in line to become the first woman Chief Justice of India in September 2027 if appointments go as per the seniority turn. Justice Bela M Trivedi, the first woman judge from the Gujarat High Court to be appointed as the Supreme Court judge. At the Supreme Court, she will have a term till June 10, 2025.

The first 34 CRPF women commandos inducted into elite anti-Maoist CoBRA unit

Women Patrol at 14,500 feet

In a first, Durga Sati, 32, Roshni Negi, 25, and Mamta Kanwasi, 33, became the

first women guards to be deployed in the treacherous forests of the country's second highest mountain, Nanda Devi, over 25,000 feet high.

They patrol the mountains to protect rare animals and plants. There is always the threat of poachers, even at these altitudes. They also check water sources and see if anything appears amiss from a security point of view – ensure our territory is safe.

Their deployment came about with a chance conversation and initiative on their part. Women forest guards would usually go up to Lata, at 11,150 feet, but would be asked not to go further. But they thought, if not now, when? They believe strongly that they joined this service to serve the country and nature.

Captain Zoya Aggarwal, Captain Papagari Thanmai, Captain Akansha Sonaware, Captain Shivani Manhas – an all-women pilot team of Air India flew over North Pole air route. The flight from San Fransico (SFO) to Bengaluru covered a distance of about 16,000 kilometres.

Female Heavy Vehicle Driver Carry Hazardous Goods

Delisha Davis, 24-year-old MCom student in Thrissur, was passionate about driving from an early age and her father Davis P A, who has been a tanker driver for the past 42 years, had no qualms about encouraging his daughter. Now, she drives her father's tanker truck, carrying hazardous goods, with each trip extending up to 300km. For the past three years, Delisha has been driving the tanker from Kochi to Malappuram thrice a week to transport fuel from the refinery in Irumbanam to a petrol bunk in Tirur.

Delisha's story came to light two weeks ago after a motor vehicle department official stopped her tanker when she was driving to Tirur with the fuel. This happened after the department was informed by someone who saw 'a young girl driving a tanker through the national highway during the lockdown'. The official was surprised when she showed him her heavy vehicle driving licence and the licence to carry hazardous goods.

The officials congratulated her passion and informed the media. Her story would motivate women who are scared of driving. Delisha probably would be the only woman in Kerala who has a licence to carry hazardous goods.

Kamla Bhasin - a Beacon of Hope

The voice of eminent feminist icon, poet and author Kamla Bhasin was a prominent one in the women's movement in India, as well as in other South Asian countries. She brought a vigour to the feminist movement in the 1970s, and inspired a generation. Bhasin wrote extensively on gender issues and emphasised how feminism is not a war between men and women, but a fight between two ideologies. She fought for equal rights for over four decades, and was best known for her work with South Asian feminist network Sangat, which has trained several thousand women on gender issues. Bhasin also authored several books on the feminist movement, including Understanding Gender and What is Patriarchy. Bhasin passed away at the age of 75.

Indian-origin Student Elected Oxford Student Union President

Indian-origin student Anvee Bhutani has been elected as the president of the Oxford Student Union (SU) in a byelection.

She was elected at Stage 11, amassing 655 votes and narrowly beating out Yannis Baur, who amassed 649 votes.

Bhutani is a Human Sciences student from Magdalen College at the University of Oxford. She is also the Co-Chair Campaign for Racial Awareness and Equality (CRAE) at Oxford SU and President of the Oxford India Society. According to the Oxford student newspaper, the voter turnout was the highest ever for a byelection with 2,506 people voting, a jump of 146% from the last byelection in 2019.

SKILL DEVELOPMENT

- Personality Development
- The Trick Before a Tick
- Skill Mapping
- Effective Problem Solving
- Decision Making
- Attitude Towards Aptitude
- Job Oriented Skillsets

Personality Development

Personality development encompasses the dynamic construction and deconstruction of integrative characteristics that distinguish an individual in terms of interpersonal behavioural traits - Wikipedia

How to Make Your Personality Vibrant?

Discover the hidden aspects of your personality

Everybody possesses certain personality traits that set us apart from the rest. These traits define how we respond to situations and people.

Traits are not fixed! A research study by psychologists at the University of Illinois suggests that we can change our traits if we want to change them. In fact. we can become the best version of ourselves if we want to.

Here are some personality development tips:

Personality Development : The How's!

1. You are Unique

Lower your self-esteem down by comparing yourself with others that shrivels your personality and does not let your strengths blossom. Know that you and the other person are unique and are just can not be compared.

2. Do Yourself a Favour

From our childhood we are taught to be kind to others. Yet, many of us fail to be kind to ourselves. Studies show that self-compassion brings positive traits like optimism, extroversion, wisdom, happiness, positivity and resilience.

According to Emma Seppala, research psychologist at Stanford University, Self-Compassion involves 3 Steps:

- Recognise that you deserve care and concern like anyone else and that is why you must be kind and understanding with oneself.
- Recognise that making mistakes and failing is part of life. So, do not be hard on yourself when you commit a mistake or fail and indulge in self-critical thoughts.

Contrary to popular belief, self-compassion means taking corrective action, albeit without being too self-critical.

•Be aware of one's emotions and feelings.

3. Have Space for Imperfection

People and situations always do not fit in your frame of perfection. Often, that makes one agitated and angry, eventually diminishing the strength of their personality. So, find your peace amidst the world's flaws even as you strive to make a change.

Acceptance of imperfection allows you to be patient and calm.

4. Have Spontaneity

Spontaneity is the key to success, and being impulsive can be disastrous. Be cent percent aware or focussed in the present moment.

5. Light in Mind and Heart

Don't overthink and overanalyze. Neither let any negativity like shame, anger, jealousy or greed stay in your consciousness for too long. Instead, learn to take it easy; forgive easily and drop grudges against people as soon as they pop up. Being light in mind and heart makes you truly happy from within. And who does not like happy people?

6. Be Enthusiastic

Enthusiasm is infectious and appealing. That is why everyone loves kids. Despite adversity in life, one must never give up their enthusiasm.

7. Be a Communicator

Words can create laughter and can also create enmity. A skillful communicator can win over people and adverse situations. Try to bring clarity in your communication.

8.Warm and Approachable

We all like people with whom we can easily mingle and talk to. No one likes a person who responds with a straight face. So, learn to be warm. Flash that smile more often. Be friendly and be ready to share and help.

9. Have a Style in Work

Doing things with style adds zing to your personality. The secret to doing things with style lies in working with passion and a relaxed mind. So, while you work at something, don't let anything distract you from putting all your energy into it. At the same time, stay relaxed.

10. Leting Go

After you're done with a task, let go of your attachment with the result. When you let go, you become free, calm and relaxed - attributes of a strong personality.

11. Be Bold

Don't give into pressure and face every challenge confidently. Either you will overcome the adversity or learn something invaluable.

12. Stay Cool

Being calm strengthens one's personality. However, staying calm can be difficult when you have a terrible headache and have an urgent deadline to meet. In such situations, tap the power of breath. As soon as you become aware of it, your stress will diminish!

13. The Proton Principle

A proton can never lose its positivity. Nor can you! Stress may affect us on the outside. However, your inner core continues to radiate positivity like a proton. It stays unaffected, happy and peaceful. Tune into this part of yourself again and again with the help of meditation. The process energises and brings out positive traits like enthusiasm.

The Trick Before a Tick

Baskaran Krishnamurthy
Writer and Colomnist

Any numerical problem dwells in and is confined to the basic principles and the core concept of what Mathematics is all about. That is why it is very important to explore the ways to understand the underlying mathematical principle in every problem one is attempting to solve. This Article focusses on how to come to grip with it so that one can emerge successful.

Test on Numerical ability is something that poses the toughest challenge to the candidates of competitive examinations. Surprisingly, candidates with mathematics background are equally 'affected' too. What is more interesting is that numerical ability test remains challenging at all levels, right from Gr. 4 exam. It is understandable if it is a 'threat' at advanced levels. But how come, at every level it is a difficult one?

The problem is akin to the problem of acquiring proficiency in English language. Having studied in English medium does not come to the 'rescue' in English language tests. Same is the case with Mathematics. In spite of having been with Mathematics for at least 10 years in school, a test on numerical ability has never been anyone's cup of tea / coffee. Why so? Simple. We had studied to be good in the 'subject' whereas it should have been 'catching the concept' and progress.

If one had approached English as a language (what it is really), one would have learnt the nuances of it so easily and effortlessly that a test on English would have been as interesting as watching a movie. Similarly our knowledge of mathematics is limited to working out sums and finding the right answer.

The moment we start seriously or funnily look into the ways and methods employed to arrive at the answer, we almost conquer it. Yes. The process of exploring is where one's power of comprehending things in proper perspective begins. This is what is expected of the candidates and this is what the test of numerical test is all about.

Exploring is not a difficult job at all. It is more like correlation of various inputs; it is an exercise to put our 'experienced results' all together and find out an easier way of understanding things and arriving at the answer in a much faster way.

For example, a question reads thus: What is 4x7x3x5x5x5? Without actually working out, by merely looking at the question, we ought to know that when a number ending 5 is multiplied by any number(s), the last digit of the answer should be either 5 or zero. Similarly when an even number is multiplied, either by an odd or even number the last digit must be even number too. As usual 4 options are given; right? The options with other than 5 or zero in the first case; and the options ending with an odd number could be eliminated straightaway. Is it not? It means that almost 50% of the 'problem' is gone even before we sit down to work on it!

The Handy Tables

Tables play a major role in arithmetic sums. It would be great if one could master maximum number of tables; would be as much easier if one could by-heart

tables up to 100 (x100) This would immediately place this candidate above all others division / multiplication involving 2 digits could be done instantly. What is the problem in mastering the tables? To know something by-heart does not amount to rote learning by itself. The ability to calculate quickly and precisely comes only from one's mastery over tables that ensures accuracy and helps in error-free workings. To gain mastery over the tables may take time but it is worth trying since it would save so much of time crucial in the competitive examinations.

To excel in numerical tests, proper application of various formulas is very much required. A formula is nothing but a much shorter route that has been proven and accepted that can never go wrong. The challenge is in identifying the correct formula connected with a given problem since most of the times it is in a hidden form and is difficult to 'locate' and fix the formula into the sum. Once this is done, rest becomes much easier.

Patterns and Principles

Numerical sums follow a specific pattern, a certain procedure and a set principle. It is only the numbers that are changed. A sum on simple or compound interest at any level in any examination can never go beyond the frontiers of the formula for calculation of simple / compound interest. Any mathematical problem for that matter dwells in and is confined to the basic principles and the core concept of what Mathematics is all about. That is why it is all the more important to explore the ways to comprehend the underlying mathematical principle in every sum that is being practiced at home.

One can take guidance from the ones who have this ability to comprehend and explain the principle in simple terms. Without this, merely working out more and more sums, doing hundreds or thousands of exercises would do no good ever.

In what way would the concept help solve the problems in arithmetic? It is strongly advised that one should strictly adhere to the 'steps' or methods while working out a mathematical sum. Yet in a competitive examination one may have to take a route that is not generally prescribed by purists of the subject. This is only for the purpose of a tick against the right answers among the given options in a competitive examination.

Let us see some questions from numerical tests of various competitive examinations in the past and see what exactly these sums demand from us and how precisely we could tackle them too. These are sums from various examinations chosen with the view to know that there indeed are pretty simple questions and that one need not be apprehensive of facing the numerical ability test.

Central Armed Police Forces (ACs) Examination, 2021

• The ratio of monthly incomes of A and B is 7:10. The ratio of their expenditures is 2:3. If each of A and B saves ₹1000/- per month, then what will be the monthly income of B?

(A) ₹9,000/- (B) ₹10,000/-
(C) ₹15,000/- (D) ₹12,000/-

It might not be a bad idea to choose at random an option and see what happens. In this sum, of the 4 options given, option

(C) should be the easiest one to 'experiment'. If income of B is 10,000, at the ratio of 7:10, income of A would be 7000. They save ₹1000 which means that A has spent (7000- 1000) ₹6000 while B has spent (10000 – 1000) ₹9000. What is the ratio of expenditure now? 6000:9000 i.e. 2:3. This is what the sum says too. So that is the answer too – option B – 10,000.

Trick: choose an easy option from the list and see how much it deviates. On this basis we can pick the right one.

• A, B and C start a business by investing ₹7,000, ₹8000 and ₹12,000 respectively. After a year, B gets ₹3,200 as his share of profit. What is the total profit?

(A) ₹16,600/- (B) ₹10,000/-
(C) ₹21,600/- (D) ₹10,800/-

This again is from CAPF examination 2021. The ratio of investments is 7000:8000:12000 i.e. 7:8:12. Total – 27 units. B's share 8 units gets 3200. One unit works out to 400. This is to be multiplied by 27. (27x4=108) So the answer is 10800. One can do it by heart. Isn't it? .

National Defence Academy and Naval Academy Examination (I), 2021

The numbers of Science, Arts and Commerce graduates working in a company are 30, 70 and 50 respectively. If these figures are represented by a pie chart,

extra

Effective Skills

Effective writing skills and good verbal communication skills go hand-in-hand. The first impression is the best impression and many fail this test due to various impediments such as stage fright, lack of self-confidence and performance anxiety.

then what is the angle corresponding to Science graduates?

(A) 36 (B) 72 (C) 120 (D) 168

Total number of graduates (30+70+50 =150) Science graduates – 30 i.e. 1/5 of the total. In a pie chart of 360 degrees, 1/5 would be 72. So the answer is B. Just a mind work would do if Science graduates form 1/5th of total strength. Rest is simple.

UPSC - Engineering Services (Preliminary) Examination, 2021

• The population of a village is 5500. If the number of males increases by 11% and the number of females increases by 20% then the population becomes 6330. The population of female in the village is

(A) 2000 (B) 2500
(C) 3000 (D) 3500

Here again, a random pick would do. Let us consider 3000 (an easy number) . If females are 3000, males should be 2500. Increase in that case – males @ 11% - 275; females @ 20% - 600. Total increase comes to 875 whereas as per the sum it is 830 (6330 – 5500) So I the answer should be less than 3000. (either 2000 or 2500) What could be seen here is that it can not be 2000 either because that would leave males at 3500 resulting in a number ending 5 while we calculate the increase by 11. Hence the answer should be 2500.

Combined Defence Services Examination (I), 2021

• A trader gives successive discounts of 20%, 10% and 5% respectively. What is the overall discount?

(A) 30% (B) 31.6%
(C) 32.8% (D) 35%

A proper understanding of the sum would do. There are discount amounts. We need to know the total of them. First discount @20% - Rs 20. Balance amount is 80.Second discount @ 10% (of 80) ₹8. Third amount 80-8=72. This discount @5% (of 72) is ₹3.60. Hence the total discount should be 20+8+3.6= 31,6. Option B is the right answer. In this sum we start from the question and move towards the answer.

•A sum of money was invested at simple interest at a certain rate for 5 years. Had it been invested at a 5% higher rate, it would have fetched ₹500/- more. What was the principal amount?

(A) 2000 (B) 1800
(C) 1600 (D) 1200

This is again from the Combined Defence Services Examination 2021. If the rate for one year is higher by 5%, for 5 years it would be 25%.i.e, ¼ of the total amount. So the principal would be

500x4=2000. No need to work out. Just understanding the sum in proper perspective is what is needed.

• The difference between the compound interest (compounded annually) and the simple interest on a certain sum of money at 12% per annum for 2 years is ₹72. What is the principal amount?

(A) 6500 (B) 6000
(C) 5500 (D) 5000

For the first year simple interest and compound interest would be same. So the difference of ₹72 would have come from the interest added for the second year. How much is the amount? If 12% is 72, 100% is 600. This is the interest for the first year. This is 12% of the principal.

If 12%is 600 what would be 100% (the principal) 600/12x100=5000. Answer is D.

• A train travelled 600 km in 5 hours and the next 900 km in 10 hours. What is the average speed of the train?

(A) 80 km/hr (B) 90 km/hr
(C) 100 km/hr (D) 120 km/hr

In this sum many candidates would start working out the average speed at first level;and then the next level. It is not at all required. What was the total distance covered? (600+900) 1500km, What was the total time spent? 5+10=15hrs. So the average is 1500/15=100. Hence C is the answer.

• In a mixture of 80 litres of a liquid and water, 25% of the mixture is the liquid. How much water should be added to the mixture so that the liquid becomes 20% of the mixture?

(A) 15 litres (B) 20 litres
(C) 24 litres (D) 25 litres

At present @25%, the liquid is 20 litres; If this 20 litres is 1/5th (20%) of the mixture, total mixture should be 100 litres. To reach 100 litres, 20 litres of more water is required. Answer is B. The concept to bear in mind is that the liquid will remain 20 litres; only by adding water, the equation / ratio changes. .

20 persons can clean 20 floors in 20 days, then in how many days can 16 persons clean 16 floors?

(A) 25 days (B) 24 days
(C) 20 days (D) 16 days

It is a very interesting one. In the above sum what could be seen is that for one person to clean one floor, it takes 20 days. Now we have 16 people for 16 floors. This means for each floor there is one person. So naturally it would take same 20 days here too. When two of three components are in same proportion, the third will remain as it is. Got it?

Staff Selection Commission - Model Question Paper (from Official Website)

• The boys of a class are made to stand in a queue. Amit is standing at 15th place from both ends. How many boys are there in the queue?

(A) 31 (B) 30
(C) 29 (D) 28

Staff Selection Commission has given this as one of the model questions. Amit is 15th meaning there are 14 boys on either side i.e. there are 28 apart from him. Add him too since he is also in the queue. Answer is 29.

We have so far seen a few sums from the previous question papers of leading competitive examinations. It might be clear by now that numerical tests have a part that is easy, simple and encouraging too. All we need to do is to be strong in the basics and apply our mind to catch the concept behind the sum. It is then a child's game to play, to enjoy and to be happy about.

Cheer up – mathematics is very much our domain too!

extra

NASA can Basically "email" Tools to Astronauts

Getting new equipment to the Space Station used to take months or years, but the new technology, 3D Printing, means the tools are ready within hours.

Aptitude On Test

In India, the process of recruitment for an entry into Public service remains by and large the same for many decades. The changes that are being made are often towards toughening the questions or amending the pattern rather than changing the concept or the subject as such. Except the current affairs related questions, rest of the syllabus remains the same as it existed many years ago. This is primarily because the basis of testing one's knowledge has always been the same all over.

The advent of National Recruitment Agency again does not promise any change in the syllabus but reinforces more or less same pattern that has become synonymous with any competitive examination in India today. This 'stability' should be in a way an advantage to the aspiring youth because they can start preparing for the exams on their own with a clear cut approach and strategy.

The idea of a candidate being tested before being selected for a job emanates from the need to choose the best among many contenders. This necessitates a procedure that is fool proof in picking up the really right candidate in every perspective. The traits or skills that are expected of an examinee include accuracy, swiftness and mental ability.

The best way of examining, evaluating and judging one's suitability to a particular job is to challenge his/her grasping power and presence of mind that play a vital role in carrying out the given task. Here comes the role of a test that would truly bring out and identify the best among the lot. As such, the scope of a competitive exam goes far beyond testing one's knowledge and enters into the area of individual skills and talents in effectively tackling various problems in a given situation.

In this regard, the purpose of selecting the most talented person is best served through what is called – 'Aptitude tests'. These are the most effective way of testing one's brilliance and capacity to solve a problem.

Of all the segments in aptitude tests, Numerical Reasoning is perhaps the easiest one provided one gets to know the nuances of it.

Candidates are required to apply certain basic mathematic principles and do a little bit of working to find out the answers. Here it is not the best answer; but the correct answer that has to be found. This means that one need not imagine or presume but has to work out mathematically to arrive at the answer.

The topics that are normally found in these tests include Average, Percentage, Simple/Compound Interest, Work&Time. Time &Speed, Ratio & Proportion, Data Interpretation, Coding and decoding.

Questions on numerical reasoning might 'look' difficult whereas in practice they are much easier to answer.

Let us see this example:
Find out the sum of $93^2 - 7^2$.

If we can apply the appropriate mathematical formula, the answer could be

Liberal Arts Education

extra

The history of liberal arts education dates back to classical antiquity. Stemming from the Latin word "liberalis" meaning "appropriate for free men." A liberal arts education was a course of study considered essential for free citizens of Greece and Rome.

found in seconds. It should be 8600. We need not find the squares of 93 & 7 then deduct. It is enough we apply the formula: $a^2 - b^2 .= (A+B) (A-B)$ i.e. (93+7) (93-7) = 100 X 86 = 8600.

Sometimes we will have to apply certain logic to find the answer. See this question from CSAT Prelims – 2019:

A and B are two heavy steel blocks. If B is placed on the top A, the weight increases by 60%. How much weight will reduce with respect to the total weight of A and B, if B is removed from the top of A?

(A) 60% **(B)** 45.5% **(C)** 40% **(D)** 37.5%

Answer should be 37.5%

Explanation: If the weight of A is 100, on placing B on top, it becomes 160. When it is removed now, we have to work out its weight (60) proportionate to 160 (combined weight) i.e. 60 / 160 of 100 = 37.5% Instead of 160, many would be tempted to take 100 and land in wrong answer.

Let us Consider Another One

CSAT Prelims – 2019 Qn. No. 15
In a school every student is assigned a unique identification number. A student is a football player if and only if the identification number is divisible by 4, whereas a student is a cricketer if and only if the identification number is divisible by 6. If every number from 1 to 100 is assigned to a student, then how many of them play cricket as well as football?

(A) 4 **(B)** 8 **(C)** 10 **(D)** 12

Answer should be 8.

Explanation: One who plays both cricket and football must have a number divisible by both 4 and 6. LCM for 4 and 6 is 12. To see how many numbers in 100 are divisible by 12 is very simple – 100 / 12. Let us leave the fraction. The answer is 8.

Process of elimination: In any test, the most effective way of answering objective type questions is to resort to what is called 'the process of elimination'. More often than not, it so happens that the candidate does not know the right answer to the question; yet, he / she would be able to pick the right answer by removing the wrong options.

For example - 733 = ?

Here, we need not multiply it to the last digit. First, let us find out the last digit. 3 X 3 X 3 = 27. So the last digit should be 7. Options with other than 7 as the last number could be eliminated. Next stage is to multiply 70 X 70 X 70 = 343000. Hence the answer should be a little above 3,43,000 with the last digit being 7. This must have helped us land at the correct answer.

This method of arriving at the correct answer by eliminating the wrong options is most needed in Aptitude tests. This would come handy only if one is used to applying this principle at the practice sessions.

We need to mention it here that many of the candidates in their preparations arein the habit of 'working out' every sum. This tendency would follow them in the original test as well which is not good where the elimination process would have been enough. This process would save precious time and also ensure the correctness in choosing the right answer.

Logical reasoning - is classified into two types:

Verbal Reasoning: It is the ability to logically understand the concepts / problems explained in words. It tests the ability to understand the given information and the implications thereof.

Non-verbal Reasoning: It is the ability to logically understand the concepts / problems expressed in numbers/letters/ figures. There could be verbal explanation too. It tests the ability to find out the logic that the given information carries and the implications thereof.

To solve questions on Logical Reasoning, we should read the information, word by word, critically analyse it and weigh all possible solutions. This segment is more about being judgemental rather than being factual or accurate. It means that one has to apply his / her mind and see what could be the best among the given options in the question.

Logical Reasoning may include the following areas: Statement analysis – assumptions and conclusions, Odd one out, Paper folding, Picture series, Coding and decoding, alphanumeric series, analogies, blood relations and data interpretation.

Consider the following pattern of numbers:

8	10	15	13
6	5	7	4
4	6	8	8
---	---	---	---
6	11	16	X

What is the number at X in the above pattern?

(A) 17 **(B)** 19 **(C)** 21 **(D)** 23

Answer (A) 17 (Put a minus mark before the middle number in each row)

Verbal Reasoning

Another model is to present a passage followed by certain statements. We are asked to decide whether the statement is true, false or cannot say. Let us consider this example. (source could not be confirmed)

A state government has chalked out a plan for its underdeveloped districts where 66% of the funds will be placed in the hands of a committee of local representatives.

Courses of action:

I. The 'A' state government should decide guidelines and norms for the functioning of the committee.

II. Other state government may follow similar plan if directed by the Central government.

A. If only I follows
B. If only II follows
C. If either I or II follows
D. If neither I nor II follows
E. If both I and II follow

Answer: There is only in the above two sentences that follows the passage naturally. The other one is a 'development' rather than a conclusion. Hence, A must be the answer.

RRB 2016

Given below a statement followed by some conclusions. You have to take the given statement to be true even if it seems to be at variance with the commonly known facts and then decide which of the given conclusion logically follow (s) from the given statements.

Statement:

High risks yield higher returns.

Conclusion:

I. No risks yield no returns.

II. Everyone should take risks in life.

A. Only conclusion I follows
B. Only conclusion II follows
C. Both I and II follow
D. Neither of them follows

Answer: D. 'Conclusion' should naturally flow from the given sentence; it is not something that is 'understood' or inferred. As that is not the case above, D should be the answer.

For the Non - Verbal Reasoning segment, candidates may try as many problems as possible in the following areas:

Series, Classification, Mirror images, shapes, cubes and dice, paper folding, pattern reading, figure matrix etc.

Questions based on Diagram test one's logical, non verbal reasoning ability. One should try to infer a set of rules from the chart / diagram and apply those rules to the given situation.

In this segment, the candidate is required to compare different figures of different shape, find out the uniformity or otherwise and choose the right answers from the options given in the question. A definite mode / sequence would have been applied in the problem and the candidate has to apply his mind and catch the sequence; there ends the challenge.

Let us consider this example.

Combined Graduate Level Examination – 2019 (Tier-1)

Select the figure that can replace the question mark (?) in the following series.

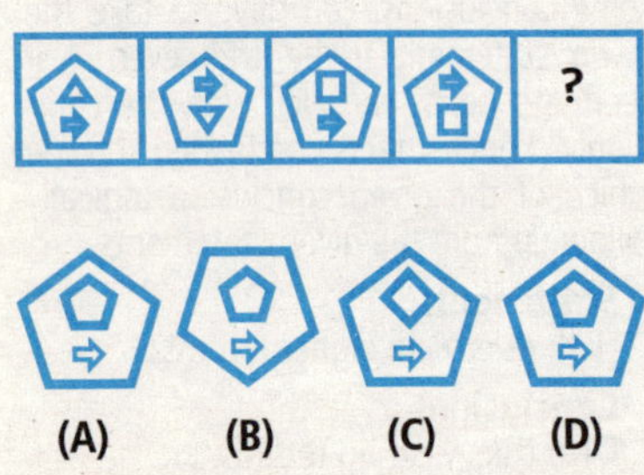

Explanation: The question carries four figures in a particular sequence followed by four options one of which would fit into the 5th box. The examinee should try to find out the logical sequence in the diagram. Once done, the answer would be readily available.

Each box has 3 figures. One should start from the largest figure that keeps rotating upwards and downwards. Sequentially the 5th one should look upward. The second large figure is triangle that swings once and then adds one side more to it becoming a square. Hence sequentially the next one in the 5th box should be of 5 sides looking upward. Third figure is an arrow that changes its direction; which should be showing the right side in the 5th box.

Among the four options given, option A is the one that fulfils the conditions. Hence the answer is A.

Let us see one more in the same segment.

Combined Graduate Level Examination – 2019 (Tier-1)

Select the figure that can replace the question mark (?) in the following series.

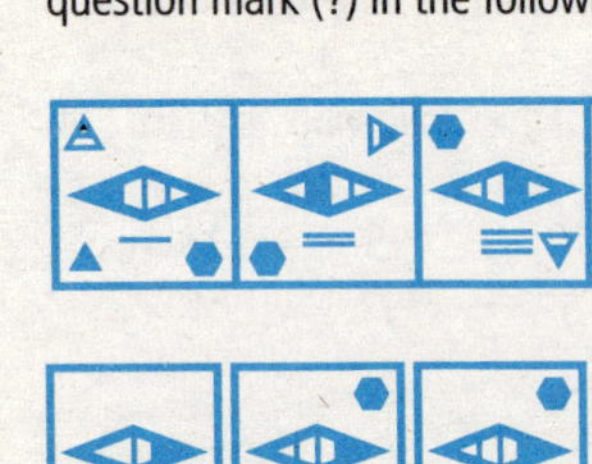

(A) (B) (C) (D)

Method of finding the answer:

When we have many figures in a box, we have to go by the sequence of each unit – starting from left, moving clockwise. A triangle on the top left moving to next side of the box; as such, the triangle should be facing the 4th side of the 4th box. This eliminates figures (A) and (C). Next comes the black dot which is place in the same position in both (B) and (D) and so need not be compared. The 3rd figure is horizontal line that adds one

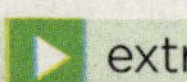

The Phrase "Democratic Recession"

The phrase was coined by the Hoover Institution's Larry Diamond to describe an erosion of civil liberties around the globe. He notes a worrying trend where more countries in the last five years have abandoned democracy.

more in each box starting from 1 to 3. So, the next box must have 4 lines. On this ground, Option (D) is the answer.

Note: since the answer is arrived, we need not spend time in comparing the 4th figure in the box. (remember - the method of elimination)

Candidates taking on aptitude tests are required to be fully focused and apply various principles to understand the concept and answer the question. Though one needs to be 'logical' and judgemental, the scope is really limited to a set 'pattern'. It is more about being on the right path rather than trying anything new or different. Because, 'pattern' always means a definite method, a common factor that is to be identified and followed.

The Key Points

1. No need to spend too much of time on any single question. All questions carry equal marks and hence do not devote relatively much longer time on any single question.

2. No need to keep re-verifying the chosen answer. Generally candidates have a tendency to do the working at least two or three times on each question to doubly ensure the correctness of the answer. This must be avoided very strictly. Once an option is chosen, the candidate should immediately mark the answer and move on to the next question. Staying on at the same question even after choosing the answer is a grave mistake. This would take away precious minutes and would lead to paucity of time in completing the question paper.

3. One has to instantly decide whether the answer has to be worked out or the

process of elimination would do. Under no circumstances, a candidate should try both methods.

4. Where at a simple glance, the question is found to be incomprehensible, one should decide whether a random selection of an answer is ok or to leave it out. No purpose would be served in struggling with a question where it is all dark and nothing could be derived out of it.

5. Finally, in competitive exams, in Aptitude Tests, one has to tackle the time constraint. Same candidate who finds the paper difficult would find it much easier if enough time is available at his / her disposal. This means that it is all about being fast and accurate rather than being slow and steady.

One should be like a runner in the 100m race – never having time to think or to look around. The moment whistle goes off, one must start running and should be on toes till the race is over.

Being strong in 'basics' with a focused mind and a determined approach, a candidate would be able to perform very well in the Aptitude tests and that would be sufficient to be successful in the examination.

All the best!

extra

Idi Amin's Ouster

In 1978, Uganda seized the small territory known as the Kagera Salient from Tanzania. Rather than accept the loss, Tanzanian forces attacked, retook it, and then continued on to Uganda's capital of Kampala, where they ousted the infamous dictator.

Job Oriented Skillsets

For many people today, a career for life is no longer an option. Most people will hold jobs with a variety of employers and move across different employment sectors through their working life. A skill is an ability to perform an activity in a competent manner. Skills can be classified into three main types: Transferable/Functional, Personal Traits/Attitudes, and Knowledge-based.

Employability is: "a set of achievements – skills, understandings, and personal attributes – that makes graduates more likely to gain employment and be successful in their chosen occupations, which benefits themselves, the workforce, the community, and the economy."It is not just about getting a job, it is about a broader set of skills and attributes that will enable a graduate to be successful throughout their working life.

What are Employability Skills?: These are the Skills You Need to Get a Job.

What skills do employers want? How do these skills match those that youth and adults are developing through their school and work experiences? How can education and training programs prepare individuals to enter a rapidly changing workplace?

The American Society for Training and Development (ASTD) emphasised 6 skill groups across all job families:

1. Basic Competency Skills - of reading, writing, computation
2. Communication Skills -of speaking, listening;
3. Adaptability Skills- of problem solving, thinking creatively;
4. Developmental Skills -of self-esteem, motivation, and goal-setting, career planning;
5. Group Effectiveness Skills- of interpersonal skills, teamwork, negotiation
6. Influencing Skills- of understanding organisational culture, sharing leadership

Employers are often looking for skills that go beyond qualifications and experience. Your education and experience may make you eligible to apply for a job but, to be successful in most roles, you will need skills that you are likely to develop over time. Some will be specific to the job, but the vast majority will be so-called 'soft skills' that can be used in any job or employment sector.

As a general rule, employers are willing to teach someone the job-specific skills required, such as how to operate particular pieces of machinery, or use particular computer packages that are very specific to that role or company. However, they usually want to see that you already have the other 'soft skills' before hiring, because they are much harder to teach.

Hard Skills vs. Soft Skills

One considerable difference between hard skills and soft skills during the hiring process is that you can list and verify hard skills, while soft skills are typically displayed during in-person interviews

Soft Skills generally pertain to interpersonal skills and other personality traits that allow you to communicate and work with others. Soft skills are also transferable, which means they are valuable for any job, no matter which industry.

Examples of Soft Skills

- Adaptability
- Communication
- Conflict resolution
- Creativity
- Decision making
- Leadership
- Motivation
- Teamwork

Hard Skills, also known as technical skills, are capabilities you use to perform a task related to a specific job. You can gain or improve these skills through training, tutorials and practice.

Examples of Hard Skills

- Accounting
- Copywriting
- Data analysis
- Event planning
- Foreign language fluency

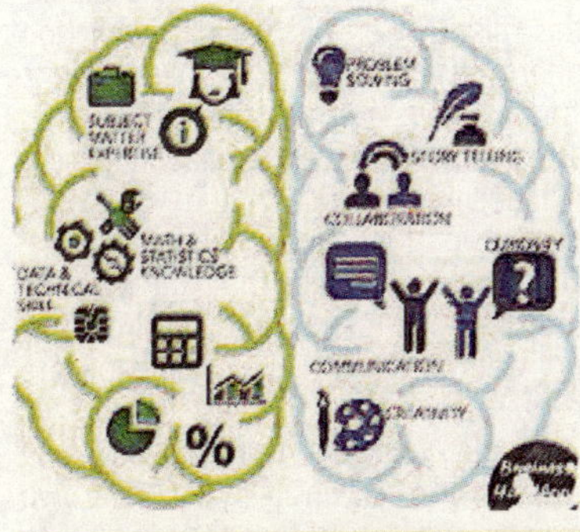

- Graphic design
- Information technology
- Mathematics
- Time management

Hard and soft skills can be further broken down into the following groups:

Hybrid Skills are a combination of hard and soft skills—many employers expect individuals to have both to succeed. A good example of a hybrid skill is customer service. While you need to have exceptional soft skills such as communication and conflict resolution, you might also be expected to be proficient with spreadsheets or a specific customer service management system.

Transferable Skills are skills that apply to any job, no matter the level or industry. Transferable skills are typically soft skills such as problem-solving and communication, and sometimes hard skills, such as mathematics and writing.

Job-specific Skills are the capabilities required for a certain position including both hard and soft skills. You usually gain these through education or on-the-job experience. Pay attention to the job description when searching for jobs to understand what job-specific skills an employer expects from their ideal candidate.

The most important employability skills are in the areas of:

- Getting along with and working well with other people, such as communication skills and other interpersonal skills;
- Being reliable and dependable: doing what you say you will by the deadline you have agreed, and turning up when you are meant to be there; and
- A willingness to learn new skills, whether those are job-specific or more general.

extra

Seizing Islands in Peacetime

Since 1918, there have been 28 instances of a country seizing one or more islands from another in peacetime. Only one—Argentina's ill-fated attempt to take the Falkland Islands in 1982—led to war.

Interpersonal Skills

Good interpersonal skills allow you to participate effectively as a member of a team, satisfy customers' and clients' expectations, negotiate, make decisions and solve problems with other people, and generally, work effectively with other employees. Well-honed interpersonal skills allow us to empathise and build rapport with colleagues and clients, leading to a better and less stressful working environment.

There are a range of areas covered by interpersonal skills, including:

1. Communication Skills these are the skills required to transmit or receive messages accurately to and from other people by speaking or in writing, without misunderstandings. These skills include:

Verbal Communication– or the words that we use, whether face-to-face or in writing. The balance between face-to-face and in writing is likely to vary in different jobs, but few, if any, will not want at least some of each type of communication;

Non-Verbal Communication– or what we communicate without words, for example through body language, tone of voice, or even emojis; and

Listening– how we take in and then interpret the verbal and non-verbal messages sent by others.

Emotional intelligence– or the ability to recognise, understand and manage your own and others' emotions, and use them positively to achieve the desired outcomes.

Team-working– the ability to work with others in groups and teams, both formal and informal. Not everyone is required to work in a close-knit team—despite the language used in many organisations—but the ability to function well in a group is a vital skill in most jobs.

Negotiation, persuasion and influencing skills– these skills all relate to finding mutually agreeable solutions to problems or situations, whether by persuading others that your solution is best, or finding a better alternative by sharing ideas.

Conflict resolution and mediation– or the skills required to resolve disagreements in a positive way, whether your own disagreements or those involving other people. These skills are often underrated until there is a problem.

Problem-solving and decision-making– or the skills needed to work effectively with others to identify, define and solve problems, including making decisions about the best course of action. Of course, it is also possible to make decisions and solve problems on your own, but being required to do so with others adds an extra dimension to the situation.

2. Being Reliable and Dependable

Being reliable and dependable are complimentary traits that would cause one to deliver what is required, expected, assigned, appointments and meeting deadlines. This sounds simple, but it requires a wide range of skills, mostly personal rather than interpersonal.

Being reliable also means being trustworthy and conscientious. For example, this might mean not leaving work (too often) when things still need doing. Trustworthiness and conscientiousness are both parts of self-regulation or self-management, which in turn is an important part of emotional intelligence. Self-regulation means that you have the self-discipline to do things that you may not want to do, but which you know are necessary.

People who are self-regulated and reliable take responsibility for their own actions and ensure that they live up to their values. They keep track of deadlines and deliver to them without needing to be chased up.

Being reliable does not, however,

mean that you have to do everything yourself. Sometimes, it may mean asking for help when you see that you are not going to be able to meet a deadline otherwise.

The final element of being reliable is using your initiative to identify where work needs doing, and getting on and doing it. Daniel Goleman, who developed the concept of emotional intelligence, identified initiative as a key part of self-motivation. He defined it as 'readiness to act on opportunities'. To develop your ability to use your initiative, you may find it helpful to work on some techniques for creative thinking, which are also helpful in addressing the final area: a willingness to learn.

3. A Willingness to Learn

A willingness to learn means being open to new ideas and experiences, and always looking to improve your skills and knowledge. Sometimes this is referred to as personal development, but that term is also used for a more formal process, of goal-setting, action and reflection. Whether you choose to make your learning process formal or informal, there is no question that the modern world requires all of us to continually update and revise our skills.

Communication Skills

1. Oral Communication is not merely the ability to speak, but also the capacity to listen. It is an art that can be learned and polished through reading, presentation skills and practice. A good communicator is one who is attuned to the audience and is able to calibrate his message accordingly. An aspiring oral communicator should be willing to acquire and hone his

listening skills over a period of time.

An oral communicator should have intellectual curiosity. A well-educated mind would be able to communicate better as content is the soul of the communication process. With an attitude of discussion and deliberation one can improve intellectual capabilities and thereby contribute to effective communication.

Effective writing skills and good verbal communication skills go hand-in-hand. The age-old dictum 'Practice makes a person perfect' makes perfect sense in the world of oral communication. The first impression is the best impression and many fail this test due to various impediments such as stage fright, lack of self-confidence and performance anxiety. A person can conquer his fears and master the art of oral communication by participating in many real and mock presentations, and speech-based activities.

Active participation in the community would transform a student into a good communicator by honing his linguistic abilities.

2. Written Communication

Written communication skills are those necessary to get your point across in writing. While they share many of the same features as verbal communication skills, there are some important differences.

Stanford University

Stanford University was founded in 1891 by California senator and railway magnate Leland Stanford in honour of his deceased son, with the promise that "the children of California shall be our children."

Where verbal communication uses body language and tone of voice to express meaning and tone, written communication relies on grammar, punctuation and word choice. Developing written communication skills requires practice and fine attention to detail.

In some ways, effective written communication is even more important than spoken communication. Unless it is being recorded, regular speech does not last. However, written communication is a record, and people may refer back to it later. This means that in addition to creating a connection with your audience, you need to consider the lasting impact of what you write. Think about how it will be perceived by your audience initially, as well as the impact it will leave.

Good written communication depends on the audience, the topic, your purpose in communicating, and other factors. However, all effective written communication has some characteristics in common:

5 Cs of Effective Written Communication

Connection- Good written communication forms a connection between the reader and the writer.

Clarity- Effective written communication is clear and easy to understand.

Cause- The cause or reason for writing needs to be clear to both the writer and the reader, including any specific actions you need from your audience.

Conciseness Good written communication sticks to the point and doesn't meander around or include lots of extraneous information.

Correctness To be effective, written communication should use the correct tone, inoffensive language, and appropriate grammar.

Here are a few tips that will help you in communicating effectively in writing

- Know Your Goal and State It Clearly
- Use the Correct Tone for Your Purpose
- Keep Language Simple
- Stay on Topic and Keep It Concise
- Use Active Voice
- Have Someone Proofread Your Writing

Adaptability Skills

Adaptability skills are skill sets that encompass a person's ability to adjust to changes in their environment. Being adaptable in one's career can mean to be able to respond quickly to changing ideas, responsibilities, expectations, trends, strategies and other processes at work.

Adaptability in the workplace plays a vital role when working on projects, developing strategies and implementing different approaches to doing your job. By showing your employers your adaptability skills, you are revealing how motivated you are to try new things and learn new skills.

Examples of adaptability skills

Adaptability skills can include a variety of skill sets that can essentially help you adapt to and deal with change in a positive and proactive way. Some of these important soft skills include:

- Communication skills
- Interpersonal skills
- Problem-solving skills
- Creative and strategic thinking skills
- Teamwork skills
- Organisational skills

Communication Skills

Being adaptable can depend on how effectively you communicate with your teammates and managers. Being able to ask for clarification during transitions or seeking out additional information or resources for a new and unfamiliar project can show your team leaders how motivated you are to learn and ask for help when you need it.

Active listening and other forms of communication like nonverbal communication are also equally important aspects

of adaptability. Active listening shows you are attentive and ready to take new direction, and developing your nonverbal communication skills can help you navigate changes in team relationships or dynamics in the workplace.

Interpersonal Skills

Similar to effectively communicating with others, having excellent interpersonal skills can also play a key role in your overall adaptability. Being able to interact with others in healthy and positive ways can help you avoid miscommunication and conflict during operational shifts.

Problem-solving Skills

Adapting to change can also rely on problem-solving skills. You might use your problem-solving skills to find creative solutions to challenging topics, and being able to observe and analyse how you might approach solving a new problem can show your managers your willingness to make adjustments or improvements to the way you approach solving problems at work.

Creative and Strategic Thinking Skills

Adaptability can also require creative thinking and the ability to think strategically. For instance, developing new ideas to market products, finding ways to adapt to a changing market and implementing methods to improve and develop new strategies can all showcase your overall adaptability skills.

Teamwork Skills

Teamwork skills can be essential to being able to adapt to different personalities and working dynamics. Your colleagues can be a combination of different skills, backgrounds and experiences. Being able to work on a diverse team of people and deal with conflict, differing ideas and other dynamics that can occur can positively benefit how adaptive you are in a team environment.

Organisational Skills

Organisation can include several different aspects that can make this skill necessary to develop your adaptability skills. When you maintain an organised work area, paperwork and other aspects of your job, you can be better prepared in the event that operational changes happen at work.

How to Improve Adaptability Skills?

Being adaptable and open to change may not always be easy, however, you might consider the following steps to help you develop and improve your adaptability skills:

- Be aware of changes in your environment
- Develop a growth mindset
- Set goals for yourself
- Ask for feedback
- Learn to acknowledge and accept change

Collaborative Skills

What is collaboration?

Collaboration means working together

extra

First Chief Minister of Jammu and Kashmir

Jammu and Kashmir had its own Prime Minister till 1965, when the post was abolished and the title was amended to Chief Minister. Ghulam Mohammed Sadiq was the last PM and the first CM of J & K.

with one or more people to complete a project or task or develop ideas or processes. In the workplace, collaboration occurs when two or more people work together towards a common goal that benefits the team or company. Workplace collaboration requires interpersonal skills, communication skills, knowledge sharing and strategy, and can occur in a traditional office or between members of a virtual team.

Successfully collaborating with your coworkers can also increase your motivation and level of engagement at work. Additionally, sharing ideas and brainstorming is helpful for developing unique solutions to complex challenges. There are many ways to collaborate effectively at work, and the skills and techniques you rely on when you collaborate can lead to greater efficiency and success.

The Benefits of Collaboration

- Being collaborative has several advantages for you as well as your team and employer:
- Solving problems and examining the big picture
- Collaboration results in together a significant amount of talent, including professionals across a wide range of skills and knowledge. When you can leverage multiple peoples' expertise, you'll likely solve problems faster and drive better outcomes long-term.

Inspiring Self-analysis

Working collaboratively can help you become more aware of your strengths as well as your weaknesses. This will help you leverage your best skills, and identify which areas you may need assistance from people with different expertise. As a result, you and your teammates can work better together to fill in competency gaps.

Teaching and Learning

You learn things from other team members every time you come together to collaborate. An organization that values collaboration encourages constant teaching and learning.

Increasing Efficiency

Mulltiple people working together can divide tasks in a way that leverages each individual's greatest strengths. Instead of struggling through tasks you're not comfortable doing, you can focus your energy where you excel and get immediate feedback on your ideas from other team members.

How to Improve your Collaboration Skills

Here are a few ways you can improve your ability to collaborate in the workplace:

1. Set clear goals and objectives

When you're leading a project, it's essential you start by setting measurable goals and clear objectives. Everyone should understand the purpose and vision behind the project, as well as how you'll be determining success.

2. Communicate your intentions

When working with others, always be sure to state your intentions before you begin tackling a task or assignment. Let your teammates know what you're doing and set realistic expectations regarding your timeline. Then, be sure to follow through on your promise.

Listen and learn to compromise

When you're working closely with others, it's essential you listen closely to each team member's ideas, feedback and advice — and be considerate and respectful when responding.

Overcome challenges and solve problems without assigning blame

To enhance collaboration, it's important you're willing to forgive mistakes when others make them and take responsibility when you make an error. This helps build trust between team members and ensures everyone feels comfortable communicating, even if they do something wrong.

Be open-minded

To be a successful collaborator, you must remain open to new ideas. Often, your peers will come to different conclusions than you, or develop a different approach to projects. It's critical you acknowledge others' contributions and consider their ideas without judgment.

Celebrate collaboration and the successes it brings

Taking time to recognize results and celebrate positive outcomes as a group is essential for effective collaboration.

If collaboration is a skill, then you can hone it. In order to, you must become proficient in a variety of areas:

- Communication
- Tolerance
- Compromise
- Authenticity
- Teamwork
- Consistency
- Reliability

Organisational Skills

Organisational skills are crucial for many work experiences - so it's imperative that you showcase them on your resume. Your sense of organisation shows that you have the focus, clarity, and strategic ability to fulfill a variety of tasks successfully. The following are important organisational skills

Time Management Skills

The point of a deadline is to keep tasks and projects under control so that business operations can flow smoothly. In retail or restaurant jobs, time management is crucial for serving customers promptly and keeping them pacified even when it is busy. Time management is an important skill employers look for because without it, a business can lose clients, miss goals, fail in efficiency, or miss important time-specific opportunities. Time management requires a good sense of work gauge so that you can correctly allot the time needed for a task. But it's not just about scheduling. Good time management also requires discipline, quick thinking, knowing how and when to delegate, and knowing when to use strategies for dealing with procrastination, distraction, and even unplanned events.

A person with great time management skills can adapt to new problems and readjust as needed to complete an assignment. This combination of planning, scheduling, strategy, delegation, and adaptability are the kinds of traits that make an employee dependable and employers look out for that. How do you list these types of skills on your resume?

Terms related to time management:

- Creating and keeping deadlines
- Delegation
- Goal setting and meeting goals
- Decision making
- Managing appointments
- Team management
- Project management
- Making schedules
- Coordinating events
- Problem solving
- Productivity
- Teamwork
- Team leadership
- Multitasking
- Strategic thinking

The Only Person to Have Held the Office of Acting PM

For 13 days, Gulzarilal Nanda was the acting Prime Minister of India after the death of Jawaharlal Nehru in 1964. He again took over as acting PM after the death of Lal Bahadur Shastri in Tashkent in January 1966.

- Implementing strategy
- Mental organisational Skills

Many jobs demand strong focus, concentration, clear, coherent thinking, and a good memory - all traits of a mentally adept and alert person. Mental organisation skills allow you to process information quickly, translate thoughts to clear and articulate communication, and focus on fine details correctly. Mental organisation can also apply to the way you use tools and strategies to aid mental tasks.

Keeping a special notebook on your desk is a useful strategy for storing spontaneous information that might otherwise escape your mind later on. You can jot down notes, inspirations, ideas, or things to remember. Experience working with a scheduler or calendar are other examples of mental organising. Working with databases is an example of an activity that requires the keen focus of an organised mind.

Examples of organisational skills related to mental efficiency:

- Analysis
- Assessment and evaluation
- Listening skills
- Communication
- Creative thinking
- Working with data
- Design
- Taking notes
- Documentation
- Identifying problems
- Conflict resolution
- Multitasking
- Developing strategies
- Developmental planning
- Public speaking
- Reviewing, reporting, and research
- Attention to detail
- Making presentations

Physical Organisation Skills

Keeping your workspace neat and functional is another important organisational skill. Clutter all over your desk spells

coming trouble. Physical organisation includes not just a tidy desk, but also the layout of rooms, floors, and whole building and it goes well beyond maintaining a neat appearance. A poorly organised space leads to physical discomfort, wasted time, lost objects, and even lost people. The space people work in has a lot to do with how well they work. Someone must design these spaces, and then everyone else must maintain order. Examples of physical organisation skills are keeping track of items as they're used, returning items to their places after use, and creating and developing sensible strategies and physical solutions for facilitating workflow, cleanliness, and efficiency in a workspace. Skills you could put on your resume that show physical organisation include:

- Filing
- Record keeping
- Office solutions
- Office management
- Resource management
- Stock inventory
- Multitasking
- Responsibility for office materials and equipment
- Office maintenance
- Coordinating and executing events

Employers often screen candidates for the ability to handle large workloads or stressful, fast-paced environments. By polishing your resume to advertise your successful organisational abilities, you greatly increase your hireability.

Managers look for employees who can

not only keep their work and their desk organised, but for those who can also adjust quickly to the organisation structure of a company.

Develop these skills and emphasise them in job applications, resumes, cover letters, and interviews. Showing that you have the skills a company is seeking will help you get hired and promoted.

Resource Management

Resource management is acquiring, allocating and managing the resources, such as individuals and their skills, finances, technology, materials, machinery and natural resources required for a project. Resource management ensures that internal and external resources are used effectively on time and to budget. Resources may be obtained internally from the host organisation or procured from external sources.

Resource management is important because:

- It provides you with an overview of everyone and everything involved in your project;
- It enables utilisation planning;
- It makes the planning and management process more transparent;
- It helps you see problems before they start;
- It gives you control over your project.

Planning

For any project, planning means anticipating which resources will be necessary and how long the project will take, then assembling those resources and blocking out the necessary time. If necessary, a worker may even have to alter the plan based on resource availability and time constraints.

Skills related to planning can be described using the following keywords:

- Analysis
- Analysing Issues
- Budgeting
- Business Intelligence
- Data
- Data Trends
- Deadlines
- Decision Making
- Design
- Development
- Forecasting
- Information Gathering
- Metrics
- Organizational Skills
- Development Planning
- Development Predicting
- Problem Solving
- Program Management
- Project Management
- Research
- Review
- Scheduling
- Strategic Planning
- Strategy Development
- Structural Planning
- Succession Planning
- Trends

Skillsets

A skillset is a combination of abilities, qualities and experiences you can apply to perform tasks well. Each person has a different skill set depending on their interests, natural abilities, personal qualities and technical skills. Skills can expand your professional competency and allow you to perform your job well.

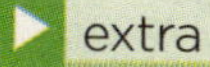

Yale Report of 1828

It is a document written by the faculty of Yale College in staunch defense of the classical curriculum. The report argued that Yale should continue to require all of its students to follow a single thorough curriculum, with Latin and Greek literature at its core.

How to Determine your Skills?

When searching for a job, displaying your most advanced, relevant skills on your resume will help employers understand why you are a good fit for the job. If you are not sure what skills you have, consider spending time answering the following questions:

- What do you enjoy? The tasks that come easily to you or that you enjoy often translate into useful skills.
- Do you receive praise or compliments on certain abilities? Consider the skills your managers or colleagues have noticed or complimented in the past. You should also take note of what people come to you for help.
- What previous accomplishments do you have? You might have won an award or simply completed a project that had better-than-expected results. What skills helped you to do those things?

How to develop new skills

If you want a job in an industry that requires different skills than those you currently have, there are many ways to expand your skill set or to develop your current skills for a better chance at promotions or raises.

- Set goals for yourself. Setting specific goals to improve your career helps you stay on track with your development. Make sure your goals are measurable, achievable and relevant to your profession or your goals. Then, consider organising a timeline to achieve your goal by setting a beginning and end date, as well as smaller goals to achieve along the way.
- Find a mentor. A professional mentor is typically a superior you respect and trust.
- Seek feedback about strengths and weaknesses. You can ask superiors, colleagues or even friends or family about your strengths and areas for improvement.
- Review job descriptions for positions you want. These job descriptions will give you an idea of the transferable skills you have, as well as the job-specific skills you will need.
- Enroll in an online degree program. Companies often encourage employees to further their education with a degree, and some offer tuition assistance or reimbursement.
- Take continuing education courses in career-related fields.
- Take advantage of company training.
- Participate in job shadowing. Job shadowing is a great way to learn more about the day-to-day responsibilities of another profession and to learn new skills. Generally, it is best to choose individuals who are experienced or perform well in their positions.
- Join a professional association in your field.

Which skills to include on your resume

Carefully review the job description. This will include both the technical and soft skills the employer is looking for in their ideal candidate. Include the technical skills they list if they align with your own personal skill set.

Technical skills show your potential employer that you have the necessary training or education for a particular role. Depending on the role, you might also list relevant soft skills on your resume.

Include any skills that you feel set you apart from other candidates. For example, you might include that you have strong relationship-building skills. While this skill might not necessarily be required for an IT job, for example, IT administrators can be even more successful with strong interpersonal skills.

Include the most relevant skillsets for the job role you seek. Include accomplishments that verify these skills in your professional history section.

Skills Mapping Tips

Skills mapping provides a whole host of benefits. The best way to visualise proficiency levels is by using skills matrices. A skills matrix is a snapshot of all the employees' skills laid out in matrix form. Create one skills matrix for each department or team. •List all the employees' names, or their roles, down the left-hand column and all their skills across the top row (or vice versa). • Enter the proficiency levels for each employee for each skill until the matrix is filled.

Follow the tips below:

1. Start with a skills assessment
Before you can determine proficiency levels, you'll first have to define which skills you actually want to assess. So, the first step you'll need to take is to perform an assessment to map your employees' skills.

Read our article, 4 popular employee self-assessment tools, to find out more.

2. Don't add too many people to any one matrix The biggest advantage of skills mapping is the clarity it provides. So, don't tackle all your staff and every possible skill in one go. Split your employees into teams or departments and select the skills relevant to each group. It's also advisable to create separate matrices for soft and hard skills. Show skills both Qualitatively and Quantitatively. Skill levels range from Nonexistent or Complete beginner to Advanced or Expert. It should show what skills are needed for a given role and how far along the required skill progression for any given person is.

3. Employee interest levels: If a specific technical skill is required for a role that an individual does not have but is interested in obtaining, that person may be better suited than someone who is uninterested in learning that skill. This is important when considering which employees fit into new roles.

4. Don't forget Soft Skills. One can train for many types of soft skills, and they're often critical to success. Things like empathy, communication, and the ability to take direction are important. Incorporate technical skills, behavioural components, soft skills, and even interpersonal skills. •This can assist in creating individualised employee development programs. It could be done on a team level or an organisational level to assess what training programs may need to be offered in the future.

5. Stick to the most important issues
The possible uses for skills matrices are virtually limitless but don't make them more complex. So, stick to the most important skills, competences, tasks, and qualifications for each position to maintain clarity.

6. Be objective: Consider getting input from multiple sources, both for the skills required for the role and for the skill level of any given individual. This can help to make the most accurate representation—which likely would not occur with just one person making the assessment.

Skill Matrix Defined

You can assess the skills of your team with an effective tool – skill matrix. You can also map the essential skills of your employees using the competency matrix. For any data-driven pro, skill matrix allows him or her to view the following successfully:

- Available skills
- Required skill of the company
- Missing skills

HR professionals need to follow two

steps to implement a skill matrix:

• Create an overview of the required skill that is essential in completing a task (In doing so, the HR professional could outline the skills needed in each activity of the team)

• Define the skills that each employee has Here's an example: An upcoming company project requires data analysis in order to make it successful. The company HR expert needs to find an employee that has excellent data analysis skills. If there's no available employee who matches the skill level, HR will hire an applicant with the required skill.

Steps for Creating a Skill Matrix

A competency matrix doesn't only need to be easy to apply so that you can create the tool: You also need to follow 5 effective steps such as the following:

(a) Choose an Evaluator

The HR professional can let each team member evaluate themselves.

(b) Define the Essential Skills

A project will be successful if you define the required or essential skills for the project. Avoid trivial or additional skills of an employee and focus only on the needed skills.

(c) Use a Scoring System

You can best assess the skills of each team through a scoring system. You can choose from two options: numeric or the descriptive scoring system. The latter has four levels, such as:

• Advanced level • Intermediate level

• Basic level • No capability

HR teams often rely on a 180-degree feedback tool that evaluates an employee through his or her manager, coworkers, or themselves. A 360–degree feedback tool is also used that has additional customer assessment, reports, and feedback from the bosses.

(d) Compare Employees Scores

For you to know the rank of each employee, compare their scores. Employees with longer experience would get higher ranks, while newbie employees would rank lower.

(e) Analyse the Skills Matrix •Shows an employee's strengths and weaknesses •Identifies the areas need training •Manage the company successfully

The Advantage

Clients have the assurance that their projects wouldn't have any delays because the team is working as one. Also, clients would be happy with the result of the project and be happy to work again with the company in the future. The result – both

company and clients, would have a harmonious business partnership for many years.

Conclusion

Skill mapping is an essential tool so that a company reaches its goals. An HR professional determines the skills present and missing in a team. Once these skills are identified, employees can work on their strengths and improve their weaknesses.

In turn, the company can hire additional employees to fill the skills gap in the organization. Managers and HR professionals can also use a skill mapping software to assist them in successful skills mapping. With the skill matrix, companies don't only travel on the right path but also develop stronger connections with clients.

So, come now and use skill mapping to your company's advantage!

Effective Problem Solving

Dr Valson Thampu
Former Principal, St. Stephen's College, New Delhi

This write-up talks about a skill that is very important not only in life but also in accomplishing tasks in a work environment. Here you will find seven simple steps that will help you become a more effective, efficient problem solver in your organisation.

Effective problem solving is one of the key attributes that separate great leaders from average ones.

Being a successful leader doesn't mean that you don't have any problems. Rather, it means that you know how to solve problems effectively as they arise. If you never had to deal with any problems, chances are pretty high that your company doesn't really need you. They could hire an entry-level person to do your job!

Unfortunately, there are many examples of leaders out there who have been promoted to management or leadership positions because they are competent and excel in the technical skills needed to do the work. These people find themselves suddenly needing to "think on their feet" and solve problems that are far more high-level and complicated than they've ever really had to deal with before. Are there tools available to these people to help them solve the problem correctly and effectively? Absolutely!

Key Leadership Skill

There are Seven Steps of Effective Problem Solving managers are learning about, developing, and implementing in their teams.

Step 1: Identify the Problem

What are things like when they are the way we want them to be?

This question helps you find the standard against which we're going to measure where we are now. If things were going the way we want them to go, what does that look like? If this person were doing the job we want him or her to do, what would they be doing?

And then ask this important question: How much variation from the norm is tolerable?

Therein lies the problem. From an engineering perspective, you might have very little tolerance. From a behavioral perspective, you might have more tolerance. You might say it's okay with me when this person doesn't do it exactly as I say because I'm okay with them taking some liberty with this. Some other issue you may need 100% compliance.

Step 2: Analyze the Problem

At what stage is this problem? This helps you identify the urgency of the problem, and there are generally three stages.

The emergent stage is where the problem is just beginning to happen. It does not cause an immediate threat to the way business operates every day. It is just beginning to happen and you have time on your side to be able to correct it without it causing much damage to the processes it is affecting.

The mature stage is where this problem is causing more than just minor damage. Some amount of damage has been done, and you need to jump on it immediately to fix it before it becomes a problem where the consequences may be greater, deeper, and more expensive if we don't solve this problem fast.

The third stage is the crisis stage, when the problem is so serious it must be corrected immediately. At this stage, real damage has been done to company processes, reputation, finances, etc. that will have potentially long-term effects on your ability to do business.

Step 3: Describe the Problem

You should be able to describe a problem by writing it in the form of a statement and you should do it in 12 words or less, assuming it's not a complicated, scientific problem. This way, you have clarity exactly what the issue is. Then, perhaps try distributing it to your team to ensure they agree that this is the root of the problem, that it makes sense, and everyone that is working toward a solution is working toward the same goal.

The Most Important Question of All, When describing our problem: Is your premise correct?

Let me give you an example of what I mean. We've all heard – or read – the story of the engineer's take on the old "half empty, half full" question. A speaker holds up the glass of water and asks

extra

Ignorance About Political System

A 2016 poll conducted for the Annenberg Public Policy Centre found that a quarter of American adults could not name the three branches of government.

if the glass is half empty or half full, a discussion within the group ensues, and you generally expect some sort of lesson in optimism, etc. from it. In this version, an engineer is in the room and answers, "I see this glass of water as being twice the size it needs to be."

You see, sometimes when you are the one in charge of the problem, you tend to set the premise of the problem from your own perspective. But, that premise may not be accurate, or it may just need an alternate perspective from which to see it. If your premise is not correct, or at least incomplete, you are not fully understanding the problem and considering all the best options for a solution.

Step 4: Look for Root Causes

This step involves asking and answering a lot of questions. Ask questions like: What caused this problem? Who is responsible for this problem? When did this problem first emerge? Why did this happen? How did this variance from the standard come to be? Where does it hurt us the most? How do we go about resolving this problem?

Also, ask the most important question: Can we solve this problem for good so it will never occur again? Because an important aspect to leadership is coming up with solutions that people can use for a long-term benefit, rather than having to deal with the same problems over and over and over.

Step 5: Develop Alternate Solutions

Just about any problem you have to deal with has more solutions to it than the one that you think of first. So, it is best to develop a list of alternate solutions that you and your team can assess and decide which one will be the best for the particular problem. I often use the ? + 1 Rule to create consensus around one – or the top two or three solutions – that will be best for everyone involved.

Then rank those solutions based on

efficiency, cost, long-term value, what resources you have and that you can commit to the solution of the problem. Then, look at every one of those solutions carefully and decide what you believe to be the best solution to this problem at this time.

Effective Problem Solving Includes an Implementation Plan

Step 6: Implement the Solution

Implementing the solution you decide on can include creating an implementation plan. It could also include planning on what happens next if something goes wrong with the solution if it doesn't work out the way you thought it would. Implementation means that everyone on your team knows and understands their part in making the solution work, that there are timelines for execution, and also that you have a system in place to track whether or not the solution has corrected the problem.

Step 7: Measure the Results

From your implementation plan in step 6, make sure you track and measure the results so you can answer questions such as: Did it work? Was this a good solution? Did we learn something here in the implementation that we could apply to other potential problems?

These seven simple steps will help you become a more effective, efficient problem solver in your organization. As you practice this process and develop the skills, these steps will become more natural to you until the point that you are using them without noticing!

Skill Mapping

Skills mapping refers to creating a visual representation of the skills needed to perform well in any given role and comparing that with the existing skills held by employees throughout the organisation. This comparison allows gaps to be identified and remedied. •Skills maps can provide a view of the entire team–how each person on the team contributes and the skills he or she is best at. •Skills mapping is also sometimes called competency mapping, esp. when put together for an entire group, though some would argue that competency mapping is more comprehensive, as it includes things beyond skills, like behaviours.

Why Do We Need Skill Mapping ?

Skill mapping doesn't only show the strengths and weaknesses of a team but also benefits the company as a whole. Organisations or companies need skills of employees mapped and present them visually because it helps create greater clarity and insight. This has several benefits:

- Sometimes, only a select group of employees can perform a certain task to a required level. Skills mapping pinpoints exactly which tasks and requirements are crucial to the organisation.
- It highlights which employees could benefit from additional training.
- Identify who are the most valuable employees and who are the specialists and who are the generalists.
- Find suitable replacements for employees when fallen sick, in a blink of an eye, or HR can create a candidate profile to replace an employee who suddenly leaves the company.
- It allows tracking the progress for each departments, teams, and individuals.

Team Benefits : Skill matrix benefits a company's employees as a whole. A HR professional can identify the skills required

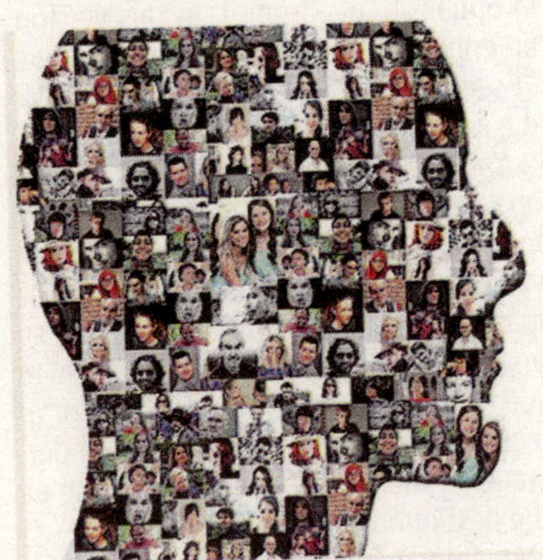

so that a project becomes successful. You would know at once if a skill in your team is required or not before a project begins.

Employee Benefits : Skill mapping allows employees to discover their strong and weak sides. Once they identify these, it's a starting point for them to improve their skills. The skill matrix also allows each employee to focus further on learning and development. Thus, they can be more reliable in the work they're doing.

Company Benefits : Through skill mapping, the company sees a clear picture of the available skills and missing skills within the organization. Then, the company can further excel in employee learning and development that contributes to reaching company goals. If there are lacking skills in the team, the company can hire applicants who have the required skill. Also, the company can place employees in areas where additional technical skills, are essential.

Client Benefits : A team that's aware of their strengths and weaknesses can work successfully. The company can hire new employees to level up the company's excellence further. The company benefits mean good news to the clients.

Decision Making

Much of what people do is solve problems and make decisions. Often, they are "under the gun", stressed and very short for time. Consequently, when they encounter a new problem or decision they must make, they react with a decision that seemed to work before. It's easy with this approach to get stuck in a circle of solving the same problem over and over again. Therefore, it's often useful to get used to an organized approach to problem solving and decision making. Not all problems can be solved and decisions made by the following, rather rational approach. However, the following basic guidelines will get you started. Don't be intimidated by the length of the list of guidelines. After you've practiced them a few times, they'll become second nature to you -- enough that you can deepen and enrich them to suit your own needs and nature.

(Note that it might be more your nature to view a "problem" as an "opportunity". Therefore, you might substitute "problem" for "opportunity" in the following guidelines.)

1. Define the problem

This is often where people struggle. They react to what they think the problem is. Instead, seek to understand more about why you think there's a problem.

Define the problem: (with input from yourself and others). Ask yourself and others, the following questions: •What can you see that causes you to think there's a problem? •Where is it happening?•How is it happening? •When is it happening?•With whom is it happening? (HINT: Don't jump to "Who is causing the problem?" When we're stressed, blaming is often one of our first reactions. To be an effective manager, you need to address issues more than people.)

Why is it happening?
Write down a five-sentence description of the problem in terms of "The following should be happening, but isn't ..." or "The following is happening and should be: ..." As much as possible, be specific in your description, including what is happening, where, how, with whom and why. (It may be helpful at this point to use a variety of research methods.

Defining complex problems:
If the problem still seems overwhelming, break it down by repeating steps 1-7 until you have descriptions of several related problems.

Verifying your understanding of the problems:
It helps a great deal to verify your problem analysis for conferring with a peer or someone else.

Prioritize the problems:
If you discover that you are looking at several related problems, then prioritize which ones you should address first.

Note the difference between "important" and "urgent" problems. Often, what we consider to be important problems to consider are really just urgent problems. Important problems deserve more attention. For example, if you're continually answering "urgent" phone calls, then you've probably got a more "important" problem and that's to design a system that screens and prioritizes your phone calls.

Understand your role in the problem:
Your role in the problem can greatly influence how you perceive the role of others. For example, if you're very stressed out, it'll probably look like others are, too, or, you may resort too quickly to blaming and reprimanding others. Or, you are feel very guilty about your role in the problem, you

may ignore the accountabilities of others.

2. Look at potential causes for the problem

It's amazing how much you don't know about what you don't know. Therefore, in this phase, it's critical to get input from other people who notice the problem and who are effected by it.

It's often useful to collect input from other individuals one at a time (at least at first). Otherwise, people tend to be inhibited about offering their impressions of the real causes of problems.

Write down what your opinions and what you've heard from others.

Regarding what you think might be performance problems associated with an employee, it's often useful to seek advice from a peer or your supervisor in order to verify your impression of the problem.

Write down a description of the cause of the problem and in terms of what is happening, where, when, how, with whom and why.

3. Identify alternatives for approaches to resolve the problem

At this point, it's useful to keep others involved (unless you're facing a personal and/or employee performance problem). Brainstorm for solutions to the problem. Very simply put, brainstorming is collecting as many ideas as possible, then screening them to find the best idea. It's critical when collecting the ideas to not pass any judgment on the ideas -- just write them down as you hear them. (A wonderful set of skills used to identify the underlying cause of issues is Systems Thinking.)

4. Select an approach to resolve the problem

When selecting the best approach, consider:

Which approach is the most likely to solve the problem for the long term?

Which approach is the most realistic to accomplish for now? Do you have the resources? Are they affordable? Do you have enough time to implement the approach?

What is the extent of risk associated with each alternative?

(The nature of this step, in particular, in the problem solving process is why problem solving and decision making are highly integrated.)

5. Plan the implementation of the best alternative (this is your action plan)

Carefully consider "What will the situation look like when the problem is solved?"

What steps should be taken to implement the best alternative to solving the problem? What systems or processes should be changed in your organization, for example, a new policy or procedure? Don't resort to solutions where someone is "just going to try harder".

How will you know if the steps are being followed or not? (these are your indicators of the success of your plan)

What resources will you need in terms of people, money and facilities?

How much time will you need to implement the solution? Write a schedule that includes the start and stop times, and when you expect to see certain indicators of success.

Who will primarily be responsible for ensuring implementation of the plan?

Write down the answers to the above questions and consider this as your action plan.

Communicate the plan to those who will involved in implementing it and, at least, to your immediate supervisor.

(An important aspect of this step in the problem-solving process is continually observation and feedback.)

6. Monitor implementation of the plan

Monitor the indicators of success:

Are you seeing what you would expect from the indicators?

Will the plan be done according to schedule?

If the plan is not being followed as expected, then consider: Was the plan realistic? Are there sufficient resources to accomplish the plan on schedule? Should more priority be placed on various aspects of the plan? Should the plan be changed?

7. Verify if the problem has been resolved or not

One of the best ways to verify if a problem has been solved or not is to resume normal operations in the organization. Still, you should consider:

What changes should be made to avoid this type of problem in the future? Consider changes to policies and procedures, training, etc.

Lastly, consider "What did you learn from this problem solving?" Consider new knowledge, understanding and/or skills.

Consider writing a brief memo that highlights the success of the problem solving effort, and what you learned as a result. Share it with your supervisor, peers and subordinates.

Rational Versus Organic Approach to Problem Solving

Rational

A person with this preference often prefers using a comprehensive and logical approach similar to the guidelines in the above section. For example, the rational approach, described below, is often used when addressing large, complex matters in strategic planning.

Define the problem.

Examine all potential causes for the problem. • Identify all alternatives to resolve the problem.

- Carefully select an alternative.
- Develop an orderly implementation plan to implement that best alternative.
- Carefully monitor implementation of the plan.
- Verify if the problem has been resolved or not.

A major advantage of this approach is that it gives a strong sense of order in an otherwise chaotic situation and provides a common frame of reference from which people can communicate in the situation. A major disadvantage of this approach is that it can take a long time to finish. Some people might argue, too, that the world is much too chaotic for the rational approach to be useful.

Organic

Some people assert that the dynamics of organizations and people are not nearly so mechanistic as to be improved by solving one problem after another. Often, the quality of an organization or life comes from how one handles being "on the road" itself, rather than the "arriving at the destination." The quality comes from the ongoing process of trying, rather than from having fixed a lot of problems. For many people it is an approach to organizational consulting. The following quote is often used when explaining the organic (or holistic) approach to problem solving.

"All the greatest and most important problems in life are fundamentally insoluble ... They can never be solved, but only outgrown. This "outgrowing" proves on further investigation to require a new level of consciousness. Some higher or wider interest appeared on the horizon and through this broadening of outlook, the insoluble lost its urgency. It was not solved logically in its own terms, but faded when confronted with a new and stronger life urge."

From Jung, Carl, Psychological Types (Pantheon Books, 1923)

A major advantage of the organic approach is that it is highly adaptable to understanding and explaining the chaotic changes that occur in projects and everyday life. It also suits the nature of people who shun linear and mechanistic approaches to projects. The major disadvantage is that the approach often provides no clear frame of reference around which people can communicate, feel comfortable and measure progress toward solutions to problems.

Hybrid World of Work

About two years after the pandemic most of us have become used to a hybrid work environment. Business houses are in the process of updating everything from meeting rooms to open-plan work areas to outdoor gathering spots. A mix of work days spent at home and in the office has become the new normal for occupations where it's an option. It is therefore important to know how to switch between the two.

Enter the Hybrid Work Reality

Absorb the lessons of work-from-home

Try to replicate your productivity wins when you return to the office. For a lot of people, working from home gave them some flexibility in how they divided their time and attention throughout the day. They found their natural work rhythms, blocked off their calendars during peak focus times, and tackled emails and meetings during a different chunk of the day.

But many of us couldn't quite conquer our calendars. Our work days became longer and more fragmented. Video meetings—with more frequency, attendees, and time zones—stretched our days at both ends, and as the personal and the professional melded, we saw more interruptions. When your child's learning device disconnects from WiFi, or the doorbell rings, you have to step away from the virtual office.

So, as many of us prepare to shift to a hybrid model of working, the first thing to do is make an inventory of everything

that worked (and didn't work) for you during work-from-home. For example, did you find that working earlier in the morning and taking a midday workout break made you more or less productive?

Plan and Theme Your Days

Planning and theming your days will help you maximize your time in both places. For example: Your team might designate two days a week where everyone comes into the office. These are the days to schedule bigger group meetings, 1:1 coffee chats to maintain and build relationships, and catch-ups on shared projects. At least one day of the week could be a no-meetings day, affording everyone some focused time to concentrate without the distraction of running between rooms or logging into virtual meetings. You might want to also designate your own work-from-home days—perhaps when you're responsible for picking your kids up from school and need to maximize your working hours.

If you're given the choice of which days you spend where, think carefully about your productive rhythm through-

extra

The Brothers Grimm

Jacob Ludwig Karl and Wilhelm Carl were born in the town of Hanau in Germany and dedicated their life to research the folk history of German literature. They are famous for their fairy tales like *Cinderella, Sleeping Beauty* and *Snow White*.

out the week. If Monday is your "ramp-up" day and it's heavy on meetings to begin with, that might be best spent in the office. On the other hand, if Friday is your "consolidation" day, work from home and tackle those heads-down tasks such as responding to non-urgent emails or writing a blog post. A lot depends on your specific home and office environments. Your themes should make the most of what each place has to offer.

Know your tools and spaces

Last year, many of us began to take greater advantage of the different settings in our video conferencing software, calendars, and inboxes. We learned how to record meetings, blur backgrounds, or set up custom rules and filters for our emails. Being tool-savvy will continue to be important as we bridge two very different contexts. Consider setting working hours and availability in your calendar, so that your colleagues know when you can best be reached.

Likewise, as you head to the office again, take time to assess your new workspace. Many businesses are in the process of updating everything from meeting rooms to open-plan work areas to outdoor gathering spots. Be sure to know how your workplace is changing and what tools are available to you. Will you need to book your desk? Will it have the same setup you're using at home? Are collaboration spaces available for team brainstorming? How will your team agree on how, when, and where they come together?

Understand how you and your team work

Now is the time to establish fresh ways of working and collaborating that cater to different time zones, as well as respect individual working styles and personal obligations.

One positive development in our nearly year-long experiment in remote working has been the way video meetings became more inclusive of global, remote teams. With the shared informality of seeing each other's homes and exchanging ideas about how to work better, we gained empathy for our colleagues. As we glimpsed each other's lives—babies on laps, dogs on couches, or maybe grandparents making guest appearances—we got a new perspective on our teammates as whole human beings. As you head back to the office part-time, see if you can find ways to sustain the camaraderie and empathy that came out of this shared experience.

As we all gear up for the next phase in the evolution of work, it's a great opportunity to develop habits that help us deliver our best.

Planning and intention

At Google, we already have some good data on how to bring out the best in your teams. Some years ago, Google completed a multi-year research study into high-performing teams and found that they all had five elements in common: psychological safety, dependability, structure and clarity, meaning, and impact. As you bridge the remote and in-person worlds, are you setting yourself and your team up for success? Do you have a set of team norms? Do you understand each other's working styles and productivity zones?

Maybe you start offering two options for training and all-hands meetings, each at a different end of the work day. Maybe you implement "No-Meeting Fridays."

Not only do these changes cater to different time zones, they respect our individual working styles and personal obligations. As teams come back together in the office—at least part of the time—it's a chance to establish fresh ways of working and collaborating that are based on the lessons of the last year.

Allow for free time

A lot of us are terrible at taking breaks when we work from home. We bridge the physical distance by staying plugged-in all the time. Much research suggests, however, that you're more productive when you take regular breaks to recharge. I like to use the pour-over coffee analogy: when you let things steep a little, you end up with a richer, deeper experience. The same is true for getting work done.

As you think about setting up your hybrid work week, don't forget to budget some blank space on your calendar. I'm not a fan of scheduling breaks, since it can feel like yet another obligation. But make sure you have some time in your day for lunch, to take a quick walk, or grab a coffee—whether it's in the office or while you're at home.

As we all gear up for the next phase in the evolution of work, it's a great opportunity to develop habits that help us deliver our best. Planning and intention go a long way. I often remind friends and colleagues that personal productivity is not just about how much you get done in a day. It's about getting the things done that matter most for your day.

25×2025 Model

According to Tata Consultancy Services, one of the largest IT service companies, has declared that the corporation intends to switch to a hybrid model 25x25 in the future. The company's strategy for 2025 is – just 25% of its over 500,000 worldwide employees will be in office locations at any given time, with associates spending only 25% of their time in the office. Furthermore, only 25 per cent of staff in project teams can be co-located. Additionally, employees will not be required to work for more than 25% of their time.

India may make up 25% of world's workforce by 2025

India can boast of a quarter of the world's workforce by 2025, provided the country harnesses the potential of its young and productive population, a study by TeamLease Services.

A conducive labour situation could also help push the nation's per capita income to $4,100 (around ₹3,00,000 at the current exchange rate of ₹74 per dollar) by 2025. This would rise to $9,802 in 2040 and $20,836 in 2050. This will finally put poverty in the museum it belongs.

The report, however, stated that a radical reform of the country's labour market ecosystem (including labour demand, labour supply and labour laws) is required for converting individuals into productive people comprising the workforce. The population of productive people is referred to as the demographic dividend of the country.

The report, however, cautioned that the demographic dividend would become a disaster if India does not radically overhaul the labour ecosystem to enhance the productivity of the growing workforce.

23 INTERNATIONAL RELATIONS

- The Changing World Geopolitics
- India-Israel Relations: From No-Relations to Strategic Partnership
- The Ministry of External Affairs
- Indian Foreign Service
- Foreign Policy
- Quadrilateral Security Dialogue -QUAD
- Act East Policy
- Indian Diaspora

The Changing World Geopolitics

Prof. (Dr.) Pranav N. Desai

Director, Centre for Research in Environment, Science and Technology Policy (CREST), New Delhi; Member, South Asia Sustainability Hub & Knowledge Network (SASH&KN), Trans-disciplinary Research Cluster on Sustainability Studies (TRCSS), Jawaharlal Nehru University, New Delhi

If the past is any indicator of the future, most of the globalising or proto globalising orders have risen and collapsed due to a combination of factors. In different phases of history, there were different driving forces for global integration. In this article we take a look at where does the world stand now.

At the beginning of the twenty-first century, the world witnessed the acceleration of globalisation. The Covid-19 pandemic has brought this process of globalisation to a screeching halt, altering geopolitics and the interrelationship between the state, markets, and society. The world faces greater pressures on the healthcare system and challenges of tackling global climate change with greater urgency and economic revival. The world economy is expected to contract by 5.2 per cent, and economies heavily dependent on trade, tourism and commodity exports will be more vulnerable.

With the end of the cold war by 1989, the bipolar world order also collapsed, giving way to a multipolar world where the USA emerged as the hegemon or the most dominant power. During this phase, freer trade, cheaper travel, faster communication led to the unfolding of the globalisation process. There was an intertwined process of the international environmental movement and the emergence of bio, nano and information and communication technologies (ICT). There was increased S & T collaboration with new partners, and the collaboration was not restricted to the triad countries like the USA, European countries and Japan. Several countries experienced rapid economic growth, including China and India. This process was only punctuated in the year 2007-08 due to the global economic crisis. Due to rapid economic growth, millions of people rose above absolute poverty. With biodiversity hotspots and the emergence of biotechnology, the Global South gained greater significance and bargaining power with the technologically advanced countries. Another noteworthy phenomenon was the rise of China as a significant global economic power and as a rival to the existing dominant power, the USA. The current pandemic crisis further intensifies this rivalry.

In the preceding context, questions arise whether the existing international order, globalisation and the geopolitical factors that shape the same will continue or collapse in the wake of the COVID-19 pandemic? Will the factors that influence geopolitics continue to exert the same or more influence or decline in the age of information and communication technologies and the declining importance of geographical proximity? Geopolitics is commonly understood as international relations influenced by geographical factors including climate, demography, natural resources, topography and political power linked to geography.

If history is any pointer to the future, most of the globalising or proto globalising orders have risen and collapsed due to a combination of factors. In different phases of history, there were different driving forces for global integration. First, there were horses and swords, battleships and guns and then the ICT. This process helped evolve new networks, economic centres and also brought miseries, migrations, violence, slavery, pandemics. Along with this, some countervailing forces also emerged, and all these global orders have risen and collapsed.

US-China Rivalry

The US-China strategic rivalry deserves the main focus here is as pandemic has affected their power competition the most along with the global geostrategic balance. However, many other important powers that have a role are Russia, Japan, Korea, India, Brazil, South Africa and many other regional associations and informal groups. In the post-pandemic period, as the USA and China seek geopolitical and geoeconomic autonomy more assertively, there is a greater likelihood of geopolitical upheaval. After the end of the cold war, the predominance of the liberal policies of the USA provided a greater impetus to a globalising world. The emergence of China as a global economic power next to the USA was an outcome of globalisation. This process has helped China emerge as a low-wage manufacturing powerhouse and the ease of exports. With the rising economic prowess, China has become more assertive. China has started pursuing more aggressive policies as reflected in aggressive territorial claims in the South China Sea, along the Indo-China and Sino-Russian borders, over Taiwan and repressive policies against Hongkong. These policies are also aimed at suggesting declining US power. China's global ambitions of Sinocentric global system are not restricted to the preceding policies. More examples are One Belt One Road (OBOR), aiming to extend influence through infrastructure development in 70 countries and international organisations. The bifurcat-

ed internet with economic and security implications opposed by the USA and Europe, pervasive intellectual property theft, 'dual use' digital technologies and civil-military fusion are all but examples of challenging US geopolitical strategy. During the Pandemic, Chinese policies were termed "Wolf warrior diplomacy" as the Chinese diplomats used confrontational rhetoric and tried to rebuff criticism of China and court controversy in interviews and social media.

Though the US and China have deep economic integration and are globalised across the system with different security implications, the USA treats the Chinese challenges more seriously than the Soviet Union during the Cold War.

It is unlikely that the USA could be displaced by China as the most dominant power with a strong economic and military base and having powerful allies. As against this, China is surrounded by more enemies than friends. Moreover, the Chinese ambitions are at the moment limited to Asian supremacy. Despite this, China's expansionist role will trigger new strategic realignments in different geographies in the aftermath of the pandemic.

The QUAD Dialogue

World history also indicates that against every hegemon and globalising force, there have been countervailing forces. Against the Chinese global ambitions and specifically aggressive postures in the Indo-Pacific region, the Quadrilateral Security Dialogue (QUAD) has emerged since 2007. The QUAD is a strategic dialogue between the United States, Japan, Australia, and India maintained by talks between member countries against the Chinese territorial claims in the South-China Sea. The Chinese claims affect several countries in the East-Asia around China. The QUAD is further likely to be strengthened by the member countries in the post-pandemic scenario. It is also possible that with the increasing Chinese influence, some of the regional or international organisations might get diluted like BRICS, IBSA or BIMSTEC.

EU, China and USA

With the worsening US-China relationship, the European Union (EU) reveals discomfort with both. The EU does not share identical views with the USA on China on the entire range of policy issues. The EU wants to take advantage of Chinese economic growth and benefit from trade and investment. The EU wishes to continue with a "multi-faceted" approach with China, and China is happy to create a wedge between the EU and the USA. The Chinese companies enjoy free access to the European markets, including controversial companies like Huawei in Germany and Peace Cable in France. At the same time, the EU joined hands with the USA in sanctioning four individuals involved in repression in Xinjiang. There was a tit for tat response from the Chinese government imposing sanctions on European diplomats. This strong reaction has made the European Parliament difficult to ratify the Comprehensive Agreement on Investment (CAI). The EU also supports the US policy on Indo-Pacific to uphold international law and freedom of navigation.

Global Scenario

The world economy has shrunk after global lockdowns, unscheduled industrial closures and restrictions on trade, travel and tourism, labour shortages, shrinking of international education; it is uncertain whether the global powers will cooperate in the fight against the pandemic. Instead of outward-looking economies during globalisation, most countries are now looking inward for rejuvenating their economies with national resources. China announced policies of "made in China 2025" by having 70 per cent self-reliance by 2025. Similarly, Indian Prime Minister Modi announced his government's mission of "Atmanirbhar Bharat," along the same lines as "Make in India." These policies are expected to reduce imports and international trade. India had surplus trade in 2020, suggesting reduced import demands.

China is also trying to extend its influence over International Organisations like the WHO. In response, the United States, the largest single financial contributor to WHO, has notified its intention to withdraw from the body. This withdrawal will have the twin effect of crippling the organisational efficacy and leaving the field open for further manipulation by China. The possibilities of greater opportunities for distributing largesse will also rise as most countries seek new funding to revive their economies in the post-pandemic period. However, the Chinese "free COVID vaccine diplomacy" does not seem to be working at the moment. There is a general feeling of hostilities the world over against China for mishandling the coronavirus outbreak and the delayed response in intimating the WHO.

Like most of the world's regions, the West-Asian region is also facing healthcare and economic pressures narrowing their space to play a confrontational role against Israel and the USA. Iran is the country affected most by the pandemic and is already facing the heat of

Global Geopolitical Challenges

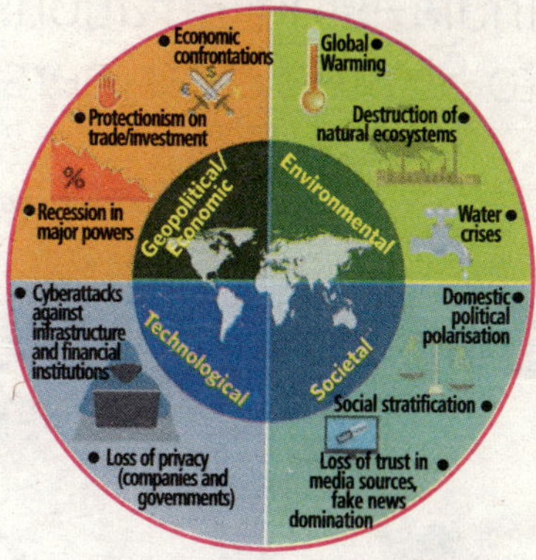

the US sanctions making her economy more vulnerable. There is a global reduction in the demand for oil because of industrial closure and a reduction in trade and travel. Moreover, there is changing geopolitics in this region, with many Gulf countries patching up with Israel due to various foreign policy objectives. Nonetheless, India, benefitting from the reduced oil prices, faces challenges of the job security of roughly eight million migrant workers and the reduced remittances.

With ideological concerns of a multipolar world, Russia will stand out clearly in operating her foreign policy objectives and play a more balanced role vis-à-vis the USA, China and India.

Finally, the pandemic has brought significant upheaval in the geopolitical landscape, intensifying existing trends and new challenges. There are some positive outcomes with a greater boost to eCommerce and health product manufacturing and exports, wider connectivity with ICT and new ways of learning. India will have to sail smoothly to deal with the complex geopolitical situation and take advantage of a positive outcome of the pandemic.

India-Israel Relations: From No-Relations to Strategic Partnership

Dr. Khinvraj Jangid
Associate Professor and Director, Jindal Centre for Israel Studies,
OP Jindal Global University, Sonipat

This article focuses on the ideological alignment between India and Israel around cultural-religious nationalism coupled with neo-liberal free market economy is which is an important driving force today. The way each state defines its national-identity has direct links with the attitudes towards the other. The significant rise of BJP, therefore, asserted and continues to assert closer relations with Israel.

India and Israel will be completing thirty years of their diplomatic relations in January 2022. The story of Israel in Indian foreign policy is enigmatic as India did not recognise Israel whereas Israel wanted to have friendship with India when it was established in May 1948. V K Krishna Menon and Jawaharlal Nehru decided to recognise Israel in 1950 but avoided diplomatic relations. India normalised its relations with Israel on 22 January 1992 under the government of PV Narsimha Rao.

Before 1992

India's diplomatic choices before and after independence were guided by the principles of anti-imperialism, anti-colonialism and Third World solidarity. Having sought British support through the Balfour Declaration in 1917 and great power politics, the Zionist movement (political movement for the Jewish nationalism led by Theodor Herzl and David Ben-Gurion) was 'contaminated' by colonialism and as such, poles apart from how the Indian national movement saw itself. The anti-Zionist notions were further strengthened by the choice of Zionist leaders to build strong relations with the West, particularly the imperialist West, instead of choosing solidarity with the struggling Asian national liberation movements. The one small window when Nehru considered opening full diplomatic relations with Israel was in March 1952, he instructed civil servants to prepare the budget for establishing a resident mission in Tel-Aviv but it did not develop much. At first, India's first national elections, due in 1952, delayed the exchange of diplomatic representatives. Thereafter, financial constraints caused more delay but essentially it was Nehru's apprehensions about public opinion, the Arab world and India's immediate interests that made him set the matter aside. Israel's involvement in the Suez Crisis of 1956, and its "collusion" with the ex-imperial powers like Britain and France to attack Egypt for denting the rising leadership of Abdul Gamal Nasser was a turning point against Israel.

Self-determination for the Palestinian people was also a significant issue for Nehru, who gave them strong support and turned away from relations with Israel. The Palestine question was deeply engaged by Mahatma Gandhi as well and Nehru's India saw it part of the Third World solidarity. In addition to these principles, there was a regional political consideration and strategic calculation for India in the 1950s: the Kashmir dispute with Pakistan. Comparing to the larger Arab world, Israel was a small state and could hardly promise some tangible benefits for Indian foreign policy. India hoped for Arab support for the its case against Pakistan over disputed Kashmir by extending its strong support to the Palestinians and not towards Israel hence. However, India's support for the Palestinian cause or solidarity with the greater Arab world did not result into any tangible diplomatic gain for India from the Arab world either.

PM Indira Gandhi and PV Narasimha Rao MoEA with Yasser Arafat, PLO chairman on March 3, 1980

It wasn't until January 1992 that India established full diplomatic relations and an exchange of ambassadors with Israel. Global external factors more than domestic change facilitated this about-turn. First, the end of the Cold War and the collapse of Soviet Union created a new diplomatic matrix for India. As a result, Indian foreign policy had to be revised and the issue of Israel was an important case as India was inclined to liberalise its economy as well as seek greater alliance with United States.

Second, Israel was an excellent source for armaments and defense systems just as the Soviet Union and its associated weapons industries were crumbling. India's poor military capabilities played a crucial role in opening relations with Israel. Israel supplied arms to India in 1962 during its war with China; Nehru himself wrote a letter to Ben-Gurion asking for help and he was more than happy to assist India.

Third, Israel was negotiating, for the first time, with Palestinian leaders like Yasser Arafat on the basis of a two-state solution during 1991-1993. The fact that Israeli and Palestinian leaders were recognising each other and making an effort for peace, even though it didn't lead to Palestinian self-determination, neutered some of India's long-held reservations about dealing with Israel.

After 1992

India-Israel relations have grown increasingly close since 1992 and Israel is a strategic partner for India now. In three decades Israel has emerged as one of India's core diplomatic allies and the second most important supplier for defense and military needs. Both are developing common ground beyond strategic defense and security collaboration issues, including technology transfers in agriculture and water conservation. India is Israel's third-largest trade partner in Asia and seventh largest globally. In recent years, bilateral trade has diversified into several sectors such as pharmaceuticals, agriculture, water, IT and telecom. Indian software companies, notably TCS, Infosys, Tech Mahindra and Wipro are expanding their presence in Israel. Similarly, Israeli companies have invested in India in renewable energy, real estate, water technologies and are also setting up research-and-development centers and production units in India. In agriculture, they both have active interest and it is benefitting more India than Israel when it comes to drip irrigation, crop diversification or having high yield crops such as dates and pomegranate with Israeli knowhow. Israel is working with Indian farmers in more than twelve states of India where it has established around 30 centres of excellence in horticulture.

The strategic partnership between India and Israel is fuelled by political pragmatism and mutual interests, and as such, it offers a win-win situation for both. No wonder, it has hardly mattered which government has been in power in the last thirty years in India, its relations with Israel have been expanding steadily and much beyond the headlines. This kind of pragmatism was impossible back in 1950s, when the challenging dynamics of newly decolonized states meant strategic partnerships were based on strict political affinity. There were few supplementary or alternative cultural or intellectual routes for finding common ground. Today, however, the transnational requirements of trade and commerce have somewhat flattened older political oppositions, and relations between India and Israel are built on these kinds of mutual interests. To some extent this has been India's instrumental approach towards Israel.

Ideas Driving National-interests

Ideas such as anti-Colonialism and Third World activism mattered in the past and current ideas such as neo-liberal free market economy and religious-cultural nationalism matter now. National interests are not given in international politics but constantly constructed by the leaders who define what is good for a nation based on their personal values and assumptions.

The ideological alignment between India and Israel around cultural-religious nationalism coupled with neo-liberal free market economy is an important driving force today. The way each State defines its national-identity has direct links with the attitudes towards the other. The significant rise of BJP, therefore, asserted and continues to assert closer relations with Israel.

It should not be a surprise, hence, that the period 1998-2004, when BJP was in power, was instrumental in the evolution of the ties between the two states. The current ideological alignment matters in their ongoing bilateral relations as much as the Nehruvian ideology mattered in the past.

Another important commonality between Indian and Israeli leaders is the growing view that the state should be militarily capable, nuclear powered and aggressive/retaliatory. The idea of a strong state, at least in militaristic/security sense, is an ideological notion with which the BJP wants India to be identified with. A strong state that follows the dictum 'offence is the best defence', which is an masculine obsession, is making more ground for military collaborations with Israel. One wishes such flawed assumptions do not succeed further. Once upon a time, Indian leaders like Jayprakash Narayan (JP) advocated friendship with Israel because it presented democratic and socialist society to emulate. After he visited Israel for a week in 1958, he said that he saw in the people of Israel 'an unconquerable spirit' which refused to take defeat, whether it was in reclaiming sandy deserts and rocky lands, or converting them into smiling orchards.

PM Narendra Modi and Israeli PM Benjamin Netanyahu Elevated their Ties to the "Strategic Partnership"

India Trade (All units in USD Million)

	Last	Previous	Highest	Lowest
Balance of Trade	-22940.00	-13810.00	790.00	-22940.00
Current Account	6500.00	-8134.78	19083.03	-31857.18
Current Account to GDP	0.90	-0.90	2.30	-4.80 % of GDP
Imports	56380.00	47.09	56380.00	46.40
Exports	33440.00	33280.00	35430.00	59.01
External Debt	570000.00	569985.00	570000.00	96392.00
Foreign Direct Investment	2235.00	-692.00	17689.00	-2891.00
Capital Flows	-61.71	-38.46	766.97	-822.33
Remittances	14354.76	14035.31	16373.32	5999.10
Tourist Arrivals	0.00	0.00	1225672.00	0.00
Gold Reserves	703.71	695.31	703.71	357.75 Tonnes
Crude Oil Production	586.45	619.97	813.00	526.00 BBL/D/1K
Terrorism Index	7.35	7.52	8.09	7.22
Weapons Sales	151.00	18.00	151.00	0.00 SIPRI TIV Million
Auto Exports	32247.00	34933.00	63693.00	4034.00 units

Indian Diaspora

The overseas Indians extends the borders of the Republic of India. According to MEA, the diaspora is currently estimated to number over 32.1 million, composed of "NRIs" and "PIOs" in 2021 [17.5m (6.4% of global migrants or 0.4% of Indian population)]. It numbers more than a million each in 11 countries, while 22 countries have concentrations of at least 100,000 ethnic Indians.

Role and Importance

• Promotes India's interest abroad •Act as India's unnamed ambassadors in the fields of culture, education, economic development and health and arts. •Helps India by investing in industry and infrastructure to encourage its economic growth. • NRI's are major source of Direct Foreign Investment, market development (outsourcing), technology transfer, charity, tourism, and political contributions in India. •The NRI-NGOs (non-governmental organisations) help in array of developmental, educational and social projects, health care and developmental activities like water management, rural development, environmental issues, self-help programs etc. •The diaspora's scientific achievements, particularly in India's IT sector is evident in its symbiotic relationship with the Silicon Valley in California. •Indian diaspora even shapes India's foreign policy. With huge remittances, overseas Indians play an important role in India's foreign exchange management and success of Indians in the developed world, esp. in knowledge industries, medical profession and academia have transformed India's image.

Pravasi Bharatiya Divas

Pravasi Bharatiya Day: 09 January (it was on this day Gandhiji, the greatest Pravasi, returned to India from South Africa).

Fifteen PBDs To connect India to its vast overseas diaspora and bring their knowledge, expertise and skills on a common platform, the PBD Convention - the flagship event of MOIA is organized from 7th-9th January every year since 2003. These conventions provide a platform to the overseas Indian community to engage with the government and people of the land of their ancestors for mutually beneficial activities, useful in networking among the overseas Indian community residing in various parts of the world and enable them to share their experiences in various fields. During the event, individuals of exceptional merit are honoured with the prestigious Pravasi Bharatiya Samman Award to appreciate their role in India's growth. The event also provides a forum for discussing key issues concerning the Indian Diaspora.

Non-resident Indian (NRI) refers to a person who, as per section 6 of the Income-tax Act of 1961, did not stay in India of at least 182 days in a financial year or 365 days spread out over four consecutive years and at least 60 days in that year.

Person of Indian Origin (PIO) refers to a foreign citizen who (Indian acquired the citizenship of another country), at any time held an Indian passport or either of their parents/ grandparents/ great-grandparents were born before independence and permanently resident in India or other territories that became part of India or is a spouse of a citizen of India.

Overseas Citizenship of India refers to a long-term visa, with restrictions on voting rights and government jobs. OCI card is available to certain PIOs, which affords holders residency and other rights, with restrictions. It is not equivalent to Indian citizenship, constitutionally.

Countrywise Overseas Indians

Country	Indian Population
Indians in Asia	
Nepal	6 M
UAE	3.1 M
Malaysia	2.9 M
Saudi Arabia	2.8 M
Myanmar	2.0 M
Sri Lanka	1,6 M
Kuwait	929,903
Qatar	692,000
Oman	689.145
Singapore	650,700
Bahrain	316,175
Thailand	195,000
Philippines	150,000
Indonesia	107,500
Israel	45,000
Japan	22,335
Hong Kong	20,444
China	15,051
Lebanon	11,000
S & N Korea	10,317
Maldives	9,000
Yemen	9,000
Brunei	8,600
Syria	1,800
Pakistan	1,184
Bhutan	1,500
Cambodia	1,500
Kazakhstan	1,200
Vietnam	1,000
Afghanistan	1,000
Iran	800
Uzbekistan	700
Turkmenistan	700
Turkey	300
Cyprus	300
Laos	125
Kyrgyzstan	100
Indians in Europe	
Netherlands	235,000
United Kingdom	1,825,000
Italy	197,301
Germany	146,090
France	109,000
Republic of Ireland	91,520
Portugal	70,000
Russia	40,000
Spain	29,000
Norway	14,695
Switzerland	13,500
Austria	11,945
Sweden	11,000
Belgium	7,000
Greece	7,000
Denmark	5,500
Ukraine	3,500
Poland	2,000
Romania	1,200
Finland	1,170
Slovakia	100
Lithuania	100
Bulgaria	20
Indians in N America/Caribbean	
United States	5,402,362
Canada	1,016,000
Trinidad and Tobago	556,800
Jamaica	90,000
Guadeloupe (France)	55,000
Cuba	34,000
Saint Vincent and the Grenadines	21,500
Grenada	12,000
Martinique (France)	43,600
Saint Lucia	4,700
Puerto Rico (US)	4,500
Guatemala	2,300
Barbados	2,200
Mexico	2,000
Saint Kitts and Nevis	1,100
Netherlands Antilles	600
Belize	500
Antigua and Barbuda	300
Haiti	200

Population of Overseas Indians

Country	NRIs	PIOs	Overseas Indian
Afghanistan	3087	19	3106
Argentina	800	1800	2600
Armenia	1477	23	1500
Australia	241000	255000	496000
Austria and Montenegro	13000	18000	31000
Azerbaijan	953	24	977
Bahamas	250	50	300
Bahrain	323292	3366	326658
Bangladesh	10385	6	10391
Barbados	600	2500	3100
Belgium	12386	8250	20636
Bhutan	60000	0	60000
Botswana	9000	3000	12000
Brazil	4729	344	5073
Brunei Darussalam	11500	269	11769
Canada	178410	1510645	1689055
Central African Republic	100	0	100
China	55500	550	56050
China (Hong Kong)	31569	7160	38729
China (Rep. Of Taiwan)	3068	378	3446
Colombia	450	89	539
Cuba	600	1	601
Denmark	12685	2315	15000
Egypt	3950	351	4301
Fiji	1400	313798	315198
Finland	5652	7739	13391
France	19000	90000	109000
Germany	1,42,585	42500	1,85,085
Greece	12300	1089	13389
Haiti	580	0	580
Holy See	NA	0	0
Indonesia	8500	111500	120000
Iran	4000	337	4337
Iraq	18000	7	18007
Ireland	15000	25000	40000
Israel	12467	85000	97467
Italy	157695	45357	203052
Jamaica	5000	75000	80000
Japan	37933	686	38619
Kenya	20000	60000	80000
Korea (S)	13236	349	13585
Kuwait	1028274	1587	1029861
Malaysia	227950	2760000	2987950
Maldives	25000	108	25108
Mauritius	10500	884000	894500
Myanmar	9207	2000000	2009207
Nepal	600000	0	600000
Netherlands	40000	200000	240000
New Zealand	80000	160000	240000
Nigeria	40000	35	40035
Oman	779351	1790	781141
Pakistan	0	0	0
Russia	21354	2236	23590
Saudi Arabia	2592166	2781	2594947
Singapore	350000	300000	650000
South Africa	60000	1500000	1560000
Sri Lanka	14000	1600000	1614000
Sweden	15349	10370	25719
Switzerland	17403	7164	24567
Tanzania	10000	50000	60000
Thailand	20000	175000	195000
Trinidad & Tobago	1800	555000	556800
Turkey	1609	99	1708
Uganda	23500	6500	30000
UAE	3419875	5269	3425144
UK	351000	1413000	1764000
USA	1280000	3180000	4460000
Zimbabwe	500	9000	9500
Total	**13459195**	**18683645**	**32100340**

The Visa

Visa is an official document or a stamp put in your passport which allows you to enter or leave a particular country.

Visa Granted by India

- Visa Categories

Transit Visa
Tourist Visa
Medical Visa
Medical Attendant V.
Business Visa
Employment Visa
Project Visa
Intern Visa
Film Visa
Student Visa
Research Visa
Conference Visa
Mountaineering V.
Missionary Visa
Journalist visa
Entry Visa
Diplomat Visa
Official / Niscellaneous Visa
UN Diplomat Visa
UN Official Visa
Visa on Arrival
Long Term Visa
SAARC Visa
Overseas Citizen of India (OCI)
Cisitor (only for Pakistal Nationals)
Double Entry (only for Bangladeshi Nationals)

Visa Requirement Code

Countries and territories with visa-free or visa-on-arrival entries for holders of regular Indian passports

- India
- Visa free/ Visa not required
- Visa issued upon arrival
- Electronic Travel Authorisation/ Pre-Arrival Authorisation or eVisa
- Visa required prior to arrival
- Visa required
- Permit required - for visiting disputed areas abroad, partially recognised countries and restricted zones.

Tourist e-Visa: At present, travelers from more than 160 countries can apply for a Tourist e-Visa, Business e-Visa or Medical e-Visa, depending on the purpose of their visit to India. Travelers who use the e-Visa program apply, pay a fee online and receive their electronic visa online before traveling to India.

The Indian e-Visa allows for double entry, with a maximum stay of 60 days per entry.

eVISA in India

The e-visa can only be used at 24 airports: Ahmedabad, Amritsar, Bagdogra, Bengaluru, Calicut, Chennai, Chandigarh, Cochin, Coimbatore, Delhi, Gaya, Goa, Guwahati, Hyderabad, Jaipur, Kolkata, Lucknow, Mangalore, Mumbai, Nagpur, Pune, Tiruchirapalli, Trivandrum, Varanasi and 3 seaports: Cochin, Goa, and Mangalore.

Business e-Visa allows for double entries within 120 days from issuance. The cost of an India Business e-Visa is US$27, $51.50, or $102.50, depending on your NATIONALITY. The India Business e-Visa is valid for entry through 25 designated Airports and 5 designated seaports Cochin, Goa, Mangalore, Mumbai, Chennai).

Medical e-Visa The Medical e-Visa is valid for 120 days after issue. This means you must enter India within 120 days of issuance. The cost of an Indian Medical e-Visa is US$27, $51.50, or $102.50, depending on your nationality. Medical e-Visa allows for 3 entries.

Indians can travel Visa-free: Indonesia, Bhutan, Maldives, Mauritius, Nepal, Seychelles, Fiji.

Cheapest Countries Indians can visit: Vietnam, Bhutan, Sri Lanka, Bangladesh, Laos, Thailand, Singapore, Malaysia, Indonesia, Maldives, Seychelles, Cambodia, Philippines, Turkey, Myanmar, Lebanon, Hong Kong, Kenya, Taiwan.

e-Visa Fee Indian Government e-Visa Fee: It is the obligation fee to apply for the travel authorization at India Immigration Department for its processing. Visa Service fee: The applicant pay it in advance at the time of filling the online Indian visa application.

US Visa Types

There are about 185 types of US visas, grouped into two main categories: •Nonimmigrant visas. Issued for temporary visits to the United States such as for tourism, business, employment, family visit, and studying. •Immigrant visas. Issued to people who will move permanently to the United States under immigrant investor schemes or family reunion.

Here are the main types of US visas:

Visitor Visas The US visitor visas are issued to those who want to go to the United States to visit for a maximum of six months and are divided into: •B1 visa for business visits.• B2 visas for tourism visitors.

Student Visas The F and M visas are for academic and vocational purposes. Depending on your school and your field of study, you will have to get either the F1 or the M1 visa. •F1 visa.visa for students.

•F2 visa. dependents of F1 visa holders.

•M1 visa. visa for vocational purposes.

Exchange Visitor Visas The exchange visitor visas are targeted to those who participate in exchange programs and some type of practical training and employment within the United States. These visas are divided into: •J1 visa •Q Visa

Temporary Work Visas These visas are issued for temporary work in the United States. Here are the categories of work visas: •H1B visa. For persons who have been employed in highly specialized fields. •H1B1 visa. For nationals of Chile and Singapore.•H-2A visa. Granted to temporary agricultural workers from selected countries in whom the US has some type of interest.•H-2B visa. Given to other types of temporary seasonal workers, who do non-agricultural work.

•H-3 visa. Obtained by those who want to take advantage of training and education opportunities. •L1 visa. Issued to intracompany managers or executives.

People who have what is called an extraordinary ability in Arts, Science, Business, Education, or Athletics and want to temporarily work in their field of expertise need an O visa. There are three types of O visas: •O1 visa – for persons with extraordinary abilities.•O2 visa – for the assistants of O1 visa holders.•O3 visa – for dependents of O1 visa holders. •P visas. are issued to sportspersons and their coaching teams.

Temporary Religious Workers who want to practice within the US in religious capacities need to get the R1 visa type.

TN/TD visas are for citizens of Canada or Mexico who will be working in the NAFTA organisation.

E3 visas For nationals of Australia. who will be working in specialty occupations.

I visa For representatives of foreign media and journalists part of the press, film, radio, or print industries, who are visiting the US to work or participate in educational media activities.

Treaty Trader and Investor Visas The E visas are called Treaty Trader and Treaty Investor visas respectively, are for those who have treaties of commerce and navigation in the US. There are two types of this visa: •E1 Visa – treaty trader visa.•E2 Visa – treaty investor visa

Diplomatic and Official Visas Categories of official and diplomatic visas are the following: •The A1 visa is for diplomats or foreign government officials who are travelling to the US on official duties or representing their government. •The A2 NATO1-6 visa is designed only for foreign military personnel who are about to serve or be stationed within the United States.

If you have been **employed in an international organisation in the United States,** you will need to get a G-1 to G-5 visa. Those who will work for NATO, will get the NATO visa.

Visas for Victims of Crime and Human Trafficking. The following visas are part of this type of visa: •T visas are for victims of human trafficking who have severe trauma, but can also assist in investigating crimes related to human trafficking. •The U visa is for those who have been a victim of certain criminal activities and that can aid in the investigation or prosecution of those criminals.

Transit and Crewmember Visas Here are the categories of this type of visa: •The C Visa is a Transit Visa USA. •The D visa is for crew members who will work on a sea vessel or international airline.

Immediate Relative & Family Sponsored Visas Here are the categories of the Immediate relative and Family Sponsored visas: •The F2A and F2B visas are for the families of Lawful Permanent Residents, more specifically their spouses, minor children, or unmarried sons and daughters aged 21 and above.

•IR-2 visa – for unmarried children under 21 years old •IR5 visa – for parents of US Citizens who are at least 21 years old

•The IR3, IH3, IR4, IH4 visas are for children from other countries who will be adopted by US citizen parent(s)

•F1 visa– for unmarried sons and daughters and their minor children •F3 visa – for married sons and daughters and their minor children •F4 visa – for brothers and sisters of US Citizens, and their spouses and minor children. •The SQ visa is for Iraqi or Afghan citizens who will be working for or on behalf of the US government and get Special Immigrant Visas (SIVs).

Fiancie and Spouse Visas Here are the categories: •K3 visas are for spouses of US citizens who are in the process of obtaining permanent immigration status.

• The IR1 and CR1 visas are for spouses of US Citizens.•Children of the K-3 visa applicants are eligible to receive K-4 visas

Employer-Sponsored Visas The following visas are issued for immigrant employees: •The EB1 visa is called an Employment First Preference Priority Workers visa. •Employment Second Preference Professionals Holding advanced Degrees and Persons of Exceptional Ability visas are for those who have labor certification and a job offer in the US. •The Employment Third Preference Skilled Workers, Professionals, and Unskilled Workers visa are for those who have an approved Petition for Alien Worker filed by their employers.•Eb-5 visa for immigrant investors.

•The SI visa is for Iraqi and Afghan Translators or Interpreters working with the US military and who meet certain requirements.

Other Type of Immigrant Visa

•The SB visa or Returning Resident Visa is for permanent US residents who for reasons beyond their control have remained outside the country for more than a year or their re-entry permit is not valid anymore.

Schengen

Schengen refers to the EU passport-free zone that covers most of the European countries. It's the largest free travel area in the world. It is a short-stay visa that allows a person to travel to any members of the Schengen Area, per stays up to 90 days for tourism or business purposes. There are another 19 other countries that are not part of the Schengen Zone, yet they allow foreign citizens of other non-Schengen countries to enter and stay in their territories, only by showing a valid multiple-entry Schengen Visa. **Schengen Countries:** Austria,Belgium, Czech Rep., Denmark, Estonia, Finland, France, Germany, Greece, Hungary, Iceland, Italy, Latvia, Lithuania, Luxembourg, Malta, Netherlands, Norway, Poland, Portugal, Slovakia, Slovenia, Spain, Sweden, Switzerland, Liechtenstein. Over 15 million people used their Schengen visa in 2019 to travel around Europe.

The Ministry of External Affairs

The Ministry of External Affairs is largely located in South Block, a building that also houses the Prime Minister's Office and the Ministry of Defence.Offices of Ministry of External Affairs are also housed in Jawahar Lal Nehru Bhavan, Shastri Bhavan, Patiala House and ISIL Building.

External Affairs Minister: Dr. S. Jaishankar

Min. of State for External Affairs: V. Muraleedharan

Min. of State for External Affairs: Smt. Meenakashi Lekhi

Min. of State for External Affairs: Dr. Rajkumar Ranjan Singh

Foreign Secretary: Shri Harsh Vardhan Shringla

Secretary (East): Ms. Riva Ganguly Das

Secretary (CPV & OIA): Shri Sanjay Bhattacharyya

Secretary (West): Mrs. Reenat Sandhu

Secretary (ER): Shri Dammu Ravi

Foreign Diplomatic Missions in India: https://meaprotocol.nic.in/?a1

Indian Missions Abroad
https://www.mea.gov.in/indian-missions-abroad-new.htm#B

Locate Mission/Post Abroad:
https://passportindia.gov.in/AppOnlineProject/mission/locateMission

Online NRI Passport Application: https://passport.gov.in/nri/

Quick Guides: https://passportindia.gov.in/AppOnlineProject/online/QuickGuide

Sushma Swaraj Institute of Foreign Service (SSIFS)

Sushma Swaraj Institute of Foreign Service was established in 1986 by the Ministry of External Affairs, to cater to the professional training needs of the Indian Foreign Service (IFS) officers inducted via UPSC every year.

SSIFS is anchored in philosophy of Government's flagship programme 'Skill India' in the realm of foreign policy and diplomacy. SSIFS provides quality training by way of essential knowledge and diplomatic skills, striving to be a state-of-the-art centre of excellence.

SSIFS is headed by the Dean, a senior Foreign Service Officer of the rank of Secretary in the Ministry of External Affairs.

Activities: Training Programmes for •different Mid-Career levels •First Time Heads of Mission •Commercial Representatives posted in Indian Missions abroad •Defence Attaches posted to join our Embassies around the world •Orientation courses for deputationists and members of other Civil Services •non-Representational Grade officials of the Ministry for foreign diplomats as a way to build bridges of friendship and cooperation with countries around the world.

SSIFS Location: Baba Gangnath Marg, Old JNU Campus, New Delhi in 2007.

Website of SSIFS: https://meafsi.gov.in/

SSIFS Alumni Portal: https://SSIFSalumni.gov.in/

SSIFS's Twitter: https://twitter.com/SSIFS_MEA

SSIFS's Facebook Page: https://www.facebook.com/SSIFS.MEA.NEWDELHI/

Indian Foreign Service

The Indian Foreign Service (IFS) can be traced back to the British rule when the Foreign Department was created to conduct business with the "Foreign European Powers". In fact it was on Sep. 13, 1783, when the East India Company passed a resolution at Fort William, now Kolkata, to create a department, to ease Warren Hastings administration in conducting its "secret and political business". The Government of India Act, 1935 delineated more clearly functions of the "Foreign" and "Political" wings of the Foreign Department.

In Sep 1946, on the eve of India's independence, the GoI decided to create a service called the Indian Foreign Service for India's diplomatic, consular and commercial representation overseas.

In 1947, there was a near seamless transformation of the Foreign and Political department of the British India government into what then became the new Ministry of External Affairs and Commonwealth Relations and in 1948 the first batch recruited under the combined Civil service examination system of the UPSC joined the service.

Selection to the IFS

The Indian Foreign Service selection are through the combined Civil Services examination The new entrants undergo a multi-faceted and comprehensive training programme to give them a thorough diplomatic knowledge, diplomatic qualities and diplomatic skills. The probationers' training begins with their colleagues from the other All India Services, at the Lal Bahadur Shastri National Academy of Administration, Mussourie. Thereafter, the probationers join the Foreign Service Institute in New Delhi and undergo focused training in the various disciplines that a career diplomat needs. The Foreign Service Institute course aims to inculcate in the diplomatic recruit a strong sense of history, knowledge of diplomacy and international relations and a grasp of general economic and political principles.

At the end of the training programme the officer is assigned his compulsory foreign language (CFL) to develop proficiency in his CFL and pass the requisite examination before he is confirmed in service.

Career

A Foreign Service Officer begins his career abroad as a Third Secretary and is promoted to Second Secretary as soon as he is confirmed in service. Subsequent promotions are to the levels of First Secretary, Counsellor, Minister and Ambassador/ High Commissioner/Permanent Representative. Officers can also be posted to Indian Consulates abroad where the hierarchy is Vice-Consul, Consul and Consul General. The hierarchy at the Ministry of External Affairs includes 6 stages: Under Secretary, Deputy Secretary, Director, Joint Secretary, Additional Secretary and Secretary.

Functions

As a career diplomat, the Foreign Service Officer is required to project India's interests, both at home and abroad on a wide variety of issues. These include bilateral political and economic cooperation, trade and investment promotion, cultural interaction, press and media liaison as well as a whole host of multilateral issues.

The functions of an Indian Diplomat: •Representing India in its Embassies, High Commissions, Consulates, and Permanent Missions to multilateral organisations like UN •Protecting India's national interests in the country of his/ her posting •Promoting friendly relations with the receiving state as also its people, including NRI / PIOs •Reporting accurately on developments in the country of posting which are likely to influence the formulation of India's policies •Negotiating agreements on various issues with the authorities of the receiving state; and Extending consular facilities to foreigners and Indian nationals abroad.

At home, MoEA is responsible for all aspects of external relations. Territorial divisions deal with bilateral political and economic work while functional divisions look after policy planning, multilateral organizations, regional groupings, legal matters, disarmament, protocol, consular, Indian Diaspora, press and publicity, administration and other aspects.

Strength

Annual intake into the IFS : 8-15 persons. Present cadre strength of the service: 600 officers manning around 162 Indian missions and posts abroad and the various posts in the Ministry at home.
Foreign Service Institute: meafsi.gov.in

PM's Foreign Tour Diplomacy

2019: PM Modi made 59 foreign trips, visiting 63 countries. Oct 2019: Single visits: 38 countries, Double visits: 12 countries, 5 times: visited China, France and Russia and USA 6 times.

2020-2021: mostly cancelled due to Covid-19

Country	Places visited	Date(s)	Purpose(s)
Bangladesh	Dhaka, Ishwaripur	26 Mar.	State visit (See India–Bangladesh relations)
UN	USA, Washington D.C.,	22-25 Sep.	General debate of the United Nations General September Assembly, Participation in Quad
USA	New York City		Leaders' Summit & State Visit *PM Narendra Modi held bilateral talks with Quad leaders

Multilateral Meetings

Group	2021	2022
BIMSTEC	-	TBD, Colombo
BRICS	9 Sep., India	TBD, China
CHOGM	TBD, Kigali	-
EAS(ASEAN)	Nov., Bandar Seri Begawan	-
FIPIC	-	-
G-7	11–13 June, Carbis Bay	-
G-20	30–31 Oct., Rome	TBD, Labuan Bajo
IEUS	8 May, Lisbon	-
NAM	-	-
NSS	-	-
SAARC	-	TBD, Islamabad
SCO	16–17 Sep., Dushanbe	November, Samarkand
UNFCCC	31 Oct.–12 Nov., Glasgow	TBD
UNGA	Sep., New York City	September, New York City
Others	Quad 24 Sep., Washington D.C.	

Bureau of Immigration

Bureau of Immigration (BoI) was set-up in 1971 by Government of India to undertake Immigration function in the country. BoI is headed by Commissioner of Immigration and assisted by FRROs for immigration facilitation service at airports and work relating to registration of foreigners under various Acts and Rules. Altogether, there are 86 Immigration Check Posts all over India, catering to international traffic. Out of these, 37 ICPs are functioning under the BoI, while the remaining are being managed by the concerned State Governments. At present, there are 12 FRROs in major cities i.e. Delhi, Mumbai Kolkata, Chennai, Amritsar, Bengaluru, Hyderabad, Calicut, Kochi, Trivandrum, Lucknow and Ahmedabad. Apart from this, there are 12 Chief Immigration Officers in the cities i.e. Goa, Jaipur, Gaya, Varanasi, Nagpur, Pune, Mangalore, Trichy, Coimbatore, Bagdogra, Chandigarh and Guwahati. At remaining places District Superintendent of Police (SP) or the prescribed authority functions as FRO to facilitate foreigners.

Aim To strengthen the Immigration system, a modernization programme viz. Mission Mode Project on Immigration, Visa Foreigners' Registration and Tracking (IVFRT) has been undertaken by MHA/BoI, with the assistance of National Informatics Center(NIC). Under the project, all the Indian Missions, Immigration Checkposts (ICPs), FRRO/FRO offices are being computerized and networked to develop a secure and integrated delivery framework to facilitate legitimate travelers. MISSION STATEMENT - " Vision, Mission and Values"

Helpline :

Email id : support.covid19-boi[at]gov.in

- For all immigration, registration, visa, ECNR etc. related queries Email may be sent on Support Centre's email id support-boi[at]mha[dot]gov[dot]in
- Phone Numbers of BOI Support Centre 011-26711443 and 011-26713851
- For PIO,OCI related queries can be done on 011-26184824
- For eVIsa related queries please dial 011-24300666
- BOI Commissioner email-id comm.boi-mha[at]nic[dot]in

Indian Passport

India has started issuing biometric e-passport for Diplomatic passport holders in India and abroad which has a 4-second response time. It is a bilingual (Hindi, English) official document provided by Indian government to prove a citizen's identity, which is necessary when leaving the country and entering another. Passport Seva Kendras (PSK) provide passport-related services across India. It is issued at 93 passport offices and 162 Indian diplomatic missions abroad.

Types of Passport

Ordinary: Type "P" - for personal.
Official: Type "S" for Service (in govt).
Diplomatic: Type "D" for Diplomats.

• Global Passport Ranking 2019: India ranks 140 with a score of 65. The number of destinations the holders can access without a prior visa has ranked India 86th in 2019. Total Passport Holders 65M, 2016.

Passport Fees •₹1000 for minors below 18 years and 5 year validity.

• Fresh passport/re-issue of passport including additional booklet due to exhaustion of visa pages (36pages) of 10 years validity. ₹1500. Tatkaal: ₹3500 • Duplicate of passport (36 pages) in lieu of lost, damaged or stolen passport ₹3,000

• Expiry: 10 years – Adult; 5 or 10 years –age 15- 18 and 5 years for Minor.

• The passport services are being provided through India's 183 diplomatic missions abroad and one lakh common service centres in the country.

• **Changes** (i) End of mandatory requirement of producing the birth certificates as proof of date of birth. (ii) Separated or divorced applicants need not mention the name of their former spouse in the form. (iii) Documents for Tatkal Passport: Ration card / Aadhaar card/ PAN, Voters ID and self-declaration of no criminal complaint.

Date of Birth Proof Transfer/school leaving/matriculation certificate, PAN card, Aadhaar card, driving license, voter ID card, LIC policy bonds, extracts of service/pension records, letter from orphanage. ***Not needed*** Birth certificate, divorce decree, adoption certificate.

Passport Validity Many countries require passport validity of not less than 6 months and one or two blank pages.

Restrictions • Indian citizens who are not native of Arunachal Pradesh, Nagaland or Mizoram - require an Inner Line Permit (ILP) if they are travelling to the North East India. ILP can be obtained online or at the airports of these states on arrival.

• Many Arab League countries refuse entry to travelers whose passports show evidence of entry into Israel or hold an unused Israeli visa.

Vaccination Many African countries require incoming passengers to have a current International Certificate of Vaccination. Some other countries require vaccination only if the passenger is coming from an infected area.

Fingerprinting Several countries including Argentina, Cambodia, Japan, Malaysia, Saudi Arabia, South Korea and the United States demand all passengers to be fingerprinted on arrival.

Know Everything about Passport: (official website of the Consular, Passport and Visa (CPV). https://passportindia.gov.in/AppOnlineProject/online/welComeMessage

Everything about Indian Passport : https://passportindia.gov.in/AppOnlineProject/pdf/Citizen_Charter.pdf
https://passportindia.gov.in/AppOnlineProject/pdf/Dissemination_of_Information.pdf

For applying Passport services www.passportindia.gov.in. Alternatively, can also use official mobile App mPassport Seva (Android and iOS App stores).

How to fill the Passport Form: https://passportindia.gov.in/AppOnlineProject/pdf/ApplicationformInstructionBooklet-V3.0.pdf

Locate Passport Seva Kendra: https://passportindia.gov.in/AppOnlineProject/locatePSK/locatePFCInp

Locate District Passport Cell: https://passportindia.gov.in/AppOnlineProject/locateDPCSPC/locateDpcSpc

Students Traveling Abroad
Indian students intending to travel abroad for the purpose of study are advised to –

• Register themselves on this site - https://portal2.madad.gov.in/AppConsular/user/RegistrationBaseAction?request_locale=en

• Obtain an appropriate visa for study abroad from the foreign Embassy/Consulate in addition to other important and relevant information for study in the foreign country

• Check that the foreign University/College is accredited and recognised.

Familiarise with the relevant rules, laws, living conditions etc of the foreign country for the purpose of study and subsequent job prospects.

• Read the general advice on do's and dont's for foreign travel - http://mea.gov.in/dos-and-donts-for-foreign-travel.htm

• For more information and details, in addition to the foreign Embassy/Consulate concerned, the relevant Indian Embassy/Consulate could also be contacted. Also please read the information provided by the Indian Embassies/Consulates at this link – click here (coming soon).

Overseas Citizen of India (OCI)

Who is an OCI? A foreign national, - (i) who was a citizen of India at the time of, or at any time after 26th January, 1950; or (ii) who was eligible to become a citizen of India on 26th January, 1950; or (iii) who belonged to a territory that became part of India after 15th August, 1947; or (iv) who is a child or a grandchild or a great grandchild of such a citizen; or (v) who is a minor child of such persons mentioned above; or (vi) who is a minor child and whose both parents are citizens of India or one of the parents is a citizen of India - is eligible for registration as OCI cardholder.

• Spouse of foreign origin of a citizen of India or spouse of foreign origin of an Overseas Citizen of India Cardholder and whose marriage has been registered and subsisted for a continuous period of not less than two years immediately preceding the presentation of the application is also eligible for registration as OCI cardholder.

• No person, who or either of whose parents or grandparents or great grandparents is or had been a citizen of Pakistan, Bangladesh or such other country as the Central Government may, by notification in the Official Gazette, specify, shall be eligible for registration as an OCI Cardholder.

• Foreign nationals cannot apply for OCI in India while on Tourist Visa, Missionary Visa and Mountaineering Visa. Moreover, the foreigner has to be ordinarily resident of India to be eligible to apply for OCI registration in India.

Note: 'ordinarily resident' will mean a person staying in a particular country or in India for a continuous period of 6 months.

Online OCI Registration Application

New OCI Registration: https://ociservices.gov.in/welcome

Apply For Special Permission : https://ociservices.gov.in/welcome

Apply for permission for any Activity Must be a OCI Card Holder. List of activities: • research •to undertake any Missionary or Tabligh or Mountaineering or Journalistic activities• internship in any foreign Diplomatic Missions or foreign Government organisations in India •employment in any foreign Diplosmatic Missions in India; • to visit any place which falls within the Protected or Restricted or prohibited areas as notified by the Union Govt or competent authority.

Foreign Policy

The year 2021 threw a bunch of challenges and opportunities in pursuit of fulfilling foreign policy objectives. For instance, the rise of China and its influence in India's neighbourhood is a cause of worry for Indiaesp. Afghanistan. Again, conclusion of EU-China Comprehensive Agreement on Investment debunks the myth of Chinese isolation after Covid-19 pandemic and further strengthened China's position. Moreover, India's foreign policy decisions like growing convergence with the US have led to weakening its links with traditional friends like Russia and Iran.

Historically, India's foreign policy is shaped by several factors such as history, culture, geography and economy which will cater to the requirements of 21st C.

Our first Prime Minister, Jawaharlal Nehru, gave a definite shape to the country's foreign policy. So did Manmohan Singh. Presently PM Narendra Modi is steering it with a new outlook and his visits to about 90 countries gives India a new look. India's foreign policy from, the post-WW-II, Cold War period, has evolved from being pro-Soviet, contrasted to Western interests, to currently becoming a Western strategic partner and providing a counterweight to China.

Panchsheel (The Five Principles (Signed on April 28, 1954) – It is the centre-piece of the Confidence and Security Building Measures (CSBMs). • Respect for each other's territorial integrity and sovereignty • Non-aggression against anyone • Non-interference in each other's internal affair • Equality and mutual benefit • Peaceful co-existence. (Chinese intruded into the Indian territory 3 months after signing the agreement).

Non-alignment

Non-alignment, avoiding any politico-military alliance with USA or Soviet Union, (but taking an independent stand on international issues according to the merits of each case.) is regarded as one of the most important features of India's foreign policy.

Cold War was intense rivalry between USA and Soviet Union without fighting a direct war to attract allies in Africa, Asia and Latin America. It started soon after the Second World War and continued for 45 years These two big county blocs became two opposite poles known as East and West. The world politics revolved around these two poles–making the world bipolar.

Era of Globalisation

Globalization and the rapid emergence of market economies all over the world, from Southeast Asia to Latin America, resulted in the spectacular emergence of regional cooperation, integration and the widespread emergence of market economies.

Post Cold War Foreign Policy • India's search for its identity in the international order which is largely dominated by the US; • An accommodation with the global nuclear order as the international system comes to terms with 'nuclear' India; • India's balancing act of tackling the challenge of global terrorism without alienating its Islamic minority; • And India's search for energy security to ensure its current rate of economic growth.

The Gujral Doctrine

This doctrine was an expression of the foreign policy initiated by Inder Kumar Gujral, the Foreign Minister in Deve Gowda Government which assumed office in June 1996. The Gujral Doctrine is a set of five principles to guide the conduct of foreign relations with India's immediate neighbours as spelt out by IK Gujral, first as India's External Affairs Minister and later as the Prime Minister.

These Principles are: •With neighbours like Bangladesh, Bhutan, Maldives, Nepal and Sri Lanka, India does not ask for reciprocity, but gives and accommodates what it can in good faith and trust. •No South Asian country should allow its territory to be used against the interest of another country of the region. •Non interference in the internal affairs of another. •All South Asian countries must respect each other's territorial integrity and sovereignty. • Settle all disputes through peaceful bilateral negotiations.

Digital Diplomacy

The consistent efforts to use of digital technologies and social media platforms to engage with the public has helped in shaping up the foreign policy narrative, communicating with the interlocutors, connecting with Indian diaspora, extending support in crisis situations and interaction with several partners. Indian diplomacy handle is also focused on creating a positive cultural narrative for Brand India. It follows an eclectic mix of content comprising of press statements, speeches, joint statements, appointments of new ambassadors, soft stories on Indian arts and culture, achievements by Indians across the world, bilateral and international relations, strides by India across various platforms as well as plethora of human-interest stories that captures the interests of its visitors and followers.

The Modi Doctrine

The foreign policy and the policy initiatives made towards other countries by the Indian government since PM Narendra Modi assumed office on 26 May 2014, is focused on improving relations with neighbouring countries in South Asia, engaging the extended neighbourhood in SE Asia and the major global powers.

The Doctrine: is one of "strategic incoherence", executed without an "overarching conceptual framework."

The Keys: • Improving relations with immediate neighbours for peace and tranquility in South Asia for realising faster development. •The concept of para diplomacy envisages each state and city to have liberty to forge special relation with foreign countries or federal states or even cities of their interest. •Bilateral trade to improve relations with most countries except few important global powers with which India shares a strategic partnership.

Policy Initiative

Fast-track Diplomacy: (Three angles - proactive, strong and sensitive) • Para Diplomacy •Link West policy • Asian Foreign Policy (*Act East policy contrary to India's previous "Look East Policy"); *South Asia policy; *West Asia policy; *Overseas Indian crisis) •Neighbourhood first policy •Indian Ocean outreach; Project Mausam (trade and cultural linkages and stress on future maritime cooperation). •Cooperation with Pacific Islands •Forum for India-Pacific Islands cooperation: To partner with the region to advance their development and improve their quality of life.

Vaccine Diplomacy

Through 2020-21, India's public articulation of "self-reliance" and refusal to sign trade pacts with RCEP countries was widely perceived as "isolationist" and "inward-looking". India did step up to supply medicines and protective kits to more than 150 countries. But India could not emerge as the global leader the world needed at this time. Lack of resources, a contracting economy and its populist politics made it come about only as an aspirational power.

Quadrilateral Security Dialogue -QUAD

The Quad is a forum comprising four democratic nations – United States of America (USA), India, Australia and Japan. The grouping known as the quadrilateral security dialogue (QSD) or quad, was first mooted by Japanese PM Shinzo Abe in 2007. However, the idea couldn't move ahead with Australia pulling out of it, apparently due to Chinese pressure. But the United States has been moving in all directions to make allies to contain China's rise. The attempts to engage more with the east through Obama's 'Pivot to Asia' and 'Indo-Pacific' partnerships besides India's 'Look East policy', a major forum was taking shape. All four nations have a common ground of being democratic and common interests of unhindered maritime trade and security. With the additional aim to counter China's aggressive behaviour in the Indo-Pacific region, the "quadrilateral" coalition was established on November 12, 2017. It held a meeting a day before the ASEAN Summit. This was the first meeting of the group after its 're-organisation' and Australia showed willingness to join the group. It was agreed that a free, open, prosperous and inclusive Indo-Pacific region serves the long-term interests of all countries in the region and of the world at large. They agreed on addressing common challenges of terrorism and proliferation linkages impacting the region as well as on enhancing connectivity. Thus it underlined the rising significance of maritime geopolitics in an increasingly integrated world. Economically, the strategy is regarded as an answer to China's Belt and Road Initiative, which is establishing a China-centric trade route.

The China Question The most significant outcomes of the March 12 summit meeting of the Quad summit were related to COVID-19 vaccine production, facilitating cooperation over emerging technologies, and mitigating climate change.

The threat posed by China is at one level military, as evidenced by its proactive pursuit of territorial claims in South Asia, the South China Sea, and the East China Sea. At another, it is economic and technological. China is a pivotal player in global supply chains, most visible today in its major role as a vaccine supplier, a major investor of surplus capital globally through the Belt and Road Initiative, and a rapidly rising technological power. It is this broader aspect of global order that the Quad aims to address, as is clear from two of the joint statement's specifics, which focus on the establishment of working groups on vaccine development and critical technologies. Both these efforts seek to constrain China's central position in the global system, but also to develop a world order that is broad-based and inclusive. The third working group being set up is on climate change, an area in which China is a cooperative player and not a competitor, and thus downplays the notion that the Quad is simply an instrument of containment. Together, three initiatives have been designed to create an environment that encourages China to be a positive player and persuades other states to shed their hesitancy toward the Quad.

Military Initiatives Though the summit focused on non-military initiatives, the Quad by no means downplays the military dimension. Its members have established the basis for regular defense cooperation through naval exercises, and the sharing of intelligence and military logistics. Adding further heft to previous bilateral efforts, the trilateral India-U.S.-Japan Malabar naval exercises expanded to include Australia in 2020. The Quad consolidated their military responses of nested strategic partnerships: linking their bilateral relationships with the India-Japan-U.S., India-Australia-Japan, and U.S.-Japan-Australia trilaterals. The Quad is a logical extension of this network and has the potential to build a "Quad Plus" arrangement involving Canada, France, and perhaps New Zealand and the United Kingdom.

Technological Process The Quad has the bandwidth to focus on countering the challenging non-security frontiers of Beijing's influence. To addressing it, the group has promoted Japan's Partnership for Quality Infrastructure – rechristened the Expanded Partnership for Quality Infrastructure – and introduced the multi-stakeholder *Blue Dot Network* process, both intended to create a globally recognised evaluation and certification system for investments in sustainable developmental projects in the Indo-Pacific region.

Restructuring Supply Chains The Quad has also prioritised restructuring supply chains to wean them away from Chinese interference. With China leveraging vaccine diplomacy to a large number of recipient states, the four members have decided to test the Resilient Supply Chain Initiative (conceived by the India-Australia-Japan trilateral) through vaccine production with India as their production hub. If the vaccine initiative is to counter China's vaccine diplomacy and influence, their cooperation over critical technologies is a second non-military action aimed to undercut the potential of China to achieve a dominant role in telecom and biotech (both mentioned in the joint statement) and other strategically significant areas.

What does India Stand to Gain?

First, the security dividend will be significant, though not immense since India can take care of the more severe threats to its security, as is evident from the Ladakh crisis, and is already benefiting from bilateral U.S. arms transfers. The Quad will bring additional gains from sharing of intelligence and logistics and from the skills obtained through military exercises. Second, greater gains can be expected from the steady restructuring of regional and global trade and investment relationships, which will reduce India's dependence on China and bring in increased investment and manufacturing activity. Third, India's status as a major power will be further enhanced through its expanded role in the making of a redesigned world order less susceptible to Chinese power and associated with more widely accepted values. Above all, India stands to gain from the creation of a more stable, cooperative world which it has the capacity to shape in unprecedented ways.

The First Physical Summit: 2021

On September 24, President Biden hosted PM Scott Morrison of Australia, PM Narendra Modi of India, and PM Yoshihide Suga of Japan at the White House for the first-ever in-person Leaders' Summit of the Quad.

The Quad Vision: • Global Health : Help Vaccinate the World – to donate more than 1.2 billion vaccine doses globally. QUAD delivered nearly 79 million safe and effective vaccine doses to the Indo-Pacific region •Enhance key investments of approx. $100 million in the healthcare sector related to COVID-19, including vaccine and treatment drugs •Establish a Clean-Hydrogen Partnership •Enhance Climate Adaptation, Resilience, and Preparedness •Build Better Health Security: to better preparing our countries and the world for the next pandemic – 100-Day Mission—to have safe and effective vaccines, therapeutics, and diagnostics available within 100 days—now and into the future • high-standards infrastructure • Green-Shipping Network – by inviting ports (Los Angeles, Mumbai Port Trust, Sydney (Botany), and Yokohama, to form a network dedicated to greening and decarbonising the shipping value chain.

Act East Policy

India's Act East Policy, originally conceived as an economic initiative, has gained political, strategic and cultural dimensions including establishment of institutional mechanisms for dialogue and cooperation. It focuses on the extended neighbourhood in the Asia-Pacific region. India has upgraded its relations to strategic partnership with Indonesia, Vietnam, Malaysia, Japan, Republic of Korea, Australia, Singapore and Association of South East Asian Nations (ASEAN) and forged close ties with all countries in the Asia-Pacific region. Apart from ASEAN, ASEAN Regional Forum (ARF) and East Asia Summit (EAS), India has also been actively engaged in regional fora such as Bay of Bengal Initiative for Multi-Sectoral Technical and Economic Cooperation (BIMSTEC), Asia Cooperation Dialogue (ACD), Mekong Ganga Cooperation (MGC) and Indian Ocean Rim Association (IORA). Act East Policy has placed emphasis on India-ASEAN cooperation in our domestic agenda on infrastructure, manufacturing, trade, skills, urban renewal, smart cities, Make in India and other initiatives. Connectivity projects, cooperation in space, S&T and people-to-people exchanges has become a springboard for regional integration and prosperity.

The Objective It aims to promote economic cooperation, cultural ties and develop strategic relationship with countries in the Asia-Pacific region through continuous engagement at bilateral, regional and multilateral levels thereby providing enhanced connectivity to the States of North Eastern Region including Arunachal Pradesh with other countries in our neighbourhood. The North East of India has been a priority in our Act East Policy (AEP). AEP The connectivity of Northeast with the ASEAN region include trade, culture, people-to-people contacts and physical infrastructure (road, airport, telecommunication, power, contacts between academic and cultural institutions etc.). Some major projects: Kaladan Multi-modal Transit Transport Project, the India-Myanmar-Thailand Trilateral Highway Project, Rhi-Tiddim Road Project, Border Haats, etc.

The Three Pillars The ASEAN-India Plan of Action identifies initiatives and areas of cooperation in political-security, economic and socio-cultural. India has stepped up its efforts to forge closer partnership with regional and Multilateral organisation like ASEAN, BIMSTEC, IORA etc. On the cultural front, Buddhist and Hindu links gave new connectivity between people and linking ASEAN with our North East. The ASEAN-India Agreement on Trade in Service and Investments has entered into force for India and seven ASEAN countries. India invited ASEAN member states to participate in the International Solar Alliance. On strategic issues, India has increased convergence on security interests with key partners in terms of combating terrorism, collaborating for peace and stability in the region and promotion of maritime security based on international laws.

Neighbourhood First

The "neighborhood first" policy is the striking feature of Modi-2 government's diplomatic approach. PM's foreign policy initiatives to some extent are governed by India's rising concern over rapid expansion of China's economic clout and military might in Asia, esp. dominating India's immediate neighborhood. To promote regional peace and economic integration in South Asia, based on India's natural geographical advantages, economic complementarity, shared cultural heritage, and preeminent strategic position, New Delhi is developing a regional strategy. By focusing in the neighborhood, India has gained greater strategic confidence in South Asian-geopolitics as it resolves its differences with its small neighbours. It has in turn provided ability to deal with Washington and Beijing. If India fails, it will only pave the way for China to exert growing influence in the region.

In a diplomatic first by inviting the leaders from the South Asian subcontinent to attend Government's swearing-in ceremony in 2014 and in 2019, and PM's travel to almost all of India's neighbours was an attempt to establish India as a dominion. India's "neighborhood first" policy is now not a mere political rhetoric but a strategic necessity. In fact, the entire neighbourhood, minus one, has turned out to be a fairly good story of regional cooperation.

Afghanistan Afghanistan underwent a change in its political leadership when Ashraf Ghani got elected president in 2014 and 2019. India's assistance for reconstruction and development in Afghanistan stands at $2 billion. It is evident from construction of the Afghan Parliament building with Indian assistance and Salma Dam in Herat. Again, reaching through Afghanistan into Central Asia's road and railway network, India has the potential to shape events as a counterweight to Pakistani and Chinese influence. The first phase of Iranian Chabahar port is an important milestone in India's foreign policy when the first consignment of wheat from India entered Afghanistan through Chabahar. In view of Pakistan denying access through its territory, India and Afghanistan have also launched an air freight corridor–giving a boost to bilateral trade, education and medical treatment in India.

Bangladesh Indian "neighborhood first" policy's success is that Bangladesh has provided great strategic opportunity to change South Asia's geopolitical situation. In July 2014, New Delhi and Dhaka accepted the judgment of International Tribunal for the Law of the Sea and settled a long-standing maritime order dispute. In June 2015, the two countries exchanged the instruments of ratification on the historic land boundary agreement, exchanged enclaves. In 2019 PM Sheikh Hasina visited India, during which India announced a new credit line of $4.5 billion with an additional $500 million for Bangladesh's defense hardware purchase. The volume of trade between both the countries is worth $10 B.

Sheikh Hasina

Bhutan Bhutan has been a time-tested friend for India. PM Modi visited Bhutan for the second time on August 17-18, 2019, said that "Bhutan has a special place in the heart of 130 crores Indians." The two countries signed 10 MoUs to further boost the ties. The two side trade have reached ₹92.28 B ($1.2 billion) in

2018. RuPay Card has been introduced to ease financial transitions. India has committed to assist Bhutan in developing a minimum of 10,000 MW of hydropower by 2020 and import the surplus electricity. The coming of the Tshering Tobgay government in 2013 and the Modi government in India in 2014 minimised China's role in adversely affecting the India-Bhutan relations. This was evident during the Doklam crisis between India and China in 2017, when Bhutan fully supported India's stand, refusing to accept an offer of $10 billion from China as economic assistance.

Dr. Lotay Tshering

Sri Lanka Sri Lanka has long been in India's geopolitical orbit, but its relationship with China has strengthened in recent years. During the final stages of the civil war with LTTE, China extended billions of dollars of loans to the Sri Lankan government for new infrastructure projects. In February 2015, Sri Lanka's newly elected President Maithripala Sirisena undertook his first official visit to India. Beset by China's offensive in its strategic backyard, Modi visited Colombo thrice: in 2015 (made a trip to Jaffna), 2017 (inaugurated a specialty hospital built with Indian assistance and visited the Indian-origin Tamil community) and 2019 (visited the Church that was bombed). Earlier Sri Lankan PM Ranil Wickremeshinghe attended the Belt and Road summit, and had a strategic port of Hambantota, (a key role in China's BRI), leased to China for 99-years. Now, India is very likely to invest in Mattala airport in Hambantota district.

N G Rajapaksa

Maldives Maldives is one South Asian country that Modi has not visited since taking office. PM Modi's visit in March 2015 during the Indian Ocean tour, was canceled due to domestic political turbulence in Maldives. However, Maldivian President Abdulla Yameen visited India in April 2016 and the two countries signed agreements in the fields of defense, taxation, tourism, conservation of mosques, and space research. But Maldives has a Free Trade Agreement (FTA) with China, Yameen has also pledged full backing for China's Maritime Silk Road (MSR), (part of the BRI). Interestingly, the Chinese embassy in Colombo managed Maldivian affairs until 2011. India's foreign ministry reminded Maldives about 1988 Maldives coop d'etat and India's concerns.

Ibrahim Solih

Nepal Due to inconsistent policies, conflicting priorities of India, the emergence of sleft coalition in Nepal's parliamentary elections, and making a new constitution reduced India's leverage in Nepal's internal politics. Kathmandu has already signed on to the BRI plan, which is cementing China's communication links with Nepal.

Pakistan India-Pakistan relations have always been facing deadlock. It got hightened by Phulwama attack and the India's reciprocal Balakot airstrike. The Modi government's policy of diplomatically isolating Pakistan has succeeded only in a small way but Islamabad has stepped up its diplomatic efforts to engage Beijing, Moscow, and Tehran. Indo-Pak relations always has a drag of Kargil war, Mumbai Parliament terror attack and the past wars.

Imran Khan

India-Afghan Relations

Afghanistan and India, geographically, are neighbours, and share cultural ties through Bollywood and cricket. Historically, relations between Afghanistan and India traces to the Indus Valley Civilisation. Following Alexander the Great's brief occupation, the successor state of the Seleucid Empire controlled the region known today as Afghanistan. In 305 BCE, they ceded much of it to the Indian Maurya Empire as part of an alliance treaty.

The Mauryans controlled the area south of the Hindu Kush, and during this period Hinduism and Buddhism prevailed. Their decline began 60 years after Ashoka's rule ended, leading to the Hellenistic reconquest of the region by the Greco-Bactrians. Much of it soon broke away from the Greco-Bactrians and became part of the Indo-Greek Kingdom. The Indo-Greeks had been defeated and expelled by the Indo-Scythians in the late 2nd century BCE.Much of Afghanistan has been influenced by Buddhist, Hindu and Zoroastrian cultures until the arrival of Islam in the 7th century. But despite many Afghans converting to Islam, the Muslims and Hindus lived side by side. Many of the kingdoms that ruled over present-day Afghanistan between the 8th century BCE and the 10th century A.D like the Greco-Bactrian kingdom, Indo-Greek Kingdom, Mauryan Empire, Indo-Scythians, Huns and at last the Kabul Shahis were made up of adherents of Greek polytheism, Zoroastrianism (in the northwest region) and Buddhism-Hinduism (in the southeast region).

Between the 10th century to the mid 18th century, northern India has been invaded by a number of invaders based in what today is Afghanistan. Among them were the Ghaznavids, Ghurids, Khaljis, Suris, Mughals and Durranis. During these eras, especially during the Mughal period (1526–1858), many Afghans began immigrating to India due to political unrest in their regions.

Fast-forwarding, Khan Abdul Ghaffar Khan and Khan Sahib were prominent leaders of the Indian independence movement and active supporters of the Indian National Congress. Although the NWFP became part of Pakistan in 1947, active Pashtun support for the Indian freedom struggle led to great sympathy in India for the cause of Pashtun autonomy and freedom. The Indian government continued to support Pashtun leader Khan Abdul Ghaffar Khan in lobbying for greater Pashtun freedom in the NWFP. According to the MEA, the friendly relations can be traced back to January 1950 when a five-year Treaty of Friendship was signed by then Prime Minister of India Jawaharlal Nehru and Afghan's then Ambassador to India Mohammad Najibullah in New Delhi. Other than affirming "everlasting peace and friendship between the two Governments", the treaty provided for establishment of diplomatic and consular posts in each other's territories.

India recognised the new Republic of Afghanistan on July 19, 1973. Indian foreign minister Swaran Singh visited Afghan President Mohammed Daoud Khan in October that year, and Khan visited India in March 1975. On July 7, 1974, the two countries signed a trade protocol.

The Diplomatic Relations

India was the only South Asian country to recognise the Soviet-backed Democratic Republic of Afghanistan in the 1980s. India and Afghanistan are also a part of several regional partnerships, including the South Asian Association for Regional Cooperation (SAARC). Anyway relations became cold during the 1990s Afghan civil war and the Taliban forming government. However, relations between Afghanistan and India received a major boost in 2011 with the signing of a strategic partnership agreement, Afghanistan's first since the Soviet invasion of 1979. India aided the overthrow of the Taliban and became the largest regional provider of humanitarian and reconstruction aid to the former Islamic Republic of Afghanistan. Indians are working in various construction projects, as part of India's rebuilding efforts in Afghanistan. Shaida Mohammad Abdali, Afghanistan's ambassador to India, in April 2017 pointed out that India "is the biggest regional donor to Afghanistan and fifth largest donor globally with over $3 billion in assistance. India has built over 200 public and private schools, sponsors over 1,000 scholarships, hosts over 16,000 Afghan students. Indians are working in various construction projects, as part of India's rebuilding efforts in Afghanistan. These workers are estimated to be anywhere between 3,000 and 4,000. India also witnessed its nationals stationed in Afghanistan often facing continuous security threats, with kidnappings and many attacks (such as the February 2010 Kabul attack) deliberately carried out on them.

Infrastructure Development

The new Afghan Parliament building

The foundation stone for the new Afghan Parliament was laid a 100-acre plot in the famous Darulaman section of Kabul in August 2005 by the last king of Afghanistan, Zahir Shah, in the presence of Hamid Karzai and Manmohan Singh.India's Central Public Works Department (CPWD) was the consultant for the project and the contract was awarded to an Indian infrastructure company in 2008. The main attraction of the building is a bronze dome of 32 meter diameter and 17.15 meter height is considered to be the largest dome in Asia. On December 25, 2015, during a state visit of Indian PM Narendra Modi, the $90millon new Parliament building was inaugurated along with President Ashraf Ghani.

Afghan-India Friendship Dam

Indian Prime Minister Narendra Modi and Afghan President Ashraf Ghani inaugurating the Salma Dam.

Salma Dam, officially the Afghan-India Friendship Dam, is a hydroelectric and irrigation dam project located on the Hari River in Chishti Sharif District of Herat Province in western Afghanistan. The hydroelectric plant produces 42 MW of power in addition to providing irrigation for 75,000 hectares of farmland. The dam was opened on 4 June 2016 by Indian PM Narendra Modi along with Afghan President Ashraf Ghani.

Military Since 2011, around 700 Afghans train in India every year in institutions such as the National Defence Academy, Indian Military Academy, Officers Training Academy, Infantry School in Mhow and the Counter-Insurgency and Jungle Warfare School in Mizoram.

Exit US - Enter Taliban

The Taliban swept across Afghanistan in August, seizing control of almost all key towns and cities, including Kabul, against the backdrop of the withdrawal of US forces. With the US exit from Afghanistan India is concerned about reemergence of hostility in the region and the role of Pakistan and China. Under the government's 'Operation Devi Shakti' India evacuated people on military transport aircraft. As Taliban rolled into Kabul on 15 August, they promised safety of Indian diplomats provided India maintained the embassy in Kabul. In the meantime, on 17th August India evacuated its diplomats and closed all its consulates and embassy. Since the Taliban assumed power in Kabul after the collapse of the Ashraf Ghani government on August 15, the group's spokesmen Suhail Shaheen and Zabiullah Mujahid spoke about the group's views on relations with India. However, Stanekzai is the first senior leader to make a statement on relations with key countries in the region – India, Pakistan, China and Russia. India is regarded as important for the subcontinent and Taliban wants to continue cultural, economic and trade ties with India like in the past.

Indian Ocean Rim Association (IORA)

Indian Ocean Rim Association (IORA) was formerly known as Indian Ocean Rim Association for Regional Cooperation (IOR-ARC). The name IORA was adopted in November 2013 in Perth, Australia during the 13th meeting of Foreign Ministers.

Members: Currently represents a grouping of 23 (of 36) countries (Australia, Bangladesh, Comoros, India, Indonesia, Iran, Kenya, Malaysia, Madagascar, Mauritius, Mozambique, Oman, Seychelles, Singapore, Somalia, South Africa, Sri Lanka, Tanzania, Thailand, UAE and Yemen) whose shores are washed by the Indian Ocean and collectively aims at enhancing economic cooperation for sustained development and balanced economic growth of its members.

Partners It has 9 Dialogue Partners: China, Egypt, Japan, Korea, UK, USA, Germany, Italy and Turkey.

Secretariat: Port Louis, Mauritius

The first IORA Leaders' Summit was held on March 7, 2017 at Jakarta, Indonesia to commemorate the 20th Anniversary of the Association. The specialised mechanisms of the IORA created for the benefit of Member States include: • IORA Special Fund • IORA Sustainable Development Programme • Chair of Indian Ocean Studies • 2 IORA Specialised Agencies: Regional Centre for Science and Technology Transfer (RCSTT) HQ: Iran and the Fisheries Support Unit (FSU) HQ: Oman.• 4 ministerial levels of specialised engagement – Trade, Blue Economy, Renewable Energy and Tourism.

The Arctic Council

The Arctic Council is the leading intergovernmental forum promoting cooperation, coordination and interaction among the Arctic States, Arctic indigenous communities and other Arctic inhabitants on common Arctic issues, in particular on issues of sustainable development and environmental protection in the Arctic.

Formation of Arctic Council Establishment of the Arctic Environmental Protection Strategy (AEPS) in 1991 as a framework for intergovernmental cooperation on environmental protection initiatives among the Arctic States including Canada, Denmark, Finland, Iceland, Norway, Sweden, Russia, and the United States. As of May 2019, thirteen non-Arctic states have Observer status. Germany, Netherlands, Poland, UK, France, Spain, China, India, Italy, Japan, South Korea,Singapore, Switzerland.

India was reelected as an Observer to AC in 2019 though joined it in 2013.

The SAARC

The South Asian Association for Regional Cooperation (SAARC) was established with the signing of the SAARC Charter in Dhaka on 8 December 1985.

The Objectives • To promote the welfare of the peoples of South Asia and to improve their quality of life • to accelerate economic growth, social progress and cultural development in the region and to provide all individuals the opportunity to live in dignity and to realise their full potentials • to promote and strengthen collective self-reliance among the countries of South Asia • to contribute to mutual trust, understanding one another's problems • to strengthen cooperation among themselves in international forums on matters of common interests •and to cooperate with international and regional organisations with similar aims and purposes.

•Member States: Afghanistan, Bangladesh, Bhutan, India, Maldives, Nepal, Pakistan and Sri Lanka. •The Secretariat: Kathmandu (17 Jan 1987) •Secretary-General: Sri Lanka Esala Ruwan Weerakoon (3 March 2020 – present).• Area: • Total 5,099,611 km^2; • Water (%). 6.8. Population: • 2015–1,713,870,000 • Density: 336.1/km^2 •GDP (PPP) 2017–Total: US$11.64 tn GDP (nominal) 2017–Total: $3.31 tn.

The ASEAN Engagement

The ASEAN-India Summit basically aims at creating opportunities for the leaders to interact in a multilateral setting, as well as for informal interactions on a one-to-one basis. Earlier on 25 January 2018, New Delhi hosted the ASEAN-India Commemorative Summit themed "Shared Values, Common Destiny", attended by the leaders of the ten ASEAN States. The Delhi Declaration covered the entire spectrum of political-security, economic, socio-cultural and development cooperation. PM Modi visited Singapore in May 2019 to attend the Shangri-La Dialogue, where he spoke about India's vision of the Indo-Pacific. India's Act East Policy was unveiled at the 12th ASEAN-India Summit in 2014 held in Nay Pyi Taw. In his Opening Statement on the occasion, PM Modi said: "A new era of economic development, industrialisation and trade has begun in India. Externally, India's 'Look East Policy' has become 'Act East Policy'."

Motto: "One Vision, One Identity, One Community" **Anthem**: The ASEAN Way **Establishment**: •Bangkok Declaration 8 Aug. 1967 •Charter: 16 Dec. 2008
Area: 4,522,518 km^2 **Population** 2020 est.: 661m **Density**: 144/km^2 **GDP (PPP)** 2020 est. • Total $9.727 trillion• **Per capita**: $14,025 •**GDP** (nominal) 2020 est. Total: $3.317 trillion • Per capita: $5,017. **Time zone:** UTC+6:30 to +9 (ASEAN)

The Far East Move

About 48 years ago, during the India-Pakistan war in 1971, when the US and British Navies tried to threaten Indian security, the Soviet Union dispatched nuclear-armed flotilla from its Pacific Fleet based at Vladivostok in support of India. Since then, the city of Vladivostok, located in Russia's Far East, has had a special place in the hearts of Indians. When PM Narendra Modi visited the city as the guest of honour at Eastern Economic Forum (EEF), he announced $1bn support and India's plans to invest in Russia's Far East – paying back the long-held Indian debt to Vladivostok.

The Far East lies in the Asian part of Russia and is less developed than the country's European areas. As part of his 'Pivot to Asia' strategy, President Vladimir Putin has invited foreign countries to invest in this region.

The idea of an 'Indo-Pacific region', signals India's willingness to work with the US mainly to counter China's assertive maritime rise, has also left Russia concerned. Moscow is apprehensive that the US would exert pressure on India's foreign policy choices and that it could lose a friendly country and one of the biggest buyers of Russian military hardware.

Multipolar Indo-Pacific

Russia wants to make sure that China does not become a hegemon in the Eurasian region and is hence deepening cooperation with countries like India, Vietnam and Indonesia. The Far East has the potential to become an anchor in deepening India-Russia cooperation; more so considering that New Delhi has expanded the scope of its 'Act East policy' to also include Moscow.

At least 17 countries have invested in the Far East which, with its investment-friendly approach and vast reserves of natural resources, has the potential to strengthen India-Russia economic partnership in areas like energy, tourism, agriculture, diamond mining and alternative energy.

A bilateral business dialogue was included in the business programme of EEF in 2017 and, in 2018, India was one of the 18 countries for which Russia simplified electronic visas to encourage tourism in the Far East.

A lack of manpower in the Far East attracts Indian professionals like doctors, engineers and teachers who can help in the region's development and their presence will help in balancing Russian concerns over Chinese migration into the region. India, being one of the largest importers of timber, can find ample resources in the region. Japan and South Korea have also been investing and New Delhi may explore areas of joint collaboration.

Paradiplomacy India has given lot of significance to 'paradiplomacy' where Indian States are being encouraged to develop relations with foreign countries. States like UP, Gujarat, Maharashtra, Haryana and Goa would be collaborating with Russian Provinces to increase trade and investments. Earlier, Commerce and Industry Minister led a delegation to Vladivostok that included CMs of these States and representatives from about 140 companies. For India, there is immense potential for mid-sized and small businesses who needs be assisted to overcome language and cultural barriers so that they successfully adopt local business practices. India and Russia are also looking at the feasibility of Chennai-Vladivostok sea route that would allow India access to Russia's Far East in 24 days, compared to the 40 days taken by the current route via Suez Canal and Europe. This route would add the required balance to peace and prosperity in South China Sea and could open new vistas for India, like the India-Russia-Vietnam trilateral cooperation.

Power Puzzle In international politics, great power rivalry is back, making it more unpredictable. In times when US President Trump is interested in 'deglobalisation' and China is promoting 'globalisation 2.0 with Chinese characteristics', it makes sense for India and Russia to increase their areas of cooperation and trade in order to build a hedge against disruptive forces and make their ties sustainable.

Shanghai Cooperation Organisation The Shanghai Cooperation Organisation (SCO) is a 8-member multilateral organization, established on 15 June 2001 in Shanghai, China by the leaders of China, Kazakhstan, Kyrgyzstan, Russia, Tajikistan and Uzbekistan. Shanghai Five group was formed on 26 April 1996 with the signing of the Treaty on Deepening Military Trust in Border Regions. India got Observer status: July 2005 Astana Summit. Full member: 9 June 2017.

India in Central Asia

The breakup of the Soviet Union led to the formation of the independent republics of Kazakhstan, Kyrgyzstan, Tajikistan, Turkmenistan, and Uzbekistan. Due to its strategic location and rich natural reserves, CA is an important player in global politics. Consequently, the "New Great Game," has seen fierce competition between global players to increase influence, hegemony and power over the region. The growing geostrategic and security concerns regarding the China–Pakistan Economic Corridor (CPEC)–China's flagship venture with Pakistan under the Belt and Road Initiative (BRI)–forced New Delhi to fix its ineffectual strategy. Soon after assuming office, PM Modi visited all the CA countries in July 2015, boosting the momentum of the "Connect Central Asia" Policy of 2012 and setting in motion the next stage of international cooperation. Eventually, the CA became the link that also placed the Eurasian region firmly in New Delhi's zone of interest. India and CA signed several deals on a range of issues including security, energy, trade and culture, with the prime minister reiterating the region's importance to India's future.

The reciprocal high-level state visits by the presidents of Tajikistan, Kyrgyzstan and Uzbekistan highlight the evolution of the India–CA dynamics through bilateral and trilateral arrangements. India's Central Asia Policy received a significant boost in 2018, when New Delhi's diplomatic efforts paid dividends in the form of admission into the Ashgabat Agreement, signed in 2011 between Iran, Oman, Turkmenistan and Uzbekistan and Qatar, for the establishment of an international transport and transit corridor. This agreement allows India to use the existing land connectivity networks to facilitate trade and commercial interaction with both CA and Eurasia, by exploiting the natural resources of the region and exporting products to CA. High-level engagement is reflected in increased trade between India and CA countries. Chabahar and Bandar Abbas are part of one project in reality. Chabahar will be completed, they (Kazakhstan) will construct a railway from Chabahar to the Iranian railway network; it will later go to Turkmenistan and Kazakhstan." A direct access to CA will help India to establish itself as one of the major players in the New Great Game and also undermine China's much-hyped BRI flagship projects.

24

GENERAL KNOWLEDGE

- Major Books of 2021
- Books, Authors and Their Nationalities
- Words and Phrases Invented by Shakespeare
- Latin Words and Abbreviations
- Famous Founders
- Deities of Classical Mythology
- 100 Documents that Changed the Course of History
- Awards and Honours
- Multilingualism: Boon or Bane

Major Books of 2021

Albert Camus once said that 'fiction is the lie through which we tell the truth', and with these words he perfectly encapsulated the immense power of the novel. The year 2021 brought us some incredible titles. 2021 saw Simone de Beauvoir's never-before-published novel *Inseparable*, released 35 years after her death. The year also saw the release of the great American writer Richard Wright's previously unpublished novel *The Man Who Lived Underground*. Jhumpa Lahiri, Chitra Banerjee Divakaruni, Salman Rushdie, Amitav Ghosh, Joan Didion and Bill Gates had standout books published during the year.

Our major books of the year feature authors both emerging and established, meditating on everything from life online to life in the intersections of identity. Given below are some of the best fiction and non-fiction books of 2021.

Fiction

A Town Called Solace

by Mary Lawson

Set in the frozen north of Canada in 1972, this is a beautiful novel about painful histories that need reckoning with and the moments in life when we can change for the better. By turns gripping and darkly funny, it uncovers the layers of grief and remorse and love that connect us, but shows that sometimes a new life is possible.

Appleseed *by* Matt Bell

In this epic speculative novel, Bell braids three narrative strands: the eighteenth-century rise of a proto-Johnny Appleseed, a portrait of civilization on the brink of ecological collapse fifty years from now, and the tale of the next millennium's inhospitable Earth, plunged into a new Ice Age. Together, these narrative threads coalesce into a gripping meditation on manifest destiny and humanity's relationship to this endangered planet, making for a breathtaking novel of ideas unlike anything you've ever read.

Asoca: A Sutra *by* Irwin Allan Sealy

Asoca-often spelled Ashoka-was hailed as Ashoka the Great, the emperor who ruled most of the Indian Subcontinent and was pivotal in the spread of Buddhism from India to other parts of Asia in the third century BC. In this novel, Sealy returns to familiar territory with an imagined

memoir of Ashoka the Great, tracing the life and times of one of history's most enigmatic characters.

China Room *by* Sunjeev Sahota
A multi-generational novel of love, oppression, trauma and the pursuit of freedom, inspired in part by the author's own family history, *China Room* twines together the stories of a woman and a man separated by more than half a century but united by blood.

Chronicles from the Land of the Happiest People on Earth *by* Wole Soyinka
The first Black winner of the Nobel Prize in Literature, Wole Soyinka's first novel in 48 years is both a whodunit and a satirical critique of individual and political greed. Written during lockdown and set in contemporary Nigeria, this book is a savagely satiric, gleefully irreverent, rollicking fictional meditation on how power and greed can corrupt the soul of a nation.

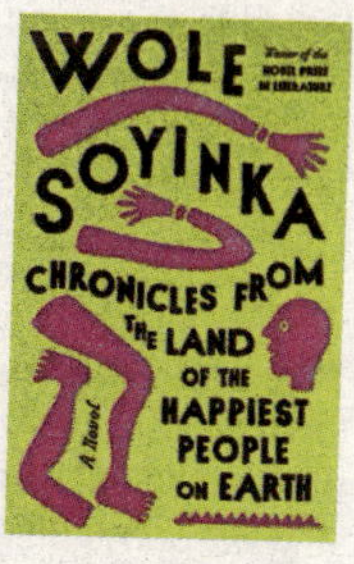

Club You to Death *by* Anuja Chauhan
Anuja Chauhan's latest novel is a murder mystery, where the death of a handsome personal trainer in a posh Delhi club sets off a chain of events that only the most intrepid of investigators can unravel.

The Committed *by* Viet Thanh Nguyen
In this blistering sequel to 2015's Pulitzer Prize-winning *The Sympathizer*, Nguyen's nameless North Vietnamese spy, last seen speeding across the sea to an uncertain future, washes up as a refugee in Paris, where he embeds himself in the French criminal underworld of the 1980s.

Detransition, Baby *by* Torrey Peters
In this electrifying debut novel, three lives coalesce around an unexpected pregnancy, forcing a bittersweet examination of identity, parenthood, and family. When Ames learns that his boss-turned-lover is pregnant, he confesses that he once identified as a trans woman, then hatches a plan for his lover to co-parent with his ex-girlfriend, a lonesome "trans elder" yearning to become a mother. In this compassionate, gut-punching story, Peters leans all the way into the tragicomedy of how families and identities are formed, making for a deeply searching novel that resists easy answers.

Gold Diggers *by* Sanjena Sathian
This debut novel is part examination of the immigrant experience, part exploration of the dark underbelly of suburbia,

all with a dash of magical realism thrown in. Two second-generation Indian Americans discover the secret to success is drinking a lemonade made from literal gold, and their lives are forever fused together and altered.

Great Circle *by* **Maggie Shipstead**
Longlisted for the 2021 Booker Prize, this *New York Times* bestseller weaves together the stories of two women living decades and continents apart: Marian Graves, an intrepid pilot whose plane goes missing while she attempts to circle the globe, and Hadley Baxter, a scandal-racked Hollywood actress recently sacked from a Twilight-alike movie franchise, who is drawn to Graves's story.

Harlem Shuffle *by* **Colson Whitehead**
Whitehead's latest showcases yet more of his range as a storyteller, following a furniture salesman leading a double life of crime. It's part heist novel, part family drama, all set against the rich backdrop of 1960s Harlem.

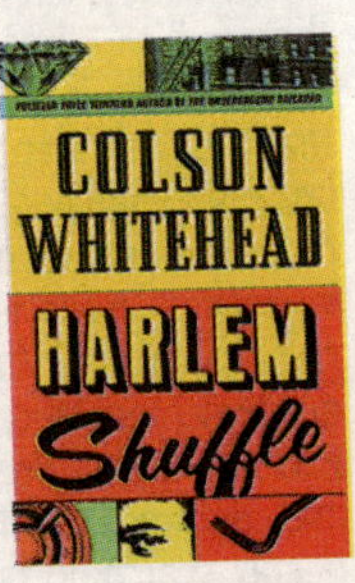

Jungle Nama *by* **Amitav Ghosh**
Jungle Nama is Amitav Ghosh's verse adaptation of an episode from the legend of Bon Bibi, a tale popular in the villages of the Sundarban, which also lies at the heart of the novel *The Hungry Tide*. It is the story of the avaricious rich merchant Dhona, the poor lad Dukhey, and his mother; it is also the story of Dokkhin Rai, a mighty spirit who appears to humans as a tiger, of Bon Bibi, the benign goddess of the forest, and her warrior brother Shah Jongoli.

Inseparable *by* **Simone de Beauvoir**
Thirty-five years after the iconic French philosopher's death, her unpublished novel was finally released to the world. it's a vibrant exploration of female will and friendship in a world that is still, too often, intent on constraining both.

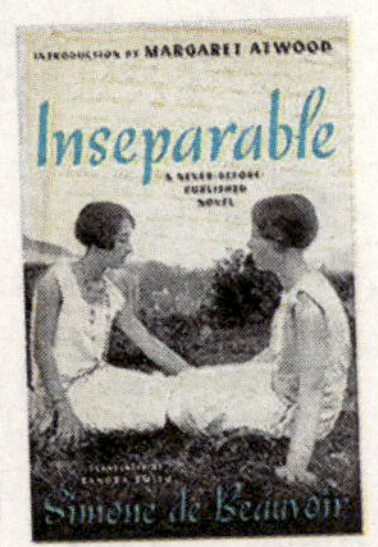

Klara and the Sun *by* **Kazuo Ishiguro**
The acclaimed *Klara and the Sun* is Ishiguro's eighth novel – and his first since being awarded the Nobel Prize for Literature in 2017. The narrator is Klara, an "Artificial Friend" who observes the world around her with an android mix of intelligence and naivety. When she is chosen by a family to live with them, she must adjust her thinking – and the novel's underlying theme of what it means to love is explored.

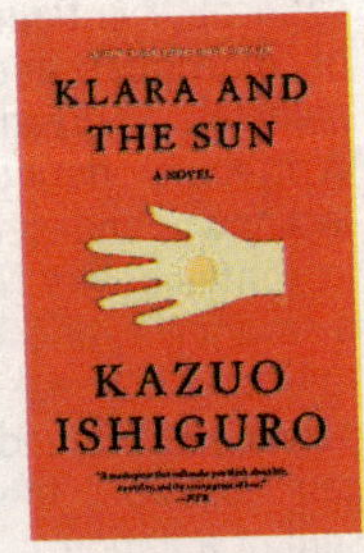

Land of Big Numbers *by* **Te-Ping Chen**

In 10 short stories set in contemporary China, Te-Ping Chen evokes the lives of various characters, from an anti-government blogger and her twin brother, a competitive gamer, to a call-centre worker and a young woman thwarted in her real ambition and working as a florist. The stories mix sharp social observation with magical realism.

The Last Queen *by* Chitra Banerjee Divakaruni

Chitra Banerjee Divakaruni's novel *The Last Queen* brings to life the youngest queen of the greatest Sikh ruler, Maharaja Ranjit Singh. Daughter of a kennel keeper, Jindan Kaur became a member of the royalty, gave birth to the King's heir, found love again after she was widowed at 21, and valiantly fought the British.

Leave the World Behind *by* Rumaan Alam

In his third novel, US writer Rumaan Alam conjures up an apocalyptic novel with a twist, subverting genre expectations by never revealing the true nature of the disaster that unfolds. We follow a middle-class white family from their Brooklyn home to an idyllic holiday Airbnb on Long Island, whose owners – a rich black couple in their 60s – knock at the door late at night asking to shelter from a cataclysmic event in the city. What follows is a neatly plotted and cuttingly observed drama about race and class, interrogating how people really act in a crisis.

The Man Who Lived Underground *by* Richard Wright

What if you could look at life from outside of life? What would you see? That's the provocative question posed in this previously unpublished novel from one of the twentieth century's greatest writers, wherein a Black man named Fred Daniels is apprehended by the police, brutally tortured, and forced to sign a confession for a violent crime he did not commit. To escape his captors, Daniels flees into the city's underground sewers, where he transforms into someone else entirely. Beneath an unfair world, Daniels tunnels into the basements of local establishments, leading him to startling truths about morality, injustice, and what matters most when the world's systems are stripped away.

Milk Blood Heat *by* Dantiel W. Moniz

The haunting debut short story collection from Dantiel W. Moniz finds a cast of characters navigating life's biggest challenges: heartbreak, inheritance, grief and growing up. Through these intergenerational narratives all set against the swampy backdrop of Florida, Moniz creates a portrait of women taking stock of their lives and what matters most to them.

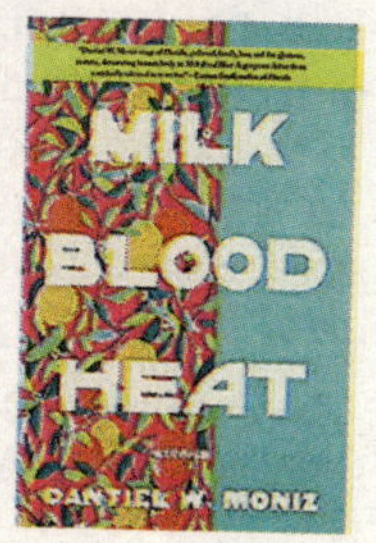

There are sisters, daughters and mothers all grappling with crises, from a 13-year-old on the cusp of becoming a teenager who is rocked by tragedy to siblings who are brought together by a trip across the country with their father's ashes. Quiet and unnerving, *Milk Blood Heat* explores the most sacred relationships, and the lingering effects of loss and loneliness.

The Other Black Girl *by* Zakiya Dalila Harris

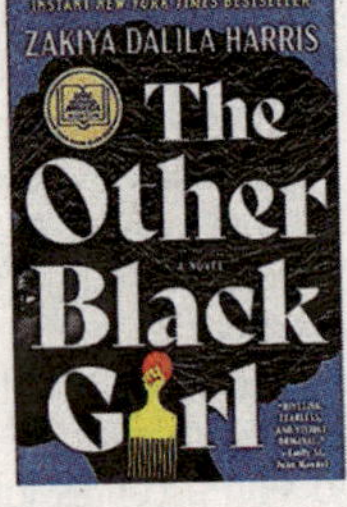

Harris's debut novel – about two young black women working in the all-white office of an upmarket US publishing house – is a fast-paced, gripping read that mixes horror and satire with sci-fi and biting social commentary.

Peaces *by* Helen Oyeyemi

In her fiction, award-winning British-Nigerian author Helen Oyeyemi playfully reinvents genres and tropes – the realms of magic and the real world frequently merge. Her latest novel *Peaces* is set on a whimsically ramshackle train, the Lucky Day, and centres around five enigmatic individuals and two pet mongooses. As the complex trajectory of the characters' interaction gradually moves towards a denouement, secrets are revealed, and a puzzle falls into place.

The Promise *by* Damon Galgut

Novelist and playwright Damon Galgut's latest centres on the decline of The Swarts – a white South-African family living on a farm outside Pretoria in the 1980s. After the death of the family's matriarch Rachel, it follows the fortunes of its three children; the "promise" of the title relates to a forsaken vow made to their black servant, Salome and the grim legacy of apartheid.

The Rules of Revelation *by* Lisa McInerney

Irish author Lisa McInerney won the Women's Prize for her novel *The Glorious Heresies*, the first in a trilogy about the criminal underworld of modern-day Cork. Her latest, *The Rules of Revelation* is the last instalment, and focuses on the habits and philosophical ruminations of drug dealer Ryan Cusack, the son of an alcoholic gangster. The result, says *The Spectator* is a novel that is "sardonic, sexy, witty, lanky with a winsome smirk, which breaks into a long-stride run for the pure pleasure of it – and it is a pleasure to observe".

Silverview *by* John le Carre

When he died in 2020, legendary British spy novelist le Carre had left behind an unpublished full-length novel. *Silverview* follows a bookseller living in a seaside town and the spy chief who arrives to investigate a potential leak.

State of Terror *by* Hillary Rodham Clinton and Louise Penny

Clinton pairs up with powerhouse mystery novelist Penny to create a heart-pounding thriller about terrorism, corruption and diplomacy, promising details only someone on the inside could contribute.

Third Eye Rising *by* Murzban F. Shroff

In these warm and wise parables of an ever-changing India, Shroff explores the tension between spiritual faith and modern life.

Whereabouts *by* Jhumpa Lahiri

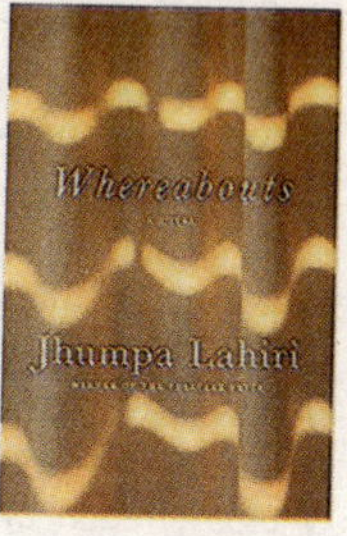

This is Lahiri's first novel written in Italian and translated to English. The story of a woman in search of change, yet not quite, this is also Lahiri's first novel since *The Lowland,* published in 2013.

Who Is Maud Dixon? *by* Alexandra Andrews

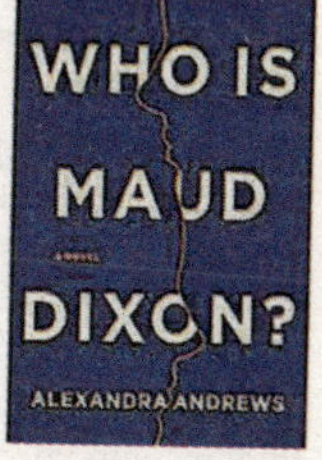

In Alexandra Andrews' propulsive debut, an ambitious editorial assistant finds herself working for the anonymous writer of a huge bestseller—and in way over her head when a research trip to Morocco turns into a deadly misadventure.

Non-Fiction

1000 Years of Joys and Sorrows *by* Ai Weiwei

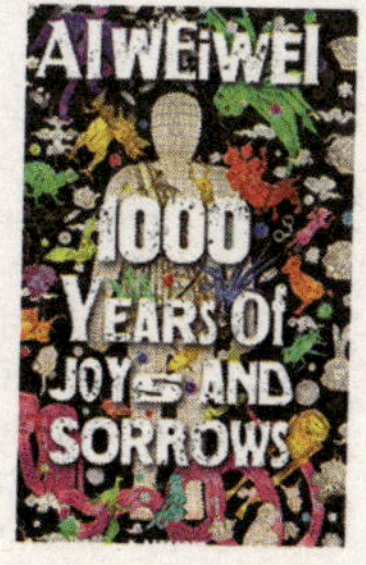

In his highly anticipated memoir, the renowned artist and political activist describes his complicated relationship with his home - from his upbringing in exile, to his decision to study art in the U.S., to his return to China as he grew into international fame.

Aftershocks *by* Nadia Owusu

Aftershocks: Dispatches from the Frontlines of Identity tells the true story of Owusu's peripatetic upbringing, as she moves across the globe – to Tanzania, England, Italy, Ethiopia and Uganda among others – with her diplomat father. The narrative sweeps forward and back in time, and the thematic structure echoes an earthquake, as each upheaval forces the ground beneath her to shudder.

A Little Devil in America: Notes in Praise of Black Performance, *by* Hanif Abdurraqib

The celebrated author of *Go Ahead in the Rain* returns with a far-reaching collection of twenty essays, each one a remarkable synthesis of criticism, autobiography, and cultural study about Black performance in America. Abdurraqib meditates on performances past and present, spotlighting everything from Soul Train to Whitney Houston, Josephine Baker to the Wu-Tang Clan. He illuminates what's personal and political about Black performance, weaving a jubilant love letter to the resilient entertainers who've graced stages both big and small.

A Swim in a Pond in the Rain *by* George Saunders

George Saunders, the acclaimed US novelist, short story writer and Booker prize-winning author of 2017's *Lincoln in the Bardo*, has been teaching creative writing at Syracuse University for the past 20 years. A condensation of Saunders' course on the 19th-Century Russian short-story in translation, *A Swim in a Pond in the Rain* takes the reader through seven stories by Tolstoy, Chekhov, Gogol and Turgenev with a line-by-line analysis that is part writing seminar, part humorous and optimistic life philosophy.

Believing *by* Anita Hill

Blending memoir with social and cultural analysis, Hill dissects gender-based violence in the U.S. and outlines three decades of history to show how it is a systemic problem in the country.

By Many A Happy Accident: Recollections of a Life *by* M. Hamid Ansari

By Many a Happy Accident is an account of a life of unplanned happenings that took M. Hamid Ansari away from his preferred fancy for academia to professional diplomacy and then be co-opted in public life and catapulted to the second highest office in the land for two consecutive terms.

The Code Breaker: Jennifer Doudna, Gene Editing, and the Future of the Human Race
by Walter Isaacson

Isaacson, famous for writing *Steve Jobs* and *Leonardo da Vinci,* writes about the 2020 Nobel Prize winner in Chemistry, biochemist Jennifer Doudna, who co-developed the gene editing technology CRISPR. CRISPR could open some of the greatest opportunities, and most troubling quandaries, of this century.

The Copenhagen Trilogy *by* Tove Ditlevsen (translated *by* Tiina Nunnally and Michael Favala Goldman)

The translated trilogy of memoirs from Danish writer Tove Ditlevsen, published as a single volume, takes a startling look inside the mind of an artist.

Dear Senthuran: A Black Spirit Memoir *by* Akwaeke Emezi

Akwaeke Emezi is the author of three novels, and their latest work, a memoir, is structured as a collection of letters addressed to friends and family – both biological and chosen – and fellow writers. The gradual unfolding of identity is at its centre, as the writer describes the experience of a non-binary life lived in parallel realities.

Eden: An Indian Retelling of Jewish, Christian and Islamic Lore *by* Devdutt Pattanaik

In his uniquely Indian style of storytelling, intimate but not irreverent, Devdutt Pattanaik introduces the readers to the many tales of angels, demons, prophets, patriarchs, judges and kings. It also retells stories from Mesopotamian, Egyptian and Zoroastrian mythologies that influenced Abrahamic monotheism in its long 5000-year-old history.

Empire of Pain *by* Patrick Radden Keefe

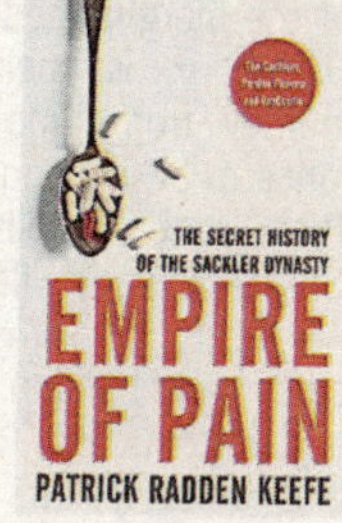

Opioid and other drug overdoses killed more than 90,000 Americans in 2020. To understand the origins of this deadly 20-plus-year epidemic, Patrick Radden Keefe, one of the top narrative nonfiction authors of his generation, offers an engrossing and deeply reported book about the Sackler family, the owners of Purdue Pharma. Their company created Oxycontin, the opioid introduced in the mid-90s that sent a wave of addiction and death across the country. Unlike previous books on the epidemic, *Empire of Pain* is focused on the wildly rich, ambitious and cutthroat family that built its empire first on medical advertising and later on painkillers.

Enter Stage Right: The Alkazi/Padamsee Family Memoir *by* Feisal Alkazi

The history of theatre, indeed of the arts, in Independent India is incomplete without a homage to the Alkazis and the Padamsees. In this memoir, Feisal Alkazi attempts a history of the first families of theatre, weaving them with anecdotes, insider accounts and some never-seen-before photographs.

Fractured Freedom: A Prison Memoir *by* Kobad Ghandy

Kobad Ghandy's prison memoir, *Fractured Freedom*, is a story of two people — Ghandy and his wife, Anuradha, who dedicated their lives in the service of the marginalised. The book is their journey from ignorance to awakening. The book details Ghandy's early life — from his time studying in London to his return to India and introduction to the Dalit Panthers and radical politics — and gives an insight into his decade-long journey of arrests and time in prisons across India.

The Good Girls *by* Sonia Faleiro

In May 2014, two teenaged Dalit girls — cousins — were found hanging from a tree in UP's Katra village. They had been sexually abused before being murdered. Faleiro, author of *Beautiful Thing: Inside the Secret World of Bombay's Dance Bars* (2010), pieces together the case and its dark aftermath in her new book.

How the Word is Passed *by* Clint Smith

In this new work of non-fiction, subtitled *A Reckoning with the History of Slavery Across America*, the poet, scholar and *Atlantic* staff writer Smith visits nine key sites linked with the legacy of slavery in the US, from Thomas Jefferson's Monticello in Charlottesville, Virginia to Angola, a Louisiana penitentiary and former plantation where inmates work the land for next-to-no payment. Blending academic research with a vast array of in-person interviews, Smith's sweeping survey is "a reckoning with reckonings" and "an extraordinary contribution to the way we understand ourselves."

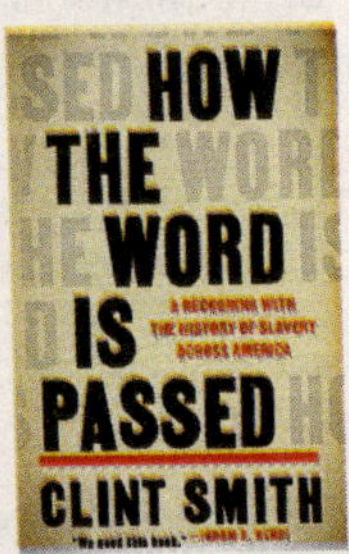

How to Avoid a Climate Disaster *by* Bill Gates

Bill Gates has spent a decade investigating the causes and effects of climate change. With the help of experts in the fields of physics, chemistry, biology, engineering, political science, and finance, he has focused on what must be done in order to stop the planet's slide to certain environmental disaster. In this book, he not only explains why we need to work toward net-zero emissions of greenhouse gases, but also details what we need to do to achieve this profoundly important goal.

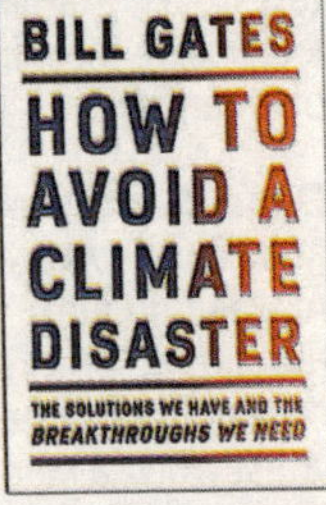

India after Liberalisation *by* Bimal Jalan

The 1991 liberalisation was India's biggest moment in its economic history after independence. As its effects began to percolate into how India lived and worked, the potential it had to lift the country and its millions out of the 'Hindu' rate of growth began to become apparent. Thirty years later, we seem to be on the cusp of a different story. In *India after Liberalisation*, Bimal Jalan offers a wide-angle view of

how liberalisation has shaped up over the intervening decades. What emerges is the story of a country best placed to catch the tide to high growth and a system that, time after time, fails to live up to the challenge of decision making.

Languages of Truth *by* Salman Rushdie

in his latest collection of nonfiction, Salman Rushdie brings together insightful and inspiring essays, criticism, and speeches that focus on his relationship with the written word and solidify his place as one of the most original thinkers of our time. Gathering pieces written between 2003 and 2020, *Languages of Truth* chronicles Rushdie's intellectual engagement with a period of momentous cultural shifts. Immersing the reader in a wide variety of subjects, he delves into the nature of storytelling as a human need, and what emerges is, in myriad ways, a love letter to literature itself. Rushdie explores what the work of authors from Shakespeare and Cervantes to Samuel Beckett, Eudora Welty, and Toni Morrison mean to him, whether on the page or in person. He delves deep into the nature of "truth," revels in the vibrant malleability of language and the creative lines that can join art and life, and looks anew at migration, multiculturalism, and censorship.

Let Me Tell You What I Mean *by* Joan Didion

Twelve pieces written between 1968 and 2000 by one of America's most revered and influential writers are brought together here for the first time. They include descriptions of trips to William Randolph Hearst's San Simeon castle and a Gamblers Anonymous meeting in Las Vegas, along with essays on Ernest Hemingway, Nancy Reagan and the photographer Robert Mapplethorpe. The volume also includes Didion's iconic 1975 Berkeley lecture 'Why I write', in which she explained: "I write entirely to find out what I'm thinking, what I'm looking at, what I see and what it means".

The Light of Asia: The Poem that Defined The Buddha *by* Jairam Ramesh

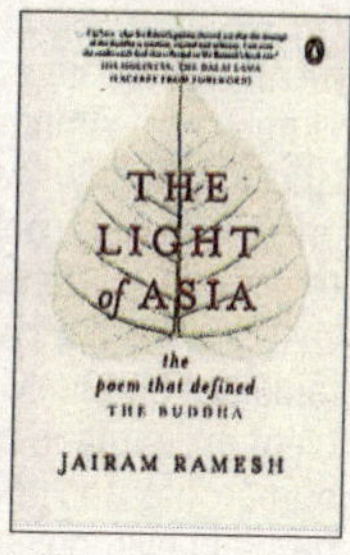

The Light of Asia is an epic poem by Sir Edwin Arnold that was first published in 1879. It is a narrative of the life and message of the Buddha. Weaving together literary, cultural, political and social history, Jairam Ramesh uncovers and narrates the fascinating story of this deeply consequential and compelling poem that has shaped our thinking of an ancient sage and his teachings. Jairam Ramesh brings into this unusual narrative the life of the multi-faceted poet himself who, among other things, was steeped in Sanskrit literature.

Love Is an Ex-Country *by* Randa Jarrar

Through the lens of a transformative cross-country road trip from California to Connecticut, Jarrar recounts her lifelong hunger for liberation from the forces of domestic violence, doxxing, and systemic racism. Along the interstate, she tangles with racist truck drivers, destroys Confederate flags in the desert, and pays a visit to the Chicago neighbourhood where her immigrant parents lived when they first touched down in the United States. This visceral, unforgettable memoir is Jarrar's barbaric yawp, asserting her triumphant choice to live joyfully in a hostile world.

The Nutmeg's Curse: A Parable for a Planet in Crisis *by* Amitav Ghosh

In this ambitious successor to *The Great Derangement,* acclaimed writer Amitav Ghosh finds the origins of our contemporary climate crisis in Western colonialism and its violent exploitation of human life and the natural environment. In the book, Ghosh follows the nutmeg's journey across the world to reflect on the trajectory of exploitation of both human resources and nature, made possible by the existing geopolitical hierarchy.

On Freedom *by* Maggie Nelson

Looking at freedom through the realms of art, sex, drugs and climate, the author of *The Argonauts* explores the contradictions, complexities and rhetoric that surround the term.

On Juneteenth *by* Annette Gordon-Reed

On June 19, 1865, in Galveston, Texas, Maj. Gen. Gordon Granger read out a declaration telling the enslaved people in Texas that they were finally emancipated, two long months after Appomattox. Juneteenth was a day long-celebrated by many Black communities in Texas and across America, but only in the past year or two has it become a more widely recognized holiday. In her slim but potent book, Pulitzer Prize- and National Book Award-winning historian and Harvard professor Annette Gordon-Reed explores the story of that day and all the ways that Black and Native people's lives have been obscured in culture.

Poet Warrior *by* Joy Harjo

The U.S. poet laureate delivers a soulful and celebratory memoir that, in lyrical terms, tells the story of her relationship to poetry and music.

Real Estate *by* Deborah Levy

The third and final instalment of her genre-bending "living autobiography" trilogy, Levy follows *Things I Don't Want to Know* and *The Cost of Living* with another impressive and immersive blend of memoir,

cultural analysis and feminist critique. In *Real Estate*, we find the writer approaching 60, travelling the world, reflecting on her past, the writers who have influenced her, and women's status in a patriarchal society.

Rememberings *by* Sinéad O'Connor

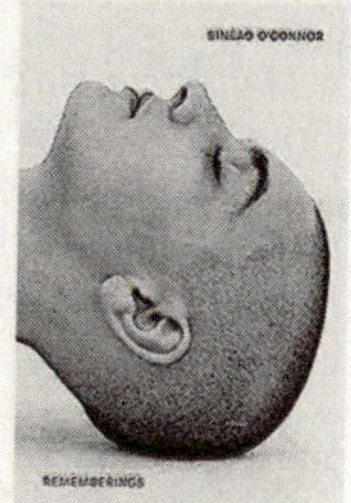

"A tremendous catalogue of female misbehaviour," is how *The Guardian* describes Irish musical artist Sinéad O'Connor's memoir *Rememberings*. In an episodic style, O'Connor candidly recounts her brutal childhood, rise to fame, and her experience of motherhood and mental health struggles.

Spy Stories : Inside the Secret World of the R.A.W. and the I.S.I. *by* Cathy Scott-Clark Adrian Levy

With unprecedented access to the R.A.W. and the I.S.I., the world's most inscrutable spy agencies, Adrian Levy and Cathy Scott-Clark describe the workings of bitter rivals, mapping their complicated history from the 1960s to the present day.

"Think Again: The Power of Knowing What You Don't Know" *by* Adam Grant

Adam Grant is an organisational psychologist who studies how people find motivation and meaning. In this book, Grant encourages people to not only learn from being wrong, but explore how it makes us feel. He examines why we're uncomfortable "thinking again," how we can develop greater introspection, and how we can teach others to think again in a way that is often more productive than getting everything right the first time.

This Life at Play: A Memoir *by* Girish Karnad; *Translated from the Kannada by Srinath Perur and Girish Karnad*

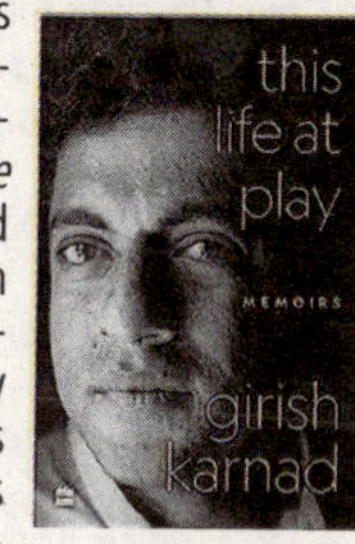

Girish Karnad was one of modern India's greatest cultural figures. *This Life at Play*, translated from the Kannada in part by Karnad himself and in part by Srinath Perur, covers the first half of his remarkable life - from his childhood in Sirsi and his early engagement with local theatre, his education in Dharwad, Bombay and Oxford, to his career in publishing, his successes and travails in the film industry, and his personal and writerly life.

Unfinished: A Memoir *by* Priyanka Chopra Jonas

A remarkable life story rooted in two different worlds, *Unfinished* offers insights into Priyanka Chopra Jonas's childhood in India; her formative teenage years in the United States; and her return to India, where against all odds as a newcomer to the pageant world, she won the national and international beauty competitions that launched her global acting career.

Books, Authors and Their Nationalities

A Bend in the River: V.S. Naipaul (Ind-Br)
A Brief History of Time: Stephen Hawking (Br)
A Bright Shining Lie: Neil Sheehan (US)
A Case of Exploding Mangoes: Mohammed Hanif (Pak)
A China Passage: John Kenneth Galbraith (US)
Accidental Death of an Anarchist: Dario Fo (It)
A Clockwork Orange: Anthony Burgess (Br)
A Corner of a Foreign Field: Ramachandra Guha (Ind)
A Critique of Pure Reason: Immanuel Kant (Ger)
A Doll's House: Ibsen (Nor)
A Farewell to Arms: Ernest Hemingway (US)
A Fine Balance: Rohinton Mistry (Ind-Can)
Against Interpretation: Susan Sontag (US)
A Grief Observed : CS Lewis (Br)
A Hero Ain't Nothin' But a Sandwich: Alice Childress(US)

A Handful of Dust: Evelyn Waugh (Br)
A Hearbraking Work of Staggering: Genius-Dave Eggers (US)
A House for Mr. Biswas: V.S.Naipaul (Ind-Br)
A Mathematician's Apology: G.H. Hardy (Br)
Ambiguity Machines and Other Stories: Vandana Singh (Ind)
A Million Mutinies Now: V.S. Naipaul (Ind-Br)
A Midsummer Night's Dream: William Shakespeare (Br)
A Modest Proposal: Jonathan Swift (Ir)
Ammi: *Letter to a Democratic Mother*: Saeed Mirza (Ind)
Amongst Women: John McGahern (Ir)
A Passage to England: Nirad C. Chaudhuri (Ind-Br)
A Passage to India: E.M. Forster (Br)
Areopagitica: John Milton (Br)
Ariel: Sylvia Plath (US)
A Room of One's Own: Virginia Woolf (Br)
A Sense of Time: H.S. Vatsyayan (Ind)
A Short History of Nearly Everything: Bill Bryson (US)
A Strange and Sublime Address: Amit Chaudhary (Ind)
A Streetcar Named Desire: Tennesse Williams (US)
A Study of History: Arnold J. Toynbee (Br)
A Suitable Boy: Vikram Seth (Ind-US)
A Suitable Girl: Vikram Seth (Ind-US)
A Tale of Two Cities: Charles Dickens (Br)
A Theory of Justice: John Rawls (US)
A Thousand Splendid Suns: Khaled Hosseini (Afg-US)
A Thousand Days: Arthur M. Schlesinger (US)

extra

The Oldest Novel in the World

Chariton's *Chaireas & Callirhoe*, subtitled *Love Story in Syracuse*, was written in the first century AD and it is considered to be the oldest novel in the world, according to the *Guinness Book of World Records*.

A Thousand Suns: Dominique Lapierre (Fr)
A Town like Alice: Nevil Shute (Br)
A Treatise of Human Nature: David Hume (Scot)
A Tree Grows in Brooklyn: Betty Smith (US)

A Vindication of the Rights of Woman: Mary Wollstonecraft (Br)
A Village by the Sea: Anita Desai (Ind-US)
A Voice for Freedom: Nayantara Sehgal (Ind)
A Week with Gandhi: Louis Fischer (Fr)
A Woman's Life: Guy de Maupassant (Fr)
A Wrinkle in Time: Madeleine L'Engle (US)
About a Boy: Nick Hornby (Br)
Absolute Friends: John le Carre (Br)
Absolute Power: David Baldacci (US)
Adam Bede: George Eliot (Br)
Adonis: P.B. Shelley (Br)
Adventures of Tom Sawyer: Mark Twain (US)
Afternoon Raag: Amit Chaudhari (Ind)
Agni Veena: Kazi Nazrul Islam (Ind)
Akbarnama: Abdul Fazal (Ind)
Alice in Wonderland: Lewis Carroll (Br)
All Quiet on the Western Front: Erick Maria Remarque (Ger-Swi-US)
All Things Bright and Beautiful: James Herriot (Br)
All's Well that Ends Well: William Shakespeare (Br)
Amar Kosh: Amar Singh (Ind)
American Pastoral: Philip Roth (US)
An American Dilemma: Gunnar Myrdal (Swe)
An American Tragedy: Theodore Dreiser (US)
An Area of Darkness: V.S. Naipaul (Ind-Br)
An Artist of the Floating World: Kazuo Ishiguro (Br)
An Autobiography: Jawaharlal Nehru (Ind)
An Equal Music: Vikram Seth (Ind-US)
An Idealist View of Life: Dr. S. Radhakrishnan (Ind)
An Uncertain Glory: India and its Contradictions: Amartya Sen & Jean Dreze
Anandmath: Bankim Chandra Chatterjee (Ind)
And Quiet Flows the Don: Mikhail Sholokhov (Rus)
And The Mountains Echoed: Khaleid Hosseini (Afg-US)
Angels & Demons : Dan Brown (US)
Angels in America: Tony Kushner (US)
Animal Farm: George Orwell (Br)
Animal's People: Indra Sinha (Ind)
Anna Karenina: LeoTolstoy (Rus)
Anne of Green Gables: L.M. Montgomery (Can)

Antony and Cleopatra: William Shakespeare (Br)
Ape and Essence: Aldous Huxley (Br)
Are you There, God? It's me, Margaret: Judy Blume (US)
Around the World in Eighty Days: Jules Verne (Fr)
Arrowsmith: Sinclair Lewis (US)
As I Lay Dying: William Faulkner (US)
As You Like It: W. Shakespeare (Br)
Asian Drama: Gunnar Myrdal (Swe)
Atonement: Ian Mcewan (Br)
A True Story of a Man, his People and an Empire: Mohandas Rajmohan Gandhi (Ind)
August 1914: Alexander Solzhenitsyn (Rus)
Aunt Julia and the Scriptwriter : Mario Vargas Llosa (Peru)
Austerlitz: WG Sebald (Ger)
Autobiography: William Butler Yeats (Ir)
Autobiography of an Unknown Indian:

Nirad C. Chaudhuri (Ind-Br)
Babbit: Sinclair Lewis (US)
Back to Methuselah: George Bernard Shaw (Br)
Bad Science: Ben Goldacre (Br)
Bandicoot Run: Manohar Malgonkar (Ind)
Beloved: Toni Morrison (US)
Ben Hur: Lewis Wallace (US)
Berlin Alexanderplatz: Alfred Doblin (Ger)
Beyond the Horizon: Eugene O'Neill (US)
Bharat Bharati: Maithili Saran Gupta (Ind)
Biographia Literaria: Samuel Taylor Coleridge (Br)
Birthday Letters: Ted Hughes (Br)
Black Boy: Richard Wright (US)
Bleeding Edge: Thomas Pynchon (US)
Blindness: Jose Saramago (Por)
Bliss was it in that Dawn: Minoo Masani (Ind)
Blink: Malcolm Gladwell (Br-Can)
Blood, brain and beer: David Ogilvy (Br)
Brave New World: Aldous Huxley (Br)
Bread, Beauty and Revolution: Khwaja Ahmad Abbas (Ind)
Breakfast at Tiffany's : Truman Capote (US)
Breakfast of Champions: A Novel: Kurt Vonnegut (US)
Breakthrough: Gen. Moshe Dayan (Isr)
Breathing Lessons: Anne Tyler (US)
Brick Lane: Monica Ali (Ban-Br)
Bridget Jones Diary: Helen Fielding (Br)
Brief Lives: John Aubrey (Br)
Bring on the Apocalypse: Six Arguments for Global Justice: George Monbiot (Br)
Bubble, The: Mulk Raj Anand (Ind)
Business Adventures: Twelve Classic *Tales from the World of Wall Street*: John Brooks (US)
Buddha: Deepak Chopra (Ind-US)
Business @ the Speed of Thou-ght: Bill Gates (US)
By God's Decree: Kapil Dev (Ind)
Byzantium: W.B. Yeats (Ir)
Cadillac Desert: Marc Reisner (US)
Caesar and Cleopatra: George Bernard Shaw (Ir)
Candida: George Bernard Shaw (Ir)
Candide: Voltaire (Fr)
Capital in the Twenty-first Century: Thomas Piketty (Fr)
Captain Corelli's Mandolin: Louis de Bernieres (Br)
Cash: The Autobiography: Johnny Cash
Catch-22: Joseph Heller (US)
Centennial: James A. Michener (US)
Charlotte's Web: E B White (US)
Checkmate: Malorie Blackman (UK)
Chemmeen: Thakazhi Sivasankara Pillai (Ind)
Cherry Orchard: Anton Chekov (Rus)
Chidambara: Sumitranandan Pant (Ind)
Childe Harold's Pilgrimage: Lord Byron (Br)
Children of Gebelawi: Naguib Mahfouz (Egy)

Chithirappaavai: P.V. Akilandam (Ind)
Chitra: Rabindra Nath Tagore (Ind)
Choma's Drum: K. Shivaram Karanth (Ind)
Chronicles: Bob Dylan (US)
Chronicle of a Death Foretold: Gabriel Garcia Marquez (Col)
Chronicles of Wasted Time: Malcolm Muggeridge (Br)
Circle of Reason: Amitav Ghosh (Ind)
Circles of Silence: Preeti Singh (Ind)
City of Joy: Dominique Lapierre (Fr)
City of Djinns: William Dalrymple (Scot)
Clarissai: Samuel Richardson (Br)
Clear Light of Day: Anita Desai (Ind-US)
Climbing the Mango Trees: Madhur Jaf-

frey (Ind)
Comedy of Errors: William Shakespeare (Br)
Coming of Age in Samoa: Margaret Mead (US)
Common Sense: Thomas Paine (Br-US)
Communist Manifesto: Karl Marx (Ger)
Confessions: J.J. Rousseau (Swi-Fr)
Confessions of a Lover: Mulk Raj Anand (Ind)
Confessions of an English Opium Eater: Thomas De Quincey (Br)
Confessions of Zeno: Italo Stevo (Ita)
Confidential Clerk: T.S. Eliot (US-Br)
Conquest of Self: Mahatma Gandhi (Ind)
Coolie: Mulk Raj Anand (Ind)
Count of Monte Cristo: Alexander Dumas (Fr)
Country Driving: Peter Hessler (US)
Coverly Papers: Joseph Addison (Br)
Creation: Gore Vidal (US)
Crescent Moon: Rabindra Nath Tagore (Ind)
Crime and Punishment: Feodor Dostoyevsky (Rus)
Crisis into Chaos: E.M.S. Namboodiripad (Ind)
Crusader or Conspirator: Coalgate and other Truths: P.C. Parikh (Ind)
Cry, the Beloved Country: Alan Paton (SA)
Culture and Anarchy : Matthew Arnold (Br)
Curfewed Night: Basharat Peer (Ind)
Cyrano de Bergerac: Edmond Rostand (Fr)
Dark Horse : Tami Hoag (US)
Darkness at Noon: Arthur Koestler (Hun-Br)
Darkness Visible: William Styron (US)
Das Kapital: Karl Marx (Ger)
Daughter of the East: Benazir Bhutto (Pak)
David Copperfield: Charles Dickens (Bri)
Days of Grace: Arthur Ashe (US) & Arnold Rampersad (Tri-US)
Dead Souls: Nikolai Gogol (Rus)
Death in Venice: Thomas Mann (Ger)

Death of a City: Amrita Pritam (Ind)
Death of a Salesman: Arthur Miller (US)
The Debacle: Emile Zola (Fr)
Decline and Fall of the Roman Empire: Edward Gibbon (Bri)
Democrats and Dissenters: Ramachandra Guha (Ind)
De Profundis : Oscar Wilde (Ir)
Descent of Man: Charles Darwin (Br)
Deserted Village: Oliver Goldsmith (Ir-Br)
Devdas: Sharat Chandra Chatterjee (Ind)
Diamond Dust: Anita Desai (Ind-US)
Diary of a Madman and other Stories: Lu Xun (Ch)
Diplomacy: Henry Kissinger (US)
Discovery of India: Jawaharlal Nehru (Ind)
Dispatches: Michael Herr (US)
Distant Drums: Manohar Malgonkar (Ind)
Divine Comedy: Dante Alighieri (It)
Divine Life: Swami Sivananda (Ind)
Doctor Sleep: Stephen King (US)
Doctor Zhivago: Boris Pasternak (Rus)
Doctor's Dilemma: George Bernard Shaw (Ir)
Don Juan: Lord Byron (Br)
Don Quixote: Miguel de Cervantes (Spa)
Down Under: Bill Bryson (US)
Dreams from My Father: A Story of Race and Inheritance: Barack Obama (US)
Dr. Jekyll and Mr. Hyde: Robert Louis Stevenson (Scot)
Dune: Frank Herbert (US)
Durgesh Nandini: Bankim Chandra Chatterjee (Ind)
Dust to Dust: Tami Hoag (US)

Earth: Emile Zola (Fr)
Eats, Shoots & Leaves: Lynne Truss (Br)
Elegy written in a Country Churchyard: Thomas Gray (Br)
Em and the Big Hoom : Jerry Pinto (Ind)
Eminent Victorians: Lytton Strachey (Br)
Emma: Jane Austen (Br)
Enchantress of Florence: Salman Rushdie (Ind-Br)
Ends and Means: Aldous Huxley (Br)
Enemies of Promise: Cyril Connolly (Br)
English August: Upamanyu Chatterjee (Ind)
Essays of Elia: Charles Lamb (Br)
Essays on Gita: Sri Aurobindo Ghosh (Ind)
Eternal Himalayas: Major H.P.S. Ahluwalia (Ind)
Ethics for the New Millennium: the Dalai Lama (Tib)
Everybody Loves a Good Drought: P. Sainath (Ind)
Family Matters: Rohinton Mistry (Ind-Can)
Family Reunion: T.S. Eliot (US- Br)
Far from the Madding Crowd: Thomas Hardy (Br)
Farewell the Trumpets: Jan Morris (Br)
Fast Food Nation: Eric Schlosser (US)
Fathers and Sons: Ivan Turgenev (Rus)
Fault Lines: Raghuram G Rajan (Ind-US)
Faust: J.W. Von Goethe (Ger)
Fifty Shades of Grey: E L James (Br)
Fingersmith: Sarah Wateres (Br)
First Circle: Alexander Solzhenitsyn (Rus)
First Sight : Danielle Steel (US)
Forever: Judy Blume (US)
For Whom the Bell Tolls: Ernest Hemingway (US)
Forsyth Saga: John Galsworthy (Br)
Fortynine Days: Amrita Pritam (Ind)
Frankenstein: Mary Shelley (Br)
Freedom at Midnight: Larry Collins (US) & Dominque Lapierre (Fr)
Freedom in Exile: Dalai Lama (Tib)
French Revolution: Thomas Carlyle (Scot)
Friends and Foes: Sheikh Mujibur Rahman (Ban)
Friends Not Masters: Ayub Khan (Pak)
From Here to Eternity: James Jones (US)
Ganadevata: Tara Shankar Bandopadhyaya (Ind)
Gandhi and Stalin: Louis Fisher (Fr)
Gardener: Rabindra Nath Tagore (Ind)
Gargantua and Pantagruel: Francois Rabelais (Fr)

The Gathering Storm: Winston Churchill (Br)
Gentleman Prefer Blondes: Anita Loos (US)
Ghasiram Kotwal: Vijay Tendulkar (Ind)
Gifted: Nikita Lalwani (Ind-Br)
Gitanjali: Rabindra Nath Tagore (Ind)
Glimpses of World History: Jawaharlal Nehru (Ind)
Godan: Prem Chand (Ind)
Godel, Escher, Bach: Douglas Hofstadter (US)
Golden Girl: P.T. Usha (Ind)
Golden Threshold: Sarojini Naidu (Ind)
Gone With The Wind: Margaret Mitchell (US)

extra

J. R. R. Tolkien as a Scholar of Languges

Lord of the Rings author J. R. R. Tolkien worked as both a scholar of languages and on the *Oxford English Dictionary* before writing his best-selling novels. He researched and explained the etymology of words starting with 'W'.

Good Earth: Pearl S. Buck (US)

Good Times, Bad Times: Harold Evans (Br)

Goodbye, Mr. Chips: James Hilton (Br)

Goodbye to All That : Robert Graves (Br)

Goodbye to Gandhi? - Travels in the New India: Bernard Imhasly (Swi)

Goodnight Mister Tom : Michelle Magorian (Br)

Go Tell It on the Mountain: James Baldwin (US)

Grammar of Politics: Harold Joseph Laski (Br)

Great Expectations: Charles Dickens (Br)

Growth of the Soil: Knut Hamsun (Nor)

Gulag Archipelago: Alexander Solzhenitsyn (Rus)

Gulliver's Travels: Jonathan Swift (Ir)

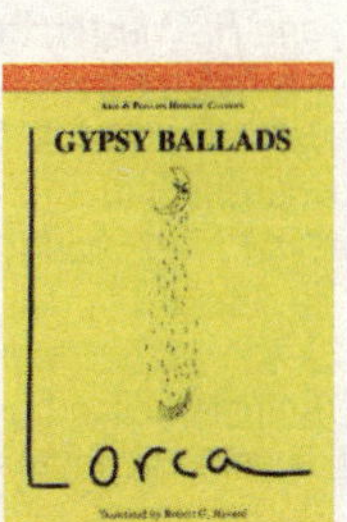

Gypsy Ballads: Federico Garcia Lorca (Spa)

Half a Life: V S Naipaul (Ind-Br)

Half of a Yellow Sun: Chimamanda Ngozi Adichie (Nig)

Hamlet: William Shakespeare (Br)

Harvest: Manjula Padmanabhan (Ind)

Harvest: Jim Crace (Br)

Harry Potter and the Goblet of Fire: J.K. Rowling (Br)

Heart of Darkness: Joseph Conrad (Pol-Br)

Heat and Dust: Ruth Prawer Jhabwala (Ger-Br)

Heir Apparent: Dr. Karan Singh (Ind)

Heritage: Anthony West (US)

Heroes and Hero Worship: Thomas Carlyle (Scot)

Herzog: Saul Bellow (US)

Himalayan Blunder: Brigadier J.P. Dalvi (Ind)

Hindu View of Life: Dr. S. Radhakrishnan (Ind)

Hinduism: Nirad C. Choudhuri (Ind-Br)

Hiroshima: John Hersey (US)

History: Elsa Morante (It)

Homage to Catalonia: George Orwell (Br)

Homegoing : Yaa Gyasi (Gha-US)

Homo Deus - A Brief History of Tomorrow: Yuval Noah Harari (Isr)

Hope against Hope: Anna Akhmatova (Ukr)

Household Education: Hariet Martineau (Br)

Housekeeping: Marilynne Robinson (US)

How to Cook A Wolf: MFK Fisher (US)

How To Know God: Deepak Chopra (Ind-US)

How to Win Friends And Influence People: Dale Carnegie (US)

Hullabaloo in a Guava Orchard: Kiran Desai (Ind)

Hunchback of Notre Dame: Victor Hugo (Fr)

Hunger: Knut Hamsun (Nor)

Hungry Stones: Rabindra Nath Tagore (Ind)

Iacocca: Lee Iacocca (US)

I am My Own Model: B.D. Jatti (Ind)

Ideas and Opinions: Albert Einstein (Ger-Swi-US)

I follow the Mahatma: K.M. Munshi (Ind)

Idols: Sunil Gavaskar (Ind)

If I am Assassinated: Z.A. Bhutto (Pak)

If Only: Geri Halliwell (Br)

If on a Winter's Night a Traveller: Italo Calvino (It)

Ignited Minds: A.P.J. Abdul Kalam (Ind)

Implosion: India's Tryst with Reality: John

Elliott (Br)
In Defence of Globalisation: Jagdish Bhagwati (Ind-US)
In Evil Hour: Gabriel Garcia Marques (Col)
In Memoriam: Alfred Lord Tennyson (Br)
In Retrospect: The Tragedy and Lessons of Vietnam: McNamara (US)
In Search of Gandhi: Richard Attenborough (Br)
Independent People: Halldor K Laxness (Ice)

India After Gandhi: The World's Largest Democracy : Ramachandra Guha (Ind)
India: A Million Mutinies Now: V S Naipaul (Ind-Br)
India Changes: Taya Zinkin (Fr)
India Discovered:John Keay (Br)
India Divided: Rajendra Prasad (Ind)
India: Emerging power: Stephen Philip Cohen (US)
India-Another Millennium: Romila Thapar (Ind)
Indian Food: A Historical Companion (Ind)
India Unbound: Gurcharan Das (Ind)
Indian War of Independence: V.D. Savarkar (Ind)
India Wins Freedom: Abul Kalam Azad (Ind)
India's Priceless Heritage: N.A. Palkhivala (Ind)
Indian Philosophy: Dr. S. Radhakrishanan (Ind)
Indica: A Deep Natural History of the Indian Subcontinent: Pranay Lal (Ind)
Indira: The Life of Indira Nehru Gandhi: Katherine Frank (US)
Inferno: Dan Brown (US)
Infidel: Ayaan Hirsi Ali (Du-US)
Inscrutable Americans: Anurag Mathur (Ind)
Inside Asia, Inside Europe, Inside Africa, etc: John Gunther (US)
In Spite of the Gods - The Strange Rise of Modern India: Edward Luce (US)
Interpreter of Maladies: Jhumpa Lahiri (Ind-US)
Intimacy: Jean Paul Sartre (Fr)
Invisible Man: H.G. Wells (Br)
Iran Awakening: Shirin Ebadi (Ira)
Is New York Burning?: Larry Collins (US) & Dominique Lapierre (Fr)
Is Paris Burning? Larry Collins (US) & Dominique Lapierre (Fr)
Isabella: John Keats (Br)
Jacques the Fatalist and His Master: Denis Diderot (Fr)
Jai Somnath: K.M. Munshi (Ind)
Jane Eyre: Charlotte Bronte (Br)
Jean Christophe: Romain Rolland (Fr)
Jejuri: Arun Kolatkar (Ind)

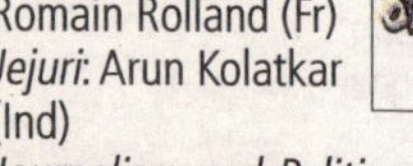

Journalism and Politics: Chalapathi Rau, M. (Ind)
Journey to the End of the Night: Louis-Ferdinand Celine (Fr)
Joy in the Morning: PG Wodehouse(Br)
Julius Caesar: William Shakespeare (Br)
Jungle Book: Rudyard Kipling (Br)
Junglee Girl: Ginu Kamani (Ind)
Jurassic Park: Michael Crichton (US)
Kamasutra: Vatsyayana (Ind)
Kane and Abel: Jeffrey Archer (Br)
Kanthapura: Raja Rao (Ind)
Kashmir: A Tragedy of Errors: Tavleen Singh (Ind)
Kayar: Thakazhi Sivasankara Pillai (Ind)
Kenilworth: Sir Walter Scott (Scot)
Kidnapped: Robert Louis Stevenson (Scot)
Kim: Rudyard Kipling (Br)
King Lear: William Shakespeare (Br)

Kubla Khan: Samuel Taylor Coleridge (Br)
Ladies Coupe: Anita Nair (Ind)
La Peste: Albert Camus (Alg-Fr.)
Lady Chatterley's Lover: D.H. Lawrence (Br)
Lajja: Taslima Nasreen (Ban)
Last Burden: Upamanyu Chatterjee (Ind)
Last Things: C.P. Snow (Br)
Le Contract (Social Contract): J.J. Rousseau (Fr.)
Lead Kindly Light: Vincent Sheean (US)
Lean In: Sheryl Sandberg (US)
Leaves of Grass: Walt Whitman (US)
Les Miserables: Victor Hugo (Fr.)
Leviathan: Thomas Hobbes (Br)
Life Divine: Sri Aurobindo (Ind)
Life After Life: Kate Atkinson (Br)
Life is Elsewhere: Milan Kundera (Cze-Fr.)
Life of Pi: Yann Martel (Can)
Life of Samuel Johnson: James Boswell (Scot)
Life on the Mississippi: Mark Twain (US)
Little Women: Louisa M Alcott (US)
Living to Tell the Tale: Gabriel Garcia Marquez (Col)
Lolita: Vladimir Nabakov (Rus-US)
London Labour and the London Poor: Henry Mayhew (Br)
Loneliness of the Long Distance Runner: Allan Sillitoe (Br)
Long Day's Journey into Night: Eugene O'Neill (US)
Long Walk to Freedom: Nelson Mandela (SA)
Look Back in Anger: John Osborne (Br)
Love Story: Erich Segal (US)
Macbeth: W. Shakespeare (Br)
Mahatma Gandhi and his Apostles: Ved Mehta (Ind-US)
Mahatma Gandhi: Romain Rolland (Fr)
Main Street: Sinclair Lewis (US)
Malgudi Days: R.K. Narayan (Ind)
Man and Superman: George Bernard Shaw (Ir)
Man of Property: John Galsworthy (Br)
Man, Beast and Virtue: Luigi Pirandello(Br-Ita)
Man-eaters of Kumaon: Jim Corbett (Br)
Mankind and Mother Earth: Arnold Toynbee (Br)
Many Worlds: K. P. S. Menon (Ind)
Mao - The Unknown Story : Jung Chang and Jon Halliday (Br)
Matterhorn: Karl Marlantes (US)
Maximum City: Bombay Lost and Found: Suketu Mehta (Ind-US)
Mayor of Casterbridge: Thomas Hardy (Br)
Meena Kumari: Vinod Mehta (Ind)
Mein Kampf: Adolf Hitler (Ger)
Memoirs: Ulysses S. Grant (US)
Memoirs of Hope: Gen. Charles de Gaulle (Fr)
Men are from Mars, Women are from Venus: John Gray (US)
Metamorphoses: Ovid (It)

Middle March: George Eliot (Bri)
Midnight in the Garden of Good and Evil: John Berendt (US)
Midnight's Children: Salman Rushdie (Ind-Br)
Mill on the Floss: George Eliot (Br)
Minorities in a Democracy: Humayun Kabir (Ind)
Mistaken Modernity: India Between Worlds: Dipankar Gupta (Ind)
Moby Dick: Hermann Melville (US)
Mohandas: A True Story of a Man, his *People and an Empire*: Rajmohan Gandhi (Ind)
Money: A Suicide Note: Martin Amis (Br)
Moonglow: Michael Chabon (US)

Moonwalk: Michael Jackson (US)
Mother India: Katherine Mayo (US)
Mother: Maxim Gorky (Rus)
Mrs. Dalloway: Virginia Woolf (Br)
Much Ado About Nothing: William Shakespeare (Br)
Murder in the Cathedral: T. S. Eliot (US-Br)
Musicophilia: *Tales of Music and the Brain*: Oliver Sacks (US)
My Country, My Life: L.K. Advani (Ind)
My Days: R. K. Narayan (Ind)
My Early Life: A Roving Commission: Winston Churchill (Br)
My India: S. Nihal Singh (Ind)
My Life: Bill Clinton (US)
My Life in France: Julia Child (US)
My Life and Times: V. V. Giri (Ind)
My Life, My Way : Cliff Richard (Br)
My Music, My Life: Pt. Ravi Shankar (Ind)
My Name is Red: Orhan Pamuk (Turk)
My Own Boswell: M. Hidayatullah (Ind)
My Presidential Years: R. Venkataraman (Ind)
My Reminiscences: R.N. Tagore (Ind)
Mystic River: Dennis Lehane (US)
My Son's Father: Dom Moraes (Ind)
My Story: Kamala Das (Ind)
My Story: Jackie Chan (Ch)
My Truth: Indira Gandhi (Ind)
Nana: Emile Zola (Fr)
Never At Home: Dom Moraes (Ind)
Never Let Me Go: Kazuo Ishiguro (Jap)
New Grub Street: George Gissing (Br)
Nice Guys Finish Second: B.K. Nehru (Ind)
Nineteen Eighty Four: George Orwell (Br)
Nisheeth: Uma Shankar Joshi (Ind)
No Country for Old Men: Cormac McCarthy (US)
No Full Stops in India: Mark Tully (Br)
No Logo: Naomi Klein (Can)
Nonsense Songs: Edward Lear (Br)
North: Seamus Heaney (Ir)
Northern Lights: Philip Pullman (Br)
Nostradamus and his Prophecies: Edgar Leoni (Fr.)
Nostromo: Joseph Conrad (Pol-Br)
Notes of A Native Son: James Baldwin (US)
O Jerusalem: Larry Collins (US) & Dominique Lapierre (Fr)
Odakkuzhal: G. Shankara Kurup (Ind)
Of Human Bondage: W. Somerset Maugham (Br)
Oliver Twist: Charles Dickens (Br)
On Chesil Beach: Ian McEwan (Br)
On Liberty: John Stuart Mill (Br)
On The Threshold of Hope: Pope John Paul II (Pol)
One Hundred Years of Solitude: Gabriel Garcia Marquez (Col)
One World and India: Arnold Toynbee (Br)
One World: Wendell Wilkie (US)
Operation Shylock: Philip Roth (US)
Orientalism: Edward Said (US)
Our Trees still Grow in Dehra: Ruskin Bond (Ind)
Oscar and Lucinda: Peter Carey (Austral)
Othello: William Shakespeare (Br)
Our Films, Their Films: Satyajit Ray (Ind)
Out of Africa: Isak Dinesen (Dan)
Out of My Life and Thought: Albert Schweitzer (Fr-Ger)
Painter of Signs: R. K. Narayan (Ind)
Pakistan Cut to Size: D. R. Mankekar (Ind)
Pakistan: The Gathering Storm: Benazir Bhutto (Pak)
Pale Blue Dot: Carl Sagan (US)
Pale Fire: Vladimir Nabokov (Rus-US)
Panchatantra: Vishnu Sharma (Ind)
Paradise: A History of the Idea that Rules the World: Kevin Rushby (Br)
Paradise Lost: John Milton (Br)
Pather Panchali: Bibhuti Bhushan (Ind)
Patriotic Gore: Edmund Wilson (US)

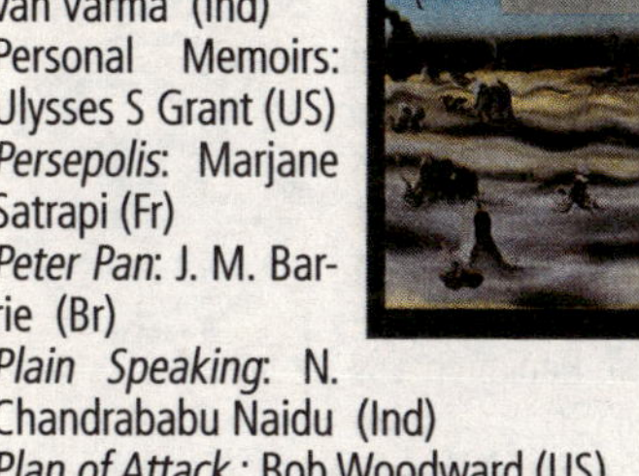

Pedro Paramo: Juan Rulfo (Mex)
People Like Us: Pavan Varma (Ind)
Personal Memoirs: Ulysses S Grant (US)
Persepolis: Marjane Satrapi (Fr)
Peter Pan: J. M. Barrie (Br)
Plain Speaking: N. Chandrababu Naidu (Ind)
Plan of Attack : Bob Woodward (US)
Pleading Guilty: Scott Turow (US)
Pond: Claire-Louise Bennett (Ir)
Portrait of India: Ved Mehta (Ind-US)
Post Office: Rabindra Nath Tagore (Ind)
Prelude: William Wordsworth (Br)
Preoccupations: Seamus Heaney (Ir)

Present at the Creation: Dean Acheson (US)
Prey: Michael Crichton (US)
Pride and Prejudice: Jane Austen (Br)
Prince: Niccolo Machiavelli (It)
Principia Mathematica: Bertrand Russell (Br)
Prison Diary: Jayaprakash Narayan (Ind)
Private Lives: Noel Coward (Br)
Profiles in Courage: John F. Kennedy (US)
Pygmalion: George Bernard Shaw (Ir)
Rabbit, Run: John Updike (US)
Rangbhoomi: Prem Chand (Ind)
Ravan & Eddie: Kiran Nagarkar (Ind)
Rebecca: Daphne du Maurier (Fr)
Rebel, The: Albert Camus (Alg-Fr)
Red Badge of Courage: Stephen Crane (US)
Red Earth and Pouring Rain: Vikram Chandra (Ind)
Red Star Over China: Edgar Snow (US)
Reflections on the French Revolution: Edmund Burke (Br)
Remembering Babylon: David Malouf (Austral)
Rendezvous with Rama: Arthur C. Clark (Br)
Revolution from Within: Gloria Steinem (US)
Riding the Storm: Harold MacMillan (Br)
Riot: A Novel: Shashi Tharoor (Ind)
Rise and Fall of the Third Reich: William L. Shirer (US)
Robinson Crusoe: Daniel Defoe (Br)
Romeo and Juliet: William Shakespeare (Br)
Room at the Top: John Braine (Br)
Rosencrantz and Guildenstern are Dead: Tom Stoppard (Br)
Rubaiyat-i Omar Khayyam: Edward Fitzgerald (Br)
Sacred Games: Vikram Chandra (Ind)
Saket: Maithili Sharan Gupta (Ind)
Sanctuary: William Faulkner (US)
Sapiens- A Brief History of Humankind: Yuval Noah Harari (Isr)
Scarlet Letter: Nathaniel Hawthorne (US)
Scoop : Evelyn Waugh (Br)
Sea of Poppies: Amitav Ghosh (Ind)

Season of Migration to the North: Tayeb Salih (Sud)
Secrets and Lies: Dilip Hiro (Ind-Br)
Seven Lamps of Architecture: John Ruskin (Br)
Seven Summers: Mulk Raj Anand (Ind)
Sexual Behaviour in the Human Male: Alfred Kinsey (US)
Shadow and Act: Ralph Ellison (US)
Shadow from Ladakh: Bhabani Bhattacharya (Ind)
Shalimar the Clown: Salman Rushdie (Ind-Br)
Shantaram: Gregory David Roberts (Ind-Br)

Shape of Things to Come: H. G. Wells (Br)
She Stoops to Conquer: Oliver Goldsmith (Ir-Br)
Siddharta: Hermann Hesse (Ger)
Silent Spring: Rachel Carson (US)
Six Characters in Search of an Author: Luigi Pirandello (It)
Six Easy Pieces: Richard P. Feynman (US)
Skinny Dip: Carl Hiaasen (US)
Slaughter House Five: Kurt Vonnegut (US)
Slow Man: J.M. Coetzee (Aus)
Small is Beautiful: A study of Economics as if People Mattered: Ernst Schumacher (Ger-Br)
Small Island: Andrea Levy (Br)
Snakes and Ladders: Essays on India: Gita Mehta (Ind-US)
Snow Country: Yasunari Kawabata (Jap)
Sofie's World: Jostein Gaarder (Nor)
Sohrab and Rustam: Matthew Arnold (Br)
So Many Cinemas: The Motion Picture in India: B.D. Garga (Ind0
Song of Solomon: Toni Morrison (US)

Sons and Lovers: D. H. Lawrence (Br)
Sophie's Choice: William Styron (US)
Soul and Structure of Governance in India: Jagmohan (Ind)
Speak, Memory: Vladimir Nabokov (Rus-US)
S.P.Q.R.: A History of Ancient Rome: Mary Beard (Br)
Steppenwolf: Hermann Hesse
Story of My Life: Moshe Dayan (Isr)
Strangers and Brothers: C. P. Snow (Br)
Strangers in the Land: John Higham (US)
Strife: John Galsworthy (Br)
Stupid White Men: Michael Moore (US)
Sun Stone: Octavio Paz (Mex)

Sunny Days: Sunil Gavaskar (Ind)
Swami and Friends: R. K. Narayan (Ind)
Sweetbitter: Stephanie Danler (US)
Sybil: Benjamin Disraeli (Br)
Talisman: Sir Walter Scott (Scot)
Tarzan of the Apes: Edgar Rice Burroughs (US)
Teacher Man: Frank McCourt
Tempest: William Shakespeare (Br)
Ten Days that Shook the World: John Reed (US)
Tender is the Night: F.Scott Fitzgerald (US)
Tenth of December: George Saunders (US)
Tenth Insight: James Redfield (U.S)
Testament of Youth: Vera Brittain (Br)
Thank You, Jeeves: P. G. Wodehouse (Br-US)
The Absolutely True Diary of a Part-Time Indian: Sherman Alexie (US)
The Adventures of Sherlock Holmes: Arthur Conan Doyle (Br)
The Affluent Society: John Kenneth Galbraith (US)
The Age of Reason: Jean Paul Sartre (Fr)
The Age of Siva: Manil Suri (Ind)
The Agenda: Bob Woodward (US)
The Agony and the Ecstasy: Irving Stone (US)
The Alchemist: Paulo Coelho (Bra)
The Algebra of Infinite Justice: Arundhati Roy (Ind)
The Ambassadors: Henry James (US-Br)

extra

Milton's *Areopagitica*

John Milton, author of *Paradise Lost*, had a huge influence on America's Founding Fathers. His political pamphlet *Areopagitica*, which argued in favour of the freedom of the press, was a key influence on the U.S. Constitution's First Amendment.

The American Language : HL Mencken (US)
The Anatomy of Melancholy: Robert Burton (Br)
The Applecart: George Bernard Shaw (Ir)
The Argumentative Indian: Amartya Sen (Ind)
The Arrangement: Elia Kazan (US)
The Art of Happiness: Dalai Lama (Tib) & Howard C. Cutler (US)
The Autobiography of Malcom X, As told to Alex Haley: Malcolm X (US)
The Banyan Tree: Hugh Tinker (Br)
The Awakening: Kate Chopin (US)
The Best and the Brightest: David Halberstam (US)
The Better Man: Anita Nair (Ind)
The Big Fisherman: Lloyd Douglas (US)
The Big Short: Michael Lewis (US)
The Black Hole: Richard Preston (US)
The Blind Assassin: Margaret Atwood (Can)
The Bonfire of the Vanities: Tom Wolfe (US)
The Book of Common Prayer: Thomas Cranmer (Br)
The Bride's Book of Beauty: Mulk Raj Anand (Ind)
The *Bridges of Madison County*: R.J. Waller (US)
The Brief Wondrous Life of Oscar Wao: Junot Diaz (Dom-US)
The Brothers Karamazov: Fyodor Dostoyevsky (Rus)
The Bully Pulpit: Doris Kearns Goodwin (US)
The Cancer Ward: Alexander Solzhenitsyn (Rus)
The Call of the Wild: Jack London (US)
The Canterbury Tales: Geoffrey Chaucer (Br)
The Cardinal: Henry Morton Robinson (US)

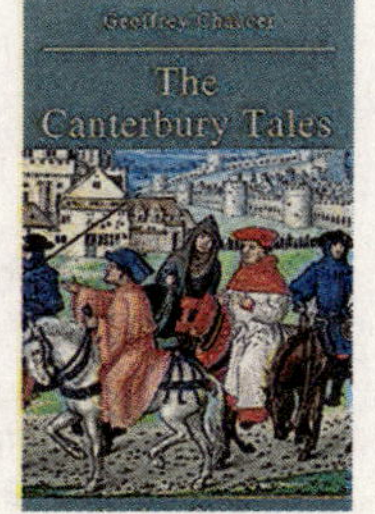

The Caretaker: Harold Pinter (Br)
The Castle: Franz Kafka (Cze)
The Cat and Shakespeare: Raja Rao (Ind)
The Catcher in the Rye: J.D. Salinger (US)
The Circle: Dave Eggers (US)
The City in History: Lewis Mumford (US)
The Civil War: Shelby Foote (US)
The Clown: Heinrich Boll (Ger)
The Common Sense Book of Baby and Child Care: Dr. Benjamin Spock (US)
The *Count of Monte Cristo*: Alexandre Dumas (Fr)
The Country without a Post Office: Agha Shahid Ali (Ind-US)
The Coup: John Updike (US)
The Court Dancer: Rabindra Nath Tagore (Ind)
The Cuckoo's Calling: J. K. Rowling (Br)
The Crucible: Arthur Miller (US)
The Curse of Cash: Kenneth Rogoff (US)
The Da Vinci Code: Dan Brown (US)
The Day of the Locust: Nathaniel West (US)
The Death of Vishnu: Manil Suri (Ind)
The Decameron: Giovanni Boccaccio (It)
The Degeneration of India: T.N. Seshan (Ind)
The Diary of a Young Girl: Anne Frank (Ger)
The Diary of Fanny Burney: Fanny Burney (Br)
The Difficulty of Being Good: Gurcharan Das (Ind)
The Double Helix: James D. Watson (US)
The Economic Consequences of the Peace: John Maynard Keynes (Br)
The Elements of Style: William Strunk (US) and EB White (US)
The End of a Beautiful Era: Joseph Brodsky (Rus-US)
The End of Food: Paul Roberts (US)
The End of History and the Last Man: Francis Fukuyama (US)
The English Roses: Madonna (It-US)
The Executioner's Song: Norman Mailer (US)

The Eye of the Storm: Patrick White (Austral)
The Far Field: Madhuri Vijay (Ind)
The Far Pavilions: M.M. Kaye (Br)
The Federalist Papers: Publius
The Female Eunuch: Germaine Greer (Austral)
The Feminine Mystique: Betty Friedan (US)
The Fifth Horseman: Larry Collins (US) and Domnique Lapierre (Fr)
The Fire Next Time: James Baldwin (US)
The First Muslim: The Story of Muhammad: Lesley Hazleton (Br-US)
The Forbidden Sea: Tara Ali Baig (Ind)
The French Lieutenant's Woman: John Fowles (Br)

The Fury: Salman Rushdie (Ind-Br)
The Future of Life: Edward O. Wilson (US)
The Gathering: Anne Enright (Ir)
The Ginger Man: J.P. Donleavy (US)
The Girl with the Dragon Tattoo: Stieg Larsson (Swe)
The Glass Palace: Amitav Ghosh (Ind)
The God Delusion: Richard Dawkins (Br)
The God of Small Things: Arundhati Roy (Ind)
The Godfather: Mario Puzo (US)
The Goldfinch: Donna Tartt (US)
The Golden Gate: Vikram Seth (Ind-US)
The Golden Notebook: Doris Lessing (Br)
The Grapes and the Wind: Pablo Neruda (Chi)
The Grapes of Wrath: John Steinbeck (US)
The Great Challenge: Louis Fischer (Fr)
The Great Gatsby: F. Scott Fitzgerald (US)
The Great Indian Novel: Shashi Tharoor (Ind)
The Great Tamasha: James Astill (Br)
The Great Tradition: F.R.Leavis (Br)
The Great Unravelling: Paul Krugman (US)
The Green Knight: Iris Murdoch (Br)
The Guide: R.K. Narayan (Ind)
The Guns of August: Barbara Tuchman (US)
The Heart of the Matter: Graham Greene (Br)
The Heart of a Woman: Maya Angelou (US)
The Heart is a Lonely Hunter: Carson McCullers (US)
The Hedgehog and the Fox: Isaiah Berlin (Rus-Br)
The History of the World: Walter Raleigh (Br)
The Hitchhiker's Guide to the Galaxy: Douglas adams (Br)
The Hornet's Nest: Jimmy Carter (US)
The Horse Whisperer: Nicholas Evans (Br)
The Hot Zone: Richard Preston (US)
The House on Mango Street: Sandra Cisneros *(US)*

The House of the Spirits: Isabel Allende (Chi)
The Humboldt Gift: Saul Bellow (US)
The Hungry Tide: Amitav Ghosh (Ind)
The Idiot: Fyodor Dostoyevsky (Rus)
The Immortal Life of Henrietta Lacks: Rebecca Skloot (US)
The Imperfectionists: Tom Rachman (Br-Can)
The Importance of Being Earnest: Oscar Wilde (Ir)
The Inheritance of Loss: Kiran Desai (Ind-US)
The Interpreters: Wole Soyinka (Nig)
The Inscrutable Americans: Anurag Mathur (Ind)
The Insider: P.V. Narasimha Rao (Ind)
The Invention of Nature - The Adventures

of Alexander Humboldt (Br)
The Invisible Man: Ralph Ellison (US)
The Ivory Throne: Manu S. Pillai (Ind)
The Joke: Milan Kundera (Cze-Fr)
The Judgement: Kuldip Nayar (Ind)
The Keeper of the Keys: Milan Kundera (Cze-Fr)
The Kite Runner: Khaled Hosseini (Afg-US)
The Prisoner of the Caucasus: Alexander Pushkin (Rus)
The Last Days of Hitler: Hugh Trevor-Roper (Br)
The Last Song of Dusk: Sidharth Sanghvi (Ind)
The Last Temptation of Christ: Kazantzakis (Gk)
The Legends of Khasak: O.V. Vijayan (Ind)
The Life of Charlotte Bronte: Elizabeth Gaskell (Br)
The Liberal Imagination: Lionel Trilling (US)
The Line of Beauty: Alan Hollinghurst (Br)
The Little Prince: Antoine de Saint-Exupery (Fr.)
The Lord of the Flies: William Golding (Br)
The Lovely Bones: Alice Sebold (US)
The Lowland: Jhumpa Lahiri (Ind-US)
The Magic Lantern: Ingmar Bergman (Swe)
The Magic Mountain: Thomas Mann (Ger)
The Making of the English Working Class: EP Thompson (Br)
The Man Without Qualities: Robert Musil (Aus)
The Mandarin: Simone de Beauvoir (Fr)
The Masters: C. P. Snow (Br)
The Medium is the Message: Marshall Mcluhan (Can)
The Men Who Killed Gandhi: Manohar Malgonkar (Ind)
The Merchant of Venice: William Shakespeare (Br)
The Middle Ground: Margaret Drabble (Br)
The Mind of the C.E.O: Jeffrey E. Garten (US)
The Miniaturist: Kunal Basu (Ind)
The Miser: Moliere (Fr)
The Moon and Sixpence: W. Somerset Maugham (Br)
The Moor's Last Sigh: Salman Rushdie (Ind-Br)
The Music Room: Namita Devidayal (Ind)
The Namesake: Jhumpa Lahiri (Ind-US)
The Name of the Rose, The Mysterious Flame of Queen Loana: Umberto Eco (It)
The Narrows: Michael Connelly (US)
The Night Manager: John le Carre (Br)
The Nude: A Study of Ideal Art: Kenneth Clark (Br)
The Oath of The Vayuputras: Amish (Ind)
The Old Man and the Sea: Ernest Hemingway (US)
The Omnivore's Dilemma: Michael Pollan (US)
The Open Society And Its Enemies : Karl Popper (Au-Br)
The Origin of Species: Charles Darwin (Br)
The Other Side of Midnight: Sidney Sheldon (US)
The Painted Veil: W. Somerset Maugham (Br)
The Palace of Illusions: Chitra Banerjee Divakaruni (Ind-US)
The Pickwick Papers: Charles Dickens (Br)
The Pilgrim's Prog-

 extra

Words Popularised by Coleridge

English Romantic poet Samuel Taylor Coleridge is credited with the first printed use of the words "selfless," "psychosomatic," "bipolar," and "bisexual." Coleridge is also responsible for the now famous phrase "suspension of disbelief."

ress: John Bunyan (Br)
The Power and the Glory: Graham Greene (Br)
The Power of Positive Thinking: Norman Vincent Peale (US)
The Pregnant King: Devdutt Pattanaik (Ind)
The Prime of Life: Simone de Beauvoir (Fr)
The Prime of Miss Jean Brodie: Muriel Spark (Scot)
The Private Life of Chairman Mao: Dr.Li Zhisui (Chi)
The Proper Study of Mankind: Isaiah Berlin (Br)
The Rain King: Saul Bellow (US)
The Rape of the Lock: Alexander Pope (Bri)
The Republic: Plato (Gk)
The Return of the Native: Thomas Hardy (Br)
The Rights of Man: Thomas Paine (Br-US)
The Right Stuff: Tom Wolfe (US)
The Road: Cormac McCarty (US)
The Road to Oxiana: Robert Byron (Br)
The Road to Wigan Pier: George Orwell (Br)
The Road Ahead: Bill Gates (US)
The Robe: Lloyd C. Douglas (US)
The Roots: Alex Haley (US)
The Satanic Verses: Salman Rushdie (Ind-Br)
The Sea: John Banville (Ir)
The Second World War: Winston Churchill (Br)
The Secret Life of Bees: Sue Monk (US)
The Selfish Gene : Richard Dawkins (Br)

The Seven Spiritual Laws of Success: Deepak Chopra (Ind-US)
The Shadow Lines: Amitav Ghosh (ind)
The Sheltering Sky: Paul Bowles (US-Mor)
The Shoes of the Fisherman: Morris L. West (Austral)
The Signature of All Things: Elizabeth Gilbert (US)
The Sixth Extinction: Elizabeth Kolbert (US)
The Song of Susannah: Stephen King (US)
The Songs of India: Sarojini Naidu (Ind)
The Souls of Black Folk: WEB Du Bois (US)
The Sound and the Fury: William Faulkner (US)
The Sound of the Mountain: Yasunari Kawabata (Jap)

The Spirit of Indian Painting: B N Goswamy (Ind)
The Spirit of the Age: William Hazlitt (Br)
The State of a Nation: Fali S. Nariman (Ind)
The Story of My Experiments with Truth: Mahatma Gandhi (Ind)
The Story of My Life: Helen Keller (US)
The Story of the Integration of the Indian States: V.P. Menon (Ind)
The *Strange and Sublime Address*: Amit Chaudhuri (Ind)
The Stranger: Albert Camus (Fr)
The Structure of Scientific Revolutions: Thomas S Kuhn (US)
The Struggle and the Triumph: Lech Walesa (Pol)
The Struggle in My Life: Nelson Mandela (SA)
The Sword and the Sickle: Mulk Raj Anand (Ind)

Aphra Behn as a Spy

Aphra Behn wasn't only a revolutionary Restoration writer; she also served as a spy under Charles II. In fact, "Aphra Behn" was her codename. Behn was actually born Eaffrey Johnson in 1640.

The Tale of Genji: Shikibu Murasaki (Jap)
The Testament: John Grisham (US)
The Third Wave: Alvin Tofler (US)
The Thirteenth Sun: Amrita Pritam (Ind)
The Three Mistakes in My Life: Chetan Bhagat (Ind)
The Time of the Hero: Mario Vargas Llosa (Peru)
The Tin Drum: Gunter Grass (Ger)
The Total Zone: Martina Navaratilova (Cze-US)
The Travels of Marco Polo: Marco Polo (It)
The Tree of Man: Patrick White (Austral)
The Trial: Franz Kafka (Cze)
The Trotter–Nama: Allan Sealy (Ind)
The Unfurnished Man: Nizzim Ezekiel (Ind)
The Universe in a Single Atom: Dalai Lama (Tib)
The Uprooted: Oscar Handlin (US)
The Uses of Literacy: Aspects of Working-Class Life: Richard Hoggart (Br)
The Varieties of Religious Experience: William James (US)
The Vegetarian: Han Kang (S. Kor)
The Vendor of Sweets: R.K. Narayan (Ind)
The Vicar of Wakefield: Oliver Goldsmith (Ir-Br)
The Victim: Saul Bellow (US)
The Volcano Lover: Susan Sontag (US)
The Wangs Vs. The World: Jade Chang (US)
The Wasteland: T.S. Eliot (US-Br)
The Way of all Flesh: Samuel Butler (Br)
The Way to Paradise: Mario Vargas Llosa (Peru)
The Wealth of Nations: Adam Smith (Scot)
The White Mughals: William Darymple (Scot)
The World is Flat: Thomas Friedman (US)
The World is What It Is: Patrick French (Br)
Thesaurus: Dr Peter Mark Roget (Br)
The Year of Magical Thinking: John Didion (US)
The Zahir: Paulo Coelho (Bra)
Their Eyes were Watching God: Zora Neale Hurston (US)
Theory of War: Joan Brady (US)
Things Fall Apart: Chinua Achebe (Nig)
Thorn Birds: Colleen McCullough (Ir- Austral)
Thousand Cranes: Yasunari Kawabata (Jap)
Thus Spake Zarathustra: Friedrich Wilhelm Nietzsche (Ger-Swi)
Time Machine: H.G. Wells (Br)
Tinker, Tailor Soldier: John Le-Carre (Br)
Tom Jones: Henry Fielding (Br)
To Kill a Mocking Bird: Harper Lee (US)
To the Lighthouse: Virginia Woolf (Br)
Train to Pakistan: Khushwant Singh (Ind)
Transmission: Hari Kunzru (Ind-Br)
Travels with a Donkey in the Cevennes: Robert Louis Stevenson (Scot)
Treasure Island: Robert Louis Stevenson (Scot)
Tropic of Cancer: Henry Miller (US)
True History of Kelly Gang: Peter Carey (Austral)
Truth, Love and a Little Malice: Khushwant Singh (Ind)
Tryst with Destiny: S. Gopalan (Ind)
Twelfth Night: W. Shakespeare (Br)
Two Leaves and a Bud: Mulk Raj Anand (Ind)
Ulysses: James Joyce (Ir)
Unaccustomed Earth: Jhumpa Lahiri (Ind-US)
Uncle Tom's Cabin: Harriet Beecher

Joseph Heller as a Writer of Screenplays

Catch-22 author Joseph Heller worked on many major screenplays in Hollywood to earn a living. A few major movies Heller worked on include *Sex and the Single Girl* and the first film adaptation of Ian Fleming's *Casino Royale.*

Stowe (US)
Under the Net: Iris Murdoch (Br)
Unless: Carol Shields (US)
Unsafe at Any Speed: Ralph Nader (US)
Unto The Last: John Ruskin (Br)
Up from Slavery: Booker T. Washington (Br)
Utopia: Thomas More (Br)
Valley of the Dolls: Jacqueline Susann (US)
Vanity Fair: William Thackeray (Br)
Vernon God Little: DBC Pierre (Austral)
Voss: Patrick White (Austral)
Waiting for Godot: Samuel Beckett (Ir)
Waiting for the Mahatma: R.K. Narayan (Ind)
Wake Up India: Annie Besant(Ir)
Walden: Henry David Thoreau (US)
War and Peace: Leo Tolstoy (Rus)
Watchmen: Alan Moore (Br)
We Love You, Charlie Freeman: Kaitlin Greenidge (US)
Westward Ho: Charles Kingsley (Br)
We Need New Names: NoViolet Bulawayo (Zim)
What is Not Yours is Not Yours: Helen Oyeyemi (Br)
What is Rememberd: Suketu Mehta (Ind-US)
What They Don't Teach You at Harvard Business School: Mark H. McCormack (US)
Where Have All the Leaders Gone?: Lee Iacocca (US)
White Noise: Don DeLillo (US)
White Teeth: Zadie Smith (Br)
Who Moved My Cheese?: Dr. Spencer Johnson (US)
Wide Sargasso Sea: Jean Rhys (Dom)
Wild Swans: Jung Chang (Chin-Br)
Wings of Fire: A.P.J. Abdul Kalam (Ind)
Winning: Jack Welch, Suzy Welch (US)
Winter Solstice: Rosamunde Pilcher (Scot)
Without Fear - The Life and Trial of Bhagat Singh: Kuldip Nayar (Ind)
Witness to an Era: Frank Moraes (Ind)
Wolf Hall: Hilary Mantel (Br)
Women in Love: D.H. Lawrence (Br)
World Within Worlds: Stephen Spender (Br)
Wuthering Heights: Emily Bronte (Br)
Yayati: V.S. Khandekar (Ind)
Yesterday and Today: K.P.S. Menon (Ind)
You Can Win: Shiv Khera (Ind)
Zen and the Art of Motorcycle Maintenance: Robert Pirsig (US)
Zorba the Greek: Nikos Kazantzakis (Gk)
Zuleika Dobson: Max Beerbohm (Br)

Nationalities: Afg: Afghan; Alg: Algerian; Austral: Australian; Aus: Austrian; Ban: Bangladeshi; Br: British; Bra: Brazilian; Can: Canadian; Ch: Chinese; Chi: Chilean; Col: Columbian; Cze: Czech; Dan: Danish; Dom: Dominican; Du: Dutch; Egy: Egyptian; Fr: French; Ger: German; Gha: Ghanaian; Gk: Greek; Hun: Hungarian; Ice: Icelander; Ind: Indian; Ir: Irish; Ira: Iranian; Isr: Israel; It: Italian; Jap: Japanese; Mex: Mexican; Mor: Moroccan; Nig: Nigerian; Nor: Norwegian; Pak: Pakistani; Peru: Peruvian; Pol: Polish; Por: Portuguese; Rus: Russian; Scot: Scottish; Spa: Spanish; SA: South African; S. Kor: South Korea; Sud: Sudanese; Swe: Swedish; Swi: Swiss; Tib: Tibetan; Tri: Trinidadian; Turk: Turkish; US: American; Zim: Zimbabwean.

Inspiration Behind Agatha Christie's Plots

When asked where she came up with the plots for her famous murder mysteries, Agatha Christie said she liked to think out her stories while eating apples and relaxing in a warm bath.

Words by William Shakespeare

The *Oxford English Dictionary* has verified that Shakespeare originated the following words or, at the very least, was the first to use them in print.

- Admirable, Aerial, Amazement, Arch-villain, Arouse, Auspicious.
- Barefaced, Bedazzle, Besmirch, Birth Place, Bloodstained, Bloodsucking
- Castigate, Clutch, Cold-blooded, Colourful, Comply, Countless, Critical
- Denote, Disgraceful, Dishearten, Distrustful, Domineering, Downstairs
- Educate, Employer, Engagement, Enmesh, Eventful, Exposure
- Fairyland, Fashionable, Fortune-teller, Foul-mouthed, Freezing, Frugal
- Generous, Go-between, Grime, Grovel
- Hostile, Hot-blooded, Hurry
- Ill-tempered, Impartial, Impede, Invitation, Invulnerable
- Lament, Lapse, Laughable, Leapfrog, Lonely, Love Letter, Lustrous
- Majestic, Manager, Marketable, Misquote, Monumental, Motionless
- Negotiate, Never-ending
- Obscene, Ode, Operate, Overrate
- Pageantry, Pander, Paternal, Perplex, Petition, Pious, Puke
- Quarrelsome
- Rant, Reclusive, Reinforcement, Reliance, Remorseless, Restoration, Retirement
- Sanctimonious, Savage, Scuffle, Shipwrecked, Shooting star, Silliness, Soft-hearted, Squabble, Stealthy, Successful, Swagger
- Tardiness, Torture, Tranquil
- Uncomfortable, Uneducated, Unhelpful, Unwillingness
- Vulnerable
- Well-behaved, Well-bred, Well-educated, Well-read
- Zany

Phrases Invented or popularised by William Shakespeare

- 'A fool's paradise' *(Romeo and Juliet)*
- 'A tower of strength ' *(Richard III)*
- 'Breath'd his last' *(Henry VI, Part 3)*
- 'Come full circle' *(King Lear)*
- 'Dead as a doornail' *(Henry VI, Part 2)*
- 'Eaten me out of house and home' *(Henry IV, Part 2)*
- Elbow-room *(King John)*
- Give the devil his due' *(Henry IV, Part I)*
- 'Hoist with his own petard' *(Hamlet)*
- 'Let slip the dogs of war' *(Julius Caesar)*
- 'Love is blind' *(The Merchant of Venice)*
- Milk of human kindness' *(Macbeth)*
- My own flesh and blood' *(The Merchant of Venice)*

- Neither a borrower nor a lender be' *(Hamlet)*
- 'Once more unto the breach' *(Henry V)*
- 'One fell swoop *(Macbeth)*
- 'Murder most foul' *(Hamlet)*
- 'Play fast and loose' *(Love's Labour's Lost)*
- 'Something in the wind' *(The Comedy of Errors)*
- 'Stood on ceremonies' *(Julius Caesar)*
- 'Strange bedfellows' *(The Tempest)*
- 'The be-all and the end-all' *(Macbeth)*
- 'The course of true love never did run smooth' (*A Midsummer Night's Dream)*
- 'The naked truth' *(Love's Labour's Lost)*
- 'The world's mine oyster' *(The Merry Wives of Windsor)*
- 'Tis neither here nor there' *(Othello)*
- 'To make a virtue of necessity' *(The Two Gentlemen of Verona)*
- 'Too much of a good thing' *(As you Like It)*
- "We are such stuff as dreams are made on' *(The Tempest)*
- 'Wear my heart upon my sleeve *(Othello)*
- 'What the dickens' *(The Merry Wives of Windsor)*
- What's in a name? *(Romeo and Juliet)*

Things That are not What they Seem

Rice paper contains not a grain of rice

French fries originated in Belgium, not France

Great Dances come from Germany, not Denmark

Ten-gallon hats hold only about six pints of water

Koala bears aren't bears, they're marsupials

Mountain goats aren't goats, they're small antelopes

Fireflies aren't flies, they're beetles

The **funny bone** isn't a bone, it's a nerve

Jackrabbits aren't rabbits, they're hares

Prairie dogs aren't dogs, they're rodents

Guinea pigs aren't pigs and nor are they from Guinea - they're South American rodents

Catgut isn't made from cats, it's made from sheep

Lead pencils contain no lead, only graphite

Glow-worms aren't worms, they're beetles

Horned toads aren't toads, they're lizards

Bombay duck isn't duck, it's dried fish

Turkish baths originated in Ancient Rome, not in Turkey

Silkworms aren't worms, they're caterpillars

Shooting stars are meteors.

The Origin of the Word 'Syphilis'

The 16th-century poet Girolamo Fracastoro is only well-known today for one word: syphilis. We get the word for this devastating sexually transmitted disease from one of Fracastoro's poems.

Sawed-Off Latin Words and Abbreviations

ad hoc "For this thing," said of something impromptu, improvised, for the matter at hand and that matter only. An ad hoc committee will probablylast out only the season (or the problem); an ad hoc solution implies that somebody is - or ought to be - working on a permanent one. Cf. *pro tem*, short for *pro tempore*, "for the time being."

ad lib. "To the desire"; in music, a sign that somebody can play a passage, or an entire piece, as loud and as fast as he wants. In show business, and without the period, a sign that somebody forgot his lines.

c Used to show that a date is approximate: "Died c. 1950.' Short for *circa*, round. Also sometime ca. Pronounced 'SIR-ka.'

cf. Meant to get you to compare something to something else: 'cf. page 30,' that is, look at it with an eye to the issue at hand. From the Latin *confer*, meaning 'consult.' If you pronounce it, say the letters, 'cee eff' page thirty.'

d.v. God willing, from *Deo volente*.

e.g. For when you're about to give (or be given) a bunch of examples: 'citrus fruits, e.g. orange, lemon, lime." Does not guarantee completeness of list (no grapefruit, for instance, above). Short for *exempli gratia*, "for the sake of example."

ergo "Therefore," "hence.". Unforgettable in Descartes' formulation *Cogito, ergo sum*, "I think, therefore I am" and unavoidable in various mathematical proofs.

et al. "And others," short for both et *alia*, "and other things," and *et alii*, "and other people." More specific than *etc.*, short for *et cetera*, and the rest," "and so forth," and can, unlike *etc.*, be used of people.

fl. From *floruit*, "he (or she) flourished. Shows up on the brass name-plates of old paintings when it's known when an artist worked but not when he was born (for the record, n., from *natus*) or died (*ob.*, from *obiit*, literally 'went to meet'). And while we're on the subject, note also: *aet.*, from *aetatis*, "at the age of," for when they know how old the artist was when he did it but not the calendar year it was done, or want to emphasize the former.

ibid "In the same book, chapter, or passage" (i.e., the one referred to in the note immediately preceding). Short for *ibidem*, "in the same place." Doesn't, unlike *op. cit.*, short for *opere citato*, "in the work cited," require an author's name, just a page number, and doesn't send you scrolling up through the 200 preceding footnotes.

i.e. For when you're about to explain (or have explained to you) the nature of something: "citrus fruits, i.e., those from trees of the family *Citrus*, with an inedible rind, juicy flesh, usually in segments, and a high vitamin C content." Short for *id est*, "that is." More authoritative, less chatty than *e.g.*

ms. The abbreviation for *manuscriptum*, manuscript, in a footnote or bibliography. Not to be confused with *Ms.*, the magazine and form of address. More than one manuscript? MSS

N.B. For *nota bene*, "note well." Calls your attention to something the writer thinks you might miss or not see the, in his opinion, enormous significance of.

op. The abbreviation for *opus*, work, used in cataloguing musical works, and designating either a single composition or a group of them that stand as a unit.

pace "With all due respect to" or "with the permission of," as in "Pace Mies, there are times when more is more." Used to express polite, or ironically polite, disagreement. Pronounced "PAY-see" (preferred by academicians) or "PAH-chay" (less correct, but more common).

passim Scattered, occurring throughout. Applied to a word, passage, or reference occurring here and there, over and over, in a specific book or author.

per se "Through itself"; intrinsically, by dint of its very nature.

Q.E.D. The capital letters printed triumphantly by a person who thinks he's convincingly proven what he set out to prove. Short for *quod erat demonstrandum*, "which was to be shown." A favourite of geometry teachers and miscellaneous pedants.

qua. "In the capacity of," "considered as, "as in "the film qua film" — the film not as a story or an evening's entertainment, but as an act of movie — making, as cinema, as art. Pronounced 'kway' or 'kwah.' From a Latin relative - pronoun form. User stands to reveal self as pretentious.

re Shorthand (and memorandumese) for 'about, 'concerning': 'Re your comment yesterday.' From *in re*, in this matter. Pronounced 'ray'.

R.I.P. Right, on all the old tombstones. But it's short for *Requiescat in pace*, "May he (or she) rest in peace."

sic A nudge, usually parenthetical, often gloating, pointing out how a third party got something wrong or gave himself away: "In his review of the new Sylvester Stallione (*sic*) movie..." From *sic*, "thus."

stet "Let it stand," "ignore all previous instructions to alter or correct," "this is, after all, how we want it." A printer's term, but one useful to anybody in a position to make — or not make— final changes. From a form of *stare*, "to stand." The opposite: *dele*, from the Latin word for 'delete.)

vide In reference to a passage in a book, means "see" or "consult." A shortened version of *quod vide*, "which see," sometimes also abbreviated as *q.v.*

viz. Used after a word or expression clearly requiring itemization. Equivalent to "namely" or "to wit": "The citrus fruits , viz., orange, lemon, lime, grapefruit, tangerine, kumquat."(No mention of tangelo, unfortunately, but you get the point.) An abbreviation of *videlicet*, "it is permitted to see." Likewise, *sc* or *scil.*, from *scilicet*, "it is permitted to know." Both *viz.* and *sc.*, unlike *e.g.*, guarantee they're giving you a complete rundown.

vs. Against, in the courtroom as the stadium. From "versus," also abbreviated v.

What Does 'Ad Hominem' Mean?

Short for *argumentum ad hominem* (literally meaning 'argument against the person'), it refers to a rhetorical strategy where the speaker attacks the other person rather than the substance of the argument itself.

Double-Barrelled Latin Phrases

bona fide (BOH-na-FIDE or BOH-na-FIE-deh): Done or made "in good faith"; sincere, genuine.

casus belli (KAH-sus-BELL-ee): "Occasion of war." An event that justifies or precipitates war.

cui bono (KWEE-BOH-noh): "For whom (is it) good?" Question first posed by a Roman magistrate to make the point that one way to approach a crime is to determine who stood to gain from it. Often wrongly used to mean "For what purpose?"

de facto (deh-FAK-toh): "From the fact." In reality; actual, actually in power. A de facto government is not formally elected or installed, but is firmly in control; cf. *de jure*, following.

de jure (deh-YOO-reh): "From the law." According to law; in principle. A de jure government is duly elected and installed, but exercises no real power; cf. *de facto*, previously.

ex post facto (EKS-post-FAK-toh): "From what is done afterward." Formulated, enacted, or operating retroactively.

in medias res (in-MAY-dee-ahs-RACE): "Into the midst of things." Into the middle of a story or narrative; without background or preamble. A convention of the classical epic, first formulated by the poet Horace. The opposite approach is *ab ovo*, "from the egg."

memento mori (meh-MEN-toh-MOR-ee): "Remember you must die." A reminder or warning of death; a death's head.

mutatis mutandis (moo-TAH-tees-moo-TAHN-dees): "The things that ought to have been changed having been changed." With the necessary substitutions having been made, the indicated variances considered.

ne plus ultra (nay-ploos-UL-trah): "Not further beyond," said to have been inscribed on the Pillars of Hercules (today's Strait of Gibraltar), as a warning to ships. A farthest point, a highest pitch, a culmination; an impassable obstacle; and, implicitly, a suggestion to stay put or, better yet, turn black.

obiter dictum (OH-buh-ter-DIK-tum): "Thing said by the way." Any incidental or parenthetical remark. In law, something the judge says in arguing a point, but that has no bearing on his decision. Plural: *obiter dicta*.

pari passu (PAH-ree-PAH-soo): "With equal pace." Simultaneously, equally, proceeding alongside.

persona non grata (per-SOH-na-nohn-GRAH-ta): "Person not pleasing." Someone unacceptable within a given context.

quid pro quo (kwid-proh-KWOH): "Something for something." A compensation, an even exchange; tit for tat.

sine qua non (sin-neh-kwah-NOHN): "Without which not." The indispensable element, condition, or quality.

sub rosa (sub-ROH-sah): "Under the rose." "sub rosa" means "in confidence," with secrecy expressed or implied; "clandestinely."

sui generis (SOO-ee-JEN-Er-is): "Of its own kind." Peculiar, unique, not to be analyzed or catalogued along standard lines.

terra firma (TERR-uh-FUR-muh): dry land; the ground as opposed to the air or sea.

tu quoque (TOO-KWOH-kweh): "You also." The ancient Roman version of "So are you." A response to an accusation directed personally.

ultra vires (UL-trah-VEER-ayz): "Beyond (one's) authority." Also, outside one's jurisdiction. It's well known that several successive administrations behaved *ultra vires* in Vietnam.

vice versa (VY-si-VER-sah): The other way around.

Words from Everywhere

Over the last 400 years, as British influence has spread around the world, through trade and the acquiring of a vast overseas empire in the 18th and 19th centuries, English has taken in words from just about every language it has come into contact with. Some of these words have been adopted directly; others have come into English via one of the other European languages. Here are some of the words borrowed at various times. It will give you an idea of the extraordinary variety that English has to offer.

Languages of the British Isles

Scots and Irish Gaelic: banshee, bard, blarney, bog, brat, cadge, galore, plaid, slogan, smithereens, spree, Tory, trousers, whisky

Welsh: coracle, corgi, flannel, flammery

Other European Languages

Modern French: ballet, brochure, camouflage, chic, cliche, elite, etiquette, garage, gourmet, liaison, menu, native, pate, police, prestige, rendezvous, ricochet, suede, verve.

In addition, English uses many French words and phrases with little attempt at integrating them into English speech patterns: à la carte, bète noire, coup d'ètat, cul de sac, fait accompli, hors d'oeuvre, nouveau riche.

Spanish: bonanza, canyon, cockroach, fiesta, macho, paella, rodeo, salsa, sombrero

Portuguese: albino, corral, marmalade, rusk, vindaloo

Dutch: beleaguer, boom, boss, brandy, coleslaw, cruise, drill, excise, gin, groove, hoist, kit, loiter, luck, poppycock, skate, sledge, splinter, split, waffle, wagon.

Afrikaans: aardvark, apartheid, boer, commandeer, commando, trek, veld

German: blitz, delicatessen, dollar, kindergarten, kitsch, lager, nickel, rucksack, snorkel, spanner, swindle, waltz, zinc

Yiddish: bagel, chutzpah, maven, nosh, schlep, schmaltz

Scandinavian Languages: fjord, geyser, mink, ombudsman, rug, saga, ski, walrus

Czech: howitzer, pistol, pram, polka, robot

Hungarian: coach, goulash, hajduk, hussar, paprika, sabre

Russian: balalaika, commissar, glasnost, knout, mammoth, perestroika, pogrom, samovar, troika

Eastern Languages

Turkish: bosh, caviar, coffee, horde, kebab, kiosk, yoghurt

Arabic: admiral, cipher, crimson, ghoul, harem, hazard, lute, magazine, masquerade, racket, saffron, sash, sherbet, tariff, zero

Persian: bazaar, candy, caravan, check, divan, jackal, jasmine, lemon, lilac, magic, orange, paradise, shawl, spinach, tale, tulip, turban

Hindi: bangle, bungalow, chintz,, chit, cot, cushy, dinghy, jungle, loot, pyjamas, shampoo, thug, toddy, verandah

South Indian Languages: betel, congee, curry, mongoose, mulligatawny, pariah, teak

Malay: (run) amok, bamboo, (tea) caddy, gingham, gong, (motor) launch, paddy, sago

Chinese: ketchup, kowtow, kung fu, silk, soya, tea, typhoon, wok

Japanese: bonsai, futon, judo, kamikaze, karate, kimono, origami, rickshaw, tycoon

Australian Aboriginal Languages: boomerang, budgerigar, dingo, kangaroo, wallaby

Polynesian and other Pacific Languages: Kiwi, mana, taboo, tattoo (on the skin), ukulele

African Languages

Banana, banjo, chimpanzee, cola, guinea, okra, raffia, voodoo, yam, zombie

American Languages

Inuit (Eskimo): anorak, igloo, kayak, parka

North American Indian Languages: chipmunk, hickory, moccasin, moose, powwow, raccoon, skunk, toboggan, tomahawk, totem

Aztec: avocado, cocoa, chilli, chocolate, coyote, tomato

Caribbean Languages: barbecue, cannibal, hammock, hurricane, maize, tobacco

South American Languages: alpaca, cashew, cocaine, condor, guano, jaguar, toucan.

British and American English

Word list of British and American differences should be treated with care. Sometimes a difference is absolute. sometimes it is a mere tendency. Words pass between dialects freely and rapidly and very often speakers of other dialects have a range of expression to choose from.

The list below gives only a few samples. For instance, thay ignore more slang expressions and new coinings. The charts have two coloumns: the first gives British preference and the second the usual form in American.

British	American
adhesive tape	sticking plaster
aerial	antenna
agony aunt	advice columnist
aeroplane	airplane
aluminium	aluminum
anticlockwise	counterclockwise

British	American
appetizer	starter
aubergine	eggplant
autumn	fall
baking tray	cookie sheet
bank holiday	legal or public holiday
beetroot	beet

British	American
biscuit sweet tasting	cookie
bonnet of car	hood
boot of car	trunk
bowler hat	derby
braces	suspenders
bumbag	fanny pack
burgle	burglarize
bury the hatchet	bury the tomahawk
call box	telephone booth
candy floss	cotton candy
caravan	trailer, mobile home
car park	parking lot
catapult	slingshot
chest of drawers	bureau
chips	french fries
Christian name, first name, forename	given name
condom	rubber
cooker	stove
cot	crib
courgettes	zucchini
crash barrier	guardrail
crisps	potato chips
crotchet	quarter note
cutlery	silverware
current account	checking account
diamante	rhinestone
dinner jacket	tuxedo
doll's house	doll house
drawing pin	thumbtack
dressing gown	robe; bathrobe
dummy (for baby)	pacifier
dungarees	overalls
dustbin	garbage can, trashcan
earth(electrical)	ground
engaged (telephone)	busy
estate agent	real-estate agent, realtor
faith school	parochial school
faucet	tap
flat (housing)	apartment
flyover	overpass
football	soccer
footway	sidewalk
fortnight	two weeks
frying pan	skillet
full stop	period
(back) garden	(back) yard
gents	men's room
to grill	to broil
guard's van	caboose
hair slide	barrette
handbag	purse
hen night	bachelorette party
hoarding	billboard
homely	homey
indicator	turn signal (on a car)
interval (in a performance)	intermission
jeans	blue jeans
jelly babies	jelly beans
jumper	sweater
jewellery	jewelry
jug	pitcher
ladies	women's room
launderette	laundromat
lavatory	washroom
level crossing	grade crossing
lift	elevator
lolly	lollipop
lorry	truck
luggage	baggage
mackintosh	raincoat
maize	corn
mangetart	snowpea
maths	math
milometer	odometer
minim	half note

British	American
monkey trick	monkey shines
motorway	expressway, freeway
mudguard	fender
mum (my)	mom (my)
nappy	diaper
noughts and crosses	tick-tac-toe
paracetamol	acetaminophen
paraffin	kerosene
pavement	sidewalk
peg	clothespin
pelmet	valance
pernickety	persnickety
petrol	gas, gasoline
pillar box, postbox	mailbox
pinafore dress	jumper
plimsolls	gym shoes
postcode	zip code
postman	mailman
powerpoint	electrical outlet
pram	baby carriage
public building	restroom
puncture	blow-out
pylon	utility pole
quaver (music)	eighth note
queue	line
railway	railboard
reverse charge	collect (call)
ring road	beltway
roundabout	traffic circle, rotary
rowing boat	rowboat
rubber	eraser
saloon (car)	sedan
sandpit	sandpile
sellotape	Scotch tape
semibreve (music)	whole note
serviette	napkin
shop assistant	sales clerk
silencer (on a car)	muffler
silverside	rump roast
single (ticket)	one-way
skeleton in the cupboard	skeleton in the closet
skipping rope	jumb rope
sledge	sled
snakes and ladders	chutes and ladders
spanner	wrench
spring onion	scallion
stag night	bachelor party
storm in a teacup	tempest in a teapot
swede (vegetable)	rutabaga
sweets	(hard) candy
tap	faucet
term	semester
tick	check mark
tie	necktie
timber	lumber
tin (of food)	can
ticket tout	scalper
toll motorway	turnpike
torch	flashlight
touch wood	knock on wood
traffic light	stoplight
trainers	sneakers
tram	streetcar, trolley (car)
tramp	hobo
undertaker	mortician
unit trust	mutual fund
vacuum flask	thermos bottle
vest	undershirt
wardrobe	closet
wastepaper	wastebasket
white (coffee)	'with milk'
windscreen	windshield
wing (of car)	fender
zebra crossing	crosswalk
zed (letter z)	zee
zip	zipper

Important Days

January

4 World Braille Day

9 NRI Day (Return of Mahatma Gandhi from South Africa in 1915)

12 National Youth Day (Birthday of Swami Vivekananda)

14 World Logic Day

15 Army Day

24 National Girl Child Day; International Day of Education; World Day for African and Afrodescendant Culture

25 National Tourism Day, National Voters' Day

26 India's Republic Day, International Customs Day

27 Day to Remember the Victims of the Holocaust

28 Data Protection Day

29 National Newspaper Day

30 Martyrs' Day (Assassination of Mahatma Gandhi)

Last Sunday World Leprosy Eradication Day

February

1 World Hijab Day

2nd Sunday World Marriage Day

2 World Wetlands Day

4 World Cancer Day

6 International Day of Zero Tolerance to Female Genital Mutilation

10 World Pulses Day

11 International Day of Women and Girls in Science

13 World Radio Day

14 St Valentine's Day

20 World Day of Social Justice

21 World Mother Language Day

24 Central Excise Day

28 National Science Day (This day in 1928 marked the discovery of 'Raman Effect' by Dr C V Raman).

March

Second Monday Commonwealth Day

Second Thursday World Kidney Day

1 Zero Discrimination Day

3 National Defence Day, World Wildlife Day

4 March

World Engineering Day for Sustainable Development

4 National Security Day; World Engineering Day for Sustainable Development

8 International Women's Day

10 Central Industrial Security Force (CISF) Raising Day

12 Mauritius Day

14 International Day of Mathematics; Pi Day [Observed on March 14 (3/14 in the month/day date format) since 3, 1 and 4 are the three significant digits of Pi].

15 World Disabled Day; World Consumer Rights Day

16 National Vaccination Day

20 International Day of Happiness; International Francophonie Day

21 World Forestry Day; International Day for the Elimination of Racial Discrimination; International Day of Nowruz; World Poetry Day; World Down Syndrome Day

22 World Water Day

23 World Meteorological Day

24 World Tuberculosis Day

27 World Theatre Day

April

2 World Autism Awareness Day

4 International Day for Mine Awareness and Assistance in Mine Action

5 National Maritime Day; International Day of Conscience

6. International Day of Sport for Development and Peace

7 World Health Day

12 International Day of Human Space Flight

14 World Chagas Disease Day

15 World Art Day

17 World Haemophilia Day

18 World Heritage Day

21 Secretaries' Day, National Civil Services Day

22 Earth Day

23 World Book and Copyright Day; English Language Day

25 World Malaria Day

26 World Intellectual Property Day

28 World Day for Safety and Health at Work

29 Day of Remembrance for All Victims of Chemical Warfare, International Dance Day

30 World Jazz Day

May

1 Workers' Day (International Labour Day)

2 World Tuna Day

3 International Energy Day, World Press Freedom Day

1st Tuesday World Asthma Day

2nd Saturday World Migratory Bird Day

2nd Sunday Mother's Day

4 Coal Miners' Day

5 African World Heritage Day; World Portuguese Language Day

8 World Red Cross Day; World Thalassaemia Day

11 National Technology Day

12 International Nurses Day

15 International Day of Families

16 International Day of Light; International Day of Living Together in Peace

17 World Hypertension Day; World Telecommunication and Information Society Day

20 World Bee Day

21 World Day for Cultural Diversity for Dialogue and Development; International Tea Day

22 International Day for Biological Diversity

25 World Thyroid Day

29 International Day of United Nations Peacekeepers

31 World No-Tobacco Day

June

1 Global Day of Parents, World Milk Day

3 World Bicycle Day

4 International Day of Innocent Children Victims of Aggression

5 World Environment Day

7 World Food Safety Day

8 World Oceans Day

3rd Sunday Father's Day

12 World Day Against Child Labour

13 International Albinism Awareness Day

14 World Blood Donor Day

15 World Elder Abuse Awareness Day

16 International Day of Family Remittances

17 World Day to Combat Desertification and Drought

19 International Day for the Elimination of Sexual Violence in Conflict

20 World Refugee Day

21 International Yoga Day

23 United Nations Day for Public Service; International Widows' Day

25 Day of the Seafarer

26 International Day against Drug Abuse and Illicit Trafficking

29 National Statistics Day (Birthday of PC Mahalanobis, who founded the Indian Statistical Institute)

30 International Asteroid Day; International Day of Parliamentarism

July

1 National Doctors' Day (Birthday of BC Roy)

First Saturday International Day of Co-operatives

6 World Zoonoses Day

11 World Population Day

12 Malala Day

15 World Youth Skills Day

18 Nelson Mandela International Day

20 World Chess Day

26 Kargil Victory Day; International Day for the Conservation of the Mangrove Ecosystem

26 July

International Day for the Conservation of the Mangrove Ecosystem

28 World Hepatitis Day

30 International Day of Friendship, World Day against Trafficking in Persons

August

First Sunday International Friendship Day

6 Hiroshima Day

7 National Handloom Day

8 World Senior Citizens' Day

9 Quit India Day, Nagasaki Day; International Day of the World's Indigenous Peoples

12 International Youth Day

15 Indian Independence Day

19 World Photography Day; World Humanitarian Day

20 Sadbhavana Diwas (Birthday of Rajiv Gandhi)

23 International Day for the Remembrance of the Slave Trade and its Abolition

23 August

International Day for the Remembrance of the Slave Trade and its Abolition

29 National Sports Day (Birthday of Dhyan Chand, the hockey wizard); International Day against Nuclear Tests

30 Small Industry Day; International Day of the Victims of Enforced Disappearances

September

2 World Coconut Day

5 Teachers' Day (Birthday of Dr S Radhakrishnan); International Day of Charity

7 International Day of Clean Air for Blue Skies

8 World Literacy Day (UNESCO)

10 World Suicide Prevention Day

12 United Nations Day for South-South Cooperation

15 Engineers' Day; International Day of Democracy.

16 World Ozone Day

17 World Patient Safety Day

18 World Bamboo Day: International Equal Pay Day

20 International Day of University Sport

21 Alzheimer's Day; Day for Peace & Non-violence (UN)

22 Rose Day (Welfare of cancer patients)

25 Social Justice Day,

26 International Day for the Total Elimination of Nuclear Weapons

27 World Tourism Day

28 World Rabies Day; International Day for Universal Access to Information

29 World Heart Day

30 International Translation Day

Last Sunday Day of the Deaf

Last Thursday World Maritime Day

October

1 International Day for the Elderly, World Vegetarian Day

2 Gandhi Jayanthi, International Day of Non-Violence, World Farm Animals Day

First Monday World Habitat Day, World Architecture Day

First Friday World Smile Day

4 World Animal Day

5 World Teachers' Day

7 World Day for Decent Work

8 Indian Air Force Day

9 World Post OfficeDay

10 World Mental Health Day

11 International Day of the Girl Child

2nd Thursday World Sight Day

2nd Friday World Egg Day

2nd Saturday World Migratory Bird Day

13 UN International Day for Natural Disaster Reduction

14 World Standards Day

15 World White Cane Safety Day; International Day of Rural Women, Global Handwashing Day; International Day of Rural Women

16 World Food Day; World Anaesthesia Day

17 International Day for the Eradication of Poverty

20 National Solidarity Day, World Statistics Day, World Osteoporosis Day

21 World Iodine Deficiency Disorders Prevention Day

24 UN Day; World Development Information Day

27 World Day for Audiovisual Heritage

28 International Animation Day

30 World Thrift Day

31 National Unity Day; World Cities Day

November

First Thursday International Day against Violence and Bullying at School including Cyberbullying

2 International Day to End Impunity for Crimes against Journalists

5 World Tsunami Awareness Day; World Day of Romani Language

6 International Day for Preventing the Exploitation of the Environment in War and Armed Conflict

7 Infant Protection Day; National Cancer Awareness Day

9 Legal Services Day

10 World Science Day for Peace and Development

Second Thursday World Quality Day

11 National Education Day (Birthday of Maulana Abul Kalam Azad)

14 Children's Day (Birthday of Jawaharlal Nehru); World Diabetes Day; International Day against Illicit Trafficking in Cultural Property

16 National Press Day; International Day for Tolerance

17 National Epilepsy Day, International Students' Day

18 Sappers' Day, International Day of Islamic Art

Third Thursday World Philosophy Day

Third Sunday World Day of Remembrance for Road Traffic Victims

19 World Day for Prevention of Abuse and Violence Against Children; World Citizens' Day, International Men's Day; World Toilet Day; Women's Entrepreneurship Day; National Integration Day

20 Universal Children's Day; Africa Industrialisation Day

21 World Television Day; World Hello Day

25 International Day for the Elimination of Violence against Women

26 Constitution Day; National Milk Day (Birthday of Verghese Kurien, father of white revolution in India); World Olive Tree Day

29 International Day of Solidarity with the Palestinian People

30 Flag Day

December

1 World AIDS Day

2 International Day for the Abolition of Slavery

3 World Day of the Handicapped

4 Indian Navy Day; International Day of Banks

5 World Soil Day, International Volunteer Day for Economic and Social Development

7 Indian Armed Forces Flag Day; International Civil Aviation Day

9 International Anti-Corruption Day

10 Human Rights Day

11 UNICEF Day; International Mountain Day

12 International Day of Neutrality

14 National Energy Conservation Day

16 Nirbhaya Day

18 International Migrants Day; Minorities Rights Day (India); Arabic Language Day

20 International Human Solidarity Day

22 National Mathematics Day

23 Farmers' Day (Birthday of Chaudhary Charan Singh)

25 Good Governance Day (Birthday of AB Vajpayee)

Deities of Classical Mythology

Greek Gods and Godesses

Name	Realm, Position, or Symbolism
Aeolus	god of the winds
Amphitrite	goddess of the oceans
Ares	god of war
Asclepius	god of medicine and healing
Athena	goddess of wisdom
Carpo	goddess of summer fruit
Chaos	personification of confusion
Chloris	goddess of flowers
Demeter	goddess of grains and harvest
Dionysus	god of wine
Enyo	goddess of war
Eos	goddess of the dawn
Eris	goddess of discord
Eros	god of love
Hermes	messenger of the gods
Hestia	goddess of the hearth
Hygeia	goddess of health
Hymen	god of marriage
Hypnos	god of sleep
Irene (or Eirene)	goddess of peace
Iris	goddess of the rainbow
Morpheus	god of dreams
Nemesis	goddess of vengeance
Persephone	queen of the underworld; goddess of spring
Selene	goddess of the moon
Zeus	chief god of Olympus

Roman Gods and Godesses

Name	Realm, Position, or Symbolism
Aesculapius	god of medicine and healing
Aurora	goddess of the dawn
Bacchus (or Liber)	god of wine
Bellona	goddess of war
Ceres	goddess of grains and harvest
Coelus	god of heaven
Cupid (or Amor)	god of love
Jupiter (or Jove)	chief of all gods
Juturna	goddess of springs of water
Juventas	goddess of youth
Juventus	god of youth
Lemures	spirits of the dead
Libitina	goddess of the under-world
Lacina	goddess of childbirth
Luna	goddess of the moon
Mars	god of war
Mercury	messenger of the gods
Minerva	goddess of wisdom
Mors	god of death
Neptune	god of the oceans
Nox	goddess of night
Pomona	goddess of fruit trees and their fruit
Salacia	goddess of the oceans
Somnus	god of sleep
Vesta	goddess of the hearth
Vulcan	god of fire and the forge

List of Firsts in India

First Chinese pilgrim to visit India .... Fa-Hien/Faxian
The first and last Muslim woman ruler of India ....Razia Sultan
First English Ambassador to the court of a Mughal Emperor ....Thomas Roe
The first British Governor-General of Bengal ....Lord Warren Hastings(1773-1785)
The first British Governor-General of India .... Lord William Bentinck(1828-1835)
The first British Viceroy of India .... Lord Canning
First Post Office Opened in India ....Kolkata (1727)
First Wax statue of a Living Indian ....Mahatma Gandhi at Madame Tussaud's in 1939
India's First Open University ....Dr B.R Ambedkar Open University, Hyderabad
India's First University ....Nalanda University
India's first man in Space .... Rakesh Sharma
The first Speaker of the Lok Sabha .... Ganesh Vasudeva Mavalankar
First Indian to reach Antarctica .... Lt. Ram Charan
First Muslim President of the Indian National Congress .... Badruddin Tyabji
The first and the last Indian to be Governor-General of free India .... C. Rajagopalachari
The first Chief Election Commissioner ....Sukumar Sen
The first Chief Justice of Supreme Court .... Justice Harilal J. Kania
The first Education Minister .... Abdul Kalam Azad
The first Defence Minister of India...Baldev Singh
The first Law Minister of India... Dr B R Ambedkar
The first Railway Minister of India ....John Mathai
The first Finance Minister of India ....R K Shanmukham Chetty
The first Minister of Food and Agriculture in India...........................Rajendra Prasad
The first Field Marshal of India .... S.H.F. Manekshaw
The first Governor-General of free India ....Lord Mountbatten
The first Home Minister of India .... Sardar Vallabh Bhai Patel
The first Indian Air Chief Marshal ....Subroto Mukerjee
The first Indian Commander-in-Chief of India .... General Cariappa
The first Indian Member of the Viceroy's Executive Council .... S P Sinha
The first Indian Naval Chief .... Vice-Admiral R.D. Katari
The first Indian Pilot ....J.R.D. Tata (1929)

The first Indian to cross English Channel .... Mihir Sen
The first Indian to get Nobel Prize in Physics .... C.V. Raman
The first Indian to join the Indian Civil Services .... Satyendra Nath Tagore
The first Indian to win Nobel Prize .... Rabindranath Tagore
The first Indian lady to become Miss World .... Rita Faria
The first Indian Judge of International Court of Justice .... Dr. Nagendra Singh
The first person to reach Mt. Everest without oxygen .... Sherpa Ang Dorjee
The first woman Lieutenant General .... Puneeta Arora

Dr. Nagendra Singh

Sherpa Ang Dorjee

Puneeta Arora

Somnath Sharma

The first person to get Param Vir Chakra .... Major Somnath Sharma
The first Muslim President of India .... Dr. Zakir Hussain
The first person of Indian origin to receive
Nobel Prize in Medicine .... Hargovind Khurana
The first Person to receive Jnanpith award .... G Shankara Kurup
The first Indian to receive Magsaysay Award .... Acharya Vinoba Bhave
The first Indian to receive Nobel Prize in Economics .... Amartya Sen
The first Indian to receive Stalin Prize .... Saifuddin Kitchlu
The first person to resign from the
Central Cabinet .... Shyama Prasad Mukherjee
The first President of India who died while in office .... Dr. Zakir Hussain
The first President of Indian National Congress .... W.C. Banerjee
The first President of Indian Republic .... Dr. Rajendra Prasad
The first Prime Minister of free India .... Pt. Jawahar Lal Nehru
The first Prime Minister of India who
did not face the Parliament .... Charan Singh
The first Prime Minister of India who resigned
without completing the full term .... Morarji Desai
The first Vice-President of India .... Dr. Radhakrishnan

The first woman Air Vice Marshal .... P. Bandopadhyaya
The first Indian woman to pilot an aircraft........ Sarla Thukral
The first Indian woman commercial Pilot .... Durba Banerjee
The first woman Ambassador .... Miss C.B. Muthamma
The first woman Asian Games Gold Medal Winner .... Kamaljeet Sandhu
The first woman Chairman of Union Public Service Commission .... Rose Millian Bathew
The first woman chairperson of Indian Airlines .... Sushma Chawla
The first woman Cheif Justice of High Court........ Leela Seth (Himachal Pradesh High Court)
The first woman Chief Minister of an Indian State .... Sucheta Kripalani
The first woman Director General of Police .... Kanchan Chaudhary Bhattacharya
The first woman Governor of a state in free India .... Sarojini Naidu
The first woman Graduates .... Kadambini Ganguly and Chandramukhi Basu, 1883
The first woman Honours Graduate .... Kamini Roy, 1886
The first woman IPS officer .... Kiran Bedi
The first woman Judge .... Anna Chandy (She became judge in a district court in 1937)
The first woman Judge in Supreme Court of India .... M. Fathima Beevi
The first woman Lawyer .... Cornelia Sorabjee
The first woman Minister in the Union Cabinet .... Rajkumari Amrit Kaur
The first woman Olympic medal Winner .... Karnam Malleswari, 2000
The first woman pilot to fly solo in the Indian Air Force .... Harita Kaur Deol
The first woman President of Indian National Congress .... Annie Besant
The first woman President of United Nations General Assembly .... Vijaya Lakshmi Pandit
The first woman Prime Minister .... Indira Gandhi
The first woman Speaker of a State Assembly .... Shanno Devi
The first woman to climb Mount Everest .... Bachhendri Pal
The first woman to climb Mount Everest twice .... Santosh Yadav
The first woman to cross English Channel .... Arati Saha
The first woman to receive Ashoka Chakra .... Neerja Bhanot
The first woman to receive Bharat Ratna .... Indira Gandhi
The first woman to receive Jnanpith Award .... Ashapurna Devi
The first woman to receive the Nobel Prize .... Mother Teresa

Mnemonic Devices

Mnemonic devices are memory aids that help you remember a specific thing. Mnemonic devices can be special rhymes and poems, acronyms, images, songs, outlines, and other tools. Mnemonic (pronounced ni-mon-ik) is derived from the Greek phrase mimneskesthai meaning to "remember."

1. The order of the planets from the sun outward: **M**y **V**ery **E**arnest **M**other **J**ust **S**erved **U**s **N**ine **P**ickles (Mercury, Venus, Earth, Mars, Jupiter, Saturn, Uranus, Neptune, Pluto).

2. The seven hills of Rome: **P**oor **Q**ueen **V**ictoria **E**ats **C**row **A**t **C**hristmas (Palatine, Quirinal, Viminal, Esquiline, Capitoline, Aventine, Caelian)

3. The twelve cranial nerves: **O**n **o**ld **O**lympus' **T**owering **T**op, **A** **F**at-Assed **G**erman **V**iewed **A** **H**op (olfactory, optic, oculomotor, trochlear, trigeminal, abducens, facial, acoustic, glossopharyngeal, vagus, accessory, hypoglossal).

4. The Linnaean system of classification: **K**ing **P**eter **C**ame **O**ver **F**rom **G**ermany **S**eeking **F**ortune (kingdom, phylum, class, order, family, genus, species, form).

5. Ranking order of the British peerage: **D**o **M**en **E**ver **V**isit **B**oston? (duke, marquess, earl, viscount, baron)

6. Colours of the rainbow: **R**ichard **O**f **Y**ork **G**ave **B**attle **i**n **V**ain (Red, Orange, Yellow, Green, Blue, Indigo, Violet)

7. The order of geological time periods: **C**ows **o**ften **S**it **D**own **C**arefully. **P**erhaps **T**heir **J**oints **C**reak? **P**ersistent **E**arly **O**iling **M**ight **P**revent **P**ainful **R**heumatism (Cambrian, Ordovician, Silurian, Devonian, Carboniferous, Permian, Triassic, Jurassic, Creataceous, Paleocene, Eocene, Oligocene, Miocene, Pliocee, Pleistocene, Recent)

8. The Countries of Central America: **B**ig **G**orillas **E**at **H**otdogs, **N**ot **C**old **P**izza (Belize, Guatemala, El Salvador, Honduras, Nicaragua, Costa Rica, Panama)

9. The order of notes to which guitar strings should be tuned: **E**aster **B**unnies **G**et **D**runk **A**t **E**aster (EBGDAE)

10. The order of taxonomy in biology: **K**ids **P**refer **C**heese **O**ver **F**ried **G**reen **S**pinach (Kingdm, Phylum, Class, Order, Family, Genus, Species)

11. The great lakes: **HOMES** (Huron, Ontario, Michigan, Erie, Superior)

12. The Great Lakes in order of size: **S**am's **H**orse **M**ust **E**at **O**ats (Superior, Huron, Michigan, Erie, Ontario)

13. The order of the first five books of the Old Testament: **G**od **E**quals **N**ight, **N**ot **D**arkness (Genesis, Exodus, Leviticus, Numbers, Deutoronomy)

14. The first batch of Roman emperors: **A**nother **T**om **C**at, **C**aught **N**apping (Augustus, Tiberius, Caligula, Claudius, Nero)

15. The first 8 presidents of the USA **W**ill **A** **J**olly **M**an **M**ake **A** **J**olly **V**isitor? (George **W**ashington, John **A**dams, Thomas **J**efferson, James **M**adison, James **M**onroe, John Quincy **A**dams, Andrew **J**ackson, Martin **V**an Buren)

16. The royal houses of the kings and queens of England (and Great Britain): **N**o **P**lan **L**ike **Y**ours **T**o **S**tudy **H**istory **W**isely (**N**orman, **P**lantagenet, **L**ancaster, **Y**ork, **T**udor, **S**tuart, **H**anover, **W**indsor)

17. Henry VIII's Wives: **A** **B**ig **S**ecret **C**onceals **H**er **P**ast (Catherine of **A**ragon, Anne **B**oleyn, Jane **S**eymour, Anne of **C**leves, Catherine **H**oward, Catherine **P**arr)

Important International Borders

Important International Borders

Name of Lines/ Boundaries	Between	Features/ Description
17th Parallel	South Vietnam and North Vietnam It was demarcated based on the 1954 Geneva Accords.	The 17th latitude from the equator divided erstwhile North and South Vietnam.
20th Parallel	Libya and Sudan	It is located at the 20th northern latitude which is used as the border between Sudan and Libya.
22nd Parallel	Egypt and Sudan	The 22nd latitude north of the equator marks a major portion of the Sudan-Egypt border.
25th Parallel	Mauritania and Mali	The northernmost section of the Mali-Mauritania border is marked using this line.
31st Parallel	Iran and Iraq It also demarcates the border between the US states of Louisiana and Mississippi.	The 31st northern latitude marks the border between Iraq and Iran.
38th Parallel	South Korea and North Korea	The 38th parallel is used to demarcate the central part of the Demilitarized zone between North and South Korea.
49th Parallel	The USA and Canada Demarcated after the Anglo-American Convention of 1818 and the Oregon Treaty of 1846, it forms the international border between the northern USA (Excluding Alaska) and Canada.	It is located 49 degrees north of the equator.
Durand Line	Pakistan and Afghanistan Present-day Afghanistan does not recognize the Durand line.	Delimited by Sir Mortimer Durand with the agreement of the erstwhile Amir of Afghanistan in 1893.

Hindenburg Line	Poland and Germany It was rendered irrelevant by the treaty of Versailles in 1919.	It was a German Defensive line in French territory during World War I
McMahon Line	China and India	It was drawn by Sir Henry McMahon in consultation with Tibetan representatives in 1914.
Maginot Line	Germany and France	It was a defensive line at the French border towards Germany before World War II. The Maginot line was rendered obsolete following the successful invasion of France by Germany following the outbreak of World War II
Mannerheim Line	Russia and Finland	Finland built this as a defensive line against the Soviet Union for the Winter War during World War II.
Oder-Neisse Line	Poland and Germany It demarcates the Polish-German border according to the Potsdam Conference. It was recognized by a unified Germany in 1990.	It runs along the rivers Oder and Lusatian Neisse rivers.
Radcliffe Line	India and Pakistan It includes present-day India, Bangladesh and Pakistan.	It was demarcated by Sir Cyril Radcliffe for the Partition of India and the formation of East and West Pakistan.
Siegfried Line	France and Germany	It was built as an extension of the Hindenburg defensive line on the western front of World War I by the Weimar Republic and later the Third Reich of Germany in the 1930s.
Blue Line	Lebanon and Israel	A border demarcation between Lebanon and Israel published by the United Nations on 7 June 2000 for the purposes of determining whether Israel had fully withdrawn from Lebanon.

Green Line / Attila Line / UN Buffer Zone	The Republic of Cyprus and Turkish Cyprus	A demilitarized zone, patrolled by the United Nations Peacekeeping Force in Cyprus (UNFICYP), that was established in 1964 and extended in 1974 after the ceasefire of 16 August 1974

Indian Military Exercises

The Indian military exercises are classified into the following types:

- Domestic exercises
- Bilateral exercises
- Multilateral exercises

Domestic Exercises – These exercises aim to improve internal engagements and there can be inter-services or intra-services depending on nature and its application.

List of Domestic Military Exercises: Gandiv Vijay, Paschim Lehar, Vayu Shakti, Vijay Prahar

Bilateral Exercises: These exercises are conducted between two countries.

The following table provides you with a list of important Indian bilateral army exercises.

Exercise Name	Participant Nations
CORPAT	India & Thailand
Dharma Guardian	India & Japan
Garuda Shakti	India & Indonesia
Hand in Hand Exercise	India & China
Maitree Exercise	India & Thailand
Mitra Shakti	India & Sri Lanka
Nomadic Elephant	India & Mongolia
Sampriti	India & Bangladesh
SIMBEX	India & Singapore
Shakti Exercise	India & France
Surya Kiran	India & Nepal
Vajra Prahar	India & the US
Yudh Abhyas	India & the US

Multilateral Exercises: These exercises are conducted by the military including more than one partner nation.

List of major multilateral exercises conducted by the military are given below:

Multilateral Exercise	No of Participating Countries
COBRA-GOLD	Asia – Pacific countries
MALABAR	4 (Australia, India, Japan, the US)
RIMPAC	26
Samvedna	South Asian Region Nations

Latest Military Exercises

The latest editions of all the important military exercises of India with other nations are mentioned in the next page.

High Altitude Warfare School (HAWS)

The Indian army's High Altitude Warfare School (HAWS) in Gulmarg is one of the most elite military training centres in the world and is frequented by Special Operations teams from the U.S, U.K and Russia.

Exercise name	Country participated with India	Latest Date/ Year/Edition	Held at
Al Nagah-III	Oman	• 12th March 2019 • 3rd Edition	Jabal AL Akhdar training camp, Oman
Bold Kurukshetra	Singapore	• 9th April 2019 • 12th Edition	Babina Military Station in Jhansi district of Uttar Pradesh
Ekuverin	Maldives	• 7th October 2019 • 10th Edition	Pune, Maharashtra
Garuda Shakti IV	Indonesia	• 19th February 2018 • 6th Edition	Bandung, Indonesia
Hand in Hand	China	• 7th December 2019 • 8th Edition	Umroi, Meghalaya
Indra	Russia	• 4th September 2020 • 11th Edition	Andaman Sea
Khanjar V	Kyrgyzstan	• April 2021 • 5th Edition	Kyrgyzstan
Lamitye	Seychelles	• 2018 • 8th Edition	Mahe Island in Seychelles
Maitree	Thailand	• 16th September 2019 • 14th Edition	Umroi, Meghalaya
Mitra Shakti-VIII	Sri Lanka	• 4th October 2021 • 8th Edition	Ampara, Sri Lanka
Multi-national Field Training Exercise(FTX)/ Exercise Force 18	18 ASEAN Plus countries	• 2nd March 2016	Pune, India
Nomadic Elephant	Mongolia	• 5th October 2019 • 14th Edition	Bakloh Cantonment, Himachal Pradesh
Prabal Dostyk	Kazakhstan	• 2nd November 2017 • Second Edition	Himachal Pradesh
Sampriti-IX	Bangladesh	• 3rd February 2020 • 9th Edition	Umroi, Meghalaya
Surya Kiran XV	Nepal	• 21st September 2021 • 15th Edition	Pithoragarh, Uttarakhand
Yudh Abhyas	United States	• 8th February 2021 • 16th Edition	Rajasthan

110 Documents That Changed the Course of History

Historical documents are original documents that contain important historical information about a person, place, or event. *110 Documents That Changed the Course of History* brings together the most important written agreements, declarations and statements in history. The documents included here have changed the course of history by rewriting laws, granting freedoms and laying out constitutions. But as well as official charters and presidential proclamations, there are also the hand-written documents that have gone on to shape the way we think, the scrawled notes that mark breakthroughs in the worlds of science and technology, and the annotated manuscripts that have become literary landmarks. The messianic power to convey a vital message at the right moment is an instance of a document as was proved by Mahatma Gandhi's Salt Satyagraha.

Documents presented here include: The Exaltation of Inanna (2300 BCE); Magna Carta (1215); Shakespeare's First Folio (1623); Declaration of independence (1776); Salt Satyagraha (1930); Indian Independence Act (1947); Apollo 11 Flight Plan (1969); COVID-19 (2019).

2300 BCE The Exaltation of Inanna A then-untitled, 153-line hymn since labelled the Exaltation of Inanna, composed by the high priestess Enheduanna in the Sumerian city-state of Ur, in about the year 2300 BCE, might be the first-ever creative work to have a claim of authorship. Inanna was the mythical Sumerian Queen of Heaven and goddess of love whom Enheduanna praised in the work and asked for help with vengeance after a political exile.

The Disk of Enheduanna Shows the High Priestess Making an Offering to Her God

Diorite Stela with the Code of Hammurabi

1754 BC Hamurabi's Code When the nearly 4000-year-old stone that contained these laws is unearthed by French archaeologists in 1901, it becomes the oldest nearly-complete ancient code of laws that the modern world has seen. This status has made Hammurabi's Code key for understanding the history and development of western systems of justice.

12th–9th Century BC I Ching *I-Ching* or the Book of Changes is an ancient Chinese divination manual and a book of wisdom which interprets hexagrams (symbols made up of six stacked horizontal lines) formed by tossed coins to form answers to questions about the future. The ancient book is a study of change in human life. The belief is that understanding the pattern and cycle of change will prepare the person for future events and help with making right decisions. The influence of the *I Ching* is still felt even today as many concepts that characterize the traditional Chinese world view, including Yin and Yang, Qi, and the Five Elements are expounded in this ancient text.

c. 750 BC Homer's The Iliad and The Odyssey Preserved for 3,000 years by memory, writing and print, the two greatest epic poems from ancient Greek culture have served for millennia as a pillar of Western literature, leaving scholars to speculate about the genius or geniuses who created these timeless classics.

512 BC The Art of War An ancient Chinese military treatise ranks as the greatest primer ever written on warfare strategy and tactics, providing a timeless and savvy guide for many field generals over the ages. It is also consulted by corporate executives, trial lawyers and other serious competitions.

408 BC-AD 318 Dead Sea Scrolls Discoveries in caves of the Judean Desert yield caches of ancient manuscripts containing

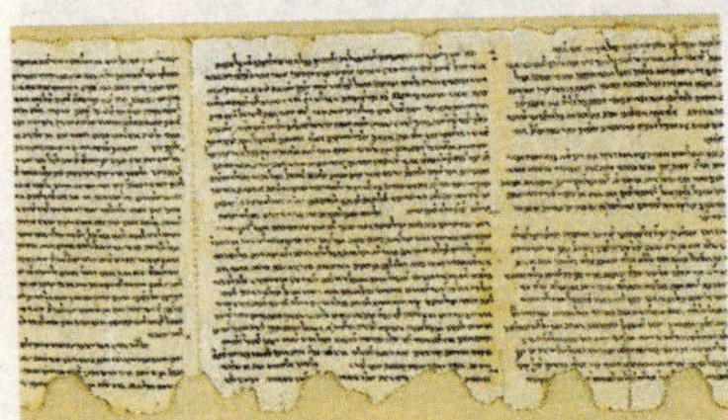

Dead Sea Scrolls

some of the earliest known pieces of the Old Testament and other writings from early Hebrew culture. Their ownership and meaning can prove controversial.

c. 400 BC Mahabharata The world's longest epic poem, which includes Hinduism's most widely read sacred scripture, the *Bhagavad Gita,* as one of its seven principal parvas (sections), ranks as one of the greatest literary achievements in history - one of the high points of Indian culture for more than 2,000 years.

400 BC - AD 200 Kama Sutra Written in Sanskrit, it is one of the world's oldest textbooks of erotic love. Very little of it, in fact, concerns the sexual act. The real *Kamasutra* is about the art of living–finding a partner, maintaining power in a marriage, using drugs and more. It tells us that anyone can live the life of pleasure–if they have money.

c. 380 BC Plato's Republic The Athenian thinker Plato– a student of Socrates and mentor of Aristotle– is credited with one of the most influential works of philosophy and moral / political theory ever written. Presented as a dialogue, it examines such core issues as the meaning of justice and the immortality of the soul.

AD 50 Gandharan Buddhist Texts Buddhist monks' scriptures, inscribed on birch bark scrolls and buried in the desert

Gandhara Buddhist Scroll

of eastern Afghanistan 2,000 years ago, are the earliest known Buddhist texts and the oldest documents extant from South Asia. They are the Indian Buddhist equivalent of the Dead Sea Scrolls.

AD 609-632 The Quran Over a period of 23 years, the word of Allah is revealed to the Prophet Muhammad through the angel Gabriel, in the form of sacred verses, and Muhammad later recites every word to his followers. Believers in the sacred religious text of Islam today comprise one-sixth of the world's population.

1215 Magna Carta Agreed between King John and his barons at Runnymede, as the first document to limit the power

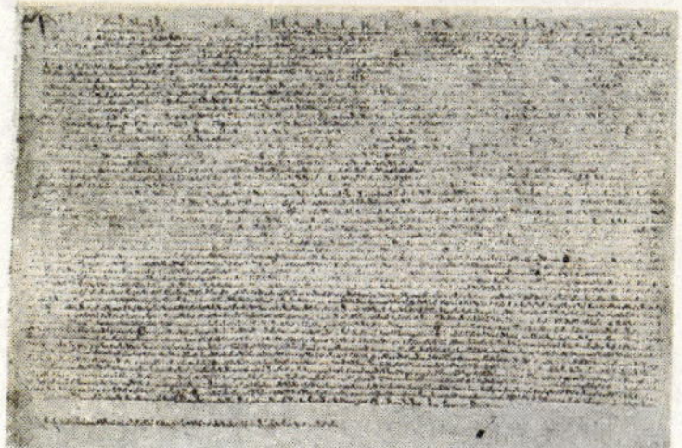

Opening of the Preamble to Magna Carta

of the monarchy and assert the certain liberties granted to free men, the medieval Great Charter of 1215 is considered the foundation of English common law.

1252 Ad Extirpanda Ad extirpanda was a papal bull promulgated on Wednesday, May 15, 1252 by Pope Innocent IV which authorized in limited and defined circumstances the use of torture by the Inquisition for eliciting confessions from heretics. The bull was issued in the wake of the murder of the papal inquisitor of Lombardy, St. Peter of Verona, who was killed by a conspiracy of Cathar sympathizers on 6 April 1252. The bull argued that as heretics are "murderers of souls as well as robbers of God's sacraments and of the Christian faith," they are "to be coerced - as are thieves and bandits - into confessing their errors and accusing others, although one must stop short of danger to life or limb."

1265-74 Summa Theologica Thomas Aquinas is the greatest Catholic philosopher and theologian of the high Middle Ages and his masterpiece, *Summa Theologica*, offers what is perhaps the finest explanation of Christian faith, although he dies before completing it. The work is considered one of the most influential works of Western literature.

1280-1300 Hereford Mappa Mundi Drawn on a large hide, the encyclopae-

Hereford Mappa

dic *Hereford Mappa Mundi* depicts the world as it appears to educated Europeans in the late 13th century, showing everything from geography and biblical lore to exotic animals, strange peoples from foreign lands and images from classical mythology - making it a mapped storehouse of medieval knowledge.

1450s Gutenberg Bible Although the first inventions occurred much earlier in

A Copy of Gutenberg Bible

China and Korea, the genesis of modern printing by means of a printing press using metal movable type is rightly traced to Gutenberg's publication of the Bible, which changed the nature of document production - and transformed the world.

1478-1519 Leonardo da Vinci's Notebooks Leonardo da Vinci's notebooks

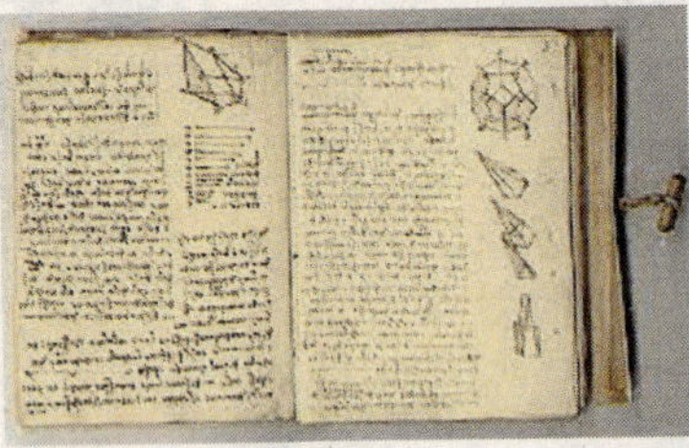

Leonardo da Vinci's Notebook

are the living record of a universal mind. They encompass all the interests and experiments of this self-taught polymath, from mathematics to flying machines. His notebooks contain diagrams, drawings, personal notes and observations, providing a unique insight into how he saw the world.

1492 Alhambra Decree In the most cataclysmic event in Jewish history since the second century AD, Spain's Catholic joint monarchs, Ferdinand and Isabella, issue an edict expelling all of the kingdom's Jews unless they convert to Christianity– a milestone in the history of intolerance.

1493 Christopher Columbus's Letter On the return leg of his first voyage of discovery to the New World, Christopher Columbus writes a letter to Spanish king Ferdinand and queen Isabella describing what he had found. It creates a sensation throughout Europe, and until the 19th century, it remains his only known

¶ Epistola Christofori Colom: cui etas nostra multum debet: de Insulis Indie supra Gangem nuper inventis. Ad quas pergrendas octavo antea mense auspiciis et ere invictissimorum Fernandi et Helisabet Hispaniarum Regum missus fuerat: ad magnificum dominum Gabrielem Sanchis eorundem serenissimorum Regum Tesaurarium missa: quam nobilis ac litteratus vir Leander de Cosco ab Hispano idiomate in latinum convertit tertio kalendas Maii. M.cccc.xciii. Pontificatus Alexandri Sexti Anno primo.

Quoniam suscepte provintie rem perfectam me consecutum fuisse gratum tibi fore scio: has constitui exarare: que te uniuscuiusque rei in hoc nostro itinere geste inventeque admoneant: Tricesimotertio die postquam Gadibus discessi in mare Indicum perveni: ubi plurimas insulas innumeris habitatas hominibus reperi: quarum omnium pro felicissimo Rege nostro preconio celebrato et vexillis extensis contradicente nemine possessionem accepi: primeque earum divi Salvatoris nomen imposui: cuius fretus auxilio tam ad hanc quam ad ceteras alias pervenimus. Eam vero Indi Guanahanin vocant. Aliarum etiam unamquamque novo nomine nuncupavi: quippe aliam insulam Sancte Marie Conceptionis. aliam Fernandinam. aliam Hysabellam. aliam Joanam. et sic de reliquis appellari iussi. Cum primum in eam insulam quam dudum Joanam vocari diximus appulimus: iuxta eius litus occidentem versus aliquantulum processi: tamque eam magnam nullo reperto fine inveni: ut non insulam: sed continentem Chatai provinciam esse crediderim: nulla tamen videns oppida municipiave in maritimis sita confinibus preter aliquos vicos et predia rustica: cum quorum incolis loqui nequibam. quare simul ac nos videbant surripiebant fugam. Progrediebar ultra: existimans aliquam me urbem villasve inventurum. Denique videns quod longe admodum progressis nihil novi emergebat: et huiusmodi via nos ad Septentrionem deferebat: quod ipse fugere exoptabam: terris etenim regnabat bruma: ad Austrumque erat in voto contendere

Christopher Columbus's Letter to Ferdinand and Isabella

written first person account of the historic events of 1492-93.

1501 Petrucci's Harmonice Musices Odhecaton A Ottaviano Petrucci is remembered for his inventions in fine music printing using movable type. In 1501, Petrucci publishes a magnificent collection of music, mostly Flemish chansons that had been written by leading composers of the time, which he titled *Harmonice Musices Odhecaton A*. The anthology included 96 secular and polyphonic songs for three or four voice parts, written in strict fixed forms.

1517 Martin Luther's 95 Theses An Augustinian monk posts a document containing 95 criticisms of the practices of the Catholic Church on a church in Saxony - thereby unintentionally providing the catalyst for a series of world-changing events that will become known as Europe's Protestant Reformation.

1521 Edict of Worms The Holy Roman

Emperor Charles V issues a decree at Worms in Germany, labelling the Church critic Martin Luther as a heretic and banning his writings. But the document has the opposite effect, elevating the dissident's stature within the growing Protestant Reformation.

1522-25 Journal of Magellan's Voyage A scholarly shipmate of Ferdinand Magellan documents the events of their epic around-the globe voyage that have cost the explorer his life and changed the course of world history. Of the 237 mariners who embarked, only 18 have survived the three-year ordeal.

1542 Destruction of the Indies A short account written by the Spanish Dominican friar Bartolomé de las Casas in 1542 about the mistreatment of and atrocities committed against the indigenous peoples of the Americas in colonial times and sent to then Prince Philip II of Spain. It is written to persuade the Spanish king to act in response to the Spanish conquistadors' abuse of the indigenous population. It is one of the most influential sources used to attempt to improve colonial conditions for the indigenous people.The book is also one of the first texts that reveal the devastation caused by Old World diseases in the New World.

1582 Gregorian Calendar (Inter Gravissimas) The Gregorian calendar, the calendar system we use today, is first introduced in 1582. Its predecessor, the Julian calendar, is replaced because it does not correctly reflect the actual time it takes the Earth to circle once around the Sun, known as a tropical year. In the Julian calendar, a leap day is added every four years, which is too frequent. Although it is not perfect either, today's Gregorian calendar uses a much more accurate rule for calculating leap years. The papal bull issued by Pope Gregory XIII in 1582 decrees that 10 days be skipped when switching to the Gregorian calendar. However, only five countries adopt the new calendar system that year—namely, Italy, Poland, Portugal, Spain, and most of France.In total, more than three centuries passed until the Gregorian calendar had been adopted in all countries, from 1582 to 1927.

1611 King James Bible In 1604, England's King James I authorizes a new translation of the Bible aimed at settling some thorny religious differences in his kingdom – and solidifying his own power. But in seeking to prove his own supremacy, King James ends up democratising the Bible instead. Thanks to emerging printing technology, the new translation brings the Bible out of the church's sole control and directly into the hands of more people than ever before, including the Protestant reformers who settled England's North American colonies in the 17th century. Even now, more than four centuries after its publication, the King James Bible (a.k.a. the King James Version, or simply the Authorized Version) remains the most famous Bible translation in history–and one of the most printed books ever.

King James Bible

1620 Mayflower Compact Before venturing ashore into an unsettled and lawless land in America, a majority of passengers aboard the Mayflower form a compact that binds the signers into a 'Civil Body Politic' that will enact 'just and equal Laws... for the general good of the Colony' — an agreement to live together under the rule of law.

1623 Shakespeare's First Folio Seven years after his death, John Heminge and Henry Condell, two of William Shakespeare's closest stage friends, strive to preserve his amazing legacy. The resulting collection of his masterful plays will go on to become what one appraiser will call the 'most documented book in the world', without which the playwright's work may have sunk into obscurity.

Shakespeare First Folio

1632 Galileo's Dialogue In presenting the theory that the Sun, not the Earth, is the centre of the universe, the greatest scientist of his day tries to dramatize his argument as a witty dialogue poking fun at Church dogma. But Galileo ends up being brought before the Roman Inquisition.

1649 Death Warrant of King Charles I This evocative document, a flat parchment containing seals and signatures, is handwritten in iron gall ink and leads to the execution of Charles I and subsequent rule of Oliver Cromwell, one of the 59 signatories. Charles is tried in the House of Commons and executed on 30 January 1649, outside Banqueting House in Whitehall. Following the Restoration of the monarchy in 1660, the Death Warrant is used to identify the commissioners who had signed it (the 'regicides') and prosecute them for treason. Even

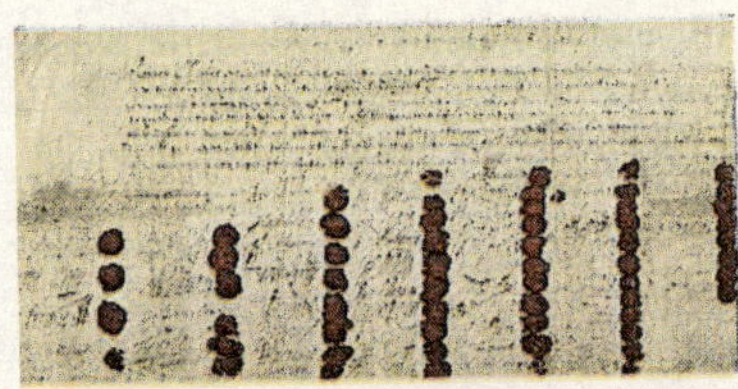

Death Warrant of King Charles I

the signatories, who had died, including Cromwell, are dug up and their bodies hanged. The House of Lords order the return of the Death Warrant from Charles' executioner who was imprisoned in the Tower of London. It is returned on 31 July 1660 and it has been in the custody of British Parliament ever since.

1660-69 Samuel Pepys's Diary A portrait of an extraordinary Englishman, whose scintillating first-hand accounts of Restoration England are reported alongside his rampant sexual exploits. The diary by which Pepys is chiefly known is kept between his 27th and 36th years. Written in Thomas Shelton's system of shorthand, or tachygraphy, with the names in longhand, it extends to 1,250,000 words, filling six quarto volumes in the Pepys Library. It is far more than an ordinary record of its writer's thoughts and actions; it is a supreme work of art, revealing on every page the capacity for selecting the small, as well as the large, essential that conveys the sense of life.

1660s-1727 Isaac Newton Papers The most influential scientist in history leaves

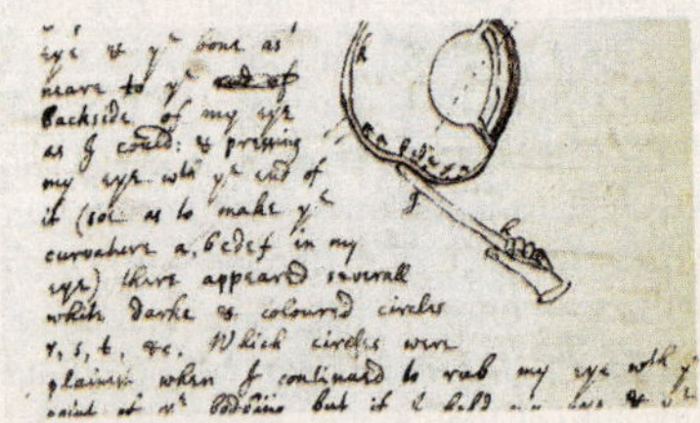

Isaac Newton Papers

behind one of the world's largest collections of precious original scholarly manuscripts, but for centuries is restricted to some of the papers because of Newton's unorthodox ideas about certain subjects.

1665 First Printed Newspaper in English The first real newspaper, other than a newsletter, to be published in England. It appears in Nov. 1665, and is started

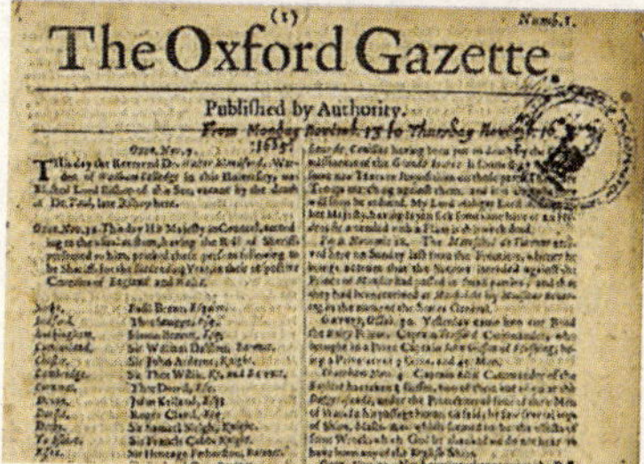

(1) Numb. 1.

The Oxford Gazette.

Published by Authority.

From Monday November 13 to Thursday November 16. 1665.

First Issue of The Oxford Gazette

by H. Muddiman. It becomes the *London Gazette* in 1666. It survives now as a record of official appointments, notices of bankruptcy, etc., having passed in 1923 into the keeping of the Stationery Office.

1689 English Bill of Rights After decades of bloody conflict, the most important document of the Glorious Revolution is an act of Parliament that spells out new limits on the powers of the Crown and establishes the supremacy of Parliament, proclaiming that all Englishmen posses certain inalienable rights under law.

1755 Samuel Johnson's Dictionary Samuel Johnson's *A Dictionary of the English Language* is one of the most famous dictionaries in history. First published in 1755, the dictionary took just over eight years to compile, required six helpers and listed 40,000 words. Each word was defined in detail, the definitions illustrated with quotations covering every branch of learning. It was a huge scholarly achievement, a more extensive and complex dictionary than any of its predecessors – the comparable *French Dictionnaire* had taken 55 years to compile and required the dedication of 40 scholars.

A copy of the First Edition of Dr. Johnson's Dictionary

1776 Declaration of Independence Drafted in the language of the Enlightenment by Thomas Jefferson between 11 June and 28 June 1776, *the Declaration of Independence* formally dissolves Great Britain's political control over the American colonies, advancing a revolutionary charter intended to unite Americans under the banner of liberty and the consent of the governed.

1776 The Wealth of Nations Adam Smith, the Scottish intellectual, single-handedly invents modern political economy with *An Inquiry Into the Nature and Causes of the Wealth of Nations* which swiftly becomes established in the minds of intelligent readers as *The Wealth of Nations.* Although it provids a comprehensive and magisterial treatment of its subject, it is also a work of robust common sense, intelligible to any careful reader, braiding history, philosophy, psychology, and sociology in a compelling tapestry of theory and experience. At the heart of *The Wealth of Nations* is the provocative suggestion that self-interest is perhaps the only criterion of economic behaviour, and that the universal, unfettered pursuit of self-advantage is the only sure guarantee of general welfare.

1787 Constitution of the United States After a five-month-long discussion, a Federal Convention at Philadelphia's Independence Hall produces a four-page parchment document which is signed by 39 of the 55 attending delegates. *The Constitution of the United States,* describing how the new national government shall operate, begins with the words, 'We the people...'

1789 Declaration of the Rights of Man and of the Citizen Inspired by the American Revolution, a group of French nobles led by General Lafayette drafts a political manifesto declaring universal rights built upon liberty, property, security and resistance to oppression - the founding text of the French Revolution.

1791 Declaration of the Rights of Woman and of the Female Citizen Angry that France's lofty Declaration of the Rights of Man and of the Citizen and the new Constitution both ignore women's rights, Olympe de Gouges, a courageous feminist writer and activist, presents her own radical declaration demanding equal treatment.

1803 Louisiana Purchase By means of fortuitous circumstances, the young United States stands to significantly increase its size by acquiring from Napoleon a vast expanse of France's colonial holdings in North America for a bargain sum. The Louisiana Purchase of 1803 brings into the United States about 828,000 square miles of territory from France, thereby doubling the size of the young republic. Part or all of 15 states are eventually created from the land deal, which is considered one of the most important achievements of Thomas Jefferson's presidency.

1803 Meriwether Lewis's List of Expenses Before setting off with William Clark on his epic overland expedition westward to the Pacific, Jefferson's protege prepares a detailed list of all the equipment and supplies that Congress will need to authorize for purchase. Nearly

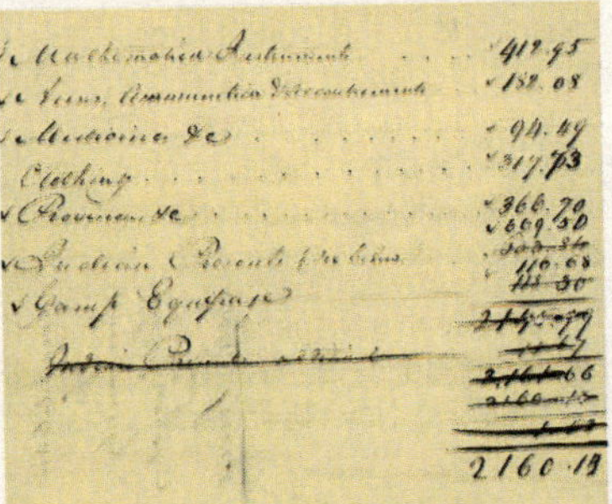

Mathematical Instruments 417.95
Medicine &c 94.49
Clothing 317.73
Camp Equipage
2160.1[illegible]

Meriwether Lewis's List of Expenses

one-third of the total projected cost is for 'Indian presents'.

1804 Napoleonic Code Napoleon Bonaparte establishes a comprehensive civil code that abolishes feudalism, fosters religious tolerance and enacts other liberal reforms across Europe. Building on Roman law and principles of the French Revolution, it proves to be one of the most influential legal codes in world history.

1822 Deciphering the Rosetta Stone The Rosetta Stone is a text written by a group of priests in Egypt to honour the Egyptian

Deciphering the Rosetta Stone

pharaoh. It lists all of the things that the pharaoh has done that are good for the priests and the people of Egypt. Many people work on deciphering hieroglyphs over several hundred years. However, the structure of the script is very difficult to work out. After many years of studying the Rosetta Stone and other examples of ancient Egyptian writing, Jean-François Champollion, a young Frenchman, deciphers hieroglyphs in 1822.

1826 First Photograph Joseph Nicéphore Niépce, a brilliant French inventor, labours for more than a decade to capture

Joseph Nicéphore Niépce's "View from the Window at Le Gras."

real-life images as lasting records by means of a process he calls Heliographie; his first surviving effort, depicting the country scene outside his workshop window, is considered the first permanent photographic image.

1833 Slavery Abolition Act Pressured by slave revolts and abolitional agitation, Parliament finally outlaws slavery in the British Empire, with some exceptions and caveats. The act includes a provision for huge compensation, not for the slaves, but for the slave owners - reparations for the wealthy.

1837-59 Charles Darwin on Natural Selection Twenty-two years after his first epiphany on the subject and 17 years after he coins the term 'natural selection', an English naturalist finally gets around to publishing his revolutionary theory. Documents show how his thinking has evolved, providing a paper trail of his development.

1844 First Telegram On May 24, 1844, Samuel F. B. Morse dispatches the first telegraphic message over an experimental line from Washington, D.C., to Baltimore. The message "What hath God wrought?," taken from the Bible, Numbers 23:23 and recorded on a paper tape, is suggested to Morse by Annie Ellsworth, the young daughter of a friend.

1848 The Communist Manifesto A 12,000-word pamphlet written by two young German philosophers offers a radical new interpretation of history and political economy - and forms the basis for a movement which will later sweep the world 'WORKERS OF THE WORLD UNITE!'

1851 The New York Times The first issue of *The New York Daily Times*– the word "Daily" is dropped from the title in 1857–is dated September 18, 1851, and announces an editorial policy that would

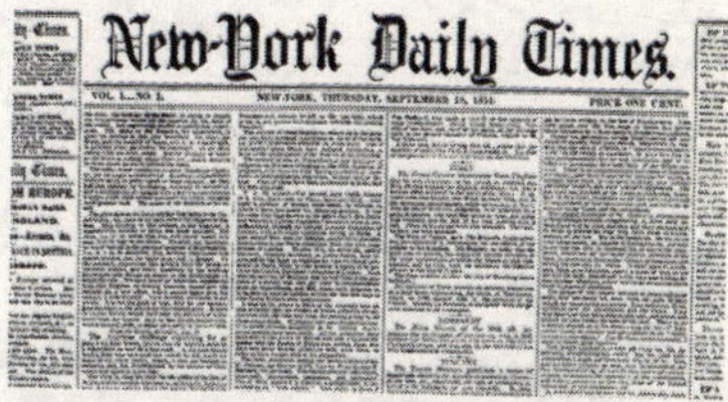

New-York Daily Times.

VOL. I....NO. 1. NEW-YORK, THURSDAY, SEPTEMBER 18, 1851. PRICE ONE CENT.

First Issue of The New York Daily Times

emphasize accurate reporting and moderation of opinion and expression. The newspaper's founders, Henry Jarvis Raymond and George Jones, in the first issue announce : "We publish today the first issue of *the New-York Daily Times*, and we intend to issue it every morning (Sundays excepted) for an indefinite number of years to come." The newspaper began publishing a Sunday edition in April of

1861.The paper's iconic slogan, "All the News That's Fit to Print", is coined in 1896 by Adolph S. Ochs, who acquires the publication in the same year.

1852 Roget's Thesaurus In 1852, Peter Mark Roget eclipses a rich tradition of topically based dictionaries with the publication of his *Thesaurus of English Words and Phrases, Classified and Arranged so as to Facilitate the Expression of Ideas.* Based on intuition as much as on specific linguistic principles, Roget's book has been a bestseller ever since and is one of the most widely used reference works ever published.

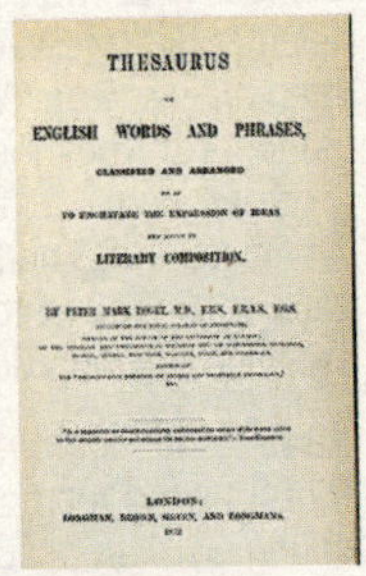
THESAURUS

ENGLISH WORDS AND PHRASES,

LITERARY COMPOSITION.

LONDON:

First Edition of Roget's Thesaurus

1854 John Snow's Cholera Map An independent-minded physician uses empirical methods to identify the source of a

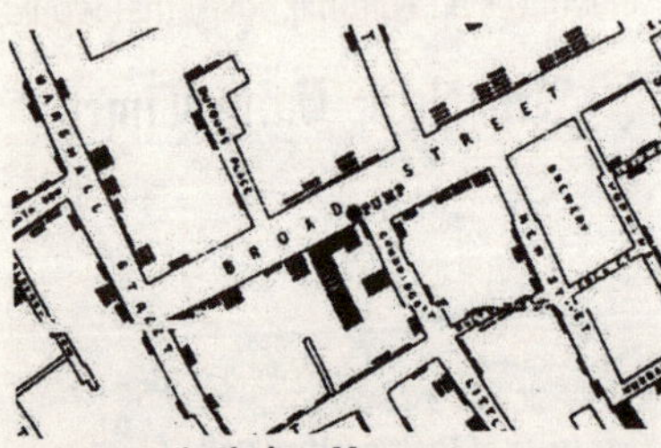

John Snow's Cholera Map

deadly cholera outbreak, thereby revolutionizing theories about the way that some diseases are transmitted. His findings prompt sweeping changes in public health and help to establish the new life-saving field of epidemiology.

1854-63 First Underground Train System The first subway system was proposed for London by Charles Pearson, a city solicitor, as part of a city-improvement plan shortly after the opening of the Thames Tunnel in 1843. The London Underground, which opened in 1863, was the world's first underground railway system. More than 30,000 passengers tried out the Tube on the opening day and it was hailed by the *Times* as "the great engineering triumph of the day".

1861 Fort Sumter Telegram The commander of a bombarded Army fort in Charleston Harbor sends a hurried message to the Secretary of War in Washington, informing him of his garrison's surrender. It means that Confederacy has staged an attack against the United States. The War Between the States has begun.

1863 Emancipation Proclamation From 1 January 1863, President Abraham Lincolon declares free all slaves residing in territory that is in rebellion against the federal government. The Emancipation Proclamation doesn't outlaw slavery, but it shows that the Civil War is being fought over slavery and the Confederates will have to pay a price for their assaults against the Union.

1868 Alaska Purchase Cheque After many years of negotiations with the Tsar, the United States buy Russia's huge

Alaska Purchase Cheque

frozen chunk of North America for two cents per acre, leaving some Americans to question if Alaska is worth that much. But the cheque is, as they say, in the mail - for more than a year.

1869 War and Peace *War and Peace*

(1869) is a novel by Russian writer Leo Tolstoy. Serialized between 1865 and 1867, it was published in book form in 1869 and has since been recognized as a masterpiece of world literature.

1878 Phonograph The phonograph was developed as a result of Thomas Edison's work on two other inventions, the telegraph and the telephone. In 1877, Edison was working on a machine that would transcribe telegraphic messages through indentations on paper tape, which could later be sent over the telegraph repeatedly.This development led Edison to speculate that a telephone message could also be recorded in a similar fashion. The patent on the phonograph was issued on February 19, 1878. The invention was highly original.

1895 Alfred Nobel's Will Alfred Nobel is remembered as the Swedish fellow who instituted the famous annual prizes. But had it not been for his confused and incomplete last will and testament, Nobel's name might be remembered differently – because he is also the inventor of dynamite who became rich on the development of lethal explosives. Regardless of his motivation for writing it, Nobel's rambling, four-page third and final will ultimately set the annual prizes into motion by stating the bulk of his money be invested in a fund the interest of which "shall be annual distributed in the form of prizes to those who, during the preceding year, shall have conferred the greatest benefit to mankind."

Testament

Alfred Nobel's Will

1899 The Interpretation of Dreams What are the most common dreams and why do we have them? What does a dream about death mean? What do dreams of swimming, failing, or flying symbolize? First published by Sigmund Freud in 1899, *The Interpretation of Dreams* considers why we dream and what it means in the larger picture of our psychological lives.

1905 Alfred Binet's IQ test With the 30-question intelligence test, "gauged to what would be 'normally' expected at certain ages," the lawyer-turned-psychologist Alfred Binet along with collaborator Theodore Simon create a test that leads to the Binet-Simon scale for measuring intelligence. Binet publishes the scale in 1905 in a journal he founded and edited called *L'Annee psychologique*. The scale becomes widely used, and a version is still in use today.

1912 Sinking of the Titanic On the night of 14 April 1912, the cramped message room of the largest and most luxurious vessel afloat turns into a maelstrom of frantic wireless activity as two young telegraphists issue a flurry of desperate distress calls - the unsinkable ship has struck an iceberg and she is going down.

The Titanic

1916 Sykes - Picot Agreement Even before the final outcome of the Great War has been determined, Great Britain, France and Russia secretly discuss how

Map Signed by Sykes and Picot

they will carve up the Middle East into 'spheres of influence' once the Ottoman Empire is defeated. Their controversial secret treaty will alter the geography of the region for decades to come.

1917 Balfour Declaration A letter written by British Foreign Secretary Arthur Balfour to Lionel Walter Rothschild–a prominent Jewish leader–in which he expresses the British government's support for a Jewish homeland in Palestine. The long-term effects of the Balfour Declaration, and the British government's involvement in Palestinian affairs, are felt even today.

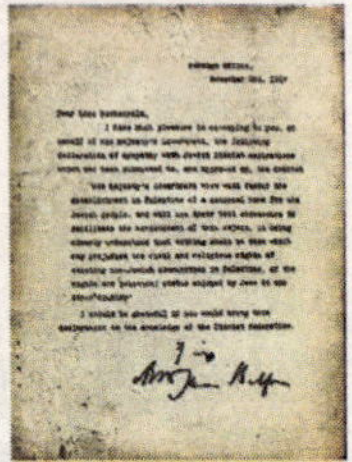
Balfour Declaration

1917 The Zimmermann Telegram After British code-breakers discover a secret German plot against the still- neutral United States, and Germany's own ambassador confirms the telegram's authenticity, it pushes America to join the Allied cause in the Great War.

1918 Wilson's 14 Points Speaking before a joint session of Congress, US President Woodrow Wilson offers his high-minded and detailed plan for ending World War I and establishing a new international order that can ensure postwar peace.

1919 19th Amendment After eight decades of struggle by women suffragists, an all-male Congress finally passes legislation for a constitutional amendment forbidding the federal government or the states from abridging the right of US citizens to vote based on gender, and it is ratified - yet women are still excluded from an historic signing ceremony.

1919 Treaty of Versailles Signed in June 1919 at the Palace of Versailles in Paris at the end of World War I, it codifies peace terms between the victorious Allies and Germany. It holds Germany responsible for starting the war and imposes harsh penalties in terms of loss of territory, massive reparations payments and demilitarization.

1920 Hitler's 25-Point Programme In February 1920, Hitler presents a 25-point Programme to a Nazi Party meeting. In the meeting, Nazi Party members publicly declare their intention to segregate Jews from "Aryan" society and to abrogate Jews' political, legal and civil rights.

1922 1922 Tutankhamun's Tomb King Tutankhamun ruled Egypt as pharaoh for

Carter and an Egyptian workman examine the third (innermost) coffin made of solid gold, inside the case of the second coffin

10 years until his death at age 19, around 1324 B.C. Although his rule was notable for reversing the tumultuous religious reforms of his father, Pharaoh Akhenaten, Tutankhamun's legacy was largely negated by his successors. He was barely known to the modern world until 1922, when British archaeologist Howard Carter chiseled through a doorway and entered the boy pharaoh's tomb, which had remained sealed for more than 3,200 years. The tomb's vast hoard of artifacts and treasure, intended to accompany the king into the afterlife, revealed an incredible amount about royal life in ancient Egypt, and quickly made King Tut the world's most famous pharaoh.

1929-31 Empire State Building Conceived and built according to masterful plans, the tallest building of its day shoots up to become the world's most famous skyscraper - an architectural marvel and astonishing feat of engineering and construction that remains an American icon.

Empire State Building

1930 The Salt Satyagraha Led by Mahatma Gandhi, 78 people start the Salt Satyagraha on March 12, 1930, from Gandhi's Sabarmati Ashram. It is a part of Mahatma Gandhi's non-violent protest against the British monopoly over the production of salt. The march ends on April 5, 1930, in Dandi where Gandhi defies the salt law by picking a lump of salt. After this, millions of people break the salt law as salt depots are raided everywhere and the manufacture of salt is undertaken. In response, the British

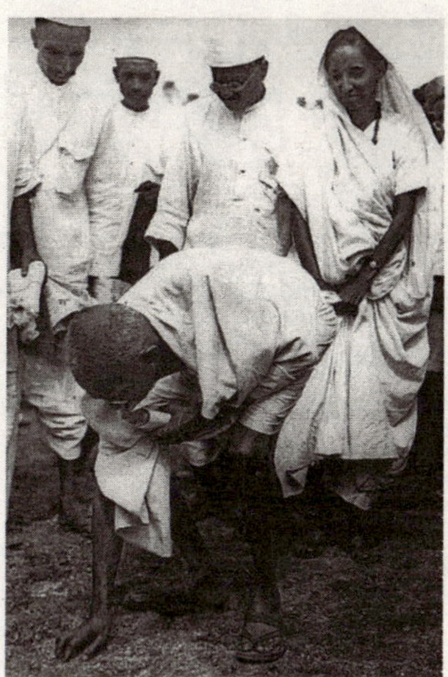

Gandhi Picking Salt at Dandi Beach at the Culmination of the Salt March

government arrests more than 95,000 people by March 31. After making salt at Dandi, Gandhi heads to Dharasana salt works and is arrested on May 5, 1930, and taken to the Yerwada central prison. But the salt satyagraha spreads nationwide, becoming the first call for civil disobedience and thus, one of the most important chapters of India's Independence struggle.

1935 Charles Richter's seismic scale Richter is a theoretical physicist who drifts into seismology to make it his calling. He starts by measuring earthquakes to find their location, then discovers that the shaking from a quake reduces as you get further from the site. This in turn leads to his development of a simple scale to quantify the amount of energy released by a quake, which he first refers to as a 'magnitude'. Richter begins using his scale in 1932 and publishes it as a paper in the *Bulletin of the Seismologi-*

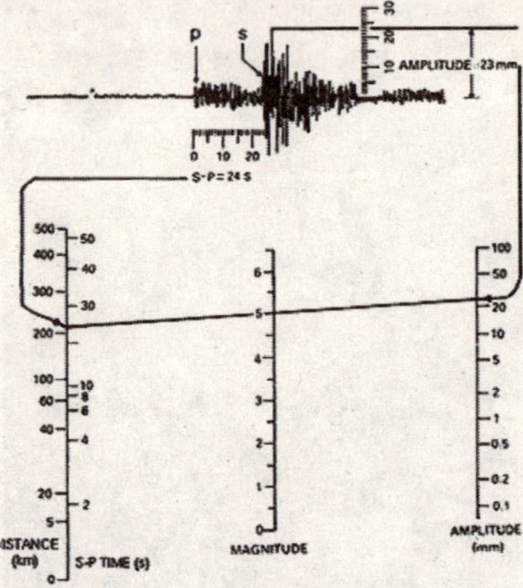

Richter Scale

cal Society of America in 1935, where it seems to have caught on.

1936 Edward VIII's Instrument of Abdication After ruling for less than one year, Edward VIII becomes the first English monarch to voluntarily abdicate the throne. He chooses to abdicate after the British government, public, and the Church of England condemn his decision to marry the American divorcée Wallis Warfield Simpson.

1938 Munich Agreement In an attempt to forestall an immediate European war, Prime Minister Chamberlain of Great Britain sign an agreement with Germany, France, and Italy, allowing the Nazi annexation of a German speaking part of Czechoslovakia (the Sudetenland).The ceded territory contains military emplacements designed to repel a German attack. The agreement strengthens the German military position and fails to halt a war.

1941 Declaration of War Against Japan In the wake of Japan's surprise attack on Pearl Harbor, President Franklin D. Roosevelt crafts one of the most effective speeches in American history, declaring, 'December 7, 1941 - a date that will live in infamy... The facts of yesterday and today speak for themselves. The people of the United States have already formed their opionions and well understand the implications to the very life and safety of our nation.'

1942 Manhattan Project Notebook The Manhattan Project is a highly secret effort to build an atomic bomb by the US. On December 2, 1942, a group of distinguished physicists, working under top-secret conditions in an unpretentious laboratory at the University of Chicago, take a crucial step towards this goal: they create the world's first controlled, self-sustaining nuclear chain reaction.

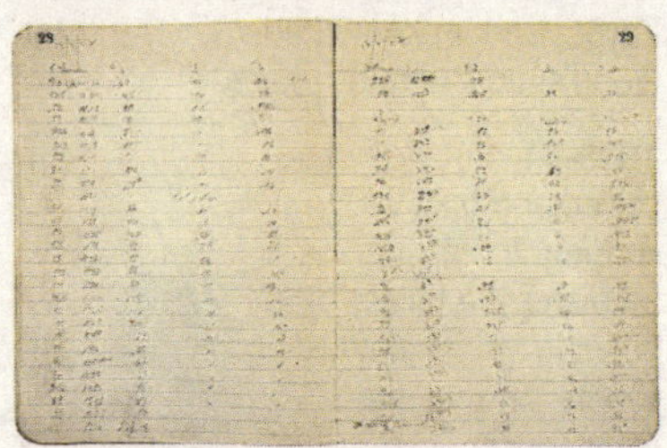

Manhattan Project Notebook

1942 Wannsee Protocol A select group of Hitler's henchmen meet at a mansion outside Berlin to coordinate plans for the implementation of the 'Final Solution of the Jewish Question', taking special security measures to cover their tracks. But an incriminating document survives.

1942-44 Anne Frank's Diary Anne Frank is a teenage Jewish girl who keeps a diary while her family is in hiding from the Nazis during World War II. For two years, she and seven others live in a "Secret Annex" in Amsterdam before being discovered and sent to concentration camps. Anne dies in the Bergen-Belsen camp in 1945. Frank's father is the family's

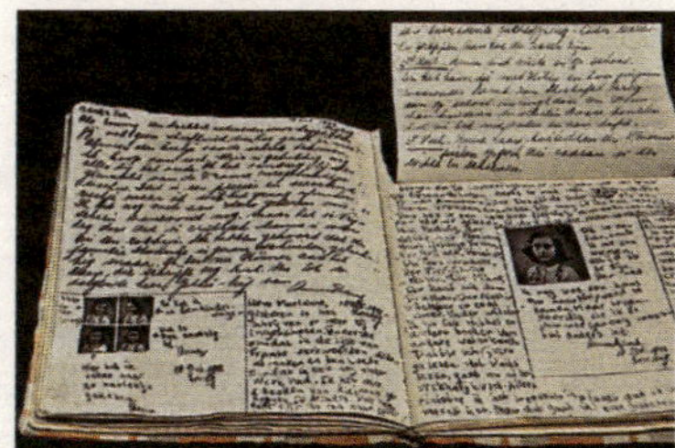

Diary of Anne Frank

sole survivor. He decides to publish the diary, which gives a detailed account of Anne's thoughts, feelings and experiences while she is in hiding. It has been an international bestseller for decades and a key part of Holocaust education programmes.

1945 Germany's Instrument of Surrender Solemn-faced generals from the victors and the vanquished convene at a table in Gen. Dwight D. Eisenhower's headquar-

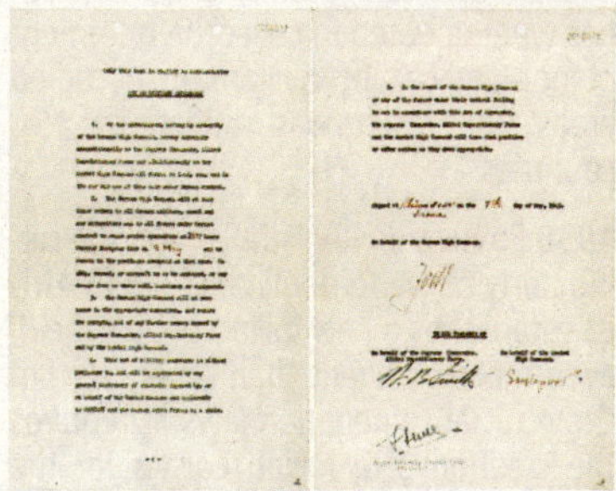

Germany's Instrument of Surrender

ters in northeastern France for Germany's unconditional surrender. But after the document signing, the Soviets demand a more formal surrender in Berlin the next day.

1945 United Nations Charter In the closing weeks of World War II, representatives of 46 governments gather in San Francisco to draft the charter for an effective replacement for the League of Nations - an international body that will help to maintain peace and security in the world.

1946-49 George Orwell's 1984 A determined author - sick, impoverished and pursued by demons - struggles in a remote Scottish farmhouse to complete his bleak dystopian novel about life in a totalitarian state. 'BIG BROTHER IS WATCHING YOU', he warns. The future has arrived.

1947 Marshall Plan Addressing Europe's utter devastation from World War II, a former US Army military commander turned Secretary of State proposes an ambitious blueprint for European recovery that entails unprecedented financial aid from the United States.

1947 Indian Independence Act Unable to overcome the resistance to their governance due to the nonviolent freedom movement led by Mahatma Gandhi, the British finally decide to bow down and grant independence to India. The final stages of transfer of power begin with Lord Mountbatten, the Governor-General, announcing "June 3 Plan". Lord Listowel, who was last Secretary of States for India and a minister in British cabinet, introduces the Indian Independence Bill in the British Parliament on July 3, 1947, and the Bill is passed on July 16, 1947. The Royal assent is granted on July 17,

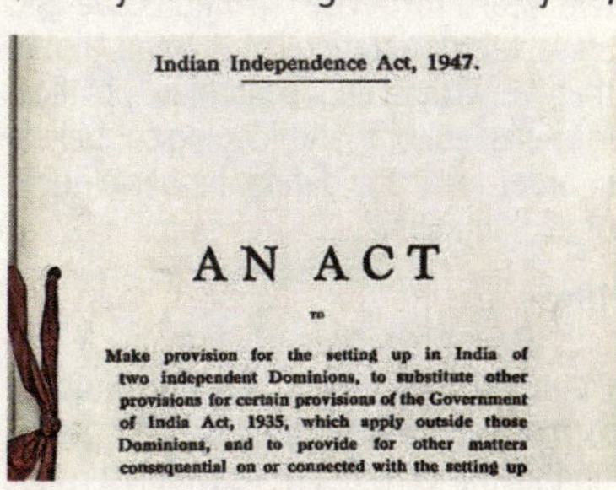

Indian Independence Act, 1947.

AN ACT

TO

Make provision for the setting up in India of two independent Dominions, to substitute other provisions for certain provisions of the Government of India Act, 1935, which apply outside those Dominions, and to provide for other matters consequential on or connected with the setting up

Indian Independence Act

1947, enforcing the Indian Independence Act, 1947. The act creates two new independent dominions; India and Pakistan. The Bengal and Punjab provinces are partitioned between the two new countries. The Act repeals the use of 'Emperor of India' as a title for the British Crown and ends all existing treaties with the princely states. Lord Mountbatten continues as Governor-General and Jawaharlal Nehru is appointed India's first Prime Minister, Muhammad Ali Jinnah becomes Pakistan's Governor-General and Liaquat Ali Khan its Prime Minster. The 15th August 1947 has since become celebrated as India's Independence Day.

1948 Universal Declaration of Human Rights Activists from different nationalities and backgrounds work together for

Eleanor Roosevelt Holding the English Version of the Universal Declaration of Human Rights

two years to devise an unprecedented universal declaration of human rights that will transcend parochial, political, religious, cultural and ideological beliefs in order to clearly define the basic rights of all humankind.

1949 Adoption of the Indian Constitution B.R. Ambedkar, Chairman of the Drafting Committee of the Constitution, formally introduces the Draft Constitution in the constituent Assembly on 4th November 1948. This 'formidable' (as Ambedkar referred to it) document, containing 315 Articles and 8 Schedules, is the culmination of the Assembly's work, particularly its committees, that began on 9th December 1946. From this point onwards, all of the Assembly's debates – 114 out of 165 sittings – centres around this Draft. These debates mark the most intense phase of Indian constitution-making. After around 10 days of general discussions on the Draft, the Assembly on 15th November 1948 begins a more focused exercise of debating and considering amendments around each Article of the Draft Constitution – a process that would go on till 17th October 1949. The Assembly finally adopts the Constitution on 26th November 1949 which comes into effect on 26th January 1950.

1949 Geneva Convention In the wake of World War II's unparalleled atrocities against non-combatants, existing treaties were updated to cover the treatment of non-combatant civilians in occupied areas. The result was ratified by 196 countries.

1950 Population Registration Act The ruling party of white-dominated South Africa establishes a new 'pillar' of apartheid, even more stringent than America's Jim Crow racial segregation laws. It requires the creation of a racial register for the nation's entire population, represented in a unique document for each individual.

1953 DNA On March 19, 1953, an eager Francis Crick, still reeling with excitement from his lab work, sits down to write his son a letter. He cuts right to the chase. "Jim Watson and I have probably made a most important discovery," he tells Michael, then 12 years old and studying at Bedales, a boarding school in southern England.Crick and James Watson, a fellow biologist at Cavendish Laboratory at

Watson and Crick with the DNA Model

University of Cambridge, had discovered the double-helix structure of DNA. In the endearing seven-page note, written clearly but with high expectations of his young son, Crick describes DNA as being "like a code" and explained how its bases—guanine, adenine, thymine and cytosine–pair up to hold together two twisting strands of molecules. He also spells out how DNA replicates itself. "Read this carefully so that you understand it. When you come home we will show you the model."

1957 Treaty of Rome The Treaty of Rome, which is signed in 1957 by the original six member states, lays much of the groundwork for the EU as it is today. It establishes the European Economic Community and Euratom, which are later brought together with the European Coal and Steel Community to form the European Communities, and later the European Union.

1958 Airline 'Black Box' Flight Data Recorder Although there is no "clear, single inventor" of the flight data recorder, many trace its origin to a certain fuel chemist named David Warren, then working for the Australian Department of Defence, who gets to daydreaming one day during a meeting about a plane crash. "He lets his mind wander to a wire recorder he'd recently seen and how, if it had been in the cockpit, that might have helped them determine if the plane had been hijacked." Warren's epiphany is followed by "a long and onerous odyssey over five years, beset with indifference and bureaucracy, strongly flavoured with gumption and stick-to-it-iveness" that yields a prototype in 1958. But Warren and colleagues neither file for a patent nor profit much from the invention, which they call the "Flight Memory."

Dave Warren with BlackBox Prototype

1961 John F. Kennedy's Inaugural Address On January 20, 1961, President John F. Kennedy delivers his inaugural address in which he announces that "we shall pay any price, bear any burden, meet any hardship, support any friend, oppose any foe to assure the survival and success of liberty."It is a meticulously crafted piece of oratory that dramatically announced a generational change in the White House and called on the nation to combat "tyranny, poverty, disease, and war itself." Kennedy wrote his thoughts in his nearly indecipherable longhand on a yellow legal pad. The climax of the speech and its most memorable phrase, "Ask not what your country can do for you–ask what you can do for your country," was honed down from a thought about sacrifice that Kennedy had long held in his mind and had expressed in various ways in campaign speeches.

1962 Beatles' Recording Contract with EMI The Beatles is an English rock and pop group formed in Liverpool in 1960. The group consists of John Lennon, Paul McCartney, George Harrison and Ringo Starr. In 1962, the group appoints Brian Epstein manager, and he negotiates a record contract with EMI's George Martin, which would revolutionize music.

1963 Martin Luther King, Jr., "I Have a Dream' On August 28, 1963, in front of a crowd of nearly 250,000 people spread

Martin Luther King Jr.

across the National Mall in Washington, D.C., the Baptist preacher and civil rights leader Rev. Dr. Martin Luther King, Jr. delivers his now-famous "I Have a Dream" speech from the steps of the Lincoln Memorial. A call for equality and freedom, it becomes one of the defining moments of the civil rights movement and one of the most iconic speeches in American history. The one-day event both protested racial discrimination and encouraged the passage of civil rights legislation.

1964 Quotations from Chairman Mao Tse-tung The ageing Chairman of China's Communist Party issues a small primer of selected inspirational quotations for soldiers that helps to fuel the cultural Revolution and quickly becomes the best-selling book in the world-Mao's *Little Red Book*.

1964 Gulf of Tonkin Resolution A joint resolution of US Congress authorizes President Lyndon B. Johnson to use conventional military force in southeast Asia, thereby providing legal cover for the US to wage in Vietnam - but the document is based on distortion and lies, showing that Congress and the American people were misled.

1969 Apollo 11 Flight Plan In preparation for the first manned moon landing, NASA produces a detailed Flight Plan

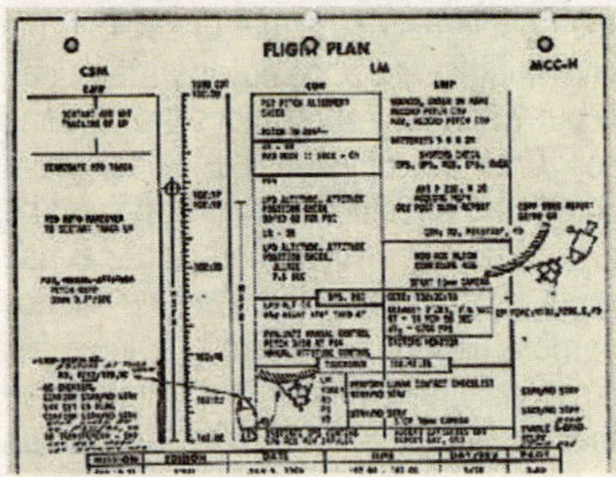

Apollo 11 Flight Plan

featuring a minute-by-minute timeline of activities by the spaceship and its three-member crew, from the launch at Cape Kennedy to the capsule's scheduled splashdown in Pacific four days later - a meticulous astronautical manual for one of the greatest technological achievements in history.

1971 The *Pentagon Papers* *The New York Times* begins publishing the *Pentagon Papers* - the Defense Department's secret history of the Vietnam War.

Officially called *The History of the U.S. Decision Making Process on Vietnam*, the *Pentagon Papers* discloses closely guarded communiques, recommendations, and decisions concerning the US military role in Vietnam during the Kennedy and John-

The New York Times

Tricia Nixon Takes Vows in Garden at White House

Vietnam Archive: Pentagon Study Traces 3 Decades of Growing U. S. Involvement

Vast Review of War Took a Year

New York Times' First Coverage of the Pentagon Papers

son administrations, along with the diplomatic phase in the Eisenhower years. The publication of the papers creates a nationwide furore, with congressional and diplomatic reverberations as all branches of the government debate over what constitute "classified" material and how much should be made public. On June 30, the Supreme Court rules that the *Times* had the right to publish the material.

1972 The Watergate Scandal The Watergate scandal is uncovered in a series of 1972 investigative articles by Carl Bernstein and Bob Woodward that eventually earns the *Washington Post* a Pulitzer. "Five Held in Plot to Bug Democratic Offices Here," says the headline at the bottom of page one in the *Washington Post* on Sunday, June 18, 1972. The story reports that a team of burglars had been arrested inside the offices of the Democratic National Committee in the Watergate office complex in Washington.

So begins the chain of events that would convulse Washington for two years, and change American politics forever. On August 9, 1974, facing likely impeachment for his role in covering up the scandal, Nixon becomes the only U.S. president to resign.

June 19, 1972

GOP Security Aide Among 5 Arrested In Bugging Affair

The Washington Post

Nixon Resigns

Ford Assumes Presidency Today

The Nixon Years

Washington Post's Coverage of the Watergate Scandal

1976 Apple Computer Company Apple Company is founded on April 1, 1976, by college dropouts Steve Jobs and Steve Wozniak, who bring to the new company a vision of changing the way people view computers. They want to make computers small enough for people to have them in their homes or offices. Their original partnership agreement and incorporation papers establish a venture that will change the world.

1981 Internet Protocol In 1981 Jon Postel writes a 45-page technical document titled 'RFC: 791' - the Internet Protocol for short - which builds on the work of his fellow computer scientists Robert Kahn and Vinton Cerf, and it is approved by the Internet Engineering Task Force as the Transfer Control Protocol (TCP/IP).

There already exists a means of sending messages from one computer to another via a small network of linked computers. However, that activity is originally intended to carry out only a limited set of activities. All of network's members are involved in government work. Under Postel's TCP/IP, the 'Internet' is transformed into a network connecting networks that freely move data around, unchanged and unexamined, according to basic standards that give it structure and make it function efficiently.

1990 Two Plus Four Treaty On 12 September 1990, the foreign ministers of the Federal Republic of Germany, the GDR, France, Russia, the UK and the USA signed the treaty that sealed the foreign policy aspects of German reunification. Until the very last minute it remained unclear whether the treaty would be adopted.

1991 First Website The beginning of the Web as a publicly available service on the Internet arrives on August 6, 1991, when Berners-Lee publishes the first-ever website. Fittingly, the site is about the World Wide Web project, describing the Web and how to use it. Hosted at CERN on Berners-Lee's NeXT computer, the site's URL was http://info.cern.ch. Berners-Lee doesn't try to cash in on his invention and rejects CERN's call to patent his Web technology. He wants the Web to be open and free so it could expand and evolve as rapidly as possible. As he later said, "Had the technology been proprietary, and in my total control, it would probably not have taken off. You can't propose that something be a universal space and at the same time keep control of it."

World Wide Web

First Website

2001 September 11 Attacks On September 11, 2001, 19 militants associated with the Islamic extremist group al Qaeda hijack four airplanes and carry out suicide attacks against targets in the United States. Two of the planes are flown into the twin towers of the World Trade Center in New York City, a third plane hits the Pentagon in Arlington, Virginia, just outside Washington, D.C., and the fourth plane crashes in a field in Shanksville, Pennsylvania. Almost 3,000 people are killed during the 9/11 terrorist attacks, which triggers major U.S. initiatives to combat terrorism and defines the presidency of George W. Bush.Osama bin Laden, the mastermind behind the September 11 attacks, remains at large until May 2, 2011, when he is finally tracked down and killed by US forces at a hideout in Abbottabad, Pakistan.

September 11 Attacks

2002 Iraq War Resolution In the frenzied aftermath of the 9/11 attacks, the Bush administration wins a joint resolution from Congress which spells out the authorization for military action against Iraq. Viewed in hindsight, the document's case for war may not appear as strong as it did then.

2006 First Tweet Ever The origins of Twitter come out of a brainstorming session at the podcasting company Odeo. The initial concept is to share short mes-

just setting up my twttr

First Tweet Ever

sages via SMS text messaging with a small group. Jack Dorsey is the primary designer of what was then code-named "twttr" and sends the first message at 9:50am on March 21st, 2006 - "just setting up my twttr." On July 15, 2006, the San Francisco-based company officially releases Twttr—later changed to Twitter—its short messaging service (SMS) for groups, to the public.

2007 Wikileaks Prompted by the failure of the mainstream news media to report important, in-depth information to the public, a shadowy shoestring alliance of brazen computer nerds takes matters into their own hands and revolutionizes the nature of investigative journalism in the digital age.

2011 3D Map of the Universe Using light from 14,000 distant yet powerful cosmic beacons, astronomers piece together the largest and most detailed 3-D map of the ancient universe. Previous versions plotted the locations of galaxies within 7

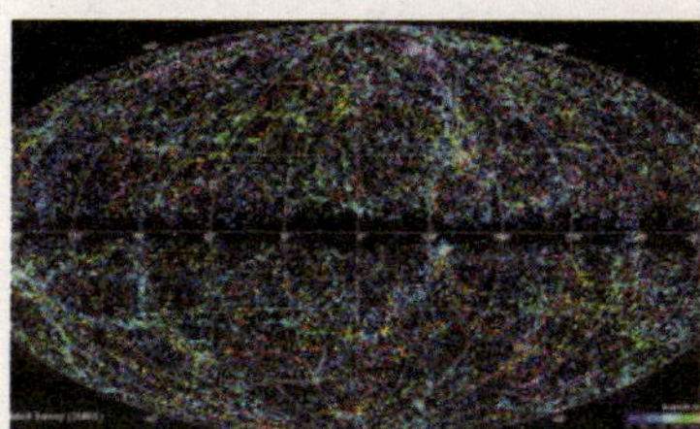

3D Map of the Universe

billion light-years of Earth. The new version, however, charts clouds of hydrogen in a swathe between 10 billion and 12 billion light-years away – farther in distance and deeper in time than any 3-D map before it. The hydrogen clouds could help answer some of astronomers' more profound questions about the universe, including the nature of dark energy.

2013 Edward Snowden Files In June 2013, *The Guardian* reports the first leak based on top-secret documents that then 29-year-old Edward Snowden stole from the National Security Agency. That leak would certainly not be the last. In the years since, journalists have released more than 7,000 top-secret documents that Snowden entrusted them with, which some believe is less than 1% of the entire archive.

He will go down in history as one of America's most consequential whistleblowers, alongside Daniel Ellsberg and Bradley Manning. He is instrumental in handing over material from one of the world's most secretive organisations – the NSA.

2019 COVID-19 The first documented coronavirus pandemic in history. The novel human coronavirus disease COVID-19 becomes the fifth documented pandemic since the 1918 flu pandemic. COVID-19 is first reported in Wuhan, China, and subsequently spreads worldwide. The coronavirus is officially named severe acute respiratory syndrome coronavirus 2 (SARS-CoV-2) by the International Committee on Taxonomy of Viruses based on phylogenetic analysis. SARS-CoV-2 is believed to be a spillover of an animal coronavirus and later adapts the ability of human-to-human transmission. Because the virus is highly contagious, it rapidly spreads and continuously evolves in the human population.

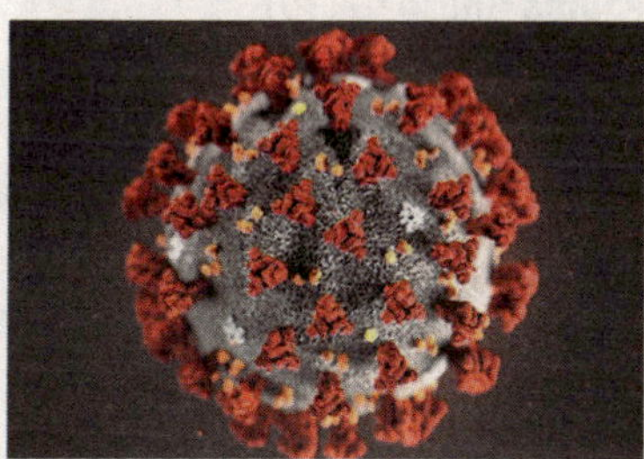

A Model of Corornavirus

Awards and Honours

Padma Awards 2021

Padma Vibhushan (7)

Shinzo Abe (Public Affairs-Japan); S P Balasubramaniam ((Posthumous) Art, Tamil Nadu); Dr. Belle Monappa Hegde (Medicine, Karnataka); Narinder Singh Kapany ((Posthumous) Science and Engineering, United States of America); Maulana Wahiduddin Khan (Others-Spiritualism, Delhi); B. B. Lal (Others - Archaeology, Delhi); Sudarshan Sahoo (Art, Odisha).

Shinzo Abe

Padma Bhushan (10)

Ms. Krishnan Nair Shantakumari Chithra (Art, Kerala); Tarun Gogoi ((Posthumous) Public Affairs, Asom); Chandrashekhar Kambara (Literature and Education, Karnataka); Sumitra Mahajan (Public Affairs, Madhya Pradesh); Nripendra Misra (Civil Service,Uttar Pradesh); Ram Vilas Paswan ((Posthumous)— Public Affairs, Bihar); Keshubhai Patel ((Posthumous) Public Affairs, Gujarat); Kalbe Sadiq ((Posthumous) Others-Spiritualism, Uttar Pradesh); Rajnikant Devidas Shroff (Trade and Industry, Maharashtra); Tarlochan Singh (Public Affairs, Haryana).

K S Chithra

Rajnikant Devidas Shroff

Padma Shri (102)

Gulfam Ahmed (Art, Uttar Pradesh); Ms. P. Anitha (Sports, Tamil Nadu); Rama Swamy Annavarapu (Art, Andhra Pradesh); Subbu Arumugam (Art, Tamil Nadu); Prakasarao Asavadi (Literature and Education, Andhra Pradesh); Bhuri Bai (Art, Madhya Pradesh); Radhe Shyam Barle (Art, Chhattisgarh); Dharma Narayan Barma (Literature and Education, West Bengal); Ms. Lakhimi Baruah (Social Work, Asom); Biren Kumar Basak (Art, West Bengal); Rajni Bector (Trade and Industry, Punjab); Peter Brook (Art, United Kingdom); Ms. Sangkhumi Bualchhuak (Social Work, Mizoram); Gopiram Bargayn Burabhakat (Art, Assam); Bijoya Chakravarty (Public Affairs, Assam); Sujit Chattopadhyay (Literature and Education, West Bengal); Jagdish Chaudhary ((Posthumous) Social Work, Uttar Pradesh); Tsultrim Chonjor

P Anitha

Subbu Arumugam

Lakhimi Baruah

Rajni Bector

(Social Work, Ladakh); Ms. Mouma Das (Sports, West Bengal); Srikant Datar (Literature and Education, United States of America); Narayan Debnath (Art, West Bengal); Chutni Devi (Social Work, Jharkhand); Ms. Dulari Devi (Art Bihar); Ms. Radhe Devi (Art, Manipur); Ms. Shanti Devi (Social Work, Odisha); Wayan Dibia (Art, Indonesia); Dadudan Gadhavi (Literature & Education, Gujarat); Parshuram Atmaram Gangavane (Art, Maharashtra); Jai Bhagwan Goyal (Literature and Education, Haryana); Jagadish Chandra Halder (Literature and Education, West Bengal); Mangal Singh Hazowary (Literature and Education, Assam); Ms. Anshu Jamsenpa (Sports, Arunachal Pradesh); Ms. Purnamasi Jani (Art, Odisha); Matha B. Manjamma Jogati (Art, Karnataka); Damodaran Kaithapram (Art, Kerala); Namdeo C Kamble (Literature and Education, Maharashtra); Maheshbhai & Shri Nareshbhai Kanodia (Duo) * ((Posthumous) Art Gujarat); Rajat Kumar Kar (Literature and Education, Odisha); Rangasami Lakshminarayana Kashyap (Literature and Education, Karnataka); Ms. Prakash Kaur (Social Work, Punjab); Nicholas Kazanas (Literature and Education, Greece); K Kesavasamy (Art, Puducherry), Ghulam Rasool Khan (Art, Jammu and Kashmir); Lakha Khan (Art, Rajasthan); Ms. Sanjida Khatun (Art, Bangladesh); Vinayak Vishnu Khedekar (Art, Goa); Ms. Niru Kumar (Social Work, Delhi); Ms. Lajwanti (Art, Punjab); Rattan Lal (Science and Engineering, United States of America); Ali Manikfan (Others-Grassroots Innovation, Lakshadweep); Ramachandra Manjhi (Art, Bihar); Dulal Manki (Art, Asom); Nanadro B Marak (Others- Agriculture, Meghalaya); Rewben Mashangva (Art, Manipur); Chandrakant Mehta (Literature and Education, Gujarat); Dr. Rattan Lal Mittal (Medicine, Punjab); Madhavan Nambiar (Sports, Kerala); Shyam Sundar Paliwal (Social Work, Rajasthan); Dr. Chandrakant Sambhaji Pandav (Medicine, Delhi); Dr. J N Pande ((Posthumous) Medicine, Delhi); Solomon Pappaiah (Literature and Education- Journalism Tamil Nadu); Ms. Pappammal (Others-Agriculture, Tamil Nadu); Dr. Krishna Mohan Pathi (Medicine, Odisha); Ms. Jaswantiben Jamnadas Popat (Trade and Industry, Maharashtra); Girish Prabhune (Social Work, Maharashtra); Nanda Prusty (Literature and Education, Odisha); K K Ramachandra Pulavar (Art, Kerala); Balan Putheri (Literature and Education, Kerala); Ms. Birubala Rabha (Social Work, Assam); Kanaka Raju (Art, Telangana); Ms. Bombay Jayashri Ramnath (Art, Tamil Nadu); Satyaram Reang (Art, Tripura); Dr. Dhananjay Diwakar Sagdeo (Medicine, Kerala); Ashok Kumar Sahu (Medicine, Uttar Pradesh); Dr. Bhupendra Kumar Singh Sanjay (Medicine, Uttarakhand); Ms. Sindhutai Sapkal (Social Work, Maharashtra); Chaman Lal Sapru ((Posthumous) Literature and Education, Jammu and Kashmir); Roman Sarmah (Literature and Education-Journalism, Assam); Imran Shah (Literature and Education, Asom); Prem Chand Sharma (Others-Agriculture, Uttarakhand);

Rattan Lal

Prakash Kaur

Niru Kumar

Arjun Singh Shekhawat (Literature and Education, Rajasthan); Ram Yatna Shukla (Literature and Education,Uttar Pradesh); Jitender Singh Shunty (Social Work, Delhi); Kartar Paras Ram Singh (Art, Himachal Pradesh); Kartar Singh (Art, Punjab); Dr. Dilip Kumar Singh (Medicine, Bihar); Chandra Shekhar Singh (Others-Agriculture, Uttar Pradesh); Ms. Sudha Hari Narayan Singh (Sports, Uttar Pradesh); Virender Singh (Sports, Haryana); Ms. Mridula Sinha ((Posthumous) Literature and Education,Bihar); K C Sivasankar ((Posthumous) Art ,Tamil Nadu); Guru Maa Kamali Soren (Social Work, West Bengal); Marachi Subburaman (Social Work, Tamil Nadu); P Subramanian ((Posthumous) Trade and Industry, Tamil Nadu); Ms. Nidumolu Sumathi (Art, Andhra Pradesh); Kapil Tiwari (Literature and Education, Madhya Pradesh); Father Vallés ((Posthumous) Literature and Education,Spain); Dr. Thiruvengadam Veeraraghavan ((Posthumous) Medicine, Tamil Nadu); Sridhar Vembu (Trade and Industry, Tamil Nadu); K Y Venkatesh (Sports, Karnataka); Ms. Usha Yadav (Literature and Education, Uttar Pradesh); Col Quazi Sajjad Ali Zahir (Public Affairs, Bangladesh).

Sudha Hari Narayan Singh

Film and Music Awards

International

Oscar

Picture: *Nomadland*; **Director: Chloé Zhao** (*Nomadland*); **Actor: Anthony Hopkins** (*The Father*); **Actress: Frances McDormand**(*Nomadland*); **Supporting Actor: Daniel Kaluuya** (*Judas and the Black Messiah)*; **Supporting Actress: Youn Yuh-jung** (*Minari*); **Original Screenplay:** *Promising Young Woman*; **Adapted Screenplay:** *The Father*; **Animated Feature Film:** *Soul;* **International Feature Film:** *Another Round* (**Denmark**); **Documentary Feature:** *My Octopus Teacher;* **Documentary Short Subject:** *Colette;* **Live Action Short Film:** *Two Distant Strangers;* **Animated Short Film:** *If Anything Happens I Love You*; **Original Score :** *Soul*; **Original Song: *"Fight for You"*** (*Judas and the Black Messiah*); **Sound:** *Sound of Metal;* **Production Design:** *Mank;* **Cinematography:** *Mank;* **Makeup and Hairstyling:** *Ma Rainey's Black Bottom;* **Costume Design:** *Ma Rainey's Black Bottom;* **Film Editing:** *Sound of Metal;* **Visual Effects:** *Tenet;* **Jean Hersholt Humanitarian Award: Tyler Perry.**

Usha Yadav

Chloé Zhao

Anthony Hopkins

Grammy Awards 2021

Song of the year: *I Can't Breathe* by Dernst Emile II, H.E.R. and Tiara Thomas; **Pop solo performance:** *Watermelon* by Harry Styles; **Pop duo/group performance:** *Rain on Me* by Lady Gaga and Ariana Grande; **R&B album:** *Bigger Love* by John Legend; **Traditional R&B performance:** *Anything For You* by Ledisi; **Progressive R&B album:** *It is what* *it is* by Thundercat; **R&B song:** *Better Than I Imagined* by Robert Glasper, Meshell Ndeogeocello & Gabriella Wilson; **New artist:** Megan Thee Stallion; **Rap performance:** *Savage* by Megan Thee Stallion featuring Beyonce; **Rap song:** *Savage* by Megan Thee Stallion featuring Beyonce; **Rap album:** King's Disease by Nas; **Melodic rap performance:** Lockdown by Anderson .Paak; **Traditional Pop Vocal Album:** *American Standard* by James Taylor; **Music Video:** *Brown Skin Girl* by Beyonce; **Song Written for Visual Media:** *No Time to Die* by Billie Eilish; **Compilation Soundtrack for Visual Media:** Jojo Rabbit; **Score Soundtrack for Visual media:** Joker by Hildur Guonadottir; **Global Music Album:** *Twice as Tall* by Burna Boy; **Dance Recording:** 10% by Kaytranada featuring Kali Uchis; **Dance/electronic Album:** *Bubba* by Kaytranada; **Rock Album:** *The New Abnormal* by The Strokes; **Best Rock Song:** *Stay High* by Brittany Howard; **Alternative Music Album:** *Fetch the Bolt Cutters* by Fiona Apple; **Country Solo Performance:** *When My Amy Prays* by Vince Gill; **Country Duo/group Performance:** *10,000 Hours* by Dan + Shay & Justin Bieber; **Country album:** *Wildcard* by Miranda Lambert; **Country Song:** *Crowded Table* by Brandi Carlile, Natalie Hemby & Lori McKenna; **New Age Album:** *More Guitar Stories* by Jim "Kimo" West; **Jazz Vocal Album:** *Secrets Are the Best Stories* by Kurt Elling Featuring Danilo Perez; **Improvised Jazz Solo:** *All Blues* by Chick Corea, Soloist Track From: Trilogy 2 (Chick Corea, Christian Mcbride & Brian Blade); **Jazz Instrumental Album:** T*rilogy 2* by Chick Corea, Christian McBride & Brian Blade; **Large Jazz Ensemble Album:** *Data Lords* by Maria Schneider Orchestra; **Latin Jazz Album:** *Four Questions* by Arturo O'farrill & The Afro Latin Jazz Orchestra: **Gospel Performance/song:** *Movin' On* by Jonathan McReynolds & Mali Music

James Taylor

Brittany Howard

Golden Globe Awards

Film (Drama):*Nomadland;* **Film (Musical/Comedy):***Borat Subsequent Movie film*; **Director**: Chloe Zhao (*Nomadland*); **Actress (Drama):** Andra Day (*The United States vs. Billie Holiday);* **Actor(Drama):** Chadwick Boseman (*Ma Rainey's Black Bottom)*; **Actress (Musical/Comedy):** Rosamund Pike (*I Care A Lot*); **Actor (Musical/Comedy):** Sacha Baron Cohen (*Borat Subsequent Movie film*): **Supporting Actress:** Jodie Foster (*The Mauritanian*); **Supporting Actor:** Daniel Kaluuya (*Judas And The Black Messiah*); **Screenplay:** Aaron Sorkin (*The Trial of the Chicago 7*); **Foreign Language Film:** *Minari;* **Animated Feature:** *Soul;* **Original Score:** *Soul*; **Original Song:** 'Io Si (Seen)' (*The Life Ahead*).

Andra Day

Chadwick Boseman

Cannes Film Festival 2021

Palme d'Or: Julia Ducournau (*Titane*, France); **Grand Prix (TIE):** Ashgar Farhadi (*A Hero*, Iran) and Juho Kuosmanen (*Compartment No.6*, Finland); **Director:** Leos Carax Annette (France); **Actress:** Renate Reinsve (*Worst Person in the World*, Norway); **Actor:** Caleb Landry Jones (*Nitram*, US); **Screenplay:** Hamaguchi Ryusuke and Takamasa Oe (*Drive My Car*, Japan); **Jury Prize (TIE):** Shared by Nadav Lapid (*Ahed's Knee*, Israel) and Apichatpong Weerasethakul (*Memoria*, Thailand); **First Film:** Antoneta Kusijanovic (*Murina*, Croatia); **Short Film:** Hong Kong's *All The Crows In The World Tang Yi;* **Short Film Palme d'Or:** *Tian Xia Wu Ya* by Tang Yi; **Special Jury Mention for Short Film:** *Ceu de Agosto* by Jasmin Tenucci.

Julia Ducournau

Caleb Landry Jones

National

Dadasaheb Phalke Award 2019: Rajinikanth

National Film Awards

Feature Film: *Marakkar: Lion of the Arabian Sea* (Malayalam); **Actor** (shared): Manoj Bajpayee (*Bhonsle*, Hindi); Dhanush (*Asuran*, Tamil); **Actress:** Kangana Ranaut (*Panga*, Hindi and *Manikarnika: The Queen of Jhansi*, Hindi); **Supporting Actress:** Pallavi Joshi (*The Tashkent Files*, Hindi); **Supporting Actor:** Vijay Sethupathi (*Super Deluxe*, Tamil); **Director:** Sanjay Puran Singh Chauhan (*Bahattar Hoorain*, Hindi); **Debut Film of a Director:** Mathukutty Xavier (*Helen*, Malayalam); **Child Artist:** Naga Vishal (*KD*, Tamil); **Action Direction:** Vikram Mor (*Avane Srimannarayana*, Kannada); **Choreography:** Raju Sundaram (*Maharishi*, Telugu), **Special Effects:** Siddharth Priyadarshan (*Marakkar: Lion of the Arabian Sea*, Malayalam); **Special Jury Award:** Radhakrishnan Parthiban (*Oththa Seruppu Size 7* (Tamil); **Lyrics:** Prabha Varma (*Kolaambi*, Malayalam); **Music Direction:** D. Imman (*Viswasam*,Tamil); **Background Music:** Prabuddha Banerjee (*Jyeshthoputro*, Bengali); **Make-up Artist:** Ranjith (*Helen*, Malayalam); **Costumes:** Sujith Sudhakaran and V. Sai (*Marakkar: Lion of the Arabian Sea*, Malayalam); **Production Design:** Sunil Nigwekar and Nilesh Wagh (*Anandi Gopal*, Marathi); **Audiography (Location Sound Recordist):** Debajit Gayan (*Iewduh*,Khasi); **Audiography (Re-recordist of final mixed track):** Resul Pookutty (*Oththa Seruppu Size 7*, Tamil); **Screenplay (Original):** Kaushik Ganguly (*Jyeshthoputro,* Bengali), **Screenplay (Adapted):** Srijit Mukherji (*Gumnaami*, Bengali); **Screenplay (Dialogue Writer):** Vivek Ranjan Agnihotri (*The Tashkent Files*, Hindi); **Cinematography:** Gireesh Gangadharan (*Jallikattu*, Malayalam); **Editing:** Navin Nooli (*Jersey*,Telugu), **Children's Film:** *Kastoori* (Hindi); **Film on Environment Conser-**

Manoj Bajpayee

Kangana Ranaut

vation: *Water Burial* (Monpa); **Film on Social Issues:** *Anandi Gopal* (Marathi); **Film on National Integration:** *Tajmahal* (Marathi); **Popular Film Providing Wholesome Entertainment:** *Maharishi* (Telugu); **Female Playback Singer:** Savani Ravindra (*Bardo*, Marathi);

Savani Ravindra

B Praak

Male Playback Singer: B Praak (*Kesari*,Hindi); **Best Films in Each Language: Hindi Film:** *Chhichhore*; **Telugu Film:** *Jersey*; **Malayalam Film:** *Kalla Nottam*; **Tamil Film:** *Asuran*; **Paniya Film:** *Kenjira*, **Mishing Film:** *Anu Ruwad*, **Khasi Film:** *Iewduh*, **Chattisgarhi Film:** *Bhulan the Maze*, **Haryanvi Film:** *Chhoriyan Chhoron Se Kam Nahi Hoti*, **Tulu Film:** *Pingara*, **Punjabi Film:** *Rab Da Radio 2*, **Odia Film:** *Kalira Atita and Sala Budhar Badla* (shared), **Manipuri Film:** *Eigi Kona*; **Marathi Film:** *Bardo*; **Konkani Film:** *Kaajro*; **Kannada Film:** *Akshi*; **Bengali Film:** *Gumnaami*; **Assamese Film:** *Ronuwa - Who Never Surrender*, **Special Mentions:** *Biriyani* (Malayalam), *Jonaki Porua* (Assamese), *Lata Bhagwan Kare* **(Marathi) and** *Picasso* **(Marathi)**

Non-Feature Film Awards

David Attenborough

Voice-over/Narration: Sir David Attenborough (*Wild Karnataka*, English); **Music Direction:** Bishakhjyoti (*Kranti Darshi Guruji — Ahead of Times*, Hindi); **Editing:** Arjun Gourisaria (*Shut Up Sona* (Hindi/ English); **Audiography:** Allwin Rego and Sanjay Maurya, *Radha* (Musical); **On-Location Sound Recordist:** Saptarshi Sarkar (*Rahas*,Hindi); **Cinematography:** Savita Singh (*Sonsi*,Hindi); **Direction:** Sudhanshu Saria (Knock Knock Knock, English/ Bengali); **Film on Family Values:** *Oru Paathira Swapnam Pole* (Malayalam); **Short Fiction Film:** *Custody* (Hindi/ English); **Special Jury Award:** *Small Scale Societies* (English); **Animation Film:** *Radha* (Musical); **Investigative Film:** *Jakkal* (Marathi); **Exploration Film:** *Wild Karnataka* (English); **Educational Film:** *Apples and Oranges* (English); **Film on Social Issues:** *Holy Rights* (Hindi) and *Ladli* (Hindi); **Environment Film:** *The Stork Saviours* (Hindi); **Promotional Film:** *The Shower* (Hindi); **Arts and Culture Film:** Shrikshetra-Ru-Sahijata (Odia); **Biographical Film:** *Elephants Do Remember* (English); **Ethnographic Film:** Charan-Atva *The Essence of Being a Nomad* (Gujarati); **Debut Non-Feature Film of a Director:** Raj Pritam *More for Khisa* (Marathi); **Non-Feature Film:** *An Engineered Dream* (Hindi).

Savita Singh

Literature

International

International Booker prize 2021 (for best author and translator of a work translated into English): David Diop, the French writer (*At Night All Blood Is Black*) and his translator Anna Moschovakis.

Pulitzer Prizes for Books, Drama & Music
The Night Watchman, by Louise Erdrich **(Fiction)**; *The Hot Wing King*, by Katori Hall **(Drama)**; *Franchise: The Golden Arches in Black America*, by

Katori Hall

Natalie Diaz

Marcia Chatelain **(History)**; *The Dead Are Arising: The Life of Malcolm X*, by the late Les Payne and Tamara Payne **(Biography)**; *Postcolonial Love Poem*, by Natalie Diaz **(Poetry)**; *Wilmington's Lie: The Murderous Coup of 1898 and the Rise of White Supremacy*, by David Zucchino **(General Nonfiction)**; *Stride*, by Tania León **(Music)**

Tania León

Susanna Clarke

Booker Prize 2020: Douglas Stuart (Shuggie Bain)
Women's Prize for Fiction 2021: Susanna Clarke (*Piranesi*)

PEN Pinter prize 2021: Tsitsi Dangarembga, Zimbabwean novelist

National

Vyas Samman 2020: Prof. Sharad Pagare
Saraswati Samman, 2020: Dr Sharankumar Limbale, the noted Marathi writer.

Sharad Pagare

Humanism/Community

International

Ramon Magsaysay Award 2021
Bangladesh's Dr. Firdausi Qadri (Affordable Vaccine Champion), Pakistan's Muhammad Amjad Saqib (Poverty Alleviation Visionary), Filipino fisherman and community environmentalist Roberto Ballon, American Steven Muncy (humanitarian work and refugee assistance and Indonesian torch bearer for investigative journalism, Watchdoc).

Gandhi Peace Prize for 2019: Qaboos bin Said Al Said, the late Sultan of Oman

Gandhi Peace Prize for 2020: Sheikh Mujibur Rahman, the father of the nation of Bangladesh

Journalism

International

Pulitzer Prizes
The New York Times **(Public Service)**; Staff of the *Star Tribune* **(Breaking News Reporting)**; Matt Rocheleau, Vernal Coleman, Laura Crimaldi, Evan Allen, and Brendan McCarthy of *The Boston Globe* **(Investigative Reporting)**; An-

The Most Oscars Ever extra

Walt Disney has won more Oscars than anyone else. He was nominated for 64 awards, and won 26!

drew Chung, Lawrence Hurley, Andrea Januta, Jaimi Dowdell and Jackie Botts of Reuters. Ed Yong of *The Atlantic* **(Explanatory Reporting)**; Kathleen McGrory and Neil Bedi of the *Tampa Bay Times* **(Local Reporting)**; Staffs of The Marshall Project; AL.com, Birmingham; *IndyStar,* Indianapolis; and the Invisible Institute, Chicago **(National Reporting);** Megha Rajagopalan, Alison Killing and Christo Buschek of BuzzFeed News **(International Reporting)**; Mitchell S. Jackson, freelance contributor, *Runner's World* Nadja Drost, freelance contributor, *The California Sunday Magzine* **(Feature Writing)**; Michael Paul Williams of the *Richmond* (Va.) *Times-Dispatch* **(Commentary)**; Wesley Morris of *The New York Times* **(Criticism)**; Robert Greene of the *Los Angeles Times* **(Editorial Writing)**; No award given **(Editorial Cartooning)**; Photography staff of Associated Press **(Breaking News Photography)**; Emilio Morenatti of Associated Press **(Feature Photography)**; Lisa Hagen of WABE, Atlanta, Chris Haxel of KCUR, Kansas City, Graham Smith, and Robert Little of National Public Radio **(Audio Reporting)**; Darnella Frazier **(Special Citation)**.

Megha Rajagopalan

2020 UNESCO/ Guillermo Cano World Press Freedom Prize: Maria Ressa

Maria Ressa

Science & Technology

International

2022 Breakthrough Prize:
Jeffery W. Kelly, Katalin Karikó, Shankar Balasubramanian, David Klenerman, Pascal Mayer **(Life Sciences);** Hidetoshi Katori, Jun Ye **(Fundamental Physics:);** Takuro Mochizuki **(Mathematics)**

Shankar Balasubramanian

2022 New Horizons Physics Prize: Suchitra Sebastian; Alessandra Corsi, Gregg Hallinan, Mansi Manoj Kasliwal, Raffaella Margutti, Vedika Khemani, Haruki Watanabe, Norman Y. Yao
Mathematics: Aaron Brown, Sebastian Hurtado Salazar, Jack Thorne, Jacob Tsimerman

2022 Maryam Mirzakhani New Frontiers Prize: Sarah Peluse, Hong Wang, Yilin Wang

2021 Michael and Sheila Held Prize: Nikhil Srivastava, Adam Marcus, Daniel Alan Spielman

2021 George Pólya Prize in Applied Combinatorics: Professor Fredrik Manne, Assefaw Gebremedhin and Alex Pothen

International Eni Award 2020 (also called the Energy Frontier award): Prof. C.N.R. Rao

C.N.R. Rao

First African American to Win Best Actor Oscar

After Hattie McDaniel's groundbreaking win for Best Supporting Actress in *Gone with the Wind* (1939), Sidney Poitier made history as the first African American to win Best Actor for *Lilies of the Field* (1963).

Millennium Technology Prize: Shankar Balasubramanian and David Klenerman.

National

Shanti Swarup Bhatnagar Prize (SSB): Dr Amit Singh& Dr Arun Kumar Shukla (**Biological Sciences**); Dr Kanishka Biswas & Dr T Govindaraju (**Chemical Sciences**); Dr Binoy Kumar Saikia (**Earth, Atmosphere, Ocean and Planetary Sciences**); Dr Debdeep Mukhopadhyay (**Engineering Sciences**); Dr Anish Ghosh & Dr Saket Saurabh (**Mathematical Sciences**); Dr Jeemon Panniyammakal; Dr Rohit Srivastava (**Medical Sciences**); Dr Kanak Saha (**Physical Sciences**).

Binoy Kumar Saikia

Debdeep Mukhopadhyay

Jeemon Panniyammakal

Rohit Srivastava

Kanak Saha

Miscellaneous

International

Pritzker Architecture Prize 2021: Anne Lacaton and Jean-Philippe Vassal

Ibrahim African leadership prize: Mo Ibrahim (for good governance in Africa)

Fukuoka Grand Prize for 2021: Palagummi Sainath (The award is given to individuals and organisations for their work in preserving Asian culture).

Palagummi Sainath

2020 ACM Turing Award (known informally as the "Nobel Prize of computing"): Alfred V. Aho and Jeffrey David Ullman.

World Food Award 2021: Dr Shakuntala Hark Singh Thilsted

Andrea Meza

Shree Saini

Miss Universe 2020: Andrea Meza (Mexico)

Miss World America 2021: Shree Saini

National

Prof. C.R. Rao Centenary Gold Medal award: Jagdish Bhagwati and C Rangarajan

Lokmanya Tilak National Award for 2021: Dr Cyrus Poonawalla, Chairman of the Pune-based vaccine maker Serum Institute of India (SII).

Important Offices

President of India: Ram Nath Kovind
Vice President: Venkaiah Naidu
Prime Minister: Narendra Modi
Chief Justice : N.V. Ramana

N.V. Ramana

Speaker, Lok Sabha: Om Birla
Dy. Speaker, Lok Sabha: vacant
Chairman, Rajya Sabha: Venkaiah Naidu
Dy. Chairman, Rajya Sabha: Harivansh Narayan Singh
Chairman, NITI Aayog: Narendra Modi
Vice Chairman, NITI Aayog: Rajiv Kumar
Attorney General: K K Venugopal
Solicitor General: Tushar Mehta
Chief of Defence Staff: General Bipin Rawat
Chief of the Army Staff: General Manoj Mukund Naravane
Chief of the Naval Staff: Admiral Karambir Singh
Chief of the Air Staff: Air Chief Marshal Vivek Ram Chaudhari

Vivek Ram Chaudhari

Comptroller and Auditor-General: Girish Chandra Murmu
Chief Election Commissioner: Sushil Chandra
Election Commissioners: Rajiv Kumar, Anup Chandra Pandey
Principal Secretary to the Prime Minister: Pramod Kumar Mishra
National Security Adviser: Ajit Kumar Doval
Principal Scientific Adviser to the Govt.: K. Vijay Raghavan
Registrar-General & Census Commissioner: Vivek Joshi
Secretary-General, Lok Sabha: Utpal Kumar Singh
Secretary-General, Rajya Sabha: Dr. P.P.K. Ramacharyulu
Governor, Reserve Bank of India: Shaktikanta Das
Cabinet Secretary: Rajiv Gauba
Home Secretary: Ajay Kumar Bhalla
Finance Secretary : T.V. Somanathan
Defence Secretary: Ajay Kumar
Surveyor General of India: Naveen Tomar
Central Vigilance Commissioner: Suresh N Patel
Chairperson, Prasar Bharti: Vacant
Chairperson, UPSC: Pradeep Kumar Joshi
Chairman, Atomic Energy Commission: Kamlesh Nilkanth Vyas
Chairperson, CBSE: Manoj Ahuja
Chairman, Central Administrative Tribunal (CAT): Manjula Das
Chairperson, Central Board of Direct Taxes: J. B. Mohapatra
Chairman, Central Board of Indirect Taxes and Customs: M. Ajit Kumar
Chairperson, Central Board of Film Certification: Prasoon Joshi
Chairman, NABARD: G R Chintala
Chairman, Audit Bureau of Circulation (ABC): Debabrata Muckerjee
Chairman, Central Electricity Regulatory Commission: P K Pujari
Chairman, Food Corporation of India: Atish Chandra
Chairman, Air India: Rajiv Bansal
Chairman, ISRO: K. Sivan

Chairman, Law Commission: B.S. Chauhan
Chairman, Life Insurance Corporation of India: M.R. Kumar
Chairman, National Book Trust: Govind Prasad Sharma
Chairman, National Commission on Farmers: Dr M.S. Swaminathan
Chairman, National Commission for SCs: Vijay Sampla
Chairman, National Commission for Backward Classes: Bhagwan Lal Sahni
Chairman, NHRC: Arun Kumar Mishra
Chairman, Press Council of India: Chandramauli Kumar Prasad
Chairman, Press Trust of India: Aveek Sarkar
Chairman, Securities & Exchange Board of India: Ajay Tyagi
Chairman, State Bank of India: Dinesh Khara
Chairman, Telecom Regulatory Authority of India: P D Vaghela
Chairman, University Grants Commission: D P Singh
Chairman & MD, ONGC: Subhash Kumar
Chairman, IRDA: Subhash Chandra Khuntia
Chairman, Staff Selection Commission: Sujata Chaturvedi
President, Indian Council for Cultural Relations: Vinay Sahasrabuddhe
Chairman, ICHR: Arvind Jamkhedkar
Chairman, Indian Farmers Fertiliser Cooperative Limited (IFFCO): Balvinder Singh Nakai
Chairman, Indian Council of Social Science Research: Bhushan Patwardhan
Chairman, Bombay Stock Exchange: Justice Vikramjit Sen
Chairman, Railway Board: Suneet Sharma
Chairman, Coir Board: D. Kuppuramu
Chairperson, Rubber Board: K N Raghavan
Chairman, Coal India: Pramod Agrawal
Chairman, SAIL: Soma Mondal
Chairperson, Sangeet Natak Akademi: Shekhar Sen
Chairman, National School of Drama: Paresh Rawal
Chairperson, Public Enterprises Selection Board (PESB): Mallika Srinivasan
CEO, Children's Film Society of India: Smita Vats Sharma

Mallika Srinivasan

Chairperson, NASSCOM: Rekha M. Menon
Chairperson, National Commission for Women: Rekha Sharma
Chairman, DRDO: G Satheesh Reddy
MD & CEO, IDBI Bank: Rakesh Sharma
Director, BARC: Dr. Ajit Kumar Mohanty
Director General CBI: Subodh Kumar Jaiswal
Director, VSSC: S. Somanath
Director, Intelligence Bureau: Arvind Kumar
Secretary, Research and Analysis Wing (RAW): Samant Goel
D-G, Border Roads Organisation: Lt. Gen. Rajeev Chaudhary
D-G, BSF: Pankaj Kumar Singh
D-G, Coast Guard: Krishnaswamy Natarajan
D-G, CRPF: Kuldiep Singh
D-G, CSIR: Shekhar C Mande
D-G, ICMR : Balram Bhargava
D-G, ASI: V Vidyavathi
D-G, National Cadet Corps: Lt. General Gurbirpal Singh
President, Assocham: Vineet Agarwal
President, BCCI: Sourav Ganguly
President, FICCI: Uday Shankar
President, Indian Newspaper Society: Shailesh Gupta
President, NASSCOM: Debjani Ghosh

Important Addresses

President of India Rashtrapati Bhavan, New Delhi-110004, EPABX : 23025321, Fax : 23017290 & 23017824, E-mail : presidentofindia@rb.nic.in, Website : www.presidentofindia.nic.in

Vice President of India 6, Maulana Azad Road, New Delhi - 110011, Tel: 23016422, 23016344, Fax: 23018124, E-mail:vpindia@nic.in, E-mail: vicepresidentofindia.nic.in

Prime Minister Office : Room No. 148 B, South Block, New Delhi, 110001, Office Tel: 23012312, Fax : 23016857, Website: www.pmindia.nic.in

Lok Sabha Speaker's Office Parliament House Address Room No. 17, Parliament House, New Delhi-110001, +91 11 23017914 (Tel), +91 11 23017795 (Tel), +91 11 23792927 (Fax), E-mail: speakerloksabha@sansad.nic.in

Supreme Court of India The Registrar, Supreme Court of India, Tilak Marg, New Delhi-110 001 (India) PABX Nos.23388922-24,23388942-44, Fax Nos.23381508, 23381584, 23384336/23384533/23384447, E-mail at : supremecourt@nic.in

Election Commission of India Nirvachan Sadan, Ashoka Road, New Delhi-110001 Tel: 011-23717391 Fax: 011-23713412 feedback@eci.gov.in

Central Bureau of Investigation (CBI) Block no. 4, 6th Floor, CGO Complex, Lodhi Road, New Delhi - 110003

Central Information Commission (CIC) August Kranti Bhavan, Bhikaji Cama Place, New Delhi - 110 066 & Old JNU Campus, New Delhi - 110 067. Tel: 26161137 Fax: 26186536

National Human Rights Commission Faridkot House, Copernicus Marg, New Delhi - 110 001. Facilitation Centre (Madad): (011) 23385368 Mobile No. 9810298900 (For complaints-24 hrs.) Fax: (011) 23386521 (complaints) / 23384863 (Administration) / 23382734 (Investigation) Email: covdnhrc@nic.in. (General)/ jrlaw@nic.in (For complaints) resnhrc@nic.in (Research Division) Web site: www.nhrc.nic.in

University Grants Commission (UGC) Bahadur Shah Zafar Marg, New Delhi, Pin: 110 002, India E-mail: webmaster @ ugc.ac.in Web: www.ugc.ac.in/ Tel: and Fax: EPABX Nos. 23232701/ 23236735/ 23239437/ 23235733/ 23237721/ 23232317/ 23234116/ 23236351/ 23230813/ 23232485 UGC reception 23239627 Fax. Nos. 23231797/ 23232783/ 23239659/ 23231814

Union Public Service Commission Dholpur House, New Delhi - 110-069, Tel: 011-23098543, 23385271 Fax: 23381125

National Commission For Women 4, Deen Dayal Upadhayaya Marg, New Delhi-110 002. Tel: 91-11-23237166, 91-11-23236988 Fax : 91-11-23236154 Complaints Cell : 91-11-23219750. E-mail: ncw@nic.in

National Commission For Minorities 5th Floor, Lok Nayak Bhavan, Khan Market, New Delhi 110 003 Tel. 24615583 Fax 24693302, 24642645, 24698410 Toll Free Number: 1800110088. E-mail: ro-ncm@nic.in

NITI Aayog (formerly Planning Commission of India) Yojana Bhavan, Sansad Marg, New Delhi -110 001. E-mail: plancom@nic.in For general queries and information Tel.: 011-23096620

Central Administrative Tribunal (CAT) 61/35 Copernicus Marg, New Delhi - 110 001, India. E-mail ID: cat-delhi@nic.in

Council of Ministers

Narendra Modi: Prime Minister and also in-charge of Ministry of Personnel, Public Grievances and Pensions; Department of Atomic Energy; Department of Space; All important policy issues and all other portfolios not allocated to any Minister

Cabinet Ministers

Amit Shah: Home Affairs and Cooperation

Amit Shah

Raj Nath Singh: Defence

Nitin Jairam Gadkari: Road Transport and Highways

Nirmala Sitharaman: Finance; Corporate Affairs

Narendra Singh Tomar: Agriculture & Farmers Welfare

Dr Subrahmanyam Jaishankar: External Affairs

Arjun Munda: Tribal Affairs

Smriti Zubin Irani: Women and Child Development

Piyush Goyal: Commerce and Industry; Consumer Affairs, Food and Public Distribution; Textiles

Dharmendra Pradhan: Education and Skill Development and Entrepreneurship

Pralhad Joshi: Parliamentary Affairs; Coal; Mines

Narayan Tatu Rane: Micro, Small and Medium Enterprises

Sarbananda Sonowal: Ports, Shipping and Waterways; AYUSH

Mukhtar Abbas Naqvi: Minority Affairs

Virendra Kumar: Social Justice and Empowerment

Giriraj Singh: Rural Development; Panchayati Raj

Jyotiraditya M Scindia: Civil Aviation

Ramachandra Prasad Singh: Steel

Ashwini Vaishnaw: Railways; Communications; Electronics and Information Technology

Pashu Pati Kumar Paras: Food Processing Industries

Gajendra Singh Shekhawat: Jal Shakti

Kiren Rijiju: Law and Justice

Raj Kumar Singh: Power, New and Renewable Energy

Hardeep Singh Puri: Petroleum and Natural Gas; Housing and Urban Affairs

Mansukh Mandaviya: Health and Family Welfare; Chemicals and Fertilizers

Bhupender Yadav: Environment, Forest and Climate Change; Labour and Employment

Dr. Mahendra Nath Pandey: Heavy Industries

Parshottam Rupala: Fisheries, Animal Husbandry and Dairying

G. Kishan Reddy: Culture; Tourism; and Development of North Eastern Region

Anurag Singh Thakur: Information and Broadcasting; Youth Affairs and Sports

Ministers of State
(Independent Charge)

Rao Inderjit Singh: Statistics and Programme Implementation; Planning and Corporate Affairs

Dr. Jitendra Singh: Science and Technology; Earth Sciences; Prime Minister's Office; Personnel, Public Grievances and

Pensions; Department of Atomic Energy; and Department of Space

Ministers of State

Shripad Yesso Naik: Ports, Shipping and Waterways; Tourism
Faggansingh Kulaste: Steel; and Rural Development
Prahalad Singh Patel: Jal Shakti and Food Processing Industries
Ashwini Kumar Choubey: Consumer Affairs, Food and Public Distribution; Environment, Forest and Climate Change
Arjun Ram Meghwal: Parliamentary Affairs and Culture
General (Retd.) V. K. Singh: Road Transport and Highways; Civil Aviation
Krishan Pal: Power and Heavy Industries
Danve Raosaheb Dadarao: Railways; Coal and Mines
Ramdas Athawale: Social Justice and Empowerment
Sadhvi Niranjan Jyoti: Consumer Affairs, Food and Public Distribution and Rural Development
Sanjeev Kumar Balyan: Fisheries, Animal Husbandry and Dairying
Nityanand Rai: Home Affairs
Pankaj Chaowdhary: Finance
Anupriya Singh Patel: Commerce and Industry
Prof. S. P. Singh Baghel: Law and Justice
Rajeev Chandrasekhar: Skill Development and Entrepreneurship and Electronics and Information Technology
Sushri Shobha Karandlaje: Agriculture and Farmers Welfare
Bhanu Pratap Singh Verma: Micro, Small and Medium Enterprises
Darshana Vikram Jardosh: Textiles; and Railways
V. Muraleedharan: External Affairs; Parliamentary Affairs
Meenakashi Lekhi: External Affairs; Culture
Som Parkash: Commerce and Industry
Renuka Singh Saruta: Tribal Affairs
Rameswar Teli: Petroleum and Natural Gas and Labour and Employment
Kailash Choudhary: Agriculture and Farmers Welfare
Annpurna Devi: Education
A. Narayanaswamy: Social Justice and Empowerment
Kaushal Kishore: Housing and Urban Affairs

Annpurna Devi

Ajay Bhatt: Defence and Tourism
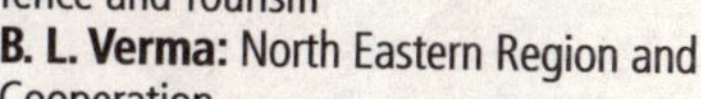
B. L. Verma: North Eastern Region and Cooperation
Shri Ajay Kumar: Home Affairs
Devusinh Chauhan: Communications
Bhagwanth Khuba: New and Renewable Energy and Chemicals and Fertilizers
Kapil Moreshwar Patil: Panchayati Raj
Sushri Pratima Bhoumik: Social Justice and Empowerment
Dr. Subhas Sarkar: Education
Dr. Bhagwat Kishanrao Karad: Finance
Dr. Rajkumar Ranjan Singh: External Affairs and Education
Bishweswar Tudu: Tribal Affairs and Jal Shakti
Shantanu Thakur: Ports, Shipping and Waterways
Dr. Munjapara Mahendrabhai: Women and Child Development and AYUSH
John Barla: Minority Affairs
Dr. L. Murugan: Fisheries, Animal Husbandry and Dairying; Information and Broadcasting
Nisith Pramanik: Home Affairs; Youth Affairs and Sports

Multilingualism: Boon or Bane

Dr. Pichirikkat Bhaskaran Nayar

The whole world is becoming smaller, and inter-communal and hence inter-lingual contacts and communication have become more common and more vitally important. Here is a look at the psycho-social, political and techno-economic global implications of multilingualism in an ever-shrinking world.

The billions of members of our species *Homo sapiens* may all look different but there are many features that they all share: they are all featherless bipeds; they are all social and sociable beings; they all live in an organised manner; and most important of all perhaps, they all use their vocal organs to produce sounds to communicate with each other. Although it is difficult to be precise about the how and when of the evolution of this particular communicative attribute, this faculty of 'languaging' now appears to be an inevitable, instinctive and congenital ability, unique to the species of the 'featherless bipeds' universally. More interestingly, in most parts of the modern world, more and more people are finding that they need, of necessity, to have and handle more than just one language even for basic survival. What is often not realised is that having to use more than one language is not a simple issue of shifting into different speech patterns but has many significant dimensions and implications.

The What and How of Language(s) and Languaging

There are thousands of different languages in the world even today although many of them are progressively on their way to death owing to various political, and anthropological reasons. It is impossible to say when or how humans first started a system of meaningful oral signals amounting to what can be called 'language'. Most scholars agree that it must have evolved more than at least a hundred thousand years ago. How languages came about as established systems of human communication and at what stage of Darwinian development it happened are also not certain. Also, languaging must have evolved in different parts of the human habitation independently as is shown by the remarkably varied and dissimilar verbal and structural patterns of different languages.

Language is primarily vocal/oral in nature and its graphic representation in writing came centuries later, and as we know, more than half the languages in the world still have no written form. There were several speculative and perhaps near-risible theories about the origin of language and its essential vocal nature. For instance, the Bow Wow Theory attributes it to humans trying to orally imitate the animals initially perhaps to signify them, the Dig Dong Theory attributes it to a natural correspondence between human sense reactions to perception of objects, while the Gesture Theory argues that language was born as a result of coordination between human bodily gestures and congruent oral gestures. All we know is the fact that the same object or event or concept can be depicted or represented by totally dissimilar heterogenous sets of expressions in different languages, and that there seems to be no rational or essential connection between what is said and what it denotes. Even the few onomatopoeic forms for an object or event (like 'bang' and 'moo' in English) are often different in different languages. This indicates that the relation between any object/event and its linguistic representation (in laymen's terms the connection between the word and the thing) has to be purely unpredictable, arbitrary, and language-specific.

The several salient facts that emerge are: 1) There are no humans in this world without at least ONE language; 2) There are thousands of languages in the world, most of them mutually unintelligible; 3) Each community has at least one language that it invariably associates and

identifies itself with although some may have more than one; 4) Every language is potentially good and competent enough to grow and develop to fulfil the requirements and demands put on it and no language is inherently or intrinsically better than or superior to any other; and 5) Most important of all, because of all the rapid technological changes in the world in the last century, the whole world is becoming smaller, and inter-communal and hence inter-lingual contacts and communication have become more common and more vitally important. Hence one should be basically aware of some of the psycho-social, political and techno-economic global implications of multilingualism in an ever-shrinking world.

Nature of Multilingualism – Language Families and Divisions

When a community of people who share a language expands and splits up into sub-communities, the dispersed language also tends to split up and differ, and eventually, if there is not much active inter-community communication, breaks up into several versions. Also, these versions may eventually become different

languages and this break up of versions into independent languages can also motivate as well as be motivated by ethno-political distinctions. In simple terms, a version or dialect of a language becomes and gets accepted as an independent language when the speaking community feels the need for it and has an army or enough political power behind it. The various languages in the world are thus assigned to various families. In India itself there are languages attributable to several (originally unrelated) families like Indo-European, Munda and Sino-Tibetan in the north and Dravidian in the south. Family semblances are sometimes obvious like say, between Hindi and Punjabi or Tamil and Malayalam, but are not often clearly or easily identifiable for the common man. For instance, though most of the languages in northern India and most of the languages in Iran and Europe belong to the same family, they hardly reveal such relationship easily through surface semblance except to linguists.

Acquisition Vs Learning – Mono-, Bi- and Multilinguals

It is now a known fact that all normal humans are genetically conditioned to spontaneously pick up and learn any language(s) they are exposed to without any explicit instruction or tutoring. If children grow up in the natural environment of even more than one language, they will acquire them all up and will develop the required competence in all. The use of this instinctive ability, called language acquisition, is universal and language independent, but psychologists have found that this can happen only before maturation (roughly pre-teenage). Once past maturation, this ability seems to flag and eventually disappear. After maturation, languages have to be learned and this involves a different mental process. The set patterns of language(s) already acquired will often interfere with (or alternatively facilitate) the learning process of further languages and it will not be easy for the learner to acquire native-like fluency in learnt languages. (*See below for the importance of this.*)

Languages are patterned and structured very differently from each other and so learning a new language and communicating effectively in it is not often an easy process for the learner. The mentally established patterns and speech habits of one's (acquired) first language (L1) usually interferes in the post-maturity learning of a new language (L2) and the learner will always tend to transfer his L1 habits onto L2 (e,g, the use of retroflex /t/ and /d/ and of the universal question tag or an expression like 'your good name' in Indian English). On the other hand, If L1 and L2 are genetically related, often it may be easy to transfer from L1 to L2, but there is always the danger of transferring speech patterns incorrectly. The typological differences between L1 and L2 can also be a hindrance to easy learning. For instance, a Malayalee, whose L1 has a rational gender system may be totally nonplussed by the irrational grammatical gender system if his L2, for instance, is Hindi, just as in a vice versa situation a Hindi speaker may find the agglutinative Malayalam structure problematic.

A fact that is often grossly ignored at worst and underrated at best is the role that an L1 has in the formation and retention of the psychic persona of an individual and in the ethnic psyche of a community for whom it is the acquired first language (mother tongue). The common notion or definition of a language as a means of communicating ideas or thoughts further reinforces this fallacious underrating. The fact is completely overlooked that one's initially acquired language is not just a means of communicating ideas but equally importantly, it is also a means of forming ideas, that is, of the very process of ideation. It is through the vocabulary and structure of the first language that individuals often form as well as give structure and meaning to the objects and events around them. In other words, people generally see, conceptualise and perceive events and objects of the world through the abstractions and categories that are permitted and shaped by the way their language system encodes and categorises them, and different languages do this in different ways.

Multilingualism and Mindset

A language creates and sustains what is called one's weltanschauung (world view, roughly), and different languages do this in different ways. These are then

embedded in the cultural patterns and codes of the speakers as 'normal'. Thus, things that are pleasant and delightful are 'warm' for an English speaker and Shakespeare can compare his beloved 'to a summer's day' in his sonnet, whereas many speakers of languages from the tropics would probably prefer a 'cool' day and an Indian would associate romance not with a sunny warm day but with provocative clouds. For a British female, someone who is tall, dark and handsome is romantically attractive but one wonders how many Indians would go along with the middle adjective in that phrase. It is also interesting that in most Bollywood movies, characters have to say 'sorry' and 'I love you' in English since the Indian language equivalents, even if and when they do exist, would sound funny, and also since most Indian languages encode love in the psyche not as an agentive/ performative but as something that transpires or happens.

Sometimes the perceptual mindset between two languages can be more complex. For example, unlike most other Indians, the Malayalam speakers make a mental and ideational distinction between existential and factual matters and use different affirmations and negations for them. In almost all Indian languages, like in English, the verb is the same in two statements like "He is here" and "He is smart", while in Malayalam (and in the Ethiopian language of Amharic) one has to use different forms

of affirmative verbs, as the former statement is perceived as existential and the latter as factual. This applies to the negative forms as well and there are different mutually irreplaceable words for their negative forms as well. Needless to say, moving from one language into another is just not a matter of finding and using new sounds, and words and a different syntax but switching on to an entirely new weltanschauung and ideation structure.

Getting used to the Deep and Surface Structures of Languages

It is sometimes argued that all languages possibly have the same underlying deep structure, that is to say, all humans perceive and conceptualise nature and natural phenomena in the same manner but organise them in different ways when languaging, resulting in the surface structures of languages differing widely. There are objects in the world and there are happenings involving the objects. These are visualised along four dimensions: there is (a) an event; (b) an agency that is the cause/doer of the event; (c) often a victim/patient who sustains/endures the event, and (d) the circumstances leading on to or affecting the event. Different languages then relate the four and connect them to each other in different ways and decide how they should appear on the surface utterance. Grammarians in many languages chose to call them Verb, Subject, Object and Adverb. English prefers to order them SVO, while several Indian languages prefer SOV, and some others decide on free order and so on. (In Hindi, for instance, if the event has a victim, the speaker perceives the event differently and so is forced to modify the form of the agent with a 'ne' added.) Different languages decide how the surface structure should connect these four dimensions together to make a meaningful utterance (syntax). So, a multilingual no doubt, has to have a more complex language brain as he has to get used to the different ways of relationships between the deep and surface structures in different languages,

An interesting communication pattern common among of bi- and multilinguals bring out some puzzling points about how language is invariantly connected with information storage and retrieval in the human brain. It also might bring out some differences in thought structure between compound bilinguals and coordinate bilinguals. (A compound bilingual acquires both languages and so thinks independently in both languages while a coordinate bilingual learns L2 after maturation and hence his weltanschauung may well be primarily in his L1 albeit near-native proficiency in L2.) A lot of information storage and retrieval forms will depend upon which language has been the vehicle for the initial input of what information. An average university-educated Indian is perhaps an ideal example of a coordinate bilingual and one from outside the Hindi belt will be a good example of a tri- or multilingual. One can notice that the surface linguistic pattern of an Indian's interaction can often be a true reflection of his linguistic domain and consequent multifaceted mindset. While interacting with his multilingual peers basically in their shared L1, it is almost difficult for him to be totally monolingual. He often unconsciously brings in words/expressions felt to be from English and mixes them with his L1 diction, shifts into English if the talk gets technical or a bit intellectually heavy and switches consciously into English if he wants to show authority and power distance.

In fact, in a community where the language available or chosen for education and public life is not the L1 but a cultivated L2, the bilinguals may have a double persona, one in private life and emotional participation informed and influenced by L1, and another in intellectual and public pursuits, informed and influenced by the L2. This may well be true with the population of most of the former British and French colonies. It is also worth mentioning here that each language carries with it its own chosen and consensual style of discourse structure, small talk, politeness modes and overall verbal behaviour rules. In the days of the Cold War, it was sometimes felt that most peace talks on the Middle East often failed at least partly because of the different discourse styles of the parties involved – the Western factual-inductive style, the Soviet axiomatic-deductive style and the Middle Eastern intuitive-affective style.

The Politics of Multilingualism

Multilingualism has substantial and supremely important political dimensions and it has mostly to do with the international geo-political status and ethnolinguistic vitality of the involved languages on the one hand, and on the other, with the role of the language in culture, in ethnicity, and in the perception and representation of statehood or nationhood.

At the root of the modern notion of statehood and national identity lies a sense of community based on a sense on ethnicity, which again is engendered and supported through and by a linguistic identity. Traditionally, communities derived and formed their individual differential identity through the language (e.g. Indian revised statehood on the basis of main languages). Right from the days of Greco-Persian wars through the great Anglo-French war days (where Joan of Arc's watch words were 'France for the French and England for the English') ethno-linguistic identity was an essential and crucial part of modern statehood. It was primarily through linguistic identity that great leaders like Bismarck and Mazzini integrated several kingdoms into the nations of Germany and Italy. Even in multi-ethnic immigrant states like Australia and the United States, linguistic loyalty and fealty to English overrides anthropological diversity. Thus, the identity of a modern nation state is invariably felt

to be linked with the notion of a 'national language', symbolising ethno-national uniformity of identity. Unfortunately, this can create huge power crises in multilingual modern post-colonial states in Asia and Africa, in particular those with democratic systems. Whichever language gets designated as the National Language automatically assumes and obtains special status and power and is accepted as the main symbol of national character and identity. Knowledge of and affiliation to the national language (and not necessarily any other official language) is primarily equated with patriotism and all nationals are automatically expected to be not only communicatively proficient in but also ethnically loyal to the national language. The 'other' languages and speakers are treated with unimportance at worst and patronization at best.

In a multilingual situation, most often, not all involved languages will have the same power and prestige and acceptability. Invariably, one of the languages (officially called National Language) will be deemed as superordinate and the others will be subordinate and the reasons often can be more political and historic than linguistic. it is very possible that the power thus allotted to the superordinate language will covertly be extended also to the native speakers of the language too. Besides, the ever-increasing dominance of the superordinate language poses a threat even to the survival of other languages, irrespective of historical and literary strength or linguistic antiquity.

Again, in multi-ethnic communicative situations, intra-national or international, assumed proficiency pre-eminence in the chosen lingua franca will give native speakers of the chosen language an advantage over the others. This makes the choice of the lingua franca a very crucial factor in terms of national dominance since the person for whom the chosen language is the L1 has an inherent linguistic as well as status advantage. In discussions, often the assumed verbal power claim of (native) acquisition can override the factual power of L2 (learnt) as the non-native can never truly claim the same verbal nuancing competence or syntactic dexterity. Besides, the onus of communicative accommodation will also totally and completely fall on the subordinate language speakers. An English speaker in most parts of the world, a Mandarin speaker anywhere in China and a Hindi speaker anywhere in India are supreme examples of this solipsistic linguistic importance and the communicative power it creates. An English speaker in officially bilingual Canada might have a better acceptance for talking in English in Quebec than a Québécois would have for talking in French in, say, Ontario. This power situation can be unfair on the subordinate language speakers, particularly if the communication is in their own linguistic territory. There is also the eventual danger of the cultural presumptions and eventually the linguistic domination of the super stratum language being slowly imposed on the 'other' languages. In India and Papua New Guinea, several languages are already dying or dead. On the other hand, in countries like Nigeria and South Africa, where there are several languages, all with equal status, the superordinate status given to English (a language with no historic local ethnic identity) as a national language helps out to neutralize the dominance of any local language.

Multilingualism is an accepted phenomenon globally but the significance of its international phenomenality and implications is very different from its intra-national presence if and when nation states decide to base their national identity on any one of its multiple languages. For the retention of national integrity, it may well be a good idea if the national language status assumed a 'first among equals' role and status, and stayed careful not to dominate and threaten the existence and importance of other major languages. So if multilingualism is a boon or bane is indeed a moot question.

25 ART, CULTURE AND HERITAGE

- Dances of India
- Indian Music
- Famous Indian Painters
- Popular Styles In Indian Architecture
- Ancient Indian Schools of Art
- Modern Indian Theatre
- Indian Writing in English

Dances of India

Dance in India has an unbroken tradition of over 2000 years. Two main divisions of its forms are classical and folk.

The criteria for being considered as classical is the style's adherence to the guidelines laid down in Natyashastra, which explains the Indian art of acting. The Sangeet Natak Akademi currently confers classical status on eight Indian classical dance styles: Bharatanatyam (Tamil Nadu), Kathak (North India), Kathakali (Kerala), Kuchipudi (Andhra Pradesh), Manipuri (Manipur), Mohiniyattam (Kerala), Odissi (Odisha), and Sattriya (Asom).

Folk dances of India vary according to the region and have no specific grammar. They fit in with the scheme of festivals in each region.

Bharatanatyam

Bharatanatyam originated in Tamil Nadu and was earlier known as Daasiyattam. This dance form has been handed down through the centuries by dance teachers (or gurus) called nattuwanars and the temple dancers, called devadasis. In the sacred environment of the temple these familes developed and propagated their heritage. The training traditionally took around seven years under the direction of the nattuwanar who were scholars and persons of great learning.

Instruments Used: Mridangam, Violin, Veena, Flute and Talam (Nattuvangam/ cymbals)

Famous Artists: Balasaraswati, C.V. Chandrasekhar, Leela Samson, Mrinalini Sarabhai, Padma Subrahmanyam, Rukmini Devi, Sonal Mansingh, Yamini Krishnamurthi, Mallika Sarabhai.

Kathak

Kathak means 'to tell a story'. This north Indian dance form is inextricably bound with classical Hindustani music, and the rhythmic agility of the feet is accompanied by the table or pakhvaj. Traditionally the stories were of Radha and Krishna, in the Natwari style (as it

was then called) but the Mughal invasion of North India had a serious impact on the dance. The dance was taken to Muslim courts and thus it became more entertaining and less religious in content. More emphasis was laid on nritha, the pure dance aspect and less on abhinaya (expression and emotion).

Instruments Used: Pakhvaj, Tabla, Harmonium, Sarengi and Talam (cymbals)

Famous Artists: Bharti Gupta, Birju Maharaj, Damayanti Joshi, Durga Das, Gopi Krishna, Kumudini Lakhia, Shambhu Maharaj, Sitara Devi

Kathakali

Kathakali (katha, "story"; kali, "performance") is a highly stylised classical dance-drama form which originated from Kerala in the 17th century. This classical dance form is particularly noticed for dancer's elaborate costume, towering head gear, billowing skirts, and long silver nails. Recent developments in Kathakali over the years include improved looks, refined gestures and added themes besides more ornate singing and precise drumming. Kathakali is performed regularly at festivals in temples, at cultural shows for connoisseurs and also at international events, occasionally in fusion dance experiments.

Instruments Used: Chenda, maddalam, chengila, ilathalam, idakka and shankhu

Famous Artists: Vazhenkada Kunchu Nair, Kottakkal Sivaraman, Kalamandalam Gopi, Kalamandalam Ramankutty Nair, Kalamandalam Vasu Pisharody

Kuchipudi

Kuchipudi derives its name from the village Kuchipudy (Kuchelapuram) in Andhra Pradesh from where it originated. The dance drama that still exists today and can most closely be associated with the Sanskrit theatrical tradition is Kuchipudi which is also known as Bhagavata Mela Natakam. The actors sing and dance, and the style is a blend of folk and classical. Arguably this is why this technique has greater freedom and fluidity than other dance styles.

Instruments Used: Mridangam, Violin, Veena, Flute and Talam (Nattuvangam/ cymbals)

Famous Artists: Josyula Seetharamaiah, Vempati Chinna Sathyam, Yamini Reddy, Prateeksha Kashi.

Manipuri

Manipuri is one of the six classical dance styles of India. It is indigenous to the state of Manipur. The roots of the dance is the ancient Sanskrit text Natya Shastra. The love story of Radha and Krishna are commonly acted out in the dance drama performance.

The Manipuri dance is a team performance, with its own unique costumes, aesthetics, conventions and repertoire. It is, for most part, marked by a performance that is graceful, fluid, sinuous with greater emphasis on hand and upper body gestures. It is accompanied with devotional music created with many instruments, with the beat set by cymbals (kartal or manjira) and double-headed drum (pung or Manipuri mrdanga) of sankirtan.

The Manipuri dance was popularised througout India when, in 1917, Rabindranath Tagore saw demonstrations of the art and brought back dance teachers to serve in his Viswa-Bharati University at Santiniketan.

Instruments Used: Pung and cymbals

Famous Artists: Guru Bipin Sinha, Jhaveri Sisters, Nirmala Mehta, Savita Mehta

Mohiniyattam

The theme of Mohiniyattam dance is love and devotion to god. Vishnu or Krishna is most often the hero. The spectators can feel His invisible presence when the heroine or her maid details dreams and ambitions through circular movements, delicate footsteps and subtle expres-

sions. Through slow and medium tempos, the dancer is able to find adequate space for improvisations and suggestive bhavas or emotions.

The basic dance steps are the Adavus which are of four kinds: Taganam, Jaganam, Dhaganam and Sammisram. These names are derived from the nomenclature called vaittari.

The Mohiniyattam dancer maintains realistic make-up and adorns a simple costume, in comparison to costumes of other dances, such as Kathakali. The dancer is attired in a beautiful white with gold border Kasavu saree of Kerala, with the distinctive white jasmin flowers around a French bun at the side of her head.

Instruments Used: Chenda, Maddalam, Cymbals and Ela taalam.

Famous Artists: Kalamandalam Kshemavati, Kanak Rele, Kalamandalam Satyabhama, Bharati Sivaji, Sunanda Nair.

Odissi

Odissi, the dance form from Odisha, is supposed to be the oldest surviving classical dance form from India. Odissi is based on the popular devotion to Lord Krishna and the verses of the Sanskrit play Geet Govinda are used to depict the love and devotion to God. The Odissi dancers use their head, bust and torso in soft flowing movements to express specific moods and emotions.

The form is curvaceous, concentrating on the tribhang or the division of the body into three parts, head, bust and torso; the mudras and the expressions are similar to those of Bharatnatyam. Odissi performances are replete with lores of the eighth incarnation of Vishnu, Lord Krishna. It is a soft, lyrical classical dance which depicts the ambience of Odisha and the philosophy of its most popular deity, Lord Jagannath, whose temple is in Puri. On the temple walls of Bhubaneshwar, Puri and Konark the dance sculptures of Odissi are clearly visible.

Instruments Used: Pakhvaj, tabla, harmonium, flute and cymbals.

Famous Artists: Debaprasad Das, Dhirendra Nath Pattnaik, Indrani Rahman, Kelucharan Mohapatra, Priyambada Mohanty, Sonal Mansingh.

Sattriya

Sattriya Nritya emerged from the sanctum of Asom's sattras in the latter half of the 19th century. Until the first half of the 19th century this dance style was performed in a highly ritualistic manner

by male dancers alone as the sattras had maintained certain rigid disciplines and austerities within their walls. On 15 November 2000, the Sangeet Natak Akademi recognised Sattriya Nritya as one of the classical dance forms of India. The classical rigidity, the strict adherence to certain principles, and the non-engagement of academic research on the dance form all contributed to the recognition and acceptance of Sattriya Nritya as one of the eight classical dance forms of India.

The core of Sattriya Nritya has usually been mythological stories. This was an artistic way of presenting mythological teachings to the people in an accessible, immediate, and enjoyable manner. Traditionally, Sattriya was performed only by bhokots (male monks) in monasteries as a part of their daily rituals or to mark special festivals. Today, in addition to this practice, Sattriya is also performed on stage by men and women who are not members of the sattras, on themes not merely mythological.

Instruments used: Khols, Talas or cymbals, flute

Famous Artists: Ghanakanta Bora, Ananda Mohan Bhagawati, Sarodi Saikia, Bhabananda Barbayan, Jatin Goswami

Indian Music

Music has always been an integral part of our culture. Indian music embraces everything from simple folk songs to refined classical music. The evolution of Indian classical music traces back to the Vedic hymns in Hindu temples. The two main genres of Indian classical music are Hindustani and Carnatic. However, our music taste has broadened and transitioned over time.

Carnatic Music

Carnatic music, one of the two major streams of Indian music, is indigenous to southern India. It flourished under

the patronage of Krishnadevaraya in Vijayanagar, the capital city of Vijayanagara Empire. Purandara Dasa, also known as 'pithamaha (father) of Carnatic music', had made great contributions to this genre. He is one of the persons who devised a basic scale for teaching Carnatic music.

Even though instruments are used, Carnatic music is basically a vocal art. The golden period of south Indian classical music was during the time of Tyagaraja, Muthuswami Dikshitar and Syama Sastri. These contemporaries are called the 'musical trinity'.

Famous Carnatic Musicians

Thyagaraja, Syama Sastri, Muthuswami Dikshitar, Chembai Vaidyanatha Bhagavatar, Semmangudi R Srinivasa Iyer, M S Subbulakshmi, M Balamurali Krishna, DK Pattammal

Hindustani Music

Hindustani is a continuously evolving classical music genre of northern India. Until the 13th century, music of the whole nation remained the same. It was after the Mughal invasion that the north Indian expression became copiously influenced by Persian and Arabic music.

Hindustani music has several sub-styles and improvisations. This genre incorporates many instruments, musical forms and ragas from other music traditions.

Pandit VN Bhatkhande is known for his major contribution of compiling Hindustani musical compositions, and publishing the reference series –*Hindustani Sangeet Kramik Pusthak Malika*. Amir Khusrau, a prolific musician, is believed to have developed the khayal, tarana and qawwali styles of music. He is often called the 'father of qawwali' (Indian sufi form). Other artists like Ravi Shankar and

Ali Akbar Khan popularised Hindustani music around the world.

Famous Hindustani Musicians
Abdul Rashid Khan, Ustad Amir Khan, Pandit Jasraj, Bade Ghulam Ali Khan, Bhimsen Joshi, Mallikarjun Mansur, Begum Akhtar, Zakir Hussain, Girija Devi, Ravi Shankar, Shubha Mudgal, Kishori Amonkar

Regional Music

Regional music in India is as diverse as the nation's cultural traditions.

Folk music is an inevitable part of Indian culture. Different types of musical instruments are used by people of different geographical and cultural groups.

Rasiya Geet: It is a kind of popular folk music from the Braj region of Uttar Pradesh. Rasiya means 'filled with rasa or emotions' and Geet means 'song'. These songs are sung in the regional Hindi dialect called Braj Basha. Braj is where Lord Krishna spent most of his childhood and youth. The usual theme of Rasiya music is the love and life of Krishna.

Pankhida: Pankhida music originated in the villages of Rajasthan. These songs are sung by peasants to ease their gruelling work in the fields. The literal meaning of the word 'Pankhida' is lover.

Lotia: It is another style of folk music from Rajasthan. Lotia songs are sung by the rural women during the festival of Lotia. They bring decorated vessels named lotas and kalash filled with water from ponds, which they carry back after the worship.

Pandwani: Pandwani is a popular musical form of Chhattisgarh. The word Pandwani means 'songs about pandavas'. These folk ballads recite stories from Mahabharata, mainly the legends of pandava brothers. A singer-narrator leads the performance. Pandwani artists don't stick to any rigid style; they always bring in something new. Impromptu lyrics and gestures are very common in this genre.

Shakunakhar: Shakunakhar is 'Uttarakhandi mangal geet' sung on many occasions like baby shower, birth of a baby, Ganesh Puja, etc, in the foothills of Himalayas. Shakunakhar songs are sung by women, not accompanied by any instruments. These charming songs are basically prayers for good fortune.

Mando: This Goan genre of music is a blend of western and Indian styles. Its origin traces back to the 19th century. Mando is popular among the Catholics of Goa. The major theme is love; there are also historical narratives and grievance against injustice.

Alha-Udal: Alha-Udal ballads of Bundelkhand narrates the legends of the valiant warrior-brothers Alha and Udal. They served the Chandel King Paramardideva, popularly known as Paramal. Alha songs mostly highlight the principles of morality, nobility and chivalry.

Hori: They are cheerful songs associated with the 'festival of colours-Holi'. Popular in Uttar Pradesh and Bihar, these semi-classical songs are mostly about the love life of Krishna and Radha.

Teej songs: Singing Teej songs to rejoice the arrival of monsoon is a tradition followed by Rajasthani women. Monsoon festivals in the state are closely associated with Lord Shiva and Goddess Parvathi. So, the themes of Teej songs revolve around the union of the divine couple. They are customarily sung on the third day after Amavasya (new moon).

Sohar: Sohar songs are traditionally sung in order to rejoice the birth of a child. Though these songs are more popular in Uttar Pradesh, they are sung in other regions too.

Qawwali: These enthralling, soulful poems aiming spiritual nourishment are of Persian origin. They have been a part

of Hindustani music since the 13th century. Qawwali ensemble usually includes single or multiple vocalists, a few instrumentalists and a small group for rhythmic handclapping. Amir Khusrow, a prolific Sufi singer and poet, is considered as the 'father of Qawwali'.

Chhakri: It is the most popular traditional music form of Jammu and Kashmir. Chhakri songs are sung by the natives during religious festivals and other celebrations. They are usually accompanied by 'rouf', a dance form, in the end. Some of the instruments used in Chhakri performances are harmonium, sarangi, rubab etc. Famous love stories like Laila and Majnu are common themes in Chhakri songs.

Laman: Laman is an interesting style of Himachali folk music originated in the Kullu Valley region. These melodious songs are sung by native women on wedding eves or other such special occasions. Tonal simplicity and rhythmic patterns followed in Laman songs make them delightful.

Kajri: Kajri songs are semi-classical songs popular in Uttar Pradesh and Bihar. They are usually sung by women during monsoon. It is a traditional practice to perform Kajri on the third day of the second half of 'bhadra' (a month in Hindu calendar). On such occasions, women dance gracefully to these songs.

Tappa: They are impassioned love songs that originated in Punjab. This genre is largely influenced by the folk music of camel riders in Sindh-Punjab region. Vibrant and fast-paced rhythmic pattern makes Tappa stand out in Hindustani genre. They are semi-classical songs, which were initially sung only in royal courts.

Powada: They are Marathi ballads praising a hero or a place. The term Powada means 'glorious narration of a story'. The chief narrator, who plays the *duff* (a drum), is called shahir. 'Afzal Khanacha Vadh', about the encounter between Afzal Khan and Shivaji, is believed to be the earliest Powada.

Bhakha: Bhakha is a melodious harvest song prevalent in Jammu. They are usually sung with the accompaniment of a harmonium.

Daskathia: It is a genre of folk songs popular in Odisha. The name Daskathia is derived from two words- 'Das', the devotee on behalf of whom the worship is done and 'Kathi', the clappers used while singing Daskathia songs. This religious art form is usually performed by two people.

extra

First Woman Shehnai Player

The first woman shehnai player of India is Bageshwari Qamar. She made her debut in the year 1983. Apart from her solo recordings, she has also recorded "jugal-bandi" with her teacher Ustad Bismillah Khan.

Burrakatha: It is a power-packed musical narrative indigenous to Andhra Pradesh. The literal meaning of the word burra is 'tambura' (a musical instrument similar to veena). The lead performer uses tambura throughout the recital of the story. The panoramic range of themes stretches from mythological tales to social issues. It is said that Burrakatha had a major role in acting as bulwark against colonialism. These performances also include a lot of gestures and dance moves to emphasise the content.

Bihu songs: They are songs sung as part of Bihu festivals like Assamese New Year, arrival of spring, etc. These songs are an indispensable part of many tribal groups in Asom. These love songs actually denote the fertility of mother nature to provide a good harvest.

Songs of Lai Haraoba Festival: Lai Haraoba is a Manipuri festival celebrated to revere the forest deities. This festival is traditionally celebrated among the Meitei ethnic group of Manipur. The main highlights of this festival are the tuneful songs and the dainty-graceful dance performances. Ougri Hangen (song of creation) and Heijing Hirao (a ritualistic song) are the two popular Lai Haraoba songs sung on the last day of the festival.

Villu Paatu: This ancient musical-story telling form is from Tamil Nadu. It is called Villu Paatu because the lead vocalist/narrator holds a villu (bow) shaped instrument while performing the song. Both historical and social themes are chosen for Villu Paatu.

Chai Hia: They are songs sung during the Chapchar Kut festival of Mizoram. Chapchar Kut is the spring festival of the region, celebrated after 'forest clearing'.

Basant Geet: The basant (spring) festival songs of Garhwal are called Basant Geet. Goddess Saraswati is worshipped during Basant festival. Floors decorated with patterns made of rice flour are a usual scene in Garhwali homes during Basant Panchami. People wear bright yellow clothes for the occasion.

Ghasiyari Geet: These are dance-songs Garhwali women of Uttarakhand sing when they walk to the forest to collect grass for their cattle. They are melodious and rhythmic songs.

Sukar ke Biah: They are Bhojpuri songs about common man and his day to day life. These songs include a lot of minute observations about the villagers, especially their perceptions and beliefs.

Ammanaivari: This is another form of folk song prevalent in Tamil Nadu. They are songs about the chivalry and bravery of Chola rulers. Usually, women sing these songs while playing with an Ammanai (wooden ball).

Lavani: This genre of music native to Maharashtra is a combination of traditional dance and song. It is usually performed to the beats of the percussion instrument 'dholki'. The songs sung in a quick tempo with a powerful rhythm have contributed greatly to the development of Marathi folk theatre.

Oldest Gharana

extra

Gwalior Gharana is the oldest gharanas in Hindustani Music. There are many Gharans that actually originated from Gwalior Gharana. Nathan Peer Baksh and Nathe Khan were the musicians who founded Gwalior Gharana in the 16th century.

Famous Indian Painters

Abanindranath Tagore

(7 Aug. 1871 - 5 Dec. 1951)

Abanindranath Tagore was the principal artist and creator of 'Indian Society of Oriental Art' and the first major exponent of swadeshi values in Indian art, thereby founding the influential Bengal school of art,which led to the development of modern Indian painting. The National Gallery of Modern Art (NGMA), New Delhi organised a virtual tour titled "The Great Maestro-Abanindranath Tagore" to commemorate the 150th birth anniversary of Abanindranath Tagore on 7th August 2020.

Asoka's Queen by Abanindranath Tagore

Famous Paintings: *Bharat Mata, My Mother, Journey's End, The Passing of Shah Jahan, Asoka's Queen.*

Amrita Sher-Gil

(Jan. 30, 1913 - Dec. 5, 1941)

Sher-Gil first received recognition at the age of 19 through her painting *Young Girls*. It won her many accolades including a gold medal and election as an Associate of the Grand Salon in Paris. She was the youngest ever member and the only Asian to have received this recognition. Amrita's work can be defined as a bridge between western and Indian art style.

Young Girls by Amrita Sher-Gil

Famous Paintings: *Three Girls, Self-Portrait, Brahmacharis, Siesta, Village Scene, In the Ladies Enclosure, Young Girls.*

Francis Newton Souza

(12 Apr. 1924 - 28 Mar. 2002)

Over the course of his six-decade career, Souza experimented with a number of genres and styles, but it's probably his strong figurative practice, his line drawings and series of 'black paintings' produced in London during the 1950s and '60s for which he is most famous. He's also revered for his repetitive use of themes and motifs, including Catholicism, the female nude, and the dichoto-

Degenerates by F N Souza

my between good and evil.

Famous Paintings: *Birth, Crufixion, Man and Woman Laughing, Words and Lines, Degenerates.*

V S Gaitonde

(1924 - Aug. 10, 2001)

Vasudev S. Gaitonde is one of India's most prominent abstract artists. Gaitonde graduated from the J.J. School of Art, Bombay (Mumbai), in 1948. Shortly thereafter he became associated with the Progressive Artists' Group founded in 1947 by artists K.H. Ara, S.K. Bakre, H.A. Gade, M.F. Hussain, S.H. Raza, and F.N. Souza. The group, based in Mumbai, aimed at breaking away from all clichéd representations in Indian art.

Greatly influenced by Zen Buddhism, Gaitonde shunned the limelight, and his earlier figurative work was soon replaced by meditative nonrepresentational paintings. He rejected application of the word abstract to his work and instead referred to it as "nonobjective"–an entirely personal encounter on canvas. Gaitonde's paintings, often compared with those of many well-known Western artists, are widely exhibited.

Untitled by V S Gaitonde

Famous Paintings: *Untitled (1995), The Bird and an Egg, Painting in White.*

Ganesh Pyne

(11 June 1937 – 12 March 2013)

Pyne is one of the most notable contemporary artists of the Bengal School of Art, who had also developed his own style of "poetic surrealism", fantasy and dark imagery, around the themes of Bengali folklore and mythology.Pyne started as a watercolourist in the Bengal school mode, and gradually shifted to gouache and finally to tempera, for his subsequent abstract and surrealist work period, in ochre, black and blue shades.

Lady with Flower by V S Gaitonde

Famous Paintings: *The Reticent, Woman and the Bird, Lady with flower, The Wooden Horse.*

S L Haldankar

(25th November 1882- 1968)

Sawlaram Lakshman Haldankar was a well-known Indian painter. Haldankar was born into a family from Sawantwadi, which was then a Princely State and

Glow of Hope by S L Haldankar

is located today in Maharashtra state. He showed early talent in the arts and this was noticed by the headmaster of his school in Sawantwadi. He received a scholarship to study at the Sir J.J. School of Art, Bombay.

His most famous painting is Glow of Hope, also known as Woman With the Lamp.The young girl in that painting is none other than his own daughter Gita Haldankar. Haldankar made another painting with his second daughter Lilavati known as the Divine Flame also under the same concept of Glow of Hope.

Famous Paintings: *Glow of Hope, the Divine Flam*

M.F. Husain

(Sept. 17, 1915 - Jun. 9, 2011)

Husain is most known for his bold and vibrantly coloured narrative paintings in a modified Cubist style. His art captures a

Horses by M F Husain

wide variety of subjects including Mahatma Gandhi; Mother Teresa; the Ramayana; the Mahabharata; the British raj; and motifs of Indian urban and rural life.

Famous Paintings: *Horses, Ganesh, Three Dynasties, Mother Teresa, the Mahabharata, the Ramayana.*

Manishi Dey

(22 Sept.1909 - 31 Jan.1966)

Manishi Dey was the student of Abanin-

Bengal Women by Manishi Dey

extra

Pattachitra Painting

Pattachitra is one of the oldest and most popular art forms of Odisha. The name comes from the Sanskrit words "patta" (canvas) and "chitra" (picture). It is made by using completely natural ingredients like tamarind paste, tree gum, conch shells and lamp soot.

dranath Tagore in Shantiniketan. Abanindranath Tagore laid emphasis on traditional Indian culture art forms. And hence, Dey's paintings centred around promoting the traditional Indian Cultural Heritage.Manishi Day painted Bengal Women around 1950. It captures the essence of rural Bengali women.
Famous Paintings: *Daughter of the Soil, Bengal women*

Jamini Roy

(Apr. 11, 1887 - Apr. 24, 1972)

Jamini Roy began his career as a painter of Post-Impressionist landscapes and portraits. The European influences in his art were much in keeping with his training in a British academic system. However, in mid-1920s, Roy completely changed

Goddess Durga with Lakshmi, Saraswati and Ganesha by Jamini Roy

his style from his academic Western training to a new style which was based on Bengali folk traditions
Famous Paintings: *Mother and Child, Three Pujarins, Krishna.*

Nandalal Bose

(Dec. 3, 1882 - Apr. 16, 1966)

Nandalal Bose was one of the pioneers of modern Indian art and a key figure of Contextual Modernism. As the movement for independence raged on in India, Nandalal Bose, along with other prominent artists, worked towards moving

Dolan Champa by Nandalal Bose

the Indian art scene away from western influences that had been prevalent in art schools of the time.
Famous Paintings: *Bapu, Dandi March, Darjeeling and Fog, New Clouds, Dolan Champa.*

Rabindranath Tagore

(May 7, 1861 - Aug. 7, 1941)

Though best known as a poet and as

Dancing Woman by Rabindranath Tagore

winner of the Nobel Prize for Literature, Rabindranath Tagore was also an artist. He began painting late in his career when he was in his sixties.
Famous Paintings: *Self Portrait, Dancing Woman, Head Study (Geometric).*

Raja Ravi Varma

(Apr. 29, 1848- Oct. 2, 1906)

His works are regarded as among the best examples of the fusion of European techniques with a purely Indian sensibility. Varma also made affordable lithographs of his paintings, making them available to the public. This in turn enhanced his reach and reputation as a painter.
Famous Paintings: *Shakuntala, Woman Holding a Fruit, Stolen Interview, There Comes Papa, The Maharashtrian Lady.*

Shakuntala by Raja Ravi Varma

There Comes Papa by Raja Ravi Varma

Satish Gujral

(25 Dec. 1925 - 26 Mar. 2020)

Gujral is known for his diversity as an artist; and he has created works in paint-

Days of Glory by Satish Gujral

extra

Madhubani Painting

Madhubani painting, also known as Mithila painting, is an art form popular in the state of Mithila in Nepal and Bihar in India. While we can't be sure of the exact origins of the art form, it can be traced back to the Ramayana period.

ing, graphics, mural, sculpture, architecture and interior design. He is also a writer. One of the prominent themes he has explored in his art is the agony faced by the people during the partition of India.
Famous Paintings: *Days of glory, Mourning en masse, Tree of Life, Raising of Lazarus.*

Sayed Haider Raza

(Feb. 22, 1922 - Jul. 23, 2016)

S. H. Raza began as a painter of expressionistic landscapes. He moved to France

La Terre by Sayed Haider Raza

in October 1950 where he continued his experiments with Western Modernism. In the 2000s, Raza delved deeper into Indian spirituality creating works around the Kundalini, Nagas and the Mahabharat.
Famous Paintings: *Saurashtra, Composition Geometrique, Ankuran, La Terre, Bindu.*

Tyeb Mehta

(July 25, 1925 - July 2, 2009)

A painter, sculptor and film-maker, Tyeb Mehta was part of the Progressive Artists' Group (PAG) in Mumbai. Here, he interacted with many artists who would later be renowned like S. H. Raza and

La Terre by Tyeb Mehta

M. F. Husain.
Famous Paintings: *A Figure on a Rickshaw, Kali, Untitled, Mahishasura, Gesture, Girl in Love.*

Girl in Love by Tyeb Mehta

Popular Styles In Indian Architecture

Of all its artistic achievements, architecture in India perhaps occupies pride of place. Indian architecture has a long and rich history dating back thousands of years. The earliest buildings in India were made of wood and then brick. Few early buildings, especially those made of wood, survive. By about the 6th century BC, stone architecture was being created on the subcontinent. Indian architects soon became highly skilled in the carving and construction of stone buildings. By the 7th century AD, the use of stone had become popular for important buildings of great size. Numerous stone temples from the medieval period still stand in India. Most surviving examples of Indian architecture before the thirteenth century are religious structures. They consist mainly of Buddhist shrines, or stupas, and of Buddhist, Hindu, and Jain temples. The residences of monks give some idea of how non-religious architecture must have appeared. However, surprisingly few examples of palaces and ordinary houses of the time have been found.

India has seen a variety of architectural styles throughout its history. Given below are a few of the most popular styles that have characterised Indian architecture from the ancient age to the modern.

Temple Architecture

Temple architecture in India developed in almost all the regions during the ancient period. Across the country distinct architectural styles in temple construction can be seen. This differentiation in styles arise out of the geographical, climatic, racial, ethnic, linguistic, and historical diversities. Ancient Indian temples are classified into three broad categories, i.e. Nagara or the Northern style, Vesara or Mixed style, and Dravida or the Southern style. Apart from the broad classification, Kerala, Bengal, and the Himalayan areas also display their regional styles in temple architecture which are equally unique.

Nagara Style

The Nagara style is associated with the land between the Himalayas and Vindhyas and developed regionally in Northern parts of India. In this style, the structure comprises two buildings, the main taller shrine and an adjoining *mandapa* which is short.The foremost difference between these two buildings is the shape of the *shikhara*. In the main shrine, a bell-shaped structure is added. The temples are mainly formed of four chambers. They are Garbhagriha, Jagmohan, Natyamandir, Bhogamandir.

Kandariya Mahadev Temple at Khajuraho

Two distinguishing features of the Nagara style are its planning and elevation. The plan is square with a number of gradual projections in the middle of each side which imparts it a cruciform shape.

There are four projection types. When there is

- One projection on each side- 'triratha'
- Two projections – 'Pancharatha'
- Three projections – 'Saptharatha'
- Four projections –'Navaratha'

It exhibits Shikhara-A tower, in elevation which is progressively inclining to in a convex curve.

The projections in the plan are also carried upwards to the top of the Shikhara.

Originally in Nagara style, there were no pillars.

Kandariya Mahadev Temple in Madhya Pradesh is a classic example of Nagara style of temple architecture. It was also included in the UNESCO World Heritage List in 1986. Other examples are Sun Temple at Modhera, Lakshman Temple of Khajuraho, Sun Temple at Konark, Jagannath Temple at Puri, etc.

Vesara Architecture

Vesara style of Architecture evolved in the state of Karnataka in the region between the Krishna River and Vindhy during the medieval centuries. This style combines both the Dravida and the Nagara architectural styles. In such form of construction, the height of the temple towers reduced even though the numbers of tiers are retained. This is attained by decreasing the height of individual tiers. The semi-circular erections of the Buddhist chaityas are also copied in this style. In this style structures are finely finished, figures are much decorated and well-polished.

Temple at Badami

Examples: Dodda Bassapa Temple at Dambal, Ladkhan Temple at Ainhole and temples at the Chalukya capital Badami.

Dravidian Architecture

Dravida style advanced in the South, throughout the Chola Empire, between 9th–12th Century AD. It is seen in the region between the Krishna and Kaveri rivers. The two most important characteristics of Dravida temple architecture are that temples have more than 4 sides in the sanctum and the Tower or Vimana are pyramidals. In Dravida style temple is situated within an ambulatory hall. There are multiple storeys called Vimana, built above the Garbhagriha. Pillars and pilasters are massively used in this architectural style. Circular passageway around the Garbhagriha (chief deity's room) to permit devotees to do Pradakshina. Mandapa is a pillared hall with decoratively carved pillars. The entire structure was encircled within a courtyard surrounded by high walls. Gopuram is the high gates in this courtyard which allow passage of people. The Kailasanatha temple is a major example of the Dravida Architecture.

Kailasanatha Temple at Kanchipuram

Mughal Architecture

The Mughal architectural style is a unique blend of Islamic, Persian and Indian styles. Starting from the 16th century until the early 18th century, Mughal ar-

Humayun's Tomb in Delhi

chitecture flourished largely in the Indian subcontinent.

Some features common to many buildings are: Large bulbous onion domes, sometimes surrounded by four smaller domes.

- Use of white marble and red sandstone.
- Use of delicate ornamentation work, including pachin kari decorative work and jali-latticed screens.
- Monumental buildings surrounded by gardens on all four sides.
- Mosques with large courtyards.
- Persian and Arabic calligraphic inscriptions, including verses from the Quran.
- Large gateways leading up to the main building.
- Iwans on two or four sides.
- Use of decorative chhatris.
- Use of jalis and jharokhas.

Mughal architecture has also influenced later Indian architectural styles, including the Indo-Saracenic style of the British Raj, the Rajput style and the Sikh style.

Some of the finest structures in the country like Humayun's Tomb, Akbar's Tomb, Fatehpur Sikri, Red Fort at Delhi, Jama Masjid Delhi and the Taj Mahal at Agra are a few examples of Mughal architecture

Kalinga Architecture

The Kalinga architecture is a style which flourished in the ancient Kalinga region. This form of style can be seen in the eastern Indian state of Odisha and also in northern parts of Andhra Pradesh. Kalinga architectural style consists of three different types of temples, i.e. Rekha Deula, Khakhara Deula and Pidha Deula. The diverse aspects of a typical Kalinga Temple consist of Architectural stipulations, historical connotations, Iconography. It also honours the custom, traditions, and connected legends.

Lingaraj Temple in Bhubaneswar

Sun Temple at Konark is one of the finest examples of Kalinga Architecture. Built with sandstone and laterite, Lingaraj Temple in Bhubaneswar marks the quintessence of Kalinga Architecture.

Sikh Architecture

This is one of those styles that have gained immense popularity across the globe. Sikh architecture is characterized by exquisite intricacy, values of progressiveness, austere beauty, and coherent flowing lines. This is one particular architectural form which managed to evolve due to its Modernism or progressive style. Sikh architecture is all about beautiful curves and straight lines; that is exactly what sets it apart from other architectural styles.

Sikh Architecture is heavily influenced

Golden Temple in Amritsar

by Mughal and Islamic styles. The onion dome, frescoes, in-lay work, and multi-foil arches are Mughal influences, more specially from Shah Jahan's period, whereas chattris, oriel windows, bracket supported eaves at the string-course, and ornamented friezes are derived from elements of Rajput architecture.

Apart from religious buildings, Sikh architecture includes secular forts, bungas (residential places), palaces, and colleges. Shri Keshgarh Sahib and the Sri Harmandir Sahib (Golden Temple) are prime examples.The most important of the complex of shrines at Sri Anandpur Sahib is Gurudwara Keshgarh Sahib, which stands on the place where the "Khalsa" was born.

Indian Vernacular Architecture

The vernacular style of architecture refers to the informal building of structures done by local builders using traditional building methods. This is one of the most widespread forms of architectural style not only in India but across the globe. The builders who construct such structures are unschooled in formal architectural design; their work typically reflects the rich multiplicity of our country's climate, locally available construction materials, and the complex variations in local social customs and craftsmanship.

Cave Architecture

The cave architecture in India is believed to have started in the third century BC. Such structures were used by the Jain monks and the Buddhist typically as a place of residence and worship. Some examples of this type of cave structure are Chaityas and Viharas of Buddhists. Caves in India are usually linked with three different religions, namely Hinduism, Buddhism, and Jainism; hence they reflect the architectural difference in accordance with respective religions.

The earliest caves carved by Buddhist monks belonged to the Hinayana Buddhist path. In this style of architecture, which prevailed from 200 BC to 200 AD, only symbols of the Buddha were used. No personal icon was used. After this era, Mahayana Buddhism flourished in India and the cave temples made in this period showed the Buddha in many poses. The idol of Buddha became a major feature of all temples of this period. The caves at Karla – which boast the single largest cave hall with well-formed pillars and an

Karla Caves

ornate entrance in the world – are one of the best examples of Hinayana cave architecture. While there are figures of human beings, celestial beings and animals on the entrance arch and the walls and designs with animals on the rounded columns, which allow the devotees to circumambulate the stupa, the Buddha is represented only by the stupa. Bhaja caves, which lie on the opposite side of Karla, are in the same category. As the number of monks increased, the caves also increased. Some were only living quarters, with no embellishments and most were dug by the monks themselves.

Rock-Cut Architecture

The Rock-cut structures in India display the most impressive piece of ancient Indian art specimen. Rock-cut architecture is the art of creating a structure by carv-

Ajanta Caves in Maharashtra

ing it out of a solid natural rock. Most of the rock-cut structures in our country were related to different religious communities. India has more than 1,500 known rock-cut structures and many of these structures contain artworks which are of global importance, and most are festooned with wonderful stone carvings.

Ajanta, Ellora and Elaphanta caves in Maharashtra are finest examples of rock-cut architecture in India.

Colonial Architecture

The colonial architecture spanning about 150 to 200 years under the British Empire attained its golden age in the second half of the 19th century.

Characteristics of Colonial architecture

The British viewed themselves as the successors to Mughals and used architectural style as a symbol of power.

The buildings they constructed in India were the direct reflection of their achievements in architecture back home.

The aim of colonial architecture under British rule was to build structures to house their people and their organisations to control Indian empire.

Under colonial architecture, new residential areas like Civil Lines and Cantonments came up in towns.

Colonial architectural style in British India witnessed another feature of rare usage of stone especially marble.

Later stone was replaced by brick as the prime material of British architecture in India; slate, machine-made tiles and steel girders came in vogue; galvanised iron revolutionised the Anglo-Indian roof.

Neo-classical Style

This architectural style is reflected in the late 19th century structures in British India.

It is an imitation of the classical Greeko-Roman style of architecture.

It involved recreation, revival, re-adaptation of building architecture in ancient Greece and Rome.

Townhall in Mumbai

The Mediterranean origins of this architecture were thought to be suitable for Indian tropical climate.

It was characterised by the construction of geometrical structures fronted with lofty pillars.

An early example of this style is Town Hall in Bombay.

Neo-Gothic Style

The neo-Gothic style was a revival of the early Gothic style of architecture which had its roots in buildings, especially churches, built in northern Europe during the medieval period.

Chhatrapati Terminus in Mumbai

It was characterised by high-pitched roofs, pointed arches and detailed decoration.

This style was adapted for building infrastructure in Bombay.

An impressive group of buildings facing the seafront including the Secretariat, University of Bombay and High Court were all built in this style.

Many Indians merchants gave money for some of these buildings. They were happy to adopt the neo-Gothic style since they believed it was progressive and would help make Bombay, a modern city.

The British invested a lot in the design and construction of railway stations in this style, an example of which is Chhatrapati Shivaji Terminus in Mumbai.

Indo-Saracenic Revival Style

It was a hybrid of Indian and European style which developed in an early twentieth century.

Indo was shorthand for Hindu and Saracen was a term Europeans used to designate Muslim.

Taj Hotel in Mumbai

The Indo-Saracenic revival architecture drew elements from native Indo-Islamic architecture and combined it with Neo-Classical styles favoured in Victorian Britain.

The inspiration for this style was medieval buildings in India with their domes, chhatris, jalis, and arches etc.

Chepauk Palace situated in Chennai (erstwhile Madras) was the first Indo-Saracenic revival building.

The Gateway of India is the most famous example of this style. The industrialist Jamsetji Tata built the Taj Mahal Hotel in the similar style.

Art-Deco Style

Art Deco in India (and especially in Mumbai) evolved into a unique style that came to be called Deco-Saracenic.

Bombay High Court

Essentially, it was a combination of the Islamic and the Hindu architectural styles.

Art Deco is one of Mumbai s least noticed architectural styles, though Mumbai and its suburbs possibly have the largest number of Art Deco buildings in the world.

Deco details touch every architectural aspect flooring, wood panelling, railings, weather shades, verandahs, balconies and facades that are very airy and built in stepped -back style, etc.

The interiors have Victorian influences while the exterior was Indian.

Art Deco architecture in Mumbai developed during the 1930s and produced facades.

The Art Deco style is also extremely popular amongst various Cinema halls that sprung up in the early to mid 20th Century including Metro Cinema, Eros Cinema etc.

Some examples of this style are - The Mahalakshmi Temple, Regal Cinema, The High Court building in Mumbai

Architects of Modern India

Contributions of Sir Edwin Lutyen and Sir Herbert Baker

The British government, experiencing a sense of crisis due to rising anti-imperialist wave in India, declared Delhi to be its new capital in 1911.

Rashtrapati Bhavan in Delhi

Thus the British leading architects Edwin Lutyens and Herbert Baker were invited to design the city of New Delhi and its important edifices.

The architects designed a monumental urban street complex that was essentially alien to Indian cities.

Their architectural style involved a fusion of classical European and Indian elements.

Lavish colonnades, open verandas, tall, slender windows, chhajjas (wide roof overhangs) and cornices jaalis (circular stone apertures) and chhatris (free-standing pavilions) were used at the same time as decorative elements from typical historic Indian architecture.

Lutyen designed Rashtrapati Bhavan, formerly the Viceroy s residence. It is built of sandstone and has design features like canopies and jaali from Rajasthan

Lutyen designed many other monuments in Delhi including India gate. In recognition of his contributions, New Delhi is also known as Lutyens Delhi.

Similarly, Baker, who came to India to work with Lutyen, had also designed many buildings in New Delhi such as Central Secretariat building, Parliament House, Bungalows of MPs etc.

Architecture after Independence

On India getting independence from the British Empire in 1947, Indian architecture immediately extricated itself from European classical styles and rushed into modernism. Modern Indian architecture still honours and upholds the traditions of India, but the architectural form works to better meet the needs of modern-day society. Modern Indian architecture reflects its various socio-cultural sensibilities which vary from region to region.

Characteristics of post-independence architecture

Today we see a traditional character in Indian architecture, but with modern form and style.

- Buildings are less ornate and more utilitarian and expressive in form.
- Building materials used in construction are a basic and locally available but cutting edge. The use of steel and glass to erect innovative building forms is very popular and striking in the landscape.
- Urban centres in India are booming, bringing along with it a rise in population and property demand.
- High rise buildings have also become very common in these dense urban areas where space must be maximized.
- Another modern characteristic in India is building of structures which are more responsive to its ecology and climate.

Also, many architects in India including Laurie Baker and Charles Correa have concerned themselves with building low-cost housing for poor households.

Le Corbusier

• He was a Switzerland-born French architect

• His largest and most ambitious project was the design of Chandigarh. It was one of the early planned cities in post-independent India. The master-plan for Chandigarh was prepared by Le Corbusier. Chandigarh's Capitol Complex, designed by Corbusier was declared by UNESCO as World Heritage in 2016.

Capital Complex in Chandigarh

• Le Corbusier's design called for the use of raw concrete, whose surface not smoothed or polished and which showed the marks of the forms in which it dried.

Not only his radical reimagination of urban life left its imprint all over the world, but also the architectural work of Le Corbusier is an outstanding contribution to the Modern Movement in Indian architecture.

Post-1947, Indian architecture was at a standstill in terms of progression; there was no unique identity being formed. However, when the Indian Punjab government took on world famous architect Le Corbusier to design the city of Chandigarh, an architectural breakthrough began.

Architects working in India began to draw inspiration in the years following Le Corbusier's work, and thus began a more rapid evolution of modern architecture.

B V Doshi

He is considered an important figure of South Asian architecture and noted for his unfathomable contributions to the evolution of architectural discourse in India.

IIM Bangalore

He contributed significantly in the development of modern Indian architecture.

In his initial years, he worked for Le Corbusier in his projects.

His noted works include Indian Institute of Management Bangalore, Amdavad ni Gufa and Tagore Hall in Ahmadabad etc.

Charles Correa

He was a Secunderabad born Indian architect

Correa was a major figure in contemporary Indian architecture. With his extraordinary and inspiring designs, he played a pivotal role in the creation of post-Independence Indian architecture.

He is known for his adaptation of Modernist tenets to local climates and building styles.

In the realm of urban planning, he is particularly noted for his sensitivity to the needs of the urban poor and for his use of traditional methods and materials.

Correa's work in India shows a careful

Gandhi Memorial in Ahmedabad

fusion of local vernacular tradition with a modernist approach

Correa's urban planning projects and land use planning present a solution to third world problems and try to go beyond that.

His famous works in India include Mahatma Gandhi Memorial in Ahmedabad, the Jawahar Kala Kendra in Jaipur, the planning of Navi Mumbai etc.

Laurie Baker

He was a British-born Indian architect. He became an Indian citizen in 1989.

He was Influenced by Mahatma Gandhi in his life and work.

Due to his social and humanitarian efforts to bring architecture and design to the common man, his belief in simplicity in design and in life, he has been called the "Gandhi of architecture."

His work follows economical, ecological and sustainable criteria in building and is devoted to people in lower income groups.

He is known for his initiatives in cost-effective energy-efficient architecture and designs that maximized space, ventilation and light.

He promoted the revival of regional building practices and use of local materials.

He was a pioneer of sustainable architecture as well as organic architecture.

Indian Coffee House in Thiruvananthapuram

Hafeez Contractor

Hafeez Contractor was born in Mumbai in a Parsi family. He earned his graduate diploma in architecture from the University of Mumbai in 1975 and completed his graduation and MS in Architecture from Columbia University, New York City

Imperial I and II in Mumbai

on a Tata scholarship. He designed The Imperial I and II, the tallest buildings in India.

extra

First Journalism Course in India

Dr Annie Besant initiated the first journalism course in India at the National University at Adyar, Madras under the aegis of Theosophical Society, in 1920. Initially, it was a bachelor's degree under the Faculty of Arts in the Department of English.

Ancient Indian Schools of Art: Gandhara, Amaravati and Mathura

The three prominent and distinct ancient schools of art in India were the Gandhara School of Art, Mathura School of Art and Amaravati School of Art.

Gandhara School of Art

- A combination of Hellenistic, West Asiatic and native elements.
- Greek and Roman techniques, modified according to Indian requirements, were employed in fashioning the Gandhara sculpture which truly represents Indian culture in a Western garb.

- Its area extended from Takshila in India to the Swat Valley in Pakistan and northwards to areas in Afghanistan.
- The Gandhara sculptors made images of Lord Buddha in the Greco-Roman style. The images of Buddha resembled Greek God Apollo. It gave more stress to the bodily features and external beauty.
- Most characteristic trait - depiction of Lord Buddha in the standing or seated positions.
- Seated Buddha is always shown cross-legged in the traditional Indian way.
- Tallest rock-cut statue of Lord Buddha - Bamiyan (Afghanistan) - 3-4 century AD.
- Early Gandhara School used bluish-grey sandstone while the later period saw the use of mud and stucco

Amaravati School of Art

- It evolved during Satavahna period.
- The sculptures of Amaravati School were made using white marbles.
- This school of art developed at Amravati, on the banks of the Krishna River in modern Andhra Pradesh.
- Construction began in 200 B.C. and was completed in 200 A.D.
- This school of art had great influence on art in Sri Lanka and South-East Asia as products from here were carried to those countries.
- Lord Buddha is depicted in the form of `Swastika` mark. This has been carved out on the cushioned seat over a throne that is situated under the Bodhi tree.
- Its ruins are preserved in the London Museum.

Mathura School of Art

- Mathura School of art is purely indigenous style. Mathura art developed during post Maurya period (mainly during Shunga period) and reached its peak during the Gupta period (AD 325 to 600).
- The sculptures of Mathura School were made using spotted red sandstone.
- The traditional centre, Mathura, remained the main art production site whereas Sarnath and Kosambi also emerged as important centres of art production. Spotted red sandstone has been used in this school.
- Themes in the Mathura Art vary from Buddhist to Brahmanical to sometimes secular. More stress was given to the inner beauty and facial emotions rather than bodily gesture.
- Buddha's first image can be traced to Kanishka's reign (about 78 A.D.).
- Under the Mathura Art images of Vishnu and Shiva, Buddha, Yakshas, Yakshinis, Shaivite and Vaishnavite deities were found.

Modern Indian Theatre

Indian Theatre, since time immemorial, has had some kind of theatrical expressions that have undergone wide–ranging changes during the last two to three thousand years. Even today, many tribes in our country perform ritually related acts during marriages, birth, death and times of propitiation to gods. There are references to dramas, dances and actors in Valmiki Ramayana and certain other puranas. Works of Panini (4th century B.C), Patanjali and Kautilya have also referred to performances and performers. All performing arts are well structured in Natyashastra of Bharatamuni, which gives numerous production manuals about theatre, music, dance and poetry.

Evolution of Sanskrit Theatre

Sanskrit Theatre, which was the first to evolve, depicted many layered images of social, cultural and mental pictures of those times through the glorious works of Kalidasa (Abhijnana Shakumthalam), Bhavabhooti (Uttararama Charitam), Bhasa (Urubhangam) etc. among others, with a view to accomplishing a state of bliss, ie, known as theory of 'Rasa'. Compared to Western theatrical concept Sanskrit Theatre treated Time, Place and Action as imaginative and created Rasa through acting, which is different from the Aristotelian concept of 'catharsis', which is intense emotions of fear or pity. Folk and traditional theatrical forms have flourished in our regional languages that too with innumerable elements of Sanskrit Theatre. These forms have separate characteristics from both Sanskrit and modern theatres.

Natyashastra itself speaks of 400 styles specified according to the regions of North, East, West and South. Along with these, ballad singers or the wandering minstrels started spreading devotional stories and musical dramas in the forms of Harikatha and Keertana rendition, that continued till 19th century. When Bhakti movement of 14 to 17th century produced great language poets,

Sanskrit theatre was very secular in its content. Ramalila and Rasalila of Uttar Pradesh, Bhagavata Mela of Tamil Nadu and Dasavatara of Maharashtra were some of them. By 17th century, Shaiva cult influenced the Jatra folk theatre of Bengal. Along with these, some non-religious folk theatres emerged like Tamasha, Bhavai, Nautanki, Therukuthu etc.

In the medieval period, theatre actor, speech and music were the domineering factors and witnessed the absence of women performers. Even though, all these were open-air performances, Koodiyattam of Kerala and Bhaona of Asom were performed in Koothambalams and Bhaona Ghars respectively. However, during British regime, this theatre reached Kolkata, Mumbai and Chennai, before reaching almost all parts of India. For Bengali aristocrats their Jatra, might have appeared backward and therefore they were attracted to the novelty of Western theatre. Many talented theatre artistes including playwrights (Girishchandra Ghosh, Rabindra Nath Tagore, Badal Sarkar) carried Bengali Theatre to its present glory.

Theatre in Maharashtra

Like in Bengal, the new theatrical activities became very popular in Maharashtra (Vasant Panduranga, Mama Warerkar, Vijay Tendulkar) and Gujarat where the impact of Western education and culture was great and formed professional theatre companies of Western type due to the efforts of enterprising Parsi Community. Some of the outstanding theatre personalities were C.C. Mehta, Jaisankar Sundary, Nassurudin Shah etc.

Vijay Tendulkar

In Oriya Rameswar Roy, Gopal Dey, Pravin Joshi were noted for their commercialism and modernity, whereas in Manipur Ratan Thiyyam, Kanhailal, Lokendra Arambham etc. contributed a lot and particularly Ratan's productions were acclaimed nationally and internationally. Modern Kannada Theatre was enriched by Adya Rangacharya, B.V. Karanth, Girish Karnad etc. The Actor / Manager dominated Tamil commercials that had veteran actors like Samband Mudaliar, T.K.S. Brothers, M.G. Ramachandran etc.

Malayalam Theatre

Even though Malayalam Theatre was flourishing under the shadow of Tamil musicals, stalwarts like Oachira Velukutty, Sebastian Kunjukunju Bhagavatar, Thikkurissi Sukumaran Nair, Thoppil Bhasi, C.N. Sreekantan Nair, G. Sankara Pillai, Kavalam Narayana Panikker, N.N. Pillai etc. enriched theatre largely. Regarding Hindi, Parsi Theatre met the entertainment needs of the urban audiences and Indian People's Theatre Association (IPTA) brought some freshness in many parts of Hindi region. Some important theatre personalities and institutions of those days were Prithwi Theatre, poet Bharathendu Harichandra, Master Madan, Agha Harsha, Radheshyam etc. who provided a West oriented Indian theatre.

Kavalam Narayana Panikker

Modern Theatre

From 20th century onwards, authentic translations and adaptations of the Western playwrights like Euripides, Shakespeare, Tolstoy, Brecht etc. were made available to Indian language theatres. The activities of National School of Drama for the last 53 years, through the directors like E. Alkazi, B.V. Karanth, Kirti Jain, Ramgopal Bajaj, Anuradha Kapur etc. gave a national character to Indian theatre. Meanwhile, for the last half century, realistic theatre was taking a back seat world over, where international Directors like Grotowski, Eugnio Barba, Richard Shechner, Peter Brook etc. opened up new vistas of theatre after learning from Asian countries and particularly from India. Use of myths or folk tales has modern metaphor with super-naturals, animals, masques, puppets, Poetry, stylized speeches etc. became very common along with rituals, tantric, martial-arts etc. Thus, a total theatre emerged with the participation of audience in the performance bending fully towards Indianness. Of course, Western theatre has provided us modern sound and lighting technology and in turn, numerous Indian plays were translated and produced in other Asian, African and Western countries.

English drama in India, which was once just the illustration of British mistreatment, tried to highlight Indian tradition, folklore, custom, rituals, conventions, and rites. Dramatists with substantial output include the poet Nissim Ezekiel (1924-2004), Dina Mehta and Manjula Padmanabhan. The saga of English theatre, which began long back during the British Imperialism, continued further and is still an eminent part of various forms of theatre in India. Continuous study, deep understanding and above all the tuneful blend of the west and East have helped English drama in India as a distinct art form whilst aiding it to stand apart with pride and dignity.

Manjula Padmanabhan

National School of Drama

After independence, theatre artistes felt the necessity of addressing the concerns of an independent nation and Chathopadhyay argued in a Bombay seminar (1956) for a middle ground between revivalism and Westernization for making the future National Indian Theatre. Consequent on this, the National School of Drama was set up in 1959 and its multifarious theatre activities were in full swing during the last 53 years, under the stewardship of veteran directors like E. Alkazi and B.V. Karanth among others. Reviving the Sanskrit tradition to the contemporary Indian audience is a strong movement towards return to the theatre of roots that caught its energy in local, traditional, rural and folk performances. Such revival rejected the imitation of decadent realistic moulds devised for entertainment or distorting Western theatrical practices. Even though the Root's Movement has an appearance of an anti–modern outlook, it has all the Indianness, authenticity, originality and creativity.

Renaissance Period

These theatre makers redefined modern, traditional, classical, folk, urban and rural as being inseparable and mutually influencing. If one wants to know our mythology, he has to follow certain signals of the West as also to negotiate with our cultural and colonial past. The period 1965-75, considered as the 'Renaissance of our Theatre', saw intense experimentation and engaging with Brechtian theatre that combined with local forms, which appeared similar to that of roots movement. Here the contribution of Kavalam Narayana Panikkar is noteworthy because he is the one who integrated the chorographical components of Kalaripayattu, Sanskrit and folk theatre elements in his productions. Along with Kavalam, Habib Tanvir mixed folk artistes of Chathishgarh with urban, B.V. Karanth used Yakshagana in his Shakesperean production, and Ratan Theyyam's creations reflected Manipur's rich folk and martial elements.

Habib Tanvir

The focus of these directors was changing 'times and spaces' which was shown in Kavalam's Avanavan Katamba, Tanvir's Charandas Chor, Tendulkar's Ghasiram Kothwal, G. Sankara Pillai's Karutha Daivathe Thedi etc. In Bengal Utpal Dutt brought a theatrical form with elaborate spectacles taken from rich Jatra plays. However, this experimentation could recast theatre not only with form, content and space but also in the productional styles.

Indian Writing in English

The beginnings of Indian Writing in English (IWE) can be traced to the nineteenth century, to the time of Raja Ram Mohan Roy (1774-1833), the enlightened social reformer who emphasized the importance of education in English if India wished to be a leading nation of the world. To Sake Dean Mahomet, an Indian traveller and entrepreneur, goes the credit of writing *Travels of Dean Mahomet* (1794), the first book in English by an Indian author.

The century also produced outstanding poets like Henry Derozio, (1809-1831), Michael Madhusudan Dutt (1824-1873), and Toru Dutt (1856-1877) who wrote poetry in English and French. Both Derozio and Toru Dutt showed great promise and tragically died very young. Toru Dutt's poem, *Our Casuarina Tree,* is believed to be autobiographical. Sarojini Naidu, Tagore's contemporary and an active figure in politics, left her mark in literature too by writing romantic poetry that earned her the sobriquet 'The Nightingale of India'. Her brother Harindranath Chattopadhyay was another renowned poet. Sri Aurobindo (1872-1950), mystic, philosopher and poet, wrote his highly rated epic *Savitri: A Legend and a Symbol* (1950-51), one of the longest poems in IWE.

Toru Dutt

The outstanding names in later IWE poetry are Nissim Ezekiel, Dom Moraes, A.K Ramanujan, Kamala Das and Vikram Seth. Other famous names include Jayanta Mahapatra, Gieve Patel, Keki Daruwalla, Eunice De Souza, P.Lal, R.Parthasarathy, Kersi Katrak, Sujata Bhatt, Hoshang Merchant, Smita Agarwal, Ranjit Hoskote, Arundhathi Subramaniam and Sudeep Sen.

First Nobel Prize

Bankim Chandra Chatterjee's work, *Rajmohan's Wife* (serialized in 1834 but published in book form posthumously in 1864), is acknowledged to be the first Indian novel in English. Rabindranath Tagore (1861-1941), the pride of India, is the outstanding literary figure of this age. He was awarded the Nobel Prize for Literature in 1913 and remains the only Indian to have won the coveted award for Literature.

Dhan Gopal Mukherji (1890-1936), was one of the first popular Indian writers in English and won the Newbery Medal in the US for his *Gay Neck, the Story of a Pigeon* (1927). An important contribution to IWE was made by P.Lal (1929-2010), a poet, essayist, translator and publisher, who established 'Writers Workshop', a press for Indian English writing, in 1958.

Dhan Gopal Mukherji

The 1930s saw the emergence of the formidable trio of novelists, Raja Rao, R.K Narayan and Mulk Raj Anand who went on to gain international fame and prestige. The novels of Raja Rao (1908-2006) with their rural settings won praise for the Indianness of their themes and his *Kanthapura* (1938) wooed the West with its unique story telling methods. His later works like the semi autobiographical *The Serpent and the Rope* (1960) and *Cat and Shakespeare* (1965) established his credentials as one of India's finest stylists. R.K Narayan (1906-2001) was introduced to the western world by Graham Greene who found great talent in his first novel *Swami and Friends* (1935) and helped him find a publisher. R.K Narayan created a fictional town, Malgudi, as the locale for most of his novels and his simple style and realistic narration won him many admirers. *The Bachelor of Arts* (1937), *The Guide* (1958), *The Man-eater of Malgudi* (1961) and *Grandmother's Tale* (1992) are some of his famous novels. The realistic novels of Mulk Raj Anand (1905-2004) like *The Untouchable* (1935) and *Coolie* (1936) reflect the harsh social divides that are the bane of India.

R.K Narayan

G V Desani (1909-2000) is another important IWE writer whose cult novel *All About H. Hatterr* (1948) about an Anglo-Malay man in search for enlightenment took the world by storm and was compared to James Joyce's *Ulysses*.

The spirit of an independent India that was struggling to establish an identity of its own was captured by later novelists like Manohar Malgonkar in his Distant Drum and The Devil's Wind, Kamala Markandaya in Some Inner Fury, Anita Desai in *Clear Light of Day* and Nayantara Sahgal in *From Fear Set Free.*

Manohar Malgonkar

Booker of Bookers

The Grand Old Man of IWE, Khushwant Singh, born in 1915, attracted notice with his 1956 novel, *Train to Pakistan* about the violent aftermath of partition and has held public attention since. His prodigious output includes short stories, novels, plays and nonfiction. *The Sunset Club* (2010) was his last literary offering. The entry of Salman Rushdie into the literary scene marked the beginning of a new era in IWE. His path breaking novel *Midnight's Children* (1981) became a book for the Booker, winning the Booker Prize in 1981, Booker of Bookers in 1992 and the Best of the Bookers in 2008. Rushdie used an innovative hybrid language in which English mingled easily with Indian terms to represent the complexities of India. His style has been described as magic realism and his other novels are *The Satanic Verses* (1988), *The Moor's Last Sigh* (1995), *Fury* (2001), *The Golden House* (2017) and *Two Years Eight Months and Twenty-eight Nights.* His latest novel is *Quichotte* (2019).

Booker Prizes

Rushdie triggered off a Booker Prize rush and since then three Indians have won the Booker – Arundhati Roy for *The God of Small Things* (1997), Kiran Desai for *The Inheritance of Loss* (2006) and Aravind Adiga for *The White Tiger* (2008). Jhumpa Lahiri, the Indian American writer won the Pulitzer Prize for Fiction in 2000 for *Interpreter of Maladies* (1999) and V.S Naipaul, the Trinidadian-British writer of Indian descent won the Nobel Prize for Literature in 2001.

A host of names jostle for attention in the Indian literary pantheon. Shashi Tharoor's *The Great Indian Novel* (1989) is a satirical take on the Mahabharata. Vikram Seth's *A Suitable Boy* (1993) at 1474 pages is one of the longest novels. Anita Desai, Shashi Deshpande, Ruskin

Kiran Nagarkar

Bond, Ruth Prawer Jhabvala, Ved Mehta, Manoj Das, Gita Mehta, Bharati Mukherjee, Namita Gokhale, Manju Kapur, Allan Sealy, Arun Joshi, Vikram Chandra, Chitra Banerjee Diwakaruni, Rohinton Mistry, Upamanyu Chatterjee, Raj Kamal Jha, Amit Chaudhuri, Gita Hariharan, Tarun Tejpal, Kiran Nagarkar, Manjula Padmanabhan, Ashok Banker, David Davidar, Hari Kunzru, Kalpana Swaminathan, Pinky Virani, Vikas Swaroop, Namita Devidayal, Shobha De, Jaishree Misra, Anita Nair and Anurag Mathur are some of the names that have made their mark in IWE.

Amitav Ghosh was conferred the 54th Jnanpith award in December 2018 and is the first Indian writer in English to have been chosen for this honour.Ghosh is the author of *The Circle of Reason* (his 1986 debut novel), *The Shadow Lines* (1998), *The Calcutta Chromosome* (1995), *The Glass Palace* (2000), *The Hungry Tide* (2004), and *Sea of Poppies* (2008), the first volume of The Ibis trilogy, set in the 1830s, just before the Opium War, which encapsulates the colonial history of the East. Ghosh's *River of Smoke* (2011), is the second volume of The Ibis trilogy. The third, *Flood of Fire*, completing the trilogy, was published 28 May 2015 to positive reviews.

Chetan Bhagat deserves special mention for the phenominal success of his popular novels. He is the author of bestselling novels *Five Point Someone* (2004), *One Night @ the Call Center* (2005), *The 3 Mistakes of My Life* (2008), *2 States* (2009), *Revolution 2020* (2011), *Half Girlfriend* (2014), *One Indian Girl* (2016) and *The Girl in Room 105* (2018).

Amish Tripathi, the author we instantly associate with mythological fiction, is best known for writing the Shiva trilogy. His debut novel, *The Immortals of Meluha*, made a record-breaking sale within a few weeks of its launch, and Amish became an internationally acclaimed Indian author. Amish Tripathi is known for his novels *The Immortals of Meluha, The Secret of the Nagas, The Oath of the Vayuputras, Ram: Scion of Ikshvaku, Sita: Warrior of Mithila* and *Raavan: Enemy of Aryavarta*. The first three books collectively comprise the Shiva trilogy and the later three are the first three books of the Ram Chandra series which is going to be a collection of five books.The Shiva trilogy was the fastest selling book series in Indian publishing history while the Ram Chandra series was the second fastest selling book series in Indian publishing history. Amish recently launched his first non-fiction book called *Immortal India*.

Manu Joseph's debut novel *Serious Men* (2010) won The Hindu Literary Prize and the PEN/Open Book Award. His semi-autobiographical second novel, *The Illicit Happiness of Other People* (2012), was described by The Wall Street Journal as a work that "injects dark, rueful laughter into an immensely touching story of loss". Jeet Thayil's second novel, *The Book of Chocolate Saints* (2018), is a hypnotic story of literature, coloured individuals and their fragmented dreams.

Manu Joseph

Exciting new names that have entered the fray recently include Meghna Pant, Janice Pariat and Kanishk Tharoor. Multiple award-winning author, journalist and speaker Meghna Pant's writing is a competent blend of inspiring and insightful. Her debut novel, *One & a Half Wife*, came out in 2012 and was a bestseller, whilst her latest book is *The Trouble with Women* (2016). In 2013, Janice Pariat's debut collection of short stories, *Boats on Land,*

Janice Pariat

won the Sahitya Akademi Young Writer Award, which made her the first writer from Meghalaya to receive an award from the Sahitya Akademi for a work in English. Kanishk Tharoor released *Swimmer Among the Stars* in 2016, wherein he weaves a heady blend of mythology, fantasy and fable into a collection of stories you'll be hard pressed to forget.

In the field of drama, IWE may not have created the ripples it did in fiction and poetry but it has creditable exponents. Krishna Mohan Banerjee's *The Persecuted* (1831) is considered the first Indian English play though Michael Madhusudan Dutt's *Is This Called Civilization?* (1871) is believed to be the play that gave direction to Indian English drama. Major IWE playwrights of the pre independence era include Tagore, Sri Aurobindo, Harindranath Chattopadhyay, A S P Ayyar, T.P Kailasam, Bharati Sarabhai, and J.M Lobo Prabhu. The names of Asif Currimbhoy, Pratap Sharma, Gurucharan Das, G.V.Desani, Lakhan Deb and Pritish Nandy rank high among the playwrights of the post independence era.

Two promising contemporary dramatists who have already made their presence felt are Mahesh Dattani (*Final Solutions, Dance Like a Man, Tara*), the first playwright in English to be awarded the Sahitya Akademi Award and Manjula Padmanabhan whose play *Harvest* reaped her the rich harvest of the Onassis Prize in 1997.

Important nonfiction IWE of early 20th century includes Jawaharlal Nehru's *Glimpses of World History,* a collection of letters written by Nehru to his daughter from various prisons in British India between 1930- 33, *The Discovery of India* (1946) and Dr S. Radhakrishnan's *Eastern Religion and Western Thought* (1939). The works of Nirad C. Chaudhuri (1897-1999) gained great acclaim and include *The Autobiography of an Unknown Indian* (1951), *A Passage to England* (1959) and *The Continent of Circe* (1965). Following the tradition of Nirad Chaudhuri by using fine prose to explore and describe contemporary Indian reality is a group of very competent nonfiction writers. They include Pankaj Mishra, Arundhati Roy, Ramachandra Guha, Mukul Kesavan and Sudhir Kakar, Suketu Mehta, Shashi Tharoor and Manu S. Pillai.

The year 2021 saw works from famous writers like Jhumpa Lahiri, Amitav Ghosh and Chitra Banerjee Divakaruni. *Whereabouts* is Jhumpa Lahiri's first book in Italian, which she herself has translated into English. *Languages of Truth* is a compilation of celebrated storyteller Salman Rushdie's essays from 2003 to 2020. *The Last Queen* by Chitra Banerjee Divakaruni focuses on Punjabi history, in specific, on Jindan Kaur, wife of Maharaja Ranjit Singh. Amitav Ghosh, who is a master storyteller, has now come out with his newest novel *Jungle nama.*

Suketu Mehta

The Year 2021 also saw debutants managing to craft masterpieces in English. *Rumours of Spring* by Farah Bashir is set against the polaroid-like backdrop of 1990s Srinagar. This poignant coming of age memoir is teeming with tenderness and innocence. *A Map of Longings* by Manan Kapoor is the first definitive biography of Agha Shahid Ali, the great poet of the 20th century. A superbly nuanced work of fiction, Anindita Ghose's first novel *The Illuminated* revolves around two women: Shashi and Tara.

26

SPORTS

- First Indian to Win Olympic Gold in Athletics: Neeraj Chopra
- Tokyo 2020
- Olympics
- World Athletics Records
- Grand Slam Winners
- FIFA World Cup
- Stop Press
- Index 2022

First Indian to Win Olympic Gold in Athletics

Neeraj Chopra

Ramesh Mathew
Former Staff Correspondent, Gulf Times, Qatar

India's century-old waiting for an elusive medal in the track and field part of the 125-year-old Modern Olympic history came to a happy conclusion on August 7, 2021, when the 24-year-old Neeraj Chopra hurled the spear to clinch the gold in an absorbing contest.

Chopra, who is undoubtedly the greatest discovery in the annals of athletics in India since phenomenal Milkha Singh, has shown enormous promise after he hit the gold in the International Association of Athletics Federations World (Under-20) Championship in Poland, in 2016. The historic Olympic achievement by an Indian sportsperson in an athletic event has certainly generated unprecedented interest among Indians across the field and the country's athletics stand to gain considerably in the forthcoming years through sponsorships and other rewards and incentives.

With his somewhat steadily improving performances and remarkably good consistency at various levels over the last three years Chopra, no doubt, had already emerged as the greatest Indian medal hope at the Olympic Games. Prior to the Tokyo event, which was postponed by a year owing to situations beyond the world's control, a remarkably large number of passionate sport lovers in India were certainly expecting the young army man to figure in the medal bracket after watching his consistent performances at the international level. And true to their expectations Chopra was in a class of his own on the 'D' day, giving absolutely no chance to the other competitors, who included among others Germany's Johannes Vetter who had five astonishing throws exceeding 90 metres in the four years preceding the Olympic Games.

However, an overconfident German athlete got himself narrowly eliminated in the qualification level prior to the final and this apparently seemed to have reduced to a large extent the immense pressure on the other competitors, including Chopra. Even on the days ahead of the competition, Vetter was so optimistic about his gold medal and was on the record more than once about his advantages against Chopra, and obviously also about his overall supremacy in the event. Like some other athletes from

Europe, the overwhelming favourite later blamed the "unhelpful' weather conditions in Tokyo for his disappointing performance.

Contrary to earlier expectations, another top contender Keshorn Walcott of Trinidad & Tobago, who was the bronze medallist at the previous Rio Olympics (2016), too failed to qualify for the final in Tokyo. Such unexpected reverses of famed athletes were shocking indeed but turned out to be a big relief for the Indian star when it mattered the most.

Julian Weber, who too had several better performances than Chopra in the last two years also failed to impress and was only fourth behind the Indian athlete and two Czech throwers, Jakus Vadlejch and Vitezslay Vasely, who were second and third respectively. Pakistani athlete Arshad Nadeem, as expected before the event, managed to remain in the medal contention until the gold was finally won by Chopra.

Chopra, who had been under the tutelage of late Garry Calvert for almost three years became a disciple of Klaus Bartonietz, a biomechanics expert from Germany who has been working with both coaches and athletes for more than four decades. Needless to be mentioned, a large section of the Indian sport aficionados feel these two trainers, without any doubt, were primarily responsible for what Chopra was between his achievements starting from 2016 Under-20 World Championship to his gold success under the simmering conditions in Tokyo last August. Chopra's gold medals at the Commonwealth Games and Asian Games, both of 2018, came from the inspirational support he received from Bartonietz and also from the lessons former world record holder Uwe Hohn imparted to him.

In the two years prior to a shoulder injury and resultant surgery Chopra underwent in the middle of 2019, Hohn was in charge of the Olympian champion and other Indian javelin throwers.

Though the athlete from Panipat had succeeded in becoming the first ever Indian collegian to cross the 80-metre mark in javelin throw a year earlier (2015) at the All India Inter University Athletics Championship, it was doubtful if so many Indians had been aware of this athlete's class, talent and potential until his achievement at the World (U-20) championship held in Bydgoszcz, in the Eastern Europe in July, 2016. His gold achievement at that championship was backed by a record breaking throw of 86.48 metres.

Will India be able to repeat in the coming years the kind of performances Chopra, and juniors like walker Amit Kumar (10 km walk, silver) and long jumper Shaili Singh (silver) delivered at the Under-20 World Championship, held in Nairobi. What is in the store for other junior athletes, aiming high and glory and are undergoing coaching in different centres, spread across the country.

At the junior level, it was the first ever time Indian athletes were winning three medals at a single edition, as one saw in the Kenyan capital. Besides Kumar and Singh, India's mixed 1600 m quartet also finished in the medal bracket, clinching a bronze.

At this juncture, India's athletics fraternity also needs to seriously introspect as to why a track star like Hima Das, who clinched the 400 m gold at the U-20 World Championship in 2018, is unable to follow up her triumph with similar successes at the World level afterwards. Such an initiative from the country's sport mandarins would certainly yield the answers to many of the unsolved questions of the previous years.

Are our athletes and their patrons content with the laurels achieved in the recent years. Along with the apparent innovations happening in coaching areas, the system in place also needs to be receptive to effecting changes as and when it needs.

TOKYO 2020

Ramesh Mathew

In the 120 years since India or Indians started participating in the Olympic Games, only 35 medals have been won by our sportspersons. Whereas Croatia, a small East European country that declared its independence from the now defunct Yugoslavia only 30 years ago (in 1991) has already captured 41 medals, including 14 gold medals. This comparison may possibly help one realise understand where India really stands at the global level in its overall sport abilities and activities.

As many of us may be aware, a handful of sportspersons who were either born in India or lived in the country had participated at the Olympic Games on their own before the 1920 edition at Antwerp. The Games hosted in the Belgian city, a year after the World War 1, had India as one of the 29 official contingents and that was the country's debut at the Games.

Though India has always been in the Olympic news, at least among our own people for one reason or the other over the last 100 years, our contingents to various editions of the Games were relatively smaller in composition compared to the size of the participating teams from many countries that have got a better track record in sport. More often than not, contingents for Olympics from India had received brickbats from sports lovers for the presence of too many officials and "less number of sports persons" a fact that cannot be completely overlooked so easily.

Coming to the 2020 Olympic Games in Tokyo, held one year behind its actual schedule, because of reasons known to one and all, India's performance, shortly speaking, was almost at par with the hopes and expectations of a large number of passionate sport lovers who had made a realistic assessment before the curtains went up.

Tokyo Olympics Closing Ceremony

Other than the shooters, most other "real" medal hopefuls in other events did reasonably well and seven medals, including a rare gold through javelin thrower Neeraj Chopra in athletics, came to our kitty for the first time. In the process, India bettered its previous best of 6 medals at a single Olympics, achieved at the 2012 Olympic Games in London.

Perhaps more than the historic gold triumph of Chopra, what actually turned the entire country euphoric was the memorable bronze achieved by Indian men's hockey team - a medal that eluded India in the last 41 years. If one looked at the results of all matches played at Tokyo, it could easily be concluded that only Belgium and Australia, the two teams that were apparently better and stronger than India alone could get the better of our boys. The bronze medal is sure to help revive the sport in a big way in its traditional centres and also outside if awards declared by various state governments after the medal winning performance were any indication of the things in shape.

As it were during the salad days of our hockey prior to the mid-1970s, Punjab contributed considerably to the success at Tokyo and no less than almost 50% of the men's hockey team comprised players from the northern state.

Considering that India hockey teams did not figure among any medals in the last 9 editions of the Olympic Games (including the 2002 Olympics in Beijing where India were not even among the qualifiers), the bronze achieved by the team at Tokyo is worth a gold indeed for the hockey lovers of the country who were all along complaining of the step motherly attitude towards the game notwithstanding the impressive records of the hockey teams prior to early 1970s.

With the bronze in Tokyo, India's medals count in the Olympic hockey has risen to 12, including 8 gold, 3 bronze and one silver.

Indian women hockey team, though unlucky to lose a medal, won the praise of the whole country with some spirited displays. Sjoerd Marijne, the Dutch coach who transformed the team into a combination of born fighters from being minnows all through the tournament deserves a special mention for his gallant efforts. Marinjne's active involvement and wholehearted commitment to the team were there to see throughout the Olympics. The bunch showed a lot of promise as each match passed and were almost within the sight of medal until their heart breaking loss against experienced Great Britain.

Inspired by their impressive show, more youngsters are expected to take up the sport seriously in the forthcoming years, especially in such states as Odisha, Bihar and Jharkhand, which are identified these days as the areas blooming with real and raw talents.

As in London Olympics (2012), two free-style wrestlers returned with medals from Tokyo. While Bajrang Punia's (65 kilos) bronze was no surprise to those who had closely followed the 27-year-old grappler's fortunes in the last 5 years, Ravikumar Dahiya's silver performance in the 57 kilo category was certainly more stunning. A gold winner at the Asian Championships twice, Dahiya was a bronze medallist at the World Championship in 2019 as well.

Deepak Punia (86 kilos) was a little unlucky to lose a bronze in his category after looking like a "certain medal" in his crucial bout against an experienced American wrestler who switched over two years ago to represent San Marino.

While three Indian male wrestlers rose to the expectations of sport buffs, bagging two medals the country's best medal hope among women Vinesh Phogat (57 kilos) caved in without a fight in her second round bout. A medallist at the Asian Games, Commonwealth and also the World Championship, Vinesh was considered a "sure medal bet" by both by the media and also those following her fortunes in sport for a long time. To compound her woes, the Wrestling Federation of India initiated action against the wrestler for a series of indiscipline(s).

Meerabhai Chanu Saikhom became the second Indian weightlifter after Karnam Malleswari (69 kg class, bronze, Sydney 2000) to win an individual medal in her pet event, when she clinched the silver in the 49 kilo class on the first day of competitions. The weightlifter also became the second from Manipur to win an Olympic medal after world champion boxer M C Mary Kom. Her success proves in no uncertain terms the hidden talents in weightlifting among Manipuri women. Manipur had the distinction of producing a world medallist in women's weightlifting in Kunjurani Devi more than 25 years ago.

Though India earned an unexpected medal in women's boxing through Lovlina Borgohain (69 kilos), the country paid a heavy price for its excessive reliance on an ageing Marycom in her 51 kg class. The 39-year-old pugilist who had done India proud at the 2012 Olympics, bagging a bronze and also winning gold medals at the World Championships as many as six times was eliminated in the quarterfinals by her Colombian opponent Ingrit Valencia in a close match.

Borgohain, who was the first sportsperson from Asom to win an Olympic medal, was also the third Indian to bring an Olympic boxing medal, others being Virender Singh (2008, bronze) and Marycom (2012, bronze).

World No.2 Pusarla Venkata Sindhu's second successive individual Olympic medal in women's badminton singles is a record for any Indian women. Though the shuttler could not repeat the silver she achieved in Rio five years ago, the bronze medal in the event not only kept her track intact but made her also richer by at least 20 million rupees. With her achievement she has also remained the only second Indian badminton player to win medals in the history of Olympics after Saina Nehwal, winner of a bronze in London (2012).

No one had spoken much about golfer Aditi Ashok before the Olympics. However, like gymnast Deepa Karmarkar who came close to a bronze in 2016, this Bengaluru lady who had trained on her own in the last four years was almost in sight of a medal until the last round of her competitions. Though she lost a medal between the cup and lip, Aditi's scintillating fourth place finish has now made her one of the most talked about persons in the Indian sport fraternity. For this golfer, it was a steep climb in her event, reaching almost to the level of a medal from her unimpressive 41st position in Rio.

Other than Neeraj Chopra, two other good performances also came from our track and field performers. Discus thrower Kamalpreet Kaur gave a good account of herself, finishing a creditable sixth with a hurl of 64 metres, which however was at least 2.5 metres behind her personal best.

The first Indian woman to cross the 65-metre mark in discus, Kamalpreet is a beneficiary of the ongoing Athlete Mentorship Programme, launched by ex Indian cricket captain Rahul Dravid.

Similarly, though the Indian 4x400 m men's relay squad could not reach the final in an extremely competitive field, the quartet consisting of Mohamed Anas Yahya, Noah Nirmal Tom, Amoj Jacob and Arogiya Raju bettered the Asian record of 3:00.56 held by Qatar, with a superb effort of 3:00.25, on the penultimate day of the Games.

True to earlier expectations Indian performers in such events as shooting, archery, artistic gymnastics, fencing, rowing, swimming, and table tennis could not make any impression and were nowhere in the reckoning in their respective events.

Shooters, as usual, made a lot of tall claims and counter claims and sections of the media were in their feet in the months preceding the Games with projections of "sure medals" for our marksmen and women. However, the entire contingent cut a very sorry figure and most of our shooters barring one or two put up a very pathetic display at the Games, often finding themselves in the rock bottom.

One wonders why our shooters are performing so miserably at the Olympic Games since their double medal performance in 2012 where Gagan Narang and Vijaya Kumar picked up medals.

Every time a failure occurs at a high magnitude event a number of reasons are discovered and attributed for our debacles. However more failures continue to happen and more reasons are rediscovered again and again at different levels. The scenario is changing indeed but it is doubtful if the pace of change is adequate enough to meet the growing challenges in sports these days.

Olympics

All Sports statistics updation by **Jojo Xaviour**

Medal Tally

Country	Gold	Silver	Bronze	Total
1. USA	39	41	33	113
2. China	38	32	18	88
3. Japan	27	14	17	58
4. UK	22	21	22	65
5. ROC	20	28	23	71
6. AUS	17	7	22	46
7. NED	10	12	14	36
8. FRA	10	12	11	33
9. GER	10	11	16	37
10. ITA	10	10	20	40
11. CAN	7	6	11	24
12. BRA	7	6	8	21
48. India	1	2	4	7

Olympic Medal Individual Winners for India

1. Norman Pritchard	Athletics- 200m	1900 Paris	Silver
2. Norman Pritchard	Athletics- 200m Hurdles	1900 Paris	Silver
3. KD Jadhav	Wrestling-Bantamweight Freestyle	1952 Helsinki	Bronze
4. Leander Paes	Tennis	1996 Atlanta	Bronze
5. Karnam Malleswari	Weightlifting- 69 kg	2000 Sydney	Bronze
6. RS Rathore	Shooting- Double Trap	2004 Athens	Silver
7. Abhinav Bindra	Shooting- 10m Air Rifle	2008 Beijing	Gold
8. Vijender Singh	Boxing	2008 Beijing	Bronze
9. Sushil Kumar	Wrestling	2008 Beijing	Bronze
10. Sushil Kumar	Wrestling	2012 London	Silver
11. Vijay Kumar	Shooting	2012 London	Silver
12. Gagan Narang	Shooting	2012 London	Bronze
13. Saina Nehwal	Badminton	2012 London	Bronze
14. Mary Kom	Boxing	2012 London	Bronze
15. Yogeshwar Dutt*	Wrestling	2012 London	Silver*
16. PV Sindu	Badminton	2016 Rio	Silver
17. Sakshi Malik	Wrestling	2016 Rio	Bronze
18. Neeraj Chopra	Javelin	2020 Tokyo	Gold
19. Saikhom Mirabai Chanu	Weight lifter	2020 Tokyo	Silver
20. Ravikumar Dahiya	Wrestler	2020 Tokyo	Silver
21. Hockey men	Hockey	2020 Tokyo	Bronze
21. P.V. Sindhu	Badminton	2020 Tokyo	Bronze
22. Lovlina Borgohain	Boxing	2020 Tokyo	Bronze
23. Bajrang Punis	Wrestling	2020 Tokyo	Bronze

India's Olympics Balance Sheet

For a country of over 1.31bn people, India's record in the Olympics paints a dismal picture. In over a century India has managed to win only 35 medals and just 30 since Independence.

Year	Gold(10)	Silver (9)	Bronze (16)
1900	-	2 Athletics	
1928	1 Hockey		
1932	1 Hockey		
1936	1 Hockey		
1948	1 Hockey		
1952	1 Hockey	1 Wrestling	
1956	1 Hockey		
1960		1 Hockey	
1964	1 Hockey		
1968			1 Hockey
1972			1 Hockey
1980	1 Hockey		
1996			1 Tennis
2000			1 Weight lifting
2004		1 Shooting	
2008	1 Shooting	1 Boxing,	
			1 Wrestling
2012		1 Wrestling	1 Shooting
		1 Shooting	1 Badminton 1 Wrestling 1 Boxing
2016		1 Badminton	1 Wrestling
2020	Javelin	Weightlifting	Hockey(men)
			Badminton
		Wrestling	Boxing
			Wrestling

Summer Olympic Winners by Total Medals (Total medals won)

1896 to 2020

Country	Medals	Country	Medals	Country	Medals	Country	Medals
USA	2,673	Japan	497	Switzerland	193	Turkey	104
Russia	1,010	Canada	326	Spain	168	S. Africa	89
GBR	916	Netherlands	321	Norway	160	Austria	87
France	750	Romania	308	Belgium	155	Jamaica	87
Germany	652	Finland	305	Brazil	150	Belarus	85
China	634	Poland	298	Ukraine	139	Argentina	77
Italy	618	S. Korea	287	Greece	121	Iran	76
Australia	547	Cuba	241	N. Zealand	117	Mexico	73
Hungary	511	Bulgaria	224	Kenya	113	Kazakhstan	72
Sweden	503	Denmark	205	Serbia	110	Czech Rep.	67

World Athletics Records

World Outdoor Track & Field: Selected Records (Men)

Event	Record	Athlete	Year
100 Metres	9.58 s	Usain Bolt (Jamaica)	2009
200 Metres	19.19 s	Usain Bolt (Jamaica)	2009
400 Metres	43.03 s	Wayde van Niekerk (S. Africa)	2016
800 Metres	1m 40.91 s	David Lekuta Rudisha (Kenya)	2012
1000 Metres	2:11.96	Noah Ngeny (Kenya)	1999
2000 Metres	4m 44.79 s	Hicham El Guerrouj (Morocco)	1999
5000 Metres	12m 35.36 s	Joshua Cheptegei Uganda)	2020
10,000 Metres	26m17.53 s	Kenenisa Bekele (Ethiopia)	2005
(confirmation awaited)	26:11.00 *	Joshua Cheptegei Uganda)	2020
20,000 Metres	5:26.0h #	Haile Gebrselassie (ETH)	2007
25,000 Metres	1:12:25.4h #	Moses Mosop (KEN)	2011
110 Metres Hurdles	12.80 s	Aries Merritt (US)	2012
400 Metres Hurdles	46.70 s	Karsten Warholm (Norway)	1992
4 x 100 Metres Relay	36.84 s	Usain Bolt, Yohan Blake, Nesta Carter, Michael Frater (Jamaica)	2012
4x200 Metres Relay	1:18.63	Jamaica	2014
4 x 400 Metres Relay	02 m 54.29 s	Andrew Valmon, Quincy Watts, Butch Reynolds,Michael Johnson (US)	1993
4x800 Metres Relay	7:02.43	Kenya	2006
4x1500 Metres Relay	14:22.22	Kenya	2014
Road Relay	1:57:06	Kenya	2005
Distance Medley Relay	9:15.50	United States	2015
3000 Metres Steeplechase	7m 53.63 s	Saif Saaeed Shaheen (Qatar)	2004
Marathon	2 h 01m 39 s	Eliud Kipchoge (Kenya)	2018
Half Marathon	58:01	Geoffrey Kamworor (Kenya)	2019
One Hour	21330	Mo Farah (GBR)	2020
One Mile	3:43.13	Hicham EL Guerrouj (MAR)	1999
100 Kilometres	6:09:14	Nao kazami (Japan)	2018
20 Km Walk (road)	1 h 16 m 36 s	Yusuke Suzuki (Japan)	2015
Pole Vault	6.18 (i)	Armand Duplantis (SWE)	2020
High Jump	2.45 m	Javier Sotomayor (Cuba)	1993
Long Jump	8.95 m	Mike Powell (US)	1991
Triple Jump	18.29 m	Jonathan Edwards (GB)	1995
Shot Put	23.12 m	Randy Barnes (US)	1990
Discus Throw	74.08 m	Jürgen Schult (East Germany)	1986
Hammer Throw	86.74 m	Yuriy Sedykh (Soviet Union)	1986
Javelin Throw	98.48 m	Jan Zelezny (Czech Republic)	1996
Decathlon	9126	Kevin Mayer (FRA)	2018

World Athletics Records

World Outdoor Track & Field: Selected Records (Women)

Event	Record	Athlete	Year
100 Metres	10.49 s	Florence Griffith Joyner (US)	1988
200 Metres	21.34 s	Florence Griffith Joyner (US)	1988
400 Metres	47.6 s	Marita Koch (East Germany)	1985
800 Metres	1m 53.28 s	Jarmila Kratochvílová (Czechoslovakia)	1983
2000 Metres	5 m 23.75 s	Genzebe Dibaba (Ethiopia)	2017
5000 Metres	14 m11.15 s	Tirunesh Dibaba (Ethiopia)	2008
10,000 Metres	29 m 17.45 s	Almaz Ayana (Ethiopia)	2016
20,000 Metres	1:05:26.6h #	Tegla Loroupe (KEN)	2000
100 m Hurdles	12.20 s	Kendra Harrison (US)	2016
400 m Hurdles	52.16	Dalilah Muhammad (USA)	2019
4 x 100m Relay	40.82 s	Tianna Madison, Allyson Felix, Bianca Knight, Carmelita Jeter (US)	2012
4x200 Metres Relay	1:27.46	United States Blue	2000
4 x 400 m Relay	3 m15.17 s	Tatyana Ledovskaya, Olga Nazarova, Mariya Pinigina, Olga Bryzgina (Soviet Union)	1988
4x800 Metres Relay	7:50.17	Soviet Union	1984
4x1500 Metres Relay	16:33.58	Kenya	2014
4x1500 Metres Relay	16:27.02*	Nike/Bowerman Track Club	2020
Mixed 4x400 Relay	3:09.34m	Wil L, Allyson F, Courtney O, Michael C.(USA)	2019
3000 Metres Steeplechase	8:44.32	Beatrice Chepkoech (KEN)	2018
20 Km Walk (Road)	1hr 54 m38 s	Florence Kiplagat (Kenya)	2015
Pole Vault	5.06 m	Yelena Isinbayeva (Russia)	2009
High Jump	2.09 m	Stefka Kostadinova (Bulgaria)	1987
Long Jump	7.52 m	Galina Chistyakova (Soviet Union)	1988
Triple Jump	15.50 m	Inessa Kravets (Ukraine)	1995
Shot Put	22.63 m	Natalya Lisovskaya (Soviet Union)	1987
Discus Throw	76.80 m	Gabriele Reinsch (East Germany)	1988
Hammer Throw	82.29 m	Anita Wlodarczyk (Poland)	2016
Javelin Throw	72.28 m	Barbora Spotákova (Czech Republic)	2006
Decathlon	8358 points	Austra Skujyte (Lithuania)	2005
Heptathlon	7291 points	Jackie Joyner-Kersee (USA)	1988
One Mile	4:12.33	Sifan Hassan	2019
One Hour	18930	Sifan Hassan	2020
Marathon	2 hr 15 m 25 s	Mary Jepkosgei Keitany (Kenya)	2017
Half Marathon	1:05:34 Wo	Peres Jepchirchir (KEN)	2020
Half Marathon Mx	1:04:31 Mx	Ababel YESHANEH	2020

* Pending ratification. Mx: mixed gender race

Tennis 2021

Grand Slam Winners

Tournament	Winner	Runner-up	Score
US Open : Date: Aug.31 – Sep 13. **Edition:** 141. **Prize:** $53,402,000 **Court:** Hard **Venue:** USTA Billie Jean King National Tennis Center, New York			
Men Singles	Daniil Medvedev	Novak Djokovic	6–4, 4 6–4, 6–4
Doubles	Rajeev Ram & Joe Salisbury	Jamie Murray & Bruno Soares	[3–6, 6–2, 6–2]
Women Singles	Emma Raducanu	Leylah Fernandez	6–4, 6–3
Doubles	Samantha Stosur & Zhang Shuai	Coc Gauff & Caty Mcnally	[3–6, 6–3, 6–3]
Mixed Doubles	Desirae Krawezyk & Joe Salisbury	Giuliana Olmos & Marcelo Arevalo	[7–5, 6–2]
Australian Open Date: Feb 08 – Feb. 21, 2021. **Edition:** 109. **Prize:** A$80,000,000 **Court:** Hard. **Venue:** Melbourne Park			
Men Singles	Novak Djokovic	Daniil Medvedev	[7–5, 6–2, 6–2]
Doubles	Ivan Dodig/ Filip Polasek	Rajeev Ram/ Joe Salisbury	[6–3, 6–4]
Women Singles	Naomi Osaka	Jennifer Brady	[6–4, 6–3]
Doubles	Elise Mertens/ Aryna Sabalenka	Barbora Krejcikova/ Katerina Siniakova	[6–2, 6–3]
Mixed Doubles	Barbora Krejíková (Czech Rep.) & Rajeev Ram (USA)	Samantha Stosur & Matthew Ebden (Australia)	[6–1, 6–4]
French Open Date: May 30–June 13, 2021 **Edition**:125 **Prize:Date:** €34,367,215 **Court**: Clay. **Venue**: Roland Garros, Paris, France			
Men Singles	Novak Djokovic	Stefanos Tsitsipas	6–7, 2–6, 6–3, 6–2,6–4
Doubles	Pierre Herbert / Nicolas Mahut	Alexander Bublik/ Andrey Golubev	4–6, 7–6, 6–4
Women Singles	Barbora Krejcikova	Anastasia Pavlyuchenkova	6-1, 2-6, 6-4
Doubles	Barbora Krejcikova / Katerina Siniakova	Bethanie Mattek-Sands/ Iga Swiatek	6-4, 6-2
Mixed Doubles	Desirae Krawezyk & Joe Salisbury	Elena Vesnina & Aslan Karatsev	[2–6, 6–4, 10–5]

Wimbledon **Date:** 28 June- 11 July **Edition:** 134 **Prize:** £ 35,016,000
Court: Grass **Venue**: All England Lawn Tennis and Croquet Club

Men Singles	Novak Djokovic	Matteo Berrettini	6–7, 6–4, 6–4, 6-3
Doubles	Nikola Mektic & Mate Pavic	Marcel Granollers & Horacio Zeballos	[6–4,7–6,2–6,7–5]
Women Singles	Ashleigh Barty	Karolina Pliskova	[6–3, 6–7,3 6–3]
Doubles	Hsieh Su-Wei / Elise Mertens	Veronika Kudermetova/ Elena Vesnina	[3–6, 7–5, 9–7]
Mixed Doubles	Neal Skupski& Desirae Krawczyk	Joe Salisbury & Harriet Dart	[6–2, 7–6]

All-time Most Grand Slam Singles Titles (Top 5 Men)

Total	Name	Australian	Wimbledon	French	US
20	Roger Federer (Switzerland)	6	8	1	5
20	Rafael Nadal (Spain)	1	2	13	4
20	Novak Djokovic (Serbia)	9	6	2	3
14	Pete Sampras (USA)	2	7	0	5
12	Roy Emerson (Australia)	6	2	2	2

Most Grand Slam Singles Titles (Open Era Top 5 Women)

Total	Name	Australian	Wimbledon	French	US
24	Margaret Court (AUS)	11	3	5	5
23	Serena Williams (USA)	7	7	3	6
22	Steffi Graf (Germany)	4	7	6	6

Previous Years

Men

Year	Australian Open	French Open	Wimbledon	US Open
2015	Novak Djokovic	Stan Wawrinka	Novak Djokovic	Novak Djokovic
2016	Novak Djokovic	Novak Djokovic	Andy Murray	Stan Wawrinka
2017	Roger Federer	Rafael Nadal	Roger Federer	Rafael Nadal
2018	Roger Federer	Rafael Nadal	Novak Djokovic	Novak Djokovic
2019	Novak Djokovic	Rafael Nadal	Novak Djokovic	Rafael Nadal
2021	Novak Djokovic	Novak Djokovic	Novak Djokovic	Daniil Medvedev

Women

2015	Serena Williams	Serena Williams	Serena Williams	Flavia Pennetta
2016	Angelique Kerber	Garbine Muguruza	Serena Williams	Angelique Kerber
2017	Serena Williams	Jelena Ostapenko	Garbine Muguruza	Sloane Stephens
2018	Caroline Wozniacki	Simona Halep	Angelique Kerber	Naomi Osaka
2019	Naomi Osaka	Ashleigh Barty	Simona Halep	Bianca Andreescu
2021	Naomi Osaka	Barbora Krejcikova	Ashleigh Barty	Emma Raducanu

Football

FIFA World Cup

Adriel Mathew Biju
Football Freelancer and Enthusiast

Qatar 2022 FIFA World Cup

The 22nd edition of the quadrennial international men's football championship will be held from 21st November to 18 December 2022 in Qatar. This will only be the 2nd time that the tournament is held entirely in Asia (after the 2002 tournament in South Korea and Japan) and the first time it's held in the middle east. In addition, this would be the last world cup involving 32 national teams, as the 2026 world cup to be held in USA, Canada and Mexico will feature 48 teams.

The schedule was shifted to late November owing to Qatar's intense summer heat with temperatures touching 50 degrees Celsius. With an estimate of over $200 billion on infrastructure projects alone, the 2022 world cup is set to be the most expensive world cup to date; 7 out of the 8 stadiums are being newly constructed in the country, all of them air-conditioned to combat the extreme weather conditions.

Year	Host	Winner	Runner-up	Top Scorer	Golden Ball Award
1930	Uruguay	Uruguay	Argentina	8 Goals-Guillermo Stabile (Argentina)	Jose Nasazzi (Uruguay)
2002	Korea Republic & Japan	Brazil	Germany	8- Ronaldo (Br)	Oliver Khan (Germany)
2006	Germany	Italy	France	5. Miroslav Klose (Ger)	Zinedine Zidane (Fr)
2010	S Africa	Spain	The Netherlands	5-Thomas Muller (Ger) David Villa (Spain) Weslen Sneijder (Netherlands) Diego Forlan (Uruguay)	Diego Forlan (Uruguay)
2014	Brazil	Germany	Argentina	6- James Rodriguez (Colombia)	Lionel Messi (Arg)
2018	Russia	France	Croatia	4 Goals	Luka Modric
2022	Qatar				

* FIFA World Cup football championship was not held in 1942 and 1946 due to World War-II.

UEFA Euro 2020

The 2020 UEFA European Football Championship, commonly referred to as UEFA Euro 2020 was the 16th UEFA European Championship, the quadrennial international men's football championship of Europe. To celebrate the 60th anniversary of the European Championship competition, the tournament was hosted in several nations with 11 cities in 11 UEFA countries each providing venues for the tournament from 11 June to 11 July 2021.

Italy won their second European Championship title by beating England on penalties in the final following a 1–1 draw after extra time. With an average of 2.78 goals per match, the tournament had the highest goal average since UEFA Euro 1976, prior to the introduction of the group stage. Eleven own goals were scored in the tournament, two more than at all the previous tournaments combined.

Top scorer award: Cristiano Ronaldo (Portugal)

Player of the Tournament: Gianluigi Donnarumma (Italy)

Young Player of the Tournament: Pedri (Spain)

Copa America 2021

The 2021 Copa América was the 47th edition of the Copa América, the international men's football championship organised by South America's football ruling body CONMEBOL. The tournament took place in Brazil from 13 June to 10 July 2021, postponed by almost a year due to the COVID-19 pandemic in South America. Argentina won the title after defeating Brazil 1–0 in the final, their first senior title since the 1993 edition of the same tournament, thus equalling Uruguay's overall record of 15 Copa América titles.

Golden Ball Award: Lionel Messi (Argentina)

Golden Boot Award: Lionel Messi (Argentina)

Golden Glove Award: Emiliano Martínez (Argentina)

Fair Play Award: Brazil

UEFA Champion's League

The UEFA Champions League (abbreviated as UCL) is an annual club football competition organised by the Union of European Football Associations (UEFA) and contested by top-division European clubs, deciding the competition winners through a round-robin group stage to qualify for a double-legged knockout format, and a single leg final. It is one of the most prestigious football tournaments in the world, being played by the national league champions (and, for some nations, one or more runners-up) of their national associations.

The 2020–21 UEFA Champions League was the 66th season of Europe's premier club football tournament organised by UEFA, and the 29th season since it was renamed from the European Champion Clubs' Cup to the UEFA Champions League. Chelsea defeated Manchester City 1–0 in the final, which was played at the Estádio do Dragão in Porto, Portugal.

Founded: 1955.

Most succaessful club: Real Madrid (13 titles)

Premier League

The Premier League, often referred to as the English Premier League or the EPL is the top level of the English football league system which operates on a system of promotion and relegation with the English Football League (EFL). The Premier League is the most-watched sports league in the world, broadcast in 212 territories to 643 million homes

and a potential TV audience of 4.7 billion people.
Founded: 20 February 1992
Number of teams: 20
Most championships: Manchester United (13 titles)
Current champion: Manchester City (5th title)
Golden Boot award: Harry Kane – 23
Playmaker of the Season: Harry Kane – 14
Golden Glove award: Ederson – 19

Serie A

Serie A (also called Serie A TIM for sponsorship reasons) is a professional league competition for football clubs located at the top of the Italian football league system and the winner is awarded the Scudetto and the Coppa Campioni d'Italia.
Founded: 20 February 1992
Number of teams: 20
Most championships: Juventus (36 titles)
Current champion: Internazionale (19 titles)
Most Goals: Cristiano Ronaldo - 29

La Liga

LaLiga is the men's top professional football division of the Spanish football league system; Administered by the Liga Nacional de Fútbol Profesional, it is contested by 20 teams, with the three lowest-placed teams at the end of each season relegated to the Segunda División and replaced by the top two teams and a play-off winner in that division.
Founded: 1929
Number of teams: 20
Most championships: Real Madrid (34 titles)
Current champion: Atlético Madrid (11 titles)
Most Goals: Lionel Messi - 30

Bundesliga

The Bundesliga, sometimes referred to as 1. Bundesliga, is a professional association football league in Germany. At the top of the German football league system, the Bundesliga operates on a system of promotion and relegation with the 2. Bundesliga. The Bundesliga is the number one football league in the world in terms of average attendance.
Founded: 24 August 1963
Number of teams: 18
Most championships: Bayern Munich (30 titles)
Current champion: Bayern Munich (30 titles)
Most Goals: Robert Lewandowski - 41

Ligue 1

Ligue 1 (officially known as Ligue 1 Uber Eats for sponsorship reasons) is a French professional league for men's association football clubs. At the top of the French football league system, it is administrated by the Ligue de Football Professionnel and operates on a system of promotion and relegation from and to Ligue 2.
Founded: 1930
Number of teams: 20
Most championships: Saint-Étienne (10 titles)
Current champion: Lille (4 titles)
Most Goals: Kylian Mbappé - 27

2021 Summer Transfer Window

One of the most eventful transfer windows in the history of the sport saw both Messi and Ronaldo on the move for new challenges. Messi, who spent 21 years at Barca, after joining at age 13 was forced to join the French club Paris Saint-Germain as economic obstacles in the form of financial fair play rules prevented Barcelona from formalising the five-year contract they had agreed with the player.

Ronaldo meanwhile sealed a return to an adoring public at Manchester United, where he rose to world-class status in a first stint from 2003-2009 after 3 years at Serie A giants, Juventus. The first 24 hours of Ronaldo's shirt sales was reported to have broken the all-time record following a transfer, overtaking Messi after his move to Paris Saint-Germain.

The most expensive transfer of the window, however, was neither of these as Manchester City struck a deal of £100m with Aston Villa to sign their captain, Jack Grealish. Other prominent names that made the move include Romelu Lukaku (Inter to Chelsea), Jadon Sancho (Borussia Dortmund to Manchester United), Raphaël Varane (Real Madrid to Manchester United), Sergio Ramos (Real Madrid to Paris Saint-Germain), etc.

Top 10 Most International Goals
(as of 11 Oct. 2021)

Player	Goals	Matches
Cristiano Ronaldo, Portugal	115	182
Ali Daei of Iran*	109	149
Mokhtar Dahiri, Malaysia*	89	142
Ferenc Puskas, Hungary*	84	85
Lionel Messi, Argentina	80	156
Sunil Chhetri, India	80	125
Godfrey Chitalu, Zambia	79	111
Hussein Saeed, Iraq	78	137
Pele, Brazil*	77	92
Ali Mabkhout, UAE	77	94

* retired

All-time Top Scorers as of 28 Oct. 2021

Rank Player	Goals	Club(s)-Goals
1 Cristiano Ronaldo	135	Manchester United-15, Real Madrid -105, Juventus-10
2 Lionel Messi	120	Barcelona
3 Robert Lewandowski/ Bayern	73	Borussia D -17, Munich-51
4 Raúl Gonzalez	71	Real Madrid-66, Schalke 04 (5)
5 Karim Benzema	66	Lyon-12, Real Madrid-54

Champions League Top Goal Scorers
(as on Aug 19, 2020)

Ps Player /Club	Goals
1 Robert Lewandowski Bayern Munich	15
2 Erling Salzburg/Borussia Dortmund	10
3 Serge Gnabry Bayern Munich	9
=4 Dries Mertens Napoli	6
=4 Harry Kane Tottenham	6

as of games played on May 8, 2019.

Ps Player/Club	Goals
1 Lionel Messi/Barcelona	12
2 Robert Lewandowski/ Bayern Munich	8
=3Cristiano Ronaldo/ Juventus	6
=3 Moussa Marega/ Porto	6
=3 Dusan Tadic/Ajax	6

as on 2019/2020

# Player/Team	Goals
1. Marcus Rashford/Manchester United	4
2. Duvan Zapata /Atalanta	3
3. Álvaro Morata /Juventus	2

Cricket

Cricket Test: Results Summary

Team	Match	Won	Lost	Draw	Tie
England	1040	378	311	351	–
Australia	834	394	226	212	2
West Indies	558	178	202	177	1
India	555	164	171	219	1
New Zealand	449	107	175	167	–
South Africa	445	169	152	124	–
Pakistan	439	143	134	162	–
Sri Lanka	297	93	113	91	–
Bangladesh	124	15	92	17	–
Zimbabwe	115	13	74	28	–
Afghanistan	6	3	3	–	–
Ireland	3	–	3	–	–

Most Runs (10,000 runs & above)

Batsman	Match	Runs
Sachin Tendulkar	200	15921
Ricky Ponting	168	13378
Jack Kallis	166	13289
Rahul Dravid	164	13288
Alastair Cook	161	12472
Kumar Sangakkara	134	12400
Brian Lara	131	11953
Chander Paul	164	11867
Jayawardena	149	11814
Allan Border	156	11174
Steve Waugh	168	10927
Sunil Gavaskar	125	10122
Younis Khan	118	10099

Most Wickets (500 & above)

Bowler	Match	Wickets
M. Muralidharan	133	800
S. Warne	145	708
J. Anderson	166	632
A. Kumble	132	619
G. Magrath	124	563
Stuart Broad	149	524
C. Walsh	132	519

Sachin Tendulkar

Most Career Matches	Sachin Tendulkar	200
Most Centuries	Sachin Tendulkar	51
Most Fifties	Sachin Tendulkar	119
Most Ducks	Courtney Walsh	43
Most Fours	Sachin Tendulkar	2058
Most Sixes	Brendon Mccullum	107
" Highest Team Total	Sri Lanka vs India	952/6 (SL)
" Lowest Team Total	New Zealand vs England	26 (Nz)
" Most Played Team	England	1039
" Most Matches Won	Australia	394

Most Test Matches as Captain

Captain	Country	Tests	Won	Lost	Drawn	Tied	Win %	Period
Graeme Smith	South Africa*	109	53	29	27	0	48.62	April 24,2003-March 5, 2014
Allan Border	Australia	93	32	22	38	1	34.41	Dec.7, 1984 - March 29, 1994
Stephen Fleming	New Zealand	80	28	27	25	0	35.00	Feb 14, 1997 - Dec 18, 2006
Ricky Ponting	Australia	77	48	16	13	0	62.34	March 8,2004 - Dec 29, 2010
Clive Lloyd	West Indies	74	36	12	26	0	48.65	Nov 22, 1974 - Jan 2, 1985
Virat Kohli	India	65	38	16	11	0	58.46	Dec 9, 2014
- M.S. Dhoni	India	60	27	18	15	0	45.00	Apr. 11, 2008 - Dec 30, 2014

*Smith's tally includes one test match as ICC World XI captain in 2005 (match lost)

Most Test Matches as Captain for Asian Sides

Captain	Country	Test	Won	Lost	Drawn	Win %	Period
Virat Kohli	India	65	38	16	11	58.46	Dec 9, 2014 - ....
M.S. Dhoni	India	60	27	18	15	45.00	Apr 11,2008-Dec 30, 2014
Arjuna Ranatunga	Sri Lanka	56	12	19	25	21.43	Dec 8, 1989 - Feb 28, 1999
Misbah-ul-Haq	Pakistan	56	26	19	11	46.43	Nov 12, 2010 - May 14, 2017
Sourav Ganguly	India	49	21	13	15	42.86	Nov 10, 2000 - Sept 22, 2005
Imran Khan	Pakistan	48	14	8	30	19.15	July 29, 1982 - Jan 7, 1992
Sunil Gavaskar	India	47	9	8	30	19.15	Jan24, 1976 - Feb 5, 1985
Mohammad Azharuddin	India	47	14	14	19	29.79	Feb 2, 1990 - Feb 28, 1999
Mansoor Ali Khan Pataudi	India	40	9	19	12	22:50	Mar 23, 1962 - Jan 29, 1975

Neutral Test Matches

The number of neutral test matches played so far in men's cricket, with the Southampton game between India and New Zealand being the latest in the last 144-years of Test cricket. Incidentally, it was the first ever neutral Test match played by India since its inaugural Test match in June 1932. Among the 12 Test-playing sides, Bangladesh is the only team not to play at a neutral venue, although it has hosted neutral Test matches. Pakistan by virtue of being forced to play away from home, i.e. in the United Arab Emirates, has appeared in most neutral Test matches.

First Neutral Test Matches Played by Each Team

Team	Dates	Opponent	Venue	Result
Australia	May 27-28,1912	South Africa	Manchester	Won by innings and 88 runs
South Africa	May 27-28, 1912	Australia	Manchester	Lost by an innings and 88 runs
Pakistan	Mar 12-15, 1999	Sri Lanka	Dhaka	Won by innings and 175 runs
Sri Lanka	Mar 12-15, 1999	Pakistan	Dhaka	Lost by an innings and 175 runs
West Indies	Jan 31-Feb 4, 2002	Pakistan	Sharjah	Lost by 170 runs
England	Jan 17-19, 2012	Pakistan	Dubai	Lost by 10 wickets
New Zealand	Nov 9-13, 2014	Pakistan	Abu Dhabi	Lost by 248 runs
Afghanistan	Mar 15-18,2019	Ireland	Dehradun	Won by seven wickets
Ireland	Mar 15-18, 2019	Afghanistan	Dehradun	Lost by seven wickets
Zimbabwe	Mar 2-3, 2021	Afghanistan	Abu Dhabi	Won by 10 wickets
India	June 18-23, 2021	New Zealand	Southampton	Lost by eight wickets

World Test Champions

New Zealand triumphed over India by 8 wickets to win the inaugural ICC World Test Championship, a two-year league competition that began with the Aug. 2019 Ashes series. In the final, played at Southampton's Rose Bowl, Kyle Jamieson who took five wickets for 31 in the first innings, was man of the match. Winning their first major ICC title the Kiwis received $1.6 million and the Test Mace -formerly awarded to the top side in the ICC ranking. India won 8,00,000

Score
India 217, 170
NZ 249, 140/2
Most Runs - Joe Root
Most Wickets - R. Ashwin

Historic Day-Night Pink-ball Test at Eden Gardens

India's Landmark Tests in Eden

1962: India's first Test victory at Eden. Beat England by 187 runs.
2001: India became the only third side, after England (twice), to win a Test (vs Aus, by 171 runs) after being made to follow-on

2001: India's 50th Test victory at home (vs Aus).
2005: India's 200th Test match at home (beat Pak by 195 runs)
2016: India 250th Test match at home (beat NZ by 178 runs)
2017: The only home Test match (vs SL) where Indian spinners did nto claim a single wicket, while pacers took 17 wickets!
2019: Nov 22-26, Ind vs Bangla at Eden. India won inns 46 runs.

Cricket ODI (as on Oct. 10.2021) Results Summary

Team	Match	Won	Lost	Tie	NR
India	996	518	428	9	41
Australia	958	581	334	9	34
Pakistan	936	490	417	9	20
Sri Lanka	867	393	431	5	38
West Indies	831	405	386	10	30
New Zealand	775	354	374	7	40
England	761	384	339	9	29
South Africa	634	388	221	6	19
Zimbabwe	538	139	379	8	12
Bangladesh	388	136	245	–	7
Ireland	173	72	88	3	10
Kenya	154	42	107	–	5
Afghanistan	129	62	63	1	3
Scotland	121	46	67	1	7

Pollard Hits Six Sixes

West Indies Kieron Pollard became only the 3rd man to hit six sixes in an international cricket. Pollard followed in the footsteps of South Africa's Herschelle Gibbs against the Netherlands in the 2007 World Cup and India's Yuvraj Singh, who also achieved the feat in the 2007 Twenty20 World Cup against England.

Six Sixes in an Over International Cricket

ODIs

Batsman	Bowler	Match	Venue	Year
Herschelle Gibbs	Daan Van Bunge	South Africa v Netherlands	St. Kitts	2007

T20Is

Batsman	Bowler	Match	Venue	Year
Yuvraj Sing	Stuart Broad	India v England	Durban	2007
Kieron Pollard	Akila Dananjaya	West Indies v Sri Lanka	Antigua	2021

Domestic Cricket First Class

Batsman	Bowler	Match	Venue	Year
Sir Garfield Sobers	Malcolm Nash	Nottinghamshire v Glamorgan	Swansea	1968
Ravi Shastri	Tilak Raj	Bombay v Baroda	Bombay	1985

T20s First Class Matches

Batsman	Bowler	Match	Venue	Year
Ross Whiteley	Karl Carver	Worcestershire Rapids v Yorkshire Vikings	Headingley	2017
Hazratullah Zazai	Abdullah Mazari	Kabul Zwanan v Balkh Legends	Sharjah	2018
Leo Carter	Anton Devcich	Canterbury Kings v Borthern Knights	Christchurch	2020

Most Runs (10,000 runs and more)

Player	Matches	Runs
Sachin Tendulkar (Ind)	463	18426
Kumar Sangakkara (SL)	404	14234
Ricky Ponting (Aus)	375	13704
Sanath Jayasurya (SL)	445	13430
Mahela Jayawardane (SL)	448	12650
Virat Kohli (Ind)	245	12169
Inzamam-ul-Haq (Pak)	378	11739
Jacques Kallis (SA)	328	11579
Saurav Ganguly (Ind)	311	11363
Rahul Dravid (Ind)	344	10889
Mahendra Dhoni (Ind)	350	10773
Chris Gayle (WI)	301	10480
Brian Lara (WI)	299	10405
Tilakratna Dilshan (SL)	330	10290

Most ...

Career matches: Sachin Tendulkar : 463
Centuries - Sachin Tendulkar: 49 matches
Fifties: Sachin Tendulkar (Ind): 145
Ducks: Sanath Jayasurya (SL): 34
Fours : Sachin Tendulkar (Ind): 2016
Sixes : Sahid Afridi (Pak): 351
Highest Team Total - Eng 481/6 vs Aus 2018 Nottingham
Lowest Team Total: Zim 35 vs SL 2004 Harare
Matches won - 581 Australia

Most Wickets (300 wkts or more)

Player	Matches	Runs
M. Muralitharan (SL)	350	534
W. Akram (Pak)	356	502
W. Younis (Pak)	262	416
C. Vaas (SL)	322	400
S. Afridi (Pak)	398	395
S. Pollock (SA)	303	393
G. McGrath (Aus)	250	381
B. Lee (Aus)	221	380
S. Malinga (SL)	226	338
A. Kumble (Ind)	271	337
S. Jayasurya (SL)	445	323
J. Srinath (Ind)	229	315
D. Vettori NZ)	295	305

IPL 2021 Dates: April 9 – Oct 15, 2021

Host: India & UAE
Champions: Chennai Super Kings
Runners up: Kolkata Knight Riders
Man of the match: Faf du Plessis
Orange Cap: Ruturaj Gaikwad (635 runs)
Purple Cap: Harshal Patel (32 wickets)
Perfect Catch: Ravi Bishnoi
Super Striker: Shimron Hetmyer
Game Changer: Harshal Patel
Most Sixes: KL Rahul (30)
Power Player: Venkatesh Iyer
Valuable Player: Harshal Patel
Fair Play: Rajasthan Royals

National Athletics Records, India

The following are the national records in athletics in India.

Outdoor

Men

Event	Record	Athlete	Year	Meet Place
Track Events				
100 m	10.26	Amiya Kumar Mallick	2016	Nati. Fed. Cup New Delhi, India
10.21	X	Anil Kumar Prakash	2000	Bangalore, India
200 m	20.63	Muhammed Anas	2018	Jablonec nad Nisou, Czech Rep.
	20.45 X	Dharambir Singh	2016	3rd Indian Grand Prix Bangalore, India
400 m	45.24	Muhammed Anas	2018	Cena Noveho Mesta nad Metuji meet Nové Mésto nad Metují, Czech Rep.
	45.21	Muhammed Anas	2019	Kladno Athletics meet, Czech Rep.
800 m	1:45.65	Jinson Johnson	2018	Nat. Inter-State Champ., Guwahati
1500 m	3:37.86	Jinson Johnson	2018	CW Games,Gold Coast, Australia
	3:37.62	Jinson Johnson	2019	Next Generation Meet, Netherlands
	3:35.24	Jinson Johnson	2019	ISTAF Berlin Berlin, Germany
3000 m	7:50.31	Surendra Singh	2008	Twickenham, United Kingdom
5000 m	13:29.70	Bahadur Prasad	1992	Birmingham, United Kingdom
10000 m	28:02.89	Surendra Singh	2008	Spanish Olympic Trials Vigo, Spain
110 m hurdles	13.48	Siddhanth Thingalaya	2017	Altis Invitational Mesa, United States
400 m hurdles	48.96	Ayyasamy Dharun	2018	Asian Games Jakarta, Indonesia
	48.80	Ayyasamy Dharun	2019	23rd Federation Cup Patiala, India
3000 m steeplechase	8:29.80	Avinash Sable	2018	58th National Open Championships Bhubaneswar, India
	8:28.94	Avinash Sable	2019	23rd Federation Cup India Patiala, India
	8:25.23	Avinash Sable	2019	World Championships Doha, Qatar
	8:21.37	Avinash Sable	2019	World Championships Doha, Qatar
20000m walk	1:20:22.52	Gurmeet Singh	2012	77th All-India Railway Championships Bhubaneswar, India
4×100m relay	38.89	Rahamatulla Molla, Suresh Sathya, Shameer Mon, A. Qureshi	2010	CW Games New Delhi, India
4×400m relay	3:00.91	Kunhu Muhammed, Muhammed Anas, Ayyasamy Dharun, Arokia Rajiv.	2016	3rd Indian Grand Prix Bangalore
Road Events				
10 km run	29:43	Kashinath Aswale	30 November 2008	India Hyderabad, India
Half marathon	1:03:53	Nitendra Singh Rawat	19 November 2017	Delhi
Half Marathon		Govindan Lakshmanan	19 November 2017	India New Delhi
Marathon	2:12:00	Shivnath Singh	1978	India Jalandhar, India
10 km walk	40:18+	Gurmeet Singh	2016	Asian Race Walking Championships Nomi, Japan
20 km walk	1:20:21	Irfan Kolothum Thodi	2012	Olympic Games,London, Great Britain
		Devender Singh	2016	Asian Race Walking Championships Nomi, Japan

50 km walk 3:55:59.5 Sandeep Kumar 2017 Indian Racewalking Championships New Delhi, India

Field Events

High jump 2.29 m Tejaswin Shankar 2018 Texas Tech Corky/Crofoot Shootout Lubbock, United States

Pole vault 5.30m Subramani Siva 2018 68th Inter-Services Championships Bangalore, India

Long jump 8.20m Sreeshankar Murali 2018 58th National Open Championships Bhubaneswar, India

Triple jump 17.30m Renjith Maheswary 2016 3rd Indian Grand Prix India Bangalore,

Shot put 20.75 m Tejinder Toor 2018 Asian Games, Jakarta, Indonesia

20.92 m Tejinder Toor 2019 59th National Open Championships Ranchi, India

Discus throw 66.28 m Vikas Gowda 2012 Old Style Discus Challenge, USA

Hammer throw 70.73 m Neeraj Kumar 2016 56th National Interstate Champion ships Hyderabad, India

72.86 m # Kamalpreet Singh 2015 Tucson Elite Classic, Tucson, USA

Javelin throw 88.06 m Neeraj Chopra 2018 Asian Games Jakarta, Indonesia

Combined Events

Decathlon 7658 pts Bharatinder Singh 2011 Indian Inter-State Championships. Bangalore, India

Women

Event	Record	Athlete	Year Meet	Place
Track Events				
100 m	11.29	Dutee Chand	2018 58th National Inter State Champion ships Guwahati, India	
	11.24	Dutee Chand 2	2016 26th G. Kosanov Memorial	Almaty, Kazakhstan
	11.26 #	Rachita Mistry	2000 National Circuit Meet	Bangalore, India
11.28		Dutee Chand	2019 Asian Championships	Doha, Qatar
11.26 Dutee Chand			2019 Asian Championships	Doha, Qatar

11.22 Dutee Chand 11 October 2019 59th National Open Championships Ranchi, India [44]

200 m 22.82 Saraswati Saha 2002 National Circuit Meet Ludhiana, India

400 m 50.79 Hima Das 26 August 2018 Asian Games Jakarta, Indonesia

800 m 1:59.17 Tintu Luka 4 September 2010 Continental Cup Split, Croatia

1500 m 4:05.39 Harmilan Bains 2021National Open Championship in Warangal

3000 m 9:04.5 (ht) Suriya Loganathan 2016 New Delhi, India

5000 m 15:15.89 Preeja Sreedharan 2010 Asian Games Guangzhou, China

10000 m 31:50.47 Preeja Sreedharan 2010 Asian Games Guangzhou, China [50]

100 m hurdles 13.38 Anuradha Biswal 2002 DDA-Raja Bhalendra Singh National Circuit meet New Delhi, India

400 m hurdles 55.42 P. T. Usha 1984 Olympic Games Los Angeles, USA

3000 m steeplechase 9:19.76 Lalita Babar Rio de JaneiroOlympic Games, Brazil

10000 m walk Gaurav Kumari 2012 Police Championships New Delhi

20000 m walk 1:40:35.70 Sapna Punia 2015 National Games, Thiruvananthapuram

4 × 100 m relay 43.42 Merlin Joseph, H. M. Jyothi, Srabani Nanda, Dutee Chand 2016 Kazakhstani Championships Almaty, Kazakhstan

4 × 400 m relay 3:26.89 Chitra K. Soman, Rajwinder Kaur, K. M. Beenamol, Manjit Kaur 2004 Olympic Games Athens, Greece

Road Events

10 km run 34:32 Kavita Raut 2009 Bangalore, India

Half marathon 1:10:31 Suriya Loganathan 2017 Delhi Half Marathon New Delhi, India

Marathon 2:34:43 O. P. Jaisha 2015 World Championships Beijing, China

10 km walk 44:42+ Khushbir Kaur 2014 IAAF World Race Walking Cup, Taicang, China

20 km walk 1:31:29 Baby Soumya 2018 National Race Walking Champion ships New Delhi, India

1:29:54 Bhawanja Jat 2020 Indian Championships Ranchi, India

Field Events

High jump 1.92 m Sahana Kumari 2012 National Inter-State Championships Hyderabad, India

Pole vault 4.15 m V. S. Surekha 2014 National Open Championships, New Delhi, India

Long jump 6.83 m Anju Bobby George 2004 Olympic Games Athens, Greece

Triple jump 14.11 m Mayookha Johny 2011 Asian Championships Kobe, Japan

Shot put 18.86 m Manpreet Kaur 2017 Asian Grand Prix Jinhua, China

Discus throw 64.84 m # Seema Antil 2004 Kiev, Ukraine

64.76 m Krishna Poonia 2012 Altius Track Crew Throwdown Maui, USA

Hammer throw 65.25 m Sarita Singh 2017 21st Federation Cup National Cham pionships Patiala, India

Javelin throw 61.86 m Annu Rani 2017 21st Federation Cup National Cham pionships Patiala, India

62.34 m 2019 23rd Federation Cup National Cham pionships Patiala, India

62.43 m 2019 World Championships Doha, Qatar

Formula F1: Lewis Hamilton became the first Formula 1 driver to have 100 creer wins, after winning Russian Grand Prix on September 26, 2021 surpassing Michael Schumacher.

China Claims Uber Cup: Beating Japan in the final with a 3-1 victory. (China's 15th victory)

Khelo India Youth Games Rescheduled

The Haryana government has decided to postpone the 2021 edition of the Khelo India Youth Games as a precautionary measure against a possible third wave of COVID-19. The event, which was scheduled to take place in November in Ambala, Chandigarh, Delhi, Panchkula and Shahbad, will now take place in February 2022.

The fourth edition of the youth championships will be held in the under-18 age group and will involve 25 sports competitions, including five indigenous games.The competition was to be held in in five cities.

Around 8,500 players are expected to participate in the competition. There could be a possibility of hosting some events of the Games in Himachal Pradesh.

The 3rd edition of the Khelo India Youth Games was held in Guwahati, Asom in January 2020. from 10 January 2020 and 22 January 2020 in Guwahati, Asom, India. Website www.kiyg2020guwahati.in

Haryana won the inaugural edition of the Khelo India Youth Games in 2018 and finished runner-up behind Maharashtra last year.

Medals Tally 2020

Rank	State	G	S	B	Total
1	Maharashtra	78	77	101	256
2	Haryana	68	60	72	200
3	Delhi	39	36	47	122
4	Karnataka	32	26	22	80
5	Uttar Pradesh	29	28	30	87
6	Tamil Nadu	22	32	22	76
7	Asom* (Host)	20	22	34	76
8	West Bengal	19	14	20	53
9	Gujarat	16	16	20	52
10	Punjab	16	15	28	59
11	Rajasthan	15	24	12	51
12	MP	15	11	20	46
13	Kerala	15	5	20	40
14	Manipur	14	20	20	54
15	Telangana	7	6	8	21
16	Chandigarh	6	2	9	17
17	Odisha	5	8	8	21
18	A&N Islands	5	2	1	8
19	Uttarakhand	4	4	11	19
20	Tripura	4	1	0	5
21	Jharkhand	3	9	7	19
22	Andhra Pradesh	3	7	7	17
23	Arunachal	3	5	4	12
24	Mizoram	3	2	5	10
25	Himachal	2	3	2	7
26	J&K	2	3	1	6
27	Chhattisgarh	1	2	4	7
28	Bihar	1	1	7	9
29	Goa	0	3	9	12
30	Daman-Diu	0	1	0	1
31	Ladakh	0	0	1	1
32	Puducherry	0	0	1	1
33	Sikkim	0	0	1	1
34	D&N Haveli	0	0	0	0
	Lakshadweep	0	0	0	0
	Meghalaya	0	0	0	0
	Nagaland	0	0	0	0
Totals		**447**	**445**	**554**	**1446**

Stop Press

- Sudan's military seizes power from a transitional government.
- The Supreme Court appoints a committee of experts to inquire into the alleged use of Israeli spyware Pegasus for surveillance of Indian citizens.
- The government appoints veteran banker K V Kamath as the chairperson of newly set up ₹20,000-crore development finance institution (DFI), National Bank for Financing Infrastructure and Development (NaBFID).
- James Michael Tyler, most famous for playing Gunther, the manager of Central Perk in the hit sitcom *Friends*, died on October 24 aged 59.
- Ila Ganesan becomes Manipur Governor
- 2 Oct. Najla Bouden Romdhane is Tunisia's first woman PM

Errata:

- Page790: Kindly read Option D as 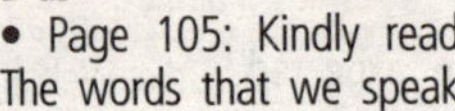
- Page 105: Kindly read The words that we speak have creative ability and it is reflected in our lives, surroundings and relationships. It can either build and motivate a person or shatter that person. The words we speak have considerable influence on our lifestyle and even our destiny.
- Page 724: Kindly read ASIA after Zimbabwe (under Africa) and before Afghanistan.
- Page 813: Para 3 - Read : "Understand how you and your team work" as a subheading
- Saamarth Yojana p. 108.

Index 2022

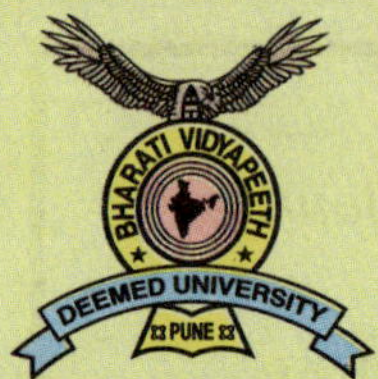

Bharati Vidyapeeth

(Deemed to be University), Pune (India)

Bharati Vidyapeeth Bhavan, Lal Bahadur Shastri Road, Pune - 411 030 (Maharashtra, India)
Phone No. : **020-24407100** Fax : **020-24339121** Website : **www.bvuniversity.edu.in**

A University, Nationally and Internationally Acclaimed for Academic Excellence and Pioneering Research...

BVU for You.

Accredited with A+ Grade by NAAC (2017)

68th Rank among Universities by NIRF 2021

Category-I Deemed to be University Grade by UGC

'A' Grade by Ministry of HRD, Government of India

Ranked in
TOP 100
Universities in India

consecutively for **5** Years

Major Educational Campuses

Pune | Navi Mumbai | New Delhi
Sangli | Karad | Kolhapur | Solapur

THE UNIVERSITY OFFERS FOLLOWING COURSES THROUGH ITS CONSTITUENT UNITS

NAME OF THE CONSTITUENT UNIT	COURSES
Medical College, Pune and Sangli	M.B.B.S., M.D./M.S. (20 specialities) M.Ch./D.M. Super Speciality (6 Specialities) M.Sc. (5 Specialitie
Dental College & Hospital, Pune, Navi Mumbai and Sangli	B.D.S. M.D.S. (8 Specialities)
College of Ayurved, Pune	B.A.M.S., P.G. Diploma, M.D./M.S. (Ayurved) (7 Specialities)
Homoeopathic Medical College, Pune	B.H.M.S., M.D. Homoeopathy (5 Specialities)
Poona College of Pharmacy, Pune NIRF - 2021 Rank 17	B.Pharm., M.Pharm. (7 Specialities) Pharm.D., Pharm.D. (Post Baccalaureate)
Nursing College, Pune, Sangli & Navi Mumbai	B.Sc. (Nursing), Post Basic B.Sc. (Nursing) M.Sc. (Nursing) (5 Specialities)
College of Engineering, Pune NIRF - 2021 Rank 96	B.Tech. (12 Specialities) M.Tech. (8 Specialities)
Department of Engineering & Technology, Navi Mumbai	B.Tech. (5 Specialities)
Institute of Management Pune, New Delhi, Navi Mumbai, Kolhapur, Karad, Sangli, Solapur	M.B.A., M.C.A., B.B.A., B.C.A.
Department of Management Studies off Campus Navi Mumbai	M.B.A.
New Law College, Pune	LL.B. (3 Years), B.A. LL.B. (5 Years) B.B.A. LL.B. (5 Years), LL.M. (2 Years)
Department of Law, New Delhi	LL.B. (3 Years), B.B.A. LL.B. (5 Years)
Yashwantrao Mohite College of Arts, Science and Commerce, Pune	B.A. (2 Specialities), B.Sc. (6 Specialities) B.Com. B.Lib. & I.Sc. M.Sc. (4 Specialities), M.Com., M.A. (2 Subjects), M.Lib. & I.Sc.
School of Visual Arts	Bachelor of Visual Arts (Applied Arts)
Social Sciences Center, Pune, Solapur	M.S.W., M.Phil. in Social Work
Rajiv Gandhi Institute of Information Technology & Biotechnology, Pune	B.Sc. Biotechnology, M.Sc. Biotechnology (3 Specialities) Advance Diploma in Bioinformatics
School of Optometry, Pune, Sangli	B.Optom., M.Optom.
School of Audiology & Speech Language Pathology, Pune	B.A.S.L.P, M.Sc. (Audiology) M.Sc. (Speech Language Pathology)
College of Physical Education, Pune	B.A. (Physical Education and Sports) B.P.Ed., M.P.Ed., M.Phil. (Physical Education)
Institute of Environment Education and Research, Pune	M.Sc. (Environment Science) (2 Specialities)
Centre for Health Management, Pune	MHA (Master in Hospital Administration)
College of Architecture, Pune	B.Arch., M.Arch. (2 Specialities)
Hotel Management and Catering Technology, Pune	B.H.M.C.T. (Bachelor of Hotel Management & Catering Technology) B.Sc. H&HA (Bachelor in Science Hospitality Management and Hotel Administration)
Department of Photography, Pune	B.A. (Commercial Photography) B.A. (Photography & Cinematography)
School of Performing Arts, Pune and Sangli	B.A. (Music), B.A. (Dance), M.A. (Music), M.A. (Dance) Diploma in Kirtan (Naradiya & Varkari Styles)
School for Skill Development and Allied Health Sciences, Pune	B.P.T.

FACULTIES / DISCIPLINES

Medicine | Dentistry | Ayurved | Homoeopathy | Pharmacy | Nursing | Engineering | Management | law | Hotel Management | Architecture | Social Sciences | Social Work | Environmental Sciences | Physical Education | Performing Arts | Science | Commerce | Photography